The Future of Business Student

(**http://gitmanxtra.swlearning.com**)

The student Web site offers interactive learning experiences that reinforce business concepts. Highlights of the Web site include the following:

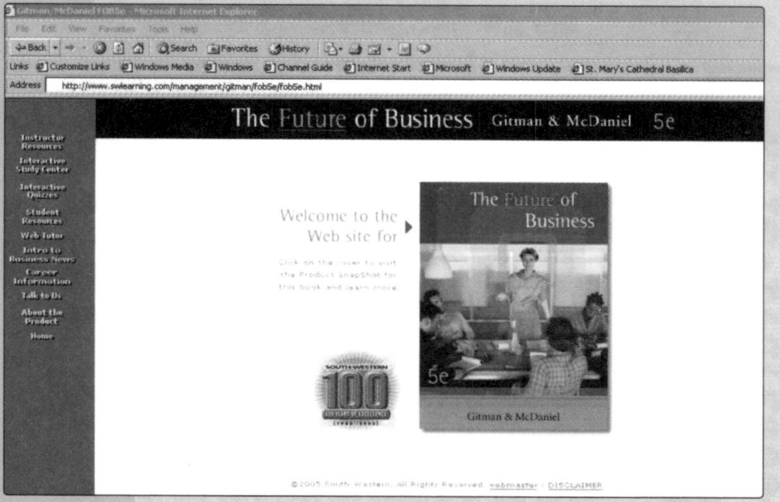

- Internet exercises that explore e-business activities.
- Crossword puzzles of key business terminology.
- Chapter quizzes that test comprehension and provide customized feedback.
- *Intro to Business News*, a continuously refreshed supply of timely news stories, all organized by chapter topic.
- Online chapter "Using the Internet for Business Success" provides the latest insights on starting and managing an e-business.
- Downloadable PowerPoint® slides.

WebTutor® Advantage

WebTutor® Advantage is designed to help you grasp complex concepts and provide several forms of interactive learning and reinforcement. This rich collection of content, customized for *The Future of Business,* Fifth Edition, is available online. In addition, **WebTutor ToolBox** may be bundled with each new copy of the textbook. Available for WebCT™ and Blackboard®, WebTutor® ToolBox includes the course management system found in WebTutor® Advantage with links to the content from our book companion web sites.

InfoTrac® College Edition

With InfoTrac® College Edition, you get complete access to full-text articles from hundreds of scholarly journals and popular periodicals such as *Newsweek, Time,* and *USA Today.* Thousands of full-length, substantive articles spanning the past four years are updated daily, indexed, and linked. And because they're online, the articles are accessible from any computer with Internet access.

The Future of Business

5e

Lawrence J. Gitman
San Diego State University

Carl McDaniel
University of Texas, Arlington

THOMSON
SOUTH-WESTERN

The Future of Business, 5e
Lawrence J. Gitman and Carl McDaniel

VP/Editorial Director:
Jack W. Calhoun

VP/Editor-in-Chief:
Michael P. Roche

Sr. Publisher:
Melissa Acuña

Sr. Acquisitions Editor:
Steve Hazelwood

Developmental Editor:
Mary H. Draper

Marketing Manager:
Nicole Moore

Production Editor:
Robert Dreas

Media Developmental Editor:
Kristen Meere

Media Production Editor:
Karen Schaffer

Manufacturing Coordinator:
Diane Lohman

Production House:
Pre-Press Company, Inc.

Printer:
Quebecor World
Versailles, Kentucky

Design Project Manager:
Anne Marie Rekow

Sr. Internal Designer:
Anne Marie Rekow

Cover Designer:
Anne Marie Rekow

Cover Images:
© PhotoDisc

Photography Manager:
Deanna Ettinger

Photo Researcher:
Terri Miller/
E-Visual Communications

Printed in the United States of America
1 2 3 4 5 07 06 05 04

ISBN: 0-324-27252-9; 0-324-20713-1

Library of Congress Control Number: 2003112533

For more information
contact South-Western,
5191 Natorp Boulevard,
Mason, Ohio 45040.
Or you can visit our Internet site at:
http://www.swlearning.com

Your Future.

It starts NOW.

Gitman and McDaniel's *The Future of Business, 5e*, solidly grounded in best practices and the latest technology, offers a wealth of practical information. The text is supported by real-world examples to introduce today's students to tomorrow's business careers. The fully-updated fifth edition, written in a friendly and conversational style, helps instructors prepare students of all interests and abilities for future achievements with the information, skills, and techniques they need to get to work and jump on the fast-track to success.

Topics. Trends. Principles. Practices.

Revised in response to extensive reviews and focus group studies, *The Future of Business, 5e* identifies and examines in depth the major issues that will shape the future of business:

- Customer Satisfaction and Quality
- Ethics
- Career Development
- Entrepreneurship and Small Business Management
- Global Business Opportunities
- Impact of Technology

The text also offers a contemporary review of all key business topics and trends, and encourages students to consider the limitless possibilities of a career in business.

Gitman and McDaniel have authored the most readable and enjoyable textbook in business — one that will engage students in interactive learning, prompt critical thinking through real-world examples, and prepare them for a wide-open future in the often chaotic but always exciting world of business.

PTi — SIMPLE AS 1 2 3

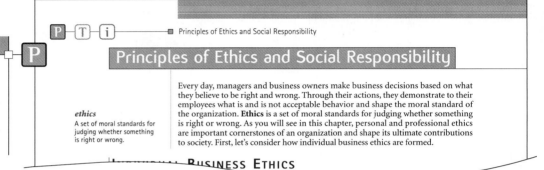

ORGANIZATION MATTERS! EACH CHAPTER OF *THE FUTURE OF BUSINESS* USES A UNIQUE THREE-PART STRUCTURE THAT LINKS PRINCIPLES, TRENDS, AND IDEAS.

PRINCIPLES OF BUSINESS

gives students a comprehensive overview of current business practices, and teaches key principles through real-world examples from the largest global corporate giants to the smallest family start-ups.

P T i — Principles of Ethics and Social Responsibility

Principles of Ethics and Social Responsibility

ethics
A set of moral standards for judging whether something is right or wrong.

Every day, managers and business owners make business decisions based on what they believe to be right and wrong. Through their actions, they demonstrate to their employees what is and is not acceptable behavior and shape the moral standard of the organization. **Ethics** is a set of moral standards for judging whether something is right or wrong. As you will see in this chapter, personal and professional ethics are important cornerstones of an organization and shape its ultimate contributions to society. First, let's consider how individual business ethics are formed.

Individual Business Ethics

TRENDS IN BUSINESS

explores the fundamental factors and emerging trends that are reshaping today's business world and altering tomorrow's competitive environment. This preview of the future gives students a keen advantage when entering the workplace.

i T P

Trends in Human Resource Management

9 learning goal

Protecting whistleblowers, the growth of minority recruiting, proactive management of diversity, advancing technology, and global competition are driving the trends in human resource management in the 21st century.

Protecting Whistleblowers

An employee "blows the whistle" when he or she discloses some wrongdoing and/or illegal behavior or practice committed by another person in the firm. Some companies have an "ethics" hotline that can be used to make this disclosure, or someone can report misconduct to legal authorities, or even the news media. If the reported wrongdoing is investigated and corrective action taken, the whistleblower has benefited the organization. On the other hand, the whistleblower could suffer if a higher authority in the organization retaliates against the whistleblower for reporting the improper behavior.

In recent years whistleblowers, such as Sherron Watkins at Enron and Cynthia ... Worldcom, have received national attention for their reports of ill...

GREAT IDEAS TO USE NOW

brings chapter topics to life with relevant and interesting tips for making the most of a professional career or becoming a smart consumer. Students develop skills that are applicable immediately.

P T i — Great Ideas to Use Now

Great Ideas to Use Now

In many situations, there are no right or wrong answers. Instead, organizations must provide a process to resolve the dilemma quickly and fairly. Two approaches for resolving ethical problems are the "three-questions test" and the newspaper test.

... Problems in Business

New!

And even better than before.

The Future of Business, 5e **RETAINS ITS HALLMARK COMPREHENSIVE COVERAGE OF THE TOPICS FUNDAMENTAL TO AN INTRODUCTORY BUSINESS COURSE WHILE KEEPING PACE WITH NEW BUSINESS INITIATIVES, BREAKTHROUGHS IN TECHNOLOGY, AND ECONOMIC CYCLES.**

CUSTOMER SATISFACTION AND QUALITY

Because satisfied customers who experience quality products and services become the loyal customers that are the foundation of success in all business endeavors, customer satisfaction and quality are addressed in every chapter of the text. A new boxed feature further demonstrates how these concepts are applied in actual companies.

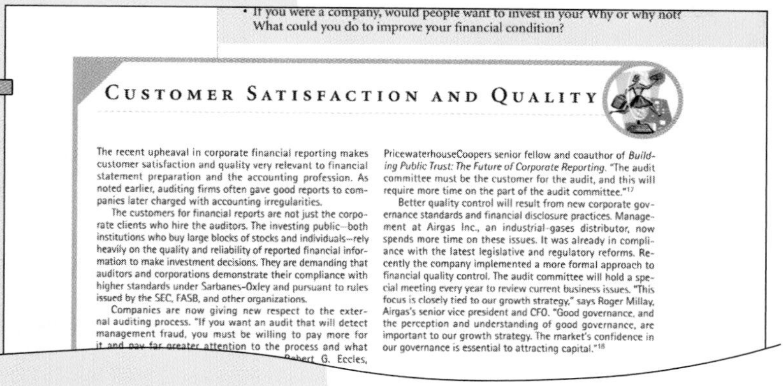
• If you were a company, would people want to invest in you? Why or why not? What could you do to improve your financial condition?

CUSTOMER SATISFACTION AND QUALITY

The recent upheaval in corporate financial reporting makes customer satisfaction and quality very relevant to financial statement preparation and the accounting profession. As noted earlier, auditing firms often gave good reports to companies later charged with accounting irregularities.

The customers for financial reports are not just the corporate clients who hire the auditors. The investing public—both institutions who buy large blocks of stocks and individuals—rely heavily on the quality and reliability of reported financial information to make investment decisions. They are demanding that auditors and corporations demonstrate their compliance with higher standards under Sarbanes-Oxley and pursuant to rules issued by the SEC, FASB, and other organizations.

Companies are now giving new respect to the external auditing process. "If you want an audit that will detect management fraud, you must be willing to pay more for it and pay far greater attention to the process and what ... Robert G. Eccles, PricewaterhouseCoopers senior fellow and coauthor of *Building Public Trust: The Future of Corporate Reporting.* "The audit committee must be the customer for the audit, and this will require more time on the part of the audit committee."[17]

Better quality control will result from new corporate governance standards and financial disclosure practices. Management at Airgas Inc., an industrial-gases distributor, now spends more time on these issues. It was already in compliance with the latest legislative and regulatory reforms. Recently the company implemented a more formal approach to financial quality control. The audit committee will hold a special meeting every year to review current business issues. "This focus is closely tied to our growth strategy," says Roger Millay, Airgas's senior vice president and CFO. "Good governance, and the perception and understanding of good governance, are important to our growth strategy. The market's confidence in our governance is essential to attracting capital."[18]

ETHICS

The scandals that have rocked the business world in recent years have touched off a wave of reform and renewed emphasis on ethical business behavior. *The Future of Business, 5e* has an entire chapter devoted to business ethics and social responsibility. Interactive ethics activities in each chapter are included on Xtra!.

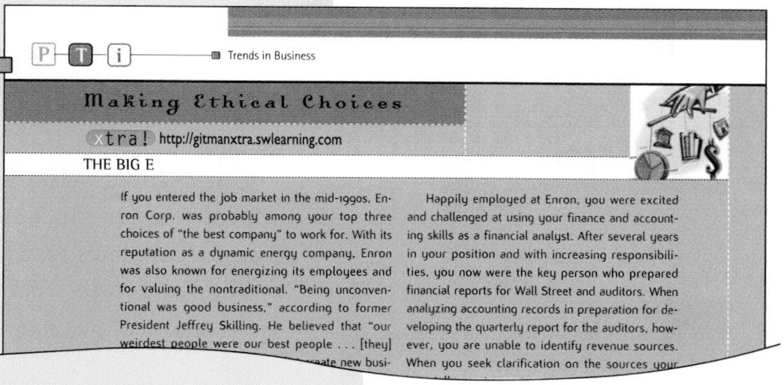
P T i Trends in Business

Making Ethical Choices

Xtra! http://gitmanxtra.swlearning.com

THE BIG E

If you entered the job market in the mid-1990s, Enron Corp. was probably among your top three choices of "the best company" to work for. With its reputation as a dynamic energy company, Enron was also known for energizing its employees and for valuing the nontraditional. "Being unconventional was good business," according to former President Jeffrey Skilling. He believed that "our weirdest people were our best people . . . [they] ... create new busi-

Happily employed at Enron, you were excited and challenged at using your finance and accounting skills as a financial analyst. After several years in your position and with increasing responsibilities, you now were the key person who prepared financial reports for Wall Street and auditors. When analyzing accounting records in preparation for developing the quarterly report for the auditors, however, you are unable to identify revenue sources. When you seek clarification on the sources your

ENTREPRENEURSHIP AND SMALL BUSINESS MANAGEMENT

Small businesses have had a large impact on today's economy and job market. Because many students will open their own businesses or go to work for small organizations, the text discusses entrepreneurship and small business principles in depth. In addition to an expanded chapter on starting and managing a small business, features throughout the text offer practical insight into the challenges and rewards of entrepreneurship, and real-world tips for success.

i T P

FOCUSING ON SMALL BUSINESS

Finding the Sweet Spot

From Wall Street to Candy Land may seem like an unusual career path, but former securities broker turned entrepreneur Jeff Rubin loves his sweet new life. He and partner Dylan Lauren took an ordinary idea and transformed it into a unique retailing concept.

Candy-themed décor and background music greet 8,000 customers a day at Dylan's Candy Bar in New York City. Shoppers browse their way through 5,000 varieties of candy and candy-themed products, many exclusive to Dylan's. The price range is equally large; you'll find Pez dispensers for $1.99 or $5,000 (for rare collectibles), $200 white-chocolate carousels, and $10,000 candy artwork. You can eat at the café or rent the party room, where kids and adults enjoy candy-themed games and crafts. On a diet? The store will tempt you with candy-shaped jewelry ... spa products, as well as a ... the Dylan's

the advice of Lauren senior, the pair used their respective talents to create a unique brand and identity. Rubin's candy business connections were invaluable in finding exclusive products, while Lauren focused on creating the right environment to showcase them. "M&Ms/Mars created 16 colors of Skittles only available at Dylan's Candy Bar," says Rubin. He also convinced other vendors to join the Dylan's team. Hershey produces 10 special Hershey Kisses just for Dylan's, and Double Bubble makes bubble gum bath products.

The store was an instant success from the moment it opened in October 2001. With sales pushing the $5 million level in 2002, Rubin and Lauren were ready to take the candy bar concept to Los Angeles, San Francisco, and Chicago and open smaller stores in other locations.

CRITICAL THINKING QUESTIONS

1. Are Rubin and Lauren entrepreneurs or small-business owners? Explain your answer.

TECHNOLOGY. YES.

THE BOOK IS JUST THE BEGINNING. ***THE FUTURE OF BUSINESS, 5E,*** **IS FULLY SUPPORTED WITH COMPLIMENTARY TEACHING AND LEARNING RESOURCES THAT GET BOTH INSTRUCTORS AND STUDENTS OFF THE PAGE AND INTO THE FUTURE.**

FOR instructors

Enhance classroom instruction with Web resources, expand learning opportunities, create an online course, or extend the boundaries of the classroom with new ways to teach, learn, conduct research, and build skills. Innovative technology lets you take learning to the next level.

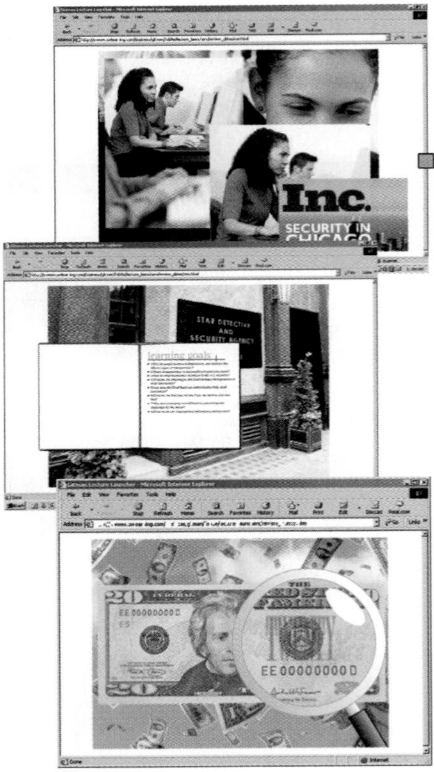

NEW! Lecture Launcher with Flash clips. Designed to capture and focus the students' attention in the critical first few minutes of class, Lecture Launchers are quick and dynamic presentations that open each PowerPoint demonstration.

Complete Video Package and Video Guide Created to enrich and support chapter concepts, these 22 professionally-produced videos present actual business issues faced by a variety of service and manufacturing organizations. The video cases challenge students to study business topics and develop solutions to real business problems.

PowerPoint Lecture System This completely redesigned PowerPoint lecture system now includes Web links, instructor teaching notes, and thorough coverage of key concepts and terminology.

The Future of Business* Web Site (http://gitman.swlearning.com)** Developed to support your course objectives, the text Web site is a rich source of downloadable supplements. Plus ***"Intro to Business News" provides a continuously refreshed supply of current event features, organized by chapter.

WebTUTOR™ Advantage

WebTutor Advantage Available for WebCT and Blackboard, WebTutor harnesses the power of the Internet to deliver innovative learning aids that actively engage students, improve comprehension of complex concepts, and reinforce learning, with content customized for *The Future of Business, 5e.*

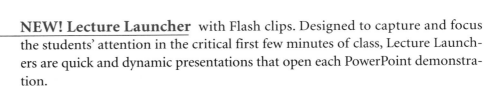

FOR

students

Develop familiarity with the technology and skills that will play an important part in your future success through interactive online resources that inform, educate, and entertain.

Xtra! The interactive materials in this Web-based learning environment get students involved in the course topics, deepen their interest, and even improve course grades.

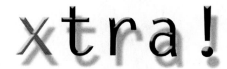

- Every chapter includes a "Making Ethical Choices" activity that provides a one-of-a-kind interactive learning experience. Students play the role of an employee of a well-recognized company, responding to a series of prompts to make choices on the best, most ethical course of action. Once they choose a strategy, students immediately learn the consequences of their actions and are given additional opportunities to learn from their experience.

- *Xtra! Quizzing* lets students self-test their knowledge as they prepare for midterms and final exams. Each question includes feedback for right and wrong answers plus textbook page references to encourage review and further study.

- And much more.

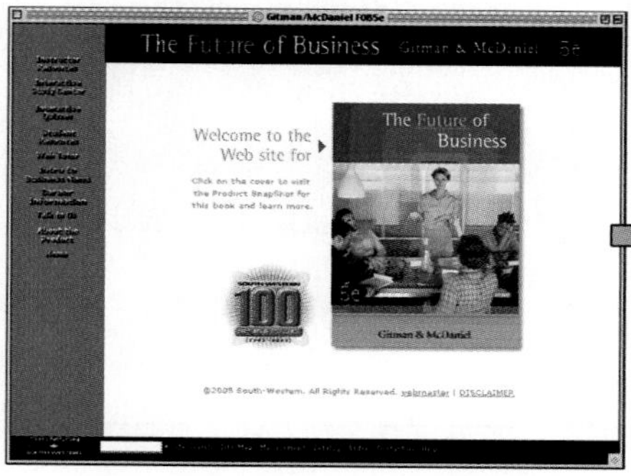

***The Future of Business* Student Web Site (http://gitman.swlearning.com)** Developed to maximize student success in the course and build online skills, the student portion of the text's Web site includes quizzes for each chapter, more than 80 Internet exercises, links to related Web sites, hundreds of PowerPoint slides that overview the important concepts and principles of each chapter, crossword puzzles of key business terms that make learning business vocabulary fun, and more. The Web site also offers extensive support resources for students seeking career information, with links to helpful sites.

InfoTrac With the College Edition of InfoTrac, students get complete, 24 hour-a-day access to full-text articles from hundreds of scholarly journals and popular periodicals such as *Newsweek, Time,* and *USA Today.*

GET IT TOGETHER.

The Future of Business, 5e features a unique **Integrated Learning System** that

anchors chapter concepts — provides a framework for study — links all of the instructor and student supplements, including the instructor's manual, test bank, and PowerPoint

The Integrated Learning System is also used throughout the supplements. Each piece of the Integrated Learning System reinforces the other components to help students learn quickly and study efficiently and to facilitate lecture preparation for instructors.

Learning goals at the beginning of each chapter outline the key concepts in the chapter.

learning goals

1 Why do people become entrepreneurs, and what are the different types of entrepreneurs?
2 Which characteristics do successful entrepreneurs share?
3 How do small businesses contribute to the U.S. economy?
4 What are the advantages and disadvantages facing owners of small businesses?
5 How does the Small Business Administration help small businesses?
6 What are the first steps to take if you are starting your own business?
7 Why does managing a small business present special challenges for the owner?
8 What trends are shaping entrepreneurship and small-business ownership?

Entrepreneurship Today

1 learning goal

From experiments with cardboard and tape, 20-something Mike Pratt pieced together a company that today has revenues of about $50 million. Frustrated with trying to cram his gym bag into a too-small locker, he went home and built a model of his ideal duffel bag. It fit into standard fitness-club lockers and kept all his supplies easily accessible in its rigid-framed interior. Retailers considered The Original Locker Bag too cumbersome. Customers, however, loved the bag that carried like a duffel and worked like a locker. In one weekend, they snapped up the 50 bags that Pratt convinced Foot Locker to take on consignment, and soon Pratt's bags were featured at elite stores like Nordstrom.

Not content to limit OGIO International's fortunes to one bag, Pratt and his employees "geared up" to produce duffels and backpacks with patented design features. His next breakthrough product was the Rig, a protective golf bag designed to

182| Part 2 Business Ownership

Major headings within the chapter are identified by learning goal icons and supported with concept checks that allow students to self-check their knowledge.

The chapter summary capsulizes key concepts to provide easy review of the chapter's content.

Summary of Learning Goals

1 **Why do people become entrepreneurs, and what are the different types of entrepreneurs?**

Entrepreneurship involves taking the risk of starting and managing a business to make a profit. Entrepreneurs are innovators who start firms either to have a certain lifestyle or to develop a company that will grow into a major corporation. People become entrepreneurs for four main reasons: the opportunity for profit, independence, personal satisfaction, and lifestyle. Classic entrepreneurs may be micropreneurs, who plan to keep their businesses small, or growth-oriented entrepreneurs. Multipreneurs start multiple companies, while intrapreneurs work within large corporations.

2 **Which characteristics do successful entrepreneurs share?**

Successful entrepreneurs are ambitious, independent, self-confident, creative, energetic, passionate, and committed. They have a high need for achievement and a ... moderate risks. They have good interpersonal and ...

Help. HERE

The Future of Business, 5e IS ALSO SUPPORTED BY A FULL RANGE OF SUPPLEMENTAL MATERIALS IN A VARIETY OF MEDIA.

FOR instructors

- **Comprehensive Instructor's Manual with Transparency Masters** follows the integrated learning system and includes full lecture enhancement and support, a comprehensive video guide, a guide to teaching a distance learning course, and a complete set of transparency masters to create overhead acetates.
- **PowerPoint Lecture System** illustrates key chapter concepts.
- **Lecture Launchers** dynamically introduce chapter topics to stimulate student interest.
- **Instructor's Resource CD** includes the instructor's manual, Lecture Launchers, PowerPoint slides, test bank, and the ExamView Testing System.
- **Color Acetate Transparencies** feature key concepts and exhibits from the text.
- **ExamView Testing Systems** create, deliver, and customize print and online tests in minutes.
- **Test Bank**, available in print and in new Windows software formats, provides over 2,000 true/false, multiple-choice, fill-in-the-blank, and short-answer questions, organized by learning goals.
- **Instructor Web site** offers a wealth of resources and links.
- **Video Package and Guide** reinforces chapter concepts and challenges students to develop problem-solving skills.
- **WebTutor Advantage** combines online learning aids with customized content.
- **WebTutor Toolbox** provides an online course management tool.

FOR students

- **Student Study Guide**, designed to reflect the integrated learning system, tests student comprehension of concepts through the use of multiple-choice questions and matching exercises, plus offers a vocabulary builder that reinforces the specialized terms used within the text.
- **Xtra!** provides an interactive Web-based learning environment that gets students directly involved in course topics and improves comprehension.
- **InfoTrac** gives 24 hour-a-day access to full-text articles from academic journals and popular periodicals.
- **Student Web site** includes quizzes and exercises, crossword puzzles and other vocabularly builders, career information, and links to other useful sites.

Big Finish.

Reflection and review are critical elements of the learning process — so Gitman and McDaniel consider the study materials at the end of a chapter as important as the chapter content itself. *The Future of Business, 5e* offers particularly robust end-of-chapter activities and exercises that not only reinforce learning, but also address SCANS competencies. Below are just some of the materials to help students develop real skills that they can carry out of the classroom and into their future careers.

PREPARING FOR TOMORROW'S WORKPLACE

These highly practical exercises develop real-world business skills that will give students a meaningful advantage over fellow graduates in the workplace.

Preparing for Tomorrow's Workplace

1. Bridget Jones wants to open her own business selling her handmade chocolates over the Internet. Although she has some money saved and could start the business on her own, she is concerned about her lack of bookkeeping and management experience. A friend mentions he knows an experienced businessman seeking involvement with a start-up company. As Bridget's business consultant, prepare recommendations for Bridget regarding an appropriate form of business organization, including outlining the issues she should consider and the risks involved, supported by reasons for your suggestions.
2. You and a partner co-own Swim-Clean, a successful pool supply and cleaning service. Because sales have tapered off, you want to expand your operations to another town 10 miles away. Given the high costs of expanding, you decide to sell Swim-Clean franchises. The idea takes off and soon you have 25 units throughout the region. Your success results in an invitation to speak at a local Rotary Club luncheon. Prepare a brief presentation describing how you evaluated the benefits and risks of becoming a franchisor, the problems you have ... and how you've established good working relationships with ...

TEAM ACTIVITIES

These exercises teach students to work collaboratively, helping them build communication and interpersonal skills. Team Activities are included in the *Preparing for Tomorrow's Workplace* and identified by a team icon.

VIDEO CASES

Video cases in each chapter feature a variety of interesting businesses and describe their strategies for growing, managing, and achieving customer satisfaction. Over half of the video cases are new in this edition.

E-COMMERCE CASES

Gitman and McDaniel include an inside look at 22 different organizations that use state-of-the-art information technology to launch online business ventures. In these e-commerce cases, students explore the business strategies of various companies and then analyze business decisions and prepare open-response comments.

E-Commerce Case

Geekcorps: Spreading the (IT) Gospel

A Peace Corps for techies? Ethan Zuckerman had a mission—to bring the technology revolution to developing countries such as Rwanda, Mongolia, Lebanon, Bulgaria, and Ghana, via techno-savvy volunteers. Zuckerman, a 1993 graduate of Williams College, became an instant millionaire in 1999 when Lycos bought the online company where he served as vice president of research and development. A self-confessed Net head, he wanted to do something he believed was important.

Geekcorps (**http://www.geekcorps.com**) was started in February 2000 with $100,000 of Zuckerman's own money. Seven months later, its first team of volunteers were at work in Accra, Ghana, where Zuckerman had spent time on a Fulbright fellowship. Geekcorps now delves into a database of 1,100 volunteers from 11 different countries to select teams of seven or eight rigorously screened volunteers, who are given four months to prepare for their stint abroad. Geekcorps pays for travel and provides lodging and a small stipend. On sabbatical from their jobs ... of one to four months, volunteers are trained to teach their skills to ...

CRITICAL THINKING ACTIVITIES

Designed to amplify and reinforce concepts presented in the chapter and to challenge students to think in-depth about chapter concepts, these exercises generate lively class discussion while developing the students' analytical and critical thinking skills.

But it's just the beginning ...

preface

Business in the 21st Century

The Future of Business, Fifth Edition, provides a personal roadmap for understanding and navigating the future of business. The Fifth Edition builds on the tremendous success of prior editions with thorough coverage of business principles and leading-edge practices adopted by business innovators, all illustrated with relevant and interesting business examples. Because the future of business is approaching us at warp speed, the Fifth Edition has been written with the goal of making you the winner in tomorrow's fast-paced marketplace. Each chapter will help you understand what is happening and what will happen in the sometimes chaotic and always exciting world of business.

If you ask successful business people what enables an organization to achieve its goals, you will inevitably receive a variety of opinions. Yet aside from "following sound accounting principles" and "having high ethical standards," two other criteria are always mentioned. These two fundamental concepts include "satisfying the customer" and "delivering quality products and services." Therefore, *customer satisfaction* and *quality* represent important themes in the Fifth Edition. However, this philosophy of satisfying customers and delivering quality products has been the guiding principle of this textbook in past editions and continues to be the mantra we embrace for this new edition. You have helped us define customer satisfaction and quality for an introduction to business textbook, and we have responded with new content and innovative features for this Fifth Edition. Thank you for your guidance and for the tremendous success of this textbook. We believe we have continued to make great strides with the Fifth Edition in preparing you for futures in business.

WHAT'S NEW IN THE FIFTH EDITION?

Keeping pace with new business initiatives, breakthroughs in technology, and the economic cycles requires careful monitoring of the business landscape. The process of sorting through these developments and determining which to include in this new edition was guided by instructor and student feedback. The result is a carefully and thoroughly updated Fifth Edition that covers the most important principles of business, preparing you for success in business today and tomorrow. Highlights of new content to the Fifth Edition include the following:

- A new prologue in the Fifth Edition, *Fast Forward to the Future: Strategies for Success in School and Business,* offers practical and inspiring advice for developing test-taking, interpersonal, time management, and planning skills. The prologue also features suggestions for finding the right career and succeeding in that first professional job.
- New content in Chapter 1 (Participating in the Dynamic Business Environment) includes workplace diversity and the aging population in the United States. This chapter also describes how advances in technology and communications are allowing more companies to enter the global arena.
- Chapter 3 (Making Ethical Decisions and Managing a Socially Responsible Business) takes a close look at recent developments in business ethics, with special sections on ethics on the Internet, training programs for employees, recent corporate scandals, and corporate giving.

- Chapter 4 (Competing in the Global Marketplace) provides new coverage of the impact of terrorism on global trade and the growth of the European Community. This chapter also presents new coverage on the fears of trade and globalization while recognizing the benefits of a global marketplace. It also explores how the Internet has opened up global business opportunities and simplified access to the global marketplace.
- Chapter 5 (Forms of Business Ownership) includes new coverage of women and minorites as franchise owners. It also addresses strategies that franchisors use to differentiate themselves as more franchise systems crowd into growing industry categories.
- Chapter 6 (Entrepreneurship: Starting and Managing Your Own Business) takes a new look at how small businesses make major contributions to the U.S. economy and the reasons behind their successes. Fascinating examples illustrate how small businesses showed resiliency after September 11 and the economic slump that followed. The Trends section of this chapter spotlights hot spots for entrepreneurial activity, the increasing role of women and minorities as entrepreneurs, and the affect of the Internet on small businesses.
- Chapter 7 (Management and Leadership in Today's Organization) reflects the impact of environmental influences on business by highlighting the skills required to manage a multinational culture and also managing during a crisis. A new section on stress management offers practical tips for managers.
- Chapter 8 (Designing Organizational Structures) reveals how technology is enabling corporations to create virtual work teams. This chapter also addresses committee, matrix, and global structures. It also includes the controversial issues surrounding executive compensation.
- Chapter 9 (Managing Human Resources) spotlights the importance of managing diversity within the firm—creating a multicultural organization with a culture that values diversity. This chapter recognizes that diversity can be a competitive advantage and identifies the companies that are best at managing diversity. This chapter also offers expanded coverage of the Equal Employment Opportunity Commission, the role of affirmative action officers, and the protection of whistleblowers who disclose wrongdoing within the firm. In addition, the chapter addresses the growth of minority recruiting and the trend toward proactive management of diversity.
- Chapter 10 (Motivating Employees and Creating Self-Managed Teams) includes a fresh perspective on Maslow's theory of motivation and new discussion of Theory Z. This chapter recognizes the role of culture on motivation and nurturing knowledge workers. Recognizing the problem of absenteeism in business today, the chapter addresses HR strategies to minimize this escalating problem.
- Chapter 12 (Achieving World-Class Operations Management) takes you behind the scenes of operations management. In this chapter, you learn how e-procurement is improving communications with suppliers and strengthening the effectiveness of the supply chain. This chapter also covers reverse auctions, electronic data interchange (EDI), new coverage of value-stream mapping, and expanded coverage of quality control, including the Six Sigma quality program and Malcolm Baldrige National Quality Award.
- A thoroughly updated Chapter 13 (Understanding Customers and Creating Marketing Strategy) includes comprehensive coverage of buyer behavior with a full review of the consumer decision-making process. New coverage includes the cultural, social, individual, and psychological factors that impact buyer behavior from the time a person recognizes a need through post-purchase behavior. This chapter includes new coverage of the types of consumer buying

decisions, more on innovative techniques for collecting customer information (scanner-based research and loyalty cards), and one-to-one marketing.

- Chapter 14 (Developing and Pricing Quality Products and Services) features new coverage on brand loyalty, global labeling, and the Internet's role in speeding new product development. This chapter also addresses yield management systems used to adjust prices and the use of color in creating brand imagery, conveying moods, and responding to ethnic differences.
- Chapter 15 (Distributing Products in a Timely and Efficient Manner) addresses the use of category management by the nation's retailers to improve sales.
- Chapter 16 (Using Integrated Marketing Communications to Promote Products) recognizes the explosive growth of Web advertising and technology in promotion. It also addresses the increased use of global labeling, comparative advertising, the use of technology in promotion, and guerilla marketing.
- Chapter 17 (Using Technology to Manage Information) provides a thoroughly up-to-date coverage of today's management information systems, virtual private networks, knowledge management, enterprise portals, and unified communications.
- In Chapter 18 (Using Financial Information and Accounting), you gain a basic understanding of accounting principles but also study the latest issues in the accounting profession including the recently passed Sarbanes-Oxley Act, designed to address the investing public's lack of trust in corporate America and make public accounting firms subject to formal regulation for the first time. This chapter emphasizes the importance of corporate governance and internal controls.
- Chapter 19 (Understanding Money and Financial Institutions) highlights the changes in the structure of the financial services industry and the growth of the mega-bank.
- Chapter 20 (Managing the Firm's Finances) includes new coverage of the role of technology in improving the efficiency in which financial managers run their operations. It addresses the central role of CFOs in re-establishing public trust. In the chapter appendix, risk management is introduced as a new initiative to manage risk exposure during times of economic or global turmoil.
- Chapter 21 (Understanding Securities and Securities Markets) spotlights the reform of the SEC, both in how it operates and its regulatory activities. It features the new Regulation FD (Fair Disclosure) requiring public companies to share information with all investors at the same time.
- Chapter 22 (Managing Your Personal Finances) gives new advice on protection from identity fraud and avoiding the Gen-X debt trap.

THE INTERACTIVE PERSPECTIVE: MAJOR BUSINESS TOPICS UP CLOSE

Today's most important business topics and trends are thoroughly covered in the Fifth Edition—this means more insight into the key economic and business developments that shape the future. Topics at the forefront of business covered in this edition include:

- Customer satisfaction and quality
- Relationship management
- Changing U.S. population
- Impact of terrorism on business

- Corporate ethics scandals
- Enlargement of the European Union
- Managing multinational cultures in the workplace
- Crisis management
- Virtual teams and corporations
- Protecting whistleblowers
- Nurturing knowledge workers
- Global management skills
- Executive compensation
- Concession bargaining
- Internet marketing research
- E-retailing
- Category management
- Database marketing
- Growth in Web advertising
- Guerrilla marketing
- One-to-one marketing
- E-procurement
- GE's Six Sigma Quality
- Reform in the SEC

Through extensive reviews and focus groups, we discovered that instructors teaching the introduction to business course place considerable importance on these business topics: ethics, customer satisfaction and quality, the role of technology in business, e-commerce, entrepreneurship and small business management, global business opportunities, and careers. Therefore, we gave these topics special emphasis.

Ethics

The business world has been rocked in the past few years by ethics scandals that led to bankruptcies for major organizations and jail terms for top executives. Well-publicized scandals have touched off a wave of reform and renewed emphasis on ethical business behavior. A paramount theme of this text is that business must be conducted in an ethical and socially responsible manner.

Chapter 3 (Making Ethical Decisions and Managing a Socially Responsible Business) is completely devoted to business ethics and social responsibility. We discuss techniques for setting personal ethical standards, how managers influence organizational ethics, tools for creating employee ethical awareness, and the concept of social responsibility. The Fifth Edition also offers a brand new approach to the process of evaluating ethical dilemmas. Interactive features, called "Making Ethical Choices," allow you to evaluate actual business dilemmas, select an ethically-sound response, and see the consequences of your choices. Although it's hard to teach morality, these short, interesting, and controversial ethical dilemmas will generate class debate and point out behaviors that cross the line. The interactive component of these activities is available with Xtra! at **http://gitmanxtra.swlearning.com**

Customer Satisfaction and Quality

We believe that delivering superior customer value, satisfaction, and quality are essential to attracting and keeping customers. Because customer satisfaction and quality are the foundation of all business principles, we have addressed these important topics in every chapter. Each chapter concludes by stressing that satisfied customers who experience quality products and services become loyal customers. Summarized in a new feature called "Customer Satisfaction and Quality," we demonstrate how these concepts are applied in actual companies.

Technology and E-Commerce

Technology not only touches all areas of business; it often revolutionizes it. Each chapter addresses how businesses are applying technology to improve processes and maximize value to the customer. In addition, Online Chapter 23 (Using the Internet for Business Success) looks at the impact of the Internet on business operations and describes the growth of e-commerce in both consumer and business-to-business markets. This chapter also explores the process for launching an e-business and looks ahead to the future of the Internet in business. No other introduction to business textbook offers such comprehensive coverage of the profound impact of the Internet on business. This chapter is located at the companion Web site at **http://gitman.swlearning.com** so that we can keep this timely topic continuously updated.

The "Applying Technology" feature provides detailed examples of how businesses are using technology to gain a competitive advantage. For example, the Applying Technology box in Chapter 12 (Achieving World-Class Operations Management) describes how fast-food chains like McDonald's, Arby's, and Burger King are hoping technology can put the "fast" back into fast food by automating many of the processes used in taking and preparing food orders.

Entrepreneurship and Small Business Management

Because many of you will either open your own businesses or go to work for small organizations, entrepreneurship and small business principles are presented throughout the text. Chapter 6 (Entrepreneurship: Starting and Managing Your Own Business) delivers insightful discussions on issues related to starting and managing a small business including the advantages and disadvantages of small business ownership.

In addition, each chapter contains a feature called "Focusing on Small Business" that offers practical insights into the challenges and rewards of actually owning and managing a small business. In Chapter 5 (Forms of Business Ownership), for example, you learn how an S corporation was the ideal form of organization for Michelle Hebert who launched a popcorn chain that offers a kaleidoscope of colors and 20 different flavors. In Chapter 6, the "Focusing on Small Business" feature explains how a former securities broker took an ordinary idea and transformed it into a unique retailing concept by opening Dylan's Candy Bar in New York City.

Global Business Economy

Chapter 4 (Competing in the Global Marketplace) offers a complete and exciting picture of competition in the global marketplace. We discuss why global trade is important to the United States, why nations trade, barriers to international trade, how companies enter the global marketplace, and a host of other international concepts and topics.

You will also find coverage of global issues throughout the text. The Trends section of each chapter frequently includes a discussion of how globalization will affect specific business activities. For example, the Trends section in Chapter 13 (Understanding Customers and Creating Marketing Strategy) examines the unique problems faced by human resource managers as more and more companies "go global." In addition, a new global business box demonstrates how businesses are expanding their workforce, products, and customer base throughout the world in order to grow. In chapter 9 (Managing Human Resources), The "Expanding Around the Globe" feature describes the human resource challenge of assigning expatriates to overseas assignments.

Careers in Business

The Future of Business, Fifth Edition is a rich source of career guidance for you. Any businessperson knows that the only thing certain about the business environment is that it always changes. With this in mind, Chapter 1 (Participating in the Dynamic Business Environment) describes the business trends altering the business landscape. The value for you is not only learning what trends influence business, but how these trends will influence business and careers within it. The Fifth Edition features this valuable career information:

- **The Prologue.** A new prologue, *Fast Forward to the Future: Strategies for Success in School and Business,* explores the interpersonal, time management, and planning skills every student needs for success in school. In the prologue, we also offer career advice and recommendations for finding and landing that first professional job. The prologue addresses how to use the Internet to jump-start a job search, prepare a cyber résumé, and research potential employers. In addition, the prologue shows you how to discover economic, demographic, and climatic information about cities in which they might work. We close the prologue with tips on interviewing and winning that first promotion.
- **Career Appendices for Each Part.** At the end of Parts 2 through 6, you can explore the career opportunities in small businesses, management, marketing, technology and information, and finance. These appendices describe the different types of employment available, positions in demand, skills required, salary expectations, and employment outlook through the next several years.
- **Integrated Career Guidance.** Career information is often the emphasis in the third section of each chapter, called Great Ideas to Use Now. For example, in Chapter 4 (Competing in the Global Marketplace), you are given insights into the importance of developing global management skills. Try It Now! boxes also emphasize career development. For instance, Try It Now! in Chapter 11 (Understanding Labor–Management Relations) explains how to negotiate for compensation and benefits. Try It Now! in Chapter 17 (Using Technology to Manage Information) tells you how to stay tuned to the latest information technology developments to enhance employment opportunities. The Hot Links Address Book, included at the end of every chapter, also provides extensive Web resources for those of you beginning a job search.

AN INNOVATIVE THREE-PART CHAPTER STRUCTURE

P T i

The new shape, pace and spirit of the global economy require new ways of looking at business and careers. We've organized every chapter of *The Future of Business,* Fifth Edition with a unique chapter structure to support three essential themes:

P **PRINCIPLES OF BUSINESS.** Each chapter delivers a comprehensive overview of current business principles and practices. You will learn what is happening in today's businesses with examples from the largest global corporate giants, such as Ford and Airbus Industries, to the smallest family start-ups.

T **TRENDS IN BUSINESS.** The second part of each chapter explores new business trends and how they are reshaping today's business and altering tomorrow's competitive environment. Technology and the global economy are covered extensively in every Trends section. We expose you to the fundamental factors that are reshaping the business world in which they will soon begin professional careers. With this preview of the future, you gain a keen advantage when entering the workplace.

i **GREAT IDEAS TO USE NOW.** This unique feature, found only in *The Future of Business,* Fifth Edition, brings the chapter topics to life with relevant and interesting tips for making the most of a professional career or becoming a smart consumer. You can utilize these suggestions throughout their careers; many are applicable immediately after reading the chapter. In Chapter 5 (Forms of Business Ownership), you can explore your readiness for starting a franchise or learn how to protect your job during a merger.

A UNIQUE STUDENT-ORIENTED PEDAGOGY

The Future of Business, Fifth Edition, is designed to engage you and arouse interest in all facets of business. Delivered in a precise, crisp writing style, each chapter includes many applications to strengthen your understanding and involve them in actual business practices.

Integrated Learning System

To anchor chapter concepts, provide a framework for study, and link all of the instructor and student supplements, the Integrated Learning System helps you learn quickly and study efficiently. It also helps ease lecture preparation. Learning goals at the beginning of each chapter outline the key concepts in the chapter and provide structure for lesson plans and help exam preparation. Major headings within the chapter are identified by icons and supported with concept checks and a chapter summary. Every supplement is also organized by learning goal to ensure that each piece of the Integrated Learning System reinforces the other components. For example, you can easily check your grasp of each learning goal by reading the text sections, reviewing the corresponding summary section, answering the Study Guide questions for the objective, and returning to the appropriate text sections for further review if necessary. You can quickly identify all material relating to an objective by simply looking for the learning goal icon.

Student-Friendly Approach

To make the content more inviting and appealing, the writing style is friendly and conversational. Instead of formal language that can often be stilted, chapter titles, headings, and chapter text are written in a relaxed, inviting manner. Ample photographs and ads aid visual learners, and captions reinforce major points of the chapters.

Hundreds of Actual Business Applications Hold Student Interest and Clarify Concepts

We focused this book on the needs, abilities, and experience of the typical student. We drew on our experiences inside and outside the classroom to create the most readable and enjoyable introduction to business textbook. We believe that the actual business applications that are interspersed throughout the chapters set the standard for readability and lucid explanation of key concepts.

Opening Vignettes that Connect

Many texts use short stories to open the chapters, but fail to make connections to these stories elsewhere in the chapters. We take a different approach. We begin each chapter with a vignette about a prominent, easily recognized company that previews that chapter's content. We then provide several questions to prompt critical thinking about the chapter. At the end of the chapter, we provide an update on the company featured in the opening vignette and offer suggestions on how it may have to adapt to meet emerging trends.

Videos Cases Introduce Actual Businesses to the Classroom

Developed by business instructors, in conjunction with a professional video studio, 22 video segments and video cases reinforce chapter concepts. These video segments feature companies such as ESPN, The Geek Squad, SAS, IBM, Polaroid, Fisher-Price, and more.

Tools for Mastering Business Vocabulary

Every key business term is carefully defined within the text. Terms are in bold type throughout the chapter to make them easier to identify. Terms are also defined in the margin where first introduced. We also include a complete glossary of all key terms at the end of the book. We deliver extra value by featuring two online quizzes for each chapter that test your comprehension of chapter terminology along with customized feedback to guide you in strengthening your business vocabulary.

Skill-Building for the Interactive Workplace

Instructors consistently tell us that one of their course goals is to strengthen research, communication, business writing, Web, and teamwork skills. In addition, some markets require that their textbook address SCANS competencies. *The Future of Business* continues to offer a variety of activities that help you develop those skills identified by SCANS. The SCANS skills include resource skills (allocating time, money, etc.), interpersonal skills (teamwork, negotiating), information ability (acquiring and evaluating data, using computers), systems understanding (operating within an organizational or social system), and technology ability (selecting equipment, tools, and applying technology to specific tasks). To aid in the development of skills, *The Future of Business,* Fifth Edition, integrates the following features in each chapter:

1. Preparing for Tomorrow's Workplace and Team Activities. These activities are designed to help you build your business skills and practice working in teams. These highly practical exercises give you a meaningful advantage over fellow graduates in the workplace. New Team activities in every chapter give you an opportunity to work with other students, building communication skills and interpersonal skills.
2. Working the Net Activities. These guide you through a step-by-step analysis of actual e-business practices and give you opportunities to build online skills.
3. Critical Thinking Activities. Each boxed feature has two purposes—to amplify and reinforce concepts presented in the chapter and to challenge you to think

in-depth about chapter concepts. Critical thinking questions can be used to generate class discussion or prompt further analysis.

4. Try It Now! This feature will help you apply the chapter topics and become better employees or consumers and also help you develop business/life skills described in the prologue.
5. Cases. Critical Thinking Cases, Video Cases, and E-Commerce cases invite you to explore business strategies of various companies, analyze business decisions, and prepare open-response comments. Because leading-edge companies are quickly embracing e-commerce as an avenue for future growth and profitability, *The Future of Business,* Fifth Edition, takes a peak inside 22 different organizations that use state-of-the-art information technology to launch online business ventures.
6. Hot Links Address Book. These activities, found at the end of every chapter, take you to the Web sites of well-known companies and show you how to find the Web's most reliable and valuable business resources. These Hot Links demonstrate actual e-commerce practices and policies, covering issues as diverse as online security, new distribution systems, mass customization and more.

A NETWORK OF GREAT RESOURCES TO MEET A VARIETY OF TEACHING NEEDS

Business success is stimulated by access to and mastery of vital resources. The same is true for the classroom. Whether teaching an online course or simply enhancing your course with Web resources, *The Future of Business,* Fifth Edition, offers a vast, complementary system of teaching and learning resources.

Each component of the comprehensive supplements package has been carefully crafted by outstanding teachers, with guidance from the textbook authors, to ensure this course is a rewarding experience. The supplements package includes excellent time-tested teaching tools as well as new supplements designed for the electronic classroom.

The Most Innovative Instructor's Supplements Ever Created

NEW LECTURE LAUNCHERS. These short chapter introductions include an audio-enhanced, attention-getting story with dynamic, interesting images. Available with the instructor's PowerPoint Lecture System, the Lecture Launchers set the stage for an interesting class lecture.

COMPREHENSIVE INSTRUCTOR'S MANUAL. At the core of the integrated learning system for *The Future of Business* is the instructor's manual prepared by Linda Hefferin, Elgin Community College. Developed in response to numerous suggestions from instructors teaching this course, each chapter is designed to provide maximum guidance for delivering the content in an interesting and dynamic manner. Each chapter begins with learning goals that anchor the integrated learning system. A lecture outline guides instructors through key terminology and concepts. Lecture enhancers provide additional information and examples from actual businesses to illustrate key chapter concepts. Each chapter includes lecture support for teaching the cases and guidance for integrating PowerPoint™ slides and other visuals that illustrate and reinforce the lecture. A comprehensive video guide includes the running time of each video, concepts illustrated in the video, teaching objectives for the case, and solutions for video case study questions. A complete set of transparency masters is available to create overhead acetates. The transparency masters include exhibits from the text and additional teaching notes designed to add fresh examples to lectures. The Instructor's Manual also includes a guide for teaching a distance learning course.

PowerPoint Lecture System. The PowerPoint Lecture System includes hundreds of slides that illustrate key chapter concepts and actual business examples, many not included in the text. Many of the full-color images provided with *The Future of Business,* 5e contain valuable teaching notes to guide instructors through lectures. These slides will help improve lecture organization and reduce preparation time. The PowerPoint™ slides were prepared by Deb Baker, Texas Christian University.

Instructor's Resource CD. For maximum convenience, the Instructor's Manual, the Lecture Launchers, the PowerPoint™ slides, the Test Bank, and the ExamView Testing System are all available on a CD.

Color Acetate Transparencies. Color acetate transparencies feature key concepts, exhibits from the text, and additional examples and exhibits not found in the text.

ExamView Testing Software. Create, deliver, and customize print and online tests in minutes with this easy-to-use Windows-based testing and assessment system. ExamView offers both a Quick Test Wizard and an Online Test Wizard that guide you step-by-step through the process of creating tests. With ExamView's complete word processing capabilities, you can enter an unlimited number of new questions or edit existing questions.

Test Bank. The comprehensive test bank, written by Tom and Betty Pritchett, Kennesaw State University, is organized by learning goal to support the integrated learning system. With over 2,000 true/false, multiple-choice, fill-in-the-blank, and short-answer questions, tests can be customized to support a variety of course objectives. The test bank is available in print and electronic formats.

Complete Video Package and Video Guide. Designed to enrich and support chapter concepts, each of the 22 videos presents real business issues faced by a variety of service and manufacturing organizations. The video cases challenge you to study business issues and develop solutions to business problems. The instructor's video guide, included in the instructor's manual, outlines the key teaching objectives of each video case and suggests answers to the critical thinking questions.

***The Future of Business* Web Site (http://gitman.swlearning.com).** Designed to support your course objectives, the text Web site is a source of downloadable supplements and over 80 Internet exercises organized by chapter. Online quizzes are designed to test student comprehension and provide customized feedback. A new Web feature, Intro to Business News, provides a continuously refreshed supply of relevant news stories that demonstrate the application of key business topics. This valuable resource organizes news stories by topic and chapter to save research time. Available at **http://gitman.swlearning.com**, Intro to Business News will have a library of news stories and will be refreshed monthly with new, current events and applications.

INTERACTIVE STUDENT SUPPLEMENTS

The Future of Business, Fifth Edition, offers innovative student resources to help ensure success in the classroom and help you learn fundamental business terminology and key business concepts.

XTRA! FOR THE FUTURE OF BUSINESS (HTTP://GITMANXTRA.SWLEARNING.COM). *The Future of Business,* Fifth Edition, features Xtra!, a Web-based learning environment that reinforces the educational experience. With access to Xtra!, you get an interactive learning experience that will help you improve course grades. Xtra! includes these features:

- **Interactive Ethics Activities.** Innovative and unique, these interactive ethics activities provide an interactive, educational learning experience. These activities, which support the Making Ethical Choices box found in each chapter, place you in the role of an employee of well-known companies. By responding to a series of prompts, you make choices on the best, most ethical course of action. Once you choose a strategy, you immediately learn the consequences of your choices and are given additional opportunities to learn from your experience.
- **Xtra! Quizzing.** These practice exams give you an opportunity to test your knowledge in preparation for midterms and final exams. Each question includes feedback for right and wrong answers and textbook page references to ease further study.
- **Chapter Case Video Segments.** These video segments bring the chapter video cases to life.
- **Business Plan Template.** A business plan template helps organize and develop a professional business plan.

WEBTUTOR ADVANTAGE. WebTutor Advantage harnesses the power of the Internet to deliver innovative learning aids that actively engage you. WebTutor is designed to help you grasp complex concepts and provide several forms of interactive learning and reinforcement. This rich collection of content, customized for *The Future of Business,* Fifth Edition, is available to you online. In addition, **WebTutor ToolBox** may be bundled with each new copy of the textbook. Available for WebCT and Blackboard, WebTutor ToolBox is the course management system found in WebTutor Advantage, with links to the content from our book companion web sites.

Thomson Learning has partnered with two of the leading course management systems available today—Blackboard and WebCT—to deliver WebTutor content cartridges to instructors around the world.

STUDENT STUDY GUIDE. Designed using the integrated learning system, the Student Study Guide, written by Jonas Falik and Brenda Hersh of Queensborough Community College, tests student comprehension of concepts through the use of multiple-choice questions, and matching exercises. A vocabulary builder reinforces business and non-business terms used within the text.

THE FUTURE OF BUSINESS STUDENT WEB SITE (HTTP://GITMAN.SWLEARNING.COM). *The Future of Business* Web site provides rich content to maximize student learning and build online skills.

- Each text chapter is supported by online quizzes that test student understanding and offer clear, customized feedback for incorrect answers.

- The Web site includes over 80 Internet Exercises that demonstrate how actual companies are applying key chapter concepts. These exercises are organized by chapter and include discussion questions and links to related Web sites.
- Hundreds of PowerPoint™ slides overview the important concepts and principles in each chapter.
- Crossword puzzles of key terms from the chapters make learning business vocabulary more fun and interactive.
- The Web site also offers voluminous support resources for students seeking career information and links to helpful sites.

INFOTRAC COLLEGE EDITION. With InfoTrac College Edition, you get complete, 24 hour-a-day access to full-text articles from hundreds of scholarly journals and popular periodicals such as Newsweek, Time, and USA Today. Thousands of full-length, substantive articles spanning the past four years are updated daily, indexed, and linked. And because they're online, the articles are accessible from any computer with Internet access. InfoTrac College Edition is perfect for all students, from dorm-dwellers to commuters and distance learners.

ACKNOWLEDGMENTS

We are exceedingly grateful to the many reviewers who offered suggestions and recommendations for enhancing the coverage, pedagogy, and support package of the Fifth Edition. The feedback from these instructors helped guide our efforts and ensure that this new edition surpassed expectations for customer satisfaction and quality. We are deeply appreciative of the insights of the following reviewers:

Andrew Johnson
Bellevue Community College

Bonnie R. Chavez
Santa Barbara City College

Janice M. Feldbauer
Austin Community College

Jerome M. Kinskey
Sinclair Community College

James P. Hess
Ivy Tech State College

Jonas Falik
Queensborough Community College

Melvin O. Hawkins
Midlands Technical College

Merrily Joy Hoffman
San Jacinto College

Ralph F. Jagodka
Mount San Antonio College

Evelyn Delaney
Daytona Beach Community College

Susan Thompson
Palm Beach Community College

Mary E. Gorman
University of Cincinnati

Charlane Bomrad Held
Onondaga Community College

Linda M. Newell
Saddleback College

Carnella Hardin
Glendale Community College

Jude A. Rathburn
University of Wisconsin–Milwaukee

David Oliver
Edison College

Linda Hefferin
Elgin Community College

Kathryn E. Dodge
University of Alaska, Fairbanks

Reviewers of the prior editions of this textbook were instrumental in launching this textbook into a strong market position. We are profoundly appreciative of the advice and recommendations of these instructors who reviewed prior editions:

Joseph H. Atallah
Devry Institute of Technology

Herm Baine
Broward Community College

Harvey Bronstein
Oakland Community College

Bonnie R. Chavez
Santa Barbara City College

M. Bixby Cooper
Michigan State University

Jonas Falik
Queensborough Community College

Janice M. Feldbauer
Austin Community College–Northridge

Dennis Foster
Northern Arizona University

James Giles
Bergen Community College

Carnella Hardin
Glendale College

Frederic H. Hawkins
Westchester Business Institute

Connie Johnson
Tampa College

Jerry Kinskey
Sinclair Community College

Raymond T. Lamanna
Berkeley College

Carol Luce
Arizona State University

Carl Meskimen
Sinclair Community College

Andrew Miller
Hudson Valley Community College

H. Lynn Moretz
Central Piedmont Community College

Joseph Newton
Bakersfield College

Teresa Palmer
Illinois State University

Robert F. Reck
Western Michigan University

Ann Squire
Blackhawk Technical College

Ron Weidenfeller
Grand Rapids Community College

This book could not have been written and published with the generous expert assistance of many people. First, we wish to thank Marlene Bellamy, Writeline Associates, for her major and outstanding contributions to numerous aspects of this text. Special appreciation goes to Carolyn Lawrence, Linda Ravden, and Renee Barnow for their contributions to the fifth edition. We wish to thank Linda Hefferin, Elgin Community College, for her creative work on the Instructor's Manual and Lecture Launchers; Deb Baker, Texas Christian University, for developing highly comprehensive, full-color PowerPoint™ slides; Jonas Falik and Brenda Hersh, Queensborough Community College, for their innovative ideas in developing the study guide; and Tom and Betty Pritchett, Kennesaw State University, for designing a highly accurate and extensive variety of test bank questions.

A special word of appreciation goes to the editorial team at South-Western, including Steve Hazelwood, Senior Acquisitions Editor; Nicole Moore, Marketing Manager; Bob Dreas, Production Editor; Deanna Ettinger, Photo Manager; Mary Draper, Developmental Editor; and Annie Marie Rekow, cover and Senior Internal Designer.

Lawrence J. Gitman
Carl McDaniel

Dedicated to the memory of my mother,
Dr. Edith Gitman, who instilled in me the
importance of education and hard work.

—Lawrence J. Gitman

To my Administrative Assistant
RoseAnn Reddick. You have been a
treasure to work with all of these years.

—Carl McDaniel

BRIEF contents

PREFACE xi
Prologue Fast Forward to the Future: Strategies for Success in School and Business 1

Part 1 The Business Environment

1 Participating in the Dynamic Business Environment 22
2 Understanding Evolving Economic Systems and Competition 48
3 Making Ethical Decisions and Managing a Socially Responsible Business 78
APPENDIX: UNDERSTANDING THE LEGAL AND TAX ENVIRONMENT 104
4 Competing in the Global Marketplace 114

Part 2 Business Ownership

5 Forms of Business Ownership 148
6 Entrepreneurship: Starting and Managing Your Own Business 180
YOUR CAREER AS AN ENTREPRENEUR 214

Part 3 Business Management

7 Management and Leadership in Today's Organizations 216
8 Designing Organizational Structures 244
9 Managing Human Resources 270
10 Motivating Employees and Creating Self-Managed Teams 306
11 Understanding Labor–Management Relations 336
12 Achieving World-Class Operations Management 366
YOUR CAREER IN MANAGEMENT 400

Part 4 Marketing Management

13 Understanding the Customer and Creating Marketing Strategy 404
14 Developing Quality Products at the Right Price 436
15 Distributing Products in a Timely and Efficient Manner 472
16 Using Integrated Marketing Communications to Promote Products 502
YOUR CAREER IN MARKETING 533

Part 5 Technology and Information

17 Using Technology to Manage Information 536
18 Using Financial Information and Accounting 568
YOUR CAREER IN THE INFORMATION AGE 603

Part 6 Finance

19 Understanding Money and Financial Institutions 606
20 Managing the Firm's Finances 634
APPENDIX: MANAGING RISK AND INSURANCE 664
21 Understanding Securities and Securities Markets 670
22 Managing Your Personal Finances 704
YOUR CAREER IN FINANCE 738

contents

P Principles
T Trends
i Ideas

PREFACE xi

Prologue

Fast Forward to the Future: Strategies for Success in School and Business 1

YOUR FUTURE IN BUSINESS: BEGIN WITH A COLLEGE DEGREE 1
- Learning the Basics of Business 1
- Choosing a Career 1

SUCCESS IN BUSINESS: IMPROVING YOUR INTERPERSONAL SKILLS 2

MAKE YOUR FUTURE HAPPEN: LEARN TO PLAN 5
- What Is a Plan? 5 The Planning Process 5 An Example of Planning 6 Planning for Your Life 6 Dreams and Plans 7 Directions for Your Life 7

GOING TO COLLEGE IS AN OPPORTUNITY OF A LIFETIME—GRAB IT AND DON'T LET GO 8
- Learn to Concentrate 8 Learn to Manage Your Time 9 Solve the Money Problem 9 Study Smart 10 Become a Master at Taking Tests 11

GETTING YOUR CAREER OFF ON THE RIGHT TRACK 12
- Think Positively 12 Take a Good Look at Yourself 13 Understand What Employers Want 14 Finding My First Professional Job 14 Using the Internet to Jump-Start Your Job Search 16 *Oh My Gosh—I've Got a Job Interview* 17 Interview Like a Pro 18 Selecting the Right Job for You 20 Starting Your New Job 20 Movin' On Up 21

Part 1 The Business Environment

1 Participating in the Dynamic Business Environment 22

P — Principles of Business 24

THE NATURE OF BUSINESS 24
- Not-for-Profit Organizations 25 Factors of Production: The Building Blocks of Business 25

T — Trends in Business 27

SOCIAL TRENDS 28
- The Growth of Component Lifestyles 29
- Two-Income Families 29

DEMOGRAPHIC TRENDS 30
- Generation Y 30 Generation X 31 Baby Boomers—America's Mass Market 31 Older Consumers—Not Just Grandparents 31 Americans on the Move 32 Diversity in America 32

EVOLVING GLOBAL ECONOMIC SYSTEMS 33
- Capitalism 34 The Command Economy 35
- Socialism 35 Mixed Economic Systems 36

TECHNOLOGICAL TRENDS 36

TRENDS IN GLOBAL COMPETITION 38
- Technology and Global Communications 38
- Improvements in Productivity 38
- The Impact of Terrorism on Global Business 39

i — Great Ideas to Use Now 40
- The Coming Talent War 40 Choosing the Right Job for You 42

PREPARING FOR TOMORROW'S WORKPLACE 43
WORKING THE NET 44
CREATIVE THINKING CASE 45
VIDEO CASE 45
E-COMMERCE CASE 46
HOT LINKS ADDRESS BOOK 47

2 Understanding Evolving Economic Systems and Competition 48

P — Principles of Economics and Competition 50

HOW BUSINESS AND ECONOMIES WORK 50
- Macroeconomics and Microeconomics 50
- Economics as a Circular Flow 51

MACROECONOMICS: THE BIG PICTURE 52
- Striving for Economic Growth 52
- Keeping People on the Job 53
- Keeping Prices Steady 55

ACHIEVING MACROECONOMIC GOALS 56
- Monetary Policy 56 Fiscal Policy 57

MICROECONOMICS: ZEROING IN ON BUSINESSES AND CONSUMERS 59
- The Nature of Demand 60 The Nature of Supply 60 How Demand and Supply Interact to Determine Prices 61

©EYEWIRE / GETTY IMAGES

Competing in a free market 64
Perfect Competition 64 Pure Monopoly 65 Monopolistic Competition 65 Oligopoly 66

T — Trends in Economics and Competition 67

Creating long-term relationships 67

Creating a competitive workplace 68

Entrepreneurial spirit in former command economies 68

Big government returns 69

i — Great Ideas to Use Now 69

PREPARING FOR TOMORROW'S WORKPLACE 73
WORKING THE NET 73
CREATIVE THINKING CASE 74
VIDEO CASE 74
E-COMMERCE CASE 75
HOT LINKS ADDRESS BOOK 77

3 Making Ethical Decisions and Managing a Socially Responsible Business 78

P — Principles of Ethics and Social Responsibility 80

Individual business ethics 80
Utilitarianism—Seeking the Best for the Majority 80 Individual Rights 80 Justice—The Question of Fairness 81 Recognizing Unethical Business Activities 81

How organizations influence ethical conduct 83
Leading by Example 83 Offering Ethics-Training Programs 83 Establishing a Formal Code of Ethics 85

Managing a socially responsible business 85
Understanding Social Responsibility 88

Responsibilities to stakeholders 89
Responsibility to Employees 89 Responsibility to Customers 89 Responsibility to Society 90 Responsibilities to Investors 93

T — Trends in Ethics and Social Responsibility 93

Trends in corporate philanthropy 93

A new social contract trend between employer and employee 94

Global ethics and social responsibility 94

i — Great Ideas to Use Now 96

Resolving Ethical Problems in Business 96
Front Page of the Newspaper Test 97

PREPARING FOR TOMORROW'S WORKPLACE 99
WORKING THE NET 100
CREATIVE THINKING CASE 100
VIDEO CASE 101
E-COMMERCE CASE 102
HOT LINKS ADDRESS BOOK 103

APPENDIX: UNDERSTANDING THE LEGAL AND TAX ENVIRONMENT 104

4 Competing in the Global Marketplace 114

P — Principles of Global Competition 116

America goes global 116
The Importance of Global Business to the United States 117 The Impact of Terrorism on Global Trade 117

Measuring trade between nations 118
Exports and Imports 118 Balance of Trade 119 Balance of Payments 120 The Changing Value of Currencies 120

Why nations trade 120
Absolute Advantage 121 Comparative Advantage 121 The Fear of Trade and Globalization 121 Benefits of Globalization 122

Barriers to trade 122
Natural Barriers 122 Tariff Barriers 122 Nontariff Barriers 123

Fostering global trade 124
Antidumping Laws 124 The Uruguay Round and the World Trade Organization 124 The World Bank and International Monetary Fund 125

International economic communities 126
North American Free Trade Agreement (NAFTA) 126 The European Union 126

Participating in the global marketplace 129
Exporting 129 Licensing 130 Contract Manufacturing 131 Joint Ventures 131 Direct Foreign Investment 132 Countertrade 132

Threats and opportunities in the global marketplace 133
Political Considerations 133 Cultural Differences 133 Economic Environment 134

The impact of multinational corporations 136
The Multinational Advantage 137

Trends in Global Competition 138

MARKET EXPANSION 138

RESOURCE ACQUISITION 138

THE IMPACT OF THE INTERNET 138

TECHNOLOGICAL CHANGE 139

GOVERNMENT ACTIONS 139

Great Ideas to Use Now 140

Continue Your Education 140
Study the Role of a Global Manager 141

PREPARING FOR TOMORROW'S WORKPLACE 144
WORKING THE NET 144
CREATIVE THINKING CASE 145
VIDEO CASE 146
E-COMMERCE CASE 146
HOT LINKS ADDRESS BOOK 147

Part 2 Business Ownership

5 Forms of Business Ownership 148

Principles of Business Ownership 150

GOING IT ALONE: SOLE PROPRIETORSHIPS 150

Advantages of Sole Proprietorships 151
Disadvantages of Sole Proprietorships 151

PARTNERSHIPS: SHARING THE LOAD 152

Advantages of Partnerships 153
Disadvantages of Partnerships 153

CORPORATIONS: LIMITING YOUR LIABILITY 155

The Incorporation Process 156 The Corporate Structure 156 Advantages of Corporations 158 Disadvantages of Corporations 158 Types of Corporations 159

SPECIALIZED FORMS OF BUSINESS ORGANIZATION 160

Cooperatives 160 Joint Ventures 162

FRANCHISING: A POPULAR TREND 162

Advantages of Franchises 164 Disadvantages of Franchises 164 Franchise Growth 165 International Franchising 165

MERGERS AND ACQUISITIONS 166

Merger Motives 167 Types of Mergers 168

Trends in Business Ownership 169

FRANCHISING: CHANGING DEMOGRAPHICS 169

FRANCHISE INNOVATIONS 169

MERGERS: EMERGING TRUTHS 170

Great Ideas to Use Now 171

Is Franchising in Your Future? 172
Mergers and You 173

PREPARING FOR TOMORROW'S WORKPLACE 176
WORKING THE NET 177
CREATIVE THINKING CASE 177
VIDEO CASE 178
E-COMMERCE CASE 179
HOT LINKS ADDRESS BOOK 179

6 Entrepreneurship: Starting and Managing Your Own Business 180

Principles of Entrepreneurship and Small-Business Management 182

ENTREPRENEURSHIP TODAY 182

Entrepreneur or Small-Business Owner? 183 Types of Entrepreneurs 183
Why Become an Entrepreneur? 184

CHARACTERISTICS OF SUCCESSFUL ENTREPRENEURS 185

The Entrepreneurial Personality 186
Managerial Ability and Technical Knowledge 186

SMALL BUSINESS: DRIVING AMERICA'S GROWTH 187

What Is a Small Business? 188 Small Business, Large Impact 188 Why Stay Small? 190

THE SMALL BUSINESS ADMINISTRATION 191

Financial Assistance Programs 191
SCORE-ing with Management Assistance Programs 192 Assistance for Women and Minorities 192

READY, SET, START YOUR OWN BUSINESS 192

Getting Started 192 Developing the Business Plan 194 Financing the Business 196 Buying a Small Business 196
Risky Business 197

MANAGING A SMALL BUSINESS 198

Using Outside Consultants 198 Hiring and Retaining Employees 198 Going Global 199

Trends in Entrepreneurship and Small-Business Ownership 200

REDUCED NUMBER OF NEW BUSINESSES 201

©PHOTODISC GREEN / GETTY IMAGES

HOT SPOTS FOR NEW BUSINESSES 201
OPPORTUNITIES FOR ALL 201
LOW- OR NO TECH TAKES OVER 203
Great Ideas to Use Now 204
Taking the First Steps 205 Working at a Small Business 205
PREPARING FOR TOMORROW'S WORKPLACE 209
WORKING THE NET 210
CREATIVE THINKING CASE 210
VIDEO CASE 211
E-COMMERCE CASE 212
HOT LINKS ADDRESS BOOK 213
YOUR CAREER AS AN ENTREPRENEUR 214

Part 3 Business Management

7 Management and Leadership in Today's Organizations 216
Principles of Management and Leadership 218
THE ROLE OF MANAGEMENT 218
PLANNING 218
ORGANIZING 222
LEADING, GUIDING, AND MOTIVATING OTHERS 223
Leadership Styles 224 Employee Empowerment 226 Corporate Culture 226
CONTROLLING 228
MANAGERIAL ROLES 229
Managerial Decision Making 229
MANAGERIAL SKILLS 231
Technical Skills 231 Human Relations Skills 232 Conceptual Skills 232 Global Management Skills 232
Trends in Management and Leadership 234
MANAGERS EMPOWERING EMPLOYEES 234
MANAGERS AND INFORMATION TECHNOLOGY 234
MANAGING MULTINATIONAL CULTURES 234
CRISIS MANAGEMENT 235
Great Ideas to Use Now 235
Effective Time Management 236
Stress Management 237
PREPARING FOR TOMORROW'S WORKPLACE 239
WORKING THE NET 240
CREATIVE THINKING CASE 240
VIDEO CASE 241
E-COMMERCE CASE 242
HOT LINKS ADDRESS BOOK 243

8 Designing Organizational Structures 244
Principles of Organizational Structures 246
STRUCTURAL BUILDING BLOCKS 246
Division of Labor 246 Departmentalization 247 Managerial Hierarchy 248 Span of Control 251 Centralization of Decision Making 252
MECHANISTIC VERSUS ORGANIC STRUCTURES 253
COMMON ORGANIZATIONAL STRUCTURES 255
Line Organization 255 Line-and-Staff Organization 255 Committee Structure 256 Matrix Structure 257
REENGINEERING ORGANIZATIONAL STRUCTURE 258
THE INFORMAL ORGANIZATION 259
Functions of the Informal Organization 259
Trends in Organizational Structures 260
THE VIRTUAL CORPORATION 260
VIRTUAL TEAMS 261
STRUCTURING FOR GLOBAL MERGERS 262
Great Ideas to Use Now 263
PREPARING FOR TOMORROW'S WORKPLACE 266
WORKING THE NET 266
CREATIVE THINKING CASE 267
VIDEO CASE 267
E-COMMERCE CASE 268
HOT LINKS ADDRESS BOOK 269

9 Managing Human Resources 270
Principles of Human Resource Management 272
DEVELOPING PEOPLE TO HELP REACH ORGANIZATION GOALS 272
HUMAN RESOURCE PLANNING 273
Job Analysis and Design 274 Human Resource Planning and Forecasting 275
EMPLOYEE RECRUITMENT 276
Recruiting from the Internal Labor Market 276 Recruiting from the External Labor Market 276 Using Technology to Recruit Applicants 277
EMPLOYEE SELECTION 277
EMPLOYEE TRAINING AND DEVELOPMENT 280
On-the-Job Training 281 Off-the-Job Training 282
PERFORMANCE PLANNING AND EVALUATION 282

EMPLOYEE COMPENSATION AND BENEFITS 283
Types of Compensation or Pay 284
Executive Compensation 286

ORGANIZATIONAL CAREER MANAGEMENT 287
Job Changes within the Organization 287
Separations 288

MANAGING DIVERSITY WITHIN THE ORGANIZATION 289
Diversity as a Competitive Advantage 290
The Best Companies for Managing Diversity 291

LAWS AFFECTING HUMAN RESOURCE MANAGEMENT 291
The Role of Government Agencies in Human Resource Management 293
Making Affirmative Action Work 294

T Trends in Human Resource Management 295
PROTECTING WHISTLEBLOWERS 295
THE GROWTH IN MINORITY RECRUITING 295
PROACTIVE MANAGEMENT OF DIVERSITY 296
ADVANCING TECHNOLOGY 296
GLOBAL COMPETITION 296

i Great Ideas to Use Now 297
Human Resources Decision Making 297

PREPARING FOR TOMORROW'S WORKPLACE 301
WORKING THE NET 301
CREATIVE THINKING CASE 302
VIDEO CASE 303
E-COMMERCE CASE 304
HOT LINKS ADDRESS BOOK 305

10 Motivating Employees and Creating Self-Managed Teams 306

P Principles of Employee Motivation 308
THE EVOLUTION OF MOTIVATION THEORY 308
Frederick Taylor's Scientific Management 308 The Hawthorne Studies 309 Maslow's Hierarchy of Needs 310 McGregor's Theories X and Y 312 Theory Z 312 Herzberg's Motivator-Hygiene Theory 313

CONTEMPORARY VIEWS ON MOTIVATION 315
Expectancy Theory 316 Equity Theory 316 Goal-Setting Theory 317 Motivation Is Culture Bound 318

FROM MOTIVATION THEORY TO APPLICATION 319
Motivational Job Design 319 Work-Scheduling Options 319 Recognition, Empowerment, and Economic Incentives 320

USING TEAMS TO ENHANCE MOTIVATION AND PERFORMANCE 321
Understanding Group Behavior 321
Work Groups versus Work Teams 323
Types of Teams 323 Building High-Performance Teams 324

T Trends in Employee Motivation 325
EDUCATION AND TRAINING 325
EMPLOYEE OWNERSHIP 326
WORK-LIFE BENEFITS 326
NURTURING KNOWLEDGE WORKERS 326
COPING WITH THE RISING COSTS OF ABSENTEEISM 327

i Great Ideas to Use Now 327
PREPARING FOR TOMORROW'S WORKPLACE 331
WORKING THE NET 332
CREATIVE THINKING CASE 332
VIDEO CASE 333
E-COMMERCE CASE 334
HOT LINKS ADDRESS BOOK 335

11 Understanding Labor–Management Relations 336

P Principles of Labor–Management Relations 338
THE EMERGENCE OF UNIONS AND COLLECTIVE BARGAINING 338
American Federation of Labor 338
Congress of Industrial Organizations 339
The AFL and CIO: Rivalry and Merger 340
The Labor Movement Today 340

THE LEGAL ENVIRONMENT OF UNIONS 341
Norris-LaGuardia Act (Anti-Injunction Act) 341 Wagner Act (National Labor Relations Act) 342 Taft-Hartley Act (Labor-Management Relations Act) 343 Landrum-Griffin Act (Labor-Management Reporting and Disclosure Act) 345

©COURTESY OF JACK IN THE BOX INC.

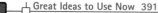

Union organizing 345
Negotiating union contracts 347
Union Security 348 Management Rights 348 Wages 349 Benefits 350 Job Security and Seniority 350
Grievance and arbitration 350
Managing labor-management conflict 351
Union Strategies 352
Employer Strategies 354
T Trends in Labor–Management Relations 355
Union organizing and membership 356
Shortages of skilled labor 356
Concession bargaining 356
i Great Ideas to Use Now 357
PREPARING FOR TOMORROW'S WORKPLACE 361
WORKING THE NET 362
CREATIVE THINKING CASE 362
VIDEO CASE 363
E-COMMERCE CASE 364
HOT LINKS ADDRESS BOOK 365
12 Achieving World-Class Operations Management 366
P Principles of Operations Management 368
Production and operations management—an overview 368
Gearing up: production planning 369
The Production Process: How Do We Make It? 370 Location, Location, Location: Where Do We Make It? 372 Designing the Facility 375 Pulling It Together: Resource Planning 377 Keeping the Goods Flowing: Supply Chain Management 380
Production and operations control 381
Routing: Where to Next? 381 Scheduling: When Do We Do It? 382
Looking for a better way: improving production and operations 384
Putting Quality First 384 Lean Manufacturing Trims the Fat 386 Transforming the Factory Floor with Technology 386 Technology and Automation at Your Service 388
T Trends in Production and Operations Management 389
Asset management 389
Modular production 390
Designing products for production efficiency 390
i Great Ideas to Use Now 391
PREPARING FOR TOMORROW'S WORKPLACE 394
WORKING THE NET 395
CREATIVE THINKING CASE 396
VIDEO CASE 397
E-COMMERCE CASE 398
HOT LINKS ADDRESS BOOK 399
YOUR CAREER IN MANAGEMENT 400
Part 4 Marketing Management
13 Understanding the Customer and Creating Marketing Strategy 404
P Principles of Marketing 406
The marketing concept 406
Customer Value 407 Customer Satisfaction 407 Building Relationships 407
Creating a marketing strategy 409
Understanding the External Environment 409 Defining the Target Market 410 Creating a Competitive Advantage 411
Developing a marketing mix 413
Product Strategy 413 Pricing Strategy 413 Distribution Strategy 414 Promotion Strategy 414 Not-for-Profit Marketing 414
Buyer behavior 415
Influences on Consumer Decision Making 415 Types of Consumer Buying Decisions 418 Business-to-Business Purchase Decision Making 419
Market segmentation 420
Demographic Segmentation 420 Geographic Segmentation 421 Psychographic Segmentation 422 Benefit Segmentation 422 Volume Segmentation 422
Using marketing research to serve existing customers and find new Customers 423
Define the Marketing Problem 423 Choose a Method of Research 423 Collect the Data 424 Analyze the Data 424 Make Recommendations to Management 425
T Trends in Marketing 425
Scanner-based research 426
Capitalizing on loyalty cards 427
Growth of one-to-one marketing 428
i Great Ideas to Use Now 429
Participate in Marketing Research Surveys 429 Understand Cognitive Dissonance 429

PREPARING FOR TOMORROW'S WORKPLACE 431
WORKING THE NET 432
CREATIVE THINKING CASE 433
VIDEO CASE 433
E-COMMERCE CASE 434
HOT LINKS ADDRESS BOOK 435

14 Developing Quality Products at the Right Price 436

Principles of Developing Products and Pricing 438

WHAT IS A PRODUCT? 438
Classifying Consumer Products 439
Classifying Business Products 440

BUILDING BRAND EQUITY AND MASTER BRANDS 441
Benefits of Branding 441 Building Repeat Sales with Brand Loyalty 442 Facilitating New-Product Sales 443 Types of Brands 444

THE IMPORTANCE OF PACKAGING IN A SELF-SERVICE ECONOMY 444
The Functions of a Package 444
Labeling 445 Adding Value through Warranties 446

CREATING PRODUCTS THAT DELIVER VALUE 447
Organizing the New-Product Effort 447
How New Products Are Developed 447
The Role of the Product Manager 451

THE PRODUCT LIFE CYCLE 451
Stages of the Life Cycle 451 The Product Life Cycle as a Management Tool 452

PRICING PRODUCTS RIGHT 452
Pricing Objectives 454 Maximizing Profits 454 Achieving a Target Return on Investment 455 Value Pricing 455

HOW MANAGERS SET PRICES 455
Markup Pricing 456 Breakeven Analysis 456

PRODUCT PRICING 457
Price Skimming 457 Penetration Pricing 457 Leader Pricing 458 Bundling 458 Odd-Even Pricing 459 Prestige Pricing 459

Trends in Developing Products and Pricing 459

NEW-PRODUCT DEVELOPMENT MOVES TO THE INTERNET 459
YIELD MANAGEMENT SYSTEMS HELP COMPANIES MAXIMIZE THEIR REVENUES 460
COLOR MOVES TO THE FOREFRONT 460

Great Ideas to Use Now 463
A Buyer's Guide 463 A Seller's Guide 464

PREPARING FOR TOMORROW'S WORKPLACE 468
WORKING THE NET 468
CREATIVE THINKING CASE 469
VIDEO CASE 469
E-COMMERCE CASE 470
HOT LINKS ADDRESS BOOK 471

15 Distributing Products in a Timely and Efficient Manner 472

Principles of Distribution 474

THE ROLE OF DISTRIBUTION 474
THE NATURE AND FUNCTIONS OF DISTRIBUTION CHANNELS 474
Marketing Intermediaries in the Distribution Channel 474 The Functions of Distribution Channels 475

HOW CHANNELS ORGANIZE AND COVER MARKETS 478
Vertical Marketing Systems 478
The Intensity of Market Coverage 479

WHOLESALING 480
Types of Wholesalers 481

THE COMPETITIVE WORLD OF RETAILING 483
Types of Retail Operations 483
Components of a Successful Retailing Strategy 485

USING SUPPLY CHAIN MANAGEMENT TO INCREASE EFFICIENCY AND CUSTOMER SATISFACTION 488
Managing the Logistical Components of the Supply Chain 489 Sourcing and Procurement 490 Production Scheduling 490 Choosing a Warehouse Location and Type 491 Setting Up a Materials-Handling System 491 Making Transportation Decisions 491

©PHOTODISC GREEN / GETTY IMAGES

Trends in Distribution 492

Category management 492

Sharing information and the load 492

Great Ideas to Use Now 493

Flying in Europe? Go Cheap 493
The Point of No Return 494

PREPARING FOR TOMORROW'S WORKPLACE 497
WORKING THE NET 497
CREATIVE THINKING CASE 498
VIDEO CASE 498
E-COMMERCE CASE 499
HOT LINKS ADDRESS BOOK 501

16 Using Integrated Marketing Communications to Promote Products 502

Principles of Integrated Marketing Communications 504

Promotional goals 504

The Promotional Mix and Integrated Marketing Communications 505

Advertising builds brand recognition 506

Types of Advertising 507 Choosing Advertising Media 508 Advertising Agencies 509 Advertising Regulation 509

The importance of personal selling 512

The Professional Salesperson 513 Sales Positions 513 The Selling Process 514

Sales promotion 516

Public relations helps build goodwill 519

New-Product Publicity 520
Event Sponsorship 520

Factors that affect the promotional mix 520

The Nature of the Product 520 Market Characteristics 520 Available Funds 521 Push and Pull Strategies 521

Trends in Promotion 522

The growth of web advertising 522

Growing use of technology in promotion 523

Guerilla marketing 523

Great Ideas to Use Now 524

Advertising Will Be More Beneficial to You 524 Always Sell Yourself 524

PREPARING FOR TOMORROW'S WORKPLACE 528
WORKING THE NET 528
CREATIVE THINKING CASE 529
VIDEO CASE 530
E-COMMERCE CASE 530
HOT LINKS ADDRESS BOOK 532

YOUR CAREER IN MARKETING 533

Part 5 Technology and Information

17 Using Technology to Manage Information 536

Principles of Information Technology 538

Transforming businesses through information 538

Linking up: computer networks 539

Connecting Near and Far with Networks 540 An Inside Job: Intranets 541 No More Tangles: Wireless Technologies 542
Private Lines: Virtual Private Networks 542
Software on Demand: Application Service Providers 543

Management information systems 544

Transaction Processing Systems 546
Decisions, Decisions: Management Support Systems 547 Decision Support Systems 548
Executive Information Systems 549
Expert Systems 549 Office Automation Systems 549

Technology management and planning 550

Optimize IT! 550 Managing Knowledge Resources 551 Technology Planning 551

Protecting computers and information 552

Data Security Issues 553 Preventing Problems 554 Keep IT Confidential: Privacy Concerns 555

Trends in Information Technology 556

Enterprise portals open the door to productivity 556

On-demand computing solves grid-lock 557

Great Ideas to Use Now 559

Preparation Pays Off 559
Protect Your Good Name 559

PREPARING FOR TOMORROW'S WORKPLACE 563
WORKING THE NET 563
CREATIVE THINKING CASE 564
VIDEO CASE 565
E-COMMERCE CASE 566
HOT LINKS ADDRESS BOOK 567

18 Using Financial Information and Accounting 568

Principles of Accounting 570

ACCOUNTING: MORE THAN NUMBERS 571

Who Uses Financial Reports? 571

THE ACCOUNTING PROFESSION 573

Public Accountants 574 Private Accountants 574 Refiguring the Accounting Environment 574 Bending the Rules 575 Better Numbers Ahead 575

BASIC ACCOUNTING PROCEDURES 577

The Accounting Equation 577 The Accounting Cycle 578 Computers in Accounting 578

THE BALANCE SHEET 579

Assets 580 Liabilities 582 Owners' Equity 583

THE INCOME STATEMENT 583

Revenues 583 Expenses 583 Net Profit or Loss 585

THE STATEMENT OF CASH FLOWS 585

ANALYZING FINANCIAL STATEMENTS 586

Liquidity Ratios 587 Profitability Ratios 588 Activity Ratios 589 Debt Ratios 589

Trends in Accounting 590

ACCOUNTANTS STICK TO THE NUMBERS 591

HOLDING ACCOUNTANTS ACCOUNTABLE 591

NEW GOVERNANCE RESPONSIBILITIES 592

CLOSING THE GAAP 592

Great Ideas to Use Now 593

PREPARING FOR TOMORROW'S WORKPLACE 597
WORKING THE NET 598
CREATIVE THINKING CASE 599
VIDEO CASE 600
E-COMMERCE CASE 601
HOT LINKS ADDRESS BOOK 602

YOUR CAREER IN THE INFORMATION AGE 603

Part 6 Finance

19 Understanding Money and Financial Institutions 606

Principles of Money and Financial Institutions 608

SHOW ME THE MONEY 608

Characteristics of Money 608 Functions of Money 608 The U.S. Money Supply 609

THE FEDERAL RESERVE SYSTEM 609

Carrying Out Monetary Policy 610 Setting Rules on Credit 611 Distributing Currency: Keeping the Cash Flowing 612 Making Check Clearing Easier 612

U.S. FINANCIAL INSTITUTIONS 613

Depository Financial Institutions 613 Nondepository Financial Institutions 616

INSURING BANK DEPOSITS 618

The Role of the FDIC 618 Enforcement by the FDIC 618

INTERNATIONAL BANKING 619

Trends in Financial Institutions 621

THE GROWTH OF THE MEGA-FINANCIAL INSTITUTION 621

THE MODERNIZATION OF FINANCIAL SERVICES: INTEGRATING BANKING, BROKERAGE, AND INSURANCE SERVICES 623

DELIVERING FINANCIAL SERVICES WITH "CLICKS AND BRICKS" 623

Great Ideas to Use Now 625

Finding Financing for Small Businesses 625

PREPARING FOR TOMORROW'S WORKPLACE 628
WORKING THE NET 629
CREATIVE THINKING CASE 630
VIDEO CASE 631
E-COMMERCE CASE 632
HOT LINKS ADDRESS BOOK 633

20 Managing the Firm's Finances 634

Principles of Financial Management 636

THE ROLE OF FINANCE AND THE FINANCIAL MANAGER 636

The Financial Manager's Responsibilities and Activities 637 The Goal of the Financial Manager 638

FINANCIAL PLANNING: LOOKING AHEAD 638

Forecasting the Future 639 Budgets 639

HOW ORGANIZATIONS USE FUNDS 640

Short-Term Expenses 640 Long-Term Expenditures 642

©DIGITAL VISION / GETTY IMAGES

Obtaining short-term financing 643
Unsecured Short-Term Loans 643
Secured Short-Term Loans 645

Raising long-term financing 645
Debt versus Equity Financing 645 Long-Term Debt Financing 646 Equity Financing 647

T Trends in Financial Management 651
The changing role of the CFO 652
Weighing the risks after September 11, 2001 653

i Great Ideas to Use Now 654
PREPARING FOR TOMORROW'S WORKPLACE 658
WORKING THE NET 659
CREATIVE THINKING CASE 660
VIDEO CASE 661
E-COMMERCE CASE 662
HOT LINKS ADDRESS BOOK 663

APPENDIX: MANAGING RISK AND INSURANCE 664

21 Understanding Securities and Securities Markets 670

P Principles of Securities and Securities Markets 672
Investor's choice: stocks and bonds 672
Sharing the Wealth—and the Risk: Stocks 672 Cashing In with Bonds 675

Playing the market with other types of securities 677
Mutual Funds 677 Futures Contracts 678 Options 678

On the training floor: securities markets 678
The Role of Investment Bankers and Stockholders 679 Online Investing 679 Types of Markets 680

Buying and selling at securities exchanges 680
U.S. Stock Exchanges 681 Global Trading and Foreign Exchanges 682 The Over-the-Counter Market 683 Market Conditions: Bull Market or Bear Market? 683 Regulation of Securities Markets 684

Popular sources of investment information 685
Company Financial Reports 686 Economic and Financial Publications 686 Online Information Resources 687 Security Price Quotations 687 Market Averages and Indexes 690

T Trends in Securities and Securities Markets 691
A stronger role for the SEC 693
Rebuilding investor trust 693

i Great Ideas to Use Now 694
The Time Is Now 694

PREPARING FOR TOMORROW'S WORKPLACE 698
WORKING THE NET 699
CREATIVE THINKING CASE 700
VIDEO CASE 700
E-COMMERCE CASE 702
HOT LINKS ADDRESS BOOK 703

22 Managing Your Personal Finances 704

P Principles of Personal Finance 706
Financial planning: the first steps 707
Cash management: where's the money? 709
Checking Accounts 709
Savings Instruments 710

Using consumer credit 711
The Pros and Cons of Using Credit 711
Credit Cards 713 Other Card Tricks 715
Loans 715 Credit History and Credit Ratings 716

Managing taxes 717
Income Taxes 717 Social Security and Medicare Taxes 719 Sales and Property Taxes 720

Selecting insurance 720
Setting Insurance Priorities 720 Property and Liability Insurance 720 Health Insurance 721 Disability Income Insurance 723 Life Insurance 723

Making investment decisions 724
Investment Goals 725 Developing an Investment Strategy 725

Securities transaction basics 727

T Trends in Personal Finance 727
Getting downright personal 728
For the Gen-X generation the future is now 729

i Great Ideas to Use Now 729
PREPARING FOR TOMORROW'S WORKPLACE 733
WORKING THE NET 734
CREATIVE THINKING CASE 734
VIDEO CASE 735
E-COMMERCE CASE 736
HOT LINKS ADDRESS BOOK 737

YOUR CAREER IN FINANCE 738

Glossary 741
Endnotes 761
Subject Index 771
Company Index 785

authors

Lawrence J. Gitman

Lawrence J. Gitman is a professor of finance at San Diego State University. He received his Bachelor's Degree from Purdue University, his M.B.A. from the University of Dayton, and his Ph.D. from the University of Cincinnati. Professor Gitman is a prolific textbook author and has over 50 articles appearing in *Financial Management, Financial Review, Financial Services Review, Journal of Financial Planning, Journal of Risk and Insurance, Journal of Financial Research, Financial Practice and Education, Journal of Financial Education,* and other publications.

His singly authored major textbooks include *Principles of Managerial Finance: Brief,* Third Edition, *Principles of Managerial Finance,* Tenth Edition, and *Foundations of Managerial Finance,* Fourth Edition. Other major textbooks include *Personal Financial Planning,* Tenth Edition, and *Fundamentals of Investing,* Ninth Edition, both co-authored with Michael D. Joehnk. Gitman and Joehnk also wrote *Investment Fundamentals: A Guide to Becoming a Knowledgeable Investor,* which was selected as one of 1988's ten best personal finance books by *Money* magazine. In addition, he co-authored *Introduction to Finance* with Jeff Madura and *Corporate Finance* with Scott B. Smart and William L. Meggison.

An active member of numerous professional organizations, Professor Gitman is past president of the Academy of Financial Services, the San Diego Chapter of the Financial Executives Institute, the Midwest Finance Association, and the FMA National Honor Society. In addition he is a Certified Financial Planner (CFP)® and a Certified Cash Manager (CCM). Gitman served as Vice-President, Financial Education of the Financial Management Association, as a Director of the San Diego MIT Enterprise Form, and on the CFP® Board of Standards. He and his wife have two children and live in La Jolla, California, where he is an avid bicyclist.

Carl McDaniel

Carl McDaniel is a professor of marketing at the University of Texas–Arlington, where he is Chairman of the Marketing Department. He has been an instructor for more than 20 years and is the recipient of several awards for outstanding teaching. McDaniel has also been a District Sales Manager for Southwestern Bell Telephone Company. Currently, he serves as a board member of the North Texas Higher Education Authority, a 1.5 billion member organization that provides immediate financing for student loans across America.

In addition to this text, McDaniel has also co-authored a number of textbooks in marketing. McDaniel's research has appeared in such publications as *Journal of Marketing, Journal of Business Research, Journal of the Academy of Marketing Science,* and *California Management Review.*

McDaniel is a member of the American Marketing Association, Academy of Marketing Science, Society for Marketing Advances, and Southwestern Marketing Association.

Besides his academic experience, McDaniel has business experience as the co-owner of a marketing research firm. Recently, McDaniel served as senior consultant to the International Trade Centre (ITC), Geneva, Switzerland. The ITC's mission is to help developing nations increase their exports. McDaniel also teaches international business each year in France. He has a Bachelor's Degree from the University of Arkansas and his Master's Degree and Doctorate from Arizona State University.

The Future of Business

5e

Prologue

Fast Forward to the Future: Strategies for Success in School and Business

YOUR FUTURE IN BUSINESS: BEGIN WITH A COLLEGE DEGREE

What makes someone a winner in life? A winner is someone who goes through the various stages of life content in knowing that they have done their best. Their best at work, home, and in all pursuits of life. A big part of having a happy life is pursuing a career that offers job satisfaction and financial rewards. If you are going to "be all that you can be," you need a good education.

A college degree unlocks doors to economic opportunity. Why get a degree?

- **Get and keep a better job.** Because the world is changing rapidly, and many jobs rely on new technology, more jobs require education beyond high school. With a college education, you will have more jobs from which to choose.

- **Earn more money.** People who go to college usually earn more than those who do not. Currently, a bachelor's degree is worth a minimum of $25,000 a year more than a high school diploma. If your career spans 45 years, you will earn $1,125,000 more than a high school graduate!

- **Get a good start in life.** A business college education helps you acquire a wide range of knowledge in many subjects as well as an advanced understanding of your specialized area of business. College also trains you to express your thoughts clearly in speech and in writing and to make informed decisions.

Simply stated, a degree in business gives you the chance to achieve the quality of life you deserve. The lifestyle, the new friends, the purchasing power of a degree won't guarantee happiness but will put you well on the road to finding it.

Learning the Basics of Business

You might want to pursue a career as a physician, florist, game warden, systems analyst, or any of a thousand other opportunities. One thing that all careers have in common is that you need to have a basic understanding of business. We hope that you will consider a career in business, but if not, your success in whatever you choose will partially depend on your basic business skills. And that is why this course is so important.

There is no other class that presents all the fundamental areas of business and then links them together like this course. This is where you get the big picture as well as an introduction to fundamental components of business. Learn it well because it will be invaluable throughout your life.

Choosing a Career

Because this course gives you a detailed overview of all of the areas of business, it will guide you in selecting a major should you select to get a degree in business. Choosing a major in college is one of life's true milestones. Your major essentially determines how you will spend the next four decades of your life! A marketing major will find a career in sales, marketing research, advertising, or other marketing-related field. An accounting major (you guessed it) will become an accountant. *Never* take selecting a major lightly. If you work 40 hours a week for the next 45 years (less vacations), you will put in about 90,000 hours on the job. Don't you think that you should choose something that you will enjoy?

Success in Business: Improving Your Interpersonal Skills

A degree in business is going to offer you many great career opportunities. Once you take your first job, how rapidly you move up the ladder is up to you. People with great interpersonal skills will always do better on and off the job than those who lack them. It has been estimated that up to 95 percent of our workplace success depends on an understanding of other people.[1] Here's how to enhance your interpersonal skills:

1. **Build your people skills.** Learn to build alliances in a group and establish harmony. Make a concerted effort to know what is happening in the lives of those on your team at school and work. About once a month get together with your group and pass out a list of issues, concerns, fears, and potential problems. Then invite everyone to give input to solve little problems before they become big. If something goes wrong, try to find out where things are not running smoothly and improve them. Be sure to compliment someone in your group who is doing an exemplary job.

   Become a good listener. When you listen well, you are in effect telling the other person that he or she is worth listening to. Listening well includes listening to both what is said and not said. Learn to read unspoken gestures and expressions. When giving feedback, plan what you will say in advance. Be positive and be specific. Ask the person receiving the feedback if they would like to discuss your comments further.

2. **Understand how to persuade others.** Remember, we all must sell ourselves and ideas to get ahead in life and business. Influencing others means overcoming objectives, igniting passions, or changing minds. The first step is to build *esprit de corps,* a shared enthusiasm and devotion to the group. Make your vision their vision so that everyone is working toward a common goal. Praise the team as a whole, but recognize the unique contributions different team members have made. The trick is to praise everyone, yet for different reasons. When you and your team successfully solve a problem, change will result.

   Persuasion rests on trust. You can build trust by being honest, fulfilling your commitments, being concerned about others, and minimizing problems and pain for others whenever possible. In short, if you have integrity, building trust becomes a simple task.

   When people raise objections to your plans or ideas, try to fully understand their comments and the motivation for making them. When you feel that you understand the true objection, answer the objection in the form of a benefit: "Yes, you will need to work next Saturday, but then you can have compensatory time off anytime you wish next month."

3. **Learn to think on your feet.** Top executives, like former Chrysler Chairman Lee Iacocca, say that "speaking well on your feet" is the best thing that you can do for your career. If you cannot quickly express yourself with confidence, others will lose confidence in you.

   It will not happen overnight, but you can become an outstanding thinker and speaker. A simple technique is to set a timer for two minutes and ask a friend to begin speaking. When the timer goes off, your friend stops speaking and you begin talking. The challenge is to use the final thought that your friend spoke as the first word of your two-minute talk. Another technique is to have someone supply you with a series of quotes. Then, without hesitation, give your interpretation.

4. **Empower yourself.** No matter who you are, what position you will hold, or where you will work, you probably will have to report to somebody. If you are

fortunate enough to work in a culture of empowerment, you are allowed control over your job (not complete control, but enough control to make you feel your opinion matters). When you are not given an opportunity to provide input, you will eventually lose interest in your job. When empowered, you have the confidence to do something to alter your circumstances. On the job, empowerment means that you can make decisions to benefit the organization and its customers.

If you want to gain empowerment in your life and work, here are a few tips: Be assertive, ask for credit for yourself when it is due, propose ideas to your group and your supervisor, initiate projects without being asked, tie your personal goals to those of the organization, develop your leadership skills, plan to learn on a continuous basis, be informed, don't let others intimidate you, and don't complain about a bad situation. Instead, take action to improve it.

5. **Acquire political savvy.** Politics is an inevitable part of every organization in the United States, including your school. Politics has always been a part of the workplace and always will be. The trick is to learn to play the political game to your own advantage *and* to the advantage of others without causing harm to anyone else. Being political means getting along with others in order to move them toward accomplishing a specific goal. It does not mean maneuvering for selfish purposes, manipulating in order to deceive, or scheming so others lose while you win.

   Here are some tips and techniques to be an effective player in the political game:

   - *Think about what you say.* Understand the effect your words will have on others before you say or write them.
   - *Empathize.* Try to think of a situation from the other person's perspective.
   - *Suggest a trial period, if you meet opposition to an idea you're proposing.* If you are as successful as you are confident, you can then ask to have the trial period extended.
   - *Learn about the political climate in which you are working.* This means knowing, among other things, what actions have led to failure for others, knowing who is "in" and why, determining who is "out" and why, and learning what behaviors lead to promotion.
   - *Volunteer to do the jobs no one else wants to do.* Occasionally pitching in shows your willingness to get the job done. However, do not make this your trademark; you do not want others to think they can take advantage of you.
   - *Work hard to meet the needs of those in authority.* Make certain you fully understand management's requirements; then go out of your way to meet them. If in time you do not think you are getting the recognition or respect you deserve, make your own needs known.
   - *Give credit.* You never know who may be in a position to hurt or harm you. Consequently, the best policy is to treat everyone with respect and dignity. Show your appreciation to everyone who has helped you. Do not steal credit that belongs to someone else.
   - *Learn your supervisor's preferences.* The more you are in sync with your supervisor's style, wishes, and preferences, the better you can do your job. However, do not be a rubber stamp. Rather, work the way your manager works. When necessary, suggest better ways of doing things.
   - *Keep secrets—your own and others'.* Resist the temptation to tell all. Not only do you run the risk of being labeled a gossip, but if you share too much about yourself, your words can come back to haunt you. If you are revealing information told to you in confidence, you are bound to lose the trust and respect of those who originally confided in you.

If you are asked to lead a team, you will need to involve all members in discussions, know how to manage conflict, understand team dynamics, and assess the team's success.

© PHOTODISC GREEN / GETTY IMAGES

6. **Become a team builder.** Throughout your college and business career you will participate on teams. Ninety-five percent of U.S. business organizations employ teamwork. An effective team is one that meets its goals on time and, if a budget is involved, within budget. The first step in creating an effective team is to have goals that are clear, realistic, supported by each team member, and parallels the larger organization goals. Exhibit 1 lists the questions that teams should answer to ensure their success.

7. **Handle conflict well.** Let's face it. The world is not a perfect place and there are no perfect people inhabiting it. The best we can hope for is people's willingness to improve life's circumstances. If we are truly committed to the idea of reducing school and workplace conflict, there is much we can do to inspire such willingness in others. Bringing conflict into the open has its advantages. Talking about conflict often helps to clear the air, and thinking about the possibility of conflict often helps to avoid it.

Exhibit 1 | Key Questions That Teams Should Answer Before Starting a Project

1. What are the goals?
2. Who provides the mission statement?
3. What are our limits?
4. Where will support come from? Who will be our sponsor?
5. Who will be team leader? How is he or she selected?
6. What are the deadlines we face?
7. What resources are available?
8. What data will we need to collect?
9. For how long will our team exist?
10. Who are the customers for our team results? What do they expect of us?
11. Will our team responsibilities conflict with our regular jobs?
12. What is the reward for success?
13. How will decisions be made?
14. How will our efforts be measured?
15. Will our intended success be replicated? If so, how and by whom?

When conflicts occur, try the K-I-N-D technique. The letters stand for:

K = Kind
I = Informed
N = New
D = Definite

The technique involves your requesting a meeting with the difficult person, whether he or she is having a conflict with you or with others. Start off with kind words, words that encourage cooperation, words that show your determination to make the conflict situation better. Next, demonstrate that you have taken the time to learn more about the person, what is important to him or her, what he or she prefers in terms of work. Show by your words that you have taken the time to become informed about the individual.

The third step requires you to do something novel, something you have not tried before. Put your creativity to work, and discover a plan to which you can both subscribe (for example, keeping a journal regarding the problem and possible solutions).

Finally, do not permit the exchange to conclude until you have made a definite overture to ensure future success. What can you promise the other person you will do differently? What are you asking him or her to do differently? Set a time to meet again and review your individual attempts to achieve collective improvement.

Make Your Future Happen: Learn to Plan[2]

There is a natural conflict between planning and being impulsive, between pursuing a long-range goal and doing what you feel like doing right now. If you have ever had to study while the rest of the family was in the living room watching television, you know what that conflict feels like. If you have ever been invited to go to the mall to eat pizza and hang out with friends, but stayed home to work on a class assignment, you know that sticking to a plan is not easy.

Of course, planning and being impulsive are both good. They both have a place in your life. You need to balance them. Having a plan does not mean that you can't act on the spur of the moment and do something that was not planned. Spontaneous events produce some of the happiest, most meaningful times of your life. Problems arise when you consistently substitute impulsive actions for goal-oriented planning. Success in life requires a balance between the two.

If you do not engage in long-range planning and lack the discipline for it, you may limit your opportunities to be impulsive. You are not going to take a weekend fun trip just because you need a break, if you have not saved the money to do it. In the short run, planning involves sacrifice, but in the long run, it gives you more options.

What Is a Plan?

A **plan** is a method or process worked out in advance that leads to the achievement of some goal. A plan is systematic, which means it relies on using a step-by-step procedure. A plan also needs to be flexible so that it may be adapted to gradual changes in your goal.

The Planning Process

Whether choosing a college or finding financial aid, you should understand how the planning process helps you accomplish your goals. The following steps outline the planning process.

Step 1: Set a Goal. Identify something you want to achieve or obtain, your **goal.** The goal, which is usually longer term in nature, will require planning, patience, and discipline to achieve. Just living in the present moment is not a goal.

Step 2: Acquire Knowledge. Gain an understanding of your goal and what will be required to achieve it. Gather information about your goal through research, conversation, and thought.

Step 3: Compare Alternatives. Weigh your options, which are the different paths you might take to achieve your goal. Analyze the pluses and minuses of each—the costs, the demands, the likelihood of success.

Step 4: Choose a Strategy. Select one option as the best plan of action. The choice is based on sound information, the experience of others, and your own interests and abilities.

Step 5: Make a Commitment. Resolve to proceed step-by-step toward achieving your goal. Keep your eyes on the prize.

Step 6: Stay Flexible. Evaluate your progress, and when necessary, revise your plan to deal with changing circumstances and new opportunities.

An Example of Planning

The following example illustrates the process of buying a new stereo using this planning process.

Step 1: Set a Goal. Purchase a stereo system.

Step 2: Acquire Knowledge. Visit friends to hear their systems. Study standards and specifications. Check on dealers, brands, models, and prices. Consult *Consumer Reports.*

Step 3: Compare Alternatives.

Alternative 1: Purchase a stereo from an online auction like e-Bay.

Pro: Affordable high-end equipment. Can buy right now.

Con: Uncertain condition of equipment. Limited warranty.

Alternative 2: Buy a compact shelf system for $325.

Pro: Can afford now. New equipment with warranty.

Con: Not suitable for adding extra speakers or using with television. Not the best sound quality.

Alternative 3: Buy a high-quality component system for $775.

Pro: Excellent sound. Greatest flexibility. New equipment with warranty.

Con: Costs more than prepared to pay now.

Step 4: Choose a Strategy. Decide to buy the high-quality system, but rather than using a credit card and paying interest, will delay the purchase for six months in order to save for it.

Step 5: Make a Commitment. Give up going to the movies for the six-month period, carry a lunch and stop eating out, and place the savings in a stereo fund.

Step 6: Keep Flexible. Four months into the plan, a model change sale provides an opportunity to buy comparable equipment for $550. Make the purchase, paying cash.

Planning for Your Life

Using the planning process to make a buying decision is a simple exercise. Making a decision about major parts of your life is far more complex. You will see that no part of life is exempt from the need for planning. It is important to apply thought,

Every aspect of your life deserves some type of planning. One decision you will need to make is how to spend your time and money. Will volunteering be one of your priorities?

creativity, and discipline to all the interrelated phases of our lives. These phases include the following:

- **Career** Choosing a field of work and developing the knowledge and skills needed to enter and move ahead in that field. We will offer you some tips to get started on a great career later in the Prologue.
- **Self** Deciding who you are and what kind of person you want to be, working to develop your strengths and overcome your weaknesses, refining your values.
- **Lifestyle** Expressing yourself in the nature and quality of your everyday life, your recreation and hobbies, how you use your time and money.
- **Relationships** Developing friendships and learning to get along with people in a variety of contexts. Building family and community ties.
- **Finances** Building the financial resources and the economic security needed to pursue all the other dimensions of your life. We will give you some tips in Chapters 21 and 22 on planning for financial security.

Dreams and Plans

People are natural dreamers. Dreams give us pleasure. They are also part of making a future. If you do not have dreams or think that you are not worthy of dreaming, something very important may be missing from your life. You have a right to your dreams, and you need them—even if there is little possibility that they will ever come true.

Planning is not the same as dreaming, but it uses dreams as raw materials. It translates them into specific goals. It tests them. It lays out a course of action that moves you toward realizing these goals and sets up milestones you need to achieve. Planning brings dreams down to earth and turns them into something real and attainable. For example, assume you have a dream to visit Spain as an exchange student. To translate this dream into a specific goal, you will need to follow the planning process—gather information about the exchange process, discuss the program with parents and teachers, and improve your Spanish-language skills.

Directions for Your Life

One of the best things about pursuing our dreams is that, even when you fall short, the effort leads to growth, and opens a path to other opportunities. The person who practices the piano every day may not achieve the dream of becoming a concert pianist but may eventually put appreciation of music to work as the director of an arts organization. A basketball player may not make it to a professional team but may enjoy a satisfying career as a coach or a sports writer. Without a plan, dreams simply dissolve. With a plan, they give shape and direction to our lives.

Planning involves a lot of thinking and finding answers to lots of questions. The answers and even the plan will change over time as you gain more knowledge and life experience. Planning is a skill that is useful in every area of your life. It is something you have to pursue consciously and thoughtfully. When you plan, you translate your goals and dreams into step-by-step strategies, specific things you can do to test your goals and bring them to reality. You often have to revise your plans, but even when your plans are not fulfilled, planning will have a positive effect on the course of your life.

Going to College Is an Opportunity of a Lifetime—Grab It and Don't Let Go[3]

You have already had one of your dreams come true—you are in college. It is indeed a rare privilege because far less than 1 percent of traditional college-age people around the world get to attend college. You're lucky! So make the best of it by learning the following college skills.

Learn to Concentrate

Concentration is the art of being focused, the ability to pay attention. Without concentration, you have no memory of what you hear, see, and read. Concentration is a frame of mind that enables you to stay centered on the activity or work you are doing. You know when you're concentrating because time seems to go by quickly, distractions that normally take you off task don't bother you, and you have a lot of mental or physical energy for the task.

You are ultimately in charge of how well you concentrate. Here are some ways to make it happen:

- *Choose a workplace.* Avoid the bed—you associate it with relaxing or sleeping. Try a desk or table for studying; you will concentrate better and accomplish more in less time. You will also have a convenient writing space and plenty of space to spread out. Be sure to have good lighting.
- *Feed your body right.* What you eat plays an important role in how well or how poorly you concentrate. Protein foods (such as cheese, meat, fish, and vegetables) keep the mind alert, while carbohydrates (such as pasta, bread, and processed sugars) make you sleepy. Caffeine (commonly found in coffee, tea, soft drinks, and chocolate) acts as a stimulant in low doses.
- *Avoid food.* Food and serious learning don't mix well. Think about it. When you try to eat and study at the same time, which gets more of your concentration? The food, of course! You will be more effective if you eat first, then study.
- *Listen to your own thoughts.* Listening to anything but your own thoughts interferes with good concentration. Eliminating distractions such as music, television, cell phones, e-mail beeps, and other people can greatly increase the amount of studying you can accomplish. Hold all calls and let e-mail wait.

Choose a study location that is free from distractions so you can concentrate better and accomplish more in less time.

© NICK DOLDING / TAXI / GETTY IMAGES

- *Make a to-do list.* If you are trying to study but get distracted by all of the things you need to do, take time to make a to-do list. Keeping track of your thoughts on paper and referring to the paper from time to time can be very effective for clearing your mind and focusing on your task.
- *Take short, frequent breaks.* Since people concentrate for about 20 minutes or less at a time, it would make sense to capitalize on your natural body rhythms and take a short break every 20 to 30 minutes. If you feel you are fully concentrating and involved in a task, then work until a natural break occurs.

Learn to Manage Your Time

There are two ways to make sure you have more time in a day. *The first and most important way to gain more time is to plan it!* It's like getting in a car and going somewhere. You need to know where you are going and have a plan to get there. Without a plan, you will waste your time and take longer to get to your destination—if you get there at all!

A **weekly project planner** will allow you to keep track of your assignments in more detail. It contains a to-do list specific to one day. It looks like a calendar but is divided into five, one-day periods with plenty of space to write. Using a weekly project planner is an effective way to keep track of assignments and plan study time according to the school calendar. Free calendars are available at **http://www.calendar.yahoo.com**.

A second way to gain more time in a day is to do more in less time. This can be as simple as doubling up on activities. For example, if you have three errands, you might try to combine them instead of doing one at a time, making one round-trip instead of three. If you commute on a bus or train or carpool, you can study during your ride. At lunch, you can review notes. Use your imagination as to how you can get more done in less time.

Here are some ideas to help you master your time:

- *Prepare for the morning the evening before.* Put out your clothes; make lunches; pack your books.
- *Get up 15 minutes earlier in the morning.* Use the time to plan your day, review your assignments, or catch up on the news.
- *Schedule a realistic day.* Avoid planning for every minute. Leave extra time in your day for getting to appointments and studying.
- *Leave room in your day for the unexpected.* This will allow you to do what you need to do, regardless of what happens. If the unexpected never happens, you will have more time for yourself.
- *Do one thing at a time.* If you try to do two things at once, you become inefficient. Concentrate on the here and now.
- *Learn to say "No!"* Say no to social activities or invitations when you don't have the time or energy.

Solve the Money Problem

You can get college money from three different sources:

- **Grants and Scholarships.** This refers to aid you do not have to repay. Grants are usually based on need while scholarships are frequently based on academic merit and other qualifying factors.
- **Educational Loans.** These are usually subsidized by federal and state governments or by the colleges themselves. Generally the loans carry lower interest rates than commercial loans, and you do not have to pay them off until after graduation.

- **Work Aid.** This is financial aid you have to work for, frequently 10 or 15 hours a week on campus.

There are many ways to cut the cost of going to college. Consider these:

- going to a community college for the first two years and then transferring to a four-year institution
- attending a nearby college and living at home
- enrolling in one of the 1,000 college and universities with cooperative educational programs that alternate between full-time studies and full-time employment
- taking a full-time job at a company that offers free educational opportunities as a fringe benefit

To learn about college costs and financial-aid, the first source to consult is *The College Board College Costs and Financial Aid Handbook*, which is probably available in the reference section of your local library. The handbook contains extensive tables outlining expenses and financial-aid programs at approximately 3,000 colleges and universities. It describes various kinds of financial aid, and since most financial aid is determined by need, it provides information for calculating your financial-aid eligibility. It also contains bibliographical information. The Web also offers information on financial aid, such as these sites:

- **http://www.fastweb.com** Fastweb has a database of more than 180,000 private sector scholarships, grants, and loans.
- **http://www.easi.ed.gov** This is the U.S. Department of Education information site for federal aid programs.

Study Smart

The first key to doing well in a subject is to complete your assignments on time. Most instructors base their assignments on what they will be discussing in class on a given day. So, if you read the pages you are assigned for the day they are due, you will better understand the day's lecture. If you don't complete an assignment when it is due, not only will you be at a disadvantage in the class, but you will have twice as much work to do for the following class.

Second, know what material to study. This may sound simple, but all too often students do not ask what material they should study and find out too late that they studied the wrong information. The easiest and most accurate way to learn what will be covered on a test is to ask your instructor or read the syllabus.

Tests measure your working memory and knowledge base. To help yourself remember, you can use several **memory devices** to recall the information you need to study. Here are a few memory devices that have been proven to work:

- *Recite information using your own words.* You will learn more when you reinforce your learning in as many ways as possible. You can reinforce your learning through hearing, writing, reading, reviewing, and reciting.
- *Develop acronyms.* **Acronyms** are words or names formed from the first letters or groups of letters in a phrase. Acronyms help you remember because they organize information according to the way you need or want to learn it. When you study for a test, be creative and make up your own acronyms. For example, COD means "cash on delivery," and GDP refers to "gross domestic product."
- *Try mnemonic sentences, rhymes, or jingles.* **Mnemonic sentences** are similar to acronyms; they help you organize your ideas. But, instead of creating a word, you make up a sentence. Creating a rhyme, song, or jingle can make the information even easier to remember. The more creative and silly the sentence, the

easier it is to remember. Take, for example, the nine planets listed in order according to their distance from the sun:

Mercury Venus Earth Mars Jupiter Saturn Uranus Neptune Pluto

The first letters of these words are: M V E M J S U N P.

An acronym using these letters would be difficult to remember. But if you create a sentence using the letters in order, you will remember the sequence better. For example: My Very Educated Mother Just Served Us Nine Pizzas

- *Visualize.* Visualization refers to creating or recalling mental pictures related to what you are learning. Have you ever tried to remember something while taking a test and visualized the page the information was on? This is your visual memory at work. Approximately 90 percent of your memory is stored visually in pictures, so trying to visualize what you want to remember is a powerful study tool.

Become a Master at Taking Tests

Taking a formal test is like playing a game. The object is to get as many points as possible in the time that you are allowed. Tests are evaluations of what you know and what you can do with what you know. Here are the rules of the test-taking game:

Rule 1: Act as If You Will Succeed. Thought is powerful. When you think negative thoughts, your stress level rises. Your confidence level may drop, which often leads to feelings of failure. When this happens, think about success. Smile and take deep, slow breaths. Close your eyes, and imagine getting the test back with a good grade written at the top.

Rule 2: Arrive Ahead of Time. Being on time or early for a test sets your mind at ease. You will have a better chance of getting your favorite seat, relaxing, and preparing yourself mentally for the game ahead.

Rule 3: Bring the Essential Testing Tools. Don't forget to bring the necessary testing tools along with you, including extra pens, sharpened pencils, erasers, a calculator, dictionary, and other items you may need.

Rule 4: Ignore Panic Pushers. Some people become nervous before a test and hit the panic button, afraid they don't know the material. **Panic pushers** are people who ask you questions about the material they are about to be tested on. If you know the answers, you will feel confident; however, if you don't, you may panic and lose your confidence. Instead of talking with a panic pusher before a test, spend your time concentrating on what you know, not on what you don't know.

Rule 5: Preview the Playing Field. Here's how to do a preview:

- Listen to instructions, and read directions carefully.
- Determine the point spread. Look at the total number of questions and the point value of each. Decide how much time you can spend on each question and still finish the test on time.
- Budget your time. If you budget your time and stick to your time limits, you will always complete the test in the amount of time given.
- Use the test as an information tool. Be on the lookout for clues that answer other questions. Frequently, instructors will test you on a single topic in more than one way.

Rule 6: Write in the Margin. Before you begin the test, write key terms, formulas, names, dates, and other information in the margin so you won't forget them.

Rule 7: Complete the Easy Questions First. Answering easy questions first helps build your confidence. If you come across a tough question, mark it so you can come back to it later. Avoid spending so much time on a challenging question that you might run out of time to answer the questions you do know.

Rule 8: Know If There Is a Guessing Penalty. Chances are your tests will carry no penalty for guessing. If your time is about to run out and there is no penalty, take a wild guess. On the other hand, if your test carries a penalty for guessing, choose your answers wisely, and leave blank the answers you do not know.

Rule 9: Avoid Changing Your Answers. Have you ever chosen an answer, changed it, and learned later that your first choice was correct? Research indicates that three out of four times your first choice is usually correct; therefore, you should avoid changing an answer unless you are *absolutely sure* the answer is wrong.

Rule 10: Write Clearly and Neatly. If you are handwriting your test (versus using a computer), imagine your instructor reading your writing. Is it easy to read or difficult? The easier your test is for the instructor to read, the better your chances of getting a higher grade.

Here are some Web sites to help you learn more about taking tests:

Essay tests and a checklist for essay tests

http://www.calpoly.edu/~sas/asc/ael/tests.essay.html

http://www.utexas.edu/student/utlc/handouts/1446.html

Checklist for essay tests

http://www.mtsu.edu/~studskl/essay.html

General test taking

http://www.calpoly.edu/~sas/asc/ael/tests.general.html

Posttest analysis

http://www.calpoly.edu/~sas/asc/ael/tests.post.test.analysis.html

Objective tests

http://www.utexas.edu/student/utlc/handouts/1444.html

Getting Your Career Off on the Right Track

Mark this section of the text with a permanent bookmark because you are going to want to refer back to it many times during the remainder of your college career. Yes, we are going to give you a road map to find, keep, and advance in that job that is perfect for you.

Think Positively

To be successful in life and in a career you need to be positive. *Positive thinking* is making a conscious effort to think with an optimistic attitude and to anticipate positive outcomes. *Positive behavior* means purposely acting with energy and enthusiasm. When you think and behave positively, you guide your mind toward your goals and generate matching mental and physical energy.

Positive thinking and behavior are often deciding factors in landing top jobs: your first job, a promotion, a change of jobs—whatever career step you are targeting. That's because the subconscious is literal; it accepts what you regard as fact.

Follow these steps to form the habit of positive thinking and to boost your success:

1. **Deliberately motivate yourself every day.** Think of yourself as successful, and expect positive outcomes for everything you attempt.
2. **Project energy and enthusiasm.** Employers hire people who project positive energy and enthusiasm. Develop the habit of speaking, moving, and acting with these qualities.

3. **Practice this positive-expectation mind-set until it becomes a habit.** Applicants who project enthusiasm and positive behavior generate a positive chemistry that rubs off. Hiring decisions are influenced largely by this positive energy. The habit will help you reach your peak potential.
4. **Dwell on past successes.** Focusing on past successes to remind yourself of your abilities helps in attaining goals. For example, no one is ever born knowing how to ride a bicycle or how to use a computer software program. Through training, practice, and trial and error, you master new abilities. During the trial-and-error phases of development, remind yourself of past successes; look at mistakes as part of the natural learning curve. Continue until you achieve the result you want, and remind yourself that you have succeeded in the past and can do so again. You fail only when you quit trying![4]

Take a Good Look At Yourself

Once you've developed a positive, "can do" attitude, the next step is to better understand yourself. Ask yourself two basic questions: "Who am I?" and "What can I do?"

Who Am I? The first step is to ask "Who am I?" This question is the start of *self-assessment*, examining your likes and dislikes and basic values. You may want to ask yourself the following questions:

- Do I want to help society?
- Do I want to help make the world a better place?
- Do I want to help other people directly?
- Is it important for me to be seen as part of a big corporation?
- Do I prefer working indoors or outdoors?
- Do I like to meet new people, or do I want to work alone?

What Can I Do? After determining what your values are, take the second step in career planning by asking "What can I do?" This question is the start of *skill assessment*, evaluating your key abilities and characteristics for dealing successfully with problems, tasks, and interactions with other people. Many skills—for instance, the ability to speak clearly and strongly—are valuable in many occupations.

Part-time jobs can teach you valuable business skills that will make you more attractive to employers. Choose a job, if possible, that gives you experience related to your chosen field.

Be sure to consider the work experience you already have including part-time jobs while going to school, summer jobs, volunteer jobs, and internships (short-term jobs for students, related to their major field of study). These jobs teach you skills and make you more attractive to potential employers. It's never too early or too late to take a part-time job in your chosen field. For instance, someone with an interest in accounting would do well to try a part-time job with a CPA (certified public accountant) firm.

In addition to examining your job-related skills, you should also look at your leisure activities. Some possible questions: Am I good at golf? Do I enjoy sailing? Tennis? Racquetball? In some businesses, transactions are made during leisure hours. In that case, being able to play a skillful, or at least adequate, game of golf or tennis may be an asset.

It's hard to like your job if you don't like the field that you're in. Most career counselors agree that finding work you're passionate about is one of the critical factors behind career success. That's why so many career counselors love all those diagnostic tools that measure your personality traits, skill levels, professional interests, and job potential.

The Web is virtually exploding with tests and assessments that you can take. Try, for example, **http://www.self-directed-search.com**. This test is based on the theory that people and work environments can be classified into six basic types: realistic, investigative, artistic, social, enterprising, and conventional. The test determines which three types best describe you, and it suggests occupations that could be a good match. The **Keirsey Character Sorter (http://www.keirsey.com)** is a first cousin of Myers-Briggs. It sorts people into four temperaments: idealists, rationals, artisans, and guardians. Like Myers-Briggs, it not only places you in an overall category, but it also offers a more detailed evaluation of your personality traits. To find a bunch of tests in one place, visit **Yahoo!** and type "online personality tests" in the search field.

Understand What Employers Want[5]

Employers want to hire people who will make their businesses more successful. The most desirable employees have the specific skills, transferable career competencies, work values, and personal qualities necessary to be successful in the employers' organizations. The more clearly you convey your skills as they relate to your job target, the greater your chance of landing your ideal job.

Job-Specific Skills. Employers seek job-specific skills (skills and technical abilities that relate specifically to a particular job). Two examples of job-specific skills are using specialized tools and equipment and using a custom-designed software program.

Transferable Skills and Attitudes. Change is a constant in today's business world. Strong transferable career skills are the keys to success in managing your career through change. The most influential skills and attitudes are the abilities to:

- Work well with people.
- Plan and manage multiple tasks.
- Maintain a positive attitude.
- Show enthusiasm.

Employers need workers who have transferable career competencies—basic skills and attitudes that are important for all types of work. These skills make you highly marketable because they're needed for a wide variety of jobs and can be transferred from one task, job, or workplace to another. Examples include these:

- Planning skills
- Research skills
- Communication skills
- Human relations and interpersonal skills
- Critical thinking skills
- Management skills

Take, for example, a construction supervisor and an accountant. Both must work well with others, manage time, solve problems, read, and communicate effectively—all transferable competencies. They both must be competent in these areas even though framing a house and balancing a set of books (the job-specific skill for each field, respectively) are not related. In every occupation, transferable competencies are as important as technical expertise and job-specific skills.[6]

Finding My First Professional Job

The next step is landing the job that fits your skills and desires. You need to consider not only a general type of work but also your lifestyle and leisure goals. If you like to be outdoors most of the time, you might be very unhappy spending eight hours a

Exhibit 2 | Where the Jobs Are: Projected U.S. Employment, 1998–2010

WHERE THE JOBS ARE
(projected U.S. employment, 1998-2010)
-10 to 2 percent
3 to 8 percent
9 to 16 percent
17 to 58 percent
Note: White denotes missing data.
Big growth in employment is projected for counties in the West, where tourism economies and mountain views are drawing willing workers.
Source: Woods & Poole Economics, Washington, DC

SOURCE: Reprinted from *American Demographics* magazine. Reprinted with permission of Primedia Business Magazines & Media. All Rights Reserved.

day in an office. Someone who likes living in small towns may dislike working at the headquarters of a big corporation in Los Angeles or New York City or Chicago. But make sure that your geographic preferences are realistic. Some parts of the country will experience much greater growth in jobs than others (see Exhibit 2).

You might start answering the question "What will I do" by studying the *Career Employment Opportunities Directory—Business Administration.* The directory lists several hundred up-to-date sources of employment with businesses, government agencies, and professional organizations.

Another important source of job information is the *Occupational Outlook Handbook*, published every two years by the U.S. Department of Labor. The introduction in the current *Handbook* projects job opportunities by industry through the year 2002. The *Handbook* is divided into 19 occupational clusters describing 200 jobs (with a section on military careers). Among the clusters are education, sales and marketing, transportation, health, and social services. Each job description tells about the nature of the work, working conditions, required training, other qualifications, chances for advancement, employment outlook, earnings, related occupations, and sources of more information. Two other good sources of job information are *Changing Times Annual Survey: Jobs for New College Graduates* and *Peterson's Business and Management Jobs.* If you are a member of a minority group, you might want to check out **http://www.black-collegian.com**, or **http://www.saludos.com**.

The career appendixes at the end of each part of this book are another good source of career information. They contain short job descriptions and explain what parts of the country are most likely to have openings in certain fields, the

When preparing your résumé, use descriptive, action words rather than vague words to describe your work experience. Also, highlight exceptional skills that are relevant to your targeted job. And always be completely honest in describing your educational and work experiences.

skills required, the employment outlook through 2010, and salary information. Each career appendix features a "dream career," a career worth striving for.

Using the Internet to Jump-Start Your Job Search

There are about 100,000 job-related sites and over 3 million résumés on the Internet. To break through the clutter, you must start with a great résumé—a written description of your education, work experience, personal data, and interests. Professional web resume software (available through **http://www.web-resume.org**) can make your résumé preparation task a lot easier. WebResume software not only helps you format your résumé but also lets you control who sees it. A "confidential" option enables you to create a two-tiered résumé. The first tier offers professional information but doesn't include your name or address. The second tier contains contact information but is password protected—and you decide who can get the password. WebResume understands what's different about looking for a job online. Its "Search Engine Keywords" function inserts the "tags" that major search engines use to index résumés. And WebResume will submit your résumé to 11 job sites, including CareerMosaic, JobTrak, and IntelliMatch. Exhibit 3 offers seven tips for preparing your cyber résumé.

Once you have created a great résumé, the next step is to get it noticed. A few tips for getting noticed are:

- Post a digital version of your résumé with examples of past work experience on your own home page. Many colleges and professional associations offer free or low-cost Web space and resources for posting résumés.

Exhibit 3 | Tips for Preparing Your Cyber Résumé

- Use key words to define your skills, experience, education, professional affiliations, and so on.
- Use concrete words rather than vague descriptions to describe your experience. For example, use "managed a team of software engineers" rather than "responsible for managing and training."
- Be concise and truthful.
- Use jargon and acronyms specific to your industry (spell out the acronyms for a human reader).
- Increase your list of key words by including specifics. For example, list the names of software that you use, such as Microsoft Word.
- Use common headings, such as Objective, Experience, Work History, Skills, Education, Professional Affiliations, Licenses, and References.
- Describe your interpersonal traits and attitude. Key words can include *dependable, high energy, leadership, sense of responsibility,* and *good memory.*

SOURCE: "Resume Tool Kit," http://www.thespectrum.com (January 2003).

- Place the word *résumé* in the Web site address to increase your chances of being caught by Internet recruiters.
- Place plenty of links to Web sites of present and former employers, colleges, professional associations, and publications on your digital resume.
- Create a simpler version of your résumé to send to a recruiter or potential employer and let them know a longer version is available.
- Read the privacy policies of online job boards to prevent unwanted eyes from viewing your résumé. Some companies have "Web scavengers" who check for their own employees' résumés online. In turn, some job boards let users "block" certain companies from seeing their postings.
- Use niche job boards in your field. Smaller, targeted boards can sometimes be more effective than the big brand-name sites.[7]

There are tens of thousands of places to send your résumé; Exhibit 4 suggests several great places to begin and their rankings by users. Don't neglect using the Internet. In the past five years 60 percent of Americans did not use the Internet in their job search. Yet, 83 percent of the corporate recruiters use the Internet to advertise their jobs.[8]

Oh My Gosh—I've Got a Job Interview

If some of the companies you contacted want to speak with you, your résumé achieved its goal of getting you a job interview. Look at the interview as a chance to describe your knowledge and skills and interpret them in terms of the employer's specific needs. To make this kind of presentation, you need to do some research on the company. A great place to start looking is **http://www.hoovers.com**. This site offers profiles and financial data on more than 12,000 companies worldwide. It also provides links to other sites where you can dig further. Hoovers.com allows you to search for companies using the following categories:

- company name
- geographic location
- industry

Exhibit 4 | Some Places to Send Your Cyber Résumé and Their Ratings by Users

Monster.com	★★★★
HotJobs (hotjobs.yahoo.com)	★★★★
America's JobBank (americasjobbank.com)	★★★★
monsterTRAK (monstertrak.com)	★★★★
ExecuNet.com	★★★★
careerbuilder.com	★★★★
Careernet.com	★★★★
Jobhunt.com	★★★
CareerSite.com	★★
Job.com	★★

SOURCE: http://www.Epinions.com (January 28, 2003).

- stock index
- news stories

Another great place to get company information is **http://www.wetfeet.com**. You can check out hundreds of companies in over 35 different industries. Want to know what it's really like to work in the automobile industry? Check out its **Industry Profiles** section. You'll find out who the major players are and what they do. The site's **What's Great and What's to Hate** section tells you just that. And the **Real People Profile** section offers an interview with—you guessed it—a real person in a specific industry. Interviews provide valuable insights from those with experience: how they got their job, what a typical day is like for them, what career aspirations they have for the future, and the biggest misconceptions about their business.[9]

As you do your information search, you should build your knowledge in these three areas:

1. **General Information About the Occupational Field.** Learn about the current and predicted industry trends, general educational requirements, job descriptions, growth outlook, and salary ranges in the industry.
2. **Information About Prospective Employers.** Learn whether the organization is publicly or privately owned. Verify company names, addresses, products or services (current and predicted, as well as trends); history; culture; reputation; performance; divisions and subsidiaries; locations (U.S. and global); predicted growth indicators; number of employees; company philosophies and procedures; predicted job openings; salary ranges; and listings of managers of your targeted department within the organization. Also learn about the competitors and customers.
3. **Information About Specific Jobs.** Obtain job descriptions; identify the required education and experience; and determine prevalent working conditions, salary, and fringe benefits.[10]

Interview Like a Pro

An interview tends to have three parts: icebreaking (about five minutes), in which the interviewer tries to put the applicant at ease; questioning (directly or indirectly) by the interviewer; and questioning by the applicant. Almost every recruiter you meet will be trying to rate you in 5 to 10 areas. The questions will be designed to assess your skills and personality.

© DIGITAL VISION / GETTY IMAGES

One-on-one interviews are the most common and may include interviews with managers in different departments. Showing enthusiasm and interest in the job projects a positive impression.

Many firms start with a *screening interview*, a rather short interview (about 30 minutes) to decide whether to invite you back for a second interview. Only about 20 percent of job applicants are invited back. The second interview is a half day or a day of meetings set up by the human resource department with managers in different departments. After the meetings, someone from the human resource department will discuss other application materials with you and tell you when a letter of acceptance or rejection is likely to be sent. (The wait may be weeks or even months.) Many applicants send follow-up letters in the meantime to show they are still interested in the firm.

For the interview you should dress conservatively. Plan to arrive about 10 to 15 minutes ahead of time. Try to relax. Smile and make eye contact with (but do not stare at) the interviewer. Body language is an important communicator. The placement of your hands and feet and your overall posture say a good deal about you. Here are some other tips for interviewing like a pro:

1. **Concentrate on being likable.** As simplistic as it seems, research proves that one of the most essential goals in successful interviewing is to be liked by the interviewer. Interviewers want to hire pleasant people others will like working with on a daily basis. Pay attention to the following areas to project that you are highly likable:
    - Be friendly, courteous, and enthusiastic.
    - Speak positively.
    - Smile.
    - Use positive body language.
    - Make certain your appearance is appropriate.
2. **Project an air of confidence and pride.** Act as though you want and deserve the job, not as though you are desperate.
3. **Demonstrate enthusiasm.** The applicant's level of enthusiasm often influences employers as much as any other interviewing factor. The applicant who demonstrates little enthusiasm for a job will never be selected for the position.
4. **Demonstrate knowledge of and interest in the employer.** "I really want this job" is not convincing enough. Explain why you want the position and how the position fits your career plans. You can cite opportunities that may be unique to a firm or emphasize your skills and education that are highly relevant to the position.
5. **State your name and the position you're seeking.** When you enter the interviewer's office, begin with a friendly greeting and state the position you're interviewing for: "Hello, Ms. Levine, I'm Bella Reyna. I'm here to interview for the accounting position." If someone has already introduced you to the interviewer, simply say, "Good morning, Ms. Levine." Identifying the position is important because interviewers often interview for many different positions.
6. **Focus on how you fit the job.** Near the beginning of your interview, as soon as it seems appropriate, ask a question similar to this: "Could you describe the scope of the job and tell me what capabilities are most important in filling the position?" The interviewer's response will help you focus on emphasizing your qualifications that best match the needs of the employer.
7. **Speak correctly.** Grammatical errors can cost applicants the job. Use correct grammar, word choice, and a businesslike vocabulary, not an informal, chatty one. Avoid slang. When under stress, people often use pet phrases (such as *you know*) too often. This is highly annoying and projects immaturity and insecurity. Don't use *just* or *only.* "I just worked as a waiter." Don't say "I guess." Avoid the word *probably* because it suggests unnecessary doubt. Ask a friend or family

member to help you identify any speech weaknesses you have. Begin eliminating these speech habits now.[11]

Also, you should avoid these "disqualifiers" at all costs. Any one of these blunders could cost you your dream job:

1. Don't sit down until the interviewer invites you to; waiting is courteous.
2. Don't bring anyone else to the interview; it makes you look immature and insecure.
3. Don't smoke.
4. Don't put anything on or read anything on the interviewer's desk; it's considered an invasion of personal space.
5. Don't chew gum or have anything else in your mouth; this projects immaturity.
6. If you are invited to a business meal, don't order alcohol. When ordering, choose food that's easy to eat while carrying on a conversation.
7. Don't offer a limp handshake; it projects weakness. Use a firm handshake.[12]

Selecting the Right Job for You

Hard work and a little luck may pay off with multiple job offers. Your happy dilemma is deciding which one is best for you. Start by considering the FACTS:

- *Fit.* Do the job and the employer fit your skills, interests, and lifestyle?
- *Advancement and growth.* Will you have the chance to develop your talents and move up within the organization?
- *Compensation.* Is the employer offering a competitive salary and benefits package?
- *Training.* Will the employer provide you with the tools needed to be successful on the job?
- *Site.* Is the job location a good match for your lifestyle and your pocketbook?

A great way to evaluate a new location is through HOMEFAIR (**http://www.homefair.com**). This site offers tools to help you calculate the cost of moving, the cost of living, and the quality of life in various places. The **Moving Calculator** helps you figure out how much it will cost to ship your worldly possessions to a particular city. The **Relocation Crime Lab** compares crime rates in various locations. The **City Snapshots** feature compares demographic, economic, and climate information for two cities of your choosing. The **Salary Calculator** computes cost-of-living differences between hundreds of U.S. and international cities and tells you how much you'd need to make in your new city to maintain your current standard of living.

Starting Your New Job

No time is more crucial, and possibly nerve-racking, than the first few months at a new job. During this breaking-in period, the employer decides whether a new employee is valuable enough to keep and, if so, in what capacity. Sometimes the employee's whole future with the company rides on the efforts of the first few weeks or months.

Most firms offer some sort of formal orientation. But generally speaking, they expect employees to learn quickly—and often on their own. You will be expected to become familiar with the firm's goals; its organization, including your place in the company; and basic personnel policies, such as coffee breaks, overtime, and parking.

Here are a few tips on making your first job rewarding and productive:

- *Listen and learn:* When you first walk into your new job, let your eyes and ears take everything in. Do people refer to one another by first names, or is the company more formal? How do people dress? Do the people you work with drop into one another's open offices for informal chats about business matters? Or have you entered a "memo mill," where anything of substance is put on e-mail and talks with other employees are scheduled through secretaries? Size up where the power lies. Who seems to most often assume a leadership role? Who is the person others turn to for advice? Why has that person achieved that position? What traits have made this person a "political leader"? Don't be misled by what others say, but also don't dismiss their evaluations. Make your own judgments based on what you see and hear.
- *Do unto others:* Be nice. Nice people are usually the last to be fired and among the first to be promoted. Don't be pleasant only with those who can help you in the company. Be nice to everyone. You never know who can help you or give you information that will turn out to be useful. Genuinely nice people make routine job assignments, and especially pressure-filled ones, more pleasant. And people who are dealt with pleasantly usually respond in kind.
- *Don't start out as a maverick:* If every new employee tried to change tried-and-true methods to suit his or her whims, the firm would quickly be in chaos. Individual needs must take a back seat to established procedures. Devote yourself to getting things done within the system. Every manager realizes that it takes time for a new person to adjust. But the faster you start accomplishing things, the faster the boss will decide that you were the right person to hire.
- *Find a great mentor:* The leading cause of career unhappiness is working for a bad boss. Good jobs can easily be ruined by supervisors who hold you back. In contrast, your career will soar (and you will smile every day) when you have a great mentor helping you along the way. If you find a job with a super mentor, jump at the chance to take it.

Movin' On Up

Once you have been on the job for a while, you will want to get ahead and be promoted. Exhibit 5 offers several suggestions for improving your chances of promotion. The first item might seem a bit strange, yet it's there for a practical reason. If you don't really like what you do, you won't be committed enough to compete with those who do. The passionate people are the ones who go the extra mile, do the extra work, and come up with fresh out-of-the-box ideas.

So there you have it! In the next chapter we will begin our journey through the world of business so that you can determine what areas of business are most interesting to you. Remember, it's never too early to begin planning your career—the future is now.

Exhibit 5 How to Move Up

- Love what you do, which entails first figuring out who you are.
- Never stop learning about new technologies and new management skills.
- Try to get international experience even if it is only a short stint overseas.
- Create new business opportunities—they could lead to a promotion.
- Be really outstandingly terrific at what you're doing now, this week, this month.

Chapter 1

Participating in the Dynamic Business Environment

learning goals

1. How do businesses and not-for-profit organizations help create our standard of living?
2. How are social trends, such as more women entering the workforce, affecting business?
3. How are demographic trends creating new opportunities for business?
4. What are the primary features of the world's economic systems?
5. How can technological effectiveness help a firm reach its goals?
6. What are the trends in global competition?

Wow!! A Frozen Peanut Butter and Jelly Sandwich—Just What the Market Wanted

A frozen, individually wrapped peanut butter and jelly sandwich. Surely no one would want *that,* thought executives at jam maker J.M. Smucker Company (**http://www.smuckers.com**). After all, there's nothing easier for someone to slap together than PB&J.

But after testing a hockey puck–shaped, plastic-wrapped sandwich in several midwestern states and generating $20 million in sales, Smucker's now is shipping frozen PB&J, called UnCrustables®, almost everywhere. Television advertising boasts that the crusts are cut off, perfect for the youthful palate. Parents can put a frozen sandwich in their child's lunch box in the morning and it will thaw by noon.

What people want from their food is changing. These days they want it prepackaged, and they don't want to share. Years ago only school-lunch milk cartons and candy bars were sized for one person. Then came potato chips and juice boxes for little ones. Now businesses, ever on the hunt for the latest food fad, are taking food-for-one to the extreme. They're prepackaging everything from breakfast to fried chicken and repackaging food so that it is easier to eat in the car. Single-size food packs have become the major source of financial growth for the food industry. And for consumers, they are substituting for traditional after-school snacks and even dinner.

Meanwhile, increasing the size of the product helps spur sales, says Paul Merage, chief executive of Chef America Inc. (**http://www.chefamerica.com**), which makes Hot Pockets, the microwavable sandwiches. In the six months since his company started adding 10 percent more filling to Hot Pockets, keeping the price stable, sales have increased 32 percent, he says.

Even food companies that have been selling individual-packaging for a long time are looking for ways to make their products easier to eat. Frito-Lay (**http://www.fritolay.com**) recently started selling its Doritos and other chips in easy-access cans, called Go Snacks. At $1.29 each, Go Snacks are considered "single serve," and cost 30 cents more than a traditional bag, according to a Frito-Lay spokeswoman. She notes that the tops screw on and off for stop-and-go eating.[1]

Critical Thinking Questions

As you read this chapter, consider the following questions:

1. What other emerging trends might impact food packaging?
2. How can a firm position itself so that it can respond rapidly to changing trends?
3. What factors might decrease the sales of single-serving packages?

Principles of Business

Each day in America thousands of new businesses are born and a rare few will become the next Microsoft or e-Bay. Unfortunately, many others will never see their first anniversary. The survivors are those that understand the trends that affect all businesses and then successfully adapt to those trends. Smucker's survives and prospers because it capitalizes on evolving trends. We begin our study of business by explaining what a business does and how it is created. Next, you will discover the key trends of this century that will have an impact on all business organizations.

The Nature of Business

1 learning goal

business
An organization that strives for a profit by providing goods and services desired by its customers.

goods
Tangible items manufactured by businesses.

services
Intangible offerings of businesses that can't be held, touched, or stored.

standard of living
A country's output of goods and services that people can buy with the money they have.

A **business** is an organization that strives for a profit by providing goods and services desired by its customers. Businesses meet the needs of consumers by providing movies, medical care, autos, and countless other goods and services. **Goods** are tangible items manufactured by businesses, such as desks. **Services** are intangible offerings of businesses that can't be held, touched, or stored. Physicians, lawyers, restaurants, car washes, and airlines all provide services. Businesses also serve other organizations, such as hospitals, retailers, and governments, by providing machinery, goods for resale, computers, and thousands of other items.

Thus, businesses create the goods and services that are the basis of our standard of living. The **standard of living** of any country is measured by the output of goods and services people can buy with the money they have. The United States has one of the highest standards of living in the world. Several countries such as Switzerland and Germany have higher wages than the United States, but their standard of living isn't higher. The reason is that prices are so much higher in those countries that people are able to purchase less than people in the United States with the same amount of money. For example, a "Real Meal Deal" at McDonald's in Geneva, Switzerland, costs about $10 compared to less than $4 in the United States.

The United States has one of the highest standards of living in the world. The standard of living is measured by the output of goods and services people can buy with the money they have.

quality of life
The general level of human happiness based on such things as life expectancy, educational standards, health, sanitation, and leisure time.

risk
The potential to lose time and money or otherwise not be able to accomplish an organization's goals.

revenue
The money a company earns from providing services or selling goods to customers.

costs
Expenses incurred in creating and selling goods and services.

profit
The money left over after all expenses are paid.

Businesses play a key role in determining our quality of life by providing jobs and goods and services to society. **Quality of life** refers to the general level of human happiness based on such things as life expectancy, educational standards, health, sanitation, and leisure time. Zurich, Switzerland, is ranked as having the world's highest quality of life followed by Vienna, Austria, and Vancouver, Canada. Cities in Europe, Australia, and New Zealand generally rank closest to the top. The least appealing cities were Brazzaville, Congo, and Khartoum, Sudan.[2] Building a high quality of life is a combined effort of businesses, government, and not-for-profit organizations.

Creating a quality of life is not without risks. **Risk** is the potential to lose time and money or otherwise not be able to accomplish an organization's goals. Without enough blood donors, for example, the American Red Cross faces the risk of not meeting the demand for blood by victims of disaster. Businesses like Microsoft face the risk of falling short of its revenue goals. **Revenue** is the money a company earns from providing services or selling goods to customers. **Costs** are expenses for rent, salaries, supplies, transportation, and many other items that a company incurs from creating and selling goods and services. Some of the costs incurred by Smucker's (featured in our opening) include expenses for fruit, sugar, jars, labels, building rental or purchase, advertising, and transportation. **Profit** is the money left over after all expenses are paid.

When a company like Smucker's uses its resources intelligently, it can often increase sales, hold costs down, and earn a profit. Not all companies earn profit, but that is the risk of being in business. In American business today, there is generally a direct relationship between risks and profit: the greater the risks, the greater the potential profit (or loss). WebVan, an online home-delivery grocer, received hundreds of millions of dollars from investors who were convinced that WebVan had the potential for success. Despite WebVan's very efficient computerized distribution system, the company failed to convince enough people to change their grocery-shopping habits. WebVan is no longer in business.

Not-for-Profit Organizations

not-for-profit organization
An organization that exists to achieve some goal other than the usual business goal of profit.

Not all organizations strive to make a profit. A **not-for-profit organization** is an organization that exists to achieve some goal other than the usual business goal of profit. The United Way, Keep America Beautiful, the American Cancer Society, Greenpeace, and the Sierra Club are all not-for-profit organizations. Most hospitals, zoos, museums, and charities are also not-for-profit organizations. Government is our largest and most pervasive not-for-profit group. Not-for-profit organizations (not including government expenditures) now account for over 28 percent of the economic activity in the United States.

Successful not-for-profit organizations follow sound business principles. These groups have goals they hope to accomplish, but the goals are not focused on profits. For example, a not-for-profit organization's goal might be feeding the poor, stopping destruction of the environment, increasing attendance at the ballet, or preventing drunk driving. Reaching such goals takes good planning, management, and control. Not-for-profit organizations do not compete directly with each other as, for example, Ford and Honda do, but they do compete for people's scarce volunteer time and donations.

Factors of Production: The Building Blocks of Business

factors of production
The resources used to create goods and services.

Factors of production are the resources used to create goods and services. By using the factors of production efficiently, a company can produce more output with the same resources. Four traditional factors of production are common to

© GARY LANDERS / CINCINNATI ENQUIRER

Ricardo Johnson, Rachetta Johnson, and Charlene Monroe established Electrical Innovations based on career goals that went beyond mastery of the electrical trade. Holding onto their dream of running their own company, these entrepreneurs are strengthening their competitive position through networking, certification programs, and fortitude.

all productive activity: natural resources, labor, capital, and entrepreneurship. A fifth factor, knowledge, is gaining in importance.

Commodities that are useful inputs in their natural state are known as natural resources. They include farmland, forests, mineral and oil deposits, and water. Sometimes natural resources are simply called *land,* although, as you can see, the term means more than just land. Today, urban sprawl, pollution, and limited resources have raised questions about resource use. Conservationists, ecologists, and government bodies are proposing laws to require land-use planning and resource conservation.

The economic contributions of people working with their minds and muscles are called labor. This input includes the talents of everyone—from a restaurant cook to a nuclear physicist—who performs the many tasks of manufacturing and selling goods and services. The tools, machinery, equipment, and buildings used to produce goods and services and get them to the consumer are known as **capital.** Sometimes the term *capital* is also used to mean the money that buys machinery, factories, and other production and distribution facilities. However, because money itself produces nothing, it is *not* one of the basic inputs. Instead, it is a means of acquiring the inputs. Therefore, in this context, capital does not include money.

Entrepreneurs are people who combine the inputs of natural resources, labor, and capital to produce goods or services with the intention of making a profit. These people make all the decisions that set the course for their firms; they create products and production processes. Because they are not guaranteed a profit in return for their time and effort, they must be risk takers. Of course, if their firms succeed, the rewards may be great.

Today, many Americans want to start their own businesses. They are attracted by the opportunity to be their own boss and reap the financial rewards of a successful firm. Many start their first business from their dorm rooms, like Michael

Focusing on Small Business

Searching for Gold on Miami's South Beach

When Wenceslao Casares was a college student in Buenos Aires, he put together a business plan for a financial-services Web site. From the beginning, he was thinking big: The company would cater to the young and affluent of Latin America, a vast region that stretches from the U.S. border to the edge of Antarctica, spans two oceans, and encompasses everything from the maquiladoras of Mexico to the beaches of Rio. But when it came to choosing where to base the company, Casares picked a city in the United States that he had never been to: Miami.

"Latin America doesn't exist," Casares says. "It's a nice concept, but Brazil is Brazil, Mexico is Mexico, and Argentina is Argentina. Miami is the only place on Earth where Latin America exists."

Welcome to Miami, the dot-com capital of Latin America. Over the last few years, scores of Internet start-ups focused on Spanish and Portuguese speakers have opened offices in Miami. A city better-known for the model business than business models, Miami has suddenly become the epicenter for young entrepreneurs from all over Latin America. Some call it Silicon Barrio; others dub it—redundantly—Silicon Beach; but almost everyone agrees it's the hub for building a regional Net company.

"The idea is finally taking hold that you can do more in Miami than go out at night in South Beach or be a model," says Ignacio Vidaguren, the vice president for business development at MercadoLibre.com, a panregional auction site that launched in Argentina in 1999 and moved its headquarters to Miami in 2000.

The attractions are legion: proximity to Wall Street and the respectability of U.S. accounting rules; direct flights to the region's major markets; a locale that doesn't incite nationalist rivalries; and a multicultural Latin local society that appeals to a hip dot-com workforce and creates a critical mass for networking. The entire seaboard from Boca Raton through Fort Lauderdale to Miami bills itself as the "Internet Coast." (There's even a Web site devoted to the concept: **http://www.internetcoast.com.**)[3]

CRITICAL THINKING QUESTIONS

1. Why do you think Miami attracts so many Latin American entrepreneurs?
2. Do you think that being in Miami lowers the risk for young entrepreneurs?
3. What are some of the potential risks for anyone starting a new dot-com?

capital
The inputs, such as tools, machinery, equipment, and buildings, used to produce goods and services and get them to the customer.

Dell of Dell Computers, or while living at home, so their cost is almost zero.

Entrepreneurs include people like Bill Gates, the founder of Microsoft, who is now one of the richest people in the world. The list of entrepreneurs also includes countless thousands of individuals who have started small companies that, while remaining small, still contribute to America's economic well-being. Miami has proven to be a magnet for young Latino entrepreneurs, as described in the Focusing on Small Business box.

A number of outstanding managers and noted academics are beginning to emphasize a fifth factor of production—knowledge. **Knowledge** is the combined talents and skills of the workforce. As the world becomes ever more uncertain, the very nature of work, organizations, and management is changing. The new competitive environment places a premium on knowledge and learning. Lester Thurow, a leading world expert on economic issues, says that "the dominant competitive weapon of the twenty-first century will be the knowledge of the work force."[4] The companies that will become and remain successful will be the ones that can learn fast, assimilate this learning, and develop new insights. Pfizer and SAP Software are two firms often cited as learning-based organizations because they utilize their human resources so effectively.

concept check

Explain the concepts of revenue, costs, and profit.

What are the five factors of production?

What is the role of an entrepreneur in society?

Trends in Business

entrepreneurs
People who combine the inputs of natural resources, labor, and capital to produce goods or services with the intention of making a profit or accomplishing a not-for-profit goal.

knowledge
The combined talents and skills of the workforce.

Business owners and managers use their skills and resources to create goods and services that will satisfy customers and prospective customers. Owners and managers have a wide latitude of control over day-to-day business decisions such as which supplies are purchased, which employees are hired, what products are sold, and where they are sold. However, certain environmental conditions that affect a business cannot be controlled. These conditions are constantly changing and include social change, demographics, economic conditions, technology, and global competition, as shown in Exhibit 1.1. Successful owners and managers must continuously study these conditions and adapt their businesses, or they will lose their ability to compete.

Consider two examples of how companies have responded to changes in the business environment:

- The fast-food industry's traditional diner is male, between 5 and 24 years old, and typically short on cash. This youthful segment of the population is expected to grow by only 5 percent over the next decade, while the 45- to 64-year-old population will grow about 30 percent, according to the U.S. Census Bureau. In addition, baby boomers (persons born between 1946 and 1964) are more likely to eat out compared with previous generations in their age group. Pressed for time, they want food fast. Moreover, the growing availability of healthier and higher-quality sandwiches has eroded their loyalty to fast-food burgers.

  Lately, small restaurant chains have responded to this change in demographics and racked up impressive sales by offering Americans upscale sandwiches as an alternative to burgers and fries. Some of those outlets, such as Cosi and Briazz, have names designed to convey European sophistication. Others, such as Corner Bakery Cafe and Panera Bread Co., have names that emphasize their use of fresh bread. All of them hope to win a big following among the nation's aging and increasingly health-conscious baby boomers.[5]
- BMW noticed that consumers are beginning to get fed up with gas-guzzler vehicles that make parking a nightmare. Many auto buyers were ready for something small but didn't want to give up the luxury to which they had

Exhibit 1.1 | The Environment of Business

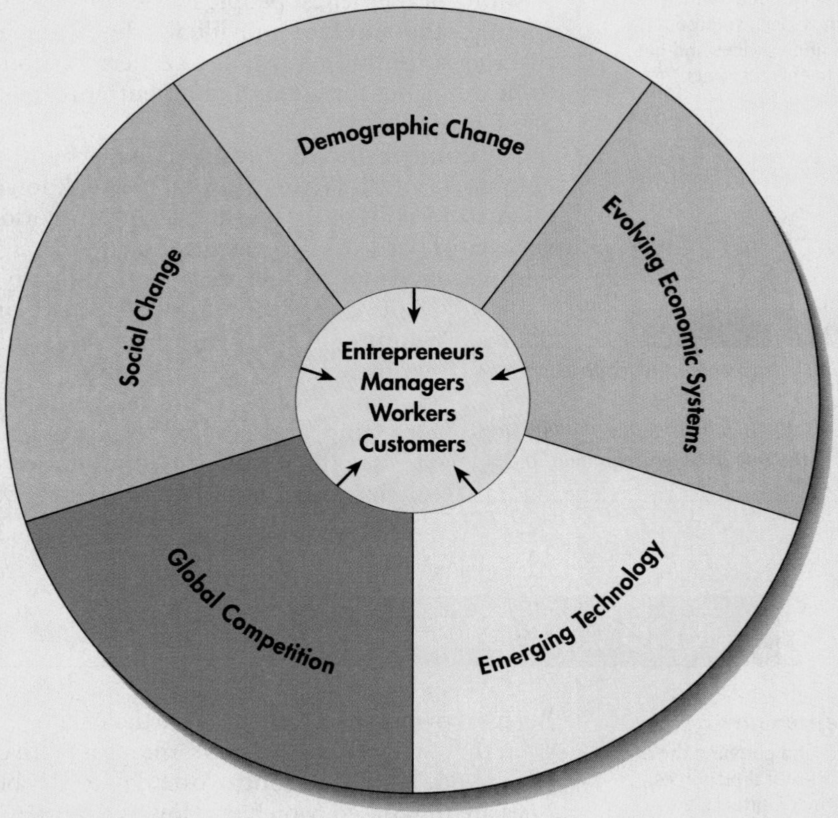

become accustomed. Enter BMW's Mini Cooper, the $20,000-plus tiny compact packed with high-tech features and high-style interiors. "This is a global trend," says Wolfgang Reitzle, head of Fort Motors' luxury division, which aims to use its Volvo brand to expand into the premium compact market. Mini Coopers have been in such demand that some dealers were asking $5,000 above the sticker price. In 2003, the Mini Cooper won the "best car" award in the North American Car and Truck of the Year awards.[6]

No one business is large or powerful enough to create major changes in the external environment. Thus, managers are basically adapters to rather than agents of change. For example, despite the huge size of General Motors, Ford, and DaimlerChrysler, these companies have only recently been able to stem the competitive push by the Japanese for an ever growing share of the U.S. automobile market. Global competition is basically an uncontrollable element in the external environment. The following section examines trends in the business environment that are reshaping today's business landscape.

Social Trends

2 learning goal

Social change is perhaps the most difficult environmental factor for owners and managers to forecast, influence, or integrate into business plans. Social factors include our attitudes, values, and lifestyles. Social factors influence the products people buy, the prices paid for products, the effectiveness of specific promotions, and how, where, and when people expect to purchase products.

© TERRI L. MILLER / E-VISUAL COMMUNICATIONS, INC.

Panera Bread appeals to busy, health-conscious baby-boomers by combining freshly baked bread and a friendly gathering place to appeal to consumers looking for a healthy alternative to a fast-food lunch.

The Growth of Component Lifestyles

People in the United States today are piecing together component lifestyles. A lifestyle is a mode of living; it is the way people decide to live their lives. A **component lifestyle** is a lifestyle made up of a complex set of interests and choices. In other words, people are choosing products and services that meet diverse needs and interests rather than conforming to traditional stereotypes.

In the past, a person's profession—for instance, banker—defined that person's lifestyle. Today a person can be a banker, gourmet, fitness enthusiast, dedicated single parent, and conservationist—all at once. Each of these lifestyles is associated with different goods and services and represents a unique market. For example, businesses advertise cooking utensils, wines, and exotic foods through magazines like *Bon Appétit* and *Gourmet* for the gourmets. The fitness enthusiast buys Adidas equipment and special jogging outfits and reads *Runner's World* magazine. Component lifestyles increase the complexity of consumers' buying habits. The banker may own a BMW but change the oil herself. She may buy fast food for lunch but French wine for dinner, own sophisticated photographic equipment and a low-priced home stereo, and shop for hosiery at Wal-Mart and suits at Brooks Brothers.

component lifestyle
A lifestyle made up of a complex set of interests and choices.

Two-Income Families

Component lifestyles have evolved because consumers can choose from a growing number of goods and services, and most have the money to exercise more options. The growth of dual-income families has resulted in increased purchasing power. Approximately 64 percent of all females between 16 and 65 years old are now in the workforce, and female participation in the labor force is expected to grow to 66 percent by 2005.[7] Today, there are more than 9 million women-owned businesses in the United States, and women are pursuing independent business ventures at twice the rate of men.[8] The phenomenon of working women has probably had a greater effect on marketing than has any other social change.

As women's earnings grow, so do their levels of expertise, experience, and authority. Working-age women are not the same group businesses targeted 30 years ago. They expect different things in life—from their jobs, from their spouses, and from the products and services they buy.

The automotive industry has finally begun to realize the power of women in vehicle purchase decisions. Women are the principal buyers or influencers for 54 percent of all cars and trucks sold in the United States.[9] Toyota has found that women influence 8 out of 10 of all vehicle purchases. Armed with this information, Toyota has set up a hotline just for women. It has also created a Web site just for female car buyers and owners. The site avoids male-oriented jargon and offers helpful hints on safety, maintenance, and financing. The limited-edition Toyota Roxy Echo is targeted at female buyers aged 18 to 32.[10]

In a recent survey, two-thirds to three-fourths of women said they are making many major economic decisions either independently or equally with a spouse. Few of the women said they left important marketplace decisions to others.[11] When it comes to big-ticket, long-term items, women remain active in the decision-making process, though most say they are more likely to make these decisions with a spouse. Life experience is an important factor in women's independence in long-term planning; married women over age 55 are more likely to make these decisions on their own than their younger counterparts are.

concept check

Why are social changes the most difficult environmental factor to predict?

How do component lifestyles make it more difficult to predict a consumer's buying habits?

What social change has had the greatest impact on business?

Saturn honors outstanding women with its "Saturn Women at Their Best Awards." Saturn is also highly responsive to women customers who are the principal buyers for over 54 percent of all cars and trucks sold in the United States.

Demographic Trends

3 learning goal

demography
The study of people's vital statistics, such as their age, race and ethnicity, and location.

Generation Y
Americans born after 1979.

Demographic trends—another uncontrollable factor in the business environment—are also extremely important to managers. **Demography** is the study of people's vital statistics, such as their age, race and ethnicity, and location. Demographics are significant because the basis for any market is people. Demographics also determine the size and composition of the workforce. Let's begin by taking a closer look at key age groups.

Generation Y

Those designated by demographics as **Generation Y** were born between 1979 and 1994. They are about 60 million strong, more than three times as large as Generation X. And though Generation Y is much smaller than the baby boom, which lasted nearly 20 years and produced 78 million children, its members are plentiful enough to put their own footprints on society.

The marketing impact of Generation Y has been immense. Companies that sell toys, videos, software, and clothing to kids have boomed in recent years. Nine of the 10 best-selling videos of all time are animated films from Walt Disney Co. Club Med, the French vacation company, now earns half its U.S. revenues from family resorts. The members of Generation Y were born into a world vastly different from the one their parents entered. The changes in family, the workforce, technology, and demographics in recent decades will no doubt affect their attitudes, but often in unpredictable ways.

Unlike the "party-a-go-go" ads aimed at them, Gen Yers lead relatively quiet lives: "listening to music, hanging with friends, going to movies, dining out, and watching TV. They rarely participate in high-action activities such as tennis and motorcycling." Most are pragmatic, like convenience, and are value oriented.

Gen Y appears to be a "notoriously fickle" consumer group, demanding the latest trends in record time. Communicators wanting to reach these teens have "to embrace that type of fast change." A critical consumer group, they "don't like a hard sell." They are "brand and fashion-conscious," but as one advertising manager has learned, you have to get the "merchandise in front of them without being in their face."[12]

Many Gen Yers are still in their teenage years. And they have money to spend on things they like. Teenagers are projected to spend $190 billion annually by 2006.[13]

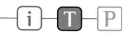

© COURTESY OF KEDS CORPORATION

Generation Y, born between 1979 and 1994, are about 60 million strong and are brand and fashion conscious. Smart marketers like Keds will monitor this segment of the market and continue to develop products that appeal to them.

Generation X
Americans born between 1965 and 1978.

baby boomers
Americans born between 1946 and 1964.

Generation X

Generation X—people born between 1965 and 1978—consists of 40 million consumers. It is the first generation of latchkey children—products of dual-career households or, in roughly half of the cases, of divorced or separated parents. Gen Xers have been bombarded by multiple media since their cradle days, thus they are savvy and cynical consumers.

With careers launched and families started, Generation X is at the stage in life when there are suddenly a host of demands competing for their time—and their budgets. As a result, Gen X spending is quite diffused: food, housing, transportation. Time is at a premium for harried Gen Xers, so they're outsourcing the tasks of daily life, which include everything from domestic help to baby-sitting. Xers spend 78 percent more than average on personal services, more than any other age group, and therefore spend 15 percent less than average on housekeeping supplies.[14]

Baby Boomers—America's Mass Market

Baby boomers represent 42 percent of all U.S. households and control 50 percent of all consumer spending.[15] This group totals nearly 78 million people, so it's useful to divide Boomers into two subgroups: the Younger Boomers, ages whose spending is still directed by their children; and the Older Boomers, ages 50 to 59 in 2005, who are in their empty-nesting years. For Younger Boomers, the home is still the castle, and family is the priority. For the first time at this stage of life, a majority (69 percent) of householders own their homes instead of renting them.[16] So it's no surprise that the Younger Boomers are directing a larger share of their budgets to their homes than all the other age groups. Spending on kids is also shaping the Younger Boomer's budget. This household devotes a significant amount of money toward keeping a growing family busy. This group spends 11 percent more than average on pets, toys, and playground equipment.[17]

Now that the kids are grown, Older Boomers are directing their funds to upgrading their homes in small ways, spending 50 percent more than average on housewares, such as china and silverware, for example.[18] They're also taking a new look at their own wardrobes, spending 13 percent more than average on adult women's apparel and 11 percent more than average on adult male apparel. Looking for a way to show off their new clothes, Older Boomers are also planning vacations; they spend 23 percent more than the average household on hotels and vacation homes.[19]

Older Consumers—Not Just Grandparents

The oldest baby boomers have already crossed the 60-year threshold that many demographers use to define the "mature market." Yet today's mature consumers are wealthier, healthier, and better educated than those of earlier generations. Fixed incomes mean tighter budgets, and as many seniors transition into their retirement years, average household income and spending declines substantially. But while spending among seniors reflects this reality, they are far from being out of the consumer marketplace. Seniors spend money maintaining what they've already accumulated. Preserving the home, for example, eats up a large share of the budget—86 percent more than in the average household.[20] Given the amount of time they now spend at home, these consumers also direct a larger chunk of their budgets to food to be eaten there. For example, they spend 50 percent more than average on fresh fruits and vegetables, 33 percent more than average on fresh milk and cream, and 25 percent more than average on baked goods.

Businesspeople who want to actively pursue the mature market must understand it. Aging consumers create some obvious opportunities. For example, JC Penney's Easy Dressing clothes feature Velcro fasteners for women with arthritis or other ailments who may have difficulty with zippers or buttons.

Americans on the Move

The average U.S. citizen moves every six years. This trend has implications for business. A large influx of new people into an area creates many new opportunities for all types of businesses. Conversely, significant out-migration from a city or town may force many of its businesses to move or close down because they can't find qualified employees. The cities with the greatest projected population growth from 1995 to 2005 are Houston, Atlanta, San Diego, Phoenix, Orlando, Dallas, and Washington, D.C.

The United States experiences both immigration from other countries and migration within its borders. The six states with the highest levels of immigration from abroad are California, New York, New Jersey, Illinois, Texas, and Massachusetts. The six states with the greatest population increases due to interstate migration are Florida, Georgia, North Carolina, Virginia, Washington, and Arizona. Areas with large numbers of immigrants face increased costs of public services, but the influx benefits the U.S. economy overall.

Diversity in America

By 2007, Hispanics will wield more than $900 billion in spending power, an increase of 315 percent since 1990. By that same year, African Americans' spending will top the $850 billion mark, and Asians' spending power will have soared 287 percent since 1990, to $455 billion—far outpacing total U.S. growth in buying power.[21]

Hispanics overtook African Americans in 2003, to become America's largest minority group with 12.5 percent of the population. In 2004, African Americans will compose 12.3 percent of the population and Asians 3.6 percent.[22] America's growing ethnic diversity is having a profound impact on business.

Firms like Ford Motor Company market their products to the growing number of Spanish-speaking immigrants, whose buying power boosts the U.S. economy.

Fuerza Ford para tu vida.
Con sus convenientes cuatro puertas estándar, toda la familia está invitada a pasear.
Ford
Espíritu de Superación
www.fordespiritu.com

© SPENCER GRANT / PHOTO EDIT

Companies across the United States have recognized that decades of diversity are resulting in bottom-line benefits. More than ever, diversity is emerging as a priority goal for visionary leaders who embrace the incontestable fact that the United States is becoming a truly multicultural society. Data from the 2000 U.S. Census confirmed that minorities now constitute one-third of the nation's population and control $1 trillion in annual spending—an increase of more than $420 billion since 1990, according to the Selig Center for Economic Growth at the University of Georgia. For businesses that seek to tap this bulging consumer purse, the latest census data paints a portrait of a multicultural marketplace that's more diverse than ever. Businesses can no longer assume that all minorities are concentrated in a handful of metropolitan areas—or that one strategy for a particular ethnic group will be effective in reaching all members of the same group.

The Impact of Immigration Part of the reason for the tremendous shift in American demographics is immigration. Thirty years ago, 8 out of 10 Californians were white.

Employees from different ethnic and racial backgrounds will continue to enrich the workplace with their diverse views and ideas.

© PHOTODISC

There has been a huge influx of immigrants, mostly from Mexico and the rest of Latin America. A further 5 million immigrants have settled in the state since 1980. Sometime around 2040, when whites will make up less than a third of California's projected 52 million people, Hispanics are projected to form a majority. California is also home to huge immigrant communities from other countries. Los Angeles hosts the largest communities of Koreans and Iranians outside their native lands. Since 1980, the United States has admitted roughly 15 million immigrants.

There is no doubt that immigrant entrepreneurs, from the corner grocer to the local builder, are creating jobs for other immigrants and for those born in the United States. Vibrant immigrant communities are revitalizing cities and older suburbs that would otherwise be suffering from a shrinking tax base. And the immigrants' links to their old countries are boosting U.S. exports to such fast-growing regions as Asia and Latin America.

The United States is also reaping a bonanza of highly educated foreigners. High-tech industries, from semiconductors to biotechnology, are depending on immigrant scientists, engineers, and entrepreneurs to remain competitive. In Silicon Valley, California, much of the technical workforce is foreign-born. At Du Pont Merck Pharmaceutical, a joint venture based in Delaware, a new antihypertensive drug was invented by a team that included two immigrants from Hong Kong and a scientist whose parents immigrated from Lithuania.

The next generation of scientists and engineers will be dominated by immigrants. The number of native-born citizens getting science PhDs has remained about the same, but the number of foreign-born students receiving science doctorates more than doubled between 1980 and 2005.

Regardless of their educational level, immigrants tend to join their peers, and their peers tend to live in large coastal cities. California, New York, Texas, Florida, Illinois, and New Jersey are expected to be home to three of every four new immigrants, who will be joining already-large minority populations in those states.

concept check

How has the changing role of women affected business?

Explain how Generation X, Generation Y, and baby boomers differ.

How is diversity changing the marketplace?

Evolving Global Economic Systems

4 learning goal

In addition to social and demographic factors, managers must understand and adapt to the economic system or systems in which they operate. Economic systems found in the world today include capitalism, command economies, socialism, and mixed economies.

Making Ethical Choices

xtra! http://gitmanxtra.swlearning.com

THE BIG E

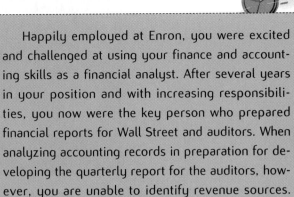

If you entered the job market in the mid-1990s, Enron Corp. was probably among your top three choices of "the best company" to work for. With its reputation as a dynamic energy company, Enron was also known for energizing its employees and for valuing the nontraditional. "Being unconventional was good business," according to former President Jeffrey Skilling. He believed that "our weirdest people were our best people . . . [they] come up with weird ideas . . . that create new businesses." Considered "The World's Coolest Company" and "nirvana," Enron offered employees exciting enticements, such as the opportunity to create their own business area. Founder Kenneth L. Lay grew the company by expanding its business to include areas outside its core. "If the idea was great enough, it didn't matter whether you ever actually did it. It was more like, 'Let's book $3 trillion in revenue and move on.'"

Happily employed at Enron, you were excited and challenged at using your finance and accounting skills as a financial analyst. After several years in your position and with increasing responsibilities, you now were the key person who prepared financial reports for Wall Street and auditors. When analyzing accounting records in preparation for developing the quarterly report for the auditors, however, you are unable to identify revenue sources. When you seek clarification on the sources your boss tells you to create your own.

ETHICAL DILEMMA

1. Do you have an obligation to obey your boss and falsify revenue sources?

SOURCES: Peter Behr and April Witt, "Visionary's Dream Led to Risky Business," July 28, 2002, "Dream Job Turns Into a Nightmare," July 29, 2002, and "Concerns Grow Amid Conflicts," July 30, 2002, *Washington Post*, downloaded from http://www.washingtonpost.com; and Friedman, Charles, "What If You'd Worked at Enron?" *Fast Company*, May 2002.

Capitalism

capitalism
An economic system based on competition in the marketplace and private ownership of the factors of production (resources); also known as the *private enterprise system.*

A remarkable trend in global economies today is the move toward capitalism. Sometimes, as in the case of the former East Germany, the transition to capitalism has been painful, but fairly quick. In other countries, such as Russia, the movement has been characterized by false starts and backsliding. **Capitalism,** also known as the *private enterprise system,* is based on competition in the marketplace and private ownership of the factors of production (resources). In a competitive economic system, a large number of people and businesses buy and sell products freely in the marketplace. In pure capitalism all the factors of production are owned privately, and the government does not try to set prices or coordinate economic activity.

A capitalist system guarantees certain economic rights: the right to own property, the right to make a profit, the right to make free choices, and the right to compete. The right to own property is central to capitalism. The main incentive in this system is profit, which encourages entrepreneurship. Profit is also necessary for producing goods and services, building plants, paying dividends and taxes, and creating jobs. The freedom to choose whether to become an entrepreneur or to work for someone else means that people have the right to decide what they want to do on the basis of their own drive, interest, and training. The government does not create job quotas for each industry or give people tests to determine what they will do.

In a capitalist system, competition is good for both businesses and consumers. It leads to better and more diverse products, keeps prices stable, and increases the efficiency of producers. Producers try to produce their goods and services at the lowest possible cost and sell them at the highest possible price. But when profits are high, more firms enter the market to seek those profits. The resulting competition among firms tends to lower prices. Producers must then find new ways of operating more efficiently if they are to keep making a profit—and stay in business.

The Command Economy

command economy
An economic system characterized by government ownership of virtually all resources and economic decision making by central-government planning; also known as *communism.*

The complete opposite to capitalism is a command economy. A **command economy, or communism**, is characterized by government ownership of virtually all resources and economic decision making by central-government planning. The government decides what will be produced, where it will be produced, how much will be produced, where the raw materials and supplies will come from, and who will get the output.

Pure capitalism and the command economy are extremes; real-world economies fall somewhere between the two. The U.S. economy leans toward pure capitalism, but government policies are used to promote economic stability and growth. Also, through policies and laws, the government transfers money to the poor, the unemployed, and the elderly. American capitalism has produced some very powerful organizations in the form of huge corporations, such as General Motors and Microsoft. Laws have been enacted to help smaller firms and entrepreneurs by requiring that the giants compete fairly against weaker competitors.

Before the Soviet Union collapsed in 1991, it had a command economy, but even so it relied to some extent on market-determined prices and allowed some private ownership. Recent reforms in Russia, China, and most of the eastern European nations have moved these economies toward more capitalistic, market-oriented systems. North Korea and Cuba are the best remaining examples of command economies.

Socialism

socialism
An economic system in which the basic industries are owned either by the government itself or by the private sector under strong government control.

Socialism is an economic system in which the basic industries are owned by the government or by the private sector under strong government control. A socialist state controls critical, large-scale industries such as transportation, communications, and utilities. Smaller businesses may be privately owned. To varying degrees the state also determines the goals of businesses, the prices and selection of goods, and the rights of workers. Socialist countries typically provide their citizens with a higher level of services, such as health care and unemployment benefits, than do most capitalist countries. As a result, taxes and unemployment may also be quite high in socialist countries.

Many countries, including Great Britain, Denmark, Israel, and Sweden, have socialist systems, but the systems vary from country to country. In Denmark, for example, most businesses are privately owned and operated, but two-thirds of the population is sustained by the state through government welfare programs.

Socialism is proving to be surprisingly resilient in western Europe. France, for example, inched toward a capitalistic form of government after the presidency of François Mitterrand ended in 1995. Yet several years later the country elected Lionel Jospin, who won the election based upon a pledge of more government control and intervention in the workplace. Now, Jacques Chirac has moved the country back toward a more capitalistic type of government. Tony Blair, Great Britain's prime minister, is a member of the Labour Party, which historically has stood for the preeminence of government, nationalized industry, extraordinary social regulation, and massive taxation to support it all.

Mixed Economic Systems

mixed economies
Economies that combine several economic systems; for example, an economy where the government owns certain industries but others are owned by the private sector.

Canada, Great Britain, and Sweden, among others, are also called **mixed economies;** that is, they use more than one economic system. Sometimes, the government is basically socialist and owns basic industries. In Canada, for example, the government owns the communications, transportation, and utilities industries, as well as some of the natural-resource industries. It also supplies health care to its citizens. But most other activity is carried on by private enterprises, as in a capitalist system.

The few factors of production owned by the government include some public lands, the postal service, and some water resources. But the government is extensively involved in the economic system through taxing, spending, and welfare activities. The economy is also mixed in the sense that the country tries to achieve many social goals—income redistribution and Social Security, for example—that may not be attempted in purely capitalist systems. Exhibit 1.2 summarizes key factors of the world's economic systems.

concept check

What is capitalism and why is it growing?
What is socialism and why is it still popular?
Why are most economies mixed?

TECHNOLOGICAL TRENDS

5 learning goal

technology
The application of science and engineering skills and knowledge to solve production and organizational problems.

productivity
The amount of goods and services one worker can produce.

The application of technology can stimulate growth under capitalism or any other economic system. **Technology** is the application of science and engineering skills and knowledge to solve production and organizational problems. New machines that improve productivity and reduce costs can be one of a firm's most valuable assets. **Productivity** is the amount of goods and services one worker can produce. Our ability, as a nation, to maintain and build wealth depends in large part on the speed and effectiveness with which we invent and adopt machines that lift productivity. For example, coal mining is typically thought of as unskilled, backbreaking labor. But visit Cyprus Amax Mineral Co.'s Twenty-mile Mine near Oak Creek, Colorado, and you will find workers with push-button controls who walk along massive machines that shear 30-inch slices from an 850-foot coal wall. Laptop computers help miners track equipment breakdowns and water quality.

American business is becoming better at using technology to create change. The development pipelines at many high-tech companies already showcase a whole new

FedEx uses digital technology to track every package from pickup to delivery. Bar codes scan every package, recording its place in the delivery cycle online as it moves down the conveyor belt. This efficient technology allows FedEx to pass cost savings onto its customers.

© MARK RICHARDS / PHOTO EDIT

Exhibit 1.2 The Basic Economic Systems of the World

	Capitalism	Command Economy	Socialism	Mixed Economy
Ownership of Business	Businesses are privately owned with minimal government ownership or interference.	Government owns all or most enterprises.	Basic industries such as railroads and utilities are owned by government. Very high taxation as government redistributes income from successful private businesses and entrepreneurs.	Private ownership of land and businesses but government control of some enterprises. The private sector is typically large.
Control of Markets	Complete freedom of trade. No or little government control.	Complete government control of markets.	Some markets are controlled and some are free. Significant central-government planning. State enterprises are managed by bureaucrats. These enterprises are rarely profitable.	Some markets such as nuclear energy and the post office are controlled or highly regulated.
Worker Incentives	Strong incentive to work and innovate because profits are retained by owners.	No incentive to work hard or produce quality products.	Private-sector incentives the same as capitalism and public-sector incentives the same as a planned economy.	Private-sector incentives the same as capitalism. Limited incentives in the public sector.
Management of Enterprises	Each enterprise is managed by owners or professional managers with little government interference.	Centralized management by the government bureaucracy. Little or no flexibility in decision making at the factory level.	Significant government planning and regulation. Bureaucrats run government enterprises.	Private-sector management similar to capitalism. Public sector similar to socialism.
Forecast for 2020	Continued steady growth.	No growth and perhaps disappearance.	Stable with probable slight growth.	Continued growth.

breed of miniaturized inventions with capabilities well beyond today's computer chips. During the next five years, these microelectromechanical systems (MEMS)—which combine sensors, motors, and digital smarts on a single sliver of silicon—are likely to replace more expensive components in computer hardware, automobile engines, factory assembly lines, and dozens of other processes and products. The operating software for these devices is now being written.

High-tech visionaries foresee far more radical developments in the next 15 to 20 years. Scientists anticipate using nature's own creative machinery. In medicine, this means replacing the body's failing organs. In manufacturing, it means creating innovative, new devices that will save time and money. The coming wave of miniaturization and molecular electronics—sometimes called "nanotechnology"—is taking shape at the intersection of chemistry, physics, biology, and electrical engineering.[23] And if it works as many scientists predict, it will bring a wholesale industrial transformation that will be more dramatic than the growth of microelectronics in the late 20th century.

concept check

What is technology?

What benefits can businesses experience through the application of technology?

What technology is having the most impact on business today?

The technology that has had a tremendous impact on consumers and businesses in the past decade is the Internet. Although some say that the Internet has not lived up to its promise, there is no doubt that it is changing the way companies conduct their business and the way many people shop. You can learn more about the Internet and its impact on business in the Online chapter: "Using the Internet for Business Success" at **http://gitman.swlearning.com**. We have only begun to see how the Internet and technology will change how we shop.

TRENDS IN GLOBAL COMPETITION

6 learning goal

Global competition is another element of the external business environment that is driving changes in the way business is conducted. Agreements among nations and laws of individual countries have generally been supportive of global competition and trade. If current trends continue, world **exports** (goods and services sold outside a firm's domestic market) will reach $11 trillion by 2005, or 28 percent of world gross domestic product.

exports
Goods and services sold outside a firm's domestic market.

gross domestic product (GDP)
The total market value of all final goods and services produced within a nation's borders in a year.

Gross domestic product (GDP) is the total market value of all final goods and services produced within a nation's borders in a year. World gross domestic product is the sum of all countries' GDP. The GDP of countries around the world are included in the world map on the inside front cover.

Because global competition is fiercer than ever, businesses must watch out for competitors around the world as well as across town. In addition, businesses must often seek out suppliers from around the world to create world-class products. For example, we usually think of Boeing airplanes as a uniquely American product. Yet firms from around the world play a role in producing the Boeing 777. Boeing has led the world in the production of commercial aircraft for over 40 years. Now, Airbus Industries, a European consortium, is set to take over the number one spot.

Chinese companies are beginning to become global competitors as economic reforms have unfolded. China's first global brand is discussed in the "Expanding Around the Globe" box.

Technology and Global Communications

Advances in technology and communications have allowed more companies than ever before to participate in the world arena. Large U.S.-based multinational corporations have operations in many countries. For example, Gillette manufactures in 57 locations in 28 countries and markets in over 200 countries. When companies like Gillette have offices all over the world, they can pick up winning ideas for new products just about anywhere. For example, Häagen-Dazs began serving a new flavor called *dulce de leche* at its sole ice-cream shop in Buenos Aires. Named after the caramelized milk that is one of the most popular flavors in Argentina, the locally developed line was an immediate hit. Within weeks, the supersweet, butterscotch-like confection was the store's best-seller.

Just one year later, consumers from Boston to Los Angeles to Paris could find *dulce de leche* at the supermarket or in one of Häagen-Dazs's 700 retail stores. In U.S. stores that carry it, only vanilla sells better. In Miami, *dulce* sells twice as fast as any other flavor. In the United States, it does over $1 million a month in revenue. And in Europe, it has moved up from a seasonal flavor to year-round status.

Improvements in Productivity

Good planning and efficient use of resources have made American companies world-class competitors. American businesses are now the most productive in

Expanding Around the Globe

China's Haier Set to Become a Global Brand

There's little about Zhang Ruimin's appearance that betrays his blossoming prominence. His blunt haircut mocks the stylish coiffures of today's executive. His pale-blue dress shirt needs pressing. And his wrists are Rolex free.

Compared with some moguls, whose lavish lifestyles and run-ins with the taxman make headlines, Zhang looks downright dowdy. But don't be misled: The CEO of Chinese appliance-maker Haier Group is arguably China's leading corporate helmsman. In November, 2002, he became the first businessman elected to the Chinese Communist Party's Central Committee.

The United States has General Electric; Germany, Mercedes-Benz; Japan, Toyota. Fast-growing China, however, has yet to produce a comparable global competitor. But with more than $7 billion in annual sales and 13 overseas factories, including a South Carolina refrigerator plant and assembly lines in Italy, Pakistan, and Iran, Haier is among the best-positioned Chinese companies to bid for global stature.

The sprawling company makes everything from cellphones and air conditioners to microwave ovens and electric razors. Haier ranks fifth in global appliance sales behind General Electric, Whirlpool, Electrolux, and Siemens. In the United States, Haier sells room air conditioners and laundry machines, as well as a "wine cooler," a compact refrigerator for aspiring sommeliers that retails for $599 to $3,660.

In the early days of China's capitalist experimentation, Zhang enjoyed wide latitude to overhaul the inefficient state-owned appliance makers he acquired. Among his first steps was partnering with Liebherr, a German appliance maker that became a key source of technology. It was also the inspiration for Haier's name (pronounced higher), a Chinese approximation of the German original.

Foreign technology would have been wasted without Zhang's overhaul of factory practices. To promote quality, he once ordered workers to destroy 76 defective refrigerators using sledgehammers. Zhang linked key employees' pay to sales of their products and required mistake-prone employees to stand before their colleagues and explain what went wrong. A ban on workplace drinking also improved productivity.

He scrapped the one-size-fits-all mentality he inherited from China's central planners. After tracing low sales of washing machines in Sichuan province to villagers' practice of using the machines to clean sweet potatoes, which clogged the washer's drain, he had a part modified to handle produce as well as clothes. Sales soared.[24]

CRITICAL THINKING QUESTIONS

1. Why have Chinese manufacturers not developed global brands in the past?
2. Do you think that economic reforms in China will ultimately lead to a democratic form of government?
3. China still has many state-owned factories that are grossly inefficient but provide jobs for millions of workers. What should be done about these factories?

the world. During the 1990s American businesses downsized to become more efficient. Downsizing means terminating employees, or laying off workers, to reduce costs and become more efficient. The goal is to produce as many or more goods and services with fewer employees. Many companies including AT&T, Boeing, and General Motors laid off tens of thousands of workers to become more competitive.

Often downsizing has been coupled with a greater use of technology, thereby greatly increasing productivity. Today, for example, there are about 65 personal computers per 100 workers in the United States. In Japan there are 20 personal computers per 100 workers. Contrary to popular belief, American businesses are much more productive than are Japanese. American manufacturers are 20 percent more productive than Japanese manufacturers, and American service providers are 50 percent more productive than Japan's service sector.

The relentless drive for efficiency has made many American firms leaders around the globe. Coca Cola, Microsoft, Wal-Mart, McDonald's, and Exxon are truly world leaders in their fields. Other, less well known American firms are just as effective in their markets against global competitors. Though American companies lead the way in the world marketplace, one thing is certain—competition from domestic and foreign competitors is only going to get tougher.

The Impact of Terrorism on Global Business

While we hate to call terrorism a "trend in business," it must be acknowledged that terrorism has profoundly impacted American business and commerce around the globe. The horrendous events of September 11, 2001, created a feeling of uncertainty among both businesses and consumers. It severely impacted industries such as tourism and the airlines. Most important, however, the American system worked. The resiliency, flexibility, and strength built into the American political and economic systems carried the country through its darkest times since World War II.

Public demand brought government back to its traditional role as guardian of the country's safety. In turn, government spending on defense increased more percentage-wise than any year since 1982.[25] Now, we have more regulation and more government intervention in business and the economy than at any time since the 1970s.

concept check

How have U.S. companies improved productivity?

How has the threat of terrorism impacted global business?

Great Ideas to Use Now

Terrorism and the general malaise of the economy in 2002–2003 resulted in an unemployment rate of around 6 percent. This was the highest level in a decade. Yet by the time you graduate things will change and change fast.

The Coming Talent War

As the economy continues to strengthen, a shortage of qualified workers will quickly return. Moreover, this shortage may persist for decades because huge numbers of baby boomers will soon be retiring and there will be fewer new workers to fill the pipeline. With more than two-thirds of women already working, and with immigration at record highs, the growth of the labor force will remain extremely low for decades to come.[26]

The big winner in all of this is you! A survey of 77 large companies and almost 6,000 managers found that they believe the most important resource over the next 20 years will be talent. And even as the demand for talent goes up, the supply will be going down. In a report entitled "The War for Talent," McKinsey Consulting

Try It Now

1. **Start a business.** It's never too early to start your own business. People as young as 14 have become successful entrepreneurs. Each year 2 million businesses are started by people under 35 years old. The average young entrepreneur now employs 18 people with sales of approximately $1 million. You can be next! For start-up help, check out the Young Americans Business Trust at **http://www.ybiz.net** and the Young Entrepreneurs Network at **http://www.youngandsuccessful.com**.
2. **Assess Your Skills.** The earlier you choose a major field, the more efficiently you can plan your college course work. Make sure you don't end up taking a lot of courses that won't count toward your degree. Do a self-assessment and skills assessment right now. Next, go to the Career Mosaic at **http://www.careerbuilder.com**. This site offers thousands of job postings as well as information about companies. Use this information to help you decide on a career field and major. Do you want to stay in your home state? This site will break down job postings by city and even zip code, so you can find a job in any part of town, like the north side of St. Louis.

Customer Satisfaction and Quality

A theme that you will find running throughout the text is the importance of excellent customer service and quality. At the end of each chapter, we will tie the material that you have just read back to a focus on quality and customer service. The reason for our focus is simple. If an organization delivers the highest quality in everything they do and provides excellent customer service, the chances of reaching the organization's goals increase dramatically.

When we speak of quality, we are not simply referring to product quality or service quality. We are also talking about having the highest quality personnel operations, financial operations, sales activities, and anything else with which the organization is involved. General Electric is the pioneer of a concept called "Six Sigma." Although created by Motorola, GE made it a religion throughout its operations. A company that adheres to Six Sigma will only have 3.4 defects per 1 million opportunities to experience failure. The company uses statistical models to measure performance in a variety of areas, including many that would appear at first difficult to quantify. Companies like 3M, Home Depot, Ford, and many others have adopted Six Sigma. Six Sigma is one example of how companies are devising strategies that improve customer satisfaction and quality. You'll learn more about the Six Sigma program in Chapter 12.

predicts that the search for the best and the brightest will become a constant, costly battle, a fight with no final victory. Not only will companies have to devise more imaginative hiring practices, but they will also have to work harder to keep their best people. Today competition is global, ideas are developed quickly and cheaply, and people are willing to change jobs often.

Only 60 percent of the corporate officers at the companies in the McKinsey report said that they were able to pursue most of their growth opportunities. They have good ideas, they have money—they just don't have enough talented people to pursue those ideas. They are "talent constrained." The leaders at Johnson & Johnson, a world-class firm, said that they never used to go outside the company to recruit top-level managers. Now they have to go outside as often as 25 percent of the time—because they are talent-constrained.

Looking Ahead at the Personal-Size Snack Food Market

J.M. Smucker Company spotted a social trend toward single-serving foods and successfully launched UnCrustables. By keeping a close watch on this and other business trends, Smucker's and other companies have an opportunity to react quickly to changing customer needs, develop new product ideas, and get them to market before competitors do.

Some markets embrace new products faster than others. For example, Europeans buy their milk in nonrefrigerated containers. U.S. consumers still find nonrefrigerated milk a little suspicious. If opinion leaders in the United States begin to accept milk sold in asceptic cartons (nonrefrigerated), however, the mass market will soon follow.

New technology may be the key to more successes in the personal-size food market. For example, scientists have yet to perfect microwave frozen French fries that taste like they just came from the fryer. When they do, it will be a huge market success.

As Smucker's enjoys the success of UnCrustables, they will need to keep a close eye on the factors that may hurt long-term sales. Some factors that could cause the decrease in sales of single-serving containers might be an increase in unemployment, rapid price increases of single-serving containers, and changing consumer preferences.

Choosing the Right Job for You

A recent survey found that 92 percent of employed adults "find meaning and purpose in their work."[27] This sentiment was especially widespread among educated workers. Among respondents age 21–35, 77 percent said "success is finding a company where you went to work for a long time."[28] It seems that the old trend toward job hopping is on the decline.

Job hopping can often lead to a promotion and a raise in salary. It can also take a lot of energy, require a continual relearning of a corporate culture, and may lead to jobs that turn out to be less than you expected. Many traditional industries such as banking and heavy-equipment manufacturing still put a premium on company loyalty. High-tech firms, in contrast, may not expect a long-term commitment. A corporate recruiter for one of America's largest and most dynamic high-tech firms recently said, "If you stay with us longer than three years, we begin to wonder what's wrong with you." Was this said in jest? Probably, but there may be an element of truth in her statement.

Summary of Learning Goals

1

How do businesses and not-for-profit organizations help create our standard of living?

Businesses attempt to earn a profit by providing goods and services desired by their customers. Not-for-profit organizations, though not striving for a profit, still deliver many needed services for our society. Our standard of living is measured by the output of goods and services. Thus, businesses and not-for-profit organizations help create our standard of living. Our quality of life is not simply the amount of goods and services available for consumers but rather the society's general level of happiness.

Economists refer to the building blocks of a business as the factors of production. To produce anything, one must have natural resources, labor, capital, and entrepreneurship to assemble the resources and manage the business. The competitive environment of our new millennium is based upon knowledge and learning. The companies that will succeed in this new era will be those that learn fast, use knowledge effectively, and develop new insights.

2

How are social trends, such as more women entering the workforce, affecting business?

The business environment consists of social, demographic, economic, technological, and competitive trends. Also, terrorism has had a negative impact on business and resulted in a major increase in government spending and activities. Managers cannot control environmental trends. Instead, they must understand how the environment is changing and the impact of those changes on the business. Several social trends are currently influencing businesses. First, people of all ages have a broader range of interests, defying traditional consumer profiles. Second, changing gender roles are bringing more women into the workforce. This trend is increasing family incomes, heightening demand for time-saving goods and services, and changing family shopping patterns.

3

How are demographic trends creating new opportunities for business?

Businesses today must deal with the unique shopping preferences of Generations X and Y and the baby boomers. Each must be appealed to in a different way with different goods and services. Generation Y, for example, is the most computer literate and the most interested in computers and accessories. And because the population is growing older, businesses are offering more products that appeal to middle-aged and elderly markets.

4 What are the primary features of the world's economic systems?

Today there is a global trend toward capitalism. Capitalism, also known as the *private enterprise system,* is based upon marketplace competition and private ownership of the factors of production. Competition leads to more diverse goods and services, keeps prices stable, and pushes businesses to become more efficient.

In a command economy, or communism, the government owns virtually all resources, and economic decision making is done by central-government planning. Governments have generally moved away from command economies because they are inefficient and deliver a low standard of living. Socialism is an economic system in which the basic industries are owned by the government or by the private sector under strong government control. The state is also somewhat influential in determining the goals of business, the prices and selection of products, and the rights of workers. Most economies are a mix of socialism and capitalism.

5 How can technological effectiveness help a firm reach its goals?

The application of technology by a firm can increase efficiency, lower costs, and help the firm grow by producing higher-quality goods and services. New technologies such as miniaturization and microelectromechanical systems are changing the world as we know it. The Internet is changing how companies sell and communicate. It is also changing how and what consumers buy. Technology enables continuous improvement.

6 What are the trends in global competition?

The world is becoming more competitive. Exports continue to rise as a percentage of world gross domestic product. As countries open their markets, U.S. firms are finding greater opportunities abroad, but free trade also means that U.S. firms will face tougher competition at home. Nevertheless, efficient U.S. companies are meeting the global challenge.

Preparing for Tomorrow's Workplace

1. Form small groups with three or four members each. Each group should then go to a small business that has opened in the past two years. Ask the owner to describe (1) the most important lesson learned since opening the business, (2) unexpected pitfalls the business encountered, and (3) the information that helped the most prior to opening the business.
2. Every country has its own customs, beliefs, and social trends. Talk to several international students at your college. Ask them to identify five customs that make doing business in their country different from the United States.
3. Create two teams of four people each. Have one side choose a command economy and the other capitalism. Debate the proposition that "capitalism/a command economy is good for developing nations."
4. Form five teams. Each team is responsible for one of the five major types of trends in business discussed in the chapter (social, demographic, evolving economic systems, technology, and global competition). Your boss, the company president, has asked each team to provide a forecast of how the trend you have chosen will affect the firm over the next five years. The firm

KEY TERMS

baby boomers 31
business 24
capital 27
capitalism 34
command economy 35
component lifestyle 29
costs 25
demography 30
entrepreneurs 27
exports 38
factors of production 25
Generation X 31
Generation Y 30
goods 24
gross domestic product (GDP) 38
knowledge 27
mixed economies 36
not-for-profit organization 25
productivity 36
profit 25
quality of life 25
revenue 25
risk 25
services 24
socialism 35
standard of living 24
technology 36

is the Boeing Company. Each team should use the library, Internet, and other data sources to make its projections. Each team member should examine at least one data source. The team should then pool the data and prepare its response. A spokesperson for each team should present the findings to the class.

Working the Net

1. Knowledge is an important asset in today's business environment. Go to the Intellectual Property Owners' site, **http://www.ipo.org/**. What is intellectual property? What kinds of information does the site provide, and how might a business use it? Be sure to provide an example.
2. How do you find what you need from among the billions of Web pages on the Internet? You'll need to use search engines and Internet directories to identify sites that contain the terms you enter in the search box. However, each search engine/directory takes a different approach to your query. Knowing how several present information and rank searches will help you decide which work best for your various information needs. In addition, there are mega-search engines that compile search results from several individual engines.

   Choose two of the following search sites. Using these two search sites, research one of these topics from the chapter: GDP, Generation Y, or baby boomers. Compare your search experience, including the follwing: design of the opening screen, ease of use, presentation of results. Which made it easiest to find what you needed, and why?

   Altavista: **http://www.altavista.com**
   Excite: **http://www.excite.com**
   Google: **http://www.google.com**
   Teoma: **http://www.teoma.com**
   Yahoo!: **http://www.yahoo.com**
   Lycos: **http://www.lycos.com**
   Dogpile: **http://www.dogpile.com** (meta-search)
   Metacrawler: **http://www.metacrawler.com** (meta-search)
   All the Web: **http://www.alltheweb.com** (meta-search)

3. North Korea is probably the best example of a command economy in the world. Go to an Internet search engine, such as Excite, Infoseek, Lycos, or Altavista, and look up the "North Korean economy." Write a report on the current economic conditions in North Korea.
4. Using the Internet search engine you liked best after your research in Activity 2, look up "résumé preparation." What types of sources do you find? Check out several sites until you find three that are useful to you. Prepare a report for the class on the different categories of sites and the best ones for assistance in writing a résumé.
5. How do leading online job-posting services compare? Look at three such sites—for example, The Monster Board (**http://www.monster.com**), 4Work (**http://www.4work.com**), Careerbuilder.com (**http://www.careerbuilder.com**), America's Job Bank (**http://www.ajb.dni.us**), and your local newspaper's classifieds. Compare them as to ease of use, breadth of listings, search features, extra features, etc. Develop a table that summarizes your findings. Which would be the most useful to an entry-level job seeker? To a midlevel manager? Why?

Creative Thinking Case

What Exactly Is a Spin Cycle?

When Whirlpool Corporation started studying how it could sell appliances to the 18-to-24-year-old crowd, it dared to watch how young people do their laundry. The Benton Harbor, Michigan, company put cameras in dorm rooms and apartments. It interviewed young adults. And a few things came out in the wash.

Sometimes, doing the laundry meant rinsing jeans in the sink and leaving them to drip. Sometimes, it meant spraying a shirt with deodorant. Unlike those over 30, who often own houses and have families, 20-somethings couldn't care less about spin cycles and water temperatures, said Charles Jones, Whirlpool's vice president of global consumer design. Their ideal machine would have just a single push button. "If you talk to a Gen Yer about laundry and washing and drying clothes, their eyes glaze over and you immediately lose them," he said.

With its traditional market saturated and sales slowing, Whirlpool is looking for ways to reach a relatively untapped group who has been ignored for good reasons: young adults, who rarely have much money, floor space, or interest in appliances. The nation's largest appliance maker is hoping to appeal to young buyers with well-designed products.

The company is testing a sleek and small silver refrigerator, as well as a microwave oven and an air purifier with orange-colored accents, in Best Buy stores in Dallas, Chicago, and Los Angeles. It has other items on the drawing board, including a microwave dryer just big enough for a pair or two of jeans.

In addition to discovering that washing clothes is rare, it learned that leftover pizza is a real problem to store. So an orange refrigerator in the works for the "Pla" (as in "play") line features special internal handles to hold a large pizza box and wheels to make the fridge more portable.[29]

CRITICAL THINKING QUESTIONS

1. Why do you think Whirlpool is interested in the 18-to-24-year-old market?
2. Do any of these products appeal to you? Would you purchase them? Why or why not?
3. How could Whirlpool tailor its products for older baby boomers?

Video Case

Burton Snowboards Rides the Peak of Success

Burton Snowboards (**http://www.burton.com**), founded by Jake Burton in the winter of 1978–1979, is a successful, privately held manufacturer and distributor of snowboards, snowboarding accessories, and apparel. The Burton name is synonymous with premier-quality snowboarding products, and the Burton Way emphasizes "knowing and respecting the consumer while keeping one eye on the market and another on the product," both key components in the company's formula for success.

Another major factor has been the company's response to trends influencing the external business environment, namely their commitment to developing snowboarding as a sport. Until the 1980s, snowboarding was not permitted at ski resorts, so Burton Snowboards spearheaded the effort to legalize snowboarding at ski resorts. According to Jake Burton, "While other companies were saying 'our boards are great,' we were saying 'snowboarding is great.'"

By focusing on the sport, Burton Snowboards helped create a growth market for snowboarding equipment. Traditionally, snowboarding appealed to males in their teens and early 20s, but in recent years the market changed significantly to include middle-aged enthusiasts and women, who buy almost half the snowboards sold. While remaining committed to its traditional core customers, the company also caters to this new, more diverse clientele.

The three major markets for snowboarding equipment, North America, Europe, and Japan have seen snowboarding grow as a sport. While Burton Snowboards is sensitive to consumers' expectations, it has not developed different product lines for each of these markets. Instead the company has focused on a global line with products that appeal to a variety of markets. Jake Burton also encourages employees at the Burlington, Vermont, operation to "spend as much time as possible overseas because it's such a great place to learn."

Will the Burton Way enable Burton Snowboards to continue being successful as a privately held company? Jake Burton thinks so. He has no plans to take the company public and expects to continue to expand and diversify by knowing and respecting his customers.

CRITICAL THINKING QUESTIONS

1. Describe some of the key external environmental conditions that are influencing Burton Snowboards.
2. How does the Burton Way address the external environmental conditions identified in question (1)?
3. Explain how a business can help shape the external environment in which it operates.

SOURCES: Adapted from material in the video: A Case Study in the Business Environment: Burton Snowboards and on the Burton Snowboards corporate Web site, http://www.burton.com; Tom Farrell, "A Ticket to Ride: The Rapid Rise of Snowboarding," *USA Today Magazine,* March 2002 and Jill Lieber, "Pioneer Burton Riding Snowboarding Avalanche," USA TODAY, February 6, 2002, both downloaded from http://www.usatoday.com.

E-Commerce Case

Powell's Books Has Staying Power

Amazon.com may tout itself as "the world's biggest bookstore," but when it needs to find an out-of-print book for a customer, it often turns to Powell's Books in Portland, Oregon. The independent retailer carries over 1.5 million new and used books in its seven stores and stocks several hundred thousand more in a local warehouse, so it's usually able to help supply the book Amazon.com needs.

Founded in the 1970s by Michael Powell and his father Walter, Powell's Books quickly built an international reputation as the place to call if you were looking for a rare or hard to find book. The firm's enormous main store in downtown Portland became something of a tourist attraction long before chains like Barnes & Noble and Borders launched "superstores."

In 1993, a man in England e-mailed Powell's with a request to buy a book on electronics. Powell's e-mailed back that the book was available and shipped it to England the next day. Powell's first online order had occurred.

Intrigued, Michael Powell decided to launch a full-fledged Web site (**http://www.powells.com**) in 1994. Rather than compete directly with large online book retailers like Amazon.com and Barnes & Noble that sold new books at steeply discounted prices, Powell decided to focus on building the online market for used books. He assigned two full-time employees to the Internet business. One employee handled programming while the other packaged and shipped orders. The site made just over $1,000 in its first month.

Michael Powell made another early critical decision. He would shun venture capital or outside financing. The online store would grow only as profits permitted, even if that meant Powells.com might grow slowly or miss market opportunities.

The contrast between Amazon.com and Powell's is startling. Amazon.com has poured millions into ads on the Web, television, magazines, and newspapers. Powell's spends just $300,000 a year, running ads only in selected magazines. Powell's runs its online business with a staff of 60. Amazon has thousands. While Amazon.com also sells CDs, software, electronics, and other products at its site, Powell's still sells only books. Amazon.com has gone public, selling shares of its stock to raise capital to fuel growth. Powell's online remains financed by its own profits, and online sales now account for 30 percent of all books sold by Powell's.

To serve a larger customer base, Powell partnered with Half.com, an eBay unit. "Our customers online and in our stores have come to expect big discounts on a wide selection of titles," explains Michael Powell. "Now Half.com shoppers will be finding those great deals, too. And, with Half.com's reach, we'll be able to serve more readers than ever before."

CRITICAL THINKING QUESTIONS

1. List the factors of production needed to operate an online bookstore. Compare the strengths and weaknesses of the factors of production used by Amazon.com and Powell's online stores. How does this influence each retailer's electronic commerce operation?
2. Do you agree with Michael Powell's strategic decision not to use outside financing to fund the online operation even if it meant slower growth and missed opportunities? Explain.
3. Explain how Powell's may be affected by several of the trends discussed in this chapter. What advice would you give to Michael Powell about dealing with these issues?

SOURCES: "Legendary Independent Bookseller, Powell's Books, Joins the Growing Roster of Sellers on eBay's Half.com," *Business Wire*, February 12, 2001, downloaded from http://www.findarticles.com; Adam L. Penenberg, "Crossing Amazon," *Forbes*, April 17, 2000, downloaded from http://www.forbes.com/forbes/00/0417/6509168a.htm; "Powells.com Expands, Purchases Additional Warehouse," Powell's Books press release, November 12, 2002, downloaded from http://www.powellsbooks.com, and "Powells.com History," Powell's Books corporate web site, http://www.powellsbooks.com.

Hot Links Address Book

Interested in the current status of companies mentioned in our book's examples? Get business headlines, reports on individual businesses, and industry overviews at
http://www.hoovers.com

Knowledge gives businesses a competitive edge. Brint.com, a business technology portal, offers insight into how companies are turning themselves into knowledge-based organizations:
http://www.brint.com

Be inspired by reading stories of up-and-coming entrepreneurs in *Entrepreneur* magazine,
http://www.entrepreneur.com

Which country has the largest GDP? The answer is at
http://www.zurich-base-line.com

Get the scoop on the latest technologies affecting our lives at
http://www.cnet.com

Want to check out the Occupational Outlook Handbook online? Go to
http://www.bls.gov/oco

Chapter 2

Understanding Evolving Economic Systems and Competition

learning goals

1. What is economics, and how are the three sectors of the economy linked?
2. How do economic growth, full employment, and price stability indicate a nation's economic health?
3. What is inflation, how is it measured, and what causes it?
4. How does the government use monetary policy and fiscal policy to achieve its macroeconomic goals?
5. What are the basic microeconomic concepts of demand and supply, and how do they establish prices?
6. What are the four types of market structure?
7. Which trends are reshaping micro- and macroeconomic environments?

PA

Need an $8,000 Conversation Piece?

For years, Internet enthusiasts and digital marketers have dreamed about kitchen appliances that could be made smarter by connecting them directly to the Internet. Endowed with the power of the Net, these appliances would supposedly help cook and preserve your food, diagnose their own malfunctions, and more. Well, thanks to the Korean giant LG Electronics, you can have the king of these Internet appliances: the 26-cubic-foot, Titanium-clad, LG Internet Refrigerator. At $8,000, this behemoth, with a built-in Windows PC on top and a 15.1-inch color flat-panel screen in the door, is probably the largest, least-mobile digital gadget in the world.

Once you hook up your cable TV and broadband Ethernet connections to handy ports on the back, this fridge can be a computer for e-mail and Web browsing; a television; a music player; a digital still and movie camera; an address book; and a calendar.

The biggest problem with using the Internet on the fridge is that entering text for Web addresses and e-mails is uncomfortable, slow, and frustrating. There's no actual keyboard. By clicking the "text" button, a "virtual" keyboard appears on the screen so you can type Web addresses by touching letters with either a finger or the included stylus, which tucks into the side of the screen. You can also try to enter text in the same fashion as you would with a personal digital assistant, by using handwriting recognition, but this method is even slower than the keyboard.

Perhaps the strangest function of the fridge is a "stored food" program. This calls up a diagram of the fridge and lets you manually record the various foods that you're putting in different compartments. The refrigerator is programmed to know how long food will last from the date you enter your purchases, and it notifies you when food may be spoiling with a message on the main screen.

One can't imagine anyone standing in front of a fridge and typing in this information, especially with the annoying virtual keyboard. Besides, do you really need a fridge to notify you that your milk is sour? Isn't that why you have a kitchen staff? At the very least, for $8,000, the fridge could come with a bar-code reader you could use to swipe the frozen-pizza box.

You can purchase your very own Internet refrigerator by accessing LG's Web site at **http://www.lgappliances.com**, and entering a zip code to find a store near you that's upscale enough to carry one.[1]

Critical Thinking Questions

As you read this chapter, consider the following questions as they relate to the Internet refrigerator:

1. What factors determine the price of the Internet refrigerator?
2. In what type of economic environment does LG Electronics compete?
3. How can the changing economic environment affect the demand for the Internet refrigerator?

Principles of Economics and Competition

economic system
The combination of policies, laws, and choices made by a nation's government to establish the systems that determine what goods and services are produced and how they are allocated.

Whether or not the Internet refrigerator described in the opening story will be a success will depend in part on the economic systems of the countries where it is marketed. A nation's **economic system** is the combination of policies, laws, and choices made by its government to establish the systems that determine what goods and services are produced and how they are allocated. Capitalism and a planned economy, which we discussed in Chapter 1, are examples of economic systems. In a planned economy, government bureaucrats would determine whether to build an Internet refrigerator. Historically, planned economies have done a much worse job of stimulating economic growth and creating a higher standard of living for their citizens than capitalist economies have. The Internet refrigerator is very expensive, and most people in planned economies like Cuba and North Korea could not afford one.

This chapter will help you understand how economies provide jobs for workers and also create and deliver products to consumers and businesses. You will also learn how governments attempt to influence economic activity through policies such as lowering or raising taxes. Next, we discuss how supply and demand determine prices for goods and services. We conclude by examining trends in evolving economic systems and competition.

How Business and Economies Work

1 learning goal

economics
The study of how a society uses scarce resources to produce and distribute goods and services.

Economics is the study of how a society uses scarce resources to produce and distribute goods and services. The resources of a person, a firm, or a nation are limited. Hence, economics is the study of choices—what people, firms, or nations choose from among the available resources. Every economy is concerned with what types and amounts of goods and services should be produced, how they should be produced, and for whom. These decisions are made by the marketplace, the government, or both. In the United States the government and the free-market system together guide the economy.

You probably know more about economics than you realize. Every day many news stories deal with economic matters: a union wins wage increases at General Motors; the Federal Reserve Board lowers interest rates; Wall Street has a record day; the president proposes a cut in income taxes; consumer spending rises as the economy grows; or retail prices are on the rise, to mention just a few examples.

Macroeconomics and Microeconomics

The state of the economy affects both people and businesses. How you spend your money (or save it) is a personal economic decision. Whether you continue in school and whether you work part-time are also economic decisions. Every business also operates within the economy. Based on their economic expectations, businesses decide what products to produce, how to price them, how many people to employ, how much to pay these employees, how much to expand the business, and so on.

macroeconomics
The subarea of economics that focuses on the economy as a whole by looking at aggregate data for large groups of people, companies, or products.

microeconomics
The subarea of economics that focuses on individual parts of the economy such as households or firms.

Economics has two main subareas. **Macroeconomics** is the study of the economy as a whole. It looks at *aggregate* data, data for large groups of people, companies, or products considered as a whole. In contrast, **microeconomics** focuses on individual parts of the economy, such as households or firms.

Both *macroeconomics* and *microeconomics* offer a valuable outlook on the economy. For example, Ford might use both to decide whether to introduce a new line of cars. The company would consider such macroeconomic factors as the national level of personal income, the unemployment rate, interest rates, fuel costs, and the national level of sales of new cars. From a microeconomic viewpoint, Ford would judge consumer demand for new cars versus the existing supply, competing models, labor and material costs and availability, and current prices and sales incentives.

Economics as a Circular Flow

circular flow
The movement of inputs and outputs among households, businesses, and governments; a way of showing how the sectors of the economy interact.

Another way to see how the sectors of the economy interact is to examine the **circular flow** of inputs and outputs among households, businesses, and governments as shown in Exhibit 2.1. Let's review the exchanges by following the purple circle around the inside of the diagram. Households provide inputs (natural resources, labor, capital, entrepreneurship) to businesses, which convert these inputs into outputs (goods and services) for consumers. In return, consumers receive income from rent, wages, interest, and ownership profits (green circle). Businesses receive income from consumer purchases of goods and services.

The other important exchange in Exhibit 2.1 takes place between governments (federal, state, and local) and both individuals and businesses. Governments supply many types of publicly provided goods and services (highways, schools, police, courts, health services, unemployment insurance, Social Security) that benefit individuals and businesses. Government purchases from businesses also contribute to business profits. The contractor who repairs a local stretch of state highway, for example, is paid by government for the work. As the diagram shows, government receives taxes from individuals and businesses to complete the flow.

Changes in one flow affect the others. If government raises taxes, households have less to spend on goods and services. Lower consumer spending causes businesses to reduce production, and economic activity declines; unemployment may rise. In contrast, cutting taxes can stimulate economic activity. Keep the circular flow in mind as we continue our study of economics. The way economic sectors interact will become more evident as we explore macroeconomics and microeconomics.

concept check

What is economics?

What is the difference between macroeconomics and microeconomics?

How do resources flow among the household, business, and government sectors?

Exhibit 2.1 | Economics as a Circular Flow

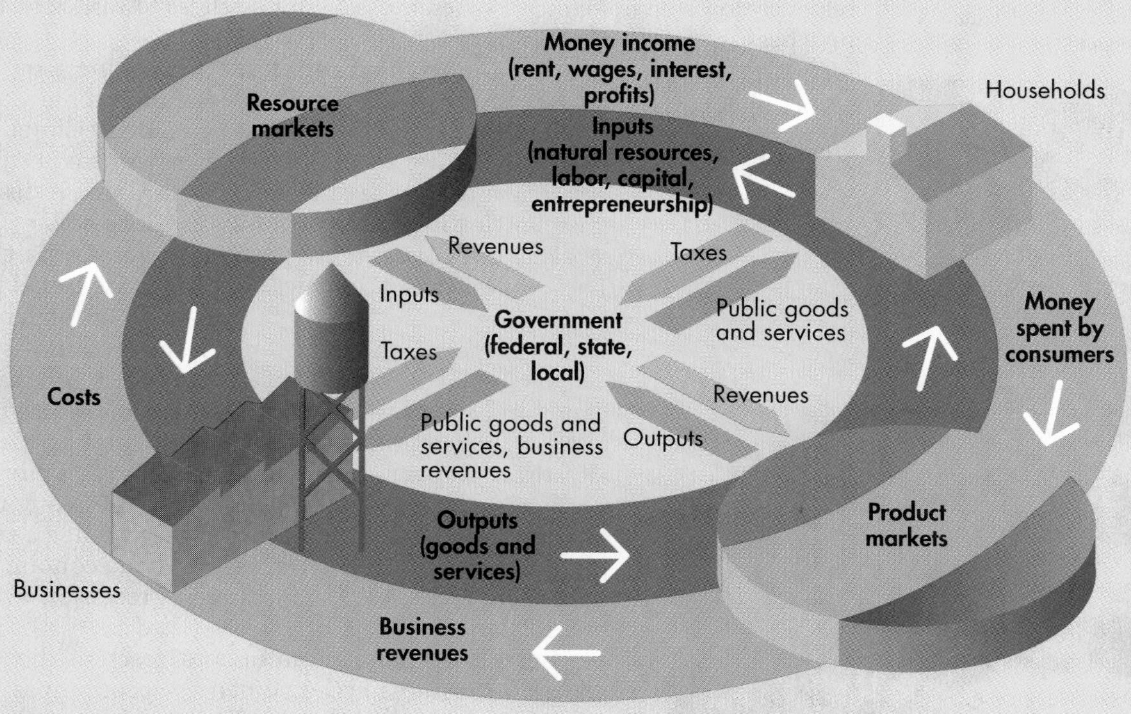

Macroeconomics: The Big Picture

2 learning goal

Have you ever looked at CNN's Headline News on the Internet or turned on the radio or television and heard something like, "Today the Labor Department reported that for the second straight month unemployment declined"? Statements like this are macroeconomic news. Understanding the national economy and how changes in government policies affect households and businesses is a good place to begin our study of economics.

Let's look first at macroeconomic goals and how they can be met. The United States and most other countries have three main macroeconomic goals: economic growth, full employment, and price stability. A nation's economic well-being depends on carefully defining these goals and choosing the best economic policies to reach them.

Striving for Economic Growth

Perhaps the most important way to judge a nation's economic health is to look at its production of goods and services. The more the nation produces, the higher its standard of living. An increase in a nation's output of goods and services is **economic growth.**

economic growth
An increase in a nation's output of goods and services.

business cycles
Upward and downward changes in the level of economic activity.

Economic growth is usually a good thing, but it also has a bad side. Increased production yields more pollution. Growth may strain public facilities, such as roads, electricity, schools, and hospitals. Thus, the government tries to apply economic policies that will keep growth to a level that does not reduce the quality of life.

As we saw in Chapter 1, the most basic measure of economic growth is the *gross domestic product (GDP).* GDP is the total market value of all final goods and services produced within a nation's borders each year. It is reported quarterly and is used to compare trends in national output. When GDP rises, the economy is growing.

The *rate* of growth in real GDP (GDP adjusted for inflation) is also important. Recently, the U.S. economy has been growing at about 2 percent or less annually. This growth rate has meant a steady increase in output of goods and services and relatively low unemployment. When the growth rate slides toward zero, the economy begins to stagnate and decline.

The housing industry is a leading economic indicator. A rise in new home construction typically translates into a robust economy.

© PHOTODISC

One country that continues to grow more rapidly than most is China. Today there are few things in the global marketplace that are not or cannot be made in China. The primary contributor to China's rapid growth has been technology. The importance of technology to China is discussed in the following Expanding Around the Globe box.

The level of economic activity is constantly changing. These upward and downward changes are called **business cycles.** Business cycles vary in length, in how high or low the economy moves, and in how much the economy is affected. Changes in GDP trace the patterns as economic activity expands and contracts. An increase in business activity results in rising output, income, employment, and prices. Eventually, these all peak, and output, income, and employment decline. A decline in GDP that lasts for two consecutive quarters (each a three-month period) is called a **recession.** It is followed by a recovery period when economic activity once again increases. The most recent recession was in 2001 and 2002.

Businesses must monitor and react to the changing phases of business cycles. When the economy is growing, companies often have a difficult time hiring good employ-

Expanding Around the Globe

Technology Powers China's Economic Growth

China has become the world's factory floor, with an output so massive and wide-ranging that it exerts downward pressure on prices around the globe on everything from textiles to TVs, mobile phones to mushrooms.

China is the world's fourth-largest industrial base, in terms of value of goods produced, behind the United States, Japan, and Germany. These days, China makes more than 50 percent of the cameras sold worldwide, 30 percent of the air conditioners and televisions, 25 percent of the washing machines, and nearly 20 percent of the refrigerators. A private Chinese company, Guangdong Galanz Enterprise Group Co., now accounts for 40 percent of all microwave ovens sold in Europe. The city of Wenzhou, in eastern China, sells 70 percent of the world's metal cigarette lighters.

Technology will continue to pave the way for a larger piece of the global technology pie. Consider these milestones in China's science and technology base:

- Chinese universities granted 465,000 science and engineering degrees in 2002—approaching the total for the United States.
- There are plans to crank out chips from seven new semiconductor plants by 2004, putting China on track to be the world's second-largest chip producer.
- A team at the Beijing Genomics Institute was among the first of several scientific teams to decode the rice genome, landing on the cover of the journal *Science*.
- Two homegrown vendors of network switches, Huawei Technologies Co. and ZTE Corp., have opened offices in the United States and Europe and snatched contracts from the likes of Cisco Systems and Nortel Networks.
- China has been launching satellites for years and intends to begin manned space missions soon.[2]

CRITICAL THINKING QUESTIONS

1. What does China's growth in technological prowess mean for U.S. companies?
2. Will China's technological growth be good or bad for U.S. consumers?
3. It has been said that "China is the most vigorous market for the United States and its most vigorous competitor." Explain.

recession
A decline in GDP that lasts for at least two consecutive quarters.

ees and finding scarce supplies and raw materials. When a recession hits, many firms find they have more capacity than the demand for their goods and services requires. During the recession of the early 1990s, many firms operated at 75 percent or less of their capacity. When plants use only part of their capacity, they operate inefficiently and have higher costs per unit produced. Let's say that Mars Corp. has a plant that can produce 1 million Milky Way candy bars a day, but because of a recession Mars can sell only half a million candy bars a day. Mars has a huge plant with large, expensive machines designed to produce a million candy bars a day. Producing Milky Ways at 50 percent capacity does not efficiently utilize Mars's investment in the plant and equipment.

Keeping People on the Job

full employment
The condition when all people who want to work and can work have jobs.

Another macroeconomic goal is **full employment,** or having jobs for all who want to and can work. Full employment doesn't actually mean 100 percent employment. Some people choose not to work for personal reasons (attending school, raising children) or are temporarily unemployed while they wait to start a new job. Thus, the government defines full employment as the situation when about 94 to 96 percent of those available to work actually have jobs. During the early 2000s, the economy operated at less than full employment.

unemployment rate
The percentage of the total labor force that is actively looking for work but is not actually working.

Measuring Unemployment To determine how close we are to full employment, the government measures the **unemployment rate.** This rate indicates the percentage of the total labor force that is not working but is *actively looking for work*. It excludes "discouraged workers," those not seeking jobs because they think no one will hire them. Each month the Department of Labor releases statistics on employment. These figures help us understand how well the economy is doing. In the past two decades, unemployment rose as high as 9.7 percent in 1982, which was a recession year. It then declined steadily through the remainder of the 1980s and most of the 1990s. In 2000, the rate fell to under 4 percent, which was

Employment in business services, especially in computer and data processing services, is projected to grow by 86 percent between 2000 and 2010, ranking as the fastest growing industry in the economy (http://www.bls.gov).

© AMY ETRA / PHOTO EDIT

concept check

How do businesses adapt to periods of contraction and expansion?

Why is full employment usually defined as a target percent below 100?

the lowest rate in almost 30 years. However, the recession of 2001–2002 drove unemployment to over 6 percent.

Types of Unemployment Economists classify unemployment into four types: frictional, structural, cyclical, and seasonal. The categories are of small consolation to someone who is unemployed, but they help economists understand the problem of unemployment in our economy.

frictional unemployment
Short-term unemployment that is not related to the business cycle.

Frictional unemployment is short-term unemployment that is not related to the business cycle. It includes people who are unemployed while waiting to start a better job, those who are reentering the job market, and those entering for the first time such as new college graduates. This type of unemployment is always present and has little impact on the economy.

structural unemployment
Unemployment that is caused by a mismatch between available jobs and the skills of available workers in an industry or region; not related to the business cycle.

Structural unemployment is also unrelated to the business cycle but is involuntary. It is caused by a mismatch between available jobs and the skills of available workers in an industry or a region. For example, if the birthrate declines, fewer teachers will be needed. Or the available workers in an area may lack the skills that employers want. Retraining and skill-building programs are often required to reduce structural unemployment.

cyclical unemployment
Unemployment that occurs when a downturn in the business cycle reduces the demand for labor throughout the economy.

Cyclical unemployment, as the name implies, occurs when a downturn in the business cycle reduces the demand for labor throughout the economy. In a long recession, cyclical unemployment is widespread, and even people with good job skills can't find jobs. The government can partly counteract cyclical unemployment with programs that boost the economy.

In the past, cyclical unemployment affected mainly less skilled workers and those in heavy manufacturing. Typically, they would be rehired when economic growth increased. During the 1990s and early 2000s, however, competition forced many American companies to downsize so they could survive in the global marketplace. Motorola cut 15,000 jobs, or 10 percent of its workforce, to lower costs so that it could compete with Asian, European, and other U.S. semiconductor and telecommunications firms.

seasonal unemployment
Unemployment that occurs during specific seasons in certain industries.

The last type is **seasonal unemployment,** which occurs during specific seasons in certain industries. Employees subject to seasonal unemployment include retail workers hired for the Christmas buying season, lettuce pickers in California, and restaurant employees in Aspen during the summer.

3 learning goal

Keeping Prices Steady

The third macroeconomic goal is to keep overall prices for goods and services fairly steady. The situation in which the average of all prices of goods and services is rising is called **inflation.** Inflation's higher prices reduce **purchasing power,** the value of what money can buy. If prices go up but income doesn't rise or rises at a slower rate, a given amount of income buys less. For example, if the price of a basket of groceries rises from \$30 to \$40 but your salary remains the same, you can buy only 75 percent as many groceries (\$30 ÷ \$40). Your purchasing power declines by 25 percent (\$10 ÷ \$40).

inflation
The situation in which the average of all prices of goods and services is rising.

purchasing power
The value of what money can buy.

Inflation affects both personal and business decisions. When prices are rising, people tend to spend more—before their purchasing power declines further. Businesses that expect inflation often increase their supplies, and people often speed up planned purchases of cars and major appliances.

During the mid-2000s and late 1990s, inflation in the United States was in the 1.5 to 4 percent range. This level is generally viewed as quite low. In the 1980s we had periods of inflation in the 12 to 13 percent range. Some nations have had triple-digit inflation or even higher in recent years. In the late 1990s, Bulgaria had an annual rate of inflation of 123 percent; Turkmenistan, 992 percent; and Angola, 4,145 percent!

demand-pull inflation
Inflation that occurs when the demand for goods and services is greater than the supply.

cost-push inflation
Inflation that occurs when increases in production costs push up the prices of final goods and services.

TYPES OF INFLATION There are two types of inflation. **Demand-pull inflation** occurs when the demand for goods and services is greater than the supply. Would-be buyers have more money to spend than the amount needed to buy available goods and services. Their demand, which exceeds the supply, tends to pull prices up. This situation is sometimes described as "too much money chasing too few goods." The higher prices lead to greater supply, eventually creating a balance between demand and supply.

Cost-push inflation is triggered by increases in production costs, such as expenses for materials and wages. These increases push up the prices of final goods and services. Wage increases are a major cause of cost-push inflation, creating a "wage–price spiral." For example, assume the United Auto Workers union negotiates a three-year labor agreement that raises wages 3 percent per year and increases overtime pay. Car makers will then raise car prices to cover their higher labor costs. Also, the higher wages will give auto workers more money to buy goods and services, and this increased demand may pull up other prices. Workers in other industries will demand higher wages to keep up with the increased prices, and the cycle will push prices even higher.

© AP / WIDE WORLD PHOTOS

The CPI is an index of the prices paid for a variety of everyday products purchased by consumers in urban areas. The cost of women's clothing, for example, is compared to the price of women's clothing in the base period, 1982–1984.

consumer price index (CPI)
An index of the prices of a market basket of goods and services purchased by typical urban consumers.

producer price index (PPI)
An index of the prices paid by producers and wholesalers for various commodities such as raw materials, partially finished goods, and finished products.

How Inflation Is Measured The rate of inflation is most commonly measured by looking at changes in the **consumer price index (CPI),** an index of the prices of a "market basket" of goods and services purchased by typical urban consumers. It is published monthly by the Department of Labor. Major components of the CPI, which are weighted by importance, are food, clothing, transportation, housing, health, and recreation. Data are collected from about 23,000 retail and service businesses in 87 areas around the country.

The CPI sets prices in a base period at 100. The base period, which now is 1982–1984, is chosen for its price stability. Current prices are then expressed as a percentage of prices in the base period. A rise in the CPI means prices are increasing. For example, the CPI was 182.2 in late 2002, meaning that prices had increased 82.2 percent from the 1982–1984 base period.

Changes in wholesale prices are another important indicator of inflation. The **producer price index (PPI)** measures the prices paid by producers and wholesalers for such commodities as raw materials, partially finished goods, and finished products. The PPI is actually a family of indexes for many different product categories. For example, the PPI for chemicals was 134.2 in September 2002. Examples of other PPI indexes include containers, fuels and lubricants, and construction. Because the PPI measures prices paid by producers for raw materials, energy, and other commodities, it may foreshadow subsequent price changes for businesses and consumers.

concept check

What is a business cycle? How do businesses adapt to periods of contraction and expansion?

Why is full employment usually defined as a target percentage below 100 percent?

What is the difference between demand-pull and cost-push inflation?

The Impact of Inflation Inflation has several negative effects on people and businesses. For one thing, inflation penalizes people who live on fixed incomes. Let's say that a couple receives $1,000 a month retirement income beginning in 2004. If inflation is 10 percent in 2005, then the couple can buy only 90 percent of what they could purchase in 2004. Similarly, inflation hurts savers. As prices rise, the real value, or purchasing power, of a nest egg of savings deteriorates.

Achieving Macroeconomic Goals

4 learning goal

To reach macroeconomic goals, countries must often choose among conflicting alternatives. Sometimes political needs override economic ones. For example, bringing inflation under control may call for a politically difficult period of high unemployment and low growth. Or, in an election year, politicians may resist raising taxes to curb inflation. Still, the government must try to guide the economy to a sound balance of growth, employment, and price stability. The two main tools it uses are monetary policy and fiscal policy.

Monetary Policy

monetary policy
A government's programs for controlling the amount of money circulating in the economy and interest rates.

Federal Reserve System (the Fed)
The central banking system of the United States.

Monetary policy refers to a government's programs for controlling the amount of money circulating in the economy and interest rates. Changes in the money supply affect both the level of economic activity and the rate of inflation. The **Federal Reserve System (the Fed),** the central banking system, prints money and controls how much of it will be in circulation. The money supply is also controlled by the Fed's regulation of certain bank activities.

When the Fed increases or decreases the amount of money in circulation, it affects interest rates (the cost of borrowing money and the reward for lending it). The Fed can change the interest rate on money it lends to banks to signal the banking system and financial markets that it has changed its monetary policy. Banks, in turn, may pass along this change to consumers and businesses that receive loans from the banks. If the cost of borrowing increases, the economy slows because interest rates affect consumer and business decisions to spend or invest. The housing industry, business, and investments react most to changes in interest rates.

As you can see, the Fed can use monetary policy to contract or expand the economy. With **contractionary policy,** the Fed restricts, or tightens, the money supply by selling government securities or raising interest rates. The result is slower economic growth and higher unemployment. Thus, contractionary policy reduces spending and, ultimately, lowers inflation. With **expansionary policy,** the Fed increases, or loosens, growth in the money supply. An expansionary policy stimulates the economy. Interest rates decline, so business and consumer spending go up. Unemployment rates drop as businesses expand. But increasing the money supply also has a negative side: More spending pushes prices up, increasing the inflation rate.

contractionary policy
The use of monetary policy by the Fed to tighten the money supply by selling government securities or raising interest rates.

expansionary policy
The use of monetary policy by the Fed to increase the growth of the money supply.

Fiscal Policy

fiscal policy
The government's use of taxation and spending to affect the economy.

The other economic tool used by the government is **fiscal policy,** its program of taxation and spending. By increasing its spending or by cutting taxes, the government can stimulate the economy. Look again at Exhibit 2.1. The more government buys from businesses, the greater business revenues and output are. Likewise, if consumers or businesses have to pay less in taxes, they will have more income to spend for goods and services. Tax policies in the United States therefore affect business decisions. High corporate taxes can make it harder for U.S. firms to compete with companies in countries with lower taxes. As a result, companies may choose to locate facilities overseas to reduce their tax burden.

Nobody likes to pay taxes, although we grudgingly accept that we have to. Although most U.S. citizens complain that they are overtaxed, we pay lower taxes per capita (per person) than citizens in many countries similar to ours, as Exhibit 2.2 shows.

Taxes are, of course, the major source of revenue for our government. Every year the president prepares a budget for the coming year based upon estimated revenues and expenditures. Congress receives the president's report and recommendations and then, typically, debates and analyzes the proposed budget for several months. The president's original proposal is always modified in numerous ways. Exhibit 2.3 shows sources of revenue and expenses for the U.S. budget.

Exhibit 2.2 Tax Revenues, by Country (Per Capita and Percentage of GDP)

	Per Capita	Percentage of GDP
United States	$ 7,234	27.6%
Japan	10,434	27.8
Australia	5,589	29.9
United Kingdom	5,968	34.1
Canada	6,858	36.1
Germany	12,197	39.3
Norway	11,706	41.2
Italy	7,416	41.7
France	10,129	44.1
The Netherlands	9,983	45.9
Belgium	10,500	46.6
Sweden	11,481	51.0
Denmark	14,460	51.6

Exhibit 2.3 | Revenues and Expenses for the Federal Budget

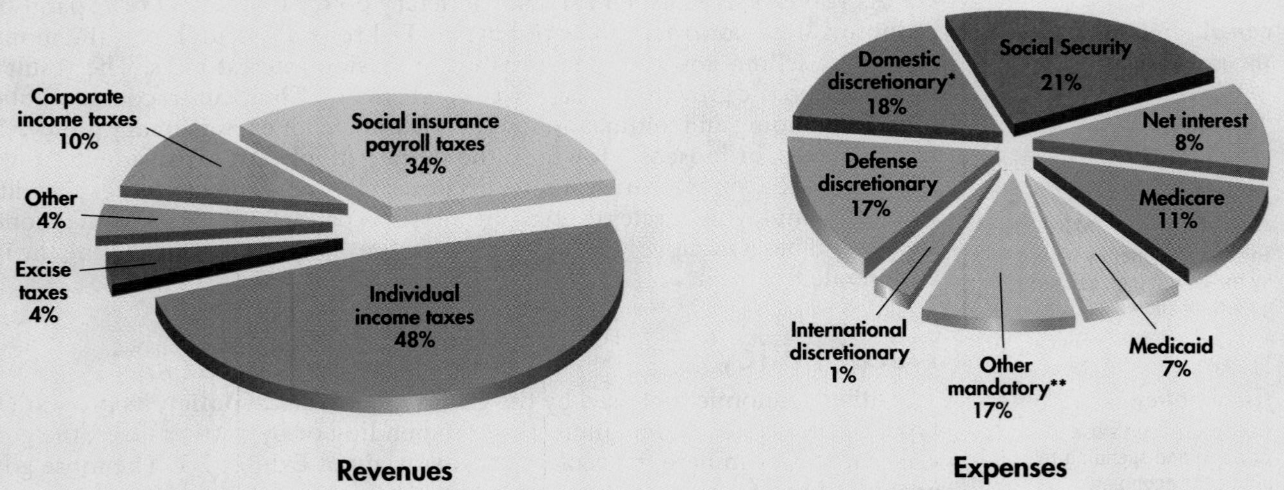

* Includes items such as expenditures for education, community development, agriculture, science, and commerce.

**Includes items such as veterans benefits and administration of justice.

crowding out
The situation that occurs when government spending replaces spending by the private sector.

While fiscal policy has a major impact on businesses and consumers, continual increases in government spending raise another important issue. When government takes more money from businesses and consumers (the private sector) and uses these funds for increased government spending (the public sector), a phenomenon known as **crowding out** occurs. Here are three examples of crowding out:

1. The government spends more on public libraries, and individuals buy fewer books at bookstores.
2. The government spends more on public education, and individuals spend less on private education.
3. The government spends more on public transportation, and individuals spend less on private transportation.

In other words, government spending is crowding out private spending.

federal budget deficit
The condition that occurs when the federal government spends more for programs than it collects in taxes.

If the government spends more for programs (social services, education, defense) than it collects in taxes, the result is a **federal budget deficit.** To balance the budget, the government can cut its spending, increase taxes, or do some combination of the two. When it cannot balance the budget, the government must make up any shortfalls by borrowing (just like any business or household).

In 1998, for the first time in a generation, there was a federal budget surplus (revenue exceeded spending) of about $71 billion. By 2002, there was once again a deficit ($159 billion). Whenever the government finds itself with a surplus, Congress begins an often heated debate about what to do with the money. Some members of Congress, for example, want to spend more on social programs or for defense. Others say that this money belongs to the people and should be returned in the form of tax cuts. Another alternative is to reduce the national debt.

national debt
The accumulated total of all of the federal government's annual budget deficits.

The U.S. government has run budget deficits for many years. The accumulative total of these past deficits is the **national debt,** which now amounts to about $6.2 trillion or about $21,660 for every man, woman, and child in the United

States. Interest on the debt is more than $180 billion a year. To cover the deficit, the U.S. government borrows money from people and businesses in the form of Treasury bills, Treasury notes, and Treasury bonds. These are federal IOUs that pay interest to the owners.

The national debt is an emotional issue debated not only in the halls of Congress, but by the public as well. Some believe that deficits contribute to economic growth, high employment, and price stability. Others have the following reservations about such a high national debt.

Not Everyone Holds the Debt One concern about a high national debt is who actually bears the burden of the national debt. If only the rich were bondholders, then they alone would receive the interest payments. Depending on how many bonds they held, they could end up receiving more in interest than they paid in taxes. In the meantime, poorer people, who held no bonds, would end up paying taxes that would be transferred to the rich as interest. Under these conditions, the debt would indeed be a burden to some.

The government is very conscious of this burden effect and has kept a watchful eye on who holds what bonds. For example, it has at times instructed commercial banks to reduce their total debt by divesting some of their bond holdings. That's also why the Treasury created **savings bonds.** Because these bonds are issued in relatively small denominations, they allow more people to buy and hold government debt.

savings bonds
Government bonds of relatively small denominations.

Crowding Out Private Investment Another concern is the effect of the national debt on private investment. If, to sell its bonds, the government raises the interest rate on the bonds it offers, it forces private businesses, which must stay competitive as suppliers of bonds in the bond market, to raise the rates they offer on their corporate bonds (long-term debt obligations issued by a company). In other words, financing government spending by government debt makes it more costly for private industry to finance its own investment. As a result, government debt may end up crowding out private investment and slowing economic growth in the private sector.

concept check

What are the two kinds of monetary policy?

What fiscal policy tools can the government use to achieve its macroeconomic goals?

What problems can a large national debt present?

Microeconomics: Zeroing in on Businesses and Consumers

5 learning goal

Now let's shift our focus from the whole economy to *microeconomics,* the study of households, businesses, and industries. This field of economics is concerned with how prices and quantities of goods and services behave in a free market. It stands to reason that people, firms, and governments try to get the most from their limited resources. Consumers want to buy the best quality at the lowest price. Businesses want to keep costs down and revenues high to earn larger profits. Governments also want to use their revenues to provide the most effective public goods and services possible. These groups choose among alternatives by focusing on the prices of goods and services.

As consumers in a free market, we influence what is produced. If Mexican food is popular, the high demand attracts entrepreneurs who open more Mexican restaurants. They want to compete for our dollars by supplying Mexican food at a lower price, of better quality, or with different features such as Santa Fe Mexican food rather than Tex-Mex. This section explains how business and consumer choices influence the price and availability of goods and services.

The Nature of Demand

demand
The quantity of a good or service that people are willing to buy at various prices.

demand curve
A graph showing the quantity of a good or service that people are willing to buy at various prices.

Demand is the quantity of a good or service that people are willing to buy at various prices. The higher the price, the lower the quantity demanded, and vice versa. A graph of this relationship is called a **demand curve.**

Let's assume you own a store that sells jackets for snowboarders. From past experience you know how many jackets you can sell at different prices. The demand curve in Exhibit 2.4 depicts this information. The *x*-axis (horizontal axis) shows the quantity of jackets, and the *y*-axis (vertical axis) shows the related price of those jackets. For example, at a price of $60, customers will buy (demand) 500 snowboard jackets.

In the graph the demand curve slopes downward and to the right. This means that as the price falls, people will want to buy more jackets. Some people who were not going to buy a jacket will purchase one at the lower price. Also, some snowboarders who already have a jacket will buy a second one. The graph also shows that if you put a large number of jackets on the market, you will have to reduce the price to sell all of them.

Understanding demand is critical to businesses. This is because demand tells you how much you can sell and at what price—in other words, how much money the firm will take in that can be used to cover costs and hopefully earn a profit. Gauging demand is difficult even for the very largest corporations, but particularly for small firms. The "Focusing on Small Business" box illustrates how Sara Blakely believed that there was a demand for her idea when no one else did.

supply
The quantity of a good or service that businesses will make available at various prices.

supply curve
A graph showing the quantity of a good or service that a business will make available at various prices.

The Nature of Supply

Demand alone is not enough to explain how the market sets prices. We must also look at **supply,** the quantity of a good or service that businesses will make available at various prices. The higher the price, the greater the amount a jacket manufacturer is willing to supply, and vice versa. A graph of the relationship between various prices and the quantities a manufacturer will supply is a **supply curve.**

Exhibit 2.4 | Demand Curve for Jackets for Snowboarders

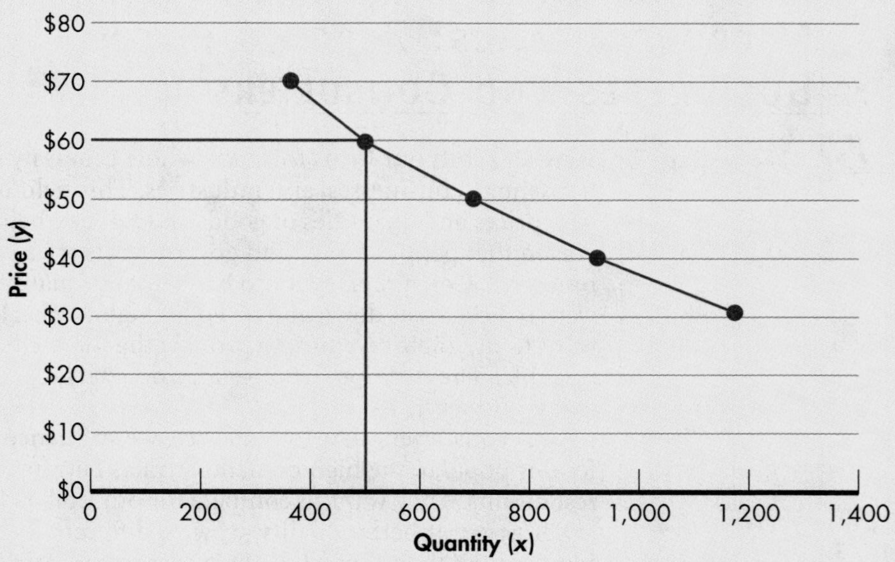

Focusing on Small Business

Making Money Without Feet

Sara Blakely was ready to pack it in. It had been a year since she'd thought up the idea for Spanx, a footless panty hose, and she had gotten nowhere with it. She was sure women would snap up a product that gave their buttocks the slimming effect of traditional hosiery but that didn't show in open-toe shoes. The people she needed to help create Spanx, though, didn't see it as the breakthrough Blakely saw it as. In fact, they thought it was a joke.

To get started, Blakely needed to patent Spanx's design. But lawyers she met with in her hometown of Atlanta—all men—thought she was crazy. "Most of them laughed out loud," she says. "They didn't understand the concept."

She had similar luck calling on hosiery mills. Blakely needed one to make a small run of Spanx that she could show to stores. She phoned 15 or so mill owners—again, nearly all men—but to no avail.

Blakely worked and traveled as a sales trainer. During one business trip, she caught the last 15 minutes of *Oprah* in her hotel room. The talk show host was chastising a model for wearing stockings with open-toe shoes. Then Oprah lifted up one of her own pant legs to reveal hose with the feet cut off. "I sprung up off the bed in my hotel room and said, 'Okay, that's my sign, I'm going for it,'" Blakely says.

She wrote her own patent essay and this ultimately convinced a lawyer to handle the patent application. Blakely then went from mill to mill until she talked a small-mill owner into making 3,000 pairs of Spanx. Spanx now has 12 full-time employees. Besides the original Spanx, which retails for $20, Blakely also sells control-top fishnets and body-shaping underwear. Today Spanx is sold at Bergdorf Goodman, Nordstrom, Bloomingdale's, Neiman Marcus, Saks Fifth Avenue, and more than 1,200 boutiques in the United States and Canada, as well as on QVC and online.[3]

Critical Thinking Questions

1. Why do you think Blakely had such a hard time convincing people that there was demand for her idea?
2. What could she have done to make it easier to convince the mills to produce her product?
3. Do you think that understanding demand is really necessary if you truly believe that you have a good idea?

We can again plot the quantity of jackets on the *x*-axis and the price on the *y*-axis. As Exhibit 2.5 shows, 900 jackets will be available at a price of $60. Note that the supply curve slopes upward and to the right, the opposite of the demand curve. If snowboarders are willing to pay higher prices, manufacturers of jackets will buy more inputs (Gore-Tex®, dye, machinery, labor) and produce more jackets. The quantity supplied will be higher at higher prices, because producers can earn higher profits.

How Demand and Supply Interact to Determine Prices

In a stable economy, the number of jackets that snowboarders demand depends on the jackets' price. Likewise, the number of jackets that suppliers provide depends on price. But at what price will consumer demand for jackets match the quantity suppliers will produce?

To answer this question, we need to look at what happens when demand and supply interact. By plotting both the demand curve and the supply curve on the same graph in Exhibit 2.6, we see that they cross at a certain quantity and price. At that point, labeled E, the quantity demanded equals the quantity supplied. This is the point of **equilibrium.** The equilibrium price is $50; the equilibrium quantity is 700 jackets. At that point there is a balance between the amount consumers will buy and the amount the manufacturers will supply.

equilibrium
The point at which quantity demanded equals quantity supplied.

Market equilibrium is achieved through a series of quantity and price adjustments that occur automatically. If the price increases to $70, suppliers produce more jackets than consumers are willing to buy, and a surplus results. To sell more jackets, prices will have to fall. Thus, a surplus pushes prices downward until equilibrium is reached. When the price falls to $40, the quantity of jackets demanded

Exhibit 2.5 Supply Curve for Jackets for Snowboarders

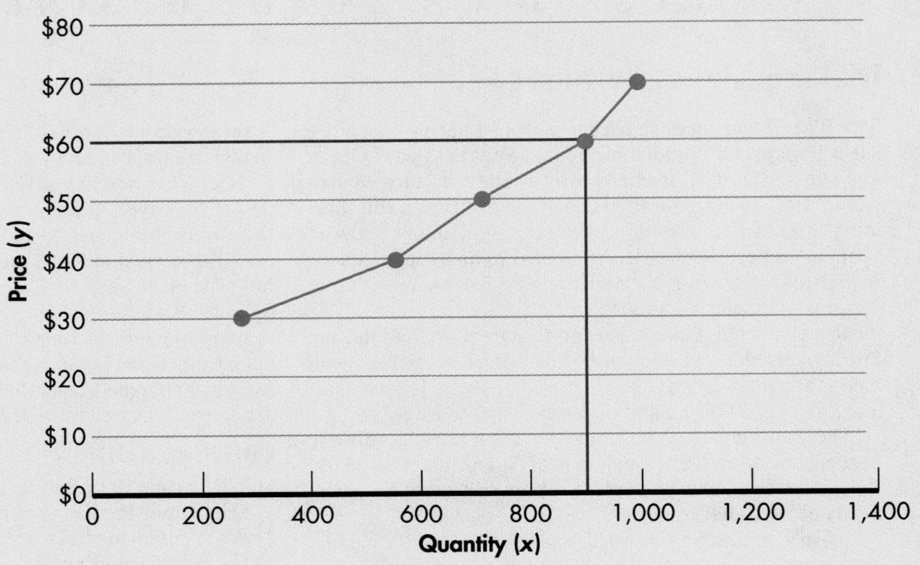

Exhibit 2.6 Equilibrium Price and Quantity

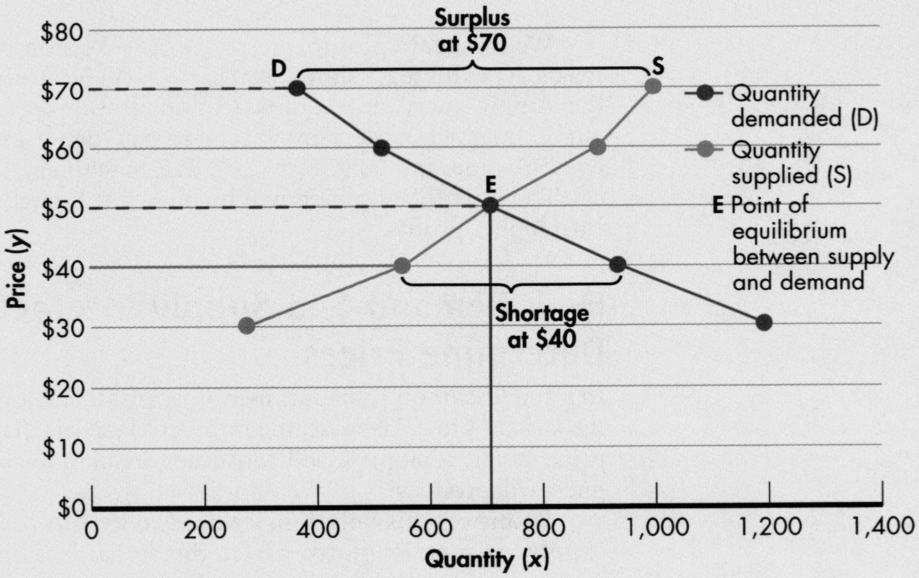

rises above the available supply. The resulting shortage forces prices upward until equilibrium is reached at $50.

The number of snowboarder jackets produced and bought at $50 will tend to rest at equilibrium unless there is a shift in either demand or supply. If demand increases, more jackets will be purchased at every price, and the demand curve shifts to the right (as illustrated by line D_2 in Exhibit 2.7). If demand decreases, less will be bought at every price, and the demand curve shifts to the left (D_1). When de-

Exhibit 2.7 | Shifts in Demand

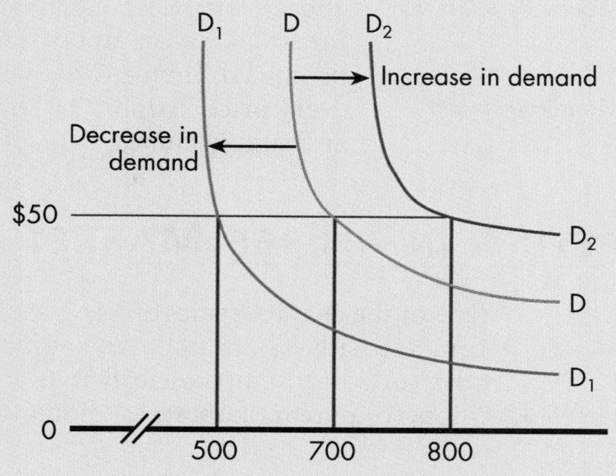

mand decreased, snowboarders bought 500 jackets at $50 instead of 700 jackets. When demand increased, they purchased 800.

When Tom Ridge, Homeland Security Secretary advised that homeowners use duct tape in a biological terrorist attack, the Henkel Consumers Adhesive company experienced an unprecedented and short-lived run on their "Duck" brand duct tape. They increased production 40 percent to meet the market's demand for duct tape. http://www.duckproducts.com

Changes in Demand A number of things can increase or decrease demand. For example, if snowboarders' incomes go up, they may decide to buy a second jacket. If incomes fall, a snowboarder who was planning to purchase a jacket may wear an old one instead. Changes in fashion or tastes can also influence demand. If snowboarding were suddenly to go out of fashion, demand for jackets would decrease quickly. A change in the price of related products can also influence demand. For example, if the average price of a snowboard rises to $1,000, people will quit snowboarding and jacket demand will fall.

Another factor that can shift demand is expectations about future prices. If you expect jacket prices to increase significantly in the future, you may decide to go ahead and get one today. If you think prices will fall, you will postpone your purchase. Finally, changes in the number of buyers will affect demand. Snowboarding is a young person's sport. The number of teenagers will increase in the next few years. Therefore, the demand for snowboarding jackets should increase.

Changes in Supply New technology typically lowers the cost of production. For example, North Face, a manufacturer of ski and snowboarder jackets, has just purchased laser-guided pattern-cutting equipment and computer-aided pattern-making equipment. Each jacket is now cheaper to produce, resulting in a higher profit per jacket. This becomes an incentive to supply more jackets at every price. If the price of resources such as labor or fabric goes up, North Face will earn a smaller profit on each jacket, and the amount supplied will decrease at every price. The reverse is also true. Changes in the prices of other goods can also affect supply.

Let's say that snow skiing becomes a really hot sport. The number of skiers jumps dramatically and the price of ski jackets soars. North Face can use its machines and fabrics to produce either ski or snowboard jackets. If the company can make more profit from ski jackets, it will produce fewer snowboarding jackets at every price. Also, simply a change in the number

concept check

What is the relationship between prices and demand for a product?

How is market equilibrium achieved?

Draw a graph that shows an equilibrium point.

of producers will shift the supply curve. If the number of manufacturers increases, more jackets will be placed on the market at every price and vice versa. Taxes can also affect supply. If the government decides, for some reason, to tax the manufacturer for every snowboard jacket produced, then profits will fall and fewer jackets will be offered at every price. Exhibit 2.8 summarizes the factors that can shift demand and supply curves.

Competing in a Free Market

6 learning goal

One of the characteristics of a free-market system is that suppliers have the right to compete with one another. The number of suppliers in a market is called **market structure.** Economists identify four types of market structures: (a) perfect competition, (b) pure monopoly, (c) monopolistic competition, and (d) oligopoly.

market structure
The number of suppliers in a market.

perfect (pure) competition
A market structure in which a large number of small firms sell similar products, buyers and sellers have good information, and businesses can be easily opened or closed.

Perfect Competition

Characteristics of **perfect (pure) competition** include:

- A large number of small firms are in the market.
- The firms sell similar products; that is, each firm's product is very much like the products sold by other firms in the market.
- Buyers and sellers in the market have good information about prices, sources of supply, and so on.
- It is easy to open a new business or close an existing one.

In a perfectly competitive market, firms sell their products at prices determined solely by forces beyond their control. Because the products are very similar and because each firm contributes only a small amount to the total quantity supplied by the industry, price is determined by supply and demand. A firm that raised its price even a little above the going rate would lose customers. In the wheat

Exhibit 2.8 Factors That Cause Demand and Supply Curves to Shift

	Shift Demand	
Factor	**To the Right If:**	**To the Left If:**
Buyers' incomes	increase	decrease
Buyers' preferences/tastes	increase	decrease
Prices of substitute products	increase	decrease
Expectations about future prices	will rise	will fall
Number of buyers	increases	decreases
	Shift Supply	
Technology	lowers cost	increases cost
Resource prices	fall	increase
Changes in prices of other products that can be produced with the same resources	profit of other product falls	profit of other product increases
Number of suppliers	increases	decreases
Taxes	lowered	increased

market, for example, the product is essentially the same from one wheat producer to the next. Thus, none of the producers has control over the price of wheat.

Perfect competition is an ideal. No industry shows all its characteristics, but the stock market and some agricultural markets, such as those for wheat and corn, come closest. Farmers, for example, can sell all of their crops through national commodity exchanges at the current market price.

Pure Monopoly

pure monopoly
A market structure in which a single firm accounts for all industry sales and in which there are barriers to entry.

barriers to entry
Factors, such as technological or legal conditions, that prevent new firms from competing equally with a monopoly.

At the other end of the spectrum is **pure monopoly,** the market structure in which a single firm accounts for all industry sales. The firm is the industry. This structure is characterized by **barriers to entry**—factors that prevent new firms from competing equally with the existing firm. Often the barriers are technological or legal conditions. Polaroid, for example, has held major patents on instant photography for years. When Kodak tried to market its own instant camera, Polaroid sued, claiming patent violations. Polaroid collected millions of dollars from Kodak. Another barrier may be one firm's control of a natural resource. DeBeers Consolidated Mines Ltd., for example, controls most of the world's supply of uncut diamonds.

Public utilities like gas and water are pure monopolies. Some monopolies are created by a government fiat that outlaws competition. The U.S. Postal Service is currently one such monopoly.

Monopolistic Competition

monopolistic competition
A market structure in which many firms offer products that are close substitutes and in which entry is relatively easy.

Three characteristics define the market structure known as **monopolistic competition:**

- Many firms are in the market.
- The firms offer products that are close substitutes but still differ from one another.
- It is relatively easy to enter the market.

Under monopolistic competition, firms take advantage of product differentiation. Industries where monopolistic competition occurs include clothing, food, and similar consumer products. Firms under monopolistic competition have

To distinguish its products in a monopolistic competitive environment, some companies like Heinz have reinvented the rules of the market with products that are clearly differentiated from competitors.

© DAVID YOUNG-WOLFF / PHOTO EDIT

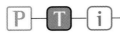

Making Ethical Choices

xtra! http://gitmanxtra.swlearning.com

PURCHASING POWER

As a child you coveted your weekly allowance and delighted in scouting out the best deals. You ended up with more toys than your friends, while spending the same amount of money. Your keen sense of the price of goods and ability to buy more quality products for the same money made your college friends envious. Finally they convinced you to take their money to purchase needed items. You were a natural purchasing agent.

You understood the relationship between supply and demand and the price you were willing to pay for goods. Shortly after graduating, you accepted a position as chief purchasing agent for the New York State–run hospital near your hometown.

In the hospital, you became concerned that prices paid for pharmaceutical goods seemed out of alignment with the laws of supply and demand. No more best deals. Perhaps even "a crisis with regard to . . . the cost of prescription drugs." Two companies—Pharmacia and GlaxoSmithKline—seemed to be inflating their drug prices. Your sense about overcharging proved correct. New York State filed a lawsuit against the companies, accusing them of offering drugs to physicians at deeply discounted prices as a way to sell more. Part of the issue involved the government's wholesale price system. Could the government be impeding your purchasing power at the hospital? The companies' pricing policy seems to involve inflating the price reported to the government and then offering the doctors an opportunity to make money on the difference between the higher reimbursement and promised lower prices from the companies.

All of this is troubling because you haven't been able to identify manufacturers of equivalent drugs at competitive prices.

ETHICAL DILEMMA

Would you purchase drugs that were not exactly the same to save the hospital money?

SOURCES: Christopher Bowe, "NY Attorney General Targets Drugmakers," *FT.com*, February 23, 2003. Downloaded from http://www.FT.com; and Hollister H. Hovey, "New York State Sues Pharmacia, Glaxo, Alleging Pricing Scheme," *Wall Street Journal*, February 14, 2003, p. B5.

more control over pricing than do firms under perfect competition because consumers do not view the products as exactly the same. Nevertheless, firms must demonstrate those product differences to justify their prices to customers. Consequently, companies use advertising to distinguish their products from others. Such distinctions may be significant or superficial. For example, Nike says "Just Do It," and Tylenol is advertised as being easier on the stomach than aspirin.

oligopoly
A market structure in which a few firms produce most or all of the output and in which large capital requirements or other factors limit the number of firms.

relationship management
The practice of building, maintaining, and enhancing interactions with customers and other parties in order to develop long-term satisfaction through mutually beneficial partnerships.

Oligopoly

An **oligopoly** has two characteristics:

- A few firms produce most or all of the output.
- Large capital requirements or other factors limit the number of firms.

Boeing and McDonnell Douglas (aircraft manufacturers) and USX (formerly U.S. Steel) are major firms in different oligopolistic industries.

With so few firms in an oligopoly, what one firm does has an impact on the other firms. Thus, the firms in an oligopoly watch one another closely for new technologies, product changes and innovations, promotional campaigns, pric-

Exhibit 2.9 | Types of Market Structures

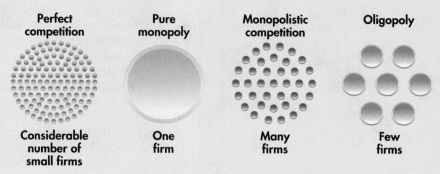

ing, production, and other developments. Sometimes they go so far as to coordinate their pricing and output decisions, which is illegal. Many antitrust cases—legal challenges arising out of laws designed to control anticompetitive behavior—occur in oligopolies. Exhibit 2.9 summarizes the primary types of market structures.

concept check

What is meant by market structure?

Describe the four types of market structure.

Trends in Economics and Competition

7 learning goal

Trends in business occur at both the macroeconomic and the microeconomic level. We will begin by taking a look at some microeconomic trends.

Creating Long-Term Relationships

Starbucks strives to build strong customer relationships and retain loyal customers with the Starbucks Card. It offers the convenience of shopping online and making purchases with a quick, easy-payment method.

© TERRI L. MILLER / E-VISUAL COMMUNICATIONS, INC.

Today, companies are focusing on **relationship management,** which involves building, maintaining, and enhancing interactions with customers and other parties so as to develop long-term satisfaction through mutually beneficial partnerships. In general, the longer a customer stays with a company, the more that customer is worth. Long-term customers buy more, take less of a company's time, are less sensitive to price, and bring in new customers. Best of all, they require no acquisition or start-up costs. Good long-standing customers are worth so much that in some industries, reducing customer defections by as little as five points—from, say, 15 percent to 10 percent per year—can double profits.

Travelodge practices relationship management by launching Travelodge Miles, a guest rewards program featuring swipe-card technology. The program thanks frequent Travelodge and Thriftlodge guests for their patronage with value-added rewards such as frequent-flyer miles, free hotel nights, free rental cars, and other travel perks. Guests earn one Travelodge Mile for each qualified lodging dollar spent at participating economy Travelodge and Thriftlodge properties. When 250 Miles have been accumulated, members can redeem them for Sleepy Bear dolls, T-shirts, or a road atlas, or keep saving the Miles for other rewards at higher levels. The enhanced

SAS customer intelligence software helps companies build strong, long-term customer relationships.

level is already paying off with an increase in the average stay of preferred guests—almost a full night longer per stay. The system makes it easy to track and gather data on the company's best customers and enabled the creation of a "Gold Level" for preferred customers. These Gold Level customers receive preferred rates and free local phone calls.

Relationship management also means creating long-term relationships with suppliers. Suppliers are making major adjustments in their thinking, management styles, and methods of responding to purchasers' standards and operational requirements. A satisfied customer is one of the best sources of new business because the customer already knows that the supplier can meet expectations and deliver on its promises. Thus, the supplier has created trust, and trust is the foundation of most successful relationships.

A **strategic alliance,** sometimes called a strategic partnership, is a cooperative agreement between business firms. The trend toward forming strategic alliances is accelerating rapidly, particularly among high-tech firms. These companies have realized that strategic partnerships are more than just important—they are critical. Nike, the largest producer of athletic footwear in the world, does not manufacture a single shoe. Gallo, the largest wine company on earth, does not grow a single grape. Boeing, the preeminent aircraft manufacturer, makes little more than cockpits and wing bits. "How can this be?" you ask. These companies, like many other companies these days, have entered into strategic alliances with their suppliers to do much of their actual production and manufacturing for them.

Creating a Competitive Workforce

strategic alliance
A cooperative agreement between business firms; sometimes called a *strategic partnership.*

Creating and building long-term relationships require a world-class workforce. The goal of leading companies such as Pfizer and Intel is for all workers to add value to every job they do every day. Such firms place a strong emphasis on training and the use of technology to improve worker productivity.

For example, the state of California employs around 200,000 workers who, for the most part, stay and build their careers in state government. Taxpayer investment in training state workers can result in significant savings for the state. California is one of the first states to offer Internet courses for its employees. Now workers are getting high-quality training from their computers at either work or home.

Entrepreneurial Spirit in Former Command Economies

A key trend in macroeconomics is the surprising entrepreneurial spirit among many citizens of former command economies.

Russia and China have inched away from planned economies. Today, China has a population of 1.3 billion and they all want more and better goods and services. Already there are 21 million *ge-ti-hu* (entrepreneurs) in China.

One example of a Russian entrepreneur is Olga Chudakova, who founded Epic Rus, a software firm in Moscow. Olga has a PhD in economics from Moscow State University. She thinks that Russian entrepreneurs are broader, more intuitive, and more philosophical than those in the United States.[4] This, she claims, is because of their mind-set. Russian education is more comprehensive, whereas education in America is more specialized. Olga notes that her staff of 150 are loyal and highly trained. Recently Epic Rus moved to a large, beautifully renovated building and invested in the most advanced computers for all its employees.

BIG GOVERNMENT RETURNS

Another trend in economics is the return of big government in the United States. When countries go to war, government spending increases for military supplies, more soldiers, and so forth. Most people think that America's war on terrorism is the reason for increased government spending and renewed deficits. It isn't. Only about a third of the additional spending is related to more defense spending; the remainder is the return of big government.

Of the programs that Congress and the president control directly, spending was up 13.9 percent in the 2002–2003 fiscal year. And that's not a new phenomenon. Soon after Bill Clinton declared, "The era of big government is over," in 1996, expenditures started to zoom. Such spending is rising so briskly that, for the first time since the late 1960s, annually appropriated programs have been growing faster than formula-driven entitlement programs like Social Security and Medicare.

Nondefense spending has been increasing so rapidly lately that 2000–2003 represented the largest four-year spending spree in a generation, even if military expenditures hadn't gone up a penny. During that period farm subsidies doubled; unemployment compensation and health programs (other than Medicare and Medicaid) jumped 50 percent; education outlays rose by a third.

Ever since Ronald Reagan's war against government in the 1980s, every president has talked big about making government small. Bush is no exception. He told reporters, "It is important for this country to be fiscally disciplined as our economy begins to recover." But federal spending has risen every year since 1965—including under Reagan—and no one is predicting that trend will end.

concept check

How do businesses provide customer value?

How does relationship management make a business more competitive?

Explain the entrepreneurial movement in former command economies.

Great Ideas to Use Now

As you study micro- and macroeconomics, remember that economics is not something you should learn for an exam and then forget. Economics is an analytical science that will help you understand the world around you. It can help you be more imaginative and insightful in everyday life. You should now better understand why prices are going up or down, when interest rates will fall, and when and why the unemployment rate will fall.

Understanding these basic economic concepts can help you decide whether to change jobs (and how much money to ask for) and whether to buy a car now or wait until next year. When you hear that Ford Motor Co. has 115 days of inventory, understanding supply and demand will tell you that now may be the time to buy that new car.

Try It Now

1. **Understand your tax commitment.** Soon you will enter the permanent job market, if you are not there already. Typically, your earnings will rise over the next 35 years, but as your earnings increase, so will your taxes. The average American works five months out of every year just to cover taxes. Are taxes too high in our country? Since taxes will be a major part of your financial life for the next 35 to 45 years, you need to be informed. Visit a few organizations that advocate tax reform, such as Americans for Tax Reform (**http://www.atr.org/**) and Citizens for Tax Justice (**http://www.ctj.org/**).
2. **Learn a foreign language.** Consider taking a job outside the United States for a while. If you decide to work overseas, having basic skills in a second language will go a long way toward ensuring that you have a rewarding and pleasant experience. Learning a second language can also bring a lot of self-satisfaction. Go to **http://www.learnalanguage.com** and learn more about learning a foreign language.

Similarly, economics will help you become a better-informed citizen. Almost every political issue is, in some way, grounded in economic concepts. You should now know what it means to balance the budget and what problems occur with monopoly power. In short, economics can help you make more thoughtful and informed decisions.

Economics not only can help you understand what is happening in other countries but also can help raise your awareness of opportunities in those countries. As more and more countries have moved away from command economies, American and foreign multinational firms are moving in to take advantage of ground-floor opportunities. Consider accepting a foreign assignment. It's a wonderful way to

Customer Satisfaction and Quality

We spoke earlier in this chapter about China's tremendous growth as a producer of goods and services for the world marketplace. The reason for that growth is that buyers are willingly purchasing the Chinese products because they deliver quality and value.

Customer value is the customer's perception of the ratio of benefits to the sacrifice necessary to obtain those benefits. Customers receive benefits in the form of functionality, performance, durability, design, ease of use, and serviceability. To receive those benefits, they give up money, time, and effort.

Customer value is not simply a matter of high quality. A high-quality product that is available only at a high price will not be perceived as a value. Nor will bare-bones service or low-quality goods selling for a low price. Instead, customers value goods and services of the quality they expect that are sold at prices they are willing to pay. Value marketing can be used to sell a $150,000 Rolls Royce as well as a $3 Tyson frozen chicken dinner.

Businesses provide customer value by:

- *Offering products that perform.* This is the bare minimum. Consumers have lost patience with shoddy merchandise.
- *Giving consumers more than they expect.* Soon after Toyota launched Lexus, the company had to order a recall. The weekend before the recall, dealers personally phoned all the Lexus owners in the United States and arranged to pick up their cars and provide replacement vehicles.
- *Avoiding unrealistic pricing.* Consumers couldn't understand why Kellogg's cereals commanded a premium over other brands, so Kellogg's market share fell 5 percent.
- *Giving the buyer facts.* Today's sophisticated consumer wants informative advertising and knowledgeable salespeople.

Looking Ahead at LG Electronics' Internet Refrigerator

Consider the opening story about the Internet refrigerator. The two basic determinants of price for the refrigerator are demand and supply: the number of people who want to purchase the product at various prices, and the number LG Electronics is willing to produce at various price points. LG Electronics produces large, consumer electronic household products. The firm competes in a market with a relatively few large competitors. Therefore, LG Electronics competes in an oligopolistic market. How will changes in the economy, such as inflation or recession, affect the Internet refrigerator? During a recession, demand for the Internet refrigerator might decline. Yet purchasers of such a product are probably quite wealthy, and wealthy people are often not as bothered by a recession as the rest of us. With inflation, prices of resources used to manufacture the Internet refrigerator will increase, so LG Electronics would probably raise the price of the refrigerator.

experience other cultures and, at the same time, get ahead in your career. More and more large organizations are requiring that their middle and upper-level managers have foreign field experience. When you have an opportunity for a foreign assignment, don't let it slip by.

In today's business world, if a firm doesn't deliver customer value it doesn't survive. Firms that provide customer value end up with satisfied customers. Some companies that are especially good at satisfying customers are: Mercedes-Benz, H. J. Heinz, Lexus, Colgate-Palmolive, MARS, Maytag, Quaker Oats, Hershey Foods, Toyota, and Cadbury Schweppes. All of the companies have won either quality or customer satisfaction awards at one time or another.

Summary of Learning Goals

1 What is economics, and how are the three sectors of the economy linked?

Economics is the study of how individuals, businesses, and governments use scarce resources to produce and distribute goods and services. The two major areas in economics are macroeconomics, the study of the economy as a whole, and microeconomics, the study of households and firms. The individual, business, and government sectors of the economy are linked by a series of two-way flows. The government provides public goods and services for the other two sectors and receives income in the form of taxes. Changes in one flow affect the other sectors.

2 How do economic growth, full employment, and price stability indicate a nation's economic health?

A nation's economy is growing when the level of business activity, as measured by gross domestic product, is rising. GDP is the total value of all goods and services produced in a year. The goal of full employment is to have a job for all who can and want to work. How well a nation is meeting its employment goals is measured by the unemployment rate. There are four types of unemployment: frictional, structural, cyclical, and seasonal. With price stability, the overall prices of goods and services are not moving very much either up or down.

3 What is inflation, how is it measured, and what causes it?

Inflation is the general upward movement of prices. When prices rise, purchasing power falls. The rate of inflation is measured by changes in the consumer price index (CPI) and the producer price index (PPI). There are two main causes of inflation. If the demand for goods and services exceeds the supply, prices will rise. This is called demand-pull inflation. With cost-push inflation, higher production costs, such as expenses for materials and wages, increase the final prices of goods and services.

4 How does the government use monetary policy and fiscal policy to achieve its macroeconomic goals?

Monetary policy refers to actions by the Federal Reserve System to control the money supply. When the Fed restricts the money supply, interest rates rise, the inflation rate drops, and economic growth slows. By expanding the money supply, the Fed stimulates economic growth.

The government also uses fiscal policy—changes in levels of taxation and spending—to control the economy. Reducing taxes or increasing spending stimulates the economy; raising taxes or decreasing spending does the opposite. When the government spends more than it receives in tax revenues, it must borrow to finance the deficit. Some economists favor deficit spending as a way to stimulate the economy; others worry about our high level of national debt.

5 What are the basic microeconomic concepts of demand and supply, and how do they establish prices?

Demand is the quantity of a good or service that people will buy at a given price. Supply is the quantity of a good or service that firms will make available at a given price. When the price increases, the quantity demanded falls but the quantity supplied rises. A price decrease leads to increased demand but a lower supply. At the point where the quantity demanded equals the quantity supplied, demand and supply are in balance. This equilibrium point is achieved by market adjustments of quantity and price.

6 What are the four types of market structure?

Market structure is the number of suppliers in a market. Perfect competition is characterized by a large number of buyers and sellers, very similar products, good market information for both buyers and sellers, and ease of entry and exit into the market. In a pure monopoly, there is a single seller in a market. In monopolistic competition, many firms sell close substitutes in a market that is fairly easy to enter. In an oligopoly, a few firms produce most or all of the industry's output. An oligopoly is also difficult to enter and what one firm does will influence others.

7 Which trends are reshaping the micro- and macroeconomic environments?

Companies are establishing long-term relationships with both customers and suppliers. To compete in today's environment, companies and industries must build a competitive workforce. At the macro level, budding entrepreneurial spirit in former command economies is sparking wealth among individual business owners and fueling the growth of capitalism. The era of big government spending has returned.

KEY TERMS

barriers to entry 65
business cycles 52
circular flow 51
consumer price index (CPI) 56
contractionary policy 57
cost-push inflation 55
crowding out 58
cyclical unemployment 54
demand 60
demand curve 60
demand-pull inflation 55
economic growth 52
economic system 50
economics 50
equilibrium 61
expansionary policy 57
federal budget deficit 58
Federal Reserve System (the Fed) 56
fiscal policy 57
frictional unemployment 54
full employment 53
inflation 55
macroeconomics 50
market structure 64
microeconomics 50
monetary policy 56
monopolistic competition 65
national debt 58
oligopoly 66
perfect (pure) competition 64
producer price index (PPI) 56
purchasing power 55
pure monopoly 65
recession 53
relationship management 66
savings bonds 59
seasonal unemployment 54
strategic alliance 68
structural unemployment 54
supply 60
supply curve 60
unemployment rate 53

PREPARING FOR TOMORROW'S WORKPLACE

1. If a friend claimed, "Economics is all theory and not very practical," how might you counter this claim?
2. Use the Internet or go to the library and determine the current trends in GDP growth, unemployment, and inflation. What do these trends tell you about the level of business activity and the business cycle? If you owned a personnel agency, how would this information affect your decision making?
3. As a manufacturer of in-line roller skates, you are questioning your pricing policies. You note that over the past five years, the CPI increased an average of 2 percent per year, but the price of a pair of skates increased an average of 8 percent per year for the first three years and 2 percent for the next two years. What does this information tell you about demand, supply, and other factors influencing the market for these skates?
4. Write a paper describing an occasion when you received outstanding customer value and an occasion when you received very poor customer value.
5. Divide the class into four teams. One pair of teams will debate the pros and cons of airline deregulation. The other pair will debate electric-utility deregulation. One team should take the pro and the other the con for each issue. If you have Internet access, use the Dow Jones news service or Lexis-Nexis to obtain current articles on the subjects.

WORKING THE NET

1. Point your browser to the Bureau of Economic Analysis Regional Accounts Data at **http://www.bea.doc.gov/bea/regional/data.htm**. Find the historical information for your state's gross domestic product (GDP). What trends do you see? Can you identify any reasons behind these trends? Compare your state's GDP to the U.S. GDP overall, which you will find at **http://www.bea.doc.gov/bea/dn1.htm.**
2. Read more about how the Consumer Price Index (CPI) is computed at the Bureau of Labor Statistics site, **http://stat.bls.gov/cpi/.** Look at the relative importance of each category included in the CPI. How well do these weightings match your own expenditures on each of these categories? What are some of the drawbacks on computing the CPI this way? Do you think these categories give a realistic picture of how most Americans spend their money? Explain your answer.
3. Still confused about the various economic indicators, GDP, and productivity measures? Go to the ABC News site's Business section (**http://abcnews.go.com/sections/business/**) and click on Guide to the Economy, which you'll find under Tools and Resources. How did it clarify your understanding of these areas?
4. Ever think about what you'd do if you were president? Here's your chance to find out how your ideas would affect the federal budget. The National Budget Simulator, at **http://www.budgetsim.org/nbs/**, lets you see how government officials make trade-offs when they prepare the federal budget. Experiment with your own budget ideas at the site. What are the effects of your decisions?

Creative Thinking Case

Inside Intel It's About Copying—Exactly

Intel Corporation has more than 2,000 PhDs on staff to cultivate new ideas. But innovation also depends on people like Trish Roughgarden, an Air Force veteran whose job is to copy slavishly. Ms. Roughgarden is known inside Intel as a "seed," an unofficial title for technicians who transfer manufacturing know-how from one Intel chip factory to another. Her job: to help ensure that Intel's latest plant works just like an identical plant in Hillsboro, Oregon. Several hundred other seeds will copy the same techniques to a third plant in Ireland.

It is all part of a major Intel strategy known as "Copy Exactly," which discourages experimentation at individual factories. Instead, engineers and technicians painstakingly clone proven Intel manufacturing techniques from one plant to the next—down to the color of workers' gloves, wall paint, or other features that would seem to have no bearing on efficiency.

The strategy emerged after Intel's last disastrous slump, when maddening variations between factories in the early 1980s hurt productivity and product quality. Japanese competitors nearly drove Intel out of business. Today, Copy Exactly shapes Intel's response to the latest economic downturn, helping accelerate the relentless pace of technology improvements known as Moore's Law, after former Intel Chairman Gordon Moore.

Intel's newest plant contains 200,000 square feet of new factory space, linked to an existing 300,000-square-foot facility to create what Intel believes is the world's largest semiconductor "clean room." One corridor stretches 900 feet, an avenue of white, ventilated flooring intersecting side streets called bays and chases. The price: more than $2 billion, roughly the same as the Oregon and Ireland additions.

While it prohibits willy-nilly changes, the Copy Exactly methodology encourages Intel workers to come up with ideas to boost productivity or make chip features smaller. But the ideas must pass a committee called the "Process Change Control Board," which requires workers to come up with tests to prove the value of their suggestions.

That bureaucracy "creates frustration" for some engineers, concedes Youssef Aly El-Mansy, an Intel vice president in charge of developing manufacturing processes. "We've lost some people from that."[5]

Critical Thinking Questions

1. Explain the link between quality and "Copy Exactly."
2. How important is technology to a global competitor like Intel? What about product quality?
3. Most management consultants claim that employees are happiest when they have freedom to make decisions in the work environment. How does this fit with "Copy Exactly"? What can be done to let employees exercise their creativity?

Video Case

Black Forest Motors: A Triple Whammy that Works

Headquartered in Germany, Mercedes-Benz (**http://www.mercedes-benz.com**) manufactures luxury automobiles for distribution in Germany, the United States, and elsewhere. To increase sales and perceived customer value in the United States, Mercedes-Benz initiated the "Customer Value Triad," a corporate strategy comprising three key components: quality goods, quality service, and value-based pricing. While quality goods and value-based pricing are generated by the manufacturer, the 310 independently owned U.S. dealerships and their 16,000 employees are the most important element when it comes to providing customers with quality service.

Black Forest Motors, a Mercedes-Benz dealership in North Acme, Michigan, is a prime example of Mercedes-Benz's corporate strategy in action. Black Forest prides itself on exceeding customers' expectations with fair pricing and quality goods and services. Dedicated employees, who have been with Black Forest Motors since its founding, translate directly into quality customer service, ensuring that the dealership is not only a great place to work but "a great place to buy a car." Enjoying the benefits of the Customer Value Triad initiative, Black Forest's customer base, their "family of owners," continues to grow.

The sales, service, and parts departments all powerfully demonstrate Black Forest's commitment to quality service, quality goods, and value-based pricing. The sales department's sole purpose is to exceed customer expectations, from test drive to vehicle delivery. Customers can schedule their test drive online through Black Forest's Web site, meet with a sales staff committed to providing the information they need to make an educated buying decision, and drive away in the Mercedes-Benz perfect for them.

The service department is a state-of-the-art facility featuring the latest diagnostic and repair equipment used by highly trained factory technicians. This department operates on the basis that "you and your vehicle deserve only the best of care." Quality goods and quality service are also emphasized in the parts department, which is stocked with a large inventory of the same high-quality parts used in manufacturing Mercedes-Benz vehicles.

Committed to the Customer Value Triad of quality goods, quality service, and value-based pricing, Black Forest Motors asks only one thing of its clients: "If you were treated well, your expectations met, and the service good, please tell your friends."

SOURCE: Downloaded from http://www.mecedes-benz.com, February 2003.

CRITICAL THINKING QUESTIONS

1. Do you think the Mercedes-Benz Customer Value Triad is an effective corporate strategy?
2. How might a strategy based on the Customer Value Triad help Mercedes-Benz and its dealerships compete effectively in the American marketplace?
3. Why are product and service quality important elements of operating a successful business? What is the impact on the price of cars?
4. Does Mercedes-Benz operate in an oligopolistic marketplace?

E-Commerce Case

Travels With Orbitz

In 2000, five major airlines—American, United, Continental, Delta, and Northwest—announced plans to launch a new online travel site called Orbitz (**http://www.orbitz.com**). Like online travel pioneer sites Travelocity and Expedia, Orbitz would let consumers search for the best airfares. Thirty other airlines quickly agreed to post their fares on the Orbitz site. Each participating airline had to agree to publish its lowest fares on the Orbitz site. The airlines, however, weren't prevented from offering the same low fares elsewhere on the Internet. One airline that decided not to join Orbitz was Southwest. The company explained that it didn't feel comfortable providing information on its fares to a company run by its top competitors.

Even before Orbitz officially opened, controversy arose. The Interactive Travel Services Association (ITSA), a trade association of online travel sites whose membership includes both Travelocity and Expedia, said the airline industry was jealous of the profits being made by online travel sites and that Orbitz was an organized effort by the airlines to "cash in" on those profits by wiping out competitive travel-booking sites. Orbitz would give airlines an unfair advantage, said the ITSA, by encouraging price fixing between airlines.

After an initial investigation, the U.S. Department of Transportation agreed that Orbitz could provide the potential for unfair competition but it didn't stop the company's launch. Instead, it agreed to review the case again after Orbitz was in operation for six months. At that point, the Department of Transportation said it hadn't found any unfair trade practices in the Orbitz operation, nor did it see any negative effect on competition or consumer choice. At the ITSA's urging, Orbitz has come under federal scruntiny several times since then, but the government has not found Orbitz in violation of any anti-competition laws.

Antonella Pianalto, ITSA executive director, is unconvinced. "The evidence is clear: Orbitz is harming competition. Prior to Orbitz, both consumers and airlines benefited from independent distributors who fiercely negotiated for the best available fares and placed downward pressure on those fares by forcing the airlines to compete. Now airlines have little incentive to compete because they don't have to use other online sites."

Nonsense, counters Orbitz CEO Jeff Katz. "The online travel marketplace was already dominated by a 'Big Two'—Travelocity and Expedia. Their complaints about us are a little like Coke and Pepsi teaming up to run Dr Pepper out of the market."

Although still third in size behind Travelocity and Expedia, Orbitz is currently the fastest-growing online travel site, with revenues topping $1 billion a year. However, the company has not yet turned a profit. Online air ticket purchases continue to grow, with over $14 billion worth of tickets purchased last year.

CRITICAL THINKING QUESTIONS

1. Do you agree with the ITSA's position or that of Orbitz CEO Jeff Katz about the effect Orbitz is having on competition and consumer choice? Defend your answer.
2. Explain how supply and demand affect the price of airline tickets. How could a change in either supply or demand affect the growth of online travel sites? Would Orbitz be in a better position to deal with these changes than Travelocity or Expedia? Why?

SOURCES: Greg Sandoval, "Competitors Call Orbitz Tactics into Question," CNet/News.com, November 20, 2001, downloaded from http://www.news.com; Rachel Konrad, "Lawmakers Urge Stronger Orbitz Probe," CNet/News.com, April 25, 2002, downloaded from http://www.news.com; Greg Sandoval, "Agency: Orbitz Could Harm Competition," CNet/News.com, June 27, 2002, downloaded from http://www.news.com; and David Wessel, Arlines' Orbitz: Consumers' Friend or Foe?" *Wall Street Journal*, August 29, 2002, p. A2.

Hot Links Address Book

The Federal Reserve Board issues a variety of statistical information about the state of the U.S. economy. Find it at the Federal Reserve's Economic Research and Data page, **http://www.federalreserve.gov/rnd.htm**

Where does the federal government get its money, and where does it go? Find out at this site: **http://www.whitehouse.gov/omb/budget/fy2002/guide02.html**

Want to know the current public debt per citizen? Go to **http://www.publicdebt.treas.gov/opd/opdpenny.htm**

The U.S. Bureau of Economic Analysis tracks national and regional economic statistics, including the GDP. To find the latest GDP statistics, visit the BEA at **http://www.bea.doc.gov**

How are the job prospects in your area? Your region's unemployment statistics can give you an idea of how hard it will be to find a job. Find the most recent unemployment statistics from the Bureau of Labor Statistics at **http://www.bls.gov/**

Where does the consumer price index stand today? Go to **http://stats.bls.gov/cpi/**

How do the PPI and the CPI differ? Get the answers to this and other questions about the PPI by visiting the Bureau of Labor Statistics PPI site at **http://www.bls.gov/ppi/**

Chapter 3

© AP / WIDE WORLD PHOTOS

Making Ethical Decisions and Managing a Socially Responsible Business

learning goals

1 What philosophies and concepts shape personal ethical standards?
2 How can organizations encourage ethical business behavior?
3 What is social responsibility?
4 How do businesses meet their social responsibilities to various stakeholders?
5 What are the global and domestic trends in ethics and social responsibility?
APPENDIX: UNDERSTANDING THE LEGAL AND TAX ENVIRONMENT
6 How does the legal system govern business transactions and settle business disputes?
7 What are the required elements of a valid contract; and what are the key types of business law?
8 What are the most common taxes paid by businesses?

Dennis Was Living Large

Midas had his gold. Elvis had his Cadillacs. Dennis Kozlowski, former CEO of Tyco (**http://www.tyco.com**), had his $6,000 shower curtain. Yes, this is what it all comes down to. Forget Enron and WorldCom. To this day, most people have no clue what special-purpose entities are and only the vaguest notion of what sins the Andrew Fastows of the world allegedly committed. When Americans think back on the corporate scandals 25 years from now, they aren't likely to summon more than a blurry memory. What they *will* remember is the bald guy with the $6,000 shower curtain. And, say, the $15,000 dog umbrella stand. Ditto for the now infamous $2.1 million birthday bash that Kozlowski threw in Sardinia for his wife's 40th birthday.

Kozlowski's tale resonates because it appears to have been based on the classic human quality of greed. Indeed, many of the crimes he's accused of—for example, his actions to avoid paying sales tax on art—are based on acts that would not be unknown to many Americans. To an average person, of course, that might mean crossing state lines to save a few bucks on a carton of cigarettes, not shipping empty crates to New Hampshire in an apparent effort to avoid $1 million in taxes on art by the likes of Monet and Renoir. But why quibble? It's precisely the scale of Kozlowski's conduct—whatever the ultimate result of the legal proceedings against him—that takes the breath away.

Kozlowski isn't charged with tasteless spending—if that were a crime he'd really be in trouble—he's charged with conspiring with CFO Mark Swartz to loot $170 million from Tyco (or $600 million, if you include his allegedly tainted stock sales). Kozlowski's friends profess total shock and amazement that he would be accused of misappropriating money. Then again, it would be rather more surprising if they proclaimed that they'd always known he might commit a multimillion-dollar fraud. To a person, they're quick to cite myriad examples of how generous Kozlowski was with various charities and causes.

That may not be the best example of Kozlowski's good character, given that Tyco has charged him with loosening the strings on the company's corporate giving program and disbursing a whopping $106 million of shareholders' money to charity. (Tyco also charges that Kozlowski passed off as personal contributions $43 million of the company's donations.)

When it came to his friends, Kozlowski was strikingly down to earth, preferring the company of ordinary folks to CEOs. If it seems at odds that a man would prefer to have his fishing buddies with him on his historic 130-foot sailboat, well, that was Kozlowski. After all, he'd risen from humble origins in Newark, the self-made son of a school crossing guard and a cop.[1]

Critical Thinking Questions

As you read this chapter, consider the following questions as they relate to Dennis Kozlowski:

1. Was Dennis acting in an unethical manner?
2. What may be the impact on Tyco?
3. Dennis gave over $106 million of Tyco's money to charity. Doesn't this make him an ethical person?

Principles of Ethics and Social Responsibility

Every day, managers and business owners make business decisions based on what they believe to be right and wrong. Through their actions, they demonstrate to their employees what is and is not acceptable behavior and shape the moral standard of the organization. **Ethics** is a set of moral standards for judging whether something is right or wrong. As you will see in this chapter, personal and professional ethics are important cornerstones of an organization and shape its ultimate contributions to society. First, let's consider how individual business ethics are formed.

ethics
A set of moral standards for judging whether something is right or wrong.

Individual Business Ethics

1 learning goal

Individual business ethics are shaped by personal choices and the environments in which we live and work. In addition, the laws of our society are guideposts for choosing between right and wrong. This section describes personal philosophies and legal factors that influence the choices people make when confronting ethical dilemmas.

Utilitarianism—Seeking the Best for the Majority

One of the philosophies that may influence choices between right and wrong is **utilitarianism**, which focuses on the consequences of an action taken by a person or organization. The notion that "people should act so as to generate the greatest good for the greatest number" is derived from utilitarianism. When an action affects the majority adversely, it is morally wrong. One problem with this philosophy is that it is nearly impossible to accurately determine how a decision will affect a large number of people.

utilitarianism
A philosophy that focuses on the consequences of an action to determine whether it is right or wrong; holds that an action that affects the majority adversely is morally wrong.

Another problem is that utilitarianism always involves both winners and losers. If sales are slowing and a manager decides to fire 5 people rather than putting everyone on a 30-hour workweek, the 20 people who keep their full-time jobs are winners, but the other 5 are losers.

A final criticism of utilitarianism is that some "costs," although small relative to the potential good, are so negative that some segments of society find them unacceptable. Reportedly, the backs of up to 3,000 animals a year are deliberately broken so that scientists can conduct spinal cord research that could someday lead to a cure for spinal cord injuries. To a number of people, however, the "costs" are simply too horrible for this type of research to continue.

Individual Rights

In our society, individuals and groups have certain rights that exist under certain conditions regardless of any external circumstances. These rights serve as guides when making individual ethical decisions. The term *human rights* implies that certain rights—to life, to freedom, to the pursuit of happiness—are conveyed at birth and cannot be arbitrarily taken away. Denying the rights of an individual or group is considered to be unethical and illegal in most, though not all, parts of the world. Certain rights are guaranteed by the government and its laws, and these are considered *legal rights.* The U.S. Constitution and its amendments, as well as state and federal statutes, define the rights of American citizens. Those rights can be disregarded only in extreme circumstances, such as during wartime. Legal rights include the freedom of religion, speech, and assembly; protection from improper arrest and searches and seizures; and proper access to counsel, confrontation of witnesses, and cross-examination in criminal prosecutions. Also held to be fundamental is the right to privacy in many matters. Legal rights are to be applied without regard to race, color, creed, gender, or ability.

justice
What is considered fair according to the prevailing standards of society; in the 20th century, an equitable distribution of the burdens and rewards that society has to offer.

Justice—The Question of Fairness

Another factor influencing individual business ethics is **justice,** or what is fair according to prevailing standards of society. We all expect life to be reasonably fair. You expect your exams to be fair, the grading to be fair, and your wages to be fair, based on the type of work being done.

In the 21st century, we take justice to mean an equitable distribution of the burdens and rewards that society has to offer. The distributive process varies from society to society. Those in a democratic society believe in the "equal pay for equal work" doctrine, in which individuals are rewarded based on the value the free market places on their services. Because the market places different values on different occupations, the rewards, such as wages, are not necessarily equal. Nevertheless, many regard the rewards as just. A politician who argued that a supermarket clerk should receive the same pay as a physician, for example, would not receive many votes from the American people. At the other extreme, communist theorists have argued that justice would be served by a society in which burdens and rewards were distributed to individuals according to their abilities and their needs, respectively.

Recognizing Unethical Business Activities

Researchers from Brigham Young University tell us that all unethical business activities will fall into one of the following categories:

1. *Taking things that don't belong to you.* The unauthorized use of someone else's property or taking property under false pretenses is taking something that does not belong to you. Even the smallest offense, such as using the postage meter at your office for mailing personal letters or exaggerating your travel expenses, belongs in this category of ethical violations.
2. *Saying things you know are not true.* Often, when trying for a promotion and advancement, fellow employees discredit their coworkers. Falsely assigning blame or inaccurately reporting conversations is lying. Although "This is the way the game is played around here" is a common justification, saying things that are untrue is an ethical violation.
3. *Giving or allowing false impressions.* The salesperson who permits a potential customer to believe that cardboard boxes will hold the customer's tomatoes for long-distance shipping when the salesperson knows the boxes are not

After the devastation caused by corporate crime at Enron and Worldcom, more employees are sounding the alarm when they detect misconduct. Ex-Enron executive Sherron C. Watkins alerted her boss at Enron of shady accounting practices that led to the discovery of corporate crime.

© AP / WIDE WORLD PHOTOS

© AP / WIDE WORLD PHOTOS

After the Ford Explorer was linked to rollover accidents and 271 deaths nationwide, The Ford Motor Co. reached a nationwide settlement that includes a national SUV safety campaign that advises consumers on safe SUV driving and loading.

strong enough has given a false impression. A car dealer who fails to disclose that a car has been in an accident is misleading potential customers.

4. *Buying influence or engaging in a conflict of interest.* A conflict of interest occurs when the official responsibilities of an employee or government official are influenced by the potential for personal gain. Suppose a company awards a construction contract to a firm owned by the father of the state attorney general while the state attorney general's office is investigating that company. If this construction award has the potential to shape the outcome of the investigation, a conflict of interest has occurred.
5. *Hiding or divulging information.* Failing to disclose the results of medical studies that indicate your firm's new drug has significant side effects is the ethical violation of hiding information that the product could be harmful to purchasers. Taking your firm's product development or trade secrets to a new place of employment constitutes the ethical violation of divulging proprietary information.
6. *Taking unfair advantage.* Many current consumer protection laws were passed because so many businesses took unfair advantage of people who were not educated or were unable to discern the nuances of complex contracts. Credit disclosure requirements, truth-in-lending provisions, and new regulations on auto leasing all resulted because businesses misled consumers who could not easily follow the jargon of long, complex agreements.
7. *Committing improper personal behavior.* Although the ethical aspects of an employee's right to privacy are still debated, it has become increasingly clear that personal conduct outside the job can influence performance and company reputation. Thus, a company driver must abstain from substance abuse because of safety issues. Even the traditional company Christmas party and picnic have come under scrutiny due to the possibility that employees at and following these events might harm others through alcohol-related accidents.
8. *Abusing another person.* Suppose a manager sexually harasses an employee or subjects employees to humiliating corrections in the presence of customers. In some cases, laws protect employees. Many situations, however, are simply interpersonal abuse that constitutes an ethical violation.

9. *Permitting organizational abuse.* Many U.S. firms with operations overseas, such as Levi Strauss, The Gap, and Esprit, have faced issues of organizational abuse. The unfair treatment of workers in international operations appears in the form of child labor, demeaning wages, and excessive work hours. Although a business cannot change the culture of another country, it can perpetuate—or stop—abuse through its operations there.
10. *Violating rules.* Many organizations use rules and processes to maintain internal controls or respect the authority of managers. Although these rules may seem burdensome to employees trying to serve customers, a violation may be considered an unethical act.
11. *Condoning unethical actions.* What if you witnessed a fellow employee embezzling company funds by forging her signature on a check that was to be voided? Would you report the violation? A winking tolerance of others' unethical behavior is itself unethical.[2]

concept check

How are individual business ethics formed?

What is utilitarianism?

How can you recognize unethical activities?

How Organizations Influence Ethical Conduct

2 learning goal

People choose between right and wrong based on their personal code of ethics. They are also influenced by the ethical environment created by their employers. Consider the following newspaper headlines:

- New York City Sues Telecom Executives Over Stock Profits
- MCG Chief Is to Forfeit Bonuses After Misstatement Revealed
- Fastow, Former Enron Officer, Indicted by U.S.
- Here's the Retirement Jack Welch Built: $1.4 Million a Month

As these actual headlines illustrate, poor business ethics can create a very negative image for a company, can be expensive for the firm and/or the executives involved, and can result in bankruptcy and jail time for the offenders. Organizations can reduce the potential for these types of liability claims by educating their employees about ethical standards, by leading through example, and through various informal and formal programs.

Leading by Example

Employees often follow the examples set by their managers. That is, leaders and managers establish patterns of behavior that determine what's acceptable and what's not within the organization. While Ben Cohen was president of Ben & Jerry's ice cream, he followed a policy that no one could earn a salary more than seven times the lowest-paid worker. He wanted all employees to feel that they were equal. At the time he resigned, company sales were $140 million and the lowest-paid worker earned $19,000 per year. Ben Cohen's salary was $133,000 based on the "seven times" rule. A typical top executive of a $140 million company might have earned 10 times Cohen's salary. Ben Cohen's actions helped shape the ethical values of Ben & Jerry's.

Offering Ethics-Training Programs

In addition to providing a system to resolve ethical dilemmas, organizations also provide formal training to develop an awareness of questionable business activities and practice appropriate responses. Many American companies have some type of ethics-training program. The ones that are most effective, like those created by Levi Strauss, American Express, and Campbell Soup Company, begin with techniques for solving ethical dilemmas such as those discussed earlier. Next,

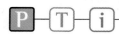

Exhibit 3.1 An Ethical Dilemma Used for Employee Training

Bill Gannon was a middle manager of a large manufacturer of lighting fixtures in Newark, New Jersey. Bill had moved up the company ladder rather quickly and seemed destined for upper management in a few years. Bill's boss, Dana Johnson, had been pressuring him about the semiannual reviews concerning Robert Talbot, one of Bill's employees. Dana, it seemed, would not accept any negative comments on Robert's evaluation forms. Bill had found out that a previous manager who had given Robert a bad evaluation was no longer with the company. As Bill reviewed Robert's performance for the forthcoming evaluation period, he found many areas of subpar performance. Moreover, a major client had called recently complaining that Robert had filled a large order improperly and then had been rude to the client when she called to complain.

Discussion Questions

1. What ethical issues does the situation raise?
2. What courses of action could Bill take? Describe the ethics of each course.
3. Should Bill confront Dana? Dana's boss?
4. What would you do in this situation? What are the ethical implications?

employees are presented with a series of situations and asked to come up with the "best" ethical solution. One of these ethical dilemmas is shown in Exhibit 3.1. Some companies have tried to add a bit of excitement and fun to their ethics-training programs by presenting them in the form of games. Citigroup, for example, has created The Work Ethic, a board game in which participants strive to correctly answer legal, regulatory, policy-related, and judgment ethics questions.

Niagara Mohawk, an electric and natural-gas utility, has an Ethics and Compliance Office that manages a company-wide ethics program, which includes a code of conduct detailing employee responsibilities and how to avoid conflicts of interest. Niagara Mohawk recently won the Better Business Bureau's International Torch Award for business ethics.[3]

© JOSE LUIS PELAEZ, INC. / CORBIS

Raytheon, one of the world's largest defense contractors, requires all of its employees to attend formal classroom ethics training each year. In addition, the company requires employees to participate in an online scenario-based ethics and business conduct training course.

Establishing a Formal Code of Ethics

code of ethics
A set of guidelines prepared by a firm to provide its employees with the knowledge of what the firm expects in terms of their responsibilities and behavior toward fellow employees, customers, and suppliers.

Most large companies and thousands of smaller ones have created, printed, and distributed codes of ethics. In general, a **code of ethics** provides employees with the knowledge of what their firm expects in terms of their responsibilities and behavior toward fellow employees, customers, and suppliers. Some ethical codes offer a lengthy and detailed set of guidelines for employees. Others are not really codes at all but rather summary statements of goals, policies, and priorities. Some companies have their codes framed and hung on office walls or printed on cards to be carried at all times by executives. The code of ethics for Costco Wholesale, the chain of membership warehouse clubs, is shown on the next page in Exhibit 3.2.

Do codes of ethics make employees behave in a more ethical manner? Some people believe that they do. Others think that they are little more than public relations gimmicks. If senior management abides by the code of ethics and regularly emphasizes the code to empoyees, then it will likely have a positive influence on behavior.

social responsibility
The concern of businesses for the welfare of society as a whole; consists of obligations beyond those required by law or contracts.

Nearly half of the respondents in a survey of 1,324 workers conducted by the Ethics Official Association and the American Society of Chartered Life Underwriters and Chartered Financial Consultants said that they had committed unethical or illegal acts on the job. Workers said that there unethical behavior was caused by pressure from overtime demands, balancing work and family, company layoffs, and other factors. The most common unethical acts were: cutting corners on quality (16%), covering up accidents (14%), abusing or lying about sick days (11%), and deceiving customers (9%).[4]

When faced with developing an ethical focus, entrepreneurs and small-business managers look at ethics a bit differently, as discussed in the Focusing on Small Business box.

concept check

What is the role of top management in organizational ethics?

What is a code of ethics?

Managing a Socially Responsible Business

3 learning goal

Acting in an ethical manner is one of the four components of the pyramid of corporate social responsibility. **Social responsibility** is the concern of businesses for the welfare of society as a whole. It consists of obligations beyond those required by law or union contract. This definition makes two important points. First, social

Focusing on Small Business

Do Ethics Just Come Naturally to Small Businesses?

In a recent survey of small-businesses, owners were asked if they have an interest in business ethics. Only 56 percent said "yes." A follow-up question was, "To what degree have you attempted to build an ethical business environment?" Surprisingly only 48 percent replied, "significant" or "some" effort. As one of the participants put it, "No one locally intentionally tries to take advantage of a customer, supplier, or employee. However, we just don't have time to worry about nonessential or fluff issues."

Tim Fulton, a small business consultant, strongly believes that small-businesses should maintain an ethical focus. He recommends: (a) be honest with your company's stakeholders; (b) keep your business simple—the more complex a business the easier for an ethical slip to occur; (c) carefully select and manage your external professionals such as your accountant, banker, and attorney; and (d) cultivate the right business culture—set the right example for employees.[5]

CRITICAL THINKING QUESTIONS

1. Do you think that small-business owners are more ethical than large-business managers?
2. Why would it make a difference if one group is more ethical than the other?
3. Do you think that Tim Fulton is giving sound ethical advice?

Exhibit 3.2 Costco Wholesale's Code of Ethics

COSTCO WHOLESALE

CODE OF ETHICS

By Jim Sinegal

OBEY THE LAW

The law is irrefutable! Absent a moral imperative to challenge a law, we must conduct our business in total compliance with the laws of every community where we do business.

Comply with all statutes.

Cooperate with authorities.

Respect all public officials and their positions.

Avoid all conflict of interest issues with public officials.

Comply with all disclosure and reporting requirements.

Comply with safety and security standards for all products sold.

Exceed ecological standards required in every community where we do business.

Comply with all applicable wage and hour laws.

Comply with all applicable anti-trust laws.

Protect information" that has not been released to the general public.

TAKE CARE OF OUR MEMBERS

The member is our key to success. If we don't keep our members happy, little else that we do will make a difference.

Provide top-quality products at the best prices in the market.

Provide a safe shopping environment in our warehouses.

Provide only products that meet applicable safety and health standards.

Sell only products from manufacturers who comply with uth in advertising/packaging" standards.

Provide our members with a 100% satisfaction guaranteed warranty on every product and service we sell, including their membership fee.

Assure our members that every product we sell is authentic in make and in representation of performance.

Make our shopping environment a pleasant experience by making our members feel welcome as our guests.

Provide products to our members that will be ecologically sensitive.

> Our member is our reason for being. If they fail to show up, we cannot survive. Our members have extended a ust" to Costco by virtue of paying a fee to shop with us. We can't let them down or they will simply go away. We must always operate in the following manner when dealing with our members:
>
> Rule #1– The member is always right.
>
> Rule #2 In the event the member is ever wrong, refer to rule #1.
>
> There are plenty of shopping alternatives for our members. We will succeed only if we do not violate the trust they have extended to us. We must be committed at every level of our company, with every ounce of energy and grain of creativity we have, to constantly strive to goods to market at a lower price."

If we do these four things throughout our organization, we will realize our ultimate goal, which is to REWARD OUR SHAREHOLDERS.

TAKE CARE OF OUR EMPLOYEES

To claim are our most important asset" is true and an understatement. Each employee has been hired for a very important job. Jobs such as stocking the shelves, ringing members' orders, buying products and paying our bills are jobs we would all choose to perform because of their importance. The employees hired to perform these jobs are performing as management's egos." Every employee, whether they are in a Costco warehouse or whether they work in the regional or corporate offices, is a Costco ambassador trained to give our members professional, courteous treatment.

Today we have warehouse managers who were once stockers and callers and vice presidents who were once in clerical positions for our company. We believe that Costco's future executive officers are currently working in our warehouses, depots, buying offices and accounting departments, as well as in our home offices.

To that end, we are committed to these principles:

Provide a safe work environment.

Pay a fair wage.

Make every job challenging, but make it fun!

Consider the loss of any employee as a failure on the part of the company and a loss to the organization.

Teach our people how to do their jobs and how to improve personally and professionally.

Promote from within the company to achieve the goal of a minimum of 80% of management positions being filled by current employees.

Create an door" attitude at all levels of the company that is dedicated to airness and listening.

RESPECT OUR VENDORS

Our vendors are our partners in business, and for us to prosper as a company, they must prosper with us. It is important that our vendors understand that we will be tough negotiators but fair in our treatment of them.

Treat all vendors and their representatives as you would expect to be treated if visiting their places of business.

Pay all bills within the allocated time frame.

Honor all commitments.

Protect all vendor property assigned to Costco as though it were our own.

Always be thoughtful and candid in negotiations.

Provide a careful review process with at least two levels of authorization before terminating business with an existing vendor of more than two years.

Do not accept gratuities of any kind from a vendor.

> These guidelines are exactly that - guidelines, some common sense rules for the conduct of our business. Intended to simplify our jobs, not complicate our lives, these guidelines will not answer every question or solve every problem. At the core of our philosophy as a company must be the implicit understanding that not one of us is required to lie or cheat on behalf of Costco. In fact, dishonest conduct will not be tolerated. To do any less would be unfair to the overwhelming majority of our employees who support and respect Costco's commitment to ethical business conduct.
>
> If you are ever in doubt as to what course of action to take on a business matter that is open to varying ethical interpretations, take the high road and do what is right.
>
> If you want our help, we are always available for advice and counsel. That's our job, and we welcome your questions or comments.
>
> Our continued success depends on you. We thank each of you for your contribution to our past success and for the high standards you have insisted upon in our company.

97HR1005

SOURCE: Reprinted by permission of Costco Wholesale.

Exhibit 3.3 The Pyramid of Corporate Social Responsibility

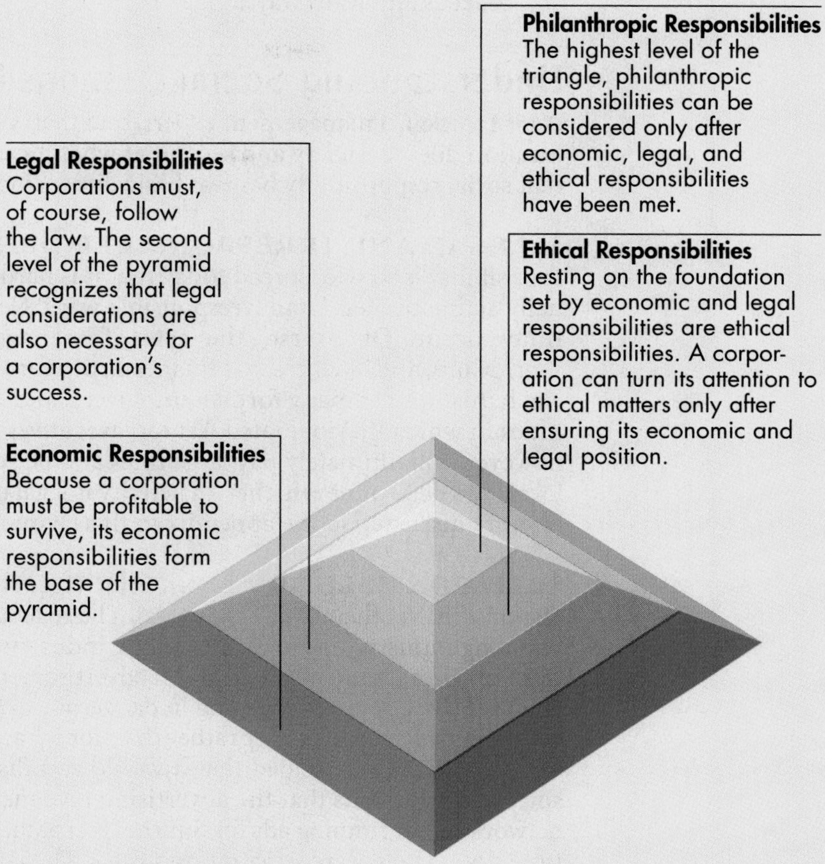

responsibility is voluntary. Beneficial action required by law, such as cleaning up factories that are polluting air and water, is not voluntary. Second, the obligations of social responsibility are broad. They extend beyond investors in the company to include workers, suppliers, consumers, and communities.

Philanthropic Responsibilities
The highest level of the triangle, philanthropic responsibilities can be considered only after economic, legal, and ethical responsibilities have been met.
Legal Responsibilities
Corporations must, of course, follow the law. The second level of the pyramid recognizes that legal considerations are also necessary for a corporation's success.
Ethical Responsibilities
Resting on the foundation set by economic and legal responsibilities are ethical responsibilities. A corporation can turn its attention to ethical matters only after ensuring its economic and legal position.
Economic Responsibilities
Because a corporation must be profitable to survive, its economic responsibilities form the base of the pyramid.

Exhibit 3.3 portrays economic performance as the foundation for the other three responsibilities. At the same time that a business pursues profits (economic responsibility), however, it is expected to obey the law (legal responsibility); to do what is right, just, and fair (ethical responsibility); and to be a good corporate citizen (philanthropic responsibility). These four components are distinct but together constitute the whole. Still, if the company doesn't make a profit, then the other three responsibilities are moot.

Many companies are already working to make the world a better place to live. Consider these examples:

- Colby Care Nurses, Inc., a home health care service located in Los Angeles County, is offering much-needed health care to predominantly African American and Hispanic communities that are often not covered by other providers. The company prides itself on giving back to the community by employing its residents and providing role models for its young people.
- Wrigley, the Chicago chewing gum maker, is producing a $10 million commercial campaign aimed at getting African, Asian, and Hispanic Americans to use doctors for regular health maintenance instead of as a last resort.

- Jantzen, the world's leading swimsuit manufacturer, makes direct grants through its clean-water campaign to organizations that preserve and clean up beaches and waterways.

Understanding Social Responsibility

Peter Drucker, a management expert, said that we should look first at what an organization does *to* society and second at what it can do *for* society. This idea suggests that social responsibility has two basic dimensions: legality and responsibility.

Illegal and Irresponsible Behavior The idea of social responsibility is so widespread today that it is hard to conceive of a company continually acting in illegal and irresponsible ways. Nevertheless, such actions do sometimes occur. Of course, the acts of managers of Global Crossing, Enron, WorldCom, and Tyco created financial ruin for their organizations, extreme financial hardships for many former employees, and general hardships for the communities in which they operated. Yet top executives walked away with millions. Some, however, will ultimately pay large fines and be sentenced to jail. Federal, state, and local laws determine whether an activity is legal or not. The laws that regulate business are discussed in the appendix to this chapter.

Irresponsible but Legal Behavior Sometimes companies act irresponsibly, yet their actions are legal. The federal government is pressuring the advertising industry and the automobile industry for more responsible advertising. The government is concerned about advertisements that place an emphasis on speed and that show vehicles engaging in dangerous driving practices. "It seems that some ads work against road safety rather than for it," according to one spokesperson.

In 2002, NBC decided that it would run distilled-liquor ads for the first time since 1948. It seems that the advertising revenue was just too good to pass up. The network began running ads for Smirnoff on Saturday Night Live and other late-night time slots. There were strict ground rules. The ads could only run after 9 P.M., when the mythical family hour ends and the audience becomes, theoretically, more than 85 percent viewers over 21. Actors featured in the ads had to be over 30. The agreement also stipulated that liquor ads would not be allowed to say or imply that consuming the hard stuff would "enhance anyone's attractiveness, personal relationships or sexual prowess."[6] However, after three months of intense pressure from Washington and various lobbying groups, NBC reversed their decision and stopped running the ads.

Legal and Responsible Behavior The vast majority of business activities fall into the category of behavior that is both legal and responsible. Most firms act legally, and most try to be socially responsible. Lucent Technologies (formerly Bell Labs) each year has 10,000 employees participate in "Global Days of Caring," assisting community projects worldwide. A recent Global Days of Caring found employees working on specific projects in 25 states and 20 countries. The projects included engaging in environmental cleanup, fixing up child care and senior citizens centers, and assisting organizations like Camp DaKaNi in Oklahoma City, home to the local Camp Fire Boys and Girls, which was significantly damaged during a tornado. Ongoing projects include painting maps on elementary school playgrounds to help teach geography and making "smart" teddy bears for children to ease the trauma of a hospital stay. Lucent gives employees paid time off for the projects and provides coordination and money. The company also engages in a number of other socially responsible activities including hiring and training the unemployed, giving equipment and grants to schools, and making grants to community agencies where Lucent employees volunteer.

concept check

What are the four components of social responsibility?

Give an example of legal but irresponsible behavior.

Yoplait's national sponsorship of the Race for the Cure represents a legal and socially responsible activity. The nationwide series of 100 running and fitness walks draw more than 1.3 million worldwide participants and benefits the Susan G. Komen Breast Cancer Foundation.

© COURTESY OF SUSAN G. KOMEN BREAST CANCER FOUNDATION

Responsibilities to Stakeholders

4 learning goal

What makes a company admired or perceived as socially responsible? Such a company meets its obligations to its stakeholders. **Stakeholders** are the individuals or groups to whom a business has a responsibility. The stakeholders of a business are its employees, its customers, the general public, and its investors.

stakeholders
Individuals or groups to whom a business has a responsibility; include employees, customers, the general public, and investors.

Responsibility to Employees

An organization's first responsibility is to provide a job to employees. Keeping people employed and letting them have time to enjoy the fruits of their labor is the finest thing business can do for society. Enron is an example of a company that violated this responsibility. Beyond this fundamental responsibility, employers must provide a clean, safe working environment that is free from all forms of discrimination. Companies should also strive to provide job security whenever possible.

Enlightened firms are also empowering employees to make decisions on their own and suggest solutions to company problems. Empowerment contributes to an employee's self-worth, which, in turn, increases productivity and reduces absenteeism.

Each year *Fortune* conducts an extensive survey of the best places to work in America. The top 10 are shown in Exhibit 3.4. Some companies offer unusual benefits to their employees. CMP Media gives employees $30,000 for infertility treatments and adoption aid. FedEx allows free rides in the jump seats of company planes. Steelcase has a 1,200-acre camping and recreational area for employee use.

Responsibility to Customers

A central theme of this text is that to be successful today a company must satisfy its customers. A firm must deliver what it promises. It must also be honest and forthright with its clients. We will discuss this in more detail in the "Customer Satisfaction and Quality" box at the end of the chapter.

Exhibit 3.4 America's Top Ten Best Places to Work

Company Headquarters (U.S. Sites) Web site	Comments
1. Edward Jones St. Louis **http://www.edwardjones.com**	No. 1 for the second straight year, this stockbroker spends 3.8% of its payroll on training, with an average of 146 hours for every employee. New brokers at the 7,781 branches get more than four times that much. Why does Jones invest so much in its people? "In order to grow, you have to be trained," says managing partner John Bachmann, "or you get trapped in the present." The company is owned by employees (25% of them have partnership stakes), and perhaps that's why they care enough to have serious profit sharing and no layoffs.
2. Container Store Dallas **http://www.containerstore.com**	Container Store continues to offer one of the highest pay scales in retail. New this year: domestic-partner benefits, free yoga classes at distribution centers, and chair massages at headquarters.
3. Alston & Bird Atlanta **http://www.alston.com**	The first law firm to crack the top five, Alston & Bird had zero layoffs and thrives on daily, weekly, monthly, and quarterly communications. Also proud of its celebrations—Bunny Brunch, Welcome Breakfasts.
4. Xilinx San Jose **http://www.xilinx.com**	Employees of the semiconductor maker have been protected from the tech downturn by the company's strict adherence to a no-layoff policy. Workers did take a 6% pay cut, but the CEO's salary was chopped 20%.
5. Adobe Systems San Jose **http://www.adobe.com**	Camaraderie is the byword at this Silicon Valley stalwart known for its graphics products: frequent all-hands meetings, job rotations, and Friday night beer bashes. Three-week paid sabbaticals every five years.
6. Amer. Cast Iron Pipe Birmingham, Ala. **http://www.acipco.com**	Turnover of less than 2% is lowest on the list, and more than a third of employees have been here for 20 years and up. On-site clinic offers free medical and dental for employees (and their families) for life.
7. TDIndustries Dallas **http://www.tdindustries.com**	Employee-owned construction firm links health insurance premiums to compensation—the less you earn, the less you pay. An entry-level worker can cover his family for $25 a week.
8. J.M. Smucker Orrville, Ohio **http://www.smuckers.com**	The addition of Jif peanut butter and Crisco shortening to Smucker's pantry of jellies, jams, and ice-cream toppings has brought on about 450 employees and doubled sales. Led by the fourth generation of Smuckers, the 105-year-old company provides health care for retirees and their spouses, as well as on-site stop-smoking classes. J.M. Smucker also offers employees unlimited paid time off to volunteer. And all employees in the Orville area have the opportunity to be taste testers.
9. Synovus Columbus, Ga. **http://www.synovus.com**	Great benefits at this Southeastern bank holding company—on-site child care, state-of-the-art gym, generous profit-sharing and pension plans—reflecting what it calls a "culture of the heart."
10. Wegmans Rochester, N.Y. **http://www.wegmans.com**	The supermarket chain lets workers take off to volunteer and to care for sick pets; employees have mentored more than 1,000 high school kids. Workers also get free ESL classes. New: up to $5,000 for adoption.

SOURCE: Robert Levering and Milton Moskowitz, "100 Best Companies to Work For," *Fortune* (January 20, 2003), pp. 128–129.

Responsibility to Society

A business must also be responsible to society. A business provides a community with jobs, goods, and services. It also pays taxes that go to support schools, hospitals, and better roads. Most companies try to be good citizens in their communities.

AT&T, for example, works to narrow the digital divide. This effort began in earnest in 1999 on the heels of a Commerce Department report that noted the

To improve senior citizens' access to the Internet, AT&T, IBM, and others contributed a $660,000 grant to simplify Internet access for older Americans in 1,000 communities. (http://www.business-ethics.com/newpage.htm)

growing disparity among minorities with regard to Internet access. Partnering with the NAACP, the National Urban League, and other organizations, AT&T has provided funding for technology centers in 20 cities to offer computer training and Internet seminars to reduce cyber-segregation.

Responsibility to society doesn't end at our shores. Global enterprises are attempting to help the public around the world as explained in the "Expanding Around the Globe" box below.

Expanding Around the Globe

Drinks for Developing Countries

Every morning a group of local nurses drove into the dusty yards of two primary schools in Gaborone, Botswana, mixed bright orange powder with processed water in big metal vats, and handed one paper cupful of the drink to each child, 250 in all. The beverage looked and tasted like Coca-Cola Company's Hi-C orange-flavored drink, but it contained extra ingredients: 12 vitamins and minerals chronically lacking in the diets of people in developing countries.

The daily ritual, a clinical test, was part of "Project Mission," a continuing Coca-Cola research-and-development effort aimed at creating a drink that could help combat anemia, blindness, and other afflictions common in poorer parts of the world. By the end of an eight-week trial, test data showed that levels of iron and zinc in the children's blood had grown. Some parents said their children, whose diets consist mostly of cornmeal and rice, had more energy and had become more attentive at school. Marvin Viekeman said his 8-year-old daughter, Anah, had gained weight by the end of five weeks. "I was suspicious about it at first," he said, "but it has helped her."

And if all goes as Coke plans, the new drink, to be called Vitango, could help boost sales at a time when growth of carbonated soft drinks is slowing.

Similarly, Proctor and Gamble (P&G) launched its product, Nutristar, in Venezuela after years of research and development and clinical tests. A powdered drink that contains eight vitamins and five minerals, Nutristar is sold at most food stores in flavors like mango and passion fruit and boldly promises "taller, stronger and smarter kids." So far, the drink is "really doing well," says Carmen Silvia Garcia, a P&G food scientist and manager for external relations for the company's operations in Venezuela.

Nutristar, selling at about 40 cents for a packet of powder that makes one liter of beverage, is priced at about 25 percent more than other powdered drinks and 30 percent below carbonated soft drinks, Ms. Garcia says.[7]

CRITICAL THINKING QUESTIONS

1. Should Coca-Cola and P&G be giving this product away to be truly socially responsible?
2. Many activists have claimed that eating at McDonald's leads to obesity. Nutristar will be available with Happy Meals. Does this make P&G socially irresponsible?
3. Coke claims that it is trying to boost overall sales with Vitango. Are boosting sales and social responsibility compatible objectives?

As the nation's largest recycler,
of course we believe
what goes around comes around.
Each year at Nucor, we keep 13 million tons of scrap steel out of America's landfills and off of her landscapes. And we turn that scrap into new steel for everything from appliances to office buildings. All the while, the neighbors near our steel recycling plants are impressed with how we preserve wetlands, enhance natural habitats and meet or exceed environmental requirements. From our well-known employee incentives to the support we provide our communities, we've always believed in sharing our success with those around us, including generations yet to come. It's just our nature.
NUCOR
It's our Nature.
Nucor, 2100 Rexford Road, Charlotte, North Carolina 28211 Phone 704/366-7000, Fax 704/362-4208, www.nucor.com

© COURTESY OF NUCOR CORPORATION

Nucor uses this advertising campaign to promote its commitment to recycling scrap into new steel. As part of its commitment to environmental protection, Nucor also has a commitment to enhancing natural habitats and meeting or exceeding environmental requirements.

ENVIRONMENTAL PROTECTION Business is also responsible for protecting and improving the world's fragile environment. The world's forests are being destroyed fast. Every second, an area the size of a football field is laid bare. Plant and animal species are becoming extinct at the rate of 17 per hour. A continent-size hole is opening up in the earth's protective ozone shield. Each year we throw out 80 percent more refuse than we did in 1960; as a result, more than half of the nation's landfills are filled to capacity.

To slow the erosion of the world's resources, many companies are becoming more environmentally responsible. Toyota is now using "renewable" energy sources to power its facilities, making it the largest single user of clean power in the world. Toyota's first step in the United States was to turn to renewable sources such as solar, wind, geothermal, and water power for the electricity at its headquarters in Torrance and Irving, California.

CORPORATE PHILANTHROPY Companies also display their social responsibility through corporate philanthropy. **Corporate philanthropy** includes cash contributions, donations of equipment and products, and support for the volunteer efforts of company employees. Corporate philanthropy totals about $9 billion a year.[8] American Express is a major supporter of the American Red Cross. The organization relies almost entirely on charitable gifts to carry out its programs and services, which include disaster relief, armed-forces emergency relief, blood and tissue services, and health and safety services. The funds provided by American Express have enabled the Red Cross to deliver humanitarian relief to victims of numerous disasters around the world. American Express has donated $3.6 million through 2002 to the Red Cross and is committed to an additional $2 million through 2004.[9] In addition, the company has given $3 million to the National Arts Marketing project, an initiative to help the Arts understand how to market themselves.

corporate philanthropy
The practice of charitable giving by corporations; includes contributing cash, donating equipment and products, and supporting the volunteer efforts of company employees.

Aetna gives away about $16.5 million in grants and sponsorships each year.[10] Adobe Systems gives away $1.5 million in product donations and $1.3 million in cash to its "community partners." The partners are nonprofit organizations and schools selected by the company. An example is City Year, a program designed to engage 17- to 27-year-olds to provide service to children and youth in support of academic and social success.[11] Adobe, Aetna, and American Express are just a few examples of how thousands of American businesses meet their social responsibilities.

The Rockefeller Foundation, one of the nation's best-known philanthropic families, offers significant aid to farmers living in developing countries to help them develop new technologies and crops that will flourish in their local conditions.

© AP / WIDE WORLD PHOTOS

Responsibilities to Investors

Companies' relationships with investors also entail social responsibility. Although a company's economic responsibility to make a profit might seem to be its main obligation to its shareholders, many investors increasingly are putting more emphasis on other aspects of social responsibility.

social investing
The practice of limiting investments to securities of companies that behave in accordance with the investor's beliefs about ethical and social responsibility.

Some investors are limiting their investments to securities that fit within their beliefs about ethical and social responsibility. This is called **social investing.** For example, a social investment fund might eliminate from consideration the securities of all companies that make tobacco products or liquor, manufacture weapons, or have a history of polluting. Not all social investment strategies are alike. Some ethical mutual funds will not invest in government securities because they help to fund the military; others freely buy government securities, with managers noting that federal funds also support the arts and pay for AIDS research. Today, about $100 billion is invested in social investment funds.

The early 2000s have been among the worst ever, in modern times, of companies failing to meet responsibilities to investors. Scandals at WorldCom, Global Crossing, Enron, and others so disturbed the investment community that they had a strong negative impact on the stock market. Investigators found companies claiming huge assets that never existed; falsified financial statements; huge loans by companies that could not be justified (or paid back); executives selling massive amounts of stock at high prices, then announcing several months later that the earnings were being restated at a much lower level, thus sending the stock crashing; and analysts making "buy" recommendations to the public while sending internal e-mails to coworkers stating that the stock was worthless. The Securities and Exchange Commission and many state attorneys general, particularly New York's, which is America's financial center, are working to enact new laws to curb these abuses.

concept check

How do businesses carry out their social responsibilities to consumers?

What is corporate philanthropy?

Is a company's only responsibility to its investors to make a profit? Why or why not?

Trends in Ethics and Social Responsibility

5 learning goal

Three important trends related to ethics and social responsibility are changes in corporate philanthropy, a new social contract between employers and employees, and the growth of global ethics and social responsibility.

TRENDS IN CORPORATE PHILANTHROPY

strategic giving
The practice of tying philanthropy closely to the corporate mission or goals and targeting donations to regions where a company operates.

Corporate philanthropy has typically involved seeking out needy groups and then giving them money or company products. Today, the focus is shifting to **strategic giving,** which ties philanthropy more closely to the corporate mission or goals and targets donations to regions where a company operates.

Stan Litow, IBM's vice president of corporate community relations, notes that the company knows it takes more than just money—checkbook philanthropy (the old model)—to have a successful giving program. "With checkbook philanthropy you could contribute a lot of money and accomplish very little," he says. "I think that in the new model, being generous is incredibly important, but the most important aspect of this new model is using our many resources to achieve something of lasting value in the communities where we live, work and do business."[12]

IBM knows throwing money at something isn't good enough, because money, in and of itself, does not do the good. It's the people, products, and programs supported by cash donations that do the worthwhile work. IBM's philanthropic donations in 2002 totaled over $126 million.[13] Of that, only 31 percent was cash. The remainder was technology and technical services—the best of what IBM has to offer.

Corporate philanthropy has also become a target for special-interest groups. AT&T, General Electric, and Eastman Kodak have come under attack by abortion foes for their donations to Planned Parenthood. The conservative Capital Research Center has criticized Anheuser-Busch, Hewlett-Packard, and other manufacturers for supporting what the center claims are radical groups seeking to undermine the capitalist system. When Philip Morris gave money to conservative political causes, the gay activist group ACT-UP encouraged consumers to stop buying its products.

A New Social Contract Trend between Employer and Employee

Another trend in social responsibility is the effort by organizations to redefine their relationship with their employees. Many people have viewed social responsibility as a one-way street that focuses on the obligations of business to society, employees, and others. Now, companies are telling employees that they also have a responsibility when it comes to job security. The new contract goes like this: "There will never be job security. You will be employed by us as long as you add value to the organization, and you are continuously responsible for finding ways to add value. In return, you have the right to demand interesting and important work, the freedom and resources to perform it well, pay that reflects your contribution, and the experience and training needed to be employable here or elsewhere." Coca-Cola, for example, requires extensive employee retraining each year. The idea, according to a Coke executive, is to become a more valuable employee by adding 25 percent to your existing knowledge every year.

Global Ethics and Social Responsibility

As U.S. businesses expand into global markets, their corporate codes of ethics and policies on social responsibility must travel with them. As a citizen of several countries, a multinational corporation has several responsibilities. These include respecting local practices and customs, ensuring that there is harmony between the

Computer firms that link their product donations to schools with their corporate goals represent the corporate philanthropic trend of strategic giving.

© PHOTODISC

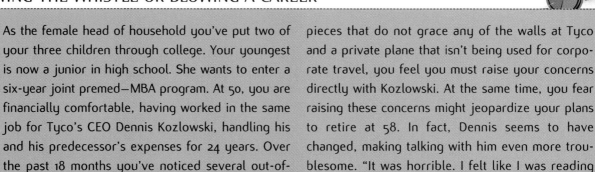

Making Ethical Choices

xtra! http://gitmanxtra.swlearning.com

BLOWING THE WHISTLE OR BLOWING A CAREER

As the female head of household you've put two of your three children through college. Your youngest is now a junior in high school. She wants to enter a six-year joint premed–MBA program. At 50, you are financially comfortable, having worked in the same job for Tyco's CEO Dennis Kozlowski, handling his and his predecessor's expenses for 24 years. Over the past 18 months you've noticed several out-of-the-ordinary expenses of large magnitude and want to discuss them with Kozlowski with whom you have an open and honest working relationship.

In fact, Kozlowski knows of your plans to retire in eight years, coinciding with graduation of your youngest. You believe that Tyco, a conglomerate of various types of industries, will always be in business and that the company's stock and retirement plan are "sacred." However, since you've paid out such large sums of money for items that you can't tie directly to the business, such as art masterpieces that do not grace any of the walls at Tyco and a private plane that isn't being used for corporate travel, you feel you must raise your concerns directly with Kozlowski. At the same time, you fear raising these concerns might jeopardize your plans to retire at 58. In fact, Dennis seems to have changed, making talking with him even more troublesome. "It was horrible. I felt like I was reading about a person I didn't know. I didn't recognize myself," he said while at a hearing about the company's fraudulent loans.

ETHICAL DILEMMA

Would you raise your concerns about the expenses directly with Dennis, knowing that doing so could create serious problems for you or for the company?

SOURCES: Anthony Bianco, William Symonds, and Nanette Byrnes, "The Rise and Fall of Dennis Kozlowski," *Business Week*, December 23, 2002, pp. 64–77; and Andrew Hill, "Kozlowski Speaks Out on Tyco Loan Deal," *Financial Times*, February 10, 2003, downloaded from **http://www.FT.com.**

organization's staff and the host population, providing management leadership, and developing a cadre of local managers who will be a credit to their community. When a multinational makes an investment in a foreign country, it should commit to a long-term relationship. That means involving all stakeholders in the host country in decision making. Finally, a responsible multinational will implement ethical guidelines within the organization in the host country. By fulfilling these responsibilities, the company will foster respect for both local and international laws.

Multinational corporations often must balance conflicting interests of stakeholders when making decisions regarding social responsibilities, especially in the area of human rights. Questions involving child labor, forced labor, minimum wages, and workplace safety can be particularly difficult. Levi Strauss was strongly praised when it announced it was leaving China in 1993 because of the country's poor human rights record. China is also an inexpensive place to manufacture clothing, and the temptation to stay there was simply too great. In fact, Levi Strauss never stopped making clothes in China; its Hong Kong subsidiary continues to manufacture clothes on a contract basis. Levi recently announced that it would begin selling clothes in China. One might argue that Levi Strauss must remain competitive and profitable, or it will not be able to be a leader in the cause of social responsibility. When the announcement came, however, human rights activists quickly set up a picket at Levi's San Francisco headquarters.

concept check

Describe strategic giving.

What role do employees have in improving their job security?

How do multinational corporations demonstrate social responsibility in a foreign country?

Great Ideas to Use Now

In many situations, there are no right or wrong answers. Instead, organizations must provide a process to resolve the dilemma quickly and fairly. Two approaches for resolving ethical problems are the "three-questions test" and the newspaper test.

Resolving Ethical Problems in Business

In evaluating an ethical problem, managers can use the three-questions test to determine the most ethical response: "Is it legal?" "Is it balanced?" and "How does it make me feel?" Companies such as Southwest Airlines, Texas Instruments, Marriott, and McDonald's rely on this test to guide employee decision making. If the answer to the first question is "no," then don't do it. Many ethical dilemmas, however, involve situations that aren't illegal. For example, the sale of tobacco is legal in the United States. But, given all the research that shows that tobacco use is dangerous to one's health, is it an ethical activity?

The second question, "Is it balanced?" requires you to put yourself in the position of other parties affected by your decision. For example, as an executive, you might not favor a buyout of your company because you will probably lose your job. Shareholders, however, may benefit substantially from the price to be paid for their shares in the buyout. At the same time, the employees of the business and their community may suffer economically if the purchaser decides to close the

Try It Now

1. **Support a good cause.** You don't have to wait until you graduate to start demonstrating your social responsibility. Also, it will look good on your resume when you need to differentiate yourself from all of the other job seekers. Go to **http://www.volunteermatch.org** and type in your zip code. You will find all sorts of organizations in your area looking for volunteers. Find one that meets your interest and that is related to your career goals and go to work. Volunteer Match has generated more than 1 million volunteer referrals with 25,000 community service organizations around the United States.
2. **Know your ethical values.** To get a better idea of your own level of ethical development, take an ethics test. Go to **http://www.ethicsandbusiness.org/stylequiz.htm**. This test will give you better insight into yourself.
3. If you are thinking about giving money to a charity, check them out first. Here are three sites that will tell you all you want to know about any charity: **http://www.give.org; http://www.charitynavigator.org;** and **http://www.charitywatch.org**.
4. **Work for a firm that cares about its social responsibilities.** When you enter the job market, make certain that you are going to work for a socially responsible organization. Ask a prospective employer "how the company gives back to society." If you plan to work for a large company, check out *Fortune*'s current list of America's most admired corporations. It appears around March 1. If you plan to work for a multinational, examine *Fortune*'s most globally admired corporations, which appears in October. The list is broken down by industry and includes 10 to 15 companies in each industry. Working for an ethical, socially responsible organization will make you proud of the place where you work.

Customer Satisfaction and Quality

Ethics and social responsibility play important roles in customer satisfaction and quality. Acting in an unethical manner, such as overcharging a client or failing to service a product properly after the sale, will normally mean losing that customer for life. Moreover, a dissatisfied customer will often tell other potential customers, resulting in further lost sales. Using cheaper, unreliable parts in the manufacturing process may save money in the short run, but will drive off customers in the long run.

People like to do business with organizations that they feel are good corporate citizens. We have given you several examples in this chapter of how companies exercise their social responsibilities. Another example is J.P. Morgan Chase & Company. In 2002, the company funded over $74 million in philanthropic gifts. J.P. Morgan Chase concentrates in three areas: community development and human services, precollegiate education, and arts and culture.[14]

business or focus its efforts in a different product area. The best situation, of course, is when everybody wins or shares the burden equally.

The final question, "How does it make me feel?" asks you to examine your comfort with a particular decision. Many people find that after reaching a decision on an issue they still experience discomfort that may manifest itself in a loss of sleep or appetite. Those feelings of conscience can serve as a guide in resolving ethical dilemmas.

Front Page of the Newspaper Test

Many managers use the "front page of the newspaper test" for evaluating ethical dilemmas. The question to be asked is how a critical and objective reporter would report your decision in a front-page story. Some managers rephrase the test for their employees: How will the headline read if I make this decision? This test is helpful in spotting and resolving potential conflicts of interest. Obviously, executives from firms like Enron and WorldCom didn't consider the front-page test when they took their actions.

Looking Ahead at Dennis Kozlowski

If the information is true, as reported in a number of media, then Dennis Kozlowski did act in an unethical manner. Kozlowski's story is far from finished, but already it is clear that his fate and that of the empire he created have diverged. Many investors and other observers believe that Tyco has a future, though new CEO Edward D. Breen, Jr., and his management team still must work their way through the massive debt left behind by Kozlowski and cope with the continuing investigations into Tyco's accounting and tax policies. No one believes that Tyco will ever regain the high growth rates that it achieved under Kozlowski. But most of the businesses that he built up—including health care and the security unit that included ADT—seem likely to survive and prosper, although as part of a far more conventional corporation.

As CEO, he had responsibilities to his stakeholders that he did not carry out. Giving money to charity, in and of itself, did not make Kozlowski an ethical person. It is further colored by information that he told those who received the funds that a large portion was coming from him personally. In fact, it came from Tyco.

Summary of Learning Goals

1 What philosophies and concepts shape personal ethical standards?

Ethics is a set of moral standards for judging whether something is right or wrong. A utilitarianism approach to setting personal ethical standards focuses on the consequences of an action taken by a person or organization. According to this approach, people should act so as to generate the greatest good for the greatest number. Every human is entitled to certain rights such as freedom and the pursuit of happiness. Another approach to ethical decision making is justice, or what is fair according to accepted standards.

2 How can organizations encourage ethical business behavior?

Top management must shape the ethical culture of the organization. They should lead by example, offer ethics-training programs, and establish a formal code of ethics.

3 What is social responsibility?

Social responsibility is the concern of businesses for the welfare of society as a whole. It consists of obligations beyond just making a profit. Social responsibility also goes beyond what is required by law or union contract. Companies may engage in illegal and irresponsible behavior, irresponsible but legal behavior, or legal and responsible behavior. The vast majority of organizations act legally and try to be socially responsible.

4 How do businesses meet their social responsibilities to various stakeholders?

Stakeholders are individuals or groups to whom business has a responsibility. Businesses are responsible to employees. They should provide a clean, safe working environment. Organizations can build employees' self-worth through empowerment programs. Businesses also have a responsibility to customers to provide good, safe products and services. Organizations are responsible to the general public to be good corporate citizens. Firms must help protect the environment and provide a good place to work. Companies also engage in corporate philanthropy, which includes contributing cash, donating goods and services, and supporting volunteer efforts of employees. Finally, companies are responsible to investors. They should earn a reasonable profit for the owners.

5 What are the global and domestic trends in ethics and social responsibility?

Today, corporate philanthropy is shifting away from simply giving to any needy group and is focusing instead on strategic giving, in which the philanthropy relates more closely to the corporate mission or goals and targets donations to areas where the firm operates. Corporate philanthropy is coming under increasing attacks from special-interest groups, however.

A second trend is toward a new social contract between employer and employee. Instead of the employer having the sole responsibility for maintaining jobs, now the employee must assume part of the burden and find ways to add value to the organization.

As the world increasingly becomes a global community, multinational corporations are now expected to assume a global set of ethics and responsibility. Global companies must understand local customs. They should also involve local stakeholders in decision making. Multinationals must also make certain that their suppliers are not engaged in human rights violations.

Appendix:

6

How does the legal system govern business transactions and settle business disputes?

Laws are the rules governing a society's conduct that are created and enforced by a controlling authority. The U.S. court system governs the legal system and includes both federal and state courts, each organized into three levels. The courts settle disputes by applying and interpreting laws. Most cases start in trial courts. Decisions can be appealed to appellate courts. The U.S. Supreme Court is the nation's highest court and the court of final appeal. To avoid the high costs of going to court, many firms now use private arbitration or mediation as alternatives to litigation.

7

What are the required elements of a valid contract; and what are the key types of business law?

A contract is an agreement between two or more parties that meets five requirements: mutual assent, capacity, consideration, legal purpose, and legal form. If one party breaches the contract terms, the remedies are damages, specific performance, or restitution. Tort law settles disputes involving civil acts that harm people or their property. Torts include physical injury, mental anguish, and defamation. Product-liability law governs the responsibility of manufacturers and sellers for product defects. Bankruptcy law gives businesses or individuals who cannot meet their financial obligations a way to be relieved of their debts. Some laws are designed to keep the marketplace free from influences that would restrict competition such as price fixing and deceptive advertising. Laws protecting consumer rights are another important area of government control.

8

What are the most common taxes paid by businesses?

Income taxes are based on the income received by businesses and individuals. Congress determines the income taxes that are to be paid to the federal government. In addition to income taxes, individuals and businesses also pay property taxes (assessed on real and personal property), payroll taxes (the employer's share of Social Security taxes and federal and state unemployment taxes), sales taxes (levied on goods), and excise taxes (levied against specific products such as gasoline, alcoholic beverages, and tobacco).

Preparing for Tomorrow's Workplace

1. Professor Joseph Badaracco of Harvard Business School believes that "real ethical dilemmas are not choices between right and wrong, but choices between right and right—cases in which both options seem correct for different reasons, yet one must be chosen and one rejected." Here is an example: Many CEOs sold shares of their company's stock when prices were near their high points. Even though their actions were legal, it soon became apparent that they knew that the stock was significantly overpriced. Was the CEO ethically obligated to tell the public that this was the case—even knowing that doing so could cause the stock price to plummet, thereby hurting someone who bought the stock earlier that day?

   SOURCE: Geoffrey Colvin, "Between Right and Right," *Fortune*, October 30, 2002, downloaded from http://www.fortune.com.

2. Your company has decided to create a new position for an ethics officer and has asked you to be part of the team that is writing the job description. Using resources such as the Web site of the Ethics Officer Association (EOA), **http://www.eoa.org**, and other materials, draft a list of job responsibilities for this new role.

KEY TERMS

code of ethics 85
corporate philanthropy 92
ethics 80
justice 81
social investing 93
social responsibility 85
stakeholders 89
strategic giving 93
utilitarianism 80

3. Boeing Corp. makes business ethics a priority, asking employees to take refresher training every year. It encourages employees to take the Ethics Challenge with their work groups and to discuss the issues with their peers. You can take the Challenge, too, by going to **http://active.boeing.com/companyoffices/ethicschallenge/cfm/initial.cfm.** Each question presents an ethical dilemma, together with three or four potential answers. Taking the Challenge will show you how Boeing approaches workplace ethics. Summarize your findings. Were there any answers that surprised you?
4. Identify the potential ethical and social responsibility issues confronting the following organizations: Microsoft, Pfizer, Nike, American Cancer Society, and R.J. Reynolds. Make recommendations on how these issues should be handled.
5. Divide the class into teams. Debate whether the only social responsibility of the employer to the employee is to provide a job. Include a discussion of the employee's responsibility to bring value to the firm.

WORKING THE NET

1. You'll find a comprehensive list of business ethics sites at **http://www.web-miner.com/busethics.htm.** Once at the site, go to the section on Corporate Codes of Ethics. Look at three examples of codes in different industries. What elements do they have in common? How are they different? Suggest how one of the codes could be improved.
2. What ethical issues arise as companies add e-business to their operations? Go to Information Week's site, **http://www.informationweek.com**, and perform a search for business ethics. What topics did you find? Identify three areas where the potential for ethical breaches could occur and briefly discuss each.
3. Visit the Fur Is Dead Web site of the people for Ethical Treatment of Animal (PETA), **http://furisdead.com.** Read about PETA's view of the fur industry. Do you agree with this view? Why or why not? How do you think manufacturers of fur clothing would justify their actions to someone from PETA? Would you work for a store that sold fur-trimmed clothing? Explain your answer.
4. Green Money Journal, **http://www.greenmoneyjournal.com**, is a bimonthly online journal that promotes social responsibility investing. What are the current topics of concern in this area? Visit the archives to find articles on socially responsible investing and two areas of corporate social responsibility. Summarize what you have learned.
5. Which companies are the most socially responsible: Find out at GiveSpot.com's link to the Business Ethics list of the 100 Best Corporate Citizens, an index of social responsibility: **http://www.givespot.com/lists/socially.htm.** Who is currently number one? How is the list determined? Then go to the GiveSpot.com home page, **http://www.givespot.com** (you can click on a link at the upper-left corner of any page) to learn more about this volunteer and philanthropy resource center. You'll find links to sites for over 700,000 nonprofits and charitable organizations, 60,000 foundations, volunteer opportunities, and social issues. Using the site, perform a brief evaluation of a charity you would consider supporting. Based on your research, would you still support it? Explain your answer.

CREATIVE THINKING CASE

Got Milk, California?

The California Milk Processor Board, creator of the "Got Milk?" advertising campaign, decided to launch a new promotion. To celebrate 10 years of "Got Milk?" advertising, the Board asked 24 small California towns to consider changing their name to Got Milk? The town would become the centerpiece of a national advertising campaign and receive free school computers, new playgrounds, a Got Milk? museum, and other goodies in exchange for changing its name.

The California towns approached by the Board were: Biggs, Vernon, Sand City, Amador, Trinidad, Point Arena, Tehama, Fort Jones, Industry, Plymouth, Etna, Isleton, Dorris, Loyalton, Bradbury, Tulelake, Maricopa, Colma, Blue Lake, Ferndale, Montague, Colfax, San Juan Bautista, and Del Rey Oaks.

Jeff Manning, the Board's executive director, stated that all he wants is to "pick up a newly printed California map and run my finger down a road and see Got Milk? California."

Officials in several towns said it would take millions of dollars to convince a town to change its name—and even then they're hesitant. Sand City Administrator Kelly Morgan, for example, said, "We're on the Monterey Peninsula and it would surely cause us to come in for some ridicule." Pam DeYoung, a resident of Industry since 1977, was even more caustic in dismissing the idea: "I think it's retarded."

Not all towns are so picky. In 2000, Halfway, Oregon, changed its name to Half.com for a year in exchange for a mere $93,000 and some computers.[15]

CRITICAL THINKING QUESTIONS

1. Do you think that the California Milk Producer Board is acting unethically? What criteria are you using to claim that their behavior is ethical or unethical? Are they being socially responsible?
2. If a town's administrators decided to accept the offer, would they be acting unethically? Would they be acting socially responsibly?
3. How would you feel about living in Got Milk? Why?

Video Case

Fair Trade Sweetens the Coffee

When you sip your morning coffee, you probably don't wonder who grew the beans. Rink Dickinson did, and when he learned that small coffee growers were at the mercy of agents and middlemen, who paid them the lowest possible prices, he decided to do something about it.

Coffee growers, receiving only 40 cents on each $8 to $9 pound of gourmet coffee sold, were fleeing from their farms to seek jobs in overcrowded cities. Others were planting illegal crops like marijuana or cocaine to generate cash for their next coffee crop. The 20 million coffee farmers who lived in poverty called the middlemen "coyotes," because they preyed on the poor.

Dickinson decided to change these unfair practices and engage in more ethically and socially responsible ways of doing business. In 1986 he cofounded Equal Exchange, a worker-owned cooperative gourmet coffee company. By buying direct and thereby eliminating middlemen, Equal Exchange was able to pay growers 50 cents per pound more.

Coffee is the leading source of foreign currency in Latin America, so this price increase had a significant impact on the economy and lifestyle of the region. Coffee growing provides jobs for people who would otherwise be unemployed. The growers' entire region benefits from projects the farm cooperatives undertake with the additional income, from reforestation programs to building new schools, day-care centers, and carpentry workshops. "We used to live in houses made of corn husks," recalls Don Miguel Sifontes, a farmer in El Salvador. "Now we have better work, better schools, homes of adobe, and a greater brotherhood of decision makers."

Fair trade underscores the idea that businesses are accountable to employees, customers, and the general public. Under exclusive agreements with farming cooperatives, Equal Exchange growers receive better prices, and customers are guaranteed high-quality coffee at fair prices. Receiving a guaranteed minimum price per pound for coffee, even when the market is lower, assures farmers of a living wage during downturns.

Following strict fair-trade guidelines, Equal Exchange enters into long-term relationships with growers, buying directly from cooperatives owned and run by farmers. The farmers themselves govern the even distribution of income and services, such as education and health care. Making credit available to farmers helps them avoid the cycle of debt. "When we sign a contract with growers, we pay up to 50 percent of the contract six months in advance," notes marketing manager Erbin Crowell. "If a hurricane hits, we share the risk." The company pays a premium price for certified organic and shade-grown coffee, and by helping growers use environmentally friendly farming methods, the environment and consumers are protected from toxic chemicals.

When specialty coffee giants Starbucks and Green Mountain announced they were entering into fair-trade agreements with farmers, Equal Exchange congratulated them. "We know these farmers and their struggles. They urgently need more importers to pay a just price, so we encourage our fellow roasters." With this statement, Dickinson raised the bar of ethical standards in the coffee business, knowing that his company can clear it with ease. With $7 million in sales, he is clearly supported by many coffee-loving consumers who do care where their beans come from.

CRITICAL THINKING QUESTIONS

1. Has Equal Exchange gone beyond other organizations to be socially and ethically responsible? Explain.
2. What are the key components of Equal Exchange's fair-trade agreement with coffee growers? How do they support the company's goals and affect coffee growers' regions and lifestyles?
3. How might Equal Exchange encourage other companies to adopt fair-trade agreements? Suggest an approach the company could use to launch such a campaign.

SOURCES: Adapted from material in the video case *The Rewards of Paying Fair: Ethics and Social Responsibility at Equal Exchange* and company Web site: http://www.equalexchange.com, accessed February 8, 2003.

E-Commerce Case

Geekcorps: Spreading the (IT) Gospel

A Peace Corps for techies? Ethan Zuckerman had a mission—to bring the technology revolution to developing countries such as Rwanda, Mongolia, Lebanon, Bulgaria, and Ghana, via techno-savvy volunteers. Zuckerman, a 1993 graduate of Williams College, became an instant millionaire in 1999 when Lycos bought the online company where he served as vice president of research and development. A self-confessed Net head, he wanted to do something he believed was important.

Geekcorps (**http://www.geekcorps.com**) was started in February 2000 with $100,000 of Zuckerman's own money. Seven months later, its first team of volunteers were at work in Accra, Ghana, where Zuckerman had spent time on a Fulbright fellowship. Geekcorps now delves into a database of 1,100 volunteers from 11 different countries to select teams of seven or eight rigorously screened volunteers, who are given four months to prepare for their stint abroad. Geekcorps pays for travel and provides lodging and a small stipend. On sabbatical from their jobs for periods of one to four months, volunteers are trained to teach their skills to people with different backgrounds.

"We never tell the volunteers to go in and do the project; they teach the in-country staff and company members to do it themselves," says Ana Marie Harkins, Geekcorps's Director of Programs. In return each business agrees to transfer the skills it acquires to the community, free of charge. "The number one asset for a Geekcorps volunteer is a good sense of humor and the ability to roll with the punches," says Peter Beardsley, 26, who spent six months in Accra. "If you let

power outages and leaky roofs get to you, you're going to have a hard time." But it is not all work and no play for the volunteers, who spend their free time exploring the host country and meeting its people.

After the dot-com bubble burst, corporate donations dwindled. The United Nations and other organizations provided some grants to help keep Geekcorps afloat. In 2002, Zuckerman joined forces with the International Executive Service Corps (IESC), an organization with a history of sending business professionals to developing countries. "We both believe that the way to transform an economy is by building small business, by bringing over skills volunteers," says Zuckerman. Thanks to the IESC partnership and private donations, Geekcorps now has enough funding for the next year and a half.

CRITICAL THINKING QUESTIONS

1. Ethan Zuckerman still hopes to attract donations from corporate sponsors. If you were Ethan Zuckerman, how would you explain to a high-technology firm why contributing to Geekcorps would be a strategic giving choice?
2. Do you think other consumer goods firms—for instance, a maker of breakfast cereals or a clothing company—would see donating to Geekcorps as an opportunity to meet their social responsibilities to employees, customers, or investors? Explain.
3. Why do you think corporate donations dwindled after the dot-com bubble burst? Do you think companies have a moral obligation to continue corporate sponsorship programs during economic downturns? Defend your answer.

SOURCES: Dawn Calleja, "Heart of Geekness," *Canadian Business Magazine*, April 20, 2002; Laurie O'Connell, "Geekcorps' Savvy Volunteers Bring the Benefits of IT to Developing Countries," *Software Development*, October 2002, downloaded from http://www.sdmagazine.com; material from Geekcorps Web site: http://www.geekcorps.org, accessed February 25, 2003; and John Yaukey, "Geekcorps Spread Computer Skills Worldwide," *Gannet News Service, HonoluluAdvertiser.com*, March 26, 2002, downloaded February 25, 2003, from http://www.honoluluadvertiser.com.

Hot Links Address Book

Find out which companies test their products on animals and which don't in the campaign section of the People for the Ethical Treatment of Animals (PETA) Web site,
http://www.peta.org

How is the International Business Ethics Institute working to promote business ethics worldwide? Find out at
http://www.business-ethics.org

Ben & Jerry's ice cream has always taken its responsibilities as a corporate good citizen seriously. Learn about the company's positions on various issues and products that support social issues at its Web site,
http://www.benjerry.com

Discover what Texas Instruments's "Ethics Quick Test" includes at
http://www.ti.com/corp/docs/company/citizen/ethics/quicktest.shtml

What does IBM Corp require from its employees in terms of ethical business conduct? It's all presented in the Business Conduct Guidelines that you will find at
http://www-1.ibm.com/partnerworld/pwhome.nsf/weblook/guide_index.html

Levi Strauss's unique corporate culture rewards and recognizes employee achievements. To learn about working for a company that values employee efforts, go to the Levi Strauss home page at
http://www.levistrauss.com

Want to see how the global environment is changing and learn the latest about global warming? Check out
http://www.climatehotmap.org

General Motors is often recognized as a top participant in philanthropic activities. Which charities and organizations does GM support, and how? Read GM's Annual Philanthropic Report online at
http://www.gm.com

appendix

UNDERSTANDING THE LEGAL AND TAX ENVIRONMENT

6 learning goal

Our legal system affects everyone who lives and does business in the United States. The smooth functioning of society depends on the law, which protects the rights of people and businesses. The purpose of law is to keep the system stable while allowing orderly change. The law defines which actions are allowed or banned and regulates some practices. It also helps settle disputes. The legal system both shapes and is shaped by political, economic, and social systems. As Judge Learned Hand wrote in *The Spirit of Liberty,* "Without [the law] we cannot live; only with it can we insure the future which by right is ours."

laws
The rules of conduct in a society, created and enforced by a controlling authority, usually the government.

In any society **laws** are the rules of conduct created and enforced by a controlling authority, usually the government. They develop over time in response to the changing needs of people, property, and business. The legal system of the United States is thus the result of a long and continuing process. In each generation new social problems occur, and new laws are created to solve them. For instance, in the late 1800s corporations in certain industries, such as steel and oil, merged and became dominant. The Sherman Antitrust Act was passed in 1890 to control these powerful firms. Eighty years later, in 1970, Congress passed the National Environmental Policy Act. This law dealt with pollution problems, which no one had thought about in 1890. Today new areas of law are developing to deal with the Internet and the recent financial scandals.

The Main Sources of Law

common law
The body of unwritten law that has evolved out of judicial (court) decisions rather than being enacted by a legislature; also called case law.

Common law is the body of unwritten law that has evolved out of judicial (court) decisions rather than being enacted by legislatures. It is also called case law. It developed in England and came to America with the colonists. All states except Louisiana, which follows the Napoleonic Code inherited from French settlers, follow the English system. Common law is based on community customs that were recognized and enforced by the courts.

statutory law
Written law enacted by a legislature (local, state, or federal).

Statutory law is written law enacted by legislatures at all levels, from city and state governments to the federal government. Examples of statutory law are the federal and state constitutions, bills passed by Congress, and ordinances, which are laws enacted by local governments. Statutory law is the chief source of new laws in the United States. Among the business activities governed by statutory law are securities regulation, incorporation, sales, bankruptcy, and antitrust.

administrative law
The rules, regulations, and orders passed by boards, commissions, and agencies of government (local, state, and federal).

Related to statutory law is **administrative law,** or the rules, regulations, and orders passed by boards, commissions, and agencies of federal, state, and local governments. The scope and influence of administrative law have expanded as the number of these government bodies has grown. Federal agencies issue more rulings and settle more disputes than all the courts and legislatures combined. Some federal agencies that issue rules are the Civil Aeronautics Board, the Internal Revenue Service, the Securities and Exchange Commission, the Federal Trade Commission, and the National Labor Relations Board.

Business Law

business law
The body of law that governs commercial dealings.

Business law is the body of law that governs commercial dealings. These laws provide a protective environment within which businesses can operate. They serve as guidelines for business decisions. Every businessperson should be familiar with the laws governing his or her field. Some laws, such as the Internal Revenue Code, apply to all businesses. Other types of business laws may apply to a specific industry, such as Federal Communications Commission laws that regulate radio and TV stations.

Uniform Commercial Code (UCC)
A model set of rules that apply to commercial transactions between businesses and between businesses and individuals; has been adopted by all states except Louisiana, which uses only part of it.

judiciary
The branch of government that is responsible for settling disputes by applying and interpreting points of law; consists of the court system.

trial courts
The lowest level of courts, where most cases begin; also called courts of general jurisdiction.

appellate courts (courts of appeals)
The level of courts above the trial courts; the losing party in a civil case and the defendant in a criminal case may appeal the trial court's decision to an appellate court.

In 1952 the United States grouped many business laws into a model that could be used by all the states. The **Uniform Commercial Code (UCC)** sets forth the rules that apply to commercial transactions between businesses and between individuals and businesses. It has been adopted by 49 states; Louisiana uses only part of it. By standardizing laws, the UCC simplifies the process of doing business across state lines. It covers the sale of goods, bank deposits and collections, letters of credit, documents of title, and investment securities. Many articles of the UCC are covered later in this appendix.

The Court System

The United States has a highly developed court system. This branch of government, the **judiciary,** is responsible for settling disputes by applying and interpreting points of law. Although court decisions are the basis for common law, the courts also answer questions left unanswered by statutes and administrative rulings. They have the power to assure that these laws do not violate the federal or state constitutions.

Trial Courts

Most court cases start in the **trial courts,** also called courts of general jurisdiction. The main federal trial courts are the U.S. district courts. There is at least one federal district court in each state. These courts hear cases involving serious federal crimes, immigration, postal regulations, disputes between citizens of different states, patents, copyrights, and bankruptcy. Specialized federal courts handle tax matters, international trade, and claims against the United States.

Appellate Courts

The losing party in a civil (noncriminal) case and a losing defendant in a criminal case may appeal the trial court's decision to the next level in the judicial system, the **appellate courts (courts of appeals).** There are 12 U.S. circuit courts of appeals. Cases that begin in a federal district court are appealed to the court of appeals for that district. These courts may also review orders from administrative agencies. Likewise, the states have appellate courts and supreme courts for cases tried in state district or superior courts.

No cases start in appellate courts. Their purpose is to review decisions of the lower courts and affirm, reverse, or modify the rulings.

The Supreme Court

The U.S. Supreme Court is the highest court in the nation. It is the only court specifically established by the U.S. Constitution. Any cases involving a state or in which an ambassador, public minister, or consul is a party are heard directly by the Supreme Court. Its main function is to review decisions by the U.S. circuit courts of appeals. Parties not satisfied with a decision of a state supreme court can appeal to the U.S. Supreme Court. But the Supreme Court accepts only those cases that it believes will have the greatest effect on the country, only about 200 of the thousands of appeals it gets each year.

Administrative Agencies

Administrative agencies have limited judicial powers to regulate their special areas. These agencies exist at the federal, state, and local levels. For example, in 1998 the Federal Trade Commission enacted the "Federal Universal Service Fund," which subjects each pager phone to an 18 cent fee. This fund was created by the Federal Trade Commission to ensure that all citizens, schools, libraries, and hospitals in rural areas have access to telecommunications service (like the Internet) at prices comparable to those charged in urban and suburban areas. A list of selected federal agencies is shown in Exhibit 3A.1.

Nonjudicial Methods of Settling Disputes

Settling disputes by going to court is both expensive and time consuming. Even if the case is settled prior to the actual trial, sizable legal expenses can be incurred in

Exhibit 3A.1 Federal Regulatory Agencies

Agency	Function
Federal Trade Commission (FTC)	Enforces laws and guidelines regarding unfair business practices and acts to stop false and deceptive advertising and labeling.
Food and Drug Administration (FDA)	Enforces laws and regulations to prevent distribution of adulterated or misbranded foods, drugs, medical devices, cosmetics, veterinary products, and hazardous consumer products.
Consumer Products Safety Commission	Ensures compliance with the Consumer Product Safety Act and seeks to protect the public from unreasonable risk of injury from any consumer product not covered by other regulatory agencies.
Federal Communications Commission (FCC)	Regulates wire, radio, and TV communication in interstate and foreign commerce.
Environmental Protection Agency (EPA)	Develops and enforces environmental protection standards and researches the effects of pollution.

preparing for trial. Therefore, many companies now use private arbitration and mediation firms as alternatives to litigation. Private firms offer these services, which are a high growth area within the legal profession.

arbitration
A method of settling disputes in which the parties agree to present their case to an impartial third party and are required to accept the arbitrator's decision.

mediation
A method of settling disputes in which the parties submit their case to an impartial third party but are not required to accept the mediator's decision.

With **arbitration,** the parties agree to present their case to an impartial third party and are required to accept the arbitrator's decision. **Mediation** is similar, but the parties are not bound by the mediator's decision. The mediator suggests alternative solutions and helps the parties negotiate a settlement. Mediation is more flexible than arbitration and allows for compromise. If the parties cannot reach a settlement, they can then go to court, an option not available in most arbitration cases.

In addition to saving time and money, corporations like the confidentiality of testimony and settlement terms in these proceedings. Arbitration and mediation also allow businesses and medical professionals to avoid jury trials, which can result in large settlements in certain types of lawsuits, such as personal injury, discrimination, medical malpractice, and product liability.

Contract Law

7 learning goal

Linda Price, a 22-year-old college student, is looking at a car with a sticker price of $16,000. After some negotiating, she and the salesperson agree on a price of $15,000, and the salesperson writes up a contract, which they both sign. Has Linda legally bought the car for $15,000? The answer is yes, because the transaction meets all the requirements for a valid contract.

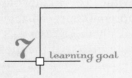

contract
An agreement that sets forth the relationship between parties regarding the performance of a specified action; creates a legal obligation and is enforceable in a court of law.

A **contract** is an agreement that sets forth the relationship between parties regarding the performance of a specified action. The contract creates a legal obligation and is enforceable in a court of law. Contracts are an important part of business law. Contract law is also incorporated into other fields of business law, such as property and agency law (discussed later in this appendix). Some of the business transactions that involve contracts are buying materials and property, selling goods, leasing equipment, and hiring consultants.

A contract can be an **express contract,** which specifies the terms of the agreement in either written or spoken words, or an **implied contract,** which depends on the acts and conduct of the parties to show agreement. An example of an express contract is the written sales contract for Linda Price's new car. An implied contract exists when you order and receive a sandwich at Jason's Grill. You and the restaurant have an implied contract that you will pay the price shown on the restaurant's menu in exchange for an edible sandwich.

Contract Requirements

Businesses deal with contracts all the time, so it's important to know the requirements of a valid contract. For a contract to be legally enforceable, all of the following elements must be present:

- *Mutual assent.* Voluntary agreement by both parties to the terms of the contract. Each party to the contract must have entered into it freely, without duress. Using physical or economic harm to force the signing of the contract—threatening injury or refusing to place another large order, for instance—invalidates a contract. Likewise, fraud—misrepresenting the facts of a transaction—makes a contract unenforceable. Telling a prospective used-car buyer that the brakes are new when in fact they have not been replaced makes the contract of sale invalid.
- *Capacity.* Legal ability of a party to enter into contracts. Under the law, minors (those under 18), mental incompetents, drug and alcohol addicts, and convicts cannot enter into contracts.
- *Consideration.* Exchange of some legal value or benefit between the parties. Consideration can be in the form of money, goods, or a legal right given up. Suppose that an electronics manufacturer agrees to rent an industrial building for a year at a monthly rent of $1,500. Its consideration is the rent payment of $1,500, and the building owner's consideration is permission to occupy the space. But if you offer to type a term paper for a friend for free and your offer is accepted, there is no contract. Your friend has not given up anything, so you are not legally bound to honor the deal.
- *Legal purpose.* Absence of illegality. The purpose of the contract must be legal for it to be valid. A contract cannot require performance of an illegal act. A contract to smuggle drugs into a state for a specified amount of money would not be legally enforceable.
- *Legal form.* Oral or written form, as required. Many contracts can be oral. For instance, an oral contract exists when Bridge Corp. orders office supplies by phone from Ace Stationery Store and Ace delivers the requested goods. Written contracts include leases, sales contracts, and property deeds. Some types of contracts must be in writing to be legally binding. In most states, written contracts are required for the sale of goods costing more than $500, for the sale of land, for contract performance that cannot be carried out within a year, and for guarantees to pay the debts of someone else.

As you can see, Linda Price's car purchase meets all the requirements for a valid contract. Both parties have freely agreed to the terms of the contract. Linda is not a minor and presumably does not fit any of the other categories of incapacity. Both parties are giving consideration, Linda by paying the money and the salesperson by turning over the car to her. The purchase of the car is a legal activity. And the written contract is the correct form because the cost of the car is over $500.

Breach of Contract

breach of contract
The failure by one party to a contract to fulfill the terms of the agreement without a legal excuse.

A **breach of contract** occurs when one party to a contract fails (without legal excuse) to fulfill the terms of the agreement. The other party then has the right to seek a remedy in the courts. There are three legal remedies for breach of contract:

- *Payment of damages.* Money awarded to the party who was harmed by the breach of contract, to cover losses incurred because the contract wasn't fulfilled. Suppose that Ajax Roofing contracts with Fred Wellman to fix the large hole in the roof of his factory within three days. But the roofing crew doesn't show up as promised. When a thunderstorm four days later causes $45,000 in damage to Wellman's machinery, Wellman can sue for damages to cover the costs of the water damage because Ajax breached the contract.

- *Specific performance of the contract.* A court order requiring the breaching party to perform the duties under the terms of the contract. Specific performance is the most common method of settling a breach of contract. Wellman might ask the court to direct Ajax to fix the roof at the price and conditions in the contract.
- *Restitution.* Canceling the contract and returning to the situation that existed before the contract. If one party fails to perform under the contract, neither party has any further obligation to the other. Because Ajax failed to fix Wellman's roof under the terms of the contract, Wellman does not owe Ajax any money. Ajax must return the 50 percent deposit it received when Wellman signed the contract.

Warranties

Express warranties are specific statements of fact or promises about a product by the seller. This form of warranty is considered part of the sales transaction that influences the buyer. Express warranties appear in the form of statements that can be interpreted as fact. The statement "This machine will process 1,000 gallons of paint per hour" is an express warranty, as is the printed warranty that comes with a computer or a telephone answering machine.

Implied warranties are neither written nor oral. These guarantees are imposed on sales transactions by statute or court decision. They promise that the product will perform up to expected standards. For instance, a man bought a used car from a dealer, and the next day the transmission fell out as he was driving on the highway. The dealer fixed the car, but a week later the brakes failed. The man sued the car dealer. The court ruled in favor of the car owner because any car without a working transmission or brakes is not fit for the ordinary purpose of driving. Similarly, if a customer asks to buy a copier to handle 5,000 copies per month, she relies on the salesperson to sell her a copier that meets those needs. The salesperson implicitly warrants that the copier purchased is appropriate for that volume.

patent
A form of protection established by the government for inventors; gives an inventor the exclusive right to manufacture, use, and sell an invention for 17 years.

copyright
A form of protection established by the government for creators of works of art, music, literature, or other intellectual property; gives the creator the exclusive right to use, produce, and sell the creation during the lifetime of the creator and for 50 years thereafter.

trademark
A design, name, or other distinctive mark that a manufacturer uses to identify its goods in the marketplace.

servicemark
A symbol, name, or design that identifies a service rather than a tangible object.

Patents, Copyrights, and Trademarks

The U.S. Constitution protects authors, inventors, and creators of other intellectual property by giving them the rights to their creative works. Patents, copyrights, and registration of trademarks and servicemarks are legal protection for key business assets.

A **patent** gives an inventor the exclusive right to manufacture, use, and sell an invention for 17 years. The U.S. Patent Office, a government agency, grants patents for ideas that meet its requirements of being new, unique, and useful. The physical process, machine, or formula is what is patented. Patent rights—pharmaceutical companies' rights to produce drugs they discover, for example—are considered intangible personal property.

The government also grants copyrights. A **copyright** is an exclusive right, shown by the symbol ©, given to a writer, artist, composer, or playwright to use, produce, and sell her or his creation. Works protected by copyright include printed materials (books, magazine articles, lectures), works of art, photographs, and movies. Under current copyright law, the copyright is issued for the life of the creator plus 50 years after the creator's death. Patents and copyrights, which are considered intellectual property, are the subject of many lawsuits today.

A **trademark** is a design, name, or other distinctive mark that a manufacturer uses to identify its goods in the marketplace. Apple Computer's multicolored apple logo (symbol) is an example of a trademark. A **servicemark** is a symbol, name, or design that identifies a service rather than a tangible object. The Travelers Insurance umbrella logo is an example of a servicemark.

Most companies identify their trademark with the ® symbol in company ads. This symbol shows that the trademark is registered with the Register of Copyrights, Copyright Office, Library of Congress. The trademark is followed by a generic description: Fritos corn chips, Xerox copiers, Scotch brand cellophane tape, Kleenex tissues.

Trademarks are valuable because they create uniqueness in the minds of customers. At the same time, companies don't want a trademark to become so well known that it is used to describe all similar types of products. For instance, Coke is often used to refer to any cola soft drink, not just those produced by the Coca-Cola Company. Companies spend millions of dollars each year to keep their trademarks from becoming *generic words,* terms used to identify a product class rather than the specific product. Coca-Cola employs many investigators and files 70 to 80 lawsuits each year to prevent its trademarks from becoming generic words.

Once a trademark becomes generic (which a court decides), it is public property and can be used by any person or company. Names that were once trademarked but are now generic include *aspirin, thermos, linoleum,* and *toll house cookies.*

Tort Law

tort
A civil, or private, act that harms other people or their property.

A **tort** is a civil, or private, act that harms other people or their property. The harm may involve physical injury, emotional distress, invasion of privacy, or *defamation* (injuring a person's character by publication of false statements). The injured party may sue the wrongdoer to recover damages for the harm or loss. A tort is not the result of a breach of contract, which would be settled under contract law. Torts are part of common law. Examples of tort cases are medical malpractice, *slander* (an untrue oral statement that damages a person's reputation), *libel* (an untrue written statement that damages a person's reputation), product liability (discussed in the next section), and fraud.

A tort is generally not a crime, although some acts can be both torts and crimes. (Assault and battery, for instance, is a criminal act that would be prosecuted by the state and also a tort because of the injury to the person.) Torts are private wrongs and are settled in civil courts. *Crimes* are violations of public law punishable by the state or county in the criminal courts. The purpose of criminal law is to punish the person who committed the crime. The purpose of tort law is to provide remedies to the injured party.

For a tort to exist and damages to be recovered, the harm must be done through either negligence or deliberate intent. *Negligence* occurs when reasonable care is not taken for the safety of others. For instance, a woman attending a New York Mets baseball game was struck on the head by a foul ball that came through a hole in the screen behind home plate. The court ruled that a sports team charging admission has an obligation to provide structures free from defects and seating that protects spectators from danger. The Mets were found negligent. Negligence does not apply when an injury is caused by an unavoidable accident, an event that was not intended and could not have been prevented even if the person used reasonable care. This area of tort law is quite controversial, because the definition of negligence leaves much room for interpretation.

Product-Liability Law

product liability
The responsibility of manufacturers and sellers for defects in the products they make and sell.

strict liability
A concept in product-liability law under which a manufacturer or seller is liable for any personal injury or property damage caused by defective products or packaging even though all possible care was used to prevent such defects.

Product liability refers to manufacturers' and sellers' responsibility for defects in the products they make and sell. It has become a specialized area of law combining aspects of contracts, warranties, torts, and statutory law (at both the state and federal levels). A product-liability suit may be based on negligence or strict liability (both of which are torts) or misrepresentation or breach of warranty (part of contract law).

An important concept in product-liability law is **strict liability.** A manufacturer or seller is liable for any personal injury or property damage caused by defective products or packaging—even if all possible care was used to prevent such defects. The definition of *defective* is quite broad. It includes manufacturing and design defects and inadequate instructions on product use or warnings of danger.

Product-liability suits are very costly. More than 100,000 product-liability suits were filed against hundreds of companies that made or used asbestos, a substance that causes lung disease and cancer but was once used widely in insulation, brake linings, textiles, and other products. Eighteen companies were forced into bankruptcy as a result of asbestos-related lawsuits, and the total cost of asbestos cases to defendants and their insurers exceeds $10 billion (most of which was paid not to the victims but to lawyers and experts).

Bankruptcy Law

bankruptcy
The legal procedure by which individuals or businesses that cannot meet their financial obligations are relieved of their debt.

Congress has given financially distressed firms and individuals a way to make a fresh start. **Bankruptcy** is the legal procedure by which individuals or businesses that cannot meet their financial obligations are relieved of their debts. A bankruptcy court distributes any assets to the creditors.

Bankruptcy can be either voluntary or involuntary. In a *voluntary bankruptcy,* the debtor files a petition with the court, stating that debts exceed assets and asking the court to declare the debtor bankrupt. In an *involuntary bankruptcy,* the creditors file the bankruptcy petition.

The *Bankruptcy Reform Act* of 1978, amended in 1984 and 1986, provides for the quick and efficient resolution of bankruptcy cases. Under this act, two types of bankruptcy proceedings are available to businesses: *Chapter 7* (liquidation) and *Chapter 11* (reorganization). Most bankruptcies, an estimated 70 percent, use Chapter 7. After the sale of any assets, the cash proceeds are given first to secured creditors and then to unsecured creditors. A firm that opts to reorganize under Chapter 11 works with its creditors to develop a plan for paying part of its debts and writing off the rest.

Laws to Promote Fair Competition

antitrust regulation
Laws that prevent companies from entering into agreements to control trade through a monopoly.

Many measures have been taken to try to keep the marketplace free from influences that would restrict competition. These efforts include **antitrust regulation,** laws that prevent companies from entering into agreements to control trade through a monopoly. The first act regulating competition was the *Sherman Antitrust Act,* passed in 1890 to prevent large companies from dominating an industry and making it hard for smaller firms to compete. This broad act banned monopolies and contracts, mergers, or conspiracies in restraint of trade. In 1914 the *Clayton Act* added to the more general provisions of the Sherman Antitrust Act. It outlawed the following:

- *Price discrimination.* Offering a customer discounts that are not offered to all other purchasers buying on similar terms.
- *Exclusive dealing.* Refusing to let the buyer purchase a competitor's products for resale.
- *Tying contracts.* Requiring buyers to purchase merchandise they may not want in order to get the products they do want.
- *Purchase of stock in competing corporations so as to lessen competition.* Buying competitors' stock in such quantity that competition is reduced.

The 1950 *Celler-Kefauver Act* amended the Clayton Act. It bans the purchase of one firm by another if the resulting merger decreases competition within the industry. As a result, all corporate acquisitions are subject to regulatory approval before they can be finalized. Most antitrust actions are taken by the U.S. Department of Justice, based on federal law. Violations of the antitrust acts are punishable by fines, imprisonment, or civil damage payments that can be as high as three times the actual damage amount. These outcomes give defendants an incentive to resolve cases.

The *Federal Trade Commission Act,* also passed in 1914, bans unfair trade practices. This act created the Federal Trade Commission (FTC), an independent five-member board with the power to define and monitor unfair trade practices, such as those prohibited by the Sherman and Clayton Acts. The FTC investigates complaints and can issue rulings called *cease-and-desist orders* to force companies to stop unfair business practices. Its powers have grown over the years. Today the FTC is one of the most important agencies regulating the competitive practices of business.

Regulation of Advertising and Pricing

A number of federal laws directly affect the promotion and pricing of products. The *Wheeler-Lea Act* of 1938 amended the Federal Trade Commission Act and gave the FTC authority to regulate advertising. The FTC monitors companies' advertisements for false or misleading claims.

The most important law in the area of pricing is the *Robinson-Patman Act,* a federal law passed in 1936 that tightened the Clayton Act's prohibitions against price discrimination. An exception is made for circumstances like discounts for quantity purchases, as long as the discounts do not lessen competition. But a manufacturer cannot sell at a lower price to one company just because that company buys all its merchandise from the manufacturer. Also, if one firm is offered quantity discounts, all firms buying that quantity of goods must get the discounts. The FTC and the antitrust division of the Justice Department monitor pricing.

Consumer Protection Laws

consumerism
A social movement that seeks to increase the rights and powers of buyers vis-à-vis sellers.

Consumerism reflects the struggle for power between buyers and sellers. Specifically, it is a social movement seeking to increase the rights and powers of buyers vis-à-vis sellers. Sellers' rights and powers include the following:

- To introduce into the marketplace any product, in any size and style, that is not hazardous to personal health or safety, or if it is hazardous, to introduce it with the proper warnings and controls.
- To price the product at any level they wish, provided they do not discriminate among similar classes of buyers.
- To spend any amount of money they wish to promote the product, so long as the promotion does not constitute unfair competition.
- To formulate any message they wish about the product, provided that it is not misleading or dishonest in content or execution.
- To introduce any buying incentives they wish.

Meanwhile, buyers have the following rights and powers:

- To refuse to buy any product that is offered to them.
- To expect products to be safe.
- To expect a product to be essentially as the seller represents it.
- To receive adequate information about the product.

Many laws have been passed to protect consumer rights. Exhibit 3A.2 lists the major consumer protection laws.

Deregulation of Industries

deregulation
The removal of rules and regulations governing business competition.

During the 1980s and 1990s, the U.S. government has actively promoted **deregulation,** the removal of rules and regulations governing business competition. Deregulation has drastically changed some once-regulated industries (especially the transportation, telecommunications, and financial services industries) and created many new competitors. The result has been entries into and exits from some industries. One of the latest industries to deregulate is the electric power industry. With almost 200 investor-owned electric utilities, it is the largest industry to be deregulated so far.

Despite the California experience, consumers typically benefit from deregulation. Increased competition often means lower prices. Businesses also benefit because they have more freedom to operate and can avoid the costs associated with government regulations. But more competition can also make it hard for small or weak firms to survive.

Regulation of the Internet

Although over 100 million Americans are signing onto the Web regularly, only a minority do so to purchase products. The majority of electronic commerce remains business-to-business transactions. Americans are still far more likely to get the latest news, rather than the latest fashions, in cyberspace. Yet there are clear successes: Amazon.com is America's biggest bookstore. EBay is a hugely successful auction site.

Exhibit 3A.2 Key Consumer Protection Laws

Mail Fraud Act (1872)	Makes it a federal crime to defraud consumers through use of the mail.
Pure Food and Drug Act (1906)	Created the Food and Drug Administration (FDA); protects consumers against the interstate sale of unsafe and adulterated foods and drugs.
Food, Drug, and Cosmetic Act (1938)	Expanded the power of the FDA to cover cosmetics and therapeutic devices and to establish standards for food products.
Flammable Fabrics Act (1953)	Prohibits sale or manufacture of clothing made of dangerously flammable fabric.
Child Protection Act (1966)	Prohibits sale of harmful toys and gives the FDA the right to remove dangerous products from the marketplace.
Cigarette Labeling Act (1965)	Requires cigarette manufacturers to put labels warning consumers about health hazards on cigarette packages.
Fair Packaging and Labeling Act (1966)	Regulates labeling and packaging of consumer products.
Consumer Credit Protection Act (Truth-in-Lending Act) (1968)	Requires lenders to fully disclose to borrowers the loan terms and the costs of borrowing (interest rate, application fees, etc.).
Fair Credit Reporting Act (1971)	Requires consumers denied credit on the basis of reports from credit agencies to be given access to their reports and to be allowed to correct inaccurate information.
Consumer Product Safety Act (1972)	Created the Consumer Product Safety Commission, an independent federal agency, to establish and enforce consumer product safety standards.
Equal Credit Opportunity Act (1975)	Prohibits denial of credit on the basis of gender, marital status, race, religion, age, or national origin.
Magnuson-Moss Warranty Act (1975)	Requires that warranties be written in clear language and that terms be fully disclosed.
Fair Debt Collection Practice Act (1978)	Makes it illegal to harass or abuse any person, to make false statements, or to use unfair methods when collecting a debt.
Alcohol Labeling Legislation (1988)	Provides for warning labels on liquor saying that women shouldn't drink when pregnant and that alcohol impairs our abilities.
Nutrition Labeling and Eduction Act (1990)	Requires truthful and uniform nutritional labeling on every food the FDA regulates.
Children's Television Act (1990)	Limits the amount of advertising to be shown during children's television programs to not more than 10.5 minutes per hour on weekends and not more than 12.0 minutes per hour on weekdays.
Americans with Disabilities Act (ADA) (1990)	Protects the rights of people with disabilities; makes discrimination against the disabled illegal in public accommodations, transportation, and telecommunications.
Brady Law (1998)	Imposes a 5-day waiting period and a background check before a gun purchaser can take possession of the gun.

Many states would like to tax commerce on the Internet. Washington, however, has promised to stop any such activity. In June 1997, the White House released "A Framework for Global Electronic Commerce," which advocated a minimalist approach to government intervention in electronic commerce. After providing a Universal Commercial Code for Electronic Commerce and protecting intellectual property, there's not much more for the government to do, according to the framework.

Taxation of Business

8 learning goal

Taxes are sometimes seen as the price we pay to live in this country. Taxes are assessed by all levels of government on both business and individuals, and they are used to pay for the services provided by government. The federal government is the largest collector of taxes, accounting for 54 percent of all tax dollars. States are next, followed closely by local government taxes. The average American family pays about 37 percent of its income for taxes, 28 percent to the federal government and 9 percent to state and local governments.

Income Taxes

income taxes
Taxes that are based on the income received by businesses and individuals.

Income taxes are based on the income received by businesses and individuals. The income taxes paid to the federal government are set by Congress, regulated by the Internal Revenue Code, and collected by the Internal Revenue Service. These taxes are *progressive,* meaning that rates increase as income increases. Most of the states and some large cities also collect income taxes from individuals and businesses. The state and local governments establish their own rules and tax rates.

Other Types of Taxes

Besides income taxes, individuals and businesses pay a number of other taxes. The four main types are property taxes, payroll taxes, sales taxes, and excise taxes.

property taxes
Taxes that are imposed on real and personal property based on the assessed value of the property.

Property taxes are assessed on real and personal property, based on the assessed value of the property. They raise quite a bit of revenue for state and local governments. Most states tax land and buildings. Property taxes may be based on fair market value (what a buyer would pay), a percentage of fair market value, or replacement value (what it would cost today to rebuild or buy something like the original). The value on which the taxes are based is the assessed value.

payroll taxes
The employer's share of Social Security taxes and federal and state unemployment taxes.

Any business that has employees and meets a payroll must pay **payroll taxes,** the employer's share of Social Security taxes and federal and state unemployment taxes. These taxes must be paid on wages, salaries, and commissions. State unemployment taxes are based on the number of employees in a firm who have become eligible for unemployment benefits. A firm that has never had an employee become eligible for unemployment will pay a low rate of state unemployment taxes. The firm's experience with employment benefits does not affect federal unemployment tax rates.

sales taxes
Taxes that are levied on goods when they are sold; calculated as a percentage of the price.

Sales taxes are levied on goods when they are sold and are a percentage of the sales price. These taxes are imposed by states, counties, and cities. They vary in amount and in what is considered taxable. Some states have no sales tax. Others tax some categories (such as appliances) but not others (such as clothes). Still others tax all retail products except food, magazines, and prescription drugs. Sales taxes increase the cost of goods to the consumer. Businesses bear the burden of collecting sales taxes and sending them to the government.

excise taxes
Taxes that are imposed on specific items such as gasoline, alcoholic beverages, airline tickets, and guns.

Excise taxes are placed on specific items, such as gasoline, alcoholic beverages, cigarettes, airline tickets, cars, and guns. They can be assessed by federal, state, and local governments. In many cases, these taxes help pay for services related to the item taxed. For instance, gasoline excise taxes are often used to build and repair highways. Other excise taxes—like those on alcoholic beverages, cigarettes, and guns—are used to control practices that may cause harm.

Chapter 4

© AP / WIDE WORLD PHOTOS

Competing in the Global Marketplace

learning goals

1 Why is global trade important to the United States and how is it measured?
2 Why do nations trade?
3 What are the barriers to international trade?
4 How do governments and institutions foster world trade?
5 What are international economic communities?
6 How do companies enter the global marketplace?
7 What threats and opportunities exist in the global marketplace?
8 What are the advantages of multinational corporations?
9 What are the trends in the global marketplace?

The Viennese Lap Up Starbucks

It takes some hubris to bring an American coffee shop to Vienna, the city of cafés, and then to ban smoking in it. But no one has ever considered Starbucks (**http://www.starbucks.com**) humble. And the move, a keystone of Starbucks's rapid expansion in Europe, appears to have paid off. Since the Karntnerstrasse coffeehouse opened in December 2001, in the smoky, beating heart of Vienna, near the Opera House, it has been a resounding success.

Many Viennese believe that their culture has been infected, that Viennese use their 1,900 or so coffee shops to linger and meet, smoke and drink, savor the wonders of pastries with cream and marzipan, ponder the world, write books and read free newspapers. They drink from china cups and order from a waiter, usually in a stained black dinner jacket.

Some Austrians say a caramel macchiato is worse than a Coca-Cola, likely to do more damage to European values (and waistlines) than a Big Mac. There was also skepticism about the Starbucks brand, associated with globalization and mass American culture. "It was the hardest part," said Franz Holzschuh, who leads the Starbucks joint venture in Austria. "People would say, 'You're the McDonald's of coffee, with paper cups.' I'd explain a hundred times that we're not McDonald's, that we're high quality and not cheap, and only use paper cups to go."

The smoking issue loomed large as well. Holzschuh, a heavy smoker, originally argued that no Austrian coffee shop could possibly ban cigarettes. "Some 40 percent of Europeans smoke and 60 percent of Italians," he said. "That's half your market!" Starbucks's American bosses were unfazed. "They said that we have 3,000 nonsmoking stores and the 3,001st will be nonsmoking too." Holzschuh conceded, but kept thinking, "OK, friends, let's wait and see."

In Austria, there is a coffeehouse for every 530 people, and Austrians drink 1,000 cups of coffee a year outside homes and offices. This is, quite simply, the densest coffee market in the world. One of the most competitive, too. "Austrians love their coffee," Holzschuh said. "We go three or four times a day to a coffeehouse to meet friends or do business."[1]

Critical Thinking Questions

1. What are some factors that can make success difficult in the global marketplace?
2. What can governments do to protect domestic competitors from firms like Starbucks?
3. What cultural differences should Starbucks consider when entering other European markets?

Principles of Global Competition

Today, global revolutions are under way in many areas of our lives: management, politics, communications, technology. The word *global* has assumed a new meaning, referring to a boundless mobility and competition in social, business, and intellectual arenas. No longer just an option, having a global vision has become a business imperative. Having a **global vision** means recognizing and reacting to international business opportunities, being aware of threats from foreign competitors in all markets, and effectively using international distribution networks to obtain raw materials and move finished products to the customer.

global vision
The ability to recognize and react to international business opportunities, be aware of threats from foreign competition, and effectively use international distribution networks to obtain raw materials and move finished products to customers.

U.S. managers must develop a global vision if they are to recognize and react to international business opportunities, as well as remain competitive at home. Often a U.S. firm's toughest domestic competition comes from foreign companies. Moreover, a global vision enables a manager to understand that customer and distribution networks operate worldwide, blurring geographic and political barriers and making them increasingly irrelevant to business decisions. The purpose of this chapter is to explain how global trade is conducted. We also discuss the barriers to international trade and the organizations that foster global trade. The chapter concludes with trends in the global marketplace.

America Goes Global

1 learning goal

Over the past two decades, world trade has climbed from $200 billion a year to more than $4 trillion. Countries and companies that were never considered major players in global markets are now contributing to this growth in world trade. Gillette, for example, derives two-thirds of its revenue from its international division. Although this has contributed tremendously to the company's growth, it has also opened the company to new problems.

A few years ago Gillette was unable to meet its 20 percent annual profit growth goal because of recessions in Asia. At the same time, global financial turmoil also presents opportunities to buy small consumer products companies outside the United States at a very good price. Gillette has agreed to an extensive licensing and

© AP / WIDE WORLD PHOTOS

On the Champ Elysees, this McDonald's is the most frequented restaurant in France. Designed to appeal to local customers, the restaurant offers a cozy Parisian atmosphere.

supply arrangement with Rocket Electric Co., one of South Korea's largest battery makers. For a payment of about $60 million, Gillette effectively doubled its share of the world's 10th-largest battery market, to about 22 percent. Although best known as a maker of razors, Gillette bought battery maker Duracell International, Inc. and is now a world leader in that industry as well.[2]

Go into a Paris McDonald's and you may not recognize where you are. There are no Golden Arches or utilitarian chairs and tables and other plastic features. The restaurants have exposed brick walls, hardwood floors, and armchairs. Some French McDonald's even have faux marble walls. Most restaurants have TVs with continuous music videos. You can even order an espresso, beer, and chicken on focaccia bread sandwich. It's not America.[3]

Global business is not a one-way street, where only U.S. companies sell their wares and services throughout the world. Foreign competition in the domestic market used to be relatively rare but now occurs in almost every industry. In fact, U.S. makers of electronic goods, cameras, automobiles, fine china, tractors, leather goods, and a host of other consumer and industrial products have struggled to maintain their domestic market shares against foreign competitors. Nevertheless, the global market has created vast, new business opportunities for many U.S. firms.

The Importance of Global Business to the United States

Many countries depend more on international commerce than the United States does. For example, France, Great Britain, and Germany all derive more than 19 percent of their gross domestic product (GDP) from world trade, compared to about 12 percent for the United States. Nevertheless, the impact of international business on the U.S. economy is still impressive:

- The United States exports about a fifth of its industrial production and a third of its farm products.
- One of every 16 jobs in the United States is directly or indirectly supported by exports.
- U.S. businesses export over $731 billion in goods to foreign countries every year, and almost a third of U.S. corporate profits is derived from international trade and foreign investment.
- Exports account for almost one-third of America's economic growth.
- Chemicals, office machinery, computers, automobiles, aircraft, and electrical and industrial machinery make up almost half of all nonagricultural exports.[4]

These statistics might seem to imply that practically every business in the United States is selling its wares throughout the world, but nothing could be further from the truth. About 85 percent of all U.S. exports of manufactured goods are shipped by 250 companies. Only the very large multinational companies have seriously attempted to compete worldwide. Fortunately, more small companies are now aggressively pursuing international markets.

The Impact of Terrorism on Global Trade

The terrorist attacks on America on September 11 changed forever the way the world conducts business. The immediate impact was a short-term shrinkage of global trade. Globalization will continue because the world's major markets are too vitally integrated for globalization to stop. Nevertheless, the growth will be slower and costlier.

Companies are paying more for insurance and to provide security for overseas staff and property. Heightened border inspections slow movements of cargo, forcing companies to stock more inventory. Tighter immigration policies curtail the

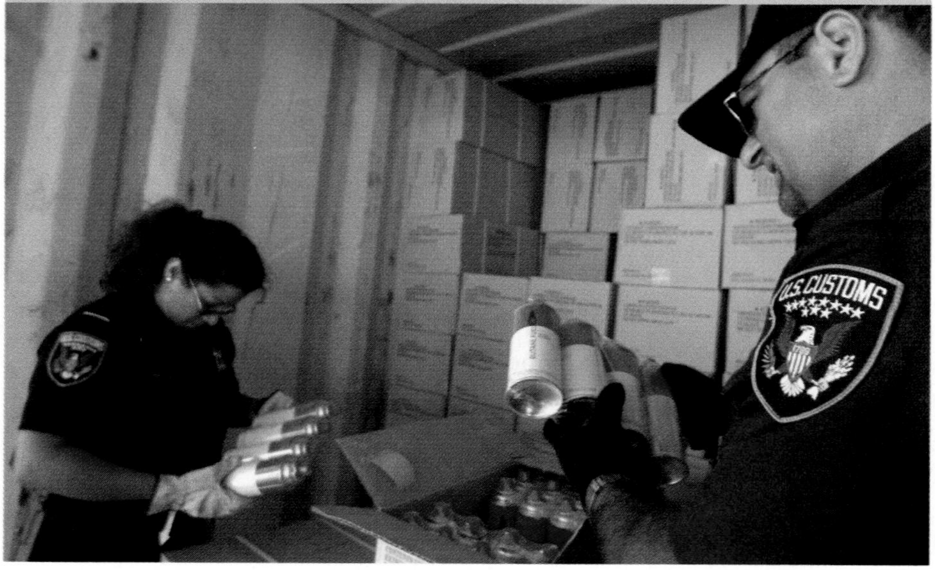

© AP / WIDE WORLD PHOTOS

Increased security measures, as a result of terrorist threats, slow the movement of cargo and increase shipping costs.

liberal inflows of skilled and blue-collar workers that allowed companies to expand while keeping wages in check. Meanwhile, greater concern about political risk is causing companies to greatly narrow their horizons when making new investments.[5] The impact of terrorism will lessen over time, but multinational firms will always be on guard.

Measuring Trade Between Nations

International trade improves relationships with friends and allies, helps ease tensions among nations, and—economically speaking—bolsters economies, raises people's standard of living, provides jobs, and improves the quality of life. The value of international trade is over $4.6 trillion a year and growing. This section takes a look at some key measures of international trade: exports and imports, the balance of trade, the balance of payments, and exchange rates.

Exports and Imports

exports
Goods and services produced in one country and sold in other countries.

imports
Goods and services that are bought from other countries.

The developed nations (those with mature communication, financial, educational, and distribution systems) are the major players in international trade. They account for about 70 percent of the world's exports and imports. **Exports** are goods and services made in one country and sold to others. **Imports** are goods and services that are bought from other countries. The United States is both the largest exporter and the largest importer in the world. During a four-year period ending in 2000, U.S. exports accounted for almost one-third of U.S. economic growth and 2.6 million additional American jobs. Exports support more than 12 million U.S. jobs.[6]

Each year the United States exports more food, animal feed, and beverages than the year before. A third of U.S. farm acreage is devoted to crops for export. The United States is also a major exporter of engineering products and other high-tech goods, such as computers and telecommunications equipment. For more than 40,000 U.S. companies (the majority of them small), international trade offers exciting and profitable opportunities. Among the largest U.S. exporters are Boeing Co., General Motors Corp., General Electric Co., Ford Motor Co., and IBM.

Despite our impressive list of resources and great variety of products, imports to the United States are also growing. Some of these imports are raw materials that we lack, such as manganese, cobalt, and bauxite, which are used to make airplane

Making Ethical Choices

xtra! http://gitmanxtra.swlearning.com

BRIBERY: JUST A COST OF DOING BUSINESS?

You serve as chief legal officer of a well-respected company that makes life-saving drugs. When the board requests your help drafting the company's strong ethics policy you are pleased to comply.

Shortly thereafter you start hearing rumors about "the Bosnia contract" and decide to investigate. You discover that the contract, to supply a million inexpensive medicine kits to war-torn regions of Bosnia, is like most of your firm's contracts with relief organizations, providing hardly any profit for your firm. But you do find it strange that a very large sum of money has been paid to a Romanian distributor to deliver the kits deep into Bosnia.

Seeking out the company executive who negotiated the contract you have one question for him—is the money a bribe of some kind? He tells you that according to the Romanian distributor, the money is needed to pay off local militia units when drivers are stopped at roadblocks. He claims that drivers without cash are taken from their trucks and shot. If the kits are to be delivered, this is a cost of doing business.

You are able to confirm through an internal investigation that none of the money has flowed back to the executive, whose only motive in agreeing to the cash payment was to get the kits delivered. And by this time the deliveries have been made. As a compassionate human being, you believe that providing medicine for the wounded is of overriding importance. But you also know that bribery, under any circumstances, is unacceptable to the board. After all, you helped draft the ethics policy yourself.

ETHICAL DILEMMA

Are you obligated to report to the board on this unorthodox contract, or should you keep silent since the delivery of medicine has already occurred?

SOURCES: "Getting Medicine to Bosnia: Acceptable Bribery?" Right vs. Right Ethical Dilemmas, Institute for Global Ethics, downloaded from http://www.globalethics.org February 25, 2003.

parts, exotic metals, and military hardware. More modern factories and lower labor costs in other countries make it cheaper to import industrial supplies (like steel) and production equipment than to produce them at home. Most of Americans' favorite hot beverages—coffee, tea, and cocoa—are imported.

Balance of Trade

balance of trade
The difference between the value of a country's exports and the value of its imports during a certain time.

trade surplus
A favorable balance of trade that occurs when a country exports more than it imports.

trade deficit
An unfavorable balance of trade that occurs when a country imports more than it exports.

The difference between the value of a country's exports and the value of its imports during a certain time is the country's **balance of trade.** A country that exports more than it imports is said to have a *favorable* balance of trade, called a **trade surplus.** A country that imports more than it exports is said to have an *unfavorable* balance of trade, or a **trade deficit.** When imports exceed exports, more money from trade flows out of the country than flows into it.

Although U.S. exports have been booming, we still import more than we export. We have had an unfavorable balance of trade throughout the 1990s and 2000s. In 2002 the United States had a trade deficit of approximately $330 billion.[7] Part of the problem is that most U.S. companies still avoid the export market. Many medium-size and small producers think "going global" is more trouble than it's worth. And as we've seen, Americans are buying more foreign goods than ever before. As long as we continue to import more than we export, the United States will continue to have a trade deficit.

Balance of Payments

balance of payments
A summary of a country's international financial transactions showing the difference between the country's total payments to and its total receipts from other countries.

Another measure of international trade is called the **balance of payments,** which is a summary of a country's international financial transactions showing the difference between the country's total payments to and its total receipts from other countries. The balance of payments includes imports and exports (balance of trade), long-term investments in overseas plants and equipment, government loans to and from other countries, gifts and foreign aid, military expenditures made in other countries, and money transfers in and out of foreign banks.

From 1900 until 1970, the United States had a trade surplus, but in the other areas that make up the balance of payments, U.S. payments exceeded receipts, largely due to the large U.S. military presence abroad. Hence, almost every year since 1950, the United States has had an unfavorable balance of payments. And since 1970, both the balance of payments *and* the balance of trade have been unfavorable. What can a nation do to reduce an unfavorable balance of payments? It can foster exports, reduce its dependence on imports, decrease its military presence abroad, or reduce foreign investment. The U.S. balance of payments deficit was over $450 billion in 2002.[8]

The Changing Value of Currencies

The exchange rate is the price of one country's currency in terms of another country's currency. If a country's currency *appreciates,* less of that country's currency is needed to buy another country's currency. If a country's currency *depreciates,* more of that currency will be needed to buy another country's currency.

How do appreciation and depreciation affect the prices of a country's goods? If, say, the U.S. dollar depreciates relative to the Japanese yen, U.S. residents have to pay more dollars to buy Japanese goods. To illustrate, suppose the dollar price of a yen is $0.012 and that a Toyota is priced at 2 million yen. At this exchange rate, a U.S. resident pays $24,000 for a Toyota ($0.012 × 2 million yen = $24,000). If the dollar depreciates to $0.018 to one yen, then the U.S. resident will have to pay $36,000 for a Toyota.

floating exchange rates
A system in which prices of currencies move up and down based upon the demand for and supply of the various currencies.

devaluation
A lowering of the value of a nation's currency relative to other currencies.

As the dollar depreciates, the prices of Japanese goods rise for U.S. residents, so they buy fewer Japanese goods—thus, U.S. imports decline. At the same time, as the dollar depreciates relative to the yen, the yen appreciates relative to the dollar. This means prices of U.S. goods fall for the Japanese, so they buy more U.S. goods—and U.S. exports rise.

Currency markets operate under a system called **floating exchange rates.** Prices of currencies "float" up and down based upon the demand for and supply of each currency. Global currency traders create the supply of and demand for a particular currency based on that currency's investment, trade potential, and economic strength. If a country decides that its currency is not properly valued in international currency markets, the government may step in and adjust the currency's value. In a **devaluation,** a nation lowers the value of its currency relative to other currencies. In August 1998, Russia devalued the ruble by 34 percent. A month later, Colombia and Ecuador also devalued their currencies but by much less than Russia. Russia not only devalued its currency but also restructured government short-term debt to long term and imposed strict financial controls on Russian banks and companies. As a result, companies and banks could not meet their foreign debt obligations.

concept check

What is global vision, and why is it important?

What impact does international trade have on the U.S. economy?

Explain the impact of a currency devaluation.

Why Nations Trade

2 learning goal

One might argue that the best way to protect workers and the domestic economy is to stop trade with other nations. Then the whole circular flow of inputs and outputs would stay within our borders. But if we decided to do that, how would we get resources like cobalt and coffee beans? The United States simply can't produce some things, and it can't manufacture some products, such as steel and most clothing, at the low costs we're used to. The fact is that nations—like people—are good at producing different things: you may be better at balancing a ledger than repairing a car. In that case you benefit by "exporting" your bookkeeping services and "importing" the car repairs you need from a good mechanic. Economists refer to specialization like this as *advantage.*

Absolute Advantage

absolute advantage
The situation when a country can produce and sell a product at a lower cost than any other country or when it is the only country that can provide the product.

A country has an **absolute advantage** when it can produce and sell a product at a lower cost than any other country or when it is the only country that can provide a product. The United States, for example, has an absolute advantage in reusable spacecraft and other high-tech items.

Suppose that the United States has an absolute advantage in air traffic control systems for busy airports and that Brazil has an absolute advantage in coffee. The United States does not have the proper climate for growing coffee, and Brazil lacks the technology to develop air traffic control systems. Both countries would gain by exchanging air traffic control systems for coffee.

Comparative Advantage

principle of comparative advantage
The concept that each country should specialize in the products that it can produce most readily and cheaply and trade those products for those that other countries can produce more readily and cheaply.

Even if the United States had an absolute advantage in both coffee and air traffic control systems, it should still specialize and engage in trade. Why? The reason is the **principle of comparative advantage,** which says that each country should specialize in the products that it can produce most readily and cheaply and trade those products for goods that foreign countries can produce most readily and cheaply. This specialization ensures greater product availability and lower prices.

For example, Mexico and China have a comparative advantage in producing clothing because of low labor costs. Japan has long held a comparative advantage in consumer electronics because of technological expertise. America has an advantage in computer software, airplanes, some agricultural products, heavy machinery, and jet engines.

free trade
The policy of permitting the people of a country to buy and sell where they please without restrictions.

protectionism
The policy of protecting home industries from outside competition by establishing artificial barriers such as tariffs and quotas.

Thus, comparative advantage acts as a stimulus to trade. When nations allow their citizens to trade whatever goods and services they choose without government regulation, free trade exists. **Free trade** is the policy of permitting the people of a country to buy and sell where they please without restrictions. The opposite of free trade is **protectionism,** in which a nation protects its home industries from outside competition by establishing artificial barriers such as tariffs and quotas. In the next section, we'll look at the various barriers, some natural and some created by governments, that restrict free trade.

The Fear of Trade and Globalization

The protests in Seattle and Genoa during meetings of the World Trade Organization and the protests in New York during the convocation of the World Bank and the International Monetary Fund (the three organizations are discussed later in the chapter) showed that many people fear world trade and globalization. What do they fear? The negatives of global trade are as follows:

- Millions of Americans have lost jobs due to imports or production shifts abroad. Most find new jobs, but those jobs often pay less.
- Millions of others fear losing their jobs, especially at those companies operating under competitive pressure.
- Employers often threaten to export jobs if workers do not accept pay cuts.
- Service and white-collar jobs are increasingly vulnerable to operations moving offshore.[9]

Benefits of Globalization

A closer look, however, reveals that globalization has been the engine that creates jobs and wealth. Benefits of global trade include:

- In China and the rest of East Asia, more people rose out of poverty between 1990 and 2000 than the entire population of the United States. The main reason was global trade.[10]
- In Africa, with its many developing economies, per capita income rose 3.6 percent per year during the 1990s, double the 1.8 percent of developed countries, and trade was the single biggest reason.[11]
- Productivity grows more quickly when countries produce goods and services in which they have a comparative advantage. Living standards can go up faster.
- Global competition and cheap imports keep down prices, so inflation is less likely to arrest economic growth.
- An open economy spurs innovation with fresh ideas from abroad.
- Export jobs often pay more than other jobs.[12]
- Relatively few American workers are in direct competition with workers from poorer countries. Most U.S. workers produce goods and services for industries that face little cross-border competition, such as healthcare and construction.[13]

concept check

Describe the policy of free trade and its relationship to comparative advantage.

Why do people fear globalization?

What are the benefits of globalization?

Barriers to Trade

3 learning goal

International trade is carried out by both businesses and governments—as long as no one puts up trade barriers. In general, trade barriers keep firms from selling to one another in foreign markets. The major obstacles to international trade are natural barriers, tariff barriers, and nontariff barriers.

Natural Barriers

Natural barriers to trade can be either physical or cultural. For instance, even though raising beef in the relative warmth of Argentina may cost less than raising beef in the bitter cold of Siberia, the cost of shipping the beef from South America to Siberia might drive the price too high. *Distance* is thus one of the natural barriers to international trade.

Language is another natural trade barrier. People who can't communicate effectively may not be able to negotiate trade agreements or may ship the wrong goods.

Tariff Barriers

A **tariff** is a tax imposed by a nation on imported goods. It may be a charge per unit, such as per barrel of oil or per new car; it may be a percentage of the value of the goods, such as 5 percent of a $500,000 shipment of shoes; or it may be a combination. No matter how it is assessed, any tariff makes imported goods more costly, so they are less able to compete with domestic products.

Protective tariffs make imported products less attractive to buyers than domestic products. The United States, for instance, has protective tariffs on imported poultry, textiles, sugar, and some types of steel and clothing. On the other side of the world, Japan imposes a tariff on U.S. cigarettes that makes them cost 60 percent more than Japanese brands. U.S. tobacco firms believe they could get as much as a third of the Japanese market if there were no tariffs on cigarettes. With tariffs, they have under 2 percent of the market.

tariff
A tax imposed on imported goods.

protective tariffs
Tariffs that are imposed in order to make imports less attractive to buyers than domestic products are.

© DOUG WILSON / CORBIS

Tariffs on the imported goods arriving on this foreign ship at a port in Seattle, Washington, make the products more expensive than those of U.S. competitors.

Arguments for and Against Tariffs. Congress has debated the issue of tariffs since 1789. The main arguments *for* tariffs include the following:

- Tariffs protect infant industries. A tariff can give a struggling new domestic industry time to become an effective global competitor.
- Tariffs protect American jobs. Unions, and others, say tariffs keep foreign labor from taking away U.S. jobs. More than 200,000 U.S. manufacturing jobs have been lost since 1997 because of high American wages.
- Tariffs aid in military preparedness. Tariffs should protect industries and technology during peacetime that are vital to the military in the event of war.

The main arguments *against* tariffs include the following:

- Tariffs discourage free trade and free trade lets the principle of competitive advantage work most efficiently.
- Tariffs raise prices, thereby decreasing consumers' purchasing power. President Bush imposed tariffs of 8 percent to 30 pecent on a wide variety of steel products. The idea was to give U.S. steel manufacturers time to modernize to better compete in the global marketplace. Within six months of imposing the tariffs, the U.S. price of cold rolled steel jumped from $210 a ton to $350 a ton. The result is that heavy users of steel, such as construction and automobile industries, have seen big increases in their costs of production.[14]

Nontariff Barriers

import quota
A limit on the quantity of a certain good that can be imported.

Governments also use other tools besides tariffs to restrict trade. One type of nontariff barrier is the **import quota** or limits on the quantity of a certain good that can be imported. The goal of setting quotas is to limit imports to the optimum amount of a given product. America protects its shrinking textile industry with quotas.

The Trade and Development Act of 2000 was passed to help economically struggling sub-Saharan African nations and Caribbean countries by bypassing U.S. textile quotas. The bill grants these nations "quota-free access for clothing assembled for U.S. companies." Without quotas, big U.S. clothing manufacturers have a great incentive to move work to those nations. In effect, the bill moves textile assembly from low-cost Asian countries to those favored under the new law.[15]

embargo
A total ban on imports or exports of a product.

A complete ban against importing or exporting a product is an **embargo.** Often embargoes are set up for defense purposes. For instance, the United States does not allow various high-tech products, such as supercomputers and lasers, to be exported to countries that are not allies. Although this embargo costs U.S. firms billions of dollars each year in lost sales, it keeps enemies from using the latest technology in their military hardware.

buy-national regulations
Government rules that give special privileges to domestic manufacturers and retailers.

customs regulations
Nonstandardized product rules and specifications created to block imports.

Government rules that give special privileges to domestic manufacturers and retailers are called **buy-national regulations.** One such regulation in the United States bans the use of foreign steel in constructing U.S. highways. Many state governments have buy-national rules for supplies and services. In a more subtle move, a country may make it hard for foreign products to enter its markets by establishing **customs regulations** that are different from generally accepted international standards, such as requiring bottles to be quart size rather than liter size. The French seem most adept at using this tactic. For example, to reduce imports of foreign VCRs, at one time France ruled that all VCRs had to enter through the customs station at Poitiers. This customs house is located in the middle of the country, was woefully understaffed, and was open only a few days each week. What's more, the few customs agents at Poitiers opened each package separately to inspect the merchandise. Within a few weeks, imports of VCRs in France came to a halt.

exchange controls
Laws that require a company earning foreign exchange (foreign currency) from its exports to sell the foreign exchange to a control agency, such as a central bank.

Exchange controls are laws that require a company earning foreign exchange (foreign currency) from its exports to sell the foreign exchange to a control agency, usually a central bank. For example, assume that Rolex, a Swiss company, sells 300 watches to Zales Jewelers, a U.S. chain, for $120,000 (U.S.). If Switzerland had exchange controls, Rolex would have to sell its U.S. dollars to the Swiss central bank and would receive Swiss francs. If Rolex wants to buy goods from abroad, it must go to the central bank and buy foreign exchange (currency). By controlling the amount of foreign exchange sold to companies, the government controls the amount of products that can be imported. Limiting imports and encouraging exports helps a government to create a favorable balance of trade.

concept check

Discuss the concept of natural trade barriers.

Describe several tariff and nontariff barriers to trade.

Fostering Global Trade

4 learning goal

From our discussion so far, it might seem that governments act only to restrain global trade. On the contrary, governments and international financial organizations work hard to increase it, as this section explains.

Antidumping Laws

dumping
The practice of charging a lower price for a product in foreign markets than in the firm's home market.

U.S. firms don't always get to compete on an equal basis with foreign firms in international trade. To level the playing field, Congress has passed antidumping laws. **Dumping** is the practice of charging a lower price for a product (perhaps below cost) in foreign markets than in the firm's home market. The company might be trying to win foreign customers, or it might be seeking to get rid of surplus goods.

When the variation in price can't be explained by differences in the cost of serving the two markets, dumping is suspected. Most industrialized countries have antidumping regulations. They are especially concerned about *predatory dumping*, the attempt to gain control of a foreign market by destroying competitors with impossibly low prices. Many businesspeople feel that Japan has engaged in predatory dumping of semiconductors in the U.S. market.

One of the most famous dumping cases in U.S. history involved Japanese color television sets during the 1960s and 1970s. In 1971 U.S. television makers filed a complaint, alleging that Japanese television makers were selling below cost and offering distributors rebates, while also restricting imports into Japan. The Treasury Department, which then enforced the antidumping laws, took no action for three years and then failed to collect duties even though it had determined that dumping was occurring. The U.S. television industry was effectively destroyed. Today, there are no U.S.-owned television makers. As a result of that experience, Congress transferred the authority to enforce antidumping laws from the Treasury Department to the Commerce Department.

The Uruguay Round and the World Trade Organization

Uruguay Round
A 1994 agreement by 117 nations to lower trade barriers worldwide.

The **Uruguay Round** of trade negotiations is an agreement to dramatically lower trade barriers worldwide. Adopted in 1994, the agreement has been now signed by 142 nations. The most ambitious global trade agreement ever negotiated, the

Uruguay Round reduced tariffs by one-third worldwide, a move that is expected to increase global income by $235 billion annually. Perhaps the most notable aspect of the agreement is its recognition of new global realities. For the first time, an agreement covers services, intellectual-property rights, and trade-related investment measures such as exchange controls.

World Trade Organization (WTO)
An organization established by the Uruguay Round in 1994 to oversee international trade, reduce trade barriers, and resolve disputes among member nations.

The **World Trade Organization (WTO)** replaces the old General Agreement on Tariffs and Trade (GATT), which was created in 1948. The GATT contained extensive loopholes that enabled countries to evade agreements to reduce trade barriers. Today, all WTO members must fully comply with all agreements under the Uruguay Round. The WTO also has an effective dispute settlement procedure with strict time limits to resolve disputes.

The WTO has emerged as the world's most powerful institution for reducing trade barriers and opening markets. The advantage of WTO membership is that member countries lower trade barriers among themselves. Countries that don't belong must negotiate trade agreements individually with all their trading partners. To date, Russia is the largest country that has not qualified for WTO membership.

The United States has had mixed results in bringing disputes before the WTO. To date, it has won slightly less than half of the cases it has presented to the WTO. America has also won about one-third of the cases brought against it by other countries. One of America's biggest losses came when a WTO panel ruled that the Japanese government's attempt to protect Fuji Film from competition by Kodak was not illegal. Recently, the United States targeted Europe, India, South Korea, Canada, and Argentina to file cases against. The disputes ranged from European aviation practices to Indian barriers affecting U.S. automakers.

The World Bank and International Monetary Fund

World Bank
An international bank that offers low-interest loans, as well as advice and information, to developing nations.

Two international financial organizations are instrumental in fostering global trade. The **World Bank** offers low-interest loans to developing nations. Originally, the purpose of the loans was to help these nations build infrastructure such as roads, power plants, schools, drainage projects, and hospitals. Now the World Bank offers loans to help developing nations relieve their debt burdens. To receive the loans, countries must pledge to lower trade barriers and aid private enterprise. In addition to making loans, the World Bank is a major source of advice and information for developing nations. The United States has granted the organization millions to create knowledge databases on nutrition, birth control, software engineering, creating quality products, and basic accounting systems.

International Monetary Fund (IMF)
An international organization, founded in 1945, that promotes trade, makes short-term loans to member nations, and acts as a lender of last resort for troubled nations.

The **International Monetary Fund (IMF)** was founded in 1945, one year after the creation of the World Bank, to promote trade through financial cooperation and eliminate trade barriers in the process. The IMF makes short-term loans to member nations that are unable to meet their budgetary expenses. It operates as a lender of last resort for troubled nations. In exchange for these emergency loans, IMF lenders frequently extract significant commitments from the borrowing nations to address the problems that led to the crises. These steps may include curtailing imports or even devaluing the currency.

Some global financial problems do not have a simple solution. One option would be to pump a lot more funds into the IMF, giving it enough resources to bail out troubled countries and put them back on their feet. In effect, the IMF would be turned into a real lender of last resort for the world economy.

The danger of counting on the IMF, though, is the "moral hazard" problem. Investors would assume that the IMF would bail them out and would therefore be encouraged to take bigger and bigger risks in emerging markets, leading to the possibility of even deeper financial crises in the future.

concept check

Describe the purpose and role of the WTO.

What are the roles of the World Bank and the IMF in world trade?

International Economic Communities

5 learning goal

preferential tariff
A tariff that is lower for some nations than for others.

free-trade zone
An area where the nations allow free, or almost free, trade among each other while imposing tariffs on goods of nations outside the zone.

North American Free Trade Agreement (NAFTA)
A 1993 agreement creating a free-trade zone including Canada, Mexico, and the United States.

Mercosur
Trade agreement between Peru, Brazil, Argentina, Uruguay, and Paraguay.

European Union
Trade agreement among fifteen European nations.

Nations that frequently trade with each other may decide to formalize their relationship. The governments meet and work out agreements for a common economic policy. The result is an economic community or, in other cases, a bilateral trade agreement (an agreement between two countries to lower trade barriers). For example, two nations may agree upon a **preferential tariff,** which gives advantages to one nation (or several nations) over others. When members of the British Commonwealth trade with Great Britain, they pay lower tariffs than do other nations. In other cases, nations may form free-trade associations. In a **free-trade zone,** few duties or rules restrict trade among the partners, but nations outside the zone must pay the tariffs set by the individual members.

North American Free Trade Agreement (NAFTA)

The **North American Free Trade Agreement (NAFTA)** created the world's largest free-trade zone. The agreement was ratified by the U.S. Congress in 1993. It includes Canada, the United States, and Mexico, with a combined population of 360 million and an economy of over $6 trillion.

Canada, the largest U.S. trading partner, entered a free-trade agreement with the United States in 1988. Thus, most of the new long-run opportunities opened for U.S. business under NAFTA are in Mexico, America's third largest trading partner. Before NAFTA, tariffs on Mexican exports to the United States averaged just 4 percent, and most goods entered the United States duty-free, so NAFTA's primary impact was to open the Mexican market to U.S. companies. When the treaty went into effect, tariffs on about half the items traded across the Rio Grande disappeared. Since NAFTA came into effect, U.S.–Mexican trade has increased by 250 percent, from $80 billion to $250 billion annually.[16] The pact removed a web of Mexican licensing requirements, quotas, and tariffs that limited transactions in U.S. goods and services. For instance, the pact allows U.S. and Canadian financial-services companies to own subsidiaries in Mexico for the first time in 50 years.

The real test of NAFTA will be whether it can deliver rising prosperity on both sides of the Rio Grande. For Mexicans, NAFTA must provide rising wages, better benefits, and an expanding middle class with enough purchasing power to keep buying goods from the United States and Canada. As of 2002, that scenario was working. Between 1993 and 2001, U.S. exports to Mexico rose 170 percent, far above the 68 percent for overall U.S. exports. Mexican exports to the United States grew 241 percent during the same period.[17] NAFTA, to date, has been very successful, displacing some workers but creating far more jobs than have been lost.

The largest new trade agreement is **Mercosur,** which includes Peru, Brazil, Argentina, Uruguay, and Paraguay. The elimination of most tariffs among the trading partners has resulted in trade revenues that currently exceed $16 billion annually. Recent recessions, in Mercosur countries, have limited economic growth, even though trade among Mercosur countries has continued to grow.

The European Union

In 1993, the member countries of the European Community (EC) ratified the Maastricht Treaty, which proposed to take the EC further toward economic, monetary, and political union. Although the heart of the treaty deals with developing a unified European Market, Maastricht was also intended to increase integration among **European Union (EU)** members.

The EU has helped increase this integration by creating a borderless economy for these 15 European nations, shown on the map in Exhibit 4.1:

Exhibit 4.1 The European Union Gets Bigger

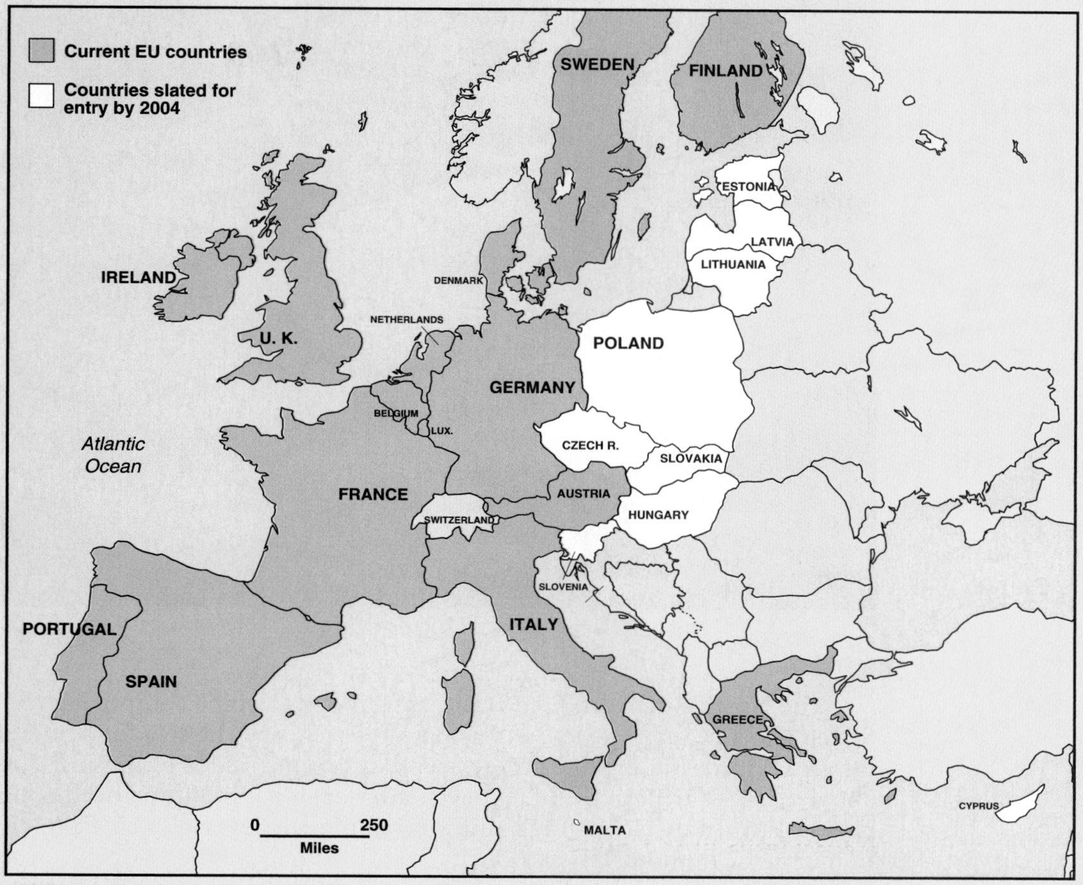

Belgium	Luxembourg
Denmark	The Netherlands
Germany	Austria
Greece	Portugal
Spain	Finland
France	Sweden
Ireland	United Kingdom
Italy	

One of the principal objectives of the European Union is to promote economic progress of all member countries. The EU has stimulated economic progress by eliminating trade barriers, differences in tax laws, and differences in product standards, and by establishing a common currency. A new European Community Bank was created along with a common currency called the euro. Together, the members of the EU have a $6.4 trillion economy, the second largest in the world.

© MATTHIAS KULKA / CORBIS

The eurodollar replaces the individual currencies of twelve European Union nations. The new common currency enables the countries to do business as a single trading bloc.

The North American Free Trade Agreement, the bloc comprising the United States, Canada, and Mexico, will remain the richer of the two for some time: total gross domestic product there stood at around $11.4 trillion in 2001, well above the $8.4 trillion of the EU even after expansion. But by head count a 25-nation European bloc of 444 million people will overtake NAFTA, currently home to 387 million.[18]

American businesses have recently been stung by aggressive antitrust actions taken by the European Commission, the European Union's executive branch. By EU law, the Commission must review any merger or acquisition involving any companies with significant revenues in the European Union. Thus, the Commission threatened to block AOL's acquisition of Time Warner unless Virgin Records was sold first. It was. The biggest action to date was denying the merger of General Electric with Honeywell, both U.S. firms. Even Jack Welch, the legendary former General Electric CEO, could not persuade the European Commission to let the merger go through.

The European Commission also sets product standards and plays a role in consumer protection. Because of the EU, Microsoft Corp. has modified contracts with software makers and Internet-service providers to give consumers a wider choice of technologies, and McDonald's Corp. has stopped serving soft-plastic toys with its Happy Meals.[19]

An entirely different type of problem facing global businesses is the possibility of a protectionist movement by the EU against outsiders. For example, European automakers have proposed holding Japanese imports at roughly their current 10 percent market share. The Irish, Danes, and Dutch don't make cars and have unrestricted home markets; they are unhappy at the prospect of limited imports of Toyotas and Hondas. Meanwhile France has a strict quota on Japanese cars to protect its own Renault and Peugeot. These local automarkers could be hurt if the quota is raised at all.

Interestingly, a number of big U.S. companies are already considered more "European" than many European companies. Coke and Kellogg's are considered

concept check

Explain the pros and cons of NAFTA.

What is the European Union? Will it ever be a United States of Europe?

classic European brand names. Ford and General Motors compete for the largest share of auto sales on the continent. IBM and Dell dominate their markets. General Electric, AT&T, and Westinghouse are already strong all over Europe and have invested heavily in new manufacturing facilities there.

Participating in the Global Marketplace

6 learning goal

Companies decide to "go global" for a number of reasons. Perhaps the most urgent reason is to earn additional profits. If a firm has a unique product or technological advantage not available to other international competitors, this advantage should result in major business successes abroad. In other situations, management may have exclusive market information about foreign customers, marketplaces, or market situations not known to others. In this case, although exclusivity can provide an initial motivation for going global, managers must realize that competitors will eventually catch up. Finally, saturated domestic markets, excess capacity, and potential for cost savings can also be motivators to expand into international markets. A company can enter global trade in several ways, as this section describes.

Exporting

exporting
The practice of selling domestically produced goods to buyers in another country.

When a company decides to enter the global market, usually the least complicated and least risky alternative is **exporting,** or selling domestically produced products to buyers in another country. A company, for example, can sell directly to foreign importers or buyers. Exporting is not limited to huge corporations such as General Motors or Westinghouse. Indeed, small companies account for 97 percent of all U.S. exporters, but only 30 percent of the export volume.[20] The United States is the world's largest exporter. Many small businesses claim that they lack the money, time, or knowledge of foreign markets that exporting requires. The U.S. Small Business Administration (SBA) now offers the Export Working Capital Program, which helps small and medium-size firms obtain working capital (money) to complete export sales. The SBA also provides counseling and legal assistance for small businesses that wish to enter the global marketplace. Companies such as American Building Restoration Products of Franklin, Wisconsin, have benefited tremendously from becoming exporters.

Procter and Gamble introduced Swiffer to a global market, appealing to consumers who share a universal desire for a simple cleaning system.

American Building is now selling its chemical products to building restoration companies in Mexico, Israel, Japan, and Korea. Exports account for more than 5 percent of the firm's total sales.

Much of what America exports is related to technology. When one thinks of technology it is often cutting-edge computer chips, aircraft or spacecraft designs, medicines, and so forth. Yet even basic technology can benefit developing countries, as explained in the "Applying Technology" box.

Licensing

Another effective way for a firm to move into the global arena with relatively little risk is to sell a license to manufacture its product to a firm in a foreign country. **Licensing** is the legal process whereby a firm (the *licensor*) agrees to let another firm (the *licensee*) use a manufacturing process, trademark, patent, trade secret, or other proprietary knowledge. The licensee, in turn, agrees to pay the licensor a royalty or fee agreed on by both parties.

licensing
The legal process whereby a firm agrees to allow another firm to use a manufacturing process, trademark, patent, trade secret, or other proprietary knowledge in exchange for the payment of a royalty.

U.S. companies have eagerly embraced the licensing concept. For instance, Philip Morris licensed Labatt Brewing Company to produce Miller High Life in Canada. The Spaulding Company receives more than $2 million annually from license agreements on its sporting goods. Fruit-of-the-Loom lends its name through licensing to 45 consumer items in Japan alone, for at least 1 percent of the licensee's gross sales.

The licensor must make sure it can exercise sufficient control over the licensee's activities to ensure proper quality, pricing, distribution, and so on. Licensing may also create a new competitor in the long run, if the licensee decides to void the license agreement. International law is often ineffective in stopping such actions. Two common ways that a licensor can maintain effective control over its licensees are by shipping one or more critical components from the United States and by locally registering patents and trademarks in its own name.

Franchising, covered in Chapter 5, is a form of licensing that has grown rapidly in recent years. Over 350 U.S. franchisors operate more than 32,000 outlets in for-

APPLYING TECHNOLOGY

Finding Technology that Benefits Developing Nations

Chickens don't eat in the dark. That is a fact of avian life. It's also an economic opportunity. If a farmer can light a chicken coop, his fowl will eat into the evening hours, consuming more and thus growing more quickly. Lighting a coop is hardly a dramatic business innovation, but it can make a big difference to the farmer, allowing him to buy more chickens or more years of schooling for his children.

Can cheap Internet access be similarly transforming? The research director of Hewlett-Packard's India laboratory, Srinivasan Ramani, thinks so. Ramani tells the story of going to Nellikuppam, in the southern state of Tamil Nadu, to check out the workings of roadside Internet kiosks—for-profit businesses that connect people to the Web for about 25 cents an hour. There he talked to a young woman, typing away. What was she doing? Chatting to her fiancé, who was working in Malaysia.

Another idea to use technology to benefit the world's poorer citizens is the Simputer. Created by four Indian scientists and on the market in early 2003, the Simputer is a handheld device with a simple touchscreen. It uses icons and can respond aloud in a number of Indian languages, allowing illiterate people access. The Simputer will sell for about $200, far more than most Indians can afford, but users will be able to buy a Smartcard for a dollar or two to rent time. The Simputer is programmed for a variety of basic uses—to consult a physician, compare commodity prices, do banking, check bus schedules, apply for government programs, or e-mail a boyfriend in Malaysia. "If we deliver the solution we hope to deliver, there is a need across the world," says CEO Swami Manohar. In that case, the Simputer could make money for its owners, as well as connect its users to the market.[21]

CRITICAL THINKING QUESTIONS

1. Do you think that the Simputer will be successful in India? What about other countries?
2. What other basic technologies might be beneficial to developing countries?

eign countries, bringing in sales of $6 billion. More than half of the international franchises are for fast-food restaurants and business services. McDonald's's international division is responsible for over 50 percent of the chain's sales and 60 percent of its profits.[22]

Contract Manufacturing

contract manufacturing
The practice in which a foreign firm manufactures private-label goods under a domestic firm's brand name.

In **contract manufacturing,** a foreign firm manufactures private-label goods under a domestic firm's brand. Marketing may be handled by either the domestic company or the foreign manufacturer. Levi Strauss, for instance, entered into an agreement with the French fashion house of Cacharel to produce a new Levi's line called "Something New" for distribution in Germany.

The advantage of contract manufacturing is that it lets a company "test the water" in a foreign country. By allowing the foreign firm to produce a certain volume of products to specification, and put the domestic firm's brand name on the goods, the domestic firm can broaden its global marketing base without investing in overseas plants and equipment. After establishing a solid base, the domestic firm may switch to a joint venture or direct investment, explained below.

Joint Ventures

joint venture
An agreement in which a domestic firm buys part of a foreign firm or joins with a foreign firm to create a new entity.

Joint ventures are somewhat similar to licensing agreements. In a **joint venture,** the domestic firm buys part of a foreign company or joins with a foreign company to create a new entity. A joint venture is a quick and relatively inexpensive way to enter the global market. It can also be very risky. Many joint ventures fail. Others fall victim to a takeover, in which one partner buys out the other.

Recently, General Motors entered into a joint venture with Avtovaz, a Soviet-era auto manufacturer in Russia, to produce a car to be called the Chevrolet Niva. Russia is expected to be one of the top 10 growth markets for cars during this decade, and GM wants to be a player. The assembly and engineering will be done at low cost in Russia. GM is providing $333 million and technology. Avtovaz offers skilled workers and a distribution system.[23]

In a successful joint venture, both parties gain valuable skills from the alliance. In the General Motors–Suzuki joint venture in Canada, for example, both parties

While pursing its global vision, Wal-Mart has tailored its products to suit the preferences of European customers. For example, German customers expect large selections of fish, sausage, and exotic fruits.

© AFP / CORBIS

have contributed and gained. The alliance, CAMI Automotive, was formed to manufacture low-end cars for the U.S. market. The plant, which is run by Suzuki management, produces the Geo Metro/Suzuki Swift—the smallest, most fuel-efficient GM car sold in North America—as well as the Geo Tracker/Suzuki Sidekick sport utility vehicle. Through CAMI, Suzuki has gained access to GM's dealer network and an expanded market for parts and components. GM avoided the cost of developing low-end cars and obtained models it needed to revitalize the lower end of its product line and its average fuel economy rating. The CAMI factory may be one of the most productive plants in North America. There GM has learned how Japanese automakers use work teams, run flexible assembly lines, and manage quality control.

Direct Foreign Investment

direct foreign investment
Active ownership of a foreign company or of manufacturing or marketing facilities in a foreign country.

Active ownership of a foreign company or of overseas manufacturing or marketing facilities is **direct foreign investment.** Direct investors have either a controlling interest or a large minority interest in the firm. Thus, they stand to receive the greatest potential reward but also face the greatest potential risk. A firm may make a direct foreign investment by acquiring an interest in an existing company or by building new facilities. It might do so because it has trouble transferring some resources to a foreign operation or obtaining that resource locally. One important resource is personnel, especially managers. If the local labor market is tight, the firm may buy an entire foreign firm and retain all its employees instead of paying higher salaries than competitors.

Sometimes firms make direct investments because they can find no suitable local partners. Also, direct investments avoid the communication problems and conflicts of interest that can arise with joint ventures. IBM, for instance, insists on total ownership of its foreign investments because it does not want to share control with local partners.

Wal-Mart has now made direct investments in nine countries with more than 1,100 stores. International sales now top $32 billion.[24] In Mexico alone, it had 579 grocery stores, wholesale-club outlets, and restaurants in 2002. Wal-Mart spent some $600 million to open 63 new Mexican units in 2003.[25] Just a decade after entering the country, Wal-Mart now captures half of all Mexican supermarket sales. And Wal-Mart's strategy of offering low prices every day is drawing more and more consumers.

Not all of its global investments have been successful. In Germany, Wal-Mart bought the 21-store Wertkauf hypermarket chain in 1997 and then 74 unprofitable and often decrepit Interspar stores in 1998. Problems in integrating and upgrading the stores resulted in at least $200 million in losses. Like all other German stores, Wal-Mart stores in Germany are required by law to close at 8 P.M. on weekdays and 4 P.M. on Saturdays and they cannot open at all on Sundays. And costs are astronomical. Derek Rowe, an American brought over to supervise the $5 million renovation of the Dortmund store, estimated that construction costs in Germany are five times what they are in the United States.[26]

Now Wal-Mart seems to be turning the corner on its international operations. It is pushing operational authority down to country managers in order to respond better to local cultures. Wal-Mart enforces certain core principles such as "everyday low prices," but country managers handle their own buying, logistics, building design, and other operational decisions.

Countertrade

countertrade
A form of international trade in which part or all of the payment for goods or services is in the form of other goods and services.

International trade does not always involve cash. Today, countertrade is a fast-growing way to conduct international business. In **countertrade,** part or all of the payment for goods or services is in the form of other goods or services. Countertrade is a form of barter (swapping goods for goods), an age-old practice whose origins have been traced back to cave dwellers. The U.S. Commerce

Department says that roughly 30 percent of all international trade involves countertrade. Each year about 300,000 U.S. firms engage in some form of countertrade.[27] American companies, including General Electric, Pepsi, General Motors, and Boeing, barter billions of goods and services every year.

concept check

Discuss several ways that a company can enter international trade.

Explain the concept of countertrade.

The Atwood Richards Co. is the world's largest countertrade organization. Atwood reviews a client's unsold products and issues trade credits in exchange. The credits can be used to obtain other products and services Atwood has acquired—everything from hotel rooms and airline tickets to television advertising time, forklift trucks, carpeting, pulp, envelopes, steel castings, or satellite tracking systems.

Threats and Opportunities in the Global Marketplace

7 learning goal

To be successful in a foreign market, companies must fully understand the foreign environment in which they plan to operate. Politics, cultural differences, and the economic environment can represent both opportunities and pitfalls in the global marketplace.

Political Considerations

We have already discussed how tariffs, exchange controls, and other governmental actions threaten foreign producers. The political structure of a country may also jeopardize a foreign producer's success in international trade.

nationalism

A sense of national consciousness that boosts the culture and interests of one country over those of all other countries.

Intense nationalism, for example, can lead to difficulties. **Nationalism** is the sense of national consciousness that boosts the culture and interests of one country over those of all other countries. Strongly nationalistic countries, such as Iran and New Guinea, often discourage investment by foreign companies. In other, less radical forms of nationalism, the government may take actions to hinder foreign operations. France, for example, requires that pop music stations play at least 40 percent of their songs in French. This law was enacted because the French love American rock and roll. Without airtime, American CD sales suffer. Coca-Cola recently attempted to purchase Orangina, France's only domestically owned and distributed soft drink. The French government blocked the sale saying that it would be "anticompetitive." The real reason was nationalism.

In a hostile climate, a government may *expropriate* a foreign company's assets, taking ownership and compensating the former owners. Even worse is *confiscation*, when the owner receives no compensation. This happened during rebellions in several African nations during the 1990s and 2000s.

Cultural Differences

Central to any society is the common set of values shared by its citizens that determine what is socially acceptable. Culture underlies the family, educational system, religion, and social class system. The network of social organizations generates overlapping roles and status positions. These values and roles have a tremendous effect on people's preferences and thus on marketers' options. Inca Kola, a fruity, greenish yellow carbonated drink, is the largest selling soft drink in Peru. Despite being described as "liquid bubble gum," the drink has become a symbol of national pride and heritage. The drink was invented in Peru and contains only fruit indigenous to the country. A local consumer of about a six-pack a day says, "I drink Inca Kola because it makes me feel like a Peruvian." He tells

3M's sensitivity to local customs has been instrumental to its worldwide success. With 35,000 employees outside of the United States all but 300 are locals who know the customs and buying habits of consumers within their country.

© AP / WIDE WORLD PHOTOS

his young daughter, "This is our drink, not something invented overseas. It is named for your ancestors, the great Inca warriors."

Language is another important aspect of culture. Marketers must take care in selecting product names and translating slogans and promotional messages so as not to convey the wrong meaning. For example, Mitsubishi Motors had to rename its Pajero model in Spanish-speaking countries because the term refers to a sexual activity. Toyota Motors's MR2 model dropped the number 2 in France because the combination sounds like a French swearword. The literal translation of Coca-Cola in Chinese characters means "bite the wax tadpole."

Each country has its own customs and traditions that determine business practices and influence negotiations with foreign customers. In many countries, personal relationships are more important than financial considerations. For instance, skipping social engagements in Mexico may lead to lost sales. Negotiations in Japan often include long evenings of dining, drinking, and entertaining; only after a close personal relationship has been formed do business negotiations begin. Exhibit 4.2 presents some cultural "dos and don'ts."

Economic Environment

The level of economic development varies considerably, ranging from countries where everyday survival is a struggle, such as the Sudan and Eritrea, to countries that are highly developed, such as Switzerland and Japan. In general, complex, sophisticated industries are found in developed countries, and more basic industries are found in less developed nations. Average family incomes are higher in the more developed countries than in the least developed markets. Larger incomes mean greater purchasing power and demand not only for consumer goods and services but also for the machinery and workers required to produce consumer goods. Exhibit 4.3 provides a glimpse of what families earn throughout the world.

infrastructure
The basic institutions and public facilities upon which an economy's development depends.

Business opportunities are usually better in countries that have an economic infrastructure in place. **Infrastructure** is the basic institutions and public facilities upon which an economy's development depends. When we think about how our own economy works, we tend to take our infrastructure for granted. It includes the money and banking system that provides the major investment loans to our nation's businesses; the educational system that turns out the incredible varieties of skills and basic research that actually run our nation's production lines; the

Exhibit 4.2 Cultural Dos and Don'ts

DO:

- Always present your business card with both hands in Asian countries. It should also be right-side up and print-side showing so that the recipient can read it as it is being presented. If you receive a business card, accept it with gratitude and examine it carefully. Don't quickly put it into your pocket.
- Dress to the culture. If you are in Switzerland, always wear a coat and tie. In other countries, a coat and tie may be viewed as overdressing and snobbish.
- Use a "soft-sell" and subtle approach when promoting a product in Japan. Japanese do not feel comfortable with America's traditional hard-selling style.
- Understand the role of religion in business transactions. In Muslim countries, Ramadan is a holy month when most people fast. During this time everything slows down, particularly business.
- Have a local person available to culturally and linguistically interpret any advertising that you plan to do. When American Airlines wanted to promote its new first-class seats in the Mexican market, it translated the "Fly In Leather" campaign literally, which meant "Fly Naked" in Spanish.

DON'T:

- Glad-hand, back-slap, and use first names on your first business meeting in Asia. If you do, you will be considered a lightweight.
- Fill a wine glass to the top if dining with a French businessperson. It is considered completely uncouth.
- Begin your first business meeting in Asia talking business. Be patient. Let your clients get to know you first.
- Kiss someone on the cheek or pat them on the shoulder in Spain before you get to know them. In Chile, expect women to greet you with a kiss on the cheek even if you are a stranger. Offer a kiss on both cheeks after you become friends with a French woman (even if you are a woman). In Switzerland, offer three kisses.
- Be on time for your appointment in some Latin American countries, but always be on time in Germany.

Exhibit 4.3 What the World Earns

High consumption levels are concentrated in a small share of households worldwide.

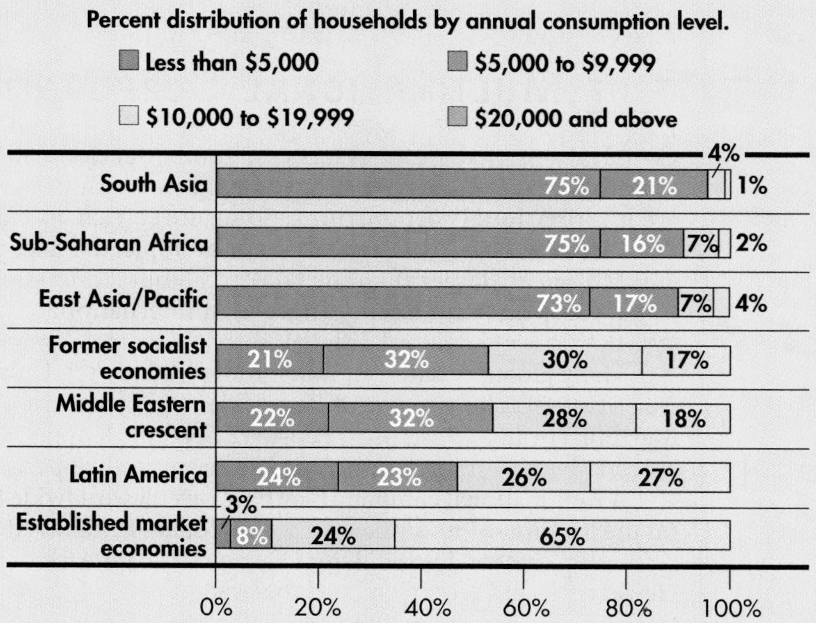

Note: Consumption is in U.S. dollars on a purchase-power-parity basis. Percentages may add to more than 100 percent due to rounding.

SOURCE: World Bank and Global Business Opportunities.

FOCUSING ON SMALL BUSINESS

Thriving on U.S. Surplus

Saad Nadhirz has launched a new retailing project: dollar stores for the emerging Mexican middle class. Forget upscale. Mr. Nadhir's new company, Waldo's $1 Mart, is all about moving things like surplus breakfast cereal and unneeded brownie mix from U.S. supermarkets to Mexican housewives.

While a lot of retailers in the "extreme value" segment have been drawn to the region—Family Dollar Stores Inc. of Matthews, North Carolina, has nearly 60 stores along the U.S. side of the Mexico border—Mr. Nadhir's stores are the first to court peso shoppers at home.

Mr. Nadhir has discovered a demographic peculiarity that many U.S. retailers covet. Besides their youth and rising incomes, Mexican consumers are among the most homogeneous on the planet. It is hard to locate a store anywhere in the United States without facing a highly fragmented client base, Mr. Nadhir explains. In Mexico, it is just the opposite: Most customers within a five-mile radius of any Waldo's store make similar salaries (about $8,000 a year), shop for similar-size households, and share nearly identical tastes.

Another difference, which can lower construction costs: Even in the poorest U.S. neighborhoods, retailers give over as much as half their space for parking, while in Mexico most shoppers walk.[28]

CRITICAL THINKING QUESTIONS

1. What might American small businesses do to meet the needs of Mexico's youthful market with rising incomes?
2. Why do you think Waldo's would not be successful in the United States?

extensive transportation and communications systems—interstate highways, railroads, airports, canals, telephones, Internet sites, postal systems, television stations—that link almost every piece of our geography into one market; the energy system that powers our factories; and, of course, the market system itself, which brings our nation's goods and services into our homes and businesses.

Industrialized countries, like the United States, often produce more than can be sold in specific markets. Selling U.S. surplus has become a real opportunity for Saad Nadhirz, as explained in the "Focusing on Small Business" box.

concept check

Explain how political factors can affect international trade.

Describe several cultural factors that a company involved in international trade should consider.

How can economic conditions affect trade opportunities?

THE IMPACT OF MULTINATIONAL CORPORATIONS

8 learning goal

Corporations that move resources, goods, services, and skills across national boundaries without regard to the country in which their headquarters are located are **multinational corporations.** Some are so rich and have so many employees that they resemble small countries. For example, the sales of both Exxon and General Motors are larger than the GDP of all but 22 nations in the world. Multinational companies are heavily engaged in international trade. The successful ones take political and cultural differences into account.

multinational corporations
Corporations that move resources, goods, services, and skills across national boundaries without regard to the country in which their headquarters are located.

Many global brands sell much more outside the United States than at home. Coca-Cola has 80 percent of its sales outside the United States; Philip Morris's Marlboro brand 67 percent; Pepsi, 42 percent; Kellogg, 50 percent; Pampers, 65 percent; Nescafe, 50 percent; and Gillette, around 62 percent.[29]

A multinational company may have several worldwide headquarters, depending on the location of its markets or technologies. Britain's APV, a maker of food-processing equipment, has a different headquarters for each of its worldwide businesses. Hewlett-Packard recently moved the headquarters of its personal computer business to Grenoble, France. Siemens A.G., Germany's electronics giant, is relocating its medical electronics division headquarters from Germany to Chicago. Honda has moved the worldwide headquarters for its power-products division to Atlanta, Georgia. The largest multinational corporations in the world are shown in Exhibit 4.4.

Exhibit 4.4 The World's Largest Multinational Corporations

Rank 2002	2001	Company Name	Country
1	1	Wal-Mart Stores	U.S.
2	3	General Motors	U.S.
3	2	ExxonMobil	U.S.
4	8	Royal Dutch/Shell Group	Netherlands/Britain
5	4	BP	Britain
6	5	Ford Motor	U.S.
7	7	DaimlerChrysler	Germany
8	10	Toyota Motor	Japan
9	9	General Electric	U.S.
10	12	Mitsubishi	Japan
11	13	Mitsui	Japan
12	18	Allianz	Germany
13	11	Citigroup	U.S.
14	15	Total	France
15	14	ChevronTexaco	U.S.
16	16	Nippon Telegraph & Telephone	Japan
17	20	ING Group	Netherlands
18	17	Itochu	Japan
19	19	International Business Machines	U.S.
20	21	Volkswagen	Germany

SOURCE: "The World's Largest Corporations," *Fortune*, July 21, 2003, p. 106. © 2003-Time Inc. All rights reserved.

The Multinational Advantage

Large multinationals have several advantages over other companies. For instance, multinationals can often overcome trade problems. Taiwan and South Korea have long had an embargo against Japanese cars for political reasons and to help domestic automakers. Yet Honda USA, a Japanese-owned company based in the United States, sends Accords to Taiwan and Korea. In another example, when the environmentally conscience Green movement challenged the biotechnology research conducted by BASF, a major German chemical and drug manufacturer, BASF moved its cancer and immune-system research to Cambridge, Massachusetts.

Another advantage for multinationals is their ability to sidestep regulatory problems. U.S. drugmaker SmithKline and Britain's Beecham decided to merge in part so that they could avoid licensing and regulatory hassles in their largest markets. The merged company can say it's an insider in both Europe and the United States. "When we go to Brussels, we're a member state [of the European Union]," one executive explains. "And when we go to Washington, we're an American company."

Multinationals can also shift production from one plant to another as market conditions change. When European demand for a certain solvent declined, Dow Chemical instructed its German plant to switch to manufacturing a chemical that had been imported from Louisiana and Texas. Computer models help Dow make decisions like these so it can run its plants more efficiently and keep costs down.

Multinationals can also tap new technology from around the world. Xerox has introduced some 80 different office copiers in the United States that were designed and built by Fuji Xerox, its joint venture with a Japanese company. Versions of the superconcentrated detergent that Procter & Gamble first formulated in Japan in response to a rival's product are now being sold under the Ariel brand name in Europe and being tested under the Cheer and Tide labels in the United States. Also, consider Otis Elevator's development of the Elevonic 411, an elevator that is programmed to send more cars to floors where demand is high. It was developed by six research centers in five countries. Otis's group in Farmington, Connecticut, handled the systems integration, a Japanese group designed the special motor drives that make the elevators ride smoothly, a French group perfected the door systems, a German group handled the electronics, and a Spanish group took care of the small-geared components. Otis says the international effort saved more than $10 million in design costs and cut the process from four years to two.

Finally, multinationals can often save a lot in labor costs, even in highly unionized countries. For example, when Xerox started moving copier-rebuilding work to Mexico to take advantage of the lower wages, its union in Rochester, New York, objected because it saw that members' jobs were at risk. Eventually, the union agreed to change work styles and to improve productivity to keep the jobs at home.

concept check

What is a multinational corporation?

What are the advantages of multinationals?

Trends in Global Competition

9 learning goal

In this section we will examine several underlying trends that will continue to propel the dramatic growth in world trade. These trends are market expansion, resource acquisition, the Internet, technological change, and governmental actions.

Market Expansion

The need for businesses to expand their markets is perhaps the most fundamental reason for the growth in world trade. The limited size of domestic markets often motivates managers to seek markets beyond their national frontiers. The economies of large-scale manufacturing demand big markets. Domestic markets, particularly in smaller countries like Denmark and the Netherlands, simply can't generate enough demand. Nestlé was one of the first businesses to "go global" because its home country, Switzerland, is so small. Nestlé was shipping milk to 16 different countries as early as 1875. Today, hundreds of thousands of businesses are recognizing the potential rich rewards to be found in international markets.

Resource Acquisition

More and more companies are going to the global marketplace to acquire the resources they need to operate efficiently. These resources may be cheap or skilled labor, scarce raw materials, technology, or capital. Nike, for example, has opened manufacturing facilities in many Asian countries in order to use cheap labor. Honda opened a design studio in southern California to put that "California flair" into the design of some of its vehicles. Large multinational banks such as Bank of New York and Citigroup have offices in Geneva, Switzerland. Geneva is the private banking center of Europe and attracts capital from around the globe.

The Impact of the Internet

In many respects "going global" is easier than it has ever been before. Opening an e-commerce site on the Internet immediately puts a company in the international marketplace. Sophisticated language translation software can make any site accessible to persons around the world. Global shippers such as UPS, FedEx, and DHL help solve international e-commerce distribution complexities. E4X, Inc. offers software to ease currency conversions. Sites that use E4X's software can post prices in U.S. dollars, then ask their customers what currency they wish to use for payment. If the answer is anything but dollars, E4X takes over the transaction and translates the price into any of 22 currencies, collects the payment from the customer, and pays the site in dollars, just as though it were any other transaction. Customers never realize they're dealing with a third party.[30]

Nevertheless, the promise of "borderless commerce" and the new "Internet economy" are still being restrained by the old brick-and-mortar rules, regulations, and habits. For example, Americans spend an average of $6,500 per year by credit card whereas Japanese spend less than $2,000. Many Japanese don't even have a credit card. So how do they pay for e-commerce purchases? 7-Eleven Japan, with over 8,000 convenience stores, has come to the rescue. eS-Books, the Japanese Web site partner of Yahoo! Japan, lets shoppers buy books and videos on the Internet, then specify to which 7-Eleven the merchandise is to be shipped. The buyer goes to that specific store and pays cash for the e-purchase.

In Germany it is typically cheaper to buy books from Amazon.com in the United Kingdom rather than the local site. Why? Germany, France, and several other European states allow publishing cartels through which groups of book publishers can legally dictate retail prices to booksellers—both online and on the ground. *Galileo's Daughter*, a biography by Dava Sobel, for example, sells at the list price of 50.24 marks ($26.99) on Germany's Amazon.de; at Amazon.co.uk, it costs 40 percent less.

The e-commerce site for the American clothing retailer Lands' End in Germany is not allowed to mention its unconditional refund policy because German retailers, which normally do not allow returns after 14 days, sued and won a court ruling blocking mention of it.

Technological Change

Both new technology in transportation systems and the expanded nature of information processing fosters continued growth in international trade. Transportation improvements from computerized container ships to cargo jetliners have dramatically improved the efficiency of distribution throughout the world. Moreover, Federal Express and other shippers use advanced computerized tracking software to tell shippers where their packages are at any point in time. Shippers can use special software that enables them to enter FedEx's database and track the packages themselves, if they so desire. It's a far cry from the sailing ships of yesteryear when voyages took weeks or months, and there was no way to communicate with the ship once it left port.

The Internet opens up the world to any seller with a Web site. Markets no longer have geographic boundaries. E-mail enables a manager in London to receive reports from Dallas, Moscow, Capetown, and Tokyo in a matter of minutes rather than days. Thus, coordinating global business strategies is now a workable reality.

Government Actions

concept check

What trends will foster continued growth in world trade?

Describe some of the ways businesses can take advantage of these trends to "go global."

Governments around the globe, working with the WTO, have significantly lowered barriers to world trade. Sellers in the global marketplace have a more level playing field than ever before. Regional trade organizations, such as the European Union, NAFTA, and Mercosur, also have reduced trade barriers in large geographic areas. As these governmental actions continue to make it easier to "go global," world trade will continue to grow.

Great Ideas to Use Now

Continue Your Education

The handwriting is on the wall. Low-skilled jobs are rapidly disappearing in America. U.S. businesses know that to compete globally, they must find cheap labor for labor-intensive businesses. This means establishing plants in Mexico, Asia, or other places in the world where labor is inexpensive. It also means that unskilled or low-skilled American workers will find it increasingly difficult to secure a permanent job. By continuing your education, you won't fall into this very undesirable trap.

Try It Now

If you travel, work, or study abroad, you are going to need to change U.S. dollars to foreign currency. Making mistakes when changing money can cost you 10 to 20 percent of your bankroll. Here are a few tips about changing money abroad.

1. Know the exchange rate between U.S. dollars and the currencies of the countries you plan to visit before you go. Go to **http://www.cnnfn.com/markets/currencies/** for the latest quotations. Keep up with the changing rates by reading *USA Today International* or the *International Herald Tribune* every day.
2. Avoid changing money at airports, train stations, and hotels. These places usually have the worst rates. Ask local people where they change money. Locals know where the best rates are.
3. Try to bargain with the clerk. Sometimes you can do better than the posted rate simply by asking.
4. Rather than making several small transactions, make one large exchange. This will often get you a better rate.
5. Don't change more than you will need. You'll pay another fee to change the foreign currency back to U.S. dollars.
6. Use a credit card. Typically, any major credit card will give you a better rate than a change booth or bank. Sometimes the spread is substantial, so minimize cash and use credit.
7. Travelers checks usually have a worse exchange rate than cash. In other words, a $100 American Express travelers check will give you less in exchange than a $100 bill. If your travelers checks are lost or stolen, however, they will be replaced, so the peace of mind is usually worth the added expense.
8. Fly cheap to Europe. To get to European destinations cheaply, consider beginning in London. The lowest price tickets from the United States to London are typically found through ticket consolidators (**http://www.twarp.com/air.htm**). Next, take a low-fare carrier to get to your final destination. Try carriers such as: easyJet, Buzz, Go, Ryanair, or Virgin Express. (Buzz now has flights to 15 airports in France for as little as $54 round-trip from London.) Although many of these aren't available on the big Internet travel sites, one independent site—**http://www.applefares.com**—specializes in searching just those airlines.

Customer Satisfaction and Quality

Determining what is *quality* is not always easy in the global marketplace. For example, a manufacturer of garden tools used very high quality tempered steel to make shovel blades and aged hickory wood for the handles. The shovel is a market leader in the United States but sold poorly in Asia despite a competitive price. The company was puzzled, so it undertook a research project to find out why the shovels weren't selling. The answer proved to be quite simple: people in Asia were of shorter stature, making the handles too long to use comfortably! The company shortened the handles and sales skyrocketed.

Quality in developing countries may mean simplifying product features and/or making the parts more durable to withstand a tougher environment. In some cases, a quality sewing machine is one that is foot-peddle operated because buyers don't have access to or can't afford electricity. Yet, companies should not assume that even the poorest people won't pay for quality. Nomads who wander the northern Sahara Desert always buy the highest quality cloth available to make their clothes. Their garments are all that stand between them and 120 degrees-plus in the summer and 10 below zero in the winter.

So to understand quality in the global marketplace a business must understand the local culture and listen to the voice of the consumer. A good example is when Universal Studios decided to build a theme park in Japan.

By surveying Japanese visitors at Universal parks in Orlando and Los Angeles, Universal gradually drew a picture of what the Japanese did and didn't like about the U.S. parks. For example, cramped in their small homes, they loved the expansive space. But accustomed to modest portions of food, many were turned off by the mountainous servings in the United States.

A marketing survey in Japan cataloged Japanese expectations for every aspect of Universal Studios Japan, from bathrooms to souvenir sales. One theme was clear, if a bit contradictory: Japanese wanted an authentic American experience, while expecting the park to cater to their own cultural preferences.

Searching for the right formula required painstaking attention to detail. Universal set up a test kitchen in Japan, where 10 Japanese and U.S. chefs tested 4,000 recipes to develop U.S.-style dishes with a touch of Japanese flavor. A seafood pizza and gumbo-style soup made the cut. A fried-shrimp concoction with colored rice crackers didn't. American tasters liked it. Japanese simply found it gross.

In a musical number based on the movie *Beetlejuice,* the main character banters away in Japanese while his sidekicks speak and sing in English. Snippets of Japanese and a Japanese stuntman were injected into a Wild West show to make the gunfight story more understandable to Japanese without ruining the effect of the U.S. performers.

Other features are uniquely Japanese. The nation's penchant for buying edible souvenirs inspired a 6,000-square-foot confection shop packed with Japanese sweets like dinosaur-shaped bean cakes. Restrooms include Japanese-style squat toilets. Even the park layout caters to the tendency of Japanese crowds to flow clockwise in an orderly manner, contrary to more chaotic U.S. crowds, which steer right.

SOURCE: Bill Spindle, "Cowboys and Samurai: The Japanizing of Universal," *Wall Street Journal* (March 22, 2001), pp. B1, B6.

Study the Role of a Global Manager

As business becomes more global, chances are that you may become a global manager. Start learning right now what this means and if it's right for you. The life of a global manager can be hectic, as these examples illustrate:

> Top overseas performers at Secure Computing, a San Jose, California, software developer, are treated to a dinner for two by Christine Hughes, senior vice president of marketing and business development. Ms. Hughes supervises a 24-person staff in North and South America and Asia. One of her missions on trips is to combat the tendency of foreign-based employees to think the organization is "U.S.-centric," she says. Because they take much longer flights than the typical corporate road warrior, global managers wind up turning airplanes into offices. When she is overseas, Ms. Hughes has her office ship her a package of paperwork overnight, so she can work on the flight home. Mr. Salzman considers flight time some of his most productive; he uses it to answer e-mail and review contracts.
>
> Indeed, a global manager's workday never really ends. Wherever they are, it's still business hours somewhere else. When she's working in Australia, Ms. Hughes usually ends her day in a hotel room, talking with someone at the home office. "I'm on the phone until two in the morning dealing with issues," she says. "You just have to accept that."[31]

Looking Ahead at Starbucks

Cultural factors, domestic competition, economic conditions, government actions, regional trade agreements, and terrorism can all make selling in the global marketplace more difficult. Governments can take a number of actions to protect domestic competitors. Some common tactics are tariffs, quotas, embargoes, exchange controls, and buy-national regulations.

There are a number of cultural factors that Starbucks should consider when entering the European market. For example, Europeans like sidewalk cafés, therefore Starbucks should have places outside to sit. Also, Europeans enjoy different pastries than Americans do, so Starbucks might consider modifying their offerings to local tastes. Europeans linger for a lengthy time when drinking coffee. This may require a larger space with more tables than in America. However, Helmut Spudich, a business editor for Vienna's *Der Standard*, has noted that Starbucks is attracting a younger crowd. "The coffeehouses in Vienna are nice, but they are old. Starbucks is considered hip," he says.[32]

In summary, Starbucks now has 5,689 outlets in 28 countries. It is one of the fastest-growing brand names in the world. The Starbucks name and image connect with consumers around the globe.

Your position may not be as hectic as that of Hughes, but you can easily see the differences between a person who is a global manager and one who is not. Is this the life for you? Would you enjoy living abroad? Can you adapt easily to other cultures?

One way to see if you might be cut out to be a global manager is to spend some time abroad. The ideal situation is to find a job overseas during the summer months. This experience will help you decide if you want to be a global manager. Also, it will look good on your résumé. One source of international jobs information is **http://www.internationaljobs.org**.

If you can't find a job overseas, save your money and travel abroad. Seeing how others live and work will broaden your horizons and give you a more enlightened view of the world. Even international travel can help you decide what you want to do in the global marketplace.

Summary of Learning Goals

1 Why is global trade important to the United States and how is trade measured?

International trade improves relations with friends and allies, eases tensions among nations, helps bolster economies, raises people's standard of living, and improves the quality of life. The United States is still the largest importer and exporter in the world. We export a fifth of our industrial production and about a third of our farm crops. One out of every 16 jobs in the United States is supported by exports.

Two concepts important to global trade are the balance of trade (the difference in value between a country's exports and its imports over some period) and the balance of payments (the difference between a country's total payments to other countries and its total receipts from other countries). The United States now has both a negative balance of trade and a negative balance of payments. Another import concept is the exchange rate, which is the price of one country's currency in terms of another country's currency. Currencies float up and down based upon the supply of and demand for each currency. Sometimes a government steps in and devalues its currency relative to the currencies of other countries.

2

Why do nations trade?

Nations trade because they gain by doing so. The principle of comparative advantage states that each country should specialize in the goods it can produce most readily and cheaply and trade them for those that other countries can produce most readily and cheaply. The result is more goods at lower prices than if each country produced by itself everything it needed. Free trade allows trade among nations without government restrictions.

3

What are the barriers to international trade?

The three major barriers to international trade are natural barriers, such as distance and language; tariff barriers, or taxes on imported goods; and nontariff barriers. The nontariff barriers to trade include import quotas, embargoes, buy-national regulations, customs regulations, and exchange controls. The main argument against tariffs is that they discourage free trade and keep the principle of comparative advantage from working efficiently. The main argument for using tariffs is that they help protect domestic companies, industries, and workers.

4

How do governments and institutions foster world trade?

The World Trade Organization created by the Uruguay Round has dramatically lowered trade barriers worldwide. For the first time, a trade agreement covers services, intellectual property rights, and exchange controls. The World Bank makes loans to developing nations to help build infrastructures. The International Monetary Fund makes loans to member nations that cannot meet their budgetary expenses. Despite efforts to expand trade, terrorism can have a negative impact on trade growth.

5

What are international economic communities?

International economic communities reduce trade barriers among themselves while often establishing common tariffs and other trade barriers toward nonmember countries. The best-known economic communities are the European Union, NAFTA, and Mercosur.

6

How do companies enter the global marketplace?

There are a number of ways to enter the global market. The major ones are exporting, licensing, contract manufacturing, joint ventures, and direct investment.

7

What threats and opportunities exist in the global marketplace?

Domestic firms entering the international arena need to consider the politics, economies, and culture of the countries where they plan to do business. For example, government trade policies can be loose or restrictive, countries can be nationalistic, and governments can change. In the area of culture, many products fail because companies don't understand the culture of the country where they are trying to sell their products. Some developing countries also lack an economic infrastructure, which often makes it very difficult to conduct business.

8

What are the advantages of multinational corporations?

Multinational corporations have several advantages. First, they can sidestep restrictive trade and licensing restrictions because they frequently have headquarters in more than one country. Multinationals can also move their operations from one country to the next depending on which location offers more favorable economic conditions. In addition, multinationals can tap into a vast source of technological expertise by drawing upon the knowledge of a global workforce.

9 What are the trends in the global marketplace?

Global business activity will continue to escalate due to several factors. Firms that desire a larger customer base or need additional resources will continue to seek opportunities outside their country's borders. The Internet offers an excellent way for firms to "go global." In addition, technological improvements in communication and transportation will continue to fuel growth in global markets by making it easier to sell and distribute products internationally.

Preparing for Tomorrow's Workplace

1. How can a country's customs create barriers to trade? Ask foreign students to describe such barriers in their country. American students should give examples of problems that foreign businesspeople might experience with American customs.
2. Should Great Britain be admitted to NAFTA? Why might Britain not wish to join?
3. Write a paper on how international economic communities may affect American business.
4. What do you think is the best way for a small company to enter international trade? Why?
5. What impact have foreign multinationals had on the U.S. economy? Give some examples.
6. Identify some U.S. multinational companies that have been successful in world markets. How do you think they have achieved their success?
7. Divide the class into teams. Each team should choose a country and research its infrastructure to determine how it will help or hinder trade. Include a variety of countries, ranging from the most highly developed to the least developed.

Working the Net

1. Go to the Trade Compliance Center site at **http://tcc.mac.doc.gov.** Click on "Research Your Country Market" and then "Search Reports." Pick a country that interests you from the index, and read the most current available reports for that country. Would this country be a good market for a small U.S. clothing manufacturer interested in expanding internationally? Why or why not? What are the main barriers to trade the company might face?
2. While still at the Trade Compliance site, **http://tcc.mac.doc.gov**, click on "Trade Agreements" and then "List All Guides." Select one guide that interests you and summarize what you learn about it.
3. Review the historical data about exchange rates between the U.S. dollar and the Japanese yen available at **http://www.x-rates.com.** Pull up charts comparing the yen to the dollar for several years. List any trends you spot. What years would have been best for a U.S. company to enter the Japanese marketplace? Given current exchange rate conditions, do you think Japanese companies are increasing or decreasing their exporting efforts in the United States?
4. Visit Foreign Trade Online, **http://www.foreign-trade.com**, and browse through the resources of this international business-to-business trade portal. What types of information does the site provide? Which would be most useful to a company

KEY TERMS

absolute advantage 121
balance of payments 120
balance of trade 119
buy-national regulations 123
contract manufacturing 131
countertrade 132
customs regulations 123
devaluation 120
direct foreign investment 132
dumping 124
embargo 123
European Union (EU) 126
exchange controls 124
exporting 129
exports 118
floating exchange rates 120
free trade 121
free-trade zone 126
global vision 116
import quota 123
imports 118
infrastructure 134
International Monetary Fund (IMF) 125
joint venture 131
licensing 130
Mercosur 126
multinational corporations 136
nationalism 133
North American Free Trade Agreement (NAFTA) 126
preferential tariff 126
principle of comparative advantage 121
protectionism 121
protective tariffs 122
tariff 122
trade deficit 119
trade surplus 119
Uruguay Round 124
World Bank 125
World Trade Organization (WTO) 125

looking to begin exporting? To a company who already exports and wants to find new markets? Rate the usefulness of the site and the information it offers.

CREATIVE THINKING CASE

Zara—The Fast Track in Retailing

Remember the shock ads from Italy's Benetton? One was a picture of a nun and priest kissing, another of a Black woman nursing a white baby. These socially-pointed messages helped turn Benetton's colorful sweaters into a casualwear empire in the 1980s, creating one of the world's best-known brands.

Now there is a new kid on the block that shuns shock and relies on digital technology to unravel Benneton and other competitors. Meet Zara, the quick-footed Spanish company that offers shoppers a steady supply of up-to-the-minute trendy clothes at affordable prices. Where many retailers operate on product lead times of six to nine months, Zara has managed, on special occasions, to stock clothes with a mere 15 days between design and window display.

Meet Esther Gomez, manager of Zara's flagship store in downtown Madrid, who is examining her dress stock a half hour before opening. Gomez spots a black dress hanging on a rack by itself. She grabs it and calculates aloud: On Monday she received four, and now, just two days later, only one remains. "I've got to make a bet on what we are going to sell next week," she says. "I'll probably order six to sell between Monday and Thursday." Thus decided, she pulls out a customized Cassiopeia handheld and, with stylus in hand, taps in an order that's beamed over the Internet to Zara headquarters in the northwestern Spanish town of La Coruña.

There, in a bright and vast white room, some 200 designers and product managers are deciding what to create. Every day they gather suggestions from Gomez and 518 other store managers worldwide—not just specific orders but ideas for cuts, fabrics, or even a new line of men's knit vests. (Gomez, for example, plans to pitch a proposal for making the hot-selling black dress in red and beige, perhaps with an asymmetrical cut exposing the left shoulder.)

After weighing the store managers' ideas, the team in La Coruña decides what to make. Designers draw up the latest ideas on their computers and send them over Zara's intranet to a smattering of its nearby factories. Within days, the cutting, dyeing, stitching, and pressing begin. And normally in just three weeks, the clothes will hang in stores from Barcelona to Berlin to Beirut.

Zara has a twice-a-week delivery schedule that not only restocks old styles but brings in entirely new designs; rival chains tend to receive new designs only once or twice a season. To make this possible, Zara's prolific design department cranks out more than 10,000 fresh items each year, far more than the competition does. "It's like you walk into a new store every two weeks," marvels Tracy Mullin, president and CEO of the National Retail Federation.

CRITICAL THINKING QUESTIONS

1. American retailers are often viewed as being on the cutting edge of retail technology. Why do you think Zara is so far ahead of U.S. fashion retailers?
2. Can Gap use this model to regain its market leadership in the United States? Why or why not?
3. Benetton's most recent ad campaign still focuses on social causes. Does this say who Benetton is or what they are trying to sell? Does it give them a competitive advantage over Zara?
4. With Zara's merchandise changing so frequently, will this increase or decrease customer loyalty? Why?

SOURCES: Jane Bainbridge, "High-Speed Retail Is Quick to Answer Customer Needs," *Marketing* (April 3, 2003); William Copacino, "The True Meaning of Supply Chain Management," *Logistics Management* (June 2003), p. 50; Miguel Helft, "Fashion Fast Forward," *Business 2.0* (May 2003), pp. 61–62; "Has Benetton Stopped Unraveling?" *Business Week* (June 30, 2003), p. 41.

Video Case

ESPN Goes Global

If your passion is Indian cricket, Argentinian soccer, or Scottish links golf, tune in to ESPN International for live coverage of your favorite international sports events. The company's initial 1989 foray into international sports broadcasting was in South America, a market that still represents 40 percent of their international business. But ESPN's international programming has since expanded to include 150–160 million households worldwide.

"Minimal data was available on basic demographics like household cable penetration, markets, or advertising," said Managing Director of ESPN International Operations, Willy Burkhart. But ESPN followed pioneers CNN and HBO into the international broadcast arena, convinced that sporting events would carry the same global appeal for viewers as news and movies. Their goal was to bring quality programming and journalistic integrity in American sports to a global audience.

Initial distribution partnerships were established with broadcast companies in Europe, Canada, and Asia, followed by penetration into Japan, Australia, New Zealand, the Middle East, Africa, and Antarctica, under ESPN's own banner. Unlike CNN's international coverage, which focuses on bringing news to an American expatriate and tourist audience, ESPN soon realized sports viewers were mainly interested in local events. They invested in the "localization" of their coverage, which included being sensitive to different languages and dialects, and hired announcers with accents unlikely to offend or insult any of their viewers.

ESPN's sales pitch to cable operators was the lure of enticing new subscribers to cable, and the promise of retaining existing users unwilling to relinquish access to first-rate, up-to-the-minute sports programming. ESPN's two revenue streams are generated from cable operators and the companies who buy ESPN advertising airtime.

Initially ESPN's own advertising was designed to encourage viewer tune-in for specific events, with little focus on building the ESPN brand or image. That has changed and the company now features stunts in their own airtime that help build ESPN brand awareness.

As the worldwide leader in sports entertainment, ESPN also recognized the need to identify and even create trends in the world of sports by producing some of their own events. Their phenomenally successful X-Games, staged each year in Thailand, features edgy "evolving sports" like ramp boarding. Retaining rights to some events is an ongoing challenge for ESPN and their own production capability provides them with greater control over some of these events.

After 10 years of successfully investing in establishing a worldwide presence, ESPN has now turned its focus to building its brand value and brand name, a name the company hopes worldwide sports viewers will continue to see as synonymous with excellence in sports broadcasting.

CRITICAL THINKING QUESTIONS

1. Why did ESPN take the risk of moving into the international broadcast arena, even though it did not have solid demographic data available?
2. What were some of the main challenges ESPN experienced in this new venture?
3. How has ESPN's international presence evolved over the past 10 years? What trends have helped it grow?

SOURCES: Adapted from material contained in the video *ESPN International* and the company Web site, http://www.international.espn.com.

E-Commerce Case

The VIP System at Your Service, Worldwide

Taking a trip? No need to worry whether you left a light on in the bedroom or forgot to turn on the security system back home. Just dial into your home's Internet site and you can automatically control what's going on in your home from anywhere in the world. That's the vision behind the VIP System from Houston-based First Capital International (**http://www.firstcap.com**). The VIP System is an interactive home management and telecommunications device installed in a home's interior walls, allowing homeowners to direct and automate lighting, security, and other home functions either at home or through the Internet.

First Capital hopes to become the global market leader in the implementation of home management and telecommunications systems. Because the system is less expensive and easier to install during home construction, the company's primary sales focus is on convincing major home construction firms to recommend it to new homebuyers. In the United States, First Capital has developed a network of sales representatives that sell the VIP System in 30 states. The company has also found that demonstrating the VIP System at building industry trade shows is a valuable sales tool.

While the company has participated in some major trade shows outside of the United States, it has decided not to build an international sales team at this point. Instead, First Capital is relying on the Internet to bring the VIP System's story to both builders and consumers. At First Capital's Web site, interested parties can take a virtual tour of a house built with the system in order to get a firsthand view of how it works.

Alex Genin, First Capital CEO and president, credits the Internet with expanding the firm's marketing reach. Using the Internet to demonstrate its product, First Capital recently signed a multimillion-dollar contract for the VIP System with a firm in Russia. "The Web has proved to be an outstanding marketing tool for us," says Genin. "In addition to Russia, we are answering requests from nearly every geographic region of the world." Europe is a primary marketing focus for the company, which also would like to expand into Asia in the future.

CRITICAL THINKING QUESTIONS

1. Do you agree with First Capital's decision to use the Internet instead of developing an overseas sales force to expand into foreign markets? What alternatives could First Capital consider?
2. What are some ways First Capital could improve the effectiveness of its global e-commerce initiative?
3. What are some barriers to trade First Capital might encounter in trying to sell its home automation system abroad?

SOURCES: Al Massey, "Houston Taps into Web to Expand Global Business," *Houston Business Journal*, April 19, 2002, downloaded from http://www.houston.bizjournals.com; "First Capital Intl Inc. Will Introduce Its VIP Systems in Florida and Europe," Company press release, March 4, 2003, downloaded from http://www.firstcap.com; and "Company's SYS Automation Software Used with Network Gateway from First Capital to Create First Web-enabled Residential Construction Project," Company press release, April 4, 2002, downloaded from http://www.firstcap.com.

Hot Links Address Book

A good starting place for help on doing business in foreign markets is the U.S. government's portal site, Export.gov. Here you'll find links to export basics, regulations, exchange rates, country and industry research, and much more:
http://www.export.gov

For links to wealth of statistics on world trade, travel to the U.S. International Trade Administration's (ITA) Office of Trade and Economic Analysis site,
http://www.ita.doc.gov/td/industry/otea/

Check out the current U.S. balance of trade with various countries at
http://www.bea.doc.gov/bea/di1.htm

Get up-to-the-minute exchange rates at
http://www.xe.com/ucc/

The World Trade Organization tracks the latest trade developments between countries and regions around the world. For the most recent global trading news, visit the WTO's site at
http://www.wto.org

Gain additional insight into the workings of the International Monetary Fund at
http://www.imf.org

Want to learn the latest info about NAFTA? Go to
http://www.NAFTA-customs.org

Chapter 5

Forms of Business Ownership

learning goals

1 What are the advantages and disadvantages of the sole proprietorship form of business organization?
2 What are the advantages of operating as a partnership, and what downside risks should partners consider?
3 How does the corporate structure provide advantages and disadvantages to a company, and what are the major types of corporations?
4 Does a company have other business organization options in addition to sole proprietorships, partnerships, and corporations?
5 What makes franchising an appropriate form of organization for some types of business, and why is it growing in importance?
6 Why are mergers and acquisitions important to a company's overall growth?
7 How will current trends affect the business organizations of the future?

Redefined Style and Function at 180°s

People laughed when Brian Le Gette and Ron Wilson quit investment banking jobs and six-figure salaries to build a better earmuff. But Le Gette and Wilson are the ones laughing now—all the way to the bank. The former business school buddies, both trained engineers, shared a vision based on a simple strategy: to innovate mundane products with redefined style and function.

It all started with the humble earmuff. While walking across campus at Virginia Tech in two feet of snow, Ron Wilson mused about keeping his ears warm without looking like a dork, and conceptualized what would later become the Ear Warmer. That was in 1986, and seven years later he and fellow Wharton Business School buddy, Brian Le Gette, designed and developed prototypes of an expandable, collapsible, fleece-covered ear warmer that wraps around the back of the head.

They charged $7,500 in start-up expenses to credit cards, and the following fall made the first sales of their ear warmers on the University of Pennsylvania campus—for $20 apiece. Then two classmates interning at QVC persuaded Le Gette and Wilson to hawk their product on the home shopping network, and the rest, as they say, is history. Their QVC debut sold 5,000 Ear Warmers in 8.5 minutes, and three years later home shoppers had bought 600,000 Ear Warmers. Their product was a winner.

Launched by this momentum, their business quickly grew into a booming product design and development company, and it was necessary to choose a form of business organization to support the company's current and future goals. Up to now, Le Gette and Wilson's informal partnership, based on not much more than shared vision and a desire to reinvent the old with new, user-friendly products, had served them well, but when it was time to formalize the company's organization they chose to become a limited liability company (LLC), a newer type of business entity that appeals to small businesses.

LLCs are easy to set up, not subject to many restrictions, and while they provide the same liability protection as corporations, they offer the option of being taxed as either a partnership or corporation. Eighteen of their fellow classmates invested in Gray Matter Holdings, the parent company of 180°s LLC (**http://www.180s.com**), "creator and marketer of innovative products for the beach and winter apparel market." Le Gette and Wilson converted a historic property in the Canton waterfront area of Baltimore into new headquarters for their rapidly growing company.

Innovation is the core of the 180°s culture. Nearly every product has multiple design and utility patents, which reflect the unique design solutions the company creates. Their world-class product design and development teams are constantly working on new innovations: a self-watering planter, a pop-open beach mat, a self-inflating foam stadium seat, to name just a few. In seven years 180°s has designed and developed over 100 new products.[1]

Critical Thinking Questions

As you review the chapter, consider these questions in relation to 180°s, LLC:

1. What made the informal partnership between Wilson and Le Gette a successful one?
2. Why did Le Gette and Wilson decide to transform their business into a limited liability company (LLC)? How did this serve their business goals?
3. Would the company's future growth and development have been well served if they had incorporated?

Principles of Business Ownership

So you've decided to start a business. You have a good idea and some cash in hand, but before you get going you need to decide what form of business organization will best suit your needs.

So first ask yourself some questions. Would you prefer to go it alone as a *sole proprietorship*, or do you want others to share the burdens and challenges of a *partnership*? Or do you prefer the limited liability protection of a *corporation*, or the flexibility of a *limited liability company (LLC)*?

Some other questions you need to consider: How easy will it be to find financing? Can you attract employees? How will the business be taxed, and who will be liable for the company's debts? If you choose to share ownership with others, how much operating control will they want, and what costs will be associated with that, or other forms of ownership? Most start-up businesses select one of the major ownership categories.

As Exhibit 5.1 illustrates, sole proprietorships are the most popular form of business ownership, accounting for 74 percent of all businesses, compared with 18 percent for corporations and 8 percent for partnerships. Because most sole proprietorships and partnerships remain small, corporations generate approximately 86 percent of total business revenues and 68 percent of total profits.

In the following pages we will discover the advantages and disadvantages of each form of business ownership and the factors that may make it necessary to change from one form of organization to another, as the needs of the business changes. As your company expands from a small to midsize or larger company, the form of business structure you selected in the beginning may no longer be appropriate.

Going It Alone: Sole Proprietorships

1 learning goal

sole proprietorship
A business that is established, owned, operated, and often financed by one person.

Mike Robson was working full-time, finishing a bachelor's degree in business, and starting work on his master's, when lunch with a fellow MBA (master of business adminstration) student changed everything. His friend mentioned that the company he worked for had trouble obtaining "toppers," metal boxes for ATM (automatic teller machine) modems. Before lunch was over, Robson decided to start a business—building toppers.

Eight months after Robson had set up business as a **sole proprietorship,** a business established, owned, operated, and often financed by one person, his $20,000 home-equity loan financing was gone, without his having sold a single box! Then he made a fateful sales call at a local credit union where they needed someone to spruce up a dilapidated ATM. Robson drew on his chemical engineering background to clean, polish, and paint the machine until it looked like new, and so his new business restoring and maintaining ATM machines was born!

Exhibit 5.1 Comparison of Forms of Business Organization

	Number	**Sales**	**Profits**
Sole Proprietorships	74%	5%	15%
Partnerships	8%	9%	17%
Corporations	18%	86%	68%

SOURCE: Internal Revenue Service, as reported in Table 699, U.S. Bureau of the Census, *Statistical Abstract of the United States, 2002*, 122nd ed. (Washington, DC: U.S. Government Printing Office, 2002), p. 471.

Robson thrived as a sole proprietor. He liked the independence of being his own boss and controlling all business decisions. When his initial idea was headed nowhere he was able to quickly change direction when a new opportunity presented itself. Many businesses in your neighborhood, including florists, dry cleaners, and beauty salons, are sole proprietorships, as are many service firms like lawyers, accountants, and realtors.

Still a sole proprietorship, Mike Robson sells very few "toppers." "We've never recouped the money we spent to develop them," he says. But with 30 employees, $2.6 million in revenues, and maintenance contracts with 10% of the nation's financial institutions, he's cleaning up anyway![2]

Advantages of Sole Proprietorships

Sole proprietorships have several advantages that make them popular:

- *Easy and inexpensive to form.* As Mike Robson discovered, sole proprietorships have few legal requirements (local licenses and permits) and are not expensive to form, making them the business organization of choice for many small companies and start-ups.
- *Profits all go to the owner.* The owner of a sole proprietorship obtains the start-up funds and gets all the profits earned by the business, so the more efficiently the firm operates, the higher the profits.
- *Direct control of the business.* All business decisions are made by the sole proprietorship owner, without having to consult anyone else. This was beneficial for Mike Robson when he needed to change the direction of his business.
- *Freedom from government regulations.* Sole proprietorships have more freedom than other forms of business with respect to government controls.
- *No special taxation.* Sole proprietorships do not pay special franchise or corporate taxes. Profits are taxed as personal income as reported on the owner's individual tax return.
- *Ease of dissolution.* With no co-owners or partners the sole proprietor can sell the business or close the doors at any time, making this form of business organization an ideal way to test new business ideas.

Disadvantages of Sole Proprietorships

Along with the freedom to operate the business as they wish, sole proprietors face several disadvantages:

- *Unlimited liability.* From a legal standpoint, the sole proprietor and the company he or she owns is one and the same, making the business owner personally responsible for all debts the company incurs, even if they exceed the company's value. The owner may need to sell other personal property—his or her car, home, or other investments—to satisfy claims against his business.
- *Difficulty in raising capital.* Business assets are unprotected against claims of personal creditors, and business lenders view sole proprietorships as high risk due to the owner's unlimited liability. Owners must often use personal funds—borrowing on credit cards, second-mortgaging their homes, or selling investments—to finance their business, and expansion plans can also be affected by an inability to raise additional funding.
- *Limited managerial expertise.* The success of a sole proprietorship rests solely with the skills and talents of the owner, who must wear many different hats and make all decisions. Owners are often not equally skilled in all areas of running a business. A graphic designer may be a wonderful artist but not know bookkeeping, how to manage production, or how to market his or her work.

- *Trouble finding qualified employees.* Sole proprietors often cannot offer the same pay, fringe benefits, and advancement as larger companies, making them less attractive to employees seeking the most favorable employment opportunities.
- *Personal time commitment.* Running a sole proprietorship business requires personal sacrifices and a huge time commitment, often dominating the owner's life with 12-hour work days and 7-day workweeks.
- *Unstable business life.* The life span of a sole proprietorship can be uncertain. The owner may lose interest, experience ill health, retire, or die. The business will cease to exist unless the owner makes provisions for it to continue operating, or puts it up for sale.
- *Losses are the owner's responsibility.* The sole proprietor is responsible for all losses, although tax laws allow these to be deducted from other personal income.

concept check

What is a sole proprietorship?

Why is this such a popular form of business organization?

What are the drawbacks to being a sole proprietor?

The sole proprietorship may be a suitable choice for a one-person start-up operation with no employees and little risk of liability exposure. For many sole proprietors, however, this is a temporary choice and as the business grows the owner may be unable to operate with limited financial and managerial resources. At this point he or she may decide to take in one or more partners to ensure that the business continues to flourish.

PARTNERSHIPS: SHARING THE LOAD

2 learning goal

Some small businesses are born when individuals turn their passion into reality. Linda Ravden's passion was to market products handcrafted by women in third-world countries to retailers in the United States. Ravden decided to import the goods directly, requiring large cash outlays as well as the challenge of inventory storage and management. She decided she needed a partner to help with an infusion of cash for initial inventory purchases, and to assist with day-to-day business operations. So friend and neighbor, Marcia Herscovitz, came on board. With complementary skills to Ravden, she handled daily operations, allowing Ravden to focus on overall business strategy, product design and development, and sales and marketing.

partnership
An association of two or more individuals who agree to operate a business together for profit.

Start-up capital came from both partners—and their **partnership,** an association of two or more individuals who agree to operate a business together for profit, was up and running, with sales of \$200,000 their first year of business.[3]

For those individuals who do not like to "go it alone," a partnership is simple to set up and offers a shared form of business ownership. It is a popular choice for

Building an effective trade show booth from scratch is time consuming and exhausting, so sharing the load made all the difference to partners, Linda Ravden and Marcia Herscovitz when promoting their products at national trade shows.

COURTESY OF BELLISSIMA DESIGNS

professional-service firms such as lawyers, accountants, architects, investment banks, stockbrokers, and real estate companies.

The parties agree, *either orally or in writing,* to share in the profits and losses of a joint enterprise. A *written partnership agreement,* spelling out the terms and conditions of the partnership, *is recommended* to prevent later conflicts between the partners. These agreements typically include the name of the partnership, its purpose, and the contributions of each partner (financial, equipment, skill/talent), as well as outline the responsibilities and duties of each partner and their compensation structure (salary, profit sharing, etc.).

It should also contain provisions for the addition of new partners, the sale of partnership interests, and the procedures for resolving conflicts, dissolving the business, and distributing the assets.

general partnership
A partnership in which all partners share in the management and profits. Each partner can act on behalf of the firm and has unlimited liability for all its business obligations.

limited partnership
A partnership with one or more general partners, who have unlimited liability, and one or more limited partners, whose liability is limited to the amount of their investment.

general partners
Partners who have unlimited liability for all of the firm's business obligations and who control its operations.

limited partners
Partners whose liability for the firm's business obligations is limited to the amount of their investment. They help to finance the business, but do not participate in the firm's operations.

There are *two basic types of partnerships: general and limited.* In a **general partnership,** all partners share in the management and the profits. They co-own the assets and each can act on behalf of the firm. Each partner also has unlimited liability for all the business obligations of the firm. A **limited partnership** has two types of partners: one or more **general partners** who have unlimited liability, and one or more **limited partners** whose liability is limited to the amount of their investment. In return for limited liability, limited partners agree not to take part in the day-to-day management of the firm. They help to finance the business but the general partners maintain operational control.

Advantages of Partnerships

Some advantages of partnerships come quickly to mind:

- *Ease of formation.* Like sole proprietorships, partnerships are easy to form. For most partnerships, applicable state laws are not complex. The partners agree to do business together and draw up a *partnership agreement.*
- *Availability of capital.* Because two or more people contribute financial resources, partnerships can raise funds more easily for operating expenses and business expansion. The partners' combined financial strength also increases the firm's ability to raise funds from outside sources.
- *Diversity of skills and expertise.* Partners share the responsibility of managing and operating the business. Ideal partnerships bring together people with complementary backgrounds rather than those with similar experience, skills, and talents. Combining partner skills to set goals, manage the overall direction of the firm, and problem solve increases the chances of the partnership's success. To find the right partner you must examine your own strengths and weaknesses, and know what you need from a partner. In Exhibit 5.2 you'll find some advice on choosing a partner.
- *Flexibility.* General partners are actively involved in managing their firm and can respond quickly to changes in the business environment.
- *No special taxes.* Partnerships pay no income taxes. A partnership must file a partnership return with the Internal Revenue Service, reporting how profits or losses were divided among the partners. Each partner's profit or loss is then reported on the partner's personal income tax return, with any profits taxed at personal income tax rates.
- *Relative freedom from government control.* Except for state rules for licensing and permits, the government has little control over partnership activities.

Disadvantages of Partnerships

Business owners must consider the following disadvantages of setting up their company as a partnership:

Exhibit 5.2 Perfect Partners

Picking a partner is both an art and a science. Be prepared to talk about everything. On paper someone may have all the right credentials, but does that person share your vision and the ideas you have for your company? Are they a straight shooter? Honesty, integrity, and ethics are equally important, as you may be liable for what your partner does. Trust your intuition and "your gut feelings—they're probably right," advises Irwin Gray, author of *The Perils of Partners*. So ask yourself the following questions and then ask a potential partner and see how well your answers match up:

1. Why do you want a partner?
2. What characteristics, talents, and skills does each person bring to the partnership?
3. How will you divide responsibilities? Consider every aspect of the business, from long-range planning to daily operations. Who will handle marketing, sales, accounting, customer service?
4. What is your long-term vision for the business (size, life span, financial commitment, etc.)?
5. What are your personal reasons for forming this company—are you looking for a steady paycheck, for independence, to create a small company, or to build a large one?
6. Are all parties willing to put in the same amount of time, and if not is there an alternative arrangement that is acceptable to everyone?
7. Do you have similar work ethics and values?
8. What requirements should be in the partnership agreement?

SOURCES: Julie Bawden Davis, "Buddy System," *Business Start Ups* (June 1998), downloaded from http://www.entreprenuer-mag.com; Azriela Jaffe, " 'Til Death Us Do Part' Is No Way to Start a Business," *Business Week Online* (October 23, 1998), downloaded from http://www.businessweek.com/smallbiz; Jerry Useem, "Partners on the Edge," *Inc.* (August 1998), pp. 54, 59.

- *Unlimited liability.* All general partners have unlimited liability for the debts of the business. In fact, any one partner can be held personally liable for all partnership debts and legal judgments (like malpractice)—regardless of who caused them. As with sole proprietorships, business failure can lead to a loss of the general partners' personal assets. To overcome this problem many states now allow the formation of *limited liability partnerships (LLPs)*, which protect each individual partner from responsibility for the acts of other partners, and limit their liability to harm resulting from their own actions.
- *Potential for conflicts between partners.* Partners may have different ideas about how to run the business, which employees to hire, how to allocate responsibilities, and when to expand. Differences in personalities and work styles can cause clashes, or breakdowns in communication, sometimes requiring outside intervention to save the business.
- *Sharing of profits.* Dividing the profits is relatively easy if all partners contribute equal amounts of time, expertise, and capital. But if one partner puts in more money and others more time it might be difficult to arrive at a fair profit-sharing formula.
- *Difficulty exiting or dissolving a partnership.* As a rule partnerships are easier to form than to leave. When one partner wants to leave, the value of his or her share must be calculated. To whom will that share be sold and will that person be acceptable to the other partners? If a partner who owns more than 50 percent of the entity withdraws, dies, or becomes disabled, the partnership must reorganize or end. To avoid these problems most partnership agree-

concept check

How does a partnership differ from a sole proprietorship?

Describe the three main types of partnerships and explain the difference between a limited partner and a general partner.

What are the main advantages and disadvantages of a partnership?

ments include specific guidelines for transfer of partnership interests, and buy–sell agreements that make provision for surviving partners to buy a deceased partner's interest. Partners can purchase special life insurance policies on each partner designed to fund such a purchase.

Business partnerships are often compared to marriages. As with a marriage, choosing the right partner is critical, so if you are considering forming a partnership, allow plenty of time to evaluate your and your potential partner's goals, personality, expertise, and working style.

Corporations: Limiting Your Liability

3 learning goal

corporation
A legal entity with an existence and life separate from its owners, who therefore are not personally liable for the entity's debts. A corporation is chartered by the state in which it is formed and can own property, enter into contracts, sue and be sued, and engage in business operations under the terms of its charter.

When people think of corporations they typically think of major, well-known companies like IBM, Microsoft, and General Electric. But corporations range in size from large multinationals with thousands of employees and billions of dollars in sales, to midsize or even smaller firms with few employees and revenues under $25,000.

A **corporation** is a legal entity with a life separate from its owners, so it is not personally liable for its debts. A corporation is subject to the laws of the state in which it is formed, where the right to operate as a business is issued by state charter. A corporation can own property, enter into contracts, sue and be sued, and engage in business operations under the terms of its charter. Unlike sole proprietorships and partnerships, corporations are taxable entities.

In launching his company, eEye Digital Security Inc., 21-year-old Mark Maiffret needed the limited liability protection of the corporate business organization model. Maiffret started hacking at age 15, learning how to mangle Web sites and breach networks. When the FBI suspected him of breaching a military network, Maiffret and Firas Bushnaq his boss (he dropped out of school to work for a software firm), decided to capitalize on his expertise. They launched eEye to outsmart the best hackers in the business by designing software to protect corporate network security.

Bearing the title "Chief Hacking Officer," Maiffret's growing company has five offices around the world and includes among their 50 employees a team of engineering hackers whose efforts bring eEye more than $1 million a month. Its unusual background makes eEye one of America's less conventional corporations.[4]

Although Michelle Hebert, founder of Pop Culture®, knew she wanted to market her gourmet popcorn using carts and kiosks, she also knew she needed the credibility and limited liability protection of a corporation to raise bank financing to expand her small business. Her chosen form of business organization, the S corporation, was an important ingredient in her recipe for success. (http://www.popcult.com)

Exhibit 5.3 The 10 Largest U.S. Corporations (ranked by 2002 sales)

	Company	Revenues ($ millions)
1	Wal-Mart Stores	246,525.0
2	General Motors	186,763.0
3	Exxon Mobil	182,466.0
4	Ford Motor	163,630.0
5	General Electric	131,698.0
6	Citigroup	100,789.0
7	ChevronTexaco	92,043.0
8	International Business Machines	83,132.0
9	American Intl. Group	67,722.8
10	Verizon Communications Group	67,625.0

SOURCE: "The Fortune 500," *Fortune* (April 14, 2003), p. F-1.

Corporations play an important role in the U.S. economy. As Exhibit 5.1 demonstrated, corporations account for only 18 percent of all businesses, but generate 86 percent of all revenues and 68 percent of all profits.

A list of the 10 largest U.S corporations, shown in Exhibit 5.3, includes many familiar names that affect our daily lives.

The Incorporation Process

Setting up a corporation is more complex than starting a sole proprietorship or partnership. Most states base their laws for chartering corporations on the Model Business Corporation Act of the American Bar Association, although registration procedures, fees, taxes, and laws regulating corporations vary from state to state.

A firm does not have to incorporate in the state where it is based and may benefit by comparing the rules of several states before choosing a state of incorporation. Although Delaware is a small state with few corporations actually based there, its pro-corporate policies make it the state of incorporation for many companies, including about half the Fortune 500. Incorporating a company involves five main steps:

- Selecting the company's name
- Writing the *articles of incorporation* (see Exhibit 5.4) and filing them with the appropriate state office, usually the secretary of state
- Paying required fees and taxes
- Holding an organizational meeting
- Adopting bylaws, electing directors, and passing the first operating resolutions

The state issues a corporate charter based on information in the articles of incorporation. Once the corporation has its charter it holds an organizational meeting to adopt bylaws, elect directors, and pass initial operating resolutions. Bylaws provide legal and managerial guidelines for operating the firm.

The Corporate Structure

As Exhibit 5.5 shows, corporations have their own organizational structure with three important components: stockholders, directors, and officers.

stockholders or shareholders
The owners of a corporation who hold shares of stock that provide certain rights.

Stockholders or shareholders are the owners of a corporation, holding shares of stock that provide them with certain rights. They may receive a portion of the

Exhibit 5.4 | Articles of Incorporation

Articles of incorporation are prepared on a form authorized or supplied by the state of incorporation. Although they may vary slightly from state to state, all articles of incorporation include the following key items:

- Name of corporation
- The company's goals
- Types of stock and number of shares of each type to issue
- Life of the corporation (usually "perpetual," meaning with no time limit)
- Minimum investment by the owners
- Methods for transferring share of stock
- Address of the corporate office
- Names and addresses of the first board of directors
- Name and addresses of the incorporators
- Other public information the incorporators wish to include

board of directors
A group of people elected by the stockholders to handle the overall management of a corporation, such as setting major corporate goals and policies, hiring corporate officers, and overseeing the firm's operations and finances.

corporation's profits in the form of dividends, and they can sell or transfer their ownership, their shares of stock in the corporation, at any time. Stockholders can attend annual meetings, elect the board of directors, and vote on matters that affect the corporation, in accordance with its charter and bylaws. Each share of stock generally carries one vote.

The stockholders elect a **board of directors** to govern and handle the overall management of the corporation. The directors set major corporate goals and policies, hire corporate officers, and oversee the firm's operations and finances. Small firms may have as few as 3 directors, whereas large corporations usually have 15 to 25.

Exhibit 5.5 | Organizational Structure of Corporations

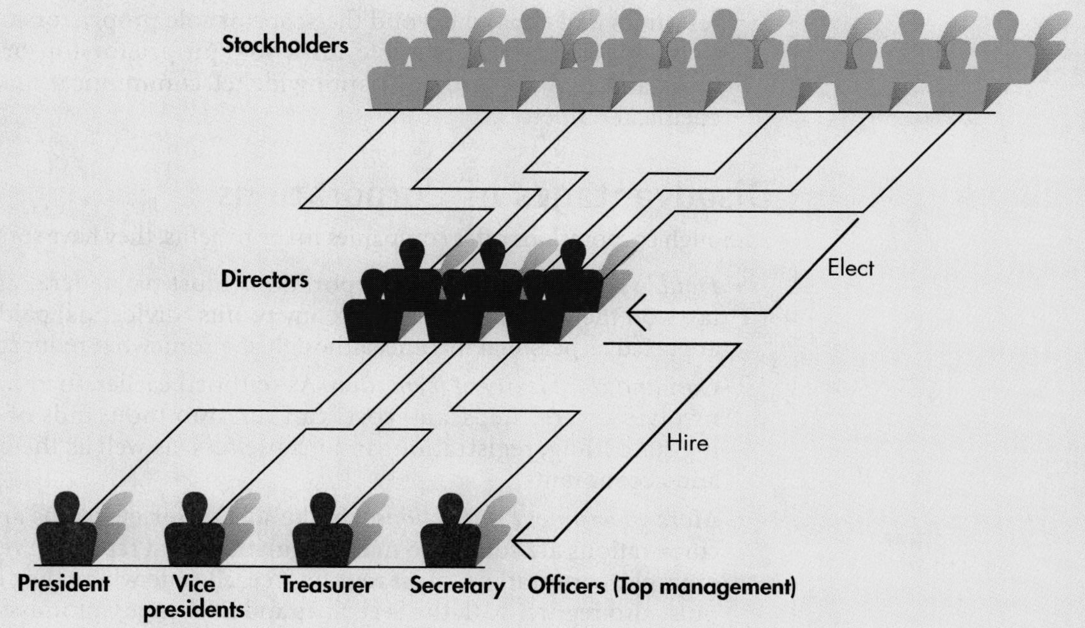

The boards of large corporations typically include both corporate executives and outside directors (not employed by the organization), chosen for their professional and personal expertise. Outside directors often bring a fresh view to the corporation's activities because they are independent of the firm. See "Making Ethical Choices" for an inside look at some of the decisions corporate boards make.

Hired by the board, the *officers* of a corporation are its top management, and include the president and chief executive officer (CEO), vice presidents, treasurer, and secretary, who are responsible for achieving corporate goals and policies. Officers may also be board members and stockholders.

Advantages of Corporations

The corporate structure allows companies to merge financial and human resources into enterprises with great potential for growth and profits:

- *Limited liability.* A key advantage of corporations is that they are separate legal entities that exist apart from their owners. An owner's (stockholder's) liability for the debts of the firm is limited to the amount of the stock they own. If the corporation goes bankrupt, creditors can look only to the assets of the corporation for payment.
- *Ease of transferring ownership.* Stockholders of public corporations can sell their shares at any time without affecting the status of the corporation.
- *Unlimited life.* The life of a corporation is unlimited. Although corporate charters specify a life term, they also include rules for renewal. Because the corporation is an entity separate from its owners, the death or withdrawal of an owner does not affect its existence, unlike a sole proprietorship or partnership.
- *Tax deductions.* Corporations are allowed certain tax deductions, such as operating expenses, which reduces their taxable income.
- *Ability to attract financing.* Corporations can raise money by selling new shares of stock. Dividing ownership into smaller units makes it affordable to more investors, who can purchase one or several thousand shares. The large size and stability of corporations also helps them get bank financing. All these financial resources allow corporations to invest in facilities and human resources and expand beyond the scope of sole proprietorships and partnerships. It would be impossible for a sole proprietorship or partnership to make automobiles, provide nationwide telecommunications, or build oil or chemical refineries.

Disadvantages of Corporations

Although corporations offer companies many benefits, they have some disadvantages:

- *Double taxation of profits.* Corporations must pay federal and state income taxes on their profits. In addition, any profits (dividends) paid to stockholders are taxed as personal income, although at a somewhat reduced rate.
- *Cost and complexity of formation.* As outlined earlier, forming a corporation involves several steps, and costs can run into thousands of dollars, including state filing, registration, and license fees, as well as the cost of attorneys and accountants.
- *More government restrictions.* Unlike sole proprietorships and partnerships, corporations are subject to many regulations and reporting requirements. For example, corporations must register in each state where they do business, and must also register with the Securities and Exchange Commission (SEC) before selling stock to the public. Unless it is closely held (owned by a small group of

Making Ethical Choices

xtra! http://gitmanxtra.swlearning.com

THE BOARD GAME

After an uninspiring and untroubled time in high school and an equally ho-hum undergraduate education during which you were content to "get by," you have found your place in the world of business. Everything clicks. You have a knack for seeing the big picture. You excel when working in multifaceted business environments—the more complex, the better. Companies value your fresh approach to structuring businesses for maximum productivity and profitability. Your adeptness has come to the attention of quite a few CEOs from a myriad of companies. In fact, you are one of the youngest people invited to serve on corporate boards of directors.

Wanting to focus most on your career, you accepted a seat on only one board—a young high-technology company, i2Technologies Inc., which has been losing money steadily. You're concerned that decisions about compensation for top executives that come before the board may further erode profitability and shareholder confidence. As a voting member, you must decide whether to approve awarding a severance package including a $500,000 consulting fee and a BMW Z-8 to Greg Brady, who was removed as CEO after a year of heavy losses. In addition to your concerns about the company's financial picture and shareholder loyalty, you wonder how your reputation as a young member of the board might be affected if you vote in favor of the award. "Many fear boards will continue to play games." How will you play?

ETHICAL DILEMMA

With your expertise in structuring for maximum profitability, would you vote in favor of the severance package and the huge bonus in the face of the company's dismal financial condition?

SOURCES: "Corporate Power, Influence, Money and Interlocking Boards of Directors Page," downloaded February 18, 2003, from http://www.verdant.net/corp.htm; and Arlene Weintraub and Ronald J. Grover, "Look Who's Still at the Trough," *Business Week*, September 9, 2002, p. 58.

stockholders), a firm must publish financial reports on a regular basis, and file other special reports with the SEC and state and federal agencies. These reporting requirements can impose substantial costs, and published information on corporate operations may also give competitors an advantage.

Types of Corporations

Three types of corporate business organization provide limited liability:

C corporation
Conventional or basic corporate form of organization.

The **C corporation** is the "basic" or conventional form of corporate organization. Small businesses may achieve liability protection through S corporations or limited liability companies (LLCs).

S corporation
A hybrid entity that is organized like a corporation, with stockholders, directors, and officers, but taxed like a partnership, with income and losses flowing through to the stockholders and taxed as their personal income.

An **S corporation** is a hybrid entity, allowing smaller corporations to avoid double taxation of corporate profits as long as they meet certain size and ownership requirements. Organized like a corporation with stockholders, directors, and officers, an S corporation is taxed like a partnership. Income and losses flow through to the stockholders and are taxed as personal income. S corporations are allowed a maximum of 75 qualifying shareholders and one class of stock. The owners of an S corporation are not personally liable for the debts of the corporation. Learn more about a company that chose to become an S corporation in the following "Focusing on Small Business" box.

Focusing on Small Business

Recipe for Success

Self-crowned Queen of Pop Michelle Hebert has always loved popcorn. When the Canadian company she worked for refused to expand to her home state of Michigan, Hebert decided to start Pop Culture, her own Detroit-based retail popcorn chain, with $8,000 of her own money. "Incredible passion and a great business plan went a long way," Hebert says, toward getting her the additional $100,000 Small Business Administration–guaranteed bank financing she needed to launch her company in 1996.

Set up as an S corporation, Hebert had "grandiose plans for Pop Culture to grow and franchise," right from the beginning. Hebert is now considering changing to the more flexible, less costly limited liability company (LLC) form of organization for her business. In addition, Hebert says she has "such lofty goals that I cannot achieve them by myself," and is looking to eventually bring in partners that will complement her strengths.

Offering a kaleidoscope of colors and 20 flavors to grab customers' attention, Hebert chose strategically placed kiosks in high-traffic malls and airports, rather than traditional retail spaces, to introduce her gourmet popcorn to the public. A good example of how an innovative concept can turn into a growth business, Hebert projects Pop Culture's current sales of $1.2 million will increase more than 100 percent this coming year.

Committed to long-term growth, Hebert has 40 employees and three retail outlets, with plans to open more stores and expand into franchising using Pop Culture's Web site (**http://www.popcult.com**) as a promotional tool. "There is no major national gourmet popcorn brand," she notes. Requests from customers for "sneak-in bags," solid-black bags of popcorn they could "sneak in" to movie theaters prompted Hebert to develop a plan for movie theaters to carry her gourmet popcorn.

Hebert has built her business presenting an old favorite with a new twist and a touch of theater, seducing her customers with Pop Culture's colorful displays and variety of flavors. Offering a product everyone loves may be a recipe for success, and Hebert's company looks like it is headed straight for the stars—five stars.[5]

CRITICAL THINKING QUESTIONS

1. Why did Michelle Hebert set up Pop Culture as an S corporation?
2. Should she change the structure of her company to a limited liability company (LLC)?

A newer type of business entity, the **limited liability company (LLC),** is also a hybrid organization. Although LLCs are not corporations, like S corporations they appeal to small businesses because they are easy to set up and not subject to many restrictions. LLCs offer the same liability protection as corporations and the option of being taxed as a partnership or a corporation. First authorized in Wyoming in 1977, LLCs became popular after a 1988 tax ruling that treats them like partnerships for tax purposes. Today all states allow the formation of LLCs.

Exhibit 5.6 summarizes the advantages and disadvantages of each form of business ownership.

concept check

What is a corporation? Describe how corporations are formed and structured.

Summarize the advantages and disadvantages of corporations. Which features contribute to the dominance of corporations in the business world?

Why do S corporations and limited liability companies (LLCs) appeal to small businesses?

Specialized Forms of Business Organization

4 learning goal

In addition to the three main forms, several specialized types of business organization play an important role in our economy. We will look at cooperatives and joint ventures in this section and take a detailed look at franchising in the following section.

limited liability company (LLC)
A hybrid organization that offers the same liability protection as a corporation but may be taxed as either a partnership or a corporation.

Cooperatives

Have you eaten a Sunkist orange or spread Land O' Lakes butter on your toast? If so, you have consumed foods produced by cooperatives. A **cooperative** is a legal entity with several corporate features, such as limited liability, an unlimited life span, an elected board of directors, and an administrative staff. Member-owners pay annual fees and share all profits, which are distributed to members in proportion to their contributions. Because they do not keep any profits, cooperatives are not subject to taxes.

Exhibit 5.6 | Advantages and Disadvantages of Major Types of Business Organization

	Sole Proprietorship	Partnership	Corporation
Advantages			
	Owner receives all profits.	More expertise and managerial skill available	Limited liability protects owners from losing more than they invest.
	Low organizational costs	Relatively low organizational costs	Can achieve large size due to marketability of stock (ownership).
	Income taxed as personal income of proprietor.	Income taxed as personal income of partners.	Ownership is readily transferable.
	Independence	Fund-raising ability is enhanced by more owners.	Long life of firm (not affected by death of owners)
	Secrecy		Can attract employees with specialized skills.
	Ease of dissolution		Greater access to financial resources allows growth.
			Receives certain tax advantages.
Disadvantages			
	Owner receives all losses.	Owners have unlimited liability; may have to cover debts of other, less financially sound partners.	Double taxation because both corporate profits and dividends paid to owners are taxed although the dividends are taxed at a reduced rate.
	Owner has unlimited liability; total wealth can be taken to satisfy business debts.	Dissolves or must reorganize when partner dies.	More expensive and complex to form
	Limited fund-raising ability can inhibit growth.	Difficult to liquidate or terminate	Subject to more government regulation
	Proprietor may have limited skills and management expertise.	Potential for conflicts between partners	Financial reporting requirements make operations public.
	Few long-range opportunities and benefits for employees	Difficult to achieve large-scale operations	
	Lacks continuity when owner dies		

cooperatives
A legal entity typically formed by people with similar interests, such as suppliers or customers, to reduce costs and gain economic power. A cooperative has limited liability, an unlimited life span, an elected board of directors, and an administrative staff; all profits are distributed to the member-owners in proportion to their contributions.

By forming cooperatives, small companies can obtain discounts to lower costs and increase purchasing power and efficiency, allowing them to compete with larger organizations. Cooperatives may be organized to provide just about any good or service, like food, childcare, business or financial services, health care, the marketing of agricultural and other products, and utilities and cablevision.

By pooling their buying power, cooperative members can purchase goods nearly as cheaply as the biggest companies do, giving the corner Ace Hardware store a chance to survive against retailing giants, Home Depot Inc. and Lowe's.

Founded in 1924, Ace Hardware is one of the nation's largest cooperatives and is wholly owned by its 5,100 independent hardware retailer members. Stores span all 50 states and 68 countries, with 50 new retail stores on the drawing board. Retail sales for the first nine months of 2002 increased 4.3 percent to $2.3 billion.[6]

© TERRI L. MILLER / E-VISUAL COMMUNICATIONS, INC.

Seller cooperatives are popular with small agricultural producers as a more effective way to compete with larger producers. Much of the food we eat today is produced by growers who belong to a cooperative.

There are two types of cooperatives. **Seller cooperatives** are popular in agriculture, as individual producers join to compete more effectively with large producers. Member dues support market development, national advertising, and other business activities. In addition to Sunkist and Land O'Lakes, other familiar cooperatives are Calavo (avocados), Ocean Spray (cranberries and juices), and Blue Diamond (nuts). Farmland Industries, the largest cooperative in the United States, sells feed, fertilizer, petroleum, and grain.

Buyer cooperatives combine members' purchasing power. Buying in volume results in lower prices. The number of U.S. businesses belonging to purchasing cooperatives has roughly doubled over the past decade to about 50,000, estimates Paul Hazen, president and chief executive officer of the National Cooperative Business Association, a Washington, DC–based trade group.[7] Food cooperatives are another example, and college bookstores may operate as buyer cooperatives. At the end of the year, members get shares of the profits based on how much they bought.

seller cooperative
Individual producers who join together to compete more effectively with large producers.

Joint Ventures

In a **joint venture** two or more companies form an alliance to pursue a specific project, usually for a specified time period. There are many reasons for joint ventures. The project may be too large for one company to handle on its own, and by forming joint ventures companies can gain access to new markets, products, or technology. Both large and small companies can benefit from joint ventures.

In December 2002, Pfizer, the world's largest pharmaceutical company, paid $400 million to a small San Diego biotechnology company, Neurocrine Biosciences, for rights to an experimental insomnia drug. The two companies will share rights in the lucrative U.S. market, while Pfizer retains exclusive rights to markets for the drug outside the United States. The deal underscores the growing importance of alliances between big companies with deep pockets and innovative but cash-poor smaller companies.

"To be set up with cash, a substantial share of profits, and a sales force from the world's top pharmaceutical company is a small biotech's dream," said analyst Matthew Geller of CIBC World Markets.[8]

concept check

Describe the two types of cooperatives and the advantages of each.

What are the benefits of joint ventures?

Franchising: A Popular Trend

5 learning goal

When the occasion calls for fewer calories than chocolate, but more taste than tulips, go for fancy fruit, artfully arranged bouquets by Edible Arrangements. Inspired by a photograph, Tariq Farid began test marketing fresh-fruit bouquet designs in 1997. Two years later he opened his first Edible store, selling colorful bouquets of florally sculpted fruit. A second store followed a year later, and by 2002 the stores showed combined revenues of $1.2 million.

On a mission to bring his healthy treats to the rest of the country, Farid sold his first two franchises in Boston and Atlanta. Costs range between $60,000 and $120,000 depending on location, with a $25,000 franchisee fee and 4 percent royalties, and there are plans to sell 30 more over the next five years. Seeking his first outside financing to fund his expansion, Farid is optimistic about the future. "We have a great name, a strategic head start, and a product that sells itself," he says. And there's always the chance that a deep-pocket national florist like FTD will want to enjoy the fruits of his labors, too.[9]

buyer cooperative
A group of cooperative members who unite for combined purchasing power.

joint venture
Two or more companies that form an alliance to pursue a specific project for a specified time period.

Jeff Sinelli projects his innovative restaurant franchise, Genghis Grill—The Mongolian Feast, will grow to between 200–300 units by 2007, thanks in part to the high number of franchisees already signed on.

COURTESY OF GENGHIS GRILL

franchising
A form of business organization based on a business arrangement between a *franchisor*, which supplies the product concept, and the *franchisee*, who sells the goods or services of the franchisor in a certain geographic area.

franchisor
In a franchising arrangement, the company that supplies the product concept to the *franchisee*.

franchisee
In a franchising arrangement, the individual or company that sells the goods or services of the *franchisor* in a certain geographic area.

As you can see, franchising comes in all sizes, from McDonald's, the world's largest food service retailer with 30,000 restaurants in 121 countries (70% are owned and operated by franchisees), to new kid on the block, Edible Arrangements. Exhibit 5.7 shows a selection of low-cost franchises, with some priced as low as $2,400.

Chances are you deal with franchise systems in your neighborhood every day. When you have lunch at Taco Bell or Jamba Juice, make copies at Kinko's, change your oil at Jiffy Lube, buy candles at Wick's 'n' Sticks, or mail a package at the UPS Store, you are dealing with a franchised business. These and other familiar name brands mean quality, consistency, and value to customers.

Providing a way to own a business without starting it from scratch, franchising is one of the fastest growing segments of the economy. **Franchising** is a form of business organization that involves a business arrangement between a **franchisor,** the company supplying the product concept, and the **franchisee,** the individual or

Exhibit 5.7 A Selection of Low-Investment Franchises (start-up cost under $50,000)

Dent Doctor (paint-free dent repair)	$49,950
Coffee News (weekly restaurant newspaper)	$ 2,400
Candy Bouquet (floral-like gourmet confections)	$ 7,300
Geeks on Call America (on-site computer support services)	$37,400
KidzArt (art training)	$ 9,900
Curves for Women (women's fitness/weight loss centers)	$25,600
Outdoor Connection (fishing/hunting trips)	$ 9,600
Bonus Building Care (commercial cleaning)	$ 7,600
Pee Wee Workout (pre-school fitness program)	$ 2,700
Rent-A-Wreck (auto leasing)	$32,800

SOURCE: "Low Investment Franchises," *Entrepreneur Magazine's 2003 Franchise 500,* http://www.entrepreneur.com. Reprinted with permission of *Entrepreneur Magazine,* Franchise 500 2003, http://www.entrepreneur.com.

company selling those goods or services in a certain geographic area. The franchisee buys a package that includes a proven product, proven operating methods, and training in managing their business.

franchise agreement
A contract setting out the terms of a franchising arrangement, including the rules for running the franchise, the services provided by the franchisor, and the financial terms. Under the contract, the franchisee is allowed to use the franchisor's business name, trademark, and logo.

A **franchise agreement** is a contract allowing the franchisee to use the franchisor's business name, trademark, and logo. The agreement also outlines the rules for running the franchise, the services provided by the franchisor, and the financial terms. The franchisee agrees to keep inventory at certain levels, buy a standard equipment package, keep up sales and service levels, follow the franchisor's operating rules, take part in franchisor promotions, and maintain a relationship with the franchisor. In return, the franchisor provides the use of a proven company name and symbols, help finding a site, building plans, guidance and training, management assistance, managerial and accounting procedures, employee training, wholesale prices for supplies, and financial assistance.

Advantages of Franchises

Like other forms of business organization, franchising offers some distinct advantages:

- *Increased ability for franchisor to expand.* Because franchisees finance their own units, franchisors can grow without making a major investment. Russ Cooper, senior vice president and general manager of franchising at GNC, was excited when franchisee Michael Taylor brought the idea of a smoothie bar to him. He says Taylor's idea was appealing because "the smoothie industry is a $1.2 billion industry with no real leader." He expects 500 to 1,000 stores will eventually have smoothie bars, and GNC is also aiming to open stand-alone smoothie bars selling blended drinks and 100 of their top-selling supplements.[10]
- *Recognized name, product, and operating concept.* The franchisee gets a widely known and accepted business with a proven track record, as well as operating procedures, standard goods and services, and national advertising. Consumers know they can depend on products from franchises like Pizza Hut, Hertz, and Holiday Inn. As a result, the franchisee's risk is reduced and the opportunity for success increased.
- *Management training and assistance.* The franchisor provides a structured training program that gives the new franchisee a crash course in how to start and operate their business. Ongoing training programs for managers and employees are another plus. In addition, franchisees have a peer group for support and sharing ideas.
- *Financial assistance.* Being linked to a nationally known company can help a franchisee obtain funds from a lender. Also, the franchisor typically gives the franchisee advice on financial management, referrals to lenders, and help in preparing loan applications. Many franchisors also offer payment plans, short-term credit for buying supplies from the franchise company, and loans to purchase real estate and equipment. Although franchisors give up a share of profits to their franchisees, they receive ongoing revenues in the form of royalty payments.

Disadvantages of Franchises

Franchising also has some disadvantages:

- *Loss of control.* The franchisor has to give up some control over operations and has less control over its franchisees than over company employees.
- *Cost of franchising.* Franchising can be a costly form of business. Costs will vary depending on the type of business, and may include expensive facilities and equipment. The franchisee also pays fees and/or royalties, which are usually tied to a percentage of sales. Fees for national and local advertising and management advice may add to a franchisee's ongoing costs.

- *Restricted operating freedom.* The franchisee agrees to conform to the franchisor's operating rules and facilities design, as well as inventory and supply standards. Some franchises require franchisees to purchase from only the franchisor or approved suppliers. The franchisor may restrict the franchisee's territory or site, which could limit growth. Failure to conform to franchisor policies could mean the loss of the franchise.

Franchise Growth

Many of today's major names in franchising, like McDonald's and Kentucky Fried Chicken, started in the 1950s, but franchising grew rapidly through the 1960s and 1970s with more types of businesses—clothing, convenience stores, business services, and many others—using franchising to distribute their goods and services. Business owners found franchising a way to expand operations quickly into new geographic areas with limited capital investment, and many are turning to technology to expand their businesses (see "Applying Technology" box on page 168).

Accounting for an estimated 50 percent of U.S. retail sales, 1,500 American companies in 75 industries use the franchise system, with 320,000 individual franchisees employing 8 million people, roughly 1 in every 17 workers.[11] Exhibit 5.8 shows some of the fastest growing franchises.

One of the fastest-growing segments in the franchise industry is women, who currently own 38 percent of all franchises, are multiple-unit owners, and are buying franchises outside of traditional women's areas. Franchising is a relationship-driven industry, and women are good at managing relationships as well as business.

With many franchisors making their recruitment a front-burner issue, women and minorities have more opportunities to get into franchising by taking advantage of special financial assistance and support programs offered to them.[12]

International Franchising

Like other forms of business, franchising is part of our global marketplace, with most franchise systems already operating units internationally, or planning to expand overseas, as international demand for all types of goods and services grows. International Franchise Association data show the number of new overseas franchise locations increased by more than 40 percent in 2000, with 300 U.S. companies (out of 1,500 total) showing an international presence.[13]

An example of this is the UPS Stores, with 1,092 of their 4,491 units located in more than 40 countries outside the United States. "The building of our brand

Exhibit 5.8 Top 10 Fastest-Growing Franchises

1.	Curves for Women	(Fitness)
2.	Subway	(Fast Food)
3.	7-Eleven Inc.	(Convenience Store)
4.	Taco Bell Corp.	(Fast Food)
5.	Jani-King	(Janitorial Services)
6.	McDonald's	(Fast Food)
7.	Jan-Pro Franchising Int'l Inc.	(Janitorial Services)
8.	Baskin-Robbins USA Co.	(Ice Cream)
9.	The Quizno's Franchise Co.	(Fast Food)
10.	KFC Corp.	(Fast Food)

SOURCE: "Fastest Growing Franchises for 2003," *Entrepreneur Magazine's 2003 Franchise 500,* http://www.entrepreneur.com. Reprinted with permission of *Entrepreneur Magazine,* Franchise 500 2003, http://www.entrepreneur.com.

outside the U.S. is a core objective for our company," says Peter Holt, executive vice president of franchise sales and development. "We see international franchising as a huge growth opportunity, and a strategic part of building our business."[14]

Restaurants, hotels, business services, educational products, car rentals, and nonfood retail stores are currently among the most popular types of international franchises. Franchisors in foreign countries face many of the same problems as other firms doing business abroad. In addition to tracking markets and currency changes, franchisors must understand local culture, language differences, and the political environment.

Franchisors in foreign countries also face the challenge of aligning their business operations with the goals of their franchisees, who may be located half a globe away.

concept check

Describe franchising and the main parties to the transaction.

Summarize the major advantages and disadvantages of franchising.

Why has franchising proved so popular?

MERGERS AND ACQUISITIONS

6 learning goal

As the 20th century drew to a close and corporations continued to merge at record levels, nearly $4 trillion worth of mergers were done from 1998 through 2000, more than in the preceding 30 years. January 2000 saw the biggest merger ever when America Online Inc. made its all-stock bid of $160 billion for Time Warner Inc.

But in the new millennium companies may be taking a more cautious approach to mergers, no longer rushing headlong into megamergers, and looking at joint venturing and other options to obtain the technology and new markets they need to expand their business. We'll discuss this trend in more detail later in this chapter.

merger
The combination of two or more firms to form a new company, which often takes on a new corporate identity.

A **merger** occurs when two or more firms combine to form one new company. Paper giant Weyerhaeuser Company snapped up Willamette Industries for $6.11 billion in February 2002, saving $1 million a year by linking operations. Mergers like this one, in well-established industries, can produce winning results in terms of improved efficiency and cost savings. Another example is the oil industry merger between Phillips and Conoco. The synergies between the companies, first estimated to produce annual savings of $750,000, were later raised to $1.25 billion per year.[15] A selection of megamergers is shown in Exhibit 5.9.

Sometimes the newly formed company assumes a completely new identity. Citibank purchased Travelers Insurance Company, Salomon Brothers (bond trad-

Conglomerate Altria Group (formerly called Philip Morris) has moved from an original focus on tobacco and beer products into multiple food categories, including cookies, coffee, cheese, and snacks, through years of mergers and acquisitions.

© TERRI L. MILLER / E-VISUAL COMMUNICATIONS, INC.

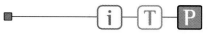

Exhibit 5.9 | Selected Megamergers, 1998–2002

Year*	Acquirer	Target	Industry	Value** ($ Billions)
2000	America Online	Time-Warner	Media/Internet	$165.9
1999	Vodafone AirTouch	Mannesmann	Telecommunications	124.8
1999	Pfizer	Warner-Lambert	Pharmaceuticals	93.9
1998	Exxon	Mobil	Oil and gas	77.2
1998	Travelers Group	Citicorp	Financial services	70.0
1998	SBC	Ameritech	Telecommunications	61.4
1999	Vodafone Group	AirTouch Communications	Telecommunications	60.3
2002	Pfizer	Pharmacia	Pharmaceuticals	59.9
1998	Nationsbank	BankAmerica	Banking	59.3
1999	AT&T	MediaOne	Telecommunications/Cable	55.8
1998	Bell Atlantic (Verizon)	GTE	Telecommunications	52.8
2001	Comcast	AT&T Broadband	Cable	47.0
1999	Viacom	CBS	Media	40.4
1999	Qwest	U.S. West	Telecommunications	40.3
1998	Daimler-Benz	Chrysler	Motor vehicles	38.6

*Announced.
**Based on stock value on announcement date. Actual price at completion may differ.

SOURCES: "Big Deals," *Business Week*, October 14, 2002, p. 64; "Ten Biggest Worldwide Deals," *The Wall Street Journal*, January 2, 2003, p. R6; "2001's Megamergers," *The Wall Street Journal*, January 2, 2002, p. R10.

ing, investment banking), and Smith Barney (retail brokerage), and merged them into a giant financial-services conglomerate called Citigroup.

acquisition
The purchase of a corporation by another corporation or by an investor group; the identity of the acquired company may be lost.

In an **acquisition**, a corporation or investor group finds a target company and negotiates with its board of directors on the acquisition. In Chevron's recent $36 billion acquisition of Texaco, Chevron was the acquirer, Texaco the target company. Sometimes the identity of the acquired business may be lost. In Chase Manhattan Bank's September 2000 takeover of JP Morgan, a small, prestigious investment bank, much of the smaller company's identity was lost under new Chase management.

Merger Motives

Although headlines tend to focus on megamergers, "merger mania" affects small companies too. General Electric has acquired a record 534 small companies over six years, more than 7 per month.[16] Roxio Inc. acquired online music service Napster Inc.'s remaining assets for stock and cash valued at around $5 million to help Roxio "expand its role in the digital-media landscape."[17]

Motives for mergers and acquisitions tend to be similar, regardless of the company's size. The goal is often strategic: to improve overall performance of the merged firms through cost savings, elimination of overlapping operations, improved purchasing power, increased market share, or reduced competition. Pacific Cycles bid $86 million for the venerable, but bankrupt Schwinn/GT Bicycle Company. Its goal was to knock out competition from Huffy and boost market share.[18]

Company growth, broadening product lines, and the ability to quickly acquire new markets, technology, or management skills are other motives for acquiring a company. Purchasing a company can offer a faster, less risky, and less costly option than developing products or markets in-house or expanding internationally. In 2002's largest deal, cable operator Comcast Corp. paid $54 billion to acquire AT&T Broadband. The new company, AT&T Comcast Corp., will be unprecedented in size and influence. Before the merger Comcast had 8.5 million customers in four major cities. Now 21 million customers in 17 cities will be hooked up to its systems. That's nearly twice as many as the next biggest cable operator, Time Warner Cable, or one in every five homes in America that has a television.[19]

Another motive for acquisitions is financial restructuring—cutting costs, selling off units, laying off employees, and refinancing the company to increase its value to stockholders. Financially motivated mergers are based not on the potential to achieve economies of scale, but rather on the acquirer's belief that the target has hidden value to be unlocked through restructuring. Most financially motivated mergers involve larger companies.

Types of Mergers

horizontal merger
A merger of companies at the same stage in the same industry; done to reduce costs, expand product offerings, or reduce competition.

vertical merger
A merger of companies at different stages in the same industry; done to gain control over supplies of resources or to gain access to different markets.

The three main types of mergers are horizontal, vertical, and conglomerate. In a **horizontal merger**, companies at the same stage in the same industry merge to reduce costs, expand product offerings, or reduce competition. Many of the largest mergers are horizontal mergers to achieve economies of scale. When Qwest acquired former regional Bell operating company U.S. West, the goal was to create a larger company to dominate the newly deregulated telecommunications industry.

In a **vertical merger**, a company buys a firm in its same industry, involved in an earlier or later stage of the production or sales process. Buying a supplier of raw materials, a distribution company, or a customer gives the acquiring firm more control. America Online (AOL) Inc. acquires companies that address different Internet-related markets and capabilities. In its $4.2 billion acquisition of Netscape Communications Corp., AOL focused on Netscape's strong presence in the corporate market and their software technology, including powerful Web browser software and behind-the-scenes software to run Web sites and conduct electronic commerce.

APPLYING TECHNOLOGY

BBQ Franchise Sizzles—on eBay

In the late 12th century, military leader Genghis Kahn created an immense empire, and Jeff Sinelli is looking to do the same with his innovative, Texas-based, restaurant franchise, Genghis Grill - The Mongolian Feast. Voted 2002 winner for most imaginative new restaurant concept by Hot Concepts, a restaurant industry event, Genghis Grill currently has four company-owned restaurants and nine others in development.

Sinelli believes technology will help his empire grow. "One of our guiding principles is to use technology to increase our presence, prosperity and profits," he says, adding that their Web site (**http://www.genghisgrill.com**) is a profit center, supported by sales of Genghis merchandise. It also offers Internet specials and birthday bowl coupons to guests who register. "We feel it is a race to 100 stores before anyone has a true brand in the Mongolian BBQ segment, and we're looking to raise awareness of the cooking style," says Sinelli, explaining that guests "build their own bowl" from a selection of meats, vegetables, and sauces.[20]

When discussing the company's growth objectives with his franchise team, Sinelli jokingly suggested selling Genghis Grill franchises on eBay. They liked the idea so much they submitted a plan to lawyers, who agreed it was feasible, and then approached eBay. eBay knows a good thing when it sees it. With dramatic increases in business-to-business (B2B) sales on the auction site, eBay unveiled a B2B auction portal in January 2003. "We're going to make it easier for businesses to find what they're looking for," says Jordan Glazier, director of B2B at eBay.[21]

Although service businesses have not sold successfully on eBay,[22] about 12,000 businesses, in manufacturing, service, and retail, are posted on eBay each month, up 35 percent from last year. When Greg Burke ran across the "businesses for sale" category on eBay, he put his leather-goods store up for auction. "It took me five minutes," he says. "I already had photos of the store." And the price is right. Sellers pay $300 for a 90-day listing, and just $3 extra for an agreement to sell.

After launching the world's first online franchise auction in the first quarter of 2003, Sinelli turned to expanding Genghis Grill's relationship with eBay—auctioning off territories, build-out, and equipment. Sinelli believes the timing is right. "It's an original idea that really fits our culture," he says.

CRITICAL THINKING QUESTIONS

1. How are some franchisors using technology to expand their businesses?
2. Name the benefits to businesses and eBay of their new B2B portal?

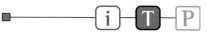

conglomerate merger
A merger of companies in unrelated businesses; done to reduce risk.

A **conglomerate merger** brings together companies in unrelated businesses to reduce risk. Combining companies whose products have different seasonal patterns or respond differently to business cycles can result in more stable sales. The Philip Morris Company, now called Altria, started out in the tobacco industry, but diversified as early as the 1960s with the acquisition of Miller Brewing Company, followed later by the purchase of General Foods, Kraft Foods, and Nabisco, among others. Current product categories include confectionery, cookies, snack foods, powdered soft drinks, convenience foods, cheese, and coffee.

A specialized, financially motivated type of merger, the **leveraged buyout (LBO),** became popular in the 1980s but is less common today. LBOs are corporate takeovers financed by large amounts of borrowed money—as much as 90 percent of the purchase price. LBOs can be started by outside investors or the corporation's management.

Believing that a company is worth more than the value of all its stock, they buy the stock and take the company private, expecting to increase cash flow by improving operating efficiency or selling off units for cash to pay off debt. Although some LBOs did improve efficiency, many did not live up to investor expectations or generate enough cash to pay their debt.

concept check

Differentiate between a merger and an acquisition.

What are the most common motives for corporate mergers and acquisitions?

Describe the different types of corporate mergers.

Trends in Business Ownership

7 learning goal

As we learned in Chapter 1, an awareness of trends in the business environment is critical to business success. Many social, demographic, and technology trends affect how businesses organize. When reviewing options for organizing a business or choosing a career path, consider the following trends in franchising and mergers and acquisitions.

Franchising: Changing Demographics

leveraged buyout (LBO)
A corporate takeover financed by large amounts of borrowed money; can be started by outside investors or by a company's own management.

Although women have been involved in franchising for years, they were unseen powers behind the scenes, running the store while their husbands did the business deals. Now franchisors want access to markets they hadn't considered and believe that women can get them there. By making more financing and loan programs available to women, they are creating opportunities for them to become franchisees in their own right. Many of the leading franchisors, like 7-Eleven, KFC, and Thrifty Car Rental, offer special programs to help women get into the franchise business.

What has prompted this turnaround? Some franchisors made recruiting women a front-burner issue in response to pressure from lawsuits, government advocacy, and civil rights groups. One study shows that 22.5 percent of franchisors offer women direct financial assistance, while another 50 percent offer indirect help. Industry insiders see this as proof that women are an increasingly valued resource for franchisors—and they are doing what is necessary to get women into their business and keep them there.[23]

Franchise Innovations

As more franchise systems crowd into growing industry categories, established franchises must find ways to differentiate themselves, such as the following:

- *Multiple-concept franchises.* What's the driving force behind the trend? "We saw we could take a competency we'd developed in one company and bridge it

© PAUL A. SOUDERS/CORBIS

Franchisees enjoy economies of scale and improved efficiency with the multiple concept franchise, by applying expertise learned in one type of restaurant franchising to other similar outlets.

over to another—the skills of franchising are transferable," says Steven Rogers, president and CEO of The Franchise Company, parent of home improvement franchises California Closets, Certa ProPainters, Paul Davis Restoration, and Stained Glass Overlay. Other multiconcept franchisors see consolidating as a way to improve efficiencies and save money. Combination franchise Molly Maid and Mr. Handyman benefit from shared marketing and promotion, hoping to appeal to a similar customer.[24]

- *Expanded product offerings.* Franchisee Greg Hund's six-year-old New York City–based Mail Boxes Etc. offers Virtual Doorman service for customers without the real thing, assuring safe deliveries of dry cleaning, floral arrangements, or packages, for a $10 per item delivery fee.[25]
- *Cross-branding.* Operating two or more franchises in one location generates more customer traffic and maximizes space, personnel, and management utilization. GNC stores now have smoothie bars, bookstores combine with coffee shops, pizza shops with ice-cream parlors.
- *New ideas.* With personalized gift giving all the rage, Steve Mandell, founder of Party City, tapped into the trend with his Pawsenclaws & Co. franchise, where customers select, stuff, and dress animals from elephants to bears, and record customized messages, played by pressing the animal's paw. The New Jersey–based company projects nine locations by year end, six of them run by franchisees.[26]

MERGERS: EMERGING TRUTHS

Size is definitely an advantage when competing in the global marketplace, but bigger does not always mean better. In a recent cover story, *Business Week* published results of an exclusive new study showing that 17 out of 20 heady megamerger "winners" were, in fact, a bust for investors who owned their shares. Their analysis showed that a full 61 percent of buyers destroyed their own shareholders' wealth. So the merger landscape is changing, with companies considering other options before stuffing their dollars in the biggest merger slot machine they can find.

But why were shareholders hung out to dry in the flood of mergers? In their eagerness to snare a deal, many buyers paid a premium that wiped out the merger's entire potential economic gain. Often managers envisioned grand synergies that proved illusory or unworkable, or bought a pig in a poke—not fully understanding what they were getting. They also underestimated the costs and logistical nightmare of consolidating the operations of merged companies with very different cultures, and failed to keep key employees aboard, sales forces selling, and customers happy. "Integrating acquisitions is both an art and a science," says Jack Levy, cochairman of mergers and acquisitions at Goldman, Sachs & Co.[27]

With a weak stock market, the total value of U.S. deals in 2002 was only $447.8 billion, the lowest level since 1994 and over 40 percent less than in 2001. When stock prices are low, acquirers' stock is no longer an attractive form of payment.[28] The number of deals dropped as well, although global merger markets were not down quite as much.

Companies will continue to seek out acquisition candidates, but the fundamental business case for merging will have to be strong. Activity is expected to come from sectors like health care, financial services, and general industry, with fewer deals in technology, telecommunications, and media. These big drivers of the past merger wave are expected to remain weak.

What should companies look for to identify mergers with a better-than-even chance of turning out well?

- A purchase price that is low enough—a 10 percent premium over the market price as opposed to 50 percent—so the buyer doesn't need heroic synergies to make the deal work.
- A target that is significantly smaller than the buyer—and in a business the buyer understands well. The more "transformational" the deal, such as entering a new business arena, the bigger the risk.
- A buyer who pays in cash and not overinflated stock. "Using stock to fund acquisitions has the same effect as using chips in a casino," says Lawrence Cunningham, author of *Outsmarting the Smart Money*. "It's the first emotional step to separating people from their money."
- Evidence that the deal isn't purely the brainchild of an egocentric CEO. Mergers are tough—culturally, commercially, and logistically. The most important quality a company can bring to a merger may be humility.[29]

concept check

What incentives are franchisors offering to women to get them involved in the franchise business?

What caused the failure of recent megamergers?

Great Ideas to Use Now

It is important to understand the benefits of different forms of business organization if you start your own company. If you decide to work for someone else, this information will help you match a business entity with your goals. Suppose you are considering two job offers for a computer-programming position: a two-year-old consulting firm with 10 employees owned by a sole proprietor, or a publicly traded software developer with sales of $500 million. In addition to comparing the specific job responsibilities, consider the following:

- Which company offers better training? Do you prefer the on-the-job training you'll get at the small company, or do you want formal training programs as well?
- Which position offers the chance to work on a variety of assignments?
- What are the opportunities for advancement? Employee benefits?
- What happens if the owner of the young company gets sick or decides to sell the company?
- Which company offers a better working environment for you?

Answering these and similar questions will help you decide which job meets your particular needs.

COURTESY OF LEARNING EXPRESS

Franchisors use ads like this one to attract new franchisees. Learning Express, a toy retailer, wants to be "Your Neighborhood Store." It offers those with a love of kids, toys, and learning an opportunity to become entrepreneurs in a fun industry.

Is Franchising in Your Future?

If the franchise route to business ownership interests you, begin educating yourself on the franchise process by investigating various franchise opportunities. You should research a franchise company thoroughly before making any financial commitment. Once you've narrowed your choices, ask for the *Uniform Franchise Offering Circular (UFOC)* for that franchisor, and read it thoroughly. The Federal Trade Commission (FTC) requires franchisors to prepare this document, which provides a wealth of information about the franchisor including its history, operating style, management, past or pending litigation, the franchisee's financial obligations, and any restrictions on the sale of units. Interviewing current and past franchisees is another essential step.

Would-be franchisees should check recent issues of small-business magazines such as *Franchise Zone, Entrepreneur, Inc., Business Start Ups,* and *Success,* for industry trends, ideas on promising franchise opportunities, and advice on how to choose and run a franchise. The International Franchise Association Web site at **http://www.franchise.org** has links to *Franchise World Magazine* and other useful sites. (For other franchise-related sites, see the "Try It Now" box and the "Working the Net" questions on page 177.)

Is franchising for you? Assertiveness, desire to be your own boss, willingness to make a substantial time commitment, passion about the franchise concept, optimism, patience, and integrity rank high on franchisors' lists. Prior business experience is also a definite plus, and some franchisors prefer or require experience in their field. The information in Exhibit 5.10 can help you make a realistic self-assessment to increase your chances of success.

Exhibit 5.10 Are You Ready to Be a Franchisee?

What can you to do to prepare when considering the purchase of a franchise? Doing your homework can spell the difference between success and failure, and some early preparation can help lay the groundwork for a successful launch of your franchised business.

Getting to know your banker at an early date should speed the loan process if you plan to finance your purchase with a bank loan. Stop by and introduce yourself. The proper real estate is a critical component for a successful retail/food franchise, so establish a relationship with a commercial real estate broker and begin scouting locations.

Professional guidance while evaluating franchise opportunities can prevent expensive mistakes, so interview advisers to find one that is right for you. Selecting an attorney with franchise experience will speed the review of your franchise agreement. Most franchise systems use computers so if you are not computer literate, take a class in the basics.

Then ask yourself some searching questions:

- Are you willing to work hard and put in long hours?
- Do you have the necessary financial resources?
- Are you excited about a specific franchise concept?
- Do you have prior business experience?
- Do your expectations and personal goals match the franchisor's?

SOURCES: Michael H. Seid and Kay Marie Ainsley, "Are You Ready to be a Franchisee?" *FranchiseZone,* December 9, 2002, downloaded from http://www.entrepreneur.com; and Thomas Love, "The Perfect Franchisee," *Nation's Business,* April 1, 1998, downloaded from http://ask.elibrary.com.

Try It Now

1. **Learn the laws.** Before starting your own company you should know the legal requirements in your area. Call the appropriate city or country departments, such as licensing, health, and zoning, to find out what licenses and permits you need, and any other requirements you must meet. Do the requirements vary depending on the type of company? Are there restrictions on starting a home-based business? Then contact your secretary of state or other agency that handles corporations to get information on how to incorporate.
2. **Study franchise opportunities.** Franchising offers an alternative to starting your own business from scratch. Do you have what it takes to be successful? Start by making a list of your interests and skills, and do a self-assessment using some of the suggestions in the last section of this chapter. Next you need to narrow a field of thousands of different franchise systems. At Franchise Handbook Online (**http://www.franchise1.com**), you'll find articles with checklists to help you thoroughly research a franchise and its industry, as well as a directory of franchise opportunities. Armed with this information, you can develop a questionnaire to evaluate a prospective franchise.

Mergers and You

Mergers and acquisitions change the business environment for employees, business owners, and customers. A merger announcement increases stress levels for all employees, and you may have to live with uncertainty for many months while the companies work out the details of integrating two operations. You may lose your job when overlapping departments are combined. According to outplacement firm, Challenger, Gray and Christmas, mergers have been responsible for huge job losses in past years.

If you work for an acquiring or target company, what does this mean careerwise? It is important to develop a portfolio of transferable skills, and keep the quality and quantity of your work at the highest possible levels. This increases your

Customer Satisfaction and Quality

Most companies allocate substantial dollars to winning new business, but rarely spend time or money trying to keep the customers they already have. Understanding the importance of satisfying today's demanding consumer can be a matter of business survival. "The fastest, least expensive way to make more money and grow your business is to become a service leader," says John Tschohl, author of *Achieving Excellence Through Customer Service.*[30]

An example of this lesson well learned is an auto repair franchise called Caliber Collision Centers. Feeling frazzled after a car accident? Let a Caliber Collision Center take care of you—and your vehicle. Offering the vehicle owner unprecedented customer service and a lifetime warranty on all work done, Caliber's innovative approach to automobile collision repair provides state-of-the-art repair work from highly skilled technical staff using sophisticated equipment.

According to Caliber's Chairman and CEO, Matthew Ohrstein, "Unparalleled customer service, superior collision repair expertise and solid relationships with insurers are some of the factors contributing to the company's remarkable growth." All Caliber Centers are affiliated with rental-car networks, ensuring customers have a car to drive while theirs is being repaired, and long-established relationships with insurers avoid the wait for an adjustor to inspect your vehicle before work can begin. An informative "preaccident" checklist of dos and don'ts posted on their Web site is just another example of how Caliber's management thinks "outside of the box," going the extra mile to take care of their customers—one car at a time.

SOURCES: Justin Martin, David Birch, "Slump? What Slump?" FSB (Fortune Small Business), December 2002/January 2003, downloaded from http://ask.elibrary.com; company Web site http://www.caliber.com accessed December 30, 2002.

Looking Ahead at 180°s

What began with two college buddies wanting to look cool while they stayed warm is today a thriving multinational consumer products company called 180°s that has a presence in more than 40 countries. Setting up the business as a limited liability company gave it credibility with their investors, enabling them to hire the talent they needed to expand their small business.

The 55-employee company concentrates on items with the greatest market potential, like ear warmers, gloves, sport sun glasses, and a line of beach gear. "We'd show top management at QVC 30 prototypes and they'd pick 10, which we'd make and sell on the show," says Wilson. The speed with which 180°s brought some of these products to market was staggering. The beach mat went from prototype to manufacturing to market in just eight weeks.

"Innovation is the easy part," says Le Gette. "Choosing the right innovation to run with is more difficult." With big-name retailers like Target, REI, Nordstrom, and Eddie Bauer lining up to sell their goods, they're clearly making the right choices. Anticipating $200 million in sales by 2005, Le Gette and Wilson are making their investors very happy. "We have an inexhaustible desire to question things most people think have already been answered," says Le Gette, "that's how we succeed in reinventing the wheel."[31]

chance of finding another job, either at the new company or at a new firm. Even if you keep your job, the corporate culture may change, whether the acquirer is a U.S. company or based overseas.

If you own a small company you may become a target, or your customers may disappear as they are acquired by other companies. Should mergers discourage you from starting your own business? Not at all! Even though size is an advantage in many industries, the worldwide economy still needs small, entrepreneurial firms.

Despite consolidation trends, large corporations still prefer to outsource certain projects to companies with specialized expertise in areas like design and technology. Also, many niche markets exist where being small provides benefits such as personal service and quick creative solutions to customer problems.

Summary of Learning Goals

1

What are the advantages and disadvantages of the sole proprietorship form of business organization?

The advantages of sole proprietorships include ease and low cost of formation, the owner's rights to all profits, the owner's control of the business, relative freedom from government regulation, absence of special taxes, and ease of dissolution. Disadvantages include owner's unlimited liability for debts, difficulty in raising capital, limited managerial expertise, difficulty in finding qualified employees, large personal time commitment, unstable business life, and the owner's personal absorption of all losses.

2

What are the advantages of operating as a partnership, and what downside risks should partners consider?

Partnerships can be formed as either general or limited partnerships. In a general partnership the partners co-own the assets and share the profits. Each partner is individually liable for all debts and contracts of the partnership. The operations of a limited partnership are controlled by one or more general partners with unlimited liability. Limited partners are financial partners whose liability is limited to their investment; they do not participate in the firm's operations. The advantages of partnerships include ease of formation, availability of capital, diversity of managerial skills and expertise, flexibility to respond to changing business conditions, no special taxes, and relative freedom from government control. Disadvantages include unlimited liability for general partners, potential for conflict between partners, sharing of profits, and difficulty exiting or dissolving the partnership.

3

How does the corporate structure provide advantages and disadvantages to a company, and what are the major types of corporations?

A corporation is a legal entity chartered by a state. Its organizational structure includes stockholders who own the corporation, a board of directors elected by the stockholders to govern the firm, and officers who carry out the goals and policies set by the board. Stockholders can sell or transfer their shares at any time, and are entitled to receive profits in the form of dividends. Advantages of corporations include limited liability, ease of transferring ownership, unlimited tax deductions, and ability to attract financing. Disadvantages include double taxation of profits at a somewhat reduced rate, the cost and complexity of formation, and government restrictions.

4

Does a company have other business organization options in addition to sole proprietorships, partnerships, and corporations?

Businesses can also organize as limited liability companies, cooperatives, joint ventures, and franchises. A limited liability company (LLC) provides limited liability for its owners, but is taxed like a partnership. These two features make it an attractive form of business organization for many small firms. Cooperatives are collectively owned by individuals or businesses with similar interests that combine to achieve more economic power. Cooperatives distribute all profits to their members. Two types of cooperatives are buyer and seller cooperatives.

A joint venture is an alliance of two or more companies formed to undertake a special project. Joint ventures can be set up in various ways, through partnerships or special-purpose corporations. By sharing management expertise, technology, products, and financial and operational resources, companies can reduce the risk of new enterprises.

5

What makes franchising an appropriate form of organization for some types of business, and why is it growing in importance?

Franchising is one of the fastest-growing forms of business ownership. It involves an agreement between a franchisor, the supplier of goods or services, and a franchisee, an individual or company that buys the right to sell the franchisor's products in a specific area. With a franchise the business owner does not have to start from scratch, but buys a business concept with a proven product and operating methods. The franchisor provides management training and assistance; use of a recognized brand name, product, and operating concept; as well as financial assistance. Franchises can be costly to start and restrict operating freedom because the franchisee must conform to the franchisor's standard procedures. The growth in franchising is attributed to its ability to expand business operations quickly into new geographic areas with limited capital investment.

6

Why are mergers and acquisitions important to a company's overall growth?

In a merger, two companies combine to form one company. In an acquisition, one company or investor group buys another. Companies merge for strategic reasons to improve overall performance of the merged firm through cost savings, elimination of overlapping operations, improved purchasing power, increased market share, or reduced competition. Company growth, broadening product lines, and the ability to quickly acquire new markets, technology, or management skills are other motives. Another motive for merging is financial restructuring—cutting costs, selling off units, laying off employees, and refinancing the company to increase its value to stockholders.

There are three types of mergers. In a horizontal merger, companies at the same stage in the same industry combine to have more economic power, to diversify, or to win greater market share. A vertical merger involves the acquisition of a firm that serves an earlier or later stage of the production or sales process, such as a supplier or sales outlet. In a conglomerate, unrelated businesses come together to reduce risk through diversification.

7

How will current trends affect the business organizations of the future?

Americans continue to open new businesses, from sole proprietorships to multiunit franchise operations. The service sector continues to grow to meet the demand for convenience from working women and two-income families. Good franchise opportunities now exist for women and minorities, supported by special financial-assistance programs. To remain competitive established franchisors are offering multiple concepts, new types of outlets, and expanded products and services. Key merger trends include a reduction in the number and size of mergers taking place, and more mergers between companies wishing to consolidate to achieve economies of scale.

Preparing for Tomorrow's Workplace

1. Bridget Jones wants to open her own business selling her handmade chocolates over the Internet. Although she has some money saved and could start the business on her own, she is concerned about her lack of bookkeeping and management experience. A friend mentions he knows an experienced businessman seeking involvement with a start-up company. As Bridget's business consultant, prepare recommendations for Bridget regarding an appropriate form of business organization, including outlining the issues she should consider and the risks involved, supported by reasons for your suggestions.
2. You and a partner co-own Swim-Clean, a successful pool supply and cleaning service. Because sales have tapered off, you want to expand your operations to another town 10 miles away. Given the high costs of expanding, you decide to sell Swim-Clean franchises. The idea takes off and soon you have 25 units throughout the region. Your success results in an invitation to speak at a local Rotary Club luncheon. Prepare a brief presentation describing how you evaluated the benefits and risks of becoming a franchisor, the problems you have encountered, and how you've established good working relationships with your franchisees.
3. Find news of a recent merger using an online search or in a business periodical like *Business Week, Fortune*, or *The Wall Street Journal*. Reseach the merger using a variety of sources including the company's Web site and news articles. Discover the motives behind the merger, the problems facing the new entity, and the company's progress toward achieving its objectives.
4. After pulling one too many all-nighters, you realize your college needs an on-campus coffee/food delivery service, and decide this might be a good business opportunity for you and some friends.

KEY TERMS

acquisition 167
board of directors 157
buyer cooperative 162
conglomerate merger 169
cooperative 161
corporation 155
C corporation 159
franchise agreement 164
franchisee 163
franchising 163
franchisor 163
general partners 153
general partnership 153
horizontal merger 168
joint venture 162
leveraged buyout (LBO) 169
limited liability company (LLC) 160
limited partners 153
limited partnership 153
merger 166
partnership 152
S corporation 159
seller cooperative 162
sole proprietorship 150
stockholders or shareholders 156
vertical merger 168

Split the class into small groups. Start by outlining the management, technical, and financial resources that are needed to start this company. Then evaluate what resources your group brings to the table, and what you will need from partners. Using Exhibit 5.2 as a guide, develop a list of questions for potential partners.

After each group presents its findings to the class, the groups should pair up with another group that seems to offer additional resources. Interview the other group's members using your questions to decide if the teams could work together and if you would proceed with this venture.

WORKING THE NET

1. Consult Entrepreneur.com's how-tos for start-ups at **http://www.entrepreneur.com/bizstartups.** Click on Business Structure and read the articles about S corporations and LLCs. If you were starting a company, which would you choose, and why?
2. Research how to form a corporation and LLC in your state using a search engine to find relevant sites. Here are two to get you started: **http://www.corporate.com** and **http://www.usa-corporate.com**. Find out what steps are necessary to set up a corporation in your state. How do the fees compare with other states? If you were incorporating a business, what state would you choose and why?
3. Select three franchises that interest you. Research them at sites such as the Franchise Handbook Online (**http://www.franchise1.com**), *Entrepreneur* magazine's Franchise 500 (**http://www.entrepreneur.com**), and Be the Boss (**http://www.betheboss.com**). Prepare a chart comparing your choices, including history, number and location of units, financial requirements (initial franchise fee, other start-up costs, royalty and advertising fees), and any other information that would help you evaluate the franchise.
4. Check out the latest merger trends at Industry Week (**http://www.industryweek.com**). Find examples of a horizontal merger and a merger that failed.

CREATIVE THINKING CASE

New Business Takes Shape

Charlie York was trying to read, but the heavy book kept slipping from her lap. She had a vision of a pyramid-shaped book rest and asked her sister, Carolyn Morton, for help designing a book rest. The result of their collaboration was The Original Peeramid Bookrest, a pyramid-shaped pillow featuring a tasseled cord "bookmark" attached to its peak. York convinced the manager of the bookstore where she worked to display the pillows, and customers bought them and made helpful suggestions for improving the design.

Once the sisters had a final prototype, they needed contract sewers to make them, and months of searching uncovered Hermell Products in Bloomfield, Connecticut, makers of durable medical equipment and pillows for use in homes and hospitals. Hermell agreed to make the pillows although "it's a very labor-intensive product and the most elaborate pillow we make," says Connie Galli, national sales manager for Hermell.

The company makes two versions of the Peeramid. One features expensive upscale fabrics provided by Morton and York for sale to their catalog, bookstore, and gift store customers, with a simpler version made by Hermell for its customers and catalog, under license from the sisters, with a royalty paid on every pillow sold.

The sisters incorporated their business, and attorneys helped them obtain a design patent on the Peeramid in 1997. Plans for an inflatable model for poolside use are on the drawing board, as well as a special marketing initiative aimed at the college market—logo'd versions of the Peeramid for their bookstores.

Recently obtained permission from the National Institute for Literacy means each Peeramid's hangtag is printed with the group's hotline number.[32] "One way to sell more book rests is to encourage more people to read," says York, and the newly established Peeramid Book Club on their Web site suggests ways to get involved in reading to others.

The sisters' parents, both entrepreneurs themselves, urge their daughters to keep going and growing. "We feel like we are in the infancy stage of the business," says York. They are learning as they go. "An aspect of our company that has been a godsend has been using Ifulfill.com to handle orders," adds Carolyn Morton. "Not having to set up shop for retail sales distribution has been a lifesaver for us!" With time and money invested and their design patent firmly in place, they are pushing forward in the hopes that their pillow will become a "must have" for book lovers everywhere.[33]

CRITICAL THINKING QUESTIONS

1. Why did Morton and York choose to incorporate instead of organizing as a partnership?
2. As the designers of their product they also need general business experience to effectively manage a growing company. Should they consider bringing in additional partners?
3. What other strategies for growth could they pursue?

VIDEO CASE

Geeks to the Rescue

If you've ever been in the middle of important projects with looming deadlines, and your computer crashes or you lose your files, you are just one of many people who would like to see someone from Robert Stephens's Geek Squad walk through your door. A quick phone call to 1-800-GEEK-SQUAD will answer three important questions: Can they fix it? When can they be there? What will it cost?

His uniformed, badge-toting "special agents" make house calls 365 days a year, providing emergency computer support to cranky clients in their homes or offices. They survey the "crime scene" and fix the problem on-site or take the computer away for repair. Either way, your computer problem is solved. Every client receives a follow-up call next day to make sure everything is still working and the client is happy with the service. The company prides itself on its rapid response time, reasonable rates, and highly skilled staff.

"I always wanted to be James Bond," says Stephens. So he introduced an element of fun and showmanship to the company in the form of "geekmobiles." These brightly painted cars displaying the company's distinctive black, orange, and white logo transport the Geek Squad's highly trained personnel around cities where the company currently operates: Minneapolis, Chicago, Los Angeles, and San Francisco. Geek Squad special agents have helped out the likes of rockers U2, Ozzy Osbourne, and the Rolling Stones, even getting to attend their concerts for free.

Stephens originally chose the name Geek Squad to suggest an "army" of employees, disguising the fact that his business originally consisted of just one person—himself. He designed the company to be different, with a unique corporate culture and branding that makes it stand out. But even though Stephens set up his business as a corporation, he believes it will continue to work best if kept small, and has no interest in franchising the company. "There is always the temptation to expand into other services, through boredom or greed or fear, but I would rather be great at one thing than mediocre at several," he says.

CRITICAL THINKING QUESTIONS

1. Why did Robert Stephens set up his company as a corporation even though he prefers to keep it small?
2. Why did he want to establish such a unique identity for his company?
3. As a service business, why did he believe it was important to convey the idea of a larger organization to prospective customers?

SOURCES: Adapted from material contained in the video *Revenge of the Nerds: People, Technology and Ethics at Geek Squad,* and the Geek Squad Web site, http://www.geeksquad.com.

E-Commerce Case

Cleaning Up on the Net

Ranked as one of 2002's "Top 30 New Franchises" by *Entrepreneur Magazine,* MaidPro (**http://www.maidpro.com**), a residential cleaning franchise, uses the Net to maintain relationships and improve communication between customers and franchisees.

Started in September 1991 by Mark Kushinsky, MaidPro's CEO, after two cleaning services did a woefully inadequate job cleaning his Boston home, MaidPro was soon voted the best maid service by *Boston Magazine.* Help was needed to manage all the customers who wanted service, so MaidPro developed proprietary software to track its growing clientele. In 1996 Kushinsky sold the first independent MaidPro franchise, and today MaidPro is one of the fastest-growing franchised cleaning companies in the nation, with 30 offices servicing 16 states.

It is also one of the most technologically advanced. To manage their MaidPro business, customers log on to the company's Web site using their e-mail address and password. They can use the enhanced Web site to check service dates, move or cancel appointments, view their billing history, or write comments on past or future jobs. Customer calls to MaidpPro's offices have decreased by 30 percent since the service has been offered, with phone tag completely eliminated. "Our staff is able to spend their time doing other things now," says Kushinsky.

A quick glance at MaidPro's Web site makes it easy to see why customers are drawn to its bright humorous graphics and user-friendly menus. And MaidPro's mission statement is nothing short of a crusade—to clean up America. "We are in the business of providing our customers with the luxury of making choices about how they spend their leisure time," says Kushinsky, "and because we provide high-quality reliable service our customers are very satisfied."

In addition to offering its customers the convenience of online access, MaidPro uses the highest quality materials and a comprehensive 49-point cleaning checklist. It also offers the convenience of credit-card payment facilities and a 24-hour guarantee, setting it apart from other cleaning services.

CRITICAL THINKING QUESTIONS:

1. How has the Internet served MaidPro's strategic growth as a franchise?
2. Evaluate how MaidPro's Web site has benefited its clients and increased its bottom line?
3. Review MaidPro's Web site. Are there other services you would offer? Explain.

SOURCES: Devlin Smith, "In Pursuit of the New Consumer," *FranchiseZone,* May 28, 2002, downloaded from http://www.entreprenuer.com, March 1, 2003; company Web site (http://www.maidpro.com) accessed March 1, 2003.

Hot Links Address Book

Which Fortune 500 company had the biggest revenue increase? The highest profits? Highest return to investors? What is the largest entertainment company? Get all the details on the largest U.S. companies at
http://www.pathfinder.com/fortune/fortune500

Confused about the differences between regular corporations, S corporations, and LLCs? Compare the three business structures at
http://www.4inc.com/compare.htm

Did you know 48,000 different cooperatives provide 120 million Americans with a wide range of goods and services? For more co-op statistics check the National Cooperative Business Association Web site at
http://www.ncba.org/stats.cfm

Want to combine your sweet tooth with your good business sense? Indulge yourself by finding out the requirements for owning a Rocky Mountain Chocolate Factory franchise at
http://www.rmcf.com

Get an international perspective on mergers and acquisitions in health care, media, and information technology at
http://www.broadview.com

Want to know what's hot and what's not in franchising? Improve your chances for success at
http://www.entrepreneur.com/franchisezone

Chapter 6

© DIGITAL VISION / GETTY IMAGES

Entrepreneurship: Starting and Managing Your Own Business

learning goals

1. Why do people become entrepreneurs, and what are the different types of entrepreneurs?
2. Which characteristics do successful entrepreneurs share?
3. How do small businesses contribute to the U.S. economy?
4. What are the advantages and disadvantages facing owners of small businesses?
5. How does the Small Business Administration help small businesses?
6. What are the first steps to take if you are starting your own business?
7. Why does managing a small business present special challenges for the owner?
8. What trends are shaping entrepreneurship and small-business ownership?

Have you Been Googled Today?

Chances are, you've used Google (**http://www.google.com**) to answer an important research question, or maybe *you* were "googled"—someone entered your name in the world's largest search engine to find information about you. First launched in 1998, Google continues to push the limits of technology, delivering amazingly accurate results to a global audience at blazing speed. Even more remarkable, Google is profitable and growing—setting it apart from most of its dot-com peers.

Cofounders Sergey Brin and Larry Page met in 1995 as Stanford computer science PhD students. Despite Brin's first reaction to Page—"He was really obnoxious"—the two became friends and collaborators. The result was Google, a play on the word *googol* (which means a huge number—1 followed by 100 zeros), to reflect their desire to find more efficient ways to search the Web's seemingly infinite information sources.

Unlike other classmates, Brin and Page had no desire to start a company and tried unsuccessfully to license their revolutionary search methodology to corporate partners. One company's CEO informed them, "Our users don't really care about search." The pair disagreed and instead followed the advice of fellow Stanford student and Yahoo! founder David Filo, who encouraged them to start Google.

They financed the new company with personal credit-card advances but soon needed more funds to expand. Postponing their graduate studies, they prepared a business plan and approached potential investors. Their first presentation, to Sun Microsystems founder Andy Bechtolsheim, netted a check for $100,000 made out to Google, Inc.—a corporation that did not yet exist. By September 1998 Brin and Page incorporated Google, Inc., arranged $1 million in start-up capital, and "headquartered" their fledgling company in a friend's garage.

Despite stiff competition, Google quickly became the favorite site for fast, accurate searches. About 97% of Google users found what they needed "every time" or "most of the time." With referrals from devoted Web surfers, not costly advertising campaigns, fueling Google's growth, the company was able to raise an additional $25 million in venture-capital funding in 1999.

Google's informal yet stimulating corporate culture was as unique as its sole focus on solving search problems. When the company moved to larger facilities in Mountain View, California, large exercise balls substituted for desk chairs, pets were welcomed, and staffers were fed by a gourmet chef. Roller hockey games and TGIF parties became hallmarks of Google's employee-friendly work environment, encouraging staffers to share ideas and continually develop technological enhancements.

Google passed the billion-pages-searched mark in 2000, becoming the world's largest search engine. As revenues from advertising and corporate clients climbed steadily, Google's young founders recognized they needed help taking the company to its next level. They recruited Eric E. Schmidt, a former executive at Novell and Sun Microsystems, to be CEO and chairman of the board, and George Reyes, another Sun alumnus, as chief financial officer of their privately held company.[1]

Critical Thinking Questions

As you read this chapter, consider the following questions as they relate to Google, Inc.:

1. Do you think Sergey Brin and Larry Page have entrepreneurial personalities? Explain your answer. What were their motives in starting Google, and what type of entrepreneurial business do you think Google is?
2. Through 2003 the company focused its efforts on becoming the best search engine. Do you think it can continue to be profitable without branching out? Why or why not?
3. What factors should Google's executive team consider in deciding whether to take Google public?

Principles of Entrepreneurship and Small-Business Management

Typical of many who catch the entrepreneurial bug, Sergey Brin and Larry Page had a vision and pursued it single-mindedly. They are joined by people from all backgrounds and age groups. Teenagers are starting fashion-clothing and high-tech companies. Recent college graduates shun the "jacket and tie" corporate world to head out on their own. Downsized employees and midcareer executives form another large group of small-business owners. Retirees who worked for others all their lives may form the company they always wanted to own.

Companies started by entrepreneurs and small-business owners make significant contributions to the U.S. and global economies. Like Google, they are hotbeds of innovation, taking leadership roles in technological change and the development of new goods and services. Small businesses (for our purposes, those with fewer than 500 employees) make a major contribution to our economy. For example, small businesses:

- Account for more than 99 percent of all employers
- Employ 51 percent of private-sector workers and 38 percent of workers in high-tech jobs
- Include the self-employed, who represent 7 percent of the workforce
- Produce 51 percent of private-sector output
- Create at least two-thirds of the net new jobs
- Represent 96 percent of all exporters of goods
- Provide economic-advancement opportunities for women and minorities
- Are 53 percent home-based and 3 percent franchises[2]

You may be one of the millions of Americans who's considering joining the ranks of business owners. As you read this chapter, you'll get the information and tools you need to help you decide whether owning your own company is the right career path for you. You'll discover why entrepreneurship continues to be one of the hottest areas of business activity, as well as the characteristics you need to become a successful entrepreneur. Then we'll look at the importance of small businesses in the economy, their advantages and disadvantages, and the role of the Small Business Administration. Next, the chapter offers guidelines for starting, managing, and growing a small business. Finally, it explores the trends that are shaping entrepreneurship and small-business ownership.

Entrepreneurship Today

1 learning goal

From experiments with cardboard and tape, 20-something Mike Pratt pieced together a company that today has revenues of about $50 million. Frustrated with trying to cram his gym bag into a too-small locker, he went home and built a model of his ideal duffel bag. It fit into standard fitness-club lockers and kept all his supplies easily accessible in its rigid-framed interior. Retailers considered The Original Locker Bag too cumbersome. Customers, however, loved the bag that carried like a duffel and worked like a locker. In one weekend, they snapped up the 50 bags that Pratt convinced Foot Locker to take on consignment, and soon Pratt's bags were featured at elite stores like Nordstrom.

Not content to limit OGIO International's fortunes to one bag, Pratt and his employees "geared up" to produce duffels and backpacks with patented design features. His next breakthrough product was the Rig, a protective golf bag designed to go from airport to course, that came to market just as golf's popularity began to rise. A complete line of golf bags followed, made in nontraditional colors and fabrics that appealed to younger players. Today OGIO's creative active gear, with aggressive designs, fabrics, and colors, ranges from motocross and golf bags to school packs.[3]

The United States is blessed with a wealth of entrepreneurs like Pratt. According to research by the Small Business Administration, 16 million Americans—about 13 percent of all nonagricultural workers—are involved in either full- or part-time entrepreneurial activities. And their ranks continue to swell as up-and-coming entrepreneurs aspire to become the next Bill Gates or Jeff Bezos (founder of Amazon.com). The desire to be your own boss runs high: In a recent survey, 71% of Americans said they'd rather work for themselves than for an employer.[4] In fact, the 2002 Panel Study of Entrepreneurial Dynamics (PSED) found that at any time, about 10 million people over 18 are trying to start new businesses in the United States. Business formation cuts across all age, gender, and ethnic lines, although men are twice as likely as women to start companies, and blacks are about 50 percent more likely to start a new business than whites. The study also revealed that about half of all new companies are started by teams—as Wilson and Le Gette's 180°s, Maiffret and Bushnaq's eEye Digital Security (both introduced in Chapter 5), and Brin and Page's Google, attest.[5]

Why has entrepreneurship remained a strong part of the foundation of the U.S. business system for so many years? Today's global economy rewards innovative, flexible companies that respond quickly to changes in the business environment. These companies are started by **entrepreneurs,** people with vision, drive, and creativity who are willing to take the risk of starting and managing a business to make a profit.

entrepreneurs
People with vision, drive, and creativity who are willing to take the risk of starting and managing a business to make a profit or of greatly changing the scope and direction of an existing firm.

Entrepreneur or Small-Business Owner?

The term *entrepreneur* is often used in a broad sense to include most small-business owners. But there is a difference between entrepreneurship and small-business management. Entrepreneurship involves taking a risk, either to create a new business or to greatly change the scope and direction of an existing firm. Entrepreneurs typically are innovators who start companies to pursue their ideas for a new product or service. Like Google's founders, they are visionaries who spot trends.

While entrepreneurs may be small-business owners, not all small-business owners are entrepreneurs. They are managers or people with technical expertise who started a business or bought an existing business and made a conscious decision to stay small. For example, the proprietor of your local independent bookstore is a small-business owner. Jeff Bezos, founder of Amazon.com, also sells books. But Bezos is an entrepreneur: he developed a new model—a Web-based book retailer—that revolutionized first the bookselling world and then moved on to change retailing in general. The two groups share some of the same characteristics, and we'll see that some of the reasons for becoming an entrepreneur or a small-business owner are very similar. However, entrepreneurs are less likely to accept the status quo and generally take a longer-term view than the small-business owner.

Types of Entrepreneurs

Entrepreneurs fall into several categories: classic entrepreneurs, multipreneurs, and intrapreneurs.

CLASSIC ENTREPRENEURS *Classic entrepreneurs* are risk takers who start their own companies based on innovative ideas. Some classic entrepreneurs are *micropreneurs* who start small and plan to stay small. They often start businesses just for personal satisfaction and the lifestyle. Her passion for food led Vanderbilt University chemistry and psychology major Katrina Markhoff to Paris to study at Le Cordon Bleu cooking school. She then took more classes while traveling in Europe, Asia, Australia, and Hawaii, attending cooking school along the way. Intrigued by the many cultures and tastes she encountered, she returned to Chicago and started Vosges Chocolate, a specialty candy company that makes chocolates in unusual flavors like curry, spicy wasabi powder from Japan, sweet dulce de leche from Argentina, and a rare white honey from Hawaii. "People are traveling a lot more and wanting more interesting experiences with food," says Markoff. "I want people to take the time to appreciate what's going on in their mouth. What better way to do that than with curry and wasabi?"[6]

In contrast, *growth-oriented entrepreneurs* want their businesses to grow into major corporations. Most high-tech companies are formed by growth-oriented entrepreneurs. Jeff Bezos recognized that with Internet technology he could compete with large chains of traditional book retailers. Bezos's goal was to build his company into a high-growth enterprise—and he even chose a name that reflected this strategy: Amazon.com. Once his company succeeded in the book sector, Bezos applied his online retailing model to other product lines, from toys and house and garden items to tools, apparel, and services. In partnership with other retailers, Bezos is well on his way to making Amazon's motto—"Earth's Biggest Selection"—a reality.[7]

MULTIPRENEURS Then there are *multipreneurs*, entrepreneurs who start a series of companies. They thrive on the challenge of building a business and watching it grow. In fact, over half of the chief executives at *Inc.* 500 companies say they would start another company if they sold their current one. Before starting Proflowers.com in 1998, Jared Polis founded, funded, and/or ran several high-tech start-ups including Bluemountain.com, American Information Systems, Inc., and Onesage.com. Today Proflowers is the largest international online flower retailer—not bad for a guy who only graduated from college in 1996![8]

INTRAPRENEURS Some entrepreneurs don't own their own companies but apply their creativity, vision, and risk taking within a large corporation. Called **intrapreneurs,** these employees enjoy the freedom to nurture their ideas and develop new products, while their employers provide regular salaries and financial backing. Intrapreneurs have a high degree of autonomy to run their own mini-companies within the larger enterprise. They share many of the same personality traits as classic entrepreneurs but take less personal risk. According to Gifford Pinchot, who coined the term *intrapreneur* in his book of the same name in 1985, 30 percent of large companies now provide seed funds that finance in-house entrepreneurial efforts. These include Intel, IBM, Texas Instruments (a pioneering intrapreneurial company), Eastman Kodak, and Xerox.[9]

intrapreneurs
Entrepreneurs who apply their creativity, vision, and risk taking within a large corporation, rather than starting a company of their own.

Whirlpool Corporation's Chairman and Chief Executive David R. Whitwam believes that encouraging employees to think like entrepreneurs is the route to higher revenues and new product offerings. "This is a stalemated industry," he says. "It's not fun slugging it out every day for incremental gains." Otherwise, Whirlpool will be faced with lower sales growth, margins, and share prices. He promotes brainstorming by reserving a significant chunk of Whirlpool's capital budget for innovations and provides "innovation consultants" and mentors to help Whirlpool employees bring their products to market. The first company-funded venture is off to a good start. Inspired Chef, in-home cooking classes taught by a branded network of chefs, is now available in 33 states and already nearing breakeven.[10]

Why Become an Entrepreneur?

As the examples in this chapter show, entrepreneurs are found in all industries and have different motives for starting companies. The most common reason cited by CEOs of the *Inc.* 500, the magazine's annual list of fastest-growing private compa-

Exhibit 6.1 | Reasons Entrepreneurs Start Companies

Reason	Percentage Citing
Wanted the challenge of building a business	31%
Wanted to be my own boss, control my own life	26
Believed it was the best route to financial independence	20
Felt frustrated or unhappy working for someone else	11
Other	12

SOURCE: "Are You Building an *Inc.* 500 Company?" *Inc.* 500, October 15, 2002, downloaded from http://www.inc.com/inc500.

nies, is the challenge of building a business, followed by the desire to control their own destiny. Other reasons, as Exhibit 6.1 shows, include financial independence and frustration of working for someone else. Two other important basic motives mentioned in other surveys are feeling personal satisfaction with your work and creating the lifestyle that you prefer.

Do entrepreneurs feel that going into business for themselves is worth it? The answer is a resounding yes. In one survey, over 80 percent said they, like Jared Polis, would do it over again.

concept check

Describe several types of entrepreneurs.

What differentiates an entrepreneur from a small-business owner?

What are some major factors that motivate entrepreneurs to start businesses?

CHARACTERISTICS OF SUCCESSFUL ENTREPRENEURS

2 learning goal

Do you have what it takes to become an entrepreneur? Being an entrepreneur requires special drive, perseverance, passion, and a spirit of adventure in addition to managerial and technical ability. Having a great concept is not enough. An entrepreneur must also be able to develop and manage the company that implements the idea. In addition, entrepreneurs *are* the company; they cannot leave problems at the office at the end of the day. Most entrepreneurs tend to work longer hours and take fewer vacations once they have their own company. They also share other common characteristics, as described in the next section.

COURTESY OF FUNKO INC.

Mike Becker has built as very successful business on fun and nostalgia. His first effort was bringing back the bobblehead doll. Many of his Wacky Wobblers have been retired and are now collector's items. He has vowed to keep his company small and fun-loving.

The Entrepreneurial Personality

Studies of the entrepreneurial personality generally find that entrepreneurs share certain key traits. Most entrepreneurs are:

- *Ambitious.* Entrepreneurs have a high need for achievement and are competitive.
- *Independent.* They are self-starters who prefer to lead rather than follow. They are also individualists.
- *Self-confident.* They understand the challenges of starting a business but are decisive and have faith in their abilities to resolve problems.
- *Risk taking.* Though they are not averse to risk, most successful entrepreneurs prefer situations with a moderate degree of risk, where they have a chance to control the outcome, over highly risky ventures that depend on luck.
- *Visionary.* Entrepreneurs' ability to spot trends and act on them sets entrepreneurs apart from small-business owners and managers.
- *Creative.* To compete with larger firms, entrepreneurs need to have creative product designs, marketing strategies, and solutions to managerial problems.
- *Energetic.* Starting a business takes long hours. Some entrepreneurs start companies while still employed full-time.
- *Passionate.* Entrepreneurs love their work. As the following "Focusing on Small Business" box describes, Jeff Rubin and Dylan Lauren turned a love of candy into a thriving and unique business.
- *Committed.* They make personal sacrifices to achieve their goals. Because they are so committed to their companies, entrepreneurs are persistent in seeking solutions to problems.

Most entrepreneurs combine many of these characteristics. Tanya York produced her first film at 19 and started York Entertainment, her film production company, two years later. The ambitious and self-confident York was persistent in her efforts to finance her company and produced seven films in just two years. "I like to always have new challenges in front of me," York says. "As soon as we have something under control and are doing well, I'll move on to setting up a new part of the business and expanding it." The strategy is working: Today she is one of *The Hollywood Reporter*'s list of 100 most powerful women in entertainment, heading a leading independent film company with 2002 sales of about $20 million.[11]

Managerial Ability and Technical Knowledge

A person with all the characteristics of an entrepreneur might still lack the business skills to run a successful business. As we'll discuss later in this chapter, entrepreneurs believe they can learn many of these technical skills.

Entrepreneurs need managerial ability to organize a company, develop operating strategies, obtain financing, and manage day-to-day activities. A survey of *Inc.* 500 executives revealed that they spend 39 percent of their time overseeing operations, 35 percent on marketing and sales, and 18 percent on hiring and managing employees.[12] Good interpersonal and communication skills are also essential in dealing with employees, customers, and other businesspeople, such as bankers, accountants, and attorneys. They also need the technical knowledge to carry out their ideas.

Mike Becker learned how to manage Funko, Inc. (**http://www.funko.com**) by trial and error. He started the company to bring back low-tech, nostalgia-

Focusing on Small Business

Finding the Sweet Spot

From Wall Street to Candy Land may seem like an unusual career path, but former securities broker turned entrepreneur Jeff Rubin loves his sweet new life. He and partner Dylan Lauren took an ordinary idea and transformed it into a unique retailing concept.

Candy-themed décor and background music greet 8,000 customers a day at Dylan's Candy Bar in New York City. Shoppers browse their way through 5,000 varieties of candy and candy-themed products, many exclusive to Dylan's. The price range is equally large; you'll find Pez dispensers for $1.99 or $5,000 (for rare collectibles), $200 white-chocolate carousels, and $10,000 candy artwork. You can eat at the café or rent the party room, where kids and adults enjoy candy-themed games and crafts. On a diet? The store will tempt you with candy-shaped jewelry and candy-scented candles and spa products, as well as a candy museum and its most popular item: the Dylan's Candy Bar T-shirt.

Rubin's entrepreneurial sweet tooth formed early: he sold bubble gum to his school friends. In 1990, after a stint in the financial world, he spent five years in Michigan helping his family run its chain of bulk candy stores. Returning to New York, he opened upscale candy stores inside FAO Schwarz, Warner Bros., Sony, and Toys "R" Us. His FAO Schweetz boutique soon accounted for almost 8 percent of the toy retailer's sales.

Rubin developed the Candy Bar with fellow sweet lover Dylan Lauren, daughter of fashion designer Ralph Lauren. On the advice of Lauren senior, the pair used their respective talents to create a unique brand and identity. Rubin's candy business connections were invaluable in finding exclusive products, while Lauren focused on creating the right environment to showcase them. "M&Ms/Mars created 16 colors of Skittles only available at Dylan's Candy Bar," says Rubin. He also convinced other vendors to join the Dylan's team. Hershey produces 10 special Hershey Kisses just for Dylan's, and Double Bubble makes bubble gum bath products.

The store was an instant success from the moment it opened in October 2001. With sales pushing the $5 million level in 2002, Rubin and Lauren were ready to take the candy bar concept to Los Angeles, San Francisco, and Chicago and open smaller stores in other locations.

Critical Thinking Questions

1. Are Rubin and Lauren entrepreneurs or small-business owners? Explain your answer.
2. What factors should they consider when deciding whether to expand their company? What business structure would you recommend they choose, and why?

SOURCES: "Dylan's Candy Bar Expands Upper East Side Flagship," Dylan's Candy Bar Web site, http://www.dylanscandybar.com; Devlin Smith, "Candy Heaven," *Entrepreneur's Start-Ups*, December 2002, downloaded from http://www.entrepreneur.com; "Sweet Spot," *People*, August 19, 2002, p. 110; and Jeannie Williams, "The Candy Is Dandy at This Store, *USA Today*, October 26, 2001, p. 4E.

based bobble-headed dolls he called Wacky Wobblers. His first character was Bob's Big Boy, the restaurant chain mascot. Putting his licensing background to work, he began producing cartoon, movie, and advertising character Wobblers—Mr. Magoo, Betty Boop, Charlie Tuna, Count Chocula, Pink Panther, and Austin Powers, for example. "[After my first order,] I still didn't understand what the heck I was doing," Becker says. "I didn't have any distribution networks, sales reps, employees, or even a place of business." He quickly had to become competent in every phase of the business, even tasks he hated, like accounting and paperwork.[13]

Entrepreneurs soon learn that they can't do it all themselves. Often they choose to focus on what they do best and hire others to do the rest. Becker learned to delegate many of the operational responsibilities so he could be "Chairman of Fun" and handle product creation and licensing.

concept check

Describe the personality traits and other skills characteristic of successful entrepreneurs.

What does it mean when we say that an entrepreneur should work on the business, not in it?

Small Business: Driving America's Growth

3 learning goal

Although large corporations dominated the business scene for many decades, in recent years small businesses have once again come to the forefront of the U.S. economy. Corporate greed and fraud have given large corporations a bad name.

© COURTESY OF BURT'S BEES, INC.

Beekeepers Roxanne Quimby (above) and her partner Burt Shavitz turned a roadside honey stand into a $45 million all-natural cosmetics company. The popularity of Burt's Bee's first skin-care product, a beeswax-based lip balm, led to multiple product lines for skin care, bath and body, cosmetics, mens' grooming, hair care, and natural remedies.

The downsizings that accompanied the economic downturn made many more people look toward smaller companies for employment. They have plenty from which to choose: 98 percent of the businesses in the United States have fewer than 100 employees, and about 80 percent of these small U.S. businesses have fewer than five employees.

What Is a Small Business?

How many small businesses are there in the United States? Estimates range from 5 million to over 22 million, depending on how government agencies and other groups define a business and the size limits they use. *Portrait of a Small Business 2001*, a study that focuses on companies with 20 employees or less, estimates that about 5 million small businesses have employees and 15.7 million are solo entrepreneurs. This group has a greater impact than you might imagine: Solo entrepreneurs and small businesses with less than 20 employees represent nearly 20 percent of GDP and 30 percent of those earning a living outside the government.[14]

So what makes a business "small"? As we've seen, there are different interpretations, and the range is extremely broad. The Small Business Administration classifies all companies with under 500 employees as a small business. In addition, a **small business** has the following characteristics:

- Independently managed
- Owned by an individual or a small group of investors
- Based locally (although the market it serves may be widespread)
- Not a dominant company (thus it has little influence in its industry)

small business
A business that is independently managed, is owned by an individual or a small group of investors, is based locally, and is not a dominant company in its industry.

Exhibit 6.2 shows some of the characteristics of the typical American small business.

Small businesses in the United States can be found in almost every industry group, as shown in Exhibit 6.3. Services dominate small businesses, accounting for about 53 percent of the total. These firms provide everything from health care to computer consulting and food and lodging. About 62 percent of small businesses focus on individuals, while the remaining 38 percent provide business-to-business goods and services. Small businesses dominate certain industries. For example, firms with fewer than 20 employees represent about 96 percent of agriculture-related companies, 90 percent of the nation's construction companies and retail firms, and 85 percent of all wholesale firms.[15]

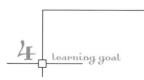

4 learning goal

Small Business, Large Impact

The sluggish economy has not stopped people from starting new companies. As leading small-business researcher David Birch points out, "We have a vibrant economy in which there are a lot of risk takers, a lot of triers, a lot of testers, a lot of experimenters. It's very different from what you find in Europe or even Japan. And I think we're blessed because of it."[16]

The National Federation of Independent Businesses reports that 85 percent of Americans view small businesses as a positive influence on American life. Not sur-

Exhibit 6.2 Snapshot of Small Business

Item	Value
Average annual revenues	$1.9 million
Average annual revenues for companies using the Internet	$3.0 million
Average profits as percentage of sales—sole proprietorships	21.5% of sales
Percentage of owners working over 40 hours a week	64%
Percentage with Internet access	84%
Percentage that maintain a Web site	51%

SOURCE: "Industry Profitability—Sole Proprietorships," Bizstats.com, downloaded from http://www.bizstats.com/spprofits current.htm; and "D&B 21st Annual Small Business Survey Summary Report," Dun & Bradstreet, downloaded from http://www.dnb.com.

prising, when you consider the many reasons that small businesses continue to thrive in the United States:

- *Independence and a better lifestyle.* Large corporations no longer represent job security or offer as many fast-track career opportunities. Midcareer employees leave the corporate world—either voluntarily or as the result of downsizing—in search of new opportunities. Many new college and business school graduates shun the corporate world altogether and start their own companies or look for work in small firms.
- *Personal satisfaction from work.* Many small-business owners cite this as one of the primary reasons for starting their companies. They love what they do.
- *Best route to success.* Small businesses offer their owners the potential for profit. Also, business ownership provides greater advancement opportunities for women and minorities, as we discuss later in this chapter.
- *Rapidly changing technology.* Advances in computer and telecommunications technology, as well as the sharp decrease in the cost of this technology, have given individuals and small companies the power to compete in industries that were formerly closed to them. The arrival of the Internet and World Wide Web is responsible for the formation of many small businesses, as we'll discuss in the trends section later in this chapter.

Exhibit 6.3 Types of Small Business, by Industry

Industry	Percentage of All Small Businesses
Services	52.9%
Retail Trade	13.0
Construction	12.4
Wholesale Trade	6.3
Manufacturing	5.5
Finance and Insurance	4.0
Agriculture, Mining, other	3.0
Transportation & Warehousing Utilities	2.9

SOURCE: "Employer Firms, and Employment by Employment Size of Firm by NAICS Codes, 1999," Office of Advocacy, U.S. Small Business Administration, based on data provided by the U.S. Census Bureau, Statistics of U.S. Businesses, downloaded from http://www.sba.gov/advo/stats/us99_n6.pdf.

COURTESY OF TASTEFULLY SIMPLE

Obtaining financing to grow can be difficult for small businesses. Jill Blashack received a loan from the Small Business Administration to start Tastefully Simple, a business that specializes in gourmet food sold through home taste-testing parties. Party attendees sample fare that includes everything from spices and soups to beer bread and dips, most priced around $6.99. Tastefully Simple now has thousands of consultants nationwide selling their gourmet food products.

- *Outsourcing.* As a result of downsizing, corporations often contract with outside firms for services they used to provide in-house. This "outsourcing" creates opportunities for smaller companies, many of which offer specialized goods and services.
- *Major corporate restructurings and downsizings.* These force many employees to look for other jobs or careers. They may also provide the opportunity to buy a business unit that a company no longer wants.

Small businesses are resilient, as they proved after September 11. They responded to changing economic conditions by refocusing their efforts on personal service and using technology more effectively. David Birch believes that most people expect that small businesses will take a serious hit—but will be surprised by how well small businesses come through the economic slump. A third of companies on the 2002 *Inc.* 500 were on the list in 2001 as well. While average sales remained about the same in 2002—$24.7 million versus $24.9 million the prior year—growth rates for this premier group of companies slipped to a still outstanding 1,500 percent, down from over 1,900 percent in 2001. Companies expressed a positive outlook for the future, with almost 80 percent planning to expand hiring, 75 percent anticipating modest to substantial growth, 60 percent introducing new products, and 56 percent moving into new markets.[17]

Why Stay Small?

Owners of small businesses recognize that being small provides special advantages. Their greater flexibility and less complex company structure allows small businesses to react more quickly to changing market forces. They can develop innovative product ideas and bring them to market more quickly, using fewer financial resources and fewer people, than big corporations. These more efficient operations keep total costs down. Small companies can serve specialized markets that may not be cost effective for a large company. Another feature is the opportunity to provide a higher level of personal service. Such attention brings many customers back to businesses like gourmet restaurants, health clubs, fashion boutiques, and travel agencies.

As a small company, Stave Puzzles of Norwich, Vermont (**http://www.stave.com**) can take chances and cultivate a free-spirited and individualistic approach to business. Since 1974, Stave has produced customized, hand-crafted mahogany jigsaw puzzles with prices from $95 to $15,000. Definitely a luxury item for a limited market—but one whose loyal following includes Bill Gates, Barbara Bush, and Stephen King—his creations include standing, 3-D, and trick puzzles. "We'll turn anything into a puzzle," claims "Chief Tormentor" and founder Steve Richardson. Stave invites its customers to "rant and rave" while reserving the right to respond in an equally outrageous fashion. Hard to imagine this happening in a large company.[18]

On the other hand, being small is not always an asset. Many small businesses encounter difficulties in obtaining adequate financing. If the founders have limited managerial skills, they may have problems growing the company. Complying with federal regulations is more expensive for small firms. Those with fewer than 20 employees spend about twice as much per employee compared to larger firms. In addition, starting and managing a small business requires a major commitment by the owner. According to Dun & Bradstreet's 21st Annual Small Business Survey, 37 percent of all entrepreneurs work more than 50 hours a week.[19] Long hours, the

Small Business Administration (SBA)
A government agency that helps people start and manage small businesses, helps small-business owners win federal contracts, and speaks on behalf of small business.

Small Business Investment Company (SBIC)
Privately owned and managed investment companies that are licensed by the Small Business Administration and provide long-term financing for small businesses.

need for owners to do much of the work themselves, and the stress of being personally responsible for the success of the business can take a toll. Joel Skolnick, cofounder of the Computer Store retail chain and then The Computer Forum training company, considers himself addicted to the entrepreneurial life. "Those entrepreneurial years were an incredible high for me," he recalls. "Every day was different—there were no rules to follow. I would wake up in the middle of the night with ideas that were out of the box, and I would try them out the next day." But by age 40 he realized that he had also sacrificed his family life and missed so much of his daughters' childhood. He sold his companies and bought a commercial-printing business. He remained a business owner, but with a more balanced life.[20]

concept check

Why are small businesses becoming so popular?

Discuss the major advantages and disadvantages of small businesses.

The Small Business Administration

5 learning goal

Many small-business owners turn to the **Small Business Administration (SBA)** for assistance. The SBA's mission is to help people start and manage small businesses, help them win federal contracts, and speak on behalf of small business. Through its national network of local offices, the SBA advises and helps small businesses in the areas of finance and management. Its toll-free number—1-800-U-ASK-SBA (1-800-827-5722)—provides general information, and its Web site at **http://www.sba.gov** offers details on all its programs.[21]

In their start-up stages, small business owners have to be masters of multitasking. Companies like business equipment manufacturer Brother target the high-growth small-business market with multifunction machines that appeal to this group.

COURTESY OF BROTHER INTERNATIONAL CORPORATION

Financial Assistance Programs

The SBA offers financial assistance to qualified small businesses that cannot obtain financing on reasonable terms through normal lending channels. This assistance takes the form of guarantees on loans made by private lenders. (The SBA no longer provides direct loans.) These loans can be used for most business purposes, including purchasing real estate, equipment, and materials. The SBA has been responsible for a significant amount of small-business financing in the United States. Between 1991 and 2000, the SBA has helped almost 435,000 small businesses get about $95 billion in loans, including substantial loans to women- and minority-owned businesses. In a recent year, the SBA backed more than $12 billion in loans to small businesses, made more than $1 billion available for disaster loans, and helped small businesses obtain more than $40 billion in federal contracts.[22] Other programs offer export financing and extra assistance to firms that suffered economic harm after the September 11 attacks.

More than 300 SBA-licensed **Small Business Investment Companies (SBICs)** provide long-term financing for small businesses. These privately owned and managed investment companies hope to earn a substantial return on their investments as the small businesses grow. For the two years ending March 31, 2002 (the SBIC program's fiscal year), SBICs invested a total of $7.5 billion in about 8,140 small businesses.[23] The SBA's Angel Capital Electronic Network (ACE-Net, **http://acenet.csusb.edu**) offers an Internet-based matching service for small businesses seeking funding of up to $5 million from individual investors. To promote economic development and job opportunities in low-income geographic areas, the SBA launched its New Markets Venture Capital Program.

COURTESY OF LA PALAPA PHOTOGRAPHER—CARINNA SALVI

Opened in November 2000 by artists Barbara Sibley and Margaritte Malfy, La Palapa attracts New York diners with its Mexico City-inspired cuisine. The pair had restaurant management experience and design talents but needed advice in how to open the business. They worked with a counselor at the Manhattan chapter of SCORE for help with their business plan and financing.

SCORE-ing with Management Assistance Programs

The SBA also provides a wide variety of management advice. Its Business Development Library has publications on most business topics. Its "Starting Out" series offers more than 30 brochures on how to start a business in different fields (from ice-cream stores to fish farms).

The Office of Business Development and local Small Business Development Centers offer advice, training, and educational programs to many thousands of businesses each year. Business development officers counsel small-business owners. The SBA also offers free management consulting through two volunteer groups, the 10,500-member Service Corps of Retired Executives (SCORE) and the Active Corps of Executives (ACE). Executives in these programs use their business background to help small-business owners. SCORE has expanded its outreach into new markets by offering e-mail counseling through its Web site (**http://www.score.org**). The SBA also offers many free online resources and courses for small business owners and aspiring entrepreneurs in its E-Business Institute, **http://www.sba.gov/training/**.

Assistance for Women and Minorities

The SBA is committed to helping women and minorities increase their business participation. It recently added new avenues such as the minority small-business program, microloans, and the publication of Spanish-language informational materials. It has increased its responsiveness to small businesses by giving regional offices more authority and creating high-tech tools for grants, loan transactions, and eligibility reviews.[24]

Through its Office of Minority Enterprise Development, the SBA offers special programs and support services for socially and economically disadvantaged persons, including women, Native Americans, and Hispanics. The SBA also makes a special effort to help veterans go into business for themselves.

concept check

Why are small businesses becoming so popular?

Discuss the reasons that small businesses have a positive impact on the U.S. economy.

What is the Small Business Administration? Describe the financial- and management-assistance programs offered by the SBA.

Ready, Set, Start Your Own Business

6 learning goal

You may have decided that you'd like to go into business for yourself. If so, what's the best way to go about it? You have three options: (a) start from scratch, (b) buy an existing business, or (c) buy a franchise. About 75 percent of business start-ups involve brand-new organizations, with the remaining 25 percent representing purchased companies or franchises. We'll cover the first two options in this section, and we discussed franchising in Chapter 5.

Getting Started

The first step in starting your own business is a self-assessment to determine whether you have the personal traits you need to succeed and, if so, what type of business would be best for you. The "Your Career" feature on pages 214 and 215

Sixteen-year old Matt Steichen's idea for a half-Titans, half-Rams jersey launched a new business, Torn Apparel. Since rap star Nelly wore the jersey during the halftime show during Super Bowl XXXIV, shown here on the far right, Torn Apparel has sold more than 3,000 special combo shirts.

includes a questionnaire and other information to help you make these decisions. Finding the idea and choosing a form of business organization come next.

FINDING THE IDEA Entrepreneurs get ideas for their businesses from many sources. It is not surprising that about 80 percent of *Inc.* 500 executives got the idea for their company while working in the same or a related industry. Starting a firm in a field where you have experience improves your chances of success. Other sources of inspiration are personal experiences as a consumer; hobbies and personal interests; suggestions from customers, family, and friends; and college courses or other education.

A good way to keep up with small-business trends is by reading entrepreneurship and small-business magazines and visiting their Web sites regularly. With articles on everything from idea generation to selling the business, they provide invaluable resources. For example, each year *Entrepreneur* publishes lists of the fastest-growing young, private companies. Reading about companies that are only a few years old but now have over $1 million in sales will inspire you. Of *Entrepreneur*'s 2002 "Hot 100" list, 31 started as home-based businesses, and 5 still are. Exhibit 6.4 lists the industry categories of the fast-growing companies on *Entrepreneur*'s 2002 list.

Ideas are all around you. Do you have a problem that you need to solve or a product that doesn't work as well as you'd like? Maybe one of your coworkers has a complaint. Raising questions about the way things are done is a great way to generate ideas. Many successful businesses get started because someone identifies needs and then finds a way to fill them.

Dave Hunegnaw was having difficulty filling jobs for his executive search firm's retailing and restaurant clients nationwide. He also recognized that many students were having problems finding jobs. With **GrooveJob.com** he solved both problems. His new Web-based job board targets two groups that big job boards such as HotJobs and Monster typically ignore: teens and college students seeking part-time work. Growing quickly since its 2001 launch, **GrooveJob.com** now lists more than 50,000 jobs and has a nationwide pool of 250,000 students. Hugenaw goes the extra mile to attract teens and 20-somethings to **GrooveJob.com,** offering free test preparation and job search tools.[25]

Exhibit 6.4 The Hot 100: 2002's Highest Growth Industries

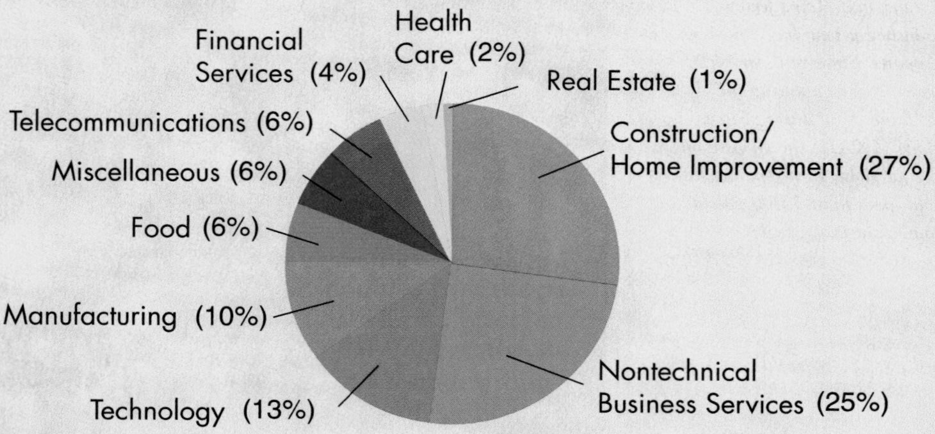

Choosing a Form of Business Organization Another key decision for a person starting a new business is whether it will be a sole proprietorship, partnership, corporation, or limited liability company. As discussed in Chapter 5, each type of business organization has advantages and disadvantages. The choice depends on the type of business, number of employees, capital requirements, tax considerations, and level of risk involved.

Developing the Business Plan

business plan
A formal written statement that describes in detail the idea for a new business and how it will be carried out; includes a general description of the company, the qualifications of the owner(s), a description of the product or service, an analysis of the market, and a financial plan.

Once you have the basic concept for a product, you must develop a plan to create the business. This planning process is one of the most important steps in starting a business and helps minimize the risks involved. A good **business plan** can be a critical determinant of whether a firm succeeds or fails. "A business plan lets you 'operate' your business on a dry-run basis without financial outlay or risk," say Douglas and Diana Gray, authors of *The Complete Canadian Small Business Guide*. "Many people do not venture out on their own because they become overwhelmed with the 'what if' syndrome." A comprehensive plan lets you run various "what if" analyses and develop strategies to overcome them—well before the business actually opens.[26]

A well-prepared, comprehensive, written business plan helps business owners take an objective and critical look at their business venture and set goals to help them manage the business and monitor its growth and performance. Writing a good business plan should take many months. Many businesspeople, in their eagerness to begin doing business, neglect planning. They immediately get caught up in day-to-day operations and have little time for planning. But taking the time to develop a good business plan pays off. Writing the plan forces them to analyze their concept carefully and make decisions about marketing, production, staffing, and financing. A venture that seems sound at the idea stage may not look so good after closer analysis. The business plan also serves as the first operating plan for the business.

The key features of a business plan are a general description of the company, the qualifications of the owner(s), a description of the product or service, an analysis of the market (demand, customers, competition), and a financial plan. The sections should work together to demonstrate why the business will be successful, focusing on the uniqueness of the business and why it will attract customers. Exhibit 6.5 provides an outline of what to include in each section of a business plan.

Exhibit 6.5 Outline for a Business Plan

Title page: Provides names, addresses, and phone numbers of the venture and its owners and management personnel; date prepared; copy number; and contact person.

Table of contents: Provides page numbers of the key sections of the business plan.

Executive summary: Provides a one- to three-page overview of the total business plan. Written after the other sections are completed, it highlights their significant points and, ideally, creates enough excitement to motivate the reader to continue reading.

Vision and mission statement: Concisely describes the intended strategy and business philosophy for making the vision happen.

Company overview: Explains the type of company, such as manufacturing, retail, or service; provides background information on the company if it already exists; describes the proposed form of organization—sole proprietorship, partnership, or corporation. This section should be organized as follows: company name and location, company objectives, nature and primary product or service of the business, current status (start-up, buyout, or expansion) and history (if applicable), and legal form of organization.

Product and/or service plan: Describes the product and/or service and points out any unique features; explains why people will buy the product or service. This section should offer the following descriptions: product and/or service; features of the product or service providing a competitive advantage; available legal protection—patents, copyrights, trademarks; and dangers of technical or style obsolescence.

Marketing plan: Shows who the firm's customers will be and what type of competition it will face; outlines the marketing strategy and specifies the firm's competitive edge. This section should offer the following descriptions: analysis of target market and profile of target customer; methods of identifying and attracting customers; selling approach, type of sales force, and distribution channels; types of sales promotions and advertising; and credit and pricing policies.

Management plan: Identifies the key players—active investors, management team, and directors—citing the experience and competence they possess. This section should offer the following descriptions: management team, outside investors, and/or directors and their qualifications, outside resource people and their qualifications, and plans for recruiting and training employees.

Operating plan: Explains the type of manufacturing or operating system to be used; describes the facilities, labor, raw materials, and product-processing requirements. This section should offer the following descriptions: operating or manufacturing methods, operating facilities (location, space, and equipment), quality-control methods, procedures to control inventory and operations, sources of supply, and purchasing procedures.

Financial plan: Specifies financial needs and contemplated sources of financing; presents projections of revenues, costs, and profits. This section should offer the following descriptions: historical financial statements for the last three to five years or as available; pro forma financial statements for three to five years, including income statements, balance sheets, cash flow statements, and cash budgets (monthly for first year and quarterly for second year); break-even analysis of profits and cash flows; and planned sources of financing.

Appendix of supporting documents: Provides materials supplementary to the plan. This section should offer the following descriptions: management team biographies, any other important data that support the information in the business plan, and the firm's ethics code.

The most common use of business plans is to persuade lenders and investors to finance the venture. The detailed information in the business plan helps them decide whether to invest. Even though the business plan may have taken months to write, it must capture the potential investor's interest in only a few minutes. For that reason, you should write the basic business plan with a particular reader in mind. Then you can fine-tune and tailor it to fit the type of investor you plan to approach and his or her investment goals.

Don't think you can set aside your business plan once you obtain financing and begin operating your the company! Entrepreneurs who think the business plan is only for raising money make a huge mistake. Business plans should be dynamic documents, reviewed and updated on a regular basis—monthly, quarterly, or annually, depending on how fast the particular industry changes.

Owners should adjust their sales and profit projections up or down as they analyze operating results. Reviewing your plan will help you identify strengths and weaknesses in marketing strategies and management and also help you evaluate possible opportunities for expansion in light of current trends and your original mission.

Many resources can help you prepare your business plan. For example, the SBA online classroom mentioned earlier offers sample business plans and online guidance for business plan preparation.

Financing the Business

Once the business plan is complete, the next step is to get the financing to set up the business. The amount required depends on the type of business and the entrepreneur's planned investment. Businesses started by lifestyle entrepreneurs require less financing than growth-oriented businesses. About half the 2002 *Inc.* 500 companies were started with $20,000 or less, with 14 percent requiring no more than $1,000![27] Of course, manufacturing and high-tech companies generally require a larger initial investment.

The two forms of business financing are **debt,** borrowed funds that must be repaid with interest over a stated time period, and **equity,** funds raised through the sale of stock (i.e., ownership) in the business. Those who provide equity funds get a share of the profits. Lenders usually limit debt financing to no more than a quarter to a third of the firm's total needs. Thus, equity financing usually amounts to about 65 to 75 percent of total start-up financing.

Two sources of equity financing for young companies are angel investors and venture-capital firms. **Angel investors** are individual investors or groups of experienced investors who provide funding for start-up businesses. Angels often get involved with companies at a very early stage. **Venture capital** is financing obtained from investment firms that specialize in financing small, high-growth companies and receive an ownership interest and a voice in management in return for their money. They typically invest at a later stage than angel investors. We'll discuss venture capital in greater detail in Chapter 20.

Who provides the start-up funding, whether debt or equity, for small companies? Over 85 percent of all business owners contribute personal savings to their new companies. Exhibit 6.6 shows how the founders of the *Inc.* 500 companies financed their start-ups. Where personal assets and money from family and friends was most important for new firms, funding from financial institutions became more important as the companies grew.

debt
A form of business financing consisting of borrowed funds that must be repaid with interest over a stated time period.

equity
A form of business financing consisting of funds raised through the sale of stock (i.e., ownership) in a business.

angel investors
Individual investors or groups of experienced investors who provide funding for start-up businesses.

venture capital
Financing obtained from investment firms that specialize in financing small, high-growth companies and receive an ownership interest and a voice in management in return for their money.

Buying a Small Business

Another route to small-business ownership is buying an existing business. Although this approach is less risky, it still requires careful and thorough analysis. The potential buyer must answer several important questions: Why is the owner selling? Does he or she want to retire or move on to another challenge, or are there some problems with the business? Is the business operating at a profit? If not, can the problems be corrected? On what basis has the owner valued the company, and is it a fair price? What are the owner's plans after selling the company? Depending on the type of business, customers may be more loyal to the owner than to the product or service. They could leave the firm if the current owner decides to open

Exhibit 6.6 | Sources of Funding of Start-Ups

Source	Percentage Using* To Start	To Grow
Owner's personal assets	87%	24%
Cofounders' personal assets	28	11
Family members or friends	19	23
Commercial bank loans	14	62
Angel investors (private equity)	8	30
Strategic partners and customers	7	12
SBA loan	3	15
Venture capital	2	19

*Multiple responses from survey participants mean that results add up to more than 100%

SOURCES: "Are You Building an *Inc.* 500 Company?" *Inc.* 500, October 15, 2002, downloaded from http://www.inc.com/inc500; and "The Numbers Game," *Inc.* 500 (October 21, 1997), p. 62.

a similar business. To protect against this situation, many purchasers include a "noncompete clause" in the contract of sale.

Many of the same steps for starting a business from scratch apply to buying an existing company. You should prepare a business plan that thoroughly analyzes all aspects of the business. Get answers to all your questions, and determine, via the business plan, that the business is a good one. Then you must negotiate the purchase price and other terms and get financing. This can be a difficult process, and it may require the use of a consultant.

Risky Business

Running your own business may not be as easy as it sounds. Despite the many advantages of being your own boss, the risks are great as well. The SBA estimates that about 10 percent of all new businesses close in an average year. Not all are failures; many businesses that close are financially successful and close for non-financial reasons. For example, the owners may decide to sell the business or move on to other opportunities. Of the 586,000 business closures in 2001, about 40,000 involved bankruptcy (financial insolvency). About one-third of new firms fail after two years, about half after four years, and almost 60 percent by the sixth year.[28]

Businesses close down for many reasons. Here are the most common causes:

- Economic factors—business downturns and high interest rates
- Financial causes—inadequate capital, low cash balances, and high expenses
- Lack of experience—inadequate business knowledge, management experience, and technical expertise

Many of the causes of business failure are interrelated. For example, low sales and high expenses are often directly related to poor management.

Inadequate planning is often at the core of business problems. As described earlier, a thorough feasibility analysis, from market assessment to financial plan, is critical to business success. And even with the best plans, business conditions change and unexpected situations arise. An entrepreneur may start a company based on a terrific new product only to find that a large firm with more marketing and distribution clout introduces a similar item.

The stress of managing a business can take its toll. The business can consume your whole life. Owners may find themselves in over their heads and unable to cope with the pressures of business operations, from the long hours to being the main decision maker. Even successful businesses have to deal with many challenges. For example, growing too quickly can cause as many problems as sluggish sales. Growth can strain a company's finances. Additional capital is required to fund the expanded operations, from hiring additional staff to purchasing more equipment. Successful business owners must respond quickly as the business changes and develop plans to manage growth.

concept check

How can potential business owners find new business ideas?

Why is it important to develop a business plan? What should such a plan include?

What financing options do small-business owners have? What risks do they face?

Managing a Small Business

7 learning goal

Whether you start a business from scratch or buy an existing one, you must be able to keep it going. The main job of the small-business owner is to carry out the business plan through all areas of the business—from personnel to production and maintenance. The small-business owner must be ready to solve problems as they arise and move quickly when market conditions change. Hiring, training, and managing employees is another crucial responsibility. Clearly, managing a small business is quite a challenge.

Over time, the owner's role will change. As the company grows, others will make many of the day-to-day decisions while the owner focuses on managing employees and making plans for the firm's long-term success. The owner must always watch performance, evaluate company policies in light of changing conditions, and develop new policies as required. She or he must nurture a continual flow of ideas to keep the business growing. The type of employees needed may also change as the firm grows. A larger firm may need more managerial talent and technical expertise.

Using Outside Consultants

One way to ease the burden of managing a business is to hire outside consultants. Nearly all small businesses need a good certified public accountant (CPA) who can help with financial record keeping, tax planning, and decision making. An accountant who works closely with the owner to help the business grow is a valuable asset. An attorney who knows about small-business law can provide legal advice and draw up essential documents. Consultants in other areas, such as marketing, employee benefits, and insurance, can be hired as needed. Outside directors with business experience are another way for small companies to get advice. Resources like these free the small-business owner to concentrate on planning and day-to-day operations.

Some aspects of the business can be outsourced, or contracted out to specialists in that area. Among the more common departments that use outsourcing are information technology, customer service, order fulfillment, payroll, and human resources. Hiring an outside company—in many cases another small business—can save money because the purchasing firm buys just the services it needs and has no investment in expensive technology. Management should review any outsourced functions as the business grows. At some point, it may be more cost effective to bring it in-house.

Hiring and Retaining Employees

Small companies may have to be creative to find the right employees and to convince applicants to join their firm. Coremetrics, a Web analytics company that tracks habits of site visitors, ran into problems when founder Brett Hurt hired the wrong person to fill a major role. "A big company won't go under because of one bad hire, but a start-up might," Hurt explains. "If you are starting your own business and you hire someone and they're not ethical, or their heart isn't in it, or they're not of the same frame of mind as you, it can crush your business."[29]

Making the decision to hire the first employee is also a major one. "I realized that it was time to hire my first employee when I could no longer do it all myself," says Deborah Wainstein, president of New York City employment agency Priority Staffing Solutions. "My business was being held back. I was working 70-hour weeks and was unable to attend conferences that would allow me to meet potential clients." Identify all the costs involved in hiring an employee to make sure your business can afford it. Help-wanted ads, extra space, taxes, and employee benefits—these will easily add about 10 to 15 percent to the salary amount. Having an employee may also mean more work for you at first in terms of training and management. It's a catch-22: To grow you need to hire more people, but making the shift from solo worker to boss can be very stressful.[30]

Attracting good employees can be hard for a small firm, which may not be able to match the higher salaries, better benefits, and advancement potential offered by many larger firms. Once they hire employees, small-business owners must promote employee satisfaction to retain them. Comfortable working conditions, flexible hours, employee benefit programs, opportunities to help make decisions, and a share in profits and ownership are some of the ways to do this. The 10 consultants who work at Analytics Operations Engineering, a Boston company, can choose the projects that appeal to them, as well as when, where, and how much they work. "I judge my employees' value by what they create," says CEO Mitchell Burman. This flexibility has helped Analytics build a loyal and dedicated workforce.[31]

Going Global

More and more small businesses are discovering the benefits of looking beyond the United States for markets. As we learned in Chapter 4, the global marketplace represents a huge opportunity for U.S. businesses, both large and small. Small businesses decide to export because of foreign competition in the United States, new markets in growing economies, economic conditions (such as recession) in the United States, and the need for increased sales and higher profits. When the value of the U.S. dollar declines against other foreign currencies, as it did after the September 11 tragedy, U.S. goods become less expensive for overseas buyers and this creates opportunities for U.S. companies to sell globally.

Small service firms are also adding international clients to their rosters. Washington, DC, attorney Harvey Jacobs was one of the first to tap into the Internet's power, putting up Jacobs & Associates's first Web site in 1995. Noticing that this global visibility was attracting a significant number of international visitors with questions about doing business online, Jacobs developed a specialty in Internet law. He has helped clients from Switzerland to Singapore with such issues as U.S. trademark, copyright infringement, royalty agreements, and domain name disputes.[32] Small businesses choosing to do business abroad may also face issues of social responsibility, as the "Making Ethical Choices" box on page 200 demonstrates.

Like any major business decision, exporting requires careful planning. Many online resources can help you decipher the complexities of preparing to sell in a foreign country and identify potential markets for your goods and services. The Small Business Association's Office of International Trade, **http://www.sba.gov/oit/**, has links to many valuable sites. The Department of Commerce also offers many services for small businesses who want to sell abroad. Its Trade Information Center, **http://www.trade.gov/td/tic/** or 1-800-USA-TRADE, and Export Center, **http://www.export.gov** are good starting places.

Many small businesses hire international-trade specialists to get started selling overseas. They have the time, knowledge, and resources that most small businesses lack. Export trading companies buy goods at a discount from small businesses and resell them abroad. Export management companies (EMCs) act on a company's behalf. For fees of 5 to 15 percent of gross sales and multiyear contracts, they handle

Making Ethical Choices

xtra! http://gitmanxtra.swlearning.com

MINDING YOUR BUSINESS

As the owner of LT Designs, a small South African company, Lisa Taylor loves her work producing competitively priced handcrafted home accessories. She is an advocate for the empowerment of women, recruiting and training workers from nearby towns. These poor rural women are often the sole supporters of their families, and they are grateful for the jobs and eager to learn new skills.

Taylor is thrilled when a U.S. textile wholesaler and distributor, attracted by her unique, well-priced products and socially responsible approach to doing business, starts buying from her. Her business triples, and she hires more workers to handle the extra load. The company is soon Taylor's single largest customer and plans an elaborate and costly marketing campaign to promote her products in the United States. The company assigns you to supervise production and work closely with Taylor on developing appropriate designs for the U.S. market.

At first Taylor welcomes your input, but her receptivity quickly turns into resentment of what she perceives as your company's attempt to "control" her business. Although she has signed an agreement with your company to approve new designs, her new sample ranges reflect none of the agreed-upon design elements. After checking with your boss, you tell Taylor that unless she agrees to follow your design standards, you will have no choice but to terminate the relationship. Taylor insists the new designs fall within agreed design specifications and that you are trying to take advantage of the workers' need for jobs to force her to compromise her artistic integrity.

If your company does not buy the products, she will have to lay off the additional workers she hired and their families will suffer. Everyone will blame the overbearing U.S. company for ruining the local economy. You are in a bind, because the company will lose its investment in the marketing campaign. It could also get negative publicity, damaging its image as a good corporate citizen.

ETHICAL DILEMMA

The U.S. company can afford to buy LT's products, and hold them in inventory, waiting for an appropriate marketing opportunity. Should they absorb the cost of doing this to protect workers' jobs?

SOURCE: Case based on experience of Linda Ravden, former owner of Bellissima Designs, as described in a personal interview February 24, 2003.

concept check

How does the small business owner's role change over time?

What role do technology and the Internet play in creating small businesses and helping them grow?

all aspects of exporting, including finding customers, billing, shipping, and helping the company comply with foreign regulations.

Trends in Entrepreneurship and Small-Business Ownership

8 learning goal

Entrepreneurship has changed since the heady days of the late 1990s, when the term seemed to imply a quick route to riches and stock options. The days of starting a dot-com while you were still in college, and making millions taking it public in a few years, are gone. A new type of entrepreneur is emerging—and we're finding that it isn't really new at all.

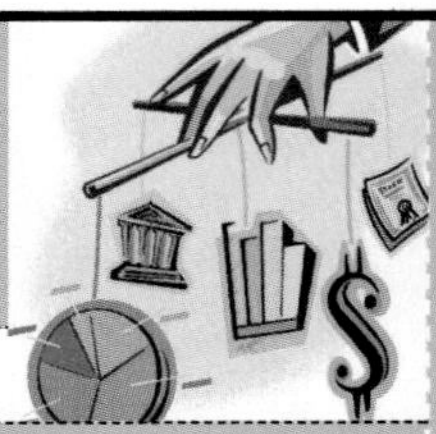

Social and demographic trends, combined with the challenges of operating in the fast-paced technology-dominated business climate of the 1990s, have changed the face of entrepreneurship and small-business ownership. New areas are emerging as entrepreneurial hot spots. Opportunities for women and minority business owners continue to grow. The role of technology in business start-ups has changed. The Internet is creating numerous opportunities for new types of small businesses.

Reduced Number of New Businesses

While the desire to strike out on your own remains strong, the number of people actually starting businesses or going solo has slowed down a bit. People are more wary of taking the plunge in the current economic climate. Reality has set in. Funding is more difficult to obtain. No longer do venture capitalists, burned in the dot-com craze, throw money at all sorts of schemes. They want to see a solid idea and a well-developed business plan. People who were eager to join the ranks of the self-employed are thinking twice before giving up the security of a regular paycheck; corporate benefits like paid vacations, subsidized health insurance, and retirement plans; and work space and equipment.

Many would-be entrepreneurs are now choosing to get hands-on experience first at larger companies. They recognize that developing their managerial and technical skills improves their chances of successful business ownership. Their employers benefit as well. Applying their entrepreneurial inclinations within existing companies, these employees open up new opportunities by creating new products and identifying new markets.[33]

That's not to say that entrepreneurship is disappearing. Those who do take the entrepreneurial route have reasonable expectations about the time and effort it takes to build a company. They are reverting to basic business management principles, core values, and core competencies. They master their primary vision before diverting money and resources into new areas.

Hot Spots for New Businesses

New geographic regions are emerging as hotbeds of entrepreneurial activity. Where the coasts and Sunbelt once dominated, the Mountain States now lead the way. The top three states in which to start a business are Nevada, Arizona, and Utah. According to small-business expert David Birch, "The Mountain States benefit from great education systems, excellent airports in places like Denver, and no industrial heritage to get rid of—because there wasn't anything there 100 years ago. Office space tends to be relatively cheap in this region, as are labor costs." These states showed significant population gains from 1990 to 1999, while California experienced a net outflow of 2.2 million. September 11 also changed where people want to live and work. Birch expects more small businesses to leave the central business district for the outskirts of cities, the suburbs, and beyond.[34] As we discuss below, technology makes this easy to do.

Opportunities for All

At one time, most entrepreneurs were career changers starting second or third careers and corporate executives deciding to go out on their own. Today, entrepreneurship cuts across all age and ethnic boundaries. Many young people are choosing entrepreneurship as their first career. For women and minorities, entrepreneurship and small-business ownership are a route to economic independence and personal and professional fulfillment. These groups are starting small businesses at rates far above

Julz Chavez started her own doll company when none of the major toy companies were interested in her multiracial line of action dolls. Today, Get Real Girl has more than $5 million in sales and boasts a board of advisors including female sports stars such as soccer player Brandi Chastain.

the general population. According to the Panel Study on Entrepreneurial Dynamics (PSED), entrepreneurship involves adults at all ages. Exhibit 6.7 shows the likelihood of starting a business depending on your age. For example, for every 1,000 women age 18 to 24, 4 will start a business. Men and women aged 25 to 34 are the most active in forming new businesses, while people over 65 are the least.[35]

Women business owners comprise one of the most dynamic small-business segments representing about one-quarter of all nonfarm businesses and almost one-third of all sole proprietorships in the United States. According to a recent report from the Center for Women's Business Research, women hold at least a 50 percent interest in 10.1 million businesses that employ 18.1 million people and generate $2.32 trillion in annual sales. "These firms represent a substantial portion—46 percent—of all privately held businesses," notes Myra M. Hart, Harvard Business School professor and chair of the Center for Women's Business Research. The Center's research also shows that the number of women-owned businesses has also been growing at higher rates than other privately-held start-ups, as have the number of employees and sales.[36]

What motivates women to start their own firms? A study sponsored by three major women's business organizations found that the two leading reasons are the inspiration of an entrepreneurial idea and frustration with their work environment. More women business owners than men report dissatisfaction with their corporate jobs, mentioning inflexibility, lack of promotional opportunities, unpleasant environment, and lack of challenge as reasons for choosing entrepreneurship. Moving company Two Men and a Truck was in fact started by a woman, Mary Ellen Sheets, in 1985 after she encountered discrimination from a trade association. Focusing on

Exhibit 6.7 | At What Age Are You Most Likely to Start a Business?

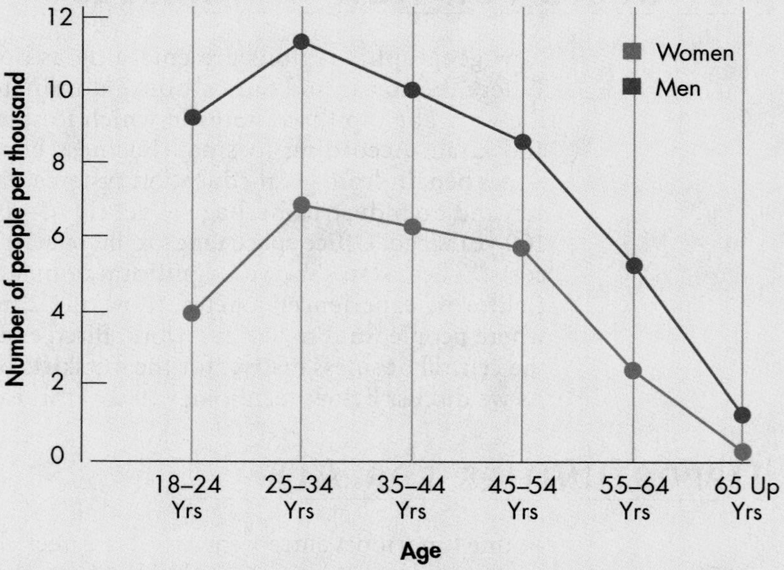

This table shows the number of people per 1,000 who will start companies.

SOURCE: Paul D. Reynolds , Nancy M. Carter, William B. Gartner, Patricia G. Greene, and Larry W. Cox. *The Entrepreneur Next Door: Characteristics of Individuals Starting Companies in America.* (Kansas City, MO: E. M. Kauffman Foundation, 2002).

customers was the key to her success. Today her daughter Melanie runs the company, which has grown to 117 franchises and $100 million in sales.[37]

The number of firms owned by minorities—nonwhite people—has more than doubled in the last two decades, and minorities now own nearly 15 percent of American businesses. Of the over 3 million firms, 99 percent are small businesses. These firms generate more than $590 billion in revenues, created more than 4.5 million jobs, and produced about $96 billion in annual payroll. Of total minority-owned businesses, the three largest ownership groups are Hispanics, 40 percent; Asians, 30 percent; and Blacks, 27 percent.[38]

In the past, Blacks were less likely than other minorities to own companies. As noted earlier, this is changing. Black men and women are about 50 percent more likely to start a business than are white men and women. Michael Parker, for example, took $3,000 in savings and personal credit-card lines to start his own general-contracting company after being laid off from a construction firm. In 10 years, ML Parker Construction, Inc. grew from 1 to 12 employees and in 2002 had about $3.5 million in revenues.[39]

Hispanic women are also making their mark in the entrepreneurial world. Former model Monica Ramirez started Zalia International to produce cosmetics formulated with more yellow- and golden-based tones for Hispanic women, a group that had been ignored by other cosmetic lines. "I found makeups from other companies had too much pink in them," she says. "I always came out feeling like I had something plastered on my face, because the colors were never right."[40]

Another boost to minority-owned enterprise is the increased availability of financing. Between 1995 and 2002, venture-capital firms have invested about $3.5 billion with minority-owned companies—more than the total for the preceding 25 years. Larry Morse's venture-capital firm Fairview Capital Partners is a specialist in minority entrepreneurship. About $350 million of the firm's $850 million portfolio is now invested with Black-, Hispanic-, and Asian-American-owned businesses—about 10 percent of all institutional funding for these companies.[41]

Low- or No Tech Takes Over

Although high-tech businesses captured the headlines, relatively few start-ups were actually in the technology sector (computers, telecommunications equipment, biotechnology). Very few entrepreneurs had the talents or financial resources to go the high-tech route. As we saw in Exhibit 6.4, only 13 of the 2002 *Entrepreneur* Hot 100 list were tech firms, compared to 36 in 2001. They were more likely to come up with better ways to make things or provide services. For example, the manufacturing sector is enjoying a rebirth as small specialty companies fill the holes left by less nimble companies that couldn't respond to changing markets. Steel and textiles are two industries where this is evident.

Technology and the Internet do, however, play a major role in creating small businesses and helping them grow. Over 70 percent of small-business owners had Internet access in 2002, up from just 47 percent in 1998, and over half of those firms have Web sites—a number that is rising quickly. Small businesses use the Internet for e-mail, to purchase goods and services, to conduct business research, and, of course, to sell their products and communicate with customers. The SBA reports that 67 percent gained new customers through their Web site and 56 percent increased their total sales.[42]

"The Internet has amazing capacities to do some very unglamorous things like reduce costs and improve customer service," says Burch LaPrade. His firm, Brightroom, takes digital photos of participants at large corporate events and sporting activities like charity runs and marathons. In a few days the photos are available for viewing and purchase on the Brightroom Web site. Using digital

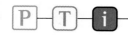

APPLYING TECHNOLOGY

Pedal Power

A passionate cyclist, Tom Medina couldn't find a bike shop that performed high-quality bicycle tune-ups. In classic entrepreneurial style—in his garage, with $300—he started Medina Cycleworks in Berkeley, California. His first goal was to be the best bicycle service shop. Soon he had an active side business building custom bicycles for his customers. "The process was fun but horribly inefficient," Medina recalls.

Medina then set forth on his second venture: creating a Web site that simplifies the custom bike-building process. The result was Wrench Science (**http://www.wrenchscience.com**), where customers can build their dream bikes for prices reaching over $5,000—expensive but well below what traditional bike shops charge. Cycle enthusiasts get the personal service of an elite bicycle shop plus the convenience of online shopping.

At the Wrench Science Web site, the customer rides smoothly along the bike-building route, receiving expert advice at each step. Enter your measurements, and Wrench Science makes sure you get properly sized products. The Web site acts like your personal master bike mechanic, letting you choose only parts that work together. Wrench Science.com automatically finds all the compatible parts for the frame, fork, and components you choose, giving you a running price and weight tally as you go. You can also save your choices and create several different models before deciding which to buy.

The site's innovative design simplifies the complex process for the customer, turning what could be a frustrating experience into an enjoyable buying trip. The time it takes customers to build custom bikes is greatly reduced as well. "Six hours [in multiple visits to a store] is literally cut down to a little bit of time," says Medina. The high degree of automation achieves Medina's efficiency objectives and gives him greater profitability than his competitors.

But the underlying proprietary WS Logic system is anything but simple. Custom-designed bicycles can have millions of possible frame/component combinations, and not all parts are compatible. These compatibility issues made developing the software particularly challenging. With the help of an experienced computer programmer, Medina was able to design the underlying personalization database and reduce his development costs from an estimated several million dollars to about $350,000.

CRITICAL THINKING QUESTIONS

1. How did Wrench Science use the Web's capabilities to develop its business? Why would customers want to substitute an online purchase for the personal attention at a bike shop?
2. What other ways can Wrench Science use technology to run and grow its business?

SOURCES: George Mannes, "Don't Give Up on the Web," *Fortune Small Business*, March 5, 2001, downloaded from Electric Library, http://ask.elibrary.com; "On the Spot: Bikesutra interviews Tim Medina of Wrench Science," *Bikesutra.com*, downloaded from http://www.Wrenchscience.com; Eric Sherman, "Size Matters: Small Is Good," *Newsweek*, May 13, 2002, pp. 40B, 40F; and "Teaming Gearheads with Geeks to Build the Perfect Bike," *Fast Company*, April 2002, downloaded from http://www.fastcompany.com.

photography reduces labor costs and allows the company to photograph more events, while distributing the photos electronically saves mailing costs. "This is just rethinking a business that's been around," says LaPrade.[43] In the "Applying Technology" box above, we'll see how the Web helps a specialized small business personalize its products to suit each customer's needs.

concept check

What significant trends are occurring in small-business management?

How is the Internet affecting small business?

Great Ideas to Use Now

After reading Chapters 5 and 6, you may be ready to go into business. Perhaps you believe you have just the product the world needs. Maybe you want to be your own boss or seek financial rewards. Quality-of-life issues may be your primary motive.

Whatever your reasons, you'll have to do a lot of groundwork before taking the plunge. Do you know what you want from life and how the business fits into your overall goals? Do you have what it takes to start a business, from personal characteristics like energy and persistence to money to fund the venture? You'll also have to research the market and financial feasibility of your product idea and develop a business plan. No question about it, becoming an entrepreneur or small-business owner is hard work.

Taking the First Steps

Maybe you know that you want to run your own business but don't know what type of business to start. In addition to the advice provided earlier in the chapter, here are some ways to gather possible ideas:

- *Brainstorm with family and friends.* Don't set any limits, and then investigate the best ideas, no matter how impossible they may seem at first.
- *Be observant.* Look for anything that catches your interest wherever you are, in your hometown or when you travel. What's special about it? Is there a niche market you can fill? Look at products that don't meet your needs and find ways to change them. Pay attention to the latest fads and trends. Amy Wolf remembered how thrilled she was to find a music store at London's Heathrow airport. Six years later, she founded AltiTunes Partners LP, a $15 million chain of music stores for travelers, with outlets in airports and a train station. Wolf knows her idea wasn't new. "I stole the idea, and then did some serious adapting," she says. She saw a need and filled it.[44]
- *Focus on your interests and hobbies.* Opportunities abound, from home-based crafts or consulting businesses to multimillion companies. Robert Tuchman turned his love of sports into a $10 million company. TSE Sports and Entertainment arranges special travel packages for corporations who want to entertain clients at major sporting and entertainment events.[45]
- *Use your skills in new ways.* Are you computer-savvy? You could start a business providing in-home consulting to novices who don't know how to set up or use their computers.

In the Career Appendix that follows this chapter, you'll find other tools to help you evaluate whether you are suited to the entrepreneurial life.

Working at a Small Business

Working for a small company can be a wonderful experience. Many people enjoy the less structured atmosphere and greater flexibility that often characterize the small-business workplace. Several years' experience at a small company can be a good stepping-stone to owning your own company. You'll get a better understanding of the realities of running a small business before striking out on your own. Other potential benefits include:

- *More diverse job responsibilities.* Small companies may not have formal job descriptions, giving you a chance to learn a wider variety of skills to use later. At a large company your job may be strictly defined.
- *Less bureaucracy.* Small companies typically have fewer formal rules and procedures. This creates a more relaxed working atmosphere.
- *Greater sense of your contribution to the business.* Your ideas are more likely to count, and you'll see how your work contributes to the firm's success. You'll have greater access to top management and be able to discuss your ideas.

However, you should also be aware of the disadvantages of being a small-business employee:

- *Lower compensation packages.* Although the gap between large and small businesses is narrowing, salaries are likely to be lower at small businesses. In

Try It Now

1. **Does it work?** Select a type of business that interests you and go through the checklist presented at **http://www.bizmove.com/starting/m1b.htm**, Starting a Business: Determining the Feasibility of Your Business Idea. Based on your feasibility study, should you continue to investigate this opportunity?
2. **Home base.** Starting a business from your home is one of the easiest ways to become self-employed. Choose an idea that you feel is suited to this type of business. What other issues do you need to investigate before startup? How feasible is your idea? Use a variety of research resources to answer these questions, including the American Association of Home-Based Businesses, Inc. (**http://jbsba.com/content/suites/hb_teleworking/message.shtml**), and *Entrepreneur*, *Inc.*, and *HomeOffice* magazines and their Web sites.

addition, there may be few, if any, employee benefits such as health insurance and retirement plans.

- *Less job security.* Small businesses may be more affected by changing economic and competitive conditions. A change in ownership can put jobs at risk as well. However, small businesses run lean to begin with, and as noted earlier, are at the forefront of job creation.
- *Greater potential for personality clashes.* Conflicts between employees are more apparent in a small company and can affect the rest of the staff. Also, if your boss owns the company, you don't have anyone to go to if you have a problem with him or her.
- *Fewer opportunities for career advancement.* After a few years, you may outgrow a small firm. There may be no chances for promotion. And with fewer people within the firm with whom to network, you'll have to join outside organizations for these connections.

Evaluating these factors will help you decide whether working at a small business is the right opportunity for you.

Customer Satisfaction and Quality

Small can be better when it comes to providing personal service and high quality. As we've discussed in Chapters 5 and 6, small businesses have an edge in tailoring their products to the customer. A quick response to customer problems is another key component of customer service, and one that can turn a complainer into a customer for life. In the construction company sector, customer satisfaction is the single most important indicator of business success. Income and profits depend on keeping customers happy. It's not enough to simply focus on customer needs. Companies must follow through and develop systems to meet those needs.

Even though customers of Timberlane Woodcrafters may consider its wooden shutters a one-time purchase, the company prides itself on keeping buyers happy. President Rick Skidmore knows that satisfied customers will refer new business his way. Timberlane immediately contacts customers with problems and promises to solve the matter promptly. Skidmore follows up with a special gift: an "Oops Kit" with a flashlight and note thanking the customer for "shedding light on the mistake." Referrals, a very cost-effective way of adding customers, are growing at 5 percent a year and now account for 25 percent of sales.[46]

Looking Ahead at Google

Receiving more than 150 million queries every day and searching over 3 billion Web pages, from more than 100 countries, Google remains the world's largest search engine. The company's reach is global: More than 50 percent of its searches originate outside the United States. Google has interfaces for 86 languages and provides results in 36 of them.

Google has stayed true to its founders' original mission: to be the best search engine. While other search sites like Excite and Yahoo! evolved into portal sites that also provide stock quotes, calendars, horoscopes, online shopping malls, and the like, Google remains dedicated only to solving search problems. The result is a series of innovative refinements to its search engine: Google Image Search, Google Wireless WebSearch, Google Toolbar, Google News Headlines, and Google Search Appliance for corporate intranets and Web servers. In late December 2002, the company introduced online shopping price-comparison service Froogle, a play on the words *frugal* and *Google*. Such tunnel vision could be the kiss of death for a company, but in Google's case, it is working, with industry watchers wondering if the company might be considering going public.[47]

Summary of Learning Goals

1 Why do people become entrepreneurs, and what are the different types of entrepreneurs?

Entrepreneurship involves taking the risk of starting and managing a business to make a profit. Entrepreneurs are innovators who start firms either to have a certain lifestyle or to develop a company that will grow into a major corporation. People become entrepreneurs for four main reasons: the opportunity for profit, independence, personal satisfaction, and lifestyle. Classic entrepreneurs may be micropreneurs, who plan to keep their businesses small, or growth-oriented entrepreneurs. Multipreneurs start multiple companies, while intrapreneurs work within large corporations.

2 Which characteristics do successful entrepreneurs share?

Successful entrepreneurs are ambitious, independent, self-confident, creative, energetic, passionate, and committed. They have a high need for achievement and a willingness to take moderate risks. They have good interpersonal and communication skills. Managerial skills and technical knowledge are also important for entrepreneurial success.

3 How do small businesses contribute to the U.S. economy?

Small businesses play an important role in the economy. They account for over 99 percent of all employers and produce 51 percent of private-sector output. Most new private-sector jobs created in the United States over the past decade were in small firms. A small business is independently owned and operated, has a local base of operations, and is not dominant in its field. The Small Business Administration further defines small business by size, according to the industry. About 98 percent of

U.S. businesses have fewer than 100 employees. Small businesses are found in every field, but they dominate the construction, wholesale, and retail categories.

4

What are the advantages and disadvantages facing owners of small businesses?

Small businesses have flexibility to respond to changing market conditions. Because of their streamlined staffing and structure, they can be efficiently operated. Small firms can serve specialized markets more profitably than large firms and provide a higher level of personal service. Disadvantages include limited managerial skill, difficulty in raising the capital needed for start-up and expansion, the burden of complying with increasing levels of government regulation, and the major personal commitment required on the part of the owner.

5

How does the Small Business Administration help small businesses?

The Small Business Administration is the main federal agency serving small businesses. It provides guarantees of private-lender loans for small businesses. The SBA also offers a wide range of management assistance services, including courses, publications, and consulting. It has special programs for veterans, minorities, and women.

6

What are the first steps to take if you are starting your own business?

After finding an idea that satisfies a market need, the small-business owner should choose a form of business organization. The process of developing a formal business plan helps the business owner to analyze the feasibility of his or her idea. This written plan describes in detail the idea for the business and how it will be implemented. The plan also helps the owner obtain both debt and equity financing for the new business.

7

Why does managing a small business present special challenges for the owner?

At first, small-business owners are involved in all aspects of the firm's operations. Wise use of outside consultants can free up the owner's time to focus on planning and strategy in addition to day-to-day operations. Other key management responsibilities are finding and retaining good employees and monitoring market conditions. Expanding into global markets can be a profitable growth strategy for small businesses.

8

What trends are shaping entrepreneurship and small-business ownership?

The tougher business climate has made many people more cautious about starting businesses. Today's entrepreneurs have reasonable expectations about the time and effort it takes to build a company. Funding is harder to secure, and investors want to see a fully developed feasibility plan. The Mountain States are now the top area for entrepreneurial companies. Opportunities continue to exist for entrepreneurs of all ages and backgrounds. The numbers of women and minority business owners continue to increase. The number of start-ups in the technology sector has declined, but Internet technology is creating numerous opportunities for new types of small-businesses and fueling small-business growth by making it easier to open Web-based businesses.

KEY TERMS

angel investors 196
business plan 194
debt 196
entrepreneurs 183
equity 196
intrapreneurs 184
small business 188
Small Business Administration (SBA) 190
Small Business Investment Company (SBIC) 190
venture capital 196

Preparing for Tomorrow's Workplace

1. After working in software development with a major food company for 12 years, you are becoming impatient with corporate "red tape" (regulations and routines). You have an idea for a new snack product for nutrition-conscious consumers and are thinking of starting your own company. What are the entrepreneurial characteristics you will need? What other factors should you consider before quitting your job? Working with a partner, choose one to be the entrepreneurial employee and one to play the role of his or her current boss. Develop notes for a script. The employee will focus on why this is a good idea, reasons he or she will succeed, and so on, while the employer will play devil's advocate to convince him or her that staying on at the large company is a better idea. Then switch roles and repeat the discussion.
2. What does it really take to become an entrepreneur? Find out by interviewing a local entrepreneur or researching an entrepreneur you've read about in this chapter or in the business press. Get answers to the following questions, as well as any others you'd like to ask:
   - How did you develop your vision for the company?
   - What are the most important entrepreneurial characteristics that helped you succeed?
   - Where did you learn the business skills you needed to run and grow the company?
   - How did you research the feasibility of your idea?
   - How did you prepare your business plan?
   - What were the biggest challenges you had to overcome?
   - Where did you obtain financing for the company?
   - What are the most important lessons you learned by starting this company?
   - What advice do you have for would-be entrepreneurs?
3. A small catering business in your city is for sale for $150,000. The company specializes in business luncheons and smaller social events. The owner has been running the business for four years from her home but is expecting her first child and wants to sell. You will need outside investors to help you purchase the business. Develop questions to ask the owner about the business and its prospects and a list of documents you'd want to see. What other types of information would you need before making a decision to buy this company? Summarize your findings in a memo to a potential investor that explains the appeal of the business for you and how you plan to investigate the feasibility of the purchase.
4. Research the various types of assistance available to women and minority business owners. Call or visit the nearest SBA office to find out what services and resources it offers. Contact trade associations such as the National Alliance of Black Entrepreneurs, the U.S. Hispanic Chamber of Commerce, the National Foundation for Women Business Owners (NFWBO), and the U.S. Department of Commerce Minority Business Development Agency (MBDA). Call these groups or use the Web to develop a list of their resources and how a small-business owner could use them.
5. Do you have what it takes to be an entrepreneur or small-business owner? You'll find many online quizzes to help you figure this out. The *Wall Street Journal* Startup Journal site offers the Entrepreneurial Motivation Quiz (**http://www.startupjournal.com/howto/soundadvice/20020430-mancuso-quiz-doc.html**). To evaluate whether you have the character traits of the entrepreneurial personality, take the quiz at the CEO Clubs site (**http://www.ceoclubs.org/main/default.htm**). What did your results tell you, and were you surprised by what you learned?

6. Your class decides to participate in a local business plan competition. Divide the class into small groups and choose one of the following ideas:
   - A new computer game based on the stock market
   - A company with an innovative design for a skateboard
   - Travel services for college and high school students

   Prepare a detailed outline for the business plan, including the objectives for the business and the types of information you would need to develop product, marketing, and financing strategies. Each group will then present its outline for the class to critique.

Working the Net

1. Visit Sample Business Plans at **http://www.bplans.com** to review sample plans for all types of businesses. Select an idea for a company in a field that interests you, and using information from this site, prepare an outline for its business plan.
2. Find a business idea you like or dislike at the American Venture Capital Exchange site (**http://www.avce.com**). Explain why you think this is a good business idea or not. List additional information the entrepreneur should have about starting this business and research the industry on the Web using a search engine.
3. Check out the U.S. Government TradeNet export portal site at **http://www.tradenet.gov.** Use Quick Links to explore three information areas, including market research and trade links. Select a trade link site from the government, university, and private categories. Compare them in terms of the information offered to small businesses that want to venture into overseas markets. Which is the most useful, and why?
4. Explore the SBA Web site at **http://www.sba.gov**. What resources are available to you locally? What classes does the E-Business Institute offer? What about financing assistance? Do you think the site lives up to the SBA's goal of being a one-stop shopping resource for the small-business owner? Why or why not?
5. You want to buy a business but don't know much about valuing small companies. Using the "Business for Sale" column in *Inc.* (also available online at **http://www. inc.com**) and resources on other small-business sites, including advertisements, develop a checklist of questions to ask when buying a business. Also summarize several ways that businesses arrive at the sale price ("Business for Sale" includes the price rationale for each profiled business).

Creative Thinking Case

Creativity Calling

Inventor Randice-Lisa (Randi) Altschul understands the formula to turn an idea into reality. She has thousands of products to her credit and holds licenses for more than 200 products, among them Turbo Fist and Racing Fist action toys and Miami Vice, Simpsons, and Teenage Mutant Ninja Turtles board games. "I can't explain why I can create things, but I can," says Altschul.

Her love of technology and creative spirit led to her latest and biggest product, a disposable cell phone that won a 2002 product of the year award. Frustrated with a bad connection, she wanted to throw her cell phone out the car window. The phone cost too much to follow through, but the concept of a disposable phone stuck with her. Convinced that the market for such a phone was huge, in 1996 she liquidated everything she owned and used numerous credit cards to raise $1.3 million to develop the prototype product.

She ran Dieceland Technologies from a bedroom in her dad's New Jersey home. With engineer Lee Volte she patented the technology for the disposable cell phone and the unique super thin technology (STT) that prints the circuits on paper. By 1999 she was almost out of money. An article in the *New York Times* set off a media blitz, caught the attention of investors, and led to a distribution agreement with GE.

The slim, patented, and trademarked Phone-Card-Phone® is about 2 inches by 3 inches will be priced at about $10 to $20, and holds an hour of outgoing calling time. After the time is gone, you can add more minutes or toss the phone. The circuit itself becomes the unit's body, as well as a tamper-proof system. Cutting it open breaks the circuits, and the phone goes dead.

As Altschul raised money to launch the phone in 2003, she rented office space and hired employees with management expertise. This lets her nurture her "toy mentality," which she considers her biggest asset. "I took the toy mentality to telecom," she says. Engineers want to make something that lasts. Kids play with a toy for about an hour, and throw it away. "I made it cheap, and I made it dumb." What's next for Altschul? She is looking for ways to incorporate STT into other products. And her nimble mind is pondering everything from a checkbook-size laptop to an interactive breakfast cereal.

CRITICAL THINKING QUESTIONS

1. "I'm nothing special," says Randi Altschul. "I just have this ability to create stuff." Explain why you agree or disagree with her statement. Why is she a successful entrepreneur?
2. The Phone-Card-Phone is designed to replace phone cards. Do you think it will be a success? Why? What market segments should Altschul target?
3. Using a Web search engine, find out if Altschul was able to raise funds to bring her phone to market.

SOURCE: Mary Bellis, "Inventor Randice-Lisa Altschul Creates the World's First Disposable Cell Phone," downloaded from http://inventors.about.com/library/weekly/aa022801a.htm; Don Debelak, "Notions in Motion," *Entrepreneur,* November 2002, downloaded from http://www.entrepreneur.com; Dieceland Technologies Web site, http://www.dtcproducts.com; and Joshua Hyatt, "Inside an Inventive Mind," *Fortune Small Business,* March 1, 2002, downloaded from Electric Library, http://ask.elibrary.com.

Video Case

Eating Healthy Annie's Way

When Annie Withey's husband suggested she create a snack food to go into the resealable bag he'd invented, she developed an all-natural, cheddar cheese-flavored popcorn. The bag never made it to market, but Annie's popcorn became Smartfood, one of the fastest-selling snack food products in U.S. history. Annie eventually left Smartfood in 1989 to found Annie's Homegrown, a pioneering company in the natural- and organic-food industry, best known for all-natural, great-tasting macaroni-and-cheese products. Annie's flagship "purple box," featuring adored mascot, Bernie the Bunny, is easily recognized by her legions of loyal customers.

Starting out with a single product, all-natural shells and cheddar, Annie's is now the fastest-growing brand in the pasta meals category (**http://www.annies.com**). They offer over 25 varieties of natural and organic pasta products, including a microwaveable version of their famous "mac and cheese," designed specifically for college dorm room convenience.

When Paul Nardone joined Annie's as sales manager in 1993, the company's $1 million in sales were predominantly from the New England market. Nardone made it his mission to make Annie's into a nationally known brand, helping Annie's become the second-largest macaroni-and-cheese brand in the United States.

Boasting of Annie's distribution in 50 states and annual sales of $20 million, Nardone—now company president—stresses that becoming successful means taking risks. For example, Withey had to be willing to personally guarantee all loans to the company. But those days are over since Solera Capital acquired a majority interest in Annie's Homegrown in September 2002. "With Solera's support, we are even better positioned to penetrate new distribution channels and develop new products to bring to market," says Nardone. One of those new products involves a licensing deal to create a pasta product in the likeness of Arthur, a young aardvark cartoon character, created by Marc Brown for a PBS show.

Founder Withey continues to fill the role of creative and inspirational leader of Annie's Homegrown Inc. Nardone describes Withey as their "quality gatekeeper—she tastes every batch of cheese they make—and the company's 'moral compass.'" For Withey, however, "the biggest struggle is that people expect me to go out and make presentations (along with other leaders in the natural-products industry) and I'm not good at that," she says, but she makes sure that others in the company are.

The Annie's Homegrown business model is unique, with day-to-day operations managed from their offices in Wakefield, Massachusetts, while Withey works from her home, a farm in Connecticut. Nardone says Withey is a very humble person whose creative instincts are "right on." When customers write to suggest new products, each idea is considered. New products are launched quickly, brought to market within 120 to 180 days.

As Withey knows from the 500-plus pieces of mail she receives every week, "It is important to customers to know there really is an Annie, that I live on a farm and have a rabbit." And they are shocked when she responds personally to most of the mail she receives. Withey never gets tired of hearing how much people enjoy her products. And reading their comments and ideas for new products helps keep her connected to her customers and the marketplace.

CRITICAL THINKING QUESTIONS

1. Does Annie Withey have the personal traits entrepreneurs need to succeed? How did her personal characteristics help shape the success of her business?
2. What long-term growth strategies is the company pursuing as it moves into the future under Solera's stewardship?
3. Explore the Annie's Web site, **http://www.annies.com**. What unique features did you find? How does this Web site expand upon Annie's mission?

SOURCES: Adapted from material contained in the video *Naturally Successful: The Entrepreneurial Advantage at Annie's Homegrown*; Chris Reidy, "N.Y. Firm Acquires Majority Stake in Annie's Homegrown," *Boston Globe*, August 13, 2002, p. C3; and from material on the Annie's Homegrown Web site, http://www.annies.com.

E-Commerce Case

Printing Money

The way Andrew Field sees it an idle printing press is like a half-full passenger jet. "When a plane takes off half full, that's revenue lost forever," says Field, founder of PrintingForLess.com (**http://www.printingforless.com**). And every hour his presses sat silent represented thousands of dollars in missed opportunity.

Founded in 1996, PrintingForLess.com (PFL) handled complex color-printing jobs in Livingston, Montana, a town of 7,000 residents. By 1998 the company was "just plugging along" with $70,000 to $80,000 per month in sales. Field's efforts to drum up business by traveling around Big Sky country failed to generate enough business to keep his single $500,000 press running.

So in 1999 Field turned to the Web to augment revenues. To minimize downtime, Field used an airline tactic—overbooking—accepting more printing jobs than his 45-employee company could handle. He relied on a Web-based service he invented called PFL-Net to manage the backlog and keep customers happy.

Field's small-business customers submit electronic files with existing designs for their print jobs. After calculating the cost with an online calculator, they can upload their files through the Web site, or mail them on CD or Zip disk.

Within two days of submitting a print job, customers can view a proof by downloading the file. After they approve it, their order is captured in a database system that tries to book printing time on a PrintingForLess.com press. If all PFL presses are booked, the system moves the job to PFL-Net where other printers can pick it up for a fixed percentage of PFL's fee. And if Field's shop is slow, he picks up excess orders from other printers, while the whole transaction remains invisible to customers.

The PrintingForLess.com Web site brings in 95 percent of the company's revenues, keeping its three printing presses busy and eclipsing their storefront-generated business. PFL-Net helped boost revenues from $1 million in 1999 to $4.3 million in 2002, with the company positioned to do $8 million to $9 million in revenues in 2003. Even his local customers prefer using the user-friendly site to place their orders. "It's become the tail that wags the dog," Field says.

CRITICAL THINKING QUESTIONS

1. Why has this printing business been such a successful e-commerce venture?
2. With his e-commerce business representing 95 percent of his company's revenues, should Andrew Field continue to keep his storefront business open? Explain your answer.
3. How have small businesses in Field's local community and around the country benefited from using PFL-Net? Why did Andrew Field create a network to share work with other printers?

SOURCES: Leigh Buchanan and Anne Stuart, "Printing Money," *Inc.* December 1, 2002, p. 74; Rich Karlgaard, "The Medium Is the Model," *Forbes Magazine*, October 14, 2002, downloaded from http://www.forbes.com; and PrintingforLess.com Web site, http://www.printingforless.com, accessed February 25, 2003.

HOT LINKS ADDRESS BOOK

Do you have a great business idea? Taking the quiz at this page at the Edward Lowe Foundation's Web site,
http://www.edwardlowe.org/aspiring.shtml,
will help you determine how feasible the idea is.

Looking for your own angel? Click on "Locate Angel Investors" in Entrepreneur.com's tools section,
http://www.entrepreneur.com/tools,
and search the database.

At the Wall Street Journal's Startup Journal,
http://www.startupjournal.com,
you'll find everything you need to know about starting, financing, and running a business, as well as a searchable database of businesses for sale.

Before your business travels to foreign shores, pay a visit to the SBA's Office of International Trade to learn the best ways to enter global markets:
http://www.sbaonline.sba.gov/OIT/

How can you find qualified overseas companies to buy your products? Find out how BuyUSA.com can help you become part of an e-marketplace:
http://www.buyusa.com

If you are considering starting a business at home, you'll find tips and advice at the American Association of Home-Based Businesses Web site,
http://www.aahbb.org

To learn about the services the U.S. Department of Commerce's Minority Business Development Agency provides for small-business owners , click over to
http://www.mbda.gov

your career

as an Entrepreneur

Do you have what it takes to own your own company? Or are you better suited to working for a corporation? To find out, you need to determine whether you have the personal traits for entrepreneurial success. If the answer is yes, you need to identify the type of business that is best for you.

Know Yourself

Owning a business is challenging and requires a great deal of personal sacrifice. You must take a hard and honest look at yourself before you decide to strike out on your own. The quiz in Exhibit YC. 1 can help you evaluate whether you have the personality traits to become a successful entrepreneur. Think about yourself and rate yourself—honestly!—on each of these characteristics.

Which Business Is for You?

If you are well suited to owning your own company, the next question is what type of business to start. You need to consider your expertise, interests, and financial resources. Start with a broad field, then choose a specific good or service. The business can involve a new idea or a refinement of an existing idea. It may bring an existing idea to a new area.

To narrow the field, ask yourself the following questions:

- What do I like to do?
- What am I good at?
- How much can I personally invest in my business?
- Do I have access to other financial resources?
- What is my past business experience?
- What are my personal interests and hobbies?
- How can I use my experience and interests in my own business?
- Do I want or need partners?

Spending time on these and similar questions will help you identify some possible business opportunities and the resources you will need to develop them.

Prior job experience is the number one source of new business ideas. Starting a firm in a field where you have specialized product or service experience improves your chances for success.

Personal interests and hobbies are another major source of ideas. Gourmet food enthusiasts have started many restaurants and specialty-food businesses. For example, Eleni Gianopulis transformed the humble cookie to a specialty-item bringing in more than $1 million in sales each year. Eleni's unique, beautifully decorated cookies come in shapes for every season and occasion, such as several series with Academy Award nominees and movie quotes. Customers, who include corporate and celebrity clients, can also place special orders. One customer ordered a cookie model of Elton John's house! Business at Eleni's NYC is growing; the cookies are now sold online (**http://www.elenis.com**) and featured in many specialty catalogs.[48]

Each January, *Entrepreneur* and *Business Start-Ups* magazines feature lists of top businesses and business trends for the coming year. Check out the current hot lists at **http://www.entrepreneur.com/hotcenter.**

Exhibit YC.1 How Do You Rate?

The following quiz will help you to assess your personality and determine if you have what it takes to start your own company. Think about yourself and rate yourself—honestly!—on each of these characteristics.

Personality Trait	**High**	**Above Average**	**Average**	**Below Average**	**Low**
Ability to handle uncertainty	○	○	○	○	○
Confidence	○	○	○	○	○
Discipline	○	○	○	○	○
Drive/ambition	○	○	○	○	○
Energy	○	○	○	○	○
Flexibility	○	○	○	○	○
Independence	○	○	○	○	○
Ability to seize opportunity	○	○	○	○	○
Persistence	○	○	○	○	○
Problem solving	○	○	○	○	○
Total					

Scoring: Give yourself 5 points for every "high," 4 points for every "above average," 3 points for every "average," 2 points for every "below average," and 1 point, for every "low."

Score results

- 50–46: You are already in business for yourself or should be!
- 45–40: Your entrepreneurial aptitude and desires are high.
- 39–30: A paid staff job and owning your own business rate equally.
- 29–20: Entrepreneurial aptitude is apparently not one of your strong suits.
- 19–10: You might find the going tough and the rewards slim if you owned your own business.

SOURCES: Eleni's NYC Web site, http://www.elenis.com; and "Got ID?" *Entrepreneur,* November 2002, dowloaded from http://www.entrepreneur.com.

Chapter 7

© AP / WIDE WORLD PHOTOS

Management and Leadership in Today's Organizations

learning goals

1. What is the role of management?
2. What are the four types of planning?
3. What are the primary responsibilities of managers in organizing activities?
4. How do leadership styles influence a corporate culture?
5. How do organizations control activities?
6. What roles do managers take on in different organizational settings?
7. What set of managerial skills is necessary for managerial success?
8. What trends will affect management in the future?

Growing Pains at Microsoft

No one questions the phenomenal success of the Microsoft Corporation (**http://www.microsoft.com**), based in Redmond, Washington. From its start in 1975, it has become the world's dominant software development company. While its image has been sullied by antitrust litigation in recent years, it is still a major force in the technology industry.

For all of its success, the company is not without internal problems. One of the most obvious is the company's difficulty in keeping professional managers at the helm. As it was at the start, the two most powerful leaders today are Bill Gates and Steve Ballmer. Until two years ago, when he passed the CEO title to Steve Ballmer, Bill Gates was intimately involved with almost every product-related decision. Delegation, under Mr. Ballmer, is still quite limited. Entrepreneurs like Gates and Ballmer frequently have trouble letting go of responsibility; however, as Microsoft matures as an organization, a more formal leadership style is necessary.

Recognizing this, the company has hired a number of established managers to occupy the number three spot. Of the five executives that have held that position, two remained about seven years and the other three have lasted less than four years each.

Leadership styles and culture clashes are frequently the cause of executive departures. When entrepreneurs and professional managers compete for power and control of today's mega corporation, it usually causes discord throughout the organization. Unfortunately for Microsoft, the transition to a mature corporation may continue to be a struggle since the current CEO, Steve Ballmer, has recently claimed that he expects to occupy that position for another 10 to 15 years.[1]

Critical Thinking Questions

As you read this chapter, consider the following questions as they relate to Microsoft:

1. What is the role of top management?
2. How are leadership styles causing problems at Microsoft?
3. What are the effects of top management on corporate culture?

Principles of Management and Leadership

Developing consistency in top leadership is critical for the successful future of Microsoft as described in the opening story. Today's companies rely on managers to guide the daily process using human, technological, financial, and other resources to create a competitive advantage. For many beginning business students, being in "management" is an attractive, but somewhat vague, future goal. This vagueness is due in part to an incomplete understanding of what managers do and how they contribute to organizational success or failure. This chapter introduces the basic functions of management and the skills required by managers to drive an organization toward its goals. We will also discuss how leadership styles influence a corporate culture and highlight the trends that are shaping the future role of managers.

THE ROLE OF MANAGEMENT

1 learning goal

management
The process of guiding the development, maintenance, and allocation of resources to attain organizational goals.

planning
The process of deciding what needs to be done to achieve organizational objectives; identifying when and how it will be done; and determining by whom it should be done.

Management is the process of guiding the development, maintenance, and allocation of resources to attain organizational goals. Managers are the people in the organization responsible for developing and carrying out this management process. Management is dynamic by nature and evolves to meet needs and constraints in the organization's internal and external environments. In a global marketplace where the rate of change is rapidly increasing, flexibility and adaptability are crucial to the managerial process. This process is based in four key functional areas of the organization: planning, organization, leadership, and control. Although these activities are discussed separately in the chapter, they actually form a tightly integrated cycle of thoughts and actions.

From this perspective, the managerial process can be described as (1) anticipating potential problems or opportunities and designing plans to deal with them, (2) coordinating and allocating the resources needed to implement plans, (3) guiding personnel through the implementation process, and (4) reviewing results and making any necessary changes. This last stage provides information to be used in ongoing planning efforts, and thus the cycle starts over again.

As shown in Exhibit 7.1, managerial work can be divided into four activities: planning, organizing, leading, and controlling. The four functions are highly interdependent, with managers often performing more than one of them at a time and each of them many times over the course of a normal workday. As you will learn in the following sections, all of the functions require sound decision making and communication skills.

concept check

Define the term management.

What are the four key functions of managers?

PLANNING

2 learning goal

strategic planning
The process of creating long-range (one to five years), broad goals for the organization and determining what resources will be needed to accomplish those goals.

Planning begins by anticipating potential problems or opportunities the organization may encounter. Managers then design strategies to solve current problems, prevent future problems, or take advantage of opportunities. These strategies serve as the foundation for goals, objectives, policies, and procedures. Put simply, planning is deciding what needs to be done to achieve organizational objectives, identifying when and how it will be done, and determining by whom it should be done. Effective planning requires extensive information about the external business environment in which the firm competes, as well as its internal environment.

There are four basic types of planning: strategic, tactical, operational, and contingency. Most of us use these different types of planning in our own lives. Some plans are very broad and long term (more strategic in nature), such as

Exhibit 7.1 What Managers Do and Why

Good management consists of these four activities:		And leads to achievement of	Which results in
Planning • Set objectives and state mission • Examine alternatives • Determine needed resources • Create strategies to reach objectives **Organizing** • Design jobs and specify tasks • Create organizational structure • Staff positions • Coordinate work activities • Set policies and procedures • Allocate resources	**Leading** • Lead and motivate employees to accomplish organizational goals • Communicate with employees • Resolve conflicts • Manage change **Controlling** • Measure performance • Compare performance to standards • Take necessary action to improve performance	→ **Organizational mission and objectives**	→ **Organizational efficiency and effectiveness**

After Disney's Magic cruise ship had a second outbreak of flu-like symptoms, 1,000 workers began cleaning and disinfecting the ship for a second time within one month. Disney Cruise Line offered free cruises to sick passengers and to travelers who stayed in the same room as sick people. This contingency plan, in the face of an unexpected crisis, helped Disney rebound and regain customer confidence.

© AP / WIDE WORLD PHOTOS

planning to attend graduate school after earning a bachelor's degree. Some plans are much more specific and short term (more operational in nature), such as planning to spend a few hours in the library this weekend. Your short-term plans support your long-term plans. If you study now, you have a better chance of achieving some future goal, such as getting a job interview or attending graduate school. Like you, organizations tailor their plans to meet the requirements of future situations or events. A summary of the four types of planning appears in Exhibit 7.2.

Strategic planning involves creating long-range (one to five years), broad goals for the organization and determining what resources will be needed to accomplish those goals. An evaluation of external environmental factors such as economic, technological, and social issues is critical to successful strategic planning. Strategic plans, such as the organization's long-term mission, are formulated by top-level managers and put into action at lower levels in the organization. For example, Carly Fiorina, CEO of Hewlett-Packard, engineered the merger with Compaq to create a vast organization that could effectively compete with Dell Computer and IBM. She believes that the merger gives her a technology company with enough products and services to satisfy all customers. "We are betting on heterogeneity," she says. "We'll be the only systems provider to support everything."[2]

An organization's **mission** is formalized in its **mission statement,** a document that states the purpose of the organization and its reason for existing. For example, Ben & Jerry's mission statement addresses three fundamental issues and states the basic philosophy of the company (see Exhibit 7.3).

In all organizations, plans and goals at the tactical and operational levels should clearly support the organization's mission statement.

Tactical planning begins the implementation of strategic plans. Tactical plans have a shorter (less than one year) time frame than strategic plans and more specific objectives

Exhibit 7.2 Types of Planning

Type of Planning	Time Frame	Level of Management	Extent of Coverage	Purpose and Goal	Breadth of Content	Accuracy/ Predictability
Strategic	1–5 years	Top management (CEO, vice presidents, directors, division heads)	External environment and entire organization	Establish mission and long-term goals	Broad and general	High degree of uncertainty
Tactical	Less than 1 year	Middle management	Strategic business units	Establish mid-range goals for implementation	More specific	Moderate degree of certainty
Operational	Current	Supervisory management	Geographic and functional divisions	Implement and activate specific objectives	Specific and concrete	Reasonable degree of certainty
Contingency	When an event occurs or a situation demands	Top and middle management	External environment and entire organization	Meet unforeseen challenges and opportunities	Both broad and detailed	Reasonable degree of certainty once event or situation occurs

Exhibit 7.3 Ben & Jerry's Mission Statement

"Ben & Jerry's is founded on and dedicated to a sustainable corporate concept of linked prosperity. Our mission consists of three interrelated parts:

Product Mission

To make, distribute and sell the finest quality all natural ice cream & euphoric concoctions with a continued commitment to incorporating wholesome, natural ingredients and promoting business practices that respect the Earth and the Environment.

Economic Mission

To operate the Company on a sustainable financial basis of profitable growth, increasing value for our stakeholders and expanding opportunities for development and career growth for our employees.

Social Mission

To operate the Company in a way that actively recognizes the central role that business plays in society by initiating innovative ways to improve the quality of life locally, nationally and internationally.

Central to the mission Of Ben & Jerry's is the belief that all three parts must thrive equally in a manner that commands deep respect for individuals in and outside the Company and supports the communities of which they are a part."

SOURCE: http://www.benjerry.com/our_company/our_mission. Reprinted with permission of Ben & Jerrry's Homemade, Inc.

mission
An organization's purpose and reason for existing; its long-term goals.

mission statement
A formal document that states an organization's purpose and reason for existing and describes its basic philosophy.

designed to support the broader strategic goals. Tactical plans begin to address issues of coordinating and allocating resources to different parts of the organization.

For an example of how planning affects an organization, look at Proctor and Gamble.[3] Prior to the tenure of the current CEO, A. G. Lafley, who took over in June 2002, Proctor and Gamble had lost $70 billion in market value in just six months. Following a strategy of aggressive new-product introduction and brand-name changes that contributed to the loss of market value, Mr. Lafley's mission was simple: turn around the current situation and grow the $40 billion company.

Innovative organizations empower their employees to present and implement, new ideas. Southwest Airlines' corporate culture, for example, encourages employees to solve problems and keep customers happy.

Unlike his predecessor, Mr. Lafley's strategy was straightforward and direct: refocus on the top brands. On a tactical level, he chose the top 10 brands and made them the highest priority. These products got most of the company's manpower and financial backing. The goal was to sell more of what was already a winner instead of trying to invest a new blockbuster product. Additionally, to reduce expenses, Mr. Lafley eliminated 9,600 jobs, shut down weak product lines, and sold product lines that were not a good strategic fit. Even in day-to-day operations, Mr. Lafley is a very hands-on CEO. He frequently visits retail stores to talk directly to both employees and customers to find out exactly what they think about his company's products. He also likes to make suggestions to store owners on where Proctor and Gamble's products will sell best.

tactical planning
The process of beginning to implement a strategic plan by addressing issues of coordination and allocating resources to different parts of the organization; has a shorter time frame (less than one year) and more specific objectives than strategic planning.

operational planning
The process of creating specific standards, methods, policies, and procedures that are used in specific functional areas of the organization; helps guide and control the implementation of tactical plans.

Operational planning creates specific standards, methods, policies, and procedures that are used in specific functional areas of the organization. Operational objectives are current, narrow, and resource focused. They are designed to help guide and control the implementation of tactical plans.

All of these types of planning are apparent in the recent history of Gillette. When Jim Kilts took over as CEO in February 2001, he inherited one of the biggest headaches in consumer products. The producer of Mach 3 razors, Duracell batteries, and Oral B toothbrushes had experienced no growth in earnings or profits for five years. By 2003, Kilts had sales growth of 5 percent to \$8.4 billion and profits up 18 percent. The first day on the job Kilts asked at a meeting of Gillette's division chiefs, "How many of you think our costs are too high?" Everyone raised their hand. He then asked, "How many of you think that the costs are too high in your department?" No one raised his or her hand. Kilts then knew that some serious planning was needed.[4]

contingency plans
Plans that identify alternative courses of action for very unusual or crisis situations; typically stipulate the chain of command, standard operating procedures, and communication channels the organization will use during an emergency.

The key to effective planning is anticipating future situations and events. Yet even the best-prepared organization must sometimes cope with unforeseen circumstances such as a natural disaster, an act of terrorism, or a radical new technology. Therefore, many companies have developed **contingency plans** that identify alternative courses of action for very unusual or crisis situations. The contingency plan typically stipulates the chain of command, standard operating procedures, and communication channels the organization will use during an emergency.

An effective contingency plan can make or break a company. Con Edison found out just how dramatically an effective contingency plan can go to change the perceptions customers have of a company.[5] Con Edison had a reputation of being called the company that New Yorkers love to hate. Following the World Trade Center attack on September 11, 2001, that reputation changed. At the time of the attack, 13,000 customers lost power and lower Manhattan's energy

concept check

What is the purpose of planning, and what is needed to do it effectively?

Identify the unique characteristics of each type of planning.

infrastructure was destroyed. Con Edison immediately put its contingency plan into effect. First, a 24-hour command center was set up. Then a team of 1,900 employees began working 24 hours per day to restore power. The team ran 36 miles of power cables and set up 100 generators to supply power to the city. Con Edison's contingency plan ensured that most people's power service was restored within one week.

ORGANIZING

3 learning goal

A second key function of managers is **organizing,** which is the process of coordinating and allocating a firm's resources in order to carry out its plans. Organizing includes developing a structure for the people, positions, departments, and activities within the firm. Managers can arrange the structural elements of the firm to maximize the flow of information and the efficiency of work processes. They accomplish this by doing the following:

organizing
The process of coordinating and allocating a firm's resources in order to carry out its plans.

- Dividing up tasks *(division of labor)*
- Grouping jobs and employees *(departmentalization)*
- Assigning authority and responsibilities *(delegation)*

These and other elements of organizational structure are discussed in detail in Chapter 8. In this chapter, however, you should understand the three levels of a managerial hierarchy. This hierarchy is often depicted as a pyramid as in Exhibit 7.4. The fewest managers are found at the highest level of the pyramid. Called **top management,** they are the small group of people at the head of the organization (such as the CEO, president, and vice president). Top-level managers develop *strategic plans* and address long-range issues such as which industries to compete in, how to capture market share, and what to do with profits. These managers design and approve the firm's basic policies and represent the firm to other organizations. They also define the company's values and ethics and thus set the tone for employee standards of behavior. For example, Jack Welch, the former CEO of General Electric, was a role model for his managers and executives. Admirers say that he had an extraordinary capacity to inspire hundreds of thousands of people in many countries and he could change the direction of a huge organization like General Electric as if it were a small firm. Following his leadership, General Electric's executives turned in impressive results. During his tenure, General Electric's average annual shareholder return was 25 percent.[6]

top management
The highest level of managers; includes CEOs, presidents, and vice presidents, who develop strategic plans and address long-range issues.

The second and third tiers of the hierarchy are called **middle management** and **supervisory management,** respectively. Middle managers (such as division heads, departmental managers, and regional sales managers) are responsible for beginning the implementation of strategic plans. They design and carry out *tactical plans* in specific areas of the company. They begin the process of allocating resources to meet organizational goals, and they oversee supervisory managers throughout the firm. Supervisors, the most numerous of the managers, are at the bottom of the managerial pyramid. These managers design and carry out *operational plans* for the ongoing daily activities of the firm. They spend a great deal of their time guiding and motivating the employees who actually produce the goods and services.

middle management
Managers who design and carry out tactical plans in specific areas of the company.

supervisory management
Managers who design and carry out operation plans for the ongoing daily activities of the firm.

concept check

Explain the managerial function of organizing.

What is the managerial pyramid?

Exhibit 7.4 | The Managerial Pyramid

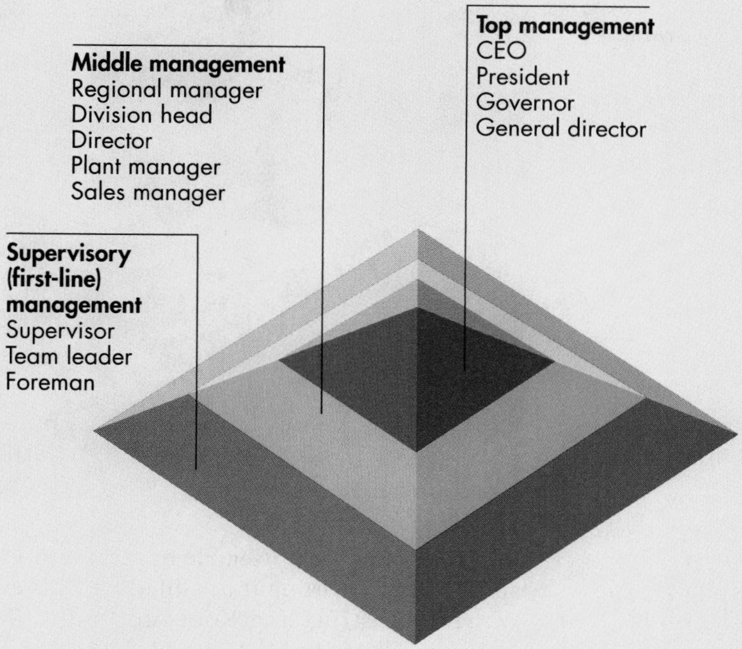

LEADING, GUIDING, AND MOTIVATING OTHERS

4 learning goal

leadership
The process of guiding and motivating others toward the achievement of organizational goals.

power
The ability to influence others to behave in a particular way.

legitimate power
Power that is derived from an individual's position in an organization.

reward power
Power that is derived from an individual's control over rewards.

Leadership, the third key management function, is the process of guiding and motivating others toward the achievement of organizational goals. Managers are responsible for directing employees on a daily basis as the employees carry out the plans and work within the structure created by management. Organizations need strong effective leadership at all levels in order to meet goals and remain competitive.

To be effective leaders, managers must be able to influence others' behavior. This ability to influence others to behave in a particular way is called **power.** Researchers have identified five primary sources, or bases, of power:

- **Legitimate power,** which is derived from an individual's position in an organization
- **Reward power,** which is derived from an individual's control over rewards
- **Coercive power,** which is derived from an individual's ability to threaten negative outcomes
- **Expert power,** which is derived from an individual's extensive knowledge in one or more areas
- **Referent power,** which is derived from an individual's personal charisma and the respect and/or admiration the individual inspires

Many leaders use a combination of all of these sources of power to influence individuals toward goal achievement. Jim Kilts gets his legitimate power from his position as CEO of Gillette. His reward power comes from turning the company around and making the stock more valuable. Also, raises and bonus for managers who meet their goals is another form of reward power. Jim Kilts is also not hesitant

Many successful organizations use participative leadership styles that involve group members in discussing issues and making decisions.

© EYEWIRE / GETTY IMAGES

to use his coercive power. He has replaced 10 of the top 14 managers in a two-year span. Kilts was brought to Gillette for his expertise in company turnarounds. He revived the struggling Kool-Aid brand, Kraft cheeses, and also a floundering Nabisco. Kilts is not the "life of the party," but he is highly respected. Investment guru Warren Buffett says, "Everything Jim Kilts says makes sense—and frankly, finding someone like that is a rarity."[7]

Leadership Styles

Individuals in leadership positions tend to be relatively consistent in the way they attempt to influence the behavior of others, meaning that each individual has a tendency to react to people and situations in a particular way. This pattern of behavior is referred to as **leadership style.** As Exhibit 7.5 shows, leadership styles can be placed on a continuum that encompasses three distinct styles: autocratic, participative, and free rein.

Autocratic leaders are directive leaders, allowing for very little input from subordinates. These leaders prefer to make decisions and solve problems on their own and expect subordinates to implement solutions according to very specific and detailed instructions. In this leadership style, information typically flows in one direction, from manager to subordinate. The military, by necessity, is generally autocratic. When autocratic leaders treat employees with fairness and respect, they may be considered knowledgeable and decisive. But often autocrats are perceived as narrow-minded and heavy-handed in their unwillingness to share power, information, and decision making in the organization. The trend in organizations today is away from the directive, controlling style of the autocratic leader.

For 41 years, Ray Wallace ran Trinity Industries of Dallas, Texas. Starting as a butane tank manufacturer, Trinity Industries grew into a multinational conglomerate making steel highway railings, barges, concrete, and railcars.[8] As the driving force behind the company's success, Ray's management style would easily be considered autocratic. He was considered to be an intimidating boss with a "shape up or ship out" personality. If someone needed a decision, he would be the one to make it. He had little trouble making difficult decisions, including the firing of his oldest son from the company.

When Ray finally turned over the company to his younger son Tim, he knew that Tim would use a very different management style. Tim believes in sharing responsibility with employees. He enlists front-line workers to help design the assem-

coercive power
Power that is derived from an individual's ability to threaten negative outcomes.

expert power
Power that is derived from an individual's extensive knowledge in one or more areas.

referent power
Power that is derived from an individual's personal charisma and the respect and/or admiration the individual inspires.

leadership style
The relatively consistent way that individuals in leadership positions attempt to influence the behavior of others.

autocratic leaders
Directive leaders who prefer to make decisions and solve problems on their own with little input from subordinates

participative leadership
A leadership style in which the leader shares decision making with group members and encourages discussion of issues and alternatives; includes democratic, consensual, and consultative styles.

Exhibit 7.5 Leadership Styles of Managers

← **Amount of authority held by the leader**

Autocratic Style	**Participative Style (democratic, consensual, consultative)**	**Free-Rein (laissez-faire) Style**
• Manager makes most decisions and acts in authoritative manner. • Manager is usually unconcerned about subordinates' attitudes toward decisions. • Emphasis is on getting task accomplished. • Approach is used mostly by military officers and some production line supervisors.	• Manager shares decision making with group members and encourages teamwork. • Manager encourages discussion of issues and alternatives. • Manager is concerned about subordinates' ideas and attitudes. • Manager coaches subordinates and helps coordinate efforts. • Approach is found in many successful organizations.	• Manager turns over virtually all authority and control to group. • Members of group are presented with task and given freedom to accomplish it. • Approach works well with highly motivated, experienced, educated personnel. • Approach is found in high-tech firms, labs, and colleges.

Amount of authority held by group members →

bly lines. He encourages less formal dress codes. He involves employees in programs to improve safety, quality, and production process efficiency. His goal is to create a business where workers are passionately involved in their work. This type of **participative leadership** has three types: democratic, consensual, and consultative.

democratic leaders
Leaders who solicit input from all members of the group and then allow the members to make the final decision through a vote.

consensual leaders
Leaders who encourage discussion about issues and then require that all parties involved agree to the final decision.

consultative leaders
Leaders who confer with subordinates before making a decision, but who retain the final decision-making authority.

free-rein (laissez-faire) leadership
A leadership style in which the leader turns over all authority and control to subordinates.

Democratic leaders solicit input from all members of the group and then allow the group members to make the final decision through a voting process. This approach works well with highly trained professionals. The president of a physicians' clinic might use the democratic approach. **Consensual leaders** encourage discussion about issues and then require that all parties involved agree to the final decision. This is the general style used by labor mediators. **Consultative leaders** confer with subordinates before making a decision, but retain the final decision-making authority. This technique has been used to dramatically increase the productivity of assembly-line workers.

The third leadership style, at the opposite end of the continuum from the autocratic style, is **free-rein** or **laissez-faire** (French for "leave it alone") **leadership.** Managers who use this style turn over all authority and control to subordinates. Employees are assigned a task and then given free rein to figure out the best way to accomplish it. The manager doesn't get involved unless asked. Under this approach, subordinates have unlimited freedom as long as they do not violate existing company policies. This approach is also sometimes used with highly trained professionals as in a research laboratory.

Although one might at first assume that subordinates would prefer the free-rein style, this approach can have several drawbacks. If free-rein leadership is accompanied by unclear expectations and lack of feedback from the manager, the experience can be frustrating for an employee. Employees may perceive the manager as being uninvolved and indifferent to what is happening or as unwilling or unable to provide the necessary structure, information, and expertise.

Each employee on the Toyota assembly line has been empowered to act as a quality control inspector, stopping the line if necessary to correct a problem.

Employee Empowerment

empowerment The process of giving employees increased autonomy and discretion to make decisions, as well as control over the resources needed to implement those decisions.

Participative and free-rein leaders use a technique called empowerment to share decision-making authority with subordinates. **Empowerment** means giving employees increased autonomy and discretion to make their own decisions, as well as control over the resources needed to implement those decisions. When decision-making power is shared at all levels of the organization, employees feel a greater sense of ownership in, and responsibility for, organizational outcomes.

Max Messmer, Chairman and CEO of Robert Half International, says: "Most people will work harder and do a better job if they feel their opinions are respected and that they are trusted to be responsible to make their own decisions. Empowering your employees will likely pay off with respect, loyalty, and the high level of productivity that comes from effective teamwork."[9] There is no one best leadership style. The most effective style for a given situation depends on elements such as the characteristics of the subordinates, the complexity of the task, the source of the leader's power, and the stability of the environment.

Corporate Culture

corporate culture The set of attitudes, values, and standards that distinguishes one organization from another.

The leadership style of managers in an organization is usually indicative of the underlying philosophy, or values, of the organization. The set of *attitudes, values,* and *standards of behavior* that distinguishes one organization from another is called **corporate culture.** A corporate culture evolves over time and is based on the accumulated history of the organization, including the vision of the founders. It is also influenced by the dominant leadership style within the organization. Evidence of a company's culture is seen in its heroes (e.g., Andy Grove of Intel), myths (stories about the company that are passed from employee to employee), symbols (e.g., the Nike swoosh), and ceremonies. Computer Associates' culture is characterized as a hard-edge corporate culture of growth at all costs. Employees are encouraged to create new ideas and turn them into a profitable reality. Mark Stabler, former senior vice president for global marketing, speaking about the culture, said: "It's a thunderously great place to work if you like extreme challenges and opportunities."[10]

Although culture is intangible and its rules are often unspoken, it can have a strong impact on a company's success. Therefore, managers must try to influence the corporate culture so that it will contribute to the success of the company. For instance, the Microsoft Corporation has committed itself to the development of a culture befitting a more mature organization. Until 2002, the company's culture was described as cowboy-like style.[11] The leadership was described as abrasive, loose, and autocratic. Employees were only recognized and rewarded for their intellect and programming skills.

The new CEO, Steve Ballmer, announced in June 2002 a new mission for the organization: "To enable people and businesses throughout the world to realize their full potential." He has committed to making strides in empowering executives to make their own decisions. He has implemented training and development, strategic planning, and formal performance evaluations. His goal is to create a great company that will be even more successful in the next 25 years than it was in the first.

concept check

How do leaders influence other people's behavior?

How can managers empower employees?

What is corporate culture?

Making Ethical Choices

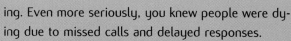

xtra! http://gitmanxtra.swlearning.com

WAITING AND WAITING AND WAITING

You've always been in a hurry, whether it's to get to a party or to find a job. You were in a hurry to land a supervisory position immediately upon college graduation, and looked for an organization that satisfied your goals of providing community service and moving up quickly. As an adept organizer, with an innate sense of the right number of people and money necessary to complete a task, you wanted your ability to plan and stay focused on goals to be recognized.

Your search led you to the police department of a major metropolitan city, as the supervisor of 911—the perfect job for someone in a hurry. Upon taking over, you analyzed the department's requirements and determined you needed more operators to service the growing call volume. You shared your findings with the chief of police, who had to approve all staffing allocations, and he agreed with your evaluation. Human resources, however, repeatedly denied your requests for more operators, even though your department received numerous complaints from callers who were left waiting and waiting. Even more seriously, you knew people were dying due to missed calls and delayed responses.

Investigating further, you discovered that although he told you otherwise, the chief of police never in fact approved your proposal so that human resources could hire the additional staff. When the mayor called to discuss complaints his office had received about poor 911 service, the chief told the mayor the call center was fully staffed and placed the blame on your department's inefficiency. Based on current call volume, your department is short approximately 25 percent of the operators needed to efficiently service the 911 calls it receives.

ETHICAL DILEMMA

When you realize your staffing proposal has been ignored and take into account the serious ramifications that result from this, do you report this to the mayor and the city's board of elected officials?

SOURCES: Mike Fitzgerald, "911 Problem Began Months Ago," *Belleville News-Democrat*, October 13, 2002, downloaded from http://www.belleville.com; and Phil Mendelson, "Want an Explanation of D.C.'s 911 Deficiencies? Hold, Please," *The Washington Post*, March 9, 2003, p. B8.

CONTROLLING

5 learning goal

controlling
The process of assessing the organization's progress toward accomplishing its goals; includes monitoring the implementation of a plan and correcting deviations from the plan.

The fourth key function that managers perform is **controlling.** Controlling is the process of assessing the organization's progress toward accomplishing its goals. It includes monitoring the implementation of a plan and correcting deviations from that plan. As Exhibit 7.6 shows, controlling can be visualized as a cyclical process made up of five stages:

1. Setting performance standards (goals)
2. Measuring performance
3. Comparing actual performance to established performance standards
4. Taking corrective action (if necessary)
5. Using information gained from the process to set future performance standards

Performance standards are the levels of performance the company wants to attain. These goals are based on its strategic, tactical, and operational plans. The most effective performance standards state a measurable behavioral objective that can be achieved in a specified time frame. For example, the performance objective for the sales division of a company could be stated as "$100,000 in gross sales for the month of January." Each individual employee in that division would also have a specified performance goal. Actual firm, division, or individual performance can be measured against desired performance standards to see if a gap exists between the desired level of performance and the actual level of performance. If a performance gap does exist, the reason for it must be determined and corrective action taken.

Feedback is essential to the process of control. Most companies have a reporting system that identifies areas where performance standards are not being met. A feedback system helps managers detect problems before they get out of hand. If a problem exists, the managers take corrective action. Toyota uses a simple but effective control system on its automobile assembly lines. Each worker serves as the customer for the process just before his or hers. Each worker is empowered to act as a quality control inspector. If a part is defective or not installed properly, the

Exhibit 7.6 The Control Process

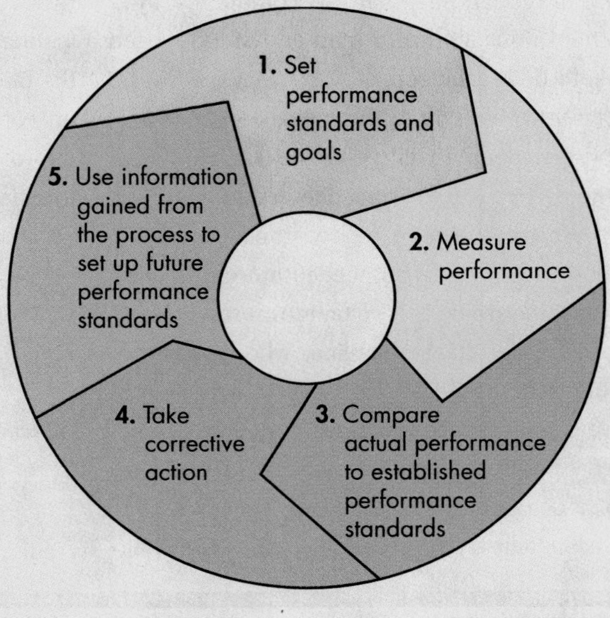
1. Set performance standards and goals
2. Measure performance
3. Compare actual performance to established performance standards
4. Take corrective action
5. Use information gained from the process to set up future performance standards

Supervisory managers need to be knowledgeable about the specific production and operation tools, techniques, and methods relevant to their specific area of the organization.

next worker won't accept it. Any worker can alert the supervisor to a problem by tugging on a rope that turns on a warning light (i.e., feedback). If the problem isn't corrected, the worker can stop the entire assembly line.

Why is controlling such an important part of a manager's job? First, it helps managers to determine the success of the other three functions: planning, organizing, and leading. Second, control systems direct employee behavior toward achieving organizational goals. Third, control systems provide a means of coordinating employee activities and integrating resources throughout the organization.

concept check

Describe the control process.

Why is the control process important to the success of the organization?

Managerial Roles

6 learning goal

In carrying out the responsibilities of planning, organizing, leading, and controlling, managers take on many different roles. A role is a set of behavioral expectations, or a set of activities that a person is expected to perform. Managers' roles fall into three basic categories: *informational roles, interpersonal roles,* and *decisional roles.* These roles are summarized in Exhibit 7.7. In an **informational role,** the manager may act as an information gatherer, an information distributor, or a spokesperson for the company. A manager's **interpersonal roles** are based on various interactions with other people. Depending on the situation, a manager may need to act as a figurehead, a company leader, or a liaison. When acting in a **decisional role,** a manager may have to think like an entrepreneur, make decisions about resource allocation, help resolve conflicts, or negotiate compromises.

informational roles
A manager's activities as an information gatherer, an information disseminator, or a spokesperson for the company.

interpersonal roles
A manager's activities as a figurehead, company leader, or liaison.

decisional roles
A manager's activities as an entrepreneur, resource allocator, conflict resolver, or negotiator.

programmed decisions
Decisions made in response to frequently occurring routine situations.

Managerial Decision Making

In every function performed, role taken on, and set of skills applied, a manager is a decision maker. Decision making means choosing among alternatives. Decision making occurs in response to the identification of a problem or an opportunity. The decisions managers make fall into two basic categories: programmed and nonprogrammed. **Programmed decisions** are made in response to routine situations that occur frequently in a variety of settings throughout an organization. For example, the need to hire new personnel is a common situation for most organizations. Therefore, standard procedures for recruitment and selection are developed and followed in most companies.

Infrequent, unforeseen, or very unusual problems and opportunities require **nonprogrammed decisions** by managers. Because these situations are unique and

Exhibit 7.7 | The Many Roles That Managers Play in an Organization

Role	Description	Example
Informational Roles		
Monitor	Seeks out and gathers information relevant to the organization.	Finding out about legal restrictions on new product technology.
Disseminator	Provides information where it is needed in the organization.	Providing current production figures to workers on the assembly line.
Spokesperson	Transmits information to people outside the organization.	Representing the company at a shareholders' meeting.
Interpersonal Roles		
Figurehead	Represents the company in a symbolic way.	Cutting the ribbon at ceremony for the opening of a new building.
Leader	Guides and motivates employees to achieve organizational goals.	Helping subordinates to set monthly performance goals.
Liaison	Acts as a go-between among individuals inside and outside the organization.	Representing the retail sales division of the company at a regional sales meeting.
Decisional Roles		
Entrepreneur	Searches out new opportunities and initiates change.	Implementing a new production process using new technology.
Disturbance handler	Handles unexpected events and crises.	Handling a crisis situation such as a fire.
Resource allocator	Designates the use of financial, human, and other organizational resources.	Approving the funds necessary to purchase computer equipment and hire personnel.
Negotiator	Represents the company at negotiating processes.	Participating in salary negotiations with union representatives.

nonprogrammed decisions
Responses to infrequent, unforeseen, or very unusual problems and opportunities where the manager does not have a precedent to follow in decision making.

complex, the manager rarely has a precedent to follow. The events on September 11, 2001, shocked America. As the events unfolded on television, many did not understand that what they were seeing were not accidents, but acts of war. Rescue and emergency workers responded to the disaster just like any other crisis. No one could have predicted that so many rescue personnel would lose their lives, because no one imagined that the structures would collapse.

Similarly, the bioterrorism attack that occurred less than one month later was not predicted.[12] President Bush publicly reassured the country that the first incident was an isolated event. Little did he realize that up and down the East Coast of the United States, more people would die and an air of panic and uncertainty would grip everyone who received mail from the U.S. Postal Service. America was simply not prepared to effectively deal with homeland attacks of this nature. The United States is still trying to figure out how to defend against both known and unknown enemies. Addressing terrorism required a systematic approach to decision making. Managers typically follow five steps in the decision-making process, as illustrated in Exhibit 7.8:

1. Recognize or define the problem or opportunity. Although it is more common to focus on problems because of their obvious negative effects, managers who do not take advantage of new opportunities may lose competitive advantage to other firms.
2. Gather information so as to identify alternative solutions or actions.

Exhibit 7.8 The Decision-Making Process

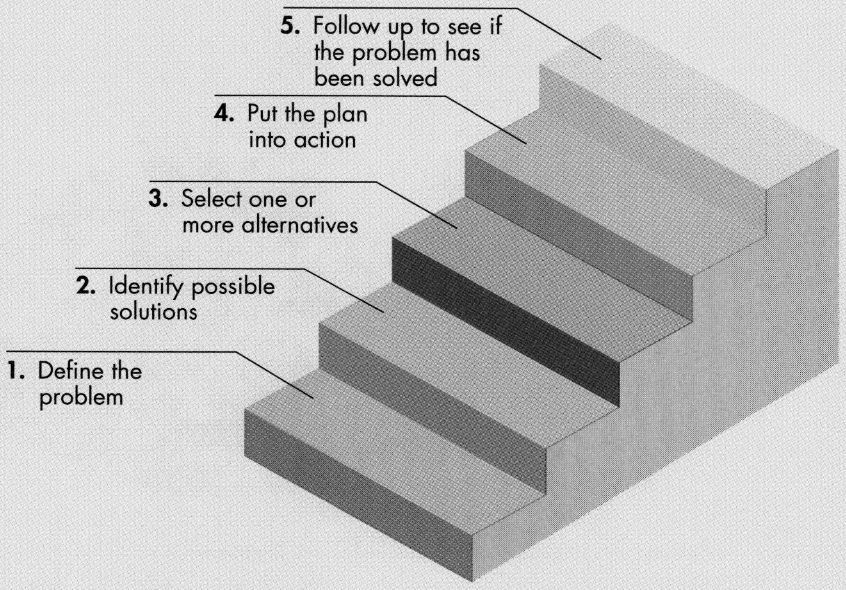
5. Follow up to see if the problem has been solved
4. Put the plan into action
3. Select one or more alternatives
2. Identify possible solutions
1. Define the problem

concept check

What are the three types of managerial roles?

Give examples of things managers might do when acting in each of the different types of roles.

List the five steps in the decision-making process.

3. Select one or more alternatives after evaluating the strengths and weaknesses of each possibility.
4. Put the chosen alternative into action.
5. Gather information to obtain feedback on the effectiveness of the chosen plan.

Managerial Skills

7 learning goal

In order to be successful in planning, organizing, leading, and controlling, managers must use a wide variety of skills. A *skill* is the ability to do something proficiently. Managerial skills fall into three basic categories: conceptual, human relations, and technical skills. The degree to which each type of skill is used depends upon the level of the manager's position as seen in Exhibit 7.9. Additionally, in an increasingly global marketplace, it pays for managers to develop a special set of skills to deal with global management issues.

Technical Skills

technical skills
A manager's specialized areas of knowledge and expertise, as well as the ability to apply that knowledge.

Specialized areas of knowledge and expertise and the ability to apply that knowledge make up a manager's **technical skills.** Preparing a financial statement, programming a computer, designing an office building, and analyzing market research are all examples of technical skills. These types of skills are especially important for supervisory managers because they work closely with employees who are producing the goods and/or services of the firm.

Exhibit 7.9 The Importance of Managerial Skills at Different Management Levels

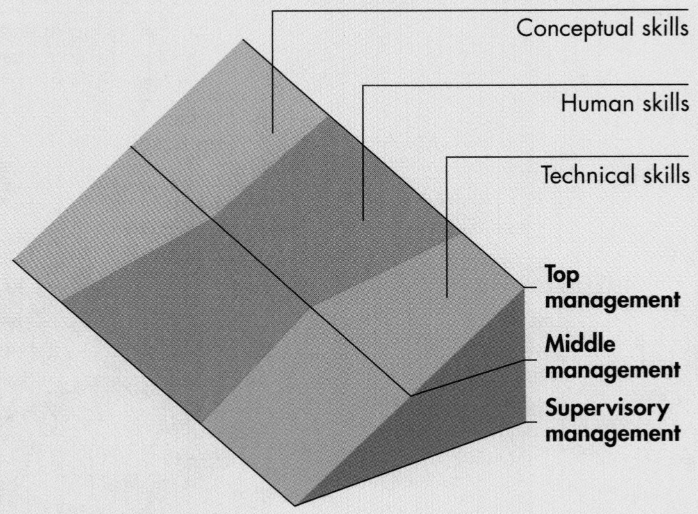

Human Relations Skills

human relations skills
A manager's interpersonal skills that are used to accomplish goals through the use of human resources.

Human relations skills are the interpersonal skills managers use to accomplish goals through the use of human resources. This set of skills includes the ability to understand human behavior, to communicate effectively with others, and to motivate individuals to accomplish their objectives. Giving positive feedback to employees, being sensitive to their individual needs, and showing a willingness to empower subordinates are all examples of good human relations skills.

At Applebee's Restaurants, one of the keys to success is genuinely friendly service.[13] To achieve their service standards requires genuinely enthusiastic staff. The capacity for such enthusiasm must be determined before the employee is hired. Prospective employees take a written test that measures skills and gives personality insights. Once an applicant is hired, the coaching process begins almost immediately. Lou Kaucic, senior vice president of Human Resources, says that new employees welcome the feedback and think that Applebee's really cares about them.

Conceptual Skills

conceptual skills
A manager's ability to view the organization as a whole, understand how the various parts are interdependent, and assess how the organization relates to its external environment.

Conceptual skills include the ability to view the organization as a whole, understand how the various parts are interdependent, and assess how the organization relates to its external environment. These skills allow managers to evaluate situations and develop alternative courses of action. Good conceptual skills are especially necessary for managers at the top of the management pyramid where strategic planning takes place.

Global Management Skills

global management skills
A manager's ability to operate in diverse cultural environments.

The increasing globalization of the world market, as discussed in Chapter 4, has created a need for managers who have **global management skills,** that is, the ability to operate in diverse cultural environments. With more and more companies choosing to do business in multiple locations around the world, employees are often required to learn the geography, language, and social customs of other cultures. It is expensive to train employees for foreign assignments and pay their relocation costs; therefore,

Focusing on Small Business

Even Highly Skilled Small-Business Owners Can't Do It Alone

Few entrepreneurs are as personally identified with the business they head as B. Thomas Golisano, founder, chairman, president, and chief executive officer of Paychex Inc., a payroll-processing firm in Rochester, New York. Mr. Golisano, now 60 years old, started Paychex in 1971, when his employer, also a payroll-processing firm, declined to pursue a market Mr. Golisano was convinced was a great opportunity: businesses with fewer than 50 workers.

Rather than quit in a huff, however, Mr. Golisano collaborated with his employer, renting office space and computer time for four years. "We had some help," he says. "It was a really great deal for both parties." Today the company is highly profitable and very successful.

Much of Paychex's success, Mr. Golisano says, is due to its ability to attract talented people from disparate backgrounds. The company was originally 17 separate operations—partnerships or franchises—which were later consolidated. Aside from Mr. Golisano, "nobody from the payroll-processing industry" was among those early 17 leaders, he says.

Over 31 years, Mr. Golisano says, he has learned his weaknesses and surrounded himself with people strong in those areas. Information technology (IT) isn't his strength, but two women, Kathy Angelidis and Judy Chapman, who were Paychex's second and third employees hired, are still around, working in IT at Paychex. "They were so dependable at what they did," he recalls. "They set a standard for everyone else. They still do that."[14]

CRITICAL THINKING QUESTIONS

1. Many times entrepreneurs are reluctant to hire new managers and give up some control. Why do you think that this is true?
2. Do you think that one managerial skill is more important for an entrepreneur than another? Why?

choosing the right person for the job is especially important. Individuals who are open-minded, flexible, willing to try new things, and comfortable in a multicultural setting are good candidates for international management positions.

concept check

Define the basic managerial skills.

How important is each of these skill sets at the different levels of the management pyramid?

What new challenges do managers face due to increasing globalization?

While a single manager may possess some or most of the skills described above, rarely does one person excel in all types of managerial skills. Every business needs a leader, but in today's marketplace things move too fast, the need for specialization is too great, and competition is too fierce for a one-man or one-woman show to survive. Even small businesses need a supporting cast, as the "Focusing on Small Business" box explains.

© AP / WIDE WORLD PHOTOS

For many managers, accepting an international position may mean helping their spouses and children adapt to the new environment.

P T i

Trends in Management and Leadership

8 learning goal

Four important trends in management today are: increasing employee empowerment, the growing use of information technology, the increasing need for global management skills, and the need to prepare for crises management.

Managers Empowering Employees

Most of the firms discussed in this chapter, including Ben & Jerry's, General Electric, and Paychex Inc., are including more employees in the decision-making process than ever before. This increased level of employee involvement comes from the realization that people at all levels in the organization possess unique knowledge, skills, and abilities that can be of great value to the company. With empowerment, managers share information and responsibility with employees at all levels in the organization. Along with the authority to make decisions, empowerment also gives employees the control over resources needed to implement those decisions. Empowering employees enhances their commitment to the organization by giving them a feeling of ownership in the firm and an increased sense of competency.

In order for empowerment to work, managers have to facilitate employee decision making by providing access to necessary information, clear expectations for results, behavioral boundaries, and the resources employees need to carry out their decisions. Empowered employees are also guided by the use of a strategic principle. A company's strategy is expressed in its strategic principle.[15] It gives immediate guidance to make decisions that advance the company's position, not undermine it. Companies like General Electric, American Online, Dell, Wal-Mart, and Southwest Airlines have successfully used this concept. When employees understand Wal-Mart's "Low Prices, Every Day," decision making gets easier.

Managers and Information Technology

The second trend having a major impact on managers is the proliferation of information technology. An increasing number of organizations are selling technology, and an increasing number are looking for cutting-edge technology to make and market the products and services they sell. A brief look at PeopleSoft, a rapidly growing provider of automated human resource functions, provides some insight into the crucial role information technology can play in today's organizations. Plenty of new technology is being used at PeopleSoft, but it is "people-oriented" technology, and it starts with a backpack. Every new employee is issued a backpack filled with a laptop, pager, cell phone, and digital assistant. Steve Zarate, chief information officer at PeopleSoft, calls it "information-to-go." Every employee has access to PeopleSoft's "massive information infrastructure that spans continents and time zones." By using the latest technology to empower people and keep members of the organization connected, PeopleSoft has grown to be a $10 billion company.

Do individuals with technical backgrounds make good managers? The answer is "yes" and "no," as discussed in the "Applying Technology" box.

Managing Multinational Cultures

As companies expand around the globe, managers will face the challenges of directing the behavior of employees around the world. They must recognize that because of cultural differences, people respond to similar situations in very different ways. Managers must decide how they are going to accomplish managing consistent employee behavior, given such diverse cultural employee backgrounds. The best way to meet this challenge of managing international employees is to develop an individual-level program that is based on values and principles.

Applying Technology

Do Techies Make Good Managers?

When Dan Fisher applied to Princeton he had to choose between two application forms: a yellow one for a traditional BA, and a green one for the engineering school. Dan was a bit of a geek: a Westinghouse science fair entrant and his high school's MVM (most valuable mathlete). So his choice seemed obvious—until his dad, a mechanical and aerospace engineer at a Long Island defense contractor, stepped in. "He said, 'Engineers are powerless drones.' So I ripped up the green form," Dan recalls. "But you know who sat near me in my Princeton eating club? Mr. Amazon himself, Jeff Bezos. He majored in electrical engineering and computer science—your quintessential nerd."

"Our concept of what general managers are needing now and in the future has put information technology right at the heart of leadership," says Kim B. Clark, dean of the Harvard Business School. Few business school deans wouldn't echo this sentiment, but Clark thinks the challenge for managers is so important that he has reshaped the Harvard experience to address it. While the case study method still rules at the B-school, "Technology and Operations Management" is now a required class for first-term MBAs.[16]

CRITICAL THINKING QUESTIONS

1. Why do you think "techies" often hire business-trained graduates to manage their companies?
2. Do you think that a lack of business training is the primary reason for the dot-com fiasco of the early 2000s?

Managers should apply three specific principles to this process: example, involvement, and trust. *Example* means that managers should set and live out the standard for others to follow. They must act as the role model for all employees of the organization. Leaders must also create personal *involvement* in the organization for all members. Involvement brings the whole person into the company's operations. People are treated like valuable partners not just as an expense to the company. Leaders must develop a culture of *trust*. This is essential to getting people to invest themselves for the mutual benefit of everyone. When these principles are applied, people are able to manage themselves and they can release incredible talent and energy.[17]

Crisis Management

Crises can occur in even the best-managed organizations. Take, for example, the power grid meltdown in 2003. No manager or executive can be completely prepared for these types of unexpected crises. However, how a manager handles the situation could mean the difference between disaster, survival, or even financial gain.

No matter what the crisis, there are some basic guidelines that managers should follow to minimize the negative outcomes. Managers should not become immobilized by the problem nor ignore it. Managers should face the problem head on. Managers should always tell the truth about the situation and then put the best people on the job to correct the problem. Managers should ask for help if they need it, and finally, managers must learn from the experience to avoid the same problem in the future.[18]

concept check

How can information technology aid in decision making?

What are three principles of managing multinational cultures?

Describe several guidelines for crisis management.

Great Ideas to Use Now

Many of the skills managers use to accomplish organizational goals can be applied outside the organizational setting. You could be using these skills in your life right now to accomplish your personal goals.

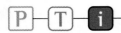

Try It Now

Save Time and Money. Successful managers use both their time and their money well. As a student, you may feel that you never have enough of either of these resources. You can save yourself some time and money by taking advantage of some of the bargains on the following Web sites:

- *Student Advantage* (**http://www.studentadvantage.com**). One way to cut costs on everything from transportation to food to clothing is to use a student discount card. The Student Advantage Card is one such discount card, accepted at over 20,000 businesses nationwide.
- *FastWeb.com* (**http://www.fastweb.com**). Save valuable time and find out about "free" money available through academic scholarships and grants. This site offers free online searches for scholarships and grants.
- *VarsityBooks.com* (**http://www.varsitybooks.com**), *Follett College Stores* (**http://www.efollett.com**), and *BigWords.com* (**http://www.Bigwords.com**). Students can spend hundreds of dollars per semester on textbooks and other course materials. Save up to 40 percent on textbooks by buying online.
- *Travelocity* (**http://www.travelocity.com**), *Expedia Travel* (**http://www.expedia.com**), *United College Plus* (**http://www.collegeplus.com**). Save time and money by using sites that make your travel arrangements for you, and do it at a discount price.
- *Apple Computer* (**http://www.apple.com/education/hed/students**) and *Campus Essentials* (**http://www.dell.com/client/edu/essentials.htm**). Take advantage of special deals (discounts and rebates) on personal computers, and then use your new computer to find even more good deals on the Internet!

Effective Time Management

Successful managers use their time wisely. Adopting the following time management techniques will help you become a more successful student now and will help prepare you for the demands of your future workplace:

- Plan ahead. This is first and most obvious. Set both long-term and short-term goals. Review your list often and revise it when your situation changes.

Customer Satisfaction and Quality

If managers are going to succeed in business, they must make certain that their companies have a laserlike focus on customer satisfaction and quality. A satisfied customer is a firm's best guarantee of reaching profit goals and gaining repeat business.

Frederick Smith, founder of FedEx, has always done everything possible to give the customer what he or she wants. Acquisitions like RPS in 1998 and American Freightways in 2001 have rounded out FedEx's offerings to include ground and freight delivery, a wise move given the corporate cost cutting that followed. "Having the ground network in place has been particularly important as the economy has slowed," says Jim Winchester, transportation analyst at Lazard Freres. "It allowed us to walk and chew gum at the same time," quips founder and CEO Fred Smith. One of FedEx's customers agrees: George Kurth, director of supply chain and logistics at Hyundai Motor America, consolidated his $450,000 monthly shipping business from a hodgepodge of companies into FedEx a few months back. "We wanted the best," he says.[19]

Looking Ahead at Microsoft

The role of top management at Microsoft is to develop strategic plans and address long-range issues. Can Microsoft evolve into the mature company that both Gates and Ballmer claim they want it to be? Integrating the formal, structured management style of a professional manager with the "cowboy" entrepreneurial management style that currently exists may be more challenging than anyone anticipates. To make this happen, Ballmer will need to stick to his guns to empower his executives. Top managers, like Bill Gates and Steve Ballmer, often set the general attitudes, values, and standards of behavior that become the foundation of a corporation's culture.

- Establish priorities. Decide what is most important and what is most urgent. Sometimes they are not the same thing. Keep in mind the 80–20 rule: 20 percent of one's effort delivers 80 percent of the results.
- Delegate. Ask yourself if the task can be accomplished as effectively by someone else. Empower other people, and you may be surprised by the quality of the outcome.
- Learn to say no. Be stingy with your time. Be realistic about how long tasks will take. Don't feel guilty when you don't have the time, ability, or inclination to take on an additional task.
- Batch. Group activities together so they take up less of your day. For example, set aside a certain time to return phone calls, answer e-mail, and do any necessary written correspondence.
- Stay on task. Learn how to handle diversions. For example, let your answering machine take messages until you finish a particular task.
- Set deadlines. Don't let projects drag on. Reward yourself each time you cross a certain number of items off your "to do" list.

Stress Management

One of the things that can stop any career in its tracks is burnout. One way to prevent burnout is to examine how well you are dealing with the current stress you are experiencing and learn how to develop coping mechanisms. To start this process, look to see if you are exhibiting any of the warning signs of being overstressed. Students under stress can have a wide range of symptoms, including headaches, asthma attacks, nailbiting, and sleep problems.[20] More serious symptoms can include stomach problems and even depression.

If you feel that you are not coping with the stress in your life, now is the time to learn some stress management skills. Here are some helpful ideas:

- Make sure to include physical exercise in your schedule. Try some mind/body work such as Yoga or stretching.
- Find someone you trust and can confide in. Talking out your problems can help a lot.
- If there is no one you feel comfortable talking to, try keeping a diary to work out your stressful situations.
- For more information visit the American Institute of Stress Web site: **http://www.stress.org**.

Summary Of Learning Goals

1

What is the role of management?

Management is the process of guiding the development, maintenance, and allocation of resources to attain organizational goals. Managers are the people in the organization responsible for developing and carrying out this management process. The four primary functions of managers are planning, organizing, leading, and controlling.

2

What are the four types of planning?

Planning is deciding what needs to be done, identifying when and how it will be done, and determining by whom it should be done. Managers use four different types of planning: strategic, tactical, operational, and contingency planning. Strategic planning involves creating long-range (one to five years), broad goals and determining the necessary resources to accomplish those goals. Tactical planning has a shorter time frame (less than one year) and more specific objectives that support the broader strategic goals. Operational planning creates specific standards, methods, policies, and procedures that are used in specific functional areas of the organization. Contingency plans identify alternative courses of action for very unusual or crisis situations.

3

What are the primary responsibilities of managers in organizing activities?

Organizing involves coordinating and allocating a firm's resources in order to carry out its plans. It includes developing a structure for the people, positions, departments, and activities within the firm. This is accomplished by dividing up tasks (division of labor), grouping jobs and employees (departmentalization), and assigning authority and responsibilities (delegation).

4

How do leadership styles influence a corporate culture?

Leading is the process of guiding and motivating others toward the achievement of organizational goals. Managers have unique leadership styles that range from autocratic to free-rein. The set of attitudes, values, and standards of behavior that distinguishes one organization from another is called corporate culture. A corporate culture evolves over time and is based on the accumulated history of the organization, including the vision of the founders.

5

How do organizations control activities?

Controlling is the process of assessing the organization's progress toward accomplishing its goals. The control process is as follows: (1) set performance standards (goals), (2) measure performance, (3) compare actual performance to established performance standards, (4) take corrective action (if necessary), and (5) use information gained from the process to set future performance standards.

6

What roles do managers take on in different organizational settings?

In an informational role, the manager may act as an information gatherer, an information distributor, or a spokesperson for the company. A manager's interpersonal roles are based on various interactions with other people. Depending on the situation, a manager may need to act as a figurehead, a company leader, or a liaison.

7

What set of managerial skills is necessary for managerial success?

Managerial skills fall into three basic categories: technical, human relations, and conceptual skills. Specialized areas of knowledge and expertise and the ability to apply that knowledge make up a manager's technical skills. Human relations skills include the ability to understand human behavior, to communicate effectively with others, and to motivate individuals to accomplish their objectives. Conceptual skills include the ability to view the organization as a whole, understand how the various parts are interdependent, and assess how the organization relates to its external environment.

8

What trends will affect management in the future?

Four important trends in management today are: increasing employee empowerment, the increasing use of information technology, the need to manage multinational cultures, and the need to prepare for crises management. Empowerment means giving employees increased autonomy and discretion to make their own decisions. Using the latest information technology, managers can make quicker, better-informed decisions. As more companies "go global," the need for multinational cultural management skills is growing. Managers must set a good example, create personal involvement for all employees, and develop a culture of trust. Crises management requires quick action, telling the truth about the situation, and putting the best people on the task to correct the situation. Finally, management must learn from the crisis in order to prevent it from happening again.

Preparing for Tomorrow's Workplace

1. Would you be a good manager? Do a self-assessment that includes your current technical, human relations, and conceptual skills. What skills do you already possess, and which do you need to add? Where do your strengths lie? Based on this exercise, develop a description of an effective manager.
2. You are planning to start one of the following companies. Develop a mission statement that defines its vision and give examples of how you would apply each of the four types of planning (strategic, tactical, operational, and contingency) in building the business.
   a. Ethnic restaurant near your campus
   b. Custom skateboard manufacturer
   c. Computer training firm
   d. Boutique specializing in Latin American clothing and jewelry
3. President Theodore Roosevelt said, "The best executive is the one who has sense enough to pick good men to do what he wants done, and self-restraint enough to keep from meddling with them while they do it." How does this statement relate to the leadership styles described in this chapter? Do you agree with Roosevelt? Is Roosevelt's definition of a good leader still appropriate today? Explain your answers.
4. Focusing on either your educational institution or a place where you have worked, prepare a brief report on its unique culture. How would you describe it? What has shaped it? What changes do you see occurring over time?
5. Divide the class into groups. Each group should visit a company and try to determine the leadership style of its managers as well as the corporate culture. Report your findings to the class.

Key Terms

autocratic leaders 224
coercive power 224
conceptual skills 232
consensual leaders 225
consultative leaders 225
contingency plans 221
controlling 228
corporate culture 226
decisional roles 229
democratic leaders 225
empowerment 226
expert power 224
free-rein (laissez-faire) leadership 225
global management skills 232
human relations skills 232
informational roles 229
interpersonal roles 229
leadership 223
leadership style 224
legitimate power 223
management 218
middle management 222
mission 220
mission statement 220
nonprogrammed decisions 230
operational planning 221
organizing 222
participative leadership 224
planning 218
power 223
programmed decisions 229
referent power 224
reward power 223
strategic planning 218
supervisory management 222
tactical planning 221
technical skills 231
top management 222

Working the Net

1. Strategic Advantage, **http://www.strategy4u.com**, offers many reasons that companies should develop strategic plans, as well as a strategy tip of the month, assessment tools, planning exercises, and resource links. Explore the site to learn the effect of strategic planning on financial performance and present your evidence to the class. Then select a planning exercise and, with a group of classmates, perform it as it applies to your school.
2. Are you leadership material? Go to the Leadership section at About.com, **http://management.about.com/cs/leadership/**. Read several articles that interest you to develop a list of characteristics of effective leaders. How do you measure up?
3. Congratulations! You've just been promoted to your first supervisory position. However, you are at a loss as to how to actually manage your staff. About.com's guide to General management, **http://management.about.com/cs/generalmanagement/**, brings together a variety of materials to help you. Check out the Essentials links, such as Management 101 and How to Manage, as well as other resources. Develop a plan for yourself to follow.
4. How do entrepreneurs develop corporate culture in their companies? Do a search on the term "corporate culture" in either *Inc.* (**http://www.inc.com**), *Entrepreneur* (**http://www.entrepreneur.com**), or Fast Company (**http://www.fastcompany.com**). Prepare a short presentation for your class that explains the importance of corporate culture and how its developed in young firms.
5. Good managers and leaders know how to empower their employees. The Business e-Coach at **http://www.1000ventures.com/business_guide/crosscuttings/employee_empowerment.html** explains why employee empowerment is so important in today's knowledge economy. After reviewing the informant at this site, prepare a brief report on the benefits of employee empowerment. Include several ideas you would like a manager to use to empower you.

Creative Thinking Case

A Ford Takes on Ford

If Bill Ford started out as a reluctant CEO, there was a good reason. He hadn't really wanted the job. His first day, he says, "was not a joyful day in my life, particularly given the ages of my [four school-age] children." He didn't want to sacrifice evenings at home with his family and time helping to manage his beloved Detroit Lions, which his family owns (and which were performing almost as badly as Ford Motor). "But," he adds, "I felt I had no choice."

The situation would be a nail-biter for any CEO. But consider this: Bill Ford is only 45 years old. Yes, he has spent 23 years at the company his great-grandfather founded, toiling away at 18 jobs, proving himself. Yes, he gets high marks for his smarts and his humility. But he is still so green. His résumé doesn't look anything like that of a Big Three CEO. Though he was the chairman of Ford Switzerland and the head of the company's climate control division—and chairman of Ford Motor since January 1999—he has never held a top operating or finance position at the company. He didn't come bulldozing into the job. He reluctantly led a coup when he and the board lost confidence in the former CEO, Jacques Nasser, in part because quality problems were soaring and morale was plummeting.

Ford has learned that his job requires him to be as much shrink as businessman—something every decent manager quickly realizes. He told some of his executives that he occasionally wondered if he should have gotten a psychology degree instead of a business degree. For instance, he found himself having to manage tension between the laid-back Nick Scheele, the former chairman of Ford Europe whom he'd tapped to be his president and COO (chief operating officer), and the more combative David Thursfield, the former CEO of Ford Europe, whom he'd made group VP (vice president) of international and global purchasing. Ford also had to fend off Wolfgang Reitzle, the head of Ford's premier automotive luxury group, who was pushing Ford for more power. Reitzle left in April 2002 with a fat consulting contract to keep him out of the arms of GM.

For now Ford plans to stay his course. By 2004, he must get his team to deliver the extra $1 billion in cuts he's promised investors. He must see to it that the problems with Jaguar are fixed and that launches of the Jaguar XJ sedan and the new F-Series pickup truck go smoothly. He must continue to boost quality and slash costs even as new contract talks loom with the United Auto Workers (UAW). A crucial part of Ford's turnaround calls for the closing of five plants by mid-decade, and Ford has said he will work with the union to get that done.[21]

CRITICAL THINKING QUESTIONS

1. How would you describe Bill Ford's leadership style?
2. Do you think Bill Ford's job entails more strategic planning than tactical planning? Why?
3. Is corporate culture important at Ford?

VIDEO CASE

SAS Knows How To Keep Employees. . . .

Insanity Inc.? "It's been called worse," says James H. Goodnight, CEO, of the company he helped cofound, SAS Institute, Inc. "If you treat people right they will make a difference. What we do here makes good business sense." The $50 to $70 million SAS saves annually, thanks to an employee defection rate of less than 4 percent, proves him right. And what does SAS do with the dollars its saves? It rewards its employees by creating a work environment that no one wants to leave.

What would keep you happy on the job? A 35-hour workweek? A health and recreational center with Olympic-size pool, gym, and basketball court? How about an on-site masseuse and free daily laundering of your workout clothes? Or unlimited sick days, with free comprehensive health insurance and access to on-site health care at a company-run clinic? And of course there are the usual financial rewards—competitive salary, bonus, and profit-sharing plan.

Impossible you say? Welcome to SAS (**http://www.sas.com**), the world's largest privately held software company and leader in e-business solutions, where every day is a dress-down day for the 4,000 people working at the company's 200-acre campus in North Carolina.

Goodnight's free-rein leadership and belief in employee empowerment reflects a corporate culture that supports employees' independent working styles. SAS "hires hard and manages easy." It makes sure employees have the technical and intellectual skills for the job, then lets them get on with it. "We are not into 'face time' here," says Goodnight. "If you need to leave at 4 P.M. on a Wednesday to go watch your child's soccer game, we trust that you will get your work done."

SAS also offers employees unlimited opportunity for growth. Many staffers come as students and stay because they are able to leapfrog around the organization, learning new skills and tackling fresh challenges. "SAS is in the intellectual-property business and our employees work on cutting-edge products. Developing employees' intellectual prowess makes them increasingly valuable to the company. It is not a disgrace to fail, as long as they learn something from it and share the information so we can all learn," says Goodnight. "Our people are our assets and we believe in taking good care of our assets."

CRITICAL THINKING QUESTIONS

1. What leadership and management styles does Jim Goodnight exhibit?
2. How do these impact the corporate culture at SAS? Explain.
3. How would you describe the corporate culture at SAS?

SOURCE: Adapted from material in the video: "Work Hard, Play Hard, and Have a Nice Lunch: Corporate Culture at SAS"; SAS Web site http://www.sas.com accessed on March 16, 2003.

E-Commerce Case

Stapling Together an E-Commerce Strategy

Wander into one of Staples's 1,040 U.S. stores and you will soon reach an Access Point. These online kiosks link you to Staples.com, where you can order products, build PCs to order, and tap into an online library with product and service information.

Why have online kiosks in the regular stores? "We're letting customers do business the way they want to do business, not the way we want them to," says Paul Gaffney, executive vice president and chief information officer (CIO) of the Framingham, Massachusetts–based office supplies superstore chain. The Access Point system increases the available products from about 7,500 stocked in the typical store to 45,000 products and dozens of business services. The build-to-order PC feature is so popular that about 35 percent of Staples' stores no longer carry computers on site.

Access Point is just one of Staples's many e-commerce initiatives. The Staples.com Web site focuses on small-business users, while 20,000 medium- to large-size companies use StaplesLink.com, their own specialized business-to-business (B2B) e-commerce site. About 70 percent of Staples Contract Division customers place orders through StaplesLink, where users can pull up real-time inventory availability, company-specific contract pricing, and order status. Corporate purchasing managers like the site, which lets them decentralize office supply purchasing while centralizing and controlling costs.

E-commerce is an integral part of Staples's long-term strategy to redefine the customer experience. The company's slogan—"Staples. that was easy"—is now guiding its business decisions. Making sure the firm's customer-focused e-commerce technology does indeed simplify purchasing for customers falls to CIO Gaffney. The behind-the-scenes integration work so that Staples's shoppers can buy online or in-store calls for a big-picture, comprehensive strategy. "To best serve our customers, we follow a disciplined approach to our technology and process integration initiatives," he explains. "That approach aligns our portfolio of projects to our overall business goals."

Gaffney has appointed several groups to help him implement his strategies. An e-commerce steering committee composed of both IT and business managers from these areas has become a primary forum for sharing technology across units and creating a common technology infrastructure. As a result, Staples.com and StaplesLink.com now share applications like order processing. Another team with people from all business areas is examining Staples's business processes and looking at how people, process, and technology relate. The goal is to identify projects that will have the greatest impact.

CRITICAL THINKING QUESTIONS

1. What special challenges does the CIO face in developing and implementing a firm's e-commerce strategy? Discuss and evaluate Gaffney's approach at Staples.
2. What managerial roles does Gaffney take? How would you describe his leadership style and the corporate culture he is promoting?
3. According to a recent article in *CIO* magazine, the CIO's role in e-commerce has passed through three stages. In the early years of e-commerce (1996–2000), the CIO took a back seat to the dedicated e-commerce business unit managers. From 2000 to 2002, as the dot-com bubble burst, the CIO moved into a major role in overall e-commerce management, focusing on execution, cost control, and consolidation. Now that e-commerce is considered an essential part of corporate strategy, many industry experts expect business unit leaders to want more control. How should the CIO's role shift to accommodate the maturing of e-commerce? What has Gaffney done to adapt his management approach to this third stage?

SOURCES: Todd Datz, "Strategic Alignment," *CIO,* August 15, 2002, downloaded from http://www.cio.com; "Staples Inc. Corporate Overview," Staples corporate Web site, downloaded from http://www.staples.com, April 20, 2003; "Staples Launches National Advertising Campaign to Introduce New Brand Promise," *Business Wire,* February 27, 2003, downloaded from http://www.staples.com; "Staples Launches New Version of StaplesLink.com B-to-B Procurement Web Site," *Business Wire,* February 18, 2003, downloaded from http://www.staples.com; "Staples Inc. Receives CIO Magazine's CIO-100 Award for Technology and Process Integration," *Business Wire,* August 15, 2002, downloaded from http://www.staples.com; Elana Varon, "The New Lords of E-Biz," *CIO,* March 15, 2003, downloaded from http://www.cio.com.

Hot Links Address Book

How does a company translate its mission statement into company action? Find out at Ben & Jerry's home page,
http://www.benjerry.com

To learn more about how firms develop contingency plans for all sorts of crises, visit *Contingency Planning* magazine's Web site at
http://www.contingencyplanning.com

What do the leaders of this year's Inc. 500 have to say about their success? Explore the Inc. 500 site at
http://www.inc.com/inc500/

Want to learn more about Bill Gates's management style? Go to his personal Web site,
http://www.microsoft.com/billgates
to read his official biography, speeches, and other information. For a different view, visit
http://www.zpub.com/un/bill

Most successful managers work hard at continually updating their managerial skills. One organization that offers many ongoing training and education programs is the American Management Association. Visit its site at
http://www.amanet.org

Search Questia's online library
http://www.questia.com
for leadership resources. You'll be able to preview a wide variety of books, journals, and other materials.

Chapter 8

© AP / WIDE WORLD PHOTOS

Designing Organizational Structures

learning goals

1 What are the five structural building blocks that managers use to design organizations?
2 What are the five types of departmentalization?
3 How can the degree of centralization/decentralization be altered to make an organization more successful?
4 How do mechanistic and organic organizations differ?
5 What is the difference between line positions and staff positions?
6 What is the goal of reengineering?
7 How does the informal organization affect the performance of the company?
8 What trends are influencing the way businesses organize?

The Restructuring of BMG

Finding the appropriate corporate structure for a multinational organization is never an easy task. However, when you're the music arm of one of the largest conglomerates in the world bent on becoming the leader in the music industry, the task is even greater. BMG's music-publishing operations are the third largest in the world and include more than 200 record labels in 41 countries, including Arista Records in New York. The careers of hundreds of artists have been launched and nurtured under BMG, including Usher, Outkast, Alan Jackson, and Santana. Reorganizing for growth is the goal of BMG (**http://www.bmg.com**), the music and entertainment division of German media giant Bertelsmann. This objective has consumed much of the time of BMG's top managers in the past few years.

In 2001, Rolf Schmidt-Holtz was appointed CEO of BMG. At that time, BMG was loosely organized and very decentralized. Many managers and workers were duplicating each other's tasks, resulting in wasted time and energy. Each of BMG's record labels, including RCA, Artista, J Records, and others, had its own management team. BMG also had regional management teams overseeing the activities of each division. One of Schmidt-Holtz's earliest objectives was to restructure BMG management units to make the company more efficient, competitive, and profitable and to create a more centralized structure.

Schmidt-Holtz restructured the organization with the intent of becoming the world's largest and most efficient music company. He cut more than 1,300 jobs and realigned or eliminated less profitable BMG markets. In Europe, Schmidt-Holtz combined some markets and in others he entered into joint ventures with other large music companies such as EMI's Capital Records. In Greece, BMG is closing shop and outsourcing its dealings to EMI's Virgin Records. In the profitable American market, BMG North America was eliminated and RCA Records's executives took over management duties. Schmidt-Holtz also created BMG Strategic Marketing Group to guide the international marketing campaigns of BMG worldwide.[1]

Critical Thinking Questions

1. How will the return to centralized decision making affect BMG?
2. Will the restructure succeed in making BMG more efficient?
3. How will the development of the specialized Strategic Marketing division affect marketing decisions within each individual unit?

Principles of Organizational Structures

In today's dynamic business environment, organizational structures need to be designed so that the organization can quickly respond to new competitive threats and changing customer needs. Future success for companies like BMG will depend on the company's ability to be flexible and respond to the needs of customers. In this chapter, we'll present the five structural building blocks of organizations and look at how each can be used to build unique organizational structures. We'll explore how communication, authority, and job specialization are combined to create both formal and informal organizational structures. Finally, we'll consider how reengineering and new business trends are changing the way businesses organize.

Structural Building Blocks

1 learning goal

As you learned in Chapter 7, the key functions that managers perform include planning, organizing, leading, and controlling. This chapter focuses specifically on the organizing function. *Organizing* involves coordinating and allocating a firm's resources so that the firm can carry out its plans and achieve its goals. This organizing, or structuring, process is accomplished by:

- determining work activities and dividing up tasks *(division of labor),*
- grouping jobs and employees *(departmentalization),* and
- assigning authority and responsibilities *(delegation).*

formal organization
The order and design of relationships within a firm; consists of two or more people working together with a common objective and clarity of purpose.

Org - inst. domination

The result of the organizing process is a formal organizational structure. A **formal organization** is the order and design of relationships within the firm. It consists of two or more people working together with a common objective and clarity of purpose. Formal organizations also have well-defined lines of authority, channels for information flow, and means of control. Human, material, financial, and information resources are deliberately connected to form the business organization. Some connections are long lasting, such as the links among people in the finance or marketing department. Others can be changed at almost any time, as when a committee is formed to study a problem.

Five structural building blocks are used in designing an efficient and effective organizational structure. They are division of labor, departmentalization, managerial hierarchy, span of control, and centralization of decision making.

Division of Labor

division of labor
The process of dividing work into separate jobs and assigning tasks to workers.

specialization
The degree to which tasks are subdivided into smaller jobs.

The process of dividing work into separate jobs and assigning tasks to workers is called **division of labor.** In a fast-food restaurant, for example, some employees take or fill orders, others prepare food, a few clean and maintain equipment, and at least one supervises all the others. In an auto assembly plant, some workers install rearview mirrors, while others mount bumpers on bumper brackets. The degree to which the tasks are subdivided into smaller jobs is called **specialization.** Employees who work at highly specialized jobs, such as assembly-line workers, perform a limited number and variety of tasks. Employees who become specialists at one task, or a small number of tasks, develop greater skill in doing that particular job. This can lead to greater efficiency and consistency in production and other work activities. However, a high degree of specialization can also result in employees who are disinterested or bored due to the lack of variety and challenge.

Specialization can have a greater downside than disinterest if employees do not work in an environment of empowerment and trust. When workers are specialists at their particular jobs, they can become extremely productive by creating innovative techniques for high-quality and -quantity output. This process can give invaluable knowledge that can be used to the workers' advantage. However, in some cases it may spell trouble for the company. Manufacturing company Boeing uses giant cutting machines run by highly specialized workers who cut metal shafts for its aircraft. The slightest deviation in accuracy can ruin the cut and create a defective product.

Some employees can outperform others hands down using the innovative techniques. Management would love to have these tricks and techniques shared among all employees. Unfortunately, the star performers sometimes refuse regardless of how much coaxing management does. These top performers cite job security, bargaining power, and insurance against reassignment as their reasons for noncompliance.[2]

Departmentalization

2 learning goal

departmentalization
The process of grouping jobs together so that similar or associated tasks and activities can be coordinated.

organization chart
A visual representation of the structured relationships among tasks and the people given the authority to do those tasks.

The second building block used to create a strong organizational structure is called **departmentalization.** After the work is divided into jobs, jobs are then grouped together so that similar or associated tasks and activities can be coordinated. This grouping of people, tasks, and resources into organizational units facilitates the planning, leading, and control processes. An **organization chart** is a visual representation of the structured relationships among tasks and the people given the authority to do those tasks. In the organization chart in Exhibit 8.1, each figure represents a job, and each job includes several tasks. The sales manager, for instance, must hire salespeople, establish sales territories, motivate and train the salespeople, and control sales operations. The chart also indicates the general type of work done in each position.

As Exhibit 8.2 shows, five basic types of departmentalization are commonly used in organizations:

1. ***Functional departmentalization,*** which is based on the primary functions performed within an organizational unit (marketing, finance, production, sales, and so on).
2. ***Product departmentalization,*** which is based on the goods or services produced or sold by the organizational unit (such as outpatient/emergency services, pediatrics, cardiology, and orthopedics).
3. ***Process departmentalization,*** which is based on the production process used by the organizational unit (such as lumber cutting and treatment, furniture finishing, shipping).
4. ***Customer departmentalization,*** which is based on the primary type of customer served by the organizational unit (such as wholesale or retail purchasers).
5. ***Geographic departmentalization,*** which is based on the geographic segmentation of organizational units (such as U.S. and Canadian marketing, European marketing, South American marketing).

Motorola sells more cell phones than anyone in China, the world's largest market with 200 million subscribers. Motorola, therefore, has a geographic departmentalization and has invested significantly in manufacturing and research and development facilities in China.

© PHOTODISC RED / GETTY IMAGES

People are assigned to a particular organizational unit because they perform similar or related tasks, or because they are jointly responsible for a product, client, or market. Decisions about how to departmentalize affect the way management assigns authority, distributes resources, rewards performance, and sets up lines of communication. Many large organizations use several types of departmentalization. For example, a global company may be - departmentalized first geographically (North American,

Exhibit 8.1 | Organizational Chart for a Typical Appliance Manufacturer

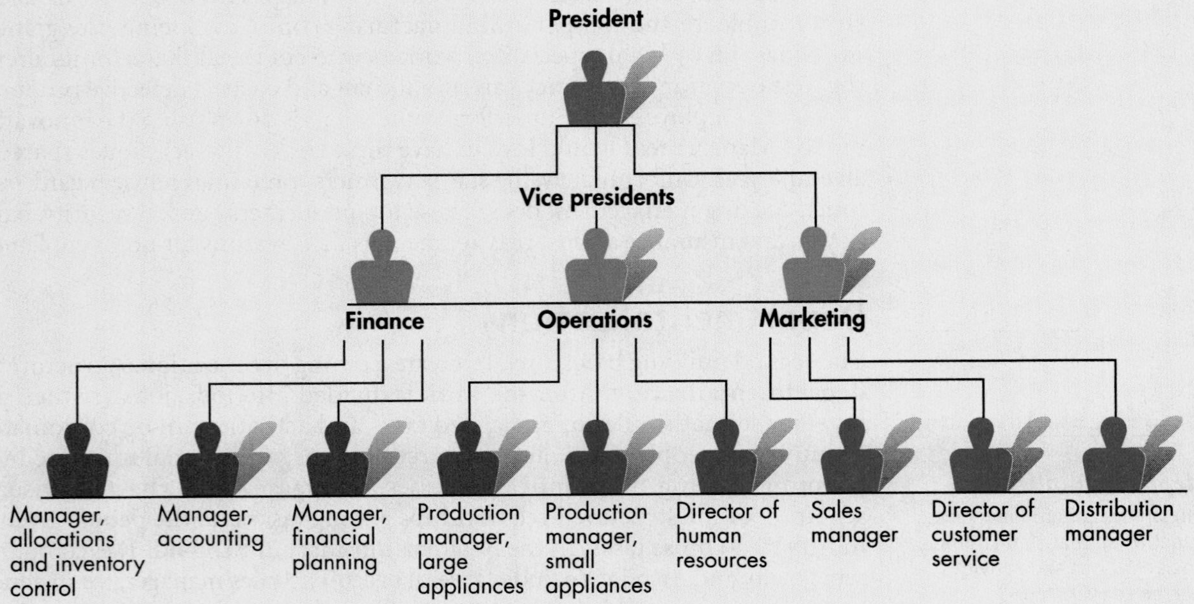

functional departmentalization
Departmentalization that is based on the primary functions performed within an organizational unit.

product departmentalization
Departmentalization that is based on the goods or services produced or sold by the organizational unit.

process departmentalization
Departmentalization that is based on the production process used by the organizational unit.

customer departmentalization
Departmentalization that is based on the primary type of customer served by the o-rganizational unit.

geographic departmentalization
Departmentalization that is based on the geographic segmentation of the organizational units.

European, and Asian units), then by product line (foods/beverages and health care), and finally by functional area (marketing, operations, finance, and so on).

Managerial Hierarchy

The third building block used to create effective organizational structure is the **managerial hierarchy** (also called the *management pyramid*), or the levels of management within the organization. Generally, the management structure has three levels: top, middle, and supervisory management. These three levels were introduced in Chapter 7.

In a managerial hierarchy, each organizational unit is controlled and supervised by a manager in a higher unit. The person with the most formal authority is at the top of the hierarchy. The higher a manager, the more power he or she has. Thus, the amount of power decreases as you move down the management pyramid. At the same time, the number of employees increases as you move down the hierarchy.

Not all companies today are using this traditional configuration. An interesting trend in designing a company's management structure is the inverted pyramid. For instance, Toronto-based Halsall Associates Ltd., an engineering firm, describes itself just that way.[3] When president of the company, Peter Halsall, discusses his management structure, he draws an upside-down pyramid. At the bottom of the pyramid, he puts himself. Above him, he lists the layers of management and finally, the front-line employees. The reason for this is to graphically show that the employees are the priority within the company. He explains: "Decisions are made so these people maximize their opportunities." This unusual view must pay off. Halsall Associates is one of Canada's leading engineering firms and is considered one of the best places to work.

An organization with a well-defined hierarchy has a clear **chain of command,** which is the line of authority that extends from one level of the organization to the

Exhibit 8.2 | Five Ways to Organize

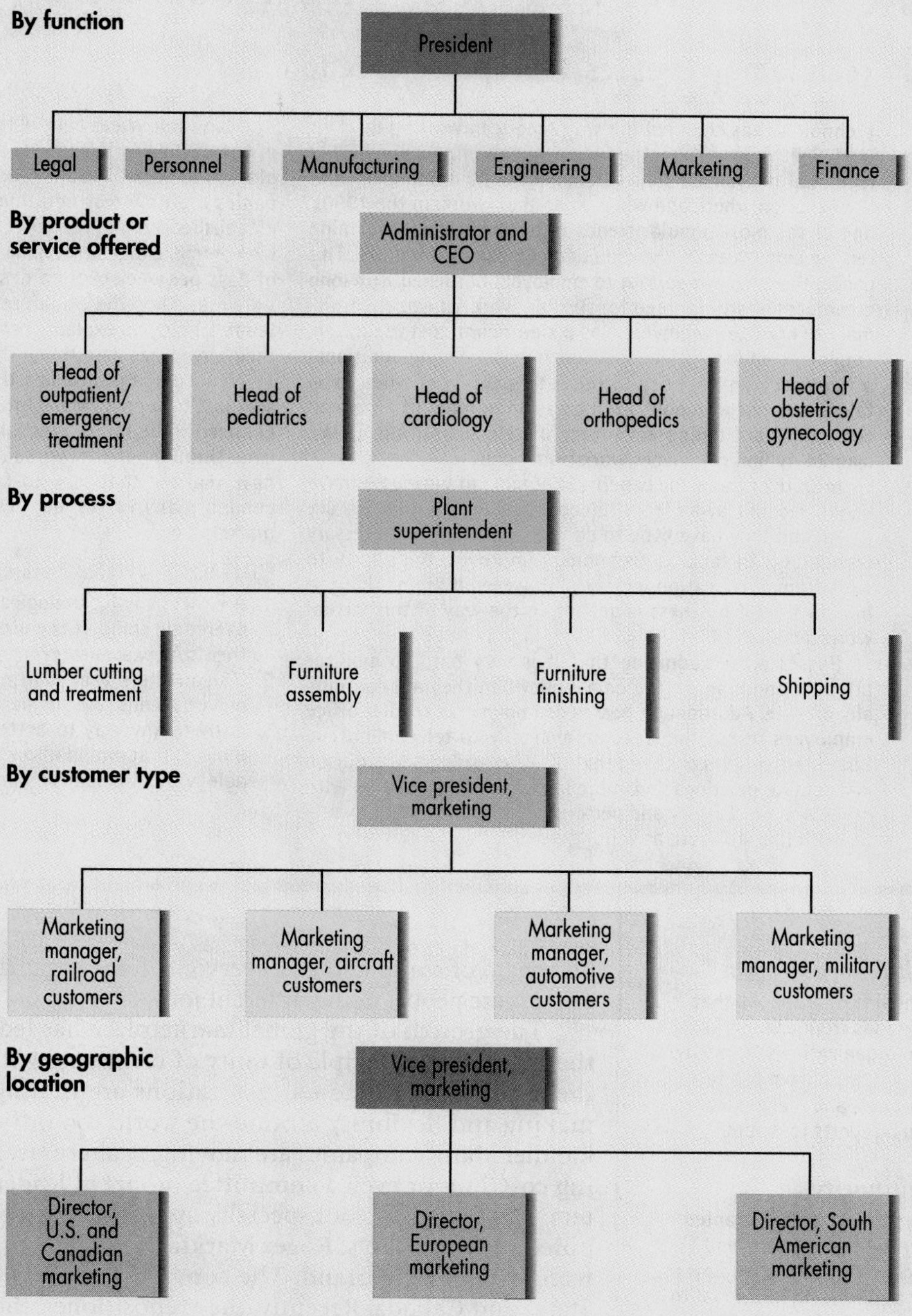

managerial hierarchy
The levels of management within an organization; typically, includes top, middle, and supervisory management.

next, from top to bottom, and makes clear who reports to whom. The chain of command is shown in the organization chart and can be traced from the CEO all the way down to the employees producing goods and services. Under the *unity of command* principle, everyone reports to and gets instructions from only one boss. Unity of command guarantees that everyone will have a direct supervisor and will not be taking orders from a number of different supervisors. Unity of command

Applying Technology

Technology Creates Workplace Freedom

Technology has changed the way American workers do their work. With computers, the Internet, cell phones, and PDAs (personal digital assistants), employees have more options than ever on where and when to do their work. In the 1990s, one of the most popular trends in business was developing remote employees as a portion of a company's workforce. This concept was very important to employees burdened with long commutes or with a need for flexible work schedules. A primary benefit to employers was a significant cost reduction. Employers no longer were burdened with needing additional office space or the need to relocate employees when local talent was not available. An increasing number of American companies are taking advantage of telecommuting. Today, over 24 million employees work from home.

In spite of the many benefits, a number of businesses have begun moving away from telecommuting. The reasons are varied and they have little to do with a lack of the necessary technology. In fact, as technology improves, the ability to work from any location improves. However, it seems that the human side of business is getting in the way of this virtual workplace.

Bosses are recognizing that it is very hard to monitor progress and manage the employee when they are continually off-site. Additionally, bosses complain that regular office employees resent the freedom available to telecommuters. Bosses are also recognizing that off-site workers miss out on last-minute meetings and, more importantly, interaction with other workers. Loyalty and personal relationships tend to suffer with this structure as well.

Many employees believe that a lack of trust is a big cause of the decline in telecommuting. Employers don't trust employees to do a full day's work. A number of American companies are now restructuring telecommuting to allow only established employees with many years of service to work from home. Other firms limit telecommuters to just a couple of days per week or for a designated period of time such as six weeks. Then the employee must join the rest of the office team. Employers explain that they want to be able to watch their employees performing their job satisfactorily.

New companies realize that all employees must be present just to survive. Many Internet start-ups know that workers need to be interacting, sharing ideas, and solving problems throughout the workday to ensure success. Employers have realized that face-to-face contact is critical to overcoming many of the hurdles faced in today's competitive marketplace.[4]

CRITICAL THINKING QUESTIONS

1. Are there any technological advancements that might help overcome some of the problems that telecommuters and their supervisors face?
2. Do you think that limiting the amount of time an employee spends telecommuting will solve the problem?
3. Is there any way to better monitor telecommuting employees that would allow employers to be more comfortable with an employee's productivity?

and chain of command give everyone in the organization clear directions and help coordinate people doing different jobs.

The growth of the global marketplace has led some companies to examine the traditional principle of unity of command with a single person at the top of the organization. These organizations are finding the need for quick decision making and flexibility around the world too difficult for any one individual to handle. Many companies are moving to alternative management models including co-CEOs or even a committee model of leadership. American Eagle Outfitters, the retailer of cool specialty apparel for men and women ages 16 to 34, has opted for duel CEOs. Roger Markfield and James O'Donnell work together as a team to build the brand. The company now has over 700 stores in the United States and Canada. Recently, they repositioned their Canadian Bluenotes brand stores from traditional jeans stores to "lifestyle stores" with more fashion-driven merchandise.

Individuals who are part of the chain of command have authority over other persons in the organization. **Authority** is legitimate power, granted by the organization and acknowledged by employees, that allows an individual to request action and expect compliance. Exercising authority means making decisions and seeing that they are carried out. Most managers *delegate*, or assign, some degree of authority and responsibility to others below them in the chain of command. The **delegation of authority** makes the employees accountable to their supervisor.

chain of command
The line of authority that extends from one level of an organization's hierarchy to the next, from top to bottom, and makes clear who reports to whom.

authority
Legitimate power, granted by the organization and acknowledged by employees, that allows an individual to request action and expect compliance.

delegation of authority
The assignment of some degree of authority and responsibility to persons lower in the chain of command.

The NFL is an organization with a well-defined hierarchy and a clear chain of command. Commissioner Paul Tagliabue oversees 32 teams and the league's total league revenue of over $4.5 billion, more than half coming from network and cable-TV contracts.

© AP / WIDE WORLD PHOTOS

Accountability means responsibility for outcomes. Typically, authority and responsibility move downward through the organization as managers assign activities to, and share decision making with, their subordinates. Accountability moves upward in the organization as managers in each successively higher level are held accountable for the actions of their subordinates.

Span of Control

The fourth structural building block is the managerial span of control. Each firm must decide how many managers are needed at each level of the management hierarchy to effectively supervise the work performed within organizational units. A manager's **span of control** (sometimes called *span of management*) is the number of employees the manager directly supervises. It can be as narrow as 2 or 3 employees or as wide as 50 or more. In general, the larger the span of control, the more efficient the organization. As Exhibit 8.3 shows, however, both narrow and wide spans of control have benefits and drawbacks.

span of control
The number of employees a manager directly supervises; also called span of management.

If hundreds of employees perform the same job, one supervisor may be able to manage a very large number of employees. Such might be the case at a clothing plant, where hundreds of sewing machine operators work from identical patterns. But if employees perform complex and dissimilar tasks, a manager can effectively supervise only a much smaller number. For instance, a supervisor in the research and development area of a pharmaceutical company might oversee just a few research chemists due to the highly complex nature of their jobs.

The optimal span of control is determined by the following five factors:

1. *Nature of the task.* The more complex the task, the narrower the span of control.
2. *Location of the workers.* The more locations, the narrower the span of control.
3. *Ability of the manager to delegate responsibility.* The greater the ability to delegate, the wider the span of control.
4. *Amount of interaction and feedback between the workers and the manager.* The more feedback and interaction required, the narrower the span of control.
5. *Level of skill and motivation of the workers.* The higher the skill level and motivation, the wider the span of control.

Exhibit 8.3 | Narrow and Wide Spans of Control

	Advantages	Disadvantages
Narrow span of control	• High degree of control. • Fewer subordinates may mean manager is more familiar with each individual. • Close supervision can provide immediate feedback.	• More levels of management, therefore more expensive. • Slower decision making due to vertical layers. • Isolation of top management. • Discourages employee autonomy.
Wide span of control	• Fewer levels of management means increased efficiency and reduced costs. • Increased subordinate autonomy leads to quicker decision making. • Greater organizational flexibility. • Higher levels of job satisfaction due to employee empowerment.	• Less control. • Possible lack of familiarity due to large number of subordinates. • Managers spread so thin that they can't provide necessary leadership or support. • Lack of coordination or synchronization.

Centralization of Decision Making

3 learning goal

centralization
The degree to which formal authority is concentrated in one area or level of an organization.

The final component in building an effective organizational structure is deciding at what level in the organization decisions should be made. **Centralization** is the degree to which formal authority is concentrated in one area or level of the organization. In a highly centralized structure, top management makes most of the key decisions in the organization, with very little input from lower-level employees. Centralization lets top managers develop a broad view of operations and exercise tight financial controls. It can also help to reduce costs by eliminating redundancy in the organization. But centralization may also mean that lower-level personnel don't get a chance to develop their decision-making and leadership skills and that the organization is less able to respond quickly to customer demands.

© CHARLES O'REAR / CORBIS

The span of control is wide for employees who have highly specialized and similar skills like these memory-chip technicians. A wide span of control means that managers can supervise more employees.

decentralization
The process of pushing decision-making authority down the organizational hierarchy.

Decentralization is the process of pushing decision-making authority down the organizational hierarchy, giving lower-level personnel more responsibility and power to make and implement decisions. Benefits of decentralization can include quicker decision making, increased levels of innovation and creativity, greater organizational flexibility, faster development of lower-level managers, and increased levels of job satisfaction and employee commitment. But decentralization can also be risky. If lower-level personnel don't have the necessary skills and training to perform effectively, they may make costly mistakes. Additionally, decentralization may increase the likelihood of inefficient lines of communication, incongruent or competing objectives, and duplication of effort.

Several factors must be considered when deciding how much decision-making authority to delegate throughout the organization. These factors include the size of the organization, the speed of change in its environment, managers' willingness to give up authority, employees' willingness to accept more authority, and the organization's geographic dispersion.

Decentralization is usually desirable when the following conditions are met:

- The organization is very large, like ExxonMobil, Ford, or General Electric.
- The firm is in a dynamic environment where quick, local decisions must be made, as in many high-tech industries.
- Managers are willing to share power with their subordinates.
- Employees are willing and able to take more responsibility.
- The company is spread out geographically, such as JC Penney, Caterpillar, or Ford.

mechanistic organization
An organizational structure that is characterized by a relatively high degree of job specialization, rigid departmentalization, many layers of management, narrow spans of control, centralized decision making, and a long chain of command.

As organizations grow and change, they continually reevaluate their structure to determine whether it is helping the company to achieve its goals. For instance, Los Angeles Police Chief William Bratton decided to reorganize the police force by granting more authority to local commanders, appointing civilians to top posts and consolidating some departments under a new Homeland Security Bureau. The chief decided to decentralize authority by granting police captains more responsibility for dealing with citizen complaints. Because of past corruption problems among the rank and file, the chief also elevated the importance of the internal affairs department.

concept check

What are the five building blocks of organizational structure?

What factors determine the optimal span of control?

What are the primary characteristics of a decentralized organization?

Mechanistic versus Organic Structures

4 learning goal

Using different combinations of the building blocks described above, organizations can build a wide variety of organizational structures. Nevertheless, structural design generally follows one of the two basic models described in Exhibit 8.4: mechanistic or organic. A **mechanistic organization** is characterized by a relatively high degree of job specialization, rigid departmentalization, many layers of management (particularly middle management), narrow spans of control, centralized decision making, and a long chain of command. This combination of elements results in what is called a tall organizational structure. The U.S. Army and the United Nations are typical mechanistic organizations.

In contrast, an **organic organization** is characterized by a relatively low degree of job specialization, loose departmentalization, few levels of management, wide spans of control, decentralized decision making, and a short chain of command. This combination of elements results in what is called a flat organizational structure. Colleges and universities tend to have flat organizational structures, with only two or three levels of administration between the faculty and the president. Exhibit 8.5 shows examples of flat and tall organizational structures.

organic organization
An organizational structure that is characterized by a relatively low degree of job specialization, loose departmentalization, few levels of management, wide spans of control, decentralized decision making, and a short chain of command.

Exhibit 8.4 Mechanistic versus Organic Structure

Structural Characteristic	Mechanistic	Organic
Job specialization	High	Low
Departmentalization	Rigid	Loose
Management hierarchy (levels of management)	Tall (many levels)	Flat (few levels)
Span of control	Narrow	Wide
Decision-making authority	Centralized	Decentralized
Chain of command	Long	Short

Exhibit 8.5 Flat versus Tall Organizational Structures

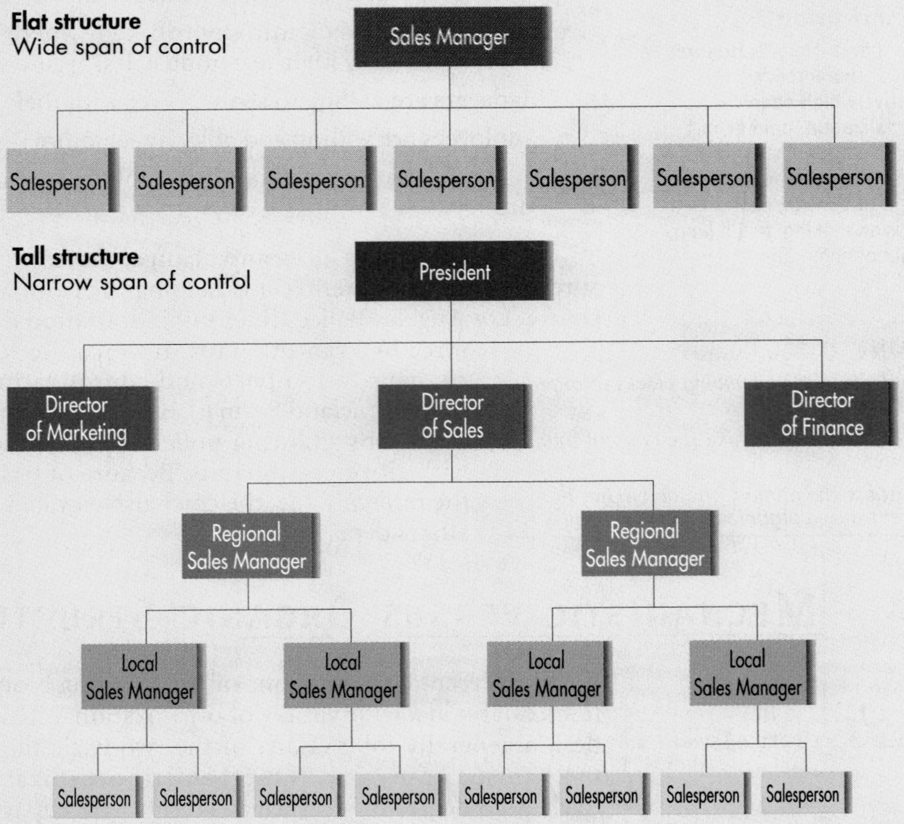

Although few organizations are purely mechanistic or purely organic, most organizations tend more toward one type or the other. The decision to create a more mechanistic or a more organic structural design is based on factors such as the firm's overall strategy, the size of the organization, the types of technologies used in the organization, and the stability of its external environment. Many e-commerce software companies and research labs are more organic than mechanistic. A few examples are: Priceline.com, PetFood Direct.com, Intel, Expedia.com, Logitech, Activision, Bio-Rad Laboratories, and Rand Corporation, the internationally known think tank.

concept check

Compare and contrast mechanistic and organic organizations.

What factors determine whether an organization should be mechanistic or organic?

Common Organizational Structures

5 learning goal

There is no single best way to design an organization. Within the basic mechanistic and organic models and the hybrids that contain elements of both, an almost infinite variety of organizational structures can be developed. Many organizations use a combination of elements from different structural types to meet their unique organizational needs. Some of the most common structural designs are discussed in this section. In addition, some companies are creating "virtual structures" for tax benefits, as discussed in the "Focusing on Small Business" box below.

Apple Computer's CEO Steve Jobs uses an organic structure to develop new products like the Imac computer. Organic structures allow firms like Apple to succeed in rapidly changing environments.

© AP / WIDE WORLD PHOTOS

Line Organization

The **line organization** is designed with direct, clear lines of authority and communication flowing from the top managers downward. Managers have direct control over all activities, including administrative duties. An organization chart for this type of structure would show that all positions in the firm are directly connected via an imaginary line extending from the highest position in the organization to the lowest (where production of goods and services takes place). This structure with its simple design, clear chain of command, and broad managerial control is often well suited to small, entrepreneurial firms.

Line-and-Staff Organization

As an organization grows and becomes more complex, the line organization can be enhanced by adding staff positions to the design. Staff positions provide specialized advisory and support services to line managers in the **line-and-staff organization,** shown in Exhibit 8.6. In daily operations, those individuals in **line positions** are directly involved in the processes used to create goods and services. Those individuals in **staff positions** provide the administrative and support services that line

Focusing on Small Business

Using a Virtual Organization to Get a Tax Break

A new business structure is gaining popularity among American entrepreneurs. It is called the offshore, virtual corporation and it offers advantages to the small-business owner as well as some large corporations. The way it works is that Internet-based companies are setting up shop outside the United States in places like Bermuda. What makes this possible is new telecommunication links to these remote locations that allow small local companies to operate like much larger international corporations.

Take, for instance, Playcentric.com, a music and video company that began operations in 2001. The company has only 10 employees, but through the virtual corporation concept, it resembles the structure of a major multinational corporation. The company's computer servers are in Bermuda, the operating unit is located in Barbados, and it has a distribution arrangement with a large Toronto record store chain.

One factor that makes this concept especially appealing to American companies is the tax-free status for many offshore countries. The virtual corporation makes potential tax savings more accessible to those who wish to take advantage of it. In the case of Playcentric.com, the owner believes that the tax advantage will allow him to undercut his competition's prices by 45 percent and still make a profit.[5]

Critical Thinking Questions

1. Are there other advantages to being a virtual company, which has no "brick and mortar" elements?
2. Is this a feasible structure for larger companies?
3. Are there any disadvantages for business owners to not be physically located in any of the geographical areas where the primary functions of the business take place?

Exhibit 8.6 | Line-and-Staff Organization

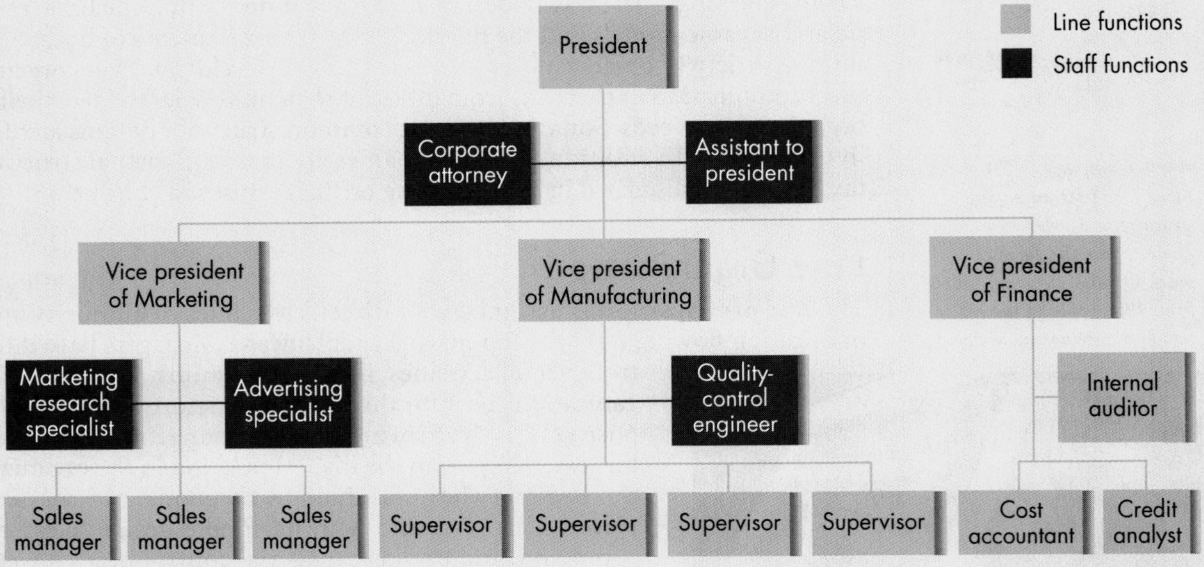

© PHOTODISC GREEN / GETTY IMAGES

The grapevine is a source of information that travels informally among employees. Although it usually carries accurate information, most employees prefer to receive work-related information from their managers.

line organization
An organizational structure with direct, clear lines of authority and communication flowing from the top managers downward.

line-and-staff organization
An organizational structure that includes both line and staff positions.

line positions
All positions in the organization directly concerned with producing goods and services and that are directly connected from top to bottom.

employees need to achieve the firm's goals. Line positions in organizations are typically in areas such as production, marketing, and finance. Staff positions are found in areas such as legal counseling, managerial consulting, public relations, and human resource management.

Committee Structure

In **committee structure,** authority and responsibility are held by a group rather than an individual. Committees are typically part of a larger line-and-staff organization. Often the committee's role is only advisory, but in some situations the

staff positions
Positions in an organization held by individuals who provide the administrative and support services that line employees need to achieve the firm's goals.

committee structure
An organizational structure in which authority and responsibility are held by a group rather than an individual.

matrix structure (project management)
An organizational structure that combines functional and product departmentalization by bringing together people from different functional areas of the organization to work on a special project.

committee has the power to make and implement decisions. Committees can make the coordination of tasks in the organization much easier. For example, Novartis, the huge Swiss pharmaceutical company, recently revamped its committee structure, which reports to its board of directors. The company hopes "to reflect best practices" in global corporate governance. Novartis will have four permanent committees reporting to the board: the chairman's committee, the compensation committee, the audit and compliance committee, and a newly created corporate governance committee. The chairman's committee will deal with business matters arising between board meetings and will be responsible for high-level appointments and acquisitions. The compensation committee looks at the renumeration of board members, while the audit and compliance committee oversees accounting and financial reporting practices. The newly created corporate governance committee's duties include focusing on board nominations, board performance evaluations, and possible conflicts of interest.

Committees bring diverse viewpoints to a problem and expand the range of possible solutions, but there are some drawbacks. Committees can be slow to reach a decision and are sometimes dominated by a single individual. It is also more difficult to hold any one individual accountable for a decision made by a group. Committee meetings can sometimes go on for long periods of time with little seemingly being accomplished.

Matrix Structure

The **matrix structure** (also called the *project management* approach) is sometimes used in conjunction with the traditional line-and-staff structure in an organization. Essentially, this structure combines two different forms of departmentalization, functional and product, that have complementary strengths and weaknesses. The matrix structure brings together people from different functional areas of the organization (such as manufacturing, finance, and marketing) to work on a special project. Each employee has two direct supervisors: the line manager from her or his specific functional area and the project manager. Exhibit 8.7 shows a matrix organization with four special project groups (A, B, C, D), each with its own project manager. Because of the dual chain of command, the matrix structure presents some unique challenges for both managers and subordinates.

Advantages of the matrix structure include:

- *Teamwork.* By pooling the skills and abilities of various specialists, the company can increase creativity and innovation and tackle more complex tasks.
- *Efficient use of resources.* Project managers use only the specialized staff they need to get the job done, instead of building large groups of underused personnel.
- *Flexibility.* The project structure is flexible and can adapt quickly to changes in the environment; the group can be disbanded quickly when it is no longer needed.
- *Ability to balance conflicting objectives.* The customer wants a quality product and predictable costs. The organization wants high profits and the development of technical capability for the future. These competing goals serve as a focal point for directing activities and overcoming conflict. The marketing representative can represent the customer, the finance representative can advocate high profits, and the engineers can push for technical capabilities.
- *Higher performance.* Employees working on special project teams may experience increased feelings of ownership, commitment, and motivation.
- *Opportunities for personal and professional development.* The project structure gives individuals the opportunity to develop and strengthen technical and interpersonal skills.

Exhibit 8.7 | Matrix Organization

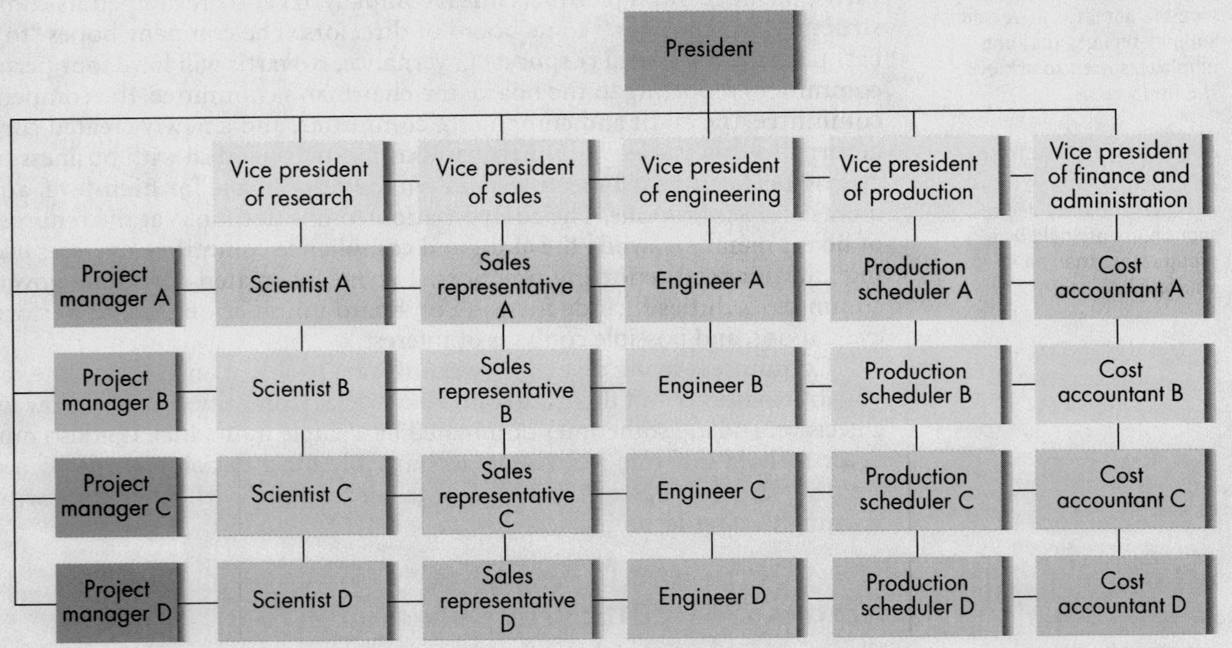

Disadvantages of the matrix structure include:

- *Power struggles.* Functional and product managers may have differing goals and management styles.
- *Confusion among team members.* Reporting relationships and job responsibilities may be unclear.
- *Lack of cohesiveness.* Team members from different functional areas may have difficulty communicating effectively and working together as a team.

reengineering
The complete redesign of business structures and processes in order to improve operations.

What benefits does a matrix structure offer a company? According to Jim Cain of the Ford Motor Company, you get the ability to leverage expertise in transactions, management, and execution.[6] In order to accomplish this goal, Ford decided to create a matrix organizational structure by integrating its treasury and finance groups with those of the Ford Motor Credit Company. The idea was to simplify access for investment bankers, commercial bankers, brokers, analysts, and others to the company's treasury. This was accomplished by creating three Assistant Treasurers who will oversee a team of directors with responsibility for specific areas such as asset management, credit, pension administration, trading, short-term funding, and risk management. Another benefit was increased responsibility in each of these areas. Through this change, the company expects great improvements in both internal and external communication.

concept check

How do line and staff positions differ?

Why does the matrix structure have a dual chain of command?

What are advantages of a matrix structure? Disadvantages?

REENGINEERING ORGANIZATIONAL STRUCTURE

6 learning goal

Periodically, all businesses must reevaluate the way they do business. This includes assessing the effectiveness of the organizational structure. To meet the formidable challenges of the future, companies are increasingly turning to **reengineering**—the complete redesign of business structures and processes in order to improve operations. An even simpler definition of reengineering is "starting over." In effect, top management asks, "If we were a new company, how would we run this place?" The purpose of reengineering is to identify and abandon the outdated rules and fundamental assumptions that guide current business operations. Every company has many formal and informal rules based on assumptions about technology, people, and organizational goals that no longer hold. Thus, the goal of reengineering is to redesign business processes to achieve improvements in cost control, product quality, customer service, and speed. The reengineering process should result in a more efficient and effective organizational structure that is better suited to the current (and future) competitive climate of the industry.

One of the most dramatic reengineering projects of recent times is that of Boeing. According to Phil Condit, Chief Executive of Boeing, he is trying to "transform" the 86-year-old defense contractor.[7] Condit's vision is to reshape Boeing into an organization that is not only a manufacturer but also a service provider. After taking office in 1996, Condit spent $16 billion to purchase McDonnell Douglas and $7 billion to buy a large portion of Rockwell International and Hughes Electronics in order to expand Boeing's involvement in the aerospace sector. In addition, Boeing is using this newly acquired technology to offer services in other industries as well. One example of this expansion is the movie industry. Boeing is using its satellite system to offer delivery of newly released movies. Instead of physically transporting canisters of celluloid, Boeing will deliver the movie digitally. The cost of digital satellite delivery of the movie runs approximately $500 compared to $2,500 per movie-viewing screen for shipping traditional canisters.

concept check

What is meant by reengineering?

What is the purpose of reengineering?

The Informal Organization

7 learning goal

Up to this point in the chapter, we have focused on formal organizational structures that can be seen in the boxes and lines of the organization chart. Yet many important relationships within an organization do not show up on an organization chart. Nevertheless, these relationships can affect the decisions and performance of employees at all levels of the organization.

informal organization
The network of connections and channels of communication based on the informal relationships of individuals inside an organization.

The network of connections and channels of communication based on the informal relationships of individuals inside the organization is known as the **informal organization.** Informal relationships can be between people at the same hierarchical level or between people at different levels and in different departments. Some connections are work related, such as those formed among people who carpool or ride the same train to work. Others are based on nonwork commonalties such as belonging to the same church or health club or having children who attend the same school. The informal channels of communication of the informal organization are often referred to as the *grapevine*, the *rumor mill*, or the *intelligence network*.

Functions of the Informal Organization

The informal organization has several important functions. First, it provides a source of friendships and social contact for organization members. Second, the interpersonal relationships and informal groups help employees feel better informed about and connected with what is going on in their firm, thus giving them some sense of control over their work environment. Third, the informal organization can provide status and recognition that the formal organization cannot or will not provide employees. Fourth, the network of relationships can aid the socialization of new employees by informally passing along rules, responsibilities, basic objectives, and job expectations. Finally, the organizational grapevine helps employees to be more aware of what is happening in their workplace by transmitting information quickly and conveying it to places that the formal system does not reach.

Although the informal organization can help the formal organization to achieve its goals, it can also create problems if not managed well. *Group norms* (commonly accepted standards of behavior) may conflict with the company's standards and cause problems. For instance, during a merger or acquisition, informal groups may strongly resist change (especially structural change), spread incorrect information through the grapevine, and foster fear and low morale among employees. With this in mind, managers need to learn to use the existing informal organization as a tool that can potentially benefit the formal organization. An excellent way of putting the informal organization to work for the good of the company is to bring informal leaders into the decision-making process.

concept check

What is the informal organization?

How can informal channels of communication be used to improve operational efficiency?

Trends In Organizational Structures

8 learning goal

To achieve long-term objectives, organizations constantly evaluate and alter their organizational structures. The increased use of information technology and globalization are creating new options for organizing a business.

THE VIRTUAL CORPORATION

One of the biggest challenges for companies today is adapting to the technological changes that are affecting all industries. Organizations are struggling to find new organizational structures that will help them transform information technology into a competitive advantage. One alternative that is becoming increasingly prevalent is the **virtual corporation,** which is a network of independent companies (suppliers, customers, even competitors) linked by information technology to share skills, costs, and access to one another's markets. This network structure allows companies to come together quickly to exploit rapidly changing opportunities. The key attributes of a virtual corporation are:

- *Technology.* Information technology helps geographically distant companies form alliances and work together.
- *Opportunism.* Alliances are less permanent, less formal, and more opportunistic than in traditional partnerships.
- *Excellence.* Each partner brings its core competencies to the alliance, so it is possible to create an organization with higher quality in every functional area and increase competitive advantage.
- *Trust.* The network structure makes companies more reliant on each other and forces them to strengthen relationships with partners.
- *No borders.* This structure expands the traditional boundaries of an organization.

Managers are taking advantage of advances in information technology to communicate with employees who work in different locations. Toughbook, by Panasonic, is designed for mobile professionals and allows for wireless communication and "anywhere" email access.

COURTESY OF PANASONIC

In the concept's purest form, each company that links up with others to create a virtual corporation is stripped to its essence. Ideally, the virtual corporation has neither central office nor organization chart, no hierarchy, and no vertical integration. It contributes to an alliance only its core competencies, or key capabilities. It mixes and matches what it does best with the core competencies of other companies and entrepreneurs. For example, a manufacturer would only manufacture,

Making Ethical Choices

xtra! http://gitmanxtra.swlearning.com

SLIPPING UP

While many of your friends like exploring boutiques, you always preferred shopping at chain stores. Walking into a Best Buy, CVS, or Staples, you know exactly where to look for the items you want. You are curious about how chain stores are structured to provide uniform customer service.

After college graduation you gain firsthand knowledge about division of labor and centralized decision making as manager of a family-owned hardware business with three local stores. After a few years in this position, a major nationwide pharmacy chain offers you a job as Middle Atlantic States regional manager which you accept. You learn that the tasks required to manage regional operations differ in some ways from those for the local stores you managed. One difference is responsibility for maintaining the exterior as well as the interior, to ensure that customers can move inside and outside safely.

In reviewing corporate policies, you discover that decisions about maintaining the exterior are the same—regardless of the stores' locations. Stores are not required to shovel snow, and management provides no resources for snow removal. This became troublesome in winter 2003, as areas that rarely get snow spent much of the winter repeatedly digging out. After the first major snowstorm, customers complained to local store managers about difficulty traversing the sidewalk in front of the store. Knowing they didn't have resources for snow removal, the managers shared their concerns with you. Your request to upper management for resources was denied, even after explaining the local legal requirement. After the second big snowstorm, several customers slip on the ice trying to enter the store.

ETHICAL DILEMMA

As a regional manager intent on providing a high level of customer service and safety, should you override upper management's decision to comply with local laws and hire a snow removal company?

SOURCES: "D.C. Snow Removal Regulations," ChevyChaseCommunity Listserv@yahoogroups.com, February 21, 2003, "DC ST 1981 § 7-901," District of Columbia Official Code 2001 Edition Division I. Government of District. Title 9. Transportation Systems. Subtitle I. Highways, Bridges, Streets, and Alleys. Chapter 6. Removal of Snow and Ice from Streets and Sidewalks. "Snow Shoveling," ChevyChaseCommunityList serv@yahoogroups.com, February 11, 2003.

virtual corporation
A network of independent companies linked by information technology to share skills, costs, and access to one another's markets; allows the companies to come together quickly to exploit rapidly changing opportunities.

while relying on a product design firm to decide what to make and a marketing company to sell the end result.

Although firms that are purely virtual organizations are still relatively scarce, many companies are embracing several of the characteristics of the virtual structure. One great example is Cisco Systems. Cisco has 34 plants that produce its products, but the company only owns 2 of them. Human hands touch only 10 percent of customer orders. Less than half of all orders are processed by a Cisco employee. To the average customer, the interdependency of Cisco's suppliers and inventory systems makes it look like one huge, seamless company.

VIRTUAL TEAMS

Technology is also enabling corporations to create virtual work teams. Geography is no longer a limitation when employees are considered for a work team. Virtual teams mean reduced travel time and costs, reduced relocation expenses, and utilization of specialized talent regardless of employee's location. Sabre, Incorporated, which processes over 400 million travel bookings each year, has created 65 permanent virtual teams with members in the United States, Canada, and several other foreign countries. Each team averages eight members.[8]

When managers need to staff a project, all they need to do is make a list of required skills and a general list of employees who possess those skills. When the pool of employees is known, the manager simply chooses the best mix of people and creates the virtual team. Special challenges of virtual teams include keeping team members focused, motivated, and communicating positively despite their location. If feasible, at least one face-to-face meeting during the early stages of team formation will help with these potential problems.

Dale Pratt doesn't share an office with her team members. She's not even in the same building or zip code. Pratt, director of Human Resources for Nortel Networks Corporation, works at company headquarters in Ontario, Canada. But as a member of a virtual team, she has colleagues as far away as Europe and China. The company creates Internet technologies, and has 80,000 employees located in 150 countries.

"We have to work in real time across the globe, really fast, and our employees have to be where our customers are," Pratt says. "For us, working with our virtual team is the same as other companies where people might sit together under a centralized roof. We simply use different tools to do our job every day." Virtual teams may be composed of full-time or part-time employees. They might have a global reach, or involve combinations of local telecommuting members and more traditional in-house workers. A senior executive might be on one planning committee for a product release, for example, another for identifying minority vendors, another to study relocating a plant, and another to evaluate software tracking. He may deal with key players who not only are out of the country but also are working for another company, or perhaps as suppliers who are on the virtual team to add information and technical support.[9]

Structuring for Global Mergers

Recent mergers creating mega firms (such as Texaco-Shell and Hewlett Packard and Compaq) raise some important questions regarding corporate structure. How can managers hope to organize the global pieces of these huge, complex new firms into a cohesive, successful whole? Should decision making be centralized or decentralized?

© AP / WIDE WORLD PHOTOS

When Hewlett Packard and Compaq merged, its management teams had to develop a new organizational structure for the newly-formed single business, while carefully blending two unique corporation cultures.

Should the firm be organized around geographic markets or product lines? And how can managers consolidate distinctly different corporate cultures? These issues and many more must be resolved if mergers of global companies are to succeed.

Beyond designing a new organizational structure, one of the most difficult challenges when merging two large companies is uniting the cultures and creating a single business. The recent merger between Pfizer and Pharmacia, makers of Dramamine and Rogaine, is no exception. Failure to effectively merge cultures can have serious effects on organizational efficiency.

In a plan scheduled to last three years, Pfizer put together 14 groups that would make recommendations concerning finances, human resources, operation support, capital improvements, warehousing, logistics, quality control, and information technology. An outside consultant was hired to facilitate the process. One of the first tasks for the groups was to deal with the conqueror (Pfizer) versus conquered (Pharmacia) attitudes. Company executives want to make sure all employees know that their ideas are valuable and they are listening.

concept check

How does technology enable firms to organize as virtual corporations?

What are some organizational issues that must be addressed when two large firms merge?

Great Ideas to Use Now

How is organizational structure relevant to you? A common thread linking all of the companies profiled in this chapter is you, the consumer. Companies structure their organizations to facilitate achieving their overall organizational goals. In order to be profitable, companies must have a competitive advantage, and competition is based on meeting customer expectations. The company that best satisfies customer wants and demands is the company that will lead the competition.

When companies make changes to their organizational structures, they are attempting to increase in some way their ability to satisfy the customer. For example, several of the companies profiled in this chapter were consolidating or centralizing parts of their operation. Why? Those companies hope to become more efficient and reduce costs, which should translate into better customer service and more reasonable prices. Some companies are decentralizing operations, giving departments or divisions more autonomy to respond quickly to changes in the market or to be more flexible in their response to customer demands. Many companies are embracing new information technology because it brings them closer to their customers faster than was previously possible. Internet commerce is benefiting consumers in a number of ways. When you buy books at **http://www.amazon.com** or use **http://www.ebay.com** to sell a used bicycle, you are sending the message that the virtual company is a structure you will patronize and support. Increasing globalization and use of information technology will continue to alter the competitive landscape, and the big winner should be the consumer, in terms of increased choice, increased access, and reduced price!

Try It Now

Evaluate Your Leadership Skills If you want to evaluate your own leadership skills, go to **http://www.humanlinks.com/skilhome.htm** and scroll down to "Managerial Skills." By taking the self-assessment quizzes offered here, you will gain insight into your ability to manage virtual teams, test your ability to think logically and analogically, and even your perceptions about management. Companies are seeking managerial leaders who have leadership traits that will guide employees through the competitive business landscape.

Customer Satisfaction and Quality

There was a time when large organizations need only open their doors and customers were waiting to do business. They didn't need to worry about being responsible to customers or having a structure flexible enough to respond to customer needs. Today, no company can afford to take its customers for granted. To keep a strong and loyal customer base, an organization structure must be created to constantly monitor the level of satisfaction the customer is experiencing and then be able to address any problems. One recent example of just how far a company is willing to go to keep its customers happy is Enterprise Rent-A-Car.

After the attacks of September 11, Enterprise found itself faced with many stranded customers. With all airports shut down, stranded travelers found themselves with no way to get home other than by car. In an unprecedented move, Andy Taylor, Chairman and CEO, told the 4,300 U.S. neighborhood locations to permit out-of-state one-way rentals for stranded travelers and waive or reimburse drop-off fees. In an e-mail message to the employees, Taylor said, "Right now, we're just concerned about taking care of our customers."[10] As a result of this decision, thousands of Enterprise's cars were displaced in other cities without any means of return. Some cars were sold, employees retrieved others, and still others were shipped back on flatbed trucks. By putting customers' needs first during this national emergency, Enterprise incurred significant costs but maintained its firm policy on customer satisfaction.

Looking Ahead at BMG

Under the leadership of Rolf Schmidt-Holtz, BMG was successful in cutting costs and becoming more effective in attracting new artists. In the United States, BMG enjoyed increased album sales during 2001 and 2002. BMG's market share has risen significantly. The reorganization in Europe and Asia is producing the same impressive results as well. Costs have been held in check, which indicates that the firm is becoming more efficient. The creation of the Strategic Marketing Group means that individual marketing group managers will have less authority than in the past.

Summary of Learning Goals

1 What are the five structural building blocks that managers use to design organizations?

The five structural building blocks that are used in designing an efficient and effective organizational structure are (1) division of labor, which is the process of dividing work into separate jobs and assigning tasks to workers; (2) departmentalization; (3) the managerial hierarchy (or the *management pyramid*), which is the levels of management within the organization; (4) the managerial span of control, which is the number of employees the manager directly supervises; and (5) the amount of centralization or decentralization in the organization, which entails deciding at what level in the organization decisions should be made.

2 What are the five types of departmentalization?

Five basic types of departmentalization (see Exhibit 8.2) are commonly used in organizations:

- *Functional.* Based on the primary functions performed within an organizational unit.
- *Product.* Based on the goods or services produced or sold by the organizational unit.
- *Process.* Based on the production process used by the organizational unit.

- *Customer.* Based on the primary type of customer served by the organizational unit.
- *Geographic.* Based on the geographic segmentation of organizational units.

3

How can the degree of centralization/decentralization be altered to make an organization more successful?

In a highly centralized structure, top management makes most of the key decisions in the organization with very little input from lower-level employees. Centralization lets top managers develop a broad view of operations and exercise tight financial controls. In a highly decentralized organization, decision-making authority is pushed down the organizational hierarchy, giving lower-level personnel more responsibility and power to make and implement decisions. Decentralization can result in faster decision making and increased innovation and responsiveness to customer preferences.

4

How do mechanistic and organic organizations differ?

A mechanistic organization is characterized by a relatively high degree of work specialization, rigid departmentalization, many layers of management (particularly middle management), narrow spans of control, centralized decision making, and a long chain of command. This combination of elements results in a tall organizational structure. In contrast, an organic organization is characterized by a relatively low degree of work specialization, loose departmentalization, few levels of management, wide spans of control, decentralized decision making, and a short chain of command. This combination of elements results in a flat organizational structure.

5

What is the difference between line positions and staff positions?

In daily operations, those individuals in line positions are directly involved in the processes used to create goods and services. Those individuals in staff positions provide the administrative and support services that line employees need to achieve the firm's goals. Line positions in organizations are typically in areas such as production, marketing, and finance. Staff positions are found in areas such as legal counseling, managerial consulting, public relations, and human resource management.

6

What is the goal of reengineering?

Reengineering is a complete redesign of business structures and processes in order to improve operations. The goal of reengineering is to redesign business processes to achieve improvements in cost control, product quality, customer service, and speed.

7

How does the informal organization affect the performance of a company?

The informal organization is the network of connections and channels of communication based on the informal relationships of individuals inside the organization. Informal relationships can be between people at the same hierarchical level or between people at different levels and in different departments. Informal organizations give employees more control over their work environment by delivering a continuous stream of company information throughout the organization, thereby helping employees stay informed.

8

What trends are influencing the way businesses organize?

The virtual corporation is a network of independent companies (suppliers, customers, even competitors) linked by information technology to share skills, costs, and access to one another's markets. This network structure allows companies to come together quickly to exploit rapidly changing opportunities.

Many companies are now using technology to create virtual teams. Team members may be down the hall or across the ocean. Virtual teams mean that travel time and expenses are eliminated and the best people can be placed on the team regardless of where they live. Sometimes, however, it may be difficult to keep virtual team members focused and motivated.

Large global mergers, like DaimlerChrysler created from the merger of America's Chrysler Corporation and Germany's Daimler Benz, raise important issues in organizational structure. The ultimate question is how does management take two huge global organizations and create a single, successful, cohesive organization? Should it be centralized or decentralized? Should it be organized along product or geographic lines? These are some of the questions management must answer.

Preparing for Tomorrow's Workplace

1. Why do you think that reengineering has become popular? Give an example of a company that has gone through reengineering.
2. Draw an organization chart of the firm you work for, your college, or a campus student organization. Show the lines of authority and formal communication. Describe the informal relationships that you think are important for the success of the organization.
3. Describe how the group norms in an informal organization with which you are familiar have influenced the company or organization. How can managers make informal organizations work for the good of the company?
4. Describe the ideal span of control for the typical middle manager. Would the manager's industry make a difference in this number? Would a manager in a service industry have a larger or smaller span of control than a manager in manufacturing?
5. How would you restructure a large mechanistic organization to be more customer friendly and increase customer satisfaction?
6. Divide the class into groups of five. Each group should be assigned a different type of organization: manufacturer, product retailer, service retailer, nonprofit organization, and governmental agency. Each group should interview managers at their assigned organization and report to the class on the structure of the organization. Be sure to ask the managers if they are satisfied with the current organizational structure and how it might be improved.

Working the Net

1. Using a search engine like Google or Yahoo! to search for the term "company organizational charts," find at least three examples of organizational charts for corporations, nonprofits, or government agencies. Analyze each entity's organizational structure. Is it organized by function, product/service, process, customer type, or geographic location?
2. At either the *Buisiness Week* (**http://www.businessweek.com**), *Fortune* (**http://www.fortune.com**), or *Forbes* (**http://www.forbes.com**) Web site, search the archives for stories about companies that have reengineered. Find an example of a reengineering effort that succeeded and one that failed and discuss why. Also visit the BPR Online Learning Center at **http://www.prosci.com** to answer the following questions: What is benchmarking and how can it help companies with business process reengineering (BPR)? What were the key findings of the best-practices surveys for change management and benchmarking?
3. Visit the *Inc.* magazine Web site (**http://www.inc.com**) and use the search engine to find articles about virtual corporation. Using a search engine, find the

Web site of at least one virtual corporation and look for information about how the company uses span of control, informal organization, and other concepts from this chapter.

4. Managing change in an organization is no easy task, as you've discovered in your new job with a consulting firm that specializes in change management. To get up to speed, go to Bpubs.com, the Business Publications Search Engine, **http://www.bpubs.com**, and navigate to the Change Management section of the Management Science category. Select three articles that discuss how companies approached the change process and summarize their experiences.
5. After managing your first project team, you think you might enjoy a career in project management. The Project Management Institute is a professional organization for project managers. Its Web site, **http://www.pmi.org**, has many resources about this field. Start at the Professional Practices section to learn what project management is, then go to the professional Development and Careers pages. What are the requirements to earn the Project Management Professional designation? Explore other free areas of the site to learn more about the job of project manager. Prepare a brief report on the career and its opportunities. Does what you've learned make you want to follow this career path?

Creative Thinking Case

Can you imagine an organization with 6,000 employees, $1.4 billion in sales, and no hierarchy structure? Then take a look at W. L. Gore & Associates. Wilbert Gore, who left Dupont to explore new uses for Teflon, started the company in 1958. Best known for its breathable, weatherproof Gore-Tex® fabric, the company is a model of unusual business practices. For instance, there is no managerial hierarchy at Gore. Employees, called associates, are treated as peers by top management. The concept fosters the idea that there are no bosses, no titles, and no formal job descriptions.

Committees, comprised of employees, are charged with making major decisions such as hiring, firing, and compensation. Even top executives' compensation is set by committee. To get a new idea implemented, all an employee need do is gain enough acceptance among fellow employees. In fact, all employees are expected to make minor decisions instead of relying on the "boss" to make them.

The company tries to maintain a family-like atmosphere by dispersing the 6,000 employees into 60 buildings, with no more than 200 employees in any one place. Since no formal lines of authority exist, employees can speak to anyone in the company at any time. This arrangement also forces employees to spend considerable time developing relationships. As one employee described it, instead of trying to please just one "boss," you have to please everyone.[11]

CRITICAL THINKING QUESTIONS

1. Given the lack of formal structure, how important do you think the informal structure becomes?
2. Do you think that Gore's reliance on committee work slows processes down?
3. How do you think this structure would affect the division of labor?

Video Case

Do You Yahoo!

Every day thousands of people do. What began as a hobby for Stanford engineering doctoral students Jerry Yang and David Filo in 1994—as a way to organize and classify Web sites they often visited—evolved into a business and quickly became the Internet's largest online navigational service.

Yahoo! was free to the consumer, attracting advertising revenues by emphasizing product innovation and the creation of new services. The company used more than 1,000 daily e-mails it received as valuable feedback for product development.

KEY TERMS

authority 250
centralization 252
chain of command 250
committee structure 257
customer departmentalization 248
decentralization 253
delegation of authority 250
departmentalization 247
division of labor 246
formal organization 246
functional departmentalization 248
geographic departmentalization 248
informal organization 259
line-and-staff organization 256
line organization 256
line positions 256
managerial hierarchy 249
matrix structure (project management) 257
mechanistic organization 253
organic organization 253
organization chart 247
process departmentalization 248
product departmentalization 248
reengineering 258
span of control 251
specialization 246
staff positions 257
virtual corporation 261

It also catered to what it identified as "defined user groups," with Beatrice's Web Guide targeted to a female audience and Yahooligans specially designed for kids.

As one of the few profitable Internet companies, Yahoo! was riding the crest of the dot-com wave when dramatic changes in the industry caused its revenues to fall precipitously. The flexible organizational structure designed by Yang and Filo needed an overhaul, and Terry Semel, a former Hollywood executive, was hired for the job. As Yahoo!'s new Chief Executive Officer, Semel streamlined the business and restored its profitability through significant restructuring of the company.

He reduced the number of Yahoo!'s businesses from more than 40 to just 6, cutting costs and sharpening the company's focus. It meant abandoning properties that had little chance of making money, like online invitations, and meant major staff changes. Nearly half of Yahoo!'s sales force and 44 percent of its top management were replaced with seasoned veterans.

In order to diversify its revenue streams, Yahoo! devised strategies to turn users into paying subscribers, tapping nonadvertising sources, such as job listings, for additional revenue. The company's acquisition of HotJobs, and a paid-search partnership with Overture, will add more than $100 million to its bottom line.

A new alliance with SBC Communications Inc. to sell broadband access is projected to generate an additional $70 million in 2003. Additionally Yahoo! will roll out its own competitively priced gateway for broadband users, charging subscribers only $5 per month compared with the $10 or $15 monthly fee charged by Microsoft Network (MSN) and America Online (AOL) respectively.

With a focus on exciting new products, supported by a corporate culture that values product integrity and customer satisfaction, Yahoo! has been able to maintain its position as one of the most recognized brand names in the world today.

CRITICAL THINKING QUESTIONS

1. How is Yahoo's! organizational structure contributing to its ongoing success?
2. What is the company doing to ensure continued revenue growth? Explain
3. Is Yahoo a mechanistic or organic organization?

SOURCES: Adapted from material in the video: "Yahoo! A Case Study in Entrepreneurship"; and from the Yahoo! Corporate Web site, http://www.yahoo.com; Ben Elgin, "Terry Semel: Rebuilding a Portal," *Business Week Online,* October 1, 2002; Ben Elgin, "Can Yahoo! Make the Bounce Last?" *Business Week,* February 17, 2003; Mylene Mangalindan, "Yahoo Breaks Dot-Com Mold, Sees a Rebound," *Wall Street Journal,* January 13, 2003, pp. B1, B12.

E-COMMERCE CASE
In Charge at Oracle

Oracle is one of the world's largest software firms, second only to Microsoft in size. Selling $9.6 billion of business software a year, Oracle has over 42,000 employees and operates around the world. The Internet has long been an integral part of founder and CEO Larry Ellison's vision for the company. Oracle introduced a line of "e-business" software applications several years ago that allow businesses to manage all of their computers and databases through the Internet. Since then, Ellison has constantly pushed the benefits of using the Web as a business tool. He claims Oracle saved $1 billion in operating costs in the first year after the firm began using its own Web-based software.

Before 2000, Ellison shared leadership of Oracle with company president Ray Lane and chief financial officer Jeff Henley. Each ran their own area—technology, sales, and finances, respectively—relatively independently. Lane was credited with helping to streamline Oracle's bloated organizational structure, opening the door for the company to compete more effectively in the e-commerce marketplace.

In 2000, however, after a power struggle with Ellison, Ray Lane abruptly resigned. Since then, Ellison has refused to name a new president. "The problem I found is that it's hard to have two leaders," Ellison says. "What happened with Oracle was we had two separate visions of where the company should go. The company was divided into two factions. It's not a healthy thing."

Many analysts, however, think Ellison needs a counterbalance, especially since Oracle's sales have been slipping. "When Ray Lane was there, he was a good complement to Larry," explains one analyst. "When he left, some of the things weren't managed quite as effectively. You don't need to have Ray Lane, but you do need that skill set."

Oracle's most pressing current problem: many customers complain that the firm's sales force has been overly aggressive and made false claims about the performance of the company's e-commerce software products. Several customers—including the state of California—have actually filed lawsuits against Oracle because of its sales practices.

Ellison says a recent company restructuring will solve the problem. Before, each salesperson was responsible for selling all of Oracle's products to customers. Now, salespeople will specialize in selling just a few particular products. Ellison says this new structure will allow salespeople to better understand and serve customer needs. "We can't possibly have salespeople who are experts in everything," Ellison says. "That's simply impossible."

CRITICAL THINKING QUESTIONS

1. Do you agree or disagree with Ellison's decision not to name a new company president? Discuss the benefits and disadvantages of centralizing company control in Ellison's hands.
2. How effective do you think Ellison's new sales force structure will be? How can the Internet help implement and support Ellison's plan?
3. What organizational structure do you think is most appropriate for Oracle? Why?

SOURCES: David Futrelle, "Jumping Ship at Oracle and Sun," *Fortune,* May 2, 2002, downloaded from http://www.business2.com; Eric Hellweg, "Oracle's Larry Ellison, a Solitary Man," *Business 2.0,* July 15, 2002, downloaded from http://www.business2.com; G. Christian Hill, "Updates: Trouble with Larry," *eCompany,* May 2001, downloaded from http://www.ecompany.com; Ian Mount, "Out of Control," *Business 2.0,* August 2002, downloaded from http://www.business2.com.

Hot Links Address Book

Has BMG's restructuring strengthened the company? Find out by checking the news releases at
http://www.bmg.com

Like corporations, government agencies have organization charts, too. Learn how the Department of Health and Human Services is structured at
http://www.hhs.gov/about/orgchart.html

How is Ford Motor Credit Company's matrix structure working? Get the latest performance statistics by clicking on "investors" at
http://www.fordcredit.com

Ford's restructuring of its worldwide treasury functions into a more streamlined and efficient operation won the company *Treasury & Risk Management* magazine's 2002 Alexander Hamilton Award. Read more about it at
http://www.treasuryandrisk.com

What benefits can a company gain by using Web-based organizational charting software? Find out the features Peopleboard.com offers companies at
http://www.peopleboard.com

What organizational changes were required when Hewlett-Packard merged with Compaq? Uncover the details at
http://www.hp.com

An excellent source of links and information about the ins and outs of the reengineering process is the Reengineering Resource Center at
http://www.reengineering.com

MouseTech LLC takes a novel approach to the virtual corporation concept, as you will see from its company profile at its Web site:
http://www.moustech.net/page2.html
and on the page about virtual corporations:
http://www.moustech.net/page4.html

Chapter 9

© DIGITAL VISION / GETTY IMAGES

Managing Human Resources

learning goals

1 What is the human resource management process, and how are human resource needs determined?
2 How do human resource managers recruit and select qualified applicants?
3 What types of training and development do organizations offer their employees?
4 How are performance appraisals used to evaluate employees' performance?
5 What are the different methods for compensating employees?
6 What is organizational career management?
7 Why does a diverse workforce lead to stronger performance in the marketplace?
8 What are the key laws and federal agencies affecting human resource management?
9 What trends are affecting human resource management?

PepsiCo Is Committed to Diversity

PepsiCo (**http://www.pepsico.com**) is the parent company of some of America's best-known brands including Pepsi, Frito-Lay, Tropicana, and Quaker Oats. With more than 140,000 employees around the world, PepsiCo employees share a common set of values and goals. Top executives and human resource managers know that success takes the work of talented and dedicated people who are committed to making an impact every day. Their ability to grow year after year is driven by their ability to attract, develop, and retain world-class people who will thrive in a dynamic environment. To achieve this, PepsiCo recognizes that they need employees who are anxious to be part of a dynamic, results-oriented company, with powerful brands and top-notch people.

Early in the firm's history—as far back as the 1940s—Pepsi-Cola acknowledged the importance of diversity within its workplaces and in the marketplace. Recognizing the importance of tailoring its marketing to minority groups, Pepsi pioneered advertising specifically to minority groups. These ads featured minority actors and actresses and focused on minority lifestyles. The company also developed education and sports programs spotlighting minorities, and sponsored major musical tours by entertainers such as Michael Jackson and Tina Turner. The firm also spends millions of dollars advertising in minority media such as *Ebony* and *Black Enterprise.*

PepsiCo has been nationally recognized as one of the top places for women and minorities to work. The firm has been hiring minorities in professional positions for over 65 years. Pepsi was the first Forture 500 Company to have an African American vice president. PepsiCo has developed a number of diversity initiatives to ensure that the firm's core value of diversity is a competitive advantage. These initiatives include the following:

- Within Pepsi-Cola, Frito-Lay, and Tropicana operating divisions, executives are completely dedicated to managing diversity in the workplace.
- Multiyear strategic plans for diversity are developed with the same vigor and goal-setting process as other business issues. Goals include turnover reduction, increased diversity hiring, and creation of an "inclusion" culture.
- An External Diversity Advisory Board consisting of educators, politicians, practitioners, and customers who advise PepsiCo senior management on how to leverage diversity in the marketplace.
- Annual employee reviews incorporate the need to "Act with Integrity," "Create a Positive Work Environment," and "Align and Motivate Teams."
- A mandatory annual Affirmative Action Planning process is in place.
- An annual organizational health survey incorporates diversity questions and requires analysis at the minority and female level. Senior management is held accountable for results.
- A corporate program is dedicated to training employees on how to work and manage in an inclusive environment.
- Employee networks mentor and support minority and female employees.

Critical Thinking Questions

As you read this chapter, consider these questions as they relate to PepsiCo:

1. How can diversity in the workplace be an advantage to PepsiCo?
2. What role does the federal government play in ensuring that diversity exists at PepsiCo and all other companies?

Principles of Human Resource Management

© PHOTODISC RED / GETTY IMAGES

As business expands around the globe, human resource managers need to develop communication systems and training strategies that build teamwork among diverse employees who may be located around the world.

Human resource management in today's organization is instrumental in driving an organization toward its objectives. Successful human resource management hinges on a company's ability to attract and hire the best employees, equip them with the skills they need to excel, compensate them fairly, and motivate them to reach their full potential. Achieving these objectives in today's business environment is made more difficult because of these challenges:

- A shortage of employees for many knowledge and highly skilled occupations is forcing organizations to compete for a limited number of employees.
- Employees are placing priority on their families and struggling to balance their home and work lives.
- Because of the worldwide expansion of business, managers are challenged to manage and communicate with employees around the globe.
- A diverse and multicultural workforce requires better workplace communication and training to maximize teamwork.
- Technology is impacting the way managers and employees make decisions, communicate with each other, and operate their business.
- Human resource laws are dictating many aspects of the employee–employer relationship.

Each day, human resource experts and front-line supervisors deal with these challenges while sharing responsibility for attracting and retaining skilled, motivated employees. Whether faced with a large or small human resource problem, supervisors need some understanding of difficult employee relations issues, especially if there are legal implications.

In this chapter, you will learn about the role of human resource management in building and maintaining an exceptional workforce. We will explore human resource planning, recruiting and selection, training, and motivating employees toward reaching organizational objectives. The chapter will also cover employee job changes within an organization, managing a diverse workforce, and the laws guiding human resource decisions. Finally, we will look at important trends influencing human resource management.

Developing People to Help Reach Organizational Goals

1 learning goal

human resource management
The process of hiring, developing, motivating, and evaluating employees to achieve organizational goals.

Human resource management is the process of hiring, developing, motivating, and evaluating employees to achieve organizational goals. Organizational strategies and objectives form the basis for making all human resource management decisions. All companies strive to hire and develop well-trained, motivated employees. The human resources management process includes these steps, illustrated in Exhibit 9.1:

- Job analysis and design
- Human resource planning and forecasting
- Employee recruitment

Exhibit 9.1 | Human Resource Management Process

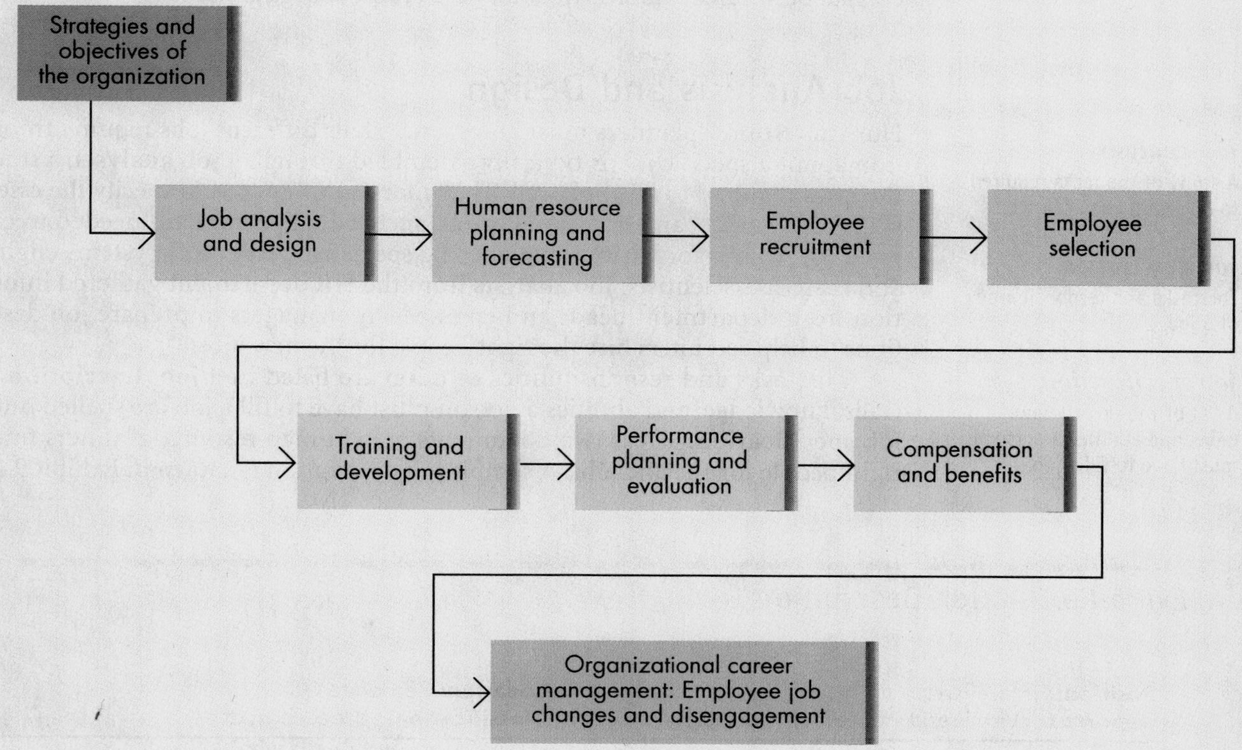

- Employee selection
- Training and development
- Performance planning and evaluation
- Compensation and benefits
- Organizational career management: employee job changes and disengagement

In the following sections, you will learn more about each of these important functions.

concept check

Define human resource management.

Describe the human resource management process.

HUMAN RESOURCE PLANNING

Firms need to have the right number of people, with the right training, in the right jobs, to do the organization's work when it needs to be done. Human resource specialists are the ones who must determine future human resource needs. Then they assess the skills of the firm's existing employees to see if new people must be hired or existing ones retrained.

human resource (HR) planning
Creating a strategy for meeting future human resource needs.

Creating a strategy for meeting future human resource needs is called **human resource (HR) planning.** Two important aspects of HR planning are job analysis and forecasting the firm's people needs. The HR planning process begins with a review of corporate strategy and policy. By understanding the mission of the organization, planners can understand its human resource needs. When Lockheed Martin was awarded the joint strikeforce contract in 2001 to produce a new generation of military aircraft, the firm had to determine the number of additional engineers and other professional employees to be hired at the various stages of aircraft development. Less than a year after receiving the contract, nearly 4,000 additional employees had been hired and nearly 1,000 were recent college graduates.

Job Analysis and Design

job analysis
A study of the tasks required to do a particular job well.

job description
The tasks and responsibilities of a job.

job specification
A list of the skills, knowledge, and abilities a person must have to fill a job.

Human resource planners must know what skills different jobs require. Information about a specific job is typically assembled through a **job analysis,** a study of the tasks required to do a job well. This information is used to specify the essential skills, knowledge, and abilities. For instance, Lockheed Martin needed to create several new jobs for various engineering specialists, especially systems engineers and materials scientists. Job analysts from the HR department gathered information from department heads and engineering managers to prepare job descriptions to help recruiters hire the right people for the new jobs.

The tasks and responsibilities of a job are listed in a **job description.** The skills, knowledge, and abilities a person must have to fill a job are spelled out in a **job specification.** These two documents help human resource planners find the right people for specific jobs. A sample job description is shown in Exhibit 9.2.

Exhibit 9.2 | Job Description

Position: College Recruiter
Reports to: Vice President of Human Resources

Location: Corporate Offices
Classification: Salaried/Exempt

Job Summary: Member of HR corporate team. Interacts with managers and department heads to determine hiring needs for college graduates. Visits 20 to 30 college and university campuses each year to conduct preliminary interviews of graduating students in all academic disciplines. Following initial interviews, works with corporate staffing specialists to determine persons who will be interviewed a second time. Makes recommendations to hiring managers concerning best-qualified applicants.

Job Duties and Responsibilities:

Estimated time spent and importance

15% Working with managers and department heads, determines college recruiting needs.
10% Determines colleges and universities with degree programs appropriate to hiring needs to be visited.
15% Performs college relations activities with numerous colleges and universities.
25% Visits campuses to conduct interviews of graduating seniors.
15% Develops applicant files and performs initial applicant evaluations.
10% Assists staffing specialists and line managers in determining who to schedule for second interviews.
5% Prepares annual college recruiting report containing information and data about campuses, number interviewed, number hired, and related information.
5% Participates in tracking college graduates who are hired to aid in determining campuses that provide the most outstanding employees.

Job Specification (Qualifications):

Bachelor's degree in human resource management or a related field. Minimum of two years of work experience with the firm in HR or department that annually hires college graduates. Ability to perform in a team environment, especially with line managers and department heads. Very effective oral and written communication skills. Reasonably proficient in Excel, Word, and Windows computer environment and familiar with PeopleSoft.

Human Resource Planning and Forecasting

Forecasting an organization's human resource needs, known as an HR *demand forecast,* is an essential aspect of HR planning. This process involves two forecasts: (1) determining the number of people needed by some future time (in one year, for example), and (2) estimating the number of people currently employed by the organization who will be available to fill various jobs at some future time. This is an *internal* supply forecast.

By comparing human resource demand and supply forecasts, a future personnel surplus or shortage can be determined and appropriate action taken. JetBlue, a low-cost airline, added planes and routes in 2003 which required adding personnel. In contrast, United Airlines reduced its flights in 2002 and decreased its employee headcount by nearly 20,000. In both cases the firms had to forecast the number of employees needed, given their respective competitive positions with the industry. Exhibit 9.3 summarizes the process of planning and forecasting an organization's people needs.

contingent workers
Persons who prefer temporary employment, either part-time or full-time.

Many firms with employee shortages are hiring **contingent workers,** or persons who prefer temporary employment, either part-time or full-time. College students and retired persons comprise a big portion of America's contingent workforce. Other people who want to work but don't want to be permanent

Exhibit 9.3 | Human Resource Planning Process

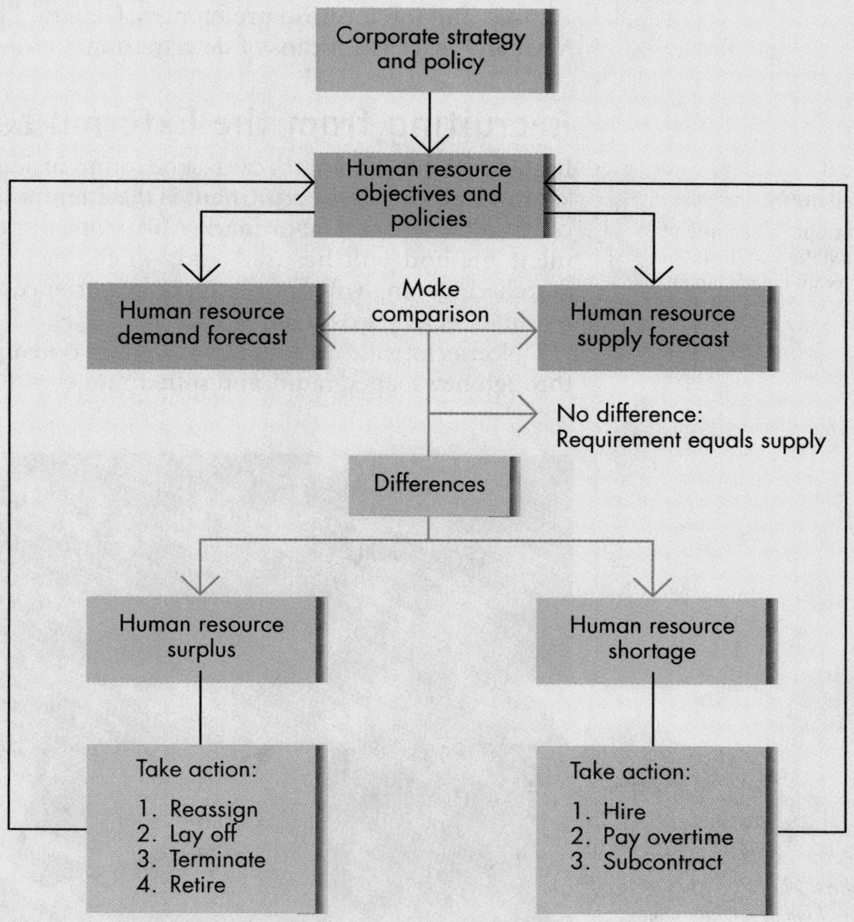

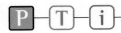

concept check

Describe the job analysis and design process.

What is the process for human resource forecasting?

employees join a professional employer organization (PEO). A PEO performs staffing, training, and compensation functions by contracting with a business to provide employees for a specified period of time. A firm with a shortage of accountants can rent or lease an accountant from the PEO for the expected duration of the shortage.

EMPLOYEE RECRUITMENT

2 learning goal

When a firm creates a new position or an existing one becomes vacant, it starts looking for people with qualifications that meet the requirements of the job. Two sources of job applicants are the internal and external labor markets. The internal labor market consists of employees currently employed by the firm; the external labor market is the pool of potential applicants outside the firm.

Recruiting from the Internal Labor Market

Most companies including UPS, Southwest Airlines, and Wal-Mart follow a policy of promotion from within and try to fill positions with their existing employees. The internal search for job applicants usually means that a person must change his or her job. People are typically either promoted or transferred. A firm's skills inventory can help find the right person for a job opening. A skills inventory is a computerized employee database containing information on each employee's previous work experience, educational background, performance records, career objectives, and job location preferences. General Electric has used a skills inventory for many years as a means of determining promotions and transfers.

Recruiting from the External Labor Market

recruitment
The attempt to find and attract qualified applicants in the external labor market.

If qualified job candidates cannot be found inside the firm, the external labor market must be tapped. **Recruitment** is the attempt to find and attract qualified applicants in the external labor market. The type of position determines which recruitment method will be used and which segment of the labor market will be searched. Boeing will not recruit an experienced engineer the same way it would recruit a secretary or clerk typist.

Nontechnical, unskilled, and other nonsupervisory workers are recruited through newspaper, radio, and sometimes even television help-wanted ads in local

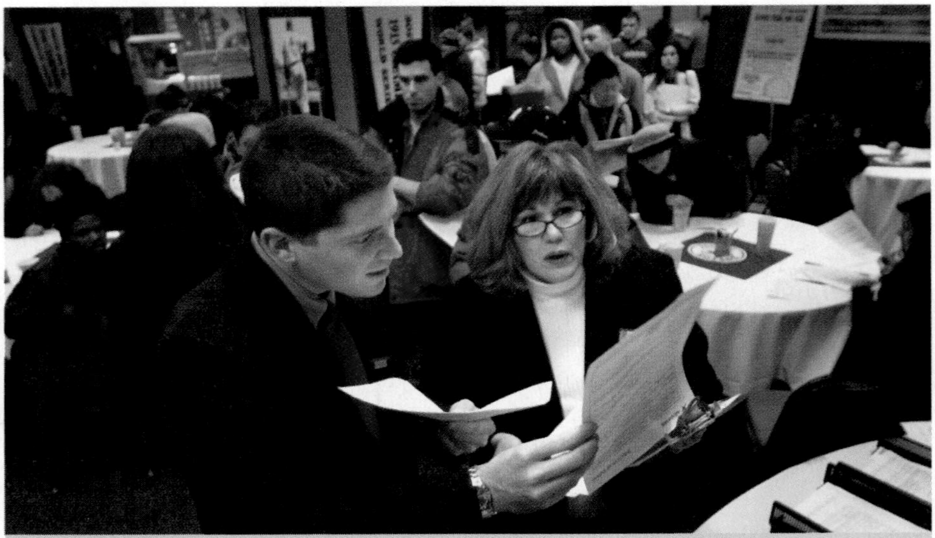

Job fairs bring together hundreds of employers and thousands of job seekers. Job fairs are one of the ways human resource managers identify employees from the external job market.

media. Starbucks placed ads in the *Beijing Youth Daily* to attract workers for its Beijing coffee shops. Entry-level accountants, engineers, and systems analysts are commonly hired through college campus recruitment efforts. Each year Texas Instruments sends recruiters to dozens of colleges across the United States that have engineering degree programs. To recruit inexperienced technicians, National SemiConductor visits junior and community college campuses with electronic and related technical programs that are within 50 to 100 miles of its facilities.

A firm that needs executives and other experienced professional, technical, and managerial employees may employ the services of an executive search firm such as Korn Ferry. The hiring firm pays the search firm a fee equivalent to one to four months of the employee's first-year salary. Many search firms specialize in a particular occupation, industry, or geographic location.

job fair
An event, typically one day, held at a convention center to bring together thousands of job seekers and hundreds of firms searching for employees.

corporate open house
Persons are invited to an open house on the premises of the corporation. Qualified applicants are encouraged to complete an application before leaving.

Many firms participate in local job fairs. A **job fair** is typically a one-day event held at a convention center to bring together thousands of job seekers and hundreds of firms searching for employees. Some firms conduct a **corporate open house.** Persons attend the open house, are briefed about various job opportunities, and are encouraged to submit a job application on the spot, or before leaving the employer's premises.

Using Technology to Recruit Applicants

An increasingly common and popular recruiting method involves using the Internet. Nearly all large, and most medium-size business firms now use online recruiting by either drawing applicants to their own Web site or utilizing the services of a job board, such as Monster.com, CareerMosaic.com, Hotjobs.com, or CareerPath.com. A firm can be assisted in these efforts by consulting an Internet recruitment directory like the Riley Guide. Some large firms, such as General Electric, receive more than 200,000 Web site visitors each month and receive as many as 10,000 résumés per month.[1]

Other firms including Coca-Cola, Paine Webber, and NationsBank utilize artificial intelligence software to scan and track résumés. Motive Communications uses Hire.com's e-Recruiter software because of its profiling capabilities. Applicant résumé information can be matched with current and future job openings. Motive Communications's applicant pool becomes a dynamic database that is constantly churning as new applicants are added. The e-Recruiter system can search and scan thousands of résumés in minutes. With such systems the words and phrases used to describe one's background and experience become very important. Technological advances, like those described in the "Applying Technology" box, aid the disabled in finding employment.

concept check

What are the two labor markets?

Describe different ways that employees are recruited.

How is technology helping firms find the right recruits?

Employee Selection

selection
The process of determining which persons in the applicant pool possess the qualifications necessary to be successful on the job.

After a firm has attracted enough job applicants, employment specialists begin the selection process. **Selection** is the process of determining which persons in the applicant pool possess the qualifications necessary to be successful on the job. The steps in the employee selection process are shown in Exhibit 9.4 and described below:

1. *Initial screening.* During the initial screening, an applicant usually completes an application form and has a brief interview of 30 minutes or less. The application form includes questions about education, work experience, and previous job duties. A personal résumé may be substituted for the application form. The interview is normally structured and consists of a short list of specific questions. For example: Are you familiar with any accounting software packages? Did you supervise anyone in your last job? Did you use a company car when making sales calls?

Applying Technology

Technology Helps the Disabled

The Americans with Disabilities Act, passed nearly 15 years ago, requires that employers not discriminate against persons with disabilities. According to the U.S. Census Bureau, approximately 54 million Americans have one or more disabilities as defined by the law.[2] Of the disabled who are capable of working, nearly two-thirds are unemployed, or significantly underemployed. The disabled as a demographic group experience the highest unemployment rate. The disabled comprise a large pool of relatively untapped talent.

Significant technological advances have been made in recent years, and will continue to be made in future years, to facilitate employment of the disabled. Sears and IBM employ many hundreds of moderately to severely disabled persons because numerous assistive devices are now available at very low to minimal cost. Many of these devices are by-products of the development of paperless information and document systems; some examples are keyboard filters and typing aids, touch screens, mouth-held electronic pointing elements, captioning and assisted listening devices, and voice recognition software.

Glenn Higgins, who is a quadriplegic, has benefited tremendously from various technological advances. He is vice president and medical director for Unum Provident Corporation in Portland, Maine. He uses a speech recognition system to operate his personal computer and a breath-activated device to move and control his electric wheelchair. He has been a very effective employee who requires very minimal help from coworkers.

CRITICAL THINKING QUESTIONS

1. The cost of assistive technology is usually perceived as a major barrier by employers to hiring those with disabilities. Do you agree with this argument? Why or why not?
2. What are some cost-free (or very minimal costs) changes or accommodations that an employer can make to facilitate employing those with physical disabilities?
3. Disabled Americans are also consumers or customers. Is it a good HR policy, and business practice, to have employees who look like their customers? Discuss.

2. *Employment testing.* Following the initial screening, an applicant may be asked to take one or more employment tests, such as the Minnesota Clerical Test or the Wonderlic Personnel Test, a mental-ability test. Some tests are designed to measure special job skills, others measure aptitudes, and some are intended to capture characteristics of one's personality. The Myers–Briggs Type Indicator is a personality and motivational instrument widely used on college campuses as an aid in providing job and career counseling as well as assisting a

Exhibit 9.4 Steps of the Employee Selection Process

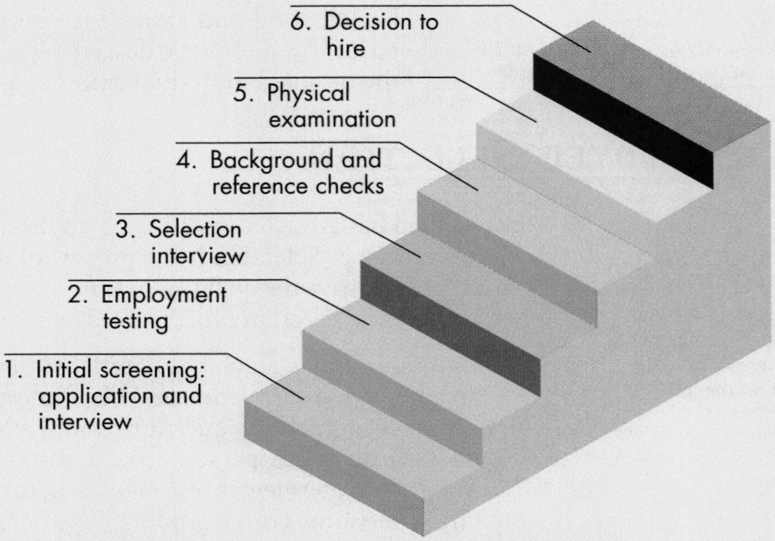

student in selecting his or her major. In recent years some firms have begun to use a test that assesses one's emotional intelligence. Frequently called the e-quotient, the emotional intelligence quotient reveals how well a person understands his or her own emotions and the emotions of others and how he or she behaves based on this understanding.

selection interview
An in-depth discussion of an applicant's work experience, skills and abilities, education, and career interests.

3. *Selection interview.* The tool most widely used in making hiring decisions by Intel, Merck, and other firms is the **selection interview,** an in-depth discussion of an applicant's work experience, skills and abilities, education, and career interests. For managerial and professional positions, an applicant may be interviewed by several persons, including the line manager for the position to be filled. This interview is designed to determine an applicant's communication ability and motivation. It is also a means for gathering additional factual information from the applicant such as college major, years of part-time work experience, computer equipment used, and reason for leaving the last job. The applicant may be asked to explain how to solve a particular management problem or how she or he provided leadership to a group in a previous work situation when an important problem had to be solved quickly. United Airlines asks prospective flight attendants how they handled a conflict with a customer or coworker in a previous job.

   Carolyn Murray, a recruiter for W. C. Gore and Associates, makers of Gore-Tex®, says she pays little attention to a candidate's carefully scripted responses to her admittedly easy questions. Instead, she listens for a casual remark that reveals the reality behind an otherwise thought-out reply. Using a baseball analogy, Carolyn gives examples of how three job candidates struck out in Exhibit 9.5.[3]

4. *Background and reference check.* If applicants pass the selection interview, most firms examine their background and check their references. In recent years an increasing number of employers such as American Airlines, Disney, and Microsoft are carefully researching applicants' backgrounds, particularly their legal history, reasons for leaving previous jobs, and even creditworthiness. Retail firms such as Men's Warehouse, JC Penney, Tandy, and TD Industries, where employees have extensive contact with customers, tend to be very careful about checking applicant backgrounds. Some checking can be easily done using the Internet. In fact, many retired law enforcement officers have started their own firms that specialize in these investigations.

Exhibit 9.5 Striking Out with Gore-Tex

The Pitch (Question to Applicant)	**The Swing (Applicant's Response)**	**The Miss (Interviewer's Reaction to Response)**
"Give me an example of a time when you had a conflict with a team member."	"Our leader asked me to handle all of the Fed Exing for our team. I did it, but I thought that Fed Exing was a waste of my time."	"At Gore, we work from a team concept. Her answer shows that she won't exactly jump when one of her teammates needs help."
"Tell me how you solved a problem that was impeding your project."	"One of the engineers on my team wasn't pulling his weight, and we were closing in on a deadline. So I took on some of his work."	"The candidate may have resolved the issue for this particular deadline, but he did nothing to prevent the problem from happening again."
"What's the one thing that you would change about your current position?"	"My job as a salesman has become boring. Now I want the responsibility of managing people."	"He's probably not maximizing his current territory, *and* he is complaining. Will he find his next role "boring" and complain about that role, too?"

Expanding Around the Globe

Americans Working Abroad

Thousands of American business firms of all sizes and shapes have some presence in other countries. In many cases the firms have facilities (manufacturing plant, sales office, or distribution center) in one or more nations. When an American firm decides to open a factory in another country, it usually temporarily assigns an American to that location. The American becomes an *expatriate* and might live and work in the other country for an extended period of time, or several years. This is an expensive arrangement for the American firm in that expatriate assignments cost an average of $1 million over a three-year period.[4] In part, because of this considerable expense, American firms attempt to have virtually all positions filled by locals once a facility is functioning effectively.

In 2001 the Air Solutions Group of Ingersoll-Rand began construction of a factory in Unocov, Czech Republic. Within a relatively short period of time, or about six months, nearly all positions were filled with Czech citizens. The only American at that point was the plant manager, and after only a few months of factory operations, he had identified a Czech whom he began to groom to replace him in two years, or less.[5] Out-of-country assignments are becoming more common and can be excellent development opportunities for managers and other professional employees. However, the failure rate for expatriate assignments can also be relatively high; a failure is usually defined as the American returning home to the United States prior to the scheduled end of the assignment.

CRITICAL THINKING QUESTIONS

1. Aside from technical knowledge and skill, what skills, knowledge, and experience do you think an employee should possess in order to increase the chances that an overseas assignment will be successful?
2. Would it be a good human resources strategy for American firms to recruit international students, following their graduation, to train for assignments back in their home countries? Why or why not?
3. What American human resources practice might be difficult to transplant in another country? Why?

5. *Physical exams.* Companies frequently require job candidates to have a medical checkup to ensure they are physically able to perform a job. Drug testing is becoming a routine part of physical exams. Companies such as American Airlines, Burlington Northern Railroad, and the U.S. Postal Service use drug testing for reasons of workplace safety, productivity, and employee health.
6. *Decision to hire.* If an applicant progresses satisfactorily through all the selection steps, a decision to hire the individual is made. The decision to hire is nearly always made by the manager of the new employee.

concept check

What are the steps in the employee selection process?

Describe some ways that applicants are tested.

The "Expanding Around the Globe" box describes how employees are chosen to fulfill jobs in overseas facilities.

Employee Training and Development

3 learning goal

training and development
Activities that provide learning situations in which an employee acquires additional knowledge or skills to increase job performance.

To ensure that both new and experienced employees have the knowledge and skills to perform their jobs successfully, organizations invest in training and development activities. **Training and development** involves learning situations in which the employee acquires additional knowledge or skills to increase job performance. Training objectives specify performance improvements, reductions in errors, job knowledge to be gained, and/or other positive organizational results. The design of training programs at General Electric, for example, includes determining instructional methods, number of trainees per class, printed materials (cases, notebooks, manuals, and the like) to be used, location of training, use of audiovisual equipment and software, and many other matters. The process of creating and implementing training and development activities is shown in Exhibit 9.6.

Training for new employees is instrumental in getting them up to speed and familiar with their job responsibilities. The first type of training that new employees experience is **employee orientation,** which entails getting the new employee ready

Exhibit 9.6 | Employee Training and Development Process

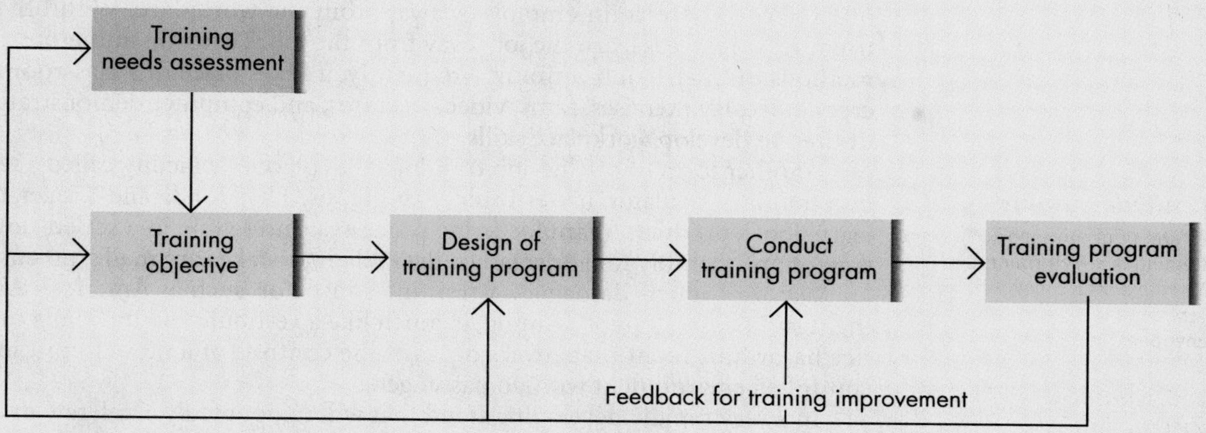

employee orientation
Training that prepares a new employee to perform on the job; includes information about job assignments, work rules, equipment, and performance expectations, as well as about company policies, salary and benefits, and parking.

to perform on the job. Formal orientation (a half-day classroom program) provides information about company policies, salary and benefits, and parking. Although this information is very helpful, the more important orientation is about job assignments, work rules, equipment, and performance expectations provided by the new employee's supervisor and coworkers. This second briefing tends to be more informal and may last for several days or even weeks. Many firms use video for employee orientation because they want a standardized message and delivery tone expressed to new employees. DSM Chemicals North America shows a video to employees about safety procedures when entering a chemical-manufacturing area. Professional videos can be expensive, costing $1,000 to $3,000 per finished minute.[6]

On-the-Job Training

on-the-job training
Training in which the employee learns the job by doing it with guidance from a supervisor or experienced coworker.

job rotation
Reassignment of workers to several different jobs over time so that they can learn the basics of each job.

apprenticeship
A form of on-the-job training that combines specific job instruction with classroom instruction.

mentoring
A form of on-the-job training in which a senior manager or other experienced employee provides job- and career-related information to a protégé.

Continuous training for both new and experienced employees is important to keep job skills fresh. Job-specific training, designed to enhance a new employee's ability to perform a job, includes **on-the-job training,** during which the employee learns the job by doing it with guidance from a supervisor or experienced coworker.

On-the-job training takes place at the job site or workstation and tends to be directly related to the job. This training involves specific job instructions, coaching (guidance given to new employees by experienced ones), special project assignments, or job rotation. **Job rotation** is the reassignment of workers to several different jobs over time. At Sears, management trainees work sequentially in two or three merchandise departments, customer service, credit, and human resources during their first year on the job.

An **apprenticeship** usually combines specific on-the-job instruction with classroom training. It may last as long as four years and can be found in the skilled trades of carpentry, plumbing, and electrical work.

With **mentoring,** another form of on-the-job training, a senior manager or other experienced employee provides job- and career-related information to a protégé. Inexpensive and providing instantaneous feedback, mentoring is becoming increasingly popular with many firms, including Federal Express, Texaco, Merrill Lynch, and Bank of America, which uses "quad squads" composed of a mentor and three new hires (a male, female, and a minority-group member). At Coca-Cola Roberto Goizueta mentored Douglas Ivester to become CEO of the company. When Goizueta died suddenly in 1997, Ivester's transition to CEO went very smoothly. The company clearly benefited from this mentoring relationship.

Off-the-Job Training

Even with the advantages of on-the-job training, many firms recognize that it is often necessary to train employees away from the workplace. With off-the-job training, employees learn the job away from the job. There are numerous popular methods of off-the-job training. Frequently, it takes place in a classroom where cases, role-play exercises, films, videos, lectures, and computer demonstrations are utilized to develop workplace skills.

vestibule training
A form of off-the-job training in which trainees learn in a scaled-down version or simulated work environment.

programmed instruction
A form of computer-assisted off-the-job training.

Another form of off-the-job training takes place in a facility called a vestibule or a training simulator. In **vestibule training,** used by Honda and Kroger, trainees learn about products, manufacturing processes, and selling in a scaled-down version of an assembly line or retail outlet. When mistakes are made, no customers are lost or products damaged. A training simulator, such as American Airlines's flight simulator for pilot training, is much like a vestibule facility. Pilots can practice hazardous flight maneuvers or learn the controls of a new aircraft in a safe, controlled environment with no passengers.

In a very rapidly developing trend that will undoubtedly accelerate in the 21st century, many companies including Compaq and Microsoft are using computer-assisted, electronically delivered training and development courses and programs. Many of these courses have their origins in **programmed instruction,** a self-paced, highly structured training method that presents trainees with concepts and problems using a modular format.

concept check

Describe several types of on-the-job training.

Explain vestibule training and programmed instruction.

Usually, off-the-job training is more expensive than on-the-job training, its impact is less direct, and the transfer of learning to the job is less immediate. Nevertheless, despite these shortcomings, some training can only be done away from the job.

Performance Planning and Evaluation

4 learning goal

performance appraisal
A comparison of actual performance with expected performance to assess an employee's contributions to the organization.

Along with employee orientation and training, new employees learn about performance expectations through performance planning and evaluation. Managers provide employees with expectations about the job. These are communicated as job objectives, schedules, deadlines, and product and/or service quality requirements. As an employee performs job tasks, the supervisor periodically evaluates the employee's efforts. A **performance appraisal** is a comparison of actual performance with expected performance to assess an employee's contributions to the organization and to make decisions about training, compensation, promotion, and other job changes. The performance planning and appraisal process is shown in Exhibit 9.7 and described below:

Exhibit 9.7 | Performance Planning and Evaluation

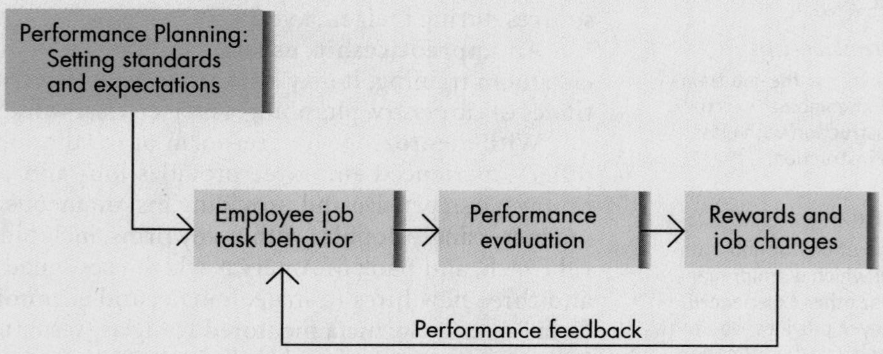

During a performance appraisal, a manager evaluates an employee's performance, comparing actual performance to expected performance goals. At General Electric, employees receive feedback from work teams, peers, and customers in order to develop perspective on their management style and skills.

© PHOTODISC BLUE / GETTY IMAGES

1. The manager establishes performance standards.
2. The employee works to meet the standards and expectations.
3. The employee's supervisor evaluates the employee's work in terms of quality and quantity of output and various characteristics such as job knowledge, initiative, relationships with others, and attendance and punctuality.
4. Following the performance evaluation, reward (pay raise) and job change (promotion) decisions can be made.
5. Rewards are positive feedback and provide reinforcement, or encouragement, for the employee to work harder in the future.

Performance appraisals serve a number of purposes, but they are most often used to make decisions about pay raises, training needs, advancement opportunities, and employee terminations.

concept check

What are the steps in the performance planning and appraisal process?

What purposes do performance appraisals serve?

EMPLOYEE COMPENSATION AND BENEFITS

5 learning goal

Compensation, which includes both pay and benefits, is closely connected to performance appraisal. Employees who perform better tend to get bigger pay raises. Several factors affect an employee's pay:

1. *Pay structure and internal influences.* Wages, salaries, and benefits usually reflect the importance of the job. The jobs that management considers more important are compensated at a higher rate; president, chief engineer, and chief financial officer are high-paying jobs. Likewise, different jobs of equal importance to the firm are compensated at the same rate. For instance, if a drill-press operator and a lathe operator are considered of equal importance, they may both be paid $21 per hour.
2. *Pay level and external influences.* In deciding how much to pay workers, the firm must also be concerned with the salaries paid by competitors. If competitors are paying much higher wages, a firm may lose its best employees. Larger firms conduct salary surveys to see what other firms are paying. Wage and

salary surveys conducted by the Chamber of Commerce or the U.S. Department of Labor can also be useful.

An employer can decide to pay at, above, or below the going rate. Most firms try to offer competitive wages and salaries within a geographic area or an industry. If a company pays below-market wages, it may not be able to hire skilled people. The level, or competitiveness, of a firm's compensation is determined by the firm's financial condition (or profitability), efficiency, and employee productivity, as well as the going rates paid by competitors. Miller Brewing Co. is considered a high-paying firm ($22–$25 per hour for production employees); McDonald's is a lower-paying company ($6–$8 per hour for counter employees).

Types of Compensation or Pay

There are two basic types of compensation: direct and indirect. Direct pay is the wage or salary received by the employee; indirect pay consists of various employee benefits and services. Employees are usually paid directly on the basis of the amount of time they work, the amount they produce, or some combination of time and output. The following are the most common types of compensation:

- *Hourly wages.* Technicians, machinists, and assembly-line workers at Briggs and Stratton are paid by the hour with wages ranging from $22.50 to $26.50 per hour.
- *Salaries.* Managerial and professional employees are paid an annual salary on either a biweekly or a monthly basis. The annual salary of the U.S. president is $200,000.
- *Piecework and commission.* Some employees are paid according to how much they produce or sell. A car salesperson might be paid $500 for each car sold or a 3 percent commission on the car's sale price. Thus, a salesperson who sold four cars in one week at $500 per car would earn $2,000 in pay for that week. Alternatively, a 3 percent commission on four cars sold with total sales revenue of $70,000 would yield $2,100 in pay.

  Increasingly, business firms are paying employees using a base wage or salary and an incentive. The incentive feature is designed to increase individual employee, work group, and/or organizational performance. Incentive pay plans are commonly referred to as variable or contingent pay arrangements.
- *Accelerated commission schedule.* A salesperson could be paid a commission rate of 3 percent on the first $50,000 of sales per month, 4 percent on the next $30,000, and 5 percent on any sales beyond $80,000. For a salesperson who made $90,000 of sales in one month, the monthly pay would be as follows:

3% ×	$50,000	=	$1,500
4% ×	$30,000	=	$1,200
5% ×	$10,000	=	$ 500
	$90,000	=	$3,200

- *Bonus.* A bonus is a payment for reaching a specific goal; it may be paid on a monthly, quarterly, or annual basis. A bank with several offices or branches might set monthly goals for opening new accounts, making loans, and customer service. Each employee of a branch that meets all goals would be paid a monthly bonus of $100. Although the bonuses are paid to the employees individually, the employees must function as an effective, high-performing group to reach the monthly goals.
- *Profit sharing.* A firm that offers profit sharing pays employees a portion of the profits over a preset level. For example, profits beyond 10 percent of gross

Making Ethical Choices

xtra! http://gitmanxtra.swlearning.com

KEEPING SECRETS

Working on national security issues for a consulting firm with U.S. Department of State contracts has been both exciting and increasingly stressful. The excitement comes from the actual work of investigating and evaluating potential terrorist threats to the United States. The stress is a result of a greatly increased workload and much closer scrutiny of your work. When you started your job in June 2000, 40- to 45-hour weeks were common. After the September 11 terrorist attacks, your workload has increased dramatically, and you now must work 55 to 65 hours per week. Managers appear to be monitoring employees' activities and paying closer attention to their mental state for evidence of instability. Along with your fellow workers, you are concerned that the heightened security measures may change the policies with regard to confidentiality of medical records.

Because the consulting firm's culture doesn't support open discussion, you don't feel comfortable talking about the stress you are experiencing with your colleagues or your supervisor. Instead, you seek counsel from HR and are given names of several psychotherapists who participate in the company's employee assistance plan. You assume that your visit to HR and the subject of that visit are as secret as the nature of your work. Your psychotherapist has advised you that your visits and the content of all sessions are confidential.

You begin to sense that your supervisor is aware of your 90-minute absences, even though you made sure to schedule visits to the therapist on a different day and different time each week. The idea that your supervisor might know you are seeking psychological counseling only increases your stress level.

ETHICAL DILEMMA

Does your employer have the right to know about your visits to a psychotherapist?

SOURCES: Tybe Diamond, "American Psychoanalytic Association Files a Lawsuit to Challenge the Bush Administration HIPPA Abuses," e-mail, April 14, 2003; "Protecting Privacy and Personal Security—Our World's Need for a Careful Balance and the 10 Commandments of Ethical Surveillance," *PRNewsire*, September 13, 2001, downloaded from http://www.findarticles.com; Jonathan A. Segal, "Security vs. Privacy: To Ensure a Secure Environment for All Workers Avoid Violating the Privacy of Any One Individual," *HR Magazine*, February 2002, downloaded from http://www.findarticles.com.

sales might be shared at a 50 percent rate with employees. The company retains the remaining profits. All employees may receive the same profit shares, or the shares may vary according to base pay.

fringe benefits
Indirect compensation such as pensions, health insurance, and vacations.

- *Fringe benefits.* **Fringe benefits** are indirect compensation and include pensions, health insurance, vacations, and many others. Some fringe benefits are required by law: unemployment compensation, worker's compensation, and Social Security, which are all paid in part by employers. *Unemployment compensation* provides former employees with money for a certain period while they are unemployed. To be eligible, the employee must have worked a minimum number of weeks, be without a job, and be willing to accept a suitable position offered by the state Unemployment Compensation Commission. Some state laws permit payments to strikers. *Worker's compensation* pays employees for lost work time caused by work-related injuries and may also cover rehabilitation after a serious injury. *Social Security* is mainly a government pension plan, but it also provides disability and survivor benefits and benefits for people undergoing kidney dialysis and transplants. Medicare (health care for the elderly) and Medicaid (health care for the poor) are also part of Social Security.

Many employers also offer fringe benefits not required by law. Among these are paid time off (vacations, holidays, sick days, even pay for jury duty), insurance (health and hospitalization, disability, life, dental, vision, and accidental death and dismemberment), pensions and retirement savings accounts, and stock purchase options.

Some firms with numerous fringe benefits allow employees to mix and match benefit items or select items based on individual needs. This is a flexible or cafeteria-style benefit plan. A younger employee with a family may desire to purchase medical, disability, and life insurance, whereas an older employee may want to put more benefit dollars into a retirement savings plan. All employees are allocated the same number of benefit dollars but can spend these dollars on different items and in different amounts.

Executive Compensation

Employees are paid different amounts according to the value of the job to the firm and the performance of the job incumbent (or employee). Persons at higher levels of the firm are paid more and generally employees with greater experience, seniority, and education are paid more than newer, inexperienced employees. Executives are the highest paid of various groups of employees. The average chief executive officer (CEO) is compensated 500 times the amount paid to the lowest paid worker.[7] This is up from 42 times in 1980. Additionally, executives are given a greater variety of fringe benefits (country club membership, car allowance, and annual physical exam with physical fitness prescription) and frequently are paid various incentives, such as bonuses, profit shares, and other benefits. While these incentives are intended to stimulate executive and firm performance as measured by increased sales, profits, market share, and stock price, there have been many examples in recent years where a CEO's pay has been significantly increased when the firm's profits declined, or the firm even lost money.

The former CEO of Kmart, Charles Conaway, whose management is now the subject of an internal inquiry, received more than $20 million in loans, cash, shares and bonuses in his first year, and he negotiated the right to fly anywhere he wanted in the company jet. James Adamson took over as CEO in 2002 and was enjoying rich perks and a $4 million pay package, even though he served on Kmart's board while the company slid toward bankruptcy and handed out millions in dubious loans to top executives. Adamson received another $3.6 million when Kmart emerged from bankruptcy in 2003 even though the 35,000 employees fired got next to nothing. So, in a period of about ten months, Adamson earned roughly $7 million—despite a 10% drop in same-store sales and a $2 billion loss in the first three quarters of his watch.[8]

Of the executive incentives mentioned above, stock options are the most controversial. A *stock option* is the right to buy company stock at a set price at a later date. An executive can be given options to buy shares of the firm's stock at a reduced price and then be allowed to sell the shares, after being held for a specified time, for a profit. In some cases the executive is given a low-interest loan by the firm to exercise the options and purchase the shares of stock. The stock option functions as an incentive because the executive is expected to manage the firm so that the stock price increases and shareholder value is enhanced. While the executive can be successful in the short run (a few months to two or three years) in raising the stock price, some short-term executive decisions can become long-term problems. But in the short term, the executive has significantly prospered through exercising stock options for thousands of shares of stock and making profits on stock sales.

Determining a CEO's fair salary isn't easy. CEOs are responsible for making decisions that can impact tens of thousands of employees and dramatically increase or decrease the value of a company. Former CEO Herb Kelleher built Southwest Airlines into a company that had a stock value greater than all other airlines combined.

©AP / WIDE WORLD PHOTOS

Another controversial element of an executive compensation package is the *golden parachute,* a very lucrative severance or retirement deal that an executive might receive even when firm performance has suffered.

In 2003 numerous large firms (American Express, Coca-Cola, Wal-Mart, General Electric, Yahoo!, and Caterpillar) were being presented shareholder resolutions to reduce golden parachutes and eliminate or tighten the use of stock options. Congressional proposals were also being made to require companies to deduct stock option costs from corporate earnings, a change that would reduce the stock options and their incentive value.

concept check

How does a firm establish a pay scale for its employees?

What is the difference between direct and indirect pay?

What makes executive compensation controversial?

Organizational Career Management

6 learning goal

An important aspect of the human resource management process is organizational career management, or facilitating employee job changes, including promotions, transfers, demotions, layoffs, terminations, and retirements.

Job Changes within the Organization

promotion
An upward move in an organization to a position with more authority, responsibility, and pay.

transfer
A horizontal move in an organization to a position with about the same salary and at about the same organizational level.

A **promotion** is an upward move in an organization to a position with more authority, responsibility, and pay. Promotion decisions are usually based on merit (ability and performance) and seniority (length of service). Union employees usually prefer a strict seniority system for employee advancement. Managers and technical employees strongly prefer promotions based on merit.

A **transfer** is a horizontal move in an organization to a position with about the same salary and at about the same organizational level. An employee may seek a transfer for personal growth, for a more interesting job, for convenience (better work hours, work location, or training opportunity), or for a job that offers more potential for advancement. Employers may transfer workers from positions where they are no longer needed to ones where they are needed. Or the goal may be to find a better fit for the employee within the firm. Sometimes transfers are made to give employees a different perspective or to reenergize them. Consider Randy Lagman, a staff support technician for Internet operations at Lands' End, a billion-dollar clothing catalog company based in Dodgeville, Wisconsin. Randy was transferred from a self-described "Web-geek" position to a job with the title "technical adventurer outfitter."

When a person is downgraded or reassigned to a position with less responsibility, it is called a **demotion.** This usually occurs when an employee isn't performing satisfactorily. In most companies, a person is given several warnings before a demotion takes place.

demotion
The downgrading or reassignment of an employee to a position with less responsibility.

Separations

A **separation** occurs when an employee leaves the company. Layoffs, terminations, resignations, and retirements are all types of separations. Sometimes separations occur because companies are trying to remain competitive in the global marketplace. When oil prices dropped significantly early in 1997, many energy firms laid off or terminated workers. UPR, Inc., an oil exploration and drilling company, initially terminated 400 employees and later offered early-retirement packages to other employees to encourage them to retire.

separation
The departure of an employee from the organization; can be a layoff, termination, resignation, or retirement.

A **layoff** is a temporary separation arranged by the employer, usually because business is slow. Layoffs can be planned, such as seasonal reductions of employees, or unplanned, as when sales unexpectedly decline. Generally, employees with the least seniority are laid off first. Within days of September 11, 2001, United Airlines issued a request to employees, particularly flight service workers, asking them to consider a three-month furlough (layoff) or leave without pay but with benefits. Several thousand employees accepted the furlough offer; however, most of them expected to be recalled to work after the three months.

layoff
A temporary separation of an employee from the organization; arranged by the employer, usually because business is slow.

There are several alternatives to a layoff. With a *voluntary reduction in pay,* all employees agree to take less pay so that everyone can keep working. Other firms arrange to have all or most of their employees take vacation time during slow periods. Major-league baseball teams, the Houston Astros, for example, encourage their full-time year-round employees to take vacations during the off-season from November through April. Other employees agree to take *voluntary time off,* or work fewer hours, which again has the effect of reducing the employer's payroll and avoiding the need for a layoff. Control Data Corporation avoids layoffs with what it calls a *rings of defense* approach. Temporary employees are hired with the specific understanding that they may be laid off at any time. When layoffs are needed, the temporary workers are the first "ring of defense." Permanent Control Data employees know they probably will never be laid off.

A **termination** is a permanent separation arranged by the employer. Reasons for terminations include failure to perform as expected, violation of work rules, downsizing (terminating workers to lower costs and become more competitive in the marketplace), dishonesty, theft, sexual harassment, excessive absenteeism, or insubordination (disobedience). Many of the three-month furloughed United employees mentioned above, along with thousands of other United employees, were terminated at the end of the furlough. They didn't lose their jobs because of poor performance, but because of significant reductions in the demand for air travel. Many air routes were discontinued and dozens of aircraft were taken out of service.

termination
A permanent separation of an employee from the organization, arranged by the employer.

Most companies follow a series of steps before terminating an employee for poor performance or violations of company rules. First, the employee is given an oral warning. The second step is a written statement that the employee's actions are not acceptable. If the employee fails to improve, he or she is suspended from work for a time. If the employee persists in wrongdoing after suspension, his or her employment is terminated.

Resignation is a permanent form of separation that is undertaken voluntarily by the employee, whereas layoff and termination are involuntary. An employee may resign for almost any reason: to seek a new career, move to a different part of the country, accept an employment offer with a significant pay raise, or join a fast-growing firm with numerous advancement opportunities.

resignation
A permanent separation of an employee from the organization, done voluntarily by the employee.

Focusing on Small Business

SIGMA's Nod to HR

Small business organizations (those with fewer than 500 employees) typically do not have a comprehensive and well-developed HR function, one that includes all of the elements included in Exhibit 9.1. A small firm, SIGMA Marketing Group, in Rochester, New York, not only places considerable importance on the HR function, but it actually won a national award from the Society for Human Resource Management (SHRM) for an innovative HR practice. SIGMA HR Director, Susan O'Connell, decided to place as much, actually more, emphasis on celebrating the hiring and orientation of a new employee as the resignation or retirement of a long-service employee. It is common for most organizations, regardless of size, to celebrate the retirement of a long-service employee. Director O'Connell felt that a newly hired employee should also receive considerable attention.

When a new employee starts work at SIGMA, O'Connell sends an e-mail announcement to all employees that welcomes the new worker. Also, a welcoming party is held one morning during the new employee's first week at his or her work station. The party includes balloons and food—bagels or muffins—for everyone who can attend. A traveler's Road Book of company information is provided the new employee and a biographical sketch of the new worker is posted on an employee bulletin board. A mentor is arranged for the new employee as well. Essentially, the celebration is designed to generate excitement for and about the new employee. This greatly speeds the process of integrating the new employee into the network of existing employees.[9]

CRITICAL THINKING QUESTIONS

1. What are the benefits to the firm and the newly hired employee of this celebration, or what value does the firm and individual receive?
2. What are the costs (financial and nonfinancial) to the firm? Do the benefits exceed the cost?
3. When you start your first (or next) professional job as an accountant, bank economist, systems analyst, or whatever, what do you expect the employer to do during the first week to help you become familiar with your job, the organization, and coworkers?

For companies in high-growth industries, keeping employees from resigning and moving to "greener pastures" is a number one priority. This is particularly true in smaller entrepreneurial firms where losing a key employee can be disastrous.

retirement
The separation of an employee from the organization at the end of his or her career.

Retirement usually ends one's career. Common retirement ages are 55, 62, 65, and 70, but no one can be required to retire, according to the Age Discrimination Act. The law does, however, allow mandatory retirement in a few occupations, such as firefighter, police officer, and commercial airline pilot. Although most organizations honor retirees with gifts or other special recognition, SIGMA Marketing Group celebrates the hiring of new employees, as described in the "Focusing on Small Business" box.

Workers in companies with too many employees may be offered early-retirement incentives. This option offers retirement benefits to younger employees or adds extra retirement benefits or both. Employees can thus retire more comfortably without working longer. Xerox, General Motors, IBM, Hewlett-Packard, and Phillips Petroleum, among others, have used early-retirement plans to reduce their workforces when economic conditions have caused declines in product demand and production schedules must be reduced.

concept check

What is organizational career management?

Define promotion, transfer, termination, and retirement.

Managing Diversity within the Organization

7 learning goal

As explained in Chapter 1, diversity refers to the blend of people with differences in ages, gender, origin, ethnicity, physical abilities, and sexual orientation. **Managing diversity** means fully utilizing the potential of all employees in a work environment that is free of diversity-related problems such as bigotry, all forms of harassment, employee turnover, absenteeism, low productivity, and poor work quality. A broad objective of managing diversity is the creation of a multicultural organization with a culture that values diversity. To achieve this, the organizational culture and its systems may need to be adapted to improve employee relationships

managing diversity
Fully utilizing the potential of all employees in a work environment.

and equip all employees to be fully productive. Companies that excel in managing diversity have found that it may add up to stronger performance in the marketplace by offering it a competitive advantage.

Diversity as a Competitive Advantage

competitive advantage
A set of unique features of an organization that are perceived by customers and potential customers as significant and superior to the competition.

A **competitive advantage**, also called a *differential advantage,* is a set of unique features of a company and its products that are perceived by the target market (the people or companies that the firm wishes to serve) as significant and superior to those of the competition. As Andrew Grove, former CEO of Intel, says, "You have to understand what it is you are better at than anybody else and mercilessly focus your efforts on it." Competitive advantage is the factor or factors that cause customers to patronize a firm and not the competition. Many things can be sources of a competitive advantage. Better utilization of technology like Intel, more efficient distribution such as Procter & Gamble, lower prices like Wal-Mart, or even a well-known brand name such as Coca-Cola can be a competitive advantage.

Many organizations now recognize diversity as a means of obtaining a competitive advantage. Exhibit 9.8 describes six ways that diversity can help create a competitive advantage.

In order to achieve these sources of competitive advantage, top management must support and be fully committed to diversity. Top managers must be champions of diversity and take a strong stand on the need to improve relationships among people who are different. Managers must put policies in place to keep the organization moving forward. Arthur Martinez, the recently retired CEO of Sears,

Exhibit 9.8 Managing Cultural Diversity Can Provide Competitive Advantage

1. Lower Costs	As organizations become more diverse, the cost of doing a poor job in integrating workers will increase. Those who handle this well will thus create cost advantages over those who don't.
2. Better Hiring	Companies develop reputations on favorability as prospective employers of women and ethnic minorities. Those with the best reputation for managing diversity will win the competition for the best personnel. As the labor pool shrinks and changes composition, this edge will become increasingly important.
3. More Effective Marketing	For multinational organizations, the insight and cultural sensitivity that members with roots in other countries bring to the marketing effort should improve these efforts in important ways. The same rationale applies to marketing to subpopulations within domestic operations.
4. Greater Employee Creativity	Diversity of perspectives and less emphasis on conformity to norms of the past (which characterize the modern approach to management of diversity) should improve the level of creativity.
5. More Effective Problem Solving	Heterogeneity in decision- and problem-solving groups potentially produces better decisions through a wider range of perspectives and more thorough critical analysis of issues.
6. Quicker Adaptation to Change	An implication of the multicultural model for managing diversity is that the system will become less determinant, less standardized, and therefore more fluid. The increased fluidity should create greater flexibility to react to environmental changes (i.e., reactions should be faster and at less cost).

SOURCE: Taylor Cox and Stacy Blake, "Managing Cultural Diversity: Implications for Organizational Competitiveness," *Academy of Management Executive* (1991, Vol. 5, No. 3). Copyright 1991 by Academy of Management. Reproduced with permission of Academy of Management in the format Textbook via Copyright Clearance Center.

was very aggressive about managing diversity. He had the chief diversity executive reporting directly to him. Sears even has a Chairman's Diversity Advisement Council that meets quarterly to work on diversity strategies.

The Best Companies for Managing Diversity

The growing recognition of the importance of diversity in the workforce is exemplified by *Fortune*'s annual list of the "Best Companies for Minorities." To compile the list, company editors examine a variety of factors. They wanted to know not just how diverse their workforce is as a whole, but also whether that diversity extends to the executive suite: How many directors and officers are black, Hispanic, Asian, or Native American? What portion of management? They also looked at compensation: Are bonuses tied to progress on diversity? How many of the 50 highest-paid employees are people of color? And they checked how a company spends its money: Does it use a minority-owned investment firm for financing? Finally, they crunched the numbers and gave each company an overall grade. (For more details, go to **http://www.fortune.com/diversity.**) A recent list of the top ten firms is shown in Exhibit 9.9.

concept check

What is involved in managing diversity?

How does a diverse workplace create a competitive advantage?

LAWS AFFECTING HUMAN RESOURCE MANAGEMENT

8 learning goal

Federal laws help ensure that job applicants and employees are treated fairly and not discriminated against. Hiring, training, and job placement must be unbiased. Promotion and compensation decisions must be based on performance. These laws help all Americans who have talent, training, and the desire to get ahead.

New legislation and the continual interpretation and reinterpretation of existing laws will continue to make the jobs of human resource managers challenging and complicated. In 1999, for example, the National Academy of Sciences reported a link between muscle and skeletal injuries and certain workplace activities, such as lifting. In response, the Occupational Safety and Health Administration (OSHA), a federal agency discussed below, issued new standards for the handling and lifting of objects by employees. Of course, human resource managers must now integrate these standards into their organizations. The key laws that currently affect human resource management are shown in Exhibit 9.10.

Several laws govern wages, pensions, and unemployment compensation. For instance, the Fair Labor Standards Act sets the minimum wage, which is periodically raised by Congress. Many minimum-wage jobs are found in service businesses, such

Exhibit 9.9 | The Top 10 Firms for Managing Diversity

Rank	Company	Location
1	McDonald's	Oak Brook, IL
2	Fannie Mae	Washington, DC
3	Denny's	Spartanburg, SC
4	Union Bank of California	San Francisco, CA
5	Sempra Energy	San Diego, CA
6	Southern California Edison	Rosemead, CA
7	SBC Communications	San Antonio, TX
8	Freddie Mac	McLean, VA
9	PepsiCo	Purchase, NY
10	PNM Resources	Albuquerque, NM

SOURCE: Jonathan Hickman, "America's 50 Best Companies for Minorities," *Fortune* (July 7, 2003), pp. 103–108.

Exhibit 9.10 Laws Impacting Human Resource Management

Law	Purpose	Agency of Enforcement
Social Security Act (1935)	Provides for retirement income and old-age health care	Social Security Administration
Fair Labor Standards Act (1938)	Sets minimum wage, restricts child labor, sets overtime pay	Wage and Hour Division, Department of Labor
Equal Pay Act (1963)	Eliminates pay differentials based on gender	Equal Employment Opportunity Commission
Civil Rights Act (1964), Title VII	Prohibits employment discrimination based on race, color, religion, gender, or national origin	Equal Employment Opportunity Commission
Age Discrimination Act (1967)	Prohibits age discrimination against those over 40 years of age	Equal Employment Opportunity Commission
Occupational Safety and Health Act (1970)	Protects worker health and safety, provides for hazard-free workplace	Occupational Safety and Health Administration
Vietnam Veterans Readjustment Act (1974)	Requires affirmative employment of Vietnam War veterans	Veterans Employment Service, Department of Labor
Employee Retirement Income Security Act (1974)—also called Pension Reform Act	Establishes minimum requirements for private pension plans	Internal Revenue Service, Department of Labor, and Pension Benefit Guaranty Corporation
Pregnancy Discrimination Act (1978)	Treats pregnancy as a disability, prevents employment discrimination based on pregnancy	Equal Employment Opportunity Commission
Immigration Reform and Control Act (1986)	Verifies employment eligibility, prevents employment of illegal aliens	Employment Verification Systems, Immigration and Naturalization Service
Americans with Disabilities Act (1990)	Prohibits employment discrimination based on mental or physical disabilities	Department of Labor
Family and Medical Leave Act (1993)	Requires employers to provide unpaid leave for childbirth, adoption, or illness	Equal Employment Opportunity Commission

as restaurants and car washes. The Pension Reform Act protects the retirement income of employees and retirees. Federal tax laws also affect compensation, including employee profit-sharing and stock purchase plans.

Employers must also be aware of changes to laws concerning employee safety, health, and privacy. The Occupational Safety and Health Act requires employers to provide a workplace free of health and safety hazards. For instance, manufacturers must require employees working on loading docks to wear steel-toed shoes so their feet won't be injured if materials are dropped. Drug and AIDS testing are also governed by federal laws.

Another employee law that continues to strongly affect the work of human resource managers is the Americans with Disabilities Act. To be considered disabled, a person must have a physical or mental impairment that greatly limits one or more major life activities. More than 54 million Americans fall into this category. Employers may not discriminate against disabled persons. They must make "reasonable accommodations" so that qualified disabled employees can perform the job, unless doing so would cause "undue hardship" for the business. Altering work schedules, modifying equipment so a wheelchair-bound person can use it, and making buildings accessible by ramps and elevators are considered reasonable. Two companies often praised for their efforts to hire the disabled are McDonald's and DuPont.

The Family and Medical Leave Act went into effect in 1993. The law applies to employers with 50 or more employees. It requires these employers to provide unpaid leave of up to 12 weeks during any 12-month period to workers who have been employed for at least a year and work a minimum of 25 hours a week. The reasons for the leave include the birth or adoption of a child; the serious illness of a child, spouse, or parent; or a serious illness that prevents the worker from doing the job. Upon return, the employee must be given her or his old job back. The worker cannot collect unemployment compensation while on leave. A company can deny leave to a salaried employee in the highest-paid 10 percent of its workforce, if letting the worker take leave would create a "serious injury" for the firm.

The state of California passed a paid family leave bill that became effective July 1, 2004. At that time nongovernmental employees become eligible for up to six weeks of paid leave, or Family Temporary Disability Insurance (FTDI) benefits, over a 12-month period. Numerous conditions are attached to paid leave eligibility, but workers will be able to receive as much as 55 percent of normal take-home pay, up to a maximum of $728 per week.[10]

The Role of Government Agencies in Human Resource Management

Several federal agencies oversee employment, safety, compensation, and related areas. OSHA sets workplace safety and health standards, provides safety training, and inspects places of work (assembly plants, construction sites, and warehouse facilities, for example) to determine employer compliance with safety regulations.

The Wage and Hour Division of the Department of Labor enforces the federal minimum-wage law and overtime provisions of the Fair Labor Standards Act. Employers covered by this law must pay certain employees a premium rate of pay (or time and one-half) for all hours worked beyond 40 in one week.

The Equal Employment Opportunity Commission (EEOC) was created by the 1964 Civil Rights Act. It is one of the most influential agencies responsible for enforcing employment laws. The EEOC has three basic functions: processing discrimination complaints, issuing written regulations, and information gathering and dissemination.

In processing discrimination complaints, the EEOC follows a three-step process:

- *Investigation.* An applicant or employee who thinks that he or she has been discriminated against begins the process by filing a complaint with the EEOC. The EEOC then notifies the company that a complaint has been filed, and the company becomes responsible for ensuring that any records relating to the complaint are kept safe. The EEOC usually finds itself with a backlog, so it may take up to two years to begin investigating the complaint.
- *Conciliation.* If the EEOC finds that an EEO law was probably violated, it attempts to resolve the case through conciliation. Conciliation consists of negotiation among the three parties involved: the complainant, the employer, and the EEOC. The goal of conciliation is to reach a fair settlement while avoiding a trial.

- *Litigation.* If conciliation is not possible, the EEOC can choose between two courses of action. The EEOC does not have the power to compel an employer to pay compensation or any other kind of damages; this can be done only as a result of a court's decision. Because pursuing a lawsuit is very expensive, the EEOC takes this course of action in only a relatively small percentage of cases. If the EEOC chooses not to pursue the case, it issues a right-to-sue letter to the complainant, who is then free to pursue court action with the blessing (if not the financial or legal support) of the EEOC.

Each year, the EEOC receives approximately 80,000 complaints from employees. The monetary benefits that the EEOC won for employees has grown substantially during the past 10 years. Large monetary settlements often occur when the EEOC files a class action suit against an employer. In a class action lawsuit, a group of similar employees (i.e., a "class") asserts that all members of an employee class suffered due to an employer's unfair policies and practices. For example, the $34 million paid by Mitsubishi Motor Manufacturing to settle several sexual harassment cases was distributed to nearly 500 former and current female employees (in addition to the lawyers). Also, Sears, Motorola, and AT&T have had to make large back-pay awards and to offer special training to minority employees after the courts found they had been discriminated against.

The Office of Federal Contract Compliance Programs (OFCCP) oversees firms with U.S. government contracts to make sure that applicants and employees get fair treatment. A big part of its job is to review federal contractors' affirmative action programs. Employers set up **affirmative action programs** to expand job opportunities for women and minorities. In the case of a major violation, the OFCCP can recommend cancellation of the firm's government contract.

affirmative action programs
Programs established by organizations to expand job opportunities for women and minorities.

Making Affirmative Action Work

Many firms have appointed an affirmative action officer to help ensure that they comply with antidiscrimination laws. At firms such as Coca-Cola, Snap-on Tools, Hilton Hotels, and the Burlington Northern-Santa Fe Railroad, the affirmative action officer makes sure that job applicants and employees get fair treatment. He or she often reports directly to the company president rather than to the vice president of human resources. Affirmative action officers watch for signs of *adverse impact,* or unfair treatment of certain classes of employees. **Protected classes** are the specific groups (women, African Americans, Native Americans, and others) who have legal protection against employment discrimination.

protected classes
The specific groups who have legal protection against employment discrimination; include women, African Americans, Native Americans, and others.

One example of adverse impact is a job qualification that tends to weed out more female applicants than male applicants. Suppose that an airline automatically rules out anyone under five feet seven inches tall who wants to be a pilot. Many more female applicants than male applicants would be rejected because women tend to be shorter than men. But height has nothing to do with a pilot's ability, so this height requirement would be discriminatory.

The overall affirmative action record of the past decade has been mixed. The employment of women in professional occupations continues to grow, but minority representation among professionals has been slow to increase, even though professional jobs have been among the fastest-growing areas. Technical jobs have the most equitable utilization rates of minorities. As the college enrollment and completion rates of racial and ethnic minority groups increase, the American workforce will be significantly more diverse. By 2005, Hispanics will be the largest minority population in the United States.[11]

concept check

What are the key federal laws affecting employment?

List and describe the functions of the two federal agencies that enforce employment discrimination laws.

What is affirmative action?

Trends in Human Resource Management

9 learning goal

Protecting whistleblowers, the growth of minority recruiting, proactive management of diversity, advancing technology, and global competition are driving the trends in human resource management in the 21st century.

Protecting Whistleblowers

An employee "blows the whistle" when he or she discloses some wrongdoing and/or illegal behavior or practice committed by another person in the firm. Some companies have an "ethics" hotline that can be used to make this disclosure, or someone can report misconduct to legal authorities, or even the news media. If the reported wrongdoing is investigated and corrective action taken, the whistleblower has benefited the organization. On the other hand, the whistleblower could suffer if a higher authority in the organization retaliates against the whistleblower for reporting the improper behavior.

In recent years whistleblowers, such as Sherron Watkins at Enron and Cynthia Cooper at Worldcom, have received national attention for their reports of illegal executive behavior. While these whistleblowers did the correct thing, they brought considerable attention, some of it negative, to themselves. Some states have passed laws in recent years that protect whistleblowers from employer retaliation. A federal statute not only protects a whistleblower who reports corruption, fraud, or financial mismanagement by a federal contracting firm, but also rewards the whistleblower with a portion of the funds associated with the mismanagement. Recently many firms have developed a whistleblower policy that provides encouragement and protection to an employee who reveals misconduct.

The Growth in Minority Recruiting

Progressive firms today have moved far beyond government mandates for hiring minorities. These organizations realize that diversity is necessary to understand and meet the needs of their customers, and diversity is an important source of competitive advantage. Nowhere is this more true than in the field of retailing.

At Home Depot's Villager's Hardware in Elizabeth, New Jersey, general store manager Tony Gonzalez discusses a popular "langosta" dish with a customer perusing food processors. Gonzalez and his customer are natives of Puerto Rico and both prepare and enjoy the island's popular foods. Gonzalez thinks a certain model would be best for the job; a passing associate, one of many bilingual employees, agrees. The customer leaves the store with the appliance and a seafood recipe.

Such in-store interactions are becoming more commonplace throughout the retail industry as companies realize they need to establish and exploit the cultural and lingual bonds between their store associates and shoppers. What's more, an increasing number of retailers are adding diversity to their corporate ranks, from buyers to the corner office, in an effort to better understand the needs of the fastest-growing segment of their customer base—the ethnic shopper.

Seventy percent of customers at the Villager's Hardware store in Elizabeth, New Jersey, are Hispanic, almost seven times the national average. The appointment of Gonzalez, an 18-year veteran of mainland U.S. retailing, is neither coincidence nor blind allegiance to political correctness. Rather, at Home Depot and other big chains, aggressive recruitment of Hispanic and African American management is becoming an increasingly effective means of gaining market share and improving profit performance. It is also a way to take the first commandment in retailing a step further: Know thy customer by becoming that customer.

Proactive Management of Diversity

In the past, most companies responded to government legislation related to diversity, such as affirmative action, out of necessity to meet federal guidelines. Organizations were reactive rather than proactive. Today there is a decided trend toward proactive management of diversity. Companies are creating initiatives to build effective multicultural organizations. This requires construction of an environment and culture in which all members can excel. Companies accomplish this by hiring and promoting people who truly believe in the firm's diversity values, reinforcing these values in performance and evaluation systems and educating all employees about diversity issues.

Being proactive also means blending the community with the organization. This involves incorporating diversity into major committees, and implementing affirmative action, education, and targeted career-development programs. ExxonMobil, IBM, Qwest, and McDonald's have started special career-development programs that are monitored and measured for members of minority groups. A proactive company must also minimize interpersonal and intergroup conflicts related to group identity and must promote understanding of cultural differences. At companies like Baxter Health Care, Coca-Cola, NationsBank, Levi Strauss, IBM, Merck, Corning, and Procter & Gamble, this goal is addressed through conflict management and resolution, adherence to Equal Employment Opportunity guidelines, and diversity training.

Advancing Technology

Advances in information technology have greatly improved the efficiency of handling many transaction-based aspects (payroll and expense reimbursement) of employee services. Technology enables instant communication of human resource data from far-flung branches to the home office. Ease of communication has also led many companies to outsource some or all of their human resource functions. **Outsourcing** is the assignment of various functions, like human resources, accounting, or legal work, to outside organizations. The National Geographic Society outsourced all of its employee benefits programs to Workforce Solutions. Without computer databases and networks, such outsourcing would be impossible.

outsourcing
The assignment of various functions, such as human resources, accounting, or legal work, to outside organizations.

telecommuting
An arrangement in which employees work at home and are linked to the office by phone, fax, and computer.

Technology has also made telecommuting a reality for millions of workers. **Telecommuting** is now commonplace. In this arrangement, employees work at home and are linked to the office by phone, fax, and computer. At Cisco Systems, a computer-networking giant based in San Jose, California, telecommuters have improved their productivity by up to 25 percent, while the company has saved about $1 million on overhead and retained key employees who might otherwise have left. What's more, those who have traded suits for sweats say they love setting their own schedules, skipping rush hour, spending more time with their kids, and working at least part-time in comfortable surroundings. Telecommuting grows when the economy is strong because employers must do what they can to attract the best and brightest workers. Telecommuting also offers environmental and political benefits as companies respond to Clean Air Act provisions aimed at reducing traffic. Furthermore, it enables businesses to cut real estate costs by creating "hoteling" arrangements in which, say, 10 people share a single cubicle on an as-needed basis.

Global Competition

As more firms "go global," they are sending an increasing number of employees overseas. Procter & Gamble, IBM, Caterpillar, Microsoft, Federal Express, and many others have tens of thousands of employees abroad. Such companies face somewhat different human resource management issues than do firms that operate only within the United States. For example, criteria for selecting employees include not only technical skills and knowledge of the business, but also the ability to adapt to a local culture and to learn a foreign language.

Once an individual is selected for an overseas assignment, language training and cultural orientation become important. Salary and benefits, relocation expenses, and special allowances (housing, transportation, and education) can increase human resource costs by as much as three times normal annual costs. After an overseas assignment of one year or more, the firm must repatriate the employee, or bring the individual back home. Job placement and career progression frequently become issues during repatriation because the firm has changed and the employee's old job may no longer exist. After spending a year in Brussels, Belgium, Mike Rocca, a financial executive with Honeywell, experienced "reentry shock" when he returned to his corporate office in Minneapolis and saw how new software had changed accounting.

concept check

Why are companies spending resources on minority recruiting?

Describe how advances in communication technology make outsourcing and telecommuting possible.

What issues does "going global" present for human resource management?

Great Ideas to Use Now

It's never too early to start thinking about your career in business. No, you don't have to decide today, but it's important to decide fairly soon how you will spend your life's work. A very practical reason for doing so is that it will save you a lot of time and money. We have seen too many juniors, seniors, or even graduate students who aren't really sure what they want to do upon graduation. The longer you wait to choose a profession, the more credit hours you may have to take in your new field and the longer it will be before you start earning real money.

A second reason to choose a career field early is that you can get a part-time or summer job and "test-drive" the profession. If it's not for you, you will find out very quickly.

Your school placement office can give you plenty of information about various careers in business. We also describe many career opportunities at the end of each part of this text. Another source of career information is the Internet. Go to any search engine, such as Excite or Lycos, and enter "careers in business," or narrow your search to a specific area such as management or marketing.

Career planning will not end when you find your first professional job. It is a life-long process that ends only with retirement. Your career planning will include conducting a periodic self-assessment of your strengths and weaknesses, gathering information about other jobs both within the firm and externally, learning about other industries, and setting career goals for yourself. You must always think about your future in business.

Human Resources Decision Making

During your professional career in business, you will likely have the opportunity to become a manager. As a manager, you will have to make many human resource decisions, including hiring, firing, promoting, giving a pay raise, sending an employee to a training program, disciplining a worker, approving a college tuition reimbursement request, and reassigning an employee to a different job. In short, you will be involved in virtually every human resource decision or activity affecting the employees you manage. Always treat people as you wish to be treated when making human resource decisions. Be fair, be honest, offer your experience and advice, and communicate frequently with your employees. If you follow this simple advice, you will be richly rewarded in your own career.

Try It Now

Make telecommuting work for you. Maybe a part-time job might require too much driving time. Perhaps there are simply no jobs in the immediate area that suit you. Try telecommuting right now. Is telecommuting for you? Many people are more satisfied with their personal and family lives than before they started working at home. But telecommuting is not for every person or every job, and you'll need plenty of self-discipline to make it work for you. Ask yourself if you can perform your duties without close supervision. Also, think about whether you would miss your coworkers. If you decide to give telecommuting a try, consider these suggestions to maintain your productivity:

- *Set ground rules with your family.* Spouses and small children have to understand that even though you're in the house, you are busy earning a living. It's fine to throw in a few loads of laundry or answer the door when the plumber comes. It's another thing to take the kids to the mall or let them play games on your office PC.
- *Clearly demarcate your work space by using a separate room with a door you can shut.* Let your family know that, emergencies excepted, the space is off-limits during working hours.
- *If you have small children, you may want to arrange for child care during your working hours.*
- *Stay in touch with your coworkers and professional colleagues.* Go into the office from time to time for meetings to stay connected.

Above all, you can make telecommuting work for you by being productive. Doing your job well whether on-site or telecommuting will help assure you of a bright future.

Looking Ahead at Pepsico

Pepsico will continue to reap the benefits of a diverse workforce. As Pepsico discovered, managing diversity and creating a harmonious work environment reduces workplace grievances and employee turnover, thus lowering costs. Pepsico now has developed a reputation for valuing diversity which enables it to attract the very best workers. Also, a diverse workforce brings a variety of points of view and creativity to the firm. New ways of thinking can solve old, unsolvable problems. Diversity brings less rigidity to the organization structure which enables Pepsico to more quickly adapt to change. Pepsico serves a diverse worldwide marketplace. Because it has a diverse workforce, it can better relate to the many different cultures that buy Pepsico drinks and snacks.

Because Pepsico has a proactive diversity policy, the company falls well within diversity guidelines provided by the federal government. Federal laws, such as the 1964 Civil Rights Act, should be viewed not as something that should be met because they are required. Instead, exceeding the minimum standards can help create a competitive advantage.

Customer Satisfaction and Quality

Employees provide most, if not all, of a firm's customer service. Usually, employees who are more experienced can provide better customer service and solve more difficult customer service problems. More experienced employees are normally persons who have worked for a firm for an extended period of time. Accordingly, employee retention is important in support of high-quality products and customer service. If an organization experiences high employee retention, or low employee turnover, it also minimizes its staffing and training costs because it doesn't need to hire as many people each year.

Nursing is a profession for which retention is a huge factor because of acute nursing shortages that have been forecast for the next 15 to 20 years. In a survey by the University of Washington School of Nursing, it was determined that retention of nurses increased with greater employee teamwork, lowering of patient–nurse ratios, and rewarding nurses with more decision-making authority. Higher pay also had a positive impact on retention.[12] Would you prefer to receive care from an experienced nurse who had worked for several years at the hospital where you might be a patient, or from an inexperienced nurse who is completing his or her first week of work?

Summary of Learning Goals

1 What is the human resource management process, and how are human resource needs determined?

The human resource management process consists of a sequence of activities that begins with job analysis and HR planning; progresses to employee recruitment and selection; then focuses on employee training, performance appraisal, and compensation; and ends when the employee leaves the organization.

Creating a strategy for meeting human resource needs is called human resource planning, which begins with job analysis. Job analysis is a process for studying a job to determine its tasks and duties for setting pay, determining employee job performance, specifying hiring requirements, and designing training programs. Information from the job analysis is used to prepare a job description, which lists the tasks and responsibilities of the job. A job specification describes the skills, knowledge, and abilities a person needs to fill the job described in the job description. By examining the human resource demand forecast and the internal supply forecast, human resource professionals can determine if the company faces a personnel surplus or shortage.

2 How do human resource managers recruit and select qualified applicants?

When a job vacancy occurs, most firms begin by trying to fill the job from within. If a suitable internal candidate is not available, the firm begins an external search. Firms use local media to recruit nontechnical, unskilled, and nonsupervisory workers. To locate highly trained recruits, employers use college recruiters, executive search firms, job fairs, and company Web sites to promote job openings.

Typically, an applicant submits an application, or résumé, and then receives a short, structured interview. If an applicant makes it past the initial screening, he or she may be asked to take an aptitude, personality, or skills test. The next step is the selection interview, which is an in-depth discussion of the applicant's work experience, skills and abilities, education, and career interests.

3 What types of training and development do organizations offer their employees?

Training and development programs are designed to increase employees' knowledge, skills, and abilities in order to foster job performance improvements. Formal training (usually classroom in nature and off-the-job) takes place shortly after being hired. Development programs prepare employees to assume positions of increasing authority and responsibility. Job rotation, executive education programs, mentoring, and special-project assignments are examples of employee development programs.

4

How are performance appraisals used to evaluate employees' performance?

A performance appraisal compares an employee's actual performance with the expected performance. Performance appraisals serve several purposes but are typically used to determine an employee's compensation, training needs, and advancement opportunities.

5

What are the different methods for compensating employees?

Direct pay is the hourly wage or monthly salary paid to an employee. In addition to the base wage or salary, direct pay may include bonuses and profit shares. Indirect pay consists of various benefits and services. Some benefits are required by law: unemployment compensation, worker's compensation, and Social Security. Others are voluntarily made available by employers to employees. These include paid vacations and holidays, pensions, health and other insurance products, employee wellness programs, and college tuition reimbursement.

6

What is organizational career management?

Organizational career management is the facilitation of employee job changes, including promotions, transfers, layoffs, and retirements. A promotion is an upward move with more authority, responsibility, and pay. A transfer is a horizontal move in the organization. When a person is downgraded to a position with less responsibility, it is a demotion. A layoff is a temporary separation arranged by the employer, usually when business is slow. A termination is a permanent separation arranged by the employer. A resignation is a voluntary separation by the employee. Retirement is a permanent separation that ends one's career.

7

Why does a diverse workforce lead to stronger performance in the marketplace?

Human resource managers should strive to create a culture that values diversity. Managing diversity means utilizing the full potential of all of the employees in the workforce. The benefits of a diverse workforce include lower costs, better hiring, more effective marketing, greater creativity, more effective problem solving, and quicker adaptation to change. These factors can give the organization a competitive advantage, a unique set of features considered superior to those of the competition.

8

What are the key laws and federal agencies affecting human resource management?

A number of federal laws (listed in Exhibit 9.10) affect human resource management. Federal law prohibits discrimination based on age, race, gender, color, national origin, religion, or disability. The Americans with Disabilities Act bans discrimination against disabled workers and requires employers to change the work environment to accommodate the disabled. The Family and Medical Leave Act requires employers, with certain exceptions, to provide employees up to 12 weeks of unpaid leave a year. The leave can be for the birth or adoption of a child or due to serious illness of a family member.

Federal agencies that deal with human resource administration are the Equal Employment Opportunity Commission (EEOC), the Occupational Safety and

Health Administration (OSHA), the Office of Federal Contract Compliance Programs (OFCCP), and the Wage and Hour Division of the Department of Labor. The EEOC and OFCCP are primary agencies for enforcement of employment discrimination laws; OSHA enforces safety regulation; and the Wage and Hour Division enforces the minimum wage and related laws. Many companies employ affirmative action and safety officers to ensure compliance with antidiscrimination and workplace safety laws.

9

What trends are affecting human resource management?

Whistleblowers report wrongdoing or illegal behavior in organizations. The actions of these people have brought down companies like Enron and WorldCom. New laws have been passed to protect whistleblowers from retaliation.

Today more and more companies are actively recruiting minorities. A diverse workforce often leads to increased market share and profits. Organizations are becoming proactive in their management of diversity. Companies are creating initiatives to build effective multicultural organizations.

Technology continues to improve the efficiency of human resource management. It also enables firms to outsource many functions done internally in the past. Telecommuting is becoming increasingly popular among employers and employees. As more firms enter the international market, they are sending an increasing number of employees overseas. In addition to normal job requirements, selected workers must have the ability to adapt to a local culture and perhaps to learn a foreign language.

Preparing for Tomorrow's Workplace

1. Would an overseas job assignment be good for your career development? If you think so, what country would you prefer to live and work in for two or three years, and what type of job would you like to have in that country?
2. The fringe benefit package of many employers includes numerous voluntarily provided items such as health insurance, life insurance, pension plan, paid vacations, tuition reimbursement, employee price discounts on products of the firm, and paid sick leave. At your age, what are the three or four most important benefits? Why? Twenty years from now, what do you think will be your three or four most important benefits? Why?
3. As a corporate recruiter, you must know how to screen prospective employees. The Integrity Center Web site at **http://www.integctr.com** offers a brief tutorial on pre-employment screening, a glossary of key words and phrases, and related information. Prepare a short report that tells your assistant how to go about this process.
4. How important is training likely to be in the future? What changes that are facing organizations will increase the importance of training?
5. Select two teams of five. One team will take the position that employees are simply a business expense to be managed. The second team will argue that employees are an asset to be developed to enable the firm to gain a competitive advantage. The remainder of the class will judge which team provided the stronger argument.

Working the Net

1. Go to the Monster Board at **http://content.monster.com/resume/** to learn how to prepare an electronic résumé that will get results. Develop a list of rules for creating effective electronic résumés, and revise your own résumé into electronic format.

KEY TERMS

affirmative action programs 294
apprenticeship 281
competitive advantage 290
contingent workers 275
corporate open house 277
demotion 288
employee orientation 281
fringe benefits 285
human resource (HR) planning 273
human resource management 272
job analysis 274
job description 274
job fair 277
job rotation 281
job specification 274
layoff 288
managing diversity 289
mentoring 281
on-the-job training 281
outsourcing 296
performance appraisal 282
programmed instruction 282
promotion 287
protected classes 294
recruitment 276
resignation 288
retirement 289
selection 277
selection interview 279
separation 288
telecommuting 296
termination 288
training and development 280
transfer 287
vestibule training 282

2. Working as a contingent employee can help you explore your career options. Visit the Manpower Web site at **http://www.manpower.com**, and search for several types of jobs that interest you. What are the advantages of being a temporary worker? What other services does Manpower offer job seekers?
3. You've been asked to give a speech about the current status of affirmative action and equal employment to your company's managers. Starting with the Web site of the American Association for Affirmative Action (**http://www.affirmativeaction.org**) and its links to related sites, research the topic and prepare an outline for your talk. Include current legislation and recent court cases.
4. Web-based training is becoming popular at many companies as a way to bring a wider variety of courses to more people at lower costs. The Web-Based Training Information Center site at **http://www.webbasedtraining.com** provides a good introduction. Learn about the basics of online training at its Primer page. Then link to the Resources section, try a demo, and explore other areas that interest you. Prepare a brief report on your findings, including the pros and cons of using the Web for training, to present to your class.
5. Your 250-employee company is considering outsourcing some of its HR functions, because it wants to offer a wider range of services. You've been asked to prepare a report on whether it should proceed and if so, how. Visit BuyerZone.com, **http://www.buyerzone.com**, click on HR Outsourcing, and then HR Outsourcing Buyer's Guide, to learn more about why companies are going outside for this important function and the advantages and disadvantages of doing so. Summarize your finding and make a recommendation. Then use a search engine to locate two to three firms that offer HR outsourcing services. Compare them and recommend one, explaining the reasons for your choice.

CREATIVE THINKING CASE

Identity Theft and Corporate Responsibility

Identity theft is rapidly becoming a widespread problem with tens of thousands of persons each year becoming victims. In some cases the crime, now a felony under the federal Identity Theft and Assumption Deterrence Act of 1998, originates with one or more employees who have access to personal employee or customer information (name, address, birthdates, and possibly Social Security numbers) and steal and use it for personal gain. The Federal Trade Commission's Identity Theft Data Clearinghouse received approximately 85,000 identity theft complaints in 2001.

In one case, an employee at Ligand Pharmaceuticals Inc. in San Diego found a box of personnel records of several dozen former workers of a firm (Glycomed Inc.) Ligand had acquired in 1995. The Ligand employee and some of her friends used information from these former Glycomed workers to obtain numerous credit cards and cell phone accounts, and even rented three apartments. The credit cards were used to purchase about $100,000 in products. It took several months before most of the victims became aware that their identities had been stolen and for them to begin to correct their credit histories and extricate themselves from the many fraudulent transactions. According to Beth Givens of the Privacy Rights Clearinghouse, a victim of identity theft spends about 175 hours investigating the crime, nearly two years working to correct credit reports, and $800 to $1,000 of various out-of-pocket expenses to restore his or her financial integrity. Unfortunately for Ligand Pharmaceuticals, 14 of the identity theft victims sued the firm and claimed that Ligand had been negligent and had not properly taken care of their personnel records. An out-of-court settlement was reached with Ligand paying a considerable sum of money to the 14 persons along with incurring significant time and resources for legal representation.[13]

Every employer has confidential, or sensitive, information about employees and most private firms have a strict secrecy policy about worker pay and benefits. Nevertheless, numerous persons (payroll clerks, benefits administrators, and the chief human resource officer) may have access to these data for appropriate and legitimate reasons, such as processing insurance claims, direct deposit of expense reimbursements, and managing employee retirement accounts.

CRITICAL THINKING QUESTIONS

1. Who should have access to employee files and sensitive (private) information?
2. How can employers safeguard employee records and prevent identification theft?
3. What action(s) should an employer take against an employee who breeches the HR records system?
4. Should an employee be able to sue his or her employer for unauthorized use of personal and employment data?

Video Case

Nurturing Individuality at Valassis

Who doesn't love a freebie? And your Sunday paper often includes one—a sachet of free shampoo, a miniature box of washing powder, a new kind of toothpaste to try—all brought to you by Valassis Communications, Inc. (**http://www.valassis.com**), a leader in marketing services for over a quarter of a century.

This publicly held company headquartered in Livonia, Michigan, employs 1,300 people across the United States and Canada, and boasts annual sales in excess of $740 million. The company's flagship product is the Free-Standing Insert (FSI), distributed through newspapers to over 57 million households every Sunday.

The FSI booklet contains coupons, refunds, and other promotional items from America's largest packaged-goods companies. Among other Valassis products are the delivery of manufacturers' product samples through Sunday newspapers and the oversight of clients' games and sweepstakes promotions. To expand their existing product base Valassis recently acquired Illinois-based NCH Marketing Services, the premier coupon-processing and promotion information management company in the United States and worldwide.

Valassis sets the standard in its industry for quality, service, reliability, and expertise with its unique corporate philosophy, titled "Change to Grow," which is based on eight fundamental principles:

- Change is good.
- Don't point fingers—solve problems.
- Go—with speed.
- Create positive energy.
- Set the bar high—don't fear failure.
- Be empowered, and be accountable.
- Communicate clearly and openly.
- Stick to fundamentals.

Executives at Valassis believe it is the company's capable and highly motivated employees who are responsible for its competitive advantage in the marketplace. With over 14,000 applicants for approximately 100 annual job openings, Valassis makes sure it hires the right people through a rigorous screening and interview process. Only those applicants most likely to embody and adhere to the principles of the company's "Change to Grow" culture, are considered for a position.

Those fortunate enough to be hired embark on career paths geared to their own unique strengths, talents, and career goals. The company also prefers to promote from within so it invests heavily in employee training, supporting independent continuing education for employees through an educational assistance reimbursement program.

There is also company-run Valassis University, offering a broad spectrum of professional and personal development courses, as well as those covering specific business functions. Employees can work toward a variety of Valassis "degrees" including a Bachelor and Master of Leadership. When it comes to managing its people, there is no doubt that Valassis means business.

CRITICAL THINKING QUESTIONS

1. Why is it advantageous for Valassis Communications to hire employees with abilities and motivation that match the company's Change to Grow culture?
2. How does the Valassis approach to training and development help reinforce the company's culture?
3. Would you like to work for a company like Valassis Communications given its Change to Grow culture? Why or why not?

SOURCE: Adapted from material in the video *Employee Recruitment and Selection: A Study of Valassis Communications;* "The 100 Best Companies to Work for in America," *Fortune,* January 20, 2003, downloaded from http://www.fortune.com; and Valassis Communications corporate Web site http://www.valassis.com, accessed March 17, 2003.

E-Commerce Case

Taco John's Fast Hiring Solution

Like most fast-food operators, Taco John's, a chain of 450 Mexican restaurants located in the West and Midwest, often has trouble with staffing. Fast-food industry turnover rates sometimes hover at 100 percent a year and finding a steady stream of applicants willing to fill low-wage hourly restaurant jobs is challenging. Many potential employees are teenagers who want to work flexible hours.

In the past, Taco John's used classified ads in local newspapers to attract applicants. The company also posted employment information on its corporate Web site. Responses to both recruiting methods, however, usually didn't fully meet staffing needs. Searching for an answer, Julie Horn, Taco John's human resources manager, turned to Youapplyhere.com, a new online recruiting site.

Run by Wyoming-based Online Reporting Services, Youapplyhere.com was created in 2002 to serve the recruiting needs of employers looking for part-time and hourly workers. At the site, job seekers can find a list of local hourly jobs and fill out an online application. In addition to the job seeker's name and contact information, the application asks three key questions: the applicant's age, whether they have U.S. citizenship, and what days and hours they're available to work. Employers, who pay $95 per job listing, can log on to the site and quickly sort applications to find candidates to fill specific time slots.

While there are many other online recruiting Web sites, Online Reporting Services believes its streamlined application process gives it a competitive advantage. "A lot of sites like Monster.com are résumé based, and résumés aren't good for selling yourself for an hourly position," says Brent Hoefler, Online Reporting vice president. "And when you're an employer looking for hourly employees, you're looking for whether they can perform for this job and not so much about their past work experience." Another advantage: Online Reporting is heavily marketing the service to high school students.

Julie Horn tested the site for two months to find employees for six corporate Taco John's stores. "I like the response it's received," she says. "We're receiving 15 to 20 applications a week. We hire a lot of 16- to 19-year-olds who have busy schedules and this site, unlike other Web sites, allows me to filter based on availability to find someone who can work weekends or nights." She's now trying to convince Taco John's 400 franchise restaurants to try out the service.

CRITICAL THINKING QUESTIONS

1. What are the advantages and disadvantages of Youapplyhere.com's streamlined application? Do you think other questions should be included? If so, which ones and why?
2. Are there other demographic groups besides high school students that You applyhere.com should be marketed to? Suggest at least three methods the company can use to attract potential job seekers.
3. Do you think that online recruiting will help solve the turnover problem faced by fast-food restaurants like Taco John's? Why or why not? What other steps should fast-food operators take to cut turnover rates?

SOURCES: Dina Berta, "Q&A: Online Reporting Services President Sees Cost Savings in Web-site Hiring," *Nation's Restaurant News,* March 17, 2003, downloaded from http://www.elibrary.com; Frank Jossi, "Youapplyhere.com Finds Gold in Low-Wage Applicants," *Quick Service Restaurant,* April 10, 2003, downloaded from http://www.qsrmagazine.com; "Online Reporting Service Awarded Contract from Taco John's International," company press release, January 7, 2003, downloaded from http://www.youapplyhere.com.

HOT LINKS ADDRESS BOOK

Does TeamStaff, a professional employer organization, live up to its motto "Simply a better way to employ people"? Find out at
http://www.teamstaff.com

Search the extensive job database of CareerBuilder.com
http://www.careerbuilder.com
for a job in a new city.

Get advice for brushing up your interview skills at the Job Hunting Advice page of the *Wall Street Journal*'s Career site,
http://www.careers.wsj.com

How does the Equal Employment Opportunity Commission promote equal opportunity in employment? Visit
http://www.eeoc.gov
to learn what the agency does.

For the latest news in the human resources field, visit the Web site of the Society for Human Resource Management at
http://www.shrm.org

Interested in a career in human resources? The Student Center in the HR Resources area of the International Public Management Association-Human Resources Web site,
http://www.ipma-hr.org
has valuable tips to point you in the right direction.

Many companies are using the Web to help manage employees. Visit ADP,
http://www.adp.com
to learn how online services can streamline their HR tasks.

Chapter 10

© WALTER HODGES / STONE / GETTY IMAGES

Motivating Employees and Creating Self-Managed Teams

learning goals

1 What are the basic principles of Frederick Taylor's concept of scientific management?
2 What did Elton Mayo's Hawthorne studies reveal about worker motivation?
3 What is Maslow's hierarchy of needs, and how do these needs relate to employee motivation?
4 How are McGregor's Theories X and Y and Ouchi's Theory Z used to explain worker motivation?
5 What are the basic components of Herzberg's motivator–hygiene theory?
6 What three contemporary theories on employee motivation offer insights into improving employee performance?
7 How can managers redesign existing jobs to increase employee motivation and performance?
8 What different types of teams are being used in organizations today?
9 What initiatives are organizations using today to motivate and retain employees?

Getting the Lead Out at UPS

Suppose your job consisted of unloading packages from a truck and placing them on a conveyor belt. After unloading the first package, you unload another and then another. You unload one box every three seconds, 1,200 every hour. This may not sound like a very exciting job. However, it is a job that is essential to United Parcel Service (**http://www.ups.com**), which hires thousands of part-time workers to move millions of packages daily. However, keeping a well-trained workforce motivated was a major problem for UPS.

When Jennifer Shroeger became district manager for UPS in Buffalo, New York, the region was experiencing a 50 percent turnover rate in its part-time employees. This was both costly and disruptive since part-time employees made up half of the Buffalo workforce. Shroeger made attracting, retaining, and motivating a part-time workforce her immediate priority. She addressed the problem by focusing on better hiring and more effective communication and by giving frontline supervisors more of the responsibility for keeping employees motivated.

Specifically, Shroeger changed the "first applicant through the door" hiring practice to targeting people whose own need for a part-time job matched the company's need. Then she identified different groups of employees by age and career stage. By tailoring her communication to each group, she was able to address those areas of concern that really affected each employee. Another initiative was to provide a positive work environment by upgrading the facilities. Employee retention committees were installed to mentor new employees through their initial hiring phase when fears and frustration were at their highest levels. Finally, to increase effectiveness, front-line supervisors were given additional training on how to communicate, listen, and solve problems facing the large and diverse workforce.[1]

Critical Thinking Questions

1. Do the new initiatives at UPS help employees feel more empowered?
2. How do you think these efforts will affect turnover?
3. Do you think that matching the employee's needs with the company's needs will increase an employee's motivation?

Principles of Employee Motivation

People can be a firm's most important resource. They can also be the most challenging resource to manage well. Employees who are motivated and work hard to achieve personal and organizational goals can become a crucial competitive advantage for a firm. The key then is understanding the process of motivation, *what* motivates individuals, and *how* an organization like UPS can create a workplace that allows people to perform to the best of their abilities. Motivation is basically a need-satisfying process. A need is the lack of something, the gap between what is and what one desires. An unsatisfied need pushes (motivates) the individual to pursue behavior that will result in the need being met.

Successful managers help employees to achieve organizational goals and guide workers through the motivation process using the leadership skills discussed in Chapter 7. To succeed, managers must understand human relations, how employees interact with one another, and how managers interact with employees to improve effectiveness. Human relations skills include the ability to motivate, lead, communicate, build morale, and teach others. This chapter presents the traditional theories on human motivation and the modern application of these theories. We also explore the use of teams in creating and maintaining a motivated workforce.

The Evolution of Motivation Theory

How can managers and organizations promote enthusiastic job performance, high productivity, and job satisfaction? Many studies of human behavior in organizations have contributed to our current understanding of these issues. A look at the evolution of management theory and research shows how managers have arrived at the practices used today to manage human behavior in the workplace. A sampling of the most influential of these theorists and research studies are discussed in this section.

Frederick Taylor's Scientific Management

1 learning goal

scientific management
A system of management developed by Frederick W. Taylor and based on four principles: developing a scientific approach for each element of a job, scientifically selecting and training workers, encouraging cooperation between workers and managers, and dividing work and responsibility between management and workers according to who can better perform a particular task.

One of the most influential figures of the *classical era* of management, which lasted from about 1900 to the mid-1930s, was Frederick W. Taylor, a mechanical engineer sometimes called the "father of **scientific management.**" Taylor's approach to improved performance was based on economic incentives and the premise that there is "one best way" to perform any job. As a manager at the Midvale and Bethlehem Steel companies in Philadelphia in the early 1900s, Taylor was frustrated at the inefficiency of the laborers working in the mills.

Convinced that productivity could be improved, Taylor studied the individual jobs in the mill and redesigned the equipment and the methods used by workers. Taylor timed each job with a stopwatch and broke down every task into separate movements. He then prepared an instruction sheet telling exactly how each job should be done, how much time it should take, and what motions and tools should be used. Taylor's ideas led to dramatic increases in productivity in the steel mills and resulted in the development of four basic principles of scientific management:

1. Develop a scientific approach for each element of a person's job.
2. Scientifically select, train, teach, and develop workers.
3. Encourage cooperation between workers and managers so that each job can be accomplished in a standard, scientifically determined way.
4. Divide work and responsibility between management and workers according to who is better suited to each task.

Employers of factory workers in the early 1900s applied scientific methods to improve productivity. During this classical era of management, employers believed performance was motivated only by economic incentives.

© MINNESOTA HISTORICAL SOCIETY / CORBIS

Taylor published his ideas in *The Principles of Scientific Management.* His pioneering work vastly increased production efficiency and contributed to the specialization of labor and the assembly-line method of production. Taylor's approach is still being used nearly a century later in companies such as United Parcel Service (UPS), where industrial engineers maximize efficiency by carefully studying every step of the delivery process looking for the quickest possible way to deliver packages to customers. Though Taylor's work was a giant step forward in the evolution of management, it had a fundamental flaw in that it assumed that all people are primarily motivated by economic means. Taylor's successors in the study of management found that motivation is much more complex than he envisioned.

The Hawthorne Studies

2 learning goal

The classical era of management was followed by the *human relations era,* which began in the 1930s and focused primarily on how human behavior and relations affect organizational performance. The new era was ushered in by the Hawthorne studies, which changed the way many managers thought about motivation, job productivity, and employee satisfaction. The studies began when engineers at the Hawthorne Western Electric plant decided to examine the effects of varying levels of light on worker productivity—an experiment that might have interested Frederick Taylor. The engineers expected brighter light to lead to increased productivity, but the results showed that varying the level of light in either direction (brighter or dimmer) led to increased output from the experimental group. In 1927, the Hawthorne engineers asked Harvard professor Elton Mayo and a team of researchers to join them in their investigation.

From 1927 to 1932, Mayo and his colleagues conducted experiments on job redesign, length of workday and workweek, length of break times, and incentive plans. The results of the studies indicated that increases in performance were tied to a complex set of employee attitudes. Mayo claimed that both experimental and control groups from the plant had developed a sense of group pride because they had been selected to participate in the studies. The pride that came from this special attention motivated the workers to increase their productivity. Supervisors who allowed the employees to have some control over their situation appeared to

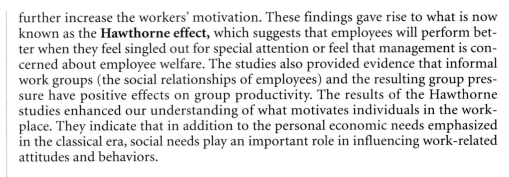

Hawthorne effect
The phenomenon that employees perform better when they feel singled out for attention or feel that management is concerned about their welfare.

further increase the workers' motivation. These findings gave rise to what is now known as the **Hawthorne effect,** which suggests that employees will perform better when they feel singled out for special attention or feel that management is concerned about employee welfare. The studies also provided evidence that informal work groups (the social relationships of employees) and the resulting group pressure have positive effects on group productivity. The results of the Hawthorne studies enhanced our understanding of what motivates individuals in the workplace. They indicate that in addition to the personal economic needs emphasized in the classical era, social needs play an important role in influencing work-related attitudes and behaviors.

Maslow's Hierarchy of Needs

3 learning goal

Another well-known theorist from the behavioral era of management history, psychologist Abraham Maslow, proposed a theory of motivation based on universal human needs. Maslow believed that each individual has a hierarchy of needs, consisting of physiological, safety, social, esteem, and self-actualization needs, as shown in Exhibit 10.1.

Maslow's theory of motivation contends that people act to satisfy their unmet needs. When you're hungry, for instance, you look for and eat food, thus satisfying a basic physiological need. Once a need is satisfied, its importance to the individual diminishes, and a higher level need is more likely to motivate the person.

Exhibit 10.1 | Maslow's Hierarchy of Needs

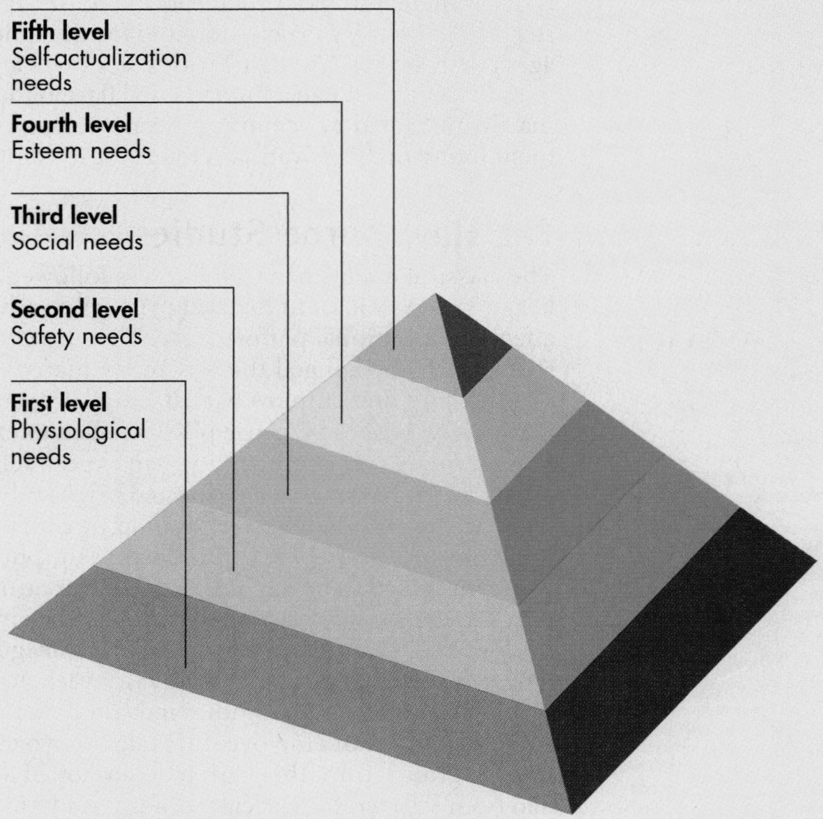

© TERRY MCCORMICK/TAXI / GETTYIMAGES

Telus, a telecommunications company, created a program called Team Machine to recognize and reward performance. The company makes everyone aware of employees who have outstanding performance and who support the company's values and strategies.

Maslow's hierarchy of needs
A theory of motivation developed by Abraham Maslow; holds that humans have five levels of needs and act to satisfy their unmet needs. At the base of the hierarchy are fundamental physiological needs, followed in order by safety, social, esteem, and self-actualization needs.

According to **Maslow's hierarchy of needs,** the most basic human needs are physiological needs, that is, the needs for food, shelter, and clothing. In large part, it is the physiological needs that motivate a person to find a job. People need to earn money to provide food, shelter, and clothing for themselves and their families. Once people have met these basic needs, they reach the second level in Maslow's hierarchy, which is safety needs. People need to feel secure, to be protected from physical harm, and to avoid the unexpected. In work terms, they need job security and protection from work hazards. Companies such as Nucor, Southwest Airlines, AFLAC, and SC Johnson provide their permanent employees the job security they need with their no-layoff policies.[2] When times are good, these companies are careful about bloating the workforce; and when times are bad, they use creative ways to keep the staff working until business improves.

Physiological needs and safety are physical needs. Once these are satisfied, individuals focus on needs that involve relationships with other people. At Maslow's third level are social needs, or needs for belonging (acceptance by others) and for giving and receiving friendship and love. Informal social groups on and off the job help people satisfy these needs. At the fourth level in Maslow's hierarchy are esteem needs, which are needs for the respect of others and for a sense of accomplishment and achievement. Satisfaction of these needs is reflected in feelings of self-worth. Praise and recognition from managers and others in the firm contribute to the sense of self-worth.

Finally, at the highest level in Maslow's hierarchy are self-actualization needs, or needs for fulfillment, for living up to one's potential, and for using one's abilities to the utmost. The Army recruiting slogan "Be all that you can be" describes the human need for self-actualization. Many mid- and upper-level managers, who have satisfied all of the lower-order needs, are driven by very personal self-actualization goals. For instance, look at Paul Allen, one of the founders of the Microsoft Corporation. Along with the other founders of Microsoft, Allen is a billionaire several times over. Although he has no financial need to work, Allen felt he had more to give professionally to the Seattle community. He maintains a Senior Strategy Advisor position at Microsoft. He also owns a venture-capital firm, an NFL football franchise, and an NBA basketball team. Given these diverse holdings, what would motivate Allen to invest in his latest venture, The Experience Music Project? Allen's motivation was his love of music and desire to share this love and his financial good fortune with others.[3] To do this, Allen invested millions to create the interactive music museum. The museum not only houses Allen's own extensive personal collection of Jimi Hendrix memorabilia, but also provides other visitors a way to experience, appreciate, and develop their own love of music.

Managers who accept Maslow's ideas attempt to improve employee motivation by modifying organizational and managerial practices to increase the likelihood that employees will meet all levels of needs. Maslow's theory has also helped managers understand that it is hard to motivate people by appealing to already satisfied needs. For instance, overtime pay may not motivate employees who earn a high wage and value their leisure time.

Maslow's theory is not without criticism. Maslow claimed that a higher-level need was not activated until a lower-level need was met. He also claimed that a satisfied need is not a motivator. A farmer who has plenty to eat is not motivated by more food (the physiological hunger need). Research has not verified these principles in any strict sense. The theory also concentrates on moving up the hierarchy without fully addressing moving back down the hierarchy. Despite these limitations, Maslow's ideas are very helpful for understanding the needs of people at work and for determining what can be done to satisfy them.

McGregor's Theories X and Y

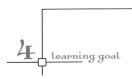

4 learning goal

Theory X
A management style, formulated by Douglas McGregor, that is based on a pessimistic view of human nature and assumes that the average person dislikes work, will avoid it if possible, prefers to be directed, avoids responsibility, and wants security above all.

Theory Y
A management style, formulated by Douglas McGregor, that is based on a relatively optimistic view of human nature; assumes that the average person wants to work, accepts responsibility, is willing to help solve problems, and can be self-directed and self-controlled.

Douglas McGregor, one of Maslow's students, influenced the study of motivation with his formulation of two contrasting sets of assumptions about human nature—Theory X and Theory Y.

The **Theory X** management style is based on a pessimistic view of human nature and assumes the following:

- The average person dislikes work and will avoid it if possible.
- Because people don't like to work, they must be controlled, directed, or threatened with punishment to get them to make an effort.
- The average person prefers to be directed, avoids responsibility, is relatively unambitious, and wants security above all else.

This view of people suggests that managers must constantly prod workers to perform and must closely control their on-the-job behavior. Theory X managers tell people what to do, are very directive, like to be in control, and show little confidence in employees. They often foster dependent, passive, and resentful subordinates.

In contrast, a **Theory Y** management style is based on a more optimistic view of human nature and assumes the following:

- Work is as natural as play or rest. People want to and can be self-directed and self-controlled and will try to achieve organizational goals they believe in.
- Workers can be motivated using positive incentives and will try hard to accomplish organizational goals if they believe they will be rewarded for doing so.
- Under proper conditions, the average person not only accepts responsibility but seeks it out. Most workers have a relatively high degree of imagination and creativity and are willing to help solve problems.

Managers who operate on Theory Y assumptions recognize individual differences and encourage workers to learn and develop their skills. An administrative assistant might be given the responsibility for generating a monthly report. The reward for doing so might be recognition at a meeting, a special training class to enhance computer skills, or a pay increase. In short, the Theory Y approach builds on the idea that worker and organizational interests are the same. The SAS Institute has successfully created a corporate culture based on Theory Y assumptions. With a 4 percent turnover rate and a recruitment ratio of 200 applicants for each open position, the success of this culture is evident. Human resource director, Jeff Chambers, claims that employee retention has more to do with the company's environment than any other factor: "The two key concepts are flexibility and trust. We have a flat organizational structure so usually an employee is no more than four to five levels away from the CEO. And we treat people like adults and allow them to do their jobs. We hire hard and then manage easy. Just leave them alone and trust them to do the right thing for the company."[4]

Theory Z

Theory Z
A theory developed by William Ouchi that combines U.S. and Japanese business practices by emphasizing long-term employment, slow career development, moderate specialization, group decision making, individual responsibility, relatively informal control over the employee, and concern for workers.

William Ouchi (pronounced O Chee), a management scholar at the University of California, Los Angeles, has proposed a theory that combines U.S. and Japanese business practices. He calls it **Theory Z.** Exhibit 10.2 compares the traditional U.S. and Japanese management styles with the Theory Z approach. Theory Z emphasizes long-term employment, slow career development, moderate specialization, group decision making, individual responsibility, relatively informal control over the employee, and concern for workers. Theory Z has many Japanese elements. But it reflects U.S. cultural values.

In the past decade, admiration for Japanese management philosophy that centers on creating long-term relationships has declined. The cultural beliefs of groupthink, not taking risks, and employees not thinking for themselves are passé.

Exhibit 10.2 | Differences in Management Approaches

Factor	Traditional U.S. management	Japanese management	Theory Z (combination of U.S. and Japanese management)
Length of employment	Relatively short term; worker subject to layoffs if business is bad	Lifetime; layoffs never used to reduce costs	Long term but not necessarily lifetime; layoffs "inappropriate"; stable, loyal workforce; improved business conditions don't require new hiring and training
Rate of evaluation and promotion	Relatively rapid	Relatively slow	Slow by design; manager thoroughly trained and evaluated
Specialization in a functional area	Considerable; worker acquires expertise in single functional area	Minimal; worker acquires expertise in organization instead of functional areas	Moderate; all experience various functions of the organization and have a sense of what's good for the firm rather than for a single area
Decision making	On individual basis	Input from all concerned parties	Group decision making for better decisions and easier implementation
Responsibility for success or failure	Assigned to individual	Shared by group	Assigned to individual
Control by manager	Very explicit and formal	More implicit and informal	Relatively informal but with explicit performance measures
Concern for workers	Focuses on work-related aspects of worker's life	Extends to whole life of worker	Is relatively concerned with worker's whole life, including the family

SOURCE: Based on information from Jerry D. Johnson, Austin College. Dr. Johnson was a research assistant for William Ouchi.

Such conformity has limited Japanese competitiveness in the global marketplace. Today there is a realization that Japanese firms need to be more proactive and nimble in order to prosper.

The average profitability of a Japanese company on the Tokyo Stock Exchange declined from about 9 percent to 1 percent in the past decade. This is often partially attributed to Japanese management philosophy. Sony, Hitachi, and other big companies are moving away from lifetime employment and now emphasize information disclosure, profitability, and management accountability.

Herzberg's Motivator–Hygiene Theory

5 learning goal

motivating factors
Intrinsic job elements that lead to worker satisfaction.

hygiene factors
Extrinsic elements of the work environment that do not serve as a source of employee satisfaction or motivation.

Another important contribution to our understanding of individual motivation came from Frederick Herzberg's studies, which addressed the question, "What do people really want from their work experience?" In the late 1950s Herzberg surveyed numerous employees to find out what particular work elements made them feel exceptionally good or bad about their jobs. The results indicated that certain job factors are consistently related to employee job satisfaction while others can create job dissatisfaction. According to Herzberg, **motivating factors** (also called *job satisfiers*) are primarily intrinsic job elements that lead to satisfaction. **Hygiene factors** (also called *job dissatisfiers*) are extrinsic elements of the work environment. A summary of motivating and hygiene factors appears in Exhibit 10.3.

One of the most interesting results of Herzberg's studies was the implication that the opposite of satisfaction is not dissatisfaction. Herzberg believed that proper management of hygiene factors could prevent employee dissatisfaction, but that these factors could not serve as a source of satisfaction or motivation. Good

Exhibit 10.3 Herzberg's Motivating and Hygiene Factors

Motivating Factors	Hygiene Factors
Achievement	Company policy
Recognition	Supervision
Work itself	Working conditions
Responsibility	Interpersonal relationships at work
Advancement	Salary and benefits
Growth	Job security

© AP / WIDE WORLD PHOTOS

According to Herzberg's motivation theory, the job factors that motivate employees, such as this Starbuck's employee, are the work itself, achievement, recognition, responsibility, advancement, and growth.

working conditions, for instance, will keep employees at a job but won't make them work harder. But poor working conditions, which are job dissatisfiers, may make employees quit. According to Herzberg, a manager who wants to increase employee satisfaction needs to focus on the motivating factors, or satisfiers. A job with many satisfiers will usually motivate workers, provide job satisfaction, and prompt effective performance. But a lack of job satisfiers doesn't always lead to dissatisfaction and poor performance; instead, a lack of job satisfiers may merely lead to workers doing an adequate job, rather than their best.

Although Herzberg's ideas have been widely read and his recommendations implemented at numerous companies over the years, there are some very legitimate concerns about Herzberg's work. Although his findings have been used to explain employee motivation, in fact his studies focused on job satisfaction, a different (though related) concept from motivation. Other criticisms focus on the unreliability of Herzberg's methodology, the fact that the theory ignores the impact of situational variables, and the assumed relationship between satisfaction and productivity. Nevertheless, the questions raised by Herzberg about the nature of job satisfaction and the effects of intrinsic and extrinsic factors on employee behavior have proved a valuable contribution to the evolution of theories of motivation and job satisfaction.

Small companies lack the resources of larger organizations, so they sometimes take a different approach in motivating workers. The "Focusing on Small Business" box explains how small organizations can raise morale, increase commitment and reduce turnover.

concept check

What did Elton Mayo's studies reveal about employee productivity?

How can a manager use an understanding of Maslow's hierarchy to motivate employees?

How do the Theory X, Theory Y, and Theory Z management styles differ?

Focusing on Small Business

You're the Boss—Now What?

Motivating workers when you have a small company requires a bit of creativity and ingenuity. Here are several low-cost ways to make employees loyal, creative, self-starters:

- Give them the freedom to choose some work projects. "When you allow them to choose their own projects, it gives them the opportunity to do something they really love and that's important to them. Then, they're going to pour so much more spirit into what they're doing."
- Give them flexible hours and benefits. "With the flexible hours you're accommodating their personal life. If you have somebody who worries about who is going to pick up their kids every day, the time loss in anxiety comes off their productivity." Consider permitting them to start earlier, get off earlier, or finish up their work at home. "You'll get more productivity in the long run."
- Let them choose the benefits they need. "Single people want very different benefits from people who have families. The one-size-fits-all just doesn't fly anymore."
- Encourage fun in the workplace. "All the research shows there's a direct correlation between having a joyful workplace and having a productive workplace. It could be a simple little thing, like every time they collect money, a horn blows. Or, play two minutes of twist music and everybody gets up and does the twist. We don't stop playing because we grow old. We grow old because we stop playing. We spend over half our lives in our places of work. It should be someplace we love."
- Tell them how their work makes someone's life better. "We all need to feel like what we're doing is important. If it's bill collecting, how is it making somebody's life better? It's helping them get their credit back in shape and helping the company because it's collecting money that's overdue. It's each individual beginning to see where they fit and how they have value. Every single job has value."
- Ask what training they'd like to receive. "One of the things workers want today is personal and professional development. They may need financial planning or a course on communicating with difficult people."
- Get to know them as individuals. They want to be respected as whole human beings with a life outside work. Say, "Let's have lunch on Friday. I want to find out about you, your family, what's important to you. I just want to know more about you." Spend one-on-one time.
- Create a good physical place to work. "The surroundings become really important. I'm seeing a lot of organizations that won't allow people to bring in personal items. It totally alienates them. Allow them to decorate [their space] in any way they choose to."
- Hold frequent grapevine meetings with employees. "People only have 'X' amount of energy. If all that energy is going into gossip and conjecture, it's not going into productivity. Head it off at the pass." Hold information sessions and tell whatever can be told at that point to allay rumors and fears. "People can take bad news. What they can't take is the not knowing."

Here are a couple of creative ways small business owners motivate their employees:

- Mark Firmaini, president of a Seattle public relations firm, closes his company every three months and takes his employees to the movies.
- At Autumn Harp, a 65-person manufacturer of skin-care products in Bristol, Vermont, founder Kevin Harper gives many employees the option to work one day a week at home. About 10 percent of his 65 employees take him up on the offer.
- Orval Madden, CEO of Hot Topic, a small chain of music related apparel and accessories stores based in Pomona, California, reimburses employees for tickets to rock concerts. The business tie-in? For Hot Topic, the shows provide important market research. To qualify for the reimbursement, employees must return with a report on the fashions that the band and the fans were wearing and with other merchandising ideas.
- Jack Schacht, president of National Trade Association (NTA), in Glenview, Illinois, provides monthly in-house luncheons for the company's 50 employees. He finds that the luncheons promote camaraderie and offer a chance to celebrate birthdays at the commercial barter company.
- Mark Zweig of Zweig White & Associates, a $3.1 million consulting and publishing firm in Natick, Massachusetts, goes even further and provides his 37 employees with free food and drink all day every day.[5]

Critical Thinking Questions

1. Do you think large companies could use the same techniques described above to motivate employees?
2. What other creative techniques could small companies use to motivate employees?
3. What might small businesses do regarding promotion policies to motivate workers?

Contemporary Views on Motivation

6 learning goal

The early management scholars laid a foundation that enabled managers to better understand their workers and how best to motivate them. Since then, new theories have given us an even better understanding of worker motivation. Three of these theories are explained in this section: the expectancy theory, the equity theory, and the goal-setting theory.

Exhibit 10.4 How Expectations Can Lead to Motivation

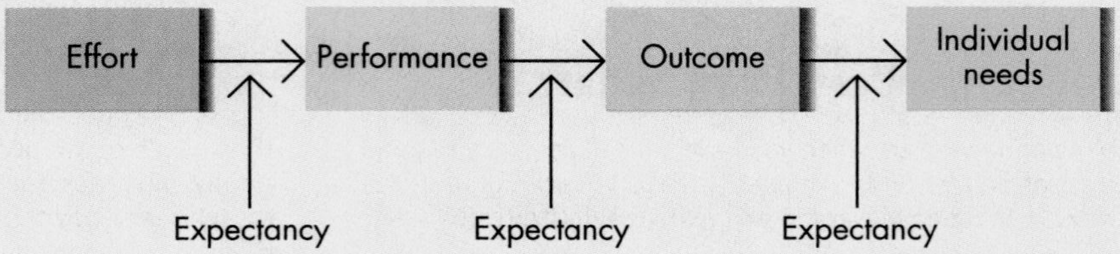

expectancy theory
A theory of motivation that holds that the probability of an individual acting in a particular way depends on the strength of that individual's belief that the act will have a particular outcome and on whether the individual values that outcome.

equity theory
A theory of motivation that holds that worker satisfaction is influenced by employees' perceptions about how fairly they are treated compared with their coworkers.

Expectancy Theory

One of the best-supported and most widely accepted theories of motivation is expectancy theory, which focuses on the link between motivation and behavior. According to **expectancy theory,** the probability of an individual acting in a particular way depends on the strength of that individual's belief that the act will have a particular outcome and on whether the individual values that outcome. The degree to which an employee is motivated depends on three important relationships, shown in Exhibit 10.4:

1. The link between *effort and performance,* or the strength of the individual's expectation that a certain amount of effort will lead to a certain level of performance.
2. The link between *performance and outcome,* or the strength of the expectation that a certain level of performance will lead to a particular outcome.
3. The link between *outcomes and individual needs,* or the degree to which the individual expects the anticipated outcome to satisfy personal needs. Some outcomes have more valence, or value, for individuals than others do.

Based on the expectancy theory, managers should do the following to motivate employees:

- Determine the rewards valued by each employee.
- Determine the desired performance level and then communicate it clearly to employees.
- Make the performance level attainable.
- Link rewards to performance.
- Determine what factors might counteract the effectiveness of an award.
- Make sure the reward is adequate for the level of performance.

Does expectancy theory work the same across cultures when workers are performing the same basic job? Some researchers say "no," as explained in the "Expanding Around the Globe" box.

Equity Theory

Another contemporary explanation of motivation, **equity theory** is based on individuals' perceptions about how fairly they are treated compared with their coworkers. Equity means justice or fairness, and in the workplace it refers to employees' perceived fairness of the way they are treated and the rewards they earn. Employees evaluate their own *outcomes* (e.g., salary, benefits) in relation to their *inputs* (e.g., number of hours worked, education, and training) and then compare the outcomes-to-inputs ratio to one of the following: (1) the employee's own past experience in a different position in the current organization, (2) the employee's own past experi-

EXPANDING AROUND THE GLOBE

Expectancy Theory in the Beauty Industry

Researchers recently conducted a study on expectancy theory attempting to determine if the level of motivation would be the same in each country. The study examined Australians and Malaysians who were employed in similar work in the beauty care industry.

The Australians were found to have significantly higher job motivation than the Malaysians. Malaysian culture dictates a strong respect for hierarchy in an organization and autocratic leadership. The Malaysian workers attach great importance to Confucian values such as the importance of the group rather than the individual. The whole notion of individuality is downplayed in this culture.

Unlike the Malaysians, Australians have strong Western values. Such values stress the importance of individualism and self-interests. Expectancy theory rests on the notion of self-interest. That is, working hard will enable me to meet my individual needs. It is not surprising that the Malaysian culture, with its emphasis on achieving harmony within the group, would be less motivated to achieve individual work goals.[6]

CRITICAL THINKING QUESTIONS

1. Will workers who are performing the same job in different cultures be motivated by the same factors? Explain using the expectancy theory.
2. In what countries would you find persons highly motivated by expectancy theory?
3. What can managers do to increase job motivation using expectancy theory?

ence in a different organization, (3) another employee's experience inside the current organization, or (4) another employee's experience outside the organization.

According to equity theory, if employees perceive that an inequity exists, they will make one of the following choices:

- *Change their work habits* (exert less effort on the job).
- *Change their job benefits and income* (ask for a raise, steal from the employer).
- *Distort their perception of themselves* ("I always thought I was smart, but now I realize I'm a lot smarter than my coworkers").
- *Distort their perceptions of others* ("Joe's position is really much less flexible than mine").
- *Look at the situation from a different perspective* ("I don't make as much as the other department heads, but I make a lot more than most graphic artists").
- *Leave the situation* (quit the job).

Managers can use equity theory to improve worker satisfaction. Knowing that every employee seeks equitable and fair treatment, managers can make an effort to understand an employee's perceptions of fairness and take steps to reduce concerns about inequity.

Goal-Setting Theory

goal-setting theory
A theory of motivation based on the premise that an individual's intention to work toward a goal is a primary source of motivation.

Goal-setting theory is based on the premise that an individual's intention to work toward a goal is a primary source of motivation. Once set, the goal clarifies for the employee what needs to be accomplished and how much effort will be required for completion. The theory has three main components: (1) specific goals lead to a higher level of performance than do more generalized goals ("do your best"); (2) more difficult goals lead to better performance than do easy goals (provided the individual accepts the goal); and (3) feedback on progress toward the goal enhances performance. Feedback is particularly important because it helps the individual identify the gap between the *real* (the actual performance) and the *ideal* (the desired outcome defined by the goal). Given the trend toward employee empowerment in the workplace, more and more employees are participating in the goal-setting process.

© AP / WIDE WORLD PHOTOS

When Michael Vick signed a multi-year contract to be quarterback for the Atlanta Falcons, his top priority was to improve his passing accuracy. Multi-million dollar contracts motivate professional athletes, but the passionate desire for meeting a specific goal is frequently a stronger motivator.

Motivation Is Culture Bound

Most motivation theories in use today were developed in the United States by Americans and about Americans.[7] Of those that were not, many have been strongly influenced by American theories. Americans' strong emphasis on individualism has led to expectancy and equity theories of motivation: theories that emphasize rational, individual thought as the primary basis of human behavior. The emphasis placed on achievement is not surprising given Americans' willingness to accept risk and their high concern for performance. But several motivation theories do not apply to all cultures.

Maslow's theory does not often hold outside the United States. For instance, in countries higher on uncertainty avoidance (such as Greece and Japan) as compared with those lower on uncertainty avoidance (such as the United States), security motivates employees more strongly than does self-actualization. Employees in high-uncertainty-avoidance countries often consider job security and lifetime employment more important than holding a more interesting or challenging job. Also contrasting with the American pattern, social needs often dominate the motivation of workers in countries such as Denmark, Norway, and Sweden that stress the quality of life over materialism and productivity.

When researchers tested Herzberg's theory outside the United States, they encountered different results. In New Zealand, for example, supervision and interpersonal relationships appear to contribute significantly to satisfaction and not merely to reducing dissatisfaction. Similarly, researchers found that citizens of Asia, Canada, Europe, Latin America, the Republic of Panama, and the West Indies cited certain extrinsic factors as satisfiers with greater frequency than did their American counterparts. The factors that motivate U. S. employees, summarized in Exhibit 10.3, may not spark the same motivation in employees in other cultures.

Even the expectancy theory, considered a well-accepted contemporary motivation theory, does not always hold up in other cultures. Some of the major differences among the cultural groups include the following:

1. English-speaking countries rank higher on individual achievement and lower on the desire for security.
2. French-speaking countries, although similar to the English-speaking countries, give greater importance to security and somewhat less to challenging work.
3. Northern European countries have less interest in "getting ahead" and work recognition goals and place more emphasis on job accomplishment. In addition, they have more concern for people and less for the organization as a whole (it is important that their jobs not interfere with their personal lives).
4. Latin American and Southern European countries find individual achievement somewhat less important; Southern Europeans place the highest emphasis on job security, while both groups of countries emphasize fringe benefits.
5. Germany ranks high on security and fringe benefits and among the highest on "getting ahead."
6. Japan, although low on advancement, also ranks second highest on challenge and lowest on autonomy, with a strong emphasis on good working conditions and a friendly working environment.

Expectancy theories are universal to the extent that they do not specify the types of rewards that motivate a given group of workers. Managers themselves must determine the level and type of rewards most sought after by a particular group.[8]

concept check

Discuss the three relationships central to expectancy theory.

Explain the comparison process that is a part of equity theory.

How does goal-setting theory contribute to our understanding of motivation?

From Motivation Theory to Application

7 learning goal

The material presented thus far in this chapter demonstrates the wide variety of theorists and research studies that have contributed to our current understanding of employee motivation. Now we turn our attention to more practical matters, to ways that these concepts can be applied in the workplace to meet organizational goals and improve individual performance.

Motivational Job Design

How might managers redesign or modify existing jobs to increase employee motivation and performance? The following three options have been used extensively in the workplace:

job enlargement
The horizontal expansion of a job by increasing the number and variety of tasks that a person performs.

job enrichment
The vertical expansion of a job by increasing the employee's autonomy, responsibility, and decision-making authority.

job rotation
The shifting of workers from one job to another; also called *cross-training.*

- *Job Enlargement.* The horizontal expansion of a job, increasing the number and variety of tasks that a person performs, is called **job enlargement.** Increasing task diversity can enhance job satisfaction, particularly when the job is mundane and repetitive in nature. A potential drawback to job enlargement is that employees may perceive that they are being asked to work harder and do more with no change in their level of responsibility or compensation. This can cause resentment and lead to dissatisfaction.
- *Job Enrichment.* **Job enrichment** is the vertical expansion of an employee's job. Whereas job enlargement addresses the breadth or scope of a job, enrichment attempts to increase job depth by providing the employee with more autonomy, responsibility, and decision-making authority. In an enriched job, the employee can use a variety of talents and skills and has more control over the planning, execution, and evaluation of the required tasks. In general, job enrichment has been found to increase job satisfaction and reduce absenteeism and turnover.
- *Job Rotation.* Also called *cross-training,* **job rotation** is the shifting of workers from one job to another. This may be done to broaden an employee's skill base or because an employee has ceased to be interested in or challenged by a particular job. The organization may benefit from job rotation because it increases flexibility in scheduling and production, since employees can be shifted to cover for absent workers or changes in production or operations. It is also a valuable tool for training lower-level managers in a variety of functional areas. Drawbacks of job rotation include an increase in training costs and decreased productivity while employees are getting "up to speed" in new task areas.

Work-Scheduling Options

As companies try to meet the needs of a diverse workforce and retain quality employees, while remaining competitive and financially prosperous, managers are challenged to find new ways to keep workers motivated and satisfied. Increasingly popular are alternatives to the traditional work schedule, such as the compressed workweek, flextime, job sharing, and telecommuting.

One option for employees who want to maximize their leisure hours, indulge in three-day weekends, and avoid commuting during morning and evening rush hours is the *compressed workweek.* Employees work the traditional 40 hours, but fit those hours into a shorter workweek. Most common is the 4-40 schedule, where employees work four 10-hour days a week. Today, over 89 percent of the Fortune 100 best companies to work for in America offer the option of a compressed workweek.[9] Organizations that offer this option claim benefits ranging from increased motivation and productivity to reduced absenteeism and turnover.

Another scheduling option, called *flextime,* allows employees to decide what their work hours will be. Employees are generally expected to work a certain number of hours per week, but have some discretion as to when they arrive at work and when they leave for the day.

job sharing
A scheduling option that allows two individuals to split the tasks, responsibilities, and work hours of one 40-hour-per-week job.

Job sharing is a scheduling option that allows two individuals to split the tasks, responsibilities, and work hours of one 40-hour-per-week job. Though used less frequently than flextime and the compressed workweek, this option can also provide employees with job flexibility. The primary benefit to the company is that it gets "two for the price of one"—the company can draw on two sets of skills and abilities to accomplish one set of job objectives. As the airlines continue to face brutal economic times many, such as United and American, have turned to job sharing to cut costs.

Telecommuting, described in Chapter 9, is a work-scheduling option that allows employees to work from home via a computer that is linked with their office, headquarters, or colleagues. It is the fastest growing of the four scheduling options.

The Stanley Group, an employee-owned international engineering, environmental, and construction services company, offers its employees a number of ways to design their jobs. Workers can opt for compressed workweeks, part-time work, job sharing, and telecommuting. The Stanley Group also provides a phased-in retirement program, offering workers either reduced-time or part-time work.

While each of these work-scheduling options may have some drawbacks for the sponsoring organizations, the benefits far outweigh the problems. For this reason, not only are the number of companies offering compressed work increasing, but so are the number of companies offering other options. Today, over 87 percent of the top companies are offering telecommuting programs, 72 percent offer job sharing, and 70 percent offer flexible schedules. All of these figures are growing, and this trend is expected to continue.[10]

Recognition, Empowerment, and Economic Incentives

All employees have unique needs that they seek to fulfill through their jobs. Organizations must devise a wide array of incentives to ensure that a broad spectrum of employee needs can be addressed in the work environment, thus increasing the likelihood of motivated employees. A sampling of these motivational tools is discussed here.

Companies around the world enhance employee motivation and job satisfaction with paid holidays and family leave. In France, for example, companies are required to give employees at least 25 days off per year, as compared to U.S. firms who offer an average of 16 days per year.

Formal recognition of superior effort by individuals or groups in the workplace is one way to enhance employee motivation. Recognition serves as positive feedback and reinforcement, letting employees know what they have done well and that their contribution is valued by the organization. Recognition can take many forms, both formal and informal. Some companies use formal awards ceremonies to acknowledge and celebrate their employees' accomplishments. Others take advantage of informal interaction to congratulate employees on a job well done and offer encouragement for the future. Recognition can take the form of an employee of the month plaque, a monetary reward, a day off, a congratulatory e-mail, or a verbal "pat on the back."

As described in Chapter 7, employee empowerment, sometimes called employee involvement or participative management, involves delegating decision-making authority to employees at all levels of the organization. Employees are given greater responsibility for planning, implementing, and evaluating the results of decisions. Empowerment is based on the premise that human resources, especially at lower levels in the firm, are an underutilized asset. Employees are capable

COURTESY OF TJX COMPANIES, INC.

Businesses use a variety of monetary incentives to motivate employees. Incentives, such as gift certificates to T.J. Maxx, help motivate top performers.

of contributing much more of their skills and abilities to organizational success if they are allowed to participate in the decision-making process and are given access to the resources needed to implement their decisions.

Any discussion of motivation has to include the use of monetary incentives to enhance performance. Currently, companies are using a variety of variable-pay programs such as piece-rate plans, profit sharing, gain sharing, and bonuses to encourage employees to be more productive. Unlike the standard salary or hourly wage, variable pay means that a portion of an employee's pay is directly linked to an individual or organizational performance measure. In *piece-rate pay plans,* for example, employees are paid a given amount for each unit they produce, directly linking the amount they earn to their productivity. *Profit-sharing plans* are based on overall company profitability. Using an established formula, management distributes some portion of company profits to all employees. *Gain-sharing plans* are incentive programs based on group productivity. Employees share in the financial gains attributed to the increased productivity of their group. This encourages employees to increase productivity within their specific work area regardless of the overall profit picture for the organization as a whole. A *bonus* is simply a one-time lump-sum monetary reward.

In the early 2000s, one of the fastest-growing employee incentive programs was stock options. This means giving employees the right to purchase company stock, typically at below-market prices. At that time the stock market and economy were booming and companies were willing to share the wealth. However, due to the negative economic impact of September 11 and the downturn in the economy, more and more executives are finding the general distribution of stock options to all employees does not make sense for the productivity of the company. Some CEOs think that stock options should be more closely tied to performance factors. For instance, Intuit's CEO, Stephen Bennett, recently slashed stock option grants by 30 percent and started basing them on job performance. Jim Grenier, vice president for human resources, said: "This was a consensus culture where rewards were spread like peanut butter."[11] Changing to a performance-based culture is seen not only in the stock option plan but also in salary increases. Employees who have top performance reviews get salary increases 2.5 times the average employee's raise.

concept check

Explain the difference between job enlargement and job enrichment.

What are the four work-scheduling options that can enhance employee performance?

Are all employees motivated by the same economic incentives? Explain.

Using Teams to Enhance Motivation and Performance

8 learning goal

One of the most apparent trends in business today is the use of teams to accomplish organizational goals. Using a team-based structure can increase individual and group motivation and performance. This section gives a brief overview of group behavior, defines work teams as specific types of groups, and provides suggestions for creating high-performing teams.

Understanding Group Behavior

Teams are a specific type of organizational group. Every organization contains *groups,* social units of two or more people who share the same goals and cooperate to achieve those goals. Understanding some fundamental concepts related to group behavior and group processes provides a good foundation for understanding

Members of formal work groups share the same organizational goals and work together to achieve these goals. Group members are guided by norms that dictate acceptable behavior to accomplish effective group performance.

© MICHAEL NEWMAN / PHOTO EDIT

concepts about work teams. Groups can be formal or informal in nature. Formal groups are designated and sanctioned by the organization; their behavior is directed toward accomplishing organizational goals. Informal groups are based on social relationships and are not determined or sanctioned by the organization.

Formal organizational groups, like the sales department at Dell Computers, must operate within the larger Dell organizational system. To some degree, elements of the larger Dell system, such as organizational strategy, Dell's company policies and procedures, available resources, and the highly motivated employee corporate culture of Dell, determine the behavior of smaller groups, like the sales department, within Dell. Other factors that affect the behavior of organizational groups are individual member characteristics (e.g., ability, training, personality), the roles and norms of group members, and the size and cohesiveness of the group. Norms are the implicit behavioral guidelines of the group, or the standards for acceptable and nonacceptable behavior. For example, a Dell sales manager may be expected to work at least two Saturdays per month without extra pay. Although this isn't written anywhere, it is the expected norm.

group cohesiveness
The degree to which group members want to stay in the group and tend to resist outside influences.

Group cohesiveness refers to the degree to which group members want to stay in the group and tend to resist outside influences (such as a change in company policies). When group performance norms are high, group cohesiveness will have a positive impact on productivity. Cohesiveness tends to increase when the size of the group is small, individual and group goals are congruent, the group has high status in the organization, rewards are group based rather than individual based, and the group competes with other groups within the organization. Work group cohesiveness can benefit the organization in several ways including increased productivity, enhanced worker self-image because of group success, increased company loyalty, reduced employee turnover, and reduced absenteeism. Southwest Airlines is known for its work group cohesiveness. On the other hand, cohesiveness can also lead to restricted output, resistance to change, and conflict with other work groups in the organization.

The opportunity to turn the decision-making process over to a group with diverse skills and abilities is one of the arguments for using work groups (and teams) in organizational settings. For group decision making to be most effective, however, both managers and group members must acknowledge its strengths and weaknesses (see Exhibit 10.5).

Exhibit 10.5 | Strengths and Weaknesses of Group Decision Making

Strengths	Weaknesses
• Groups bring more information and knowledge to the decision process.	• Groups typically take a longer time to reach a solution than an individual takes.
• Groups offer a diversity of perspectives and, therefore, generate a greater number of alternatives.	• Group members may pressure others to conform, reducing the likelihood of disagreement.
• Group decision making results in a higher-quality decision than does individual decision making.	• The process may be dominated by one or a small number of participants.
• Participation of group members increases the likelikhod that a decision will be accepted.	• Groups lack accountability, because it is difficult to assign responsibility for outcomes to any one individual.

work groups
Groups of employees who share resources and coordinate efforts so as to help members better perform their individual duties and responsibilities. The performance of the group can be evaluated by adding up the contributions of the individual group members.

work teams
Groups of employees who not only coordinate their efforts, but also collaborate by pooling their knowledge, skills, abilities, and resources in a collective effort to attain a common goal; causing the performance of the team to be greater than the sum of the members' individual efforts.

problem-solving teams
Teams of employees from the same department or area of expertise and from the same level of the organizational hierarchy who meet regularly to share information and discuss ways to improve processes and procedures in specific functional areas.

self-managed work teams
Highly autonomous teams of employees who manage themselves without any formal supervision and take responsibility for setting goals, planning and scheduling work activities, selecting team members, and evaluating team performance.

Work Groups versus Work Teams

We have already noted that teams are a special type of organizational group, but we also need to differentiate between work groups and work teams. **Work groups** share resources and coordinate efforts to help members better perform their individual duties and responsibilities. The performance of the group can be evaluated by adding up the contributions of the individual group members. **Work teams** require not only coordination but also *collaboration,* the pooling of knowledge, skills, abilities, and resources in a collective effort to attain a common goal. A work team creates *synergy,* causing the performance of the team as a whole to be greater than the sum of team members' individual contributions. Simply assigning employees to groups and labeling them a team does not guarantee a positive outcome. Managers and team members must be committed to creating, developing, and maintaining high-performance work teams. Factors that contribute to their success are discussed later in this section.

Types of Teams

The evolution of the team concept in organizations can be seen in three basic types of work teams: problem solving, self-managed, and cross-functional. **Problem-solving teams** are typically made up of employees from the same department or area of expertise and from the same level of the organizational hierarchy. They meet on a regular basis to share information and discuss ways to improve processes and procedures in specific functional areas. Problem-solving teams generate ideas and alternatives and may recommend a specific course of action, but they typically do not make final decisions, allocate resources, or implement change.

Every day select Daimler Chrysler dealers ship every part they replace on warranty to the company's Quality Engineering Center. The parts are then given to the center's problem-solving teams to examine. One team, for example, examined parts from a Jeep Wrangler that was brought to the dealer with only 5,000 miles on it. Warranty repairs on that vehicle cost $3,891.[12] Often the problem-solving team will call in the suppliers to help understand what went wrong. Using problem-solving teams has reduced warranty costs by 50 percent in the last six years.

Many organizations that experienced success using problem-solving teams were willing to expand the team concept to allow team members greater responsibility in making decisions, implementing solutions, and monitoring outcomes. These highly autonomous groups are called **self-managed work teams.** They manage themselves without any formal supervision, taking responsibility for setting

Making Ethical Choices

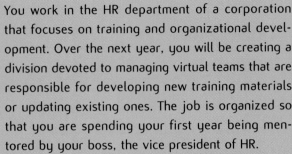

xtra! http://gitmanxtra.swlearning.com

TEAM SPIRIT—OH REALLY

You work in the HR department of a corporation that focuses on training and organizational development. Over the next year, you will be creating a division devoted to managing virtual teams that are responsible for developing new training materials or updating existing ones. The job is organized so that you are spending your first year being mentored by your boss, the vice president of HR.

With full understanding of the benefits technology brings to virtual teams, you are also aware of the essential need for trust among members of virtual teams. The first project you are following is a virtual team tasked with updating one of the corporation's most sought after guides. The HR vice president appointed all team members and assigned one person as the team leader. None of the team members knows one another, and the team leader is the only team member who has direct contact with your boss. In following the team's work, you realize that no one knows exactly what each member has contributed because members are not in contact with each other. Their only contact is with the team leader.

Your sense is that the team leader is taking full credit for all the work. Not only is she the only one with direct contact to your boss, she lives in the same area as the corporation's headquarters. The other team members are located across the United States. Your sense is confirmed when only the team leader is invited to the annual awards dinner and at the dinner receives singular acknowledgment for her work on updating the guide.

ETHICAL DILEMMA

How can the vice president of HR and eventually you determine if each team member pulled his or her own weight or that the team lead had to step in to complete or redo the guide?

SOURCES: Sirkka L. Jarvenpaa and Dorothy E. Leidner, "Communication and Trust in Global Virtual Teams," *Journal of Computer-Mediated Communication*, June 1998, downloaded from http://www.ascusc.org; Carla Joinson, "Managing Virtual Teams: Keeping Members on the Same Page without Being in the Same Place Poses Challenges for Managers," *HR Magazine*, June 2002, downloaded from http://www.findarticles.com; and Charlene Marmer Solomon, "Managing Virtual Teams," *Workforce*, June 1, 2001, downloaded from http://www.findarticles.com.

goals, planning and scheduling work activities, selecting team members, and evaluating team performance. PepsiCo, Hewlett-Packard, and Xerox are just a few of the well-known, highly successful companies using self-managed work teams.

cross-functional teams
Teams of employees who are from about the same level in the organizational hierarchy but from different functional areas; for example, engineering, finance, and marketing.

An adaptation of the team concept is called a **cross-functional team.** These teams are made up of employees from about the same hierarchical level, but different functional areas of the organization. Many task forces, organizational committees, and project teams are cross-functional. Often the team members work together only until they solve a given problem or complete a specific project. Cross-functional teams allow people with various levels and areas of expertise to pool their resources, develop new ideas, solve problems, and coordinate complex projects. Both problem-solving teams and self-managed teams may also be cross-functional teams. Bell Helicopter uses both types of teams to increase its efficiency in building helicopters.

Building High-Performance Teams

When teams are formed to address issues or solve complex problems, they often are under tight deadlines to provide effective solutions. Rarely do they spend time properly setting up the team for maximum effectiveness. Frequently, much time is lost resolving conflicts before the team refocuses on their primary focus. Here are some tips to set up the team properly to deliver the expected results:

1. Create and share the team's purpose. Discuss why the team exists.
2. Create specific and challenging goals. Discuss measurable results and expectations.
3. Create a collaborative approach. Discuss the methods and strategies for working together.
4. Define clear roles. Discuss everyone's role on the team. Resolve conflicts early.
5. Define complementary skills. Discuss what skills are present within the team. Discuss how each member can use his or her skills to ensure the team's success. Reorganize any skill gaps within the team and discuss how to resolve them.[13]

In addition to getting the team off on the right foot, there are also some pitfalls to avoid. According to team-building expert, Margrit Harris, President of Strata Team—Team Strategist Group, here are some surefire team destroyers:

1. No common objective—if you don't have a vision, you certainly won't get there.
2. Clashing personalities—when people are in conflict, cooperation and creativity are lost. This doesn't mean everyone needs to have the same personality, but everyone needs to be able to quickly resolve conflict and build a spirit of harmony.
3. Too similar expertise—when there is no diversity of skills among the team members, then the team can suffer. Complementary skill sets add strength to the overall effectiveness.
4. Questionable ethical standards—questions regarding ethical standards can destroy teams quickly. Suspicions can undo even the best of teams.
5. Different operating styles—complementary operating styles are usually best. Clashing styles can create frustration and conflict among the team members.[14]

concept check

What is the difference between a work team and a work group?

Identify and describe three types of work teams.

What are some ways to build a high-performance team?

Trends in Employee Motivation

9 learning goal

This chapter has focused on understanding what motivates people and how employee motivation and satisfaction affect productivity and organizational performance. Organizations can improve performance by investing in people. In reviewing the ways companies are currently choosing to invest in their human resources, we can spot four positive trends: (1) education and training, (2) employee ownership, (3) work–life benefits, and (4) nurturing knowledge workers. All of the companies making the *Fortunes*' annual list of the "100 Best Companies to Work For" know the importance of treating employees right. They all have programs that allow them to invest in their employees through programs such as these and many more.[15] Today's businesses also face the challenge of increased costs of absenteeism. This section discusses each of these trends in motivating employees.

Education and Training

Companies that provide educational and training opportunities for their employees reap the benefits of a more motivated, as well as a more skilled, workforce. Employees who are properly trained in new technologies are more productive and less resistant to job change. Education and training provide additional benefits by increasing employees' feelings of competence and self-worth. When companies spend money to upgrade employee knowledge and skills, they convey the message "we value you and are committed to your growth and development as an employee." The Bech Group, a construction firm in Southlake, Texas, believes strongly in providing ongoing training for its employees.[16] The company requires that every employee receive a minimum of 40 hours of training per year. However, the average employee logs 66 hours during a given year.

Employee Ownership

Behind employee ownership programs is the belief that they cause workers to act more like partners than clock watchers. The theory is that employees, who think like owners, are more motivated to take care of customers' needs, reduce unnecessary expenses, make operations smoother, and stay around longer. According to Rutgers University economist, Douglas Kruse, "On average, worker-owned companies survive longer, lose fewer workers, enjoy bigger profits, and are more productive than their non-employee-owned competitors."[17]

Most companies that have employee ownership programs have achieved positive results. In fact, for the past decade these companies, on average, have outperformed the general stock market.[18] Republic Engineered Products (formerly Republic Steel) and RTM Restaurant Group (Arby's Roast Beef, Lee's Famous Recipe Chicken, and Del Taco Mexican restaurants) have been very satisfied with the productivity and growth of their companies, partially due to employee ownership programs.[19]

Work–Life Benefits

In another growing trend in the workplace, companies are helping their employees to manage the numerous and sometimes competing demands in their lives. Organizations are taking a more active role in helping employees achieve a balance between their work responsibilities and their personal obligations. The desired result is employees who are less stressed, better able to focus on their jobs, and, therefore, more productive. Ford Motor Co. is a leader in providing work–life benefits for employees. The company offers telecommuting, part-time positions, job sharing, subsidized child care, elder-care referral, and on-site fitness centers.

Nurturing Knowledge Workers

Most organizations have specialized workers, and managing them all effectively is a big challenge. In many companies, knowledge workers (now two-fifths of the workforce) may have a supervisor, but they are not "subordinates." They are "associates." Within their area of knowledge, they are supposed to do the telling. Since knowledge is effective only if specialized, knowledge workers are not homogeneous, particularly the fast-growing group of knowledge technologists such as computer systems specialists, lawyers, programmers, and others. And because knowledge work is specialized, it is deeply splintered.

Many businesses, like hospitals, have many knowledge specialists. In financial services, too, there is increasing specialization and need for concentration on one specialty!

It is important today to pay close attention to the health and well-being of all workers. A knowledge-based workforce is qualitatively different from a less skilled workforce. True, knowledge workers are still a minority, but they are fast becoming the largest single group. And they have already become the major creator of wealth. Increasingly the success, indeed the survival, of every business will depend on the performance of its knowledge workforce. And since it is impossible for any but the smallest organization to have "better people," the only way an organization in a knowledge-based economy and society can excel is by getting more out of the same kind of people—by managing its knowledge workers for greater productivity and "to make ordinary people do extraordinary things."

Knowledge-based businesses need to be focused on the productivity of their capital, that is, of the knowledge worker. Managers need to focus on the business rather than on employment-related rules, regulations, and paperwork. To spend one-quarter of one's time on job-related paperwork is indeed a waste of precious, expensive, scarce resources. It is boring.

The only way to achieve leadership in the knowledge-based business is to spend time with the promising knowledge professionals: to get to know them and to be known by them; to mentor them and to listen to them; to challenge them and to encourage them.[20]

Coping with the Rising Costs of Absenteeism

The rate of employee absenteeism in the United States is very consistent from year to year. It averages about 1.7 percent of scheduled workdays.[21] The cost, however, continues to rise very rapidly. Short-term absence costs have doubled in the past decade. Much of this is due to the cost of health-related absences.

As American workers age, they will experience more responsibilities for caring for elderly parents. Also, an older workforce means more health-related time off. Experts speak about an "entitlement mentality" of many workers. That is, "I am entitled to take off when I want or need to." Stress-related absenteeism is also on the rise.

Companies are trying to lower absenteeism in the following ways:

- Allowing employees who arrive late, or miss a day, to do "make-up time," usually the same day or within the same week.
- Establishing a grace period of a certain number of minutes for late arrivals that won't count as tardies.
- Eliminating advance-notice requirements for tardies, which lets employees call at the last minute and be excused for a late arrival if operations won't be disrupted.
- Allowing employees to refuse mandatory overtime occasionally—for example, for 25 percent of the time.
- Eliminating formal attendance policies altogether. Instead, treat poor attendance as you do performance problems. Employees who slip receive feedback and counseling, followed by a performance or development plan. The employee is discharged if the behavior doesn't improve.[22]
- Providing on-site day care for employees' children.
- Contracting with a firm specializing in elder care to make on-site visits to employees' elderly relatives.

concept check

What benefits can an organization derive from training and educational opportunities, stock ownership programs, and work–life benefits?

How are knowledge workers different from traditional employees?

Why is the cost of absenteeism rising and what can be done about it?

Great Ideas to Use Now

We've come a long way from the days of Taylor's *scientific management.* Organizations now offer a wide variety of incentives to attract and retain high-quality employees. A knowledgeable, creative, committed, and highly skilled workforce provides a company with a source of sustainable, competitive advantage in an

Try It Now

The accompanying table lists 17 personal characteristics and 13 institutional values you might encounter at a company. Select and rank-order the 10 personal characteristics that best describe you; do the same for the 10 institutional values that would be most evident in your ideal workplace. Test your fit at a firm by seeing whether the characteristics of the company's environment match your top 10 personal characteristics.

The Choice Menu

Rank Order (1–17)	You Are	Rank Order (1–13)	Your Ideal Company Offers
______	1. Flexible	______	1. Stability
______	2. Innovative	______	2. High expectations of performance
______	3. Willing to experiment	______	3. Opportunities for professional growth
______	4. Risk taking	______	4. High pay for good performance
______	5. Careful	______	5. Job security
______	6. Autonomy seeking	______	6. A clear guiding philosophy
______	7. Comfortable with rules	______	7. A low level of conflict
______	8. Analytical	______	8. Respect for the individual's rights
______	9. Team oriented	______	9. Informality
______	10. Easygoing	______	10. Fairness
______	11. Supportive	______	11. Long hours
______	12. Aggressive	______	12. Relative freedom from rules
______	13. Decisive	______	13. The opportunity to be distinctive, or different from others
______	14. Achievement oriented		
______	15. Comfortable with individual responsibility		
______	16. Competitive		
______	17. Interested in making friends at work		

Customer Satisfaction and Quality

So often we think of employee motivation as purely an internal process. However, recent research shows that happy, satisfied employees who stay in jobs can affect an organization's level of customer satisfaction. Unifi Network, a division of PricewaterhouseCoopers, and Roper Starch Worldwide recently conducted a survey of customers of business in six different industries. Across all six industries, the survey results showed that employee turnover has a significant impact on customer satisfaction. Customers felt that employee retention affected the quality of the service they received from the organization.

Gary Wallace, CEO of Commonwealth Credit Union in Frankfort, Kentucky, recognized this connection between motivated employees and happy customers some time back. With customer satisfaction as his primary goal, Wallace first went about implementing programs to find new and better ways to serve his employees. Commonwealth redecorated the employee lounge in the colors of the local football teams and offered employees an enjoyable place to relax. It installed multimedia stations at each branch to offer motivational messages and information about employee benefits and upcoming company and community events. The company also built larger employee cubicles and constructed an outdoor patio with umbrella tables.[23]

How has all of this worked? Quite well for Mr. Wallace and the Commonwealth Credit Union. The company has expanded its market share and its assets have passed the $500 million mark. Service has improved, employee turnover is down, and customer satisfaction has never been higher.

Looking Ahead at UPS

When companies like UPS develop and implement programs that match the goals of the employee and the goals of the organization, they create employees who feel more empowered and more motivated. For UPS, the results have been extraordinary. In 2002, the turnover rate was down from 50 percent to 6 percent. Annual savings from lower hiring costs amount to $1 million. Additionally, lost workdays from injuries are down 20 percent and package delivery mistakes have dropped from 4 percent to 1 percent. Anytime a manager can match employees' needs with company needs, motivation of the workers tends to increase.[24]

increasingly competitive business environment. What does that mean to you? It means that companies are working harder than ever to meet employee needs. It means that when you graduate from college or university you may choose a prospective employer on the basis of its day-care facilities and fitness programs as well as its salaries. It means that you need to think about what motivates you. Would you forgo a big salary to work for a smaller company that gives you lots of freedom to be creative and make your own decisions?

Would you trade extensive health coverage for a share of ownership in the company? Most organizations try to offer a broad spectrum of incentives to meet a variety of needs, but each company makes trade-offs, and so will you in choosing an employer. Do a little research on a company you are interested in working for (paying particular attention to its corporate culture); then use the exercise in the "Try It Now" box to help you determine how well your values fit with the company's values.

Summary of Learning Goals

1 What are the basic principles of Frederick Taylor's concept of scientific management?

Scientific management is based on the belief that employees are motivated by economic incentives and that there is "one best way" to perform any job. The four basic principles of scientific management developed by Taylor are as follows:

1. Develop a scientific approach for each element of a person's job.
2. Scientifically select, train, teach, and develop workers.
3. Encourage cooperation between workers and managers so that each job can be accomplished in a standard, scientifically determined way.
4. Divide work and responsibility between management and workers according to who is better suited to each task.

2 What did Elton Mayo's Hawthorne studies reveal about worker motivation?

The pride that comes from special attention motivates workers to increase their productivity. Supervisors who allow employees to have some control over their situation appeared to further increase the workers' motivation. The Hawthorne effect suggests that employees will perform better when they feel singled out for special attention or feel that management is concerned about employee welfare.

3

What is Maslow's hierarchy of needs, and how do these needs relate to motivation?

Maslow believed that each individual has a hierarchy of needs, consisting of physiological, safety, social, esteem, and self-actualization needs. Managers who accept Maslow's ideas attempt to increase employee motivation by modifying organizational and managerial practices to increase the likelihood that employees will meet all levels of needs. Maslow's theory has also helped managers understand that it is hard to motivate people by appealing to already satisfied needs.

4

How are McGregor's Theories X and Y and Ouchi's Theory Z used to explain worker motivation?

Douglas McGregor influenced the study of motivation with his formulation of two contrasting sets of assumptions about human nature—designated Theory X and Theory Y. Theory X says people don't like to work and will avoid it if they can. Because people don't like to work, they must be controlled, directed, or threatened to get them to make an effort. Theory Y says that people want to be self-directed and will try to accomplish goals that they believe in. Workers can be motivated with positive incentives. McGregor personally believed that Theory Y assumptions describe most employees and that managers seeking to motivate subordinates should develop management practices based on those assumptions.

William Ouchi's Theory Z combines U.S. and Japanese business practices. Theory Z emphasizes long-term employment, slow career development, and group decision making. The long-term decline of the Japanese economy has resulted in most U.S. firms moving away from Japanese management practices.

5

What are the basic components of Herzberg's motivator–hygiene theory?

Frederick Herzberg's studies indicated that certain job factors are consistently related to employee job satisfaction while others can create job dissatisfaction. According to Herzberg, motivating factors (also called satisfiers) are primarily intrinsic job elements that lead to satisfaction, such as achievement, recognition, the (nature of) work itself, responsibility, advancement, and growth. What Herzberg termed hygiene factors (also called dissatisfiers) are extrinsic elements of the work environment such as company policy, relationships with supervisors, working conditions, relationships with peers and subordinates, salary and benefits, and job security. These are factors that can result in job dissatisfaction if not well managed. One of the most interesting results of Herzberg's studies was the implication that the opposite of satisfaction is not dissatisfaction. Herzberg believed that proper management of hygiene factors could prevent employee dissatisfaction, but that these factors could not serve as a source of satisfaction or motivation.

6

What three contemporary theories on employee motivation offer insights into improving employee performance?

According to expectancy theory, the probability of an individual acting in a particular way depends on the strength of that individual's belief that the act will have a particular outcome and on whether the individual values that outcome. Equity theory is based on individuals' perceptions about how fairly they are treated compared with their coworkers. Goal-setting theory states that employees are highly motivated to perform when specific goals are established and feedback on progress is offered.

7

How can managers redesign existing jobs to increase employee motivation and performance?

The horizontal expansion of a job by increasing the number and variety of tasks that a person performs is called job enlargement. Increasing task diversity can enhance job satisfaction, particularly when the job is mundane and repetitive in nature. Job enrichment is the vertical expansion of an employee's job to provide the employee with more autonomy, responsibility, and decision-making authority. Other popular motivational tools include work-scheduling options, employee recognition programs, empowerment, and variable-pay programs.

8

What different types of teams are being used in organizations today?

Work groups share resources and coordinate efforts to help members better perform their individual duties and responsibilities. The performance of the group can be evaluated by adding up the contributions of the individual group members. Work teams require not only coordination but also *collaboration,* the pooling of knowledge, skills, abilities, and resources in a collective effort to attain a common goal. Four types of work teams are used: problem solving, self-managed, cross-functional, and virtual teams.

9

What initiatives are organizations using today to motivate and retain employees?

Today, firms are using several key tactics to motivate and retain workers. First, companies are investing more in employee education and training, which make workers more productive and less resistant to job change. Second, managers are offering employees a chance for ownership in the company. This can strongly increase employee commitment. Enlightened employers are providing work–life benefits to help employees achieve a better balance between work and personal responsibilities. Businesses are also recognizing the importance of managing knowledge workers and reducing the growing cost of employee absenteeism.

Preparing for Tomorrow's Workplace

1. Do you think the concept of scientific management is applicable today? Why or why not?
2. How are job satisfaction and employee morale linked to job performance? Do you work harder when you are satisfied with your job? Explain your answer.
3. Review the assumptions of Theories X, Y, and Z. Under which set of assumptions would you prefer to work? Is your current or former supervisor a Theory X, Theory Y, or Theory Z manager? Explain by describing the person's behavior.
4. Think about several of your friends who seem to be highly self-motivated. Talk with each of them and ask them what factors contribute the most to their motivation. Make a list of their responses and compare them to the factors that motivate you.
5. Is money a job satisfier or a job maintenance factor for you? Explain.
6. Both individual motivation and group participation are needed to accomplish certain goals. Describe a situation you're familiar with in which cooperation achieved a goal that individual action could not. Describe one in which group action slowed progress and individual action would have been better.

KEY TERMS

cross-functional teams 324
equity theory 316
expectancy theory 316
goal-setting theory 317
group cohesiveness 322
Hawthorne effect 310
hygiene factors 313
job enlargement 319
job enrichment 319
job rotation 319
job sharing 320
Maslow's hierachy of needs 311
motivating factors 313
problem-solving teams 323
scientific management 308
self-managed work teams 323
Theory X 312
Theory Y 312
Theory Z 312
work groups 323
work teams 323

7. Using expectancy theory, analyze how you have made and will make personal choices, such as a major area of study, a career to pursue, or job interviews to seek.
8. If a famous executive or sports figure were to give a passionate motivational speech, trying to persuade people to work harder, what do you think the impact would be? Why?
9. You are the supervising manager of a group of college students. You have very limited funds but feel you need to do something to motivate your workers. What would you do?

Working the Net

1. Looking for 1,001 ways to motivate or reward your employees? Bob Nelson can help. Visit the Recognition resources section of his Nelson Motivation site at **http://www.nelson-motivation.com** to get some ideas you can put to use to help you do a better job, either as a manager or as an employee.
2. More companies are offering their employees stock ownership plans. To learn the differences between an employee stock ownership plan (ESOP) and stock options, visit the National Center for Employee Ownership (NCEO) at **http:/www.nceo.org** and the Foundation for Enterprise Development (FED) at **http:/www.fed.org**. Which stock plan would you rather have? Why? Also visit the ownership culture area of the NCEO site. What does research on employee ownership indicate? Cite specific examples.
3. Open-book management is one of the better known ways to create a participatory work environment. Over 2,000 companies have adopted this practice, which involves sharing financial information with nonmanagement employees and training them to understand financial information. Does it really motivate employees and improve productivity? Do a search for this topic at the NCEO site, **http:/www.nceo.org**. You'll find survey results, case studies, related activities, and links that will help you answer this question.
4. You've been asked to develop a staff recognition program for your company but don't have a clue where to start! Three sites with articles and other useful information are *Incentive* magazine, **http:/www.incentivemag.com**, the National Association for Employee Recognition, **http:/www.recognition.org**, and the U.S. Office of Personnel Management, **http:/www.opm.gov/perform/reward.html**. Using the material you'll find there, outline the plan you would recommend for your company.
5. Use a search engine to find companies that offer "work–life benefits." Link to several companies and review their employee programs in this area. How do they compare? Which benefits would be most important to you if you were job hunting, and why?

Creative Thinking Case

Handling Economic Downturns at TD Industries

Employee ownership programs are one method American corporations use to maximize employee productivity and motivation. The idea is that motivated employees will work harder to serve customers, produce quality products, and improve operations. Some of America's largest companies are more than 50 percent employee owned. These organizations include United Parcel Services, Avis, and Publix Supermarkets.

What happens to employee motivation when business slows down? TD Industries, a Dallas-based air-conditioning, heating, and plumbing company, is an employee-owned company that faced such a challenge. The company's backlog of projects shrank rapidly with the economic downturn in the telecom and dot-com industries located in North Dallas. Because it is employee owned, the company considered layoffs as the last step in cost-cutting measures.

In 1989, the company was forced to lay off 15 to 20 percent of its employees. The oil crisis and the savings and loan crisis in Texas destroyed the local economy and brought construction to a halt. Following the layoffs, the remaining employees agreed to loan the company $1.5 million from the employee pension fund to help the cash-strapped company.

TD Industries undertook a number of strategies to avoid layoffs to address the current reduction in business. It went after business in other industry sectors. Employees were encouraged to take vacation time and attend training sessions during this slower time. Other possible solutions presented to employees included taking a 10 percent cut in pay or a voluntary day off each week without pay.[25]

CRITICAL THINKING QUESTIONS

1. In what other way might the company address the reduced workload?
2. What might happen to employee motivation during these difficult times?
3. How might this reduction in business have been handled differently if TD Industries was not employee owned?

VIDEO CASE

Teamwork Matters At Hill, Holiday

"Teamwork helps foster the creative spirit," say Tim Jones and Marty Smith, the creative directors responsible for the coveted Dunkin' Donut account at 32-year-old advertising agency Hill, Holiday Creative, located in Boston.

"Advertising by committee doesn't work," says Jones. "Too many opinions water down the essence and energy of the work." They prefer working with autonomous creative teams, who are given their own space to work on a project. In Smith and Jones's experience this encourages "ownership" of the work, causing people to work harder and produce better results.

They review team output at the end of the workday. "People can be defensive when they've spent all day on an idea and we tell them they're heading down the wrong path," says Smith. "They may need time to think things over and regroup, so they go home and get it out of their system. Usually they are already working on new stuff by the next morning."

One exercise they found helpful was having their people review all 60 Dunkin' Donut advertising spots, which they mounted, gallery-style, on an office wall. The two creative directors "graded" each one, highlighting its strengths and weaknesses, including some they themselves had created—which received Ds and Fs. "It makes people feel better if they know you have made mistakes along the way too," says Smith.

They encourage people to be forthcoming with all their ideas, no matter how bad they think they are, because sometimes a brilliant idea comes out of a really bad one. "It doesn't matter where ideas come from," says Jones. "Sometimes writers come up with visual ideas and art directors with text suggestions." It can be tempting to put another team on a project if the ideas aren't flowing well, but competition seems to work against the creative process.

Dunkin' Donuts's TV spots air 52 weeks a year, in addition to print ads and holiday and seasonal promotions. So one team may be working on a coffee campaign, while another focuses on summer beverages, and still another on donuts. With plenty of work to go around, Smith and Jones are happy to give others the chance to work on a major account. "We bring a palpable enthusiasm to everything we do—it motivates others and helps us gel as a team," says Jones.

CRITICAL THINKING QUESTIONS

1. Distinguish between two major types of teams in the workplace. Which type does Hill, Holiday utilize?
2. Does Hill, Holiday utilize contemporary theories on employee motivation? Explain.
3. What else could Hill, Holiday do to increase employee motivation?

SOURCE: Adapted from material in the video: "Coffee Talk: Teamwork at Hill," Holiday Creative; Hill, Holiday Creative Web site, http:/www.hhcc.com, accessed March 17, 2003.

E-Commerce Case

Virtual Assistants Can Take Care of Your Business

Neal Lekwa, owner of the Calbert Group, prefers to hire multiple virtual assistants to avoid the "agony" of running a traditional office. His virtual company, which employs teams of subcontractors and virtual assistants scattered between Maine and India, provides e-commerce, Web construction, program design, photography, and consulting services to companies in the lodging and airline industries. "It is a very efficient way of delegating work," he says. "Everything is pure business."

Virtual assistants are highly motivated team players. They understand that their clients' success ultimately means their success. Its Web site (**http://www.calbertgroup.com**), states that team building "is always a matter of chance—searching in the right places, and luck." Clearly Lekwa knew where to search for his highly qualified virtual teams, who use results as their benchmark for success. State-of-the-art Web sites, insightful intuitive design, navigational efficiency, and superb software delivery systems mean a good end result.

Using virtual assistants is one way small businesses can operate and compete by containing costs. Dan Stafford, owner of PS Associates based on Vashon Island, Washington, couldn't manage without his virtual assistant, Terri Vincent, of Cody, Wyoming, who takes care of his mass mailings, travel arrangements, and other daily office operations. Vincent, a self-employed administrative professional, works from her downtown Cody office for a dozen regular clients each month, charging by the hour or by the project.

But managing a virtual workforce can present unique challenges. None of the virtual employees know one another—their only connection is through the contractor they work for. Keeping far-flung assistants in different time zones in the communication loop can be a major challenge, so superior project management skills are important to the success of operating a virtual business.

Cheryl Allin, 33, a working mother from Tacoma, Washington, signed her first client just six weeks after opening her own virtual-assistant business. "I wanted to use my experience in Internet businesses and still be available for my four children," she says. Now, thanks to technology and the growing acceptance of virtual business arrangements, a valuable and previously underutilized segment of the workforce can reap the benefits of doing useful and rewarding work, while their clients benefit from what they bring to the (virtual) table.

CRITICAL THINKING QUESTIONS

1. What are some of the benefits virtual assistants and their clients derive from this unique way of doing business?
2. What are some of the challenges of motivating and retaining a team of virtual employees?

SOURCES: Jenny Lynn Zappala, "Virtual Assistants Enjoy Flexibility, Independence," *Puget Sound Business Journal,* January 18, 2002, downloaded from bizjournals.com! April 7, 2003; International Virtual Assistants Association Web site, http://www.ivaa.org, accessed April 7, 2003; Staffcentrix Web site, accessed April 7, 2003; Calbert Group Web site, http://www.calbertgroup.com, accessed April 7, 2003.

HOT LINKS ADDRESS BOOK

Want to find out more about organizational efficiency at United Parcel Service? Visit
http://www.ups.com

What makes a company a good place to work? Find out by reading about the companies on *Fortune* magazine's "100 Best Companies to Work For" by visiting
http://www.fortune.com

Expand your knowledge about motivation in the workplace at Accel-Team's site,
http://www.accel-team.com/motivation/index.html

How do you keep employees satisfied? The Business Research Lab has a series of articles on this topic at
http://www.busreslab.com/tips/tipses.htm

Find team-building resources galore at Teambuilding, Inc.'s supersite,
http://www.teambuildinginc.com

ASTD is a professional association and leading resource on workplace learning and performance issues. Visit its site,
http://www.astd.org
to learn more about these topics.

Chapter 11

© AP / WIDE WORLD PHOTOS

Understanding Labor–Management Relations

learning goals

1 What is the historical development of American labor unions?
2 What role did federal law play in the development of the union–management relationship?
3 What is the union organizing process?
4 What is the collective bargaining process, and what key issues are included in the union contract?
5 How do employees file a grievance?
6 What economic tactics do unions and employers use in labor–management conflicts?
7 What trends will affect American workers and labor–management relations?

Lockout of West Coast Dockworkers

Although relatively uncommon, employers can lock out (or prevent from coming into work) unionized employees in an attempt to convince the union to accept the employer's labor contract proposals.

In late 2002, the Pacific Maritime Association (PMA) (**http://www.pmanet.org/**), which represents West Coast shippers and terminal operators, locked out 10,500 dockworkers who handle freight at 29 shipping/receiving ports stretching from San Diego to Seattle. Dockworkers are represented by the International Longshore and Warehouse Union (ILWU) (**http://www.ilwu.org/**). The PMA contended that dockworkers had been engaging in a work slowdown for several days. Dockworkers had been working without a labor agreement since mid-July 2002, when their most recent three-year labor contract expired.[1]

PMA and ILWU had negotiated for several months about wages, pensions, and other benefits, all very standard contract issues that are normally changed with each new contract. The most difficult issues of these negotiations, however, involved productivity and use of new cargo-handling technology. PMA port operators wanted to use the technology of bar-code scanners and "fast passes" for toll booths to enhance the efficiency of dock operations. These technological devices speed information processing, which in turn allows loading and unloading of freight to be done faster. The ILWU was willing to allow implementation of the technologies, but it didn't want any shipping clerks and other employees to lose their jobs. Also, the union wanted any new jobs associated with the technology to be under its jurisdiction. PMA had resisted the union's position because it wanted to have the flexibility to outsource (or contract out to a third party) tasks that were currently performed by shipping clerks.[2]

Each year over $300 billion of goods (perishable fruits and vegetables, frozen meats, car parts, electronic components, household appliances and entertainment gadgets, and hundreds of other items) pass through West Coast ports. A short lockout (a week or less) would have little economic impact, but losses would total $1 to $2 billion a day. A work stoppage of more than a week would result in the shutdown of some manufacturing plants that operate with very limited parts inventory.[3]

Almost immediately following the start of the lockout and shutdown, pressure began to increase on President George W. Bush to invoke the national emergency strike procedures of the Taft–Hartley Act. This law, passed in 1947, can be used only by the president of the United States in the event a work stoppage creates a significant threat to the economy and the health and safety of U.S. citizens. The president can appoint a "board of inquiry" to investigate the situation. With information from the board of inquiry report, the president can declare an 80-day cool-down (or cooling-off) period during which the workers must return to work and the adversaries, in this case the PMA and ILWU, must resume their contract negotiations.

Critical Thinking Questions

As you read this chapter, consider these questions as they relate to the West Coast work stoppage of dock operations:

1. President Bush was faced with a difficult situation. He could (a) invoke the national emergency strike procedures of the Taft–Hartley Act, or (b) intensify federal efforts to bring the two sides together, possibly even becoming directly involved in the negotiations himself, or (c) do essentially nothing and allow the dispute to continue for an extended time. What should he do and why?
2. What are the various procedures within the Taft–Hartley Act that can be used in this situation?
3. Do you think that these procedures have been used much in the past?

Principles of Labor–Management Relations

Tens of thousands of American firms are unionized and millions of American workers belong to unions. Worker organizations have existed in the United States since before the signing of the Declaration of Independence. If you work in the mining, manufacturing, construction, or transportation industries, you will probably deal with or be affected by labor unions.

labor union
An organization that represents workers in dealing with management over disputes involving wages, hours, and working conditions.

collective bargaining
The process of negotiating labor agreements that provide for compensation and working arrangements mutually acceptable to the union and to management.

A **labor union,** such as the International Brotherhood of Teamsters, is an organization that represents workers in dealing with management over disputes involving wages, hours, and working conditions. The labor relations process that produces a union–management relationship consists of three phases: union organizing, negotiating a labor agreement, and the day-to-day administering of the agreement. At phase one, a group of employees within a firm may form a union on their own or an established union (United Auto Workers, for example) may target an employer and organize many of the firm's workers into a local labor union. The second phase constitutes **collective bargaining,** which is the process of negotiating labor agreements that provide for compensation and working arrangements mutually acceptable to the union and to management.

The third phase of the labor relations process involves the daily administering of the labor agreement primarily through handling worker grievances and other workforce management problems that require interaction between managers and labor union officials.

Labor unions have a rich history in American business. We begin this chapter by exploring their historical development. Next, we discuss the critical role federal law has played and continues to play in labor–management relations. We will see how unions are organized and how they bargain with management. We then discuss important issues and items in labor agreements and the economic tactics available to unions and to management. We conclude with trends in labor–management relations.

The Emergence of Unions and Collective Bargaining

1 learning goal

Early labor organizations began to develop toward the end of the 1700s, as the United States started to shift from an agricultural to an industrial economy. Craft guilds or societies, as they were called, were made up of skilled artisans (shoemakers and tailors) who pushed for better working conditions. They resisted shop owners who wanted to lower wages. Many of the early guilds threatened to stop working unless business owners paid higher wages, provided some of the tools needed for work, and shortened the workday. Employers opposed these efforts, often successfully, and the guilds would disband.

Knights of Labor
The first important national labor organization in the United States; founded in 1869.

In 1869 a small group of clothing workers secretly founded the Noble Order of the Knights of Labor. The **Knights of Labor** was the first major national labor organization. By about 1880 its local assemblies had more than 500,000 members. But it was never very successful at improving the employment situation of working people. Instead, the organization was more concerned with broad social and economic issues such as child labor, public education, and business monopolies.

American Federation of Labor

Many of the craft groups within the Knights of Labor were unhappy with its social-reform policy and political activities. In 1881 they broke away and formed the Federation of Organized Trades and Labor Unions, which five years later was renamed

© HULTON ARCHIVE / GETTY IMAGES

Industrial unions were formed in the mid-1930s to represent workers in mass-production industries. They organized factory workers like the automotive employees shown here in 1937 protesting work conditions at General Motor's assembly plant in Flint, Michigan.

American Federation of Labor (AFL)
A national labor organization made up of numerous craft unions; founded in 1881 by splinter groups from the Knights of Labor. In 1955, the AFL merged with the Congress of Industrial Organizations (CIO) to form the AFL-CIO.

craft union
A union that represents skilled workers in a single craft or occupation such as bricklaying, carpentry, or plumbing.

industrial union
A union that represents all of the workers in a particular industry, such as auto workers or steel workers.

American Federation of Labor (AFL). Under Samuel Gompers, who was its president for more than 35 years, the AFL pressed for better recognition and more power for member unions, collective bargaining, and the right to conduct temporary work stoppages (*strikes*) to improve wages, hours, and working conditions.

The AFL consisted of numerous craft unions joined together under the banner of one large labor organization. A **craft union** represents skilled workers in a single craft or occupation, such as bricklaying, carpentry, or plumbing. Each craft union had exclusive jurisdiction over its trade or craft and respected the jurisdictions of other craft unions; that is, each had the right to organize all workers within a single skilled trade or craft. The carpenters' union, for example, represented only carpenters; it did not represent plumbers. Each union also developed its own constitution, chose its own leaders, and formulated its own strategy for collective bargaining.

Congress of Industrial Organizations

The AFL was the major force on the labor scene for nearly 50 years. But with the Great Depression of the 1930s came severe unemployment in the building and skilled trades and a loss of power for the AFL. Then, just as the economy began to improve, the AFL faced a crisis. Mass-production workers wanted to be represented by unions, but the craft unions thought the factory workers would jeopardize the high labor standards that had been gained through collective bargaining and did not want to represent them.

Under the leadership of John L. Lewis, the United Mine Workers (UMW) of America challenged the AFL's position. For several decades the UMW had been a member of the AFL. But it had developed as a mining industry union, containing both skilled and unskilled workers. Thus, it went against the AFL's doctrine of exclusive jurisdiction based on craft. Lewis argued that a union organized along industry lines would be better than a craft union for representing workers in large-scale, mass-production industries. Each industry could have its own union. Under the leadership of Lewis, Sidney Hillman, and Walter Ruether, industry-wide union membership drives began in the automobile, steel, tire, and oil industries. In each case a different **industrial union** was formed under the slogan "one industry, one union."

Congress of Industrial Organizations (CIO)
A national labor organization made up of numerous industrial unions; founded in 1935. In 1955, the CIO merged with the American Federation of Labor (AFL) to form the AFL-CIO.

In 1935 Lewis took his union and a handful of others and left the AFL. They formed the **Congress of Industrial Organizations (CIO).** As a collection of industrial unions, the CIO succeeded in organizing unions in the mass-production industries of food processing, electrical-equipment manufacturing, auto assembly, and oil refining. After a brief period, the AFL counterattacked and also recruited thousands of industrial workers to its ranks.

The AFL and CIO: Rivalry and Merger

Until the early 1950s, the AFL and the CIO competed for new members and frequently attempted to steal each other's members. Unfortunately, some workers got caught in the crossfire. These efforts cost both organizations a lot of money and produced few membership gains overall. Finally, the two decided to end their rivalry. On December 5, 1955, the AFL and CIO merged into one organization with George Meany as its president. The combined AFL-CIO spoke for more than 16 million workers.

Today, the AFL-CIO is an umbrella organization for most American labor unions. It represents about 80 unions and approximately 85 percent of all rank-and-file union members—those who are not elected officials of the union. The AFL-CIO provides research, education, legal, and public-relations services to member unions. It does not take part in collective bargaining. It does sponsor and coordinate union membership and organizes drives. Lobbying and political involvement are also prominent activities. Under the leadership of AFL-CIO President John Sweeny, the labor federation spent about $39 million in the 2002 federal and state elections to try to win more Democratic governorships, and Senate and House seats.[4] In most elections union members vote in higher percentages than the populace as a whole.

The Labor Movement Today

The basic structure of the modern labor movement consists of three parts: local unions, national and international unions, and the AFL-CIO. There are approximately 60,000 local unions and 80 national and international unions. Unions, in general, have experienced a steady decline in membership, as shown in Exhibit 11.1.

local union
A branch or unit of a national union that represents workers at a specific plant or in a specific geographic area.

LOCAL UNIONS A **local union** is a branch or unit of a national union that represents workers at a specific plant or over a specific geographic area. Local 276 of the United Auto Workers represents assembly employees at the General Motors plant in Arlington, Texas. In conformance to national union rules, local unions determine the number of local union officers, procedures for electing officers, the schedule of local meetings, financial arrangements with the national organization, and the local's role in negotiating labor agreements.

The three main functions of the local union are collective bargaining, worker relations and membership services, and community and political activities. Collective bargaining takes place every two or three years. Local union officers and shop stewards in the plant oversee worker–management relations on a day-to-day basis. A **shop steward** is an elected union official who represents union members to management when workers have complaints. For most union members, his or her primary contact with the union is through union officials at the local level.

shop steward
An elected union official who represents union members to management when workers have complaints.

national union
A union that consists of many local unions in a particular industry, skilled trade, or geographic area and thus represents workers throughout an entire country.

NATIONAL AND INTERNATIONAL UNIONS **National unions** range in size from a few thousand members (Screen Writers Guild) to more than a million members (Teamsters, with 1.4 million).

The number of national unions has steadily declined since the early 20th century. Much of this decline has resulted from union mergers. Early in 1999, for example, the United Papermakers International Union (UPIU) and the Oil, Chemical and Atomic Workers Union (OCAW) agreed to merge under the new name of PACE, or Paper, Al-

Exhibit 11.1 | Union Membership Trends, 1955–2003

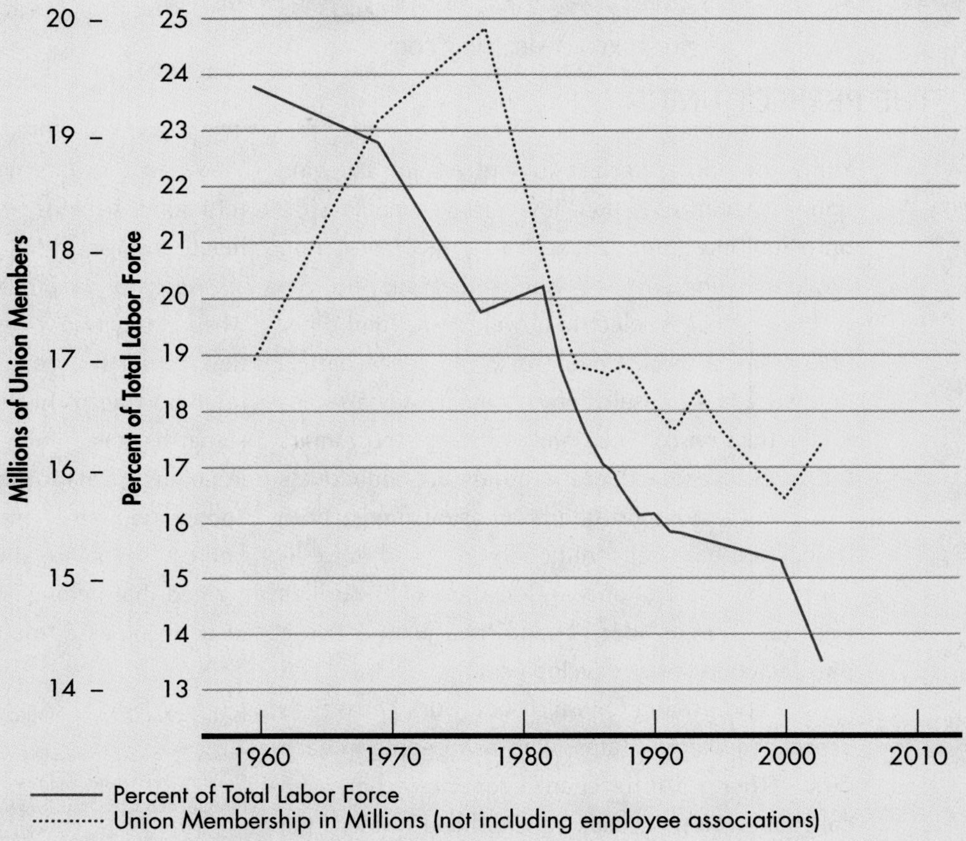

SOURCE: Bureau of Labor Statistics, Washington, D.C.: U.S. Department of Labor.

lied-Industrial, Chemical and Energy International Union. PACE has 320,000 members and has set an aggressive growth goal of adding 10,000 new members a year, according to Robert Wages, executive vice president of the new organization. In recent years merger discussions have been ongoing among the Auto Workers, Steelworkers, and Machinist unions. If these three unions merged, the resulting union would be the largest in the United States.

concept check

Trace the development of the labor movement in the United States.

What is the AFL-CIO, and how does it operate?

The Legal Environment of Unions

2 learning goal

Although today unions and employers nearly always resolve their differences without disruptions, union–management relations have not always been so peaceful and businesslike. The respectful relationship that now exists between unions and employers has resulted, in part, from laws passed from the early 1930s to the late 1950s.

Norris–LaGuardia Act (Anti-Injunction Act)

Before 1932, a company faced with striking or picketing workers could get the courts to order them back to work. It did so by requesting an **injunction,** a court order barring certain union activities. Only rarely did a judge deny the employer's request for an injunction. Union members who didn't obey could be fined or sent to prison.

injunction
A court order barring certain union activities.

Making Ethical Choices

xtra! http://gitmanxtra.swlearning.com

THE PERFECT UNION

You've found the perfect "union"—a job allowing you to capitalize on your love of investments without requiring you to make cold calls. You enjoy the opportunity to sell bonds that support the building of roads, electric-power plants, and other utilities for a foreign country. What's even better, you work in a nonsales environment, for a salary rather than on commission. Your target customers for $500 investment grade bonds are individuals and, for the $25,000 bonds, pension funds; both groups are easy sells. Although you need to be licensed by the National Association of Securities Dealers, you consider earning this qualification a plus for your career development.

The corporation for which you work has offices across the United States, with few people in each office. There is little chance for interacting with colleagues directly, making it difficult to learn the ropes or talk about the work environment. This lack of contact with other professionals soon becomes problematic.

When you interviewed for the job, you were told about benefits—35-hour workweek, amount of health insurance that you are responsible for, and six weeks of vacation in your first year. However, when you get your first paycheck you see a deduction for union dues in addition to the deduction for your portion of health insurance. This is troublesome, because philosophically you do not believe in unions. Perhaps even more distressing is the response you get from company headquarters when you call to inquire about the deduction. You are informed that belonging to a union is a requirement of your job as a "marketing representative."

ETHICAL DILEMMA

Is this condition of employment an unfair labor practice?

Sources: Personal interview with Renée Barnow, April 13, 2003; Gillian Flynn, "When Unions Come Calling," *Workforce*, November 2000, downloaded from http://www.findarticles.com; and "How to Win Past Practice Grievances," Work Rights Press, June 2001, downloaded from http://www.workrightspress.com.

yellow-dog contracts
Contracts in which employees agreed not to join a labor union as a condition of being hired.

Norris–La Guardia Act
A statute enacted in 1932 that barred the use of injunctions to prevent strikes and other union activities and made yellow-dog contracts unenforceable; also called the *Anti-Injunction Act.*

Wagner Act
A statute enacted in 1935 that established that employees have a right to organize and join labor unions and to engage in collective bargaining; also known as the *National Labor Relations Act.*

Employers also used the courts to enforce **yellow-dog contracts,** in which employees agree not to join a labor union as a condition of being hired. Employees who broke a yellow-dog contract could be fired. Blacklists of workers who were involved with unions circulated among employers to keep the workers from being hired.

The **Norris–La Guardia Act** of 1932 (also known as the Anti-Injunction Act) largely ended the use of injunctions by employers. It banned their use to prevent strikes, among other things. The act also made yellow-dog contracts unenforceable.

Wagner Act (National Labor Relations Act)

The Norris–La Guardia Act opened the door to more union organizing, especially in mass-production industries. But employers were still not obliged to bargain with unions. The unions urged Congress to pass a law that would require employers to deal with them. Congress responded with the National Labor Relations Act of 1935, commonly known as the **Wagner Act.** This law encouraged the formation of unions and the use of collective bargaining. It also provided a means for peacefully resolving disputes over union representation.

In addition to making it illegal for an employer to refuse to bargain with a union about wages, hours, and other job conditions, the Wagner Act also protected workers from unfair labor practices. For instance, an employer cannot discriminate against (or treat unfairly) an employee who is involved in union activities. Nor can an employer fire an employee for joining a union.

National Labor Relations Board (NLRB)
An agency established by the Wagner Act of 1935 to enforce the act and investigate charges of employer and union wrongdoing and supervise elections for union representatives.

The **National Labor Relations Board (NLRB)** was established to enforce the Wagner Act. Its five members are appointed by the president; the agency's main office is in Washington, DC, and regional and field offices are scattered throughout the United States. NLRB field agents investigate charges of employer and union wrongdoing (or unfair labor practices) and supervise elections held to decide union representation. Administrative law judges conduct hearings to determine whether employers and unions have violated the law. In 1998 the NLRB allowed unfair labor practice charges and election petitions to be made on its Web site.

Taft–Hartley Act (Labor–Management Relations Act)

Employers resisted the Wagner Act and in some cases disobeyed it, until the Supreme Court upheld the law in 1937. Many employers saw the Wagner Act as too pro-labor. In 1947 Congress amended it with the Labor–Management Relations Act, commonly known as the **Taft–Hartley Act**. This act:

Taft-Hartley Act
A statute enacted in 1947 that defined unfair union practices, outlined the rules for dealing with strikes of major economic impact, broadened employer options for dealing with unions, and further defined the rights of employees as individuals.

- Defined unfair union practices.
- Outlined the rules for dealing with strikes of major economic impact.
- Broadened employer options for dealing with unions.
- Further defined the rights of employees as individuals.

Among the unfair union practices banned by the Taft–Hartley Act were excessive or discriminatory fees and dues. (For example, monthly dues of $200 would be too much for a union member who earns only $2,000 per month.) Also, the act made it unlawful for picketing union members to block nonstriking employees from entering the business to go to work. Another unfair practice, is that unions cannot refuse to bargain (or negotiate) with the employer. Paying union dues may sometimes raise ethical questions such as those raised in the "Making Ethical Choices" box.

EMERGENCY STRIKE PROCEDURES Immediately after World War II, union strike activity increased dramatically. Lengthy strikes disrupted business, and many firms and citizens suffered. In response, Congress included national emergency strike procedures in the Taft–Hartley Act. Under these provisions, the president can declare a national emergency if a strike threatens the health and safety of Americans. The president can temporarily stop the strike by having a federal judge issue an injunction. The injunction forces the strikers back to work for up to 80 days (known as the *cooling-off period*) while the employer and labor negotiators try to resolve their differences. If they don't reach an agreement within 80 days, the strike can resume. The president cannot initiate procedures to have a second injunction issued; only one cooling-off period is permitted.

In the early October 2002 West Coast dockworker lockout, President George W. Bush instructed the Justice Department to obtain the 80-day injunction. This court request took place on the 10th day of the work stoppage. The Northern District Court of California issued the injunction just a few hours after receiving the request. This was the first time in 24 years that a president had made an injunction request for the purpose of ending a work stoppage.[5] The International Longshore and Warehouse Union (ILWU) opposed the president's actions, whereas the Pacific Maritime Association (PMA), the employer's association that represents the terminal operators and shippers, was supportive of President Bush's handling of the situation.[6]

FEDERAL MEDIATION AND CONCILIATION SERVICE Congress also created the Federal Mediation and Conciliation Service as part of the Taft–Hartley Act. This service helps unions and employers negotiate labor agreements. Agency specialists, who serve as impartial third parties between the union and the employer, use two processes: conciliation and mediation. In **conciliation,** the specialist helps management and the union focus on the issues and acts as a go-between, or a communication channel through which the union and employer can send messages to and share information with each other.

conciliation
A method of attempting to settle labor disputes in which a specialist from the Federal Mediation and Conciliation Service helps management and the union focus on the issues and acts as a go-between.

mediation
A method of attempting to settle labor disputes in which a specialist from the Federal Mediation and Conciliation Service serves as a mediator.

The specialist takes a stronger role in **mediation,** a process of settling disputes in which the parties present their case to a neutral mediator. The mediator (the specialist) holds talks with union and management negotiators at separate meetings and at joint sessions. The mediator also suggests compromises. Mediators cannot issue binding decisions or impose a settlement on the disputing parties. Their only tools are communication and persuasion. Mediation almost always produces a settlement between the union and a firm, but sometimes the process takes months or even a year, and either or both sides can reject the mediator's assistance. In 2002, aircraft manufacturer Boeing rejected a mediator's request to resume contract negotiations with the International Association of Machinists and Aerospace Workers, its largest union (25,000 members). Union members were in the process of voting on whether to accept the firm's last, best offer. The union failed to obtain the two-thirds majority vote that was required to reject the offer and began a strike.[7]

Another recent request for mediation involved railroad engineers and unmanned locomotives as explained in the "Applying Technology" box below.

APPLYING TECHNOLOGY

Unmanned Locomotives on the Nation's Railroads

While the nation's railroads, particularly Amtrack, still transport passengers, most of the large-scale railroad systems move freight, not passengers. Burlington Northern Santa Fe (BNSF) and Union Pacific Railroad (UPR) are two large railroads that have been experimenting with unmanned locomotives. The two firms have used about 40 3,000-horsepower unmanned locomotives in their large switching yards. The Brotherhood of Locomotive Engineers (BLE) has opposed use of unmanned locomotives because of safety concerns and the threat of job loss. If BNSF and UPR extend unmanned locomotives from the switching yards to cross-country trains, fewer onboard engineers are needed.

The unmanned locomotives are operated in switching yards by workers using hand-held controls. These workers are members of the United Transportation Union (UTU), a union that represents several groups of railroad employees. The UTU's latest contract contains provisions that permit its members to operate unmanned locomotives following a two-week training course. Railroad engineers, represented by the BLE, take up to eight months of training before being certified to operate locomotives. To complicate this situation, the Teamsters Union and the BLE have been engaged in discussions that will likely lead to the BLE being merged into the Teamsters.

The BLE has pursued this dispute to the Federal Railroad Administration and has requested the National Mediation Service to intervene and help negotiate a settlement that would ban use of unmanned locomotives on cross-country train routes. Failing this effort, the union has pledged to pursue legislation that would ban unmanned locomotives outside of switching yards. An important objective of BNSF and UPR is to gain efficiencies and increased productivity through application of technology.[8]

CRITICAL THINKING QUESTIONS

1. If you were Matt Rose, President and CEO of BNSF, would you decide to use unmanned locomotives outside switching yards? Why or why not?
2. Should railroad engineers be permitted to strike over this technological improvement? Explain your answer.
3. Assume that the BLE merges with the Teamsters Union. Could the railroad companies play one union (Teamsters) off the other (UTU) in an effort to create dissension among groups of employees? Would you consider such management action ethical? Why or why not?

Landrum–Griffin Act
A statute enacted in 1959 to regulate the internal affairs of unions; contains a bill of rights for union members, rules for electing union officers, and safeguards to keep unions financially sound.

Landrum–Griffin Act (Labor-Management Reporting and Disclosure Act)

Shortly after the merger of the AFL and the CIO in 1955, some national unions including the Teamsters and Bakery Workers were accused of poor financial management, rigged elections for officers, and bribery of union officials. After an investigation, Congress passed the Labor–Management Reporting and Disclosure Act of 1959, often called the **Landrum–Griffin Act.** Unlike the Wagner and Taft–Hartley Acts, this law deals mostly with the internal affairs of labor unions. It contains a bill of rights for union members, a set of rules for electing union officers, and safeguards to help make unions financially sound. It also requires that unions file detailed annual financial reports with the U.S. secretary of labor. The Department of Labor enforces the Landrum–Griffin Act.

concept check

Discuss the key points of the Norris-La Guardia Act and the Wagner Act.

Define mediation and conciliation.

Union Organizing

3 learning goal

A nonunion employer becomes unionized through an *organizing campaign.* The campaign is started either from within, by unhappy employees, or from outside, by a union that has picked the employer for an organizing drive. Once workers and the union have made contact, a union organizer tries to convince all the workers to sign *authorization cards.* These cards prove the workers' interest in having the union represent them. In most cases, employers resist this card-signing campaign by speaking out against unions in letters, posters, and employee assemblies. However, it is illegal for employers to interfere directly with the card-signing campaign or to coerce employees into not joining the union.

union certification election
An election in which workers vote, by secret ballot, on whether they want to be represented by a union; conducted by the National Labor Relations Board.

bargaining unit
The employees who are eligible to vote in a union certification election and who will be represented by the union if it is certified.

Once the union gets signed authorization cards from at least 30 percent of the employees, it can ask the National Labor Relations Board for a **union certification election.** This election, by secret ballot, determines whether the workers want to be represented by the union. The NLRB posts an election notice and defines the **bargaining unit**—employees who are eligible to vote and who will be represented by the particular union if it is certified. Supervisors and managers cannot vote. The union and the employer then engage in a preelection campaign conducted through speeches, memos, and meetings. Both try to convince workers to vote in their favor. Exhibit 11.2 lists benefits usually stressed by the union during a campaign and common arguments employers make to convince employees a union is unnecessary.

The election itself is conducted by the NLRB. If a majority vote for the union, the NLRB certifies the union as the exclusive bargaining agent for all employees who had been designated as eligible voters. The employer then has to bargain with the union over wages, hours, and other terms of employment. The complete organizing process is summarized in Exhibit 11.3.

decertification election
An election in which workers vote, by secret ballot, on whether they want to continue to be represented by their union.

In some situations, after one year, if the union and employer don't reach an agreement, the workers petition for a **decertification election** which is similar to the certification election but allows workers to vote out the union. Decertification elections are also held when workers become dissatisfied with a union that has represented them for a longer time. In recent years, the number of decertification elections increased to several hundred per year.

One of the largest businesses in the United States has been successful in remaining nonunion for many years. The United Food and Commercial Workers (UFCW) has been persistent in efforts to gain bargaining rights for Wal-Mart employees. One UFCU organizing drive involved 5,000 Wal-Mart workers in and around Las Vegas. The union had petitioned for an NLRB election late in 2001. Wal-Mart vigorously resisted the organizing drive. Employees became intimidated by the aggressive corporate campaign. The union withdrew its petition and filed numerous unfair labor practices against the firm claiming Wal-Mart had fired several union sympathizers, engaged in surveillance of employees, and hired anti-

Exhibit 11.2 Benefits Stressed by Unions in Organizing Campaigns and Common Arguments Against Unions

Benefits Stressed by Unions:

Almost Always Stressed	Often Stressed	Seldom Stressed
Grievance procedures	More influence in decision making	Higher-quality products
Job security	Better working conditions	Technical training
Improved benefits	Lobbying opportunities	More job satisfaction
Higher pay		Increased production

Employer Arguments Against Unionization:

- An employee can always come directly to management with a problem; a third party (the union) isn't necessary.
- As a union member, you will pay monthly union dues of $15 to $30.
- Merit-based decisions (promotions) are better than seniority-based.
- Pay and benefits are very similar to the leading firms in the industry.
- We meet all health and safety standards of the Federal Occupational Safety and Health Administration.
- Performance and productivity are more important than union representation in determining pay raises.

Exhibit 11.3 Union Organizing Process and Election

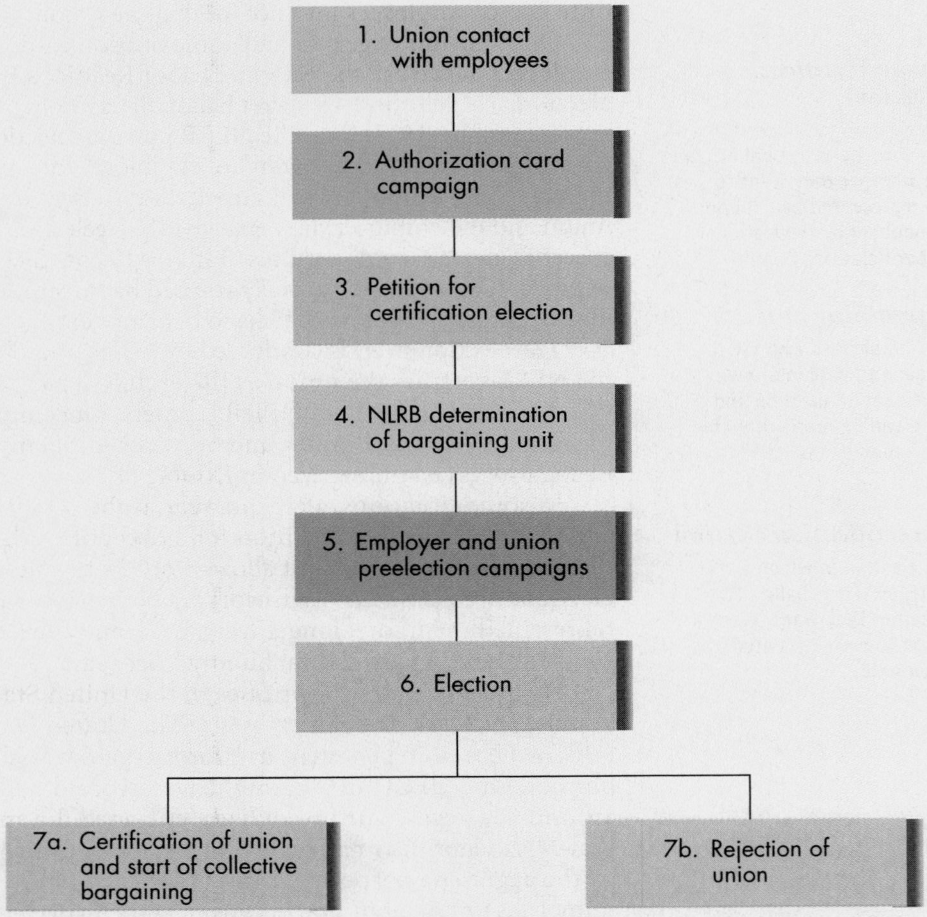

concept check

Describe the union organizing process.

What is a union certification election?

union consultants to train supervisors. While the union was not successful in the Las Vegas organizing drive, it later started a region-wide organizing effort in Michigan, Ohio, Indiana, and Kentucky at Wal-Mart facilities to gain representation rights for as many as 117,000 Wal-Mart employees.[9]

Negotiating Union Contracts

4 learning goal

A union contract is created through collective bargaining. Typically, both management and union negotiating teams are made up of a few persons. One person on each side is the chief spokesperson.

Bargaining begins with union and management negotiators setting a *bargaining agenda,* a list of contract issues that will be discussed. Much of the bargaining over the specific details takes place through face-to-face meetings and the exchange of written proposals. Demands, proposals, and counterproposals are exchanged during several rounds of bargaining. The resulting contract must then be approved by top management and by union members. The collective bargaining process is shown in Exhibit 11.4.

Exhibit 11.4 The Process of Negotiating Labor Agreements

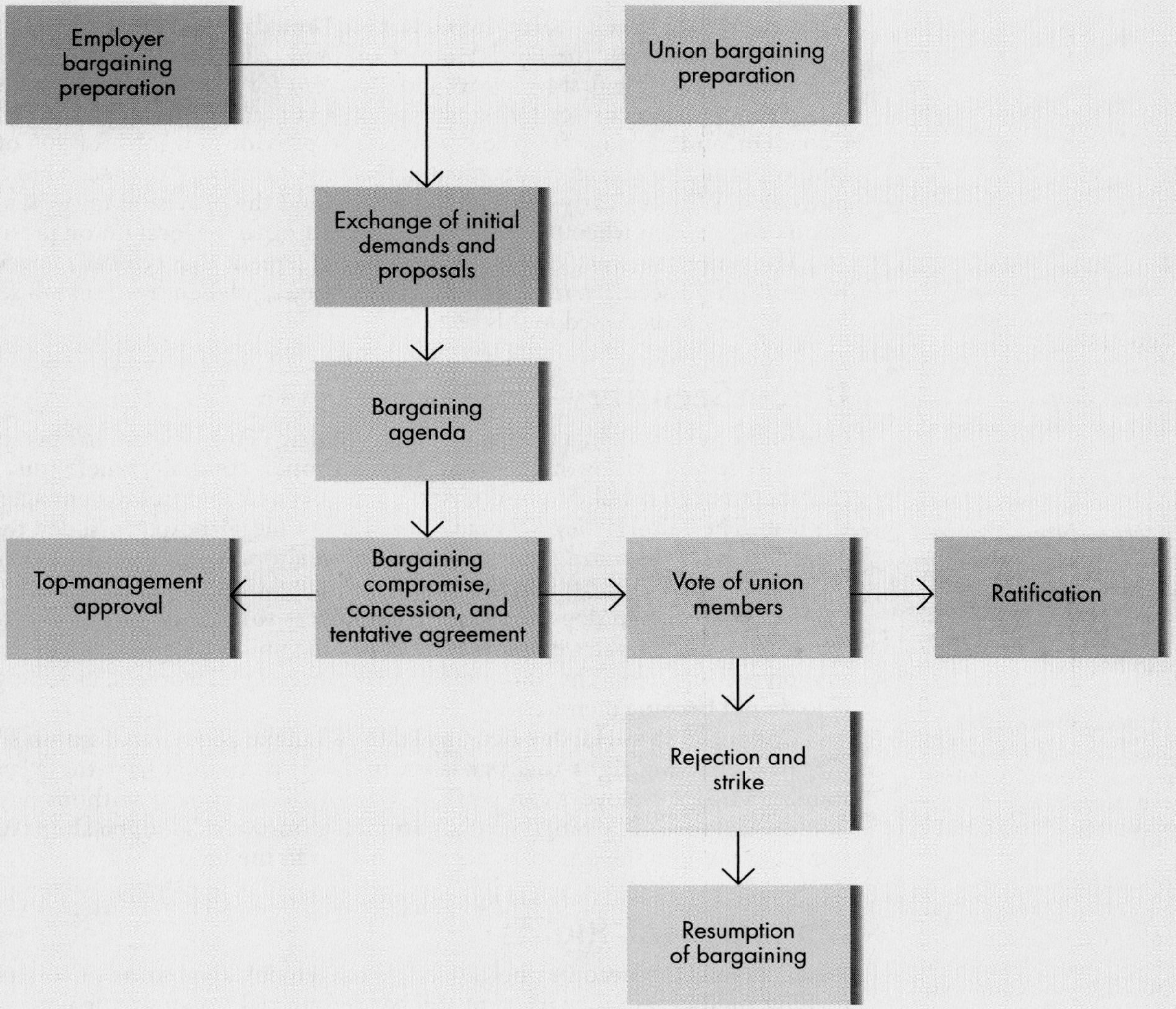

General Electric employees held strikes in 48 locations to protest the company's decision to force them to pay $200 more per year toward their health costs. Union contracts usually cover issues as job benefits, job security, union security, and management rights.

© AP / WIDE WORLD PHOTOS

Late in 2002 the Canadian division of the United Auto Workers reached a contract settlement with the Ford Motor Company. Along with wage increases of 3 percent each of the first two years and 2 percent for the third contract year, provisions included a cost-of-living allowance, a contract-signing bonus of $1,000 Canadian, and a pledge from the company to provide new jobs for 900 of 1,400 employees at a pickup assembly plant in Oakville, Ontario, that is slated to close in mid-2004. With the early-retirement package and the provision for new jobs, no layoffs will happen when the plant closes, according to the local union president.[10]

The union contract is a legally binding agreement that typically covers such issues as union security, management rights, wages, job benefits, and job security. Each of these is discussed in this section.

closed shop
A company where only union members can be hired; made illegal by the Taft–Hartley Act.

union shop
A company where nonunion workers can be hired but must then join the union.

agency shop
A company where employees are not required to join the union but must pay it a fee to cover its expenses in representing them.

right-to-work laws
State laws that allow employees to work at a unionized company without having to join the union.

open shop
A company where employees do not have to join the union or pay dues or fees to the union; established under right-to-work laws.

Union Security

One of the key issues in a contract is union security. From the union's perspective, the most secure arrangement is the **closed shop,** a company where only union members can be hired. The union serves, in effect, as an employment agency for the firm. The Taft–Hartley Act made closed shops illegal, however. Today, the most common form of union security is the **union shop.** Nonunion workers can be hired, but then they must join the union, normally within 30 or 60 days.

An **agency shop** does not require employees to join the union. But to keep working at the company, employees must pay the union a fee to cover its expenses in representing them. The union must fairly represent all workers, including those who do not become members.

Under the Taft–Hartley Act, any state can make all forms of union security illegal by enacting **right-to-work laws.** In the 21 states that have these laws (see Exhibit 11.5), employees can work at a unionized company without having to join the union. This arrangement is commonly known as an **open shop.** Workers don't have to join the union or pay dues or fees to the union.

Management Rights

When a company becomes unionized, management loses some of its decision-making abilities. But management still has certain rights that can be negotiated in collective bargaining.

Exhibit 11.5 | States with Right-to-Work Laws

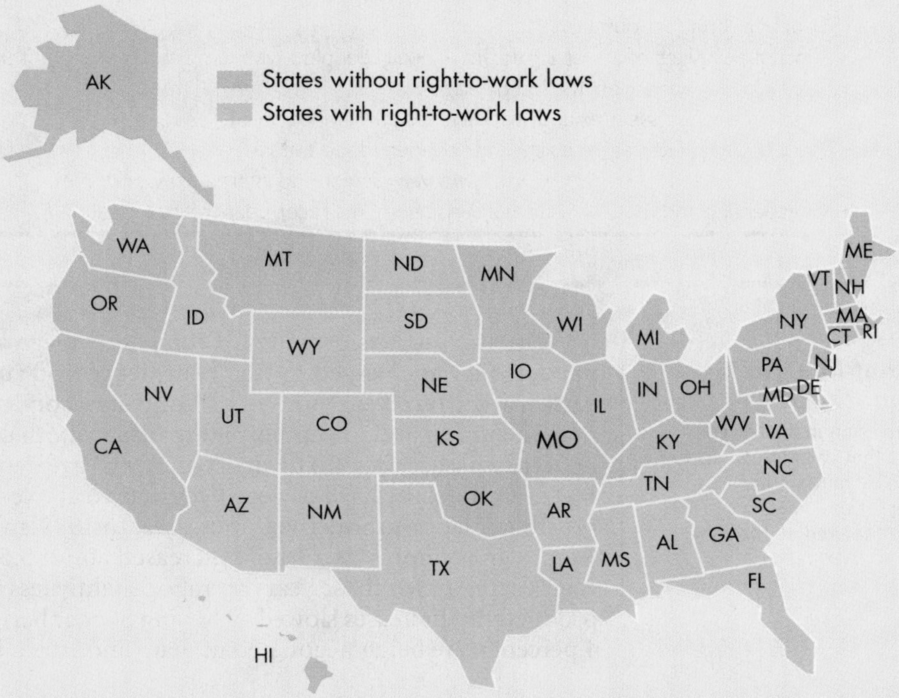

One way to resist union meddling in management matters is to put a *management rights clause* in the labor agreement. Most union contracts have one. A typical clause gives the employer all rights to manage the business except as specified in the contract. For instance, if the contract does not specify the criteria for promotions, with a management rights clause managers will have the right to use any criteria they wish. Another way to preserve management rights is to list areas that are not subject to collective bargaining. This list might secure management's right to schedule work hours, hire and fire workers, set production standards, determine the number of supervisors in each department, and promote, demote, and transfer workers.

The NFL Players Association's collective bargaining agreement includes a player's salary cap that gives the teams stability. The NFL is widely seen as having the most favorable player deal in pro sports.

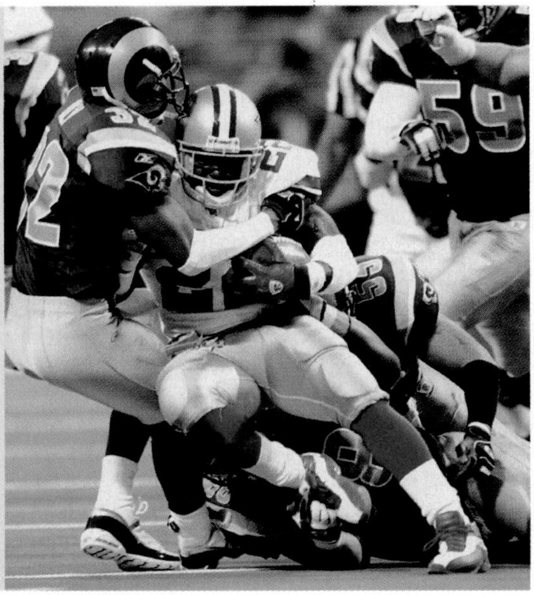

© AP / WIDE WORLD PHOTOS

Wages

Much bargaining effort goes into wage increases and improvements in fringe benefits. Once agreed to, they remain in effect for the life of the contract. In the contract mentioned earlier between the Auto Workers of Canada and Ford Motor Co., hourly wages of $27.70 Canadian will increase a compounded 8.21 percent over the contract's three-year duration. Additionally, the agreement contained an increase in paid time off (vacations, holidays, and personal days). Exhibit 11.6 provides a summary list of contract provisions and various issues covered in the Auto Workers' negotiations with American auto manufacturers in the summer of 2003.[11]

Some contracts provide for a **cost-of-living adjustment (COLA),** under which wages increase automatically as the cost of living goes up.

Exhibit 11.6 Summary of Auto Industry Issues and Agreement Provisions for 2003

- Four-year contract duration.
- Modest pay hikes of about 3 percent annually coupled with lump-sum adjustment at contract signing.
- Plant-closing worker protection packages.
- Lean production systems and worker productivity incentives.
- Production scheduling flexibility and broadened job classification.
- Early-retirement incentives to deal with very senior and aging auto workforce.
- Outsourcing and modular assembly arrangements received increased scrutiny.

cost-of-living adjustment (COLA)
A provision in a labor contract that calls for wages to increase automatically as the cost of living rises (usually measured by the consumer price index).

Other contracts provide for *lump-sum wage adjustments.* The workers' base pay remains unchanged for the contract period (usually two or three years), but each worker receives a bonus (or lump sum) once or twice during the contract.

The union and the employer are usually both concerned about the firm's ability to pay higher wages. The firm's ability to pay depends greatly on its profitability. But even if profits have declined, average to above-average wage increases are still possible if labor productivity increases. In 1999 and 2000, the productivity of the American economy as a whole increased about 3.5 percent each year. Negotiated wage increases for those years averaged slightly less than 3 percent each year. While productivity increases slowed following September 11, 2001, wage increases of 2 to 4 percent were being negotiated in many industries in 2002–2003.

Benefits

In addition to requests for wage increases, unions usually want better fringe benefits. In some industries, such as steel and auto manufacturing, fringe benefits are 40 percent of the total cost of compensation. Benefits may include higher wages for overtime work, holiday work, and less desirable shifts; insurance programs (life, health and hospitalization, dental care); payment for certain nonwork time (rest periods, vacations, holidays, sick time); pensions; and income-maintenance plans. A fairly common income-maintenance plan is a *supplementary unemployment benefits fund* set up by the employer to help laid-off workers. Unions seek benefits for their members in many countries as explained in the "Expanding Around the Globe" box.

Job Security and Seniority

Cost-of-living adjustments, supplementary unemployment benefits, and certain other benefits give employees some financial security. But most financial security is directly related to job security—the assurance, to some degree, that workers will keep their jobs. Of course, job security depends primarily on the continued success and financial well-being of the company.

Seniority, the length of an employee's continuous service with a firm, is discussed in about 90 percent of all labor contracts. Seniority is a factor in job security; usually, unions want the workers with the most seniority to have the most job security.

concept check

Explain the collective bargaining process.

What are the different forms of seniority, and why is it important to employees?

Grievance and Arbitration

5 learning goal

The union's main way of policing the contract is the grievance procedure. A **grievance** is a formal complaint, by an employee or by the union, that management has violated some part of the contract. Under a typical contract, the employee starts by presenting the grievance to the supervisor, either in person or in writing. The typical grievance procedure is illustrated in Exhibit 11.7.

Expanding Around the Globe

Union Activism Increases in Great Britain

Labor unions are not unique to the United States. Unions can be found in South Korea, Japan, Germany, France, Great Britain, Canada, and dozens of other countries. In some countries unions exert significant political as well as economic pressure. Union political involvement takes place through the Labour Party in Great Britain.

During Prime Minister Margaret Thatcher's years (1980s) in Great Britain, labor unions' political influence declined along with a significant drop in union strike activity. In recent years, however, during the administration of Tony Blair, union militancy and strike activity have increased. Bob Crow, leader of the British Rail and Maritime Transport union, has directed several, short-lived strikes of the Tube, as the London subway system is called. In 2002, the Fire Brigades Union announced plans for up to 36 days of nationwide strikes, the first in 25 years, to press for a 40 percent pay raise. Derek Simpson, a former Communist, was elected in 2002 as the leader of Britain's second-largest union of engineers. Crow, Simpson, and other newly elected labor leaders express Marxist political views, voice contempt for Britain's centrist economic policies, and exhibit a willingness to strike.[12]

CRITICAL THINKING QUESTIONS

1. The American labor movement is more conservative (politically and economically) than unions in Great Britain. Nevertheless, do you think firefighters or transit workers should be permitted to strike? Why or why not?
2. Should public-sector workers (federal and state employees) in the United States be allowed to unionize and negotiate wages and working conditions? If so, what specific items could be negotiated?
3. As an executive of a business faced with a strike, what are some things that you could do to solve the situation and minimize the strike's impact?

grievance
A formal complaint, filed by an employee or by the union, charging that management has violated the contract.

arbitration
The process of settling a labor-management dispute by having a third party—a single arbitrator or a panel—make a decision, which is binding on both the union and the employer.

If the problem isn't solved, the grievance is put in writing. The employee, one or more union officials, the supervisor, and perhaps the plant manager then discuss the grievance. If the matter still can't be resolved, another meeting takes place with higher-level representatives of both parties present. If top management and the local union president can't resolve the grievance, it goes to arbitration.

Arbitration is the process of settling a labor–management dispute by having a third party—a single arbitrator or a panel—make a decision. The decision is final and binding on the union and the employer. The arbitrator reviews the grievance at a hearing and then makes the decision, which is presented in a document called the *award.*

In a recent Citgo Refining and Chemicals Co. arbitration case, the arbitrator was presented with union and company evidence regarding firing of an employee for abuse of sick leave. The longtime employee called in sick two consecutive days over a weekend when she had been scheduled to work. The evening of the first day, or Saturday, she attended a community social function. A press photographer was present at the event and took a picture of the employee and her date. Several days after the event the picture appeared in the local newspaper. The arbitrator agreed with the company's decision to terminate the employee.[13] Firing is the most common type of case submitted for arbitration.

A second common type of grievance arbitration case involves promotion, job transfer, layoff, and other job change situations. In another recent case involving Saint-Gobain Container, Inc., a glass container manufacturer, the arbitrator ruled that a worker should be promoted because he met the "capabilities required" and "qualifications" specified by the firm. The labor agreement specified that the firm promote into a job the most senior employee with the ability to perform.[14]

concept check

Describe the grievance procedure.
In what ways do arbitrators act like judges?

Managing Labor–Management Conflict

6 learning goal

Both sides to labor–management conflicts have powerful tools for exerting economic (or financial) pressure. Unions can fight with strikes, product boycotts, picketing, and corporate campaigns. Employers can fight with lockouts, strike

Exhibit 11.7 | Typical Grievance Procedure

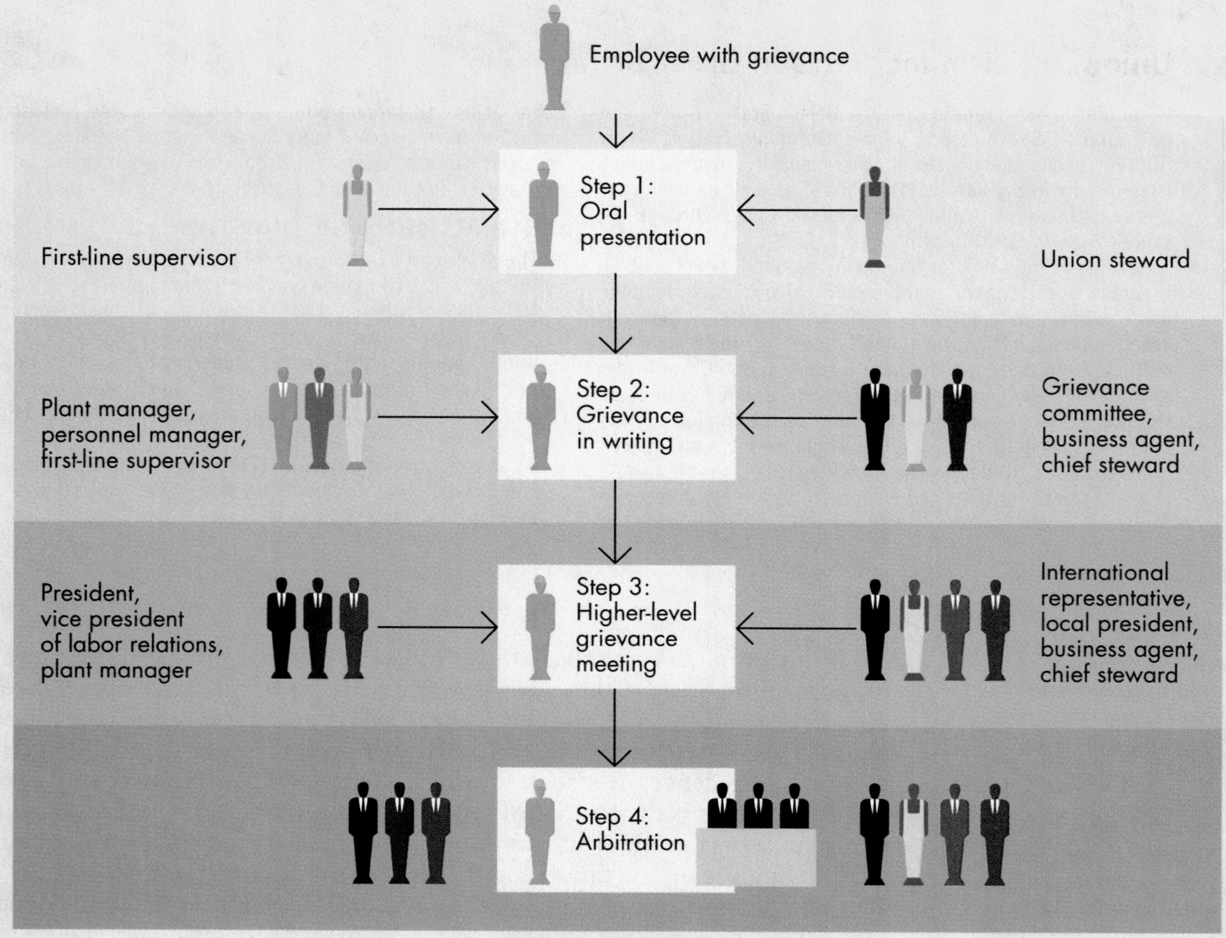

replacements, and mutual-aid pacts and can also shift production to nonunion plants or out of the country. Exhibit 11.8 lists the methods used by both sides.

Union Strategies

The strike is the most powerful union tool, but it is usually the means of last resort. Although a strike may hurt the employer, it also means loss of pay to employees. On the average, fewer than 2 percent of U.S. workers are involved in strikes each year. And with few exceptions, strikes tend to last under a month. However, strikes by the United Auto Workers at Caterpillar in 1982 and 1992 lasted many months each time.

Strikes occur most often over economic issues such as wages, pensions, vacation time, and other benefits. A strike normally starts immediately after the old union contract has expired, if management and labor can't agree on new contract terms. Sometimes a group of union members or an entire local union will strike without the approval of the national union, while the contract is still in effect. This action, which is often illegal because it violates the contract, is called a **wildcat strike.**

wildcat strike
A strike by a group of union members or an entire local union without the approval of the national union while the contract is still in effect.

Exhibit 11.8 Strategies of Unions and Employers

Union Strategies		Employer Strategies	
Strike:	Employees refuse to work.	**Lockout:**	Employer refuses to let employees enter plant to work.
Boycott:	Employees try to keep customers and others from doing business with employer.	**Strike replacements:**	Employer uses non-union employees to do jobs of striking union employees.
Picketing:	Employees march near entrance of firm to publicize their view of dispute and discourage customers.	**Mutual-aid pact:**	Employer receives money from other companies in industry to cover some of income lost because of strikes.
Corporate campaign:	Union disrupts stockholder meetings or buys company stock to have more influence over management.	**Shift production:**	Employer moves production to nonunion plant or out of country.

© AP / WIDE WORLD PHOTOS

Strikes are powerful union tools, usually used as a last resort when labor and management cannot reach agreement on issues such as wages, pensions, vacation time, and other benefits.

selective strike strategy
A union strategy of conducting a strike at (shutting down) a critical plant that supplies parts to other plants.

Another union strike strategy is to shut down (strike) a critical plant that supplies parts to other plants. Because the other plants don't receive parts from the struck plant, the firm has to curtail production and loses sales. The United Auto Workers used this **selective strike strategy** in the summer of 1998 against the General Motors stamping and parts facility in Flint, Michigan. The 54-day strike at one plant caused the company to stop production at virtually all of its assembly plants because critical parts were not available. GM lost approximately $2.2 billion during this dispute. From 1992 to early 1999, GM endured 22 strikes, losing 286 days of production, worth about $4 billion.

sick-out
A union strategy in which a group of employees claim they cannot work because of illness, thereby disrupting the company.

A different form of refusal to work is the **sick-out,** which occurs when a group of employees claim they can't work because of illness. Nearly 30 percent of American Airlines pilots called in sick on different days one week in February 1999. Flight operations were severely disrupted, tens of thousands of passengers were inconvenienced and angered, and the company lost more than $100 million.

picketing
Union members parade in front of the employer's plant carrying signs and trying to persuade nonstriking workers to stop working and customers and suppliers from doing business with the company.

The tactic most often used by unions is **picketing**. When a union calls a strike, it usually sets up picket lines to advertise the strike and discourage the employer from staying open. Union members parade back and forth in front of the employer's site, carrying signs saying the employer is unfair. The picketers try to persuade nonstriking workers to stop working and other people (customers and suppliers) to stop doing business with the company.

Another union weapon is the consumer and product boycott. If a union has a dispute with a firm that produces a consumer product, it asks its own and other union members to stop purchasing the product. Product sales drop and the company suffers financially. In the 1970s, under the leadership of Cesar Chavez, the United Farm Workers Union in California organized nationwide boycotts of table grapes and lettuce. Lettuce and grape growers lost millions because many customers supported the farm workers.

corporate campaign
A union strategy in which a union disrupts a corporation's relations with its shareholders or investors as a means of attacking the company.

The **corporate campaign** is a fairly new union strategy. With this strategy, a union may try to disrupt the stockholder meetings of a company it wants to pressure. Sometimes the union buys stock in the company so it can have more influence. The union may also threaten to withdraw great sums of money from banks that do business with the firm. Unions have recently conducted corporate campaigns against the Diamond Walnut Cooperative, Fisher Scientific, Hood Furniture Co., and the Frontier Hotel (Las Vegas).

Sometimes unions will try to draw attention to their complaints by trying to get free publicity. The "Focusing on Small Business" box explains how the Laborer's International Union tried to draw media attention.

Employer Strategies

lockout
An employer tactic in a labor dispute in which the employer refuses to allow workers to enter a plant or building to work, which means that the workers do not get paid.

strike replacements
Nonunion employees hired to replace striking union members; also known as *scabs*.

mutual-aid pact
An agreement by companies in an industry to create a fund that can be used to help cover fixed costs of any member company whose workers go on strike.

Employers have their own strategies in labor disputes. One of the most effective is the **lockout**, in which the company refuses to let workers enter a plant or building to work. If the workers can't perform their jobs, they don't get paid. Also, management can hire temporary workers during a lockout. Sometimes, however, a lockout can benefit the union. Overhead costs (costs for lease payments, insurance premiums, and management salaries) continue whether a plant is open or closed, putting pressure on management to end the lockout. One of the most widely publicized lockouts took place from August 1998 to early January 1999. NBA team owners locked out their players over player compensation issues. After six months and the cancellation of nearly 1,000 professional basketball games, NBA Commissioner David Stern and Billy Hunter, executive director of the players union, reached a contract settlement. An abbreviated 50-game schedule started in February 1999. Although both parties lost (the players lost several months of salary, and the teams lost ticket and TV revenues), the owners were considered to have won the dispute. The West Coast work stoppage on the loading docks, featured in the chapter opener, was also an employer lockout.

Strike replacements (or "scabs") are nonunion employees hired to replace striking union members. If suitable replacements can be found, the company can

Focusing on Small Business

If You Are Planning a Rally, Don't Forget the Paperwork

About 60 members of the Local 1180 of the Laborer's International Union decided to march on the Harrisburg (Pennsylvania) International Airport (HIA) to voice their complaints against Kinsley Construction Company. Kinsley had won a contract to do site preparation work as part of a major expansion of the Harrisburg airport.

A union flyer charged that Kinsley had had "numerous serious violations" of U.S. Occupational Safety and Health Administration standards and had been cited by the state Department of Environmental Protection multiple times for environmental problems. "We believe this is a union, nonunion issue," said Barbara Sardella, a Kinsley company spokesperson. She said Kinsley's environmental and safety records "equal or exceed others in the construction industry," and the company had no outstanding violations.

The union asked the Federal Aviation Administration to investigate Kinsley's record, suspend its bidding privileges, stop the bidding at HIA, and investigate the airport's prequalification process for contractors. The minority contractors and members of the Interdenominational Ministers' Conference of Greater Harrisburg were there to protest what they said were HIA's discriminatory contracting and hiring practices. "This is not just a senseless brawl. What we're saying is that we've been shut out. We want to make the playing field more level," said James White, president of the Central Pennsylvania Chapter of the National Association of Minority Contractors. The union also weighed in on concerns of the minority contractors and ministers. "Plans to use minorities at HIA should be called token at 6-1/4 percent contracting and a 4 percent hiring and not diverse," Local 1180 President Robert Disabella said.

The rally, however, fizzled when police were called. The police claimed that the protesters needed a written permit to gather on HIA property.[15]

Critical Thinking Questions

1. Since the police forced the protesters to disband, should Kinsley management go back to "business as usual"?
2. What other steps might the union take to get their grievances heard?
3. What actions could Kinsley take to protect itself?

stay open and keep making sales and earning profits. The problem with strike replacements is finding qualified people. Major-league baseball teams were ready to field minor-league players in the spring of 1995. Many fans, however, were ready to stay home and not attend the games. A settlement was reached, but some early-season games were canceled. In 1995 President Clinton signed an executive order prohibiting the hiring of replacement workers in firms with government contracts. Employers, in general, have strongly disagreed with this action.

Another strategy used by employers in some industries is the **mutual-aid pact.** Companies in an industry pool some of their financial resources in a fund that can be used to help cover costs of any member company whose workers go on strike. These pacts have been used with some success in the airline, tire, and newspaper industries.

concept check

What strategies can unions use against employers in labor conflicts?

What strategies does management have?

Whose strategies seem to be the strongest and most effective?

Trends in Labor–Management Relations

7 learning goal

Three labor–management trends that began during the last years of the 20th century have continued into the 21st century. Among the most notable is the unions' effort to reverse the decline in their memberships. Shortages of skilled labor in the unionized crafts, particularly construction, will continue to be a problem. Third, one of the fallouts of September 11, 2001, has involved layoffs in several sectors of the economy, particularly the transportation industry, which is heavily unionized. This situation, in turn, has fostered concession bargaining.

Union Organizing and Membership

Most unions saw their memberships decline in the 1980s, 1990s, and early 2000s. The greatest losses were experienced by unions that represent significant numbers of manufacturing employees (United Auto Workers, United Steelworkers, Machinists, Communication Workers, and Electrical Workers). Corporate restructuring (mergers, acquisitions, and downsizing), technological changes (automation and industrial robots), and the shifting of manufacturing offshore to countries such as Mexico, China, and Korea reduced manufacturing employment, and therefore union membership dropped. These changes will continue.

In contrast, however, many unions that represent service-sector workers increased their memberships in the late 1990s and early 2000s (Service Employees International Union [SEIU], United Food and Commercial Workers International Union, Hotel Employees and Restaurant Employees International Union, and American Federation of State, County and Municipal Employees). In particular, significant union membership gains took place in the health care industry. In 2000, for example, the SEIU unionized 1,400 nurses and 500 professional and scientific personnel at the state hospital and medical school on the campus of the University of Iowa.

While the American labor movement gained a few thousand members in the late 1990s, economic and labor market conditions began to weaken in 2001 with the unemployment rate rising from about 4 percent to 6 percent by late 2003. Many layoffs that happened during this period involved union members. Union efforts to maintain membership have focused on negotiating contract provisions that strengthen job security, encourage and increase retraining, and limit outsourcing jobs to third parties, which is another cause of worker layoffs.

Shortages of Skilled Labor

A trend that will become more pronounced as we move further into the 21st century is the developing shortage of skilled workers in nearly all of the construction crafts. Approximately 75 percent of construction firms of all sizes have reported shortages of skilled labor.[16] Most of these shortages can be traced to falling enrollments in apprenticeship programs. Many apprenticeship programs in the trades of plumbing, carpentry, painting, sheet metal work, electrical work, and tile laying are sponsored jointly by unions and management. Machinist and millwright craft workers are also in short supply in many manufacturing industries. Enrollments in apprenticeship programs in manufacturing are also declining. Unions and employers of skilled workers will need to cooperate more closely to entice sufficient numbers of young people into apprenticeship programs so that they can become journeymen and eventually master craftsmen.

Concession Bargaining

concession bargaining
Unions giving contract gains back to management.

Essentially, **concession bargaining** involves the union giving contract gains for the workers back to management. This usually occurs in two contract areas, compensation and work rules. A firm in severe financial difficulty, like United Airlines was in 2003, proposes to its unions that contract-scheduled wage increases must be eliminated and current wages decreased. In United's case, they needed to generate cost savings so that its financial situation could improve. Failing to gain wage concessions from the union(s) might cause the firm to file for bankruptcy, which would result in significant layoffs.

The other area of concessions typically entails the employer proposing to change various work rules to gain greater production efficiencies. The pilots union

To reverse the trend in shortages of skilled labor, unions and employers need to cooperate to attract more people to skilled trades. Their joint sponsorship of apprenticeship programs in skilled trades such as carpentry will help to alleviate the shortage of skilled labor.

© MICHAEL NEWMAN / PHOTOEDIT

concept check

What trends are occurring in union membership?

What can be done to alleviate shortages of skilled labor?

at United might agree that each pilot would fly up to three additional hours per month for the same pay. This change could stabilize the number of pilots needed, or eliminate the need to hire additional pilots, therefore better controlling labor costs and improving efficiency.

Great Ideas to Use Now

Even though the labor movement has declined in recent years, you are very likely to encounter unions and union members if you work in the airline, railroad, trucking, construction, health care, and various manufacturing industries, as well as the federal government. In fact, if you work in a nonsupervisory position, you may become a union member.

If you advance into a management position in a unionized firm, you will deal with union stewards and other union officials. You might even become a member of the firm's bargaining team and assist in negotiating a labor agreement. As a manager in such a situation, you need to possess and exercise effective interpersonal skills, especially communication and perceptual skills. Perceptual skill in a unionized environment is the ability to quickly understand a situation with conflict potential. Many union–management conflicts are caused by misunderstandings and lack of communication. Those who are successful in the union–management arena, whether they be managers, union officials, or mediators, are especially effective communicators with outstanding perceptual skills.

How can you develop these important interpersonal skills? These skills obviously improve with experience, but you can accelerate skill development by (1) taking courses that will challenge your oral and written communication skills, (2) joining student organizations and becoming an officer or committee chair, and (3) being an effective group member in business courses where student teams solve business problems, make investment decisions, or devise ways to implement changes in the work environment.

Try It Now

Improve Your Negotiation Skills. An important activity of the union–management relationship and collective bargaining is negotiating. Whether you pursue a career in labor relations or some other field, you will negotiate in your job. Purchasing agents, sales representatives, and stockbrokers negotiate on a daily basis. To negotiate successfully, you must be prepared. Two aspects of this preparation are (1) identifying items or aspects of a situation that are negotiable and (2) for these items, determining a range of acceptable alternatives or outcomes.

After you graduate from college and have two or three years of work experience, you will probably have several job advancement opportunities with either your current employer or other business organizations. This situation will involve a test of your negotiating skills. Start preparing now. The table lists some of the benefits that may be offered to you in your next job. First, circle the items that you think you will be able to negotiate. Second, for these negotiable items, identify possible outcomes ranging from pessimistic to realistic to optimistic. For example, a pessimistic outcome on a company car might be no car at all, a realistic outcome might be a Ford Taurus, and an optimistic outcome might be a BMW.

	Range of Alternatives/Outcomes		
Item/Consideration	**Pessimistic**	**Realistic**	**Optimistic**
Company car			
Expense account			
Travel allowance			
Salary			
Health insurance			
Training			
Bonus/other incentives			
Relocation expenses			
Work location			
Home office and equipment			
College tuition reimbursement			
Country club membership			

Customer Satisfaction and Quality

Employees (and union members) obviously can have a significant influence on customer satisfaction and the quality of a service or product. With respect to the labor relations process, a good union–management relationship, one that exhibits mutual trust and effective communication and information sharing, will lead to more highly satisfied employees. Satisfied employees will give higher-quality service (or make a better product) that will more fully satisfy customers. When the union–management relationship is not good, employees tend to be less satisfied. This situation may cause customer satisfaction and product quality to suffer.

Like all of the large U.S. air carriers, Southwest Airlines is heavily unionized. However, Southwest has always had good working relationships with its unions and its corporate culture and management practices have consistently encouraged good employee performance and satisfaction. This has resulted in Southwest employees providing the firm with a competitive advantage of great customer service. A common set of airline performance measures focus on (a) customer complaints, (b) lost baggage, and (c) on-time departure and arrival. When an airline has the best performance in these areas, it is referred to as winning the triple crown. Southwest Airlines has won the triple-crown award more often than any other airline and it has been a profitable airline for more consecutive quarters than any other airline.

Looking Ahead at West Coast Dockworkers

After about a week of work stoppage on the West Coast shipping docks, President Bush successfully activated the national emergency strike procedures of the Taft–Hartley Act. These procedures involve the president (a) appointing a board of inquiry to investigate the strike, and the (b) board filing a report with the president indicating the size, scope, and other characteristics of the strike. The president then (c) declares the strike a national emergency, and (d) through the U.S. Attorney General seeks an injunction, or court order, to stop the strike and require workers to go back to work and the union and management to continue meaningful negotiations. The injunction can last for 80 days. Hopefully, prior to the conclusion of 80 days the two sides reach an agreement. In fact, this happened. After approximately six weeks or 45 days, the International Longshore and Warehouse Union and the Pacific-Maritime Association reached a tentative agreement that resolved all issues. For the first 15 years (1947 to 1962) of Taft–Hartley, the procedures were invoked by presidents about two dozen times. The last time a president had invoked these procedures prior to President Bush was 1978, when President Carter was unsuccessful in obtaining a court order to stop the coal strike that began in the fall of 1977.

Summary of Learning Goals

1

What is the historical development of American labor unions?

In 1881 many of the craft groups left the Knights of Labor to form the American Federation of Labor (AFL). Under Samuel Gompers, the AFL pursued such practical matters as union rights and better wages, hours, and working conditions for members.

Today, the U.S. labor movement consists of the AFL-CIO labor federation, national and international unions, and local unions. A national union consists of many local unions in a particular industry, skilled trade, or geographic area. The main functions of the local unions are collective bargaining, worker relations and membership services, and community and political activities.

2

What role did federal law play in the development of the union–management relationship?

The Norris–LaGuardia Act of 1932 banned employers' use of injunctions and greatly limited yellow-dog contracts. This law essentially ended the use of the courts as a means of settling a labor dispute. In 1935 Congress passed the Wagner Act, which encouraged the formation of unions, defined unfair labor practices, and created the NLRB. The Wagner Act was amended in 1947 by the Taft–Hartley Act, which placed some constraints on labor union organizing activities. In 1959 Congress passed the Landrum–Griffin Act, which dealt mainly with the internal affairs of unions, or such things as officer elections, financial record keeping, and constitution and bylaw provisions.

3

What is the union organizing process?

A company is unionized through an organizing drive that begins either inside, with a small group of existing employees, or outside, with an established union that targets the employer. When the union gets signed authorization cards from 30 percent of the firm's employees, the NLRB conducts a union certification election. A majority vote is needed to certify the union as the exclusive bargaining agent. The union and the employer then begin collective bargaining and have one year in which to reach an agreement.

4 What is the collective bargaining process, and what key issues are included in the union contract?

Collective bargaining is the process of negotiating, administering, and interpreting labor agreements. Both union and management negotiators prepare a bargaining proposal. The two sides meet and exchange demands and ideas. Bargaining consists of compromises and concessions that lead to a tentative agreement. Top management then approves or disapproves the agreement for the management team. Union members vote to either approve or reject the contract. The key issues that are included in a union contract are wage increases, fringe benefits, and job security.

5 How do employees file a grievance?

In most labor agreements the grievance procedure consists of three or four steps. In the initial step, the employee files a grievance; this is an oral and/or written presentation to the supervisor and may involve a union steward as representative of the grievant. Steps two and three involve meetings of the employee and one or more union officials and the appropriate supervisor and one or more management officials. If the grievance is not resolved at step three, either party (union or management) can request that an arbitrator, or neutral third party, hear and decide the grievance.

6 What economic tactics do unions and employers use in labor–management conflicts?

The union's primary weapon is the strike—union members stop working. During a strike, union members may picket, or parade back and forth in front of the struck employer carrying signs that alert the public to the union's dispute with the employer. An additional union action is the product boycott where the union attempts to convince consumers to discontinue purchase of products of the firm with which the union has a dispute. Employers' weapons include the lockout, strike replacements, mutual-aid pacts, and shifting of production to nonunion locations. Of these, the lockout and strike replacements are the most common.

7 What trends will affect American workers and labor–management relations?

Decline in union members will slow, and the growth in members that began in the last half of 1998 may continue, especially in the service and health care fields. Union demands for wage increases and improvements in fringe benefits will stimulate new membership. These demands will be commonplace as long as the economy is strong. Shortages of skilled workers will likely persist further into the 21st century. To drive more interest in skilled craft positions, unions and employers will need to build strong apprenticeship programs that provide sound foundations for careers in the skilled crafts. During economic downturns, the use of concession bargaining rises.

KEY TERMS

agency shop 348
American federation of Labor (AFL) 339
arbitration 351
bargaining unit 345
closed shop 348
collective bargaining 338
concession bargaining 356
conciliation 344
Congress of Industrial Organizations (CIO) 340
corporate campaign 354
cost-of-living adjustment (COLA) 350
craft union 339
decertification election 345
grievance 351
industrial union 339
injunction 341
Knights of Labor 338
labor union 338
Landrum–Griffin Act 345
local union 340
lockout 354
mediation 344
mutual-aid pact 354
National Labor Relations Board (NLRB) 343
national union 340
Norris–LaGuardia Act 342
open shop 348
picketing 354
right-to-work laws 348
selective strike strategy 353
shop steward 340
sick-out 354
strike replacements 354
Taft–Hartley Act 343
union certification election 345
union shop 348
Wagner Act 342
wildcat strike 352
yellow-dog contract 342

PREPARING FOR TOMORROW'S WORKPLACE

1. Assume you have been asked to speak at a local meeting of human resource and labor relations professionals. The topic is whether union membership will increase or decline in the 21st century. Take either the increase or the decline position and outline your presentation.
2. Under what circumstances, if any, should police officers, firefighters, teachers, and nurses be allowed to strike? If you believe any or all of these groups should not be allowed to strike under any circumstances, how can they deal with poor supervision, low salaries, stressful job situations, and inadequate equipment?
3. Go to the government documents section in your college or university library and inspect publications of the Department of Labor (DOL), including *Employment and Earnings, Compensation and Working Conditions, Monthly Labor Review, Occupational Outlook Handbook,* and *Career Guide to Industries.* Alternatively, go to the DOL, Bureau of Labor Statistics Web site at **http://stats.bls.gov**. Access the most recent DOL publications and locate the following information:
   - Number of persons in the American workforce.
   - Unemployment rate for last year.
   - Demographic characteristics of the American workforce: race, ethnic status, age, marital status, and gender.
   - Occupations where there are projected shortages for the next 5 or 10 years.
   - Union membership by major industry category: manufacturing, banking and finance, health care, business and personal services, sports and entertainment, and any other area of interest to you.
4. Assume you are a director of labor relations for a firm faced with a union certification election in 30 days. Draft a letter to be sent to your employees in which you urge them to vote "no union"; be persuasive in presenting your arguments against the union.
5. Divide the class into four groups; each group will focus on one of the major professional sports (baseball, football, basketball, and hockey). Within each group students should engage in a discussion/debate concerning whether the athletes of that sport should unionize and engage in collective bargaining.
6. Divide the class into union and management teams and negotiate the following union demands:
   a. Wage increases of 10 percent
   b. Union shop
   c. Cost-of-living allowance or adjustment
   d. Fully paid (by employer) health insurance
   e. No outsourcing or subcontracting
7. Go to the library and skim recent issues of the *Wall Street Journal, Business Week,* and/or the *Daily Labor Report* until you find articles about either a recent strike or a labor contract settlement. Report to your class the specifics of the strike or settlement.
8. Assume you are a union member. Would you participate in an employee sick-out? Why or why not?
9. Have you or a member of your family ever been a union member? If so, name the union and describe it in terms of membership size, membership characteristics, strike history, recent bargaining issues, and employers under union contracts.
10. Divide the class into two groups. One group will take the position that workers should be required to join unions and pay dues. The other group will take the position that workers should not be required to join unions. Hold a debate in which a spokesperson from each group is given 10 minutes to present the group's arguments.

Working the Net

1. How are labor unions using the Internet to expand their influence? Use a search engine or the AFL-CIO Web site (**http://www.aflcio.org**) to find individual union Web sites. Describe in a brief report how the Internet helps three unions in different industries.
2. What are the key issues facing labor unions today? Visit Labornet, **http://www.labornet.org**, select three current topics, and summarize the key points for the class.
3. Go to the DOL, Bureau of Labor Statistics Web site at **http://stats.bls.gov**. Access the most recent DOL publications and locate the following information:
   - Number of persons in the American workforce.
   - Unemployment rate for last year.
   - Demographic characteristics of the American workforce: race, ethnic status, age, marital status, and gender.
   - Occupations where there are projected shortages for the next 5 or 10 years.
   - Union membership by major industry category: manufacturing, banking and finance, health care, business and personal services, sports and entertainment, and any other area of interest to you.

   What conclusions can you draw from your findings?
4. Not everyone believes that unions are good for workers. The National Right to Work Legal Defense Foundation offers free legal aid to employees whose "human and civil rights have been violated by compulsory unionism abuses." Visit its site (**http://www.nrtw.org**) and summarize its position on the disadvantages of labor unions.
5. Although we tend to think of labor unions as representing manufacturing employees, many office and service industry employees, teachers, and professionals belong to unions. Visit the Web sites of several nonmanufacturing unions and discuss how they help their members. Here are some suggestions: the Office and Professional Employees International Union (**http://www.opeiu.org**), the American Federation of State, County and Municipal Employees (**http://www.afscme.org**), the National Education Association (**http://www.nea.org**), Actors' Equity Association (**http://www.actorsequity.org**), and the American Federation of Musicians (**http://www.afm.org**). What are the differences, if any, between these unions and those in other industries?

Creative Thinking Case

Collective Bargaining at a Seattle Hotel

You are the manager of a large hotel (400 rooms) in Seattle. One union represents several groups of employees, including housekeeping and laundry workers, food service employees, bell hops, and various craftsmen (electricians, plumbers, and other maintenance workers). Several contracts have been peacefully negotiated, or negotiated without strikes. You have worked in the hotel for the entire 15 years the union has existed.

With the sluggish economy, occupancy rates have been down and the hotel workforce has been reduced, primarily through attrition. You have finally come to realize that labor costs must be reduced further and an employee layoff is the only option. This situation is complicated by the facts that the current labor agreement will expire in about 120 days and that the opening, or first, bargaining session is scheduled for two weeks from now. You have been preparing for negotiations for several weeks.

Yesterday you received from the union a lengthy letter in which a list of areas was presented for bargaining. The union didn't indicate its initial position for any of the items, but you can easily anticipate what the demands will be in most cases. The last paragraph of the letter informed you that a strike vote had been taken and more than 90 percent of the union members voted to strike if a new contract can't be negotiated before the expiration date of the current agreement. The union has never struck and this is the first time a strike vote has even been conducted.

CRITICAL THINKING QUESTIONS

1. How will the strike vote influence your preparation for negotiations? What bargaining strategy should you formulate?
2. While a strike, if it happens, is nearly four months into the future, how can you prepare for a work stoppage? How could you keep the hotel operating during a strike, if you chose to do so?

VIDEO CASE

Fighting for Writers' Rights

"Without the writer there'd be no movies or television shows, but because they worked behind the scenes, writers were often ignored," says Mona Mangan, Executive Director of the Writers Guild of America (East) (**http://www.wgaeast.org**), which represents writers in motion pictures, television, radio, and network news. "Producers would give their brother or girlfriend the writer's credit on a movie."

Respect is a huge issue for writers, who are proud of their words and want to receive proper credit for them. For over 50 years the not-for-profit WGA has strived to make life better for working writers, making sure they get the proper credit and payment for their work. "Labor unions used to be for miners or factory workers," says Mangan, "but the development of new jobs in new industries meant those people needed protection in the work place too."

The organization also makes sure its members are properly compensated. Writers are paid in two ways: upfront money, which is paid directly to the writer upon delivery of a script, and money paid on an ongoing basis for the reuse or syndication of a writer's work. The Writers Guild tracks all secondary uses of its members' work, and to make sure writers receive what they are entitled to, all fees from these "residuals" are paid directly to the Writers Guild on the writer's behalf.

With movies and TV shows often generating more money outside the United States from foreign-distribution rights, the Writers Guild used its collective bargaining power to negotiate payments for writers for all work distributed in foreign markets. "You never get everything you want in a negotiation," says Mangan, "and you have to decide if what's left on the table is worth putting friends and co-workers out of work for."

As difficult as strikes are to go through, they are sometimes necessary in order to get what you want. A 1988 writers strike lasted six months and meant no new TV shows for the fall season. Another writers strike protested ABC's desire to be able to fire news writers at will. The Writers Guild insisted there had to be a reason to fire someone, and members went on strike to show they were serious. They won.

Arbitration is another form of settling disputes. The WGA may file a grievance against a company that has not paid or given a writer proper credit. A panel of arbitrators will hear the matter in the form of a mini-trial and make a decision all parties must abide by. Sometimes government mediators may be brought in to settle a matter.

The Guild also offers other benefits, such as health care and pensions, as well as a quick and easy way to register literary property. Ten dollars buys you 10 years of protection and peace of mind. But mainly the organization provides solidarity—for individuals with common interests, acting as a unit, to benefit themselves and fellow members.

CRITICAL THINKING QUESTIONS

1. What function does the Writers Guild serve?
2. How does the Writers Guild achieve changes that benefit its members?
3. Why would creative people like writers consider joining a labor union? Would you join a labor union if it were available in your industry? Why or why not?

SOURCES: Adapted from material in the video: "Writers Guild: You Do the Writing, We'll Do the Fighting;" Writers Guild of America (East) Web site, http://www.wgaeast.org, accessed March 23, 2003; Dave McNary, "Moore, WGAE in Pay Rift," *Variety*, March 14, 2003, downloaded from http://www.variety.com.

E-COMMERCE CASE

Labor Movements Reinvent Themselves—on the Web

Associate-level attorneys at large firms around the country recently negotiated big, across-the-board raises, thanks in great part to the Internet. Stuck in partnerships without stock options, they felt left out of the stock market bonanza, and exchanged information about their firms' salaries and plans on Web sites. The same technology that has changed the way business works is changing the way workers organize—especially professionals for whom e-mail and Web browsing is as natural as blinking.

Of course the issue surest to raise the hackles of workers is money. When IBM announced it was changing from its traditional pension plan to a cash-balance plan, instead of taking to the barricades, employees took to the Web. Alliance@IBM, a group affiliated with the Communications Workers of America (CWA) labor union, bills itself as "The official national site for the IBM Employees' Union, CWA Local 1701." All active employees, contractors, temporary employees, and retirees are eligible to join. Even exempt employees are eligible—but no managers! With different levels of membership, monthly dues go toward producing flyers, sponsoring seminars, benefits research, and providing members with legal advice on employment issues.

The Alliance Web site is the focal point of information and communication for union members, providing regular news updates as well as links to other helpful sites, like the IBM Workers International Solidarity Web site, which serves the company's international personnel. The Alliance is also pursuing strategies to press IBM management, Congress, and the courts to correct injustices at IBM regarding the pension plan and overtime policies; and to build support for collective bargaining to guarantee employees' rights and benefits in a legally binding contract. Alliance members believe pro-union is pro-IBM. They want the company to be successful and believe their voice in the workplace will ultimately contribute to that success.

Stephen Herzenberg, executive director of Keystone Research Center, a think tank in Harrisburg, Pennsylvania, says. "The labor movement can look like it's dead because it's stuck in old forms, but then it finds a new way to reinvent itself." The Internet is giving labor unions a new way to organize—with new categories of workers as members.

CRITICAL THINKING QUESTIONS

1. How has the Internet contributed to the revival of labor movements? Explain.
2. Why is the Internet making it possible for new types of workers to join organized labor movements?
3. Would you join an organized labor movement if invited to do so? Explain why or why not.

SOURCES: David Propson, "Workers of the Web, Unite!" *Business2.0, September 2000,* downloaded from Web site http://www.business2.com, April 13, 2003; Web site Alliance@IBM downloaded from http://www.allianceibm.org, April 14, 2003; The Keystone Research Center http://www.keystoneresearch.org, downloaded April 14, 2003.

Hot Links Address Book

What diverse types of unions are affiliated with the AFL-CIO today? Visit this Web site to find out:
http://www.aflcio.org/aboutunions/unions

At the NLRB Web site,
http://www.nlrb.gov
you'll learn about the agency's many activities and how it protects workers' rights.

Visit the Social Security Administration site to track the latest cost-of-living adjustment at
http://www.ssa.gov
You'll find it in the publications section.

What product boycotts are currently in progress, and are any tied to union issues? Visit
http://www.boycotts.org
to find out.

The Communications Workers of America (CWA) is the largest telecommunications union in America. Learn about the many groups it represents, as well as industry issues, at
http://www.cwa-union.org

Harley-Davidson is proud of its labor-management relationship as you'll see from the "Determination: Our Employees" section of the 2002 annual report. Find the report in the investor relations area of
http://www.harleydavidson.com

Chapter 12

© AP / WIDE WORLD PHOTOS

Achieving World-Class Operations Management

learning goals

1 Why is production and operations management important in both manufacturing and service firms?
2 What types of production processes are used by manufacturers and service firms?
3 How do organizations decide where to put their production facilities? What choices must be made in designing the facility?
4 Why are resource-planning tasks like inventory management and supplier relations critical to production?
5 How do operations managers schedule and control production?
6 How can quality management and lean-manufacturing techniques help firms improve production and operations management?
7 What roles do technology and automation play in manufacturing and service industry operations management?
8 What key trends are affecting the way companies manage production and operations?

Building on Success at Harley-Davidson

Harley-Davidsons aren't just motorcycles. They're an American legend, known for their unique style, sound, and power ever since the first one was assembled in a backyard workshop in 1903. "People want more than two wheels and a motor," explains Harley-Davidson CEO Jeffrey Bleustein. "Harleys represent something very basic—a desire for freedom, adventure, and individualism."

Twenty years ago, Harley also represented everything that was wrong with American manufacturing. The company's production facilities were outdated and inefficient, keeping prices high. Quality was so poor that owners sometimes joked they needed two Harleys—one to ride and one for parts. As fed-up consumers turned to motorcycles made by Japanese and German manufacturers, Harley-Davidson's sales plummeted and the company teetered on bankruptcy.

Today, however, Harley-Davidson (**http://www.harley-davidson.com**) is a company reborn. The company posted its 17th consecutive year of profits in 2002. With retail sales growing at 19 percent a year, Harley-Davidson has roared off with 50 percent of the motorcycle market. How did this turnaround happen? With single-minded focus on just one thing: turning cost-effective manufacturing excellence into a company-wide passion.

The quest for excellence begins with product design. Every component in a Harley bike is put through a rigorous design process that examines its manufacturability according to quality standards. Special software estimates the cost of each design proposal so that expenses can be carefully controlled. Vendors hoping to supply various components to Harley-Davidson automatically receive this same information electronically, integrating them into the product development cycle.

Lasers and robots automate many production tasks. Components ready for assembly are loaded onto specially designed carts that swivel 360 degrees and can be lowered or raised to suit different workers or tasks. The carts then move into workstations where groups of employees assemble them into motorcycle frames. No motorcycle leaves a Harley-Davidson plant without a final quality inspection. A team of test drivers revs up and rides each motorcycle, checking operating quality and listening for the classic Harley sound.

Employees play a critical role in Harley's production facilities. Working in teams, many employees are cross-trained to perform a variety of production tasks. Each work team is asked to constantly look for ways to build better motorcycles. The company has implemented many employee-generated ideas for improving equipment, factory layout, and production processes.

Industry analysts say Harley-Davidson's rebirth and continued growth is intricately tied to its dedication to quality and efficiency in its operations and production processes. "Harley-Davidson succeeded because they aligned all stakeholders—from customers to shareholders to employees and suppliers," says consultant Stephen Shapiro. "They created the Harley-Davidson family, where everyone, including unions, are united in a common purpose."[1]

Critical Thinking Questions

As you read this chapter, consider the following questions as they relate to Harley-Davidson:

1. How has focusing on quality in its operations and production supported Harley-Davidson's growth?
2. What external factors have led to this focus?
3. What future production decisions will Harley need to make in order to continue to grow?

Principles of Operations Management

Finding the most efficient and effective methods of producing the goods or services it sells to customers is an ongoing focus of nearly every type of business organization. Today more than ever, changing consumer expectations, technological advances, and increased competition are all forcing business organizations to rethink where, when, and how they will produce products or services.

Like Harley-Davidson, manufacturers have discovered that it is no longer enough to simply push products through the factory and onto the market. Consumers demand high quality at reasonable prices. They also expect manufacturers to deliver products in a timely manner. Firms that can't meet these expectations often face strong competition from businesses that can. To compete, many manufacturers are reinventing how they make their products by automating their factories, developing new production processes, using quality control techniques, and tightening their relationships with suppliers.

Service organizations are also facing challenges. Their customers are demanding better service, shorter waits, and more individualized attention. Just like manufacturers, service organizations are using new methods to deliver what customers need and want. Banks, for example, are using technology such as ATMs and the Internet to make their services more accessible to customers. Many colleges now offer weekend and even online courses for working students. Tax services are filing tax returns via computer.

This chapter examines how manufacturers and service firms manage and control the creation of products and services. We'll discuss production planning, including the choices firms must make concerning the type of production process they will use, the location where production will occur, the design of the facility, and the management of resources needed in production. Next, we'll explain routing and scheduling, two critical tasks for controlling production and operations efficiency. Many businesses are improving productivity by employing quality control methods and automation. We'll discuss these methods before summarizing some of the trends affecting production and operations management.

Production and Operations Management—An Overview

1 learning goal

production
The creation of products and services by turning inputs, such as natural resources, raw materials, human resources, and capital, into outputs, which are products and services.

operations management
Management of the production process.

Production, the creation of products and services, is an essential function in every firm. Production turns inputs, such as natural resources, raw materials, human resources, and capital, into outputs, which are products and services. This process is shown in Exhibit 12.1. Managing this conversion process is the role of **operations management.**

In the 1980s, many U.S. industries, such as automotive, steel, and electronics, lost customers to foreign competitors because their production systems could not provide the quality customers demanded. As a result, most American companies, both large and small, now consider a focus on quality to be a central component of effective operations management.

The goal of customer satisfaction, closely linked to quality, is also an important part of effective production and operations. In the past, the manufacturing function in most companies was inwardly focused. Manufacturing had little contact with customers and didn't always understand their needs and desires. Today, however, stronger links between marketing and manufacturing have encouraged production managers to be more outwardly focused and to consider decisions in light of their effect on customer satisfaction. Service companies have also found

Exhibit 12.1 | Production Process for Products and Services

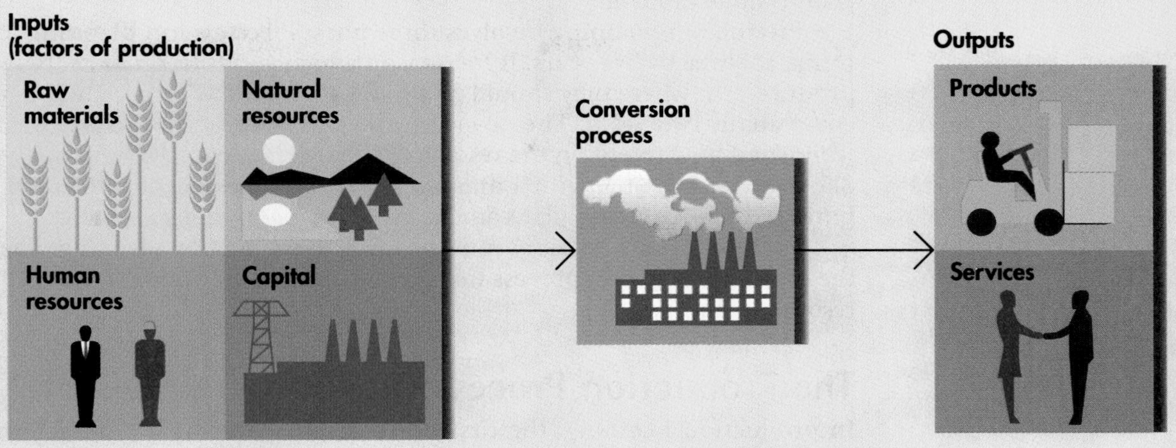

that making operating decisions with customer satisfaction in mind can be a competitive advantage.

Operations managers, the personnel charged with managing and supervising the conversion process, play a vital role in today's firm. They control about three-fourths of a firm's assets, including inventories, wages, and benefits. They work closely with other major functions of the firm, such as marketing, finance, accounting, and human resources, to help ensure that the firm produces its goods profitably and continually satisfies customers. They face the challenge of combining people and other resources to produce high-quality goods, on time and at a reasonable cost. Working with marketing, they help to decide which products to make or which services to offer. They become involved with the development and design of goods and determine what production processes will be most effective.

Production and operations management involves three main types of decisions that are made at three different stages:

1. *Production planning.* The first decisions facing operations managers come at the *planning stage.* At this stage, managers decide where, when, and how production will occur. They obtain resources and determine site locations.
2. *Production control.* At this stage, the decision-making process focuses on scheduling, controlling quality and costs, and the actual day-to-day operations of running a factory or service facility.
3. *Improving production and operations.* The final stage of operations management focuses on developing more efficient methods of producing the firm's goods or services.

These three types of decisions are ongoing and often occur simultaneously. In the following sections, we will take a closer look at the decisions and considerations firms face in each of these stages of production and operations management.

production planning
The aspect of operations management in which the firm considers the competitive environment and its own strategic goals in an effort to find the best production methods.

GEARING UP: PRODUCTION PLANNING

An important part of operations management is **production planning.** During production planning, the firm considers the competitive environment and its own strategic goals in an effort to find the best production methods. Good production planning balances goals that may conflict such as providing high-quality service while keeping operating costs down, or keeping profits high while maintaining adequate inventories of finished products. Sometimes accomplishing all of these goals is quite difficult.

Production planning involves three phases. Long-term planning has a time frame of three to five years. It focuses on which goods to produce, how many to produce, and where they should be produced. Medium-term planning decisions cover about two years. They concern the layout of factory or service facilities, where and how to obtain the resources needed for production, and labor issues. Short-term planning, with a one-year time frame, converts these broader goals into specific production plans and materials management strategies.

Four important decisions must be made in production planning. They involve the type of production process that will be used, site selection, facility layout, and resource planning.

The Production Process: How Do We Make It?

2 learning goal

production process
The way a good is made.

mass production
The ability to manufacture many identical goods at once.

mass customization
A manufacturing process in which goods are mass-produced up to a point and then custom tailored to the needs or desires of individual customers.

customization
The production of goods or services one at a time according to the specific needs or wants of individual customers.

job shop
A manufacturing firm that produces goods in response to customer orders.

In production planning, the first decision involves which type of **production process**—the way a good is made—best fits with the company's goals and customer demands. Another important consideration is the type of good or service being produced, as different goods may require different production processes. In general, there are three types of production: mass production, mass customization, and customization. In addition to production type, operations managers also classify production processes in two ways: (1) by how inputs are converted into outputs and (2) by the timing of the process.

ONE FOR ALL: MASS PRODUCTION **Mass production,** manufacturing many identical goods at once, was a product of the Industrial Revolution. Henry Ford's Model-T automobile is a good example of mass production. Each car turned out by Ford's factory was identical, right down to its color. If you wanted a car in any color except black, you were out of luck. Canned goods, over-the-counter drugs, and household appliances are examples of goods that are still mass-produced. The emphasis in mass production is on keeping manufacturing costs low by producing highly uniform products using repetitive and standardized processes. As many products become more complicated to produce, however, mass production is becoming more complex. Automobile manufacturers, for example, must now incorporate more sophisticated electronics into their car designs. As a result, the number of assembly stations in most automobile manufacturing plants has increased.

JUST FOR YOU: CUSTOMIZING GOODS In **mass customization,** goods are produced using mass-production techniques, but only up to a point. At that point, the product or service is custom tailored to the needs or desires of individual customers. American Leather, a leather-furniture manufacturer, uses mass customization to produce couches and chairs to customer specifications within 30 days. The basic frames used to make the furniture are the same, but automated cutting machinery precuts the color and type of leather ordered by each customer. They are then added to each frame, using mass-production techniques. The company manufacturers 225 finished pieces of furniture per day.[2] **Customization** is the opposite of mass-production. In customization, the firm produces goods or services one at a time according to the specific needs or wants of individual customers. Unlike mass customization, each product or service produced is unique. For example, a print shop may handle a variety of projects, including newsletters, brochures, stationery, and reports. Each print job varies in quantity, type of printing process, binding, color of ink, and type of paper. A manufacturing firm that produces goods in response to customer orders is called a **job shop.**

Some types of service businesses also deliver customized services. Doctors, for instance, usually must consider the individual illnesses and circumstances of each

Exhibit 12.2 | Classification of Production Types

Mass Production	**Mass Customization**	**Customization**
Highly uniform products or services. Many products made sequentially. Examples: Breakfast cereals, soft drinks, and computer keyboards.	Uniform and standardized production to a point, then unique features added to each product. Examples: Dell computers, tract homes, and Taylor Made Golf clubs.	Each product or service produced according to individual customer requirements. Examples: Custom homes, legal services, and haircuts.

patient before developing a customized treatment plan. Real estate agents also develop a customized service plan for each customer based on the type of house the person is selling or wants to buy. The differences between mass production, mass customization, and customization are summarized in Exhibit 12.2.

Converting Inputs to Outputs Production involves converting *inputs* (raw materials, parts, human resources) into *outputs* (products or services). In a manufacturing company, the inputs, the production process, and the final outputs are usually obvious. Harley-Davidson, for instance, converts steel, rubber, paint, and other inputs into motorcycles. The production process in a service company involves a less obvious conversion. For example, a hospital converts the knowledge and skills of its medical personnel, along with equipment and supplies from a variety of sources, into health care services for patients. Exhibit 12.3 provides examples of the inputs and outputs used by several other types of businesses.

There are two basic processes for converting inputs into outputs. In **process manufacturing,** the basic input (raw materials, parts) is *broken down* into one or more outputs (products). For instance, bauxite (the input) is processed to extract aluminum (the output). The **assembly process** is just the opposite. The basic inputs, like parts, raw materials, or human resources, are either *combined* to create the output or *transformed* into the output. An airplane, for example, is created by assembling thousands of parts. Steel manufacturers use heat to transform iron and other materials into steel. In services, customers may play a role in the transformation process. For example, a tax preparation service combines the knowledge of the tax preparer with the client's information about personal finances in order to complete tax returns.

Production Timing A second consideration in choosing a production process is timing. A **continuous process** uses long production runs that may last days, weeks, or months without equipment shutdowns. It is best for high-volume, low-variety products with standardized parts, such as nails, glass, and paper. Some services also use a continuous process. Your local electric company is one example. Per-unit costs are low and production is easy to schedule.

In an **intermittent process,** short production runs are used to make batches of different products. Machines are shut down to change them to make different products at different times. This process is best for low-volume, high-variety products such as those produced by mass customization or customization. Job shops are examples of firms using an intermittent process.

process manufacturing
A production process in which the basic input is *broken down* into one or more outputs (products).

assembly process
A production process in which the basic inputs are either *combined* to create the output or *transformed* into the output.

continuous process
A production process that uses long production runs lasting days, weeks, or months without equipment shutdowns; generally used for high-volume, low-variety products with standardized parts.

intermittent process
A production process that uses short production runs to make batches of different products; generally used for low-volume, high-variety products.

Exhibit 12.3 | Converting Inputs to Outputs

Type of Organization	Input	Output
Airline	Pilots, crew, flight attendants, reservations system, ticketing agents, customers, airplanes, fuel, maintenance crews, ground facilities	Movement of customers and freight
Grocery store	Merchandise, building, clerks, supervisors, store fixtures, shopping carts, customers	Groceries for customers
High school	Faculty, curriculum, buildings, classrooms, library, auditorium, gymnasium, students, staff, supplies	Graduates, public service
Manufacturer	Machinery, raw materials, plant, workers, managers	Finished products for consumers and other firms
Restaurant	Food, cooking equipment, serving personnel, chefs, dishwashers, host, patrons, furniture, fixtures	Meals for patrons

Although some service companies use continuous processes, most service firms rely on intermittent processes. For instance, a restaurant preparing gourmet meals, a physician performing physical examinations or surgical operations, and an advertising agency developing ad campaigns for business clients all customize their services to suit each customer. They use the intermittent process. Note that their "production runs" may be very short—one grilled salmon or one eye exam at a time.

Location, Location, Location: Where Do We Make It?

3 learning goal

A big decision that managers must make early in production and operations planning is where to put the facility, be it a factory or a service office. The facility's location affects operating and shipping costs and, ultimately, the price of the product or service and the company's ability to compete. Mistakes made at this stage can be expensive, because moving a factory or service facility once production begins is difficult and costly. Firms must weigh a number of factors to make the right decision.

© DANNY LEHMAN / CORBIS

General Motors operates a 1.2-million-square-foot plant in Silao, Mexico. The plant employs 3,000 workers and builds Chevy Suburbans. Access to low-cost labor was a major factor in GM's choice of Mexico for its plant location.

Making Ethical Choices

xtra! http://gitmanxtra.swlearning.com

SWEATING IT OUT AT NEW ERA CAP

As production manager for New Era Cap, the largest American manufacturer of ball caps, you supervise operations at three factories. The oldest plant, in Derby, New York, has 600 workers and produces 120,000 caps a week, the lowest production rate of the three plants. The Derby factory also has the highest worker absentee rate of any plant, with as many as 13 percent of workers calling in sick on any given day.

In an attempt to bring the Derby plant up to the same level of efficiency as the other two plants, you've implemented several changes in the past few years. You've introduced new production schedules, made staff cuts, and tried to reduce absentee rates.

Unhappy with the changes you've made, Derby workers went on strike 10 months ago. After New Era executives refused to settle with the striking workers' demands for reduced hours and pay raises, their union, the Communications Workers of America (CWA) issued public statements accusing the Derby plant of "sweatshop" working conditions. At the CWA's urging, the United Students Against Sweatshops (USAS) started a campaign to get colleges and universities to boycott New Era caps. Several universities have already joined the boycott.

You are convinced that the Derby plant is not a sweatshop. You've shifted most of Derby's production to New Era's other two factories with minimal problems. The union now says it will end the strike and call off the boycott if the company grants immediate pay raises and health benefit increases to all Derby workers. You feel this is blackmail.

ETHICAL DILEMMA

Should you recommend that New Era's president agree to the union's demands?

SOURCES: "New Era Union Plans Boycott," *Buffalo Business First* (July 20, 2001); "Cap Maker Shifts Production After Walkout," *Buffalo Business First* (July 16, 2001); "New Era Says 'Sweatshop' Label Is False," *Buffalo Business First* (June 4, 2002); "New Era Cap Makes New Offer to CWA Strikers," *Buffalo Business First* (February 26, 2002); all sources downloaded from http://buffalo.bizjournals.com.

Availability of Production Inputs As we discussed earlier, organizations need certain resources to produce products and services for sale. Access to these resources, or inputs, is a huge consideration in site selection. Executives must assess the availability of raw materials, parts, and equipment for each production site under consideration. The costs of shipping raw materials and finished goods can be as much as 25 percent of a manufacturer's total cost, so locating a factory where these and other costs are as low as possible can make a major contribution to a firm's success. Companies that use heavy or bulky raw materials, for example, may choose to be located near suppliers. Mining companies want to be near ore deposits, oil refiners near oil fields, paper mills near forests, and food processors near farms. Cargill Dow LLC chose Blair, Nebraska, as the site for its new chemical plant that will turn corn products into fabrics and food-packaging materials because its raw material needs could be met by corn grown within a 90-mile radius of the site.[3]

The availability and cost of labor are also very important to both manufacturing and service businesses. Payroll costs can vary widely from one location to another because of differences in the cost of living, the number of jobs available, and the skills and productivity of the local workforce. The unionization of the local labor force is another point to consider in many industries.

Low labor costs were one reason why Globe Motors, an Ohio manufacturer of motors and power steering systems for automotive, aerospace, and defense applications, chose Portugal as the site for its new production facility. In addition to low labor costs, Portugal offers manufacturers the lowest operating costs in the 15-nation European Union.[4]

MARKETING FACTORS Businesses must also evaluate how their facility location will affect their ability to serve their customers. For some firms, it may not be necessary to be located near customers. Instead, the firm will need to assess the difficulty and costs of distributing its goods to customers from the chosen location.

Other firms may find that locating near customers can provide marketing advantages. When a factory or service center is close to customers, the firm can often offer better service at a lower cost. Other firms may gain a competitive advantage by locating their facilities so that customers can easily buy their products or services. The location of competitors may also be a factor. Businesses with more than one facility may also need to consider how far to spread their locations in order to maximize market coverage. Globe Motors decided to build its new production facility in Europe because the continent is a major market for Globe's products. By building its motors closer to this large customer base, rather than exporting them to Europe after producing them in the United States, Globe believes it will be able to improve customer service and response time.[5]

MANUFACTURING ENVIRONMENT Another factor to consider is the manufacturing environment in a potential location. Some localities have a strong existing manufacturing base. When a large number of manufacturers, perhaps in a certain industry, are already located in an area, that area is likely to offer greater availability of resources, such as manufacturing workers, better accessibility to suppliers and transportation, and other factors that can increase a plant's operating efficiency.

Industry Week magazine conducts a regular survey of the manufacturing climate offered by metropolitan areas around the world. Each metropolitan area is rated on the productivity of its manufacturing sector, the percentage of the local workforce employed in manufacturing, the contribution of manufacturing to the area's overall economy, and several other factors. Though not necessarily the largest manufacturing cities in the world, the top-rated cities are considered "world-class" manufacturing cities by *Industry Week*. The most recent list included Barcelona, Spain; Houston, Texas; Milan/Turin, Italy; Osaka, Japan; Portland, Oregon; San Jose, California; and Singapore, Singapore.[6]

LOCAL INCENTIVES Incentives offered by countries, states, or cities may also influence site selection. Tax breaks are a common incentive. The locality may reduce the amount of taxes the firm will pay on income, real estate, utilities, or payroll. Local governments also sometimes offer exemption from certain regulations or financial assistance in order to attract or keep production facilities in their area. For example, Portugal helped entice Globe Motors by offering $7.6 million in financial incentives, as well as tax breaks and assistance with paying for employee-training programs.[7]

INTERNATIONAL LOCATION CONSIDERATIONS Like Globe Motors, many U.S. manufacturers have chosen to move much of their production to facilities outside of the United States in recent years. As many as 1.3 million manufacturing jobs have moved abroad since 1992, with the majority of jobs leaving since 2000.[8] There are often sound financial reasons for considering a foreign location. Labor costs are considerably lower in countries like Singapore, China, and

Exhibit 12.4 | Cost of Doing Business: Least to Most Expensive Countries

1. Canada
2. United Kingdom
3. Italy
4. Netherlands
5. France
6. Austria
7. United States
8. Germany
9. Japan

SOURCE: Jill Jusko, "U.S. Grows Less Cost Competitive, New Research Shows," *Industry Week*, January 31, 2002, downloaded from http://www.industryweek.com.

Mexico. Foreign countries may also have fewer regulations governing how factories operate. A foreign location may move production closer to new markets. As we've seen, all these considerations motivated Globe Motors to build a new production facility in Portugal.

Consulting firm KPMG LLP, Canada, recently conducted a study that examined the cost of doing business in nine industrial countries. The study measured 27 factors, including labor, taxes, government regulatory costs, and utilities. Canada was found to be the least expensive country overall, especially for the manufacturing of electronics and specialty chemicals. Germany and Japan were ranked as the most expensive, followed by the United States. Exhibit 12.4 summarizes the study's results.

Designing the Facility

After the site location decision has been made, the next focus in production planning is the facility's layout. Here, the goal is to determine the most efficient and effective design for the particular production process. A manufacturer might opt for a U-shaped production line, for example, rather than a long, straight one, to allow products and workers to move more quickly from one area to another.

Service organizations must also consider layout, but they are more concerned with how it affects customer behavior. It may be more convenient for a hospital to place its freight elevators in the center of the building, for example, but doing so may block the flow of patients, visitors, and medical personnel between floors and departments.

A product or assembly-line layout, described on page 377, is frequently used in food-processing plants. This Tyson processing plant in Springdale, Arkansas, uses a product layout. As chicken parts move through the factory, they are breaded, cooked, frozen and then boxed for shipment to supermarkets

There are three main types of facility layouts: process, product, and fixed-position layouts. All three layouts are illustrated in Exhibit 12.5. Cellular manufacturing is another type of facility layout.

Process Layout: All Welders Stand Here

The **process layout** arranges work flow around the production process. All workers performing similar tasks are grouped together. Products pass from one workstation to another (but not necessarily to every workstation). For example, all grinding would be done in one area, all assembling in another, and all inspection in yet another. The process layout is best for firms that produce small numbers of a wide variety of products, typically using general-purpose machines that can be changed rapidly to new operations for different product designs. For example, a manufacturer of custom machinery would use a process layout.

Exhibit 12.5 | Facility Layouts

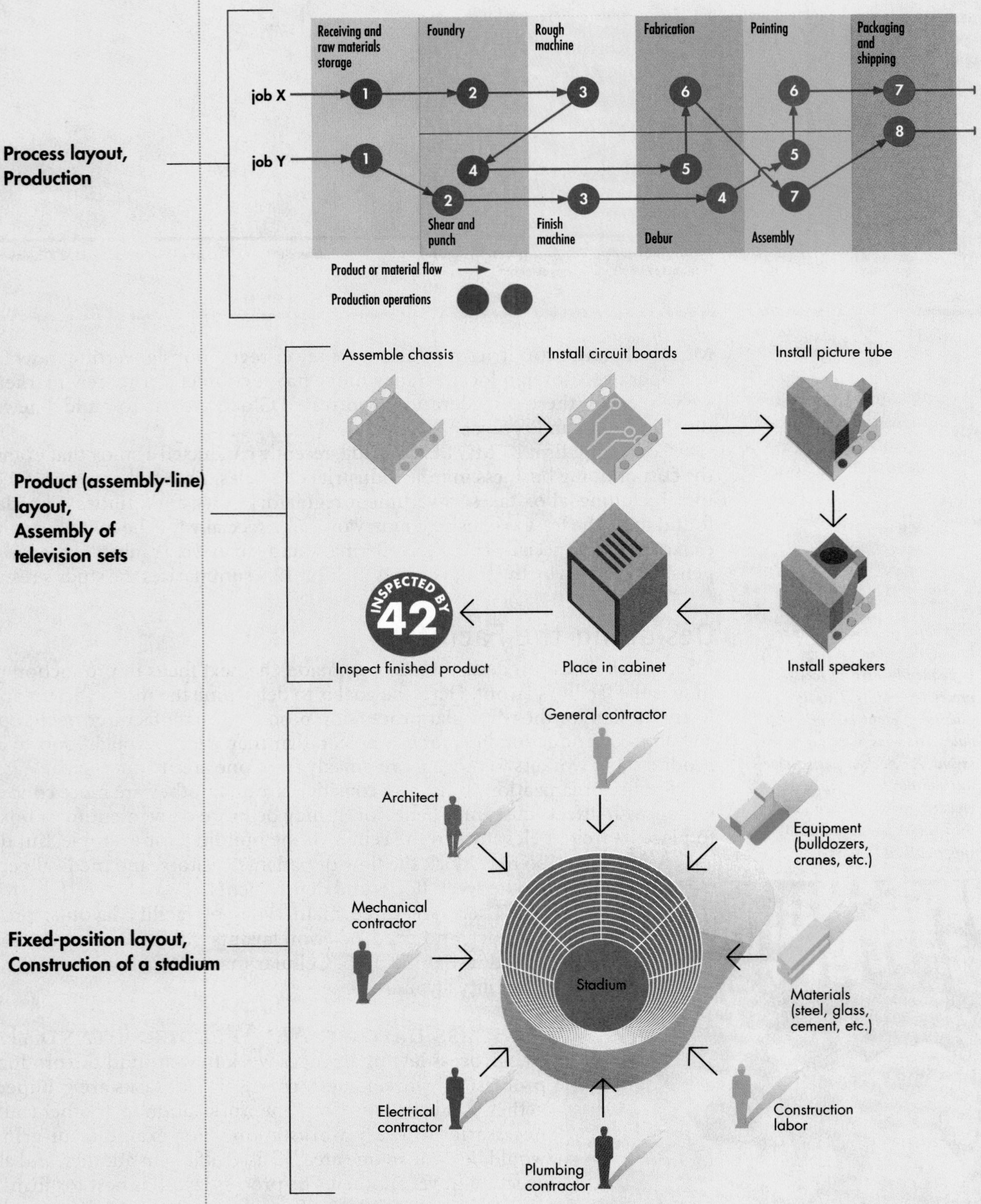

SOURCE: Top image from *Operations Management, 9th edition*, by Gaither/Frazier. © 2002. Reprinted with permission of South-Western, a division of Thomson Learning: www.thomsonrights.com. Fax 800 730-2215.

process layout
A facility arrangement in which work flows according to the production process. All workers performing similar tasks are grouped together, and products pass from one workstation to another.

product (assembly-line) layout
A facility arrangement in which workstations or departments are arranged in a line with products moving along the line.

fixed-position layout
A facility arrangement in which the product stays in one place and workers and machinery move to it as needed.

cellular manufacturing
Production technique that uses small, self-contained production units, each performing all or most of the tasks necessary to complete a manufacturing order.

PRODUCT LAYOUT: MOVING DOWN THE LINE Products that require a continuous or repetitive production process use the **product** (or **assembly-line**) **layout.** When large quantities of a product must be processed on an ongoing basis, the workstations or departments are arranged in a line with products moving along the line. Automobile and appliance manufacturers, as well as food-processing plants, usually use a product layout. Service companies may also use a product layout for routine processing operations. For example, overnight film processors use assembly-line techniques.

FIXED-POSITION LAYOUT: STAYING PUT Some products cannot be put on an assembly line or moved about in a plant. A **fixed-position layout** lets the product stay in one place while workers and machinery move to it as needed. Products that are impossible to move—ships, airplanes, and construction projects—are typically produced using a fixed-position layout. Limited space at the project site often means that parts of the product must be assembled at other sites, transported to the fixed site, and then assembled. The fixed-position layout is also common for on-site services like housecleaning services, pest control, and landscaping.

CELLULAR MANUFACTURING: A START-TO-FINISH FOCUS **Cellular manufacturing** combines some aspects of both product and fixed-position layout. Work cells are small, self-contained production units that include several machines and workers arranged in a compact, sequential order. Each work cell performs all or most of the tasks necessary to complete a manufacturing order. There are usually between 5 and 10 workers in a cell, and they are trained to be able to do any of the steps in the production process. The goal is to create a team environment where team members are involved in production from beginning to end.

Pulling It Together: Resource Planning

4 learning goal

As part of the production-planning process, firms must ensure that the resources needed for production, such as raw materials, parts, and equipment, will be available at strategic moments in the production process. This can be a huge challenge. The components used to build just one Boeing airplane, for instance, number in the millions. Cost is also an important factor. In many industries, the cost of materials and supplies used in the production process amounts to as much as half of sales revenues. Resource planning is therefore a big part of any firm's production strategy. Resource planning begins by specifying which raw materials, parts, and components will be required, and when, to produce finished goods. To determine the amount of each item needed, the expected quantity of finished goods to be produced must be forecast. A **bill of material** is then drawn up that lists the items and the number of each required to make the product. **Purchasing,** or *procurement,* is the process of buying production inputs from various sources.

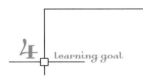

bill of material
A list of the items and the number of each required to make a given product.

purchasing
The process of buying production inputs from various sources; also called *procurement.*

make-or-buy decision
The determination by a firm of whether to make its own production materials or buy them from outside sources.

outsourcing
The purchase of items from an outside source rather than making them internally.

MAKE OR BUY? Next, the firm must decide whether to make its own production materials or buy them from outside sources. This is the **make-or-buy decision.** The quantity of items needed is one consideration. If a part is used in only one of many products, buying the part may be more cost-effective than making it. Buying standard items, such as screws, bolts, rivets, and nails, is usually cheaper and easier than producing them internally. Sometimes purchasing larger components from another manufacturing firm is cost-effective as well. Purchasing items from an outside source instead of making them internally is called **outsourcing.** Harley-Davidson, for example, purchases its tires, brake systems, and other motorcycle components from other businesses that make them to Harley's specifications. If a product has special design features that need to be kept secret to protect a competitive advantage, however, a firm may decide to produce all parts internally.

Because millions of parts are required to build a jet, inventory management is critical for aerospace manufacturers like Boeing. Computerized resource planning systems are used to help track and schedule the flow of parts, raw material, and equipment so they are available to production workers at the correct time.

© ED KASHI / CORBIS

In deciding whether to make or buy, a firm must also consider whether outside sources can provide high-quality supplies in a reliable manner. Having to shut down production because vital parts weren't delivered on time can be a costly disaster. Just as bad are inferior parts or materials, which can damage a firm's reputation for producing high-quality goods. Therefore, firms that buy some or all of their production materials from outside sources should pay close attention to building strong relationships with quality suppliers.

inventory
The supply of goods that a firm holds for use in production or for sale to customers.

INVENTORY MANAGEMENT: NOT JUST PARTS A firm's **inventory** is the supply of goods it holds for use in production or for sale to customers. Deciding how much inventory to keep on hand is one of the biggest challenges facing operations managers. On the one hand, with large inventories, the firm can meet most production and customer demands. Buying in large quantities can also allow a company to take advantage of quantity discounts. On the other hand, large inventories can tie up the firm's money, are expensive to store, and can become obsolete.

inventory management
The determination of how much of each type of inventory a firm will keep on hand and the ordering, receiving, storing, and tracking of inventory.

Inventory management involves deciding how much of each type of inventory to keep on hand and the ordering, receiving, storing, and tracking of it. The goal of inventory management is to keep down the costs of ordering and holding inventories while maintaining enough on hand for production and sales. Good inventory management enhances product quality, makes operations more efficient, and increases profits. Poor inventory management can result in dissatisfied customers, financial difficulties, and even bankruptcy.

One way to determine the best inventory levels is to look at three costs: the cost of holding inventory, the cost of reordering frequently, and the cost of not keeping enough inventory on hand. Managers must measure all three costs and try to minimize them.

perpetual inventory
A continuously updated list of inventory levels, orders, sales, and receipts.

To control inventory levels, managers often track the use of certain inventory items. Most companies keep a **perpetual inventory,** a continuously updated list of inventory levels, orders, sales, and receipts, for all major items. Today, companies often use computers to track inventory levels, calculate order quantities, and issue purchase orders at the right times. The following "Focusing on Small Business" box describes how improving inventory management saved a small company big bucks.

COMPUTERIZED RESOURCE PLANNING Many manufacturing companies have adopted computerized systems to control the flow of resources

Focusing on Small Business

Sharpening Inventory Management at Simplex Nails

Simplex Nails knows that little things can add up. The Georgia manufacturer makes roofing nails, which bring in $30 million in annual sales for the 30-employee firm. As the economy stalled, however, so did demand for roofing nails. Severe competition from foreign nail manufacturers—who could make and price nails more cheaply than Simplex—further added to the company's woes. Simplex soon found itself left with excess inventory and factory capacity. Unable to recover these costs, Simplex began losing money.

The company turned to the Georgia Tech Business Development Institute for ideas. One problem that was quickly identified was the firm's inventory levels. Simplex developed a sales forecast each year based on the previous year's sales and then the factory manufactured nails to meet that forecast. If the sales forecast proved inaccurate, however, as was often the case, Simplex was left with excess inventory that it couldn't sell.

On the other hand, the company often received orders from customers for nails that it hadn't yet produced so the factory began storing materials and supplies to be ready to produce unexpected orders. "They had a lot of work-in-progress inventory," says John Stephens, the Georgia Tech Institute engineer who worked with Simplex. "They would fill orders from scratch, and if they didn't have it in stock, they were quoting four to six weeks to fill orders. I asked them 'How long does it take to make a nail?' They said, 'Well, we can make a nail in a day.' So, I said, 'If you can make a nail in a day, why does it take four to six weeks to fill an order?'"

Stephens suggested that Simplex implement production techniques to reduce inventory, production cycle time, and manufacturing inefficiencies. The first step was switching from a "push" to a "pull" system of production. Now, instead of gearing production to forecasts based on previous sales, Simplex builds nails only when customers order them, "pulling" manufacturing according to actual orders. Stephens also helped the company identify which processes, materials, and equipment add value to the finished product, helping to reduce materials and parts inventory and eliminate waste.

"Now, if we don't need it, we don't make it," says plant manager Jeff Kurtz. "And if it doesn't add to the product in some way, we don't buy it or do it."

The results were dramatic. Simplex has reduced inventory by 52 percent, saving over $530,000 in just one year on inventory costs alone. Simplex is now able to price more competitively and customers are more satisfied. "Our cash flow all around has improved and our production is more efficient," says Kurtz.

Critical Thinking Questions

1. How might the benefits of the changes in Simplex's factory affect the firm's other business functions, such as marketing, human resources, or financial management?
2. Simplex has not had the financial resources to invest in new technologies until now. Which technologies and automated systems discussed in this chapter would you recommend Simplex investigate for further production improvements? Why?
3. What are some of the risks of manufacturing only to customer orders, not to forecasts? How can Simplex avoid these risks?

SOURCES: Tonya Vinas, "Little Things Mean a Lot," *Industry Week*, November 1, 2002, downloaded from http://www.industryweek.com; "Lean Enterprise Practices Help Simplex Nails Regain Competitive Edge," Georgia Institute of Technology press release, November 30, 2001; and "Georgia Tech Economic Development Institute—Success Stories," Georgia Institute of Technology, downloaded December 12, 2002, from http://www.industry.gatech.edu/lean/leanmauf_success.cfm.

materials requirement planning (MRP)
A computerized system of controlling the flow of resources and inventory. A master schedule is used to ensure that the materials, labor, and equipment needed for production are at the right places in the right amounts at the right times.

manufacturing resource planning II (MRPII)
A complex computerized system that integrates data from many departments to allow managers to better forecast and assess the impact of production plans on profitability.

and inventory. **Materials requirement planning (MRP)** is one such system. MRP uses a master schedule to ensure that the materials, labor, and equipment needed for production are at the right places in the right amounts at the right times. The schedule is based on forecasts of demand for the company's products. It says exactly what will be manufactured during the next few weeks or months and when the work will take place. Sophisticated computer programs coordinate all the elements of MRP. The computer comes up with materials requirements by comparing production needs to the materials the company already has on hand. Orders are placed so items will be on hand when they are needed for production. MRP helps ensure a smooth flow of finished products.

Manufacturing resource planning II (MRPII) was developed in the late 1980s to expand on MRP. It uses a complex computerized system to integrate data from many departments, including finance, marketing, accounting, engineering, and manufacturing. MRPII can generate a production plan for the firm, as well as management reports, forecasts, and financial statements. The system lets managers make more accurate forecasts and assess the impact of production plans on profitability. If one department's plans change, the effects of these changes on other departments are transmitted throughout the company.

enterprise resource planning (ERP)
A computerized resource-planning system that incorporates information about the firm's suppliers and customers with its internally generated data.

Whereas MRP and MRPII systems are focused internally, **enterprise resource planning (ERP)** systems go a step further and incorporate information about the firm's suppliers and customers into the flow of data. ERP unites all of a firm's major departments into a single software program. For instance, production can call up sales information and know immediately how many units must be produced to meet customer orders. By providing information about the availability of resources, including both human resources and materials needed for production, the system allows for better cost control and eliminates production delays. The system automatically notes any changes, such as the closure of a plant for maintenance and repairs on a certain date or a supplier's inability to meet a delivery date, so that all functions can adjust accordingly. Both large and small organizations use ERP to improve operations.

Keeping the Goods Flowing: Supply Chain Management

In the past, the relationship between purchasers and suppliers was often competitive and antagonistic. Businesses used many suppliers and switched among them frequently. During contract negotiations, each side would try to get better terms at the expense of the other. Communication between purchasers and suppliers was often limited to purchase orders and billing statements.

supply chain
The entire sequence of securing inputs, producing goods, and delivering goods to customers.

Today, however, many firms are moving toward a new concept in supplier relationships. The emphasis is increasingly on developing a strong **supply chain.** The supply chain can be thought of as the entire sequence of securing inputs, producing goods, and delivering goods to customers. If any links in this process are weak, chances are customers—the end point of the supply chain—will end up dissatisfied.

supply chain management
The process of smoothing transitions along the supply chain so that the firm can satisfy its customers with quality products and services; focuses on developing tighter bonds with suppliers.

STRATEGIES FOR SUPPLY CHAIN MANAGEMENT Ensuring a strong supply chain requires that firms implement supply chain management strategies. **Supply chain management** focuses on smoothing transitions along the supply chain, with the ultimate goal of satisfying customers with quality products and services. A critical element of effective supply chain management is to develop tighter bonds with suppliers. In many cases, this means reducing the number of suppliers used and asking those suppliers to offer more services or better prices in return for an ongoing relationship. Instead of being viewed as "outsiders" in the production process, many suppliers are now playing an important role in supporting the operations of their customers. They are expected to meet higher quality standards, offer suggestions that can help reduce production costs, and even contribute to the design of new products.

e-procurement
The process of purchasing supplies and materials online using the Internet.

TALK TO US: IMPROVING SUPPLIER COMMUNICATIONS Effective supply chain management requires the development of strong communications with suppliers. Technology, particularly the Internet, is providing new ways to do this. **E-procurement,** the process of purchasing supplies and materials online, is booming. One consulting firm predicts that the dollar value of materials purchased online will hit $3.17 trillion in 2003, up from $75 billion in 2000.[9] Some manufacturing firms use the Internet to keep key suppliers informed about their requirements. Intel, for example, has set up a special Web site for its suppliers and potential suppliers. Would-be suppliers can visit the site to get information about doing business with Intel; once they are approved, they can access a secure area to make bids on Intel's current and future resource needs.

The Internet also streamlines purchasing by providing firms with quick access to a huge database of information about the products and services of hundreds of potential suppliers. Many large manufacturers now participate in *reverse auctions* online. In an online reverse auction, the manufacturer posts its specifications for

electronic data interchange (EDI)
The electronic exchange of information between two trading partners.

routing
The aspect of production control that involves setting out the work flow—the sequence of machines and operations through which the product or service progresses from start to finish.

the materials it requires. Potential suppliers then bid against each other to get the job. Reverse auctions can slash procurement costs. Owens Corning, for example, has cut materials costs by 10 percent through online auction procurement.

However, there are risks with reverse auctions. It can be difficult to establish and build ongoing relationships with specific suppliers using reverse auctions because the job ultimately goes to the lowest bidder. Therefore, reverse auctions may not be an effective procurement process for critical production materials.[10]

Another communications tool is **electronic data interchange (EDI),** in which two trading partners exchange information electronically. EDI can be conducted via a linked computer system or over the Internet. The advantages of exchanging information with suppliers electronically include speed, accuracy, and lowered communication costs.

Dana Corporation, a California manufacturer of auto and truck frames, has only one customer, New United Motor Manufacturing Inc. (NUMMI), a joint venture between Toyota and General Motors. In the past, NUMMI could give Dana only a six-week production forecast. A fax was sent to Dana each day updating NUMMI's needs. Dana and NUMMI then installed an EDI system that continually alerts Dana about NUMMI's purchasing requirements on an hourly basis. As a result, Dana has been able to cut its inventory, smooth its production scheduling, and meet NUMMI's needs more efficiently and rapidly.[11]

concept check

What are the four types of decisions that must be made in production planning?

What factors does a firm consider when making a site selection decision?

How is technology being used in resource planning?

Production and Operations Control

5 learning goal

Every company needs to have systems in place to see that production and operations are carried out as planned and to correct errors when they are not. The coordination of materials, equipment, and human resources to achieve production and operating efficiencies is called *production control.* Two of its key aspects are routing and scheduling.

Routing: Where to Next?

Routing is the first step in production control. It sets out a work flow, that is, the sequence of machines and operations through which a product or service progresses from start to finish. Routing depends on the type of goods being produced and the facility layout. Good routing procedures increase productivity and cut unnecessary costs.

One useful tool for routing is **value-stream mapping,** where production managers "map" the flow from suppliers through the factory to customers. Simple icons represent the materials and information needed at various points in the flow. Value-stream mapping can help identify where bottlenecks may occur in the production process and is a valuable tool for visualizing how to improve production routing.

Medical manufacturer Medtronic, Inc. used value-stream mapping to better understand how materials and information were routed through its Jacksonville, Florida, production plant. The company identified 48 different streams for the different products the plant produced. From the map, Medtronic was able to determine where waste and slowdowns were most likely to occur and develop an improvement plan that reduced standard production cycle time, cut inventory levels, and improved overall productivity.[12]

Routing and scheduling is just as important to service organizations as it is to manufacturing firms. Hospitals, for instance, must carefully schedule the equipment, personnel, and facilities needed to conduct patient surgeries and other treatments.

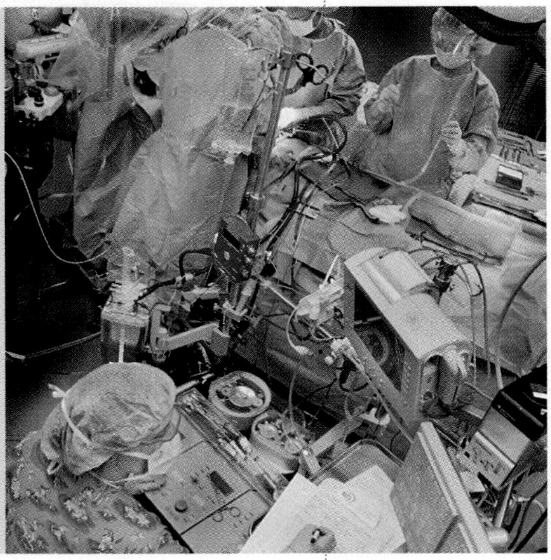

Scheduling: When Do We Do It?

value-stream mapping
Routing technique that uses simple icons to visually represent the flow of materials and information from suppliers through the factory and to customers.

scheduling
The aspect of production control that involves specifying and controlling the time required for each step in the production process.

Closely related to routing is **scheduling.** Scheduling involves specifying and controlling the time required for each step in the production process. The operations manager prepares timetables showing the most efficient sequence of production and then tries to ensure that the necessary materials and labor are in the right place at the right time.

Scheduling is important to both manufacturing and service firms. The production manager in a factory schedules material deliveries, work shifts, and production processes. Trucking companies schedule drivers, clerks, truck maintenance, and repair with customer transportation needs. Scheduling at a college entails deciding when to offer which courses, in which classrooms, with which instructors. A museum must schedule its special exhibits, ship the works to be displayed, market its services, and conduct educational programs and tours.

Scheduling can range from simple to complex. Giving numbers to customers waiting to be served in a bakery and making interview appointments with job applicants are examples of simple scheduling. Organizations that must produce large quantities of products or services, or service a diverse customer base, face more complex scheduling problems.

Three common scheduling tools used for complex situations are Gantt charts, the critical path method, and PERT.

Gantt charts
Bar graphs plotted on a time line that show the relationship between scheduled and actual production.

Tracking Progress with Gantt Charts Named after their originator, Henry Gantt, **Gantt charts** are bar graphs plotted on a time line that show the relationship between scheduled and actual production. Exhibit 12.6 is an example. On the left, the chart lists the activities required to complete the job or project. Both the scheduled time and the actual time required for each activity are shown, so the manager can easily judge progress.

Gantt charts are most helpful when only a few tasks are involved, when task times are relatively long (days or weeks rather than hours), and when job routes are short and simple. One of the biggest shortcomings of Gantt charts is that they

Exhibit 12.6 | A Typical Gantt Chart

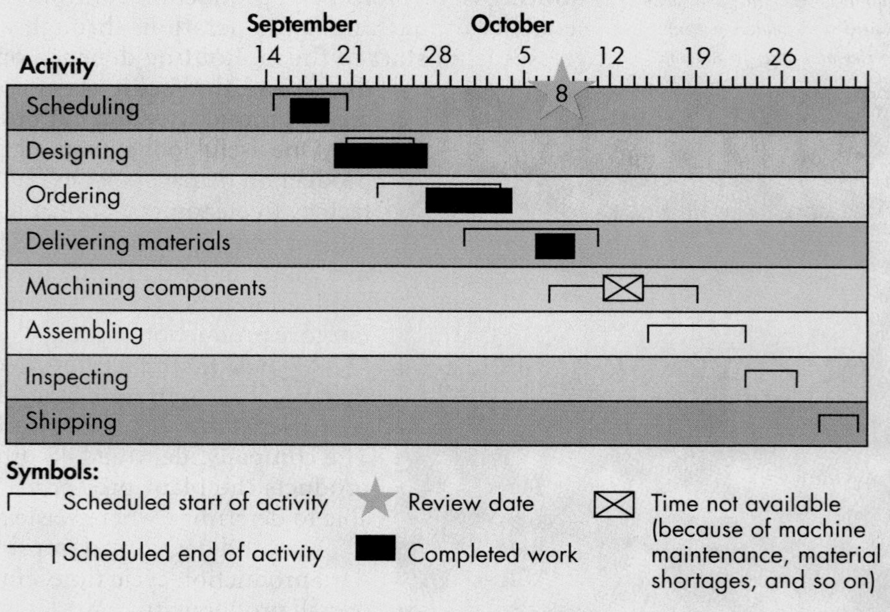

are static. They also fail to show how tasks are related. These problems can be solved, however, by using two other scheduling techniques, the critical path method and PERT.

The Big Picture: Critical Path Method and PERT

To control large projects, operations managers need to closely monitor resources, costs, quality, and budgets. They also must be able to see the "big picture"—the interrelationships of the many different tasks necessary to complete the project. Finally, they must be able to revise scheduling and divert resources quickly if any tasks fall behind schedule. The critical path method (CPM) and the program evaluation and review technique (PERT) are related project management tools that were developed in the 1950s to help managers accomplish this.

critical path method (CPM)
A scheduling tool that enables a manager to determine the critical path of activities for a project—the activities that will cause the entire project to fall behind schedule if they are not completed on time.

critical path
In a critical path method network, the longest path through the linked activities.

program evaluation and review technique (PERT)
A scheduling tool that is similar to the CPM method but assigns three time estimates for each activity (optimistic, most probable, and pessimistic); allows managers to anticipate delays and potential problems and schedule accordingly.

In the **critical path method (CPM),** the manager identifies all of the activities required to complete the project, the relationships between these activities, and the order in which they need to be completed. Then, the manager develops a diagram that uses arrows to show how the tasks are dependent on each other. The longest path through these linked activities is called the **critical path.** If the tasks on the critical path are not completed on time, the entire project will fall behind schedule.

To better understand how CPM works, look at Exhibit 12.7, which shows a CPM diagram for constructing a house. All of the tasks required to finish the house and an estimated time for each have been identified. The arrows indicate the links between the various steps and their required sequence. As you can see, most of the jobs to be done can't be started until the house's foundation and frame are completed. It will take five days to finish the foundation and another seven days to erect the house frame. The activities linked by red arrows form the critical path for this project. It tells us that the fastest possible time the house can be built is 38 days, the total time needed for all of the critical path tasks. The noncritical path jobs, those connected with black arrows, can be delayed a bit or done early. Short delays in installing appliances or roofing won't delay construction of the house because these activities don't lie on the critical path.

Like CPM, **program evaluation and review technique (PERT)** helps managers identify critical tasks and assess how delays in certain activities will affect operations

Exhibit 12.7 | A CPM Network for Building a House

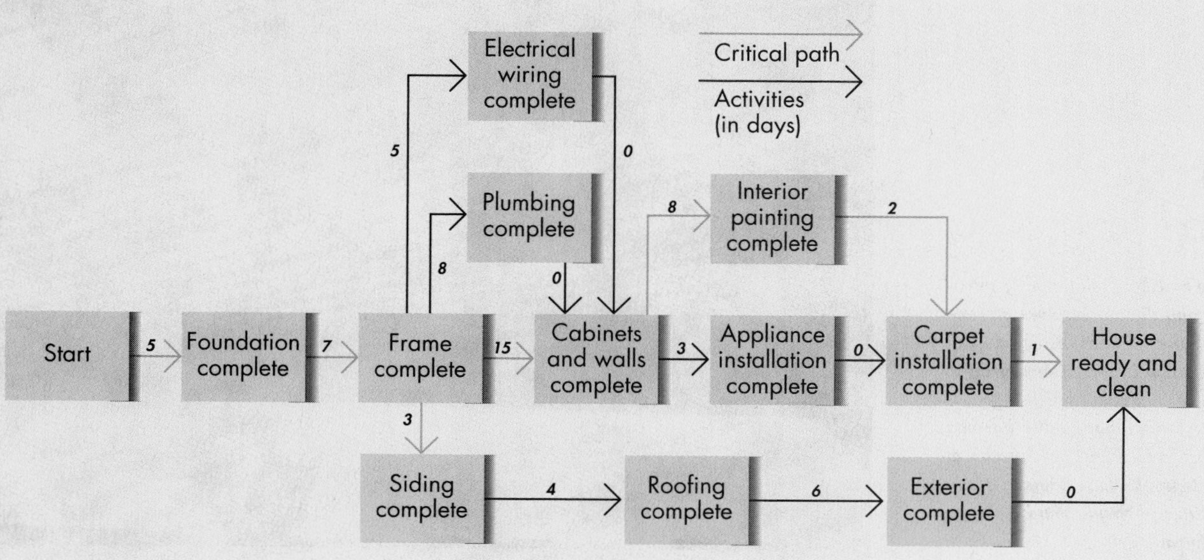

or production. In both methods, managers use diagrams to see how operations and production will flow. PERT differs from CPM in one important respect, however. CPM assumes that the amount of time needed to finish a task is known with certainty; therefore, the CPM diagram shows only one number for the time needed to complete each activity. In contrast, PERT assigns three time estimates for each activity: an optimistic time for completion, the most probable time, and a pessimistic time. These estimates allow managers to anticipate delays and potential problems and schedule accordingly.

concept check

What is production control, and what are its key aspects?

Identify and describe three commonly used scheduling tools.

Looking for a Better Way: Improving Production and Operations

6 learning goal

Competing in today's business world is challenging. To compete effectively, firms must keep production costs down. At the same time, however, it's becoming increasingly complex to produce and deliver the high-quality goods and services customers demand. Methods to help meet these challenges include quality management techniques, lean manufacturing, and automation.

Putting Quality First

quality
Goods and services that meet customer expectations by providing reliable performance.

quality control
The process of creating standards for quality, producing goods that meet them, and measuring finished products and services against them.

Successful businesses recognize that quality and productivity must go hand in hand. **Quality** goods and services meet customer expectations by providing reliable performance. Defective products waste materials and time, increasing costs. Worse, poor quality causes customer dissatisfaction, which usually means lost sales.

A consumer measures quality by how well a good serves its purpose. From the company's point of view, quality is the degree to which a good conforms to a set of predetermined standards. **Quality control** involves creating those quality standards, producing goods that meet them, and measuring finished products and services against them. It takes more than just inspecting goods at the end of the assembly line to ensure quality control, however. Quality control requires a

The Six Sigma quality program directly involves production employees in setting quality standards and in measuring and analyzing finished goods to ensure that quality has been achieved. Here, a worker in an electronics factory inspects a finished circuit board looking for any defects.

company-wide dedication to managing and working in a way that builds excellence into every facet of operations.

Dr. W. Edwards Deming, an American management consultant, was the first to say that quality control should be a company-wide goal. His ideas were adopted by the Japanese in the 1950s but largely ignored in the United States until the 1970s. Deming believed that quality control must start with top management, who must foster a culture dedicated to producing quality.

total quality management (TQM)
The use of quality principles in all aspects of a company's production and operations.

continuous improvement
A commitment to constantly seek better ways of doing things in order to achieve greater efficiency and improve quality.

Six Sigma
A quality control process that relies on defining what needs to be done to ensure quality, measuring and analyzing production results statistically, and finding ways to improve and control quality.

Deming's concept of **Total Quality Management (TQM)** emphasizes the use of quality principles in all aspects of a company's production and operations. It recognizes that all employees involved with bringing a product or service to customers—marketing, purchasing, accounting, shipping, manufacturing—contribute to its quality. TQM focuses on **continuous improvement,** a commitment to constantly seek better ways of doing things in order to achieve greater efficiency and improve quality. Company-wide teams work together to prevent problems and systematically improve key processes instead of troubleshooting problems only as they arise. Continuous improvement continually measures performance using statistical techniques and looks for ways to apply new technologies and innovative production methods.

Another quality control method is the **Six Sigma** quality program. Six Sigma is a company-wide process that focuses on measuring the number of defects that occur and systematically eliminating them in order to get as close to "zero defects" as possible. In fact, Six Sigma quality aims to have every process produce no more than 3.4 defects per million. Six Sigma focuses on designing products that not only have less defects but that also satisfy customer needs. A key process of Six Sigma is called *DMAIC*. This stands for Define, Measure, Analyze, Improve, and Control. Employees at all levels define what needs to be done to ensure quality, then measure and analyze production results using statistics to see if the standards are met. They are also charged with finding ways to improve and control quality.

General Electric was one of the first companies to institute Six Sigma throughout the organization. All GE employees are trained in Six Sigma concepts, and many analysts believe this has given GE a competitive manufacturing advantage. Service firms have applied Six Sigma to their quality initiatives as well. Bank of America Corp., for example, says it expected to save $1 billion from changes instituted from Six Sigma quality control management techniques.[13]

Malcolm Baldrige National Quality Award
An award given to recognize U.S. companies that offer goods and services of world-class quality; established by Congress in 1987 and named for a former secretary of commerce.

MALCOLM BALDRIGE NATIONAL QUALITY AWARD

The **Malcolm Baldrige National Quality Award,** named for a former secretary of commerce, was established by the U.S. Congress in 1987 to recognize U.S. companies that offer goods and services of world-class quality. The award promotes awareness of quality and allows the business community to benchmark which quality control programs are most effective.

Administered by the U.S. Department of Commerce's National Institute of Standards and Technologies (NIST), the award's most important criterion is a firm's effectiveness at meeting customer expectations. The firm must also demonstrate that it offers quality goods and services. To qualify for the award, a company must also show continuous improvement in internal operations. Company leaders and employees must be active participants in the firm's quality program and they must respond quickly to data and analysis.

Organizations in a wide variety of industries have won the Baldrige Award since it was first awarded in 1987. In 2002, for example, the Baldrige Award winners were Pal's, a southeastern fast-food chain; SSM Health Care in St. Louis, Missouri; and Motorola's Commercial, Government and Industrial Solutions division.[14] Branch-Smith Printing Division, a small family business in Fort Worth, Texas, also received the Baldrige Award in 2002.

WORLDWIDE EXCELLENCE: INTERNATIONAL QUALITY STANDARDS The International Organization for Standardization (ISO), located in Belgium, is an industry organization that has developed standards of quality that are used by businesses around the world. **ISO 9000,** introduced in the 1980s, is a set of five technical standards designed to offer a uniform way of determining whether manufacturing plants and service organizations conform to sound quality procedures. To register, a company must go through an audit of its manufacturing and customer service processes, covering everything from how it designs, produces, and installs its goods to how it inspects, packages, and markets them. Over 500,000 organizations worldwide have met ISO 9000 standards. For example, Mission Bell Winery in Madera, California, went through a one-year quality control audit and certification process that examined all areas of production, bottling, and distribution to become one of only two U.S. wineries that meet ISO 9000 requirements.[15]

ISO 14000, launched after ISO 9000, is designed to promote clean production processes in response to environmental issues like global warming and water pollution. To meet ISO 14000 standards, a company must commit to continually improving environmental management and reducing pollution resulting from its production processes.

ISO 9000
A set of five technical standards of quality management created by the International Organization for Standardization to provide a uniform way of determining whether manufacturing plants and service organizations conform to sound quality procedures.

ISO 14000
A set of technical standards designed by the International Organization for Standardization to promote clean production processes to protect the environment.

Lean Manufacturing Trims the Fat

Manufacturers are discovering that they can better respond to rapidly changing customer demands, while keeping inventory and production costs down, by adopting lean-manufacturing techniques. **Lean manufacturing** streamlines production by eliminating steps in the production process that do not add benefits that customers are willing to pay for. In other words, *non-value-added production processes* are cut so that the company can concentrate its production and operations resources on items essential to satisfying customers. Toyota was a pioneer in developing these techniques, but today manufacturers in many industries have also adopted the lean-manufacturing philosophy.

Another Japanese concept, **just-in-time (JIT),** goes hand in hand with lean manufacturing. JIT is based on the belief that materials should arrive exactly when they are needed for production, rather than being stored on site. Relying closely on computerized systems such as MRP, MRPII, and ERP, manufacturers determine what parts will be needed and when, and then order them from suppliers so they arrive "just in time." Under the JIT system, inventory and products are "pulled" through the production process in response to customer demand. JIT requires close teamwork between vendors and purchasing and production personnel because any delay in deliveries of supplies could bring JIT production to a halt.

Unexpected events can also cause problems for firms relying on JIT. For example, the September 11 terrorist attacks caused chaos in the supply chains of many manufacturers. In 2002, a shutdown of West Coast ports due to a labor dispute also affected many manufacturers. New United Motor Manufacturing Inc. (NUMMI), in Fremont, California, which receives 34 containers of supplies daily for same-day production, was forced to shut down its truck assembly plant for five days during the port closures.[16] In spite of these risks, if employed properly, a JIT system can greatly reduce inventory-holding costs and can also smooth production highs and lows.

lean manufacturing
Streamlining production by eliminating steps in the production process that do not add benefits that customers are willing to pay for.

just-in-time (JIT)
A system in which materials arrive exactly when they are needed for production, rather than being stored on site.

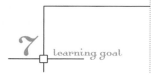

7 learning goal

Transforming the Factory Floor with Technology

Technology is helping many firms improve their operating efficiency and ability to compete. Computer systems, in particular, are enabling manufacturers to automate factories in ways never before possible.

Among the technologies helping to automate manufacturing are computer-aided design and manufacturing systems, robotics, flexible manufacturing systems, and computer-integrated manufacturing.

Computer-Aided Design and Manufacturing Systems

computer-aided design (CAD)
The use of computers to design and test new products and modify existing ones.

computer-aided manufacturing (CAM)
The use of computers to develop and control the production process.

CAD/CAM systems
Linked computer systems that combine the advantages of *computer-aided design* and *computer-aided manufacturing*. The system helps design the product, control the flow of resources, and operate the production process.

Computers have transformed the design and manufacturing processes in many industries. In **computer-aided design (CAD),** computers are used to design and test new products and modify existing ones. Engineers use these systems to draw products and look at them from different angles. They can analyze the products, make changes, and test prototypes before making even one item. **Computer-aided manufacturing (CAM)** uses computers to develop and control the production process. The systems analyze the steps required to make the product. They then automatically send instructions to the machines that do the work. **CAD/CAM systems** combine the advantages of CAD and CAM by integrating design, testing, and manufacturing control into one linked computer system. The system helps design the product, control the flow of resources needed to produce the product, and operate the production process.

Cardianove Inc., a Montreal-based manufacturer of medical and surgical equipment, used CAD software to develop the world's smallest heart pump. The company says using computer-aided design shaved two years off the normal design time for cardiac devices. The company's CAD program ran complex three-dimensional simulations to confirm that the design would function properly inside the human body. Cardionove tested over 100 virtual prototypes using the software before the top three designs were actually produced for real-life testing.[17]

robotics
The technology involved in designing, constructing, and operating computer-controlled machines that can perform tasks independently.

Robotics

Robots are computer-controlled machines that can perform tasks independently. **Robotics** is the technology involved in designing, constructing, and operating robots. The first robot, or "steel-collar worker," was used by General Motors in 1961. Today the company has over 25,000 robots at work in its plants.[18]

Robots can be mobile or fixed in one place. Fixed robots have an arm that moves and does what the computer instructs. Some robots are quite simple, with limited movement for a few tasks such as cutting sheet metal and spot welding. Others are complex, with hands or grippers that can be programmed to perform a series of movements. Some robots are even equipped with sensing devices for sight and touch.

Robots usually operate with little or no human intervention. Replacing human effort with robots is most effective for tasks requiring accuracy, speed, or strength. Although manufacturers, such as Harley-Davidson as described at the beginning of this chapter, are most likely to use robots, some service firms are also finding them useful. Some hospitals, for example, use robots to sort and process blood samples, freeing medical personnel from a tedious, sometimes hazardous, repetitive task.

flexible manufacturing system (FMS)
A system that combines automated workstations with computer-controlled transportation devices—automatic guided vehicles (AGVs)—that move materials between workstations and into and out of the system.

Adaptable Factories: Flexible Manufacturing Systems

A **flexible manufacturing system (FMS)** automates a factory by blending computers, robots, machine tools, and materials-and-parts-handling machinery into an integrated system. These systems combine automated workstations with computer-controlled transportation devices. Automatic guided vehicles (AGVs) move materials between workstations and into and out of the system.

Flexible manufacturing systems are expensive. Once in place, however, a system requires little labor to operate and provides consistent product quality. The system can be changed easily and inexpensively. FMS equipment can be programmed to perform one job and then quickly be reprogrammed to perform another. These systems work well when small batches of a variety of products are required or when each product is made to individual customer specifications.

computer-integrated manufacturing (CIM)
The combination of computerized manufacturing processes (like robots and flexible manufacturing systems) with other computerized systems that control design, inventory, production, and purchasing.

QUICK CHANGE WITH COMPUTER-INTEGRATED MANUFACTURING **Computer-integrated manufacturing (CIM)** combines computerized manufacturing processes (like robots and FMS) with other computerized systems that control design, inventory, production, and purchasing. With CIM, when a part is redesigned in the CAD system, the changes are quickly transmitted both to the machines producing the part and to all other departments that need to know about and plan for the change.

Technology and Automation at Your Service

Manufacturers are not the only businesses benefiting from technology. Nonmanufacturing firms are also using automation to improve customer service and productivity. Banks now offer services to customers through automated teller machines (ATMs), via automated telephone systems, and even over the Internet. Retail stores of all kinds use point-of-sale (POS) terminals that track inventories, identify items that need to be reordered, and tell which products are selling well. Wal-Mart, the leader in retailing automation, has its own satellite system connecting POS terminals directly to its distribution centers and headquarters. As the "Applying Technology" box discusses, the restaurant industry is also streamlining operations with automation technology.

concept check

Define total quality management, lean manufacturing, and just-in-time, and explain how each can help a firm improve its production and operations.

How are both manufacturing and nonmanufacturing firms using technology and automation to improve operations?

APPLYING TECHNOLOGY

Have It Your Way—and Fast—at Burger King

Tired of long lines at fast-food restaurants? Chains like McDonald's, Arby's, and Burger King are hoping technology can put the "fast" back into fast food by automating many of the processes used in taking and preparing food orders.

Paul Bobo, who manages six Burger King restaurants in Florida and Georgia, uses technology throughout his restaurants to keep operations running at peak speeds. An automated system called IntelliKitchen uses bar codes on food wrappers to keep track of the finished items sitting in the restaurant hot bins. When new sandwiches will be needed soon, the system automatically places an order in the kitchen for workers to start preparing replacements. Not only does IntelliKitchen use color-coded instructions to tell employees when to fire up new burgers and fries, it even tells them how many meat patties, buns, and fries to put together and specifies how much mustard and ketchup to include with an order. Because IntelliKitchen provides such detailed instructions, Bobo says employee training is easier. "The color coded instructions help them a lot. It makes life so much easier."

Bobo also uses ZEOM.net, a computer-driven management tool. ZEOM.net lets Bobo manage what's going on in all of his restaurants—seven when he's miles away at another restaurant. ZEOM.net gathers real-time data about sales, labor, and inventory from each restaurant and displays the information on Bobo's laptop computer.

Bobo can also stay on top of what is happening in each restaurant because video from security cameras is instantly available via his computer. For example, once Bobo logged on to his computer and caught an employee doing homework while on duty. He phoned the store and told her that she shouldn't be doing homework when she was supposed to be working. "The stunned look on her face was priceless," says Bobo. "I haven't had any trouble with her doing homework since then."

Bobo says service speeds have improved in all of his restaurants. "The gold standard, in terms of speed of service for Burger King, is two minutes, 30 seconds. Prior to installing these systems we were at approximately two minutes, 48 seconds. In a four-week period we shaved about four seconds off that, and expect to get to about two minutes, 20 seconds in the next four to six weeks."

CRITICAL THINKING QUESTIONS

1. How is automation like Paul Bobo uses in his restaurants likely to change customers' opinions of fast-food restaurants? Why?
2. Discuss the effect of automation and technology on the employees of fast-food restaurants.
3. Would the technology being used in fast-food restaurants work in the cafeteria of your school? How about for an expensive steakhouse? Defend your answer.

SOURCES: Chris George, "Thin, Show, Tell," *QSR* magazine, September 2001, downloaded from http://www.qsrmagazine.com; Jennifer LeClaire, "The Revolution," *QSR* magazine, November 2002, p. 44; and Jennifer LeClaire, "Get Smart," *QSR* magazine, December 10, 2002, downloaded from http://www.qsrmagazine.com.

Trends in Production and Operations Management

8 learning goal

The slowing economy has had a dramatic effect on the U.S. manufacturing sector. Fifty years ago, more than a third of U.S. employees worked in factories, but today just over 10 percent of U.S. workers hold manufacturing jobs. Although manufacturing continues to account for 20 percent of U.S. domestic product, since 2000, more than 1.9 million factory jobs—nearly 10 percent of manufacturing employment—have been eliminated as manufacturers attempted to cut operating costs in light of the weakened economy. Many of these jobs have been moved overseas, where manufacturers have opened new production facilities or contracted out production to foreign firms with lower operating and labor costs.[19] The Institute of Supply Management noted at the end of 2002 that the manufacturing sector was continuing to contract. Shipments from manufacturers to customers were 1.7 percent below 2001 levels at the end of 2002, while new orders continued to drop. Manufacturing inventories also had risen. "The manufacturing sector is feeling the brunt of the economic downturn," said Norbert Ore of the Institute of Supply Management. "Overall, there is not really any sign of potential change." [20]

These economic challenges, along with continued growth in global competition, increasingly complex products, and more demanding consumers, continue to force manufacturers to plan carefully how, when, and where they produce the goods they sell. New production techniques and manufacturing technologies are vital to keep production costs as low as possible and productivity levels high. At the same time, many firms are reevaluating the productivity of their production facilities and, in some cases, are deciding to close underperforming factories.

Nonmanufacturing firms are not immune to the sluggish economy either. Like manufacturers, they must carefully manage how they use and deploy their resources, while keeping up with the constant pace of technological change. Nonmanufacturing firms must be ever vigilant in their search for new ways of streamlining service production and operation in order to keep their overall costs down.

Asset Management

In a tight economy, businesses must be careful about how their operating assets are used. From raw materials to inventories and manufacturing equipment, wasted, malfunctioning, or misused assets are costly. For example, one telephone company reported it had lost track of $5 billion worth of communications equipment. "I would say that every big company I have worked with has lost track of many major assets and a plethora of minor ones," said one executive. In fact, when chief financial officers of large companies were surveyed by *CFO Magazine,* 70 percent reported that asset management in their firms was "inefficient" or "erratic."[21]

Asset management software systems, many of which are Internet based, are beginning to help fix this problem. These programs automatically track materials, equipment, and inventory. They also automate inventory management and maintenance and repairs scheduling.

ChevronTexaco has successfully implemented this type of system in its enormous production facility in Bakersfield, California. The facility is one of the largest outdoor factories in the world, stretching 100 miles from north to south, and contains a maze of storage tanks, filtering installations, and pipelines. In all, there are 230,000 separate pieces of equipment and machinery in hundreds of categories in the facility. To manage all of these assets, ChevronTexaco has installed an automated asset management system that schedules preventive maintenance for all equipment and tracks where surplus equipment and supplies are stored. ChevronTexaco estimates it is saving millions of dollars a year in the facility from more effective asset management.[22]

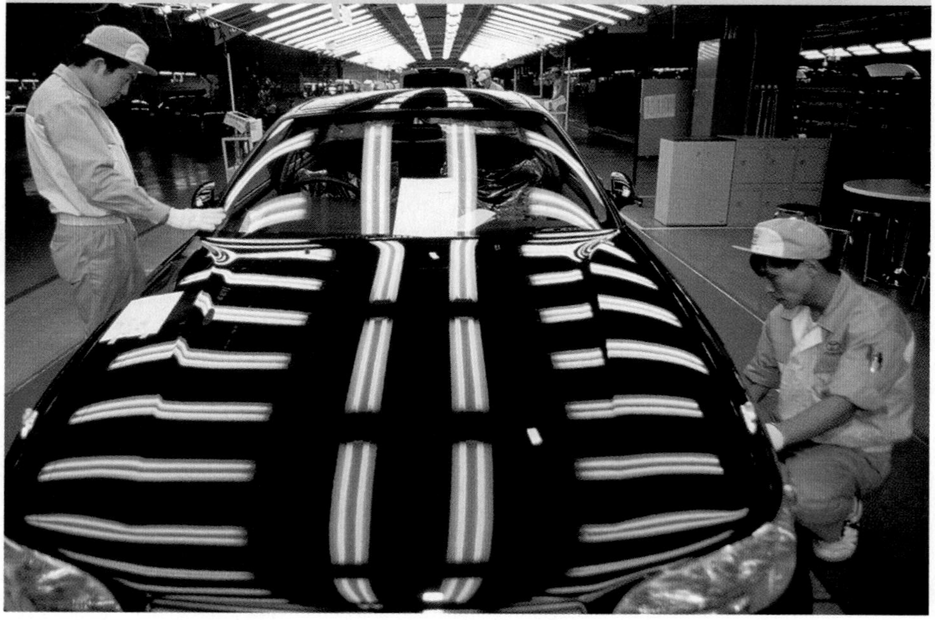

Toyota focuses design and engineering on "crossover vehicles"—car model designs that appeal to different consumer segments yet are built using many of the same components and parts. This has allowed Toyota's factories to become flexible and modular.

Modular Production

Increasingly, manufacturers are relying on *modular production* to speed and simplify production. Modular production involves breaking a complex product, service, or process into smaller pieces that can be created independently and then combined quickly to make a whole. Modular production not only cuts the cost of developing innovative products, but it also gives businesses a tool for meeting rapidly changing conditions. Modular production also makes it easier to implement mass customization or pure customization strategies.

Johnson Controls Inc. (JCI), a Michigan manufacturer, works closely with its suppliers to modularly build automotive interiors. JCI uses 11 major components from 35 different suppliers to build Jeep Liberty cockpits. The parts, designed to fit and function together, are then assembled in JCI's factory. "Our product development strategy is to build from the best capabilities and technologies in the world, but that doesn't mean they have to be owned and operated by us," says JCI vice president Jeff Edwards.[23]

Designing Products for Production Efficiency

Today's operations managers recognize that production efficiency must begin *before* the first part reaches the factory floor. As a result, many manufacturers are investing in new methods of integrating product design and engineering with the manufacturing supply chain.

DaimlerChrysler, for example, has instituted a computerized design system dubbed FastCar. FastCar links the computer-aided design process to internal business functions such as production, finance, procurement, and marketing. As cars are designed, all of these groups are immediately able to see how proposed designs will affect production costs, manufacturability, and other factors. The system also alerts suppliers to engineering and production specifications to guarantee receipt of quality parts for new components. FastCar has cut the time required to roll out new products from design to production by 70 percent.[24]

Another developing trend is the use of factory-simulation tools for product design. These tools allow product designers to see the effects their designs will have

concept check

Explain modular production.

Why does production efficiency have to begin before the first part reaches the factory floor?

on production equipment. For example, if a design calls for a specific size of drilled hole on a product, factory-simulation tools will specify which particular drill bit and machine will be necessary for the task.

Great Ideas to Use Now

As we've seen throughout this chapter, every organization produces something. Cereal manufacturers turn grains into breakfast foods. Law firms turn the skills and knowledge of attorneys into legal services. Retailers provide a convenient way for consumers to purchase a variety of goods. Colleges and universities convert students into educated individuals. Therefore, no matter what type of organization you end up working for in the future, you will be involved, to one degree or another, with your employer's production and operations processes.

In some jobs, such as plant manager and quality control manager, you will have a direct role in the production process. However, employees of manufacturing firms are not the only ones involved with production. Software developers, bank tellers, medical personnel, magazine writers, and a host of other jobs are also actively involved in turning inputs into outputs. If you manage people in these types of jobs, you'll need insight into the tools used to plan, schedule, and control production processes. Understanding production processes, resource management, and techniques for increasing productivity is vital to becoming a more valuable employee, who sees how his or her job fits into "the big picture" of the firm's operating goals.

If you plan to start your own business, you'll also face many production and operations decisions. You can use the information from this chapter to help you find suppliers, design an operating facility (no matter how small), and put customer-satisfying processes in place. This information can also help you make decisions about whether to manufacture goods yourself or rely on outside contractors to handle production.

Try It Now

Track a Project with a Gantt Chart Your teacher has just announced a huge assignment, due in three weeks. Where do you start? How can you best organize your time? A Gantt chart can help you plan and schedule more effectively. You'll be able to see exactly what you should be doing on a particular day.

- First, break the assignment down into smaller tasks: pick a topic, conduct research at the library or on the Internet, organize your notes, develop an outline, and write, type, and proofread the paper.
- Next, estimate how much time each task will take. Be realistic. If you've spent a week or more writing similar papers in the past, don't expect to finish this paper in a day.
- At the top of a piece of paper, list all of the days until the assignment is due. Along the side of the paper, list all of the tasks you've identified in the order they need to be done.
- Starting with the first task, block out the number of days you estimate each task will take. If you run out of days, you'll know you need to adjust how you've scheduled your time. If you know that you will not be able to work on some days, note them on the chart as well.
- Hang the chart where you can see it.

Customer Satisfaction and Quality

Although this chapter has talked a great deal about methods for producing products faster and less expensively, it is important to remember that the most efficient factory in the world would be deemed a failure if the products it made broke soon after customers purchased them. Underlying every production and operations management decision is a very simple question: how will this affect our customers' satisfaction? To compete in today's marketplace, businesses must make sure they have the right answer.

The Honeywell Control Products plant in Warren, Illinois, realized it didn't have the right answer. The plant makes electromechanical snap-action switches that are used in machines such as icemakers and washing machines. In the face of foreign competition in the early 1990s, the plant had developed a successful strategy to improve productivity and reduce manufacturing costs. By 1998, however, it was clear that customers weren't happy. Complaints and returns were constantly rising.

The problem? "We were driving the wrong behaviors," says Cynthia Knautz, manufacturing engineer at the plant. "All of our employee goals were set on output. Our production employees could build 36,000 bad switches in a day and still get rewarded." The plant set up new processes to help track and control quality and tied employee incentives to quality and customer satisfaction. As a result, customer reject rates have dropped dramatically while production rates have actually increased.

SOURCE: "Best Plant Winners: Honeywell Control Products," *Industry Week*, downloaded from http://www.industryweek.com.

Looking Ahead at Harley-Davidson

Like other U.S. manufacturers, Harley-Davidson has kept a close eye on recent economic developments. CEO Bleustein is optimistic about the future, however. "I think we've seen the worst of it. It's going to get better but how fast is difficult to tell," he says.

An ongoing concern for Harley-Davidson is accurately predicting how many motorcycles to produce. Although Harley-Davidson nearly doubled the production capacity of its three plants between 1995 and 2000, changing economic conditions mean production planning is more important than ever. Remembering the experience of not being able to meet customer demand in the 1990s, the company continues to plan for future growth. Bleustein expects Harley's factories to produce 289,000 motorcycles in 2003, a 10 percent increase over 2002. "Each time we make a step up in production capacity, we let things level out, and watch very carefully to see that customer demand is still out there," explains Bleustein. "We feel pretty comfortable with our capacity expansion programs."[25]

Summary of Learning Goals

1 Why is production and operations management important in both manufacturing and service firms?

In the 1980s, many U.S. manufacturers lost customers to foreign competitors because their production and operations management systems did not support the high-quality, reasonably priced products consumers demanded. Service organizations also rely on effective operations management in order to satisfy consumers. Operations managers, the personnel charged with managing and supervising the conversion of inputs into outputs, work closely with other functions in organizations to help ensure quality, customer satisfaction, and financial success.

2

What types of production processes are used by manufacturers and service firms?

Products are made using one of three types of production processes. In mass production, many identical goods are produced at once, keeping production costs low. Mass production, therefore, relies heavily on standardization, mechanization, and specialization. When mass customization is used, goods are produced using mass-production techniques up to a point, after which the product or service is custom tailored to individual customers by adding special features. When a firm's production process is built around customization, the firm makes many products one at a time according to the very specific needs or wants of individual customers.

3

How do organizations decide where to put their production facilities? What choices must be made in designing the facility?

Site selection affects operating costs, the price of the product or service, and the company's ability to compete. In choosing a production site, firms must weigh the availability of resources—raw materials, human resources, and even capital—needed for production, as well as the ability to serve customers and take advantage of marketing opportunities. Other factors include the availability of local incentives and the manufacturing environment. Once a site is selected, the firm must choose an appropriate design for the facility. The three main production facility designs are process, product, and fixed-position layouts. Cellular manufacturing is another type of facility layout.

4

Why are resource-planning tasks like inventory management and supplier relations critical to production?

Production converts input resources, such as raw materials and labor, into outputs, finished products and services. Firms must ensure that the resources needed for production will be available at strategic moments in the production process. If they are not, productivity, customer satisfaction, and quality may suffer. Carefully managing inventory can help cut production costs while maintaining enough supply for production and sales. Through good relationships with suppliers, firms can get better prices, reliable resources, and support services that can improve production efficiency.

5

How do operations managers schedule and control production?

Routing is the first step in scheduling and controlling production. Routing analyzes the steps needed in production and sets out a work flow, the sequence of machines and operations through which a product or service progresses from start to finish. Good routing increases productivity and can eliminate unnecessary cost. Scheduling involves specifying and controlling the time and resources required for each step in the production process. Operations managers use three methods to schedule production: Gantt charts, the critical path method, and program evaluation and review technique.

6

How can quality management and lean-manufacturing techniques help firms improve production and operations management?

Quality and productivity go hand in hand. Defective products waste materials and time, increasing costs. Poor quality also leads to dissatisfied customers. By implementing quality control methods, firms often reduce these problems and streamline production. Lean manufacturing also helps streamline production by eliminating unnecessary steps in the production process. When activities that don't add value for customers are eliminated, manufacturers can respond to changing market conditions with greater flexibility and ease.

7

What roles do technology and automation play in manufacturing and service industry operations management?

Many firms are improving their operational efficiency by using technology to automate parts of production. Computer-aided design and manufacturing systems, for example, help design new products, control the flow of resources needed for production, and even operate much of the production process. By using robotics, human time and effort can be minimized. Factories are being automated by blending computers, robots, and machinery into flexible manufacturing systems that require less labor to operate. Service firms are automating operations too, using technology to cut labor costs and control quality.

8

What key trends are affecting the way companies manage production and operations?

The manufacturing sector has been particularly hard hit by the economic slowdown. As a result, and faced with growing global competition, increased product complexity, and more demanding customers, manufacturers must carefully plan how, when, and where they produce the goods they sell. New production techniques and manufacturing technologies can help keep costs as low as possible. Managing assets like inventory, raw materials, and production equipment is increasingly important. Asset management software systems automatically track materials and inventory to help reduce waste, misuse, and malfunctions. Modular production allows manufacturers to produce products using high-quality parts without investments in expensive technology. Production efficiency must begin before the factory floor. Many firms are using tools that integrate product design and engineering with the manufacturing supply chain in order to understand the cost and quality implications of producing new products.

Preparing for Tomorrow's Workplace

1. Tom Lawrence and Sally Zickle are co-owners of L-Z Marketing, an advertising agency. Last week, they landed a major aerospace manufacturer as a client. The company wants the agency to create its annual report. Tom, who develops the art for the agency, needs about a week to develop the preliminary report design, another two weeks to set the type, and three weeks to get the report printed. Sally writes the material for the report and doesn't need as much time: two days to meet with the client to review the company's financial information and about three weeks to write the report copy. Of course, Tom can't set type until Sally has finished writing the report. Sally will also need three days to proofread the report before it goes to the printer. Develop either a Gantt chart or a critical path diagram for Tom and Sally to use in scheduling the project. Explain why you chose the method you did. How long will it take Tom and Sally to finish the project if there are no unforeseen delays?
2. Look for ways that technology and automation are used at your school, in the local supermarket, and at your doctor's office. As a class, discuss how automation affects the service you receive from each of these organizations. Does one organization use any types of automation that might be effectively used by one of the others? Explain.

KEY TERMS

assembly process 371
bill of material 377
CAD/CAM systems 387
cellular manufacturing 377
computer-aided design (CAD) 387
computer-aided manufacturing (CAM) 387
computer-integrated manufacturing (CIM) 388
continuous improvement 385
continuous process 371
critical path 383
critical path method (CPM) 383
customization 370
electronic data interchange (EDI) 381
e-procurement 380
enterprise resource planning (ERP) 380
fixed-position layout 377
flexible manufacturing system (FMS) 387
Gantt charts 382
intermittent process 371
inventory 378
inventory management 378
ISO 9000 386
ISO 14000 386
job shop 370
just-in-time (JIT) 386
lean manufacturing 386
make-or-buy decision 377
Malcolm Baldrige National Quality Award 385
manufacturing resource planning II (MRPII) 379
mass customization 370
mass production 370
materials requirement planning (MRP) 379
operations management 368
outsourcing 377
perpetual inventory 378
process layout 377

3. Pick a small business in your community. Make a list of the resources critical to the firm's production and operations. What would happen if the business suddenly couldn't acquire any of these resources? Divide the class into small groups and discuss strategies that small businesses can use to manage their supply chain.
4. Broadway Fashions is a manufacturer of women's dresses. The company's factory has 50 employees. Production begins when the fabric is cut according to specified patterns. After being cut, the pieces for each dress style are placed into bundles, which then move through the factory from worker to worker. Each worker opens each bundle and does one assembly task, such as sewing on collars, hemming dresses, or adding decorative items like appliqués. Then, the worker puts the bundle back together and passes it on to the next person in the production process. Finished dresses are pressed and packaged for shipment. Draw a diagram showing the production process layout in Broadway Fashion's factory. What type of factory layout and process is Broadway using? Discuss the pros and cons of this choice. Could Broadway improve the production efficiency by using a different production process or factory layout? How? Draw a diagram to explain how this might look.
5. As discussed in this chapter, many American firms have moved their manufacturing operations to overseas locations in the past decade. While there can be sound financial benefits to this choice, moving production overseas can also raise new challenges for operations managers. Identify several of these challenges and offer suggestions for how operations managers can use the concepts in this chapter to minimize or solve them.
6. Reliance Systems, headquartered in Oklahoma City, is a manufacturer of computer keyboards. The company plans to build a new factory and hopes to find a location with access to low-cost but skilled workers, national and international transportation, and favorable government incentives. As a team, use the Internet and your school library to research possible site locations, both domestic and international. Choose a location you feel would best meet the company's needs. Make a group presentation to the class explaining why you have chosen this location. Include information about the location's labor force, similar manufacturing facilities already located there, availability of resources and materials, possible local incentives, political and economic environment in the location, and any other factors you feel make this an attractive location. After all teams have presented their proposed locations, as a class rank all of the locations and decide the top two Reliance should investigate further.

WORKING THE NET

1. Find the supplier information Web sites of several firms (for example, Motorola, Northrop Grumman, Verizon, etc.) by using the Google search engine, **http://www.google.com**, to conduct a search for "supplier information." Visit two or three of these sites. Compare the requirements the companies set for their suppliers. How do the requirements differ? How are they similar?
2. Visit *Site Selection* magazine, **http://www.siteselection.com**. Under Area Spotlights, you will find articles and information about the manufacturing environment in various U.S. locations. Pick three to four areas to read about. Using this information, what locations would you recommend as a location for firms in the following industries: general services, telecommunications, automotive manufacturing, and electronics manufacturing. Explain.
3. Manufacturers face many federal, state, and local regulations. Visit the National Association of Manufacturers at **http://www.nam.org**. Pick two or three of the legislative or regulatory issues discussed under the "policy" sections and use a search engine like Yahoo (**http://www.yahoo.com**) to find more information.

KEY TERMS

process manufacturing 371
product (or assembly-line) layout 377
production 368
production planning 369
production process 370
program evaluation and review technique (PERT) 383
purchasing 377
quality 384
quality control 384
robotics 387
routing 381
scheduling 382
Six Sigma 385
supply chain 380
supply chain management 380
total quality management (TQM) 385
value-stream mapping 382

4. Using a search engine like Excite (**http://www.excite.com**) or Info Seek (**http://www.infoseek.com**), search for information about technologies like robotics, CAD/CAM systems, or ERP. Find at least three suppliers for one of these technologies. Visit their Web sites and discuss how their clients are using their products to automate production.
5. Research either the Malcolm Baldrige National Quality Award or the ISO 9000 Quality Standards program on the Internet. Write an executive summary that explains the basic requirements and costs of participating. What are the benefits of participating? Include a brief example of a company that has participated and their experiences. Include a list of relevant Web site links for further reading.

Creative Thinking Case

Shipshape Quality at Bombardier

Bombardier, a $14-billion-a-year Montreal manufacturer of jets, railcars, and snowmobiles, knew it was taking on a big risk when it bought the manufacturing operations of Outboard Marine Corp. (OMC) for $55 million in 2001. OMC, maker of Evinrude and Johnson outboard boat engines, was in a tailspin. Product quality had declined so severely that the company's share of the $2-billion-a-year outboard-engine market had plummeted from 55 percent in 1995 to just 23 percent in 2000.

OMC manufactured its components and parts at nine production facilities scattered around the United States, Mexico, and China. Engine transmission housings die-cast in Waukegan, Illinois, were shipped to Andrews, North Carolina, for machining and subassembly and then sent to the Calhoun, Georgia, plant for final assembly. It often took three weeks or more for component parts to move between plants, boosting production costs and delaying production.

Bombardier did not want to wait for OMC to turn around on its own. Bombardier sent a cross-functional team of specialists from its plant maintenance, operations, marketing, finance, and quality control departments to determine how to improve OMC's quality and operations. The first recommendation? Shut down two plants and reduce production in a third to consolidate operations and drastically shorten parts supply routes. OMC would now concentrate final assembly at its four-year-old Sturtevant, Wisconsin, plant. Bombardier would spend $50 million upgrading the plant with new technology and equipment. The team next hired a new workforce, carefully selecting workers who were team players with problem-solving skills.

The Bombardier team studied all of OMC's engineering drawings and recommended that OMC redesign many parts to improve quality control. Defective parts stored in inventory were identified and eliminated. Bombardier now requires that all assembly workers spend as much as 20 percent of their time inspecting engines for quality defects. Bombardier also set what it calls DQR—durability, quality, and reliability—standards for each unit produced.

Bombardier implemented these and other changes within 78 days after it acquired OMC. The results have been dramatic. Quality has improved enough that Bombardier offers a three-year warranty on its engines, the longest in the industry. Market share is almost back to previous levels. Bombardier plans to expand the Sturtevant plant to boost production to 60,000 engines a year, including many new models—nine times the current rate.

CRITICAL THINKING QUESTIONS

1. Could Bombardier have achieved the same results without closing any plants? How?
2. What technologies would you recommend Bombardier invest in at its Sturtevant plant? Describe what each technology could do to help meet Bombardier's goals.

3. What new challenges do you think Bombardier will face as it boosts production to nine times the current rate? How should Bombardier prepare for those challenges?

SOURCES: Gene Bylinsky, "Elite Factories: They're Setting Lofty Standards in Quality Control, Preventive Maintenance, and Automation," *Fortune*, September 2, 2002, p. 172B; "Bombardier First-Built Outboard Engines Delivered to Worldwide Market," Bombardier company press release, October 17, 2001.

VIDEO CASE

Big Blue Turns Small Businesses into Large Competitors

"It is like music, once it is in place and working," says Susan Jain, a marketing executive with IBM Global Services. She is talking about Enterprise Resource Planning or ERP, complex software modules that do just about everything to help companies run more efficiently and competitively.

"The old systems couldn't relate one piece of information to another," she says. Separate databases meant information systems weren't integrated, so day-to-day operations were cumbersome and management reporting often inaccurate. With ERP information is accessible immediately, greatly improving overall operating efficiency and speeding up and shortening internal reporting procedures, and even reducing the time it takes to bring new products to market.

ERP is a "relational database" that ties all aspects of information gathering and dissemination together in a tidy package. For example, ERP software modules can receive an order, check raw-material stocks to make sure the order can be produced, order any additional materials that may be needed, place the order in the production schedule, and send it to shipping and invoicing. Its human resources module will even help hire and train the staff needed to produce and fulfill the order.

Companies no longer need to predict way in advance what products customers might want, or keep tons of product on warehouse shelves gathering dust. ERP literally allows companies to "build to order"—in fact IBM has an automobile customer that does just that. It builds to order, one car at a time, eliminating the customary guessing games of what colors or styles may be popular at a given time.

Even small companies are investing in ERP systems to enable them to grow and compete, despite the substantial investment in time and dollars that is required. Jain is candid about the costs involved. The software costs around $1 million dollars, with an equal expenditure required for new hardware. Implementation, training, and education can cost two to three times that amount, and take years in the case of very large companies.

IBM Global Financing supports all elements of an ERP acquisition with a broad array of financing offerings with flexible payment options. But after all that expense, return on investment is difficult to measure. With so many variables driving business success, good results could be due to other factors, like changes in working styles, or a general upswing in the current business environment. IBM's promotional material asks "Are You Ready for IBM?" It's a big decision for small companies to make.

CRITICAL THINKING QUESTIONS

1. As the production manager for a large manufacturing company you recommend the acquisition of ERP software to your bosses. Be specific in describing how such a system would help your company be more competitive.
2. What kind of information would you want such a system to integrate for your company?
3. Explain how you would propose to track performance to justify the cost of installing such a system.

SOURCE: Adapted from material in the video: "Are You Ready for IBM?" Information Management Systems at IBM. Downloaded from http://www.ibm.com, April 8, 2003.

E-Commerce Case

GM Goes Digital

Six years ago, General Motors was an e-commerce dinosaur. The giant automaker was bogged down with 7,000 different information technology (IT) systems spread across the company. Communications with suppliers, dealers, and customers—as well as between the company's own divisions—often stumbled, resulting in long product development delays and an inefficient supply chain.

To solve these problems, GM had to go digital. It started by consolidating the company's telecommunications infrastructure to increase Internet bandwidth. This allowed GM to support connectivity between the company and its business partners. The next step was to reduce the number of company IT systems by nearly half, so that communications could flow freely from computer to computer via the Internet.

GM chose a single CAD program that allows 3-D design documents to be shared online by the company's 18,000 designers and engineers at its 14 different global design labs. GM also hooked more than 1,000 of its key suppliers' engineers into the same system. Now, all parties involved in the design and development process are able to view and discuss design plans online in real time. The time required to bring a new vehicle to market has been cut to just 18 months. GM purchases many of its raw materials and parts through the Internet as well, through an online joint procurement effort formed with other automakers, further streamlining production and operations.

GM also launched a consumer online shopping and buying site in 40 countries, **http://www.GMBuyPower.com**. U.S. consumers can visit the site, choose which options they want their car to have, find a dealer that has it in inventory, and shop for the best price.

Brazilian consumers can actually complete their entire sales transaction online through **http://www.GMBuyPower.com**. GM worked with its Brazilian dealers to develop a special Chevrolet model, the Celta, specifically for Internet sales. Since GM began selling the Celta online in Brazil, more than 80,000 of the cars have been sold entirely over the Internet. GM hopes to expand online sales to other countries within the next few years.

CRITICAL THINKING QUESTIONS

1. What are the benefits and disadvantages for suppliers who are connected to GM's Internet-based CAD system? How do you think GM decides which suppliers should be included?
2. If you were GM's information technology manager, what other uses of the Internet would you recommend the company pursue? Why?
3. What challenges might GM face in attempting to expand online sales globally? How can the Internet be used to overcome these challenges in various countries? Do you think GM will ever offer complete online sales transactions for car purchases in the United States? Why or why not?

SOURCES: John Teresko, "Techology Leader of the Year—Transforming GM," *Industry Week,* December 1, 2001; Missy Sullivan, Constance Gustke, and Nikhil Hutheesing, "Case Studies: Digital Do-Overs," *Forbes,* October 7, 2002, downloaded from http://www.forbes.com; "Brazil: Internet Car Sales Grow," *South American Business Information,* March 9, 2001.

Hot Links Address Book

See how American Leather brings it all together to create beautiful customized couches at
http://www.americanleather.com

Learn more about the products Globe Motors manufactures, both in the U. S. and abroad, at
http://www.globe-motors.com

What characteristics contribute to a city's manufacturing climate? Find out by reading more at *Industry Week's* Web site:
http://www.industryweek.com

How do companies decide whether to make or buy? Find out more at the Outsourcing Institute, a professional association where buyers and sellers network and connect:
http://www.outsourcing.com

Take a cyber-tour of New United Motor Manufacturing's manufacturing process at
http://www.Nummi.com

Learn how to build your own Gantt Chart at
http://www.mindtools.com/pages/article/newPPM_03.htm

What does it take to win the Malcolm Baldrige Quality Award? Get the details at
http://www.quality.nist.gov

Want to know more about how robots work? Find out at
http://electronics.howstuffworks.com/robot.htm

your career

in Management

Many students in business schools choose management as their major. Management principles and practices apply in any kind of organization, regardless of the product, service, or process. A person who wants to become a manager needs a strong background in psychology, sociology, group dynamics, social psychology, and human relations.

Managers must respect the individuality, dignity, and needs of the people who report to them. They must also be able to motivate others to perform needed tasks. In turn, good managers are always motivated to do the best possible job. They also are confident—and their confidence is based on continual self-evaluation of their abilities and past successes.

Now is a good time for college graduates to seek careers in management. However, a college degree does not lead immediately to a management position. The career path for a manager typically begins with a position as a management trainee. Trainees learn about company policy, the nature of the industry, operating procedures, and organization structures. They may also spend some time on the production line, work in a warehouse, or perform some other blue-collar job. The training program may last from several weeks to several years. After completing the program, new managers may specialize in sales, production, accounting, personnel, industrial relations, credit, finance, or research and development. Middle-level and upper-level managers are chosen from the ranks of sales managers, production managers, controllers, and so on.

If you enjoy working with people, consider human resource management. This field requires the ability to get along with different types of people and to communicate efffectively. You do not have to be outgoing to have strong interpersonal skills. In fact, a quiet, friendly manner can be an asset. Take speech, writing, and other communication courses in college to strengthen your interpersonal skills.

A career in human resource management offers many challenges and opportunities. For instance, if you choose this field, you will have a chance to help ensure that all employees are treated fairly. All decisions must be made fairly, whether they involve who to hire, promote, and train; how much to pay; or how to help dissatisfied employees. When employees sense that the employer is unfair, their work attitudes and behaviors suffer. Absenteeism, low motivation, lack of concern for the quality of products, lack of commitment, and even sabotage may result. These attitudes and behaviors affect costs, productivity, and profits. As a communicator and an advocate, the human resource professional helps the organization succeed.

Dream Career: Hotel And Motel Management

Hotel and motel management is a sophisticated field. Managers must understand computers, finance, and labor relations. They also need to know the seven other areas that make up the backbone of the operation: rooms, food and beverage, personnel, sales and marketing, hotel accounting, conventions, and catering. The emphasis in hotel and motel management has evolved from technical skills to management skills. Recently, the industry has become much more competitive because more companies are pursuing a limited number of travelers.

The preferred way to advance is through the management-training program of a major hotel chain. Prospective managers receive 6 to 15 months of intensive training, rotating through all the major departments. The fastest way to become a general manager is to specialize in room sales or food and beverage, which are the most operations-oriented areas.

- *Places of employment.* Throughout the country and abroad, with most jobs in medium-size to large cities. About 68,000 workers hold jobs in this field in the United States.
- *Skills required.* A two-year degree for some jobs, but the quickest route to management is a four-year degree. A

second language is mandatory for employment overseas, and it helps in some U.S. metropolitan areas.

- *Employment outlook through 2010.* Fair.
- *Salaries.* $22,000–$38,000 for trainees; $40,000–$55,000 for assistant managers; $70,000–100,000+ for general managers in major cities.

Where the Opportunities Are

City Manager

With the increase in urban problems—decaying inner cities, for example—cities have a great need for people with managerial skills. City managers are usually appointed by a governing body, such as a city council, and are responsible to that body. The major duties of city managers are managing tax collection and disbursement, law enforcement, and public-works projects; hiring department heads and supporting staffs; and preparing annual budgets (to be approved by city officials). Other duties may include collecting rents, designing traffic controls, and planning for expansion.

- *Places of employment.* Generally, cities with populations over 50,000, although some smaller communities now hire city managers.
- *Skills required.* Master's degree in public administration, although some cities accept people with a four-year degree and several years' experience as an assistant city manager.
- *Employment outlook through 2010.* Good. More and more cities are seeking professional managers rather than politicians to handle complex city affairs.
- *Salaries.* $30,000–$60,000 for assistant city managers; $55,000–$100,000+ for city managers, with the higher figure for medium-size to large cities.

Quality Control Manager

If significant numbers of a product break down during the warranty period, the cost of repairs eats into corporate profits. Thus many firms hire quality control employees for all phases of the design and manufacturing process. Others spend their money on inspection procedures. A quality control manager supervises quality control inspectors. The inspectors decide whether products and materials meet quality standards. To do so, they either examine every item produced or check a sample of the items.

- *Places of employment.* Everywhere, but the best opportunities are in areas where manufacturing industries are concentrated, such as Austin, Boston, Detroit, New Jersey, and California.
- *Skills required.* Two-year degree for inspectors; two-year or four-year degree plus experience for managers; four-year degree or master's degree for quality control engineers.
- *Employment outlook through 2010.* Above average.
- *Salaries.* $28,000–$44,000 for inspectors; $40,000–$60,000 for managers; $70,000+ for managers with an engineering degree and an MBA.

Purchasing Manager

If materials, supplies, and equipment are not on hand when they're needed, the entire work flow of an organization could stop. Keeping a big enough supply on hand is the purchasing manager's responsibility. It includes more than just buying goods and services, however. Market forecasting, production planning, and inventory control are all part of the job. Purchasing managers supervise purchasing agents or industrial buyers, who do the actual buying. More than half of all purchasing managers work for moderate-size to large manufacturers. The rest work in government agencies, construction companies, hospitals, and schools.

- *Places of employment.* Throughout the country, especially in large industrial and government centers, such as Washington, DC, Atlanta, Chicago, Pittsburgh, and Los Angeles. There are about 536,000 purchasing manager jobs in the United States
- *Skills required.* Generally, a two-year or four-year degree, but many employers now require an MBA.
- *Employment outlook through 2010.* Fair in general; good with MBA.
- *Salaries.* $32,000–$42,000 for junior purchasing agents (but less for entry-level purchasing agents in the federal government); $45,000–$80,000 for purchasing managers.

Industrial Production Manager

Production managers are usually responsible for all production in a factory. In large plants with several operations—aircraft assembly, for instance—a manager is in charge of each operation, such as machining, assembly, or finishing. Production managers are typically responsible for production scheduling, staffing, equipment, quality control, inventory control, and coordination with other departments. Production managers, in essence, plan the production schedule. They determine which machines will be used, whether overtime or extra shifts are necessary, the sequence of production, and related matters.

- *Places of employment.* Throughout the United States. There are about 255,000 people working in this field today.

- *Skills required.* Two-year or four-year degree, depending on employer. More are requiring a four-year degree, and some are requiring an MBA.
- *Employment outlook through 2010.* Good with undergraduate engineering degree and MBA.
- *Salaries.* $27,000–$45,000 for assistant production managers; $47,000–$81,000 for production managers. Some employers give performance bonuses.

Manager of Corporate Training

The training and development of employees is of great importance. U.S. companies spend over $270 billion a year on formal and informal training. That's only slightly less than is spent nationally each year on elementary, secondary, and higher education. Technical training in robotics and automation and basic education for those who have not finished high school are two areas of growth in the field of training.

A manager of corporate training supervises specialists who design training programs, conduct those programs, and assess them. The training manager may also oversee a reimbursement program for employees who take outside courses, arrange for special noncredit courses for employees on college campuses, and represent the firm in designing apprenticeship programs with labor unions.

- *Places of employment.* Any relatively large firm (1,000 or more employees).
- *Skills required.* Four-year or master's degree with a major in human resource management, adult education, psychology, or occupational education.
- *Employment outlook through 2010.* Very good
- *Salaries.* $28,000–$35,000 to start for corporate training specialists; $65,000–$95,000 for managers; higher salaries for those with more experience or an advanced college degree.

Plant Health and Safety Officer

The Occupational Safety and Health Act of 1970 requires that manufacturing facilities and offices be safe and healthy places to work. Virtually all firms that employee 500 or more workers have a safety officer, who conducts safety inspections, keeps accident and injury records, provides safety training, and may help design safety features into equipment.

- *Places of employment.* Any business or other type of establishment that employs several hundred or more people. Even large office buildings often have a health and safety officer.
- *Skills required.* Four-year degree with a major in industrial engineering, safety engineering, industrial hygiene, occupational nursing, industrial administration, or some area of business administration.
- *Employment outlook through 2010.* Good, especially in manufacturing firms and health care organizations.
- *Salaries.* $40,000–$75,000. The higher salaries are associated with positions requiring an engineering background.

Human Resource Development Specialist

The past decade has seen much corporate restructuring through mergers, acquisitions, and retrenchments. Some firms have created internal consulting jobs for people who can smooth corporate change and development. The duties of a development specialist include counseling employees about their performance, conducting stress management programs, mediating disputes between departments, helping employees find new jobs, and counseling employees with personal or career problems.

- *Places of employment.* Large organizations, which are most likely to be located in metropolitan areas.
- *Skills required.* Master's (even doctoral) degree in psychology, business administration, human resource management, industrial or organizational psychology, or related behavioral or social sciences.
- *Employment outlook through 2010.* Good. Only very large firms are likely to hire human resource development specialists.
- *Salaries.* $45,000–$110,000. The lower salaries are for people with a master's degree; the higher salaries are for those with experience or a doctoral degree.

College Recruiter

Many firms, especially large ones, recruit graduates from colleges and universities. A corporate college recruiter is involved in employment planning and assessing human resource needs for professional, technical, and managerial employees; selecting colleges to visit; interviewing graduating students at those colleges; performing preliminary screening of these applicants; and recommending applicants to line managers for in-depth interviews. The job can involve a lot of travel, especially in the late fall and early spring. The recruiter may also be responsible for developing recruiting brochures for distribution to applicants through college placement offices across the country.

- *Places of employment.* Any firm, government agency, or other type of organization that hires large numbers of college graduates.
- *Skills required.* Four-year college degree with almost any major. Very good oral and written communication skills are essential.

- *Employment outlook through 2010.* Good, although fewer positions are available in manufacturing firms. This job is usually reserved for those who know about the organization.
- *Salaries.* $32,000–$70,000. Larger firms in metropolitan areas pay higher salaries.

Management Careers: A Final Note

This discussion has not begun to exhaust the list of managerial positions. There are managers for every possible business function: traffic managers, public-relations managers, office managers, department managers, and administrators at all levels.

Many opportunities for advancement from line operations, sales positions, or general administrative work are available for those who wish to move up and take more responsibility. Higher-level managers need many more administrative skills than lower-level managers do, but most companies train people for those positions. Many companies also encourage potential managers to continue their education. Some even pay tuition. The future looks promising for those willing to make the effort to move into management.

Chapter 13

© AP / WIDE WORLD PHOTOS

Understanding the Customer and Creating Marketing Strategy

learning goals

1 What are the marketing concept and relationship building?
2 How do managers create a marketing strategy?
3 What is the marketing mix?
4 How do consumers and organizations make buying decisions?
5 What are the five basic forms of market segmentation?
6 How is marketing research used in marketing decision making?
7 What are the trends in understanding the consumer?

Avon Goes for the Younger Set

Avon Products Inc. (**http://www.avon.com**) is ringing the doorbells of a new customer generation: teenagers and young women. And teens are doing some of the ringing. The big direct seller of beauty products, eager to reach 16- to 24-year-old shoppers who mostly associate the Avon name with their mothers, launched a cosmetics line called Mark. The hip packaging is distinctly more upscale than other teen-focused brands, including Procter & Gamble Co.'s Cover Girl or mass-market brands such as Bonne Bell. It is also trendier than Avon's traditional look, which is aimed squarely at 25- to 55-year-old American women.

Avon is recruiting teens as sales representatives, even as it pushes ahead on efforts to boost its main U.S. sales ranks by 36 percent to 750,000 by 2007. While the company expects some door-to-door selling by its new recruits, it envisions youth sales mostly taking place among groups of friends at slumber parties and other informal gatherings. Avon hopes the opportunity to sell cosmetics to peers will prove more alluring than toiling behind the counter in fast-food restaurants.

About 17 million young women in the United States are in the 16- to 24-year-old age group, with an aggregate purchasing power of $96 billion—one-quarter of which is spent on beauty and beauty-related products, Avon says. "It's not just lip gloss," says Deborah I. Fine, the former publisher of *Glamour* magazine tapped by Avon to lead the youth charge. "It's lip gloss with an earnings opportunity."

Avon executives say research shows that young women have a "neutral to positive" image of the company. But when Mark made its debut, its own name was in lights. The name Avon appears but only in tiny letters.[1]

Critical Thinking Questions

1. Why do companies identify target customers for their products?
2. Why is it important to differentiate a product?
3. How does a company like Avon find out what customers and potential customers want in the way of cosmetics?

Principles of Marketing

marketing
The process of discovering the needs and wants of potential buyers and customers and then providing goods and services that meet or exceed their expectations.

exchange
The process in which two parties give something of value to each other to satisfy their respective needs.

Marketing played an important role in Avon's successful launch of Mark. Marketing is the process of getting the right goods or services to the right people at the right place, time, and price, using the right promotion techniques. This concept is referred to as the *"right" principle.* We can say that **marketing** is finding out the needs and wants of potential buyers and customers and then providing goods and services that meet or exceed their expectations. Marketing is about creating exchanges. An **exchange** takes place when two parties give something of value to each other to satisfy their respective needs. In a typical exchange, a consumer trades money for a good or service.

To encourage exchanges, marketers follow the "right" principle. If your local Avon rep doesn't have the right lipstick for you when you want it, at the right price, you will not exchange money for a new lipstick from Avon. Think about the last exchange (purchase) you made: What if the price had been 30 percent higher? What if the store or other source had been less accessible? Would you have bought anything? The "right" principle tells us that marketers control many factors that determine marketing success. In this chapter, you will learn about the marketing concept and how organizations create a marketing strategy. You will learn how the marketing mix is used to create sales opportunities. Next, we examine how and why consumers and organizations make purchase decisions. Then, we discuss the important concept of market segmentation, which helps marketing managers focus on the most likely purchasers of their wares. We conclude the chapter by examining how marketing research and decision support systems help guide marketing decision making.

The Marketing Concept

1 learning goal

marketing concept
Identifying consumer needs and then producing the goods or services that will satisfy them while making a profit for the organization.

If you study today's best organizations, you'll see that they have adopted the **marketing concept,** which involves identifying consumer needs and then producing the goods or services that will satisfy them while making a profit. The marketing concept is oriented toward pleasing consumers by offering value. Specifically, the marketing concept involves the following:

- Focusing on customer wants so the organization can distinguish its product(s) from competitors' offerings.
- Integrating all of the organization's activities, including production, to satisfy these wants.
- Achieving long-term goals for the organization by satisfying customer wants and needs legally and responsibly.

Today, companies of every size in all industries are applying the marketing concept. McDonald's, for example, found that burger eaters like to determine what's on their burger rather than buying a hamburger that is already dressed in a heated bin. Now, its restaurants can deliver fresh sandwiches made to order.

production orientation
An approach in which a firm works to lower production costs without a strong desire to satisfy the needs of customers.

Firms have not always followed the marketing concept. Around the time of the Industrial Revolution in America (1860–1910), firms had a **production orientation,** which meant that they worked to lower production costs without a strong desire to satisfy the needs of their customers. To do this, organizations concentrated on mass production, focusing internally on maximizing the efficiency of operations, increasing output, and ensuring uniform quality. They also asked such questions as: What can we do best? What can our engineers design? What is economical and easy to produce with our equipment? There is nothing wrong with assessing a firm's capabilities. In fact, such assessments are necessary in planning. But the production orientation does not consider whether what the firm produces most efficiently also meets the needs of the marketplace. By implementing the marketing concept, an organization looks externally to the consumers in the marketplace and commits to customer value, customer satisfaction, and relationship marketing as explained in this section.

Customer Value

customer value
The ratio of benefits to the sacrifice necessary to obtain those benefits, as determined by the customer; reflects the willingness of customers to actually buy a product.

Customer value is the ratio of benefits to the sacrifice necessary to obtain those benefits. The customer determines the value of both the benefits and the sacrifices. Creating customer value is a core business strategy of many successful firms. Customer value is rooted in the belief that price is not the only thing that matters. A business that focuses on the cost of production and price to the customer will be managed as though it were providing a commodity differentiated only by price. In contrast, businesses that provide customer value believe that many customers will pay a premium for superior customer service. Sir Colin Marshall, chairman of the board of British Airways (BA), is explicit about his commitment to superior customer service, insisting that BA can succeed only by meeting all of its customers' value-driven needs, not just price.

The automobile industry also illustrates the importance of creating customer value. To penetrate the fiercely competitive luxury automobile market, Lexus adopted a customer-driven approach, with particular emphasis on service. Lexus stresses product quality with a standard of zero defects in manufacturing. The service quality goal is to treat each customer as one would treat a guest in one's home, to pursue the perfect person-to-person relationship, and to strive to improve continually. This strategy has enabled Lexus to establish a clear quality image and capture a significant share of the luxury car market.

Customer Satisfaction

customer satisfaction
The customer's feeling that a product has met or exceeded expectations.

Customer satisfaction is a theme that we have stressed throughout the text. **Customer satisfaction** is the customer's feeling that a product has met or exceeded expectations. Lexus consistently wins awards for its outstanding customer satisfaction. JD Powers and Associates surveys car owners two years after they make their purchase. The Customer Satisfaction Survey is made up of four measures that each describe an element of overall ownership satisfaction at two years: vehicle quality/reliability, vehicle appeal, ownership costs, and service satisfaction from a dealer. Lexus continues to lead the industry. Lexus manager Stuart McCullough comments, "In close collaboration with our dealers we aim to provide the best customer service, not only in the car industry, but in any industry. The JD Powers surveys are a testament to our success in making our customers happy."[2]

At Double Tree Hotels, guests are asked to fill out a CARE card several times during their stay to let staff know how they are doing. Managers check the cards daily to solve guests' problems before they check out. Guests can also use a CARE phone line to call in their complaints at the hotel. A CARE committee continually seeks ways to improve guest services. The goal is to offer a solution to a CARE call in 15 minutes. Embassy Suites goes one step further by offering a full refund to guests who are not satisfied with their stay.

Who delivers the most customer satisfaction in America? Exhibit 13.1 reveals a number of well-known companies in select categories.

Building Relationships

relationship marketing
A strategy that focuses on forging long-term partnerships with customers by offering value and providing customer satisfaction.

Relationship marketing is a strategy that focuses on forging long-term partnerships with customers. Companies build relationships with customers by offering

Exhibit 13.1 Companies That Deliver the Highest Levels of Satisfaction in Selected Product/Service Categories

Industry/Manufacturer	Score*	Industry/Manufacturer	Score*
Personal Computers	**71**	***News and Information***	**73**
Dell Computer	76	ABCNews.com	74
Apple Computer	73	MSNBC.com	73
Gateway	72	CNN.com	72
Hewlett-Packard	71	NYTimes.com	71
Compaq Computer	68	USAToday.com	71
Household Appliances	**82**	***Food Processing***	**81**
Kenmore	83	H.J. Heinz	88
Maytag	83	Hershey Foods	87
Whirlpool	83	Quaker Oats	87
General Electric	82	Sara Lee	84
Automobiles	**80**	ConAgra Foods	83
BMW	86	General Mills	83
GM (Buick)	86	Mars	83
GM (Cadillac)	86	Nestle	83
Ford (Lincoln-Mercury)	84	Dole Food	82
DaimlerChrysler (Benz)	83	Kellogg	81
Toyota	83	Kraft Foods	81
Ford (Volvo)	82	Campbell Soup	80
Apparel	**80**	Tyson Foods	80
VF Corp.	82	***Beverages-Beer***	**81**
Liz Claiborne	80	Anheuser-Busch	82
Jones Apparel Group	87	Adolph Coors	79
Levi Strauss	78	Miller Brewing	79
Personal Care Products	**81**	***Beverages-Soft drinks***	**85**
Clorox	85	Cadbury Schweppes	86
Dial	84	PepsiCo	86
Unilever	83	Coca-Cola	85
Procter & Gamble	81		
Colgate-Palmolive	80		

*maximum score is 100—Highest satisfaction

Bold face = industry average

SOURCE: National Quality Research Center at University of Michigan, 2002.

value and providing customer satisfaction. Companies benefit from repeat sales and referrals that lead to increases in sales, market share, and profits. Costs fall because it is less expensive to serve existing customers than to attract new ones. Keeping a customer costs about one-fourth of what it costs to attract a new customer, and the probability of retaining a customer is over 60 percent, whereas the probability of landing a new customer is less than 30 percent.[3]

Customers also benefit from stable relationships with suppliers. Business buyers have found that partnerships with their suppliers are essential to producing high-quality products while cutting costs. Customers remain loyal to firms that provide them greater value and satisfaction than they expect from competing firms.

Frequent-buyer clubs are an excellent way to build long-term relationships. All major airlines have frequent-flyer programs. After you fly a certain number of miles you become eligible for a free ticket. Now, cruise lines, hotels, car rental agencies, credit-card companies, and even mortgage companies give away "airline miles" with purchases. Consumers patronize the airline and its partners because they want the free tickets. Thus, the program helps to create a long-term relationship with the customer.

If an organization is to build relationships with customers, its employees' attitudes and actions must be customer oriented. Any person, department, or division that is not customer oriented weakens the positive image of the entire organization. An employee may be the only contact a potential customer has with the firm. In that person's eyes, the employee is the firm. If greeted discourteously, the potential customer may well assume that the employee's attitude represents the whole firm.

Building long-term relationships with customers is an excellent way for small businesses to compete against the big chains. Sometimes small firms, with few employees, are in a better position to focus on a tiny segment of the market, as explained in the "Focusing on Small Business" box.

concept check

Explain the marketing concept.

Explain the difference between customer value and customer satisfaction.

What is meant by relationship marketing?

Creating a Marketing Strategy

2 learning goal

There is no secret formula for creating goods and services that provide customer value and customer satisfaction. An organization that is committed to providing superior customer satisfaction puts customers at the very center of its marketing strategy. Creating a customer-focused *marketing strategy* involves four main steps: understanding the external environment, defining the target market, creating a competitive advantage, and developing a marketing mix. This section will examine the first three steps, and the next section will discuss how a company develops a marketing mix.

Understanding the External Environment

Unless marketing managers understand the external environment, a firm cannot intelligently plan for the future. Thus, many organizations assemble a team of

Focusing on Small Business

Building Long-Term Relationships

With Wal-Marts and Home Depots overrunning the landscape, it looked as though Josh and Michael Bracken's small nursery in Dallas, Texas, would quickly wilt. So how is it that profit at the Brackens' Nicholson-Hardie Nursery & Garden Center rose 11 percent last year and the brothers are talking of expansion? Well, they make house calls, for one thing.

In industry after industry, chain competitors have driven independents into the ground. The same thing almost happened in the nursery business, where big retailers now control two-thirds of the $71 billion lawn-and-garden market. But today, many of the nation's 10,000 independent nurseries are stubbornly holding their own by stocking plants suited for local conditions, pampering customers, and luring them with inventive promotions.

Because the Brackens can't buy in bulk as the chains do, they don't even attempt to match the chains' prices. Instead, they offer superior customer service by stocking more than 1,000 plant varieties, far more than the chains carry.

To distinguish themselves, the brothers aim for the sort of customer who "would buy a Land Rover versus a Chevrolet," says Josh. Thus, the stores stock top-of-the-line tools one might find in Martha Stewart's garden, including $35 British sheep shears for trimming grass and $45 Swiss pruners.[4]

CRITICAL THINKING QUESTIONS

1. What else could the Brackens do to build long-term relationships with customers?
2. Would a frequent purchaser program work?
3. What about giving away airline miles with purchases?

specialists to continually collect and evaluate environmental information, a process called **environmental scanning.** The goal in gathering the environmental data is to identify future market opportunities and threats.

environmental scanning
The process in which a firm continually collects and evaluates information about its external environment.

For example, as technology continues to blur the lines between personal computers, television, and compact disc players, a company like Sony may find itself competing against a company like Hewlett-Packard. Research shows that children would like more games bundled with computer software, while adults desire various types of word-processing and business-related software. Is this information an opportunity or a threat to Hewlett-Packard marketing managers?

In general, six categories of environmental data shape marketing decisions:

- *Social forces* such as the values of potential customers and the changing roles of families and women working outside the home.
- *Demographic forces* such as the ages, birth and death rates, and locations of various groups of people.
- *Economic forces* such as changing incomes, inflation, and recession.
- *Technological forces* such as advances in communications and data retrieval capabilities.
- *Political and legal forces* such as changes in laws and regulatory agency activities.
- *Competitive forces* from domestic and foreign-based firms.

Defining the Target Market

target market
The specific group of consumers toward which a firm directs its marketing efforts.

Managers and employees focus on providing value for a well-defined target market. The **target market** is the specific group of consumers toward which a firm directs its marketing efforts. It is selected from the larger overall market. For instance, Carnival Cruise Lines says its main target market is "blue-collar entrepreneurs," people with an income of $25,000 to $50,000 a year who own auto supply shops, dry cleaners, and the like. Unlike other cruise lines, it does not seek affluent retirees. Quaker Oats targets its grits to blue-collar consumers in the South. Kodak targets Ektar color print film, designed for use only in rather sophisticated cameras, to advanced

MexGrocer.com *is a nationwide bilingual online grocery store for hard-to-find, nonperishable Mexican food, household products, recipes and cookbooks ideal for its target market: amateur chefs looking for authentic Mexican recipes, as well as Mexican cookbooks.*

amateur photographers. The Limited, Inc. has several different types of stores, each for a distinct target market: Express for trendy younger women, Lerner for budget-conscious women, Lane Bryant and Roaman's for full-size women, and Henri Bendel's for upscale, high-fashion women. These target markets are all part of the overall market for women's clothes.

Identifying a target market helps a company focus its marketing efforts on those who are most likely to buy its products or services. Concentrating on potential customers lets the firm use its resources efficiently. The target markets for Marriott International's lodging alternatives are shown in Exhibit 13.2. The latest in the Marriott family is SpringHill Suites. The SpringHill idea came from another Marriott chain, Fairfield Suites, an offshoot of Marriott's Fairfield Inns. The suites, opened in 1997, were roomy but devoid of most frills: The closets didn't have doors, and the lobby floors were covered with linoleum. Some franchisees complained to Marriott that the suites were *under*priced: Fairfield Suites guests were saying they would pay a little more for a few more frills. So Marriott began planning an upgrade. To create each of the first 20 or so SpringHill locations, Marriott spent $200,000 renovating an existing Fairfield Suites unit, adding ergonomic chairs, ironing boards, and other amenities. Lobbies at SpringHill hotels are fancier than the rooms themselves: The lobbies have fireplaces, breakfast rooms, crown moldings at the ceiling, and granite or ceramic tile floors.

competitive advantage
A set of unique features of a company and its products that are perceived by the target market as significant and superior to those of the competition; also called *differential advantage.*

cost competitive advantage
A firm's ability to produce a product or service at a lower cost than all other competitors in an industry while maintaining satisfactory profit margins.

Creating a Competitive Advantage

A competitive advantage, also called a differential advantage, is a set of unique features of a company and its products that are perceived by the target market as significant and superior to those of the competition. As Andrew Grove, CEO of Intel, says, "You have to understand what it is you are better at than anybody else and mercilessly focus your efforts on it." **Competitive advantage** is the factor or factors that cause customers to patronize a firm and not the competition. There are three types of competitive advantage: cost, product/service differential, and niche.

COST COMPETITIVE ADVANTAGE A firm that has a **cost competitive advantage** can produce a product or service at a lower cost than all its competitors while maintaining satisfactory profit margins. Firms become cost leaders by obtaining inexpensive raw materials, making plant operations more efficient,

Exhibit 13.2 The Target Markets for Marriott International

	Price Range	Target Market
Fairfield Inn	$45–65	Economizing business and leisure travelers
TownePlace Suites	$55–70	Moderate-tier travelers who stay three to four weeks
SpringHill Suites	$75–95	Business and leisure travelers looking for more space and amenities
Courtyard	$75–105	Travelers seeking quality and affordable accommodations designed for the road warrior
Residence Inn	$85–110	Travelers seeking a residential-style hotel
Marriott Hotels, Resorts, and Suites	$90–235	Grounded achievers who desire consistent quality
Renaissance Hotels and Resorts	$90–235	Discerning business and leisure travelers who seek creative attention to detail
Ritz-Carlton	$175–300	Senior executives and entrepreneurs looking for a unique, luxury, personalized experience

designing products for ease of manufacture, controlling overhead costs, and avoiding marginal customers.

A cost competitive advantage enables a firm to deliver superior customer value. Chapparal Steel, for example, is the leading low-cost U.S. steel producer because it uses only scrap iron and steel and a very efficient continuous-casting process to make new steel. In fact, Chapparal is so efficient that it is the only U.S. steel producer that ships to Japan. Similarly, Fort Howard Paper's competitive advantage lies in its cost-saving manufacturing process. Fort Howard Paper uses only recycled pulp, rather than the more expensive virgin pulp, to make toilet paper and other products. The quality, however, is acceptable only to the commercial market, such as office buildings, hotels, and restaurants. Therefore, the company does not try to sell to the home market through grocery stores.

Over time, the cost competitive advantage may fail. Typically, if one firm is using an innovative technology to reduce its costs, then other firms in the industry will adopt this technology and reduce their costs as well. For example, Bell Labs invented fiber optic cables that reduced the cost of voice and data transmission by dramatically increasing the number of calls that could be transmitted simultaneously through a two-inch cable. Within five years, however, fiber optic technology had spread through the industry and Bell Labs lost its cost competitive advantage. Firms may also lose their cost competitive advantage if competing firms match their low costs by using the same lower-cost suppliers. Therefore, a cost competitive advantage may not offer a long-term competitive advantage.

differential competitive advantage
A firm's ability to provide a unique product or service with a set of features that the target market perceives as important and better than the competitor's.

niche competitive advantage
A firm's ability to target and effectively serve a single segment of the market within a limited geographic area.

Differential Competitive Advantage

A product/service **differential competitive advantage** exists when a firm provides something unique that is valuable to buyers beyond simply offering a low price. Differential competitive advantages tend to be longer lasting than cost competitive advantages because cost advantages are subject to continual erosion as competitors catch up.

The durability of a differential competitive advantage tends to make this strategy more attractive to many top managers. Common differential advantages are brand names (Lexus), a strong dealer network (Caterpillar Tractor for construction equipment), product reliability (Maytag washers), image (Neiman Marcus in retailing), and service (Federal Express). Brand names such as Coca-Cola, BMW, and Cartier stand for quality the world over. Through continual product and marketing innovations and attention to quality and value, managers at these organizations have created enduring competitive advantages. Arthur Doppelmayer, an Austrian manufacturer of aerial transport systems, believes his main differential advantage, besides innovative equipment design, is his service system, which allows the company to come to the assistance of users anywhere in the world within 24 hours. Doppelmayer uses a worldwide system of warehouses and skilled personnel prepared to move immediately in emergency cases.

A differential competitive advantage offers a unique value to consumers. Keebler promises chocolate lovers that their Fudge Shoppe Clusters "don't fudge on the fudge."

Enchantingly irresistible...
...and that's just the guy who bakes 'em.
Fudge Shoppe
Clusters
We don't fudge on the Fudge.™

Niche Competitive Advantage

A company with a **niche competitive advantage** targets and effectively serves a single segment of the market within a limited geographic area. For small companies with limited resources that potentially face giant competitors, "niche-ing" may be the only viable option. A market segment that has good growth potential but is not crucial to the success of major competitors is a good candidate for a niche strategy. Once a potential segment has been identified, the firm needs to make certain it can defend against challengers through its superior ability to serve buyers in the segment. For example, STI Music Private Bank follows a niche strategy with its concentration on country music stars and entertainment industry professionals in Nashville. Its office is in the heart of Nashville's music district. STI has decided to expand its niche strategy to Miami, the "epicenter" of Latin music, and Atlanta. The latter is a longtime rhythm-and-blues capital and now is the center of contemporary "urban" music. Both new markets have the kinds of music professionals—entertainers, record executives, producers, agents, and others—that have made STI so successful in Nashville.

concept check

What is environmental scanning?

What is a target market, and why should a company have one?

Explain the three types of competitive advantages and provide examples of each.

Developing a Marketing Mix

3 learning goal

Once a firm has defined its target market and identified its competitive advantage, it can create the **marketing mix,** that is, the blend of product offering, pricing, promotional methods, and distribution system that brings a specific group of consumers superior value. Distribution is sometimes referred to as place, so the marketing mix is based on the **four Ps:** product, price, promotion, and place. Every target market requires a unique marketing mix to satisfy the needs of the target consumers and meet the firm's goals. A strategy must be constructed for each of the four Ps and blended with the strategies for the other elements. Thus, the marketing mix is only as good as its weakest part. An excellent product with a poor distribution system could be doomed to failure. A successful marketing mix requires careful tailoring. For instance, at first glance you might think that McDonald's and Wendy's have roughly the same marketing mix. After all, they are both in the fast-food business. But McDonald's targets parents with young children through Ronald McDonald, heavily promoted children's Happy Meals, and playgrounds. Wendy's is targeted to a more adult crowd. Wendy's has no playgrounds but it does have carpeting (a more adult atmosphere) and expanded its menu to include items for adult tastes.

marketing mix
The blend of product offering, pricing, promotional methods, and distribution system that brings a specific group of consumers superior value.

four Ps
Product, price, promotion, and place (distribution), which together make up the marketing mix.

Product Strategy

Marketing strategy typically starts with the product. You can't plan a distribution system or set a price if you don't know what you're going to market. Marketers use the term *product* to refer to both *goods,* such as tires, stereos, and clothing, and *services,* such as hotels, hair salons, and restaurants. Thus, the heart of the marketing mix is the good or service. Creating a **product strategy** involves choosing a brand name, packaging, colors, a warranty, accessories, and a service program.

Marketers view products in a much larger context than you might imagine. They include not only the item itself but also the brand name and the company image. The names Ralph Lauren and Gucci, for instance, create extra value for everything from cosmetics to bath towels. That is, products with those names sell at higher prices than identical products without the names. We buy things not only for what they do, but also for what they mean. Product strategies are discussed further in Chapter 14.

product strategy
Taking the good or service and selecting a brand name, packaging, colors, a warranty, accessories, and a service program.

Pricing Strategy

Pricing strategy is based on demand for the product and the cost of producing it. Some special considerations can also influence the price. Sometimes, for instance, a special introductory price is used to get people to try a new product. Some firms enter the market with low prices and keep them low, such as Carnival Cruise Lines and Suzuki cars. Others enter a market with very high prices and then lower them over time, such as producers of high-definition televisions and personal computers. You can learn more about pricing strategies in Chapter 14.

pricing strategy
Setting a price based upon the demand and cost for a good or service.

Distribution Strategy

distribution strategy
Creating the means by which products flow from the producer to the consumer.

Distribution strategy is creating the means (the channel) by which a product flows from the producer to the consumer. One aspect of distribution strategy is deciding how many stores and which specific wholesalers and retailers will handle the product in a geographic area. Cosmetics, for instance, are distributed in many different ways. Avon has a sales force of several hundred thousand representatives who call directly on consumers. Clinique and Estee Lauder are distributed through selected department stores. Cover Girl and Del Laboratories use mostly chain drugstores and other mass merchandisers. Redken sells through beauticians. Revlon uses several of these distribution channels. Distribution is examined in detail in Chapter 15.

Promotion Strategy

promotion strategy
The unique combination of personal selling, advertising, publicity, and sales promotion to stimulate the target market to buy a product or service.

Many people feel that promotion is the most exciting part of the marketing mix. **Promotion strategy** covers personal selling, advertising, public relations, and sales promotion. Each element is coordinated with the others to create a promotional blend. An advertisement, for instance, helps a buyer get to know the company and paves the way for a sales call. A good promotion strategy can dramatically increase a firm's sales. Promotion is the topic of Chapter 16.

Public relations plays a special role in promotion. It is used to create a good image of the company and its products. Bad publicity costs nothing to send out, but it can cost a firm a great deal in lost business. Good publicity, such as a television or magazine story about a firm's new product, may be the result of much time, money, and effort spent by a public-relations department.

Sales promotion directly stimulates sales. It includes trade shows, catalogs, contests, games, premiums, coupons, and special offers. McDonald's discount coupons and contests offering money and food prizes are examples of sales promotions.

The American Red Cross, a not-for-profit organization, uses social marketing to remind families to prepare their homes and families for emergencies and disasters.

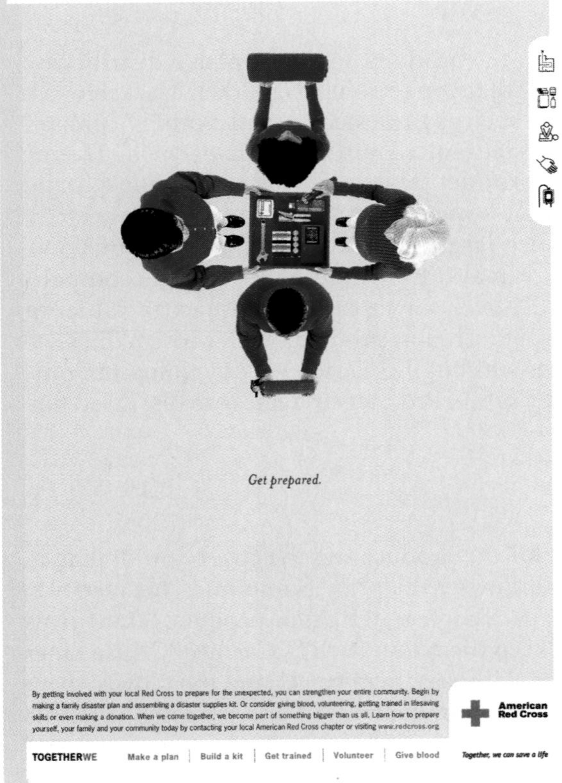

Not-for-Profit Marketing

Profit-oriented companies are not the only ones that analyze the marketing environment, find a competitive advantage, and create a marketing mix. The application of marketing principles and techniques is also vital to not-for-profit organizations. Marketing helps not-for-profit groups identify target markets and develop effective marketing mixes. In some cases, marketing has kept symphonies, museums, and other cultural groups from having to close their doors. In other organizations, such as the American Heart Association and the U.S. Army, marketing ideas and techniques have helped managers do their jobs better. The Army, for instance, has identified the most effective ways to get men and women between the ages of 18 and 24 to visit a recruiter. In the private sector, the profit motive is both an objective for guiding decisions and a criterion for evaluating results. Not-for-profit organizations do not seek to make a profit for redistribution to owners or shareholders. Rather, their focus is often on generating enough funds to cover expenses. For example, the Methodist Church does not gauge its success by the amount of money left in offering plates. The Museum of Science and Industry does not base its performance evaluations on the dollar value of tokens put into the turnstile.

Not-for-profit marketing is also concerned with social marketing, that is, the application of marketing to social issues and causes. The goals of **social marketing** are to effect social change (for instance, by creating racial harmony), further social causes (for instance, by helping the homeless), and evaluate the relationship between marketing and society (for instance, by asking whether society should allow advertising on television shows for young children). Individual organizations also engage in social marketing. The Southern Baptist Radio and Television Convention promotes brotherhood and goodwill by promoting religion and good deeds. M.A.D.D. counsels against drunk driving, and the National Wildlife Federation asks your help in protecting endangered animals and birds.

concept check

What is meant by the marketing mix?

What are the components of the marketing mix?

How can marketing techniques help not-for-profit organizations?

Define social marketing.

Buyer Behavior

4 learning goal

social marketing
The application of marketing techniques to social issues and causes.

buyer behavior
The actions people take in buying and using goods and services.

An organization cannot reach its goals without understanding buyer behavior. **Buyer behavior** is the actions people take in buying and using goods and services. Marketers who understand buyer behavior, such as how a price increase will affect a product's sales, can create a more effective marketing mix.

To understand buyer behavior, marketers must understand how consumers make buying decisions. The consumer decision-making process has several steps, which are shown in Exhibit 13.3. The entire process is affected by cultural, social, individual, and psychological factors. The buying process starts with need recognition. This may be as simple as running out of coffee. Yes, I need to purchase more coffee. Or perhaps you recently got married and recognize that you need to start building equity instead of paying rent. Perhaps you are also considering starting a family. Therefore, you decide to buy your first home (Step 1 in Exhibit 13.3).

Next, you begin to gather information about financing, available homes, styles, locations, and so forth (Step 2). After you feel that you have gathered enough information, you begin to evaluate alternatives (Step 3). For example, you might eliminate all homes that cost over $150,000 or are more than a 30-minute drive to your work. Then an offer is made and, if it is accepted, a purchase is made (Step 4). Finally, you assess the experience and your level of satisfaction with your new home (Step 5).

Merrill Lynch targets consumers reaching retirement age with this advertisement promoting its financial services. Demographic segmentation is the most common form of market segmentation.

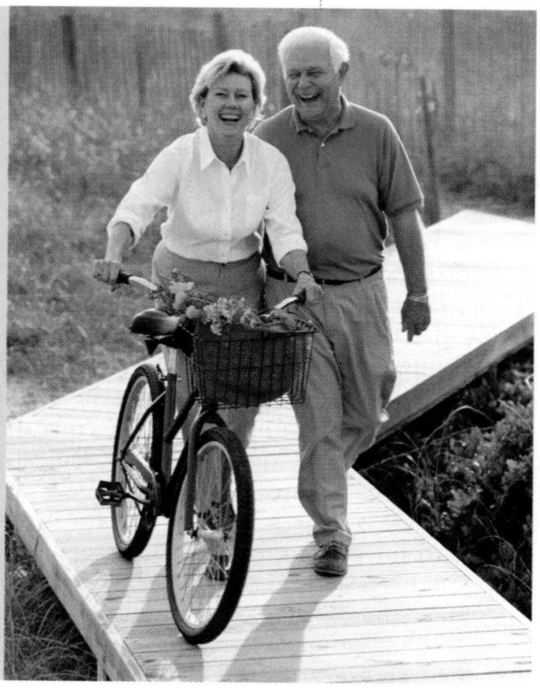

Influences on Consumer Decision Making

Cultural, social, individual and psychological factors have an impact on consumer decision making from the time a person recognizes a need through postpurchase behavior. We will examine each of these in more detail.

Culture Purchase roles within the family are influenced by culture. **Culture** is the set of values, ideas, attitudes, and symbols created to shape human behavior. Culture is environmentally oriented. The nomads of Finland have developed a culture for Arctic survival. Similarly, the natives of the Brazilian jungle have created a culture suitable for jungle living.

Culture by definition is social in nature. It is human interaction that creates values and prescribes acceptable behavior. Thus culture gives order to society by creating common expectations. Sometimes these expectations are codified into law; for example, if you come to a red light, you stop the car. As long as a value or belief meets the needs of society, it will remain part of the culture; if it is no longer functional, the value or belief recedes. The value that very large families are "good" is no longer

Exhibit 13.3 | Consumer Decision-Making Process

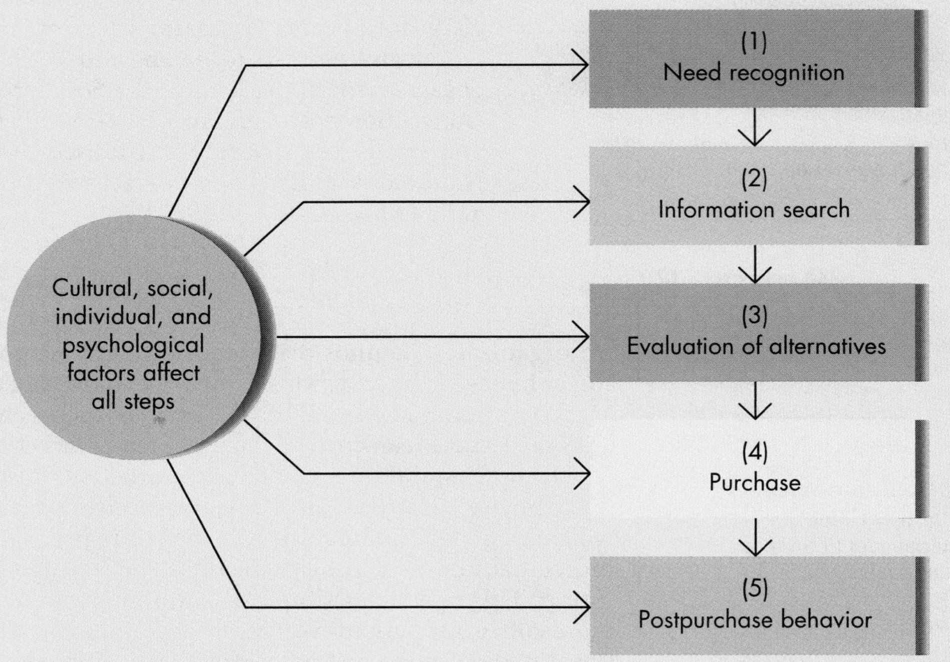

culture
The set of values, ideas, attitudes, and other symbols created to shape human behavior.

held by a majority of Americans. Since Americans live in an urban rather than a rural environment, children are no longer needed to perform farm chores.

Culture is not static. It adapts to changing societal needs and evolving environmental factors. The rapid growth of technology has accelerated the rate of cultural change. Inventions such as the elevator made possible modern high-rise cities. Television changed entertainment patterns and family communication flows, and heightened public awareness of political and other news events. The Internet has changed how we communicate and how many of us work.

SOCIAL FACTORS Most consumers are likely to seek out the opinions of others to reduce their search and evaluation effort or uncertainty, especially as the perceived risk of the decision increases. Consumers may also seek out others' opinions for guidance on new products or services, products with image-related attributes, or products where attribute information is lacking or uninformative. Specifically, consumers interact socially with reference groups, opinion leaders, and family members to obtain product information and decision approval. All the formal and informal groups that influence the buying behavior of an individual are that person's **reference groups.** Consumers may use products or brands to identify with or become a member of a group. They learn from observing how members of their reference groups consume, and they use the same criteria to make their own consumer decisions. A reference group might be a fraternity or sorority, a group you work with, or a club to which you belong.

reference groups
Formal and informal groups that influence buyer behavior.

Reference groups frequently include individuals known as group leaders, or **opinion leaders**—those who influence others. Obviously, it is important for marketing managers to persuade such people to purchase their goods or services. Many products and services that are integral parts of Americans' lives today got their initial boost from opinion leaders. For example, DVDs and sport utility vehicles were embraced by opinion leaders well ahead of the general public. Opinion leaders are often the first to try new products and services out of pure curiosity.

opinion leaders
Those who influence others.

They are typically self-indulgent, making them more likely to explore unproven but intriguing products and services.

The family is the most important social institution for many consumers, strongly influencing values, attitudes, self-concept—and buying behavior. For example, a family that strongly values good health will have a grocery list distinctly different from that of a family that views every dinner as a gourmet event. Moreover, the family is responsible for the **socialization process,** the passing down of cultural values and norms to children. Children learn by observing their parents' consumption patterns, and so they will tend to shop in a similar pattern.

socialization process
The passing down of cultural norms and values to children.

Marketers should consider family purchase situations along with the distribution of consumer and decision-maker roles among family members. Ordinary marketing views the individual as both decision maker and consumer. Family marketing adds several other possibilities: Sometimes more than one family member or all family members are involved in the decision; sometimes only children are involved in the decision; sometimes more than one consumer is involved; and sometimes the decision maker and the consumer are different people. For example, a parent will select a dentist for a child to visit.

Individual Influences on Consumer Buying Decisions

A person's buying decisions are also influenced by personal characteristics that are unique to each individual, such as gender, personality, and self-concept. Individual characteristics are generally stable over the course of one's life. For instance, most people do not change their gender, and the act of changing personality requires a complete reorientation of one's life.

Physiological differences between men and women result in different needs, such as health and beauty products. Just as important are the distinct cultural, social, and economic roles played by men and women and the effects that these have on their decision-making processes. Men and women also shop differently. Studies show that men and women share similar motivations in terms of where to shop—that is, seeking reasonable prices, merchandise quality, and a friendly, low-pressure environment—but they don't necessarily feel the same about shopping in general. Most women enjoy shopping; their male counterparts claim to dislike the experience and shop only out of necessity. Furthermore, men desire simple shopping experiences, stores with less variety, and convenience.

Each consumer has a unique personality. **Personality** is a broad concept that can be thought of as a way of organizing and grouping how an individual typically reacts to situations. Thus, personality combines psychological makeup and environmental forces. It includes people's underlying dispositions, especially their most dominant characteristics. Although personality is one of the least useful concepts in the study of consumer behavior, some marketers believe that personality influences the types and brands of products purchased. For instance, the type of car, clothes, or jewelry a consumer buys may reflect one or more personality traits.

personality
A way of organizing and grouping how an individual reacts to situations.

Self-concept, or self-perception, is how consumers perceive themselves. Self-concept includes attitudes, perceptions, beliefs, and self-evaluations. Although self-concept may change, the change is often gradual. Through self-concept, people define their identity, which in turn provides for consistent and coherent behavior.

self-concept
How people perceive themselves.

Self-concept combines the **ideal self-image** (the way an individual would like to be) and the **real self-image** (how an individual actually perceives him or herself). Generally, we try to raise our real self-image toward our ideal (or at least narrow the gap). Consumers seldom buy products that jeopardize their self-image. For example, someone who sees herself as a trendsetter wouldn't buy clothing that doesn't project a contemporary image.

ideal self-image
The way an individual would like to be.

real self-image
How an individual actually perceives him- or herself.

Psychological Influences on Consumer Buying Decisions

An individual's buying decisions are further influenced by psychological factors such as perception, and beliefs and attitudes. These factors are what consumers use to interact with their world. They are the tools consumers use to recognize their feelings, gather and analyze information, formulate thoughts and opinions, and take action. Unlike the other three influences on consumer behavior, psychological influences can be affected by a person's environment because they are applied on specific occasions. For example, you will perceive different stimuli and process these stimuli in different ways depending on whether you are sitting in class concentrating on the instructor, sitting outside of class talking to friends, or sitting in your dorm room watching television.

The world is full of stimuli. A stimulus is any unit of input affecting one or more of the five senses: sight, smell, taste, touch, hearing. The process by which we select, organize, and interpret these stimuli into a meaningful and coherent picture is called **perception.** In essence, perception is how we see the world around us and how we recognize that we need some help in making a purchasing decision. People cannot perceive every stimulus in their environment. Therefore, they use **selective exposure** to decide which stimuli to notice and which to ignore. A typical consumer is exposed to more than 250 advertising messages a day but notices only between 11 and 20.

A **belief** is an organized pattern of knowledge that an individual holds as true about his or her world. A consumer may believe that Sony's camcorder makes the best home videos, tolerates hard use, and is reasonably priced. These beliefs may be based on knowledge, faith, or hearsay. Consumers tend to develop a set of beliefs about a product's attributes and then, through these beliefs, a *brand image*—a set of beliefs about a particular brand. In turn, the brand image shapes consumers' attitudes toward the product.

An **attitude** is a learned tendency to respond consistently toward a given object, idea, or concept, such as a brand. Attitudes rest on an individual's value system, which represents personal standards of good and bad, right and wrong, and so forth; therefore, attitudes tend to be more enduring and complex than beliefs. For an example of the nature of attitudes, consider the differing attitudes of consumers around the world toward the practice of purchasing on credit. Americans have long been enthusiastic about charging goods and services and are willing to pay high interest rates for the privilege of postponing payment. To many European consumers, doing what amounts to taking out a loan—even a small one—to pay for anything seems absurd.

perception
The process by which we select, organize, and interpret stimuli into a meaningful and coherent picture.

selective exposure
The process of deciding which stimuli to notice and which to ignore.

belief
An organized pattern of knowledge that an individual holds as true about the world.

attitude
Learned tendency to respond consistently toward a given object, idea, or concept.

Types of Consumer Buying Decisions

All consumer buying decisions generally fall along a continuum of three broad categories: routine response behavior, limited decision making, and extensive decision making (see Exhibit 13.4). Goods and services in these three categories can best be described in terms of five factors: level of consumer involvement, length of time to make a decision, cost of the good or service, degree of information search, and the number of alternatives considered. The level of consumer involvement is perhaps the most significant determinant in classifying buying decisions. **Involvement** is the amount of time and effort a buyer invests in the search, evaluation, and decision processes of consumer behavior.

Frequently purchased, low-cost goods and services are generally associated with **routine response behavior.** These goods and services can also be called low-involvement products because consumers spend little time on search and decision before making the purchase. Usually, buyers are familiar with several different brands in the product category but stick with one brand. Consumers engaged in routine response behavior normally don't experience need recognition until they are exposed to advertising or see the product displayed on a store shelf.

Limited decision making typically occurs when a consumer has previous product experience but is unfamiliar with the current brands available. Limited decision making is also associated with lower levels of involvement (although higher

involvement
The amount of time and effort a buyer invests in the search, evaluation, and decision processes of consumer behavior.

routine response behavior
Purchase of low-cost, frequently bought items with little search or decision making.

limited decision making
Consumer has previous product experience but is unfamiliar with the current brands available.

Exhibit 13.4 | Continuum of Consumer Buying Decisions

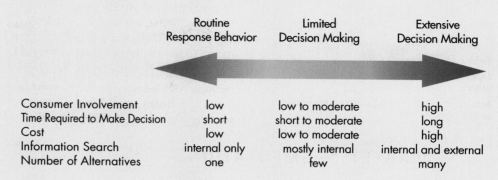

	Routine Response Behavior	Limited Decision Making	Extensive Decision Making
Consumer Involvement	low	low to moderate	high
Time Required to Make Decision	short	short to moderate	long
Cost	low	low to moderate	high
Information Search	internal only	mostly internal	internal and external
Number of Alternatives	one	few	many

than routine decisions) because consumers do expend moderate effort in searching for information or in considering various alternatives. Suppose the children's usual brand of cereal, Kellogg's Corn Flakes, is unavailable in the grocery store. Completely out of cereal at home, the parent now must select another brand. Before making a final selection, he or she may pull from the shelf several brands similar to Kellogg's Corn Flakes, such as Corn Chex and Cheerios, to compare their nutritional value and calories and to decide whether the children will like the new cereal.

extensive decision making
Purchasing an unfamiliar, expensive, infrequently bought item.

Consumers practice **extensive decision making** when buying an unfamiliar, expensive product or an infrequently bought item. This process is the most complex type of consumer buying decision and is associated with high involvement on the part of the consumer. This process resembles the model outlined in Exhibit 13.3. These consumers want to make the right decision, so they want to know as much as they can about the product category and available brands. Buyers use several criteria for evaluating their options and spend much time seeking information. Buying a home or a car, for example, requires extensive decision making.

Business-to-Business Purchase Decision Making

Business buyer behavior and business markets are different from consumer markets. Business markets include institutions such as hospitals and schools, manufacturers, wholesalers and retailers, and various branches of government. The key difference between a consumer product and a business product is the intended use. If you purchase a certain model Dell computer for your home so you can surf the Internet, it is a consumer good. If a purchasing agent for MTV buys exactly the same computer for an MTV script writer, it is a business good. Why? The reason is that MTV is a business, so the computer will be used in a business environment.

Characteristics of the Business-to-Business Market

The main differences between consumer markets and business markets are as follows:

1. *Purchase volume.* Business customers buy in much larger quantities than consumers. Think how many truckloads of sugar Mars must purchase to make one day's output of M&Ms. Imagine the number of batteries Sears buys each day for resale to consumers. Think of the number of pens the federal government must use each day.
2. *Number of customers.* Business marketers usually have far fewer customers than consumer marketers. As a result, it is much easier to identify prospective buyers and monitor current needs. Think about how few customers for airplanes or industrial cranes there are compared to the more than 80 million consumer households in the United States.

3. *Location of buyers.* Business customers tend to be much more geographically concentrated than consumers. The computer industry is concentrated in Silicon Valley and a few other areas. Aircraft manufacturing is found in Seattle, St. Louis, and Dallas/Fort Worth. Suppliers to these manufacturers often locate close to the manufacturers to lower distribution costs and facilitate communication.
4. *Direct distribution.* Business sales tend to be made directly to the buyer because such sales frequently involve large quantities or custom-made items like heavy machinery. Consumer goods are more likely to be sold through intermediaries like wholesalers and retailers.

concept check

Explain the consumer decision-making process.

How do business markets differ from consumer markets?

Market Segmentation

5 learning goal

market segmentation
The process of separating, identifying, and evaluating the layers of a market in order to identify a target market.

The study of buyer behavior helps marketing managers better understand why people make purchases. To identify the target markets that may be most profitable for the firm, managers use **market segmentation,** which is the process of separating, identifying, and evaluating the layers of a market to identify a target market. For instance, a target market might be segmented into two groups: families with children and families without children. Families with young children are likely to buy hot cereals and presweetened cereals. Families with no children are more likely to buy health-oriented cereals. You can be sure that cereal companies plan their marketing mixes with this difference in mind. A business market may be segmented by large customers and small customers or by geographic area.

The five basic forms of consumer market segmentation are demographic, geographic, psychographic, benefit, and volume. Their characteristics are summarized in Exhibit 13.5 and discussed in the following sections.

Demographic Segmentation

demographic segmentation
The differentiation of markets through the use of categories such as age, education, gender, income, and household size.

Demographic segmentation uses categories such as age, education, gender, income, and household size to differentiate among markets. This form of market segmentation is the most common. The U.S. Census Bureau provides a great deal of demographic data. For example, marketing researchers can use census data to find areas within cities that contain high concentrations of high-income consumers, singles, blue-collar workers, and so forth.

Many products are targeted to various age groups. Most music CDs, Pepsi, Coke, many movies, the Chrysler Neon, and thousands of other products are targeted toward teenagers and persons under 25 years old. In contrast, most

Exhibit 13.5 Forms of Consumer Market Segmentation

Form	General Characteristics
Demographic segmentation	Age, education, gender, income, race, social class, household size
Geographic segmentation	Regional location (e.g., New England, Mid-Atlantic, Southeast, Great Lakes, Plains States, Northwest, Southwest, Rocky Mountains, Far West); population density (urban, suburban, rural); city or county size; climate
Psychographic segmentation	Lifestyle, personality, interests, values, attitudes
Benefit segmentation	Benefits provided by the good or service
Volume segmentation	Amount of use (light versus heavy)

Exhibit 13.6 | Age Segmentation for Fritos, Doritos, and Tostitos

	Name Derivation	Year Introduced	Main Ingredients	Demographic	Snack Niche, According to Frito Lay
Frito	"Little fried bits" (Spanish)	1932	Corn, vegetable oil, salt	33- to 51-year-old males	"Hunger satisfaction"
Doritos	"Little bits of gold"	1964	Corn, vegetable oil, cheddar cheese, salt	Teens, mostly males	"Bold and daring snacking"
Tostitos	"Little toasted bits" (Spanish)	1981	White corn, vegetable oil, salt	Upscale consumers born between 1946 and 1964	"Casual interaction through friends and family . . . a social food that brings people together"

SOURCE: Frito-Lay.

cruises, medical products, fine jewelry, vacation homes, Buicks, and denture products are targeted toward people 50 years old and up. An example of how Frito Lay targets various age groups for three of its most popular products is shown is Exhibit 13.6.

Certain markets are segmented by gender. These include clothing, cosmetics, personal care items, magazines, jewelry, and footwear. Gillette, for example, is one of the world's best-known marketers of personal care products and has historically targeted men for the most part. Yet women's products have generated most of Gillette's growth since 1992. Gillette's shaving line for women has expanded into a $400 million global business, growing nearly 20 percent annually. Gillette has increased its advertising budget to help it reach a goal of over $1 billion in revenues from women's shaving products worldwide. In the United States, women's blades and disposables now make up about one-fifth of Gillette's sales.

Income is another popular way to segment markets. Income level influences consumers' wants and determines their buying power. Housing, clothing, automobiles, and alcoholic beverages are among the many markets segmented by income. Budget Gourmet frozen dinners are targeted to lower-income groups, whereas the Le Menu line is aimed at higher-income consumers.

Geographic Segmentation

geographic segmentation
The differentiation of markets by region of the country, city or county size, market density, or climate.

Geographic segmentation means segmenting markets by region of the country, city or county size, market density, or climate. *Market density* is the number of people or businesses within a certain area. Many companies segment their markets geographically to meet regional preferences and buying habits. Pizza Hut, for instance, gives Easterners extra cheese, Westerners more ingredients, and Midwesterners both. Both Ford and Chevrolet sell more pickup trucks and truck parts in the middle of the country than on either coast. The well-defined "pickup truck belt" runs from the upper Midwest south through Texas and the Gulf states. Ford "owns" the northern half of this truck belt, and Chevrolet the southern half.

Cabela's is the world's foremost outfitter serving people who love the outdoors. Psychographic segmentation is market segmentation by personality or lifestyle.

Psychographic Segmentation

psychographic segmentation
The differentiation of markets by personality or lifestyle.

Race, income, occupation, and other demographic variables help in developing strategies but often do not paint the entire picture of consumer needs. Demographics provide the skeleton, but psychographics add meat to the bones. **Psychographic segmentation** is market segmentation by personality or lifestyle. People with common activities, interests, and opinions are grouped together and given a "lifestyle name." For example, Harley-Davidson divides its customers into seven lifestyle segments, from "cocky misfits" who are most likely to be arrogant troublemakers, to "laid-back camper types" committed to cycling and nature, to "classy capitalists" who have wealth and privilege.

Benefit Segmentation

benefit segmentation
The differentiation of markets based on what a product will do rather than on customer characteristics.

Benefit segmentation is based on what a product will do rather than on consumer characteristics. For years Crest toothpaste was targeted toward consumers concerned with preventing cavities. Recently, Crest subdivided its market. It now offers regular Crest, Crest Tartar Control for people who want to prevent cavities and tartar buildup, Crest for kids with sparkles that taste like bubble gum, and another Crest that prevents gum disease. Another toothpaste, Topol, targets people who want whiter teeth—teeth without coffee, tea, or tobacco stains. Sensodyne toothpaste is aimed at people with highly sensitive teeth.

Volume Segmentation

volume segmentation
The differentiation of markets based on the amount of the product purchased.

The fifth main type of segmentation is **volume segmentation,** which is based on the amount of the product purchased. Just about every product has heavy, moderate, and light users, as well as nonusers. Heavy users often account for a very large portion of a product's sales. Thus, a firm might want to target its marketing mix to the heavy-user segment.

Retailers are aware that heavy shoppers not only spend more, but also visit each outlet more frequently than other shoppers. Heavy shoppers visit the grocery store 122 times per year, compared with 93 annual visits for the medium shopper. They visit discount stores more than twice as often as medium shoppers, and they visit convenience/gas stores more than five times as often. On each trip, they consistently spend more than their medium-shopping counterparts.[5]

concept check

Define market segmentation.

List and discuss the five basic forms of market segmentation.

USING MARKETING RESEARCH TO SERVE EXISTING CUSTOMERS AND FIND NEW CUSTOMERS

6 learning goal

marketing research
The process of planning, collecting, and analyzing data relevant to a marketing decision.

How do successful companies learn what their customers value? Through marketing research, companies can be sure they are listening to the voice of the customer. **Marketing research** is the process of planning, collecting, and analyzing data relevant to a marketing decision. The results of this analysis are then communicated to management. The information collected through marketing research includes the preferences of customers, the perceived benefits of products, and consumer lifestyles. Research helps companies make better use of their marketing budgets. Marketing research has a range of uses from fine-tuning existing products to discovering whole new marketing concepts.

For example, everything at the Olive Garden restaurant chain from the décor to the wine list is based on marketing research. Each new menu item is put through a series of consumer taste tests before being added to the menu. Hallmark Cards uses marketing research to test messages, cover designs, and even the size of the cards. Hallmark's experts know which kinds of cards will sell best in which places. Engagement cards, for instance, sell best in the Northeast, where engagement parties are popular. Birthday cards for "Daddy" sell best in the South because even adult southerners tend to call their fathers Daddy.

This section examines the marketing research process, which consists of the following steps:

1. Define the marketing problem.
2. Choose a method of research.
3. Collect the data.
4. Analyze the research data.
5. Make recommendations to management.

Define the Marketing Problem

The most critical step in the marketing research process is defining the marketing problem. This involves writing either a problem statement or a list of research objectives. If the problem is not defined properly, the remainder of the research will be a waste of time and money. Two key questions can help in defining the marketing problem correctly:

1. Why is the information being sought? By discussing with managers what the information is going to be used for and what decisions might be made as a result, the researcher can get a clearer grasp of the problem.
2. Does the information already exist? If so, money and time can be saved and a quick decision can be made.

Choose a Method of Research

survey research
A marketing research method in which data is gathered from respondents, either in person, by telephone, by mail, at a mall, or through the Internet to obtain facts, opinions, and attitudes.

After the problem is correctly defined, a research method is chosen. There are three basic research methods: survey, observation, and experiment.

With **survey research,** data is gathered from respondents, either in person or at a mall, or through the Internet, by telephone, or mail, to obtain facts, opinions, and attitudes. A questionnaire is used to provide an orderly and structured approach to data gathering. Face-to-face interviews may take place at the respondent's home, in a shopping mall, or at a place of business.

Observation research is research that monitors respondents' actions without direct interaction. In the fastest-growing form of observation research, researchers use cash registers with scanners that read tags with bar codes to identify the item being purchased. Technological advances are rapidly expanding the future of observation research. For example, A. C. Nielsen has been using black boxes for years on television sets to silently obtain information on a family's viewing habits. But what if the set is on and no one is in the room? To overcome that problem, researchers will soon rely on infrared passive "people meters" that will identify the faces of family members watching the television program. Thus, the meter will duly record when the set is on and no one is watching.

observation research
A marketing research method in which the investigator monitors respondents' actions without interacting directly with the respondents; for example, by using cash registers with scanners.

In the third research method, **experiment,** the investigator changes one or more variables—price, package, design, shelf space, advertising theme, or advertising expenditures—while observing the effects of those changes on another variable (usually sales). The objective of experiments is to measure causality. For example, an experiment may reveal the impact that a change in package design has on sales.

experiment
A marketing research method in which the investigator changes one or more variables—price, packaging, design, shelf space, advertising theme, or advertising expenditures—while observing the effects of these changes on another variable (usually sales).

Collect the Data

Two types of data are used in marketing research: **primary data,** which are collected directly from the original source to solve a problem; and **secondary data,** which is information that has already been collected for a project other than the current one but may be used to help solve it. Secondary data can come from a number of sources, among them government agencies, trade associations, research bureaus, universities, the Internet, commercial publications, and internal company records. Company records include sales invoices, accounting records, data from previous research studies, and historical sales data.

primary data
Information collected directly from the original source to solve a problem.

secondary data
Information that has already been collected for a project other than the current one, but that may be used to solve the current problem.

Primary data are usually gathered through some form of survey research. As described earlier, survey research often relies on interviews. See Exhibit 13.7 for the different types of surveys. Today, conducting surveys over the Internet is the fastest growing form of survey research, as the "Applying Technology" box describes.

Analyze the Data

After the data have been collected, the next step in the research process is data analysis. The purpose of this analysis is to interpret and draw conclusions from the mass of collected data. Many software statistical programs such as SAS and SPSS are available to make this task easier for the researcher.

© DANA WHITE / PHOTOEDIT

Interviewing people in a shopping mall is a popular survey research method that allows firms to gather information about consumer opinions and attitudes.

Exhibit 13.7 | Common Types of Survey Research

Internet surveys	Conducted on the Internet, often using respondents from huge Internet panels (persons agreeing to participate in a series of surveys).
Executive surveys	Interviews of professionals (e.g., engineers, architects, doctors, executives) or decision makers are conducted at their place of business.
Mall-intercept surveys	Interviews with consumers are conducted in a shopping mall or other high-traffic location. Interviews may be done in a public area of the mall, or respondents may be taken to a private test area.
Central-location telephone surveys	Interviews are conducted from a telephone facility set up for that purpose. These facilities typically have equipment that permits supervisors to unobtrusively monitor the interviewing while it is taking place. Many of these facilities do national sampling from a single location. An increasing number have computer-assisted interviewing capabilities. At these locations, the interviewer sits in front of a computer terminal attached to a mainframe or a personal computer. The questionnaire is programmed into the computer, and the interviewer uses the keyboard to directly enter responses.
Self-administered questionnaires	Self-administered questionnaires are most frequently employed at high-traffic locations such as shopping malls or in captive audience situations such as classrooms and airplanes. Respondents are given general information on how to fill out the questionnaire and are expected to fill it out on their own. Kiosk-based point-of-service touch screens provide a way to capture information from individuals in stores, health clinics, and other shopping or service environments. Sometimes software-driven questionnaires on diskettes are sent to individuals who have personal computers.
Ad hoc (one-shot) mail surveys	Questionnaires are mailed to a sample of consumers or industrial users, without prior contact by the researcher. Instructions are included; respondents are asked to fill out the questionnaire and return it via mail. Sometimes a gift or monetary incentive is provided.
Mail panels	Questionnaires are mailed to a sample of individuals who have been precontacted. The panel concept has been explained to them, and they have agreed to participate for some period of time, in exchange for gratuities. Mail panels typically generate much higher response rates than do ad hoc mail surveys.

Make Recommendations to Management

After completing the data analysis, the researcher must prepare the report and communicate the conclusions and recommendations to management. This is a key step in the process because marketing researchers who want their conclusions acted upon must convince the manager that the results are credible and justified by the data collected. Today, presentation software like PowerPoint and Astound provides easy-to-use tools for creating reports and presentations that are more interesting, compelling, and effective than was possible just a few years ago.

concept check

Define marketing research.

Explain the marketing research process.

What are the three basic marketing research methods?

Trends in Marketing

7 learning goal

To discover exactly what customers value most, organizations are using innovative techniques for collecting customer information. Some of the more sophisticated marketing research techniques that are growing in popularity are scanner-based research, capitalizing on loyalty cards, and one-to-one marketing.

Applying Technology

The Internet Has Completely Changed Marketing Research

By 2005, half of all marketing research expenditures will be for Internet-based marketing research. Current methods of conducting some types of research soon may seem as quaint as a steam-engine train. New techniques and strategies for conducting traditional marketing research are appearing online in increasing numbers every day. Following are some growth drivers of such research:

- The Internet provides more rapid access to business intelligence and thus allows for better and faster decision making.
- The Internet improves a firm's ability to respond quickly to customer needs and market shifts.
- The Internet facilitates conducting follow-up studies and longitudinal research.
- The Internet slashes labor- and time-intensive research activities (and associated costs), including mailing, telephone solicitation, data entry, data tabulation, and reporting.

Internet surveys have several specific advantages:

- *Rapid development, real-time reporting.* Internet surveys can be broadcast to thousands of potential respondents simultaneously. The results can be tabulated and posted for corporate clients to view as the returns arrive. Thus, Internet survey results can be in a client's hands in significantly less time than traditional survey results.
- *Dramatically reduced costs.* The Internet can cut costs by 25 to 40 percent while providing results in half the time it takes to do a traditional telephone survey. Data-collection costs account for a large proportion of any traditional market research budget. Telephone surveys are labor-intensive efforts incurring training, telecommunications, and management costs. Using the Internet eliminates these costs completely.
- *Personalization.* Internet surveys can be highly personalized for greater relevance to each respondent's own situation, thus speeding the response process. Respondents enjoy answering only pertinent questions, being able to pause and resume the survey as their schedule allows, and having the ability to see previous responses and correct inconsistencies.
- *Higher response rates.* Busy respondents are growing increasingly intolerant of "snail mail" or telephone-based surveys. Internet surveys take half the time to complete that phone interviews do, can be accomplished at the respondent's convenience (after work hours), and are much more stimulating and engaging. Graphics, interactivity, links to incentive sites, and real-time summary reports make Internet surveys more enjoyable. This results in much higher response rates.
- *Ability to contact the hard-to-reach.* Certain of the most surveyed groups are also the most difficult to reach—doctors, high-income professionals, and top management in Global 2000 firms. Many of these groups are well represented online. Internet surveys provide convenient anytime/anywhere access that makes it easy for busy professionals to participate.[6]

CRITICAL THINKING QUESTIONS

1. Do you see any disadvantages of Internet surveys?
2. What value do you see for the customer to complete market surveys?

Scanner-Based Research

scanner-based research
System for gathering information from a single group of respondents by continuously monitoring the advertising, promotion, and pricing they are exposed to and the things that they buy.

Scanner-based research is a system for gathering information from a single group of respondents by continuously monitoring the advertising, promotion, and pricing they are exposed to and the things they buy. The variables measured are advertising campaigns, coupons, displays, and product prices. The result is a huge database of marketing efforts and consumer behavior. Scanner-based research is bringing ever closer the Holy Grail of marketing research: an accurate, objective picture of the direct causal relationship between different kinds of marketing efforts and actual sales.

The two major scanner-based suppliers are Information Resources, Inc. (IRI) and the A.C. Nielsen Company. Each has about half the market. However, IRI is the founder of scanner-based research.

IRI's first product is called *BehaviorScan.* A household panel (a group of 3,000 long-term participants in the research project) has been recruited and maintained in each BehaviorScan town. Panel members shop with an ID card, which is presented at the checkout in scanner-equipped grocery stores and drugstores, allowing IRI to track electronically each household's purchases, item by item, over time. It uses microcomputers to measure TV viewing in each panel household and can

Making Ethical Choices

xtra! http://gitmanxtra.swlearning.com

HITTING THE LONG SHOT

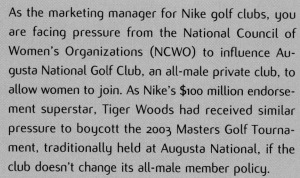

As the marketing manager for Nike golf clubs, you are facing pressure from the National Council of Women's Organizations (NCWO) to influence Augusta National Golf Club, an all-male private club, to allow women to join. As Nike's $100 million endorsement superstar, Tiger Woods had received similar pressure to boycott the 2003 Masters Golf Tournament, traditionally held at Augusta National, if the club doesn't change its all-male member policy.

You see Tiger Woods as both a magnet and a lightning rod. As reported in the *New York Times*, "Watching a Tiger Woods drive is part spectatorship, part instruction, and part wishful thinking. Therein lies the marketer's allure." Woods himself, who is rarely caught off guard on a fairway or a putting green, was surprised to find that he was a lightning rod in the divisive issue over whether women should be admitted as members of Augusta National.

NCWO chair Martha Burk challenged Nike to take a leadership role because "Nike is a company that markets aggressively to women. I think the public would applaud any companies that take a stand here." Long admired as a daring marketer for using its advertising to promote social issues, Nike has used Tiger Woods as an outspoken supporter of equal rights in Nike Golf ads and has backed women's sports by using female superstars such as Olympian Marion Jones. Woods confirms his belief in equal rights, saying, "I've always wanted to impact lives in a positive way. But I like to pick my own causes, and not be forced into having to do something."

ETHICAL DILEMMA

Do you have a social responsibility, as marketing manager for Nike golf clubs, to publicly support the membership of women at Augusta National Golf Club through promotional or public relations messages?

SOURCES: Jeff Gerth, "Personal Business; Selling Golfers the Hope of the Sweeter Swing," *The New York Times*, April 13, 2003, p. C8, downloaded from http://www.nyt.com; Jere Longman with Clifton Brown, "Debate on Women at Augusta Catches Woods Off Balance," *The New York Times*, October 20, 2002, p. C1, downloaded from http://www.nyt.com; Michael McCarthy, *USA Today*, September 23, 2002.

send special commercials to panel member television sets. With such a measure of household purchasing, it is possible to manipulate marketing variables, such as TV advertising or consumer promotions, or to introduce a new product and analyze real changes in consumer buying behavior.

IRI's most successful product is *InfoScan*—a scanner-based sales-tracking service for the consumer packaged-goods industry. Retail sales, detailed consumer purchasing information (including measurement of store loyalty and total grocery basket expenditures), and promotional activity by manufacturers and retailers are monitored and evaluated for all bar-coded products. Data are collected weekly from more than 31,000 supermarkets, drugstores, and mass merchandisers.

Capitalizing on Loyalty Cards

loyalty cards
Cards issued by a manufacturer, service organization, or retailer that give discounts to loyal and frequent shoppers.

Just swipe the card at the checkout register and get a discount on tomatoes, toothpaste, or other specials. You save money, and the store builds a record that lets it know how to serve its best customers. **Loyalty cards** are cards issued by a service organization, retailer, or manufacturer that give discounts to loyal and frequent shoppers. Most companies require the shopper to fill out a demographic profile questionnaire before the card is issued.

Loyalty cards have been around for a few years now, and supermarket and drugstore chains are beginning to reap the benefits. With a huge amount of data being collected on shoppers, from the types of soda they buy to whether they like to shop late at night, merchants are getting smarter at tracking consumer trends. And they're changing their merchandise, store layout, and advertising accordingly to keep their most loyal customers spending. A few examples:

- CVS Corp. launched its loyalty-card program and discovered that cosmetics buyers are its best customers. So beauty products have been put up front in a third of the stores, instead of being relegated to the back corners.
- Food Lion started offering loyalty cards a few years ago and now is stocking up on peppers, cactus leaves, and plantains in its Charlotte, North Carolina, stores to better serve Hispanic customers from the Caribbean.
- Winn-Dixie Stores, which began rolling out a loyalty-card program in March 2002, can now measure the effectiveness of ads on top customers and knows the 25 items that attract the most loyal shoppers.

Retailers estimate that 20 percent of their shoppers account for 80 percent of store sales, so finding out what their best customers want is essential. By simply scanning purchases, stores track what's selling, but when that information is tied to loyalty cards, merchants obtain richer information on who is buying what. This is the prized asset of supermarkets' future.[7]

GROWTH OF ONE-TO-ONE MARKETING

one-to-one marketing
Creating a unique marketing mix for every customer.

marketing database
Computerized file of customers' and potential customers' profiles and purchase patterns.

One-to-one marketing is creating a unique marketing mix for every consumer. The key to creating one-to-one marketing is a good marketing database. The information contained in a marketing database helps managers know and understand customers, and potential customers, on an individual basis. A **marketing database** is a computerized file of customers' and potential customers' profiles and purchase patterns.

In the 1960s, network television enabled advertisers to "get the same message to everyone simultaneously." Database marketing can get a customized, individual message to everyone simultaneously through direct mail. This is why database marketing is sometimes called *micromarketing*. Database marketing can create a computerized form of the old-fashioned relationship that people used to have with the corner grocer, butcher, or baker. "A database is sort of a collective memory," says Richard G. Barlow, president of Frequency Marketing, Inc., a Cincinnati-based consulting firm. "It deals with you in the same personalized way as a mom-and-pop grocery store, where they knew customers by name and stocked what they wanted."

The size of some databases is impressive: Ford Motor Company's is about 50 million names; Kraft General Foods, 30 million; Citicorp, 30 million; and Kimberly Clark, maker of Huggies diapers, 10 million new mothers. American Express can pull from its database all cardholders who made purchases at golf pro shops in the past six months, who attended symphony concerts, or who traveled to Europe more than once in the past year, as well as the very few people who did all three.

Companies are using their marketing databases to implement one-to-one marketing. For example, Novartis Seeds, Inc., a Minneapolis-based agriculture business, produces individually customized, full-color brochures for 7,000 farmers. Each piece features products selected by Novartis dealers specifically for the farmer based on information collected about the farm operation and the types of crops grown. Instead of the 30-page catalog Novartis traditionally sent, these customers get a 1-page brochure with only the five or six products they need, plus other complementary products dealers feel they should consider.

concept check

Describe how scanner-based research helps measure the effectiveness of marketing.

Explain how loyalty cards are of benefit to manufacturers and retailers.

Describe one-to-one marketing and the role of marketing databases.

Great Ideas to Use Now

As a consumer, you participate in shaping consumer products by the choices you make and the products and services you buy. You can become a better consumer by actively participating in marketing surveys and learning more about the products you buy.

Participate in Marketing Research Surveys

All of us get tired of telephone solicitations where people try to sell us everything from new carpet to chimney cleaning. Recognize that marketing research surveys are different. A true marketing research survey will *never* involve a sales pitch nor will the research firm sell your name to a database marketer. The purpose of marketing research is to build better goods and services for you and me. Help out the researchers and ultimately help yourself. The Council for Marketing and Opinion Research (CMOR) is an organization of hundreds of marketing research professionals that is dedicated to preserving the integrity of the research industry. If you receive a call from someone who tries to sell you something under the guise of marketing research, get the name and address of the organization. Call CMOR at 1-800-887-CMOR and report the abuse.

Understand Cognitive Dissonance

cognitive dissonance
The condition of having beliefs or knowledge that are internally inconsistent or that disagree with one's behavior.

When making a major purchase, particularly when the item is expensive and choices are similar, consumers typically experience **cognitive dissonance;** that is, they have beliefs or knowledge that are internally inconsistent or that disagree with their behavior. In other words, instead of feeling happy with their new purchase, they experience doubts, feel uneasy, and wonder if they have done the right thing. Understand that this feeling of uneasiness is perfectly normal and goes away over time. Perhaps the best way to avoid cognitive dissonance is to insist on a strong warranty or money-back guarantee. A second approach is to read everything you can find about your purchase. Go to the Internet and use the search engines to find articles relevant to your purchase. Find Internet chat rooms about your product and join in the discussion. And, before you buy, check out the *Consumer Reports* ratings on your product at **http://www.consumerreports.org.** For electronic products also go to **http://www.CNET.com** and **http://www.ZDNET.com.**

Try It Now

1. **Stop junk mail.** If you are upset about junk mail, contact the Direct Marketing Association and have your name removed from mailing lists. The e-mail address is **http://www.the-dma.org/**. You can also join an umbrella organization dedicated to stopping the flood of junk e-mail, intrusive telemarketing calls, and junk mail. One such organization is Zero Junk Mail. It can be found at **http://www.zerojunkmail.com**.
2. **Stop unwanted telemarketing.** If you are tired of being interrupted at dinner by annoying telemarketers join the National Do Not Call Registry. Go to **http://www.donotcall.gov**.
3. **Be a more intelligent consumer.** You can increase your standard of living by one-third by spending wisely. A good place to start is to get a free copy of the federal government's *Consumer Information Catalog* at **http://www.pueblo.gsa.gov**.

Looking Ahead at Avon

Before a company can create a marketing mix, it must identify the target market for the product. Thus, Avon had to first identify the 16- to 24-year-old target market for Mark. To be successful a company must differentiate its product from the competition. If not, the product will be perceived as generic (all products are the same) and then can compete only on the basis of price. Mark, however, has been created specifically for 16- to 24-year-old girls and is highly differentiated from the competition. Avon must continue to use marketing research to identify the ever-changing desires of the target market.

Customer Satisfaction and Quality

We have stressed the importance of product/service quality throughout the text. But how does a company know if it is offering high quality and satisfaction to its customers? The answer is marketing research. Marketing research provides the feedback to managers through customer satisfaction surveys about how well the company is doing.

Conducting a survey is a rather easy task; however, making changes based upon the research can be a different story. It all begins with the commitment of top management. If top management makes customer satisfaction a top priority, then the chance of creating satisfied customers increases greatly. For example, Jean Gourdon, General Manager of the Montreal Novotel hotel, consistently earns the highest customer satisfaction ratings in the entire Accor system (over 3,800 Novotel, Sofitel, Red Roof Inns, Ibis, and Motel 6 hotels). Jean Gourdon is devoted to satisfying customers. Interestingly, he accomplishes this by making employees number one.

"I tell my customers that it is staff first, customers second, profit third," Gourdon says. "I tell them that the management of this hotel does not spend time with customers. I have six department heads who concentrate on the staff. That means being attentive to family life as well, since I believe the organization has a role [to play] in life, not just work." As a result, it is the employees' responsibility to not only clean rooms or change menus, but also to take care of problems and represent the hotel to guests. "These people are the ambassadors of the hotel," Gourdon says. "They are extremely motivated, not just because they don't have supervision, but because they are empowered. It gives their job another dimension and also leverage in the industry." According to Gourdon, customers say it works. "They tell me that when they are here they are treated like kings," he says.[8]

Summary of Learning Goals

1 What are the marketing concept and relationship building?

Marketing includes those business activities that are designed to satisfy consumer needs and wants through the exchange process. Marketing managers use the "right" principle—getting the right goods or services to the right people at the right place, time, and price, using the right promotional techniques. Today, many firms have adopted the marketing concept. The marketing concept involves identifying consumer needs and wants and then producing goods or services that will satisfy them while making a profit. Relationship marketing entails forging long-term relationships with customers, which can lead to repeat sales, reduced costs, and stable relationships.

2 How do managers create a marketing strategy?

A firm creates a marketing strategy by understanding the external environment, defining the target market, determining a competitive advantage, and developing a marketing mix. Environmental scanning enables companies to understand the external environment. The target market is the specific group of consumers toward which a firm directs its marketing efforts. A competitive advantage is a set of unique features of a company and its products that are perceived by the target market as significant and superior to those of the competition.

3

What is the marketing mix?

To carry out the marketing strategy, firms create a marketing mix—a blend of products, distribution systems, prices, and promotion. Marketing managers use this mix to satisfy target consumers. The mix can be applied to nonbusiness as well as business situations.

4

How do consumers and organizations make buying decisions?

Buyer behavior is what people and businesses do in buying and using goods and services. The consumer decision-making process consists of the following steps: recognizing a need, seeking information, evaluating alternatives, purchasing the product, judging the purchase outcome, and engaging in postpurchase behavior. A number of factors influence the process. Cultural, social, individual, and psychological factors have an impact on consumer decision making. The main differences between consumer and business markets are purchase volume, number of customers, location of buyers, direct distribution, and rational purchase decisions.

5

What are the five basic forms of market segmentation?

Success in marketing depends on understanding the target market. One technique used to identify a target market is market segmentation. The five basic forms of segmentation are demographic (population statistics), geographic (location), psychographic (personality or lifestyle), benefit (product features), and volume (amount purchased).

6

How is marketing research used in marketing decision making?

Much can be learned about consumers through marketing research, which involves collecting, recording, and analyzing data important in marketing goods and services and communicating the results to management. Marketing researchers may use primary data, which are gathered through door-to-door, mall-intercept, telephone, the Internet, and mail interviews. The Internet is becoming a quick, cheap, and efficient way to gather primary data. Secondary data are available from a variety of sources including government, trade, and commercial associations. Secondary data save time and money, but they may not meet researchers' needs. A huge amount of secondary data is available on the Internet. Both primary and secondary data give researchers a better idea of how the market will respond to the product. Thus, they reduce the risk of producing something the market doesn't want.

7

What are the trends in understanding the consumer?

BehaviorScan uses scanners and television meters to measure the impact of marketing on sales of specific products. BehaviorScan panels can also measure the impact of coupons, free samples, store displays, new packaging, and pricing. A second trend is retailers capitalizing on shopper loyalty cards. These enable managers to make customer shopping patterns. A third trend is the growing use of one-to-one marketing by using databases to better target the needs of customers and noncustomers.

Preparing for Tomorrow's Workplace

1. Can the marketing concept be applied effectively by a sole proprietorship, or is it more appropriate for larger businesses with more managers? Explain.

KEY TERMS

attitude 418
belief 418
benefit segmentation 422
buyer behavior 415
cognitive dissonance 429
competitive advantage 411
cost competitive advantage 411
culture 416
customer satisfaction 407
customer value 407
demographic segmentation 420
differential competitive advantage 412
distribution strategy 514
environmental scanning 410
exchange 406
experiment 424
extensive decision making 419
four Ps 413
geographic segmentation 421
ideal self-image 417
involvement 418
limited decision making 418
loyalty cards 427
market segmentation 420
marketing 406
marketing concept 406
marketing database 428
marketing mix 413
marketing research 423
niche competitive advantage 412
observation research 424
one-to-one marketing 428
opinion leader 416
perception 418
personality 417
pricing strategy 413
primary data 424
product strategy 413
production orientation 406
promotion strategy 414

2. Before starting your own business, you should develop a marketing strategy to guide your efforts. Choose one of the business ideas listed below and develop a marketing strategy for the business. Include the type of market research (both primary and secondary) you will perform and how you will define your target market.
   a. Crafts store to capitalize on the renewed interest in knitting and other crafts
   b. Online corporate-training company
   c. Ethnic restaurant near your campus
   d. Another business opportunity that interests you
3. "Market segmentation is the most important concept in marketing." Why do you think some marketing professionals make this statement? Give an example of each form of segmentation.
4. Pick a specific product that you use frequently, such as a cosmetic or toiletry item, a snack food, article of clothing, book, computer program, or music CD. What is the target market for this product, and does the company's marketing strategy reflect this? Now consider the broader category of your product. How can this product be changed and/or the marketing strategy adjusted to appeal to other market segments?
5. Can marketing research be carried out in the same manner all over the world? Why or why not?
6. Divide the class into two groups. Debate the following propositions: (1) business buyer behavior can be just as emotional as consumer buyer behavior; (2) consumer buyer behavior can be just as rational as business buyer behavior.

WORKING THE NET

1. You've been hired by a snack food manufacturer that is interested in adding popcorn snacks to its product line. First, however, the company asks you to find some secondary data on the current market for popcorn. Go to the Dogpile Search Engine (**http://www.dogpile.com**) and do a search for "popcorn consumption." Can you find how much popcorn is sold annually? The geographic locations with the highest popcorn sales? The time of the year when the most popcorn is sold? What are the limitations of doing research like this on the Internet?
2. You and a friend want to start a new magazine for people who work at home. Do a search of the U.S. Census database at **http://www.census.gov** to get information about the work-at-home market. Then visit the American Association of Home Based Business site, **http://www.aahbb.org**, to expand your research. Summarize your findings.
3. Visit the SRI Consulting site, **http://www.sric-bi.com** and click on the VALS Survey link. First read about VALS survey and how marketers can use it. Describe its value. Then take the survey to find out which psychographic segment you're in. Do you agree or disagree with the results? Why or why not?
4. How good was the marketing strategy you developed in Question 2 of Preparing for Tomorrow's Workplace? Using advice from the marketing section of *Entrepreneur* (**http://www.entrepreneur.com**) or other resources, revisit your marketing strategy for the business you selected and revise the plan accordingly. (*Entrepreneur*'s article "Write a Simple Marketing Plan" is a good place to start.) What did you overlook? (If you didn't do this exercise, pick one of the businesses and draft a marketing strategy using online resources to guide you.)
5. As the number of people online continues to grow, more of the Web surfers are also buying products online. What do researchers say about the characteristics of the online market? What market segments are appearing? Visit several sites to research this topic and then prepare a report on the demographics of

KEY TERMS

psychographic segmentation 422
real self-image 417
reference groups 416
relationship marketing 407
routine response behavior 418
scanner-based research 426
secondary data 424
selective exposure 418
self-concept 417
social marketing 415
socialization process 417
survey research 423
target market 410
volume segmentation 422

online markets and other key considerations for marketers. NUA Internet Surveys is a good place to start: **http://www.nua.ie/surveys/**. You'll find summaries of the latest research studies and can search for others by category. From there, you can link to the sites of market research companies. (Many research company sites require registration or subscriptions; however, you can check press releases for summaries of research findings.) Also search for "Internet marketing" or "online marketing" using search engines and business publication sites like *Business Week, Entrepreneur,* and *Inc.*

CREATIVE THINKING CASE

Icebergs Are Hot

Scott Lundquist has a rather unusual company. His firm harvests and sells icebergs. Listen to what he says about such an unusual occupation.

"I'm the only person in Alaska with a 'glacier ice harvesting' permit. You need one. They don't want you screwing around with baby seals. My ice costs $1.56 a pound. It isn't 7-Eleven ice. I'm trying to reach the 1 or 2 percent of the population who want premium ice. In my sales pitch, I stress that my ice is 8,000 to 10,000 years old, the remnants of the last Ice Age. Glacier ice is dense, so it melts slower, chilling your beverage without diluting it. That point works. Everything cold is cool now, so I'm sure ice is going to be the next fad. Right now, I've got six customers. Lufthansa buys it for cocktail parties. One day they called up the state and asked, 'Is there any way we can get some glacier ice? Some German clients want it for their drinks.' I sold them a 5,600-pound piece. I've also sold ice to Johnnie Walker for the same thing, and I just sent a company down in Santa Barbara [California] a 25-pound sample,—by FedEx. I'm also talking with Princess Cruises, trying to get 1,000-pound pieces on their cruise ships. They could put them right on their decks. It will last five days before melting. People could reach out and touch one. Being in front of a glacier is like being in God's country. Selling isn't all I do. I have to go get the ice, and that is the hard work. We'll board a 51-foot fishing boat and steam for Blackstone Glacier. The best ice is closest to the face where it's just dropped into the water. We only take ones that are clear and pure. We wrap a chain around it and hoist it into the boat. Then it's two hours back to Whittier, where we load the ice with a forklift, onto a flatbed truck or into my one-ton pickup before driving back to my freezer in Anchorage. You gotta get back fast. You hope for cold, cloudy days and you dread the sun. You lose some. You always lose some."[9]

CRITICAL THINKING QUESTIONS

1. Is Scott following the marketing concept?
2. Is he segmenting the market?
3. Who might be some other customers for his product?
4. Can you think of any way that Scott might expand his product line?

VIDEO CASE

Building Customer Relationships—One Kid at a Time

If giving consumers what they want is an excellent way to ensure loyalty and build long-term customer relationships, Fisher-Price has the right idea. Inviting its customers to participate in product design and development studies is an integral part of its marketing research programs. It is also one way Fisher-Price makes sure that products will achieve high levels of customer acceptance and success when they finally do reach the marketplace.

Founded in 1930, Fisher-Price is the most widely recognized brand of infant and preschool toys in the industry, and a trusted name in early childhood development. The company has earned a reputation for designing and producing high-quality toys that provide both developmental benefits and fun for children from birth to age 5.

Shelly Glick Gryfe, Director of Marketing Research at Fisher-Price, is proud of its Play Lab and Mom Talks, which are conducted in-house. Drawing from a list of several thousand volunteers, Gryfe and her team invite mothers with children who meet a specific demographic requirement to spend the day at their facility. In the Play Lab children do arts and crafts, read stories, and are encouraged to interact with a selection of toys. Some of the toys are still in development, while others, including those from competing companies, are already on the market.

These sessions are designed to provide the marketing research team with "directional information." Their designers, who observe the children from behind a one-way mirror, are looking for feedback on how they can make Fisher-Price products even better. It was this level of detailed observation that was responsible for the large feet on the company's preschool-age action figures called Rescue Heroes. The designers noted how frustrated the children became when a competitor's action figures kept toppling over.

Mothers are also an important part of the process. After viewing models, videos, and photo-boards, and observing children's interactions with the toys, they are consulted on such topics as ranking products in order of desirability and giving opinions on age appropriateness and product pricing. Gryfe says parents participate because they "want to have good toys coming out for their children."

There is no doubt that kids and moms know what they like. Mothers loved the "good guy" theme of the Rescue Heroes line when it was first introduced in 1998 and declared it a winner. CBS television agreed, creating a Rescue Heroes TV series for young viewers, which has helped boost ongoing demand for the products. At Fisher-Price giving the customer a voice means everyone wins.

CRITICAL THINKING QUESTIONS

1. How does Fisher-Price's marketing research strategy help build customer loyalty?
2. What other "spin-off" benefits does it produce for the company? For the consumer?
3. Is there a downside to having customers involved in the product development process? Explain.

SOURCE: Adapted from the video "Fisher-Price: The Pre-School Boy;" and information on Fisher-Price brands downloaded from the Mattel corporate Web site, http://www.mattel.com, April 22, 2003.

E-Commerce Case

Uncle Sam Wants YOU—to Play This Game

Did you like playing with toy soldiers? Are online shoot-'em-up games now your passion? You'll love America's Army: Operations, which you can download from **http://www.goarmy.com** or one of the sites at **http://www.americasarmy.com**. The "first-person shooter" role-playing game offers cutting-edge gaming technology. Up to 26 players compete against each other, experiencing the "the closest thing to being in the U.S. Army since playing with those little green plastic soldiers," according to the overview in the IGN.com guide to the game. "You will undergo strenuous training, tests of skill and knowledge, and dangerous assignments. By playing this game, you will need to work with your teammates to achieve your goals. You must have honor, loyalty, and . . . those other things!"

How much will this very popular game set you back? Not a penny. In addition to free downloads, over half a million game CDs were distributed through *Computer Gaming World* and other magazines.

Why free? America's Army: Operations was created by the U.S. Army as a recruiting tool.

The game was the brainchild of a West Point professor, Lt. Col. Casey Wardynski, who recognized that computer gaming was a perfect way to target a recruiting-age audience. He won the approval of Army officials, who were eager to find a better way to reach potential enlistees. Designers at the Naval Postgraduate School tackled the project. The team visited 20 Army bases, where they took digital notes of everything, right down to chipped paint, weapon noises and recoil, and bullet impact on different substances. The result was a game so realistic that recruits arriving at Fort Benning, Georgia, already know their way around the base.

Within just two months of the game's July 4, 2002, debut, 2.5 million users downloaded it. Today about half a million people play each weekend, and about 28 percent of the traffic at GoArmy.com, the Army's redesigned Web site, originates at a game hosting site.

America's Army: Operations is just one component of the Army's new recruiting campaign, "An Army of One," which replaced "Be All That You Can Be." Working with a new ad agency, Leo Burnett, the Army placed the Web at the center of its recruiting efforts. GoArmy.com is action packed, with loud music and video clips profiling recruits and soldiers. A series of reality-television online episodes follows six recruits as they go through basic training. On a typical day, 750 people take part in chat rooms hosted by online recruiters, a very successful feature: About 10 percent of chat room visitors enlist.

Using the Web and videogames, along with support from other media, the new campaign has increased leads from applicants by 166 percent. In addition, these applicants have better qualifications. Online ads at sites like MTV.com and Real.com helped bring over 11 million visitors to GoArmy in 2002, up 37 percent. "We are going to where the audience is," says Chris Miller, co-CEO of Chemistri, the interactive arm of Leo Burnett. "And this audience is on the Web all the time."

CRITICAL THINKING QUESTIONS

1. Analyze the Army's new marketing strategy and discuss its effectiveness. Is the Army following the marketing concept? Explain your answer.
2. What types of marketing research would be involved in developing the new "An Army of One" campaign?
3. Visit the GoArmy.com web site (**http://www.goarmy.com**) and explore its many features. Is it an effective marketing tool for the Army? How can it improve the site?
4. Optional: If you are a gamer, download and play America's Army: Operations. Evaluate its benefits as a marketing tool to encourage young people to enlist. Are there any downsides to this method of generating interst?

SOURCES: "America's Army," IGN.com, downloaded from http://guides.ign.com/guides/482289/index.html, April 24, 2003; Steve Butts, "The Army's Making a Game of Its Own Now," IGN.com, May 30, 2002, downloaded from http://www.ign.com; Trent Gegax, "Full Metal Joystick," *Newsweek,* October 14, 2002, pp. 38R, 38T; and Thomas Mucha, "Operation Sign 'Em Up," *Business 2.0,* April 2003, downloaded from http://www.business2.com.

HOT LINKS ADDRESS BOOK

What's new at Avon since it launched its Mark. line? Browse the company's Web site at
http://www.avoncompany.com
to find out how the teen products are doing.

What's the latest in customer loyalty programs? Do a search for "loyalty programs" at SearchCRM.com,
http://searchcrm.techtarget.com
to discover the answer.

Considering a career in marketing? At the American Marketing Association site,
http://www.marketingpower.com
you can read articles about different marketing topics of interest and visit the Career Center.

What's different about business-to-business marketing? Find out at the Business Marketing Association site,
http://www.marketing.org

How satisfied are American consumers today? The American Customer Satisfaction Index (ACSI) is an economic indicator based on modeling of customer evaluations. Find the latest survey results at
http://www.theacsi.org

A good place to learn more about marketing research is Quirks Marketing research review,
http://www.quirks.com
In addition to articles, you can link to major marketing research firms.

For a quick demographic overview of your home state check out the Quick Facts page of the U.S. Census Bureau,
http://quickfacts.census.gov/qfd/
after which you can click thrugh to the main Census site,
http://www.census.gov
to access a vast array of census data.

Chapter 14

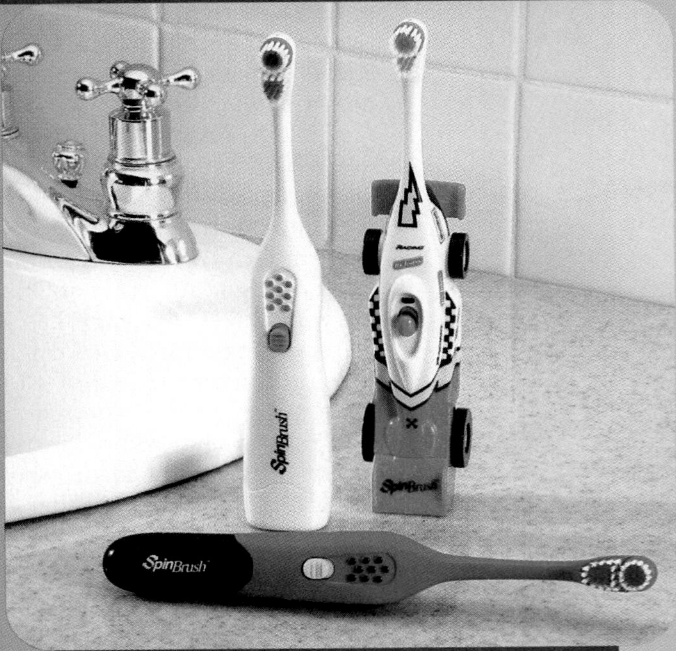

© AP / WIDE WORLD PHOTOS

Developing Quality Products at the Right Price

learning goals

1 What is a product, and how is it classified?
2 How does branding distinguish a product from its competitors?
3 What are the functions of packaging?
4 How do organizations create new products?
5 What are the stages of the product life cycle?
6 What is the role of pricing in marketing?
7 How are product prices determined?
8 What strategies are used for pricing products?
9 What trends are occurring in products and pricing?

P&G's Positive Spin on Sales

The only time he loses sleep, says A.G. Lafley, is when he thinks a competitor might beat him to a hot new product. And Lafley is sleeping pretty well these days. The soft-spoken, silver-thatched CEO is leading consumer products giant Procter & Gamble (**http://www.pg.com**) from one hit to another. Crest's battery-powered SpinBrush for dental care and its Whitestrips for tooth brightening have helped Crest global sales grow 50 percent in the past two years—a surge unheard of for such a big, mature brand. That kind of innovation has sent P&G's profits into double-digit growth.

With the SpinBrush, P&G showed that it no longer suffers from the Not-Invented-Here syndrome. Making a bet on a small Cleveland, Ohio, start-up called Dr. John's and its invention of an ingenious battery-powered toothbrush that could be sold at a profit for roughly $6, Crest bought the firm at the beginning of last year and, by applying its marketing and distribution muscle, has turned it into a $200 million category killer. Lafley hopes it can be a model for the future. "I'd love to see a third to half of 'discovery' come from outside," he says. "I really want the doors open."

Davin Yates, team leader on the new toothbrush, never imagined how successful the Crest SpinBrush would be. While most electric brushes cost more than $50, SpinBrush works on batteries and sells for just $5. Since that focus group in October, 2000, it has become the nation's best-selling toothbrush, manual or electric. In P&G's last fiscal year, it posted more than $200 million in global sales, helping Crest become the consumer product maker's 12th billion-dollar brand. It has also helped Crest reclaim the title as No. 1 oral-care brand in the United States, a position it lost to Colgate-Palmolive's Colgate brand in 1998. "It's hard for P&G's business models to conceive of a business growing as quickly as SpinBrush," Yates says.

Perhaps the biggest change for P&G was in SpinBrush's pricing. P&G usually prices its goods at a premium, based on the cost of technology. But competitors now follow new products more quickly, eroding P&G's pricing power. With SpinBrush, P&G reversed its usual thinking. It started with an aggressive price, then found a way to make a profit. If P&G had conceived SpinBrush, admits Yates, "my gut tells me we would not have priced it where we did."

That's just the opportunity John Osher and his three colleagues saw when they had the SpinBrush brainstorm back in 1998. Osher, 55, had spent most of his career inventing things and selling them to big companies. His latest creation had been the Spin Pop, a lollipop attached to a battery-powered plastic handle, in which the candy spun at the press of a button. He had teamed up on the Spin Pop with John R. Nottingham and John W. Spirk, the principals of a Cleveland industrial-design firm, and their in-house patent lawyer, Lawrence A. Blaustein. The Spin Pop had recently sold to Hasbro for millions and the men were looking for another way to utilize the technology.

They can't remember who came up with the concept, but they know it came from their group walks through the aisles of their local Wal-Mart, where they went for inspiration. They saw that electric toothbrushes, from Sonicare to Interplak, cost more than $50 and for that reason held a fraction of the overall toothbrush market. They reasoned: Why not create a $5 electric brush using the Spin Pop technology? At just $1 more than the most expensive manual brushes, they figured many consumers would trade up. They spent 18 months designing and sourcing a high-quality brush that wouldn't cost more than $5, batteries included. "If it had cost $7.99, we wouldn't have gone forward," Osher says.[1]

Critical Thinking Questions

1. How are new products usually developed?
2. Where is the SpinBrush in the product life cycle?
3. What price strategy is being used for the SpinBrush?

Principles of Developing Products and Pricing

The creation of a marketing mix normally begins with the first of the four Ps, product. Only when there is something to sell can marketers create a promotional theme, set a price, and establish a distribution channel (place). Organizations prepare for long-term success by creating and packaging products that add value and pricing them to meet the organization's financial objectives. In addition, organizations respond to changing customer needs by creating new products. This chapter will examine products, brands, and the importance of packaging. We discuss how new products are created and how they go through periods of sales growth and then decline. Next, you will discover how managers set prices to reach pricing goals. Alternative pricing strategies used to reach specific target markets are then discussed. We conclude with a look at trends in products and pricing.

What Is a Product?

1 learning goal

product
In marketing, any good or service, along with its perceived attributes and benefits, that creates value for the customer.

In marketing, a **product** is any good or service, along with its perceived attributes and benefits, that creates value for the customer. Attributes can be tangible or intangible. Among the tangible attributes are packaging and warranties as illustrated in Exhibit 14.1. Intangible attributes are symbolic, such as brand image. People make decisions about which products to buy after considering both tangible and intangible attributes of a product. For example, when you buy a pair of jeans, you consider price, brand, store image, and style before you buy. These factors are all part of the marketing mix.

Products are often a blend of goods and services as shown in Exhibit 14.2. For example, Honda Accord (a good) would have less value without Honda's maintenance agreement (a service). Although Burger King sells such goods as sandwiches and french fries, customers expect quality service as well, including quick food

Exhibit 14.1 Tangible and Intangible Attributes of a Product Create Value for the Buyer

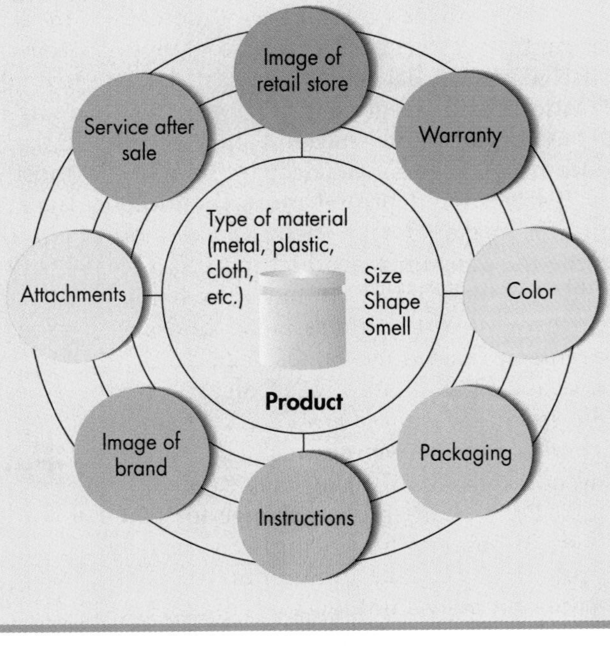

Exhibit 14.2 | Products Are Typically a Blend of Goods and Services

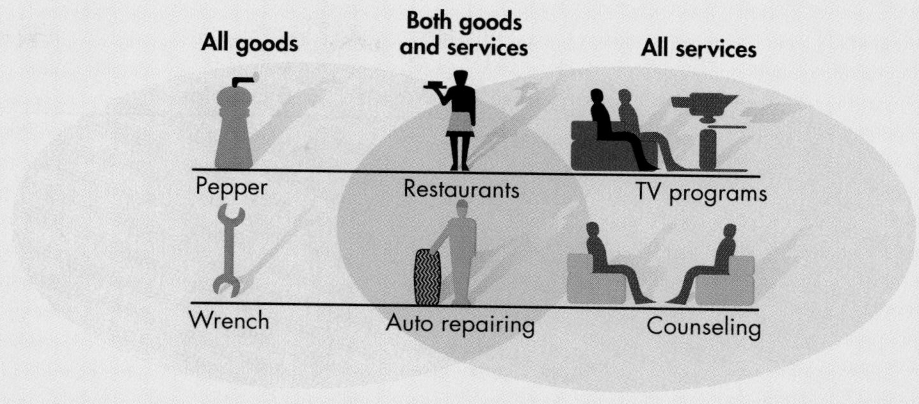

preparation and cleanliness. When developing a product, an organization must consider how the combination of goods and services will provide value to the customer.

Classifying Consumer Products

Because most things sold are a blend of goods and services, the term *product* can be used to refer to both. After all, consumers are really buying packages of benefits that deliver value. The person who buys a plane ride on Continental Airlines is looking for a quick way to get from one city to another (the benefit). Providing this benefit requires goods (a plane, food) and services (ticketing, maintenance, piloting).

Marketers must know how consumers view the types of products their companies sell so that they can design the marketing mix to appeal to the selected target market. To help them define target markets, marketers have devised product categories. Products that are bought by the end user are called *consumer products.* They include electric razors, sandwiches, cars, stereos, magazines, and houses. Consumer products that get used up, such as Breck hair mousse and Lay's potato chips, are called *consumer nondurables.* Those that last for a long time, such as Whirlpool washing machines and computers, are *consumer durables.*

Another way to classify consumer products is by the amount of effort consumers are willing to make to acquire them. The four major categories of consumer products are unsought products, convenience products, shopping products, and specialty products, as summarized in Exhibit 14.3.

unsought products
Products that either are unknown to the potential buyer or are known but the buyer does not actively seek them.

Unsought products are products unknown to the potential buyer or known products that the buyer does not actively seek. New products fall into this category until advertising and distribution increase consumer awareness of them. Some goods are always marketed as unsought items, especially products we do not like to think about or care to spend money on. Life insurance, cemetery plots, medical services, and similar items require aggressive personal selling and highly persuasive advertising. Salespeople actively seek leads to potential buyers. Because consumers usually do not seek out this type of product, the company must go directly to them through a salesperson, direct mail, telemarketing, or direct-response advertising.

convenience products
Relatively inexpensive items that require little shopping effort and are purchased routinely without planning.

Convenience products are relatively inexpensive items that require little shopping effort. Soft drinks, candy bars, milk, bread, and small hardware items are examples. We buy them routinely without much planning. This does not mean that such products are unimportant or obscure. Many, in fact, are well known by their brand names—such as Pepsi-Cola, Pepperidge Farm breads, Domino's pizza, Sure deodorant, and UPS shipping.

Exhibit 14.3 Classification of Consumer Products by the Effort Expended to Buy Them

Consumer Product	Examples	Degree of Effort Expended by Consumer
Unsought products	Life insurance Burial plots New products	No effort
Convenience products	Soft drinks Bread Milk Coffee	Very little or minimum effort
Shopping products	Automobiles Homes Vacations	Considerable effort
Specialty products	Expensive jewelry Gourmet dinners Limited-production automobiles	Maximum effort

shopping products
Items that are bought after considerable planning, including brand-to-brand and store-to-store comparisons of price, suitability, and style.

specialty products
Items for which consumers search long and hard and for which they refuse to accept substitutes.

In contrast to convenience products, **shopping products** are bought only after a brand-to-brand and store-to-store comparison of price, suitability, and style. Examples are furniture, automobiles, a vacation in Europe, and some items of clothing. Convenience products are bought with little planning, but shopping products may be chosen months or even years before their actual purchase.

Specialty products are products for which consumers search long and hard and for which they refuse to accept substitutes. Expensive jewelry, designer clothing, state-of-the-art stereo equipment, limited-production automobiles, and gourmet dinners fall into this category. Because consumers are willing to spend much time and effort to find specialty products, distribution is often limited to one or two sellers in a given region, such as Neiman-Marcus, Gucci, or the Porsche dealer.

Classifying Business Products

capital products
Large, expensive items with a long life span that are purchased by businesses for use in making other products or providing a service.

expense items
Items, purchased by businesses, that are smaller and less expensive than capital products and usually have a life span of less than one year.

Products bought by businesses or institutions for use in making other products or in providing services are called *business* or *industrial products.* They are classified as either capital products or expense items. **Capital products** are usually large, expensive items with a long life span. Examples are buildings, large machines, and airplanes. **Expense items** are typically smaller, less expensive items that usually have a life span of less than a year. Examples are printer ribbons and paper. Industrial products are sometimes further classified in the following categories:

1. *Installations.* These are large, expensive capital items that determine the nature, scope, and efficiency of a company. Capital products like General Motors' Saturn assembly plant in Tennessee represent a big commitment against future earnings and profitability. Buying an installation requires longer negotiations, more planning, and the judgments of more people than buying any other type of product.
2. *Accessories.* Accessories do not have the same long-run impact on the firm as installations, and they are less expensive and more standardized. But they are still capital products. Minolta copy machines, IBM personal computers (PCs), and smaller machines such as Black & Decker table drills and saws are typical

Component parts need to be assembled to create the finished product for the consumer. Ground beef, hamburger buns, ketchup, mustard, and pickles are all component parts for Burger King hamburgers.

© ALYX KELLINGTON / INDEX STOCK IMAGERY

accessories. Marketers of accessories often rely on well-known brand names and extensive advertising as well as personal selling.

3. *Component parts and materials.* These are expense items that are built into the end product. Some component parts are custom-made, such as a drive shaft for an automobile, a case for a computer, or a special pigment for painting U.S. Navy harbor buoys; others are standardized for sale to many industrial users. Intel's pentium chip for PCs and cement for the construction trade are examples of standardized component parts and materials.
4. *Raw materials.* Raw materials are expense items that have undergone little or no processing and are used to create a final product. Examples include lumber, copper, and zinc.
5. *Supplies.* Supplies do not become part of the final product. They are bought routinely and in fairly large quantities. Supply items run the gamut from pencils and paper to paint and machine oil. They have little impact on the firm's long-run profits. Bic pens, Champion copier paper, and Pennzoil machine oil are typical supply items.
6. *Services.* These are expense items used to plan or support company operations; for example, janitorial cleaning and management consulting.

concept check

What is a product?

What are the classes of consumer goods?

Explain how business products are classified

Building Brand Equity and Master Brands

2 learning goal

brand
A company's product identifier that distinguishes the company's products from those of its competitors.

trademark
The legally exclusive design, name, or other identifying mark associated with a company's brand.

Most industrial and consumer products have a brand name. If everything came in a plain brown wrapper, life would be less colorful and competition would decrease. Companies would have less incentive to put out better products because consumers would be unable to tell one company's products from those of another.

The product identifier for a company is its **brand.** Brands appear in the form of words, names, symbols, or designs. They are used to distinguish a company's products from those of its competitors. Examples of well-known brands are Kleenex tissues, Jeep automobiles, and IBM computers. A **trademark** is the legally exclusive design, name, or other identifying mark associated with a company's brand. No other company can use that same trademark.

Benefits of Branding

Branding has three main purposes: product identification, repeat sales, and new-product sales. The most important purpose is *product identification.* Branding allows

The Mini Cooper reflects the characteristics of an effective brand name. It's short, distinctive, easy to remember, and describes the product's benefits.

marketers to distinguish their products from all others. Exhibit 14.4 identifies the characteristics of an effective brand name. Many brand names are familiar to consumers and indicate quality. The term **brand equity** refers to the value of company and brand names. A brand that has high awareness, perceived quality, and brand loyalty among customers has high brand equity. Brand equity is more than awareness of a brand—it is the personality, soul, and emotion associated with the brand. Think of the feelings you have when you see the brand name Harley-Davidson, Nike, or even Microsoft. A brand with strong brand equity is a valuable asset. Some brands such as Coke, Kodak, Marlboro, and Chevrolet are worth hundreds of millions of dollars.

brand equity
The value of company and brand names.

A brand so dominant in consumers' minds that they think of it immediately when a product category, use, attribute, or customer benefit is mentioned is a **master brand.** Scotch tape and Kleenex tissues are examples of master brands. Exhibit 14.5 lists some of America's master brands in several product categories.

master brand
A brand so dominant that consumers think of it immediately when a product category, use, attribute, or customer benefit is mentioned.

U.S. master brands command substantial premiums in many places around the world. Band-Aids command a 500 percent premium in China.

Building Repeat Sales with Brand Loyalty

A consumer who tries one or more brands may decide to buy a certain brand regularly. The preference for a particular brand is **brand loyalty.** It lets consumers buy with less time, thought, and risk. Brand loyalty ensures future sales for the firm. It

brand loyalty
A consumer's preference for a particular brand.

Exhibit 14.4 Characteristics of Effective Brand Names

- Easy to pronounce (by both domestic and foreign buyers)
- Easy to recognize
- Easy to remember
- Short
- Distinctive, unique
- Describes the product
- Describes the product's use
- Describes the product's benefits
- Has a positive connotation
- Reinforces the desired product image
- Is legally protectable in home and foreign markets of interest

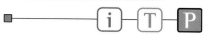

Exhibit 14.5 | America's Master Brands

Product Category	Master Brand
Adhesive bandages	Band-Aid
Antacids	Alka-Seltzer
Baking soda	Arm & Hammer
Cellophane tape	Scotch Tape
Fast food	McDonald's
Gelatin	Jell-O
Rum	Bacardi
Salt	Morton
Soft drinks	Coca-Cola
Soup	Campbell's

can also help protect a firm's share of the market, discourage new competitors, and thus prolong the brand's life. Brand loyalty even allows companies to raise prices. Quaker Oats Co., maker of Cap'n Crunch, Life, and Quaker oatmeal, recently raised its prices 3.8 percent. Analysts said that Quaker could do this, even though other cereal makers didn't raise prices, because of the strong consumer loyalty to Quaker products.[2]

What makes people loyal to a brand? Though pricing, promotion, and product quality are important, customer interaction with the company may be most important in service businesses. A recent study found that consumers have little brand loyalty when shopping for themselves and their children, with fewer than a quarter having favorite brands in most grocery categories and just 27 percent being brand loyal for baby food and baby items. But 53 percent stick to one brand of pet food. Nearly four in five consumers (78 percent) switch brands for price, 66 percent for product quality, 40 percent lured by promotional offers or coupons, and 33 percent just because of the availability of products or brands. Weekly store sale flyers generate the most consumer awareness among various promotions studies and are responsible for the most sales. Although 86 percent of grocery shoppers prepare a list, just 28 percent adhere to it after reaching the store.[3]

Brand loyalty typically builds over time. The first level is *brand recognition*, in which consumers recall having seen or heard of the brand. Companies often spend millions on promotion for new products to achieve brand recognition. A product may then achieve *brand preference* where a consumer prefers a certain brand like the SpinBrush but may buy an alternative due to lack of availability of the SpinBrush, price, or effective promotion by a competing product. The ultimate for any product manager is *brand insistence* where consumers will buy only that brand. Lexus, for example, has reached this level among some car purchasers.

Facilitating New-Product Sales

The third main purpose of branding is to facilitate *new-product sales*. Let's assume that your class forms a company to market frozen tarts and pies under the name "University Frozen Desserts." Now, assume that Pepperidge Farm develops a new line of identical frozen tarts and pies. Which ones will consumers try? The Pepperidge Farm products, without doubt. Pepperidge Farm is known for its quality frozen bakery products. Consumers assume that its new tarts and pies will be of high quality and are therefore willing to give them a try. The well-known Pepperidge Farm brand is facilitating new-product introduction.

Types of Brands

manufacturer brands
Brands that are owned by national or regional manufacturers and widely distributed; also called *national brands.*

Brands owned by national or regional manufacturers and widely distributed are **manufacturer brands.** (These brands are sometimes called national brands, but since some of the brands are not owned by nationwide or international manufacturers, *manufacturer brands* is a more accurate term.) A few well-known manufacturer brands are Ford, Maytag, Nike, and Sony.

Manufacturer brands can bring new customers and new prestige to small retailers. For instance, a small bicycle repair shop in a Midwestern college town got the franchise to sell and repair Trek bicycles. The shop's profits grew quickly, and it became one of the most successful retail businesses in the university area. Because manufacturer brands are widely promoted, sales are often high. Also, most manufacturers of these brands offer frequent deliveries to their retailers. Thus, retailers can carry less stock and have less money tied up in inventory.

dealer brands
Brands that are owned by the wholesaler or retailer rather than the name of the manufacturer.

Brands that are owned by the wholesaler or retailer, rather than that of the manufacturer, are **dealer brands.** Sears has several well-known dealer (or private) brands, including Craftsman, Diehard, and Kenmore. The Independent Grocers Association (IGA), a large wholesale grocery organization, uses the brand name Shurfine on its goods. Dealer brands tie consumers to particular wholesalers or retailers. If you want a Kenmore washing machine, you must go to Sears.

Although profit margins are usually higher on dealer brands than on manufacturer brands, dealers must still stimulate demand for their products. Sears's promotion of its products has made the company one of the largest advertisers in the United States. But promotion costs can cut heavily into profit margins. And if a dealer-brand item is of poor quality, the dealer must assume responsibility for it. Sellers of manufacturer brands can refer a disgruntled customer to the manufacturer.

generic products
Products that carry no brand name, come in plain containers, and sell for much less than brand-name products.

Many consumers don't want to pay the costs of manufacturer or dealer brands. One popular way to save money is to buy **generic products.** These products carry no brand name, come in plain containers, and sell for much less than brand-name products. They are typically sold in black-and-white packages with such simple labels as "liquid bleach" or "spaghetti." Generic products are sold by 85 percent of U.S. supermarkets. Sometimes manufacturers simply stop the production line and substitute a generic package for a brand package, though the product is exactly the same. The most popular generic products are garbage bags, jelly, paper towels, coffee cream substitutes, cigarettes, and paper napkins.

concept check

Define the terms brand *and* trademark.

Explain the differences between manufacturer brands and dealer brands.

What is a generic product?

The Importance of Packaging in a Self-Service Economy

3 learning goal

Just as a brand gives a product identity, its packaging also distinguishes it from competitors' products and increases its customer value. When you go to the store and reach for a bottle of dishwashing detergent, the package is the last chance a manufacturer has to convince you to buy its brand over a competitor's. A good package may cause you to reach for Joy rather than Palmolive.

The Functions of a Package

A basic function of packaging is to protect the product from breaking or spoiling and thus extend its life. A package should be easy to ship, store, and stack on a shelf and convenient for the consumer to buy. Many new packaging methods have been developed recently. Aseptic packages keep foods fresh for months

International Delight introduced a sleek, new package that offers consumers the convenience of opening, pouring, and closing using one hand. The flip-top spout increases the customer value.

without refrigeration. Examples are Borden's "'sipp' packs" for juices, the Brik Pak for milk, and Hunt's/Del Monte's aseptic boxes for tomato sauce. Some package developers are creating "microatmospheres," which allow meat to stay fresh in the refrigerator for weeks.

A second basic function of packaging is to help promote the product by providing clear brand identification and information about the product's features. For example, Ralston Purina Co.'s Dog Chow brand, the leading dog food, was losing market share. The company decided that the pictures of dog breeds on the package were too old-fashioned and rural. With a new package featuring a photo of a dog and a child, sales have increased.

Labeling

An integral part of any package is its label. Labeling generally takes one of two forms: persuasive or informational. **Persuasive labeling** focuses on a promotional theme or logo, and consumer information is secondary. Cheetos Crunchy, for example, features Chester Cheetah throwing a switch from "cheesy" to "dangerously cheesy." As Frito-Lay notes, "it's the taste against which all other crunchy cheese-flavored snacks are measured by." Note that the standard promotional claims—such as "new," "improved," and "super"—are no longer very persuasive. Consumers have been saturated with "newness" and thus discount these claims.

Informational labeling, in contrast, is designed to help consumers make proper product selections and lower their cognitive dissonance after the purchase. Sears attaches a "label of confidence" to all its floor coverings. This label gives such product information as durability, color, features, cleanability, care instructions, and construction standards. Most major furniture manufacturers affix labels to their wares that explain the products' construction features, such as type of frame, number of coils, and fabric characteristics. The Nutritional

persuasive labeling
A type of product label that reinforces or repeats a promotional theme or logo.

informational labeling
A type of product label that provides product information to aid consumers in making product selections and minimize cognitive dissonance after the purchase.

Informational labeling may give consumers easy-to-understand instructions, explain how to use a product, or warn about potential misuse. The labels on vitamins, for example, include a list of ingredients, supplement facts, directions for use, and consumer warnings.

Exhibit 14.6 Understanding the Global Labeling for a Computer Monitor

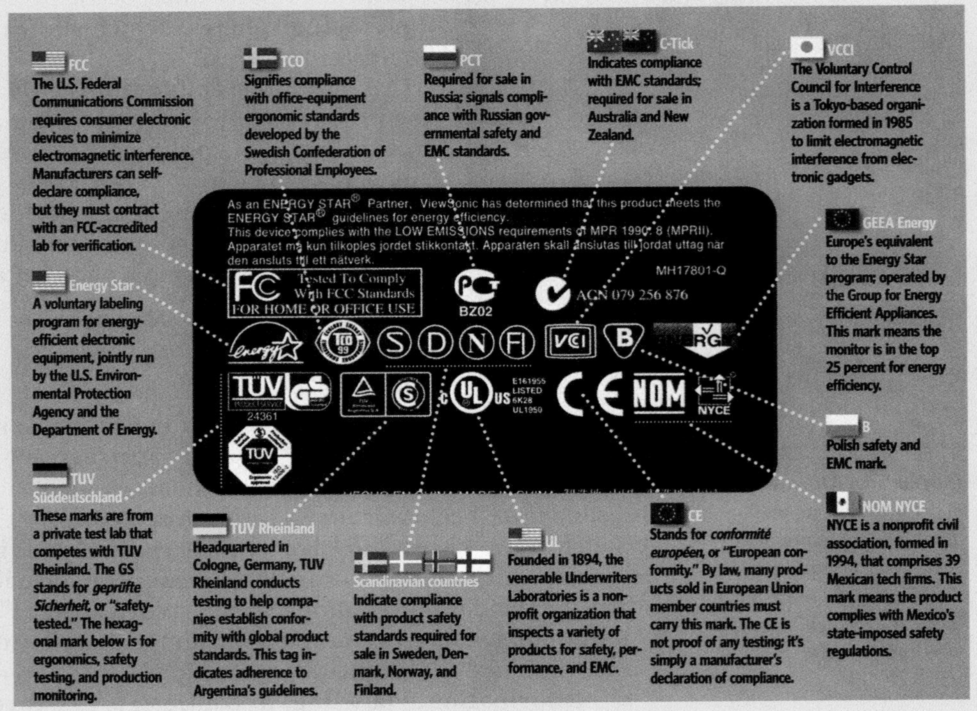

SOURCE: Reprinted with permission of ViewSonic Corporation.

The FDA requires that food packages include nutritional information. SlimFast, a replacement drink, includes daily values for vitamins, minerals, fat and protein on its label.

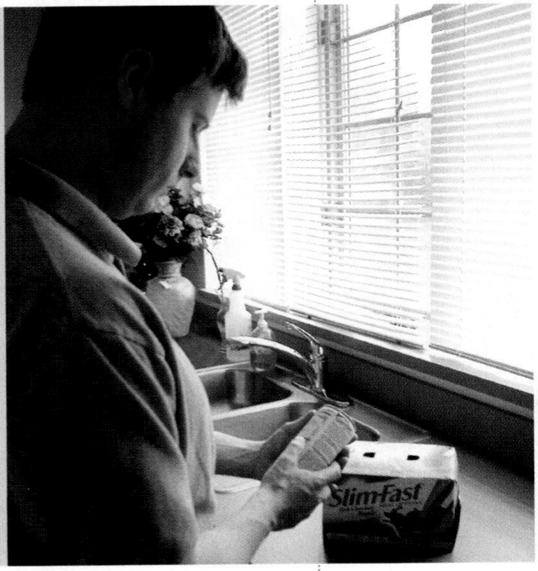

© TERRI L. MILLER / E-VISUAL COMMUNICATIONS, INC.

Labeling and Education Act of 1990 mandated detailed nutritional information on most food packages and standards for health claims on food packaging. An important outcome of this legislation is guidelines from the Food and Drug Administration for using terms like *low fat, light, reduced cholesterol, low sodium, low calorie*, and *fresh*.

Products sold in the global marketplace often have complex labels. Exhibit 14.6 decodes the label and the back of a computer monitor.

Adding Value through Warranties

A **warranty** guarantees the quality of a good or service. An **implied warranty** is an unwritten guarantee that the product is fit for the purpose for which it was sold. All sales have an implied warranty under the Uniform Commercial Code (a law that applies to commercial dealings in most states). An **express warranty** is made in writing. Express warranties range from simple statements, such as "100 percent cotton" (a guarantee of raw materials) and "complete satisfaction guaranteed" (a statement of performance), to extensive documentation that accompanies a product.

In 1975, Congress passed the Magnuson-Moss Warranty–Federal Trade Commission Improvement Act to help consumers understand warranties and to help them get action from manufacturers and dealers. A **full warranty** means the manufacturer must meet certain minimum standards, including repair of any defects "within a reasonable time and without charge" and replacement of the merchandise or a full refund if the product does not work "after a reasonable number of attempts" at repair. Under the law, any warranty that does not live up to this tough standard must be "conspicuously" promoted as a limited warranty.

concept check

What are the functions of a package?

Explain the differences between an implied warranty, an express warranty, and a full warranty.

CREATING PRODUCTS THAT DELIVER VALUE

4 learning goal

New products pump life into company sales, enabling the firm not only to survive but also to grow. Companies like Allegheny Ludlum (steel), Dow (chemicals), Hewlett-Packard (computers), Campbell Soup (foods), and Stryker (medical products) get most of their profits from new products. Companies that lead their industries in profitability and sales growth get 49 percent of their revenues from products developed within the last five years.

Marketers have several different terms for new products, depending on how the product fits into a company's existing product line. When a firm introduces a product that has a new brand name and is in a product category new to the organization, it is classified as a new product.

A new flavor, size, or model using an existing brand name in an existing category is called a **line extension.** Diet Cherry Coke and caffeine-free Coke are line extensions. The strategy of expanding the line by adding new models has enabled companies like Seiko (watches), Kraft (cheeses), Oscar Mayer (lunch meats), and Sony (consumer electronics) to tie up a large amount of shelf space and brand recognition in a product category.

warranty
A guarantee of the quality of a good or service.

implied warranty
An unwritten guarantee that a product is fit for the purpose for which it is sold.

express warranty
A written guarantee about a product, such as that it contains certain materials, will perform a certain way, or is otherwise fit for the purpose for which it was sold.

Organizing the New-Product Effort

In large organizations, such as Procter & Gamble and Kraft General Foods, new-product departments are responsible for generating new products. The department typically includes people from production, finance, marketing, and engineering. In smaller firms, committees perform the same functions as a new-product department.

For major new-product development tasks, companies sometimes form venture teams. IBM, for example, formed a venture group to create the first PC. Like a new-product department, a venture team includes members from most departments of the company. The idea, however, is to isolate the team members from the organization's day-to-day activities so that they can think and be creative. IBM is headquartered in New York, but the PC venture team was located in Florida.

Line extensions in room deodorizers include Glade's new 3-in-1 Pillar Candles. These new scents by Glade help increase its shelf space and brand recognition.

How New Products Are Developed

Developing new products is both costly and risky. New-product failure rates for household and grocery products approach 80 percent.[4] The overall failure rate is approximately 60 percent. Industrial goods failure rates tend to be lower than those for consumer goods. To increase their chances for success, most firms use the following product development process, which is also summarized in Exhibit 14.7.

1. *Set new-product goals.* New-product goals are usually stated as financial objectives. For example, a company may want to recover its investment in three years or less. Or it may want

Exhibit 14.7 Steps to Develop New Products That Satisfy Customers

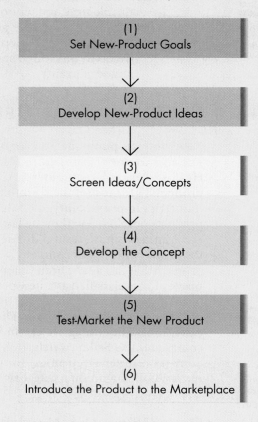

(1) Set New-Product Goals

↓

(2) Develop New-Product Ideas

↓

(3) Screen Ideas/Concepts

↓

(4) Develop the Concept

↓

(5) Test-Market the New Product

↓

(6) Introduce the Product to the Marketplace

full warranty
The manufacturer's guarantee to meet certain minimum standards, including repair or replacement of the product or refunding the customer if the product does not work.

line extension
A new flavor, size, or model using an existing brand name in an existing category.

New product ideas help solve customer problems. Chrysler developed the Voyager minivan with sliding passenger doors for families who want to load and unload from either side of the van.

to earn at least a 15 percent return on the investment. Nonfinancial goals may include using existing equipment or facilities.

2. *Develop new-product ideas.* Smaller firms usually depend on employees, customers, investors, and distributors for new ideas. Larger companies use these sources and more structured marketing research techniques, such as focus groups and brainstorming. A **focus group** consists of 8 to 12 participants led by a moderator in an in-depth discussion on one particular topic or concept. The goal of focus group research is to learn and understand what people have to say and why. The emphasis is on getting people talking at length and in detail about the subject at hand. The intent is to find out how they feel about a product, concept, idea, or organization, how it fits into their lives, and their emotional involvement with it. Focus groups often generate excellent product ideas. A few examples of focus group–influenced products are the interior design of the Toyota Rav4, Stick-Up room deodorizers, Swiffer WetJet, and Wendy's Salad Sensations. In the industrial market, machine tools, keyboard designs, aircraft interiors, and backhoe accessories evolved from focus groups.

   Brainstorming is also used to generate new-product ideas. With **brainstorming,** the members of a group think of as many ways to vary a product or solve a problem as possible. Criticism is avoided, no matter how ridiculous an idea seems at the time. The emphasis is on sheer numbers of ideas. Evaluation of these ideas is postponed to later steps of development.

3. *Screen ideas and concepts.* As ideas emerge, they are checked against the firm's new-product goals and its long-range strategies. Many product concepts are rejected because they don't fit well with existing products, needed technology is not available, the company doesn't have enough resources, or the sales potential is low.

4. *Develop the concept.* Developing the new-product concept involves creating a prototype of the product, testing the prototype, and building the marketing strategy. The type and amount of product testing vary, depending on such factors as the company's experience with similar products, how easy it is to make the item, and how easy it will be for consumers to use it. Suppose that Seven Seas is developing a new salad dressing flavor. The company already has a lot

focus group
A group of 8 to 12 participants led by a moderator in an in-depth discussion on one particular topic or concept.

brainstorming
A method of generating ideas in which group members suggest as many possibilities as they can without criticizing or evaluating any of the suggestions.

© AP / WIDE WORLD PHOTOS

The HUMMER H2 is designed for serious off-roading. With 35-inch tires and steep approach angles, the H2 can cross streams and power through two-foot-deep snow. This new product was developed for consumers who want both interior comfort and off-road capabilities.

of experience in this area, so the new dressing will go directly into advanced taste tests and perhaps home-use tests. To develop a new line of soft drinks, however, Seven Seas would most likely do a great deal of testing. It would study many aspects of the new product before actually making it.

While the product is tested, the marketing strategy is refined. Channels of distribution are selected, pricing policies are developed and tested, the target market is further defined, and demand for the product is estimated. Management also continually updates the profit plan.

As the marketing strategy and prototype tests mature, a communication strategy is developed. A logo and package wording are created. As part of the communication strategy, promotion themes are developed, and the product is introduced to the sales force.

test-marketing
The process of testing a new product among potential users.

5. *Test-market the new product.* **Test-marketing** is testing the product among potential users. It allows management to evaluate various strategies and to see how well the parts of the marketing mix fit together. Few new-product concepts reach this stage. For those that pass this stage, the firm must decide whether to introduce the product on a regional or national basis.

   Companies that don't test-market their products run a strong risk of product failure. In essence, test-marketing is the "acid test" of new-product development. The product is put into the marketplace and then the manufacturer can see how it performs against the competition. An example of a hot idea that wasn't test-marketed is discussed in the "Focusing on Small Business" box.

6. *Introduce the product.* A product that passes test-marketing is ready for market introduction, called *rollout,* which requires a lot of logistical coordination. Various divisions of the company must be encouraged to give the new item the attention it deserves. Packaging and labeling in a different language may be required. Sales training sessions must be scheduled, spare parts inventoried, service personnel trained, advertising and promotion campaigns readied, and wholesalers and re-

FOCUSING ON SMALL BUSINESS

The CueCat Didn't Have Nine Lives

It was the peak of the Internet bubble, and a former infomercial producer named J. Jovan Philyaw had the gadget that seemed to answer the prayers of old-line businesses looking for an easy way to get onto the Web.

Mr. Philyaw's device, the CueCat, is a handheld, cat-shaped scanner that attaches to a PC. Hold it up to the bar code in an ad or a catalog or a can of soup, and your computer would whisk you to a Web page connected to the product. During 1999 and 2000, as he traveled from one corporate conference room to another, Mr. Philyaw's selling skills, combined with Internet euphoria, won the CueCat a long list of investors.

At RadioShack Corp., Chief Executive David Edmondson was wowed after just a brief demo. "I went, 'Holy Toledo! This is big,'" Mr. Edmondson recalls. The Fort Worth, Texas, retailer invested heavily in CueCat as did Coca Cola and General Electric. By being keyed to a bar code, the CueCat would take consumers to the exact Web page where a company wanted them to go. "It allows you to go 20,000 leagues under the sea in one swipe," said Mr. Edmondson of RadioShack, which ended up manufacturing the product and distributing it from its stores.

Forbes magazine, which was not an investor, mailed the CueCat to subscribers and began putting bar codes in its ads for readers to swipe while looking at the magazine. The *Dallas Morning News* regularly ran codes next to stories.

The CueCat's big launch was met with a wave of consumer indifference, not to mention withering reviews. Four million CueCats were given out across the country; few, if any, are still being used. Six million more are gathering dust. Reviewers were openly contemptuous, saying Web surfers could much more easily type in a Web address than they could carry around a CueCat. Computer columnist Walter Mossberg called the device "unnatural and ridiculous" and said it "failed miserably." Perhaps the biggest problem was that the reader had to be close to a computer connected to the Internet. Instead of reading your favorite magazine in your recliner, you had to go sit at your computer desk to use the CueCat.[5]

CRITICAL THINKING QUESTIONS

1. Could marketing research have predicted CueCat's failure?
2. Why do you think so many big companies bought into the CueCat concept?
3. Would you have used CueCat? Why or why not?

tailers informed about the new item. If the new product is to be sold internationally, it may have to be altered to meet the requirements of the target countries. For instance, electrical products may have to run on different electrical currents.

product manager
The person who develops and implements a complete strategy and marketing program for a specific product or brand.

The Role of the Product Manager

When a new product enters the marketplace in large organizations, it is often placed under the control of a product or brand manager. A **product manager** develops and implements a complete strategy and marketing program for a specific product or brand. Product management first appeared at Procter & Gamble in 1929. A new company soap, Camay, was not doing well, so a young Procter & Gamble executive was assigned to devote his exclusive attention to developing and promoting this product. He was successful, and the company soon added other product managers. Since then, many firms, especially consumer products companies, have set up product management organizations.

concept check

How do companies organize for new-product development?

What are the steps in the new-product development process?

Explain the role of the product manager.

The Product Life Cycle

5 learning goal

Product managers create marketing mixes for their products as they move through the life cycle. The **product life cycle** is a pattern of sales and profits over time for a product (Ivory dishwashing liquid) or a product category (liquid detergents). As the product moves through the stages of the life cycle, the firm must keep revising the marketing mix to stay competitive and meet the needs of target customers.

Stages of the Life Cycle

As illustrated in Exhibit 14.8, the product life cycle consists of the following stages:

Exhibit 14.8 Sales and Profits During the Product Life Cycle

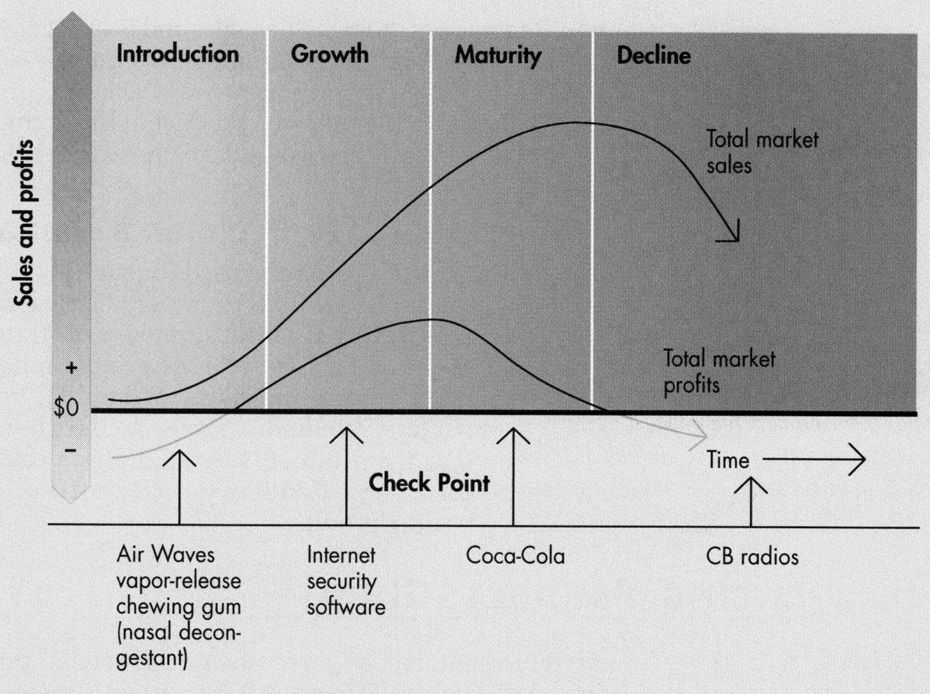

product life cycle
The pattern of sales and profits over time for a product or product category; consists of an introductory stage, growth stage, maturity, and decline (and death).

1. *Introduction.* When a product enters the life cycle, it faces many obstacles. Although competition may be light, the *introductory stage* usually features frequent product modifications, limited distribution, and heavy promotion. The failure rate is high. Production and marketing costs are also high, and sales volume is low. Hence profits are usually small or negative.
2. *Growth stage.* If a product survives the introductory stage, it advances to the *growth stage* of the life cycle. In this stage, sales grow at an increasing rate, profits are healthy, and many competitors enter the market. Large companies may start to acquire small pioneering firms that have reached this stage. Emphasis switches from primary demand promotion to aggressive brand advertising and communicating the differences between brands. For example, the goal changes from convincing people to buy compact DVD players to convincing them to buy Sony versus Panasonic or Sharp.

   Distribution becomes a major key to success during the growth stage, as well as in later stages. Manufacturers scramble to acquire dealers and distributors and to build long-term relationships. Without adequate distribution, it is impossible to establish a strong market position.

   Toward the end of the growth phase, prices normally begin falling and profits peak. Price reductions result from increased competition and from cost reductions from producing larger quantities of items (economies of scale). Also, most firms have recovered their development costs by now, and their priority is in increasing or retaining market share and enhancing profits.
3. *Maturity.* After the growth stage, sales continue to mount—but at a decreasing rate. This is the *maturity stage.* Most products that have been on the market for a long time are in this stage. Thus, most marketing strategies are designed for mature products. One such strategy is to bring out several variations of a basic product (line extension). Kool-Aid, for instance, was originally offered in three flavors. Today there are more than 10, as well as sweetened and unsweetened varieties.

   Products that are in the maturity stage in America may be at the introduction or growth phase in our countries. A good example is dishwashers in Japan, as explained in the "Expanding Around the Globe" box.
4. *Decline (and death).* When sales and profits fall, the product has reached the *decline stage.* The rate of decline is governed by two factors: the rate of change in consumer tastes and the rate at which new products enter the market. Sony VCRs are an example of a product in the decline stage. The demand for VCRs has now been surpassed by the demand for DVDs.

The Product Life Cycle as a Management Tool

The product life cycle may be used in planning. Marketers who understand the cycle concept are better able to forecast future sales and plan new marketing strategies. Exhibit 14.9 is a brief summary of strategic needs at various stages of the product life cycle. Marketers must be sure that a product has moved from one stage to the next before changing its marketing strategy. A temporary sales decline should not be interpreted as a sign that the product is dying. Pulling back marketing support can become a self-fulfilling prophecy that brings about the early death of a healthy product.

concept check

What is the product life cycle?

Describe each stage of the product life cycle.

What are the marketing strategies for each stage of the product life cycle?

PRICING PRODUCTS RIGHT

6 learning goal

An important part of the product development process is setting the right price. Price is the perceived value that is exchanged for something else. Value in our society is most commonly expressed in dollars and cents. Thus, price is typically the

EXPANDING AROUND THE GLOBE

In Japan a Dishwasher Can Create Guilt

For decades, Japanese consumers have snapped up the latest gadgets, from DVD players to camcorders to cell phones. So why not the dishwasher? Only 7 percent of Japanese households have one, compared with half the households in the United States. One reason is that Japanese kitchens are too small for bulky machines. Then there's Japan's notoriously sticky cuisine, featuring raw eggs, fermented soybeans, and glutinous rice. But the biggest obstacle might be guilt. The only thing many Japanese housewives hate more than doing dishes is the thought of having the dishes done for them. "You tend to feel that washing dishes is part of a housewife's job," says Miwa Watanabe, a writer for a Web site where housewives can share stories about their daily lives.

But prospects for the dishwasher are picking up. Ms. Watanabe, for example, finally overcame her guilty conscience and bought one. And some of Japan's biggest consumer appliance companies, not to mention the nation's leading toilet manufacturer, are gradually scrubbing away other barriers to dishwasher ownership.

Size is the first obstacle to fall. "This will fit!" exclaims an actress in a recent advertisement for models made by Matsushita Electric Industrial Co., Japan's leading dishwasher maker. The $704 machine looks like a carry-on suitcase, but holds enough plates for a family of five, the company says. Noise is no longer an issue either: Toshiba Corp. boasts that its latest machine, also $704, emits no more sound than "a quiet park." To boost awareness of dishwashers, electronics makers have designated every February 22 as Dishwasher Day. Manufacturers celebrate by giving away free dishwashers and promoting a pair of smiling cartoon plates as mascots.[6]

CRITICAL THINKING QUESTIONS

1. How might dishwasher manufacturers help Japanese housewives overcome their guilt of owning a dishwasher?
2. Dishwashers are in what stage of the product life cycle in Japan?
3. Might Japanese dishwashers find a niche in the American market?

Exhibit 14.9 Strategies for Success at Each Stage of the Product Life Cycle

Category	Introduction	Growth	Maturity	Decline
Marketing objectives	Encourage trial, establish distribution	Get triers to re-purchase, attract new users	Seek new users or uses	Reduce marketing expenses, keep loyal users
Product	Establish competitive advantage	Maintain product quality	Modify product	Maintain product
Distribution	Establish distribution network	Solidify distribution relationships	Provide additional incentives to ensure support	Eliminate trade allowances
Promotional	Build brand awareness	Provide information	Reposition product	Eliminate most advertising and sales promotions
Pricing	Set introductory price (skimming or penetration pricing)	Maintain prices	Reduce prices to meet competition	Maintain prices

amount of money exchanged for a good or service. Note that *perceived value* refers to the time of the transaction. After you've used a product you've bought, you may decide that its actual value was less than its perceived value at the time you bought it. The price you pay for a product is based on the *expected satisfaction* you will receive and not necessarily the *actual satisfaction* you will receive.

Although price is usually a dollar amount, it can be anything with perceived value. When goods and services are exchanged for each other, the trade is called *barter*. If you exchange this book for a math book at the end of the term, you have engaged in barter.

Pricing Objectives

Price is important in determining how much a firm earns. The prices charged customers times the number of units sold equals the *gross revenue* for the firm. Revenue is what pays for every activity of the company (production, finance, sales, distribution, and so forth). What's left over (if anything) is profit. Managers strive to charge a price that will allow the firm to earn a fair return on its investment.

The chosen price must be neither too high nor too low. And the price must equal the perceived value to target consumers. If consumers think the price is too high, sales opportunities will be lost. Lost sales mean lost revenue. If the price is too low, consumers may view the product as a great value, but the company may not meet its profit goals. Three common pricing objectives are maximizing profits, achieving a target return on the investment, and offering good value at a fair price.

Maximizing Profits

profit maximization
A pricing objective that entails getting the largest possible profit from a product by producing the product as long as the revenue from selling it exceeds the cost of producing it.

Profit maximization means producing a product as long as the revenue from selling it exceeds the cost of producing it. In other words, the goal is to get the largest possible profit from the product. For example, suppose Carl Morgan, a builder of houses, sells each house for $100,000. His revenue and cost projections are shown in Exhibit 14.10. Notice in column 3 that the cost of building each house drops for the second through the fifth house. The lower cost per house results from two things: First, by having several houses under construction at the same time, Morgan can afford to hire a full-time crew. The crew is more economical than the independent contractors to whom he would otherwise subcontract each task. Second, Morgan can order materials in greater quantities than usual and thus get quantity discounts on his orders.

Morgan decides that he could sell 15 houses a year at the $100,000 price. But he knows he cannot maximize profits at more than seven houses a year. Inefficiencies begin to creep in at the sixth house. (Notice in column 3 that the sixth house costs more to build than any of the first five houses.) Morgan can't supervise more than seven construction jobs at once, and his full-time crew can't handle even those

Exhibit 14.10 Revenue, Cost, and Profit Projections for Morgan's Houses

(1) Unit of Output (House)	(2) Selling Price (Revenue)	(3) Cost of Building House	(4) Profit on House	(5) Total Profit
1st	$ 100,000	$ 76,000	$ 24,000	$ 24,000
2nd	100,000	75,000	25,000	49,000
3rd	100,000	73,000	27,000	76,000
4th	100,000	70,000	30,000	106,000
5th	100,000	70,000	30,000	136,000
6th	100,000	77,000	23,000	159,000
7th	**100,000**	**90,000**	**10,000**	**169,000**
8th	100,000	115,000	(15,000)	154,000

seven. Thus, Morgan has to subcontract some of the work on the sixth and seventh houses. To build more than seven houses, he would need a second full-time crew.

The exhibit also shows why Morgan should construct seven houses a year. Even though the profit per house is falling for the sixth and seventh houses (column 4), the total profit is still rising (column 5). But at the eighth house, Morgan would go beyond profit maximization. That is, the eighth unit would cost more than its selling price. He would lose $15,000 on the house, and total profit would fall to $154,000 from $169,000 after the seventh house.

Achieving a Target Return on Investment

target return on investment
A pricing objective where the price of a product is set so as to give the company the desired profitability in terms of return on its money.

Another pricing objective used by many companies is **target return on investment** where a price is set to give the company the desired profitability in terms of return on its money. Among the companies that use target return on investment as their main pricing objective are 3M, Procter & Gamble, General Electric, and DuPont.

To get an idea of how target return works, imagine that you are a marketing manager for a cereal company. You estimate that developing, launching, and marketing a new hot cereal will cost $2 million. If the net profit for the first year is $200,000, the return on investment will be $200,000 ÷ $2,000,000, or 10 percent. Let's say that top management sets a 15 percent target return on investment. (The average target return on investment for large corporations is now about 14 percent.) Since a net profit of $200,000 will yield only a 10 percent return, one of two things will happen: either the cereal won't be produced, or the price and marketing mix will be changed to yield the 15 percent target return.

Value Pricing

value pricing
A pricing strategy in which the target market is offered a high-quality product at a fair price and with good service.

Value pricing has become a popular pricing strategy. **Value pricing** means offering the target market a high-quality product at a fair price and with good service. It is the notion of offering the customer a good value. Value pricing doesn't mean high quality that's available only at high prices. Nor does it mean bare-bones service or low-quality products. Value pricing can be used to sell a variety of products, from a $35,000 Jeep Grand Cherokee to a $2.99 package of L'eggs hosiery.

A value marketer does the following:

- *Offers products that perform.* This is the price of entry because consumers have lost patience with shoddy merchandise.
- *Gives consumers more than they expect.* Soon after Toyota launched Lexus, the company had to order a recall. The weekend before the recall, dealers phoned every Lexus owner in the United States and arranged to pick up their cars and provide replacement vehicles.
- *Gives meaningful guarantees.* DaimlerChrysler offers a 70,000-mile power train warranty. Michelin recently introduced a tire warranted to last 80,000 miles.
- *Gives the buyer facts.* Today's sophisticated consumer wants informative advertising and knowledgeable salespeople.
- *Builds long-term relationships.* American Airlines' Advantage program, Hyatt's Passport Club, and Whirlpool's 800-number hot line all help build good customer relations.

concept check

Explain the concept of price.

What is meant by target return on investment, and how does it differ from profit maximization?

What is value pricing?

How Managers Set Prices

7 learning goal

After establishing a pricing objective, managers must set a specific price for the product. Two techniques that are often used to set a price are markup pricing and breakeven analysis.

Markup Pricing

markup pricing
A method of pricing in which a certain percentage (the markup) is added to the product's cost to arrive at the price.

One of the most common forms of pricing is **markup pricing.** In this method, a certain dollar amount is added to a product's cost to arrive at the retail price. (The retail price is thus *cost plus markup.*) The cost is the expense of manufacturing the product or acquiring it for resale. The markup is the amount added to the cost to cover expenses and leave a profit. For example, if Banana Boat suntan cream costs Walgreen's drugstore $5 and sells for $7, it carries a markup of 29 percent:

Cost	$5	Cost to Walgreen's
Markup	+ 2	Walgreen's markup to cover expenses (utilities, wages, etc.)
Retail price	$7	Banana Boat suntan cream price paid by the consumer

$$\text{Walgreen's markup percentage} = \frac{\text{Markup}}{\text{Retail price}} = \frac{\$2}{\$7} = 29\%$$

Several elements influence markups. Among them are tradition, the competition, store image, and stock turnover. Traditionally, department stores used a 40 percent markup. But today competition has forced retailers to respond to consumer demand and meet competitors' prices. A department store that tried to sell household appliances at a 40 percent markup would lose customers to such discounters as Wal-Mart and Target. However, a retailer trying to develop a prestige image will use markups that are much higher than those used by a retailer trying to develop an image as a discounter.

Breakeven Analysis

breakeven point
The price at which a product's costs are covered, so additional sales result in profit.

fixed costs
Costs that do not vary with different levels of output; for example, rent.

variable costs
Costs that change with different levels of output; for example, wages and cost of raw materials.

fixed-cost contribution
The selling price per unit (revenue) minus the variable costs per unit.

total revenue
The selling price per unit times the number of units sold.

total cost
The sum of the fixed costs and the variable costs.

total profit
Total revenue minus total cost.

Manufacturers, wholesalers (companies that buy from manufacturers and sell to retailers and institutions), and retailers (firms that sell to end users) need to know how much of a product must be sold at a certain price to cover all costs. The point at which the costs are covered and additional sales result in profit is the **breakeven point.**

To find the breakeven point, the firm measures the various costs associated with the product:

- **Fixed costs** do not vary with different levels of output. The rent on a manufacturing facility is a fixed cost. It must be paid whether production is one unit or a million units.
- **Variable costs** change with different levels of output. Wages and expenses of raw materials are considered variable costs.
- The **fixed-cost contribution** is the selling price per unit (revenue) minus the variable costs per unit.
- **Total revenue** is the selling price per unit times the number of units sold.
- **Total cost** is the total of the fixed costs and the variable costs.
- **Total profit** is total revenue minus total cost.

Knowing these amounts, the firm can calculate the breakeven point:

$$\text{Breakeven point in units} = \frac{\text{Total fixed cost}}{\text{Fixed-cost contribution}}$$

Let's see how this works: Grey Corp., a manufacturer of aftershave lotion, has variable costs of $3 per bottle and fixed costs of $50,000. Grey's management believes the company can sell up to 100,000 bottles of aftershave at $5 a bottle without having to lower its price. Grey's fixed-cost contribution is $2 ($5 selling price per bottle minus $3 variable costs per bottle). Therefore, $2 per bottle is the amount that can be used to cover the company's fixed costs of $50,000.

To determine its breakeven point, Grey applies the previous equation:

$$\text{Breakeven point in bottles} = \frac{\$50{,}000 \text{ fixed cost}}{\$2 \text{ fixed-cost contribution}} = 25{,}000 \text{ bottles}$$

Grey Corp. will therefore break even when it sells 25,000 bottles of after shave lotion. After that point, at which the fixed costs are met, the $2 per bottle becomes profit. If Grey's forecasts are correct and it can sell 100,000 bottles at $5 a bottle, its total profit will be $150,000 ($2 per bottle × 75,000 bottles).

By using the equation, Grey Corp. can quickly find out how much it needs to sell to break even. It can then calculate how much profit it will earn if it sells more units. A firm that is operating close to the breakeven point may change the profit picture in two ways. Reducing costs will lower the breakeven point and expand profits. Increasing sales will not change the breakeven point, but it will provide more profits.

concept check

Explain how markups are calculated.

Describe breakeven analysis.

What does it mean to "break even"?

PRODUCT PRICING

8 learning goal

Managers use various pricing strategies when determining the price of a product, as this section explains. Price skimming and penetration pricing are strategies used in pricing new products; other strategies such as leader pricing and bundling may be used for established products as well.

Price Skimming

price skimming
The strategy of introducing a product with a high initial price and lowering the price over time as the product moves through its life cycle.

The practice of introducing a new product on the market with a high price and then lowering the price over time is called **price skimming.** As the product moves through its life cycle, the price usually is lowered because competitors are entering the market. As the price falls, more and more consumers can buy the product.

Price skimming has four important advantages. First, a high initial price can be a way to find out what buyers are willing to pay. Second, if consumers find the introductory price too high, it can be lowered. Third, a high introductory price can create an image of quality and prestige. Fourth, when the price is lowered later, consumers may think they are getting a bargain. The disadvantage is that high prices attract competition.

Price skimming can be used to price virtually any new products such as high-definition televisions, PCs, and color computer printers. For example, the Republic of Tea has launched new Imperial Republic White Tea, which it says is among the rarest of teas. Because it is minimally processed, white tea is said to retain the highest level of antioxidants and has a lower caffeine content than black and green teas. The company says the tea is picked only a few days each year, right before the leaf opens, yielding a small harvest. The product retails for $14 per tin of 50 bags. Products don't have to be expensive to use a skimming strategy.

Penetration Pricing

penetration pricing
The strategy of selling new products at low prices in the hope of achieving a large sales volume.

A company that doesn't use price skimming will probably use **penetration pricing.** With this strategy, the company offers new products at low prices in the hope of achieving a large sales volume. Procter & Gamble did this with SpinBrush. Penetration pricing requires more extensive planning than skimming does because the company must gear up for mass production and marketing. When Texas Instruments entered the digital-watch market, its facilities in Lubbock,

© AP / WIDE WORLD PHOTOS

Dell offers new products at low prices in order to achieve a high sales volume. In a successful strategy to increase market share, Dell slashed prices of personal computers requiring competitors Gateway, HP, and Compaq to do the same.

Texas, could produce 6 million watches a year, enough to meet the entire world demand for low-priced watches. If the company had been wrong about demand, its losses would have been huge.

Penetration pricing has two advantages. First, the low initial price may induce consumers to switch brands or companies. Using penetration pricing on its jug wines, Gallo has lured customers away from Taylor California Cellars and Inglenook. Second, penetration pricing may discourage competitors from entering the market. Their costs would tend to be higher, so they would need to sell more at the same price to break even.

Leader Pricing

Pricing products below the normal markup or even below cost to attract customers to a store where they wouldn't otherwise shop is **leader pricing.** A product priced below cost is referred to as a **loss leader.** Retailers hope that this type of pricing will increase their overall sales volume and thus their profit.

leader pricing
The strategy of pricing products below the normal markup or even below cost to attract customers to a store where they would not otherwise shop.

loss leader
A product priced below cost as part of a leader pricing strategy.

Items that are leader priced are usually well known and priced low enough to appeal to many customers. They also are items that consumers will buy at a lower price, even if they have to switch brands. Supermarkets often feature coffee and bacon in their leader pricing. Department stores and specialty stores also rely heavily on leader pricing.

Bundling

Bundling means grouping two or more related products together and pricing them as a single product. Marriott's special weekend rates often include the room, breakfast, and one night's dinner. Department stores may offer a washer and dryer together for a price lower than if the units were bought separately.

bundling
The strategy of grouping two or more related products together and pricing them as a single product.

The idea behind bundling is to reach a segment of the market that the products sold separately would not reach as effectively. Some buyers are more than willing to buy one product but have much less use for the second. Bundling the second product to the first at a slightly reduced price thus creates some sales that otherwise would not be made. Aussie 3-Minute Miracle Shampoo is typically bundled with its conditioner because many people use shampoo more than conditioner so they don't need a new bottle of conditioner.

odd-even (psychological) pricing
The strategy of setting a price at an odd number to connote a bargain and at an even number to suggest quality.

prestige pricing
The strategy of increasing the price of a product so that consumers will perceive it as being of higher quality, status, or value.

Odd-Even Pricing

Psychology often plays a big role in how consumers view prices and what prices they will pay. **Odd-even pricing** (or **psychological pricing**) is the strategy of setting a price at an odd number to connote a bargain and at an even number to imply quality. For years, many retailers have priced their products in odd numbers—for example, $99.95 or $49.95—to make consumers feel that they are paying a lower price for the product.

Some retailers favor odd-numbered prices because they believe that $9.99 sounds much less imposing to customers than $10.00. Other retailers believe that an odd-numbered price signals to consumers that the price is at the lowest level possible, thereby encouraging them to buy more units. Neither theory has ever been conclusively proved, although one study found that consumers perceive odd-priced products as being on sale. Even-numbered pricing is sometimes used to denote quality. Examples include a fine perfume at $100 a bottle, a good watch at $500, or a mink coat at $3,000.

concept check

What is the difference between penetration pricing and price skimming?

Explain the concept of price bundling.

Describe odd-even pricing and prestige pricing.

Prestige Pricing

The strategy of raising the price of a product so consumers will perceive it as being of higher quality, status, or value is called **prestige pricing.** This type of pricing is common where high prices indicate high status. In the specialty shops on Rodeo Drive in Beverly Hills, which cater to the super-rich of Hollywood, shirts that would sell for $15 elsewhere sell for at least $50. If the price were lower, customers would perceive them as being of low quality.

Trends in Developing Products and Pricing

9 learning goal

As customer expectations increase and competition becomes fiercer, perceptive managers will find innovative strategies to satisfy demanding consumers and establish unique products in the market. Management is under pressure to develop new products more quickly and move them to the marketplace—thus, the trend toward using the Internet for new-product development. Two other significant trends are the use of yield management systems to maximize revenues and the growing importance of color in packaging and product design.

NEW-PRODUCT DEVELOPMENT MOVES TO THE INTERNET

In the recent past big companies, like Kraft, General Motors, and Colgate Palmolive would spend five years or longer in developing a new product. Today, competitive pressures are bringing the time frame down to months instead of years.

A few cutting-edge marketing research companies are now offering new-product research on the Internet to make the new-product development process even faster. Decision Analyst, a global leader in Internet marketing research, offers "Conceptor," an Internet-based new-product concept-testing system. First, a sample of 250 is drawn from Decision Analysts 3.5 million consumers in their Internet panel. Then the respondents visit a special Web site to view a new-product concept and a complete battery of questions and diagnostic ratings. Finally, a sophisticated mathematical model is used to predict the concept's chances for success. The entire process can be completed in a couple of days.

If a product concept looks promising, then the prototype can be evaluated on Decision Analyst's Optima Internet-based product-testing system. Households are given a test product to try in their home for a few days or weeks depending on frequency of use. The consumers go to the Internet and answer a series of questions about the product including: overall rating, likes, dislikes, feelings about specific product features, and purchase interest. A sophisticated mathematical model then tells the company if the product is optimal or not, and indicates what features need to be changed to improve the product. Decision Analyst has used this new Internet research system to test many products including: soups, beer, coffee, salad dressings, restaurant entrees, breads, snacks, wine, and processed meats.[7]

Yield Management Systems Help Companies Maximize Their Revenues

yield management systems (YMS)
Mathematical software that helps companies adjust prices to maximize revenue

When competitive pressures are high, a company must know when it can raise prices to maximize its revenues. More and more companies are turning to yield management systems to help adjust prices. First developed in the airline industry, **yield management systems (YMS)** use complex mathematical software to profitably fill unused capacity. The software employs techniques such as discounting early purchases, limiting early sales at these discounted prices, and overbooking capacity. YMS now are appearing in other services such as lodging, other transportation forms, rental firms, and even hospitals.

Yield management systems are spreading beyond service industries as their popularity increases. The lessons of airlines and hotels aren't entirely applicable to other industries, however, because plane seats and hotel beds are perishable—if they go empty, the revenue opportunity is lost forever. So it makes sense to slash prices to move toward capacity if it's possible to do so without reducing the prices that other customers pay. Cars and steel aren't so perishable. Still, the capacity to make these goods is perishable. An underused factory or mill is a lost revenue opportunity. So it makes sense to cut prices to use up capacity if it's possible to do so while getting other customers to pay full price.

ProfitLogic has helped customers such as JCPenney, Gymboree, Ann Taylor, and the Gap determine the best markdown price. The software has boosted profit margins from 5 to 18 percent. KhiMetrics, used by Buy.com and others, analyzes dozens of factors such as a product's life cycle, competitors' prices, and past sales data at various price points before churning out a list of possible prices and calculating the best ones. New sales data are fed back into the formulas daily to refine the process. Systems such as this aren't cheap, however, costing from $200,000 to $500,000.[8]

Color Moves to the Forefront

In the past, color was viewed as just another design element in a package or a product. Today marketers know that colors have the power to create brand imagery and convey moods. They also know it's essential to take demographic differences into account when selecting a brand's plumage, because colors are accepted by different ages, genders, and ethnic groups in different ways.

Traditionally, men and women have had different tastes in color, with women drawn to brighter tones and more sensitive to subtle shadings and patterns. The differences are attributed in part to biology, since females see color better than males do (color blindness is 16 times more prevalent in men), and in part to socialization, with girls more likely to be steered toward coloring books and art sup-

Making Ethical Choices

xtra! http://gitmanxtra.swlearning.com

PRICING MISDIAGNOSIS

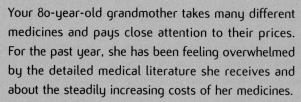

Your 80-year-old grandmother takes many different medicines and pays close attention to their prices. For the past year, she has been feeling overwhelmed by the detailed medical literature she receives and about the steadily increasing costs of her medicines.

When you last visited, she asked you, an interning pharmacist at an independent drugstore, to review the material she received. In her medical file are letters from drugstore chains. One letter promotes an alternative treatment for her diabetes. Another letter from a different chain announces an important change for people with osteoporosis who take Fosamax daily and encourages switching to the new Fosamax weekly. Your grandmother wasn't clear about the reason for doing so and was afraid she might forget to take the medicine if she took it only once a week. Neither letter mentions that the new drugs cost significantly more than the ones she is taking.

Your inquiry leads to the reason: In small print at the bottom of the letters are disclaimers from Merck, Fosamax's maker, and Eli Lilly, developer of both her current and the alternative diabetes medicine. Both companies paid the drug chains to send the letter to customers who take the particular medicine. Drugstores participate with drug manufacturers in this target marketing effort by compiling lists of names, addresses, and phone numbers with prescriptions for a specific drug. Further exploration reveals that drug companies consider such letters patient education.

When you return to your job, you receive a memo from the association of independent pharmacies to which your store belongs. The memo asks you to join drug company marketing programs that would send your customers letters similar to what your grandmother received.

ETHICAL DILEMMA

Your store manager (not a pharmacist) wants to join the program because it would generate significant additional revenue. What would you tell him or her to do in response to the memo?

SOURCES: Scott Hensley, "Drug Makers Are Boosting Prices on Key Medicines," *Wall Street Journal Online*, April 13, 2003; Denise Myshko, "Pricing—The Cost of Doing Business," PharmaVOICE, March 1, 2002, downloaded from http://www.websterconsultinggroup.com/pharmapricing; Ann Zimmerman and David Armstrong, "How Drug Makers Use Pharmacies to Push Pricey Pills," *Wall Street Journal*, May 1, 2002, pp. A1, A12.

plies. American men—compared with Europeans—have traditionally avoided brighter, more complex, and warmer hues in favor of darker, richer neutrals and blues, says Kathy LaManchusa, a color trend strategist for companies such as Kmart, Motorola, and Philip Morris.[9]

Although young people are typically more open than their elders to experimenting with color, kids today are exposed to an even wider palette from an early age. Crayola crayons come in 120 different hues, and advanced computer graphics offer a remarkably extensive selection. That makes preteen and teen preferences unusually sophisticated (in color theory, "sophisticated" describes a color created by a complex mixture of pigments, e.g., deep maroon). Preferences run to offbeat combinations and color effects such as glitter, translucence, pearlescence, and metallics.

The trend toward brighter and more complex colors (i.e., created through a mixture of multiple tones, often with special effects such as translucence or metallic sheen) also reflects the increasingly multicultural makeup of the country. Ethnic differences arising from cultural, religious, and historical experiences are also a major influence on color preferences.

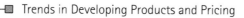

African Americans, some researchers find, are drawn to strong, saturated color, often in the red, yellow, and brown families, a preference that seems to be rooted in their African heritage. Jill Morton of Colorcom found that while working at the University of Architecture at the University of Hawaii, students from Africa constantly worked with sandy hues, primarily burnt oranges and browns.[10]

concept check

How can the Internet be used in new-product development?

What is the main advantage of a yield management system?

How can color impact a consumer's desire for a product?

Hispanics veer toward warm colors, but variations do exist. When it comes to apparel, Mexicans are more traditional (i.e., reds, blues, black) and Puerto Ricans are drawn to livelier colors (i.e., pinks, purples). In Florida, a Cuban palette of pastels, flamingo pink, and salmon dominates fashion as well as exterior and interior design. Exhibit 14.11 depicts how managers can interpret and use colors in their marketing strategies.

Exhibit 14.11 The Power of Colors

Color	Attributes	Associated with	The effect
Red	exciting, daring, dynamic, sexy, intense, impulsive, active, aggressive, passionate	blood, fire, competition, heat, emotion, optimism, life, Valentine's Day, violence, communism	arousal, stimulation, increases heart and respiration rate
Orange	in your face, vibrant, warm	extroversion, adventure, celebration	stimulating but less than red, triggers alert
Yellow	the warmest color, cheerful, happy	sunshine, creativity, imagination, optimism, futuristic, spirituality, newness, low prices	warming, cheering
Green	fresh, clean, restful	economy, nature, balance, envy, fertility, spring	stabilizing, nurturing, healing, revitalizing
Blue	calm, tranquil, holy	constancy, dependability, water, sky, holiness, protection, purity, peace, trust, loyalty, patience, hope, perseverance, sadness and depression, the future	calming, cleansing, cooling
Purple/Violet	exciting, mysterious, complex, intriguing	passion, spirituality, art, creativity, wit, sensitivity, vanity, moodiness, royalty, superiority, homosexuality, richness	inspiring, thought provoking, polarizing
Pink	warm, cheerful, simple, uncomplicated emotions	romance, sweetness, delicacy, tenderness, refinement, sentimentality, femininity, innocence	subduing, flattering
Brown	comfortable, reliable, steady, simple	earth, substance, stability, harmony, hearth, home, neutrality	comforting, soothing
Black	mysterious, elegant, sophisticated, worldly, sexy, powerful	sophistication, simplicity, death and mourning, bad luck, night, power, evil	empowering
Gray	safe, secure, practical, dependable, elegant	neutrality, boredom, coolness, safety, conservatism, ashes	reassuring, dulling
White	clean, fresh, pure, modern, neat	purity, sterility, calm, mourning (China and India), brides (West)	eyestrain, headaches, attention getting

SOURCE: Roper/Pantone, Color Matters, C.A.U.S., Supermarketguru.com.interviews, "Would You Trust IBM If It Were Big Orange?" *Business 2.0* (November 22, 2003), p. 52; "Why Does Orange Signify Decaf?" *Fortune* (May 17, 2002), p. 30; and the author's research.

Great Ideas to Use Now

Chances are that someday you will be a buyer or seller on eBay. The auction site has over 46 million users with more than 18,000 different categories of items on the auction block. Yet, finding what you want or getting the best deal can be tough. Here are a few helpful tips:

A Buyer's Guide

Browsing/Searching

- Before diving in, get a solid sense of what the items you're interested in are worth. Use the "completed items" advanced search to see the prices that similar

Preferred by	Used for	Brands
achievers, high-powered, active women, most economically stable, most secure	cars, lingerie, cosmetics, bridalwear (among Asian Americans; red is popular in Chinese and in Korean cultures, too)	Coca-Cola, Red Cross, Revlon
influentials, adolescents, bright orange is second least favorite color overall	safety color—to alert our attention; not for full-blown danger but potential danger	Cingular, Home Depot, Sanka coffee
the first color kids reach for, yet the least preferred color overall	the lead color projected for women's, men's, children's and home use through 2004	Kodak, Juicy Fruit, National Geographic
popular among influentials, opinion leaders, trendsetters; "slime green" preferred by youths; no. 2 favorite	higher-end vehicles (rich, dark hunter green); in interiors popular for bedrooms (to compensate for lack of natural light/outdoors), natural foods	John Deere, Starbucks, British Petroleum
No. 1 favorite in America	No. 1 for casual clothing; No. 2 for business clothing, not for most rooms, especially not dining room	Microsoft, American Express, Jet Blue
No. 3 favorite, popular among 18- to 29-year-olds, artists; more androgynous than other colors; loved or hated more than any other color	not used much in interiors or for clothing; Americans have gone back to purple in times of war	Sun, Yahoo, Barney
soft pink preferred overall to bright pink; preferred by women	mainstream traditional pink is still the color for little girls	Mary Kay, Barbie, Pepto Bismol
practical people; down-to-earth people; Midwesterners; noncoastals	rich earthtones and neutrals preferred for the home	UPS, Aveda shampoo
intellectuals, rebels, fashion industry, increasingly broad in appeal	No. 1 for business clothing; No. 2 for casual clothing	Frexinet Champagne
not generally chosen as a favorite; usually not a big seller, though fashionable for past few years among creative people, visual artists	men's business attire, growing popularity with women	Brite Nails, Black Pearl Resort
intellectuals, modern types, limited appeal overall	summer attire, bridal fashion though not in some parts of the world; low-fat and diet foods	Ivory Soap, Dove soap

items actually sold for, or check eBay's library for the category-specific "inside scoop," which generally features a useful page titled "Factors Influencing Value."

- Search in both related and general categories, as sellers often misclassify their wares. For example, if you're looking for a CD by Elvis Costello, check classic rock, pop, and punk in addition to alternative rock.
- Be descriptive when searching. Specify dates, colors, brands, sizes, and model numbers. Try variations—if a model number has a hyphen, search both with and without it.
- Conduct searches often, as items are constantly added and removed. Save yourself from having to monitor the site on a daily basis by using the "favorite searches" service, which will notify you by e-mail when items matching your search criteria are put up for sale.
- Think eBay for retail too. Many companies, such as Dell and Handspring, off-load surplus inventory at deep discounts, so check here before you try standard retail outlets.

Bidding

- Don't bid if you don't intend to buy, as bids are binding contracts. Bids can be retracted only under exceptional circumstances (e.g., the seller changes the product description after you've placed your bid).
- Don't bid in the first days of an auction. Doing so merely reveals your interest and increases the likelihood of other bidders joining the fray, causing the price to rise quickly. Instead, wait until the auction is near its close (10 to 30 seconds before, depending on the speed of your Internet connection) and bid the maximum amount you are willing to pay, regardless of any previous bids—a strategy known as sniping. To do this, open a second browser window and fill in all the relevant information, stopping just short of submitting your bid. Watch the auction wind down in the first window, and then, when the time is right, place your bid in the second. Don't fret—you can always use a professional sniper service to handle this for you automatically (see "Resources").
- Factor in shipping costs, which typically fall on the buyer. If the item is bulky or the seller lives overseas, your "bargain" might end up costing more than you bargained for. E-mail the seller your zip code to get an estimated shipping fee.
- Try adding a penny or two to your bid. Since many bids are placed in round-number increments, this little extra something can mean the difference between winning by a nose and coming up short.

A Seller's Guide

Listing Online auctions bring out the competitive nature in bidders, especially as the clock runs out. Bidding wars are a seller's dream; to make sure your auction gets significant play, follow these steps:

- Include specifics, such as manufacturer or product name, in both the title and description.
- Be honest in describing imperfections. This gives buyers comfort that you're being honest, and could head off conflicts later.
- Set a low initial bid amount to attract more bidders. The mere *possibility* of getting a great deal on that rare Tony Gwynn rookie card encourages competition and increases the likelihood of rival bidders driving up the price. This can also save you money, since eBay's listing fees are based on the minimum bid you set.

Try It Now

Finding bargain travel rates. A growing number of Web sites are helping travelers get unusually cheap hotels and airline tickets, even by the already heavily discounted standards of the Web. The sites, with names like Biddingfortravel.com and Flyertalk, provide advice on winning strategies (don't bid more than $35 for a room until just before leaving town) and most important, the exact price people are paying for hotels and airfare. That undercuts the heart of Priceline's system, in which travelers bid without knowing what price the site will actually accept.

Even before checking a site like Biddingfortravel, devoted bargain hunters head for a site like Farechase.com, a so-called site-scraper, which searches other sites to find the lowest rates. That information provides even more background for making an informed bid on Priceline.[11]

- Include a picture, since most buyers are reluctant to make a big purchase sight unseen. But don't overdo it: Including too many photos, or big ones with large file sizes, slows download times and tends to frustrate buyers with dial-up connections.
- Set a "buy it now" price, which allows buyers to subvert the bidding process and nab an item outright for a predetermined amount.
- Don't set a "reserve" price, which requires bidders to meet or exceed a certain minimum. Since bidders can't see this minimum price, many avoid such auctions altogether out of fear that they'll be wasting their time.
- Accept multiple forms of payment, which increases the likelihood that interested buyers will place bids.
- Pay attention to when your auction is scheduled to end. eBay auctions run 3, 5, 7, or 10 days; to get the most traffic, make sure that yours includes a full weekend and ends at a time when people will be around to bid up the price.

Closing the Deal

- Congratulate the winner by e-mail. Include the auction number, a description of the item, the amount of the winning bid, and estimated shipping charges.
- Send the item as soon as the buyer's payment clears and alert the buyer by e-mail (be sure to include the tracking number).
- Include links to your other auctions in all e-mail correspondence with the buyer; if he's satisfied with this experience, he might want to check out what else you have.[12]

Customer Satisfaction and Quality

Creating new products demands that quality be built into those items from the beginning. If a new product is of poor quality, consumers may buy it once but never a second time. Moreover, a dissatisfied customer will tell others of his or her bad experiences, which will further reduce demand. Building quality into products not only helps keep customers, but also cuts down on the expense of servicing warranty repairs.

The French automaker, Renault, sold cars in the United States in the 1960s and 1970s. Yet, the quality was not there and sales suffered. Renault found that poor quality would not let them earn a profit in the U.S. market. Renault withdrew and has not since attempted to reenter the American market.

Looking Ahead at SpinBrush

SpinBrush, one of Procter & Gamble's most successful new products in the past decade, was not created in the typical manner. In fact, it was purchased from a group of inventors. The typical approach for creating new products is shown in Exhibit 14.7. Currently the SpinBrush is in the growth phase of the product life cycle. The Spin-Brush created tremendous demand by following a penetration price strategy. It was priced far below other motorized toothbrushes such as SoniCare and Braun.

Summary of Learning Goals

1 What is a product, and how is it classified?

A product is any good or service, along with its perceived attributes and benefits, that creates customer value. Tangible attributes include the good itself, packaging, and warranties. Intangible attributes are symbolic like a brand's image. Products are categorized as either consumer products or industrial products. Consumer products are goods and services that are bought and used by the end users. They can be classified as unsought products, convenience products, shopping products, or specialty products, depending on how much effort consumers are willing to exert to get them. Industrial products are those bought by organizations for use in making other products or in rendering services and include capital products and expense items.

2 How does branding distinguish a product from its competitors?

Products usually have brand names. Brands identify products by words, names, symbols, designs, or a combination of these things. The two major types of brands are manufacturer (national) brands and dealer (private) brands. Generic products carry no brand name. Branding has three main purposes: product identification, repeat sales, and new-product sales.

3 What are the functions of packaging?

Often the promotional claims of well-known brands are reinforced in the printing on the package. Packaging is an important way to promote sales and protect the product. A package should be easy to ship, store, and stack on a store shelf. Companies can add value to products by giving warranties. A warranty guarantees the quality of a good or service.

4 How do organizations create new products?

To succeed, most firms must continue to design new-products to satisfy changing customer demands. But new-product development can be risky. Many new products fail. To be successful, new-product development requires input from production, finance, marketing, and engineering personnel. In large organizations, these people work in a new-product development department. The steps in new-product development are setting new-product goals, exploring ideas, screening ideas, developing the concept (creating a prototype and building the marketing strategy), test-marketing, and introducing the product. When the product enters the marketplace, it is often managed by a product manager.

5

What are the stages of the product life cycle?

After a product reaches the marketplace, it enters the product life cycle. This cycle typically has four stages: introduction, growth, maturity, and decline (and possibly death). Profits usually are small in the introductory phase, reach a peak at the end of the growth phase, and then decline. Marketing strategies for each stage are listed in Exhibit 14.9.

6

What is the role of pricing in marketing?

Price indicates value, helps position a product in the marketplace, and is the means for earning a fair return on investment. If a price is too high, the product won't sell well and the firm will lose money. If the price is too low, the firm may lose money even if the product sells well. Prices are set according to pricing objectives. Among the most common objectives are profit maximization, target return on investment, and value pricing.

7

How are product prices determined?

A cost-based method for determining price is markup pricing. A certain percentage is added to the product's cost to arrive at the retail price. The markup is the amount added to the cost to cover expenses and earn a profit. Breakeven analysis determines the level of sales that must be reached before total cost equals total revenue. Breakeven analysis provides a quick look at how many units the firm must sell before it starts earning a profit. The technique also reveals how much profit can be earned with higher sales volumes.

8

What strategies are used for pricing products?

The two main strategies for pricing a new product are price skimming and penetration pricing. Price skimming involves charging a high introductory price and then, usually, lowering the price as the product moves through its life cycle. Penetration pricing involves selling a new-product at a low price in the hope of achieving a large sales volume.

Pricing tactics are used to fine-tune the base prices of products. Sellers that use leader pricing set the prices of some of their products below the normal markup or even below cost to attract customers who might otherwise not shop at those stores. Bundling is grouping two or more products together and pricing them as one. Psychology often plays a role in how consumers view products and in determining what they will pay. Setting a price at an odd number tends to create a perception that the item is cheaper than the actual price. Prices in even numbers denote quality or status. Raising the price so an item will be perceived as having high quality and status is called prestige pricing.

9

What trends are occurring in products and pricing?

Because of competitive pressures to develop new products more quickly, many companies are now using the Internet for new-product development. A second trend is that many service businesses and other companies have turned to yield management systems to maximize their revenues. Finally, color is playing a key role in packaging and product design strategies.

KEY TERMS

brainstorming 449
brand 441
brand equity 442
brand loyalty 442
breakeven point 456
bundling 458
capital products 440
convenience products 439
dealer brands 444
expense items 440
express warranty 447
fixed costs 456
fixed-cost contribution 456
focus group 449
full warranty 448
generic products 444
implied warranty 447
informational labeling 445
leader pricing 458
line extension 448
loss leader 458
manufacturer brands 444
markup pricing 456
master brand 442
odd-even (psychological) pricing 459
penetration pricing 457
persuasive labeling 445
prestige pricing 459
price skimming 457
product 438
product life cycle 452
product manager 451
profit maximization 454
shopping products 440
specialty products 440
target return on investment 455
test-marketing 450
total cost 456
total profit 456
total revenue 456
trademark 441
unsought products 439
value pricing 455
variable costs 456
warranty 447
yeild management systems 460

PREPARING FOR TOMORROW'S WORKPLACE

1. Write an e-mail explaining how most products are a combination of goods and services; provide examples.
2. Your company plans to start selling gourmet frozen foods through the Internet. You are chairing a team to name this new service. Write an e-mail to team members suggesting things that they should consider in creating a brand name.
3. Divide the class into two groups. Have the two groups debate whether consumers will readily accept the following products as generic products: automobile tires, ice cream, staples, scientific calculators, running shoes, panty hose, gasoline, and men's briefs.
4. Under what circumstances would a jeans maker market the product as a convenience product? A shopping product? A specialty product?
5. Go to the library and look through magazines and newspapers to find examples of price skimming, penetration pricing, and value pricing. Make copies and show them to the class.
6. Write down the names of two brands to which you are loyal. Indicate the reasons for your loyalty.
7. Explain how something as obvious as a retail price can have a psychological dimension.
8. Divide the class into teams. Create a market list of products. Each team should go to a different supermarket chain store or an independent supermarket and write down the prices of the goods selected. Report your findings to the class.

WORKING THE NET

1. Thousands of new products are introduced each year, but many don't stay on store shelves for long. NewProductWorks, a new-product development consulting firm, uses its collection of over 70,000 new and once-new products as the foundation for its services. The site also has an online poll that gives you a chance to vote on proposed new products. Go to **http://www.newproductworks.com** and click on "Poll: Hits or Misses?" Read the descriptions of new products, rate them, and then see how your view compares to the composite rating of the product so far. Summarize your experience. Then click on "Hits & Misses." In this section you'll find products that the NPW experts expect to succeed and those that won't. Pick a product from the "We Expect Them to be Successes" or "Jury Is Out" category and find out where it currently stands.
2. You're working for a company that plans to introduce gourmet treats for pets. Your job is to determine the market for this new product and the marketing issues that may need to be addressed. Do a search online for articles on pet ownership, pet food, and pet products. In addition to search engines, include marketing magazine sites such as *Adweek* and *Brandweek* (**http://www.adweek.com** and **http://www.brandweek.com**) and an online database such as InfoTrak. Write a short report to your manager based on your research.
3. Visit an online retailer such as Amazon.com (**http://www.amazon.com**), PC-Connection.com (**http://www.pcconnection.com**), or Drugstore.com (**http://www.drugstore.com**). At the site, try to identify examples of leader pricing, bundling, odd-even pricing, and other pricing strategies. Do online retailers have different pricing considerations than "real-world" retailers? Explain.
4. Do a search on Yahoo (**http://www.yahoo.com**) for online auctions for a product you are interested in buying. Visit several auctions and get an idea of

how the product is priced. How do these prices compare with the price you might find in a local store? What pricing advantages or disadvantages do companies face in selling their products through online auctions? How do online auctions affect the pricing strategies of other companies? Why?

5. Learn more about branding strategies at the *Brandweek* magazine site, **http://www.brandweek.com**. Pick two companies featured in recent articles and search the site for more articles about them. Summarize their approach to branding their products. Do you think they have been effective in strengthening the brand? Explain.

Creative Thinking Case

How About a Peppermint Three-Piece Suit?

Not everyone would buy underwear that's coated with soil, but Chang Seong Ho is particular about his health. The 26-year-old Korean university student recently paid $12 for a pair of "yellow earth" boxer shorts, made from a fabric infused with microgranules of a yellow soil purported to emit far-infrared rays. Those rays, the low-energy waves farthest in the spectrum from visible light, cut odor and improve circulation, the maker of his shorts says. "I'm always interested in anything concerning health," says Mr. Chang.

Mr. Chang's soiled underwear isn't an outlandish wardrobe choice here. Textile innovation is a big and growing business around the world, and Asia, where consumers love both New Age gadgets and Old World naturopathy, is leading the way with some of the most unusual fabrics. In a land of conservatively dressed business professionals, South Korea's Kolon Corp. has been boosting its sales with a line of "fragrant suits," available in stress-busting lavender or peppermint. Cheil Industries Inc. is doing a brisk business with its new Rogatis brand "Ki" business suits, which have sachets of a charcoal-and-jade powder sewn into the armpits and crotch. The mixture, according to the company, blocks electromagnetic radiation emitted by computer and television screens and also gives the wearer an energy boost.

Dupont has teamed up with Levi's to product Lycra-blend jeans. Recently it launched Kevlar jeans with Polo Ralph Lauren Corp. Dupont is now making clothes that can be detected by global positioning satellites.

Asia has been leading the charge with some of the most bizarre inventions. In January, the Hong Kong unit of the United Kingdom lingerie maker Triumph International Ltd. launched in Asia the aloe vera bra and underwear set, which promises to lubricate the wearer's skin for up to 40 washes.[13]

CREATIVE THINKING QUESTIONS

1. Do you think that these products would sell well in America? Why or why not?
2. Should market research be done prior to launching such products?
3. What pricing strategy should be used for "fragrant suits"?

Video Case

The Toronto Blue Jays Hit a Home Run with Pricing

Can doubling the number of ticket categories bring more fans out to the ball game? For the Toronto Blue Jays, an improved pricing strategy and additional promotional strategies helped the team raise its profile in its home town.

Prior to the 1999 baseball season, the Toronto Blue Jays (**http://www.bluejays.ca**) had just five ticket-pricing categories. After thorough study of their ticket prices, the Blue Jays established a new pricing structure with 10 levels to provide fans different product value. From single-ticket $7 seats to season tickets costing over

$13,000 ($165 per game) for the "In the Action" seats, fans can pick the ticket program that suits them best. (These prices have been updated from the ones in the case for the 2003 season.) In between seats range from $24 to $49, depending on location. In addition to individual seats and season passes, Blue Jays fans can buy Flex-Packs with 5, 20, or 40 tickets to the games they choose. These packages sell at a discount from the single-ticket price. Group ticket sales, an important component of the Blue Jays product mix, are targeted toward the seats priced at about $40 and under.

As part of the Toronto team's effort to provide a high-quality product at a fair price, the Blue Jays added several regularly occurring special promotions during many home games. For example, every Tuesday home game is a TIM-BR Mart Tuesday. The building supplies chain collaborates with the Blue Jays in a three-part promotion. When a Toronto player hits the official TIM-BR Mart target, a fan chosen at random wins a cottage supplied and built by TIM-BR Mart. Another fan chosen at random gets to watch the game from a custom-built wood deck in the Toronto SkyDome. This fan is also provided food and beverage service. A third lucky fan wins a custom-built deck for his or her home by TIM-BR Mart.

Saturday home games have special promotions for children. On Jr. Jays Saturdays, sponsored by the Toronto Star, children 14 and under are admitted at discounted prices. The gates open early so fans can watch batting practice, and kids can participate in many activities and contests, win prizes, and get player autographs. Children can enter a drawing to throw out the ceremonial first pitch at the next Jr. Jays Saturday game; nine youngsters get to take the field along with the Blue Jays starting lineup and a child is selected to announce the Blue Jays batters for one inning. Children can also run the bases following the game. Each child 14 and under also receives Blue Jays souvenir giveaways.

The Blue Jays' marketing staff continue to add special promotions to please their fans. For example, they asked fans what they enjoy the most about attending a Blue Jays game and combined many of these elements to create Premium Games. Tickets for these games cost a few dollars more but include a pregame party, early admission to watch batting practice, autograph signing, giveaway items, and postgame entertainment. Staples's Business Depot "Deal of the Game," the FedEx Home Run Club, and Schneider's Juicy Jumbo Toss are among the team's current promotions.

This well-planned package of special promotions, along with different ticket prices for seats providing different amenities, has increased the Toronto Blue Jays' popularity. As a result, attendance at games is up and the fan base is growing.

CRITICAL THINKING QUESTIONS

1. How would you describe the Toronto Blue Jays' baseball franchise as a product?
2. What decision criteria do you think the Blue Jays used in establishing their new ticket price structure? Do you agree with this pricing strategy?

SOURCE: Toronto Blue Jays Web site, http://toronto.bluejays.mlb.com.

E-Commerce Case

A Perfect Fit for Lands' End

How do you like your chinos? That's the question Lands' End asked its customers when it began offering customized pants on its Web site about two years ago (**http://www.landsend.com**). Customers simply sign on, choose their preferred style and fit from millions of choices, enter a few details about their body shape, and in a few weeks a custom-made pair of pants is delivered to their doorstep. The customized chinos proved so successful that Lands End has since started offering made-to-order jeans, dress shirts, and twill pants on its Web site as well. About 40 percent of the firm's Web sales are now made-to-order.

Ironing out the details took some effort. Lands' End teamed with Archetype, a California technology firm specializing in mass-customization ordering systems.

At the end of every day, Lands' End electronically sends customer orders to Archetype's California offices where Archetype's software compares body measurements, factors in individual fit preferences, and adjusts the base pattern designs accordingly. The patterns are then electronically transmitted to a contract manufacturer in Mexico for production.

At the factory, each unique pattern is entered into automated equipment that cuts the fabric according to customer specifications. To control quality, Lands' End worked closely with its Mexican partner, which had to install new machinery to meet Lands' End specifications. Quality inspections are also critical. "The last person in the mod setup measures the pants. If they miss on any of five critical points, the pants are scrapped and remade," says Ron James, Lands' End customer project manager. After passing the final quality check, the clothes are bulk shipped to a distribution center in the United States, where they are packaged and mailed directly to customers.

Lands' End was an "early adopter" of the Internet, launching its Web site in 1995. Initially, the site featured 100 products as well as stories, essays, and travelogues. Today, landsend.com is the world's largest apparel Web site based on business volume. The company has also been a leader in using the Web to enhance the shopping experience and to foster one-on-one relationships with its customers.

Customer satisfaction with the custom-made clothes is high, even though they cost as much as 40 percent more than regular Lands' End products. Returns are far below those of non-customized Lands' End products. Lands' End has also been able to dramatically reduce its inventory levels. "What we've done is solve a consumer problem, which is getting a garment I want in a style that fits," says Robert Holloway, CEO of Archetype.

CRITICAL THINKING QUESTIONS

1. Evaluate Lands' End's product and pricing strategy. Do you think the custom-made clothes justify a 40 percent pricing premium? Why or why not?
2. Visit the Lands' End site and briefly discuss how Lands' End uses the Internet for the custom-clothing line and its other products. What innovative features does it offer? (Also check the landsend.com description in the "General Information" section.) Does it add value, and if so, how?
3. What role, if any, does the Lands' End brand play in this product line?

SOURCES: Anne D'Innocenzio, "Lands' End Expands Custom Clothes," *AP Online Wire,* September 4, 2002; David Drickhammer; "A Leg Up on Mass Customization," *Industry Week,* September 9, 2002, downloaded from http://www.industryweek.com; Jon Swartz, "Have It Your Way," *USA Today,* October 30, 2002, p. 3B; "Custom Pants in a Click; Lands' End Custom Gives Shoppers More Choices than Ever Before," Lands' End company press release, November 1, 2001.

HOT LINKS ADDRESS BOOK

Delve deeper into Procter & Gamble's marketing and brand management strategies at the firm's home page,
http://www.pg.com

See how one consulting firm helps clients pick the right name by pointing your Web browser to
http://www.namebase.com

Find out how to trademark a design, name or other identifying mark by visiting the U.S. Patents and Trademark Office at
http://www.uspto.gov

Curious about how generic and private label products are manufactured? Visit the Private Label Manufacturers Association at
http://www.plma.com

Protect yourself! The Federal Trade Commission has more information about warranties at
http://www.ftc.gov

For the latest trends in packaging, visit the Packaging Digest site,
http://www.packagingdigest.com

Companies are turning to Web-based smart-pricing software to improve margins on products. Find out how one company's software works at ProfitLogic, Inc.'s Web site,
http://www.profitlogic.com.

Chapter 15

© COURTESY OF JACK IN THE BOX INC.

Distributing Products in a Timely and Efficient Manner

learning goals

1 What is physical distribution?
2 What are distribution channels and their functions?
3 How are channels organized?
4 When would a marketer use exclusive, selective, or intensive distribution?
5 What is wholesaling, and what are the types of wholesalers?
6 What are the different kinds of retail operations and the components of a successful retailing strategy?
7 How can supply chain management increase efficiency and customer satisfaction?
8 What are the trends in distribution?

Jack Moves Out of the Box

Want a lottery ticket with that burger? The thin line between convenience stores and fast-food restaurants is disappearing at Jack in the Box Inc. (**http://www.jackinthebox.com**). The San Diego–based company's new locations will feature full-size hamburger joints beside 24-hour convenience stores, to be called Quick Stuff, with gas pumps in the parking lots. After testing the concept for more than three years, Jack in the Box now plans to open 100 to 150 convenience stores between 2003 and 2008.

The move to combine fast food, a convenience store, and gasoline pumps amounts to a declaration of war against the convenience store industry, which has long cooperated with fast-food operators: Thousands of convenience stores feature fast-food counters with brand names such as Wendy's, Subway, and Taco Bell. But it also comes at a time when traditional convenience retailers are facing new competition from old-line retailers: Wal-Mart Stores Inc., Costco Wholesale Corp., and Kroger Co. all are adding gasoline pumps to many of their stores, giving consumers multiple choices for buying gas and picking up a gallon of milk.

Why all the interest? To Bob Nugent, chairman and chief executive of Jack in the Box, it's open terrain because no one owns the convenience store market. In the burger market, McDonald's Corp. boasts a 43.1 percent share while Jack in the Box, with its 1,850 stores, has 4.6 percent. The single largest convenience store player, 7-Eleven Inc., has a little more than 4 percent of the market.

Jack in the Box says it has been more successful operating its own convenience stores. The company says it began the experiment in 2000 in Sacramento when faced with a piece of land too pricey to support a restaurant.

Instead of passing up prime property, Jack in the Box decided to open a convenience store and form a partnership with a fuel company to provide gas. The test grew to 12 stores before the company decided to make it part of its growth strategy. When paired with a convenience store and a gas station, a Jack in the Box generates nearly $1.25 million a year, the same as the average annual sales of a stand-alone Jack in the Box.

The gas station partners—which include ChevronTexaco, Royal Dutch/Shell, BP, and Citgo Petroleum Corp.—don't pay any development costs but sell their fuel to Jack in the Box. The two extra sources of revenue, from the convenience store and gas station, not only give the burger chain more sources of income, but allow it to buy more desirable real estate.[1]

Critical Thinking Questions

1. How important is location in determining retailing success?
2. Why are distribution and supply chain management getting more attention from top management?
3. Can you think of other partnerships such as the one Jack in the Box is forging with convenience stores and gas stations?

Principles of Distribution

physical distribution (logistics)
Efficiently managing the acquisition of raw materials to the factory and the movement of products from the producer to industrial users and consumers.

This chapter explores how organizations use a distribution system to enhance the value of a product and examines the methods they use to move products to locations where consumers wish to buy them. First, we'll discuss the functions and members of a distribution system. Next, we'll explore the role of wholesalers and retailers in delivering products to customers. We'll also discuss how supply chain management increases efficiency and customer satisfaction. Finally, we'll look at trends in distribution.

The Role of Distribution

1 learning goal

Physical distribution is efficiently managing the acquisition of raw materials to the factory and the movement of products from the producer or **manufacturer** to industrial users and consumers. Physical-distribution activities are usually the responsibility of the marketing department and are part of the large series of activities included in the supply chain. As discussed in Chapter 12, a supply chain is the system through which an organization acquires raw material, produces products, and delivers the products and services to its customers. Exhibit 15.1 illustrates a supply chain. Supply chain management helps increase the efficiency of logistics service by minimizing inventory and moving goods efficiently from producers to the ultimate users.

concept check

Define physical distribution.

Physical distribution is usually the responsibility of which department?

The Nature and Functions of Distribution Channels

2 learning goal

On their way from producers to end users and consumers, goods and services pass through a series of marketing entities known as a **distribution channel.** This section will look first at the entities that make up a distribution channel and then will examine the functions that channels serve.

Marketing Intermediaries in the Distribution Channel

A distribution channel is made up of **marketing intermediaries,** or organizations that assist in moving goods and services from producers to end users and consumers. Marketing intermediaries are in the middle of the distribution process between the producer and the end user. The following marketing intermediaries most often appear in the distribution channel:

- *Agents and brokers.* **Agents** are sales representatives of manufacturers and wholesalers, and **brokers** are entities that bring buyers and sellers together. Both agents and brokers are usually hired on commission basis by either a buyer or a seller. Agents and brokers are go-betweens whose job is to make deals. They do not own or take possession of goods.
- *Industrial distributors.* **Industrial distributors** are independent wholesalers that buy related product lines from many manufacturers and sell them to industrial users. They often have a sales force to call on purchasing agents, make deliveries, extend credit, and provide information. Industrial distributors are used in such industries as aircraft manufacturing, mining, and petroleum.

manufacturer
A producer; an organization that converts raw materials to finished products.

distribution channel
The series of marketing entities through which goods and services pass on their way from producers to end users.

marketing intermediaries
Organizations that assist in moving goods and services from producers to end users.

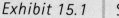

Exhibit 15.1 | Supply Chain

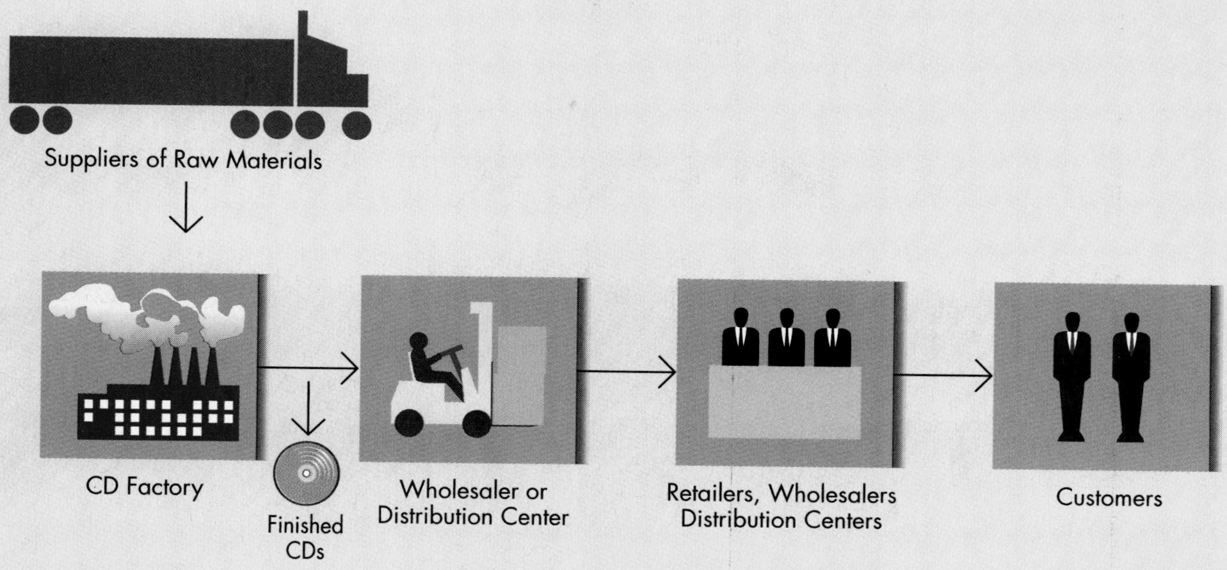

agents
Sales representatives of manufacturers and wholesalers.

brokers
Go-betweens that bring buyers and sellers together.

industrial distributors
Independent wholesalers that buy related product lines from many manufacturers and sell them to industrial users.

wholesalers
Firms that sell finished goods to retailers, manufacturers, and institutions.

retailers
Firms that sell goods to consumers and to industrial users for their own consumption.

- *Wholesalers.* **Wholesalers** are firms that sell finished goods to retailers, manufacturers, and institutions (such as schools and hospitals). Historically, their function has been to buy from manufacturers and sell to retailers.
- *Retailers.* **Retailers** are firms that sell goods to consumers and to industrial users for their own consumption.

At the end of the distribution channel are final consumers, like you and me, and industrial users. Industrial users are firms that buy products for internal use or for producing other products or services. They include manufacturers, utilities, airlines, railroads, and service institutions, such as hotels, hospitals, and schools.

Exhibit 15.2 shows various ways marketing intermediaries can be linked. For instance, a manufacturer may sell to a wholesaler that sells to a retailer that in turn sells to a customer. In any of these distribution systems, goods and services are physically transferred from one organization to the next. As each takes possession of the products, it may take legal ownership of them. As the exhibit indicates, distribution channels can handle either consumer products or industrial products.

The Functions of Distribution Channels

Why do distribution channels exist? Why can't every firm sell its products directly to the end user or consumer? Why are go-betweens needed? Channels serve a number of functions.

Channels Reduce the Number of Transactions Channels make distribution simpler by reducing the number of transactions required to get a product from the manufacturer to the consumer. Assume for the moment that only four students are in your class. Also assume that your professor requires five textbooks, each from a different publisher. If there were no bookstore, 20 transactions would be necessary for all students in the class to buy the books, as shown in Exhibit 15.3. If the bookstore serves as a go-between, the number of transactions is reduced to nine. Each publisher sells to one bookstore

Exhibit 15.2 | Channels of Distribution for Industrial and Consumer Products

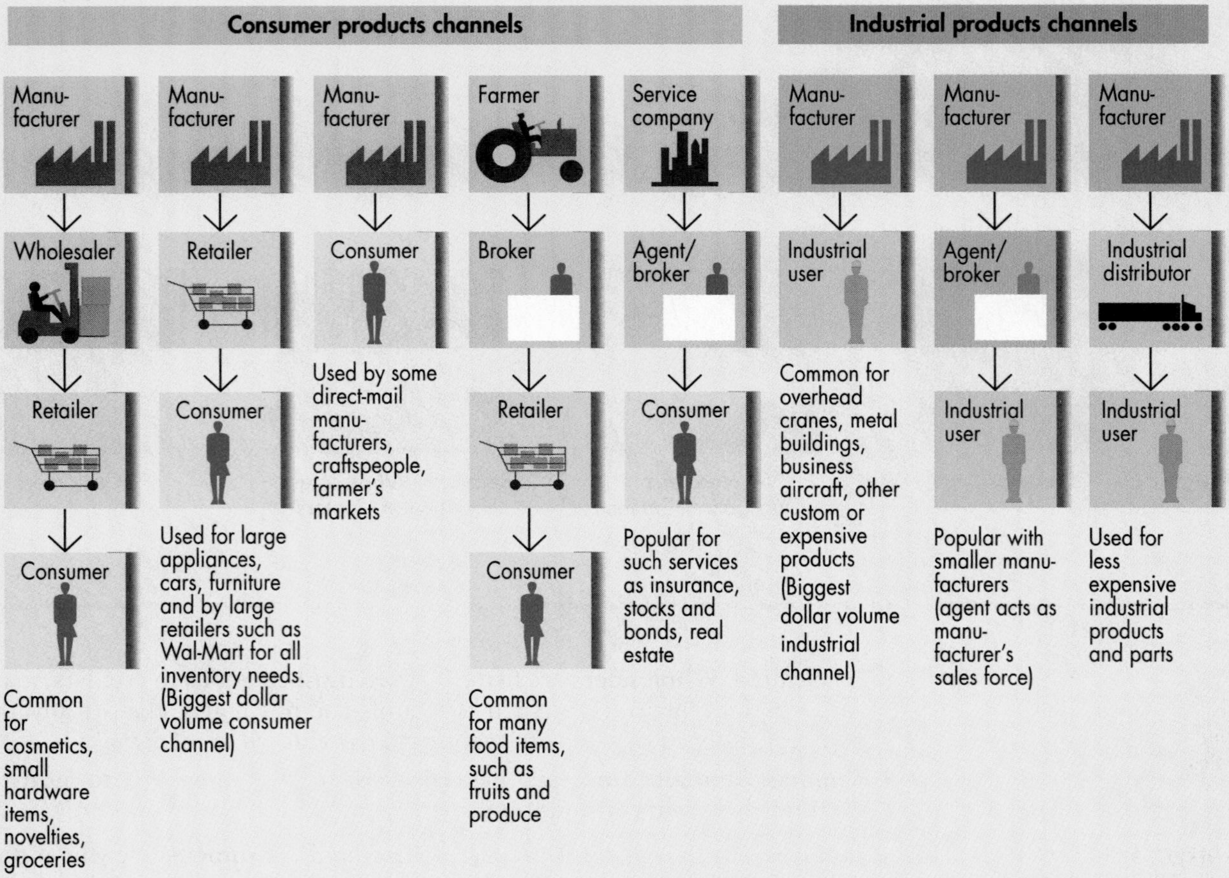

An efficient distribution system allows Home Depot to economically offer customers a vast assortment of building materials, appliances, and tools.

© MICHAEL NEWMAN / PHOTOEDIT

Exhibit 15.3 | How Distribution Channels Reduce the Number of Transactions

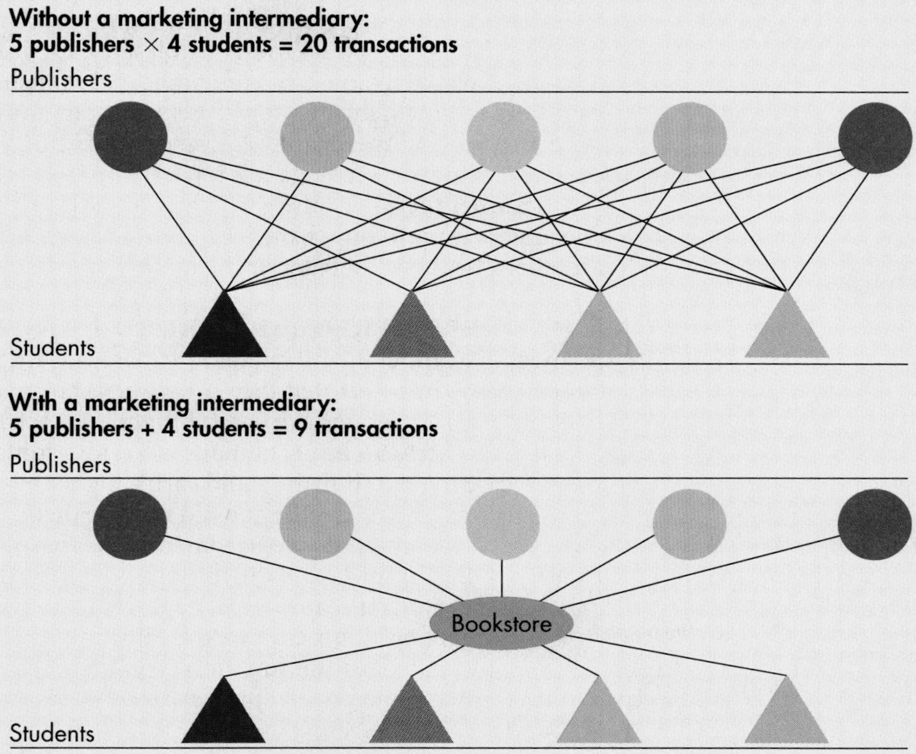

rather than to four students. Each student buys from one bookstore instead of from five publishers.

Dealing with channel intermediaries frees producers from many of the details of distribution activity. Producers are traditionally not as efficient or as enthusiastic about selling products directly to end users as channel members are. First, producers may wish to focus on production. They may feel that they cannot both produce and distribute in a competitive way. On the other hand, manufacturers are eager to deal directly with giant retailers, such as Wal-Mart. Wal-Mart offers huge sales opportunities to producers.

CHANNELS EASE THE FLOW OF GOODS Channels make distribution easier in several ways. The first is by *sorting,* which consists of the following:

- *Sorting out.* Breaking many different items into separate stocks that are similar. Eggs, for instance, are sorted by grade and size.
- *Accumulating.* Bringing similar stocks together into a larger quantity. Twelve large grade A eggs could be placed in some cartons and 12 medium grade B eggs in other cartons.
- *Allocating.* Breaking similar products into smaller and smaller lots. (Allocating at the wholesale level is called **breaking bulk.**) For instance, a tank-car load of milk could be broken down into gallon jugs. The process of allocating generally is done when the goods are dispersed by region and as ownership of the goods changes.

breaking bulk
The process of breaking large shipments of similar products into smaller, more usable lots.

Without the sorting, accumulating, and allocating processes, modern society would not exist. We would have home-based industries providing custom or semicustom products to local markets. In short, we would return to a much lower level of consumption.

A second way channels ease the flow of goods is by locating buyers for merchandise. A wholesaler must find the right retailers to sell a profitable volume of merchandise. A sporting-goods wholesaler, for instance, must find the retailers who are most likely to reach sporting-goods consumers. Retailers have to understand the buying habits of consumers and put stores where consumers want and expect to find the merchandise. Every member of a distribution channel must locate buyers for the products it is trying to sell.

Channel members also store merchandise so that goods are available when consumers want to buy them. The high cost of retail space often means that goods are stored by the wholesaler or the manufacturer.

Channels Perform Needed Functions The functions performed by channel members help increase the efficiency of the channel. Yet consumers sometimes feel that the go-betweens create higher prices. They doubt that these intermediaries perform useful functions. Actually, however, if channel members did not perform important and necessary functions at a reasonable cost, they would cease to exist. If firms could earn a higher profit without using certain channel members, they would not use them.

A useful rule to remember is that, although channel members can be eliminated, their functions cannot. The manufacturer must either perform the functions of the intermediaries itself or find new ways of getting them carried out. Publishers can bypass bookstores, for instance, but the function performed by the bookstores then has to be performed by the publishers or by someone else.

concept check

List and define the marketing intermediaries that make up a distribution channel.

How do channels reduce the number of transactions?

Define breaking bulk.

How Channels Organize and Cover Markets

3 learning goal

In an efficient distribution channel, all the channel members work smoothly together and do what they're expected to do. A manufacturer expects wholesalers to promote its products to retailers and to perform several other functions as well. Not all channels have a leader or a single firm that sets channel policies. But all channels have members who rely on one another.

Vertical Marketing Systems

To increase the efficiency of distribution channels, many firms have turned to vertical marketing systems. In a **vertical marketing system,** firms are aligned in a hierarchy (such as manufacturer to wholesaler to retailer). Such systems are planned, organized, formalized versions of distribution channels. The three basic types of vertical marketing systems are corporate, administrative, and contractual.

vertical marketing system
An organized, formal distribution channel in which firms are aligned in a hierarchy such as from manufacturer to wholesaler to retailer.

Corporate Distribution Systems In a **corporate distribution system,** one firm owns the entire channel of distribution. Corporate systems are tops in channel control. A single firm that owns the whole channel has no need to worry about channel members. The channel owner will always have supplies of raw materials and long-term contact with customers. It will have good distribution and product exposure in the marketplace.

corporate distribution system
A vertical marketing system in which one firm owns the entire distribution channel.

Examples of corporate distribution systems abound. Evans Products Co. (a manufacturer of plywood), for instance, bought wholesale lumber distributors to better market its products to retail dealers. This move was an example of forward integration. **Forward integration** occurs when a manufacturer acquires a marketing intermediary closer to the customer, such as a wholesaler or retailer. A wholesaler could integrate forward by buying a retailer. Other examples of forward

forward integration
The acquisition by a market intermediary of another marketing intermediary closer to the customer.

integration include Sherwin-Williams, a paint maker that operates over 2,000 paint stores, and Hart Schaffner and Marx, a long-established menswear manufacturer that owns more than 100 clothing outlets. Or a manufacturer might integrate forward by buying a wholesaler. For decades, Pepsi-Cola focused on supplying syrup and concentrate to independent bottlers. But in the 1980s, it decided it could best satisfy retailers' demands by serving them itself. After spending several billion dollars to buy out independent bottlers, Pepsi-Cola today owns bottling and distributing operations that account for half the soda in its system. This strategy created many opportunities for supply chain improvement through a reorganization of its bottling and distribution network. To guide those decisions, Pepsi analyzed demographic trends to identify locations that would yield long-term growth and warrant future expansion. It coupled this information with soft-drink consumption trends and marketing forecasts, thus determining when and where new plants should be located. But none of this would have been possible without the purchase of its bottling and distribution outlets.

backward integration
The acquisition of the production process by a wholesaler or retailer.

Backward integration is just the reverse of forward integration. It occurs when a wholesaler or retailer gains control over the production process. Many large retail organizations have integrated backward. Sears has part ownership of production facilities that supply over 30 percent of its inventory. Wal-Mart bought McLane Co., a Texas wholesaler with a reputation as one of the best specialty distributors of cigarettes, candy, and perishables in the United States. With McLane, Wal-Mart can avoid outside distributors and can lower overall costs.

administrative distribution system
A vertical marketing system in which a strong organization takes over as leader and sets policies for the distribution channel.

Administrative Distribution Systems In an **administrative distribution system,** a strong organization takes over as leader and sets channel policies. The leadership role is informal; it is not written into a contract. Companies such as Gillette, Hanes, Campbell's, and Westinghouse are administrative system leaders. They can often influence or control the policies of other channel members without the costs and expertise required to set up a corporate distribution system. They may be able to dictate how many wholesalers will be in the channel or, for example, require that the wholesalers offer 60-day credit to retail customers, among other things.

contractual distribution system
A vertical marketing system in which a network of independent firms at different levels (manufacturer, wholesaler, retailer) coordinate their distribution activities through a written contract.

Contractual Distribution Systems The third form of vertical marketing is a **contractual distribution system.** It is a network of independent firms at different levels (manufacturer, wholesaler, retailer) that coordinate their distribution activities through a written contract. Franchises (described in Chapter 5) are a common form of the contractual system. The parent companies of McDonald's and Chemlawn, for instance, control distribution of their products through the franchise agreement each franchisee signs.

exclusive distribution
A distribution system in which a manufacturer selects only one or two dealers in an area to market its products.

The Intensity of Market Coverage

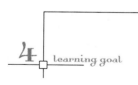

4 learning goal

All types of distribution systems must be concerned with market coverage. How many dealers will be used to distribute the product in a particular area? As Exhibit 15.4 shows, the three degrees of coverage are exclusive, selective, and intensive. The type of product determines the intensity of the market coverage.

When a manufacturer selects one or two dealers in an area to market its products, it is using **exclusive distribution.** Only items that are in strong demand can be distributed exclusively because consumers must be willing to travel some distance to buy them. If Wrigley's chewing gum were sold in only one drugstore per city, Wrigley's would soon be out of business. However, Bang and Olufsen stereo components, Jaguar automobiles, and Adrienne Vittadini designer clothing are distributed exclusively with great success.

selective distribution
A distribution system in which a manufacturer selects a limited number of dealers in an area (but more than one or two) to market its products.

A manufacturer that chooses a limited number of dealers in an area (but more than one or two) is using **selective distribution.** Since the number of retailers

Exhibit 15.4 | Different Products Require Different Degrees of Market Coverage

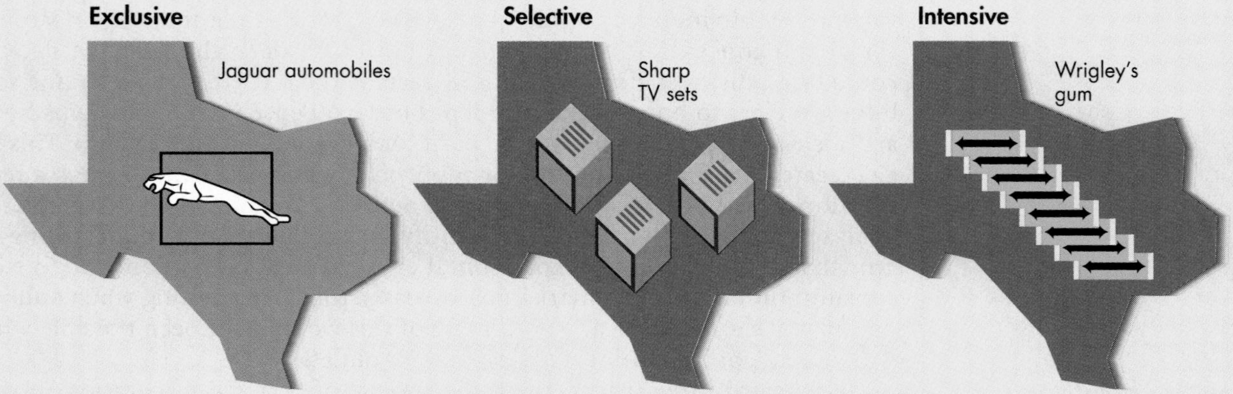

intensive distribution
A distribution system in which a manufacturer tries to sell its products wherever there are potential customers.

handling the product is limited, consumers must be willing to seek it out. Timberland boots, a high-quality line of footwear, are distributed selectively. So are Sony televisions, Maytag washers, Waterford crystal, and Tommy Hilfiger clothing. When choosing dealers, manufacturers look for certain qualities. Sony may seek retailers that can offer high-quality customer service. Tommy Hilfiger may look for retailers with high-traffic locations in regional shopping malls. All manufacturers try to exclude retailers that are a poor credit risk or that have a weak or negative image.

concept check

What is meant by an efficient channel of distribution?

Name the three degrees of market coverage.

Describe the types of products that are distributed using intensive distribution.

A manufacturer that wants to sell its products everywhere there are potential customers is using **intensive distribution.** Such consumer goods as bread, tape, and lightbulbs are often distributed intensively. Usually, these products cost little and are bought frequently, which means that complex distribution channels are necessary. Coca-Cola is sold in just about every type of retail business, from gas stations to supermarkets.

WHOLESALING

5 learning goal

Wholesalers are channel members that buy finished products from manufacturers and sell them to retailers. Retailers in turn sell the products to consumers. Manufacturers that use selective or exclusive distribution normally sell directly to retailers. Manufacturers that use intensive distribution often rely on wholesalers.

Wholesalers also sell products to institutions, such as manufacturers, schools, and hospitals, for use in performing their own missions. A manufacturer, for instance, might buy computer paper from Nationwide Papers, a wholesaler. A hospital might buy its cleaning supplies from Lagasse Brothers, one of the nation's largest wholesalers of janitorial supplies.

Sometimes wholesalers sell products to manufacturers for use in the manufacturing process. A builder of custom boats, for instance, might buy batteries from a battery wholesaler and switches from an electrical wholesaler. Some wholesalers even sell to other wholesalers, creating yet another stage in the distribution channel.

About half of all wholesalers offer financing for their clients. They sell products on credit and expect to be paid within a certain time, usually 60 days. Other wholesalers operate like retail stores. The retailer goes to the wholesaler, selects the merchandise, pays cash for it, and transports it to the retail outlet.

Exhibit 15.5 | The Two Categories of Wholesalers

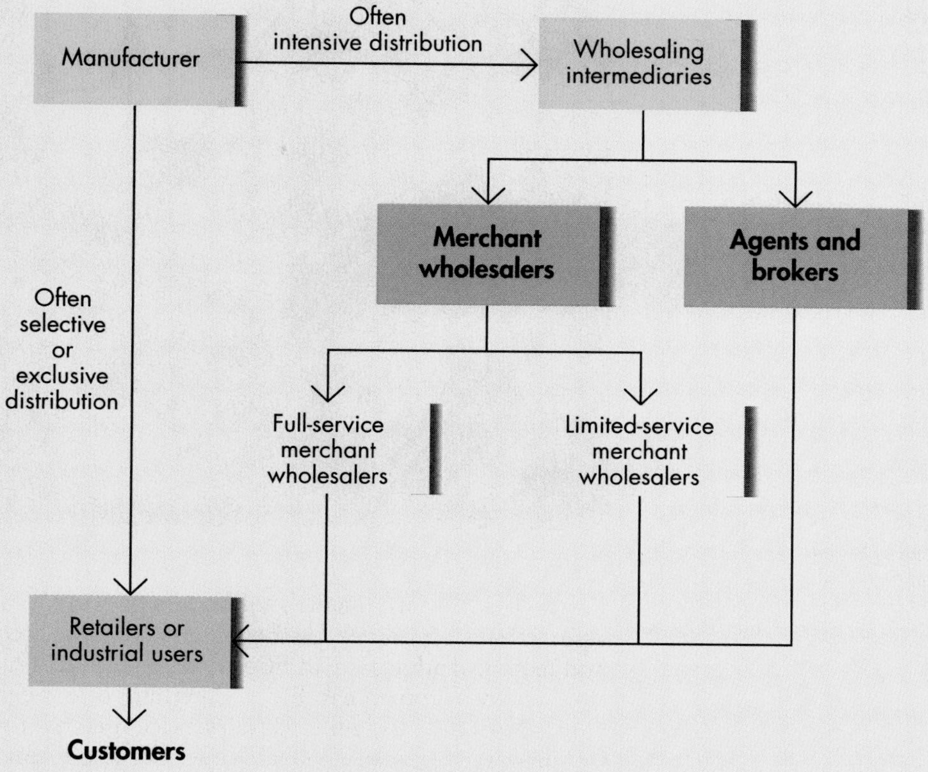

Because wholesalers usually serve limited areas, they are often located closer to retailers than the manufacturers are. Retailers can thus get faster delivery at lower cost from wholesalers. A retailer who knows that a wholesaler can restock store shelves within a day can keep a low level of inventory on hand. More money is then available for other things because less cash is tied up in items sitting on the shelves or in storerooms.

Types of Wholesalers

The two main types of wholesalers are merchant wholesalers and agents and brokers, as shown in Exhibit 15.5. Merchant wholesalers take title to the product (ownership rights); agents and brokers simply facilitate the sale of a product from producer to end user.

merchant wholesaler
An institution that buys goods from manufacturers (takes ownership) and resells them to businesses, government agencies, other wholesalers, or retailers.

MERCHANT WHOLESALERS Merchant wholesalers make up 80 percent of all wholesaling establishments and conduct slightly under 60 percent of all wholesale sales. A **merchant wholesaler** is an institution that buys goods from manufacturers and resells them to businesses, government agencies, other wholesalers, or retailers. All merchant wholesalers take title to the goods they sell. Most merchant wholesalers operate one or more warehouses where they receive goods, store them, and later reship them. Customers are mostly small or moderate-size retailers, but merchant wholesalers also market to manufacturers and institutional clients. Merchant wholesalers can be categorized as either full-service or limited-service wholesalers, depending on the number of channel functions they perform.

Business and retail customers pay cash for and carry their purchases from Sam's Club, a limited-service wholesaler that doesn't offer credit or delivery service.

full-service merchant wholesalers
Wholesalers that provide many services for their clients, such as providing credit, offering promotional and technical advice, storing and delivering merchandise, or providing installation and repairs.

limited-service merchant wholesalers
Wholesalers that typically carry a limited line of fast-moving merchandise and do not offer many services to their clients.

cash and carry wholesaler
A limited-service merchant wholesaler that does not offer credit or delivery services.

manufacturers' representatives
Salespeople who represent noncompeting manufacturers; function as independent agents rather than as salaried employees of the manufacturers.

Full-service merchant wholesalers perform many functions. They assemble an assortment of products for their clients, provide credit, and offer promotional help and technical advice. In addition, they maintain a sales force to contact customers, store and deliver merchandise, and perhaps offer research and planning support. Depending on the product line, full-service merchant wholesalers sometimes provide installation and repair as well. Full service also means "going the extra mile" to meet special customer needs, such as offering fast delivery in emergencies.

As the name implies, **limited-service merchant wholesalers** perform only a few of the full-service merchant wholesaler's activities. Generally, limited-service merchant wholesalers carry a limited line of fast-moving merchandise. They do not extend credit or supply market information. One type of limited-service merchant wholesaler is the **cash and carry wholesaler.** This wholesaler doesn't offer credit or delivery, hence the term "cash and carry" wholesaler. Sam's Clubs and Costco are nationally known cash and carry wholesalers. About 60 percent of Sam's volume is done with small businesses. These companies are unique because they are not only wholesalers but also do business with consumers. Government employees, credit union members, and employees of large corporations, among others, can pay an annual fee (usually $35) and shop at Costco or Sam's. Retail customers typically pay a 5 percent markup as well. Exhibit 15.6 lists additional types of limited-service merchant wholesalers.

AGENTS AND BROKERS As mentioned earlier, agents represent manufacturers and wholesalers. **Manufacturers' representatives** (also called **manufacturers' agents**) represent noncompeting manufacturers. These salespeople function as independent agents rather than as salaried employees of manufacturers. They do not take title to or possession of merchandise. They get commissions if they make sales—and nothing if they don't. They are found in a variety of industries, including electronics, clothing, hardware, furniture, and toys.

Brokers bring buyers and sellers together. Like agents, brokers do not take title to merchandise, they receive commissions on sales, and they have little say over company sales policies. They are found in markets where the information that would join buyers and sellers is scarce. These markets include real estate, agriculture, insurance, and commodities.

concept check

Define wholesaling and describe what wholesalers do.

Describe merchant wholesalers and the categories of merchant wholesalers.

Explain the difference between agents and brokers.

Exhibit 15.6 Limited-Service Merchant Wholesalers

Cash and carry wholesalers:	Have a limited line of fast-moving goods and sell to small retailers for cash. Normally do not deliver.
Truck wholesalers:	Perform primarily a selling and delivery function. Carry a limited line of semiperishable merchandise (such as milk, bread, snack foods), which they sell for cash as they make their rounds of supermarkets, small groceries, hospitals, restaurants, factory cafeterias, and hotels.
Drop shippers:	Operate in bulk industries, such as coal, lumber, and heavy equipment. Do not carry inventory or handle the product. Upon receiving an order, they select a manufacturer, who ships the merchandise directly to the customer on the agreed-upon terms and time of delivery. The drop shipper assumes title and risk from the time the order is accepted to its delivery to the customer.
Rack jobbers:	Serve grocery and drug retailers, mostly in the area of nonfood items. They send delivery trucks to stores, and the delivery people set up toys, paperbacks, hardware items, health and beauty aids, and so on. They price the goods, keep them fresh, set up point-of-purchase displays, and keep inventory records. Rack jobbers retain title to the goods and bill the retailers only for the goods sold to consumers. They do little promotion because they carry many branded items that are highly advertised.
Producers' cooperatives:	Owned by farmer members and assemble farm produce to sell in local markets. The co-op's profits are distributed to members at the end of the year. Co-ops often attempt to improve product quality and promote a co-op brand name, such as Sun Maid raisins, Sunkist oranges, or Diamond walnuts.

The Competitive World of Retailing

6 learning goal

Some 30 million Americans are engaged in retailing. Of this number, almost 16 million work in service businesses like barber shops, lawyers' offices, and amusement parks. Although most retailers are involved in small businesses, most sales are made by the giant retail organizations, such as Sears, Wal-Mart, Target, and JCPenney. Half of all retail sales come from fewer than 10 percent of all retail businesses. This small group employs about 40 percent of all retail workers. Retailers feel the impact of changes in the economy more than many other types of businesses. Survival depends on keeping up with changing lifestyles and customer shopping patterns.

Types of Retail Operations

There is a great deal of variety in retail operations. The major types of retailers are described in Exhibit 15.7, which divides them into two main categories: in-store and nonstore retailing. Examples of *in-store retailing* include Sears, Wal-Mart, Target, Saks, and Marshall Field's. These retailers get most of their revenue from people who come to the store to buy what they want. Many in-store retailers also do some catalog and telephone sales.

Nonstore retailing includes vending, direct selling, direct-response marketing, home shopping networks, and Internet retailing. Vending uses machines to sell food and other items, usually as a convenience in institutions like schools and hospitals.

Direct selling involves face-to-face contact between the buyer and seller, but not in a retail store. Usually, the seller goes to the consumer's home. Sometimes contacts are made at the place of work. Mary Kay Cosmetics, Avon, Herbalife, and Amway each employ over 100,000 direct salespeople. Some companies, such as

Exhibit 15.7 Retailing Takes Many Forms

Types of In-Store Retailing	Description	Examples
Department store	Houses many departments under one roof with each treated as a separate buying center to achieve economies of buying, promotion, and control	JCPenney, Saks, May Co., Rich's, Bloomingdale's
Specialty store	Specializes in a category of merchandise and carries a complete assortment	Toys "R" Us, Radio Shack, Zales Jewelers
Convenience store	Offers convenience goods with long store hours and quick checkout	7-Eleven, Circle K
Supermarket	Specializes in a wide assortment of food, with self-service	Safeway, Kroger, Winn Dixie
Discount store	Competes on the basis of low prices and high turnover; offers few services	Wal-Mart, Target
Off-price retailer	Sells at prices 25 percent or more below traditional department store prices in spartan environment	Robs, T.J. Maxx, Clothestime
Factory outlet	Owned by manufacturer; sells close-outs, factory seconds, and canceled orders	Levi Strauss, Ship 'n Shore, Dansk
Catalog store	Sends catalogs to customers and displays merchandise in showrooms where customers can order from attached warehouse	Best, Lurias
Hypermart	Offers huge selection of food and general merchandise with very low prices; sometimes called "mall without a wall"	Hypermart USA, American Fare
Types of Nonstore Retailing	**Description**	**Examples**
Vending machine	Sells merchandise by machine	Canteen
Direct selling	Sells face-to-face, usually in the person's home	Fuller Brush, Avon, Amway
Direct-response marketing	Attempts to get immediate consumer sale through media advertising, catalogs, or direct mail	K-Tel, L.L. Bean, Ronco
Home shopping networks	Selling via cable television	Home Shopping Network, QVC
Internet retailing (e-commerce)	Selling over the Internet	Bluefly.com, landsend.com, gap.com, Amazon.com, Cheapstuff.com, Dell.com

Tupperware and Longaberger baskets, specialize in parties in a person's home. Most parties are a combination social affair and sales demonstration. The hostess usually gets a discount and a special gift for rounding up a group of friends. Such parties seem to be replacing door-to-door canvassing. The sales of many direct-sales companies have suffered, however, as women continue to enter the workforce on a full-time basis.

Direct-response marketing is conducted through media that encourage a consumer to reply. Popular direct-response media are catalogs, direct mail, television, newspapers, and radio. The ads invite a person to "call the toll-free number now" or to fill out an order blank. Direct-response marketing includes K-Tel selling "golden oldies" and an ex-racecar driver touting herbal baldness remedies. It also

Focusing on Small Business

Young E-Retailers Challenge Nike

Eric Eways sits at a computer squeezed between his red bunk bed and roughly six dozen shoe boxes, scouring an inbox full of e-mails from sneaker shops in France, Kuwait, and Taiwan. The phone rings, and Mr. Eways, who is 16 years old, dictates the terms of the transaction: "Take whatever he can get. If he says he can get 17 of the Greeks, buy all 17."

The Greeks in question are Nike basketball sneakers. They are embroidered on each heel with the Greek letters Alpha Phi Alpha, the name of an African American college fraternity. Nike Inc., which makes small runs of shoes for all kinds of special events, produced a limited edition of roughly 2,000 pairs—the company won't say how many—in honor of Alpha Phi Alpha's sponsorship of Philadelphia's annual "Greek Picnic," a major summer gathering of African American fraternities and sororities that hadn't even begun as Mr. Eways closed his deal.

Beyond the college students, a far more lucrative market exists for Nike's Greeks. Around the world, sneaker fanatics are willing to pay hundreds and sometimes thousands of dollars to buy rare styles. Eways and his 27-year-old business partner, Joe Guerrero, are among the most aggressive of the dozens of middlemen who work their contacts on the Internet and among retailers, snapping up as many shoes as possible—even before some stores have had a chance to put them on their shelves—and reselling them at a profit.

From Eway's cluttered Brooklyn bedroom—where he and Guerrero operate an online store called sneakerpimp.com—the two are subverting a key marketing strategy of one of the world's most savvy consumer giants. Nike's goal is to release a limited number of hot collectibles at targeted stores on particular dates, which can generate "buzz" at those outlets and lure customers to buy other Nike products. But sneakerpimp.com and other online operators effectively hijack the process for their own ends.

Eways and Guerrero exemplify how entrepreneurs are taking advantage of technology to complicate not just the traditional distribution channels but also the marketing efforts of big companies. Others who have done so include the creators of Napster and other music-sharing Web sites. There's also Harry Knowles, an Austin, Texas, film junkie whose aintitcoolnews.com reports on movies before they are released, sometimes undermining Hollywood studios' publicity plans. Yet all these big corporations also benefit from the obsessive attention of their most mercenary fans. The independent operators generate a sense of excitement and elusiveness, and can help the big companies tap into the consumer desire for nostalgic products.[2]

Critical Thinking Questions

1. Are Eways and Guerrero demonstrating ethical business practices by snatching up Nike shoes and reselling them for a profit?
2. Should Nike try to shut down sneakerpimp.com?
3. Is e-commerce going to drive some traditional companies out of business?

includes the catalogs sent out by Land's End, L. L. Bean, J. Crew, Nordstrom's, and countless others.

Internet retailing, also called e-commerce, is the selling of merchandise over the Internet. E-commerce sales are exploding and will have a profound impact on retailers around the world. It is also going to change how you shop. Strategies for online shopping are covered later in this chapter.

Components of a Successful Retailing Strategy

Retailing is a very competitive business. Managers have to develop an effective strategy to survive. The key tasks in building a retail strategy are defining a target market, developing a product offering, creating an image and a promotional strategy, choosing a location, and setting prices.

Defining a Target Market The first and foremost task in developing a retail strategy is to define the target market. This process begins with market segmentation, the topic of an earlier chapter, and the determination of a target market. For example, Target's merchandising approach for sporting goods is to match its product assortment to the demographics of the local store and region. Target stores in the Northeast stock a variety of ski equipment to satisfy the local interest in downhill and cross-country skiing. The amount of space devoted to sporting goods, as well as in-store promotions, also varies according to each store's target market.

Target markets in retailing are often defined by demographics. Dollar General and Family Dollar stores target households earning less than $25,000 per year. Eddie Bauer targets suburban 25- to 45-year-olds. Claire's, a retailer selling inexpensive costume jewelry, such as Y-shaped necklaces, wire tricep bracelets, and headbands, targets 12- to 14-year-old girls.

Developing the Product Offering The second element in determining a retail strategy is the product offering, also called the product assortment or merchandise mix. Retailers decide what to sell on the basis of what their target market wants to buy. They can base their decision on market research, past sales, fashion trends, customer requests, and other sources. For example, after more companies began promoting office casual days, Brooks Brothers, the upscale retailer of men's and women's conservative business wear, updated its product line with khaki pants, casual shirts, and a selection of brightly colored shirts and ties.

efficient consumer response (ECR)
A method of managing inventory and streamlining the movement of products from supplier to distributor to retailer; relies on electronic data interchange to communicate information such as automatic shipping notifications, invoices, inventory data, and forecasts.

electronic data interchange (EDI)
Computer-to-computer exchange of information, including automatic shipping notifications, invoices, inventory data, and forecasts; used in efficient consumer response systems.

After determining what products will satisfy target customers' desires, retailers must find sources of supply and evaluate the products. When the right products are located, the retail buyer negotiates a purchase contract. The buying function can be performed in-house or delegated to an outside firm. The goods must then be moved from the seller to the retailer, which means shipping, storing, and stocking the inventory. The trick is to manage the inventory by cutting prices to move slow goods and by keeping adequate supplies of hot-selling items in stock.

One of the more efficient new methods of managing inventory and streamlining the way products are moved from supplier to distributor to retailer is called **efficient consumer response (ECR).** At the heart of ECR is **electronic data interchange (EDI),** the computer-to-computer exchange of information, including automatic shipping notifications, invoices, inventory data, and forecasts. In a full implementation of ECR, products are scanned at the retail store when purchased, which updates the store's inventory lists. Headquarters then polls the stores to retrieve the data needed to produce an order. The vendor confirms the order, shipping date, and delivery time, then ships the order, and transmits the invoice electronically. The item is received at the warehouse, scanned into inventory, and then sent to the store. The invoice and receiving data are reconciled, and payment via an electronic transfer of funds completes the process. Many retailers are experimenting with or have successfully implemented ECR and EDI. Dillard's, one of the fastest-growing regional department store chains, has one of the most technologically advanced ECR systems in the industry.

A retailer's image is made up of the store's merchandise mix, service level, and atmosphere. Williams-Sonoma's store image includes knowledgeable salespeople, elegant merchandise displays, and specialty bakeware.

The pioneer and market leader in ECR systems is Wal-Mart. Now, the retailing giant is carrying ECR a step further with radio ID tags, discussed in the "Applying Technology" box.

Creating an Image and Promotional Strategy The third task in developing a retail strategy is to create an image and a promotional strategy. Promotion combines with the store's merchandise mix, service level, and atmosphere to make up a retail image. We will discuss promotion in more detail in the next chapter. *Atmosphere* refers to the physical layout and décor of the store. They can create a relaxed or busy feeling, a sense of luxury, a friendly or cold attitude, and a sense of organization or clutter.

Applying Technology

This Radio Doesn't Play the Top 40

Retailers, their suppliers, and zealous techies are abuzz with the idea of slapping small devices known as radio frequency identification (RFID) tags on products to track them from the assembly line to your shopping cart.

When a tag comes in range of a reader, the radio signal powers up the tag. The computer chip on the tag then sends back a radio signal to the reader containing the data with which it has been encoded. In the systems that Wal-Mart and other retailers have begun piloting, the reader is linked to a computer network, where software is able to analyze the data sent back by the tagged object, identify it, and then issue instructions based on that. The software, for example, might charge a customer's account for the item, order a robot arm to pack the object in a specific mail-order shipment box, register in a database that the tagged item has made it from the warehouse to the store's shelves, and note that a customer had taken an item into a dressing room but decided not to buy it.

When it comes to retail, the appeal is that you won't just be able to tag a product generically as a bottle of milk, for example, as you currently would with a Universal Product Code, or UPC, bar code. You could theoretically give each bottle its own distinct code, which would let you keep track of where a given bottle is any time, where exactly it came from, and when the milk is due to expire.

The other main advantage is that you don't have to manually scan each item every time you want to check this information—wireless readers can query as many as hundreds of tags at the same time and do so from several feet away without the individual tags having to be visible. This means a whole crate-load of bottles could be scanned without removing each one. A shelf-mounted reader might provide updates on the number of bottles left. For consumers, it means the ability to speed up the checkout process by pushing your shopping cart in front of a wireless radio reader.

On top of that, a whole range of other applications will be possible once RFID becomes more common. A tagged shirt, for example, might wirelessly tell your washing machine at what temperature it needs to be cleaned—or tell your dry cleaner that the shirt belongs to you.[3]

CRITICAL THINKING QUESTIONS

1. Can you think of other uses for radio ID tags?
2. How can Wal-Mart use the tags to gain more customer satisfaction?
3. The tags currently cost about 5 cents each. Is this a problem for retailers?

These are the most influential factors in creating a store's atmosphere:

- *Employee type and density.* Employee type refers to an employee's general characteristics—for instance, neat, friendly, knowledgeable, or service oriented. Density is the number of employees per 1,000 square feet of selling space. A discounter such as Target has a low employee density that creates a "do-it-yourself" casual atmosphere.
- *Merchandise type and density.* The type of merchandise carried and how it is displayed add to the atmosphere the retailer is trying to create. A prestigious retailer such as Saks or Marshall Field's carries the best brand names and displays them in a neat, uncluttered arrangement.
- *Fixture type and density.* Fixtures can be elegant (rich woods), trendy (chrome and smoked glass), or old, beat-up tables, as in an antique store. The fixtures should be consistent with the general atmosphere the store is trying to create. By displaying its merchandise on tables and shelves rather than on traditional pipe racks, the Gap creates a relaxed and uncluttered atmosphere that enables customers to see and touch the merchandise more easily.
- *Sound.* Sound can be pleasant or unpleasant for a customer. Classical music at a nice Italian restaurant helps create ambiance, just as country and western music does at a truck stop. Music can also entice customers to stay in the store longer and buy more or encourage them to eat quickly and leave a table for others.
- *Odors.* Smell can either stimulate or detract from sales. The wonderful smell of pastries and breads entices bakery customers. Conversely, customers can be repulsed by bad odors, such as cigarette smoke, musty smells, antiseptic odors, and overly powerful room deodorizers.

Choosing a Location The next task in creating a retail strategy is figuring out where to put the store. First, a community must be chosen. This decision depends on the strength of the local economy, the nature of the competition, the political climate, and so forth. Then a specific site must be selected. One important decision is whether to locate in a shopping center. Large retailers and sellers of shopping goods like furniture and cars can use a free-standing store because customers will seek them out. Such a location also has the advantages of low-cost land or rent and no direct competitors close by. It may be harder to attract customers to a free-standing location, however. Another disadvantage is that the retailer can't share costs for promotion, maintenance, and holiday decorating, as do stores in a mall.

Setting Prices Another strategic task of the retail manager is to set prices. The strategy of pricing was presented in Chapter 14. Retailing's goal is to sell products, and the price is critical in ensuring that sales take place.

Price is also one of the three key elements in the store's image and positioning strategy. Higher prices often imply quality and help support the prestige image of such retailers as Lord & Taylor, Saks Fifth Avenue, Coach, Cartier, and Neiman-Marcus. On the other hand, discounters and off-price retailers offer good value for the money.

concept check

Describe at least five types of in-store retailing and four forms of nonstore retailing.

Discuss the components of a successful retail strategy.

Using Supply Chain Management to Increase Efficiency and Customer Satisfaction

7 learning goal

Distribution is an important part of the marketing mix. Retailers don't sell products they can't deliver, and salespeople don't (or shouldn't) promise deliveries they can't make. Late deliveries and broken promises may mean loss of a customer. Accurate order filling and billing, timely delivery, and arrival in good condition are important to the success of the product.

The goal of supply chain management is to create a satisfied customer by coordinating all of the activities of the supply chain members into a seamless process. Therefore, an important element of supply chain management is that it is completely customer driven. In the mass-production era, manufacturers produced standardized products that were "pushed" down through the supply channel to the consumer. In contrast, in today's marketplace, products are being driven by customers, who expect to receive product configurations and services matched to their unique needs. For example, Dell only builds computers according to its customers' precise specifications, such as the amount of RAM memory; type of monitor, modem, or CD drive; and amount of hard-disk space.[4]

Through the channel partnership of suppliers, manufacturers, wholesalers, and retailers along the entire supply chain who work together toward the common goal of creating customer value, supply chain management allows companies to respond with the unique product configuration and mix of services demanded by the customer. Today, supply chain management plays a dual role: first, as a *communicator* of customer demand that extends from the point of sale all the way back to the supplier, and second, as a *physical flow process* that engineers the timely and cost-effective movement of goods through the entire supply pipeline.

Accordingly, supply chain managers are responsible for making channel strategy decisions, coordinating the sourcing and procurement of raw materials, scheduling production, processing orders, managing inventory, transporting and storing supplies and finished goods, and coordinating customer service activities.

Making Ethical Choices

xtra! http://gitmanxtra.swlearning.com

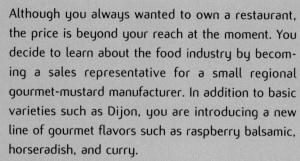

CUTTING THE MUSTARD

Although you always wanted to own a restaurant, the price is beyond your reach at the moment. You decide to learn about the food industry by becoming a sales representative for a small regional gourmet-mustard manufacturer. In addition to basic varieties such as Dijon, you are introducing a new line of gourmet flavors such as raspberry balsamic, horseradish, and curry.

You sell to a variety of food outlets: restaurants, gourmet-food stores, upscale markets, and major grocery chains such as Safeway, Giant, and Whole Foods. One of your biggest challenges is getting the chains to give you decent shelf space for your products. Your company must compete with large food manufacturers like French's and Kraft, whose Nabisco division makes the popular Grey Poupon line. Kraft's large product line and huge promotional budget give it incredible marketing clout with retailers.

Although your products are well received by consumers in smaller retail outlets, getting the chains to carry them isn't easy. It's standard practice for food manufacturers and distributors to pay retailers "slotting fees" for premium shelf position in their stores and even to limit shelf space for competing products.

Until now, your CEO has refused to pay slotting fees and considers them unethical, believing that they ultimately raise prices from consumers and curtail competition. Retailers, on the other hand, consider the fees a legitimate promotional expense and compensation for the risk of selling new products—not to mention a revenue source that can range from $5,000 to over $50,000. Your fellow specialty-food manufacturers have been hesitant to speak up in government hearings about these fees, for fear of being blackballed by supermarkets.

ETHICAL DILEMMA

Your company's three-year sales plan—and your success in meeting your sales quota—depends on getting larger distribution for your new product line. Should you recommend that your company begin to pay slotting fees to get better and more shelf space?

SOURCES: Chris Baker, "It's Yellow, but not French," *The Washington Times*, March 19, 2003, downloaded from http://www.washingtontimes.com; Brandon Copple, "Shelf-Determination," *Forbes*, April 14, 2002, downloaded from http://www.Forbes.com; "Controversial 'Slotting Fees' More Common, Costly," *Silicon Valley/San Jose Business Journal*, December 12, 2002, downloaded from http://sanjose.bizjournals.com; Eric Wieffering, "Grocery Shelves: Stock Strategies," *Minneapolis Star Tribune*, March 7, 2003, p. 1A.

Supply chain managers are also responsible for the management of information that flows through the supply chain. Coordinating the relationships between the company and its external partners, such as vendors, carriers, and third-party companies, is also a critical function of supply chain management. Because supply chain managers play such a major role in both cost control and customer satisfaction, they are more valuable than ever.

Managing the Logistical Components of the Supply Chain

Logistics, discussed earlier, is a term borrowed from the military that describes the process of strategically managing the efficient flow and storage of raw materials, in-process inventory, and finished goods from the point of origin to point of consumption. The supply chain team manages the logistical flow. Key decisions in managing the logistical flow are: finding and procuring raw materials and supplies, production scheduling, choosing a warehouse location and type, setting up a materials-handling system, and making transportation decisions.

Sourcing and Procurement

One of the most important links in the supply chain is that between the manufacturer and the supplier. Purchasing professionals are on the front lines of supply chain management. Purchasing departments plan purchasing strategies, develop specifications, select suppliers, and negotiate price and service levels.

The goal of most sourcing and procurement activities is to reduce the costs of raw materials and supplies and to have the items available when they are needed for production or for the office but not before (see just-in-time manufacturing in Chapter 12).

Production Scheduling

In traditional mass-market manufacturing, production begins when forecasts call for additional products to be made or inventory control systems signal low inventory levels. The firm then makes a product and transports the finished goods to its own warehouses or those of intermediaries, where the goods wait to be ordered by retailers or customers. Production scheduling based on pushing a product down to the consumer obviously has its disadvantages, the most notable being that companies risk making products that may become obsolete or that consumers don't want in the first place.

In a customer "pull" manufacturing environment, which is growing in popularity, production of goods or services is not scheduled until an order is placed by the customer specifying the desired configuration. This process, known as *mass customization,* or *build-to-order,* uniquely tailors mass-market goods and services to the needs of the individuals who buy them. Mass customization was explained in Chapter 14. Companies as diverse as BMW, Dell Computer, Levi Strauss, Mattel,

© AP / WIDE WORLD PHOTOS

Reliable and inexpensive water transportation is one of the five major modes of transportation that distribution managers can choose from to move products from the producer to the buyer.

and a slew of Web-based businesses are adopting mass customization to maintain or obtain a competitive edge.

Choosing a Warehouse Location and Type

Deciding where to put a warehouse is mostly a matter of deciding which markets will be served and where production facilities will be located. A *storage warehouse* is used to hold goods for a long time. For instance, Jantzen makes bathing suits at an even rate throughout the year to provide steady employment and hold down costs. It then stores them in a warehouse until the selling season.

distribution centers
Warehouses that specialize in changing shipment sizes, rather than in storing goods.

Distribution centers are a special form of warehouse. They specialize in changing shipment sizes rather than storing goods. Such centers make bulk (put shipments together) or break bulk. They strive for rapid inventory turnover. When shipments arrive, the merchandise is quickly sorted into orders for various retail stores. As soon as the order is complete, it is delivered. Distribution centers are the wave of the future, replacing traditional warehouses. Companies simply can't afford to have a lot of money tied up in idle inventory.

Setting Up a Materials-Handling System

A materials-handling system moves and handles inventory. The goal of such a system is to move items as quickly as possible while handling them as little as possible. Rite Aid, the huge drugstore chain, uses bar codes, moving carousels and eight miles of conveyors to process 60,000 cartons a day in its California distribution center. Its sophisticated materials-handling system provided 99.6 percent accuracy and a 99 percent on-time delivery to its retail drug stores.[5]

Making Transportation Decisions

Transportation typically accounts for between 5 and 10 percent of the price of goods. Physical-distribution managers must decide which mode of transportation to use to move products from producer to buyer. This decision is, of course, related to all other physical-distribution decisions. The five major modes of transportation are railroads, motor carriers, pipelines, water transportation, and airways. Distribution managers generally choose a mode of transportation on the basis of several criteria:

- *Cost.* The total amount a specific carrier charges to move the product from the point of origin to the destination.
- *Transit time.* The total time a carrier has possession of goods, including the time required for pickup and delivery, handling, and movement between the point of origin and the destination.
- *Reliability.* The consistency with which the carrier delivers goods on time and in acceptable condition.
- *Capability.* The carrier's ability to provide the appropriate equipment and conditions for moving specific kinds of goods, such as those that must be transported in a controlled environment (for example, under refrigeration).
- *Accessibility.* The carrier's ability to move goods over a specific route or network.
- *Traceability.* The relative ease with which a shipment can be located and transferred.

Using these six criteria, a shipper selects the mode of transportation that will best meet its needs. Exhibit 15.8 shows how the basic modes of transportation rank in terms of these criteria.

concept check

What is the goal of supply chain management?

Describe the key decisions in managing the logistical flow.

What factors are considered when selecting a mode of transportation?

Exhibit 15.8 Criteria for Ranking Modes of Transportation

	Highest				Lowest
Relative cost	Air	Truck	Rail	Pipe	Water
Transit time	Water	Rail	Pipe	Truck	Air
Reliability	Pipe	Truck	Rail	Air	Water
Capability	Water	Rail	Truck	Air	Pipe
Accessibility	Truck	Rail	Air	Water	Pipe
Traceability	Air	Truck	Rail	Water	Pipe

Trends in Distribution

Companies are using new distribution strategies to boost their profits and gain a competitive edge. The Internet is spurring many of these new strategies by opening up a whole new avenue for buying goods and services. In this section we'll discuss two emerging trends in distribution, category management and information sharing.

Category Management

category management
Suppliers manage the inventory of a category of products for a retailer.

Borders Books used to carry more than 10 titles about sushi in its cooking section. Now, it has cut the number to three because HarperCollins, the nation's third-largest publishing house, told Borders to do so. This is the mushrooming trend toward category management. **Category management** is where the nation's largest retailers ask one supplier in a category to determine how the retailer should best stock its shelves. Thus, HarperCollins tells Borders which cookbooks to carry from all cookbook publishers! Category management is becoming standard practice at nearly every U.S. supermarket, convenience store, mass merchant, and drug chain. The reason is that it works. Retailers attribute 14 percent sales growth to category management.

A retailer can increase profits by managing itself not as a collection of products, but product categories. People don't shop for soft drinks the way that they shop for meat. With soft drinks, it may be more effective to group brands (Pepsi, Coke, store brand) together; in another category, freshness is most important. Sophisticated computer programs and marketing research help decide which products and how much should be carried. Manufacturers that supply most of the category management are called captains. Category captains include: soft drinks—Coca-Cola; wine—E&J Gallo; Shaving—Gillette; pet food—Nestlé Purina; and detergent—Procter & Gamble.

The best retailers are far from passive when it comes to accepting category captains' recommendations. Wal-Mart runs the captain's plan by a "validator," which is a second supplier. So Dole, for example, runs a check on what Del Monte proposes.[6]

Sharing Information and the Load

General Mills had a problem that plagues most companies that use trucks to ship products: trucks that ship only air. Drivers carrying loads of Betty Crocker cake mixes, Cheerios, or Yoplait yogurt were hauling an empty trailer as often as 15 percent of the time. Once a load was delivered, the trucks had to return empty if the driver couldn't find a load. It is estimated that $30 billion a year is wasted by empty trucks.

General Mills found a solution. The company teamed with other manufacturers, such as paper-products maker Fort James, to use new logistics software to find loads for otherwise empty trucks. If General Mills has a truckload of Wheaties to send to Atlanta, but no load to fill the truck as it returns to its Minneapolis plant, the software examines the other companies' shipping schedules and finds that Fort James has a load of Brawny paper towels and Dixie cups that needs to go from Atlanta to St. Paul, Minnesota. The software alerts both companies, who have agreed in advance on terms. General Mills and Fort James pay less per mile, and General Mills does not have to find a load to haul back.

The alliance now includes General Mills, Fort James, Pillsbury, Land O' Lakes, and carton maker Graphic Packaging. General Mills is now planning to take things further by sharing warehouse space.[7]

concept check

Explain category management and why it is popular.

How does information sharing save shippers money?

Great Ideas to Use Now

This chapter covers retailing, so we decided to offer you a few shopping tips to make your life easier. Also, it may put a few extra dollars in your billfold!

Flying in Europe? Go Cheap

It used to be that flying 200 miles in Europe cost you as much or more than flying across the Atlantic. With Europe's discount airlines, that has changed. Check out these Web sites, shown on the next page:

Try It Now

1. **Comparison shop.** A beauty of the Internet is the ability to comparison shop like never before. To compare brands, features, and prices of products, go to one of these sites: **http://ww.bottomdollar.com**, **http://www.mysimon.com**, or **http://www.compare.net**. For the best bargains try **http://www.overstock.com**, **http://www.smartbargains.com**, **http://www.bluefly.com**, or **http://www.evalueville.com**.
2. **Kick the tires before you buy.** At some point you are going to buy a car. The Web can simplify the process, help you make an intelligent decision, and save you money. Start at **http://www.edmunds.com**. The online version of the respected car-buying guide is crammed with information about new and used cars. The site offers thousands of car reviews and current loan rates. Once you decide what you want, go to one or all of these sites to get the best price: **http://www.autobytel.com**, **http://www.autoconnect.com**, or **http://www.autoweb.com**. If you decide to buy a used car but are not sure about the strange sound or unexplained dent, go to **http://www.carfax.com** and plug in the car's vehicle identification number. In return you will get an immediate report of the car's public history that will tell you such things as whether the car has been auctioned and its emission test results. The report costs $20, but if there are no data, you don't pay. Once you have found the car of your dreams, go to **http://www.eloan.com**, enter the make, model, and year, and NationsBank will give you a quote for a loan or a lease plan at no charge.

Exhibit 15.9 Return Policies of Selected Retailers

Cracking Down:

Company	Return Policy
Target	Save the receipt. No store credit issued without one—only very limited exchanges.
Home Depot	New 90-day window on returns, and store credit given if you don't have a receipt.
Best Buy	Electronics buyers beware: 15 percent restocking fees on some items and short return windows of 14–30 days.
Gap	Hurry. 14-day window on returns for any reason with the receipt. After that, items must have tags and look new.
JCPenney	Strict rules on furniture, jewelry, and other items; store credit issued if you don't have a receipt.

Better Deals:

Company	Return Policy
Circuit City	A good spot for electronics—no restocking fees.
Radio Shack	Again, no restocking fees. But make returns within 30 days.
L.L. Bean	"We don't want you to have anything from L.L. Bean that is not 100% satisfactory." But they might ask a few questions.
Lands' End	"Guaranteed Period." Returns or refunds at any time, for any reason.

SOURCE: Jane Spencer, "The Point of No Return," *Wall Street Journal* (May 14, 2002), p. D2.

Ryanair
http://www.ryanair.com
$30 Dublin to Edinburg

Easy Jet
http://www.easyjet.com
$16 Amsterdam to Glasgow

Virgin Express
http://www.virgin-express.com
$63 Madrid to Brussels

The fares were the cheapest found during the summer of 2003. Book early to get the best rates.

The Point of No Return

Many companies are tightening their returns policies and the "no" word is cropping up more often. The latest policies from some of America's largest retailers are shown in Exhibit 15.9. It is always better to know the return policy before you buy.

Customer Satisfaction and Quality

Distribution is all about getting the right product to the right person, at the right place, at the right time. If only one of these things does not occur, then the firm will have a dissatisfied customer. Sophisticated supply chain management programs, using the latest software, have dramatically reduced distribution errors as well as lowered costs for the firm.

Oracle, the giant software company, has switched from an overaggressive sales force to making customer service its top priority. "It's more than just the sale," said Paul Ciandrini, an Oracle senior vice president who heads up the company's commercial sales in the western region of North America. "I can make the sale and be a hero, but I can't go back in and expand that sale if it's of no value to the customer."[8]

Even the smallest details are being reconsidered. Oracle used to offer slick presentations on its products and the features that distinguished them from those of PeopleSoft Inc. or SAP AG of Germany. Now, it uses demonstrations that map its customers' specific technology environment, so it can put itself in its customers' shoes, by focusing on problems as they see them.

Looking Ahead at Jack in the Box

You may have heard that three factors determine the success of a retailer: location, location, and location. While a bit exaggerated, location determines the type of customers you serve and the level of convenience to get to your store by the target customer. Land acquisition costs, construction costs, retail image, and a host of other factors are influenced by location. Distribution and supply chain management are getting more attention from management because they can be a source of tremendous cost savings and can enhance customer satisfaction. Jack in the Box's move into convenience stores could create several problems. First, management's expertise is in running fast-food restaurants, not convenience stores. If management takes their eye off of the ball in the cutthroat fast-food industry, they could lose profits and market share. Opening convenience stores can also create channel conflict between Jack in the Box and current convenience stores that sell Jack in the Box foods.

Summary of Learning Goals

1

What is physical distribution?

Physical distribution is efficiently managing the acquisition of raw materials to the factory and the movement of products from the producer or manufacturer, to industrial users and consumers. Physical distribution activities are usually the responsibility of the marketing department and are part of the large series of activities included in the supply chain.

2

What are distribution channels and their functions?

Distribution channels are the series of marketing entities through which goods and services pass on their way from producers to end users. Distribution systems focus on the physical transfer of goods and services and on their legal ownership at each stage of the distribution process. Channels (a) reduce the number of transactions, (b) ease the flow of goods, and (c) increase channel efficiency.

3

How are channels organized?

A vertical marketing system is a planned, hierarchical, organized distribution channel. There are three types of vertical marketing systems: corporate, administrative, and contractual. In a corporate system, one firm owns the entire channel. In an administrative system, a strong organization takes over as leader and sets channel policies. In a contractual distribution system, the independent firms coordinate their distribution activities by written contract. Forward integration occurs in a distribution channel when a marketing intermediary acquires another marketing intermediary closer to the customer, such as a retailer. Backward integration occurs when a wholesaler or retailer gains control over the production process.

4

When would a marketer use exclusive, selective, or intensive distribution?

The degree of intensity depends in part on the type of product being distributed. Exclusive distribution (one or two dealers in an area) is used when products are in high demand in the target market. Selective distribution has a limited number of dealers per area, but more than one or two. This form of distribution is used for consumer shopping goods, some specialty goods, and some industrial accessories. Intensive distribution occurs when the manufacturer sells its products in virtually every store willing to carry them. It is used mainly for consumer convenience goods.

5

What is wholesaling, and what are the types of wholesalers?

Wholesalers typically sell finished products to retailers and to other institutions, such as manufacturers, schools, and hospitals. They also provide a wide variety of services, among them storing merchandise, financing inventory, breaking bulk, providing rapid delivery to retailers, and supplying market information. The two main types of wholesalers are merchant wholesalers, and agents and brokers. Merchant wholesalers buy from manufacturers and sell to other businesses. Full-service merchant wholesalers offer a complete array of services to their customers, who are retailers. Limited-service merchant wholesalers typically carry a limited line of fast-moving merchandise and offer few services to their customers. Agents and brokers are essentially independents who provide buying and selling services. They receive commissions according to their sales.

6

What are the different kinds of retail operations and the components of a successful retailing strategy?

Some 30 million Americans are engaged in retailing. Retailing can be either in-store or nonstore. In-store retail operations include department stores, specialty stores, discount stores, off-price retailers, factory outlets, and catalog showrooms. Nonstore retailing includes vending machines, direct sales, direct-response marketing, and Internet retailing (e-commerce).

Creating a retail strategy is important in all kinds of retailing and involves defining a target market, developing a product offering, creating an image and a promotional strategy, choosing a location, and setting prices. The most important factors in creating a store's atmosphere are employee type and density, merchandise type and density, fixture type and density, sound, and odors.

7

How can supply chain management increase efficiency and customer satisfaction?

The goal of supply chain management is to coordinate all of the activities of the supply chain members into a seamless process, thereby increasing customer satisfaction. The logistical components of the supply chain include: sourcing and procurement, production scheduling, choosing a warehouse location and type, setting up a materials-handling system, and making transportation decisions.

8

What are the trends in distribution?

Two emerging trends in distribution are category management and information sharing. The former is where large retailers ask one supplier in a category of products to determine how the retailer should best stock its shelves. Nearly every supermarket chain, convenience store chain, mass merchant, and drugstore chain uses category management. Vendors use sophisticated computer programs and marketing research to determine which products and how much should be carried. The result is greater sales and higher profits.

KEY TERMS

administrative distribution system 479
agents 475
backward integration 479
breaking bulk 477
brokers 475
cash and carry wholesaler 482
category management 492
contractual distribution system 479
corporate distribution system 478
distribution centers 491
distribution channel 474
efficient consumer response (ECR) 486
electronic data interchange (EDI) 486
exclusive distribution 479
forward integration 478
full-service merchant wholesalers 482
industrial distributors 475
intensive distribution 480
limited-service merchant wholesalers 482
manufacturer 474
manufacturers' representatives (manufacturers' agents) 482
marketing intermediaries 474
merchant wholesaler 481
physical distribution 474
retailers 475
selective distribution 479
vertical marketing system 478
wholesalers 475

Information sharing among shippers by truck is resulting in fewer empty loads to haul back. By sharing their shipping needs, manufacturers have found that they can use each other's trucks to avoid making a shipment and then having to return empty. Sophisticated software helps members of the shipping alliance find loads for the return haul home. The greater the number of manufacturers in the alliance, the lower the chance that a return trip will be empty.

PREPARING FOR TOMORROW'S WORKPLACE

1. Divide the class into two groups with one taking the "pro" position and the other the "con" position on the following issue: "The only thing marketing intermediaries really do is increase prices for consumers. It is always best to buy direct from the producer."
2. Trace the distribution channel for some familiar product. Compose an e-mail that explains why the channel has evolved as it has and how it is likely to change in the future.
3. You work for a small chain of department stores (six stores total) located within a single state. Write a memo to the president explaining how e-commerce may affect the chain's business.
4. Go to a successful, independent specialty store in your area that has been in business for quite a while. Interview the manager and try to determine how the store successfully competes with the national chains.
5. Discuss why innovation is so important in retailing today. Be sure to give examples.
6. Divide the class into teams. Each team should select a local manufacturer to visit. The team should interview managers to determine how its supply chain functions. Make a report to the class.

WORKING THE NET

1. Visit *Industry Week*'s Web site at **http://www.industryweek.com**. Under archives, do a search using the search term "supply chain management." Choose an article from the results that describes how a company has used supply chain management to improve customer satisfaction, performance, or profitability. Give a brief presentation to your class on your findings.
2. What are some of the logistics problems facing firms that operate internationally? Visit the *Logistics Management* magazine Web site at **http://www.manufacturing.net/lm/** and see if you can find information about how firms manage global logistics. Summarize the results.
3. Search for information on retail careers at the About.com's retail industry information site, **http://www.retailindustry.about.com**. What types of careers are available in retailing? What skills are needed? Does a career in retailing appeal to you? Why or why not?
4. How does category management help companies? For one view, visit the InfoCenter's Category Management pages of Hershey's Vending division at **http://www.hersheysvending.com/infocenter/category.shtml**. What benefits does this system claim to offer to owners of vending machines? What are the advantages for Hershey's? Browse the rest of the Web site. What other helpful information does it provide?
5. One of the biggest challenges for retailers is integrating their various channels to provide a seamless experience for customers, regardless of the channel. Pick two

of the following companies, explore their Web sites, and compare the channel integration strategies: Staples (**http://www.staples.com**), Gap (**http://www.gap.com**), Borders (**http://www.borders.com**), Powell's Books (**http://www.Powells.com**), LLBean (**http://www.llbean.com**), or Target Stores (**http://www.target.com**). In addition to looking at the Web sites from a channel perspective, you may want to look at the company information and news sites.

Creative Thinking Case

Cabela's Targets Men Who Hate to Shop

As the largest retailer in Sidney, Nebraska, Cabela's Inc. sells the sort of products that people bought in the Old West: guns, tents, fishing lures, and such. Cabela's serves the nation's oldest market—the outdoorsman—and its numbers are shrinking.

Yet Cabela's is one of the nation's hottest retailers. Its small but growing chain of stores is a formidable economic-development force, drawing gigantic crowds to tiny towns. And Cabela's accomplishes this by appealing to a most unlikely customer—men who hate to shop. "I'll do just about anything to avoid shopping," says John Brown, a small-business owner in Cheyenne, Wyoming. In 35 years of marriage, his wife says she's persuaded him to go shopping only twice. Yet one day last month he invited her to drive 100 miles with him for a day of shopping at Cabela's. "I'm like a kid in a candy store here," he said, dropping a new tackle box into his cart.

Cabela's operates only eight stores, but they are blockbusters. The Cabela's in Michigan is that state's largest tourist attraction, drawing 6 million people a year—35 percent as many visiting shoppers as all of New York City had in 2000. In Minnesota, Cabela's is the second-largest tourist attraction, trailing only the Mall of America.

Call it the reverse-Wal-Mart effect: Instead of stealing customers from nearby retailers, Cabela's bestows them. Its secret is a philosophy that would be heretical at Wal-Mart: Spend like mad on stores. The ceilings of its buildings are as high as at indoor stadiums and feature glass tops to let in natural light. Beneath the high ceilings are nature scenes: a mountain populated with stuffed bear, caribou, and bighorn sheep; a waterfall spilling into a stream stocked with live trout.

As much as 45 percent of floor space is devoted not to selling but to hundreds of pieces of not-for-sale, museum-quality taxidermy. A stuffed polar bear alone can cost $10,000.

By selling branded clothing and other gifts that appeal to their customers' wives and children, Cabela's is also proving that rural shoppers desire more than a local discounter.[9]

CRITICAL THINKING QUESTIONS

1. Both Cabela's and its arch competitor Bass Pro Shops started out as catalog businesses. Why do you think they both started opening retail stores?
2. The old adage in retailing is that location is everything. So why would anyone open a huge store in Sidney, Nebraska?
3. What do you think might ultimately limit the growth of Cabala's?

Video Case

PING-Karsten Hits the Sweet Spot

Inventor Karsten Solheim was having trouble with his golf game, so he decided to build a better golf club. Named for the sound it makes when it strikes the ball, his PING Putter, introduced in 1959, revolutionized golf club design.

Seven years later his Anser putter clocked more than 500 wins and changed putting forever.

From humble beginnings working out of his garage, Solheim, a former engineer with General Electric, stayed ahead of the pack with his pioneering product designs. His company, Karsten Manufacturing, now employs 900 people at the company's headquarters in Phoenix, Arizona. Karsten's belief that properly fitted clubs are critical to a golfer's performance has been responsible for the company's specialization in manufacturing custom-fitted clubs. A custom set of clubs can incorporate the small modifications that make all the difference to a player's game.

Today, more than 2,200 club fitters, who have completed an intensive three-day club-fitting seminar at the company's headquarters, help customers choose the right PING clubs designed to fit their own personal specifications. After being measured by a trained professional, the customer's specifications are sent to the Karsten plant, where a set of custom clubs is made on-site in just two days. Each set of clubs has a unique serial number, and the company's revolutionary tracking system keeps tabs on all club specifications. It is a key strategy in making and keeping customers happy. If a customer loses a club, it can be quickly and easily replaced.

In late 2002 Karsten Manufacturing became the first golf equipment company to allow golfers to design clubs online. By visiting **http://www.pinggolf.com/Specify/**, customers can select the look, style, feel, and weight of their own custom-designed PING SPECIFY putter. Using the site's Retailer Locator, they can order their putter directly from their nearest retail location. "This new online program will not only help the consumer understand the concept and options available with the SPECIFY putter, it is another example of how our company supports its retailers with innovation and service," said John Solheim, PING Chairman and CEO.

Karsten Manufacturing's commitment to quality innovative products, an efficient supply and delivery system, and a uniquely personal approach to customer service, can only mean more winners for the country's 25 million golfers and the next generation of PING products.

CRITICAL THINKING QUESTIONS

1. How has PING set itself apart in the highly competitive arena of golf equipment design and manufacturing? Explain.
2. Describe the benefits of the company's unique golf club–tracking system in the context of timely and efficient distribution of products.
3. How do PING's innovative marketing concepts benefit retailers?

SOURCES: Adapted from material in the video: "PING-Karsten"; PING-Karsten corporate Web site http://www.pinggolf.com, accessed May 7, 2003; "PING Introduces Web Site for Golfers to Create Their Own Specify Putter," *PRNewswire*, December 9, 2002, downloaded from http://www.findarticles.com; and "PING Named Top Custom-Fitting Golf Equipment Company by National Survey of Golfers," *PRNewswire*, October 24, 2001, downloaded from http://www.findarticles.com.

E-Commerce Case

A Blockbuster Idea

Movies delivered right to your door? What could be more convenient? Select from 13,500 movies at the company's easy-to-use Web site. List favorites in your "movie rental queue," then sit back until the mailman arrives. Within 48 hours, your DVD movies are delivered in a prepaid return envelope. View as many movies as you like in a month, keeping them as long as you wish—no more late fees!—a maximum of three at a time. When you return a movie, your next selection is automatically plucked from your rental queue and mailed to you. And you can have all this at a cost of just $19.95 per month.

Reed Hastings, CEO of the Los Gatos, California–based company, Netflix (**http://www.netflix.com**), confidently projects continued rapid growth. American ownership of DVD players stands at 35 million, up from zero in 1997. "Over the next four years we will grow our subscriber base to 5 million," predicts Hastings. "With a billion in revenue, we'll be a 'real' media company. At $150 million in annual revenues we are still just a promising niche."

One of the few successful e-commerce public stock offerings of 2002, Netflix's second-quarter revenues doubled to $36.4 million from $18.4 million one year ago. Its earnings of $6.5 million in the second quarter compare to losses of $100,000 just one year ago.

The company is an interesting marriage of high and low tech. It uses the Internet as a cost-effective way to reach its customers. DVD delivery is by mail, however, because it only costs 37 cents to send a DVD by mail—well below the $3.50 or so that Hastings estimates it would cost to send movies over the Internet.

Now Hollywood has come calling. The studios are eager to sign deals with Netflix to counter the growing power of Blockbuster, which has launched a copycat subscription service in four metropolitan markets and plans to go national in 2004. Wal-Mart, the largest U.S. retailer of DVDs, also plans to roll out a competitive service by year-end.

While both announcements knocked down Netflix stock, Hastings isn't worried. "We've been doing this for four years and know how to do it well," he says. His plan to stay ahead of the competition is to excel at what made the company a hit—delivering an amazing assortment of movies quickly by mail. And with 10 new distribution centers on the drawing board, the company aims to deliver its DVDs in 24 hours, which should keep its 670,000 subscribers very happy.

CRITICAL THINKING QUESTIONS

1. Describe Netflix's distribution strategy and its role in the company's huge success as an e-commerce company. What function does the Netflix Web site serve in its distribution channel?
2. How will an alliance with the Hollywood studios benefit the company? Explain.
3. How can Netflix counter the impact on its business from growing competition? Do you think Blockbuster's and Wal-Mart's network of stores will give them an advantage? Explain.

SOURCES: Jane Black, "Movies by Mail," *Business Week Online,* October 1, 2002, downloaded from http://www.businessweek.com, April 14, 2003; Netflix Web site, http://www.netflix.com, accessed April 27, 2003; and Bob Tedeschi, "As Blockbuster Moseys Online, Two Competitors Are Already Running Hard. But Will That Matter?" *New York Times,* April 28, 2003, p. C 6.

Hot Links Address Book

To do business with Wal-Mart, you'll have to meet the retailer's tough supplier requirements. Go to
http://www.walmartstores.com
and click on the "Suppliers" tab to learn more.

At the National Retail Federation's Web site,
http://www.nrf.com
you'll find current retail statistics, links to retailing resources, and information about retailing careers.

The American Wholesale Marketers Association is an international trade organization for distributors of convenience products in the United States. Visit its Web site,
http://www.awmanet.org
to browse the latest issue of *Distribution Channels* magazine and learn more about this field.

Want to learn more about direct selling? Learn how people become Amway representatives and find out more about the company by visiting
http://www.amway.com

Stores magazine,
http://www.stores.org
offers hundreds of ideas for putting together a successful retail strategy.

Freightworld,
http://www.freightworld.com
offers detailed information on various modes of transportation and links to transportation companies.

The *Supply Chain Management Review*
http://www.manufacturing.net/SCM/
offers stories on supply chain management along with information on the latest technology in the field.

Chapter 16

© AP / WIDE WORLD PHOTOS

Using Integrated Marketing Communications to Promote Products

learning goals

1 What are the goals of promotional strategy?
2 What are the elements of the promotional mix, and what is integrated marketing communications?
3 What is advertising and what are the different types of advertising?
4 What are the advertising media, and how are they selected?
5 What is personal selling?
6 What are the goals of sales promotion, and what are several types of sales promotion?
7 How does public relations fit into the promotional mix?
8 What factors affect the promotional mix?
9 What are three important trends in promotion?

New Beetle Fights Bug Problem

Volkswagen (**http://www.vw.com**) is hoping its new Beetle convertible will turn its frown upside down. Europe's biggest car maker recently began promoting its new Beetle convertible in the United States with a 60-second commercial featuring a somber young man experiencing the banalities of daily life. He finally cracks a smile after seeing the new Beetle convertible. The ad was shown in movie theaters nationwide. It was also placed on "The West Wing," which is broadcast on NBC, and "Everybody Loves Raymond," which airs on CBS.

Volkswagen has a lot riding on the car, which has a starting price of $20,450. The car maker needs the new convertible to stimulate Beetle sales, which were down about 25 percent in the United States in 2002 and 2003. Still, the company has high hopes. "We think this is going to re-energize the Beetle brand overall," says Karen Marderosian, director of marketing for Volkswagen of America. The company spends about $450 million on advertising, each year, in America. "It is a tough market," says Ms. Marderosian. "We haven't had a lot of new products in the past couple of years. We are hoping that this is the thing that will bring Volkswagen more to the forefront."

To help get notices, Volkswagen dispatched "street teams" that went to such cities as Dallas, Chicago, and San Francisco. The group fed parking meters and handed out coffee coupons, newspapers, and subway tokens—all in the name of advertising. They also held car-washing events, and gave out driver "wanted" posters.

Magazine ads, running in publications such as *Vanity Fair* and *InStyle,* featured just a single word, such as "Grass" or "Beach," and offered consumers a whiff of fresh-cut grass and ocean breezes through the use of scent strips.

Volkswagen also placed classified ads in daily newspapers that included this memorable copy: "Passing smiles for sale. Ear to ear, some with dimples, most with teeth. Finger pointing included as well as prolonged stares."[1]

Critical Thinking Questions

As you read this chapter, consider the following questions as they relate to the new Volkswagen convertible:

1. Was it necessary to use any other type of promotion other than advertising to launch the new Beetle convertible?
2. What other means could be used to promote the new vehicle?
3. Could the Internet play a role in promoting the new convertible?

Principles of Integrated Marketing Communications

promotion
The attempt by marketers to inform, persuade, or remind consumers and industrial users to engage in the exchange process.

Very few goods or services can survive in the marketplace without good promotion. Marketers, such as those touting the Volkswagen convertible, promote their products to build demand. **Promotion** is an attempt by marketers to inform, persuade, or remind consumers and industrial users to engage in the exchange process. Once the product has been created, promotion is often used to convince target customers that it has a differential advantage over the competition. A *differential advantage* or competitive advantage, as explained in Chapter 13, is a set of unique features that the target market perceives as important and better than the competition's features and may result in purchase of the brand. Such features may include high quality, fast delivery, low price, good service, and the like. Lexus, for example, is seen as having a quality differential advantage over other luxury cars. Therefore, promotion for Lexus stresses the quality of the vehicle.

This chapter presents the goals of promotion, the last element of the marketing mix, and explores the elements of the promotional mix. You will also learn about advertising and how personal selling and public relations fit into the promotional mix.

Promotional Goals

1 learning goal

Most firms use some form of promotion. The meaning of the Latin root word is "to move forward." Hence actions that move a company toward its goals are promotional in nature. Because company goals vary widely, so do promotional strategies. The goal is to stimulate action. In a profit-oriented firm, the desired action is for the consumer to buy the promoted item. Mrs. Smith's, for instance, wants people to buy more frozen pies. Not-for-profit organizations seek a variety of actions with their promotions. They tell us not to litter, to buckle up, to join the army, and to attend the ballet.

Promotional goals include creating awareness, getting people to try products, providing information, retaining loyal customers, increasing the use of products, and identifying potential customers. Any promotional campaign may seek to achieve one or more of these goals:

1. *Creating awareness.* All too often, firms go out of business because people don't know they exist or what they do. Small restaurants often have this problem. Simply putting up a sign and opening the door is rarely enough. Promotion through ads on local radio or television, coupons in local papers, flyers, and so forth can create awareness of a new business or product.
2. *Getting consumers to try products.* Promotion is almost always used to get people to try a new product or to get nonusers to try an existing product. Sometimes free samples are given away. Lever, for instance, mailed over 2 million free samples of its Lever 2000 soap to target households. Coupons and trial-size containers of products are also common tactics used to tempt people to try a product. Volkswagen spent over $200 million trying to get consumers to consider the new convertible when shopping for a car.
3. *Providing information.* Informative promotion is more common in the early stages of the product life cycle. An informative promotion may explain what ingredients (like fiber) will do for your health, tell you why the product is better (high-definition television versus regular television), inform you of a new low price, or explain where the item may be bought.

These new Nike shoes are designed for tri-athletes and include "outsoles" that allow water to drain out of the bottom of the shoe, reducing blisters and keeping feet dry. This advertisement creates awareness of this new type of running shoe.

People typically will not buy a product or support a not-for-profit organization until they know what it will do and how it may benefit them. Thus, an informative ad may stimulate interest in a product. Consumer watchdogs and social critics applaud the informative function of promotion because it helps consumers make more intelligent purchase decisions. Star-Kist, for instance, lets customers know that its tuna is caught in dolphin-safe nets.

4. *Keeping loyal customers.* Promotion is also used to keep people from switching brands. Slogans such as Campbell's Soups are "M'm! M'm! Good!" and "Intel Inside" remind consumers about the brand. Marketers also remind users that the brand is better than the competition. Dodge Ram trucks claim that they have superior safety features. For years, Pepsi has claimed it has the taste that consumers prefer. Continental Airlines brags of its improvement in on-time ratings. Such advertising reminds customers about the quality of the product.

   Firms can also help keep customers loyal by telling them when a product or service is improved. Blockbuster guarantees that the hit movie you want to rent is in stock or it's free.
5. *Increasing the amount and frequency of use.* Promotion is often used to get people to use more of a product and to use it more often. When smoking was banned on domestic flights, Wrigley's began promoting its chewing gum as a good alternative to smoking. The most popular promotion to increase the use of a product may be frequent-flyer or -user programs. The Marriott Rewards program awards points for each dollar spent at a Marriott property. At the Platinum level, members receive a guaranteed room, an upgrade to their finest available accommodations, access to the concierge lounge, a free breakfast, free local phone calls, and a variety of other goodies.
6. *Identifying target customers.* Promotion helps find customers. One way to do this is to list a Web site. For instance, the *Wall Street Journal* and *Business Week* include Web addresses for more information on computer systems, corporate jets, color copiers, and other types of business equipment, to help target those who are truly interested. Fidelity Mutual Funds ads trumpet, "Solid investment opportunities are out there," then direct customers to go to **http://www.fidelity.com**. A full-page ad in the *Wall Street Journal* for Sprint unlimited wireless e-mail invites potential customers to visit **http://www.sprintpcs.com**. These Web sites typically will ask for your e-mail address.

The Promotional Mix and Integrated Marketing Communications

2 learning goal

The combination of advertising, personal selling, sales promotion, and public relations used to promote a product is called the **promotional mix.** Each firm creates a unique mix for each product. But the goal is always to deliver the firm's message efficiently and effectively to the target audience. These are the elements of the promotional mix:

promotional mix
The combination of advertising, personal selling, sales promotion, and public relations used to promote a product.

- *Advertising.* Any paid form of nonpersonal promotion by an identified sponsor.
- *Personal selling.* A face-to-face presentation to a prospective buyer.
- *Sales promotion.* Marketing activities (other than personal selling, advertising, and public relations) that stimulate consumer buying, including coupons and samples, displays, shows and exhibitions, demonstrations, and other types of selling efforts.

SANDRO MILLER PHOTOGRAPHY

PowerBar's ProteinPlus bars target health-conscious consumers who want a tasty source of protein without a lot of sugar. This advertisement provides information to explain the benefits of ProteinPlus.

- *Public relations.* The linking of organizational goals with key aspects of the public interest and the development of programs designed to earn public understanding and acceptance.

Ideally, marketing communications from each promotional-mix element (personal selling, advertising, sales promotion, and public relations) should be integrated. That is, the message reaching the consumer should be the same regardless of whether it comes from an advertisement, a salesperson in the field, a magazine article, or a coupon in a newspaper insert.

This unintegrated, disjointed approach to promotion has propelled many companies to adopt the concept of **integrated marketing communications (IMC)**. IMC involves carefully coordinating all promotional activities—media advertising, sales promotion, personal selling, and public relations, as well as direct marketing, packaging, and other forms of promotion—to produce a consistent, unified message that is customer focused. Following the concept of IMC, marketing managers carefully work out the roles the various promotional elements will play in the marketing mix. Timing of promotional activities is coordinated, and the results of each campaign are carefully monitored to improve future use of the promotional mix tools. Typically, a marketing communications director is appointed who has overall responsibility for integrating the company's marketing communications.

Pepsi relied on IMC to launch Pepsi One. The $100 million program relied on personal selling in the distribution channels, a public-relations campaign with press releases to announce the product, and heavy doses of advertising and sales promotion. The company toured the country's shopping malls setting up Pepsi One "lounges"—inflatable couches with plastic carpeting—for random taste tests. It also produced 11,000 end-cap displays for supermarket aisles and created stand-up displays for 12-packs to spark impulse purchases. It secured Oscar-winning actor Cuba Gooding Jr. as spokesperson for the ad campaign. The ads made their debut during the World Series. The tagline for the ad campaign was "Only One has it all."

The sections that follow examine the elements of the promotional mix in more detail.

concept check

List and discuss the goals of promotion.

What is the promotional mix?

What are the features of an integrated marketing communications campaign?

Advertising Builds Brand Recognition

3 learning goal

integrated marketing communications (IMC)
The careful coordination of all promotional activities—media advertising, sales promotion, personal selling, and public relations, as well as direct marketing, packaging, and other forms of promotion—to produce a consistent, unified message that is customer focused.

Most Americans are bombarded daily with advertisements to buy things. **Advertising** is any paid form of nonpersonal presentation by an identified sponsor. It may appear on television or radio; in newspapers, magazines, books, or direct mail; or on billboards or transit cards.

The money that big corporations spend on advertising is mind-boggling. Total advertising expenses in this country are estimated at more than $250 billion a year.[2] Global-advertising expenditures are approximately $321 billion annually.[3] General Motors is America's largest advertiser, spending over $3.4 billion annually. This is slightly under $400,000 per hour, seven days a week, 24 hours per day. Unilever is the largest advertiser outside the United States, spending about $3.0 billion per year. The top five advertising spending categories are: automotive, retail, department and discount stores, movies and media, food and beverages, and medicines.[4]

Super Bowl games cost about $2.1 million for a 30-second commercial. A "Monday Night Football" commercial costs about $450,000 for 30 seconds, but for

Your heart's desire.
Pepperidge Farm Natural Whole Grain does a heart good. A good source of fiber with no trans fat. What's more, this moist, robust bread makes for one great sandwich.
PEPPERIDGE FARM
Never Have An Ordinary Day.
Natural Whole Grain

COURTESY OF PEPPERIDGE FARM, INCORPORATED

Pepperidge Farm explains in this advertisement that the fiber in Natural Whole Grain is good for your heart. Informative promotion is more common in the early stages of the product life cycle.

that $450,000 the advertiser gets a chance to contact hard-to-reach men between the ages of 18 and 49. A typical Monday night spot might bring a maker of cars, beer, soft drinks, fast foods, or other products an 11.5 percent "male" rating, meaning that about 11.5 percent of the television-owning households with men in them watch the ads. That's about 11.3 million men.

In this section, you will learn about the different types of advertising, the strengths and weaknesses of advertising media, the functions of an advertising agency, and how advertising is regulated.

Types of Advertising

The form of advertising most people know is **product advertising,** which features a specific good or service. It can take many different forms. One special form is **comparative advertising,** in which the company's product is compared with competing, named products. Coca-Cola and Pepsi often use comparative advertising. Does comparative advertising work? Recent research says that comparative ads grab your attention and increase your purchase intention. Some comparative ads, however, lack believability and are not effective.[5] Another special form is **reminder advertising,** which is used to keep the product name in the public's mind. It is most often used during the maturity stage of the product life cycle. Reminder advertising assumes that the target market has already been persuaded of the product's merits and just needs a memory boost. Miller beer, V8 vegetable juice, and the FTD florist association use reminder promotion.

In addition to product advertising, many companies use **institutional advertising.** This type of advertising creates a positive picture of a company and

advertising
Any paid form of nonpersonal presentation by an identified sponsor.

product advertising
Advertising that features a specific good or service.

comparative advertising
Advertising that compares the company's product with competing, named products.

reminder advertising
Advertising that is used to keep a product's name in the public's mind.

© AP / WIDE WORLD PHOTOS

The Zoom-Zoom tagline, used to promote Mazda's line of high performance cars like this Mazda RX-8, is familiar to many customers because of Mazda's integrated marketing communications campaign.

institutional advertising
Advertising that creates a positive picture of a company and its ideals, services, and roles in the community.

advocacy advertising
Advertising that takes a stand on a social or economic issue; also called *grassroots lobbying.*

its ideals, services, and roles in the community. Instead of trying to sell specific products, it builds a desired image and goodwill for the company. For example, Weyerhaeuser ran a full-page ad in a number of publications that says, "There's a reason we'll never run out of trees. We put them back after we use them." The ad goes on to say that Weyerhaeuser plants over 100 million seedlings every year to replenish the forests. Some institutional advertising supports product advertising that targets consumers. Other institutional advertising is aimed at stockholders or the public. **Advocacy advertising** takes a stand on a social or economic issue. It is sometimes called *grassroots lobbying.* Energy companies often use this type of advertising to influence public opinion about regulation of their industry.

Choosing Advertising Media

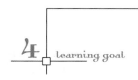

4 learning goal

advertising media
The channels through which advertising is carried to prospective customers; includes newspapers, magazines, radio, television, outdoor advertising, direct mail, and the Internet.

The channels through which advertising is carried to prospective customers are the **advertising media.** Both product and institutional ads appear in all the major advertising media. Exhibit 16.1 indicates where all of the money spent on advertising goes. Exhibit 16.2 summarizes the advantages and disadvantages of these media. Each company must decide which media are best for its products. Two of the main factors in making that choice are the cost of the medium and the audience reached by it.

Advertising Costs and Market Penetration

Cost per contact is the cost of reaching one member of the target market. Naturally, as the size of the audience increases, so does the total cost. Cost per contact enables an advertiser to compare media vehicles, such as television versus radio, or magazine versus newspaper, or, more specifically, *Newsweek* versus *Time.* An advertiser debating whether to spend local advertising dollars for TV spots or radio spots could consider the cost per contact of each. The advertiser might then pick the vehicle with the lowest cost per contact to maximize advertising punch for the money spent. Often costs are expressed on a **cost per thousand (CPM)** contacts basis.

Comparative advertising is a type of advertising where one product is compared with a competing product. The Boca Flame Grilled Burger claims to have 68% less fat than a ground beef hamburger.

TRY TO TELL THE DIFFERENCE.
Boca
Burgers
THE TASTE WILL CHANGE YOU

Reach is the number of different target consumers who are exposed to a commercial at least once during a specific period, usually four weeks. Media plans for product introductions and attempts at increasing brand awareness usually emphasize reach. For example, an advertiser might try to reach 70 percent of the target audience during the first three months of the campaign. Because the typical ad is short-lived and often only a small portion of an ad may be perceived at one time, advertisers repeat their ads so consumers will remember the message. **Frequency** is the number of times an individual is exposed to a message. Average frequency is used by advertisers to measure the intensity of a specific medium's coverage.

Media selection is also a matter of matching the advertising medium with the product's target market. If marketers are trying to reach teenage females, they might select *Seventeen* magazine. If they are trying to reach consumers over 50 years old, they may choose *Modern Maturity.* A medium's ability to reach a precisely defined market is its **audience selectivity.** Some media vehicles, like general newspapers and network television, appeal to a wide cross section of the population. Others—such as *Brides, Popular Mechanics, Architectural Digest,* MTV, ESPN, and Christian radio stations—appeal to very specific groups.

Exhibit 16.1 | Total U.S. Advertising Expenditures by Media Categories

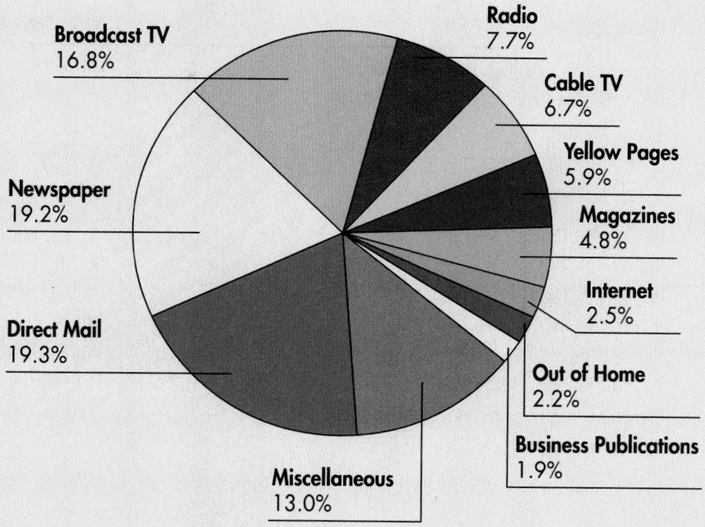

SOURCE: Reprinted with permission from the *Advertising Age Fact Pack 2002*. Copyright © Crain Communications Inc. 2002.

cost per thousand (CPM)
Cost per thousand contacts is a term used in expressing advertising costs; refers to the cost of reaching 1,000 members of the target market.

reach
The number of different target consumers who are exposed to a commercial at least once during a specific period, usually four weeks.

frequency
The number of times an individual is exposed to an advertising message.

audience selectivity
An advertising medium's ability to reach a precisely defined market.

advertising agencies
Companies that help create ads and place them in the proper media.

National Advertising Division (NAD)
A subdivision of the Council of Better Business Bureaus that investigates complaints about advertising from consumers and other advertisers.

Advertising Agencies

Advertising agencies are companies that help create ads and place them in the proper media. Many firms rely on agencies to both create and monitor their ad campaigns.

Full-service advertising agencies offer the five services shown in Exhibit 16.3. Members of the creative-services group develop promotional themes and messages, write copy, design layouts, take photos, and draw illustrations. The media-services group selects the media mix and schedules advertising. Researchers may conduct market research studies for clients or help develop new products or gauge the firm's or product's image. Merchandising advice may include developing contests and brochures for the sales force. Campaign design and planning are often wholly in the hands of the agency, although some firms prefer to do much of the work in-house, relying on the agency only for scheduling media and evaluating the campaign.

Advertising Regulation

Besides planning advertising campaigns and scheduling media, advertising agencies must also cope with the growing role and scope of advertising regulation.

SELF-REGULATION IN THE ADVERTISING INDUSTRY To avoid increasing government regulation, in 1971 advertising industry leaders set up procedures for self-regulation. The **National Advertising Division (NAD)** of the Council of Better Business Bureaus is a complaint bureau for consumers and advertisers. The **National Advertising Review Board (NARB)** is an appeals board that may be used if the NAD is deadlocked on an issue or if the losing party wishes to appeal.

After receiving a complaint about an advertisement, the NAD investigates. It collects and evaluates information and then decides whether the ad's claims are

Exhibit 16.2 Strengths and Weaknesses of Major Media

Medium	Strengths	Weaknesses
Newspapers	Geographic selectivity and flexibility Short-term advertiser commitments News value and immediacy Constant readership High individual market coverage Low cost	Little demographic selectivity Limited color facilities Short-lived
Magazines	Good reproduction, especially color Message permanence Demographic selectivity (can reach affluent audience) Regionality Local-market selectivity Special-interest possibilities Relatively long advertising life	Long-term advertiser commitments Slow audience buildup Limited demonstration capacities Lack of urgency Long lead time for ad placement May be expensive for national coverage
Radio	Low and negotiable costs High frequency Immediacy of message Relatively little seasonal change in audience Highly portable Short scheduling notice Short-term advertiser commitments Entertainment carryover	No visuals Advertising message short-lived Background sound Commercial clutter (a large number of ads in a short time)
Television	Widely diversified audience Creative visual and audio opportunities for demonstration Immediacy of message Entertainment carryover	High cost Limited demographic selectivity Advertising message short-lived Consumer skepticism about advertising claims
Network	Association with programming prestige	Long-term advertiser commitments
Local	Geographic selectivity Associated with programs of local origin and appeal Short lead time	Narrow audience on independent stations High cost for broad geographic coverage
Outdoor advertising	Repetition possibilities Moderate cost Flexibility	Short messages Lack of demographic selectivity Many distractions when observing the message
Direct mail	Very efficient with good mailing list Can be personalized by computer Can reach very specific demographic market Lengthy message with photos and testimony	Very costly with poor mailing list May never be opened
Internet	Inexpensive global coverage Available at any time Interactive personalized message via e-mail	Not everyone has access Difficult to measure ad effectiveness Pop-up clutter

substantiated. If the ad is deemed unsatisfactory, the NAD negotiates with the advertiser to obtain a change in the ad or its discontinuation.

A coalition of 15 Better Business Bureaus expressed concern about the truth and accuracy of Costco Wholesale Corporation's use of the name Costco Wholesale in advertising and signage for its chain of retail outlets. The coalition was concerned that the name Costco Wholesale, as used by Costco in its retail adver-

Exhibit 16.3 | Functions of an Advertising Agency

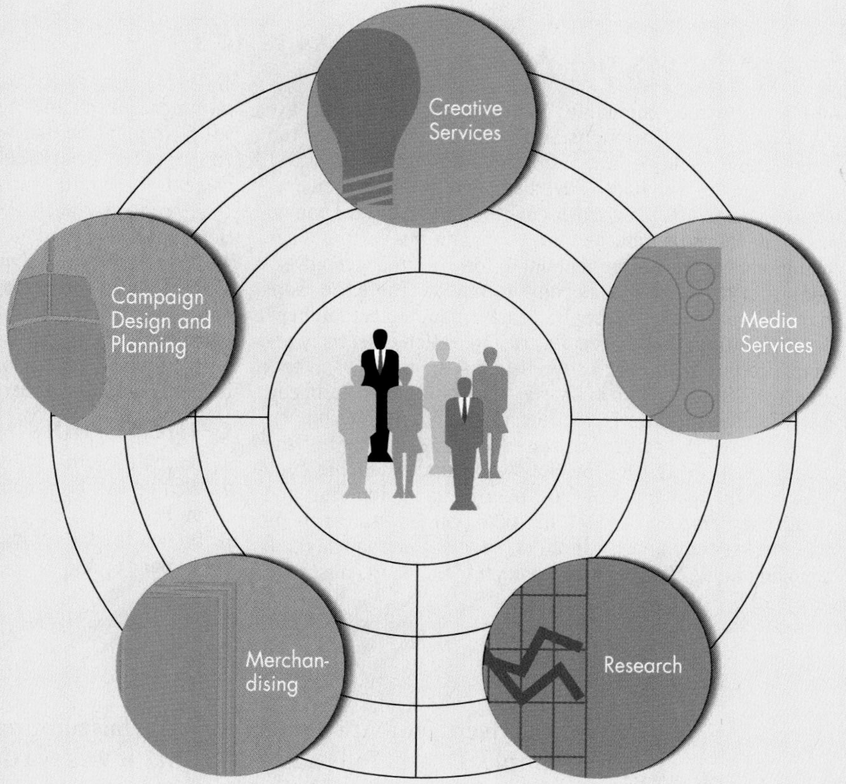

National Advertising Review Board (NARB)
A board that hears appeals from the decisions of the National Advertising Division (NAD) of the Council of Better Business Bureaus or resolves issues if the NAD is deadlocked.

Federal Trade Commission (FTC)
An agency of the U.S. government that works to prevent deception and misrepresentation in advertising.

corrective advertising
An advertisement run to correct false impressions left by previous ads.

tising, implies that Costco's prices are wholesale prices. In its review of the matter, NAD concluded that the advertiser's pricing data, business model, and consumer perception evidence were sufficient to demonstrate that its trade name Costco Wholesale is truthful and not misleading. The coalition disagreed with NAD's conclusion and appealed the matter to NARB. After careful consideration, the NARB Panel, which consisted of five industry representatives, affirmed NAD's decision, finding, "that Costco's trade name, when used in the context and manner demonstrated in this proceeding, is truthful and not misleading."[6]

Advertising managers want to avoid having to drop or modify advertisements or commercials. Not only does the controversy create ill will for the company, but the ad must be remade, which can be expensive. In addition, if a substitute commercial is unavailable, the timing of the campaign may be destroyed.

Federal Regulation of Advertising When self-regulation doesn't work, in the United States the **Federal Trade Commission (FTC)** steps in. The FTC's main concern is with deception and misrepresentation in advertising. The FTC defines deception as "a representation, omission, or practice that is likely to mislead the consumer acting reasonably in the circumstances, to the consumer's detriment." The courts have ruled that deception can include what the consumer infers from the advertisement, as well as what is literally said.

The FTC's traditional remedy for deceptive advertising is a cease-and-desist order barring use of the advertising claims found to be false or deceptive. In some cases, the FTC also requires a corrective message. **Corrective advertising** is

Expanding Around the Globe

Smoke Across the Waters

American tobacco companies frequently complain that the U.S. government restrictions on tobacco advertising are too severe. But it could be worse: This could be Europe or Asia.

In the realm of tobacco advertising, the U.S. government is almost considerate. Many other countries have placed a ban on nearly all forms of tobacco marketing, and intend to impose further limitations on the remaining forms of tobacco advertising that the industry has come to rely on. There are more than 20 countries (in Europe) that have adopted comprehensive prohibitions on tobacco advertising, which essentially attempts to outlaw tobacco advertising. A look at laws in two countries—Sweden and Malaysia—illustrates how European and Asian nations are working to curb tobacco advertising.

In Sweden, 17 percent of the men and 21 percent of the women smoke. This is low by global standards. There has been a near total ban on tobacco advertising in all print and broadcast media since 1994. In 2002, point-of-sale promotion was severely limited. In 2003, new warning labels read: "Smoking kills," "Smokers die younger," "Smoking causes fatal lung cancer," and "Smoking when pregnant harms your baby." In addition, the health warnings will have to take up 70 percent of a package's outer surface, compared to only 4 percent of the outer surface in the past.

By contrast, labels are not the focus of upcoming regulations in Malaysia, where more people smoke and their numbers apparently are rising, despite more stringent governmental controls on tobacco marketing. The Malaysian government has banned all forms of promotions using cigarette brand names, as well as sponsorships by tobacco companies. In addition, the new regulations will prohibit scenes in movies and television shows that depict people smoking.[7]

CRITICAL THINKING QUESTIONS

1. Do you think that antismoking ads motivate smokers to quit?
2. Why do you think tobacco laws are more lax in the United States?
3. Do you think that advertising causes young people to start smoking?

an advertisement run to correct the false impressions left by previous ads. For example, Doan's Pills advertised that it was particularly effective for relieving back pain, and that it contained an active ingredient not found in other over-the-counter medications. The FTC ordered $8 million be spent by the company to state "Although Doan's is an effective pain reliever, there is no evidence that Doan's is more effective than other pain relievers for back pain."[8]

The U.S. tobacco industry is viewed by some people as being highly regulated. Yet, as the "Expanding Around the Globe" box indicates, American laws are relatively lax.

concept check

Define five different types of advertising, and give examples.

Indicate some of the strengths and weaknesses of the seven main advertising media.

Name the groups that regulate advertising, and explain what remedies they may prescribe.

The Importance of Personal Selling

5 learning goal

personal selling
A face-to-face sales presentation to a prospective customer.

Advertising acquaints potential customers with a product and thereby makes personal selling easier. **Personal selling** is a face-to-face sales presentation to a prospective customer. Sales jobs range from salesclerks at clothing stores to engineers with MBAs who design large, complex systems for manufacturers. About 6.5 million people are engaged in personal selling in the United States. Slightly over 45 percent of them are women. The number of people who earn a living from sales is huge compared, for instance, with the half a million workers employed in the advertising industry. Personal selling offers several advantages over other forms of promotion:

- Personal selling provides a detailed explanation or demonstration of the product. This capability is especially desirable for complex or new goods and services.
- The sales message can be varied according to the motivations and interests of each prospective customer. Moreover, when the prospect has questions or

raises objections, the salesperson is there to provide explanations. In contrast, advertising and sales promotion can respond only to the objections the copywriter thinks are important to customers.

- Personal selling can be directed only to qualified prospects. Other forms of promotion include some unavoidable waste because many people in the audience are not prospective customers.
- Personal selling costs can be controlled by adjusting the size of the sales force (and resulting expenses) in one-person increments. In contrast, advertising and sales promotion must often be purchased in fairly large amounts.
- Perhaps the most important advantage is that personal selling is considerably more effective than other forms of promotion in obtaining a sale and gaining a satisfied customer.[9]

The Professional Salesperson

Companies that recruit college graduates to enter the field of selling want to develop professional salespeople. A professional salesperson has two main qualities: complete product knowledge and creativity. The professional knows the product line from A to Z and understands what each item can and cannot do. He or she also understands how to apply the product to meet customers' needs. For instance, a sales rep may find a way to install conveyor equipment that will lower the cost of moving products in the prospective customer's plant.

Professional salespeople develop long-term relationships with their clients. Most salespeople rely on repeat business, which depends, of course, on trust and honesty. Most professional selling is not high pressured. Instead, the sales process is more a matter of one professional interacting with another, such as a salesperson working with a purchasing agent. Professional salespeople are largely sources of information and creative problem solvers. They cannot bully a professional buyer into making an unwanted purchase.

Sales Positions

College graduates have many opportunities in sales. Among them are the following:

- *Selling to wholesalers and retailers.* When a firm buys products for resale, its main concerns are buying the right product and getting it promptly. Often retailers expect the manufacturer's salesperson to stock the merchandise on the shelves and to set up promotional materials approved by the store. Sometimes these sales jobs are entry-level training positions that can lead to better opportunities.
- *Selling to purchasing agents.* Purchasing agents are found in government agencies, manufacturing firms, and institutions (hospitals and schools). Purchasing agents look for credibility (Can the salesperson deliver merchandise of the proper quality when needed?), service after the sale, and a reasonable price. The message the salesperson must get across is one of complete dependability and reliability.
- *Selling to committees.* The form of selling that may demand the most professionalism and creativity is selling to a buying committee. When a purchase decision is so important that it will have a big impact on the buyer's long-run success, it is usually made by a committee. When United Airlines decides to order 100 new airplanes, for instance, a committee decides what type of plane to buy. A committee sales presentation requires careful analysis of the potential buyer's needs. It commonly includes an audiovisual display.

Exhibit 16.4 | Steps in Making a Successful Sale

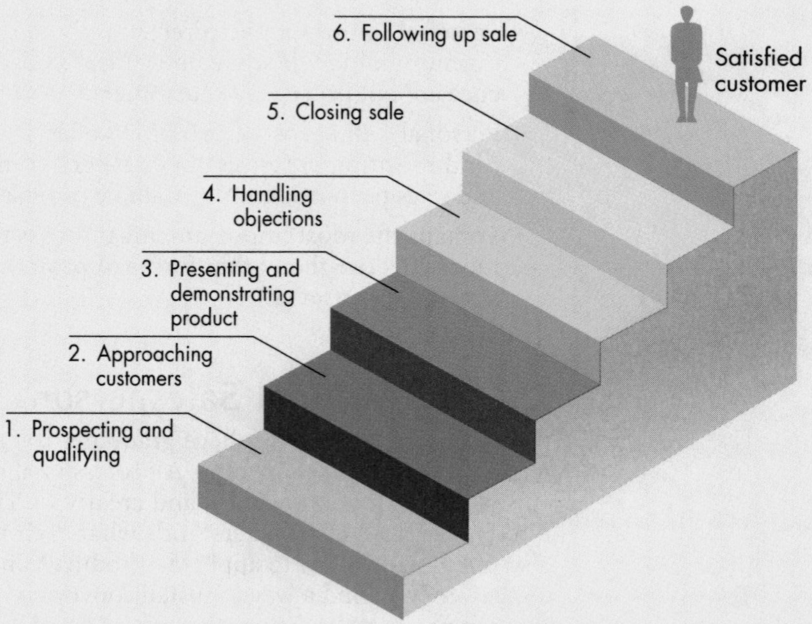

The Selling Process

Selling is a process that can be learned. Scholars have spelled out the steps of the selling process, shown in Exhibit 16.4, and professional salespeople use them all the time. These steps are as follows:

sales prospects
The companies and people who are most likely to buy a seller's offerings.

prospecting
The process of looking for sales prospects.

qualifying questions
Inquiries used by salespeople to separate prospects from those who do not have the potential to buy.

1. *Prospecting and qualifying.* To start the process, the salesperson looks for **sales prospects,** those companies and people who are most likely to buy the seller's offerings. This activity is called **prospecting.** Because there are no surefire ways to find prospects, most salespeople try many methods.

   For many companies, the inquiries generated by advertising and promotion are the most likely source of prospects. Inquiries are also known as sales leads. Leads usually come in the form of letters, cards, e-mail addresses, or telephone calls. Some companies supply salespeople with prospect lists compiled from external sources, such as Chamber of Commerce directories, newspapers, public records, club membership lists, Internet inquiries, and professional or trade publication subscription lists. Meetings, such as professional conventions and trade shows, are another good source of leads. Sales representatives attend such meetings to display and demonstrate their company's products and to answer the questions of those attending. The firm's files and records can be another source of prospects. Correspondence with buyers can be helpful. Records in the service department can identify people who already own equipment and might be prospects for new models. Finally, friends and acquaintances of salespeople can often supply leads.

   One rule of thumb is that not all prospects are "real." Just because someone has been referred or has made an inquiry does not mean that the person is a genuine prospect. Salespeople can avoid wasting time and increase their productivity by qualifying all prospects. **Qualifying questions** are used to separate prospects from those who do not have the potential to buy. The following three questions help determine who is a real prospect and who is not:

Making Ethical Choices

xtra! http://gitmanxtra.swlearning.com

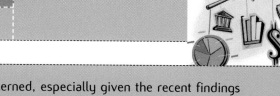

DOES IT REALLY DO THAT?

Your business and creative talents have come together in your work as a copywriter for an advertising company. In the few years since you started working, your assignments have been on products that encourage weight loss and enhance physical fitness. You've written ads for dietary supplements and diet pills guaranteeing immediate and permanent weight loss. Now you've been asked to head the creative team to promote exercise equipment from a manufacturer that guarantees toned "abs" in two weeks after using the product for only 20 minutes per day.

As an advocate for keeping fit, you are curious about the claims on the fact sheet from the maker of the exercise product for which you're the creative-team lead. You wonder how to best motivate the team when you are not sure you believe the product's claims. In addition to doing research about the claims, you buy the exercise equipment for your older sister and ask her to follow the company's recommendation. She's overweight and you are concerned, especially given the recent findings that carrying extra weight in one's midsection is a contributing factor to cancer.

After following the recommended exercise program for the machine you provide her, your sister doesn't seem to have toned up or slimmed down. Your research reveals that "spot reduction . . . isn't physiologically possible" using exercise machines. The American Council on Exercise found that most claims that ab machine manufacturers make are greatly exaggerated.

ETHICAL DILEMMA

Can you continue serving as the lead of the creative team knowing that you'd be producing false advertising?

SOURCES: "Fad Diets and Exercise Machines as They Relate to Fat Loss," *Weight Loss and Diet Facts*, 2001, downloaded from http://www.weightloss-and-diet-facts.com/exercise-machines; Nancy Hellmich, "Being Overweight Linked to Dying of Cancer," *USA Today*, April 24, 2003, downloaded from http://www.usatoday.com/life; Nat Ives, "Fast Food and the Obesity Problem," *New York Times*, December 4, 2002, downloaded from http://www.nyt.com; Joe Skorupa, "Crunch Time: Ab Machines Promise Washboard Stomachs in Minutes a Day, But Do They Really Work?" *Popular Mechanics*, downloaded from http://www.popularmechanics.com/science/sports.

- Does the prospect have a need for our product?
- Can the prospect make the buying decision?
- Can the prospect afford our product?

2. *Approaching customers.* After identifying a prospect, the salesperson explains the reason for wanting an appointment and sets a specific date and hour. At the same time, the salesperson tries to build interest in the coming meeting. One good way to do this is to impart an interesting or important piece of information—for instance, "I think my product can cut your shipping and delivery time by two days."
3. *Presenting and demonstrating the product.* The presentation and demonstration can be fully automated, completely unstructured, or somewhere in between. In a fully automated presentation, the salesperson shows a movie, slides, or uses a laptop and data projector and then answers questions and takes any orders. A completely unstructured presentation has no set format. It may be a casual conversation, with the salesperson presenting product benefits that might interest the potential buyer.

4. *Handling objections.* Almost every sales presentation, structured or unstructured, meets with some objection. Rarely does a customer say "I'll buy it" without asking questions or voicing concerns. The professional salesperson tries to anticipate objections so they can be countered quickly and with assurance.

   Often employed in business, the "higher authority" objection is frequently used when one of the parties says, "This agreement looks good, but I'll have to run it by my committee" (or wife or any other "higher authority"). The result is that that sales presentation turns out to be just a preliminary, nonbinding round. After the higher authority responds, often disapproving the agreement, the sale goes into round two or starts all over again.

   The next time you buy a house, car, or anything expensive, watch carefully how the salesperson will say, "If we find the house (or car) that you really like, is there any reason you could not make the purchase today?" Once they get the green light, the salesperson will spend whatever time it takes to find you the right product. However, if you say your uncle has to give the final approval, since he will be loaning you the money, the salesperson will try and set up an appointment when the uncle can be present.[10]

5. *Closing the sale.* After all the objections have been dealt with, it's time to close the sale. Even old pros sometimes find this part of the sales process awkward. Perhaps the easiest way to close a sale is to ask for it: "Ms. Jones, may I write up your order?" Another technique is to act as though the deal has been concluded: "Mr. Bateson, we'll have this equipment in and working for you in two weeks." If Mr. Bateson doesn't object, the salesperson can assume that the sale has been made.

6. *Following up on the sale.* The salesperson's job isn't over when the sale is made. In fact, the sale is just the start. The salesperson must write up the order properly and turn it in promptly. Often this part of the job is easy. But an order for a complex piece of industrial equipment may be a hundred pages of detail. Each detail must be carefully checked to ensure that the equipment is exactly what was ordered.

   After the product is delivered to the customer, the salesperson must make a routine visit to see that the customer is satisfied. This follow-up call may also be a chance to make another sale. But even if it isn't, it will build goodwill for the salesperson's company and may bring future business. Repeat sales over many years are the goal of professional salespeople.

concept check

What are the advantages of personal selling?
Describe the professional salesperson.
Explain the selling process.

SALES PROMOTION

6 learning goal

sales promotions
Marketing events or sales efforts—not including advertising, personal selling, and public relations—that stimulate buying.

comarketing
Where two or more companies promote each others products or services.

Sales promotion helps make personal selling and advertising more effective. **Sales promotions** are marketing events or sales efforts—not including advertising, personal selling, and public relations—that stimulate buying. Today, sales promotion is a $300 billion industry and growing. Sales promotion is usually targeted toward either of two distinctly different markets. Consumer sales promotion is targeted to the ultimate consumer market. Trade sales promotion is directed to members of the marketing channel, such as wholesalers and retailers. In a survey, 5,100 marketing managers in all industries were asked, "What sales promotion tactics are most important to your overall promotion strategy?" The replies were: comarketing (37 percent); special events (31 percent); sampling (22 percent); coupons (22 percent); games, contests, and sweepkstakes (20 percent); sponsorships (20 percent); the Internet (14 percent); trade shows (14 percent); and premiums (13 percent).[11] **Comarketing** is where two or more companies promote each others products and services. In

Frequent shopper cards and free online coupons, called U-pons, are forms of sales promotion that continue to gain popularity among retailers and consumers. Savings is still the number one reason for getting and using frequent shopper cards, like this Kroger Plus card.

© TERRI L. MILLER / E-VISUAL COMMUNICATIONS, INC.

2003, General Motors entered into a comarketing program with Genmar, the world's largest recreational-boat builder (Aquasport, Champion, Crestliner, Glastron, Ranger, and others). GM profiles Genmar boats in many of its advertising and promotion programs. Genmar is doing the same to cross-promote their respective products.[12]

The goal of the promotion tactics cited above is immediate purchase. Therefore, it makes sense when planning a sales promotion campaign to target customers according to their general behavior. For instance, is the consumer loyal to your product or to your competitor's? Does the consumer switch brands readily in favor of the best deal? Does the consumer buy only the least expensive product, no matter what? Does the consumer buy any products in your category at all?

The objectives of a promotion depend on the general behavior of target consumers as described in Exhibit 16.5. For example, marketers who are targeting loyal users of their product don't want to change behavior. Instead, they want to reinforce existing behavior or increase product usage. Frequent-buyer programs that reward consumers for repeat purchases can be effective in strengthening brand loyalty. Other types of promotions are more effective with customers prone to brand switching or with those who are loyal to a competitor's product. Cents-off coupons, free samples, or an eye-catching display in a store will often entice shoppers to try a different brand.

Sales promotion offers many opportunities for entrepreneurs. Entrepreneurs design contests and sweepstakes, fabricate displays, manufacture premiums, and deliver free samples, among other things. One successful entrepreneurial venture started when two friends were having a drink together in Paris. They created a company called Impact Diffusion, which is featured in the "Focusing on Small Business" box.

concept check

How does sales promotion differ from advertising?

Describe several types of sales promotion.

Exhibit 16.5 | Types of Consumers and Sales Promotion Goals

Type of Behavior	Desired Results	Sales Promotion Examples
Loyal customers: People who buy your product most or all of the time	Reinforce behavior, increase consumption, change purchase timing	Loyalty marketing programs, such as frequent-buyer cards or frequent-shopper clubs Bonus packs that give loyal consumers an incentive to stock up or premiums offered in return for proof-of-purchase
Competitor's customers: People who buy a competitor's product most or all of the time	Break loyalty, persuade to switch to your brand	Sweepstakes, contests, or premiums that create interest in the product.
Brand switchers: People who buy a variety of products in the category	Persuade to buy your brand more often	Sampling to introduce your product's superior qualities compared to their brand
Price buyers: People who consistently buy the least expensive brand	Appeal with low prices or supply added value that makes price less important	Any promotion that lowers the price of the product, such as coupons, cents-off packages, and bonus packs Trade deals that help make the product more readily available than competing products Coupons, cents-off packages, refunds, or trade deals that reduce the price of the brand to match that of the brand that would have been purchased

Focusing on Small Business

Turning the Tables Toward Promotion

A small Paris café . . . a table for two . . . a message . . . from Siemen's cell phones. So much for romantic imagery. France's legendary bistros and cafés are turning their tabletops into billboards for Swatch watches and an assortment of other goods and services—the idea being that while patrons sip espresso and Perrier, they can also drink in the advertiser's message.

The concept was born when Akim Rezgui and Jacques Delavault were having a drink together in Paris. As the two men talked, they examined the menu on display under the glass covering the table. "The service was so slow, I had time to read the menu twice before we got our drinks," Mr. Delavault recalls. "We thought, 'What a great place to put an ad, when you have a captive audience and people are already relaxed.'"

It's common for beer distributors and other vendors to provide logo-bearing furniture to café owners, but Impact Diffusion says its venture is the first time an independent company has put tables in French bistros to sell them as advertising space to a third party. So far the company has handled campaigns for brands such as OCB (a French company that makes cigarette rolling paper), Virgin Group's Virgin Cola, Switzerland's Swatch Group AG, the watch company, and Siemens AG, promoting new mobile phones.

The tabletops are sold in 14-day slots. An advertiser can rent as few as 10 tables; renting the entire network for the two weeks costs around $125,000, far less than most print and television campaigns and especially attractive to the explosion of Internet start-ups looking for a low-cost way to promote their new brands.[13]

Critical Thinking Questions

1. Do you think this will be an effective form of promotion? Why?
2. Would this work in the United States?
3. If you invested in this media, how would you know that it was money well spent?

PUBLIC RELATIONS HELPS BUILD GOODWILL

7 learning goal

public relations
Any communication or activity designed to win goodwill or prestige for a company or person.

publicity
Information about a company or product that appears in the news media and is not directly paid for by the company.

Like sales promotion, public relations can be a vital part of the promotional mix. **Public relations** is any communication or activity designed to win goodwill or prestige for a company or person. Its main form is **publicity,** information about a company or product that appears in the news media and is not directly paid for by the company. Publicity can be good or bad. Reports of children overeating fast food leading to obesity is an example of negative publicity.

Naturally, firms' public relations departments try to create as much good publicity as possible. They furnish company speakers for business and civic clubs, write speeches for corporate officers, and encourage employees to take active roles in such civic groups as the United Way and the Chamber of Commerce. The main tool of the public relations department is the *press release,* a formal announcement of some newsworthy event connected with the company, such as the start of a new program, the introduction of a new product, or the opening of a new plant. Public relations departments may perform any or all of the functions described in Exhibit 16.6.

Toronto, stung by the SARS outbreak and the World Health Organization's travel advisory, launched a public relations campaign in 2003 to reassure business and vacation travelers that Toronto was a safe city to visit.

© DIAPHOR AGENCY / INDEX STOCK IMAGERY

Exhibit 16.6 | The Functions of a Public Relations Department

Public Relations Function	Description
Press relations	Placing positive, newsworthy information in the news media to attract attention to a product, a service, or a person associated with the firm or institution
Product publicity	Publicizing specific products or services
Corporate communications	Creating internal and external messages to promote a positive image of the firm or institution
Public affairs	Building and maintaining national or local community relations
Lobbying	Influencing legislators and government officials to promote or defeat legislation and regulation
Employee and investor relations	Maintaining positive relationships with employees, shareholders, and others in the financial community
Crisis management	Responding to unfavorable publicity or a negative event

New-Product Publicity

Publicity is instrumental in introducing new products and services. Publicity can help advertisers explain what's different about their new product by prompting free news stories or positive word of mouth about it. During the introductory period, an especially innovative new product often needs more exposure than conventional, paid advertising affords. Public relations professionals write press releases or develop videos in an effort to generate news about their new product. They also jockey for exposure of their product or service at major events, on popular television and news shows, or in the hands of influential people.

Event Sponsorship

Public relations managers may sponsor events or community activities that are sufficiently newsworthy to achieve press coverage; at the same time, these events also reinforce brand identification. Sporting, music, and arts activities remain the most popular choices of event sponsors. For example, almost all of the major college football bowls are sponsored by a product such as the Toyota Gator Bowl, SBC Cotton Bowl, and the Tostitos Fiesta Bowl. Many sponsors are also turning to more specialized events that have tie-ins with schools, charities, and other community service organizations.

concept check

What are the functions of a public relations department?

Explain the concept of event sponsorship.

Factors That Affect the Promotional Mix

8 learning goal

Promotional mixes vary a great deal from product to product and from one industry to the next. Advertising and personal selling are usually a firm's main promotional tools. They are supported by sales promotion. Public relations helps develop a positive image for the organization and its products. The specific promotional mix depends on the nature of the product, market characteristics, available funds, and whether a push or a pull strategy is used.

The Nature of the Product

Selling toothpaste differs greatly from selling overhead industrial cranes. Personal selling is most important in marketing industrial products and least important in marketing consumer nondurables (consumer products that get used up). Broadcast advertising is used heavily in promoting consumer products, especially food and other nondurables. Print media are used for all types of consumer products. Industrial products may be advertised through special trade magazines. Sales promotion, branding, and packaging are roughly twice as important (in terms of percentage of the promotional budget) for consumer products as for industrial products.

Market Characteristics

When potential customers are widely scattered, buyers are highly informed, and many of the buyers are brand loyal, the promotional mix should include more advertising and sales promotion and less personal selling. But sometimes personal selling is required even when buyers are well informed and geographically dispersed, as is the case with mainframe computers. Industrial installations and component parts may be sold to knowledgeable people with much education and work experience. Yet a salesperson must still explain the product and work out the details of the purchase agreement.

detailing
The physical stocking of merchandise at a retailer by the salesperson who delivers the merchandise.

Salespeople are also required when the physical stocking of merchandise—called **detailing**—is the norm. Milk and bread, for instance, are generally stocked by the person who makes the delivery, rather than by store personnel. This practice is becoming more common for convenience products as sellers try to get the best display space for their wares.

Available Funds

Money, or the lack of it, is one of the biggest influences on the promotional mix. A small manufacturer with a tight budget and a unique product may rely heavily on free publicity. The media often run stories about new products.

If the product warrants a sales force, a firm with little money may turn to manufacturers' agents. They work on commission, with no salary, advances, or expense accounts. The Duncan Co., which makes parking meters, is just one of the many that rely on manufacturers' agents.

Push and Pull Strategies

push strategy
A promotional strategy in which a manufacturer uses aggressive personal selling and trade advertising to convince a wholesaler or retailer to carry and sell its merchandise.

pull strategy
A promotional strategy in which a manufacturer focuses on stimulating consumer demand for its product, rather than on trying to persuade wholesalers or retailers to carry the product.

Manufacturers may use aggressive personal selling and trade advertising to convince a wholesaler or a retailer to carry and sell their merchandise. This approach is known as a **push strategy.** The wholesaler, in turn, must often push the merchandise forward by persuading the retailer to handle the goods. A push strategy relies on extensive personal selling to channel members, or trade advertising, and price incentives to wholesalers and retailers. The retailer then uses advertising, displays, and other promotional forms to convince the consumer to buy the "pushed" products. This approach also applies to services. For example, the Jamaican Tourism Board targets promotions to travel agencies, which are members of its distribution channel.

At the other extreme is a **pull strategy,** which stimulates consumer demand in order to obtain product distribution. Rather than trying to sell to wholesalers, a manufacturer using a pull strategy focuses its promotional efforts on end consumers. As they begin demanding the product, the retailer orders the merchandise from the wholesaler. The wholesaler, confronted with rising demand, then places an order from the manufacturer. Thus, stimulating consumer demand pulls the product down through the channel of distribution. Heavy sampling, introductory consumer advertising, cents-off campaigns, and couponing may all be used as part of a pull strategy. For example, using a pull strategy, the Jamaican Tourism Board may entice travelers to come to its island by offering discounts on hotels or airfare. The push and pull promotional strategies are illustrated in Exhibit 16.7.

Rarely does a company use a pull or a push strategy exclusively. Instead, the mix will emphasize one of these strategies. For example, pharmaceutical company Marion Merrell Dow uses a push strategy, emphasizing personal selling and trade advertising, to promote its Nicoderm patch nicotine-withdrawal therapy to physicians. Sales presentations and advertisements in medical journals give physicians the detailed information they need to prescribe the therapy to their patients who want to quit smoking. Marion Merrell Dow supplements its push promotional strategy with a pull strategy targeted directly to potential patients through advertisements in consumer magazines and on television. The advertisements illustrate the pull strategy in action: Marion Merrell Dow directs consumers to ask their doctors about the Nicoderm patch.

concept check

Explain how the nature of the product, market characteristics, and available funds can affect the promotional mix.

Distinguish between push and pull strategies.

Exhibit 16.7 | Push and Pull Promotional Strategies

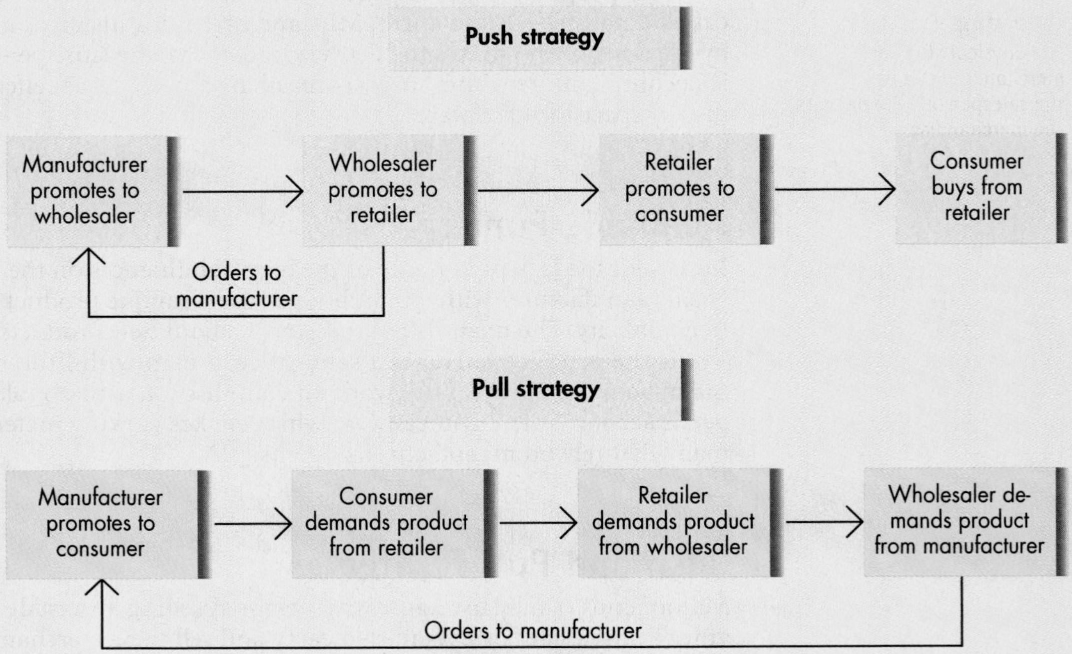

Trends in Promotion

9 learning goal

Companies are adopting new promotional strategies to hone their marketing message and reach more customers. They are also using new technology to make promotion more effective. The explosive growth of Internet advertising, the application of technology, and guerrila marketing are discussed in this section.

The Growth of Web Advertising

The explosive growth of the Internet has led to similar growth in Web advertising. For companies whose businesses are based on the Internet, building a recognized brand name is important. With nothing to pick up or touch and hundreds of similar-sounding sites to choose from, online consumers have little to go on except a familiar name. In cyberspace, anyone with enough resources to rent space on a server and build some buzz for its brand is a potentially dangerous competitor.

A new study of online advertising has shown that it can positively influence consumer perceptions of brands and can increase sales by an average of 6.6 percent for major consumer packaged goods.[14] Because online advertising does work, if it is done properly, almost all (97 percent) large traditional advertisers in the United States ran online ads in 2002.[15] Well-known companies such as Pfizer, Sara Lee, Citigroup, and Volkswagen of America more than doubled their online advertising in 2002.

Many online advertisers are moving away from the traditional small banner ads. While bigger ads, such as large rectangles or skyscrapers (large vertical ads) tend to be more effective, they are also more expensive. ESPN.com promises 4.5

million impressions (views) for a 24-hour period for a wide rectangle run along the top of its home page. The cost is $100,000 for 24 hours.

One study has shown that 12 percent of all shoppers use the Internet to download coupons.[16] Delivery methods for online coupons vary. Consumers who are willing to answer a few marketing survey questions can print them out directly from manufacturers' Web sites. Those who prefer one-stop shopping—and also don't mind answering marketing questions—can find a wide variety of coupons on Web sites such as CoolSavings.com. Another site, ValuePage.com, requires only a zip code and e-mail address. Some companies, such as clothiers Brooks Brothers Inc. and AnnTaylor Stores, invite customers to register online to receive coupons by e-mail that they can forward to friends and family.

Growing Use of Technology in Promotion

All forms of promotion are applying more and more technology to enhance effectiveness. The downtowns of European cities tend to have much greater foot traffic than those of the United States. As a result, street posters tend to be used more often. A typical size might be 12 feet tall and 6 feet wide, with full-color ads. Now, with the application of technology, the posters sing, talk, or even smell. A recent London poster ad for an energy drink called Purdey's played "chilled out" windchimes at bus stops. With the touch of a button on a poster, London pedestrians can get a whiff of Procter & Gamble's new shampoo Head & Shoulders Citrus Smell.[17]

In California, electronic billboards are profiling drivers as they go by and then instantly personalizing the freeway ads. For example, if the freeway were packed with country music listeners, the billboards might make a pitch for casinos. If National Public Radio were on, the billboards could change to ads for a high-quality car or a gourmet grocery.

The billboards pick up which radio stations are being played and then instantly access a vast databank of information about the people who typically listen to those stations. The electronic ads will then change to fit listener profiles.[18]

Guerrilla Marketing

guerilla marketing
Proactive efforts to spread positive word-of-mouth information and to encourage product usage.

Guerrilla marketing (also called *street marketing* and *diffusion marketing*) refers to proactive efforts to spread positive word-of-mouth information and to encourage product usage. Guerrilla marketing is designed to create a buzz about a product or service so that people start spreading the word. The PT Cruiser was planted in rental fleets in trendy Miami to get people talking. Vespa Scooters hired sleek-looking models to buzz up to hot cafés and clubs in trendy Los Angeles neighborhoods.

Sony Erickson used street marketing to create buzz for its T68i mobile phone that can double as a digital camera. In one initiative, dubbed Fake Tourist, 60 trained actors and actresses hung around tourist attractions such as the Empire State Building in New York and the Space Needle in Seattle. Working in teams of two or three and behaving as if they were actual tourists, the actors and actresses asked unsuspecting passersby to take their pictures. Presto: instant product demonstrations.

A second stunt involved the use of "leaners"—60 actresses and female models with extensive training in the phone's features who frequented trendy lounges and bars without telling the establishments what they were up to. The women received scripted scenarios designed to help them engage strangers in conversation. One involved having an actress's phone ring while she's in the bar—and having the caller's picture pop up on the screen. In another scenario, two women sit at opposite ends of the bar playing an interactive version of the Battleship game on their phones. Consumer activists decry the campaign as deceptive.[19]

concept check

Describe the advantages of Web advertising and why most large, traditional advertisers ran online ads in 2002.

How does technology improve the effectiveness of advertising.

When is it appropriate to use guerilla marketing?

Great Ideas to Use Now

Two important points from this chapter apply directly to you now. By understanding how advertising is changing to benefit you, you will be a better-informed consumer. By realizing the importance of selling yourself, you will be better able to take advantage of life's opportunities.

Advertising Will Be More Beneficial to You

More and more advertising dollars will be directed to online promotion in the future. For the online advertiser, the challenge is to educate, entertain, or otherwise give you a benefit. Advertisers know that no one can be compelled to pay attention online—they must deliver benefits up front. If Colgate Palmolive wants to advertise toothpaste online, it needs more than photogenic lovers with toothy smiles. Unilever has created a Web site for Mentadent toothpaste that offers potential customers the chance to order a free sample, get oral-care advice, and send questions to a dental hygienist. Every week airlines send e-mails to millions of subscribers listing rock-bottom fares for undersubscribed flights on the coming weekend. You can and should expect to receive benefits from online advertisers.

E-mail advertising is also becoming more personal and more valuable to you. Although users of e-mail have long complained about unwanted direct marketing—commonly called spam—that hasn't stopped companies from looking for new and improved ways to exploit e-mail as a marketing tool. Now, by using sophisticated data-mining techniques to develop far more tailored messages, marketers may well be succeeding. Lured by the speed, cost savings, and personalized pitches that are possible online, companies such as 1-800-Flowers, Amazon.com, and Macy's are testing the tactic. Macys.com, for example, will e-mail you to remind you of your spouse's birthday and anyone else you specify. Amazon.com e-mails you if a favorite author is conducting an online chat or has published a new work. It's a far cry from impersonal mass advertising. This is strictly for you.

Always Sell Yourself

If you stop and think about it, all of us must be salespeople. If you are going to be successful in business, and in life in general, you must be a salesperson. You must be able to effectively explain and sell your plans, ideas, and hopes. A straight "A" student who can't do this will not be successful. Conversely, a "C" student who can will be successful. *Always* be prepared to sell yourself and your ideas. It's the best way to get ahead in business and in life.

Try It Now

1. **Sell yourself.** Go to **http://www.amazon.com** and under the search engine type "selling yourself." Order one or more of the books available to improve your selling skills. Also, consider a Dale Carnegie training course. For more information, go to **http://www.dale-carnegie.com**.
2. **Protect your privacy online.** Here are some pointers to protect yourself against spam:
   - **Use free Web-based e-mail** services like Microsoft's Hotmail.com to create a second e-mail address to give out when shopping at an e-commerce site. This will prevent your corporate or primary account from being deluged with targeted spam.
   - **Use Web sites like http://www.spychecker.com** to check if you have unwittingly downloaded spyware—nettlesome programs that are secretly installed when you download many free programs. Visitors to Spychecker are prompted to enter the names of programs, and the site tells them whether the software contains spyware.
   - **Activate your Web browser's security** functions to block out cookies or alert you when a site is trying to install one on your computer. In Internet Explorer, you would go to Tools, and then click on the Internet Options command. That brings up a series of tabs, including one for Security. Moving the sliding bar to its highest setting will disable all cookies. This, however, may make it difficult to visit many popular Web sites, since the sites tend to require the ability to install cookies on your machine.
   - **Use e-mail remailers** like the one at **http://www.gilc.org/speech/anonymous/remailer.html** to bounce your message through a series of computers that forward it on, in theory making it untraceable. Sending anonymous e-mail through these remailers also reduces the odds of it being read by hackers who try to monitor data traffic to and from companies and sites like Hotmail.
   - **Use privacy software to shield** the content and addresses of the Web sites you visit from employers and other prying eyes. Two of the best such programs are those available at **http://www.anonymizer.com** and **http://www.anonymprom.com/free/nph-surf**.

Customer Satisfaction and Quality

The relationship between promotion and customer satisfaction and quality is very straightforward. If you are going to claim something about your product or service, then you had better deliver. Nothing hurts a company more than promising what it can't deliver. Many years ago, one of your authors had seen an ad for Pop Tarts when they first arrived on the market. It talked about their great taste, convenience, and so forth. He bought a box, ate one, and hasn't eaten one since. Moreover, he has told others about his experience. Certainly the product has been improved over the years, but nothing could coax him into trying one again. Unmet promises create dissatisfied customers and negative word-of-mouth promotion.

JetBlue was recently named *Advertising Age*'s "Marketer of the Year." Amy Curtis-McIntyre, Vice President of Marketing, says, "Advertising is the last thing you bring into the mix. You start by getting your product right, getting your employee attitude right, getting everyone internally understanding the mission. Then you move to telling your story through public relations. You build your advertising last."[20] JetBlue's focus is both price and great service. Offering live TV on every flight created great coverage in the media. Even offering Hain Celestial Terra Blue Chips generated a lot of free press. A *60 Minutes* producer was so impressed with JetBlue that *60 Minutes* did a segment on the company. The free publicity was worth millions.

Looking Ahead at Volkswagen's New Beetle

Volkswagen used guerrilla marketing "street teams" to help create a buzz for the new Beetle convertible. It helped generate interest and excitement in the convertible. Public relations and various forms of sales promotion such as a sweepstakes could have also been used to launch the car. Volkswagen could have launched a new Web site for the car but did not. However, the convertible is featured on the Volkswagen USA home page. A mouse click will give you a virtual tour of the vehicle at **http://www.vw.com**.

Summary of Learning Goals

1 What are the goals of promotional strategy?

Promotion aims to stimulate demand for a company's goods or services. Promotional strategy is designed to inform, persuade, or remind target audiences about those products. The goals of promotion are to create awareness, get people to try products, provide information, keep loyal customers, increase use of a product, and identify potential customers.

2 What are the elements of the promotional mix, and what is integrated marketing communications?

The unique combination of advertising, personal selling, sales promotion, and public relations used to promote a product is the promotional mix. Advertising is any paid form of nonpersonal promotion by an identified sponsor. Personal selling consists of a face-to-face presentation in a conversation with a prospective purchaser. Sales promotion consists of marketing activities—other than personal selling, advertising, and public relations—that stimulate consumers to buy. These activities include coupons and samples, displays, shows and exhibitions, demonstrations, and other selling efforts. Public relations is the marketing function that links the policies of the organization with the public interest and develops programs designed to earn public understanding and acceptance. Integrated marketing communications (IMC) is being used by more and more organizations. It is the careful coordination of all of the elements of the promotional mix to produce a consistent, unified message that is customer focused.

3 What is advertising and what are the different types of advertising?

Institutional advertising creates a positive picture of a company. Advocacy advertising takes a stand on controversial social or economic issues. Product advertising features a specific good or service. Comparative advertising is product advertising in which the company's product is compared with competing, named products. Reminder advertising is used to keep a brand name in the public's mind.

4 What are the advertising media, and how are they selected?

The main types of advertising media are newspapers, magazines, radio, television, outdoor advertising, direct mail, and the Internet. Newspaper advertising delivers a local audience but has a short life span. Magazines deliver special-interest markets and offer good detail and color. Radio is an inexpensive and highly portable medium but has no visual capabilities. Television reaches huge audiences and offers visual and audio opportunities, but it can be very expensive. Outdoor advertising requires short messages but is only moderately expensive. Direct mail can reach targeted audiences, but it is only as good as the mailing list. The Internet is global in scope and can offer a personalized message response by e-mail, but as yet not everyone is on the Net. Media are evaluated on a CPM (cost per thousand contacts) basis and by reach and frequency.

5

What is personal selling?

About 6.5 million people in the United States are directly engaged in personal selling. Personal selling enables a salesperson to demonstrate a product and tailor the message to the prospect; it is effective in closing a sale. Professional salespeople are knowledgeable and creative. They also are familiar with the selling process, which consists of prospecting and qualifying, approaching customers, presenting and demonstrating the product, handling objections, closing the sale, and following up on the sale.

6

What are the goals of sales promotion, and what are several types of sales promotion?

Immediate purchase is the goal of sales promotion whether it is aimed at consumers or the trade (wholesalers and retailers). The most popular sales promotions are coupons, samples, premiums, contests, and sweepstakes. Trade shows, conventions, and point-of-purchase displays are other types of sales promotion.

7

How does public relations fit into the promotional mix?

Public relations is mostly concerned with getting good publicity for companies. Publicity is any information about a company or product that appears in the news media and is not directly paid for by the company. Public relations departments furnish company speakers for business and civic clubs, write speeches for corporate officers, and encourage employees to take active roles in civic groups. These activities help build a positive image for an organization, which is a good backdrop for selling its products.

8

What factors affect the promotional mix?

The factors that affect the promotional mix are the nature of the product, market characteristics, available funds, and whether a push or a pull strategy is emphasized. Personal selling is used more with industrial products, and advertising is used more heavily for consumer products. With widely scattered, well-informed buyers and with brand-loyal customers, a firm will blend more advertising and sales promotion and less personal selling into its promotional mix. A manufacturer with a limited budget may rely heavily on publicity and manufacturers' agents to promote the product.

9

What are three important trends in promotion?

Web advertising can positively influence consumer perceptions of brand and has been proven to increase sales of major consumer packaged goods. Increasingly, consumers are looking to the Web for more product information and sales promotions, such as coupons. Technology will continue to improve the effectiveness of advertising by personalizing promotional messages and delivering product information. Guerilla marketing is designed to create a buzz about a product or service so that people start spreading the word.

KEY TERMS

- advertising 507
- advertising agencies 509
- advertising media 508
- advocacy advertising 508
- audience selectivity 509
- comarketing 516
- comparative advertising 507
- corrective advertising 511
- cost per thousand (CPM) 509
- detailing 521
- Federal Trade Commission (FTC) 511
- frequency 509
- guerilla marketing 523
- institutional advertising 508
- integrated marketing communications (IMC) 506
- National Advertising Division (NAD) 509
- National Advertising Review Board (NARB) 511
- personal selling 512
- product advertising 507
- promotion 504
- promotional mix 505
- prospecting 514
- public relations 519
- publicity 519
- pull strategy 521
- push strategy 521
- qualifying questions 514
- reach 509
- reminder advertising 507
- sales promotions 516
- sales prospects 514

PREPARING FOR TOMORROW'S WORKPLACE

1. Think of a product that you use regularly. Find several examples of how the manufacturer markets this product, such as ads in different media, sales promotions, and publicity. Assess each example for effectiveness in meeting one or more of the six promotional goals described in the chapter. Then analyze them for effectiveness in reaching you as a target consumer. Consider such factors as the media used, the style of the ad, and ad content. Present your findings to the class.
2. Visit the Advertising practice area at the Arent Fox Kintner Plotkin & Kahn, PLLC, law firm's Web site (**http://www.arentfox.com**). Then link to the Advertising Law site the firm maintains. What are the current issues before the FTC? Click on Laws and Regulations to read the FTC Advertising Guidelines. Do you think most advertisers would self-regulate their advertising to comply with this regulation if the FTC did not enforce it? Why or why not?
3. Choose a current advertising campaign for a beverage product. Describe how the campaign uses different media to promote the product. Which media is used the most, and why? What other promotional strategies does the company use for the product? Evaluate the effectiveness of the campaign. Present your results to the class.
4. The Promotional Products Association International is a trade association of the promotional-products industry. Its Web site, **http://www.ppa.org**, provides an introduction to promotional products and how they are used in marketing. Read its FAQ page and the Industry Sales Volume statistics (both reached through the About Us link). Then go to the Resources and Technology section and link to the most recent Golden Pyramid Competition. Choose three to four winners from different categories. Now prepare a short report on the role of promotional products in the promotional mix. Include the examples you selected and explain how the products helped the company reach its objective.
5. Apply what you learned in this chapter to a real-world business situation. Divide the class into groups of four or more. Each group will assume the role of the Marketing and Sales Department for Cameron Balloons, a company in Bristol, England. Spend some time at its Virtual Factory site (**http://www.bized.ac.uk/virtual/cb/factory/reception/intro1.htm**), where you will learn about the company and its major business functions. After familiarizing yourself with the company, focus on the marketing and sales pages. Develop a promotional strategy for the company. Be sure to explain the basis for the strategy, the target market(s), which promotional channels you will use and why (not all may be appropriate), and whether you recommend a push or a pull strategy.

WORKING THE NET

1. The Zenith Media site at **http://www.zenithmedia.com** is a good place to find links to Internet resources on advertising. At the site, click on "Leading Corporate and Brand Sites." Pick three of the company sites listed and review them, using the concepts in this chapter.
2. Go to the *Sales and Marketing* magazine site at **http://www.salesandmarketing.com**. Read several of the free recent articles from the magazine as well as online exclusives and prepare a brief report on current trends in one of the following topics: sales strategies, marketing strategies, customer relationships, or training.
3. Does a career in marketing appeal to you? Start your journey at Careers in Marketing, **http://www.careers-in-marketing.com**, and explore the five dif-

ferent areas listed there: Advertising & Public Relations, Market Research, Non-Profit, Product Management, and Retailing. Which one appeals to you most, and why? Briefly describe the type of work you would be doing, the career path, and how you will prepare to enter this field (for example, courses, part-time jobs, etc.).

4. Entrepreneurs and small businesses don't always have big sales promotion budgets. The Guerrilla Marketing Web page at **http://www.gmarketing.com** has many practical ideas for those with big ideas but small budgets. After exploring the site, explain the concept of guerrilla marketing. Then list five ideas or tips that appeal to you and summarize why they are good marketing strategies.
5. Press releases are a way to get free publicity for your company and products. Visit several of the following sites to learn how to write a press release: **http://www.ereleases.com/howtowrite.html**; **http://www.press-releases.com/write-a-press-release.html**; **http://www.publicityinsider.com**; or **http://www.netpress.org/careandfeeding.html**. Which sites were most helpful, and why? Develop a short "how-to" guide on press releases for your classmates. Then write a press release that announces the opening of your new health food restaurant, Zen Foods, located just two blocks from campus.

Creative Thinking Case

Quiksilver Goes Low Key to Stay Cool

In a 2½-minute biopic shot by the marketing department at Quiksilver Inc., surf champion Kelly Slater recalls the "heaviest" day of his life. He saw a surfer fatally swallowed by a giant wave, then realized it was his best friend. "I just want to say one last thing, man," Mr. Slater says, his voice cracking. "I should have paddled back out to get you."

Mr. Slater endorses Quiksilver wetsuits and T-shirts, but all you see is his face. The name "Quiksilver" is nowhere to be found. Still, starting in September Quiksilver will be broadcasting the vignette, and three or four others like it, on Fox Sports Network twice an hour during the day in hopes of drawing more attention to "board sports" it mentions.

Because Quiksilver is never explicitly mentioned—one of the vignettes even centers on a skateboarder who is sponsored by a competing apparel company—Fox Sports is running the spots free of charge. The video segments are part of the Huntington Beach, California, company's "tread lightly" approach to marketing. Although the company, which stated that it expects to post between $685 million and $690 million in revenue for the fiscal year ended October 2002, has been by far the biggest "breakout brand" in the close-knit, surf-shop-centric "board sports" industry, it doesn't like to draw too much attention to itself. Danny Kwock, a Quiksilver cofounder, says, "We don't want to slap our name on everything like we're this big company, you know? Big is the enemy of cool."

The goal of the Fox Sports deal, and of the entertainment division that Quiksilver launched this year to start a video-on-demand channel for extreme-sports programming, is to "grow these sports," Mr. Kwock explains.

Quiksilver has made board shorts and wetsuits since the 1970s, and it has videotaped the exploits of the surfers and skateboarders it pays to endorse their products for almost as long. The company also has pioneered some creative-marketing stunts: It branded all of the skaters in Activision Inc.'s wildly popular "Tony Hawk: Pro Skater" videogame. This year, it teamed up with Nextel Communications Inc. on a cell phone targeted at teenage girls that flips open to a pink screen emblazoned with the logo of Roxy, its surfwear line for girls.

But Quiksilver restricts its traditional promotion mainly to the sponsorship of surfing and skateboarding events and ads in magazines.[21]

CRITICAL THINKING QUESTIONS

1. Do you think that Quiksilver is promoting the brand properly?
2. Wouldn't it be better to spend more money on network television to reach a wider audience?
3. What other forms of sales promotion could Quiksilver use?

VIDEO CASE

Ready, Aim, Strategize

"This is not your father's Polaroid," is the message the company wanted to convey when launching their new i-Zone cameras. The problem was how to present the colorful instant pocket cameras with a cool, hip image from a company perceived as old and stodgy. An integrated approach combining publicity, advertising, and promotion was needed.

The first step for Mary Courville, Director of Public Relations for Polaroid's Consumer Group, was to meet with the marketing manager for the camera to obtain positioning and target-audience data. Meetings with the agencies handling advertising, publicity, and promotion followed. Their mission—to design an integrated promotional campaign that would smash all the old perceptions of Polaroid.

The film for the new cameras was so powerful and different they decided to make it the focus of the campaign. The unique "sticky film" takes postage stamp–size pictures that pop out of the camera with two colorful paper "wings" attached for messages or drawings. Removing the photo backing turns the image into a sticker.

"Where will *you* stick it?" became the campaign's slogan. The media kit Courville's team developed was a clear plastic lunch box containing a camera, film, and items like a belt buckle, key chain, and diary, demonstrating how the photo stickers can be used. Accompanying promotional materials like press releases and covering letters were written in "teen speak" to maintain the teen theme. Press kits were sent to teen, parenting, and entertainment magazines, television news and lifestyle programs, and Internet sites.

Advertising initially focused solely on television, considered the most effective way to reach the largest target audience. Through sponsorships with bands like the Backstreet Boys, Polaroid wanted to further associate the camera with its teen target market. Polaroid partnered with Sears to place giant billboards at the top 10 city venues where the band was to appear, inviting fans to leave their pictures and a message for the band on the boards. Online advertising on such Internet sites as chickclick.com were also a huge success.

Courville says this was the most successful launch of any product at Polaroid in the last 20 years. It was so successful that the company's stock jumped to a 52-week high right after the launch. "We're at the point now where people are calling us," she says.

CRITICAL THINKING QUESTIONS

1. Why did an integrated approach to launching the i-Zone camera prove to be so successful?
2. What were some of the key elements of this campaign? Explain.
3. What else could Polaroid have done to promote the i-Zone?

SOURCES: Adapted from material in the video, "Polaroid"; material downloaded from Polaroid's i-Zone Web site, http://www.i-zone.com, accessed April 24, 2003.

E-COMMERCE CASE

DoubleClick

New York–based DoubleClick (**http://www.DoubleClick.com**) is the largest Internet advertising firm, with revenues of over $300 million a year. Yet DoubleClick doesn't create ads for its clients; instead, it offers two services: Internet ad sales and ad serving.

DoubleClick sells advertising space on more than 1,500 Web sites, including Travelocity and AltaVista. The Web site owners pay DoubleClick a commission for selling ad space to advertisers. DoubleClick's proprietary technology also "serves" more than 60 billion ads per month for advertisers, making sure each ad is delivered and displayed properly on Web sites. Behind the scenes, DoubleClick's software also tracks Web surfers as they move around the Internet, click on ads, make purchases, and look at online information.

In 1999, DoubleClick purchased Abacus, the largest consumer database firm in the United States. Abacus has detailed consumer profiles of 90 percent of American households, gathered from sources like department store records and magazine subscriptions as well as a business-to-business database with information on more than 62 million business contacts. DoubleClick combined its knowledge of Web surfers' Internet behavior with Abacus' powerful consumer database to create large amounts of personal information about consumers. As a result, Web surfers would no longer be anonymous. Marketers would be able to find out their names, addresses, demographics, and actual buying habits. This transactional data would be invaluable in identifying new customers and optimizing the profitability of their existing customer base.

Consumer groups immediately cried foul, calling DoubleClick's plan an invasion of privacy. "Companies like DoubleClick are taking advantage of the technology to rob people of their privacy, causing people to distrust the Internet," said one privacy rights expert. Many advertisers, however, had a different view. "For an advertiser, if you marry Abacus information with behavioral data online, you get nirvana," said Michele Slack, an analyst with Jupiter Communications. Others pointed out that many companies already collect massive amounts of personal information about consumers.

Such attacks were nothing new to DoubleClick, whose size and clout have made it the target of privacy advocates concerned about the company's use of "cookies," files placed on Web surfers' computers to track and record their online activities. This information allows DoubleClick to target advertising to those who have an interest in relevant areas. "There are always going to be controversies when people start using new technologies," says Kevin Ryan, DoubleClick's CEO. "When credit cards were introduced, people wouldn't use them because they were worried that the credit card companies would be tracking them. But they got over it."

To appease privacy advocates, DoubleClick revised its privacy policy and requested comments from consumers, public-interest groups, and lawmakers. "DoubleClick is committed to executing its business in the most open manner possible," said DoubleClick Chief Privacy Officer Jules Polonetsky. The policy explains how the company uses cookies and includes detailed instructions for users who want to "opt out," or stop receiving cookies.

CRITICAL THINKING QUESTIONS

1. How can marketers use personal data combined with Web-use information to promote goods and services more effectively?
2. Visit DoubleClick's Web site and read the company's privacy policy statement. Do you think it goes far enough in protecting consumers' privacy? Why? What other steps can DoubleClick take to improve this policy?
3. Should businesses use information gathered on the Internet to develop customer databases for marketing purposes?

SOURCES: D. Ian Hopper, "Web Sites Give Info to Ad Cos.," *AP Online,* June 13, 2000, downloaded from http://www.business.elibrary.com; "DoubleClick Reports 4Q and Full-Year 2002 Results," Company press release, January 21, 2003, downloaded from DoubleClick Web site, http://www.doubleclick.com; M. Corey Goldman, "Unglamourous DoubleClick Clicks Along," *The Toronto Star,* April 21, 2003, downloaded from BigChalk Library, http://library.bigchalk.com; Ralph King, "Kevin O'Connor Gives People the Willies," *Ecompany.com* (October 2000), downloaded from http://www.ecompany.com; David McGuire "DoubleClick Asks for Feedback on New Privacy Policy," *Newsbytes News Network,* June 1, 2001, downloaded from http://www.newsbytes.com; and Fred Vogelstein, "The Internet's Busybody," *U.S. News & World Report,* March 6, 2000, p. 39.

Hot Links Address Book

One good site for the latest news and views on Internet advertising is the Internet Advertising section of Internet.com,
http://www.internetnews.com/IAR/

How can you find the right magazine in which to advertise? The MediaFinder Web site at
http://www.mediafinder.com
has a searchable database of thousands of magazines.

Which companies are currently the target of consumer complaints about advertising? You'll find out at the site for the National Advertising Division (NAD) of the Council of Better Business Bureaus,
http://www.nadreview.org

Want to avoid legal problems with your ad campaign? Find detailed information about advertising and trade regulation law at the site for Arent Fox, a law firm that specializes in this area:
http://www.arentfox.com

What should a media kit for the press include? 101 Public Relations,
http://www.101publicrelations.com
provides the answer, along with other good information about getting publicity for your company.

Advertising Age magazine
http://www.adage.com
has a wealth of information about the latest in advertising, including videos and ratings of new ads.

your career

in Marketing

Marketing is critically important to American businesses. Top management realizes that a company must understand the marketplace and consumer needs and wants if it is to grow and compete effectively.

Marketing offers a rich variety of career opportunities, from marketing research to creative advertising. Some positions are desk jobs—for instance, market research analyst and product manager. Others—especially those in sales, public relations, and advertising—require wide contact with the public and with other firms. The outlook for careers in marketing will continue to be very bright through the year 2010.

Dream Career: Advertising Account Manager

Advertising account managers make sales to client firms. They are also responsible for keeping clients satisfied so they will stay with the advertising agency. These managers work on a day-to-day basis with clients and serve as the link between clients and the agency's creative, media, and research departments.

Account managers must understand each client's target consumers very well. To be successful, they have to help design the best possible advertising for their clients—advertising that will make a client's business grow. They also have to be able to identify the strengths and weaknesses of the brands to which they are assigned. Identifying brand differences is important, too, because these differences help set apart a client's products.

Human nature being what it is, clients can sometimes be difficult. With tact, insight, and a little humor, account managers should always tell clients what the agency believes is right for their business, even if this is not what the clients want to hear.

- *Places of employment.* Mainly New York City and Chicago, although there are more than 8,000 moderate-size and smaller agencies found in every metropolitan area.
- *Skills required.* Four-year degree.
- *Employment outlook through 2010.* Good.
- *Salaries.* \$28,000–\$35,000 for assistant account executives; \$38,000–\$75,000 for account executives; \$50,000–\$125,000 for account supervisors (who manage several account executives).

Where the Opportunities Are

Retail Buyer

All merchandise sold in retail stores, from automobile tires to high-fashion clothing, appears through the decisions of buyers. Buyers for small stores may buy all the merchandise. Buyers for large stores often handle only one or two related lines, such as home furnishings and accessories. Buyers work with a limited budget and thus try to choose merchandise that will sell fast. They must understand customer likes and dislikes and be able to predict fashion and manufacturing trends.

- *Places of employment.* Throughout the country, with most jobs in major metropolitan areas.
- *Skills required.* Two-year degree for some jobs; four-year degree for most.
- *Employment outlook through 2010.* Fair.
- *Salaries.* \$26,000–\$85,000, plus bonuses for some buyers.

Market Researcher

Market researchers provide information that marketing managers use to make decisions. Statisticians determine sample sizes, decide who is to be interviewed, and analyze data. Account executives in research firms sell research projects to advertising agencies, manufacturers, and retailers. They also act as go-betweens for research firms and clients in planning studies, giving progress reports and presenting results. Field supervisors hire research field workers to do the interviewing. They are in charge of gathering data quickly, economically, and accurately.

- *Places of employment.* Mostly large research firms in New York City, Chicago, Dallas, and California. Other opportunities are available with manufacturers and large retailers throughout the country.
- *Skills required.* For research statisticians, an MBA; for account executives, a four-year degree; for field supervisors, usually a four-year degree but sometimes a two-year degree.
- *Employment outlook through 2010.* Very good in the places mentioned here; good elsewhere.
- *Salaries.* $38,000–$60,000 for research statisticians; $35,000–$100,000+ for account managers; $20,000–$40,000 for field supervisors.

Manufacturer's Representative

Manufacturer's sales reps sell mainly to other businesses: factories, railroads, banks, wholesalers, retailers, hospitals, schools, libraries, and other institutions. Most of these salespeople sell nontechnical products. Those who deal in highly technical goods, such as electronic equipment, are often called sales engineers or industrial sales workers. Some manufacturer's sales positions require much travel.

- *Places of employment.* Throughout the country.
- *Skills required.* For selling nontechnical products, usually a four-year degree; for selling technical products, a technical undergraduate degree and an MBA.
- *Employment outlook through 2010.* Very good.
- *Salaries.* $30,000–$65,000 for nontechnical sales reps; $40,000–$110,000+ for technical sales reps. Many companies also pay commissions or bonuses to salespeople.

Wholesaler Sales Representative

Wholesaler sales reps visit buyers for retail, industrial, and commercial firms and for schools, hospitals, and other institutions. They offer samples, pictures, or catalogs that list the items their company stocks. Some help retail store personnel improve and update systems for ordering and taking inventory. Sales reps who handle technical products, such as air-conditioning equipment, may help with installation and maintenance.

- *Places of employment.* Usually large cities (where the wholesalers are), but sales territories may be almost anywhere.
- *Skills required.* Either a two-year or a four-year degree, depending mainly on the product line and market.
- *Employment outlook through 2010.* Fair.
- *Salaries.* $30,000–$100,000, with the higher figure for experienced people in growth industries.

Public Relations Agent

Public relations agents help firms, government agencies, universities, and other organizations build and maintain a positive public image. They may handle press, community, or consumer relations; interest-group representation; fundraising; speech writing; or plant tours. They often represent employers in community projects.

- *Places of employment.* Manufacturing firms, public utilities, transportation companies, insurance companies, trade and professional associations, and government agencies, mainly in large cities. More than half of the roughly 2,000 public relations firms are in New York City, Chicago, Los Angeles, and Washington, DC. There are about 74,000 jobs in America in this field.
- *Skills required.* Four-year degree.
- *Employment outlook through 2010.* Very good.
- *Salaries.* $28,000–$75,000+, with the higher figure for public relations directors.

Product Manager

In large manufacturing firms, one key product may account for millions of dollars in sales. Such a project is too important to leave its success to chance. Product managers oversee its marketing program and are responsible for meeting profit objectives. They must coordinate the activities of the distribution department, market researchers, advertising agencies, and so on, to ensure that the product has the right marketing mix. Working with many departments without direct authority over any of them requires good human relations and planning skills.

- *Places of employment.* Major population centers and industrial centers.
- *Skills required.* Four-year degree usually, but some employers require an MBA.
- *Employment outlook through 2010.* Good.
- *Salaries.* $28,000–$90,000, with the higher figure for group product managers.

Advertising Media Planner

Advertising media planners supervise all media purchases and determine when commercials will be shown and which media will be used. They also select, recommend, and evaluate publications and programs that expose the advertising to best advantage. Media planners are responsible for achieving the right exposure in a campaign. They must be good negotiators because media rates can be flexible. Skilled planners can stretch their clients' media budgets.

- *Places of employment.* Mainly New York City and Chicago for large advertising agencies, but every metropolitan area for moderate-size and smaller agencies.
- *Skills required.* Four-year degree or MBA.
- *Employment outlook through 2010.* Fair.
- *Salaries.* $35,000–$75,000, with the higher amounts at major New York agencies.

Distribution Traffic Manager

Distribution traffic managers are responsible for inbound raw materials and products and outbound finished goods. They look for ways to avoid waste and damage and reduce time in transit, packaging costs, warehouse costs, and costs of intraplant movement. Most important, perhaps, traffic managers must understand the costs and services of the carriers so that they can reduce expense and improve service.

- *Places of employment.* Throughout the country, especially big industrial centers.
- *Skills required.* MBA.
- *Employment outlook through 2010.* Very good.
- *Salaries.* $35,000–$70,000, with the higher figure for senior traffic managers.

Chapter 17

© MICHAEL NEWMAN / PHOTO EDIT

Using Technology to Manage Information

learning goals

1 How has information technology transformed business and managerial decision making?
2 Why are computer networks an important part of today's information technology systems?
3 What types of systems make up a typical company's management information system?
4 How can technology management and planning help companies optimize their information technology systems?
5 What are the best ways to protect computers and the information they contain?
6 What are the leading trends in information technology?

Home Depot Builds a (Data) Warehouse

Home Depot Inc. (**http://www.homedepot.com**), once the high-growth leader among home improvement retailers, is in the midst of its own major remodeling project. The company was losing ground to Lowe's, its major competitor, as sales and profits dropped steadily. With both companies opening new big-box stores at a fast clip, the market was approaching the saturation point.

A key element in the plan to spruce up the country's second largest retailer is a heavy investment in information technology (IT). Ranging from new self-service checkout terminals for its customers—the first in a home improvement store chain—to new IT infrastructure, the company hopes to use technology to position itself for future success.

Although Home Depot was ahead of other retailers in some IT areas, such as using wireless applications in stores, it lagged in developing a *data* warehouse, that is: a collection of data that supports management decision making. In late 2002, Home Depot partnered with IBM to build a new Web-accessible data warehouse to give it state-of-the-art information management technology.

"We know that more timely analysis of customer's buying patterns will help us better anticipate their needs," said Bob DeRodes, Home Depot's executive vice president and chief information officer (CIO). "Now, we will be able to do a better job of predicting these needs and providing the right assortment of goods and services for each set of customers, whether they are do-it-yourself enthusiasts or professionals. This is an important component of our ongoing business strategy."

Even though the company is late in adopting data-warehousing technology, DeRodes considers it a plus. "Because of the rate of [technical] change, the last guy in has the advantage. That's us," he says. The company doesn't have to worry about integrating old systems with the newest technology. "As we begin this initiative, we know more about how to do this than anyone who previously built an enterprise-wide data warehouse, and we can do it much faster," he continues. He believes that Home Depot will be able to get better information, much faster and in much more useable fashion.

Home Depot's first purely analytical database is an expensive project, costing tens of millions of dollars and the addition of another 25 people to its 25-member database administration department. An important consideration was future growth, so the data warehouse is designed for virtually unlimited expansion. Ease of use is another factor; managers access the data warehouse through a specialized "dashboard" interface. The answers they get when they make queries results in better forecasting and planning.

The company is rolling out the new data warehouse project in stages. The initial phase focuses on human resources functions. For example, the new system will automate performance measurement of Home Depot's 300,000 employees, making it easier to retain and reward its personnel. Then the system will expand to include the Atlanta-based retailer's supply chain, inventory management, and replenishment operations. DeRodes expects the data warehouse to eventually process sales data almost in real time and use it for pricing decisions, inventory forecasting, and in-store space management.[1]

Critical Thinking Questions

As you read this chapter, consider the following questions as they relate to Home Depot:

1. How will managing information give Home Depot a competitive advantage?
2. Do you agree with Bob DeRodes that implementing the data warehouse now, instead of years ago when technology was not as advanced, will in fact be an advantage?
3. What problems might Home Depot have while implementing the data warehouse?

Principles of Information Technology

SMALL WONDER
*Actual chip size
at least 25 times smaller
You're looking at the Mu (μ)-chip, the smallest chip** on the planet. Mu-chip can be attached to most things, including passports and bank notes. It is revolutionizing security and authentication technologies with its intelligent data storage abilities. As an egg brings new life, so Hitachi is always looking to bring a new quality to life. Hitachi is working throughout the various fields of life sciences, this includes all human protein analysis through which lives can be saved and prolonged. Small wonders building big futures.
Visit Hitachi on the web and see how we're inspiring the next with our advanced technologies and innovative solutions.
*Actual chip size measures 0.4 mm x 0.4 mm **Smallest RFID (radio frequency identification) chip
HITACHI
Inspire the Next

PHOTO COURTESY OF HITACHI, LTD.

High-tech manufacturers are constantly pushing the limits on innovation. Semiconductor chips have decreased in size to a fraction of a millimeter! Hitachi's tiny radio frequency identification chip takes security and authentication capabilities to a higher level. These chips could be used on passports, charge cards, and bank notes.

As Home Depot's executives learned, harnessing the power of information technology gives a company a significant competitive advantage. **Information technology (IT)** includes the equipment and techniques used to manage and process information. The data warehouse will help the retailer in many ways, from cutting inventory costs to identifying market trends faster.

Information is at the heart of all organizations. Without information about the processes of and participants in an organization—including orders, products, inventory, scheduling, shipping, customers, suppliers, employees—a business cannot operate.

In less than 60 years, we have shifted from an industrial society to a knowledge-based economy driven by information. Businesses depend on information technology for everything from running daily operations to making strategic decisions. Computers are the tools of this information age, performing extremely complex operations as well as everyday jobs like word processing and creating spreadsheets. The pace of change has been rapid since the personal computer became a fixture on most office desks. Individual units became part of small networks, followed by more sophisticated enterprise-wide networks. Now the Internet makes it effortless to connect quickly to almost anyplace in the world. A manager can share information with hundreds of thousands of people worldwide almost as easily as with a colleague on another floor of the same office building. The Internet and the Web have become indispensable business tools that facilitate communication within companies as well as with customers. Like Home Depot, many companies entrust an executive called the **chief information officer (CIO)** with the responsibility of managing all information resources.

information technology (IT)
The equipment and techniques used to manage and process information.

Today most of us are **knowledge workers** who develop or use knowledge. Knowledge workers contribute to and benefit from information they use in performing planning, acquiring, searching, analyzing, organizing, storing, programming, producing, distributing, marketing, or selling functions. We must know how to gather and use information from the many resources available to us.

Because most jobs today depend on information—obtaining, using, creating, managing, and sharing it—this chapter begins with the role of information in decision making and goes on to discuss computer networks and management information systems. The management of information technology—planning and protection—follows. Finally, we'll look at the latest trends in information technology. Throughout the chapter, examples show how managers and their companies are using computers to make better decisions in a highly competitive world.

Transforming Businesses through Information

1 learning goal

Information systems like Home Depot's data warehouse and the computers that support them are so much a part of our lives that we almost take them for granted. These **management information systems (MIS),** methods and equipment that provide information about all aspects of a firm's operations, provide managers with the information they need to make decisions. They help managers properly categorize and identify ideas that result in substantial operational and cost benefits.

chief information officer (CIO)
An executive with responsibility for managing all information resources in an organization.

knowledge worker
A worker who develops or uses knowledge, contributing to and benefiting from information used in performing planning, acquiring, searching, analyzing, organizing, storing, programming, producing, distributing, marketing, or selling functions.

Businesses collect a great deal of *data*—raw, unorganized facts that can be moved and stored—in their daily operations. Only through well-designed IT systems and the power of computers can managers process these data into meaningful and useful *information* and use it for specific purposes, such as making business decisions. One such form of business information is the **database,** an electronic filing system that collects and organizes data and information. Using software called a *database management system (DBMS)*, you can quickly and easily enter, store, organize, select, and retrieve data in a database. These data are then turned into information to run the business and to perform business analysis.

Databases are at the core of business information systems. For example, a customer database containing name, address, payment method, products ordered, price, order history, and similar data provides information to many departments. Marketing can track new orders and determine what products are selling best; sales can identify high-volume customers or contact customers about new or related products; operations managers need order information to obtain inventory and schedule production of the ordered products; and finance needs sales data to prepare financial statements. Later in the chapter we will see how companies use very large databases called data warehouses and data marts.

Companies are discovering that they can't operate well with a series of separate information systems geared to solving specific departmental problems. It takes a team effort to integrate the systems described in Chapter 12, throughout the firm. Company-wide *enterprise resource planning (ERP)* systems that bring together human resources, operations, and technology are becoming an integral part of business strategy. So is managing the collective knowledge contained in an organization, using data warehouses and other technology tools. Technology experts are learning more about the way the business operates, and business managers are learning to use information systems technology effectively to create new opportunities and reach their goals.

concept check

What are management information systems? Why are they important to today's business organizations?

Distinguish between data and information. How are they related?

How does systems integration benefit a company?

Linking Up: Computer Networks

2 learning goal

Today most businesses use networks to deliver information to employees, suppliers, and customers. A **computer network** is a group of two or more computer systems linked together by communications channels to share data and information. Today's networks often link thousands of users and can transmit audio and video as well as data.

Networks include clients and servers. The *client* is the application that runs on a personal computer or workstation. It relies on a *server* that manages network resources or performs special tasks such as storing files, managing one or more printers, or processing database queries. Any user on the network can access the server's capabilities.

By making it easy and fast to share information, networks have created new ways to work and increase productivity. They provide more efficient use of resources, permitting communication and collaboration across distance and time. With file sharing, all employees, regardless of location, have access to the same information. Shared databases also eliminate duplication of effort. Employees at different sites can "screen share" computer files, working on data as if they were in the same room. Their computers are connected by phone or cable lines, they all see the same thing on their display, and anyone can make changes that are seen by the other participants. The employees can also use the networks for videoconferencing.

Networks make it possible for companies to run enterprise software, large programs with integrated modules that manage all of the corporation's internal operations. Enterprise resource planning systems run on networks. Typical subsystems include finance, human resources, engineering, sales and order distribution, and

management information system (MIS)
The methods and equipment that provide information about all aspects of a firm's operations.

database
An electronic filing system that collects and organizes data and information.

computer network
A group of two or more computer systems linked together by communications channels to share data and information.

order management and procurement. These modules work independently and then automatically exchange information, creating a company-wide system that includes current delivery dates, inventory status, quality control, and other critical information. ERP applications can also be integrated with Web-based resources, as explained in the Online Chapter, "Using the Internet for Business Success," at **http://gitman.swcollege.com**. Let's now look at the basic types of networks companies use to transmit data—local area networks and wide area networks—and popular networking applications like intranets and extranets.

Connecting Near and Far with Networks

local area network (LAN)
A network that connects computers at one site, enabling the computer users to exchange data and share the use of hardware and software from a variety of computer manufacturers.

wide area network (WAN)
A network that connects computers at different sites via telecommunications media such as phone lines, satellites, and microwaves.

Two basic types of networks are distinguished by the area they cover. A **local area network (LAN)** lets people at one site exchange data and share the use of hardware and software from a variety of computer manufacturers. LANs offer companies a more cost-effective way to link computers than linking terminals to a mainframe computer. The most common uses of LANs at small businesses, for example, are office automation, accounting, and information management. LANs can help companies reduce staff, streamline operations, and cut processing costs. LANs can be set up with wired or wireless connections.

A **wide area network (WAN)** connects computers at different sites via telecommunications media such as phone lines, satellites, and microwaves. A modem connects the computer or a terminal to the telephone line and transmits data almost instantly, in less than a second. The Internet is essentially a worldwide WAN. Long-distance telephone companies, such as AT&T, MCI, and Sprint, operate very large WANs. Companies also connect LANs at various locations into WANs. WANs make it possible for companies to work on critical projects around the clock by using teams in different time zones.

Several forms of WANs—intranets, virtual private networks (VPNs), and extranets—use Internet technology. Here we'll look at intranets, internal corporate networks that are widely available in the corporate world, and VPNs. Extranets are discussed in the Online Chapter, "Using the Internet for Business Success," at **http://gitman.swcollege.com**.

Although wireless networks have been around for more than a decade, they are increasing in use because of falling costs, faster and more reliable technology, and improved standards. They are similar to their wired LAN and WAN cousins, except they use radio frequency signals to transmit data. You probably use a wireless WAN (WWAN) regularly when you use your cellular phone. WANs' coverage can span several countries. Telecommunications carriers AT&T Wireless, Cingular Wireless, Sprint PCS, T-Mobile, and Verizon operaters use wireless WANs.[2]

Wireless LANs (WLANs) that transmit data at one site offer an alternative to traditional wired systems. WLANs' reach is a radius of 500 feet indoors and 1,000 feet outdoors and can be extended with antennas, transmitters, and other devices. The wireless devices communicate with a wired access point into the wired network. WLANs are convenient for specialized applications where wires are in the way or when employees are in different locations in a building. Hotels, airports, restaurants, hospitals, retail establishments, universities, and warehouses are among the largest users of WLANs.

WLANs are faster and more reliable than WANs, yet the cost is comparable to wired LANs. Boston's Care Group Health System, a hospital consortium, set up wireless LANs in the intensive care, emergency, and operating room areas. The network allowed doctors to enter patient orders electronically and to access patients' complete medical records from anywhere in the hospital. Switching to the electronic system has greatly improved patient care by eliminating errors caused by difficult-to-read handwritten orders. Installing the WLAN in a medical setting presented a challenge for the IT staff, as wireless devices must be at least three feet from patients to prevent interference with critical medical equipment such as pacemakers.[3]

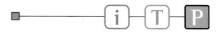

Making Ethical Choices

xtra! http://gitmanxtra.swlearning.com

BIG BROTHER IS WATCHING YOU—TACITLY

As a marketing research analyst for a software developer that makes security software like virus protection and firewalls, you must keep up with industry trends and know what your competitors are doing. Therefore you are intrigued when you learn about a new software product that keeps track of words and phrases in employee e-mails and other documents. This would allow you to look for certain target terms that might indicate that an employee has a friend working at a rival firm, or another has a cousin who works for a potential new distributor. In essence, you could use data-mining techniques to dig up a wealth of business intelligence.

The software, called KnowledgeMail, is the brainchild of a Silicon Valley start-up called Tacit Knowledge Systems. Its founder and CEO, David Gilmour, considers it an efficient and cost-effective way for companies like yours to get the information you need from your employees.

When you met with Gilmour to learn more about the program, you expressed your concern about your employees' reactions to the installation of this type of monitoring software. Gilmour acknowledged that privacy is a major issue in the workplace today and that some potential customers expressed concern that they might be subject to lawsuits for collecting employee data without specifically telling staff how it could be used.

In fact, Gilmour maintains that KnowledgeMail can improve personal privacy, because employees maintain control over their personal profiles, which stay private until the employee chooses to make all or part of it public. "The profiles are visible only to that particular employee. At the technical level, customers are not allowed to tamper with their employees' profiles," he explains. He also told you that several Fortune 100 companies are already using the product.

ETHICAL DILEMMA

Should you recommend the purchase of KnowledgeMail for your company, and on what do you base your proposal?

SOURCE: Mike Hofman, "Software to Watch over Me," *Inc.*, July 1, 2000, downloaded from http://www.inc.com; Tacit Knowledge Systems Web site, http://www.tacit.com.

An Inside Job: Intranets

intranet
An internal corporate-wide area network that uses Internet technology to connect computers and link employees in many locations and with different types of computers.

Like LANs, **intranets** are private corporate networks. Many companies use both types of internal networks. However, because they use Internet technology to connect computers, intranets are WANs that link employees in many locations and with different types of computers. Essentially mini-Internets that serve only the company's employees, intranets operate behind a *firewall* that prevents unauthorized access. Employees navigate using a standard Web browser, which makes the intranet easy to use. They are also considerably less expensive to install and maintain than other network types and can take advantage of the Internet's interactive features such as chat rooms and team work spaces. Many software providers now offer off-the-shelf intranet packages so that companies of all sizes can benefit from the increased access to and distribution of information, including multimedia, that intranets provide.

Intranets have many applications. They can be narrowly focused for specific purposes. Allied Van Lines uses an intranet for its Agent Notification System. Using the intranet, the moving company's 500 independent agents all across the country can be sure they are picking up the right items, on schedule. Mary Mancuso, manager of agent support services, expects that timely order information will save agents a total of more than $6 million annually. At the corporate level, the intranet will improve the quality of information and lead to greater customer satisfaction.

Intranets that take a broader view serve as sophisticated knowledge management tools. For example Chrysler Corp.'s Dashboard intranet is a joint effort of human resources, information systems, and corporate communications. It provides 40,000 employees with a wide range of tools for competitive intelligence, collaborative work group support, employee benefits, and financial modeling. Users can also tap into many other resources, including company news, stock and mutual fund quotes, a vehicle-build tracking system, and manufacturing quality statistics.[4]

No More Tangles: Wireless Technologies

Wireless technology has become commonplace today. We routinely use such devices as cellular phones, personal digital assistants (PDAs), garage door openers, and television remote controls—without thinking of them as examples of wireless technology. Businesses use wireless technologies to improve communications with customers, suppliers and employees. You may have seen the term Wi-Fi, which refers to wireless fidelity. When products carry the "Wi-Fi Certified" designation, they have been tested and certified to work with each other, regardless of manufacturer.

Companies in the package delivery industry were among the first users of wireless technology. Delivery personnel use handheld computers to send immediate confirmation of package receipt. UPS considers its investment in wireless technology a good one. Not only do customers get better service, but UPS keeps expenses down. Without wireless technology, UPS would have to hire more call center and service representatives. You may also have seen meter readers and repair personnel from utility and energy companies send data from remote locations back to central computers.[5]

Private Lines: Virtual Private Networks

virtual private networks (VPNs)
Private corporate networks connected over a public network, such as the Internet. VPNs include strong security measures to allow only authorized users to access the network.

Many companies use **virtual private networks (VPNs)** to connect two or more private networks (such as LANs) over a public network, such as the Internet. VPNs include strong security measures to allow only authorized users to access the network and its sensitive corporate information. Companies with widespread offices may find that a VPN is a more cost-effective option to creating a network using purchased networking equipment and leasing expensive private lines. This type of private network is more limited than a VPN, because it doesn't allow authorized users to connect to the corporate network when they are at home or traveling. The "Expanding Around the Globe" box describes how one chain of hotels uses VPNs to improve customer service.

As Exhibit 17.1 shows, the VPN uses existing Internet infrastructure and equipment to connect remote users and offices almost anywhere in the world—

Exhibit 17.1 Virtual Private Networks (VPNs)

Expanding Around the Globe

Managing IT Is Not a Luxury at Mandarin Oriental Hotel Group

As Hong Kong based Mandarin Oriental Hotel Group (MOHG) began to expand its reach beyond Asia, its computer networks also had to grow to accommodate the greater international scope. The prestigious hotel chain currently operates 20 luxury hotels including facilities in Hong Kong, Bangkok, Singapore, London, Geneva, New York, and Hawaii. For a company whose mission is to "completely delight and satisfy our guests" and that prides itself on being a leader in the hospitality industry, reliable IT systems that provide the highest level of customer service are essential.

The hotel group uses an Internet-based VPN that can handle multiple and widespread locations. Sophisticated networks pay off for the group. The dedicated online reservations service introduced in February 2001 converts rates into the guest's preferred currency. Online reservations made directly through the MOHG Web site **(http://www.mandarinoriental.com)** quickly jumped 20 percent a month. As a result, Mandarin Oriental was able to reduce the amount it paid out in third-party commissions to other Web sites and travel agents.

Upgrading and managing its rapidly growing information technology infrastructure presented management challenges for the award-winning hotel company. In addition, explains director of technology Nick Price, MOHG had to quickly build new infrastructure and remain responsive—yet minimize capital investment.

MOHG's IT management decided that outsourcing network management services would be more cost-effective than doing it in-house. It contracted with InteQ Corp., a Bedford, Massachusetts, company that specializes in infrastructure and application management solutions for corporate customers. InteQ's InfraSolve software proactively monitors the hotel group's computers, applications, and other network equipment. When a problem arises, it fixes it remotely. The Web-based interface makes it easy for MOHG managers to use a standard Web browser to check on network status and performance and receive real-time alerts.

"InteQ did what would have taken us two years to do," says Geoff McClelland, vice president of technology for hotel development, who is based in Sydney, Australia. By outsourcing, MOHG's IT personnel are free to focus on business-critical issues. Overall service levels are higher, yet costs are lower.

CRITICAL THINKING QUESTIONS

1. Was a VPN a good choice for Mandarin Oriental Hotel Group? Explain your answer.
2. Discuss the pros and cons of outsourcing some IT functions rather than doing them in-house. Can you think of any tasks that might not be appropriate for an outside firm to handle?

SOURCES: Mitch Betts, "Case Studies in Network and Systems Management," *Computerworld*, September 16, 2002, downloaded from http://www.computerworld.com; "InteQ Gains Momentum Through Series of Customer Wins," February 11, 2002, press release, InteQ Web site, http://www.inteqnet.com/press_feb1102.html; and Mandarin Oriental Hotel Group Web site, http://www.mandarinoriental.com.

without long-distance charges. In addition to saving on telecommunications costs, companies using VPNs don't have to buy or maintain special networking equipment and can outsource management of remote access equipment. VPNs are useful for salespeople and telecommuters, who can access the company's network as if they were on-site at the company's office. On the downside, the VPN's availability and performance, especially when it uses the Internet, depends on factors largely outside of an organization's control.[6]

Software on Demand: Application Service Providers

application service providers (ASPs)
A service company that buys and maintains software on its servers and distributes it through high-speed networks to subscribers, for a set period and price.

As software developers release new types of application programs and updated versions of existing ones every year or two, companies have to analyze whether they can justify buying or upgrading to the new software—in terms of both cost and implementation time. **Application service providers (ASPs)** offer a different approach to this problem. Companies subscribe to an ASP and use the applications much like you'd use telephone voice mail, the technology for which resides at the phone company. Exhibit 17.2 on page 544 shows how the ASP interfaces with software and hardware vendors and developers, the IT department, and users.

The simplest ASP applications are automated—for example, a user might use one to build a simple e-commerce site. ASPs provide three major categories of applications to users:

- Enterprise applications, including customer relationship management, enterprise resource planning (ERP), e-commerce, and data warehousing.

Exhibit 17.2 Structure of an ASP Relationship

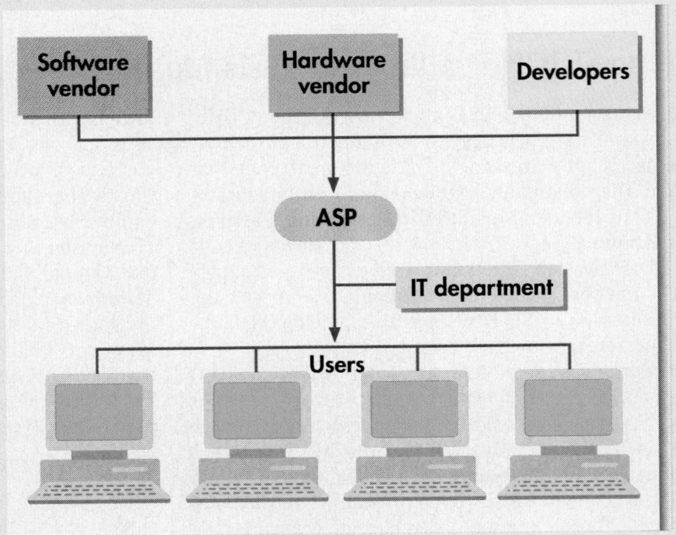

- Collaborative applications for internal communications, e-mail, groupware, document creation, and management messaging.
- Applications for personal use—for example, games, entertainment software, and home-office applications.

concept check

What is a computer network? What benefits do companies gain by using networks?

How do a LAN and a WAN differ? Why would a company use a wireless network?

What advantages do VPNs offer a company? ASPs?

The basic idea behind subscribing to an ASP is compelling. Users can access any of their applications and data from any computer, and IT can avoid purchasing, installing, supporting, and upgrading expensive software applications. ASPs buy and maintain the software on their servers and distribute it through high-speed networks. Subscribers rent the applications they want for a set period and price. The savings in infrastructure, time, and staff could be significant.

Management Information Systems

3 learning goal

While individuals use business productivity software such as word processing, spreadsheet, and graphics programs to accomplish a variety of tasks, the job of managing a company's information needs falls to *management information systems:* users, hardware, and software that support decision making. Information systems collect and store the company's key data and produce the information managers need for analysis, control, and decision making.

As we learned in Chapter 12, factories use computer-based information systems to automate production processes and order and monitor inventory. Most companies use them to process customer orders and handle billing and vendor payments. Banks use a variety of information systems to process transactions such as deposits, ATM withdrawals, and loan payments. Most consumer transactions also involve information systems. When you check out at the supermarket, book a hotel room using a toll-free hotel reservations number, or buy CDs over the Internet, information systems record and track the transaction and transmit the data to the necessary places. Health care providers and insurers use information systems to speed up claims processing, as the "Focusing on Small Business" box explains.

© AP / WIDE WORLD PHOTOS

Computer modeling helps Aventis, a major pharmaceutical company, save time and money on later stage clinical drug trials. When the simulation results in one study indicated that the drug's side effects outweighed its benefits, Aventis saved $50 to $100 million by stopping the trial and using that funding for another project that had greater potential for success.

Companies typically have several types of information systems, starting with systems to process transactions. Management support systems are dynamic systems that allow users to analyze data to make forecasts, identify business trends, and model business strategies. Office automation systems improve the flow of communication throughout the organization. Each type of information system serves a particular level of decision making: operational, tactical, and strategic. Exhibit 17.3 on page 546 shows the relationship between transaction processing and management support systems as well as the management levels they serve. Let's now take a more detailed look

Focusing on Small Business

TriZetto Writes a Technology Prescription

Health care providers and insurers are curing their claims-processing and administrative headaches with a "technology prescription" from TriZetto Group, Inc., **http://www.trizetto.com**, a growing Newport Beach, California, software and services company. TriZetto's health care information technology applications automate labor-intensive paper-based processes so that TriZetto's 500 customers, who represent about 40 percent of the U.S. population with health insurance, work more efficiently and cut costs.

TriZetto offers such products as Facets, a leading managed health care payers' system; QicLink, an application designed for benefits administrators; and HealthWeb, a Web-based platform that allows health plans and providers, members, employers, and brokers to exchange information and conduct business online. It also provides consulting to customize systems to customer requirements, as well as outsourcing and business services.

Customers like Blue Cross Blue Shield of Tennessee (BCBST) sing TriZetto's praises. After the health insurance provider implemented Facets, claims-processing time went from an average of 30 days to just 10 days. The cost savings from Facets paid for the application within just four years and now generates ongoing savings of about $5 million annually. BCBST also installed HealthWeb to improve communications both internally and externally. Now health coverage enrollments can take place online, and better access to information improves efficiency. "Our systems are more integrated, we can better leverage our data, and we can simplify everything," says Bob Worthington, senior vice president of corporate and information services for BCBST. An added plus for BCBST: customer satisfaction ratings are the highest ever.

Keeping up with regulatory changes is both a challenge and an opportunity for TriZetto. The company developed two products in response to the passage of the Health Insurance Portability and Accountability Act of 1996 (HIPAA): HIPAA Gateway to process electronic transactions and HIPAA Privacy, which manages personal health information according to HIPAA guidelines. TriZetto worked with CareSource, an Ohio health plan, to implement not only these two HIPAA applications but also Facets. "With a 200 percent enrollment increase in recent years, we required the advanced technology and productivity of Facets to help us manage growth and costs while improving work processes," said Mike Knellinger, chief information officer for CareSource. "TriZetto's comprehensive solution is integral to our smooth system migration and overall long-term success."

CRITICAL THINKING QUESTIONS

1. Why is the health care industry well suited for the application of information technology?
2. What are the special challenges facing TriZetto in developing new IT products for health care customers?

SOURCES: "TriZetto Signs Software License and Hosting Agreement with CareSource," company press release, May 6, 2003, downloaded from http://www.trizetto.com; TriZetto Web site, http://www.TriZetto.com, accessed May 24, 2003; Arlene Weintraub, "TriZetto's Rx for Health-Care Costs," *Business Week Online*, October 9, 2002, downloaded from http://www.businessweek.com.

Exhibit 17.3 | A Company's Integrated Information System

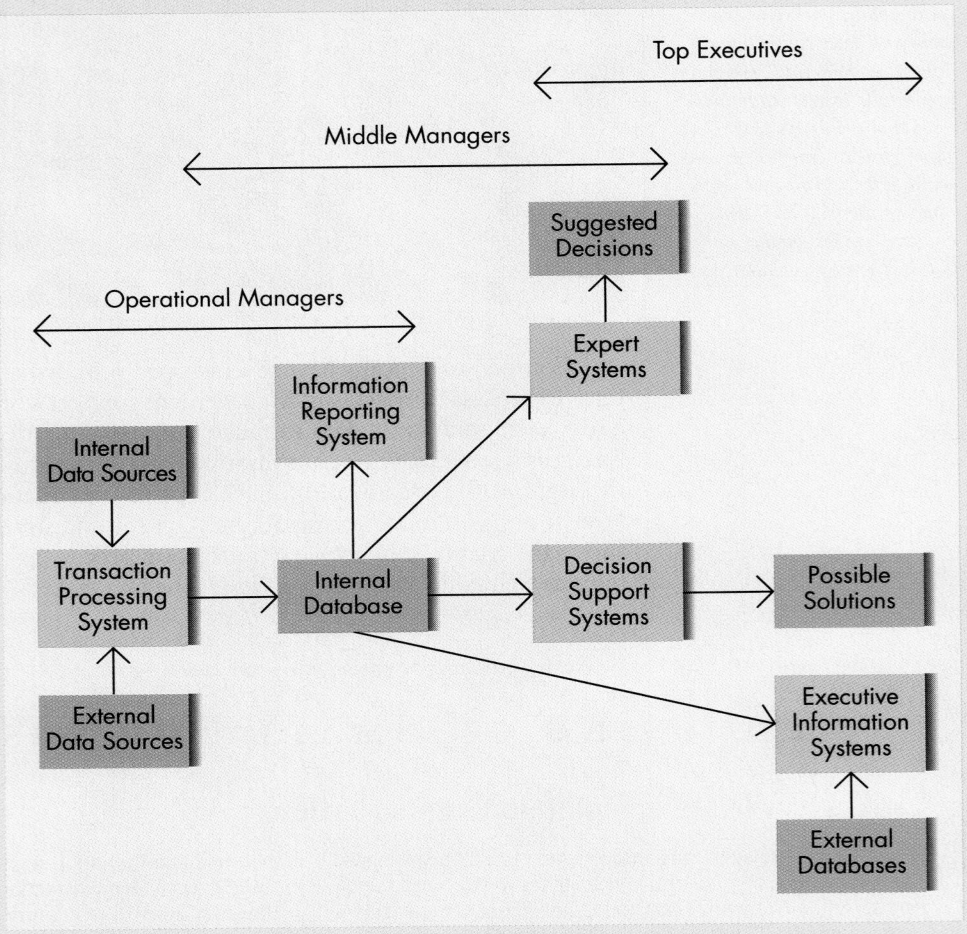

at how companies and managers use transaction processing and management support systems to manage information.

Transaction Processing Systems

transaction processing system (TPS)
An information system that handles the daily business operations of a firm. The system receives and organizes raw data from internal and external sources for storage in a database using either batch or online processing.

batch processing
A method of updating a database in which data are collected over some time period and processed together.

The firm's integrated information system starts with its **transaction processing system (TPS).** The TPS receives raw data from internal and external sources and prepares these data for storage in a database similar to a microcomputer database but vastly larger. In fact, all the company's key data are stored in a single huge database that becomes the company's central information resource. As noted earlier, the *database management system* tracks the data and allows users to query the database for the information they need.

The database can be updated in two ways: **batch processing,** where data are collected over some time period and processed together, and **online,** or **real-time, processing,** which processes data as they become available. Batch processing uses computer resources very efficiently and is well suited to applications such as payroll processing that require periodic rather than continuous processing. Online processing keeps the company's data current. When you make an airline reservation, the agent enters your reservation directly into the airline's computer and quickly receives confirmation. Online processing is more expensive than batch processing, so

Exhibit 17.4 | Accounting Information System

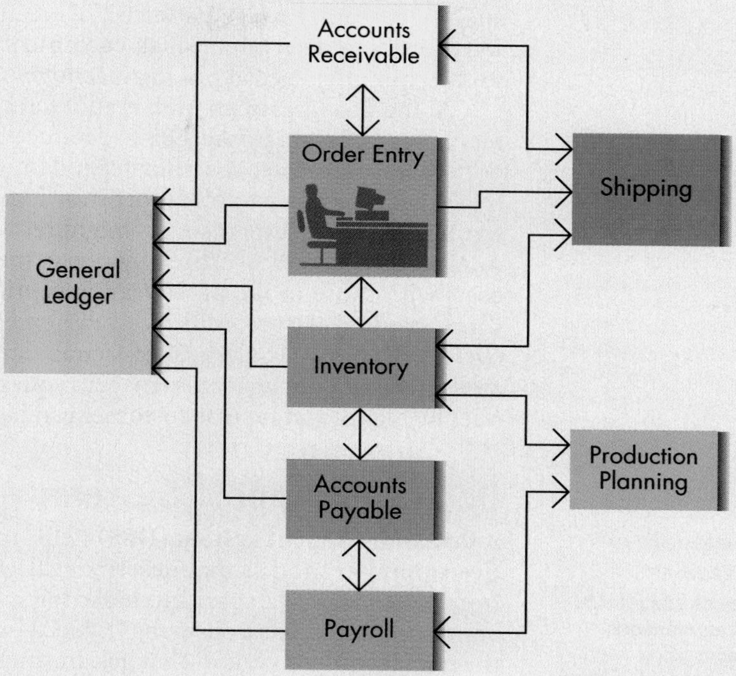

on-line (real-time) processing
A method of updating a database in which data are processed as they become available.

management support system (MSS)
An information system that uses the internal master database to perform high-level analyses that help managers make better decisions.

data warehouse
An information technology that combines many databases across a whole company into one central database that supports management decision making.

data mart
Special subset of a data warehouse that deals with a single area of data and is organized for quick analysis.

companies must weigh the cost versus the benefit. For example, a factory that operates round-the-clock may use real-time processing for inventory and other time-sensitive requirements but process accounting data in batches overnight.

The accounting information system diagrammed in Exhibit 17.4 is a typical TPS. It has subsystems for order entry, accounts receivable (for billing customers), accounts payable (for paying bills), payroll, inventory, and general ledger (for determining the financial status and profitability of the business). The accounting information system provides input to and receives input from the firm's other information systems, such as manufacturing (production planning data, for example) and human resources (data on hours worked and salary increases to generate paychecks).

Decisions, Decisions: Management Support Systems

Transaction processing systems automate routine and tedious back-office processes such as accounting, order processing, and financial reporting. They reduce clerical expenses and provide basic operational information quickly. **Management support systems (MSSs)** use the internal master database to perform higher-level analyses that help managers make better decisions.

Information technologies such as data warehousing are part of more advanced MSSs, as we learned in the Home Depot opening vignette. A **data warehouse** combines many databases across the whole company into one central database that supports management decision making. Data warehouses include software to extract data from operational databases, maintain the data in the warehouse, and provide data to users. Data warehouses may contain many **data marts,** special subsets of a data warehouse that each deal with a single area of data. Data marts are organized for quick analysis. Companies use data warehouses for many purposes, including customer relationship management systems, fraud detection, product line analysis, and corporate asset management. Retailers might wish to identify customer demographic characteristics and shopping patterns to improve direct-mailing responses. Banks can more easily spot credit-card fraud, as well as analyze customer usage patterns. Telecommunications firms tap into their data warehouses to determine which customers are likeliest to switch service providers so they can offer special pricing incentives to maintain their loyalty.[7]

At the first level of an MSS is an *information-reporting system,* which uses summary data collected by the TPS to produce both regularly scheduled and special reports. The level of detail would depend on the user. A company's payroll personnel might get a weekly payroll report showing how each employee's paycheck was determined. Higher-level mangers might receive a payroll summary report that shows total labor cost and overtime by department and a comparison of current labor costs with those in the prior year. Exception reports show cases that fail to meet some standard. An accounts receivable exception report that lists all customers with overdue accounts would help collection personnel focus their work. Special reports are generated only when a manager requests them; for example, a report showing sales by region and type of customer can highlight reasons for a sales decline.

Decision Support Systems

decision support system (DSS)
A management support system that helps managers make decisions using interactive computer models that describe real-world processes.

A **decision support system (DSS)** helps managers make decisions using interactive computer models that describe real-world processes. The DSS also uses data from the internal database but looks for specific data that relate to the problems at hand. It is a tool for answering "what if" questions about what would happen if the manager made certain changes. In simple cases, a manager can create a spreadsheet and try changing some of the numbers. For instance, a manager could create a spreadsheet to show the amount of overtime required if the number of workers increases or decreases. With models, the manager enters into the computer the values that describe a particular situation, and the program computes the results. Marketing executives at a furniture company could run DSS models that use sales data and demographic assumptions to develop forecasts of the types of furniture that would appeal to the fastest-growing population groups.

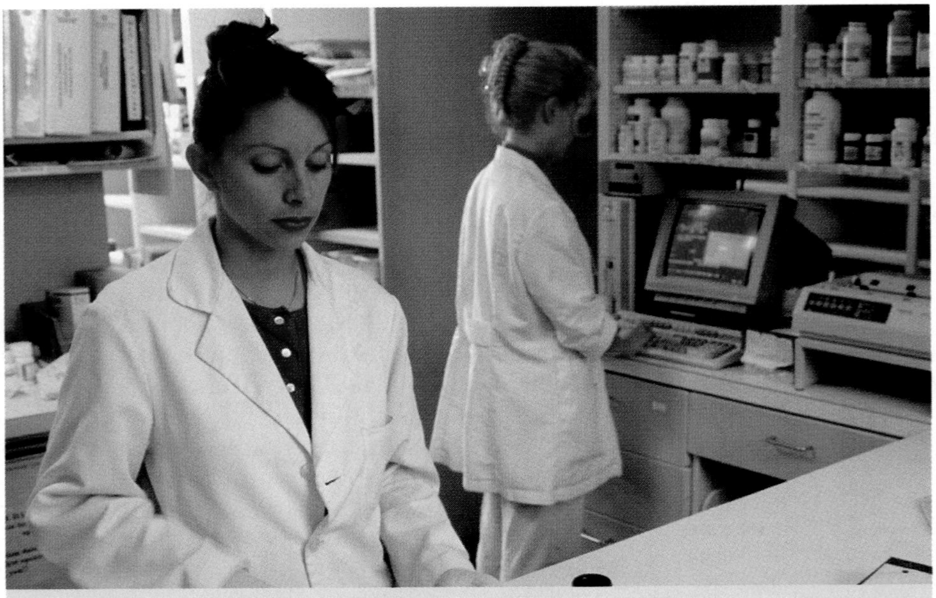

Medical professionals use expert systems to analyze patients' medications, ensuring that they do not cause allergic reactions and potentially dangerous interactions with patients' other prescriptions.

Executive Information Systems

executive information system (EIS)
A management support system that is customized for an individual executive; provides specific information for strategic decisions.

Although similar to a DSS, an **executive information system (EIS)** is customized for an individual executive. These systems provide specific information for strategic decisions. For example, a CEO's EIS may include special spreadsheets that present financial data comparing the company to its principal competitors and graphs showing current economic and industry trends.

Until it implemented a Web-based executive management information system (EMIS), Aetna Inc. lacked an automated system to provide executives with a single source of timely, reliable financial and operational information. Aetna's managers had problems getting the right information to analyze product performance. They also had to wait a month to get information from local offices, making it hard to respond to changing market conditions. The health insurance and benefits company implemented the EMIS to bring together key information that previously resided in separate systems throughout the company. Using the new system, Aetna executives can access financial information within 12 to 14 business days. Managers can now look at the market and react to pricing concerns and trends such as changing medical costs. Analytical software tools create reports of financial and operational information based on business units or geography, or broken into customer segments. The greatly improved understanding of the company's business fundamentals is credited with helping Aetna return to profitability.[8]

Expert Systems

expert system
A management support system that gives managers advice similar to what they would get from a human consultant; it uses artificial intelligence to enable computers to reason and learn to solve problems in much the same way humans do.

An **expert system** gives managers advice similar to what they would get from a human consultant. Artificial intelligence enables computers to reason and learn to solve problems in much the same way humans do, using what-if reasoning. Although they are expensive and difficult to create, expert systems are finding their way into more companies as more applications are found. Lower-end expert systems can even run on PDAs like the Palm Pilot. Top-of-the-line systems help airlines appropriately deploy aircraft and crews, critical to the carriers'efficient operations. The cost of hiring enough people to do these ongoing analytical tasks would be prohibitively expensive. Expert systems have also been used to help explore for oil, schedule employee work shifts, and diagnose illnesses.

Some expert systems take the place of human experts, while others assist them. Aim Services of Tennessee, a software and management consulting company, helped a pleasure-boat manufacturer install an expert system that could change the manufacturing runs for different boat configurations. Employees on the factory floor answer questions on their handheld devices, with the sequence of questions determined by the employee's answers. The system also gives directions to reprogram the robotic production system or for other tasks. Since the company installed the expert system, production downtime has decreased and employees experience less stress.[9]

Office Automation Systems

office automation system
An information system that uses information technology tools such as word processing systems, e-mail systems, cell phones, PDAs, pagers, and fax machines to improve communications throughout an organization.

Today's **office automation systems** make good use of the computer networks in many companies to improve communications. Office automation systems assist all levels of employees and enable managers to handle most of their own communication. Many of the newer devices now combine multiple functions. The key elements, many of which have been around for years and others that are fairly new, include:

- Word processing systems for producing written messages.
- E-mail systems for communicating directly with other employees and customers and transferring computer files.

- Departmental scheduling systems for planning meetings and other activities.
- Cell phones for providing telephone service away from the office, as in cars. Newer models can receive and send e-mail and text messages, graphics, and browse the Web.
- PDAs that replace paper personal planners and address books; these can also transfer data to and from the user's PC and run some software. Newer models can also handle e-mail and Web browsing.
- Wireless e-mail devices, such as the Blackberry.
- Pagers that notify employees of phone calls. Some pagers can display more extensive written messages sent from a computer network.
- Voice-mail systems for recording, storing, and forwarding phone messages.
- Facsimile (fax) systems for delivering messages on paper within minutes.
- Electronic bulletin boards and computer conferencing systems for discussing issues with others who are not present.

Office automation systems also make telecommuting and home-based businesses possible. An estimated 8 million people work at home, using microcomputers and other high-tech equipment to keep in touch with the office. Instead of spending time on the road twice a day, telecommuters work at home two or more days a week.

concept check

What are the main types of management information systems, and what does each do?

Differentiate between the types of management support systems, and give examples of how companies use each.

How can office automation systems help employees work more efficiently?

Technology Management and Planning

4 learning goal

With the help of computers, people have produced more data in the last 30 years than in the previous 5,000 years combined. Companies today make sizable investments in information technology to help them manage this overwhelming amount of data, convert the data into knowledge, and deliver it to the people who need it. In many cases, however, the companies do not reap the desired benefits from these expenditures. Among the typical complaints from senior executives are that the company is spending too much and not getting adequate performance and payoff from IT investments, these investments do not relate to business strategy, the firm seems to be buying the latest technology for technology's sake, and communications between IT specialists and IT users are poor.

Optimize IT!

Managing a company's enterprise-wide IT operations, especially when those often stretch across multiple locations, software applications, and systems, is no easy task. Not only must IT managers deal with on-site systems. They must also oversee the networks that connect staff working at locations ranging from the next town to another continent. Research firm Gartner Inc. estimates that about 37 percent of the workforce works remotely at least part-time. What makes the IT manager's job even more difficult is providing this technology for remote employees in the face of time constraints and lower budgets—while maintaining a cohesive corporate culture.[10] Add to these concerns the increasing use by employees of handheld devices like PDAs and cell phones that handle e-mail messaging and you have an overwhelming management task!

Growing companies may find themselves with a decentralized IT structure that includes many separate systems and duplication of efforts. A company that wants to enter or expand into e-commerce needs systems that are flexible enough to adapt to this changing marketplace. Security for equipment and data is another critical area, which we will cover later in the chapter.

The goal is to develop an integrated, company-wide technology plan that balances business judgment, technology expertise, and technology investment. IT planning requires a coordinated effort among a firm's top executives, IT managers, and business-unit managers to develop a comprehensive plan. Such plans must take into account the company's strategic objectives and how the right technology will help managers reach those goals.

Technology management and planning are not just about buying new technology. Today companies are cutting IT budgets so that managers are being asked to do more with less. They are implementing projects that leverage their investment in the technology they already have. At electronics retailer Circuit City Stores Inc., vice president of MIS William E. McCorey Jr. continually evaluates his company's existing technology infrastructure to make sure that it is optimized for maximum system availability and service levels. This is an important component in achieving a formal Six Sigma quality certification. Through projects such as hardware consolidation and installation of special software to boost performance rates on certain equipment, McCorey hopes to reduce infrastructure and administrative costs by up to 15 percent.[11]

Managing Knowledge Resources

As a result of the proliferation of information, we are also seeing a major shift from information management to a broader view that focuses on finding opportunities in and unlocking the value of intellectual rather than physical assets. Where *information management* involves collecting, processing, and condensing information, the more difficult task of **knowledge management (KM)** focuses on researching, gathering, organizing, and sharing an organization's collective knowledge to improve productivity, foster innovation, and gain competitive advantage. Some companies are even creating a new position, *chief knowledge officer,* to head up this effort. The goal of KM is to allow organizations to generate value from their intellectual assets—not just documents but also the knowledge in their employees' heads.[12]

knowledge management (KM)
The process of researching, gathering, organizing, and sharing an organization's collective knowledge to improve productivity, foster innovation, and gain competitive advantage.

Companies use their IT systems to facilitate the physical sharing of knowledge. But better hardware and software are not the answer to KM. KM is not technology based but rather a business practice that uses technology. Effective KM calls for a major change in behavior as well as technology to leverage the power of information systems, especially the Internet, and a company's human capital resources. The first step is creating an information culture through organizational structure and rewards that promotes a more flexible, collaborative way of working and communicating. However, moving an organization toward KM is no easy task, but well worth the effort in terms of creating a more collaborative environment, reducing duplication of effort, and increasing shared knowledge. The benefits can be significant in terms of growth, time, and money. A study of leading technology companies by In-Momentum, a research and consulting firm, revealed that companies with advanced networks that enabled people to share ideas both within and outside the company grew faster than companies that lacked these resources. These companies had more network interconnectivity. This strong communications system was part of a larger package of cultural characteristics that includes a customer-centered culture, strong leadership, and a lean bureaucracy. The payoff can be huge. Chief knowledge officer Jeff Stempe at ChevronTexaco estimates that his company has reduced operating expenses by over $2.5 billion a year through KM systems to share best practices.[13]

Technology Planning

A good technology plan provides employees with the tools they need to perform their jobs at the highest levels of efficiency. The first step is a general needs assessment, followed by ranking of projects and the specific choices of hardware and

Exhibit 17.5 Questions for IT Project Planning

- What are the company's overall objectives?
- What problems does the company want to solve?
- How can technology help meet those goals and solve the problems?
- What are the company's IT priorities, both short and long term?
- What type of technology infrastructure (centralized or decentralized) best serves the company's needs?
- Which technologies meet the company's requirements?
- Are additional hardware and software required? If so, will they integrate with the company's existing systems?
- Does the system design and implementation include the people and process changes, in addition to the technological ones?
- Do you have the in-house capabilities to develop and implement the proposed applications, or should you bring in an outside specialist?

concept check

What are some ways a company can manage its technology assets to its advantage?

Differentiate between information management and knowledge management. What steps can companies take to manage knowledge?

List the key questions managers need to ask when planning technology purchases.

software. Exhibit 17.5 poses some basic questions departmental managers and IT specialists should ask when planning technology purchases.

Once managers identify the projects that make business sense, they can choose the best products for the company's needs. The final step is to evaluate the potential benefits of the technology, in terms of efficiency and effectiveness. For a successful project, you must evaluate and restructure business processes, choose technology, develop and implement the system, and manage the change processes to best serve your organizational needs. Installing a new IT system on top of inefficient business processes is a waste of time and money!

PROTECTING COMPUTERS AND INFORMATION

5 learning goal

Have you ever lost a term paper you'd worked on for weeks because your hard drive crashed or you deleted the wrong file? You were upset, angry, and frustrated. Multiply that paper and your feelings hundreds of times over, and you can understand why companies must protect computers, networks, and the information they store and transmit from a variety of potential threats. For example, security breaches of corporate information systems—from human hackers or electronic versions like viruses and worms—are increasing at an alarming rate. The ever-increasing dependence on computers requires plans that cover human error, power outages, equipment failure—and, since September 11, 2001 terrorist attacks. To withstand natural disasters such as major fires, earthquakes, and floods, many companies install specialized fault-tolerant computer systems.

Disasters are not the only threat to data. A great deal of data, much of it confidential, can easily be tapped or destroyed by anyone who knows about computers. Keeping your networks secure from unauthorized access—from internal as well as external sources—requires formal security policies and enforcement procedures. The increasing popularity of mobile devices—laptops, handheld computers, PDAs, and digital cameras—and wireless networks requires calls for new types of security provisions. Rob Clyde, chief technology officer at computer security software firm Symantec, reports that half of the chief executives at a recent roundtable event cited Wi-Fi, a wireless networking technology, as a top security concern. Wireless networks with open access points, for example, can permit unauthorized entry—even if a company has methods in place to prevent this.[14]

Data Security Issues

Unauthorized access into a company's computer systems can be expensive, and not just in monetary terms. The FBI estimates that computer crime cost $450 million dollars in 2001 and is growing at an alarming rate: Incidents rose 250 percent in 2002.[15] A recent study reported that 90 percent of the participating corporations have experienced a computer break-in in the last year. In the 10-year period from 1993 to 2002, the number of crimes reported to the CERT Coordination center, a federally financed information center for computer security information, has climbed from 1,334 to more than 82,000 in 2002. Most of the increase occurred since 1998, when the number of reported crimes was only 3,734.[16]

Firms are taking steps to prevent these costly computer crimes and problems, which fall into several major categories:

- *Unauthorized access and security breaches.* Whether from internal or external sources, unauthorized access and security breaches are a top concern of IT managers. These can create havoc with a company's systems and damage customer relationships. Unauthorized access also includes employees, who can copy confidential new-product information and provide it to competitors or use company systems for personal business that may interfere with systems operation. Networking links make it easier for someone outside the organization to gain access to a company's computers. Computer crooks are getting more sophisticated all the time and find new ways to get into ultrasecure sites. In December 2000, hackers accessed the customer database of online software retailer Egghead.com, which held 3.7 million credit-card account numbers. Although Egghead maintained that its security measures prevented the hackers from stealing the data, customers and shareholders were not convinced. The stock's price quickly dropped 25 percent, customers defected to other companies, and Egghead filed bankruptcy in August 2001.[17]
- *Software piracy.* The copying of copyrighted software programs by people who haven't paid for them is another form of unauthorized use. Piracy takes revenue away from the company that developed the program—usually at great cost. It includes making counterfeit CDs to sell as well as personal copying of software to share with friends. Software firms take piracy seriously and go after the offenders. Many also make special arrangements so that large companies can get multiple copies of programs at a lower cost rather than use illegal copies. Companies are continually adding features such as antipiracy codes and "shells" to limit the use of the software on other computers and prevent unauthorized copying of CDs. Recent versions of Microsoft's Windows XP and Office require "activation" to get full use. The user is limited in the number of times he or she can start up a system without registering the software. "That's been very helpful in making it tough for counterfeiters," says Patrick Mueller, senior investigator for Microsoft.[18] Intuit requires customers to obtain a special product activation number before using its TurboTax software to prepare income taxes. While they can use the program on other computers, only the original computer can be used to print and electronically file tax returns.[19]
- *Deliberate damage to equipment or information.* For example, an unhappy employee in the purchasing department could get into the computer system and delete information on past orders and future inventory needs. The sabotage could severely disrupt production and the accounts payable system. Willful acts to destroy or change the data in computers are hard to prevent. To lessen the damage, companies should back up critical information.
- *Computer viruses.* In a recent survey of network managers, they ranked new computer viruses their top security/business threat.[20] A computer program that copies itself into other software and can spread to other computer systems,

COURTESY OF INTERNET SECURITY SYSTEMS, INC.

Protecting personal and corporate computers from invasion by hackers is critical. Because today's firewall and anti-virus software may not work on tomorrow's threats, companies now provide dynamic, round-the-clock services to identify, prevent, and resolve online attacks and unauthorized access.

computer virus
A computer program that copies itself into other software and can spread to other computer systems.

a **computer virus** can destroy the contents of a computer's hard drive or damage files. Another form is called a "worm" because it spreads itself automatically from computer to computer. Unlike a virus, a worm doesn't require e-mail to replicate and transmit itself into other systems. It can enter through valid access points. The January 25, 2003, "Slammer" worm entered computer systems through a standard entry point for queries to a Microsoft database. It not only affected computers but caused so much additional traffic volume that it clogged up the Internet as well. This brought down some types of telephone service, bank networks, and other critical Net-dependent communications systems. For example, Bank of America's teller machines were unable to dispense cash because like other banks, Bank of America sends encrypted data over the Internet.[21]

Viruses can hide for weeks or months before starting to damage information. A virus that "infects" one computer or network can be spread to another computer by sharing disks or by downloading infected files over the Internet. To protect data from virus damage, virus protection software automatically monitors computers to detect and remove viruses. Program developers make regular updates available to guard against newly created viruses. In addition, experts are becoming more proficient at tracking down virus authors, who are subject to criminal charges.

- *Spam.* Although you might think that *spam,* or unsolicited and unwanted e-mail, is just a nuisance, it also poses a security threat to companies. Viruses spread through e-mail attachments that can accompany spam e-mails. Spam presents other threats to a corporation: the cost of time lost in dealing with spam—like opening the messages, searching for legitimate messages that special spam filters keep out—is about $4 billion a year in lost productivity for U.S. businesses. Companies also spend $3.7 billion for more powerful network equipment and bandwidth capacity, and about $1.2 billion in help-desk support.[22]

Preventing Problems

Firms that take a proactive approach can prevent security and technical problems before they start. They begin by creating formal written security policies to set standards and provide the basis for enforcement. These should have the support of top management. Then they follow with procedures to implement the security policies. Because IT is a dynamic field with ongoing changes to equipment and processes, it's important to review security policies often. Some security policies can be handled automatically, by technical measures, while others involve administrative policies that rely on humans to perform them. Examples of administrative policies are "Users must change their passwords each quarter" and "End users will update their virus signatures at least once a week."[23]

Preventing costly problems can be as simple as regularly backing up applications and data. Companies should have systems in place that automatically back up the company's data every day and store copies of the backups off site. In addition, employees should back up their own work regularly. Another good policy is to maintain a complete and current database of all IT hardware, software, and user details to make it easier to manage software licenses and updates and diagnose problems. In many cases, IT staff can use remote access technology to automatically monitor and fix problems, as well as update applications and services.

Companies should never overlook the human factor in the security equation. As Kevin Mitnick, the infamous convicted hacker, told a Senate panel on government computer security, "Companies spend millions of dollars on firewalls, encryption and secure access devices, and it's money wasted, because none of these measures address the weakest link in the security chain." He first used what he called a "social engineering" attack—convincing someone over the phone through deception to reveal a password—to get into the computer systems. One of the most common ways that outsiders get into company systems is posing as an employee by getting the staffer's full name and username from an e-mail message, then calling the help desk to ask for a forgotten password. Other ways to get passwords: seeing them on sticky notes attached to a desk or computer monitor, leaving machines logged on when employees are away from their desks, and leaving laptop computers with sensitive information unsecured in public places.[24]

Handheld computers and PDAs pose security risks as well. They are often used to store sensitive data such as passwords, bank details, and calendars. Imagine the problems that could arise if an employee saw a calendar entry like "meeting re: layoffs" or an outsider saw "meeting about merger with ABC Company." PDAs can spread viruses when users download virus-infected documents to their company computers.

Companies have many other ways to avoid an IT meltdown, as Exhibit 17.6 demonstrates. Further discussion of protecting confidential data is covered in the Online Chapter, "Using the Internet for Business Success," at **http://gitman.swcollege.com**.

Keep IT Confidential: Privacy Concerns

The very existence of huge electronic file cabinets full of personal information presents a threat to our personal privacy. Until recently, our financial, medical, tax, and other records were stored in separate computer systems. Computer networks make it easy to pool these data into data warehouses. Companies also sell the

Exhibit 17.6 Procedures to Protect IT Assets

- Protect the equipment itself with stringent physical security measures to the premises.
- Protect data using special *encryption* technology to encode confidential information so only the recipient can decipher it.
- Stop unwanted access from inside or outside with special authorization systems. These can be as simple as a password or as sophisticated as fingerprint or voice identification.
- Install *firewalls,* hardware or software designed to prevent unauthorized access to or from a private network.
- Monitor network activity with intrusion-detection systems that signal possible unauthorized access, and document suspicious events.
- Train employees to troubleshoot problems in advance, rather than just react to them.
- Hold frequent staff-training sessions to teach correct security procedures, such as logging out of networks when they go to lunch and changing passwords often.
- Make sure employees choose sensible passwords, of at least six and ideally eight characters long, containing numbers, letters, and punctuation marks. Avoid dictionary words and personal information.
- Establish a database of useful information and FAQs (frequently asked questions) for employees so they can solve problems themselves.
- Develop a healthy communications atmosphere.

information they collect about you from sources like warranty registration cards, credit-card records, registration at Web sites, personal data forms required to purchase online, and grocery store discount club cards. Telemarketers can combine data from different sources to create fairly detailed profiles of consumers.

The September 11, 2001 tragedy raised additional privacy concerns. In its aftermath, the government began looking for ways to improve domestic-intelligence collection and analyze terrorist threats within the United States. Sophisticated database applications that look for hidden patterns in a group of data, a process called **data mining,** increase the potential for tracking and predicting people's daily activities. For example, the Pentagon's Total Information Awareness (TIA) program uses IT to analyze data from commercial transactions such as credit-card purchases and telephone calls. Legislators and privacy activists worry that programs like this could lead to excessive government surveillance that encroaches on personal privacy. The stakes are much higher as well: Errors in data mining by companies in business may result in a consumer being targeted with inappropriate advertising, while a governmental mistake in tracking suspected terrorists could do untold damage to an unjustly targeted person.[25]

data mining
Sophisticated database applications that look for hidden patterns in a group of data to help track and predict future behavior.

Increasingly, consumers are fighting to regain control of personal data and how that information is used. Privacy advocates are working to block sales of information collected by governments and corporations. For example, they want to prevent state governments from selling driver's license information and supermarkets from collecting and selling information gathered when shoppers use barcoded plastic discount cards. With information about their buying habits, advertisers can target consumers for specific marketing programs.

The challenge to companies is to find a balance between collecting the information they need while at the same time protecting individual consumer rights. Most registration and warranty forms that ask questions about income and interests have a box for consumers to check to prevent the company from selling their names. Many companies now state their privacy policies to ensure consumers that they will not abuse the information they collect. We'll return to the topic of protecting consumer privacy in the Online Chapter, "Using the Internet for Business Success," at **http://gitman.swcollege.com**.

concept check

Describe the different threats to data security.

How can companies protect information from destruction and from unauthorized use?

Why are privacy rights advocates alarmed over the use of techniques such as data warehouses and data mining?

Trends in Information Technology

6 learning goal

Information technology is a continually evolving field. The fast pace and amount of change, coupled with IT's broad reach, make it especially challenging to isolate industry trends. From the time we write this chapter to the time you read it—as little as six months—new trends will appear and those that seemed important may fade. However, some trends that are reshaping today's IT landscape are enterprise portals and on-demand computing.

Enterprise Portals Open the Door to Productivity

Improving communications with employees was a top priority for global information technology giant Hewlett Packard (HP). Not only was the company reinventing itself, it was also in the process of integrating its acquisition of computer manufacturer Compaq—situations that called for good channels for CEO Carly Fiorina to communicate with employees about these changes. Add to that sys-

Technology is responsible for the rapidly increasing flow of information. Technology can also provide the solutions to prevent serious communication errors and improve productivity. For example, automated order fulfillment software reduces errors, improves turnaround time, and raises customer satisfaction.

tems and procedures that differed across company divisions and geographic locations, and you have a major IT challenge on your hands.

The answer for HP was a business to employee (B2E) enterprise portal that has become the company's primary source for employee information. An **enterprise portal** is an internal Web site that provides proprietary corporate information to a defined user group. By evaluating, streamlining, and standardizing a host of separate manual transactions, the portal development team create a cohesive, unified framework for employee communications. Although the initial portal project cost about $20 million, HP saved $50 million in just the first year by reducing staffing in call centers, outsourcing benefits administration in the United States, and consolidating Web sites and servers.[26]

Portals can take one of three forms: business to employee (B2E), business to business (B2B), and business to consumer (B2C). Although this may sound much like an intranet, an enterprise portal allows individuals or user groups to customize the portal page. They can select from the available information sources and applications exactly what they need for their particular job situations and don't have to waste time searching for them. The portal gathers everything into one place, helping them to do their jobs more quickly and efficiently.

Why are more companies adopting portal technology? Portals provide:

- A consistent, simple user interface across the company
- Integration of disparate systems and multiple sets of data and information
- A single source for accurate and timely information that integrates internal and external information
- A shorter time to perform tasks and processes,
- Cost savings through the elimination of "information intermediaries"
- Improved communications within the company and with customers, suppliers, dealers, and distributors

On-Demand Computing Solves Grid-Lock

enterprise portal
A customizable internal Website that provides proprietary corporate information to a defined user group, such as employees, supply chain partners, or customers.

What do you do with 8,000 demonstration desktop computers sitting idle in your 272 retail stores? If you are Gateway Computer, you link together the processing power they represent into a grid that produces more than 14 trillion floating point operations per second at peak capacity—creating a virtual supercomputer that ranks above the world's second fastest supercomputer. Then you offer businesses Gateway Processing On Demand, a cost-effective way to access high-end computing resources on an as-needed basis for about 15 cents per processor hour—a fraction of what it would cost to have a supercomputer on-site. As a result, smaller companies and those that don't have an ongoing need for supercomputer capacity can perform extremely complex calculations in hours or days, instead of months.

With *grid computing,* users work collaboratively on a virtual supercomputer using a hardware and software infrastructure that clusters and integrates computers and applications from multiple sources, harnessing unused power in their existing PCs and networks. The grid structure distributes computational resources but maintains central control of the process. A central server acts as a team leader

Exhibit 17.7 How Grid Computing Works

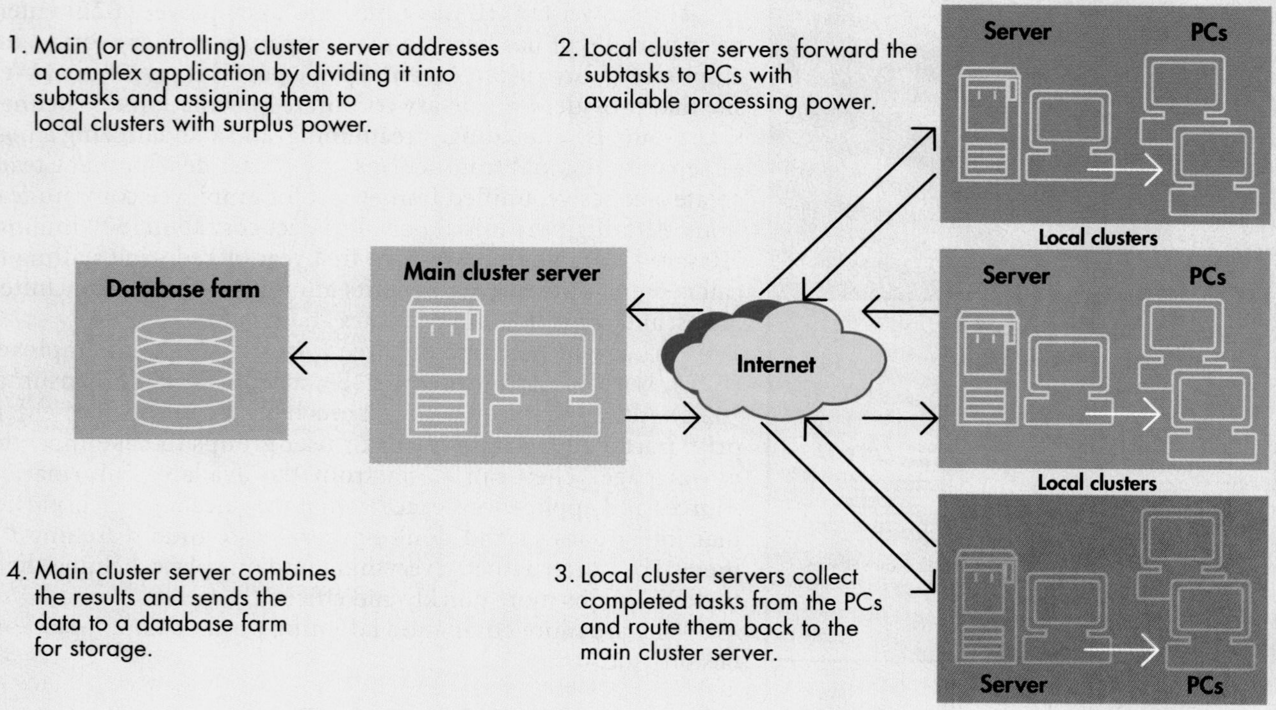
1. Main (or controlling) cluster server addresses a complex application by dividing it into subtasks and assigning them to local clusters with surplus power.
2. Local cluster servers forward the subtasks to PCs with available processing power.
3. Local cluster servers collect completed tasks from the PCs and route them back to the main cluster server.
4. Main cluster server combines the results and sends the data to a database farm for storage.
Database farm
Main cluster server
Internet
Server
PCs
Local clusters
Server
PCs
Local clusters
Server
PCs

SOURCE: Adapted from Sami Lais, "Grid Computing," *Computerworld*, December 23, 2002.

and traffic monitor. The controlling cluster server divides a task into subtasks, assigns the work to computers on the grid with surplus processing power, combines the results, and moves on to the next task until the job is finished. Exhibit 17.7 shows how a typical grid setup works.

Gateway is not alone in pursuing this largely untapped market. IBM, Sun Microsystems, and Hewlett-Packard are among the companies announcing on-demand services. IBM is hoping to generate a significant new revenue stream for the company with its on-demand e-business unit. In March 2003, Petroleum Geo-Services (PGS) became IBM's first on-demand customer. PGS, which needs massive computing power to analyze sonar data in searching for oil deposits, will now obtain about one-third of its supercomputing capacity from IBM. "PGS has been looking for a more flexible business model which addresses peak computing requirements," said PGS's Chris Usher. By outsourcing its peak needs, and buying IT infrastructure sufficient to serve only its average demand, PGS and other companies don't have lots of unused capacity going to waste.

Irving Wladawsky-Berger, general manager of IBM's "e-business on demand" initiative, expects on-demand computing to become increasingly popular. Businesses will be able to choose whether to own the hardware and applications themselves or acquire them from a service provider on a fixed- or variable-cost basis. Several factors are coming together to make on-demand computing delivered via a grid more feasible: ever-present connectivity via the Internet, improved network performance, and greater acceptance of collaborative work methods. Several industry groups are currently developing standards and security protocols to protect data.

Companies are setting up internal grids as well as tapping into the on-demand services offered by these companies. Monsanto Company scientists analyze plant genes to determine traits characteristic of better crop yields. Because this process requires manipulating huge amounts of data, researchers were able to analyze only 10 to 50 genes each year. In 2000, Monsanto decided to use grid computing rather than invest in its own supercomputers. It created a grid from hundreds of computers in its St. Louis headquarters and the Cambridge, Massachusetts offices of its Cereon subsidiary. In between doing other tasks, these computers perform a small calculation. Instead of six weeks, the gene analysis process now takes less than one day, enabling Monsanto to investigate thousands of genes each year.[27]

concept check

How do enterprise portals differ from intranets? What additional benefits do they provide to a company?

What advantages does grid computing offer a company? What are some of the downsides to using this method?

Great Ideas to Use Now

Computer literacy is no longer a luxury. To succeed in business today, almost everyone must develop technological competence. Whether you have a part-time job in a fast-food restaurant that uses computerized ordering systems or perform financial analyses that guide the future of your own company, you will depend on computers. The more you increase your knowledge of technology, the more valuable you will be as an employee in today's information-driven businesses. In addition, the shortage of qualified IT personnel opens up new career avenues to those that enjoy working with technology. You can also take steps to protect your privacy.

Preparation Pays Off

Whether you are an employee or a business owner, you need to be aware of how technology affects the way your firm operates. New applications can change fundamental company operations and employees' roles. For example, companies that install ERP systems want individual employees to make more strategic, far-reaching decisions than before. This requires a dramatic shift in employees' roles and the way they should view their jobs. For example, an accountant's responsibilities might now include analyzing budgets, not just auditing expenses. A salesperson's role might expand to include more strategic decision making about customer issues. Your company will see the business benefits sooner if you prepare for these changing roles. A manager should begin teaching employees operational procedures before implementing the new system and help them acquire the necessary analytical skills. As an employee, you can take the initiative to learn as much as possible about the new technology and how it operates.

Protect Your Good Name

Identity theft is on the rise. Consumer complaints tracked by the Federal Trade Commission jumped from 86,000 in 2001 to 162,000 in 2002. Because many victims don't report identity theft, the Justice Department says that the number could be as high as 700,000 each year. The costs of ID theft are enormous. Clearing your name once your identity is stolen can take a lot of time and money, more than 175 hours and $1,000 in out-of-pocket expenses. Credit-card companies and retailers lose billions of dollars each year due to identity theft.

"The workplace is becoming the target of choice for identity thieves," says Beth Givens, director of the Privacy Rights Clearinghouse. A dishonest employee with access to numerous employee or customer files can cause great damage. For example, a laboratory employee at a biotechnology company found personnel records of 38 former employees who had worked at a company that her employer had acquired. Before she was caught, she used the names, addresses, and

Try It Now

1. **Stay current.** Keeping up with the fast pace of technology change is a real challenge, but it is necessary if you wish to remain up-to-date on the latest IT developments. The Internet has simplified this task, however. Get into the habit of visiting news sites such as ZDNet (**http://www.zdnet.com**) for current tech news. You can also link to Ziff Davis publications such as *PC Magazine,* read product reviews, find online classes, and even compare prices on technology products. Another excellent site is CNet's News.com (**http://www.news.com**), which updates the technology news headlines throughout the day. It has sections on enterprise computing, e-business, communications, media, personal technology, and investing.
2. **What jobs are hot?** Managing information is an emerging career area. There are jobs for people to enter the information, for people to "mine" it to find the best markets as well as to assess the interest and need for new products, and for specialists who understand the complex hardware and software needed to facilitate the loading, maintenance, and use of information. As a result of the increase in outsourcing of some IT functions and the shift of many IT jobs overseas where labor costs are lower, companies now are hiring Business Analysts (BAs, also called Subject Area Experts or SAEs). BAs serve as the business liaisons and interface with the company to whom the project is outsourced and with offshore personnel. To learn more about these areas and the wide range of other IT positions currently available, read the classified employment ads in your local newspaper and *The Wall Street Journal.* Go online to browse the employment ads from almost any major newspaper and surf through the Web sites with job listings. Many technology company Web sites also post job openings. Make a list of jobs that interest you. In addition, read the general job listings to see how many require computer skills.

Social Security numbers to run up $100,000 on 25 credit cards and open 20 cell phone accounts.

Often you have no idea that your identity has been stolen. And you may not be able to prevent it, but you can reduce the chances that it will happen:

- Order your credit reports once or twice a year, one from each of the three reporting services, Equifax, TransUnion and Experian.
- Always check your monthly charge-card statements for fraudulent charges that signal that someone may have stolen your personal information. Then contact the creditors and let them know the information is not accurate.
- Contact these credit-reporting agencies to forbid prescreening credit-rating checks, to stop unsolicited credit-card offers that can fall into the wrong hands.
- Don't leave your mail to be picked up in your mailbox.
- Shred old financial records and credit-card offers that you receive.
- Make sure there is nothing in your wallet that has your Social Security number on it.

At work, find out how the company's sensitive records are discarded, both paper and computer files. Ask about security measures like password controls on computers and background checks on new hires.[28]

Customer Satisfaction and Quality

Information technology can be used in many ways to satisfy customers and improve quality. In fact, most IT systems, from customer relationship management systems to enterprise portals, are at the heart of satisfying employees, vendors, and customers. For example, with accurate and timely information company managers can make decisions that add new products in response to customer requests. Customer databases and order fulfillment systems speed products on their way to customers. Internally, better information allows production managers to accurately forecast inventory so that it is on site when needed, instead of paying for rush delivery. Automated systems improve the quality of production, ordering, administration, and finance. Pharmaceutical companies use computer modeling systems to simulate clinical trials, saving time and money when developing new drugs.

Quality, of course, has another side. IT systems must be planned, designed, and implemented to meet the highest quality standards. Many companies have rushed to implement new systems without allowing adequate time to test them before "going live"—with disastrous results.

Technology and communications tools are an important way for health care providers to improve quality. The Food and Drug Administration estimates that hospitals make more than 770,000 medication errors each year, of which at least 28 percent and as much as 98 percent can be avoided. These costly problems arise from staffing shortages, inexperienced personnel, and even illegible doctors' orders. Many hospitals use Solana Beach, California–based Bridge Medical's Medpoint bar-code and software system to reduce patient medication mistakes. Patients wear a wristband with a bar code. Scanning the bar code into a bedside computer brings up the patient's medication record, which a nurse can compare to the pharmacy order to check for differences. Medpoint also alerts medical personnel to potential problems, like incorrect dosages, drug interactions, and medications that may have similar names. Although the Medpoint system costs from $500,000 to $1 million depending on hospital size, the critical quality control it provides protects patients from injury or even death from drug errors, making this technology well worth the cost.[29]

Looking Ahead at Home Depot

Like many companies, Home Depot recognized that business intelligence applications were critical to its future. Almost 30 percent of respondents to a recent survey on IT spending by retailers ranked this area the most important IT-related strategic initiative for 2003. The company's IT plan has the support of top executives. "This is the kind of technology Home Depot needs to help make decisions that will keep us in the forefront of our industry," says CEO Bob Nardelli.

The data warehouse is just one part of the company's larger IT plan. Over the coming years, Home Depot will shift its infrastructure from a decentralized to a centralized structure "We have increased cash spending on new technology by a factor of 12 since 2000," says CIO Bob DeRodes. As the data warehouse functions come online, Home Depot can expand its IT capabilities with new point-of-sale systems and other projects.[30]

Summary of Learning Goals

1 How has information technology transformed business and managerial decision making?

Businesses depend on information technology for everything from running daily operations to making strategic decisions. Companies must have management information systems that gather, analyze, and distribute information to the appropriate parties, including employees, suppliers, and customers. These systems collect data and process it into usable information for decision making. Managers tap into databases to access the information they need, whether for placing inventory orders, scheduling production, or preparing long-range forecasts. They can compare information about the company's current status to its goals and standards. Company-wide enterprise resource planning systems that bring together human resources, operations, and technology are becoming an integral part of business strategy.

2 Why are computer networks an important part of today's information technology systems?

Computer networks link computers so they can share. Today companies use networks of computers that share data and expensive hardware to improve operating efficiency. Types of networks include local area networks (LANs), wide area networks (WANs), and wireless local area networks (WLANs). Intranets are private WANs that allow a company's employees to communicate quickly with each other and work on joint projects, regardless of their location. Companies are finding new uses for wireless technologies like handheld computers, cell phones, and e-mail devices. Virtual private networks (VPNs) give companies a cost-effective secure connection between remote locations by using public networks like the Internet.

3 What types of systems make up a typical company's management information system?

A management information system consists of a transaction processing system, management support systems, and an office automation system. The transaction processing system (TPS) collects and organizes operational data on the firm's activities. Management support systems help managers make better decisions. They include an information-reporting system that provides information based on the data collected by TPS to the managers who need it; decision support systems that use models to assist in answering "what if" types of questions; and expert systems that give managers advice similar to what they would get from a human consultant. Executive information systems are customized to the needs of top management. All employees benefit from office automation systems that facilitate communication by using word processing, e-mail, fax machines, and similar technologies.

4 How can technology management and planning help companies optimize their information technology systems?

To get the most value from information technology (IT), companies must go beyond simply collecting and summarizing information. Technology planning involves evaluating the company's goals and objectives and using the right technology to reach them. IT managers must also evaluate existing infrastructure to get the best return on the company's investment in IT assets. Knowledge management (KM) focuses on sharing an organization's collective knowledge to improve productivity and foster innovation. Some companies establish the position of chief knowledge officer to head up KM activities.

5 What are the best ways to protect computers and the information they contain?

Because companies are more dependent on computers than ever before, they need to protect data and equipment from natural disasters and computer crime. Types of computer crime include unauthorized use and access, software piracy, malicious damage, and computer viruses. To protect IT assets, companies should prepare written security policies. They can use technology such as virus protection and firewalls and employee training in proper security procedures. They must also take steps to protect customers' personal privacy rights.

6 What are the leading trends in information technology?

IT is a dynamic industry, and companies must stay current on the latest trends to identify those which help them maintain their competitive edge. Enterprise portals and on-demand grid computing are two trends that help users work more quickly and efficiently, increase employee productivity, and improve communications inside and outside the company. An enterprise portal provides users a single resource for information sources and applications. They can customize this internal Web page to gather everything into one place, helping users to do their jobs more quickly and efficiently. Portals can take one of three forms: Business to employee (B2E), business-to-business (B2B), and business to consumer (B2C). Grid computing harnesses the idle power of desktop PCs and other computers to create a virtual supercomputer. A company can access the grid on an as-needed basis instead of investing in its own supercomputer equipment. Outsourcing a portion of the company's computing needs provides additional flexibility. Companies can also set up internal grids.

KEY TERMS

application service providers (ASPs) 543
chief information officer (CIO) 539
computer network 539
computer virus 554
data mart 547
data mining 556
data warehouse 547
database 539
decision support system (DSS) 548
enterprise portal 557
executive information system (EIS) 549
expert system 549
information technology (IT) 538
intranet 541
knowledge management (KM) 551
knowledge worker 539
local area network (LAN) 540
management information system (MIS) 539
management support system (MSS) 547
office automation system 549
transaction processing system (TPS) 546
virtual private networks (VPNs) 542
wide area network (WAN) 540

Preparing for Tomorrow's Workplace

1. How has information technology changed your life? Describe at least three areas (both personal and school/work related) where having access to better information has improved your decisions. Are there any negative effects? What steps can you take to manage information better?
2. Visit or conduct a phone interview with a local small-business owner about the different ways her or his firm uses information technology. Prepare a brief report on your findings that includes the hardware and software used, how it was selected, benefits of technology for the company, and any problems in implementing or using it.
3. Your school wants to automate the class registration process. Prepare a memo to the Dean of Information Systems describing an integrated information system that would help a student choose and register for courses. Make a list of the different groups that should be involved and questions to ask during the planning process. Include a graphic representation of the system similar to Exhibit 17.4 that shows how the data become useful information. Indicate the information a student needs to choose courses and its sources. Explain how several types of management support systems could help students make better course decisions. Include ways the school could use the information it collects from this system. Have several students present their plans to the class, which will take the role of university management in evaluating them.
4. Should companies outsource IT? According to an interview in the December 9, 2002, *San Jose Mercury News,* Craig Conway, president and chief executive of PeopleSoft, believes that IT is too important to outsource and that application service providers (ASPs) don't have a future. Yet research firm IDC reports that worldwide ASP spending could exceed $20 billion by 2005, up from just $1 billion in 2000. What's your position? Divide the class into groups designated "for" or "against" outsourcing and/or ASPs. Have them research the current status of ASPs using publications like *CIO* and *Computerworld* and Web sites like ASPnews.com, **http://www.aspnews.com**.

Working the Net

1. One of the fastest-growing areas of business software is enterprise resource planning (ERP) applications. Visit the site of one of the following companies: SAP (**http://www.sap.com**); PeopleSoft (**http://www.peoplesoft.com**); Oracle (**http://www.oracle.com**); or Baan (**http://www.baan.com**). Prepare a short presentation for the class about the company's ERP product offerings and capabilities. Include examples of how companies use the ERP software.
2. What can an intranet accomplish for a company? Find out by using such resources as Brint.com's Intranet Portal, **http://www.brint.com/Intranets.htm**, and *Intranet Journal,* **http://www.intranetjournal.com/**. Look for case studies

that show how companies apply this technology. Summarize the different features an intranet provides.

3. Learn more about the CERT Coordination Center (CERT/CC), which serves as a center of Internet security expertise. Explore its Web site, **http://www.cert.org**. What are the latest statistics on incidents reported, vulnerabilities, security alerts, security notes, mail messages, and hotline calls? What other useful information does the site provide to help a company protect IT assets?
4. Research the latest developments in computer security at *Computerworld*'s site, **http://computerworld.com/securitytopics/security**. What types of information can you find here? Pick one area, such as security for wireless devices and networks, and summarize your findings.
5. How can someone steal your identity? Using information at the Federal Trade Commission's central Web site for information about identity theft, **http://www.consumer.gov/idtheft/**, compile a list of the ways thieves can access key information to use your identity. What steps should you take if you've been a victim of identity theft? Summarize key provisions of federal laws dealing with this crime and the laws in your state.

Creative Thinking Case

How Jungle Got Out of the Woods

Timing, they say, is everything, and never more so than in the case of Jungle.com's decision to beef up its IT systems in time for the anticipated 2001 Christmas rush. The United Kingdom online retailer had grown quickly and haphazardly, and so had its systems. "The computer system was held together with bits of string, the website written like spaghetti," says CEO David Oldroyd. Jungle and parent company, Argos Retail Group, hired Retek, a systems supplier specializing in retail applications, to handle the £5 million (about $8.1 million) systems overhaul, going live on September 27, 2001, after three months of testing.

Unfortunately the three main modules for customer order management, merchandising, and distribution management didn't work together for Jungle. The upgraded systems did not communicate, causing customer orders to get lost in the system and fail to reach the warehouse for processing. To make matters worse, the problem wasn't immediately apparent, masked by the expected backlog of orders caused by the changeover between systems.

The company ended up canceling 2,500 Christmas orders due in part to incorrect customer order data, out-of-stock products, and an inability to deliver by Christmas. The systems failure cost Jungle £10 million (over $16 million) in lost sales and customer goodwill. There is no bigger crime than upsetting customers through poor service, and Oldroyd estimates the systems failure cost the company at least 10 percent of its customer base.

Could it have all been avoided? The company had to balance the risk that its old system couldn't cope with the projected Christmas rush, against the risk of implementing a completely new system. "In an ideal world we would have wanted more time but we felt the risks had been identified and were being managed," Oldroyd says.

"Risk analysis is essential," says Tony Lock, senior analyst at Bloor Research (a UK financial firm). He believes Jungle's experience with Retek was a classic case of not working out the basics. "You have to identify the business issues and ask yourself which suppliers best meet your needs. Just because a supplier tells you it can be done, doesn't mean it can. You need to see that it works for a live customer."

Within 24 hours of Oldroyd's call for help, Retek flew in a team of system engineers from the United States. In eleven days they had rewritten the module interfaces, and Jungle was back in control and moving forward. In addition, Retek's engineers remained on site to help Jungle resolve any remaining business issues.

Oldroyd admits if Jungle had still been an independent company it would have been finished. As it is the systems problems "probably cost us a year in Jungle's development."

CRITICAL THINKING QUESTIONS

1. What were some of the IT problems Jungle faced as its online business grew?
2. You are Jungle.com's CIO. How would you present the business case for the IT upgrade project to CEO Oldroyd? What risks would you include?
3. How could Jungle have managed its IT systems upgrade without jeopardizing their business?

SOURCES: "Argos Selects Retek as Its Core Merchandising Solution," *PRNewswire,* July 24, 2001; Robert Blincoe, "It's a Jungle Out There," *Computer Weekly,* September 26, 2002, both downloaded from http://www.findarticles.com; and Matt Kelly, "Kelly's I: Jungle.com," *The Mirror* (Glasgow), December 10, 2001, p. 34.

VIDEO CASE

Ordering Up Fresh Sales Data at Archway Cookies

Founded by Harold and Ruth Swanson in Michigan in 1936, Archway Cookies set the standard for making one-of-a-kind cookies. The Swansons' cookies used only the finest quality ingredients and then delivered them fresh to the stores. This commitment to traditional quality and guaranteed freshness became the mission of Archway Cookies. Distributors choose from over 60 different varieties of Home Style, Gourmet, Fat Free, Sugar Free, Bag, and Holiday cookies. Archway then bakes the cookies to order and ships them within 48 hours. Today Archway is part of United States Bakery, a group of five bakery companies headquartered in the Pacific Northwest.

Bake today/ship tomorrow operations call for accurate and timely information. Archway managed its information using paper-based sales and tracking systems dating back to the 1930s. These antiquated procedures hadn't changed much over the years, so that Archway didn't have a fast, effective, and efficient flow and use of data.

The company's customers ran the gamut from convenience stores and gas stations to national chains like Kroger and Safeway and mass-merchandisers like Wal-Mart and Target. "We have to know what's selling in each district so we can maximinze promotions and sales," says Roy Jasper, the company's national sales manager. Upgraded information management systems to automate data collection, improve data flow, and create a single database were a critical component in management's plan to achieve its higher sales growth goals.

In 1991 Archway Cookies began using an integrated hardware and software system from Intermec Technologies Corp. Key components of the system were Intermec's Norand Base Bakery database software, Norand 4410 handheld computers, and mobile printers.

Prior to implementing Intermec's system, Archway's distributors wrote everything down in route books. Archway employees then entered the data manually. As a result, managers had difficulty understanding, comprehending, and analyzing data on a timely basis. This changed drastically when Archway supplied its distributors with handheld computers and began using route accounting software designed specifically for the baking industry. With the new management information system, Archway was able to track, analyze, and adjust sales to customers at the distributor level. "Today we know within 24 hours what was sold to a store by variety," says Jasper. "We can track promotion and service activity at any level, right through the ranks of our company. We have about 600 distributors and sell to about 50,000 stores. That's tracking a lot of detailed data," he adds.

According to Gene H. McKay III, Archway's chief of finance and operations, the use of information technology has produced considerable benefits. "Implementing this technology has saved the distributors an enormous amount of time on their routes, so the distributors have additional time for call-backs and for soliciting new sales," he says. Since the system was installed, Archway sales have increased 3 to 4 percent every year. The system has also provided better information access and information sharing throughout the company.

CRITICAL THINKING QUESTIONS

1. Why is timely and accurate information essential for Archway's manufacturing operations?
2. How does Archway Cookies manage information technology to its advantage?
3. Do you think Archway Cookies would be able to achieve its sales growth goals without the use of computerized information technology?

SOURCES: Adapted from material contained in "Archway Cookies Finds Automation Leads to Paperless Sales and Instant Data Access," Case Studies, Intermec.com, March 5, 2001, http://www.intermec.com; the U.S. Bakery Web site, http://www.usbakery.com, accessed August 2, 2003; and from material in the video *Management Information Systems: A Study of Archway Cookies.*

E-COMMERCE CASE

Opening the Bottleneck in Online Wine Sales

E-commerce wine sites appeal to connoisseurs and novices alike. The wealth of information and search features available online make it easy for wine lovers to get helpful advice and product information. Consumers can find a large selection of wines—from rare vintages to moderately priced bottles—and then conveniently order them.

Despite the obvious appeal of buying wine online, the growth of Internet wine sales has been hampered by legal restrictions. Archaic liquor laws dating back to Prohibition allow each state to determine who can sell alcohol directly to residents. Even counties within a state may have special laws. Some states have reciprocal agreements so that wineries, retailers, and dot-coms based within them can ship directly to consumers in those states. Other states require retailers to obtain the right sales permit to ship across state lines or make direct shipping illegal. Montana even requires the customer to buy a $50 "connoisseurs permit"! Some states have unique rules: Pennsylvanians can order wine online as long as they pick it up at a state-controlled wine and spirits store. Wine e-tailers face a logistical tangle in trying to keep track of each jurisdiction. In fact, no one can sell wine nationally; Wine.com, one of the largest wine wholesalers, operates in just 31 states plus Washington, DC.

Creative wine dot-coms have figured out how to serve customers in many states. Wineaccess.com (**http://www.wineaccess.com**), an online mall of individual shops, uses a consolidated search engine to identify stores with the desired wines. Wine.com operates as a "buyers agent" through in-state networks that join wholesalers and retailers into one large online store. It arranges order delivery or pickup with a wholesaler and retailer located in a jurisdiction that can legally sell to the customer. At the Web site, **http://www.wine.com**, enter the state to which the wine will be shipped; the online customer information system tells you whether you can proceed. It then follows up with specific screens and ordering forms based on the recipient's residence. Other databases and site links provide extensive reviews and recommendations as well as searches by region and type of wine. Developing the information system for the networks was no easy task, however. In addition to different state liquor laws, each distributor used a different inventory tracking and coding system.

CRITICAL THINKING QUESTIONS

1. What advantages do online wine sales offer wine merchants? Their customers? Are there any drawbacks to buying via the Internet?

2. Assume that you are working with Wine.com to develop its information systems project. Prepare a list of the types of information Wine.com should include in its distributor and customer databases.
3. How can Wine.com use the information in its customer and distributor databases to increase sales?

SOURCES: Katy McLaughlin, "Merlot by Mail: Ordering Wine Online Gets Easier," *The Wall Street Journal,* August 21, 2002, pp. D1, D4; Wine.com Web site, http://www.wine.com, accessed May 20, 2003; and the Wine Institute Web site, http://www.wineinstitute.org.

Hot Links Address Book

If you want to know the definition of a computer term or more about a particular topic, Webopedia has the answer:
http://www.webopedia.com

Can't tell a LAN from a WAN? Learn more about networking at About.com's Networking pages,
http://www.compnetworking.about.com/mbody.htm

To find out if that e-mail alerting you to another virus threat is real or a hoax, check out the latest information at
http://www.snopes.com

How can you "inoculate" your computer against viruses? Symantec's Security Response has the latest details on virus threats and security issues:
http://www.symantec.com/avcenter/

Darwin.com is an online magazine that offers helpful articles and Executive Guides that provide a good introduction to key IT topics.
http://www.darwinmag.com

Curious about how companies are using Unified messaging? Find case studies and discussions of current issues at UnifiedMessaging.com,
http://www.unifiedmessaging.com

Curious about how companies are using on demand grid computing? Read the Grid FAQ at the Grid Computing Technology Centre, and then check out some of the many links to other resources.
http://www.gridcomputing.com

Chapter 18

© AP / WIDE WORLD PHOTOS

Using Financial Information and Accounting

learning goals

1. Why are financial reports and accounting information important, and who uses them?
2. What are the differences between public and private accountants, and are public accountants subject to new regulations?
3. What are the six steps in the accounting cycle?
4. In what terms does the balance sheet describe the financial condition of an organization?
5. How does the income statement report a firm's profitability?
6. Why is the statement of cash flows an important source of information?
7. How can ratio analysis be used to identify a firm's financial strengths and weaknesses?
8. What major trends affect the accounting industry today?

Enron Drills through Accounting Rules

Once a high-flying energy company that ranked seventh on the 2000 Fortune 500, Enron (**http://www.enron.com**) is now the poster child for corporate financial wrongdoing. A boring pipeline company that became the world's largest wholesale energy trader, Enron was ultimately brought down by corporate greed—dragging its prestigious accounting firm, Arthur Andersen, along with it. Enron's top executives were brought to trial accused of fraud, money laundering, conspiracy, and obstruction of justice, among other charges.

Enron had a long history of playing fast and loose with accounting principles. It almost went under in 1987, when its oil traders reported $1 billion in false transactions to show higher volume and earn larger bonuses. During the 1990s, Chairman Kenneth Lay and President Jeffrey Skilling promoted a corporate culture that favored innovative new ventures, whether or not they made sound business sense. To the public, the company was a major success story.

But underneath its glitzy surface Enron was manipulating accounting rules to create the illusion of growth, enhance its bottom line, and serve its own agenda. For example, the company obtained Securities and Exchange Commission (SEC) approval to use an accounting method that allowed it to report the total amount a project was expected to earn over its lifetime as current revenue. This encouraged managers to close deals quickly and then inflate future earnings estimates to reach profit goals and fatten their bonuses. For example, in 1999 the company reported income of $65 million on projected natural gas sales from an as-yet-unbuilt pipeline project.

Enron also formed a series of special-purpose entities to cover up losses in high-risk ventures and hide massive amounts of debt. A quirk in the law allowed Enron to borrow from the partnerships and not disclose the debt on Enron's corporate financial statements. These financial games and phantom earnings made the company's financial condition look solid, and its stock price rose to more than $90 per share in August 2000. Yet during 2000, its trickery represented about 96 percent of Enron's reported net income of $979 million. The company also reported debt of only $10.2 billion, rather than the full $22.1 billion for which it was responsible.

Enron did have review procedures in place, but they were often brushed aside. Enron employees and Andersen accountants who raised concerns about accounting irregularities were considered disloyal. In fact, Enron management pressured Andersen staffers and members of its internal risk management team to sign off on complicated deals or controversial accounting practices or risk losing their jobs.

Despite quarterly profits that continued to climb through July 2001, Enron's financial house of cards began tumbling down. In November 2001, Enron admitted to overstating profits by $586 million from 1997 to 2000 and also revealed that its declining financial condition triggered repayment on $690 million of debt hidden in the off-the-books companies. Investors, alarmed at how Enron had obscured financial information in its published financial reports, questioned the overall reliability of corporate financial reporting. By December 2001, the stock was trading at 60 cents a share and the company had filed bankruptcy.[1]

Critical Thinking Questions

As you read this chapter, consider the following questions as they relate to Enron:

1. What role should Enron's independent accounting firm, Arthur Andersen, have played to stop Enron's wrongdoing? What actions could it have taken?
2. Make some recommendations to Enron's new board of directors for procedures to prevent accounting problems in the future.
3. Do you think the government should get involved in setting accounting regulations, or should the accounting profession and companies self-regulate and enforce? Explain your answer.

Principles of Accounting

The losses resulting from the Enron bankruptcy were more than $60 billion! And Enron was just the first in a series of companies whose stories hit the front pages as news of their disregard for accepted accounting procedures became public. Companies such as Adelphia, Qwest, Tyco, WorldCom, and Xerox join Enron in a rogue's gallery for their financial abuses:[2]

- Adelphia—The cable television operator made off-the-books loans to executives; executives later conspired to loot the company.
- Qwest—Executives of the phone carrier knowingly violated strict accounting rules, by booking two-year "bill and hold" transactions as current revenue to meet second-quarter 2001 revenue targets.
- Tyco—Pressured companies it was acquiring to report lower earnings just before the deal was signed, so that profits would jump once the target was part of Tyco; told employees to make up evidence to support a change in accounting to raise income.
- WorldCom—Enhanced current profits by improperly categorizing operating expenses as long-term capital expenses, instead of taking them all as a cost of business in the period when they were incurred; inflated current earnings by more than $9 billion overall. Resulted in largest bankruptcy in U.S. history—$107 billion.
- Xerox—improperly padded revenues by $3 billion between 1997 and 2000. The SEC filed civil fraud charges against KPMG, its auditor.

In addition, the Justice Department found Arthur Andersen, Enron's accounting firm, guilty of shredding documents that disclosed alleged abuses at the energy trader. Andersen, long considered the most rigorous firm in its approach to accounting standards, was forced to disband.

These cases raise critical concerns about the independence of those who audit a company's financial statements, questions of integrity and public trust, and financial reporting standards. Investors suffered as a result, because the crisis in confidence sent stock prices tumbling. Companies lost billions in value. For example, a survey of 33 public companies revealed that in the 18 months from January 2001 to June 30, 2002, their combined peak market value of $1.8 trillion plunged to $527 billion, representing almost $1.3 trillion in lost value to shareholders.[3]

So it's no surprise that more people are paying attention to accounting topics! We now recognize that accounting is the backbone of any business, providing a framework to understand the firm's financial condition. Reading about accounting irregularities, fraud, audit (financial statement review) shortcomings, out-of-control business executives, and bankruptcies, we have become very aware of the importance of accurate financial information and sound financial procedures.

All of us—whether we are self-employed, work for a local small business or a multinational Fortune 100 firm, or are not currently in the workforce—benefit from knowing the basics of accounting and financial statements. We can use this information to educate ourselves about companies before interviewing for a job or buying a company's stock or bonds. Employees at all levels of an organization use accounting information to monitor operations. They also must decide which financial information is important for their company or business unit, what those numbers mean, and how to use them to make decisions.

Financial information is central to every organization. To operate effectively, businesses must have a way to track income, expenses, assets, and liabilities in an organized manner. Financial information is also essential for decision making. Managers prepare financial reports using *accounting*, a set of procedures and guidelines for companies to

© BONNIE KAMIN / PHOTOEDIT, INC.

Financial accounting information, such as asset values, sales and inventory, helps managers in all types of organizations make business decisions that enhance organizational effectiveness and efficiency.

accounting
The process of collecting, recording, classifying, summarizing, reporting, and analyzing financial activities.

managerial accounting
Accounting that provides financial information that managers inside the organization can use to evaluate and make decisions about current and future operations.

follow when preparing financial reports. Unless you understand basic accounting concepts, you will not be able to "speak" the standard financial language of businesses.

This chapter starts by discussing why accounting is important for businesses and for users of financial information. Then it provides a brief overview of the accounting profession and recent problems in the industry, and the new regulatory environment. Next it presents an overview of accounting procedures, followed by a description of the three main financial statements—the balance sheet, the income statement, and the statement of cash flows. Using these statements, we then demonstrate how ratio analysis of financial statements can provide valuable information about a company's financial condition. Finally, the chapter explores current trends affecting the accounting profession.

Accounting: More than Numbers

1 learning goal

Accounting is the process of collecting, recording, classifying, summarizing, reporting, and analyzing financial activities. It results in reports that describe the financial condition of an organization. All types of organizations—businesses, hospitals, schools, government agencies, civic groups—use accounting procedures. Accounting provides a framework for looking at past performance, current financial health, and possible future performance. It also provides a framework for comparing the financial positions and financial performances of different firms. Understanding how to prepare and interpret financial reports will enable you to evaluate two computer companies and choose the one that is more likely to be a good investment.

As Exhibit 18.1 on page 572 shows, the accounting system converts the details of financial transactions (sales, payments, purchases, and so on) into a form that people can use to evaluate the firm and make decisions. Data become information, which in turn becomes reports. These reports describe a firm's financial position at one point in time and its financial performance during a specified period. Financial reports include *financial statements,* such as balance sheets and income statements, and special reports, such as sales and expense breakdowns by product line.

In managerial accounting, internal reports detailing financial information such as the costs of labor and material in production are shared with other managers to assess the organization's performance.

© AP / WIDE WORLD PHOTOS

Who Uses Financial Reports?

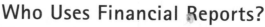

The accounting system generates two types of financial reports, as shown in Exhibit 18.2: internal and external. Internal reports are used within the organization. As the term implies, **managerial accounting** provides financial information that managers inside the organization can use to evaluate and make decisions about current and future operations. For instance, the sales reports prepared by managerial accountants show how well marketing strategies are

Exhibit 18.1 | The Accounting System

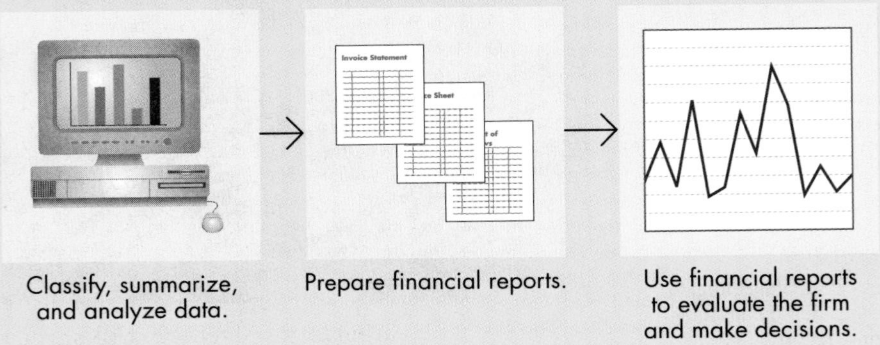
Classify, summarize, and analyze data.
Prepare financial reports.
Use financial reports to evaluate the firm and make decisions.

working. Production cost reports help departments track and control costs. Managers may prepare very detailed financial reports for their own use and provide summary reports to top management.

financial accounting
Accounting that focuses on preparing external financial reports that are used by outsiders such as lenders, suppliers, investors, and government agencies to assess the financial strength of a business.

generally accepted accounting principles (GAAP)
The financial accounting standards followed by accountants in the United States when preparing financial statements.

Financial accounting focuses on preparing external financial reports that are used by outsiders, that is, people who have an interest in the business but are not part of management. Although these reports also provide useful information for managers, they are primarily used by lenders, suppliers, investors, and government agencies to assess the financial strength of a business.

To ensure accuracy and consistency in the way financial information is reported, accountants in the United States follow **generally accepted accounting principles (GAAP)** when preparing financial statements. The **Financial Accounting Standards Board (FASB)** is a private organization that is responsible for establishing financial accounting standards in the United States.

At the present time, there are no international accounting standards. Because accounting practices vary from country to country, a multinational company must make sure that its financial statements conform to both its own country's accounting standards and those of the parent company's country. Often another country's standards are quite different from U.S. GAAP. The International Accounting Standards Committee has been working for years to develop global

Exhibit 18.2 | Reports Provided by the Accounting System

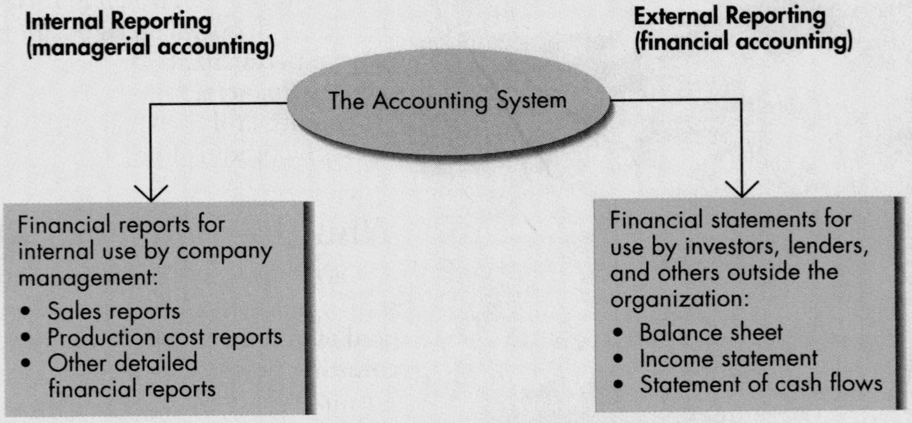
Internal Reporting (managerial accounting)
External Reporting (financial accounting)
The Accounting System
Financial reports for internal use by company management:
• Sales reports
• Production cost reports
• Other detailed financial reports
Financial statements for use by investors, lenders, and others outside the organization:
• Balance sheet
• Income statement
• Statement of cash flows

Expanding Around the Globe

One World of Numbers, for All?

Imagine being treasurer of a major multinational company with significant operations in 10 other countries. Because the accounting rules in those countries don't conform to GAAP, your staff has to prepare nine sets of financial reports that comply with the host country's rules—and also translate the figures to GAAP for consolidation into the parent company's statements. It's a massive undertaking.

If the International Accounting Standards Board (IASB) has its way, your task will be much easier in years to come. This group is developing international accounting standards that will remove disparities between national and international standards, improve the quality of financial information worldwide, and simplify comparisons of financial statements across borders.

The GAAP Convergence 2002 project of the six largest U.S. accounting firms reports that about 95 percent of respondents in a global survey said their countries are adopting uniform accounting standards. However, this happens to be the IASB's International Financial Reporting Standards (IFRS), rather than the Financial Accounting Standards Board (FASB)'s U.S. GAAP. The two groups are committed to merging IFRS and GAAP into a consistent set of international accounting standards by 2005—easier in theory than in practice because of different approaches used in the two sets.

Board staff members were asked to compare accounting rules in 15 different areas and recommend the better of the two. Nokia's chief financial officer expressed concern at this methodology. "There should be a really strong effort to make global harmonization possible," said Olli-Pekka Kallasvuo. "We need less discussion on whose rule is better . . . [and] more on how to make [harmonization] possible."

Many attributed the preference of IFRS over GAAP to the numerous accounting scandals in the United States. These critics claimed that GAAP is too specific and rigid, which allowed companies to apply rules literally, while at the same time bending them to suit their needs. They were humbled in February 2003, when Dutch grocery chain Royal Ahold Monday announced that it improperly inflated earnings by $500 million. Securities regulators were left questioning whether IFRS is really better than GAAP.

CRITICAL THINKING QUESTIONS

1. Is it important to have a single set of international accounting standards for at least publicly owned companies? Defend your answer.
2. Where do IASB and FASB efforts to merge IFRS and GAAP now stand? Use a search engine and also the archives of *CFO* magazine, **http://www.cfo.com**, to research this and summarize your findings.

SOURCES: Stephen Taub, "At FASB, IASB, the Urge to Converge," *CFO.com*, October 30, 2002; Stephen Taub, "Royal Ahold in Dutch," *CFO.com*, February 25, 2003; and Stephen Taub, "World Going IFRS," *CFO.com*, February 24, 2003, all downloaded from http://www.cfo.com.

Financial Accounting Standards Board (FASB)
The private organization that is responsible for establishing financial accounting standards in the United States.

accounting standards that make it easier to compare financial statements of foreign-based companies. The "Expanding Around the Globe" box discusses the challenges involved in this effort.

Financial statements are the chief element of the **annual report,** a yearly document that describes a firm's financial status. Annual reports usually discuss the firm's activities during the past year and its prospects for the future. Three primary financial statements included in the annual report are discussed and illustrated later in this chapter:

- The balance sheet.
- The income statement.
- The statement of cash flows.

concept check

Explain who uses financial information.

Differentiate between financial accounting and managerial accounting.

The Accounting Profession

2 learning goal

When you think of accountants, do you picture someone who works in a back room, hunched over a desk, wearing a green eye shade and scrutinizing pages and pages of numbers? While today's accountants still must love working with numbers, they now work closely with their clients to not only prepare financial reports but also help them develop good financial practices. Computers have taken the tedium out of the number-crunching and data-gathering parts of the job and now offer powerful analytical tools as well. Therefore, accountants must keep up with information technology trends. The accounting profession has grown due to the increased complexity, size, and number of businesses and the frequent changes in the tax laws. Accounting is now an over $40 billion industry. The more than 1 million accountants in the United States are classified as either public accountants or private (corporate) accountants.

Public Accountants

Independent accountants who serve organizations and individuals on a fee basis are called **public accountants.** Public accountants offer a wide range of services, including preparation of financial statements and tax returns, independent auditing of financial records and accounting methods, and management consulting. **Auditing,** the process of reviewing the records used to prepare financial statements, is an important responsibility of public accountants. They issue a formal *auditor's opinion* indicating whether the statements have been prepared in accordance with accepted accounting rules. This written opinion is an important part of the annual report.

The largest public accounting firms, called the Big Four, operate worldwide and offer a variety of business consulting services in addition to accounting services. In order of size, they are PricewaterhouseCoopers (PWC), Deloitte & Touche Tohmatsu International (DTT), KPMG International, and Ernst & Young (E&Y). A former member of this group, Arthur Andersen, disbanded in 2002 as a result of the Enron scandal.

To become a **certified public accountant (CPA),** an accountant must complete an approved bachelor's degree program and pass a test prepared by the American Institute of Certified Public Accountants. Each state also has requirements for CPAs such as several years' on-the-job experience and continuing education. Only CPAs can issue the auditor's opinion on a firm's financial statements. Most CPAs first work for public accounting firms and later may become private accountants or financial managers.

Private Accountants

Accountants employed to serve one particular organization are **private accountants.** Their activities include preparing financial statements, auditing company records to be sure employees follow accounting policies and procedures, developing accounting systems, preparing tax returns, and providing financial information for management decision making. Managerial accountants also have a professional certification program. Requirements to become a **certified management accountant (CMA)** include passing an examination.

Refiguring the Accounting Environment

While our attention was focused on big-name accounting scandals, the government's General Accounting Office was investigating the extent of accounting irregularities in the wider corporate arena. Its report revealed that there was in fact an epidemic of such problems. From 1997 to 2002, the number of companies restating reported earnings because of improper accounting procedures tripled, from just under 1 percent to 3 percent. Another study disclosed that 94 percent of the public companies later named for accounting irregularities received a good report from their auditors.

A report of the American Institute of Certified Public Accountants (AICPA) described three basic ways companies massage their financial reports with creative, aggressive, or inappropriate accounting techniques:

COURTESY OF CHEVRONTEXACO CORPORATION

The financial information contained in ChevronTexaco's Annual Report is prepared using financial accounting standards. Lenders, suppliers, investors, and government agencies refer to the annual report to assess the financial strength of a business.

annual report
A yearly document that describes a firm's financial status and usually discusses the firm's activities during the past year and its prospects for the future.

public accountants
Independent accountants who serve organizations and individuals on a fee basis.

auditing
The process of reviewing the records used to prepare financial statements and issuing a formal *auditor's opinion* indicating whether the statements have been prepared in accordance with accepted accounting rules.

certified public accountant (CPA)
An accountant who has completed an approved bachelor's degree program, passed a test prepared by the American Institute of Certified Public Accountants, and met state requirements. Only a CPA can issue an auditor's opinion on a firm's financial statements.

private accountants
Accountants who are employed to serve one particular organization.

certified management accountant (CMA)
A managerial accountant who has completed a professional certification program, including passing an examination.

- Commit fraudulent financial reporting.
- Unreasonably stretch accounting rules to significantly enhance financial results.
- Follow appropriate accounting rules, but use loopholes to manage financial results.[4]

Bending the Rules

Why did companies willfully push accounting to the edge—and over it—to artificially pump up revenues and profits? Looking at the companies involved in the recent scandals, some basic similarities have emerged.

Like Enron, these companies operated within a company culture of arrogance and were known for taking above-average risks in their business transactions. Given several possible interpretations of accounting policies, they applied the one that worked to their advantage. They manipulated the rules to get to a predetermined result and conceal negative financial information. Compensation packages were tied to financial or operating targets, making executives and managers greedy and pressuring them to find sometimes questionable ways to meet what may have been overly optimistic goals.

The checks and balances in place, such as audit committees, boards of directors, and financial control procedures, were ineffective and not independent from management. Financial reporting was highly centralized and tightly controlled by top management, increasing the opportunity for fraud. Financial performance benchmarks were often out of line with the companies' industry. Complicated business structures often made it hard to figure out how the company made its profits, and the cash flow from operations did not seem in line with reported earnings. (You'll learn about this important difference between cash and reported earnings in the sections on the income statement and statement of cash flows.) Companies made lots of acquisitions, quickly, often to show growth rather than for sound business reasons. Management focused more on buying new companies than making the existing operations more profitable.[5]

Companies focused on making themselves look good in the short term, doing whatever was necessary to top past performance and to meet the expectations of investment analysts, who project earnings, and investors, who panic when a company misses the analysts' forecasts. Executives who benefited when stock prices rose had no incentive to question the earnings increases that led to the price gains. "Corporate managers were not looking beneath the surface at how they were running their businesses," said Barry Barbash, a former SEC attorney. "Financial gymnastics outweighed solid financial practices."[6]

These number games raised serious concerns about the quality of earnings and questions about the validity of financial reports. Investors discovered to their dismay that they could neither assume that auditors were adequately monitoring their clients' accounting methods nor depend on the integrity of published financial information. "There is a crisis of confidence in my profession," said Joseph Berardino, former CEO of Arthur Andersen, during his testimony at congressional hearings about Enron Corp. "Real change will be required to regain the public's trust."[7]

The SEC made some efforts to investigate allegations of impropriety and conflicts of interest between the accounting and consulting units of audit firms. Says Isaac Hunt, a former SEC commissioner, "I don't think we had enough people who were willing to walk in there and say, 'I don't understand these numbers. What do they mean?'"[8]

Better Numbers Ahead

Since 2002 a number of accounting reforms have been put in place to set better standards for accounting, auditing, and financial reporting. Investors, now aware

© AP / WIDE WORLD PHOTOS

Following several years of big-name accounting scandals where companies pushed the limits of accounting standards, major CPA firms like PricewaterhouseCoopers are working to rebuild public trust. It has developed a Code of Conduct for all employees that provides a broad range of guidance about the standards of integrity and business conduct.

Sarbanes-Oxley Act
Act passed in 2002 that sets new standards for auditor independence, financial disclosure and reporting, and internal controls; establishes an independent oversight board; and restricts the types of nonaudit services auditors can provide audit clients.

of the possibility of various accounting shenanigans, are avoiding companies that use complicated financial structures and off-the-books financing.

On July 30, 2002, the **Sarbanes-Oxley Act** went into effect. This law, one of the most extensive pieces of business legislation ever passed by Congress, was designed to start the economy on the road to recovery and address the investing public's lack of trust in corporate America. It redefines the public corporation–auditor relationship and restricts the types of services auditors can provide to clients. The Act clarifies auditor-independence issues, places increased accountability on a company's senior executives and management, strengthens disclosure of insider transactions (an employee selling stock based on information not known by the public), and prohibits loans to executives.

For the first time, a new, independent five-member Public Company Accounting Oversight Board (PCAOB) will have the authority to set and amend auditing, quality control, ethics, independence, and other standards for audit reports. The Act specifies that all members be financially literate. Two members must have their CPA designation, while the other three cannot be or have been CPAs. Appointed and overseen by the SEC, the PCAOB can also inspect accounting firms, investigate breaches of securities law, standards, competency, and conduct, and take disciplinary action. The Board registers public accounting firms, as the Act now requires. Altering or destroying key audit documents now carries felony charges and increased penalties.

Other key provisions of the Act cover the following areas:

- *Auditing standards.* The Board must include in its standards several requirements, such as maintaining audit work papers and other documentation for audit reports for seven years, the review and approval of audit reports by a second partner, and audit standards for quality control and review of internal control procedures.
- *Financial disclosure.* Companies must clearly disclose all transactions that may have a material current or future effect on their financial condition, including those that are off the books or with unconsolidated entities (related companies whose results the company is not required to combine with its own financial statements under current accounting rules). Management and major stockholders must disclose transactions such as sales of company stock within two days of the transaction. The company must disclose its code of ethics for senior financial executives. Any significant changes in a company's operations or financial condition must be disclosed "on a rapid and current basis."

- *Financial statement certification.* Chief executive officers and chief financial officers must certify company financial statements, with severe criminal and civil penalties for false certification. If securities fraud results in restatement of financial reports, these executives will lose any stock-related profits and bonuses they received prior to the restatement.
- *Internal controls.* Each company must have appropriate internal control procedures in place for financial reporting; and its annual report must include a report on implementation of those controls to assure the integrity of financial reports.
- *Consulting work.* The Act restricts the nonauditing work auditors may perform for an auditing client. In the past, the large accounting firms had expanded their role to include a wide range of advisory services that went beyond their traditional task of validating a company's financial information. Conflicts of interest arose when the same firm earned lucrative fees for both audit and consulting work for the same client.[9]

Other regulatory organizations also took steps to prevent future abuses. In September 2002, the AICPA Auditing Standards Board (ASB) issued expanded guidelines to help auditors uncover fraud while conducting audits. The New York Stock Exchange stiffened its listing requirements so that the majority of directors at listed companies must be independent and not employees of the corporation. Nor can auditors serve on clients' boards for five years. Companies listed in the Nasdaq marketplace cannot hire former auditors at any levels for three years. We'll look at how companies are responding to the changes in audit and reporting requirements later in the chapter.

concept check

Compare the responsibilities of public and private accountants. How are they certified?

Summarize the major changes affecting accounting and corporate reporting and the reasons for them.

Basic Accounting Procedures

3 learning goal

Using generally accepted accounting principles, accountants record and report financial data in similar ways for all firms. They report their findings in financial statements that summarize a company's business transactions over a specified time period. As mentioned earlier, the three major financial statements are the balance sheet, income statement, and statement of cash flows.

People sometimes confuse accounting with bookkeeping. Accounting is a much broader concept. *Bookkeeping,* the system used to record a firm's financial transactions, is a routine, clerical process. Accountants take bookkeepers' transactions, classify and summarize the financial information, and then prepare and analyze financial reports. Accountants also develop and manage financial systems and help plan the firm's financial strategy.

The Accounting Equation

The accounting procedures used today are based on those developed in the late 15th century by an Italian monk, Brother Luca Pacioli. He defined the three main accounting elements as assets, liabilities, and owners' equity. **Assets** are things of value owned by a firm. They may be *tangible,* such as cash, equipment, and buildings, or *intangible,* such as a patent or trademarked name. **Liabilities**—also called *debts*—are what a firm owes to its creditors. **Owners' equity** is the total amount of investment in the firm minus any liabilities. Another term for owners' equity is *net worth.*

assets
Things of value owned by a firm.

liabilities
What a firm owes to its creditors; also called *debts.*

owners' equity
The total amount of investment in the firm minus any liabilities; also called *net worth.*

The relationship among these three elements is expressed in the accounting equation:

$$\text{Assets} - \text{Liabilities} = \text{Owners' equity}$$

The accounting equation must always be in balance (that is, the total of the elements on one side of the equals sign must equal the total on the other side).

Suppose you start a bookstore and put $10,000 in cash into the business. At that point, the business has assets of $10,000 and no liabilities. This would be the accounting equation:

Assets	=	Liabilities	+	Owners' equity
$10,000	=	$0	+	$10,000

The liabilities are zero and owner's equity (the amount of your investment in the business) is $10,000. The equation balances.

To keep the accounting equation in balance, every transaction must be recorded as two entries. As each transaction is recorded, there is an equal and opposite event so that two accounts or records are changed. This method is called **double-entry bookkeeping.**

double-entry bookkeeping
A method of accounting in which each transaction is recorded as two entries so that two accounts or records are changed.

Suppose that after starting your bookstore with $10,000 cash, you borrow another $10,000 from the bank. The accounting equation will change as follows:

Assets	=	Liabilities	+	Owners' equity	
$10,000	=	$0	+	$10,000	Initial equation
$10,000	=	$10,000	+	$0	Borrowing transaction
$20,000	=	$10,000	+	$10,000	Equation after borrowing

Now you have $20,000 in assets—your $10,000 in cash and the $10,000 loan proceeds from the bank. The bank loan is also recorded as a liability of $10,000 because it's a debt you must repay. Making two entries keeps the equation in balance.

The Accounting Cycle

The *accounting cycle* refers to the process of generating financial statements, beginning with a business transaction and ending with the preparation of the report. Exhibit 18.3 shows the six steps in the accounting cycle. The first step in the cycle is to analyze the data collected from many sources. All transactions that have a financial impact on the firm—sales, payments to employees and suppliers, interest and tax payments, purchases of inventory, and the like—must be documented. The accountant must review the documents to make sure they're complete.

Next each transaction is recorded in a *journal,* a listing of financial transactions in chronological order. Then the journal entries are recorded in *ledgers,* which show increases and decreases in specific asset, liability, and owners' equity accounts. The ledger totals for each account are summarized in a *trial balance,* which is used to confirm the accuracy of the figures. These values are used to prepare financial statements and management reports. Finally, individuals analyze these reports and make decisions based on the information in them.

Software programs like QuickBooks help small businesses consolidate and simplify accounting and financial tasks. These programs walk users through the basics to create financial databases, prepare a budget, design customized forms, pay bills, invoice customers, track expenses, manage inventory, and print reports.

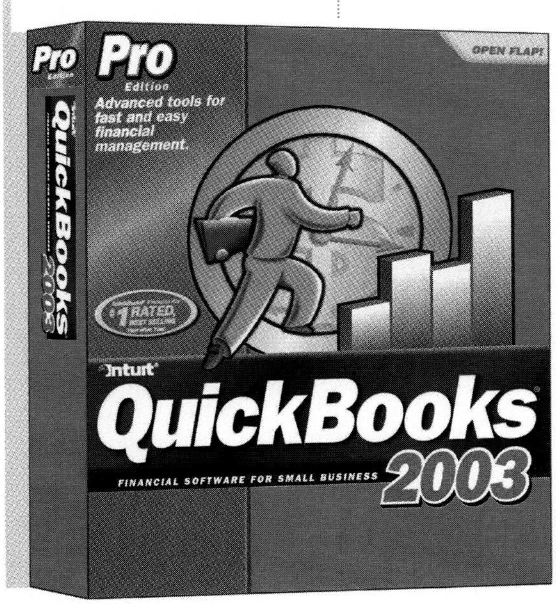

© COURTESY OF INTERNET SECURITY SYSTEMS

Computers in Accounting

Computerized accounting programs do many different things. Most accounting packages offer six basic modules that handle general ledger, sales order, accounts receivable, purchase order, accounts payable, and inventory control functions. Tax programs use accounting data to prepare tax returns and tax plans. Computerized point-of-sale terminals used by many retail firms automatically record sales and do some of the bookkeeping. The Big Four and many other large public accounting firms develop accounting software for themselves and for clients.

Exhibit 18.3 | The Accounting Cycle

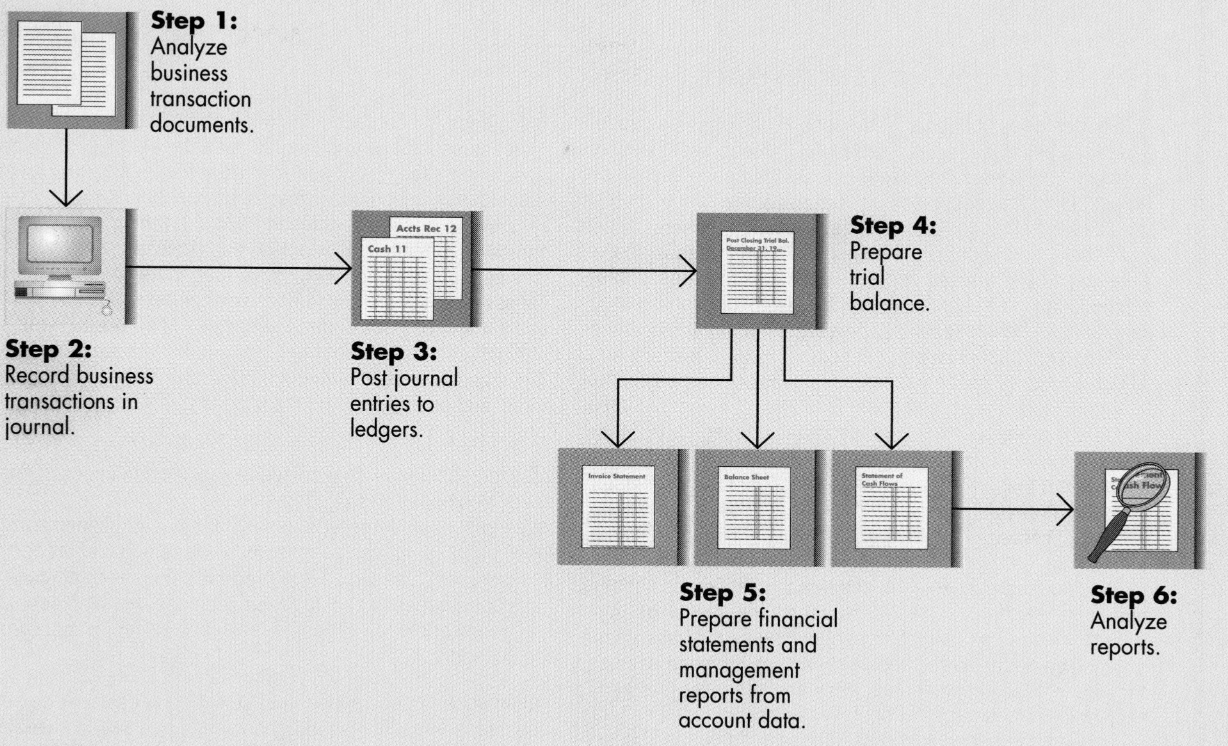
Step 1:
Analyze business transaction documents.
Step 2:
Record business transactions in journal.
Accts Rec 12
Cash 11
Step 3:
Post journal entries to ledgers.
Step 4:
Prepare trial balance.
Invoice Statement
Balance Sheet
Statement of Cash Flows
Step 5:
Prepare financial statements and management reports from account data.
Step 6:
Analyze reports.

concept check

Explain the accounting equation.

Describe the six-step accounting cycle.

What role do computers play in accounting?

Accounting and financial applications typically represent one of the largest portions of a company's software budget. Accounting software ranges from off-the-shelf programs for small businesses to full-scale customized enterprise resource planning systems for major corporations. As the "Focusing on Small Business" box explains, accounting software can help a small business manage its finances and grow successfully.

THE BALANCE SHEET

4 learning goal

balance sheet
A financial statement that summarizes a firm's financial position at a specific point in time.

liquidity
The speed with which an asset can be converted to cash.

The **balance sheet,** one of three financial statements generated from the accounting system, summarizes a firm's financial position at a specific point in time. It reports the resources of a company (assets), the company's obligations (liabilities), and the difference between what is owned (assets) and what is owed (liabilities), or owners' equity.

The assets are listed in order of their **liquidity,** the speed with which they can be converted to cash. The most liquid assets come first, and the least liquid are last. Because cash is the most liquid asset, it is listed first. Buildings, on the other hand, have to be sold to be converted to cash, so they are listed after cash. Liabilities are arranged similarly: liabilities due in the short term are listed before those due in the long term.

The balance sheet at December 31, 2005, for Delicious Desserts, Inc., an imaginary bakery, is illustrated in Exhibit 18.4 on page 581. The basic accounting equation is reflected in the three totals highlighted on the balance sheet: assets of $148,900 equal the sum of liabilities and owners' equity ($70,150 + $78,750). The three main categories of accounts on the balance sheet are explained below.

Focusing on Small Business

Fox & Hounds Collars Its Accounting

Robin Kershner started Fox & Hounds in 1996 to tap the rapidly growing market for attractive, unique, and comfortable pet accessories. Her products combined fine design and functionality, using top-quality materials like Italian calfskin with suede linings for the collars and leashes. As her products caught the attention of pet owners, sales climbed. To free up time so she and her four employees could focus on customer relationships, Kershner implemented Peachtree Complete Accounting, a software package developed for small businesses. The software automated bookkeeping and accounting tasks but also handled invoicing, purchasing, and inventory control.

Using accounting software to gain control of financial matters is a big plus for most small businesses. In the event of a tax audit, for example, having well-organized financial records can save untold hours and cost. The simplest versions function as check ledgers, while the most sophisticated handle most accounting tasks, from tracking accounts receivable and inventory to preparing financial statements. More software vendors are developing small-business versions of their high-end multiuser systems to meet the needs of high-growth companies. Another option now available to small businesses is the Web-based accounting program accessed through a Web browser. The software and your company's data reside on the application provider's server.

Fox & Hounds' vice president Mike Bennett credits the software with allowing Fox & Hounds to increase product lines from 4 to 120 styles and its customer base from 10 to 700 regional and international retailers. It recently added pet carriers, harnesses, and toys to its original products. Sales are now over $1 million. Recently the company integrated the accounting software with contact management software. The enhanced functionality lets Fox & Hounds manage its accounting, sales orders, manufacturing, and inventory more efficiently and develop customized product marketing campaigns.

Combining the accounting and customer databases has improved customer satisfaction and retention. "We now have the capability—at an extremely low cost—to compete with large manufacturers who have the capital to invest in large-scale marketing solutions, unlike most small businesses," says Bennett. "It also reduces the amount of time spent maintaining our information since we no longer have to make additions and changes in two separate systems."

CRITICAL THINKING QUESTIONS

1. How did accounting software provide the impetus for Fox & Hounds' growth?
2. You are in charge of the purchase and implementation of Fox & Hounds' accounting software. Develop a list of functions the software should handle, the types of data the company will need to input and sources, and any other information you need to evaluate different accounting packages.

SOURCES: "Accounting for Everything," Small Business Computing.com, March 14, 2002, downloaded from http://www.smallbusinesscomputing.com; Fox & Hounds company Web site, http://www.foxandhounds.com; Michele Marrinan, "Defense Mechanisms," Small Business Computing.com, January 16, 2002, downloaded from http://www.smallbusinesscomputing.com; and "Peachtree Provides a Personal Touch for Pinpointing the Perfect Pooch Products," Peachtree Success Stories, downloaded from Peachtree Web site, http://www.peachtree.com.

Assets

current assets
Assets that can or will be converted to cash within the next 12 months.

Assets can be divided into three broad categories: current assets, fixed assets, and intangible assets. **Current assets** are assets that can or will be converted to cash within the next 12 months. They are important because they provide the funds used to pay the firm's current bills. They also represent the amount of money the firm can quickly raise. Current assets include:

- *Cash.* Funds on hand or in a bank.
- *Marketable securities.* Temporary investments of excess cash that can readily be converted to cash.
- *Accounts receivable.* Amounts owed to the firm by customers who bought goods or services on credit.
- *Notes receivable.* Amounts owed to the firm by customers or others to whom it lent money.
- *Inventory.* Stock of goods being held for production or for sale to customers.

fixed assets
Long-term assets used by a firm for more than a year such as land, buildings, and machinery.

depreciation
The allocation of an asset's original cost to the years in which it is expected to produce revenues.

Fixed assets are long-term assets used by the firm for more than a year. They tend to be used in production and include land, buildings, machinery, equipment, furniture, and fixtures. Except for land, fixed assets wear out and become outdated over time. Thus, they decrease in value every year. This declining value is accounted for through depreciation. **Depreciation** is the allocation of the asset's original cost to the years in which it is expected to produce revenues. A por-

Exhibit 18.4 Balance Sheet for Delicious Desserts

Delicious Desserts, Inc.
Balance Sheet as of December 31, 2005

Assets			
Current assets:			
Cash		$15,000	
Marketable securities		4,500	
Accounts receivable	$45,000		
Less: Allowance for doubtful accounts	1,300	43,700	
Notes receivable		5,000	
Inventory		15,000	
Total current assets			$ 83,200
Fixed assets:			
Bakery equipment	$56,000		
Less: Accumulated depreciation	16,000	$40,000	
Furniture and fixtures	$18,450		
Less: Accumulated depreciation	4,250	14,200	
Total fixed assets			54,200
Intangible assets:			
Trademark		$ 4,500	
Goodwill		7,000	
Total intangible assets			11,500
Total assets			**$148,900**
Liabilities and Owners' Equity			
Current liabilities:			
Accounts payable	$30,650		
Notes payable	15,000		
Accrued expenses	4,500		
Income taxes payable	5,000		
Current portion of long-term debt	5,000		
Total current liabilities		$60,150	
Long-term liabilities:			
Bank loan for bakery equipment	$10,000		
Total long-term liabilities		10,000	
Total liabilities			**$ 70,150**
Owners' equity:			
Common stock (10,000 shares outstanding)		$30,000	
Retained earnings		48,750	
Total owners' equity			**$ 78,750**
Total liabilities and owners' equity			**$148,900**

tion of the cost of a depreciable asset—a building or piece of equipment, for instance—is charged to each of the years in which it is expected to provide benefits. This practice helps match the asset's cost against the revenues it provides. Since it is impossible to know exactly how long an asset will last, estimates are used. They are based on past experience with similar items or IRS guidelines for assets of that type. Notice that, through 2005, Delicious Desserts has taken a total of $16,000 in depreciation on its bakery equipment.

On its balance sheet, Delicious Desserts would list its bakery equipment, furniture, and fixtures as fixed assets. The amount it owes its vendors for supplies would appear as a current liability—accounts payable—and its bank loan would be under long-term liabilities. On the income statement, you'll find a summary of revenues and expenses for a particular time period.

intangible assets
Long-term assets with no physical existence, such as patents, copyrights, trademarks, and goodwill.

Intangible assets are long-term assets with no physical existence. Common examples are patents, copyrights, trademarks, and goodwill. *Patents* and *copyrights* shield the firm from direct competition, so their benefits are more protective than productive. For instance, no one can use more than a small amount of copyrighted material without permission from the copyright holder. *Trademarks* are registered names that can be sold or licensed to others. One of Delicious Desserts' intangible assets is a trademark valued at $4,500. *Goodwill* occurs when a company pays more for an acquired firm than the value of its tangible assets. Delicious Desserts' other tangible asset is goodwill of $7,000.

Liabilities

Liabilities are the amounts a firm owes to creditors. Those liabilities coming due sooner—current liabilities—are listed first on the balance sheet, followed by long-term liabilities.

current liabilities
Short-term claims that are due within a year of the date of the balance sheet.

Current liabilities are those due within a year of the date of the balance sheet. These short-term claims may strain the firm's current assets because they must be paid in the near future. Current liabilities include:

- *Accounts payable.* Amounts the firm owes for credit purchases due within a year. This account is the liability counterpart of accounts receivable.
- *Notes payable.* Short-term loans from banks, suppliers, or others that must be repaid within a year. For example, Delicious Desserts has a six-month, $15,000 loan from its bank that is a note payable.
- *Accrued expenses.* Expenses, typically for wages and taxes, that have accumulated and must be paid at a specified future date within the year although no bill has been received by the firm.
- *Income taxes payable.* Taxes owed for the current operating period but not yet paid. Taxes are often shown separately when they are a large amount.
- *Current portion of long-term debt.* Any repayment on long-term debt due within the year. Delicious Desserts is scheduled to repay $5,000 on its equipment loan in the coming year.

long-term liabilities
Claims that come due more than one year after the date of the balance sheet.

Long-term liabilities come due more than one year after the date of the balance sheet. They include bank loans (such as Delicious Desserts' $10,000 loan for bakery equipment), mortgages on buildings, and the company's bonds sold to others.

Owners' Equity

Owners' equity is the owners' total investment in the business after all liabilities have been paid. For sole proprietorships and partnerships, amounts put in by the owners are recorded as capital. In a corporation, the owners provide capital by buying the firm's common stock. For Delicious Desserts, the total common stock investment is $30,000. **Retained earnings** are the amounts left over from profitable operations since the firm's beginning. They are total profits minus all dividends (distributions of profits) paid to stockholders. Delicious Desserts has $48,750 in retained earnings.

concept check

What is a balance sheet?

What are the three main categories of accounts on the balance sheet, and how do they relate to the accounting equation?

How do retained earnings relate to owners' equity?

The Income Statement

5 learning goal

The balance sheet shows the firm's financial position at a certain point in time. The **income statement** summarizes the firm's revenues and expenses and shows its total profit or loss over a period of time. Most companies prepare monthly income statements for management and quarterly and annual statements for use by investors, creditors, and other outsiders. The primary elements of the income statement are revenues, expenses, and net income (or net loss). The income statement for Delicious Desserts for the year ended December 31, 2005, is shown in Exhibit 18.5.

retained earnings
The amounts left over from profitable operations since the firm's beginning; equal to total profits minus all dividends paid to stockholders.

income statement
A financial statement that summarizes a firm's revenues and expenses and shows its total profit or loss over a period of time.

revenues
The dollar amount of a firm's sales plus any other income it received from sources such as interest, dividends, and rents.

gross sales
The total dollar amount of a company's sales.

net sales
The amount left after deducting sales discounts and returns and allowances from gross sales.

expenses
The costs of generating revenues.

cost of goods sold
The total expense of buying or producing a firm's goods or services.

Revenues

Revenues are the dollar amount of sales plus any other income received from sources such as interest, dividends, and rents. The revenues of Delicious Desserts arise from sales of its bakery products. Revenues are determined starting with **gross sales,** the total dollar amount of a company's sales. Delicious Desserts had two deductions from gross sales. *Sales discounts* are price reductions given to customers that pay their bills early. For example, Delicious Desserts gives sales discounts to restaurants that buy in bulk and pay at delivery. *Returns and allowances* is the dollar amount of merchandise returned by customers because they didn't like a product or because it was damaged or defective. **Net sales** is the amount left after deducting sales discounts and returns and allowances from gross sales. Delicious Desserts' gross sales were reduced by $4,500, leaving net sales of $270,500.

Expenses

Expenses are the costs of generating revenues. Two types are recorded on the income statement: cost of goods sold and operating expenses.

The **cost of goods sold** is the total expense of buying or producing the firm's goods or services. For manufacturers, cost of goods sold includes all costs directly related to production: purchases of raw materials and parts, labor, and factory overhead (utilities, factory maintenance, machinery repair). For wholesalers and retailers, it is the cost of goods bought for resale. For all sellers, cost of goods sold includes all the expenses of preparing the goods for sale, such as shipping and packaging.

Delicious Desserts' cost of goods sold is based on the value of inventory on hand at the beginning of the accounting period, $18,000. During the year, the company spent $109,500 to produce its baked goods. This figure includes the cost of raw materials, labor costs for bakery workers, and the cost of operating the bakery area. Adding the cost of goods manufactured to the value of beginning inventory, we get the total cost of goods available for sale, $127,500. To determine the cost of goods sold for the year, we subtract the cost of inventory at the end of the period:

Exhibit 18.5 Income Statement for Delicious Desserts

Delicious Desserts, Inc.
Income Statement for the Year Ended December 31, 2005

Revenues			
Gross sales		$275,000	
Less: Sales discounts		2,500	
Less: Returns and allowances		2,000	
Net Sales			$ 270,500
Cost of Goods Sold			
Beginning inventory, January 1		$ 18,000	
Cost of goods manufactured		109,500	
Total cost of goods available for sale		$127,500	
Less: Ending inventory December 31		15,000	
Cost of goods sold			112,500
Gross profit			**$158,000**
Operating Expenses			
Selling expenses			
Sales salaries	$31,000		
Advertising	16,000		
Other selling expense	18,000		
Total selling expenses		$ 65,000	
General and administrative expenses			
Professional and office salaries	$20,500		
Utilities	5,000		
Office supplies	1,500		
Interest	3,600		
Insurance	2,500		
Rent	17,000		
Total general and administrative expenses		50,100	
Total operating expenses			115,100
Net profit before taxes			**$ 42,900**
Less: Income taxes			10,725
Net profit			**$ 32,175**

gross profit
The amount a company earns after paying to produce or buy its products but before deducting operating expenses.

operating expenses
The expenses of running a business that are not directly related to producing or buying its products.

$$\$127{,}500 - \$15{,}000 = \$112{,}500$$

The amount a company earns after paying to produce or buy its products but before deducting operating expenses is the **gross profit.** It is the difference between net sales and cost of goods sold. Since service firms do not produce goods, their gross profit equals net sales. Gross profit is a critical number for a company because it is the source of funds to cover all the firm's other expenses.

The other major expense category is **operating expenses.** These are the expenses of running the business that are not related directly to producing or buying its products. The two main types of operating expenses are selling expenses and general and administrative expenses. *Selling expenses* are those related to marketing and distributing the company's products. They include salaries and commissions paid to salespeople and the costs of advertising, sales supplies, delivery, and other items that can be linked to sales activity, such as insurance, telephone and other utilities, and postage. *General and administrative expenses* are the business expenses that cannot be linked to either cost of goods sold or sales. Examples of general and administrative expenses are salaries of top managers and office support staff; utilities; office supplies; interest expense; fees for accounting, consulting, and legal services; insurance; and rent. Delicious Desserts' operating expenses totaled $115,100.

net profit (net income)
The amount obtained by subtracting all of a firm's expenses from its revenues, when the revenues are more than the expenses.

net loss
The amount obtained by subtracting all of a firm's expenses from its revenues, when the expenses are more than the revenues.

Net Profit or Loss

The final figure—or bottom line—on an income statement is the **net profit** (or **net income**) or **net loss.** It is calculated by subtracting all expenses from revenues. If revenues are more than expenses, the result is a net profit. If expenses exceed revenues, a net loss results.

Several steps are involved in finding net profit or loss. (These are shown in the right-hand column of Exhibit 18.5.) First, cost of goods sold is deducted from net sales to get the gross profit. Then total operating expenses are subtracted from gross profit to get the net profit before taxes. Finally, income taxes are deducted to get the net profit. As shown in Exhibit 18.5, Delicious Desserts earned a net profit of $32,175 in 2005.

It is very important to recognize that profit does not represent cash. The income statement is a summary of the firm's operating results during some time period. It does not present the firm's actual cash flows during the period. Those are summarized in the statement of cash flows, which is discussed briefly in the next section.

concept check

What is an income statement? How does it differ from the balance sheet?

Describe the key parts of the income statement. Distinguish between gross sales and net sales.

How is net profit or loss calculated?

The Statement of Cash Flows

6 learning goal

statement of cash flows
A financial statement that provides a summary of the money flowing into and out of a firm during a certain period, typically one year.

Net profit or loss is one measure of a company's financial performance. However, creditors and investors are also keenly interested in how much cash a business generates and how it is used. The **statement of cash flows,** a summary of the money flowing into and out of a firm, is the financial statement used to assess the sources and uses of cash during a certain period, typically one year. All publicly traded firms must include a statement of cash flows in their financial reports to stockholders. The statement of cash flows tracks the firm's cash receipts and cash payments. It gives financial managers and analysts a way to identify cash flow problems and assess the firm's financial viability.

Using income statement and balance sheet data, the statement of cash flows divides the firm's cash flows into three groups:

- *Cash flow from operating activities.* Those related to the production of the firm's goods or services.
- *Cash flow from investment activities.* Those related to the purchase and sale of fixed assets.
- *Cash flow from financing activities.* Those related to debt and equity financing.

Delicious Desserts' statement of cash flows for 2005 is presented in Exhibit 18.6. It shows that the company's cash and marketable securities have increased over the last year. And during the year the company generated enough cash flow to increase inventory and fixed assets and to reduce accounts payable, accruals, notes payable, and long-term debt.

concept check

What is the purpose of the statement of cash flows?

Why has cash flow become such an important measure of a firm's financial condition? What situations can you cite from the chapter that support your answer?

Exhibit 18.6 | Statement of Cash Flows for Delicious Desserts

Delicious Desserts, Inc.
Statement of Cash Flows for 2005

Cash Flow from Operating Activities		
Net profit after taxes	$27,175	
Depreciation	1,500	
Decrease in accounts receivable	3,140	
Increase in inventory	(4,500)	
Decrease in accounts payable	(2,065)	
Decrease in accruals	(1,035)	
Cash provided by operating activities		$24,215
Cash Flow from Investment Activities		
Increase in gross fixed assets	($ 5,000)	
Cash used in investment activities		($ 5,000)
Cash Flow from Financing Activities		
Decrease in notes payable	($ 3,000)	
Decrease in long-term debt	(1,000)	
Cash used by financing activities		($ 4,000)
Net increase in cash and marketable securities		**$15,215**

Analyzing Financial Statements

7 learning goal

ratio analysis
The calculation and interpretation of financial ratios using data taken from the firm's financial statements in order to assess its condition and performance.

Individually, the balance sheet, income statement, and statement of cash flows provide insight into the firm's operations, profitability, and overall financial condition. By studying the relationships among the financial statements, however, one can gain even more insight into a firm's financial condition and performance.

Ratio analysis involves calculating and interpreting financial ratios using data taken from the firm's financial statements in order to assess its condition and performance. A financial ratio states the relationship between financial data on a

© AP / WIDE WORLD PHOTOS

How is Best Buy doing this quarter compared to historical results? With ratio analysis, managers can track performance. For example, the net profit margin shows how much profit is left after all expenses.

percentage basis. For instance, current assets might be viewed relative to current liabilities or sales relative to assets. The ratios can then be compared over time, typically three to five years. A firm's ratios can also be compared to industry averages or to those of another company in the same industry. Period-to-period and industry ratios provide a meaningful basis for comparison, so that we can answer questions such as, "Is this particular ratio good or bad?"

It's important to remember that ratio analysis is based on historical data and may not indicate future financial performance. Ratio analysis merely highlights potential problems; it does not prove that they exist. However, ratios can help managers monitor the firm's performance from period to period, to understand operations better and identify trouble spots.

Ratios are also important to a firm's present and prospective creditors (lenders), who want to see if the firm can repay what it borrows and assess the firm's financial health. Often loan agreements require firms to maintain minimum levels of specific ratios. Both present and prospective shareholders use ratio analysis to look at the company's historical performance and trends over time.

Ratios can be classified by what they measure: liquidity, profitability, activity, and debt. Using Delicious Desserts' 2005 balance sheet and income statement (Exhibits 18.4 and 18.5), we can calculate and interpret the key ratios in each group. Exhibit 18.7 summarizes the calculations of these ratios for Delicious Desserts. We'll now discuss how to calculate the ratios and, more important, how to interpret the ratio value.

Liquidity Ratios

liquidity ratios
Ratios that measure a firm's ability to pay its short-term debts as they come due.

current ratio
The ratio of total current assets to total current liabilities; used to measure a firm's liquidity.

acid-test (quick) ratio
The ratio of total current assets excluding inventory to total current liabilities; used to measure a firm's liquidity.

net working capital
The amount obtained by subtracting total current liabilities from total current assets; used to measure a firm's liquidity.

Liquidity ratios measure the firm's ability to pay its short-term debts as they come due. These ratios are of special interest to the firm's creditors. The three main measures of liquidity are the current ratio, the acid-test (quick) ratio, and net working capital.

The **current ratio** is the ratio of total current assets to total current liabilities. Traditionally, a current ratio of 2 ($2 of current assets for every $1 of current liabilities) has been considered good. Whether it is sufficient depends on the industry in which the firm operates. Public utilities, which have a very steady cash flow, operate quite well with a current ratio well below 2. A current ratio of 2 might not be adequate for manufacturers and merchandisers that carry high inventories and have lots of receivables. The current ratio for Delicious Desserts for 2005, as shown in Exhibit 18.7, is 1.4. This means little without a basis for comparison. If the analyst found that the industry average for small bakeries was 2.4, Delicious Desserts would appear to have low liquidity.

The **acid-test (quick) ratio** is like the current ratio except that it excludes inventory, which is the least-liquid current asset. The acid-test ratio is used to measure the firm's ability to pay its current liabilities without selling inventory. The name *acid-test* implies that this ratio is a crucial test of the firm's liquidity. An acid-test ratio of at least 1 is preferred. But again, what is an acceptable value varies by industry. The acid-test ratio is a good measure of liquidity when inventory cannot easily be converted to cash (for instance, if it consists of very specialized goods with a limited market). If inventory is liquid, the current ratio is better. Delicious Desserts' acid-test ratio for 2005 is 1.1. Because the bakery's products are perishable, it does not carry large inventories. Thus, the values of its acid-test and current ratios are fairly close. At a manufacturing company, however, inventory typically makes up a large portion of current assets, so the acid-test ratio will be lower than the current ratio.

Net working capital, though not really a ratio, is often used to measure a firm's overall liquidity. It is calculated by subtracting total current liabilities from total current assets. Delicious Desserts' net working capital for 2005 is $23,050. Comparisons of net working capital over time often help in assessing a firm's liquidity.

Exhibit 18.7 Ratio Analysis for Delicious Desserts at Year-End 2005

Ratio	Formula	Calculation	Result
Liquidity Ratios			
Current ratio	Total current assets / Total current liabilities	\$83,200 / \$60,150	1.4
Acid-test (quick) ratio	(Total current assets − inventory) / Total current liabilities	(\$83,200 − \$15,000) / \$60,150	1.1
Net working capital	Total current assets − Total current liabilities	\$83,200 − \$60,150	\$23,050
Profitability Ratios			
Net profit margin	Net profit / Net sales	\$132,175 / \$270,500	11.9%
Return on equity	Net profit / Total owners' equity	\$32,175 / \$78,750	40.9%
Earnings per share	Net profit / Number of shares of common stock outstanding	\$32,175 / 10,000	\$3.22
Activity Ratio			
Inventory turnover	Cost of goods sold / Average inventory		
	Cost of goods sold / (Beginning inventory + Ending inventory)/2	\$112,500 / (\$18,000 + \$15,000)/2	
		\$112,500 / \$16,500	6.8 times
Debt Ratio			
Debt-to-equity ratio	Total liabilities / Owners' equity	\$70,150 / \$78,750	89.1%

Profitability Ratios

profitability ratios
Ratios that measure how well a firm is using its resources to generate profit and how efficiently it is being managed.

To measure profitability, a firm's profits can be related to its sales, equity, or stock value. **Profitability ratios** measure how well the firm is using its resources to generate profit and how efficiently it is being managed. The main profitability ratios are net profit margin, return on equity, and earnings per share.

The ratio of net profit to net sales is the **net profit margin,** also called *return on sales.* It measures the percentage of each sales dollar remaining after all expenses, including taxes, have been deducted. Higher net profit margins are better than lower ones. The net profit margin is often used to measure the firm's earning power. "Good" net profit margins differ quite a bit from industry to industry. A grocery store usually has a very low net profit margin, perhaps below 1 percent, while a jewelry store's net profit margin would probably exceed 10 percent. Delicious Desserts' net profit margin for 2005 is 11.9 percent. In other words, Delicious Desserts is earning 11.9 cents on each dollar of sales.

The ratio of net profit to total owners' equity is called **return on equity (ROE).** It measures the return that owners receive on their investment in the firm, a major reason for investing in a company's stock. Delicious Desserts has a 40.9 percent ROE for 2005. On the surface, a 40.9 percent ROE seems quite good. But the level of risk in the business and the ROE of other firms in the same industry must also be considered. The higher the risk, the greater the ROE investors look for. A firm's ROE can also be compared to past values to see how the company is performing over time.

Earnings per share (EPS) is the ratio of net profit to the number of shares of common stock outstanding. It measures the number of dollars earned by each share of stock. EPS values are closely watched by investors and are considered an important sign of success. EPS also indicates a firm's ability to pay dividends. Note that EPS is the dollar amount earned by each share, not the actual amount given to stockholders in the form of dividends. Some earnings may be put back into the firm. Delicious Desserts' EPS for 2005 is $3.22.

Activity Ratios

Activity ratios measure how well a firm uses its assets. They reflect the speed with which resources are converted to cash or sales. A frequently used activity ratio is inventory turnover.

The **inventory turnover ratio** measures the speed with which inventory moves through the firm and is turned into sales. It is calculated by dividing cost of goods sold by the average inventory. (Average inventory is estimated by adding the beginning and ending inventories for the year and dividing by 2.) Based on its 2005 financial data, Delicious Desserts' inventory, on average, is turned into sales 6.8 times each year, or about once every 54 days (365 days ÷ 6.8). The acceptable turnover ratio depends on the line of business. A grocery store would have a high turnover ratio, maybe 20 times a year, whereas the turnover for a heavy equipment manufacturer might be only 3 times a year.

Debt Ratios

Debt ratios measure the degree and effect of the firm's use of borrowed funds (debt) to finance its operations. These ratios are especially important to lenders and investors. They want to make sure the firm has a healthy mix of debt and equity. If the firm relies too much on debt, it may have trouble meeting interest payments and repaying loans. The most important debt ratio is the debt-to-equity ratio.

The **debt-to-equity ratio** measures the relationship between the amount of debt financing (borrowing) and the amount of equity financing (owners' funds). It is calculated by dividing total liabilities by owners' equity. In general, the lower the ratio, the better. But it is important to assess the debt-to-equity ratio against both past values and industry averages. Delicious Desserts' ratio for 2005 is 89.1 percent. The ratio indicates that the company has 89 cents of debt for every dollar the owners have provided. A ratio above 100 percent means the firm has more debt than equity. In such a case, the lenders are providing more financing than the owners.

net profit margin
The ratio of net profit to net sales; also called *return on sales.* It measures the percentage of each sales dollar remaining after all expenses, including taxes, have been deducted.

return on equity (ROE)
The ratio of net profit to total owners' equity; measures the return that owners receive on their investment in the firm.

earnings per share (EPS)
The ratio of net profit to the number of shares of common stock outstanding; measures the number of dollars earned by each share of stock.

activity ratios
Ratios that measure how well a firm uses its assets.

inventory turnover ratio
The ratio of cost of goods sold to average inventory; measures the speed with which inventory moves through a firm and is turned into sales.

debt ratios
Ratios that measure the degree and effect of a firm's use of borrowed funds (debt) to finance its operations.

debt-to-equity ratio
The ratio of total liabilities to owners' equity; measures the relationship between the amount of debt financing following and the amount of equity financing (owner's funds).

concept check

How can ratio analysis be used to interpret financial statements?

Name the main liquidity and profitability ratios and explain what they indicate.

What kinds of information do activity ratios give? Why are debt ratios of concern to lenders and investors?

Making Ethical Choices

xtra! http://gitmanxtra.swlearning.com

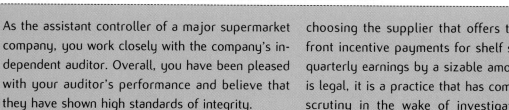

SUPERMARKETS SHELVE REVENUES AND CAN AUDITORS

As the assistant controller of a major supermarket company, you work closely with the company's independent auditor. Overall, you have been pleased with your auditor's performance and believe that they have shown high standards of integrity.

During this year's review of your firm's financial reports and its internal controls, as required under the Sarbanes-Oxley Act of 2002, the auditor raised a question about the timing of incentive payments received from vendors and when they would be recognized as revenue. The issue of such incentive payments from vendors is a big one in the grocery industry. Several of your competitors, including Albertson's and Kroger's, each booked vendor payments received of $2 billion to $3 billion in 2002—more than those companies' operating profits. You are aware that your chain uses these payment receipts to manipulate earnings, choosing the supplier that offers the largest up-front incentive payments for shelf space to boost quarterly earnings by a sizable amount. While this is legal, it is a practice that has come under closer scrutiny in the wake of investigations of other accounting irregularities.

You are called into a meeting with the CFO and the controller to discuss what to do about the warning from the audit firm that it may have a "reportable condition" relating to this situation. The CFO wants to fire the audit firm and hire another one. The controller asks for your opinion.

ETHICAL DILEMMA

Should you go along with the CFO and recommend firing the audit firm?

SOURCES: David Henry, "Accounting Games in the Grocer's Aisle," *Business Week*, April 14, 2003, p. 64; and Stephen Taub, "D&T Warned A&P Dismissed," *CFO.com*, September 19, 2002, downloaded from http://www.cfo.com.

Trends in Accounting

8 learning goal

In the past, auditors were portrayed primarily as "bean-counters" who over-analyzed financial data and were of little help to the managers and employees who produced the numbers they examined. As they began to be valued as important members the client's financial team, they took an active role advising their clients on financial systems and procedures, accounting software, and changes in accounting regulations. They kept expanding the types of nonauditing services they provided, generating high fees but also creating higher potential for conflicts of interest. Then came the high-profile fraud cases. Clearly, the existing accounting/auditing system wasn't working as intended. Investors didn't feel they could trust what they read in financial reports, even if the auditors had issued a clean opinion. Significant changes were called for to correct the wrongs and restore investor confidence.

Under the Sarbanes-Oxley Act, accounting firms will have to once again focus on their core auditing business. Accounting firms must also adapt to a new regulatory environment now that the Act ends the industry's self-regulation and sets higher standards for audit procedures. The roles of the board of directors and its audit committee are now stronger. We could also see some major changes in GAAP.

Accountants Stick to the Numbers

During the 1980s, accountants moved beyond their traditional task of auditing a company's financial information to provide additional services. Their first steps were financial services that were a logical extension of their audit assignments. They analyzed operating information to discover what's behind the numbers. By examining the risks and weaknesses in a company, they helped managers develop financial controls and procedures to prevent future trouble spots. Other related areas included tax, legal, and investment advisory services.

Starting in 1980, accounting firms moved further afield from their core businesses, developing huge consulting units that provided a wide range of information technology, business strategy, human resources, and similar management services. As a result, accountants—especially the largest firms—became more involved in the operations of their clients. This raised the question of potential conflicts of interest: Can auditors serve both the public and the client? Auditors' main purpose is to certify financial statements. Could they maintain sufficient objectivity to raise questions while auditing a client that provides significant consulting revenues? Can they review systems and methods that they designed and implemented?

By 2000, when accounting firms began reporting revenue sources to the SEC, nonaudit services accounted for 72 percent of the $5.7 billion in fees that 1,200 public companies paid their auditors. For example, Motorola paid its auditor KPMG about $4 million a year for auditing services. Yet this represented a minor portion of total fees to KPMG; in 2000 fees soared to $62.3 million because of a major IT project, and were a more normal $19 million in 2001.[10] To avoid the potential for conflict of interest, several of the largest accounting firms spun off their consulting units into separate companies. Andersen's consulting unit became Accenture; Deloitte Consulting separated from Deloitte Touche Tohmatsu in 2002 and changed its name to Braxton. Some advisory services remained with the auditing firms.

However, under Sarbanes-Oxley auditors may no longer provide eight specific types of nonaudit services to their audit clients. These include: services (like bookkeeping) related to the client's accounting records or financial statements, design and implementation of financial information systems, internal auditing, management functions, human resources, investment services, and legal services. The oversight board can amend the list as required. Corporate audit committees must preapprove all nonaudit services that auditors provide to their companies. As a result, accounting firms must evaluate potential client relationships and determine if they wish to pursue the audit business or the consulting business—but not both.

Holding Accountants Accountable

Until 2002, the accounting profession regulated its standards and practices through organizations such as the AICPA. However, its Public Oversight Board was unable to effectively enforce standards and apply sanctions when required. If problems with auditor independence arose, the accounting firms placed the organization's funding in jeopardy. "The profession has resisted meaningful self-regulation for decades," says Michael H. Sutton, a former chief accountant at the SEC.

As discussed earlier, the Sarbanes-Oxley Act made public accounting firms subject to formal regulation for the first time. Many industry observers say it's about time. "There's a void of leadership in the audit industry," says Sutton. "The firms are all in defensive mode." As a result, auditors are becoming overly conservative in how they interpret accounting rules.[11]

Auditors now understand that they must critically evaluate audit data rather than accept what a client tells them. They should take a skeptical view of a client's practices, challenge procedures, and question the assumptions behind the numbers. They must be willing to say no if they believe that a client's accounting practices are flawed. In addition, every five years the partners in charge must rotate off an audit. No longer can companies hire someone to become chief executive, financial, or accounting officer or controller if that person was an employee of the company's audit firm for the past year.

It's no surprise that the areas of professional ethics and independence are at the forefront of accounting industry initiatives. A new mind-set is taking hold in auditing firms. Integrity is the word of the day. They are strengthening codes of ethics and setting more rigorous quality standards, as the "Customer Satisfaction and Quality" box on page 594 explains. Another big change is in the area of internal audits. In the early 1990s corporations began to outsource this function, often to the same firm that performed its financial statement audit. Because this is no longer allowed, many companies are bringing internal audits in-house, which creates high demand for qualified personnel in this area.[12]

Over time, Sarbanes-Oxley should promote greater auditor independence and a willingness to ask their corporate clients hard questions about financial practices. The SEC, AICPA, FASB, and other organizations are issuing rules for compliance with provisions of the Sarbanes-Oxley Act. "It's a very different environment from nine months ago," says Ed Nussbaum, CEO of Grant Thornton LLP, the sixth-largest audit firm. "Instead of focusing on whittling down our fees, senior executives and audit committees are challenging us to make sure we're doing an adequate job."[13]

New Governance Responsibilities

An important result of the high-profile fraud cases is a new emphasis on corporate governance and internal controls. Where once boards of directors could take a passive role, they must now take greater responsibility for what happens in their companies. Executives, too, must make a commitment to high standards of corporate reporting and strong, effective internal controls. "A company's commitment at the highest levels of an organization can help ensure reliable financial reporting and increased investor confidence," said Barry Melancon, AICPA president and CEO.[14]

The audit committee takes on new importance in promoting good financial management policies and preventing accounting fraud. Sarbanes-Oxley mandates that at least one member must be a "financial expert." The committee is directly responsible for choosing the corporation's independent auditor and overseeing the auditor's work. It approves internal accounting controls, monitors the company's choice of accounting policies, and deals with accounting issues and disputes over rule interpretation. The SEC has proposed that companies include in their annual reports a report on the company's internal controls and financial reporting that assesses how effective the controls are.

For example, integrated communications services company R.R. Donnelley is promoting stronger links between the audit committee and financial management. "It is clear that we need a broader approach to evaluate the risks to the value that we can and should create for our shareholders," says Gregory A. Stoklosa, chief financial officer. "The audit committee will be more involved in developing our overall framework for risk management. In addition, it will be more involved in our earnings announcements and disclosure on a quarterly basis."[15]

Closing the GAAP

Many accounting industry experts place some of the blame for the current situation on the complexity of GAAP. "Over the last 10 years, U.S. GAAP has evolved into complex detailed rules that encourage financial engineering rather than transparency," says PricewaterhouseCoopers global CEO Samuel DiPiazza, Jr. He and former PricewaterhouseCoopers colleague Robert Herz, who is now head of FASB, would like to see a shift from standards-based to the principles-based accounting used by the International Accounting Standards Board. "It's a lot harder for me to bend a principle than to bend a rule," says DiPiazza. Instead of asking if the accounting follows the rules, executives and auditors would look at how it shows a transaction's underlying economics. "A principles-based system is one where the accounting standard simply lays out objectives of good reporting in an area," explains Herz. Standards would be broader, simpler, and more concise—12 pages instead of 200 pages. "We would tell people that, if you can't see a particular rule to fit your situation, go back to the main objective or principle." This would get rid of the many exceptions to current standards and provide fewer loopholes.[16]

concept check

Why did self-regulation of the accounting industry fail? What changes will auditing firms have to make to operate under the Sarbanes-Oxley Act?

Summarize the new guidelines for improved corporate governance.

How might GAAP be modified to reduce future rule manipulation?

Great Ideas to Use Now

By now it should be very clear that basic accounting knowledge is a valuable skill to have, whether you start your own company or work for someone else. Analyzing a company's financial statements before you take a job there can tell you quite a bit about its financial health. Once you are on the job, you need to understand how to read financial statements and how to develop financial information for business operations. It's almost impossible to operate effectively in a business environment otherwise. Especially in a small company, you will wear many hats, and having accounting skills may help you get the job. In addition, accounting will help you manage your personal finances.

If you own your own firm, you can't rely on someone else to take charge of your accounting system. You must decide what financial information you need to manage your company better and to track its progress. If you can't understand the reports your accountant prepares, you will have no idea whether they are accurate.

Managing your personal finances is also a lot easier if you understand accounting. Suppose your Great-Aunt Helen wants to buy you a few shares of stock to encourage your interest in business. Her stockbroker suggests two computer companies, and Aunt Helen asks you to choose one of them. The product lines of the companies are nearly identical. Where can you get more information to help you make your choice? Someone suggests that you should study their financial statements. The companies send you their financial statements upon request. Now that you have a basic understanding of accounting, you have an idea of what all those numbers mean and how you can use them to make your decision.

As task 2 in the preceding "Try It Now" box noted, accounting can also help you create personal financial statements. Budgeting, a key part of personal finance discussed in Chapter 22, also uses accounting concepts. And as noted above, financial statements are at the core of investment analysis.

Summary of Learning Goals

1 Why are financial reports and accounting information important, and who uses them?

Accounting involves collecting, recording, classifying, summarizing, reporting, and analyzing a firm's financial activities according to a standard set of procedures. The financial reports resulting from the accounting process give managers, employees, investors, customers, suppliers, creditors, and government agencies a way to analyze a company's past, current, and future performance. Financial accounting is concerned with the preparation of financial reports using generally accepted accounting principles. Managerial accounting provides financial information that management can use to make decisions about the firm's operations.

Try It Now

1. **Learn to read financial statements.** To become more familiar with annual reports and key financial statements, head for IBM's Guide to Understanding Financials at **http://www.ibm.com/investor/financialguide/**. The material offers a good overview of financial reporting and shows you what to look for when you read these documents.
2. **Prepare personal financial statements.** One of the best ways to learn about financial statements is to prepare them. Put together your personal balance sheet and income statement, using Exhibits 18.4 and 18.5 as samples.

You will have to adjust the account categories to fit your needs. Here are some suggestions:

- Current assets—cash on hand, balances in savings and checking accounts.
- Investments—stocks and bonds, retirement funds.
- Fixed assets—real estate, personal property (cars, furniture, jewelry, etc.).
- Current liabilities—charge-card balances, loan payments due in one year.
- Long-term liabilities—auto loan balance, mortgage on real estate, other loan balances that will not come due until after one year.
- Income—employment income, investment income (interest, dividends).
- Expenses—housing, utilities, food, transportation, medical, clothing, insurance, loan payments, taxes, personal care, recreation and entertainment, and miscellaneous expenses.

After you complete your personal financial statements, use them to see how well you are managing your finances. Consider the following questions:

- Should you be concerned about your debt ratio?
- Would a potential creditor conclude that it is safe or risky to lend you money?
- If you were a company, would people want to invest in you? Why or why not? What could you do to improve your financial condition?

Customer Satisfaction and Quality

The recent upheaval in corporate financial reporting makes customer satisfaction and quality very relevant to financial statement preparation and the accounting profession. As noted earlier, auditing firms often gave good reports to companies later charged with accounting irregularities.

The customers for financial reports are not just the corporate clients who hire the auditors. The investing public—both institutions who buy large blocks of stocks and individuals—rely heavily on the quality and reliability of reported financial information to make investment decisions. They are demanding that auditors and corporations demonstrate their compliance with higher standards under Sarbanes-Oxley and pursuant to rules issued by the SEC, FASB, and other organizations.

Companies are now giving new respect to the external auditing process. "If you want an audit that will detect management fraud, you must be willing to pay more for it and pay far greater attention to the process and what will be included and analyzed," says Robert G. Eccles, PricewaterhouseCoopers senior fellow and coauthor of *Building Public Trust: The Future of Corporate Reporting*. "The audit committee must be the customer for the audit, and this will require more time on the part of the audit committee."[17]

Better quality control will result from new corporate governance standards and financial disclosure practices. Management at Airgas Inc., an industrial-gases distributor, now spends more time on these issues. It was already in compliance with the latest legislative and regulatory reforms. Recently the company implemented a more formal approach to financial quality control. The audit committee will hold a special meeting every year to review current business issues. "This focus is closely tied to our growth strategy," says Roger Millay, Airgas's senior vice president and CFO. "Good governance, and the perception and understanding of good governance, are important to our growth strategy. The market's confidence in our governance is essential to attracting capital."[18]

Looking Ahead at Enron

Even as it tried to climb out of bankruptcy, Enron continued to make the news. Not only had it twisted accounting practices to boost energy prices and inflate profits, it also manipulated tax rules. In February 2003 a report of Congress's Joint Committee on taxation revealed that Enron devised complex tax-motivated transactions with no business purpose other than to avoid taxes and increase financial accounting income. From 1996 to 1999, these schemes generated tax losses of $3 billion, far more than its $2.3 billion in reported income. The firm paid a meager $63 million in taxes in 2000 and 2001. Enron took advantage of technical differences in tax and accounting rules to create tax losses—at the same time it was exaggerating its earnings to prop up the stock price.

The report also disclosed that in 2000 Enron paid out $1.4 billion in compensation to its 200 highest-paid employees. The company's board did not properly oversee compensation and seemingly never denied a bonus request. In setting up these tax-motivated deals, Enron paid enormous fees to attorneys, accounting firms, and banks. Lindy Paull, chief of the joint committee staff, questioned the independence of these advisors and said that the letters they provided that said the proposed transactions "should" comply with tax law avoided or skimmed over any questionable issues. "We would say at a minimum that they turned a blind eye to some critical facts," she said.

Despite these setbacks, Enron continued its efforts to restructure the company. It hoped to emerge from bankruptcy as a viable, if smaller, company.[19]

2

What are the differences between public and private accountants, and are public accountants subject to new regulations?

Public accountants work for independent firms that provide accounting services—such as financial report preparation and auditing, tax return preparation, and management consulting—to other organizations on a fee basis. Private accountants are employed to serve one particular organization and may prepare financial statements, tax returns, and management reports.

The bankruptcies of companies like Enron and WorldCom, plus widespread abuses of accounting practices, raised critical issues of auditor independence and the integrity and reliability of financial reports. To set better standards for accounting, auditing, and financial reporting and prevent future accounting irregularities, Congress passed the Sarbanes-Oxley Act in 2002. This Act establishes an independent board to oversee the accounting profession, sets stricter auditing and financial disclosure standards, and places increased accountability on a company's senior executives and management. It restricts auditors from providing certain types of consulting services to clients. Other organizations such as the SEC, the New York Stock Exchange, and accounting industry professional associations issued new regulations and guidelines related to compliance with the Act.

3

What are the six steps in the accounting cycle?

The accounting cycle refers to the process of generating financial statements. It begins with analyzing business transactions, recording them in journals, and posting them to ledgers. Ledger totals are then summarized in a trial balance that confirms the accuracy of the figures. Next the accountant prepares the financial statements and reports. The final step involves analyzing these reports and making decisions.

4

In what terms does the balance sheet describe the financial condition of an organization?

The balance sheet represents the financial condition of a firm at one moment in time, in terms of assets, liabilities, and owners' equity. The key categories of assets are current assets, fixed assets, and intangible assets. Liabilities are divided into current and long-term liabilities. Owners' equity, the amount of the owners' investment in the firm after all liabilities have been paid, is the third major category.

5

How does the income statement report a firm's profitability?

The income statement is a summary of the firm's operations over a stated period of time. The main parts of the statement are revenues (gross and net sales), cost of goods sold, operating expenses (selling and general and administrative expenses), taxes, and net profit or loss.

6

Why is the statement of cash flows an important source of information?

The statement of cash flows summarizes the firm's sources and uses of cash during a financial-reporting period. It breaks the firm's cash flows into those from operating, investment, and financing activities. It shows the net change during the period in the firm's cash and marketable securities.

7

How can ratio analysis be used to identify a firm's financial strengths and weaknesses?

Ratio analysis is a way to use financial statements to gain insight into a firm's operations, profitability, and overall financial condition. The four main types of ratios are liquidity ratios, profitability ratios, activity ratios, and debt ratios. Comparing a firm's ratios over several years and comparing them to ratios of other firms in the same industry or to industry averages can indicate trends and highlight financial strengths and weaknesses.

8

What major trends affect the accounting industry today?

The recent scandals made it clear that the current accounting/auditing system wasn't working as intended and needed an overhaul to correct the wrongs and restore investor confidence in financial reporting. To eliminate potential conflicts of interest between auditing and consulting units, the Sarbanes-Oxley Act prohibits accounting firms from providing nonaudit services in eight areas. The accounting industry's self-regulation ended under the Act, which places formal controls on accounting firms. Professional ethics and auditor independence are among the industry's priorities. Auditors will be taking a harder line when they are analyzing clients' financial reporting practices and raising questions when they are not satisfied. The roles of the board of directors and its audit committee are now stronger. We could also see some major changes in GAAP from a shift to principles-based rather than standards-based accounting.

KEY TERMS

accounting 571
acid-test (quick) ratio 587
activity ratios 589
annual report 574
assets 577
auditing 574
balance sheet 579
certified management accountant (CMA) 575
certified public accountant (CPA) 575
cost of goods sold 583
current assets 580
current liabilities 582
current ratio 587
debt ratios 589
debt-to-equity ratio 589
depreciation 580
double-entry bookkeeping 578
earnings per share (EPS) 589
expenses 583
financial accounting 572
Financial Accounting Standards Board (FASB) 573
fixed assets 580
generally accepted accounting principles (GAAP) 572
gross profit 584
gross sales 583
income statement 583
intangible assets 582
inventory turnover ratio 589
liabilities 577
liquidity 579
liquidity ratios 587
long-term liabilities 582
managerial accounting 571
net loss 585
net profit margin 589
net profit (net income) 585
net sales 583
net working capital 587
operating expenses 584
owners' equity 577
private accountants 575
profitability ratios 588
public accountants 574

PREPARING FOR TOMORROW'S WORKPLACE

1. Your firm has been hired to help several small businesses with their year-end financial statements.

   a. Based on the following account balances, prepare the Marbella Design Enterprises balance sheet as of December 31, 2005:

Cash	$30,250
Accounts payable	28,500
Fixtures and furnishings	85,000
Notes payable	15,000
Retained earnings	64,450
Accounts receivable	24,050
Inventory	15,600
Equipment	42,750
Accumulated depreciation on fixtures and furnishings	12,500
Common shares (50,000 shares at $1)	50,000
Long-term debt	25,000
Accumulated depreciation on equipment	7,800
Marketable securities	13,000
Income taxes payable	7,500

   b. The following are the account balances for the revenues and expenses of the Windsor Gift Shop for the year ending December 31, 2005. Prepare the income statement for the shop.

Rent	$ 15,000
Salaries	23,500
Cost of goods sold	98,000
Utilities	8,000
Supplies	3,500
Sales	195,000
Advertising	3,600
Interest	3,000
Taxes	12,120

2. During the year ended December 31, 2005, Lawrence Industries sold $2 million worth of merchandise on credit. A total of $1.4 million was collected during the year. The cost of this merchandise was $1.3 million. Of this amount, $1 million has been paid, and $300,000 is not yet due. Operating expenses and income taxes totaling $500,000 were paid in cash during the year. Assume that all accounts had a zero balance at the beginning of the year (January 1, 2005). Write a brief report for the company controller that includes calculation of the firm's (a) net profit and (b) cash flow during the year. Explain why there is a difference between net profit and cash flow.

3. A friend has been offered a sales representative position at Draper Publications, Inc., a small publisher of computer-related books, but wants to know more about the company. Because of your expertise in financial analysis, you offer to help analyze Draper's financial health. Draper has provided the following selected financial information:

KEY TERMS

ratio analysis 586
retained earnings 583
return on equity (ROE) 589
revenues 583
Sarbanes-Oxley Act 576
statement of cash flows 585

Account balances on December 31, 2005:

Inventory	$ 72,000
Net sales	450,000
Current assets	150,000
Cost of goods sold	290,000
Total liabilities	180,000
Net profit	35,400
Total assets	385,000
Current liabilities	75,000
Other information	
Number of common shares outstanding	25,000
Inventory at January 1, 2005	48,000

Calculate the following ratios for 2005: acid-test (quick) ratio, inventory turnover ratio, net profit margin, return on equity (ROE), debt-to-equity ratio, and earnings per share (EPS). Summarize your assessment of the company's financial performance, based on these ratios, in a report for your friend. What other information would you like to have to complete your evaluation?

4. Use the Internet and business periodicals to research how companies and accounting firms are implementing the provisions of the Sarbanes-Oxley Act. What are the major concerns they face? What rules have other organizations issued that relate to Act compliance? Summarize your findings.

5. Two years ago, Rebecca Mardon started a computer consulting business, Mardon Consulting Associates. Until now, she has been the only employee, but business has grown enough to support an administrative assistant and another consultant this year. Before she adds staff, however, she wants to hire an accountant and computerize her financial record keeping. Divide the class into small groups, assigning one person to be Rebecca and the others to represent members of a medium-size accounting firm. Rebecca should think about the type of financial information systems her firm requires and develop a list of questions for the firm. The accountants will prepare a presentation making recommendations to her as well as explaining why their firm should win the account.

WORKING THE NET

1. Do annual reports confuse you? Many Web sites can take the mystery out of this important document. See IBM's Guide to Understanding Financials at **http://www.prars.com/ibm/ibmframe.html**. Moneychimp's "How to Read an Annual Report" features an interactive diagram that provides a big picture view of what the report's financial information tells you: **http://www.moneychimp.com/articles/financials/fundamentals.htm**. Which site was more helpful to you, and why?

2. Corporate reports filed with the SEC are now available on the Web at the EDGAR (Electronic Data Gathering, Analysis, and Retrieval system) Web site, **http://www.sec.gov/edgar.shtml**. First, read about the EDGAR system; then go to the search page **http://www.sec.gov/edgar/searchedgar/webusers.htm**. To see the type of information that companies must file with the SEC, use the search feature to locate a recent filing by Microsoft. What types of reports did you find, and what was the purpose of each report?

3. Can you judge an annual report by its cover? What are the most important elements of a top annual report? Go to Sid Cato's Official Annual Report Web site, **http://www.sidcato.com**, to find his 15 standards for annual reports and read about the reports that receive his honors. Then get a copy of an annual report and evaluate it using Cato's 135-point scale. How well does it compare to his top picks?
4. Go to the Web site of the company whose annual report you evaluated in Question 3. Find the Web version of its annual report and compare it to the print version. What differences do you find, if any? Do you think companies should put their financial information online? Why or why not?
5. Was Enron successful in restructuring after bankruptcy? Use your online research skills to find out the company's current status. Does it exist as a viable company today, and what is the outlook for the future?

Creative Thinking Case

A Dishonorable Discharge for the Marine Corps of Accounting

Arthur Andersen started the accounting firm that bore his name in 1913. From the start, he embraced the highest business ethics, refusing to manipulate unsatisfactory financial results at a client's request. Andersen's motto, "Think straight, talk straight," was the foundation of the Chicago-based company's culture of honesty and integrity. This reputation earned Andersen the nickname "Marine Corps of Accounting" for its disciplined and strict attention to accounting standards.

By the 1990s, the Andersen culture had strayed far from its founder's philosophy. Andersen was "a place where the mad scramble for fees had trumped good judgment," says Barbara Ley Toffler, author of *Final Accounting: Ambition, Greed and the Fall of Arthur Andersen.* These fees came not only from auditing but increasingly from the rapidly growing consulting practices of Andersen and its industry colleagues. Business units competed with each other and were rewarded for bringing in revenues, not for evaluating a deal's riskiness.

The growth of consulting revenues was in itself a problem. Andersen often provided business services to the same companies it audited, earning as much from consulting as auditing. This conflict of interest placed pressure on the auditors to go along with aggressive accounting practices, to preserve the consulting relationships and earnings.

Andersen's culture also placed a loyalty to the firm before loyalty to clients or shareholders. Partners who raised questions were penalized. This attitude went straight down the line, as Toffler discovered when leading a meeting of young Andersen employees. She asked how they would respond if a supervisor told them to do something they consider wrong. Only one person spoke up: "If he insisted I do it, yes, I would." Toffler then asked if he would tell anyone about it: "No. It could hurt my career."

Turning a blind eye to accounting irregularities at clients was a common practice. Says Toffler, who—ironically—ran Andersen's business ethics consulting practice from 1995 to 1999, "High-level members of that organization knew much of what was going on." As Enron's wrongdoings became public, the firm's top management became Enron's partner in duplicity instead of demonstrating the industry leadership its founder would have expected.

In June 2002, Andersen was convicted of obstruction of justice in the Enron case for shredding documents. Later that summer, the doors shut at the accounting firm that once set the standards to which other firms aspired.

CRITICAL THINKING QUESTIONS

1. Toffler says that Andersen executives expected that aggressive accounting would have an impact when the economy tanked but issued few warning memos and did nothing to change the culture of greed. With the benefit of hindsight, what steps could Andersen's leadership have taken to preserve the firm as the accounting scandals unfolded?
2. Andersen's Enron audit team was aware of monkey business as early as 1987, when management covered up the oil-trading scandal mentioned in the chapter opener. It also caved in to pressure to sign off on questionable deals and participated in document destruction that led to its obstruction of justice conviction. Suggest procedures that auditors and corporations should adopt and enforce to prevent these abuses.
3. Discuss why providing consulting services to audit clients in such areas as business strategy, financial strategy, human resources, and information technology systems planning, design, and implementation can create a conflict of interest.

SOURCES: Greg Farrell, "Former Andersen Exec Tells of Stressful Internal Culture," *USA Today,* March 3, 2003, p. 3B; William J. Holstein, "Lessons of a Fallen Rival for Accounting's Big 4," *The New York Times,* February 23, 2003, p. C6; and Rob Walker, "Inside a Culture of Greed," *Newsday,* March 6, 2003, p. D33.

VIDEO CASE

The Weathervane Terrace Inn and Suites

Charlevoix is a northern Michigan resort community located in a valley between Lake Charlevoix and Lake Michigan. With its majestic maple trees, picket fences, Victorian homes, three-masted schooners and gleaming yachts, blue water, and white sand beaches, Charlevoix is reminiscent of a summer resort town from the 1800s. In the winter, it offers scenic cross-country trails for skiers and snowmobilers. In short, Charlevoix is a year-round tourist destination.

One of Charlevoix's premier lodging facilities is the Weathervane Terrace Inn and Suites (**http://www.weathervane-chx.com**). The Weathervane Inn, an architectural and historic landmark, offers its guests a special and unique lodging experience. The Inn has special guest packages such as the Charlevoix Sampler and several different golf packages. The Weathervane's staff readily accommodates guests' special requests, such as organizing special outings, making reservations with other hotels on a guest's itinerary, arranging a charter fishing expedition, or renting a sailboat.

The Weathervane Inn has an interesting, if not unique, ownership structure. The rooms and suites are essentially condominium units owned by individual investors. A management team operates the inn for the owners. The managers' duties include promoting the inn, renting units to guests when they are not being used by the owners, cleaning and maintaining the rental units, and regularly reporting operating results to the owners. The managers strive to equitably allocate rentals across all the units. By doing this, they assure that all owners receive reasonable rental income from their condominium properties.

Essentially, the Weathervane's staff are sales and management agents for the condominium owners. As agents, they have a stewardship responsibility with regard to the investors' assets. This agency relationship also imposes important financial reporting requirements on the managers.

To enable them to do an effective and efficient job of financial reporting, the Weathervane Inn's managers use a computerized accounting information system. This system tracks all the accounting and financial data for each condominium unit, including rental activity and income, operating expenses, and maintenance expenses. This information is used to generate monthly accounting reports for each condominium owner. Thus, the owners are able to monitor and evaluate the management of their investment properties.

CRITICAL THINKING QUESTIONS

1. Why is it important for the Weathervane Inn to have an effective and efficient accounting information system?
2. What types of accounting reports are likely to be most useful to the condominium owners? Explain your answer.
3. How can the condominium owners make use of financial accounting? How can they make use of managerial accounting?

E-Commerce Case

Compliance Conundrum

The Sarbanes-Oxley Act of 2002 placed new compliance and disclosure burdens on corporate executives. Not only must top executives certify their firms' financial statements, but they must also quickly publicize "on a current basis" such matters as insider transactions in the company's stock, events that require certain SEC filings, and "any material changes in their financial condition."

No wonder, then, that a company's Web site has become an important part of its investor-relations efforts. Both investors and analysts use corporate Web sites as a major source of information for quarterly earnings releases, press releases other than earnings, annual reports, SEC filings such as the 10K or 10Q, Webcasts of current conference calls with security analysts and archives of past Webcasts, and other financial and investment-related information

According to a survey of more than 200 corporate clients conducted by CCBN (**http://www.ccbn.com**), a provider of Internet-based shareholder communications services, 95 percent use their corporate Web site to communicate compliance with the Act and rebuild investor confidence. About one-quarter clearly highlighted their compliance on their investor-relations home page, while 17 percent did so on their new-release page, and 5 percent on the site's home page.

"The fact that companies are communicating compliance on their Web site without the requirement of the SEC shows that the Internet has become one of the most important channels for reaching shareholders and the institutional investor community," said Rob Adler, CCBN's cofounder and president. This is good news for CCBN, which specializes in delivering and managing online investor relations. The company builds, manages, and hosts the investor-relations sections of Web sites for more than 3,000 public companies, providing detailed shareholder information through interactive, multimedia solutions. CCBN has added new capabilities to help companies with other areas of Sarbanes-Oxley compliance, such as communicating information on corporate governance and establishing investor and governance hotlines.

CRITICAL THINKING QUESTIONS

1. Why is the Web well-suited for corporate compliance with the Sarbanes-Oxley Act?
2. Visit the CCBN site, **http://www.ccbn.com**, and read about its services. Why might a company want to outsource these services to CCBN?

SOURCES: Matthew French, "Cashing in on Compliance," *Mass High Tech,* October 21, 2002, downloaded from http://www.masshightech.com; "NIRI Releases 2002 Trends and Technology Survey," National Investor Relations Institute press release, February 11, 2003, downloaded from http://www.niri.org; and Louis M. Thompson, Jr., "The New World of Corporate Disclosure: Reg. FD, Sarbanes-Oxley and Beyond," Keynote address before the DeMarche Manager Institute Conference, Naples, Florida, February 20, 2003, downloaded from the National Investor Relations Institute Web site, http://www.niri.org.

Hot Links Address Book

What issues is the FASB working on now? Check it out at
http://www.fasb.org

Two good sites to learn about the latest news in the accounting industry are Electronic Accountant,
http://www.electronicaccountant.com
and Accounting Web,
http://www.accountingweb.com

To find out more about the accounting profession and becoming a CPA, visit the American Institute of Certified Public Accountants' Web site at
http://www.aicpa.org/
and click on "Students."

The Accounting Library site has a virtual consultant to help companies choose the best accounting applications for their needs. Check it out at
http://www.excelco.com/

At their Web sites, you can learn about the types of services the Big Four accounting firms are now offering their clients:
http://www.deloitte.com
http://www.ey.com
http://www.kpmg.com
and
http://www.pwcglobal.com

your career

in the Information Age

The fields of computers/information systems and accounting are among those growing fastest in the United States. Each offers many career opportunities at all levels.

With the increasing reliance on information technology, the number of traditional information-processing jobs—applications development, programmers, systems analysts, and computer operators, for instance—has increased. Many jobs have opened up in areas like networking, database administration, telecommunications, computer training and consulting, technical support, and microcomputer sales, service, and repair. In addition, the Internet offers many job opportunities, from Webmaster to Web site designer and software developer. Many other opportunities have been created by applying computer technology to existing jobs.

Despite the dot-com bust, the growth rate in technology fields remains high. The demand continues for people who can help businesses adapt and integrate new technologies into their organization. The increasing complexity of new technology has increased the need for support specialists who can provide users with technical assistance. Many companies now outsource IT functions to specialists, creating growth in computer services companies. The Bureau of Labor Statistics estimates that jobs in such areas as software engineering, computer support, database administration, and system administration will almost double by 2010. Another growth area is desktop publishing, as more companies use computers to produce documents in-house or by contracting with a specialist in this area.

Some degree of computer knowledge and technical literacy is essential no matter what career you choose. Now every industry has computer jobs. Computers have also changed the way managers get data, make decisions, and do their work. If you enjoy working with computers, you may wish to try a career providing the computer-related services that senior managers need, especially development of information systems, decision support systems, and Internet-related systems.

A person who chooses a computer-oriented career needs more than just computer and math skills. People skills, organizational skills, analytical skills, and communication skills are all needed to enter one of today's hottest career paths. Continuing education is important to keep up with changing technology. Many hardware and software vendors offer training seminars, as do universities and colleges. Obtaining technical or professional certification is a good way to demonstrate your capabilities.

New government regulations and the increased demand for good financial information have fueled the need for able accountants and auditors. To succeed in accounting, you need good basic math skills and an ability to analyze and interpret facts and figures. Good communication skills—both written and spoken—and computer skills are also important. Internal auditing has become a growth area as companies bring this function in-house instead of outsourcing it.

Dream Career: Web Site Designer

Professional Web site designers are responsible for most of what you see and hear on the Internet. Because having a Web presence is becoming a must, businesses now spend almost $20 billion annually on Web site development. As a result, demand for skilled Web site designers is on the rise.

Using special coding languages, Web editing and graphics software, and tools like scanners and digital cameras, Web designers create Web sites to fit the client's image. The best designers make each site unique yet strive for simple, clean designs that are easy for users to navigate. In addition to developing new sites, they also maintain sites and redesign older sites to incorporate technology such as audio, videoconferencing, and other multimedia features. Keeping Web sites fresh and entertaining so that visitors return provides a steady stream of ongoing assignments.

The job calls for creativity as well as knowledge of Internet programming languages such as HTML, XML, JavaScript, and Perl. The complexity of sites varies. As the availability of do-it-yourself resources increases, designers who can build high-end sites with e-commerce and database applications will find jobs plentiful.

Designers may work in-house for one company or for specialized design firms that serve a variety of clients. Some firms do only page design, while others offer a full range of services, including Web site hosting, design, and marketing.

- *Places of Employment:* Web site designers work both in-house and for specialized Internet services and consulting firms. Positions are available in most areas of the country.
- *Skills Required:* May require Associate's degree or its equivalent and some on-the-job experience. Proficiency in Web programming languages, design experience.
- *Employment Outlook through 2010:* Above average.
- *Salaries:* $35,250 to $54,500 for those with one to three years' experience; average compensation for experienced designers is $65,000.

Where the Opportunities Are

Systems Analyst

The people who diagnose computer-related business problems and offer solutions for them in the form of information systems are called systems analysts. They help firms maximize their efficiency using available technology, working with managers to define the problem and break it down into parts. For instance, if a firm needs a new inventory system, systems analysts will meet with purchasing and manufacturing managers to figure out what data to collect, what computer equipment will be required, and what steps to take to process the information.

Analysts use such techniques as accounting, sampling, and mathematical models to analyze a problem and design a new system. Then, they translate the system into hardware needs and instructions for computer programmers, and work with the programmers to set up the system.

Systems analysts need prior work experience. Nearly half of all systems analysts transfer from other careers, especially programming. In many industries, systems analysts begin as programmers and are promoted to systems analyst positions after gaining experience.

- *Places of Employment:* Systems analysts work in all types of organizations. Positions are available in most large urban areas throughout the country.
- *Skills Required:* Four-year degree in computer science or a related field like business or engineering. Many positions require an MBA or an advanced degree in computer science.
- *Employment Outlook through 2010:* Above average.
- *Salaries:* $37,500 to $89,000+ for experienced analysts. Median salary: $59,330.

Computer Programmer

Computer programmers work in a variety of companies. Software companies use programmers to develop packaged applications programs used by many companies and individuals. Hardware manufacturers may use programmers to write systems software for their equipment. Many companies hire programmers to develop customized computer applications. For example, a life insurance company programmer may write software to calculate policy premiums based on life expectancy tables, while a programmer at an educational software firm may develop math and reading games for elementary school children.

Computer programmers write programs based on design specifications from systems analysts. Then, they determine the steps the program must take to accomplish the desired tasks and write the program in a series of coded instructions, using one of the languages developed especially for computers. Next, programmers test the program and correct any errors, a process called "debugging." Finally, the programmer prepares instructions for those who will run the program.

- *Places of Employment:* Throughout the United States, especially in areas with many high-tech companies—including the San Francisco and Boston metropolitan areas, North Carolina, Texas, and Southern California.
- *Skills Required:* Bachelor's degree or higher, although some programmers qualify with two-year degrees or certificates. Technical or professional certification is becoming more common.
- *Employment Outlook through 2010:* Above average.
- *Salaries:* $35,000 for beginning programmers; average starting salary for programmers with bachelor's degree in computer programming or computer science, $48,600–$52,000; $35,000–$95,000+ for experienced programmers; salaries are higher for those with proficiency in certain programming languages.

Database Manager

Today companies rely heavily on databases to operate. They gather and store vast amounts of information on customers, inventory, and projects to use in marketing, production, and sales. E-commerce operations are database-dependent, creating even higher demand for database managers. The database manager normally is not involved in the design or development of the database software. Instead, these managers typically take over once the system has been installed at the organization.

A database manager is responsible for scheduling and coordinating user access as well as for overall security. The manager arranges for the preparation of backup files and emergency recovery plans. He or she advises management as to which data should be included in the database, how it should be organized, and how long it should remain. Many database managers also compile and analyze statistics on use and efficiency of the database and report these findings to management.

- *Places of Employment:* Throughout the country, with most opportunities in large urban areas.
- *Skills Required:* Bachelor's degree; many organizations also require relevant work experience and/or an MBA, as well as continuing education to upgrade technical expertise.
- *Employment Outlook through 2010:* Above average.
- *Salaries:* Database analyst: $39,100–$65,000; average: $54,700; database managers: $72,500–$105,000+; median $63,700.

Network Administrators

As more companies turn to decentralized computer systems linked into networks, the demand is growing for network administrators to facilitate communications between computers. These specialists help managers define their computing needs and integrate their department's computer systems into the larger system. They purchase the network's equipment (PCs, workstations, printers, scanners, and databases) and maintain the network.

- *Places of Employment:* Throughout the country, with most opportunities in large urban areas .
- *Skills Required:* B.S. in computer science and computer experience; certification from manufacturers of network systems hardware is desirable.
- *Employment Outlook through 2010:* Excellent.
- *Salaries:* $33,000–88,000+; median $53,300 for administrators and $61,200 for senior administrators.

Accountant

About 965,000 accountants work in the United States today. Most accountants are involved in managerial accounting for businesses. Another 25 percent work in public accounting firms. The government and educational institutions also employ many accountants.

Managerial accountants work in all types of businesses, from small firms to large multinational corporations. Many are either certified management accountants (CMAs) or certified public accountants (CPAs). They prepare financial statements and other reports for management. They may also specialize in such areas as budgeting, internal auditing, or international, tax, or cost accounting. The top positions for managerial accountants are corporate controller and treasurer. The controller manages the accounting, audit, and budget departments. The treasurer is responsible for cash management, financial planning, and other financial activities.

Public accountants earn more than managerial accountants. More than 300,000 public accountants work in accounting firms throughout the United States and abroad. All levels of government have accounting positions as well. Most of these positions carry civil-service rank, and advancement depends on education and experience.

Accountants also establish businesses of their own, hanging out their shingles as CPAs, tax accountants, and accounting consultants.

Opportunities for minorities and women are excellent in the accounting field.

- *Places of Employment:* Throughout the country, primarily in large urban areas.
- *Skills Required:* Four-year degree in accounting or related field. Many large firms prefer an M.S. in accounting or an MBA. Computer skills are also important.
- *Employment Outlook through 2010:* Average growth.
- *Salaries:* $29,250–$40,250 for beginning accountants and auditors with bachelor's degree; $33,500–$47,750 with one to three years' experience; $39,250–$59,500 for senior accountants; $46,750–$76,750 for managers, and $60,500–$106,500 for directors; $100,000–$300,000+ for partners in CPA firms. The average for general accounting is $56,000.

SOURCES: *CollegeJournal Salary Data,* http://www.collegejournal.com/salarydata/, downloaded March 17, 2003; *Occupational Outlook Handbook 2002–2003,* U.S. Bureau of Labor Statistics, http://www.bls.gov/oco; "Salary Wizard," *Business Week Online,* http://swz-businessweek.salary.com, downloaded March 17, 2003.

Chapter 19

© AP / WIDE WORLD PHOTOS

Understanding Money and Financial Institutions

learning goals

1 What is money, what are its characteristics and functions, and what are the three parts of the U.S. money supply?
2 How does the Federal Reserve manage the money supply?
3 What are the key financial institutions, and what role do they play in the process of financial intermediation?
4 How does the Federal Deposit Insurance Corporation (FDIC) protect depositors' funds?
5 What role do U.S. banks play in the international marketplace?
6 What trends are reshaping the financial institutions?

One-Stop Shopping—From Singapore to Budapest—With Citigroup

No one could ever accuse Sandy Weill of thinking small. As Chairman of Citigroup (**http://www.citigroup.com**), he oversees the world's largest financial-services firm. With assets well over $1 trillion, Citigroup is a global behemoth serving the financial needs of over 200 million customers in more than 100 countries. Perhaps most staggering, however, is the sheer number of financial products and services offered under the Citigroup umbrella: consumer banking and credit services, corporate treasury and cash management services, corporate and investment banking, insurance, and securities brokerage services. In short, you can meet every financial need—from a simple checking account to buying stock to arranging a corporate loan to setting up a Web-based cash management system—by contacting just one company.

Citigroup was formed in 1998 by the merger of Citicorp, then already a world banking powerhouse, and Travelers Group, an insurance and brokerage giant. The Citicorp/Travelers merger represented a new era in banking: the birth of the mega-financial institution able to offer one-stop shopping for financial services by integrating bank, insurance, and investment products and services within one organization. As Weill said at the time, the Citicorp/Travelers merger created "one helluva candy store."

Weill keeps adding to his candy store. Among the treats he's acquired in the past three years: banks in Japan, Poland, Mexico, and Hungary; pension funds; in Europe, Mexico, and South America; and an online brokerage firm in Japan. Cross-selling all of the company's services to all of its customers in all of its markets is a key company goal.

Using technology to build tighter customer bonds is also high on Weill's list of priorities. When a customer signs on to MyCiti.com, for example, they instantly see all of their Citigroup accounts—from home loans and insurance accounts to the frequent flyer miles they've earned using a Citibank credit card—displayed on a single screen. In Singapore, Citigroup has experimented with a cell phone service that lets customers do their banking, sell stocks, and even buy insurance from anywhere their cell phone reaches—the ultimate convenience in one-stop shopping.[1]

Critical Thinking Questions

As you read this chapter, consider the following questions as they relate to Citigroup:

1. What are the advantages and disadvantages of being a financial institution of Citigroup's size?
2. How is technology changing the way financial institutions interact with business and consumer customers?
3. How does government regulation affect the financial services industry?
4. What role do financial institutions like Citigroup play in business and the global economy?

Principles of Money and Financial Institutions

Imagine using your cell phone to open a bank account! The financial-services industry is indeed moving in new directions, as demonstrated by Citigroup. Advanced technology, globalization of markets, and the relaxation of regulatory restrictions are accelerating the pace of change in financial services. The changes are giving businesses and consumers new options for conducting their financial transactions. The competitive landscape for financial institutions is also changing as they develop new ways to increase their market share and boost profits.

Because financial institutions connect people with money, this chapter begins with a discussion of money, its characteristics and functions, and the components of the U.S. money supply. Next, it explains the role of the Federal Reserve System in managing the money supply. Then it describes different types of financial institutions and their services and the organizations that insure customer deposits. The chapter ends with a discussion of international banking and trends in the financial institutions.

Show Me the Money

1 learning goal

money
Anything that is acceptable as payment for goods and services.

Money is anything that is acceptable as payment for goods and services. It affects our lives in many ways. We earn it, spend it, save it, invest it—and often wish we had more of it. Business and government use money in similar ways. Both require money to finance their operations. By controlling the amount of money in circulation, the federal government can promote economic growth and stability. For this reason, money has been called the lubricant for the machinery of our economic system. Our banking system was developed to ease the handling of money.

Characteristics of Money

For money to be a suitable means of exchange, it should have these key characteristics:

- *Scarcity.* Money should be scarce enough to have some value but not so scarce as to be unavailable. Pebbles, which meet some of the other criteria, would not work well as money because they are widely available. Too much money in circulation increases prices (inflation, as discussed in Chapter 2). Governments control the scarcity of money by limiting the quantity of money produced.
- *Durability.* Any item used as money must be durable. A perishable item such as a banana becomes useless as money when it spoils. Even early societies used durable forms of money, such as metal coins and paper money, which lasted for a long time.
- *Portability.* Money must be easily moved around. Large or bulky items, such as boulders or heavy gold bars, cannot be transported easily from place to place.
- *Divisibility.* Money must be capable of being divided into smaller parts. Divisible forms of money help make possible transactions of all sizes and amounts.

Although the world's currencies look different, their basic characteristics and functions remain the same.

© WILLIAM WHITEHURST / CORBIS

Functions of Money

Using several types of goods as money would be confusing. Thus, societies develop a uniform money system to measure the value of goods and services. For money to be acceptable,

© CHUCK SAVAGE / CORBIS

At the end of the day, restaurant owners count the money their business has earned, demonstrating money's functions as a medium of exchange and a standard and store of value.

it must function as a medium of exchange, as a standard of value, and as a store of value.

As a *medium of exchange,* money makes transactions easier. Having a common form of payment in each country is much less complicated than having a barter system, wherein goods and services are exchanged for other goods and services. Money allows the exchange of products to be a simple process.

Money also serves as a *standard of value.* With a form of money whose value is accepted by all, goods and services can be priced in standard units. This makes it easy to measure the value of products and allows transactions to be recorded in consistent terms.

As a *store of value,* money is used to hold wealth. It retains its value over time. Someone who owns money can keep it for future use rather than exchange it today for other types of assets.

The U.S. Money Supply

The U.S. money supply is composed of currency, demand deposits, and time deposits. *Currency* is cash held in the form of coins and paper money. Other forms of currency are travelers checks, cashiers checks, and money orders. As of December 2002, the United States had about $677 billion of currency in circulation.[2]

Demand deposits consist of money kept in checking accounts that can be withdrawn by depositors on demand. Demand deposits include regular checking accounts as well as interest-bearing and other special types of checking accounts. **Time deposits** are deposits at a bank or other financial institution that pay interest but cannot be withdrawn on demand. Examples are savings accounts, money market deposit accounts, and certificates of deposit. Economists use two terms to report on and discuss trends in the U.S. monetary system: M1 and M2. **M1** (the *M* stands for money) is used to describe the total amount of readily available money in the system and includes currency and demand deposits. As of February 2003, the M1 monetary supply was $1.2 trillion. **M2** includes all M1 monies plus time deposits and other money that are not immediately accessible. In February 2003, the M2 monetary supply was $6.14 trillion.[3]

Credit cards, sometimes referred to as "plastic money," are used as a substitute for cash and checks. Credit cards are not money; they are a form of borrowing. When a bank issues a credit card to a consumer, it gives a short-term loan to the consumer by directly paying the seller for the consumer's purchases. The consumer pays the bank when it receives the monthly statement. Credit cards do not replace money; they simply defer payment.

demand deposits
Money kept in checking accounts that can be withdrawn by depositors on demand.

concept check

What is money, and what are its characteristics?

What are the main functions of money?

What are the three main components of the U.S. money supply? How do they relate to M1 and M2?

The Federal Reserve System

2 learning goal

Before the 20th century, there was very little government regulation of the U.S. financial or monetary systems. In 1907, however, several large banks failed, creating a public panic that led worried depositors to withdraw their money from other banks. Soon, many other banks had failed and the U.S. banking system was near collapse. The Panic of 1907 was so severe that Congress created the Federal Reserve System in 1913 to provide the nation with a more stable monetary and banking system.

The **Federal Reserve System** (commonly called the **Fed**) is the central bank of the United States. The Fed's primary mission is to oversee the nation's monetary and credit system and to support the ongoing operation of America's private-banking system. The Fed's actions help keep inflation under control,

time deposits
Deposits at a bank or other financial institution that pay interest but cannot be withdrawn on demand.

Exhibit 19.1 | Federal Reserve Districts and Banks

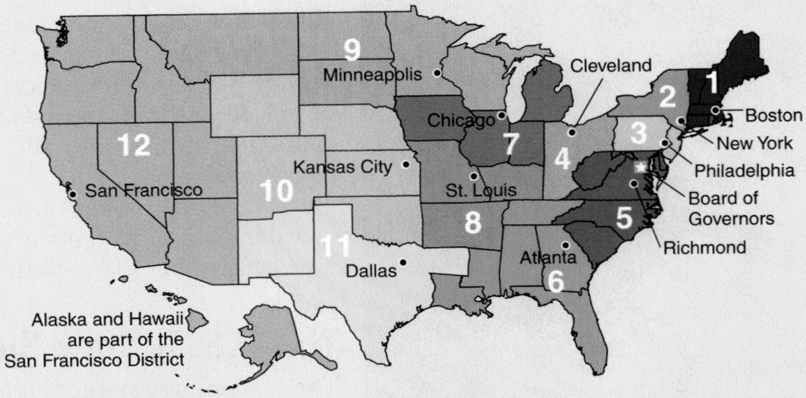

SOURCE: http://www.federalreserve.gov/otherfrb.htm

M1
The total amount of readily available money in the system, that includes currency and demand deposits.

affect the interest rates banks charge businesses and consumers, and ultimately stabilize the U.S. financial system. The Fed operates as an independent government entity. It derives its authority from Congress but its decisions do not have to be approved by the president, Congress, or any other government branch. However, Congress does periodically review the Fed's activities and the Fed must work within the economic framework established by the government.

The Fed consists of 12 district banks, each covering a specific geographic area. Exhibit 19.1 shows the 12 districts of the Federal Reserve. Each district has its own bank president who oversees operations within that district.

Alan Greenspan is the current Chairman of the Federal Reserve Board.

© MATT MENDELSOHN / CORBIS

Originally, the Federal Reserve System was created to control the money supply, act as a borrowing source for banks, hold the deposits of member banks, and supervise banking practices. Its activities have since been broadened, making it the most powerful financial institution in the United States. Today, four of the Federal Reserve System's major activities are carrying out monetary policy, setting rules on credit, distributing currency, and making check clearing easier.

Carrying Out Monetary Policy

The most important function of the Federal Reserve System is carrying out monetary policy. The Federal Open Market Committee (FOMC) is the Fed policy-making body that meets eight times a year to make monetary policy decisions. It uses its power to change the money supply in order to control inflation and interest rates, increase employment, and influence economic activity. Three tools used by the Federal Reserve System in managing the money supply are

Exhibit 19.2 The Federal Reserve System's Monetary Tools and Their Effects

Tool	Action	Effect on Money Supply	Effect on Interest Rates	Effect on Economic Activity
Open market operations	Buy government bonds	Increases	Lowers	Stimulates
	Sell government bonds	Decreases	Raises	Slows Down
Reserve requirements	Raise reserve requirements	Decreases	Raises	Slows Down
	Lower reserve requirements	Increases	Lowers	Stimulates
Discount rate	Raise discount rate	Decreases	Raises	Slows Down
	Lower discount rate	Increases	Lowers	Stimulates

M2
A term used by economists to describe the U.S. monetary supply. Includes all M1 monies plus time deposits and other money that are not immediately accessible.

Federal Reserve System (Fed)
The central bank of the United States; it consists of 12 district banks, each located in a major U.S. city.

open market operations
The purchase or sale of U.S. government bonds by the Federal Reserve to stimulate or slow down the economy.

reserve requirement
Requires banks that are members of the Federal Reserve System to hold some of their deposits in cash in their vaults or in an account at a district bank.

discount rate
The interest rate that the Federal Reserve charges its member banks.

open market operations, reserve requirements, and the discount rate. Exhibit 19.2 summarizes the short-term effects of these tools on the economy.

Open market operations—the tool most frequently used by the Federal Reserve—involve the purchase or sale of U.S. government bonds. The U.S. Treasury issues bonds to obtain the extra money needed to run the government (if taxes and other revenues aren't enough). In effect, Treasury bonds are long-term loans (five years or longer) made by businesses and individuals to the government. The Federal Reserve buys and sells these bonds for the Treasury. When the Federal Reserve buys bonds, it puts money into the economy. Banks have more money to lend so they reduce interest rates, and lower rates generally stimulate economic activity. The opposite occurs when the Federal Reserve sells government bonds.

Banks that are members of the Federal Reserve System must hold some of their deposits in cash in their vaults or in an account at a district bank. This **reserve requirement** ranges from 3 to 10 percent on different types of deposits. When the Federal Reserve raises the reserve requirement, banks must hold larger reserves and thus have less money to lend. As a result, interest rates rise and economic activity slows down. Lowering the reserve requirement increases loanable funds, causes banks to lower interest rates, and stimulates the economy; however, the Federal Reserve seldom changes reserve requirements.

The Federal Reserve is called "the banker's bank" because it lends money to banks that need it. The interest rate that the Federal Reserve charges its member banks is called the **discount rate.** When the discount rate is less than the cost of other sources of funds (such as certificates of deposit), commercial banks borrow from the Federal Reserve and then lend the funds at a higher rate to customers. The banks profit from the *spread,* or difference, between the rate they charge their customers and the rate paid to the Federal Reserve. Changes in the discount rate usually produce changes in the interest rate that banks charge their customers. The Federal Reserve raises the discount rate to slow down economic growth and lowers it to stimulate growth.

Setting Rules on Credit

Another activity of the Federal Reserve System is setting rules on credit. It controls the credit terms on some loans made by banks and other lending institutions. This

selective credit controls
The power of the Federal Reserve to control *consumer credit rules* and *margin requirements*.

power, called **selective credit controls,** includes consumer credit rules and margin requirements. *Consumer credit rules* establish the minimum down payments and maximum repayment periods for consumer loans. The Federal Reserve uses credit rules to slow or stimulate consumer credit purchases. *Margin requirements* specify the minimum amount of cash an investor must put up to buy securities, investment certificates issued by corporations or governments. The balance of the purchase cost can be financed through borrowing from a bank or brokerage firm. By lowering the margin requirement, the Federal Reserve stimulates securities trading. Raising the margin requirement slows the trading. Margin requirements are discussed further in Chapter 21.

Distributing Currency: Keeping the Cash Flowing

The Federal Reserve distributes to banks the coins minted and the paper money printed by the U.S. Treasury. Most paper money is in the form of Federal Reserve notes. Look at a dollar bill and you'll see "Federal Reserve Note" at the top. The large letter seal on the left indicates which Federal Reserve Bank issued it. For example, bills bearing a *D* seal are issued by the Federal Reserve Bank of Cleveland, and those with an *L* seal are issued by the San Francisco district bank.

Making Check Clearing Easier

Another important activity of the Federal Reserve is processing and clearing checks between financial institutions. When a check is cashed at a financial institution other than the one holding the account on which the check is drawn, the Federal Reserve's system lets that financial institution—even if distant from the institution holding the account on which the check is drawn—quickly convert the check into cash. Checks drawn on banks within the same Federal Reserve district are handled through the local Federal Reserve bank using a series of bookkeeping entries to transfer funds between the financial institutions. The process is more complex for checks processed between different Federal Reserve districts.

The time between when the check is written and when the funds are deducted from the check writer's account provides float. *Float* benefits the check writer by allowing it to retain the funds until the check clears; that is, the funds are actually withdrawn from its accounts. Businesses open accounts at banks throughout the country that are known to have long check-clearing times. By "playing the float,"

Coins for circulation in the American monetary supply are produced by the U.S. Mint, a division of the U.S. Treasury Department.

© PHOTODISC GREEN / GETTY IMAGES

firms can keep their funds invested for several extra days, thus earning more money. To reduce this practice, in 1988 the Fed established maximum check-clearing times.

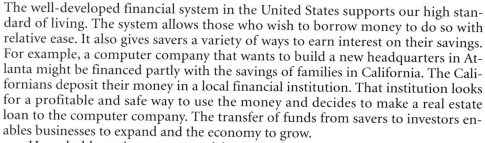

concept check

What are the four key functions of the Federal Reserve System?

What three tools does the Federal Reserve System use to manage the money supply, and how does each affect economic activity?

In 2002, about 40 billion checks were written in the United States, accounting for about 60 percent of all noncash retail payments. However, as credit cards and other types of electronic payments have become more popular, the use of checks is declining. Responding to this decline, the Federal Reserve scaled back its check-processing facilities in early 2003, closing five sites and cutting a net of 400 jobs.[4]

U.S. Financial Institutions

3 learning goal

financial intermediation
The process in which financial institutions act as intermediaries between the suppliers and demanders of funds.

The well-developed financial system in the United States supports our high standard of living. The system allows those who wish to borrow money to do so with relative ease. It also gives savers a variety of ways to earn interest on their savings. For example, a computer company that wants to build a new headquarters in Atlanta might be financed partly with the savings of families in California. The Californians deposit their money in a local financial institution. That institution looks for a profitable and safe way to use the money and decides to make a real estate loan to the computer company. The transfer of funds from savers to investors enables businesses to expand and the economy to grow.

Households are important participants in the U.S. financial system. Although many households borrow money to finance purchases, they supply funds to the financial system through their purchases and savings. Overall, businesses and governments are users of funds. They borrow more money than they save.

Sometimes those who have funds deal directly with those who want them. A wealthy realtor, for example, may lend money to a client to buy a house. Most often, financial institutions act as intermediaries—or go-betweens—between the suppliers and demanders of funds. The institutions accept savers' deposits and invest them in financial products (such as loans) that are expected to produce a return. This process, called **financial intermediation,** is shown in Exhibit 19.3. Households are shown as suppliers of funds, and businesses and governments are shown as demanders. However, a single household, business, or government can be either a supplier or a demander, depending on the circumstances.

Financial institutions are the heart of the financial system. They are a convenient vehicle for financial intermediation. They can be divided into two broad groups: depository institutions (those that accept deposits) and nondepository institutions (those that do not accept deposits).

Depository institutions like banks, thrifts, and credit unions provide savings and loan services for customers.

© DAVID YOUNG-WOLFF / PHOTO EDIT

Depository Financial Institutions

Not all depository financial institutions are alike. Most people call the place where they save their money a "bank." Some of those places are indeed banks, but other depository institutions include thrift institutions and credit unions.

Commercial Banks A **commercial bank** is a profit-oriented financial institution that accepts deposits, makes business and consumer loans, invests in government and corporate securities, and provides other financial services. There are about 7,933 commercial banks in the United States accounting for $6.9 trillion in loans and investments (a bank's

Exhibit 19.3 The Financial Intermediation Process*

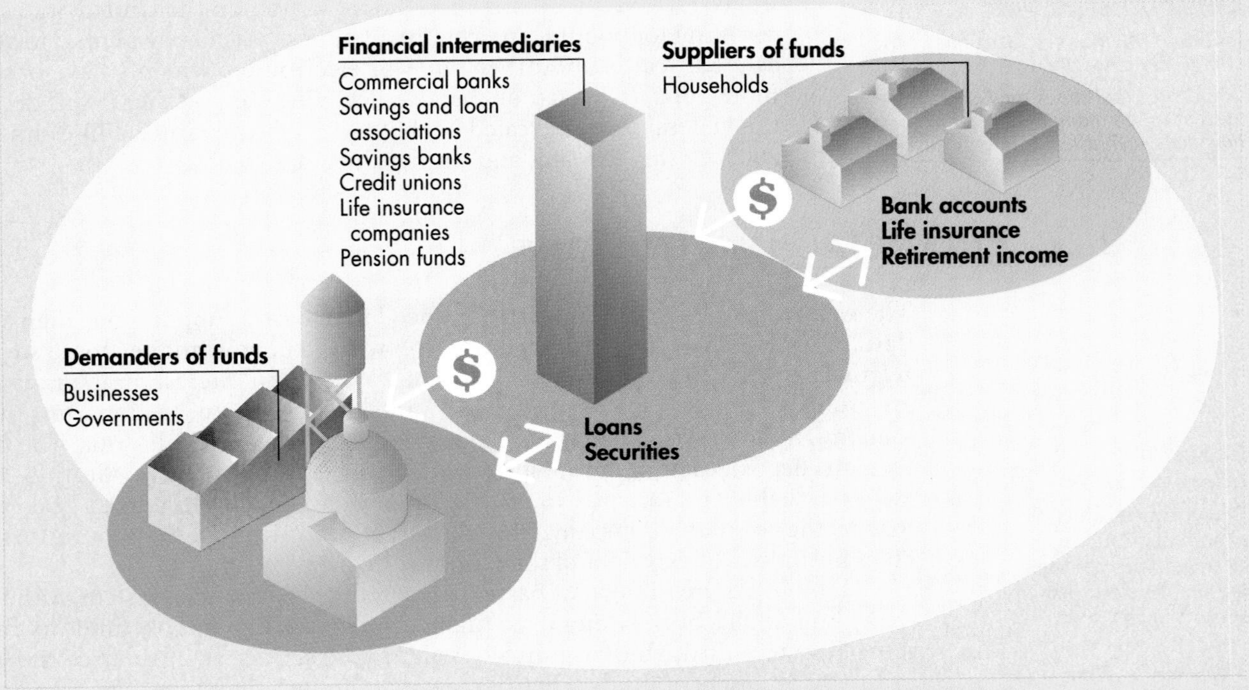

*Only the dominant suppliers and demanders are shown here. Clearly, a single household, business, or government can be either a supplier or demander, depending on circumstances.

assets) and $3.9 trillion in deposits.[5] Exhibit 19.4 lists the top 10 U.S.-owned commercial bank holding companies.

Customers' deposits are a commercial bank's main source of funds; the main use of those funds is loans. The difference between the interest earned on loans and the interest paid on deposits, plus fees earned from other financial services, pays the bank's costs and provides a profit. Commercial banks are cor-

Exhibit 19.4 Top U.S.-Owned Commercial Bank Holding Companies, Based on Assets, 2003

	Assets
1. Citigroup, Inc.	$1,031,568,000
2. J.P. Morgan Chase & Co.	741,759,000
3. Bank of America Corp.	660,007,000
4. Wells Fargo & Co.	334,250,000
5. Wachovia Corp.	333,880,000
6. Bank One Corp.	267,187,000
7. FleetBoston Financial Corp.	187,327,000
8. U.S. Bancorp	174,006,000
9. SunTrust Banks Inc.	112,422,026
10. National City Corp.	109,361,713

SOURCE: "Top U.S. Bank and Thrift Holding Companies by Assets," *American Banker* (February 10, 2003), http://www.americanbankder.com.

porations owned and operated by individuals or other corporations. To do business, they must get a **bank charter**—an operating license—from either the federal government or a state government. U.S. commercial banks can be either national or state banks.

National banks are chartered by the Comptroller of the Currency, who is part of the U.S. Treasury Department. These banks must belong to the Federal Reserve System and must carry insurance on their deposits from the Federal Deposit Insurance Corporation. *State banks* are chartered by the state in which they are based. Generally, state banks are smaller than national banks, are less closely regulated than national banks, and are not required to belong to the Federal Reserve System.

commercial banks
Profit-oriented financial institutions that accept deposits, make business and consumer loans, invest in government and corporate securities, and provide other financial services.

bank charter
An operating license issued to a bank by the federal government or a state government; required for a commercial bank to do business.

thrift institutions
Depository institutions formed specifically to encourage household saving and to make home mortgage loans.

credit unions
Not-for-profit, member-owned financial cooperatives.

THRIFT INSTITUTIONS

A **thrift institution** is a depository institution formed specifically to encourage household saving and to make home mortgage loans. Thrift institutions include *savings and loan associations (S&Ls)* and *savings banks.* S&Ls keep large percentages of their assets in home mortgages. Compared with S&Ls, savings banks focus less on mortgage loans and more on stock and bond investments. The 1,482 thrift institutions in the United States have about $1.3 trillion in assets and $851 billion in deposits.[6]

CREDIT UNIONS

A **credit union** is a not-for-profit, member-owned financial cooperative. Credit union members typically have something in common: they work for the same employer, belong to the same union or professional group, or attend the same church or school, for example. The credit union pools their assets, or savings, in order to make loans and offer other services to members. The not-for-profit status of credit unions makes them tax-exempt, so they can pay good interest rates on deposits and offer loans at favorable interest rates. Like banks, credit unions can have either a state or federal charter.

The approximately 11,000 credit unions in the United States have more than 76 million members.[7] U.S. credit unions currently have over $515 billion in assets, with the average credit union having $49 million in assets. However, although credit unions as a whole hold far less in assets than banks do, credit unions are growing faster than banks in terms of asset growth percentage rates. In 2001, for example, bank assets grew by only 5.3 percent, while the assets of credit unions grew 14.5 percent.[8] The five largest credit unions in the United States are shown in Exhibit 19.5.

Commercial banks, thrift institutions, and credit unions offer a wide range of financial services for businesses and consumers. Typical services offered by depository financial institutions are listed in Exhibit 19.6. Some financial institutions specialize in providing financial services to a particular type of customer, such as consumer banking services or business banking services. The "Focusing on Small

Exhibit 19.5 | Five Largest U.S. Credit Unions

1. Navy Federal Credit Union, Merrifield, Virginia
2. State Employees Credit Union, Raleigh, North Carolina
3. Pentagon Federal Credit Union, Alexandria, Virginia
4. Boeing Employees Credit Union, Tukwila, Washington
5. Golden 1 Credit Union, Sacramento, California

SOURCE: "Top 150 Credit Unions by Assets," *American Banker* (December 26, 2002), http://www.americanbanker.com.

Exhibit 19.6 | Services Offered by Depository Financial Institutions

Service	Description
Savings accounts	Pay interest on deposits
Checking accounts	Allow depositors to withdraw any amount of funds at any time up to the amount on deposit
Money market deposit accounts	Savings accounts on which the interest rate is set at market rates
Certificates of deposit (CDs)	Pay a higher interest rate than regular savings accounts, provided that the deposit remains for a specified period
Consumer loans	Loans to individuals to finance the purchase of a home, car, or other expensive items
Business loans	Loans to businesses and other organizations to finance their operations
Money transfer	Transfer of funds to other banks
Electronic funds transfer	Use of telephone lines and computers to conduct financial transactions
Automated teller machine (ATM)	Allows bank customers to make deposits and withdrawals from their accounts 24 hours a day
Debit cards	Allow customers to transfer money from their bank account directly to a merchant's account to pay for purchases
Smart card	Card that stores monetary value and can be used to buy goods and services instead of using cash, checks, and credit and debit cards
Online banking	Allows customers to conduct financial transactions via the Internet or through a dial-in line that operates with a bank's software

Business" box on page 617 describes how one bank targets the needs of small businesses in the local community. These services play an important role in helping to fuel the U.S. economy and foster individual financial security.

Nondepository Financial Institutions

Some financial institutions provide a few banking services but do not accept deposits. These nondepository financial institutions include insurance companies, pension funds, brokerage firms, and finance companies. They serve both individuals and businesses.

Insurance Companies Insurance companies are major suppliers of funds. Policyholders make payments (called *premiums*) to buy financial protection from the insurance company. Insurance companies invest the premiums in stocks, bonds, real estate, business loans, and real estate loans for large projects. The insurance industry is discussed in detail in the Appendix to Chapter 20, "Managing Risk and Insurance."

pension funds
Large pools of money set aside by corporations, unions, and governments for later use in paying retirement benefits to their employees or members.

Pension Funds Corporations, unions, and governments set aside large pools of money for later use in paying retirement benefits to their employees or members. These **pension funds** are managed by the employers or unions themselves or by out-

Focusing on Small Business

Front Range Bank Reaps Large Profits from Small Business

Dave Wade doesn't look like most bank presidents. He wears his shoulder-length hair pulled back in a ponytail and comes to work in cotton trousers and sweater vests instead of three-piece suits. Even his office is different. It's located right in the lobby of Front Range Bank's (**http://www.frontrangebank.com**) main branch so Wade can wave to customers as they pass by.

Wade founded the Lakewood, Colorado, bank in 1997. Previously, Wade had been president of Green Mountain Bank, another Colorado Bank. When U.S. Bancorp, one of the country's largest banking companies, purchased Green Mountain in the late 1990s, Wade left. He had no desire to work for a big bank. "After that deal, I didn't fit into the new profile," he says. "Big banks try to be everything to everyone, and we don't."

Wade has built Front Range into a three-branch community bank with $50 million in assets. The bank's primary focus is on serving the needs of mom-and-pop businesses located within three miles of its headquarters. Clients include businesses like small construction companies and delicatessens that need loans to buy equipment to keep their businesses going. Front Range customers have annual revenues of between $50,000 and $6 million.

Wade believes that Front Range is better able to understand its customers' needs and provide more personalized attention. However, he admits that Front Range may not provide as many services as a large bank. "If you're totally price-sensitive, we may not be the place for you. . . . But when someone calls us up, they get to talk to someone," he says. "If they call a big bank, they get an 800 number or are told to call Minneapolis. Rather than looking for ways to generate income, we look for solutions to customers' problems."

Front Range may face stiffer competition in the years ahead. Increasingly, large banks like Wells Fargo, U.S. Bancorp, and Bank of America are recognizing that small businesses tend to build broad and deep relationships with their financial institutions that are very profitable. As a result, big banking firms are refocusing their efforts on local marketing campaigns aimed at capturing the business of small business.

CRITICAL THINKING QUESTIONS

1. If you were a small-business owner, would you prefer to do your banking with a bank like Front Range or a larger, more comprehensive bank? Explain why.
2. How could a large out-of-state bank provide the same level of customer service and customer knowledge to a small business as a local bank like Front Range?

SOURCES: Paula Moore, "Uniquely Independent," *Denver Business Journal* (March 8, 2002), downloaded from http://denver.bizjournals.com; Charles B. Wendel, "Small Businesses Are a Big Deal, But Banks Are Giving Short Shrift," *American Banker* (February 7, 2003), downloaded from http://www.americanbanker.com.

side managers, such as life insurance firms, commercial banks, and private investment firms. Pension plan members receive a specified monthly payment when they reach a given age. After setting aside enough money to pay near-term benefits, pension funds invest the rest in business loans, stock, bonds, or real estate. They often invest large sums in the stock of the employer. U.S. pension fund assets total more than $5 trillion.

Brokerage Firms A *brokerage firm* buys and sells securities (stocks and bonds) for its clients and gives them related advice. Many brokerage firms offer some banking services. They may offer clients a combined checking and savings account with a high interest rate and also make loans, backed by securities, to them. Chapter 21 explains the activities of brokerage firms in more detail.

Finance Companies A *finance company* makes short-term loans for which the borrower puts up tangible assets (such as an automobile, inventory, machinery, or property) as security. Finance companies often make loans to individuals or businesses that cannot get credit elsewhere. To compensate for the extra risk, finance companies usually charge higher interest rates than banks do. *Consumer finance companies* make loans to individuals. Beneficial Corp. and Household International, which recently merged, are two of the largest consumer finance companies. Together, they have more than 30 million customers. Promising new businesses with no track record and firms that can't get more credit from a bank often obtain loans from *commercial finance companies.* AT&T Capital Business Finance, GE Capital Small Business Finance, and The Money Store Commercial Lending are examples of commercial finance companies.

concept check

What is the financial intermediation process?

Differentiate between the three types of depository financial institutions and the services they offer.

What are the four main types of nondepository financial institution?

Insuring Bank Deposits

4 learning goal

The U.S. banking system worked fairly well from the establishment of the Federal Reserve System in 1913 until the 1929 stock market crash and the Great Depression that followed. Business failures caused by these events resulted in major cash shortages as people rushed to withdraw their money from banks. Many cash-starved banks failed because the Federal Reserve did not, as expected, lend money to them. The government's efforts to prevent bank failures were ineffective. In the next two years, 5,000 banks—about 20 percent of the total number—failed.

President Franklin D. Roosevelt made strengthening the banking system his first priority. After taking office in 1933, Roosevelt declared a bank holiday, closing all banks for a week so he could take corrective actions. Congress passed the Banking Act of 1933, which gave the Federal Reserve System power to regulate banks and reform the banking system. The act's most important provision was the creation of the **Federal Deposit Insurance Corporation (FDIC)** to insure deposits in commercial banks. The 1933 act also gave the Federal Reserve authority to set reserve requirements, ban interest on demand deposits, regulate the interest rates on time deposits, and prohibit banks from investing in specified types of securities. In 1934 the Federal Savings and Loan Insurance Corporation (FSLIC) was formed to insure deposits at S&Ls. When the FSLIC went bankrupt in the 1980s, the FDIC took responsibility for administering the fund that insures deposits at thrift institutions. Today, the major deposit insurance funds include the following:

Federal Deposit Insurance Corporation (FDIC)
An independent, quasi-public corporation backed by the full faith and credit of the U.S. government that insures deposits in commercial banks and thrift institutions for up to a ceiling of $100,000 per account.

- *The Bank Insurance Fund (BIF).* Administered by the FDIC, this fund provides deposit insurance to commercial banks.
- *The Savings Association Insurance Fund (SAIF).* Administered by the FDIC, this fund provides deposit insurance to thrift institutions.
- *The National Credit Union Share Insurance Fund.* Administered by the National Credit Union Administration, this fund provides deposit insurance to credit unions.

Role of the FDIC

The FDIC is an independent, quasi-public corporation backed by the full faith and credit of the U.S. government. It insures about 314 million deposit accounts in commercial banks and 79 million accounts in thrift institutions against loss if the financial institution fails. The FDIC insures all member banks in the Federal Reserve System. The ceiling on insured deposits is $100,000 per account. Each insured bank pays the insurance premiums, which are a fixed percentage of the bank's domestic deposits. The FDIC charged a flat rate for deposit insurance until 1993. Then, due to the large number of bank and thrift failures during the 1980s and early 1990s, it implemented a risk-based premium system that bases each bank's premium on the risk the bank poses to the insurance fund. Some experts argue that certain banks take too much risk because they view deposit insurance as a safety net for their depositors—a view many believe contributed to earlier bank failures.

Enforcement by the FDIC

To ensure that banks operate fairly and profitably, the FDIC sets guidelines for banks and then reviews the financial records and management practices of member banks at least once a year. Bank examiners perform these reviews during unannounced visits. Bank examiners rate banks on their compliance with banking regulations. For example, banks must comply with the Equal Credit

Opportunity Act, which states that a bank cannot refuse to lend money to people because of their color, religion, or national origin. Examiners also rate a bank's overall financial condition. They focus on loan quality, management practices, earnings, liquidity, and whether the bank has enough capital (equity) to safely support its activities.

When bank examiners conclude that a bank has serious financial problems, the FDIC can take several actions. It can lend money to the bank, recommend that the bank merge with a stronger bank, require the bank to use new management practices or replace its managers, buy loans from the bank, or provide extra equity capital to the bank. The FDIC may even cover all deposits at a troubled bank, including those over $100,000, to restore the public's confidence in the financial system.

concept check

What is the FDIC, and what are its responsibilities?

What are the major deposit insurance funds?

What can the FDIC do to help financially troubled banks?

International Banking

5 learning goal

The financial marketplace spans the globe, with money routinely flowing across international borders. Multinational corporations need many special banking services, such as foreign-currency exchange and funding for overseas investments. U.S. banks play an important role in global business by providing loans to foreign governments and businesses. They also offer trade-related services. For example, they provide global cash management services that help firms manage their cash flows, improve their payment efficiency, and reduce their exposure to operational risks. Even consumers in other nations have a need for banking services that banks in their countries don't provide. Therefore, large banks often look beyond their national borders for profitable banking opportunities.

Many U.S. banks have expanded into overseas markets by opening offices in Europe, Latin America, and Asia. They often provide better customer service than local banks and have access to more sources of funding. Citibank, for example, was the first bank to offer banking-by-phone and 24-hour-a-day ATM service in Japan. International banking is a two-way street, however. Several international banks have made headway into the American consumer and business banking markets in recent years, including Germany's Deutsche Bank, Holland's ABN

Many U.S. financial institutions, including Citibank, have expanded beyond American borders. A bright Citibank sign is seen in the Shibuya district in Tokyo, Japan.

© AP / WIDE WORLD PHOTOS

Exhibit 19.7 | Seven Largest Foreign-Owned U.S. Banks

	Foreign holding company	Assets of U.S. Bank (in thousands)
1. HSBC Bank USA Buffalo, NY	HSBC Holdings PLC London, UK	$86,956,401
2. Citizens Bank Providence, RI	Royal Bank of Scotland Edinburgh, Scotland	59,371,401
3. LaSalle Bank Chicago, IL	ABN Amro Amsterdam, Holland	59,268,521
4. Union Bank of California San Francisco, CA	Mitsubishi Tokyo Financial Group Tokyo, Japan	37,028,539
5. Deutsche Bank New York, NY	Deutsche Bank Frankfurt, Germany	41,648,815
6. Harris Bancorp Chicago, IL	Bank of Montreal Montreal, Canada	37,730,710
7. Allfirst Bank Baltimore, MD	Allied Irish Banks Ltd. Dublin, Ireland	17,409,324

SOURCE: "U.S. Banks Owned by Foreign Holding Companies," *American Banker* (January 24, 2003), downloaded from http://www.americanbanker.com.

Amro, Great Britain's HSBC, and the Canadian Bank of Montreal.[9] Exhibit 19.7 lists the seven largest U.S. banks that are owned by foreign companies.

For U.S. banks, expanding internationally can be difficult. Banks in other nations are often subject to fewer regulations than U.S. banks, making it easier for them to undercut American banks on the pricing of loans and services. Some governments also protect their banks against foreign competition. For example, Citigroup has been trying to gain a larger share of the lucrative Chinese banking market but has been stymied by government red tape. The Chinese government limits the amount of deposits that foreign banks can accept from customers and imposes high fees on foreign banks. It also controls foreign-bank deposit and loan interest rates, limiting their ability to compete with government-owned Chinese banks.[10]

Political and economic uncertainty in other countries can also make international banking a high-risk venture. In the late 1990s, for example, Asian banks underwrote loans to finance highly speculative real estate ventures and corporate expansions that fueled booming economies in several Pacific Rim countries, which attracted many foreign investors. The bank loans and foreign investments made the balance sheets of the Asian banks and their customers look better than they actually were, which encouraged U.S., German, French, and other European banks to make billions of dollars worth of loans to Thailand, Indonesia, Malaysia, and Korea. When investors started taking their money out of the Asian banks, the banks' assets plummeted, forcing currency devaluations. The situation severely injured the economies of several Asian countries, resulting in high inflation and deep debt. Lacking capital, Asian banks could not get loans to conduct business, and companies couldn't get loans to finance the production and export of their products. The crisis also hurt many foreign banks, including U.S. banks such as Bank of America and Chase Manhattan. As the "Expanding Around the Globe" box discusses, FleetBoston Financial Corp. has recently faced a similar situation in Latin America and, as a result, has had to make some difficult decisions regarding its international banking operations.

concept check

What is the role of U.S. banks in international banking?

What challenges do U.S. banks face in foreign markets?

Expanding Around the Globe

FleetBoston Crashes in Argentina

For many U.S. banks, Argentina seemed like a sure bet in the late 1990s. American companies were investing heavily in Argentina, and they needed banking services. At the time, Argentina was also the wealthiest nation in Latin America, with a large middle class forming a growing market for mortgages, credit cards, and asset management services. The government of Argentina was also looking for foreign banks to underwrite its debt, which promised to pay high returns.

FleetBoston found Argentina particularly attractive. By 1999, the Boston-based bank was Argentina's third largest private-sector bank with 131 branches and 4,000 employees. In addition to corporate and government loans, the bank had the largest portfolio of consumer loans of any U.S. bank operating in Argentina. Thirteen percent of FleetBoston's assets and 4 percent of its total earnings came from its operations in Argentina.

Then, danger bells sounded. Government debt reached historic highs in 2000, just as Argentina's economy entered a severe recession. Unemployment began to rise. Some U.S. banks, like Bank of America, pulled out of Argentina, but FleetBoston believed Argentina's problems were temporary. "We're still very comfortable with our position in Argentina," a company spokesperson said in late 2000.

The situation went from bad to worse in 2001. Unemployment rose to 30 percent and the value of Argentine money fell 70 percent. Consumers stopped paying back loans. Mired in political turmoil, the government announced it was defaulting on its loans as well.

FleetBoston was hit hard. By the end of 2002, it had been forced to write off $2.3 billion in losses from its Argentina operations, including $600 million in loans to the Argentinian government. As a direct result, FleetBoston's stock prices dropped dramatically and have yet to recover.

Although FleetBoston has now stopped making new loans in Argentina, the bank remains somewhat optimistic about the country's future. "I think we're close to seeing stability there," says Charles Gifford, FleetBoston's CEO. "The overwhelming pain we have taken in the past is behind us."

Many, however, believe FleetBoston should abandon Argentina entirely. "Argentina is now the sick man of Latin America and I think FleetBoston really has to think through what they want to do there," says one financial industry analyst.

CRITICAL THINKING QUESTIONS

1. Discuss the factors that made Argentina an attractive foreign market for FleetBoston. Suggest ways FleetBoston could have avoided or minimized some of the problems it encountered in Argentina before making the decision to enter this market.
2. Why do you think FleetBoston stayed in Argentina even when there were warning signs that its economy was headed for trouble?
3. Do you think FleetBoston should continue to operate in Argentina or should it pull out of the country entirely? Why?

SOURCES: Karen Krebsbach, "Crying for Argentina: Dark Lessons from the Southern Hemisphere," *US Banker* (October 1, 2002); Laura Mandaro, "U.S. Banks Shore Up Defenses in Argentina, Brazil," *American Banker* (August 23, 2002); and Alissa Schmelkin, "U.S. Bank Exposure to Argentina Minimized," *American Banker* (October 31, 2001); all downloaded from http://www.americanbanker.com.

Trends in Financial Institutions

6 learning goal

Once a highly regulated industry offering limited services, the financial institutions industry continues to change. A dramatic increase in mergers and acquisitions throughout the industry in the past decade has helped to change the structure of the industry, sometimes creating powerful mega-financial institutions. Industry deregulation has opened the door for all kinds of financial institutions to expand into new markets and offer both consumers and businesses a broader array of products and services. Technology is also changing the way banks and other financial institutions deliver their services to customers.

The Growth of the Mega-Financial Institution

Throughout the 1990s, banks and other financial institutions merged at an unprecedented pace. In 1975, there were more than 19,000 depository institutions; by the end of 1999, there were less than 9,000. Although the pace of mergers and

Exhibit 19.8 Top Five Bank and Thrift Mergers 2002

Buyer	Seller	Price (in thousands)
1. Citigroup New York	Golden State Banc Corp. San Francisco	$5,227,237
2. Washington Mutual Seattle	Dime Bancorp New York	4,777,522
3. BNP Parisbas Paris	United California Bank Los Angeles	2,400,000
4. BB&T Corp Winston-Salem, NC	AREA Bancshares Corp Owensboro, KY	511,400
5. Marshall & Ilsley Corp. Milwaukee	Mississippi Valley BancShares St. Louis	501,942

SOURCE: "Largest U.S. Financial Institution Mergers, 2002," *American Banker Online,* downloaded from http://www.americanbanker.com.

acquisitions within the industry slowed somewhat in the first three years of this century, financial institutions continue to look at mergers as a way to expand. Exhibit 19.8 shows the top five thrift mergers in 2002.

One major effect of this merger and acquisition activity has been a notable change in the structure of the financial-services industry: greater consolidation. As already mentioned, there are now far fewer banks than there were just 30 years ago. Many banks in the past decade also used mergers and acquisitions as a way to expand across state lines. More than half of bank mergers in the 1990s occurred between banks in different states. As a result, 40 percent of all bank deposits are now controlled by banks headquartered in a different state.[11]

Mergers and acquisitions have also led to the creation of *larger* financial institutions, or mega-banks. Financial-services powerhouses, these banks operate in markets across the country and control a large share of domestic deposits and lending activity. In fact, eight mega-banking companies now hold 30 percent of domestic banking deposits, four times as much as at the beginning of 1990.[12]

Proponents of the trend toward bank consolidation believe that it strengthens the U.S. banking system. They contend that having fewer but larger financial institutions helps keep costs low and improves operating efficiency, which translates into lower costs and greater convenience for customers. They also note that larger financial institutions have better resources to meet the lending requirements of both consumers and businesses, which can help bolster the economy. Opponents of consolidation fear that it concentrates power in a few large financial institutions, giving customers less choice. They say that larger, national banks provide less personal service and knowledge of local economies than do local banks. "During the wave of mergers, all the people who went to small banks for personalized services suddenly became clients of the larger banks that had bought their institutions," notes one banking executive. "Those people were used to banks that had a more intimate relationship with customers, but you don't find that in larger banks, which take more of a mass-marketing approach."[13]

However, in an interesting countertrend to consolidation, the number of small banks has actually been increasing during recent years. According to the Independent Bankers Association of America, there's been an increase in the number of new bank charters for small banks in the past two years because many people and businesses prefer their personal service and attention to that offered by the mega-banks.

The Modernization of Financial Services: Integrating Banking, Brokerage, and Insurance Services

Depository institutions now have the ability to provide a broader array of financial services and products to consumers and businesses, thanks to the Gramm-Leach-Bliley Act of 1999, also known as the Financial Services Modernization Act. The act repealed the Glass-Steagall Act of 1933, which had prohibited banks from selling securities and insurance. Glass-Steagall was passed after the 1929 stock market crash when federal investigators determined that the banking industry's practice of buying stock in their customers' firms had contributed to the bank failures that followed the stock market crash.

In 1999, banks argued that the law was outdated and put them at a disadvantage in competing with security and investment firms that were not bound by the same laws that regulated banks. Gramm-Leach-Bliley gave expanded powers to financial institutions that apply for status as a financial holding company with the federal government. They can sell securities and insurance products, underwrite corporate and municipal bonds, offer expanded merchant banking activities, and offer other, complementary financial services.

The act has resulted in a wave of acquisitions and mergers between commercial banks and brokerage and insurance firms. For example, in early 2003, Wachovia Bank merged its brokerage division with the brokerage unit of Prudential Financial, a transaction that created the nation's third-largest brokerage firm.[14] As financial services continue to be integrated in the next few years, it is expected that both consumers and businesses will benefit by being able to have all of their financial-service needs met by one financial intermediary rather than using separate firms for their banking, investment, and insurance needs.

The act also allowed firms other than those traditionally providing banking services to enter the banking industry. Brokerage and insurance firms have moved to add banking services to their product line. E*Trade, an online brokerage firm, for example, now offers credit cards and operates an extensive ATM network for its customers. The company is also looking at cross-selling mortgages to its customer base.[15] Even nonfinancial institutions like retailers Nordstrom and Wal-Mart have investigated the possibility of obtaining bank charters and providing financial services.

The Gramm-Leach-Bliley Act also addressed important consumer privacy issues that have consequences beyond the banking industry. It requires financial institutions to annually notify consumers about their practices for handling personal information and sharing that information with third parties, and to offer consumers a way to opt out of having that information shared with third parties. However, the act specifies that its privacy provisions apply not just to banks but also to any business that is "significantly involved in financial activities." This means that these provisions also apply to businesses like real estate appraisers, insurance companies, brokers, pension funds, automobile-leasing companies, travel agencies, and retailers who issue their own credit cards, among others.

Delivering Financial Services with "Clicks and Bricks"

Today's bank customers are demanding greater convenience from their financial institutions. No longer content with limited "banker's hours," customers expect to be able to access to their accounts 24 hours a day, seven days a week. They also expect

Making Ethical Choices

xtra! http://gitmanxtra.swlearning.com

"PREYING" FOR LOANS

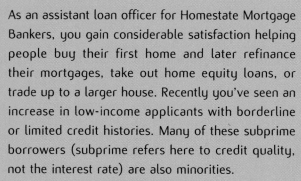

As an assistant loan officer for Homestate Mortgage Bankers, you gain considerable satisfaction helping people buy their first home and later refinance their mortgages, take out home equity loans, or trade up to a larger house. Recently you've seen an increase in low-income applicants with borderline or limited credit histories. Many of these subprime borrowers (subprime refers here to credit quality, not the interest rate) are also minorities.

In a recent meeting of lending officers, the senior vice president in charge of your area said that he would like the bank to do more with subprime borrowers. While he mentioned that it represents a way to build up Homestate's loan portfolio, he placed the emphasis on the much greater profitability from subprime lending. He encouraged loan officers to look for ways to charge higher interest rates, loan fees, and servicing costs on new loans, refinance existing loans, and push related products like credit life insurance. The higher costs are easily justified because of the greater credit risk the company is taking. He points out that your commissions will be higher as well.

However, there is a fine line between subprime lending with justifiably higher costs and what could be considered "predatory lending" that takes advantage of these less sophisticated borrowers. This troubles you. On the one hand, subprime loans help consumers with marginal credit who could not otherwise borrow. They probably carry additional risk and should be priced higher. However, you believe that the costs of many of Homestate's subprime loans aren't tied to the risk but based on how much profit the company can squeeze from the borrower.

ETHICAL DILEMMA

Should you make subprime loans, knowing that to get them approved you will have to price them with high fees that may not be totally justified?

SOURCES: "CBA Subprime Lending Issues," *Consumer Banking Association*, downloaded June 18, 2003, from http://www.cbanet.org/issues/subprime_lending/subprime_lending.html; Gordon Matthews, "Does Everyone Have the Right to Credit?" *US Banker* (April 2001), downloaded from http://www.findarticles.com; "Subprime Lending," Fair Housing and Equal Opportunity, Department of Housing and Urban Development, downloaded June 18, 2003, from http://www.hud.gov/offices/fheo/lending/subprime.cfm.

that financial institutions will provide a variety of access methods, from traditional branch offices to ATMs to the Internet.

Technology is helping financial institutions provide convenient access in new ways. The Internet lets consumers and businesses access account information with a few clicks of a mouse. About 26 million consumers—approximately 20 percent of all bank customers—now do at least some of their banking online, more than triple the number just three years ago.[16] Verifying account balances and transferring funds between accounts are the two most frequent uses of online banking services.[17] Other automated services, such as ATMs and computerized telephone systems, allow customers to access their accounts and complete various transactions electronically at any time of day or night as well.

However, most financial institutions have found that delivering services electronically isn't enough to satisfy customers. Although the number of brick-and-mortar branches dropped in the last decade, the trend has been slowly reversing as banks find customers still appreciate the ability to interact with their financial institution in the one-to-one personal environment that a branch provides. "The concept check

What are the advantages and disadvantages of bank consolidation?

What impact has the Financial Services Modernization Act had on the banking industry?

How is technology changing the way financial institutions deliver their services to customers?

branch has been rediscovered in the last few years," says Steve Davidson, an economist with America's Community Bankers, a banking trade organization. "Branches offer a unique communication and selling opportunity. The typical consumer wants to have a large network of both electronic access choices and branch locations to choose from."[18]

Great Ideas to Use Now

It's been said that money makes the world go round, and this is especially true when it comes to the world of business. Understanding how money functions and the role the U.S. monetary system plays in our economy is vital for every businessperson. In times of economic uncertainty, the actions of the Federal Reserve Board can directly affect the stability of the nation's economy, the availability of funds for loans, the interest rates paid by both consumers and businesses, and the strength of the U.S. banking system. The basic information about the Federal Reserve System and U.S. monetary system presented in this chapter can help you better understand economic policies that will directly affect your wallet.

As we've discussed throughout this chapter, the financial institution where you do your banking today is very different from the one where your parents did their banking 30 years ago. Likewise, financial institutions in 2030 will undoubtedly bear little resemblance to today's banks, thrifts, and credit unions. Deregulation, mergers, and changes in the structure of the banking industry have already given consumers and businesses more choice about where they buy financial services. Technologies like the Internet, debit cards, automated phone service, and ATMs make access immediate and constant.

However, new financial products and services mean consumers have many more choices. Not only can you choose how to access your account, you can also choose the level of relationship you want to have with your financial institution. Do you want to have a personal relationship with a small community bank that may not offer as broad an array of financial services or would a large national bank better serve your personal and business banking and financial-services needs?

Both consumers and businesses need to stay informed about the choices and options available. Smart consumers and businesses comparison-shop for financial services, evaluating not only an institution's convenience but also the fees, product range, and service levels of competitive financial institutions. Some may find that one financial institution can serve all or most of their financial service needs, including deposit and checking accounts, investment services, insurance, and lending. Others may decide that it makes sense to use different types of financial institutions for different needs. For example, they may decide to use a credit union for low-cost personal checking and savings accounts; a commercial bank for their brokerage, insurance, and small-business banking; and a savings and loan for their home mortgage.

Finding Financing for Small Businesses

A special concern of entrepreneurs and small businesses is obtaining credit. They often find they have a more difficult time obtaining funding than do large firms that have proven track records, larger asset bases, and established relationships with financial institutions. The Small Business Administration (SBA) (**http://www.sba.gov**) underwrites some loans written by financial institutions to small businesses but there are specific qualifications they must meet. In addition to large commercial banks, good sources of funding for small businesses

Try It Now

1. **Is it really free?** How much is your checking account really costing you? Maybe more than you think. Even "free" checking accounts aren't always a good deal when you add up extra costs such as ATM fees, lost interest, bounced-check charges, and other hidden expenses. Take a closer look at your current checking account and then comparison shop to see if you could be getting a better deal elsewhere. Here's how:
   a. Ask yourself how you really use your checking account. What's the average balance you keep in your account? How many checks do you write in a typical month? What time of day do you do most of your banking and where do you prefer to do it?
   b. Zero in on the real cost of your current checking account. Once you know how you use your checking account, you can get a clearer idea of its true cost—beyond just the monthly account fee. Do you write more checks per month than allowed by your "free" account? What is the cost of each check? How many times do you use the ATM instead of a branch? How much does it cost each time? Do you pay extra for overdraft protection? What does your bank charge for bounced checks? Add in any bonuses you receive with your checking account as well. For example, does your bank waive your credit card's annual fee for keeping your checking account with them?
   c. Comparison shop. Call or visit several banks and weigh prices and services. On the Internet, BankRate.com (**http://www.bankrate.com**) lets you digitally compare bank products. Could you pay lower fees elsewhere? Could you earn interest on your checking account at a credit union? Would you be better off paying a monthly fee with unlimited check-writing privileges? Crunch the numbers to find the best deal.
2. **Banking business.** Interview a local small-business owner about his or her relationship with a bank. What services does the bank provide for the owner? Why did the owner choose that particular bank over other banks?

include local community banks, which may understand local market conditions better and be eager to work with smaller firms. Credit unions are also now able to offer some types of SBA loans to small businesses.

When researching banks, entrepreneurs and small-business owners need to look at banks as more than just lending institutions. They should think in terms of establishing an ongoing relationship with a financial institution. They also need to look at the availability of other banking services and products to help improve their efficiency and profitability. They should consider the type of relationship they would like to have with their banker, the kinds of credit they'll need now and in the future, and the terms of payment they can realistically afford. When applying for small-business credit, the best way to improve your chances of getting a business loan or line of credit is to give the bank information that will help it understand the strengths of your business. Prospective bankers are impressed by well-prepared presentations that include your business plan, financial history, and a management team that's committed to helping you achieve your business goals.

Customer Satisfaction and Quality

Succeeding in the competitive financial-services industry requires more than offering the lowest interest rates on loans or paying the highest savings dividends; it requires a dedicated commitment to customer service excellence. The financial-services industry provides many lessons for all service organizations about how to achieve service quality and customer satisfaction.

Financial institutions have learned, for instance, that service quality requires an intimate knowledge of customer needs and desires. Consider the experience of Capital One Financial Corp. The credit-card issuer has used state-of-the-art computer technology to build detailed databases of all of its customers. When a customer calls the company, Capital One's high-speed computers automatically identify who is calling, predict the reason for the call, and provide the customer service representative with a detailed profile of the customer's needs—all before the phone is even answered.[19]

Banks and other financial institutions have also learned the importance of convenience in providing service quality. Although banks hoped that online banking would let them eliminate or greatly reduce the number of costly physical branch offices they operated, many quickly learned that customers prefer having a variety of service options.

Commerce Bancorp in Cherry Hill, New Jersey, has found that basic customer service principles are key to competing in a tough market. "Commerce's promise to customers is, 'I'm going to make it easy, and even a little enjoyable for you to give me your money, and for you to get it back,'" says one industry analyst. Commerce has seen 40 percent growth rates in the past three years.[20]

Looking Ahead at Citigroup

With profits in 2002 topping $15 billion, Citigroup has cash to spend, and Chairman Sandy Weill continues to look for acquisition targets in the financial-services industry. His latest focus: increasing Citigroup's share of the U.S. consumer banking market, especially in California, Florida, Illinois, and New York.

Weill has more than expansion on his mind these days, however. Citigroup found itself in the negative spotlight when news broke that the company had loaned millions to both Enron and WorldCom. When reports surfaced that investigators were probing to discover whether Citigroup had helped either firm dupe investors, Citigroup's stock tumbled and Citigroup faced regulatory problems with the Securities and Exchange Commission. Responding to the crisis, Weill instituted a number of management and internal operating changes.

More challenges may lie ahead. The world's economy is uncertain, which may limit Citigroup's growth. The political situation in Brazil, where Citigroup has invested heavily, is also a concern. "It's a tough, tough economic environment," Weill admits. Still, with a huge network of assets and a global reach, Citigroup should be positioned to ride out the challenge.[21]

Summary of Learning Goals

1

What is money, what are its characteristics and functions, and what are the three parts of the U.S. money supply?

Money is anything accepted as payment for goods and services. For money to be a suitable means of exchange, it should be scarce, durable, portable, and divisible. Money functions as a medium of exchange, a standard of value, and a store of value. The U.S. money supply consists of currency (coins and paper money), demand deposits (checking accounts), and time deposits (interest-bearing deposits that cannot be withdrawn on demand).

2 **How does the Federal Reserve manage the money supply?**

The Federal Reserve System (the Fed) is an independent government agency that performs four main functions: carrying out monetary policy, setting rules on credit, distributing currency, and making check clearing easier. The three tools it uses in managing the money supply are open market operations, reserve requirements, and the discount rate.

3 **What are the key financial institutions, and what role do they play in the process of financial intermediation?**

Financial institutions can be divided into two main groups: depository institutions and nondepository institutions. Depository institutions include commercial banks, thrift institutions, and credit unions. Nondepository institutions include insurance companies, pension funds, brokerage firms, and finance companies. Financial institutions ease the transfer of funds between suppliers and demanders.

4 **How does the Federal Deposit Insurance Corporation (FDIC) protect depositors' funds?**

The Federal Deposit Insurance Corporation insures deposits in commercial banks through the Bank Insurance Fund and deposits in thrift institutions through the Savings Association Insurance Fund. Deposits in credit unions are insured by the National Credit Union Share Insurance Fund, which is administered by the National Credit Union Administration. The FDIC sets banking policies and practices and reviews banks annually to ensure that they operate fairly and profitably.

5 **What role do U.S. banks play in the international marketplace?**

U.S. banks provide loans and trade-related services to foreign governments and businesses. They also offer specialized services such as cash management and foreign-currency exchange.

6 **What trends are reshaping the financial institutions?**

Mergers and acquisitions have consolidated the financial institutions industry, helping banks to improve their operating efficiency, reduce costs, and extend their geographic reach. Although powerful mega-banks now control much of the banking industry, many new, smaller community banks are being chartered. All kinds of financial institutions are expanding into new markets and offering a broader array of products and services thanks to the Financial Services Modernization Act. Technology is also changing the way banks and other financial institutions deliver their services to customers.

Preparing for Tomorrow's Workplace

1. You are starting a small business selling collectible books over the Internet and need to establish a business banking account that will provide the following services: business checking, credit-card processing, business savings account, and the possibility of establishing a business line of credit. Call or visit at least three local banks and gather information about their business banking services, including data about fees, service options, and other features of interest to entrepreneurs. Write a short summary of each bank's offerings and benefits and make a recommendation about which bank you would choose for your new business. Explain.

KEY TERMS

bank charter 615
commercial banks 615
credit unions 615
demand deposits 609
discount rate 611
Federal Deposit Insurance Corporation (FDIC) 618
Federal Reserve System (Fed) 611
financial intermediation 613
M1 610
M2 611
money 608
open market operations 611
pension funds 616
reserve requirement 611
selective credit controls 612
thrift institutions 615
time deposits 609

2. Do you agree or disagree with the argument that consolidation is good for the U.S. banking industry? How does your argument affect consumers? Small-business owners? Large businesses? Defend your answers with specific examples if possible.
3. If you follow business news reports, you've undoubtedly heard mention of the Fed raising or lowering interest rates. What exactly does this mean? Explain how the Fed's decision to raise and lower its discount rate might affect (a) a large manufacturer of household appliances, (b) a midsize software firm, (c) a small restaurant, (d) a family hoping to purchase their first home, and (e) a college student.
4. Research the banking system of another country and write a report on your findings. If possible, try to answer these questions: Is there a central banking system similar to the U.S. Federal Reserve system in place? Which government agency or department controls it and how does it operate? How stable is the country's central banking system? How does it compare in structure and operation to the Federal Reserve System? How much control does the government have over banks operating in the country? Are there any barriers to entry specifically facing foreign banks? What would this mean to a foreign business attempting to do business in this country?
5. A growing number of banks use databases to identify profitable and unprofitable customers. Bankers say they lose money—about $500 a year—on unprofitable customers who typically keep less than $1,000 in their checking and savings accounts, frequently call the bank to check on their accounts, and often visit the bank. Profitable customers keep several thousand dollars in their accounts and seldom visit a teller or call the bank. To turn unprofitable customers into profitable ones, banks have assessed fees on almost 300 services, including using a bank teller. Many fees are waived for customers who maintain high account balances. Bankers justify the fees by saying they're in business to earn a profit. Discuss whether banks are justified in treating profitable and unprofitable customers differently. Defend your answers.
6. During its regular meetings, the Federal Open Market Committee, the Federal Reserve's monetary policy-making body, considers a number of economic indicators and reports before making decisions. The decisions made by the Fed include: whether to sell or purchase Federal treasury bonds, whether to raise or lower bank reserve requirements, and whether to raise or lower the Federal reserve discount rate. Divide your class into groups (if possible, try to use seven members, the size of the FOMC) and assign each group one of these decisions. As a group, identify the types of information used by the Fed in making their assigned decision and how that information is used. Find the most recent information (sources may include newspapers, business publications, online databases, etc.) and analyze it. Based on this information and your group's analysis, what should the Fed do now? Present your findings and recommendations to the class.

WORKING THE NET

1. The *Washington Post* considers the Federal Reserve's decisions and actions so important that the newspaper publishes a daily update on them. Go to **http://www.washingtonpost.com/wp-dyn/business/specials/federalreserve/index.html** and read today's Federal Reserve news. Pick an article and write an executive summary that explains why this news item is important to businesspeople.
2. There is a debate within the financial industry about whether credit unions should retain their status as tax-free institutions. Visit the Web site of the

Credit Union National Association (**http://www.cuna.org**) and at least three of the following banking industry trade associations: American Bankers Association (**http://www.aba.com**), America's Community Bankers (**http://www.acbankers.org**), Consumer Bankers Association (**http://www.cbanet.org**), Independent Community Bankers of America (**http://www.icba.org**). Find information on each site regarding this debate and write a paper summarizing your opinion.

3. Using a search engine such as Google (**http://www.google.com**) or Yahoo (**http://www.yahoo.com**), use the Internet to research two of the following banking technologies: debit cards, online banking, ATMs, or smart cards. Make a presentation to your class describing future trends in the use of these technologies by the financial-services industry.
4. What are your rights to privacy when dealing with financial institutions? Research the specific privacy provisions related to banking and financial services using the Internet and write a paper on how you can use this information to protect your privacy and financial identity.
5. The federal government has established specific regulations for financial institutions providing online banking services. Research these regulations at the Controller of Currency Web site (**http://www.occ.treas.gov**) and describe how they affect a financial institution's ability to operate over the Internet.

Creative Thinking Case

ING Direct Serves Up Coffee, Tea, and Mortgages

ING Direct's mission is clear, says president and CEO Arkadi Kuhlmann: Challenge the traditional banking industry by offering consumers a new option. "Look at an airline such as Southwest," he says. "People like them because they make it easy to fly. They also make you feel as if they're on your side by cracking jokes and not wearing standard uniforms. We're trying to do that with banking. We want to make people feel proud about saving their money—even make them feel that it's a cool thing to do."

Step into one of ING Direct's three branch offices and you hardly know you're in a bank. Dubbed ING Direct cafés, their facades are made of glass and the color scheme inside is bright orange. Behind the counters, sales associates serve up cappuccino and biscotti along with information on mortgages, savings accounts, and CDs. Customers take a seat at nearby café-style tables to sip their coffee and do their actual banking at Internet stations.

The cafés are all part of a strategy that have helped ING rocket to $10 billion in assets since its founding in September 2000. With more than 1 million customers, and new assets streaming in at more than $500 million a month, the Wilmington, Delaware, financial institution is now one of the 50 biggest banks in the country.

Kuhlmann says ING focuses on the things customers really want—high interest rates on deposits and radically simplified loans—while eliminating the high-cost services that customers can do without. As a result, ING doesn't have an ATM network and customers are urged to do most of their banking via the Internet or over the phone. Marketing focuses on low-cost, high-return campaigns. Sales associates (unlike at traditional banks ING doesn't call customer contact personnel customer service representatives) are trained to develop upbeat, positive relationships with customers but also earn steep commissions. Customers are ING's biggest selling tool. Nearly 40 percent of new accounts are generated by word of mouth when happy customers tell others about ING.

CRITICAL THINKING QUESTIONS

1. Do you agree with Kuhlmann that most banking customers would choose higher interest rates and simplified loans over extra banking services? Why or why not?

2. Compare the structure and economics of the airline industry to the financial-services industry. How are they alike? How are they different? ING Direct's CEO compares the company to Southwest Airlines. Do you think this is a fair comparison? Why? What challenges might ING Direct face that are different from those encountered by Southwest Airlines in its early history?
3. How might ING Direct's current strategy affect its future growth?

SOURCES: Scott Kirsner, "Would You Like a Mortgage with Your Mocha?," *Fast Company* (March 2003), downloaded from http://www.fastcompany.com; Stephanie Milloti, "Coffee, Tea, or IRA," *Business 2.0* (June 2002), downloaded from http://www.business2.com.

Video Case

Customers Come First at Firstbank Corporation

Are small, community banks a thing of the past? Not if you live in Michigan, where Firstbank Corporation (**http://www.firstbank-corp.com**) operates. This bank holding company consists of a small network of affiliated community banks and bank service companies: Firstbank–Alma, Firstbank–Mt. Pleasant, Firstbank–West Branch, Firstbank–Lakeview, Firstbank–St Johns, 1st Armored, Inc. (West Branch), and 1st Title (West Branch).

The Alma bank dates back to 1901, when it opened its doors as First State Bank of Alma. It grew to become the major financial institution in Gratiot County and today is the lead bank in Firstbank Corporation, which was formed in 1985 as a one-bank holding company. In 1987, Firstbank Corporation expanded into a multibank holding company, to allow for new business opportunities and growth.

Offering a full range of deposit and loan products, Firstbank's affiliates seek to differentiate themselves from their banking competition by continuously focusing on exceptional customer service. The banks believe that integrity, customer satisfaction, and trust are the key elements of solid community banking. Each affiliate bank has its own president and board of directors. This helps each bank to make decisions that focus on the local community and local customers.

Firstbank–Mt. Pleasant, for instance, is headed by Thomas Sullivan, who is also president and CEO of Firstbank Corporation. He emphasizes that Firstbank customers will have a more personal and flexible banking experience because the bank strives to tailor its services to individual customer needs. The bank offers "a wide variety of checking and savings accounts to fit . . . [customers'] individual or corporate needs, and all types of consumer, mortgage, and commercial loans." The bank also has an affiliation with SII Investments, Inc. to provide customers with access to stocks, bonds, mutual funds, annuities, and insurance products.

Firstbank–Alma, another affiliate, is headed by James E. Wheeler II. Wheeler emphasizes making banking convenient for customers and knowing customers well so that the bank can recommend appropriate financial solutions—whatever a customer's banking needs happen to be.

Another unit of Firstbank Corporation is 1st Armored, Inc., which provides several armored courier services for financial institutions in Michigan. These services include Federal Reserve shipping, individual bank deliveries, coin wrapping, and automated teller machine servicing.

CRITICAL THINKING QUESTIONS

1. What role does Firstbank Corporation play in the U.S. financial system?
2. Why have the Firstbank Corporation affiliates been able to keep a strong customer base despite competition from larger banks with a national presence? How can the Internet help?
3. Visit the Firstbank–Alma Web site (**http://www.firstbank-alma.com**). If you were the owner of a restaurant in Alma, would you bank with Firstbank–Alma? Why? If you were the vice president of finance for a $250 million

manufacturing company, what services would you need? Could this bank handle those needs?

SOURCES: Adapted from the material in the video "Financial Statement Analysis/Creditor and Investor Decisions: Firstbank and Roney & Co.," and from the Firstbank corporate Web site, http://www.firstbank-corp.com, accessed June 4, 2003.

E-Commerce Case

Virtual Service at NetBank

Many banks offer online banking services, but NetBank (**http://www.netbank.com**) is different. It's a virtual bank with no physical location, no branch offices, and no tellers. It operates exclusively on the Internet, yet offers all the services of brick-and-mortar banks. NetBank customers can open checking accounts, pay their bills, get a mortgage loan, apply for credit cards, and even buy insurance, 24 hours a day, seven days a week through the Internet.

Because NetBank has no tellers or physical locations, NetBank saves on overhead costs and passes the savings on to customers by paying higher interest rates on deposit accounts and charging lower service fees. However, Douglas Freeman, NetBank's CEO, believes that the biggest appeal for NetBank's 165,000 customers is convenience. "What is attractive about NetBank to our customers is the fact that we save them time and give them control over their finances," he says. "Today, most families are two-income families and people simply do not have enough time to do everything they have to do. People are on the Internet at home anyway and going to a website like NetBank to do financial transactions literally takes a tenth of the time it does to get in a car and drive to a bank branch."

NetBank's typical customer is 42 years of age, college educated, and married with children. Most are solidly middle class and own their own homes. The majority have their paychecks deposited directly into their NetBank accounts and then access their funds through ATMs. NetBank does not charge an ATM access fee.

Strategic marketing alliances with companies like Quicken helps bring in new customers, as does Internet advertising. "We do very targeted advertising on the Internet as we are trying to attract financially savvy people that are heavy Internet users," says Freeman.

Although NetBank's deposits now top $1.7 billion, Freeman sees room for greater expansion in the future. "The biggest issue is that it takes time for customers to become comfortable and familiar with what we do. It took five to ten years for ATMs to gain mass consumer acceptance. I believe that Internet banking will just have to go through the time cycle for people to get more comfortable with how it works," he says.

CRITICAL THINKING QUESTIONS

1. Do you think NetBank's strategy of targeting Internet users only is a sound business plan? Explain.
2. Do you agree or disagree with Freeman's definition of banking convenience? What types of banking customers might NetBank not be able to serve effectively?
3. What are the advantages and disadvantages of focusing solely on the Internet as a delivery channel? Do you think that NetBank will eventually need to add other types of customer contact points? If so, what types would you recommend and why?

SOURCES: Lynn Fosse, "Douglas K. Freeman, Chief Executive Officer, NetBank, Inc. Interview," *Wall Street Corporate Reporter* (July 5, 2002), downloaded from http://www.elibrary.com; David Haffenreffer, "NetBank, Inc.," *CNN Money Morning* (November 26, 2002), downloaded from http://www.elibrary.com; Robert Luke, "NetBank Ahead of Expectations," *The Atlanta Journal and Constitution* (January 30, 2003), downloaded from http://www.elibrary.com; "NetBank, Inc. Announces Plan to Offer Insurance in all 50 States," company press release (June 5, 2002).

Hot Links Address Book

Tour the American Currency Exhibit to learn the history of our nation's money at
http://www.frbsf.org/currency/

To learn more about how the Federal Reserve System works, visit the Web site of the Federal Reserve Bank of St. Louis at
http://www.stls.frb.org/publications/pleng/

The FDIC gets so many requests about banks' insurance status that it added an option to determine "Is my bank insured?" on its Web site. Visit
http://www.fdic.gov

What goes on at a Federal Open Market Committee Meeting? Find out by reading the minutes of the Committee's latest meeting at
http://www.federalreserve.gov/fomc/

Want to know more about the relationship between Congress and the Federal Reserve? Go to
http://www.house.gov/jec/fed/fed/fed-impt.htm

How much do you know about the Federal Reserve? Test your knowledge with the *Washington Post*'s online quiz at
http://www.washingtonpost.com/wp-srv/business/quizzes/fedquiz.htm

Find out what other services the Federal Reserve provides to financial institutions at
http://www.frbservices.org

How did Abraham Lincoln do his banking? Take a cyber-tour of American banking history at
http://www.occ.treas.gov/occ140th/history.htm

To find out if you're eligible to join a credit union, visit the Credit Union National Administration's credit union locator at
http://www.cuna.org/data/consumer/culinks/cu_locator.html

Chapter 20

© TERRI MILLER / E-VISUAL COMMUNICATIONS, INC.

Managing the Firm's Finances

learning goals

1 What roles do finance and the financial manager play in the firm's overall strategy?
2 How does a firm develop its financial plans, including forecasts and budgets?
3 What types of short-term and long-term expenditures does a firm make?
4 What are the main sources and costs of unsecured and secured short-term financing?
5 How do the two primary sources of long-term financing compare?
6 What are the major types, features, and costs of long-term debt?
7 When and how do firms issue equity, and what are the costs?
8 What trends are affecting the practice of financial management?
APPENDIX: MANAGING RISK AND INSURANCE
9 What is risk and how can it be managed? What makes a risk insurable?
10 What types of insurance coverage should businesses consider?

Krispy Kreme Raises Some Dough—and Profits

Have you rushed to buy a Krispy Kreme Hot Original Glazed doughnut when the "hot" light flashes? If so, you're in good company. Krispy Kreme (**http://www.krispykreme.com**) sells more than 7.5 million doughnuts every day in its company-owned and franchise "factory" stores, where you can actually see the sweet treats being made.

Until 1995, filling your desire for a Krispy Kreme meant traveling to the Southeast, where the regional chain located its stores. Word spread about the melt-in-your-mouth confections, and in 1995, the company began a national expansion program. Krispy Kremes developed a cult-like following. By mid-2003 the company had more than 285 stores in 38 states, Canada, and Australia. Afficionados can also find Krispy Kreme doughnuts at select "off premises" locations like grocery and convenience stores.

To finance its aggressive expansion program, Krispy Kreme raised equity through an initial public offering of common stock in April 2000 at $21 a share. Investors, attracted by the company's strong financial condition, gobbled up the shares. Demand for its equity remained high, and the company was able to sell more new shares of common stock in February 2001. As a result, Krispy Kreme has mostly equity in its capital structure, the mix of debt and equity used to fund the company.

In mid-2003, its debt-to-equity ratio was 21 percent—extremely low compared to the restaurant industry average of about 80 percent. This gives the company plenty of flexibility to issue either debt or equity when it needs additional funding.

While you savor your Krispy Kreme doughnut, chief financial officer Randy Casstevens and his financial team are working behind the scenes to bring Krispy Kremes to you. Financing the company's continued growth is just one of their responsibilities. They must develop long-term financial plans and forecasts that reflect the strategic direction management wants to take the company—in Krispy Kreme's case, growing the company over the next six years to 750 stores in the United States and Canada, with another 60 in the United Kingdom, Australia, and New Zealand. Krispy Kreme also has development partners in Mexico and Asia.

Their strategic plans would show the number of new stores it expects to open each year (64 in 2003 alone), the cost of each store, and other major capital expenditures such as acquisitions, as well as the revenue, expense, and income projections for the time period. Working with managers in other departments, they prepare short-term operating plans and budgets to assure efficient use of the firm's resources.

Deciding how to invest the firm's funds is another responsibility of the company's financial executives. They must analyze proposed projects and choose those that offer solid rates of return in relationship to the risk. For example, to expand its beverage offerings, Krispy Kreme acquired Digital Java, a coffee-roasting business, and built a coffee-roasting plant.

As it moves forward with its well-planned expansion and promising financial future, Krispy Kreme can feel good about the fact that it is not just its doughnuts and coffee that are hot.[1]

Critical Thinking Questions

As you read this chapter, consider the following questions as they relate to Krispy Kreme:

1. In addition to raising and investing funds for Krispy Kreme, what other types of financial activities would its financial managers oversee?
2. What types of economic, industry, and other information would be important to Krispy Kreme's financial analysts in developing forecasts of revenues and expenses?
3. How do the actions of the company's financial managers contribute to their primary goal of maximizing the value of the firm to its owners?

Principles of Financial Management

In today's fast-paced global economy, managing a firm's finances is more complex than ever. For Krispy Kreme's financial managers, a thorough command of traditional finance activities—financial planning, investing money, and raising funds—is only part of the job. Financial managers are more than number crunchers. As part of the top-management team, chief financial officers (CFOs) need a broad understanding of their firm's business and industry, as well as leadership ability and creativity. They must never lose sight of the primary goal of the financial manager: *to maximize the value of the firm to its owners.*

Financial management—spending and raising a firm's money—is both a science and an art. The science part is analyzing numbers and flows of cash through the firm. The art is answering questions like these: Is the firm using its financial resources in the best way? Aside from costs, why choose a particular form of financing? How risky is each option?

This chapter focuses on the financial management of a firm. We'll start with an overview of the role of finance and of the financial manager in the firm's overall business strategy. Next we consider the basics of financial planning: forecasts and budgets. Discussions of short- and long-term uses of funds and sources of short- and long-term financing follow. Finally, we'll look at key trends affecting financial management. The appendix that follows discusses managing risk and insurance.

The Role of Finance and the Financial Manager

1 learning goal

financial management
The art and science of managing a firm's money so that it can meet its goals.

Finance is critical to the success of all companies. It may not be as visible as marketing or production, but management of a firm's finances is just as much a key to the firm's success.

Financial management—the art and science of managing a firm's money so that it can meet its goals—is not just the responsibility of the finance department. All business decisions have financial consequences. Managers in all departments must work closely with financial personnel. If you are a sales representative, for example, the company's credit and collection policies will affect your ability to make sales.

Any company, whether it's a two-attorney law partnership or General Motors, needs money to operate. To make money, it must first spend money—on inventory and supplies, equipment and facilities, and employee wages and salaries.

Because all business decisions have financial consequences, managers in all departments must work closely with financial personnel. A company's credit and collection policies, for example, may impact a sales representatives' ability to close a sale.

© ROYALTY-FREE / CORBIS

Exhibit 20.1 | How Cash Flows through a Business

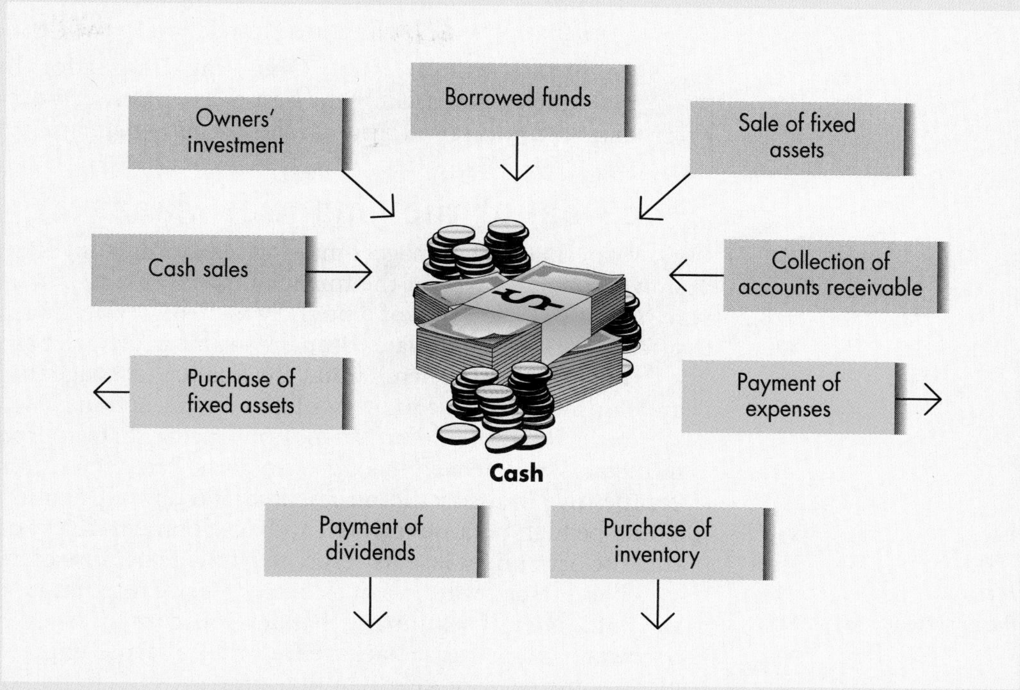

Revenues from sales of the firm's products should be the chief source of funding. But money from sales doesn't always come in when it's needed to pay the bills. Financial managers must track how money is flowing into and out of the firm (see Exhibit 20.1). They work with the firm's other department managers to determine how available funds will be used and how much money is needed. Then they choose the best sources to obtain the required funding.

For example, a financial manager will track day-to-day operational data such as cash collections and disbursements to ensure that the company has enough cash to meet its obligations. Over a longer time horizon, the manager will thoroughly study whether and when the company should open a new manufacturing facility. The manager will also suggest the most appropriate way to finance the project, raise the funds, and then monitor the project's implementation and operation.

Financial management is closely related to accounting. In most firms both areas are the responsibility of the vice president of finance or the CFO. But the accountant's main function is to collect and present financial data. Financial managers use financial statements and other information prepared by accountants to make financial decisions. Financial managers focus on **cash flows,** the inflows and outflows of cash. They plan and monitor the firm's cash flows to ensure that cash is available when needed.

cash flows
The inflows and outflows of cash for a firm.

The Financial Manager's Responsibilities and Activities

Financial managers have a complex and challenging job. They analyze financial data prepared by accountants, monitor the firm's financial status, and prepare and implement financial plans. One day they may be developing a better way to automate cash collections, the next they may be analyzing a proposed acquisition. The key activities of the financial manager are:

- *Financial planning.* Preparing the financial plan, which projects revenues, expenditures, and financing needs over a given period.
- *Investment (spending money).* Investing the firm's funds in projects and securities that provide high returns in relation to their risks.
- *Financing (raising money).* Obtaining funding for the firm's operations and investments and seeking the best balance between debt (borrowed funds) and equity (funds raised through the sale of ownership in the business).

The Goal of the Financial Manager

How can financial managers make wise planning, investment, and financing decisions? The main goal of the financial manager is *to maximize the value of the firm to its owners.* The value of a publicly owned corporation is measured by the share price of its stock. A private company's value is the price at which it could be sold.

To maximize the firm's value, the financial manager has to consider both short- and long-term consequences of the firm's actions. Maximizing profits is one approach, but it should not be the only one. Such an approach favors making short-term gains over achieving long-term goals. What if a firm in a highly technical and competitive industry did no research and development? In the short run, profits would be high because research and development is very expensive. But in the long run, the firm might lose its ability to compete because of its lack of new products.

This is true regardless of a company's size or point in its life cycle. David Deeds was cofounder of a company that developed an innovative computer-aided design hardware and software package for architects and engineers. He and his partners made some decisions early in the company's life to pursue opportunities such as consulting projects that quickly generated revenue. The company saw its profits grow, adding staff and offices to handle the increased business. But this sidetracked the founders from their initial vision: designing revolutionary new products to address client needs. "We managed ourselves into a niche where we could survive and make a little money but never offer anything unique or grow significantly," says Deeds. While they built a reasonably successful small business, the desire for the quick buck overrode the long-term goal of building a $100 million company.[2]

Financial managers constantly strive for a balance between the opportunity for profit and the potential for loss. In finance, the opportunity for profit is termed **return;** the potential for loss, or the chance that an investment will not achieve the expected level of return, is **risk.** A basic principle in finance is that the higher the risk, the greater the return that is required. This widely accepted concept is called the **risk-return trade-off.** Financial managers consider many risk and return factors when making investment and financing decisions. Among them are changing patterns of market demand, interest rates, general economic conditions, market conditions, and social issues (such as environmental effects and equal employment opportunity policies).

return
The opportunity for profit.

risk
The potential for loss or the chance that an investment will not achieve the expected level of return.

risk-return trade-off
A basic principle in finance that holds that the higher the risk, the greater the return that is required.

concept check

What is the role of financial management in a firm?

How do the three key activities of the financial manager relate?

What is the main goal of the financial manager? How does the risk-return trade-off relate to the financial manager's main goal?

FINANCIAL PLANNING: LOOKING AHEAD

2 learning goal

As we learned in Chapter 7, companies use several types of plans to determine how to achieve organizational objectives. A company's *financial plan* is part of the overall company plan and guides the firm toward its business goals and the maximization of its value. The financial plan enables the firm to estimate the amount and timing of its investment and financing needs.

To prepare a financial plan, the financial manager must first consider existing and proposed products, the resources available to produce them, and the financing needed to support production and sales. Forecasts and budgets are essential to the firm's financial planning. They should be part of an integrated planning process that links them to strategic plans and performance measurement.

Forecasting the Future

The financial-planning process starts with financial forecasts, or projections of future developments within the firm. The estimated demand for the firm's products (the sales forecast) and other financial and operating data are key inputs. At Ford Motor Company, economic analysts estimate expected production and sales for each line of cars and trucks. Then financial analysts prepare detailed short- and long-term financial forecasts based on these assumptions.

short-term forecasts
Projections of revenues, costs of goods, and operating expenses over a one-year period.

Short-term forecasts, or *operating plans,* project revenues, costs of goods, and operating expenses over a one-year period. Using short-term forecasts, Ford's financial managers estimate the next year's expenses for inventory, labor, advertising, and other operating activities. These estimates form the basis for cash budgets, described below, which forecast cash inflows and outflows over the same period.

long-term forecasts
Projections of a firm's activities and the funding for those activities over a period that is longer than 1 year, typically 2 to 10 years.

Long-term forecasts, or *strategic plans,* cover a period that is longer than 1 year, typically 2 to 10 years, and take a broader view of the firm's financial activities. With these forecasts, management can assess the financial effects of various business strategies: What would be the financial results of investing in new facilities and equipment? Of developing new products? Of eliminating a line of business? Of acquiring other firms? Long-term forecasts also show where the funding for these activities is expected to come from.

Lenders typically ask potential borrowers for forecasts that cover the period the loan will be outstanding. "We're obviously asking so we understand the risk of a deal," says John L. Daniels, senior vice president, commercial banking, at Bank of America Corp. "We're looking for the cash-flow perspective and how we're getting paid. We build our loan agreements and covenants on that information."[3] (Covenants are requirements that the company comply with certain operating and financial measures during the loan period.)

Budgets

budgets
Formal written forecasts of revenues and expenses that set spending limits based on operational forecasts; include cash budgets, capital budgets, and operating budgets.

Firms prepare **budgets** to plan and control their future financial activities. Budgets are formal written forecasts of revenues and expenses that set spending limits

© AP / WIDE WORLD PHOTOS

Companies use capital budgets to forecast the costs of equipment like that pictured here and used to make Edy's Ice Cream. Budgets of all types help companies plan and control their future financial activities.

based on operational forecasts. All budgets begin with forecasts. Budgets provide a way to control expenses and compare the actual performance to the forecast.

Firms use several types of budgets, most of which cover a one-year period:

- **Cash budgets** forecast the firm's cash inflows and outflows and help the firm plan for cash surpluses and shortages. Because having enough cash is so critical to their financial health, many firms prepare annual cash budgets subdivided into months or weeks. Then they project the amount of cash needed in each shorter time period.
- **Capital budgets** forecast outlays for fixed assets (plant and equipment). They usually cover a period of several years and ensure that the firm will have enough funds to buy the equipment and buildings it needs.
- **Operating budgets** combine sales forecasts with estimates of production costs and operating expenses in order to forecast profits. They are based on individual budgets for sales, production, purchases of materials, factory overhead, and operating expenses. Operating budgets then are used to plan operations: dollars of sales, units of production, amounts of raw materials, dollars of wages, and so forth.

Budgets are routinely used to monitor and control the performance of a division, a department, or an individual manager. When actual outcomes differ from budget expectations, management must take action.

cash budgets
Budgets that forecast a firm's cash inflows and outflows and help the firm plan for cash surpluses and shortages.

capital budgets
Budgets that forecast a firm's outlays for fixed assets (plant and equipment), typically covering a period of several years.

concept check

What is a financial plan? Name two types of financial planning documents.

Distinguish between short- and long-term forecasts. How are both used by financial managers?

Briefly describe three types of budgets.

How Organizations Use Funds

3 learning goal

To grow and prosper, a firm must keep investing money in its operations. The financial manager decides how best to use the firm's money. Short-term expenses support the firm's day-to-day activities. For instance, athletic-apparel maker Nike regularly spends money to buy such raw materials as leather and fabric and to pay employee salaries. Long-term expenses are typically for fixed assets. For Nike, these would include outlays to build a new factory, buy automated manufacturing equipment, or acquire a small manufacturer of sports apparel.

operating budgets
Budgets that combine sales forecasts with estimates of production costs and operating expenses in order to forecast profits.

Short-Term Expenses

Short-term expenses, often called *operating expenses,* are outlays used to support current selling and production activities. They typically result in current assets, which include cash and any other assets (accounts receivable and inventory) that can be converted to cash within a year. The financial manager's goal is to manage current assets so the firm has enough cash to pay its bills and to support its accounts receivable and inventory.

Cash Management: Assuring Liquidity Cash is the lifeblood of business. Without it, a firm could not operate. An important duty of the financial manager is **cash management,** or making sure that enough cash is on hand to pay bills as they come due and to meet unexpected expenses.

Businesses use budgets to estimate the cash requirements for a specific period. Many companies keep a minimum cash balance to cover unexpected expenses or changes in projected cash flows. The financial manager arranges loans to cover any shortfalls. If the size and timing of cash inflows closely match the size and timing of cash outflows, the company needs to keep only a small amount of cash on hand. A company whose sales and receipts are fairly predictable and regular throughout the year needs less cash than a company with a seasonal pattern of sales and receipts. A toy company, for instance, whose sales are concentrated in the fall, spends a great deal of cash during the spring and summer to build inventory. It has excess cash during the winter and early spring, when it collects on sales from its peak selling season.

cash management
The process of making sure that a firm has enough cash on hand to pay bills as they come due and to meet unexpected expenses.

marketable securities
Short-term investments that are easily converted into cash.

commercial paper
Unsecured short-term debt —an IOU—issued by a financially strong corporation.

Because cash held in checking accounts earns little, if any, interest, the financial manager tries to keep cash balances low and to invest the surplus cash. Surpluses are invested temporarily in **marketable securities,** short-term investments that are easily converted into cash. The financial manager looks for low-risk investments that offer high returns. Three of the most popular marketable securities are Treasury bills, certificates of deposit, and commercial paper. (**Commercial paper** is unsecured short-term debt—an IOU—issued by a financially strong corporation.)

In addition to seeking the right balance between cash and marketable securities, the financial manager tries to shorten the time between the purchase of inventory or services (cash outflows) and the collection of cash from sales (cash inflows). The three key strategies are to collect money owed to the firm (accounts receivable) as quickly as possible, to pay money owed to others (accounts payable) as late as possible without damaging the firm's credit reputation, and to turn inventory quickly in order to minimize the funds tied up in it.

accounts receivable
Sales for which a firm has not yet been paid.

MANAGING ACCOUNTS RECEIVABLE **Accounts receivable** represent sales for which the firm has not yet been paid. Because the product has been sold but cash has not yet been received, an account receivable amounts to a use of funds. For the average manufacturing firm, accounts receivable represent about 15 to 20 percent of total assets.

The financial manager's goal is to collect money owed to the firm as quickly as possible, while offering customers credit terms attractive enough to increase sales. Accounts receivable management involves setting *credit policies,* guidelines on offering credit, and *credit terms,* specific repayment conditions, including how long customers have to pay their bills and whether a cash discount is given for quicker payment. Another aspect of accounts receivable management is deciding on *collection policies,* the procedures for collecting overdue accounts.

Setting up credit and collection policies is a balancing act for financial managers. On the one hand, easier credit policies or generous credit terms (a longer repayment period or larger cash discount) result in increased sales. On the other hand, the firm has to finance more accounts receivable. The risk of uncollectible accounts receivable also rises. Businesses consider the impact on sales, timing of cash flow, experience with bad debt, customer profiles, and industry standards when developing their credit and collection policies.

Companies that want to speed up collections actively manage their accounts receivable, rather than passively letting customers pay when they want to. Companies that take this approach can collect from anyone—even a bankrupt company like Enron!—as you'll learn in the "Focusing on Small Business" box on page 642.

Technology plays a big role in helping companies improve their credit and collections performance. When the tech sector fell on hard times, Cisco saw its global days sales outstanding (DSO) climb to a high of 47 days in January 2001. The company developed Web-based reporting tools that improved overall cash management. Managers received frequently updated accounts receivable and cash collection reports, along with real-time collection and credit reports. The new system also flagged potential problems with customers. Within nine months of implementation, Cisco exceeded its goal of reducing DSO to 30 days, slashing that number to 24 days.[4]

INVENTORY Another use of funds is to buy inventory needed by the firm. In a typical manufacturing firm, inventory is nearly 20 percent of total assets. The cost of inventory includes not only its purchase price, but also ordering, handling, storage, interest, and insurance costs.

Production, marketing, and finance managers usually have differing views about inventory. Production managers want lots of raw materials on hand to avoid production delays. Marketing managers want lots of finished goods on hand so customer orders can be filled quickly. But financial managers want the least inventory possible without harming production efficiency or sales. Financial managers

Focusing on Small Business

Patience and Persistence Pay Off

Receiving a check in the mail is usually not cause for celebration—unless it's from a bankrupt company called Enron. The $1,635 payment came as no surprise to Nettie Morrison, accounts receivable specialist for Foresight, a 50-employee Ohio software firm, who applies persistence, advance planning, and other commonsense strategies to get paid. Although Enron's annual licensing contract was up for renewal in February 2002, Morrison went into action in fall 2001—as soon as she heard about the company's serious problems. She identified the person who had the authority to make the payment, calling every week to develop a relationship, and was paid on time in March 2002.

For many small businesses, getting paid is a hassle. Yet they must offer their customers trade credit, or payment terms, to survive. As Rolf Albers, head of his own electronics-manufacturing company, says, "If I went to Sears today and wanted to buy a refrigerator, they would make me pay today. But a small manufacturer with no track record can call me, wanting $1,000 worth of equipment, and they think they can wait 90 days to pay." To protect himself, Albers requires customers who fall behind to pay up-front for future orders.

Morrison also takes prompt action. She makes a "courtesy call" the day after a payment is due and follows up in a week if the check still hasn't arrived—or sooner for a larger amount. Companies that provide services often send final invoices before work on a project is complete, so they can stop work if the customer takes too long to pay.

Collection strategies should actually start before payments are late. For example, call before the bill comes due to confirm that the customer received it and has the documentation, such as purchase orders, required to process the payment. Another of Morrison's strategies is doing the math for customers. Instead of just stating the penalty interest rate of 1.5 percent per month for late payment, Foresight's bills read: "If paid by September 30, your cost is $x; if paid after September 30, your cost is $y (invoice amount plus interest)." This simple change helped customers clearly understand the payment terms and significantly increased the number of on-time payments.

Critical Thinking Questions

1. Why is managing accounts receivable such an important function for small businesses?
2. Suggest two other strategies that small businesses can use to get paid on time and two they can use to collect overdue payments.

SOURCES: Cliff Ennico, "How to Get Yourself Paid," *Entrepreneur.com* (April 22, 2002), downloaded from http://www.entrepreneur.com; Ilan Mochari, "Collection Slip-Ups," *Inc.com* (August 20, 2002), downloaded from http://www.inc.com; and Ilan Mochari, "How to Collect from Anyone (Even Enron)," *Inc.* (September 1, 2002), pp. 67–68.

must work closely with production and marketing to balance these conflicting goals. Techniques for reducing the investment in inventory—inventory management, the just-in-time system, and materials requirement planning—were described in Chapter 12.

Long-Term Expenditures

A firm also uses funds for its investments in long-lived assets, such items as land, buildings, machinery, equipment, and information systems. These are called **capital expenditures.** Unlike operating expenses, which produce benefits within a year, the benefits from capital expenditures extend beyond one year. For instance, a printer's purchase of a new printing press with a usable life of seven years is a capital expenditure. It appears as a fixed asset on the firm's balance sheet. Paper, ink, and other supplies, however, are expenses. Mergers and acquisitions, discussed in Chapter 5, are also considered capital expenditures.

capital expenditures
Investments in long-lived assets, such as land, buildings, machinery, and equipment, that are expected to provide benefits that extend beyond one year.

Firms make capital expenditures for many reasons. The most common are to expand and to replace or renew fixed assets. Another reason is to develop new products. Most manufacturing firms have a big investment in long-term assets. Boeing Company, for instance, puts millions of dollars a year into airplane-manufacturing facilities.

capital budgeting
The process of analyzing long-term projects and selecting those that offer the best returns while maximizing the firm's value.

Because capital expenditures tend to be costly and have a major effect on the firm's future, the financial manager must analyze long-term projects and select those that offer the best returns while maximizing the firm's value. This process is called **capital budgeting.** Decisions involving new products or the acquisition of another business are especially important. Managers look at project costs and forecast the future benefits the project will bring—for example, from increased productivity, staff reductions, and other cost savings—to calculate the firm's estimated return on the investment.

For example, consider the 215-foot-high Wicked Twister roller coaster at Cedar Point amusement park in Ohio. Before going ahead with the $9 million investment, president Dick Kinzel wanted to be sure the ride would pay for itself in no more than two years. His capital budgeting analysis incorporated projections of larger crowds and a $2 admission increase. When the numbers showed that the Twister met the company's test, Kinzel gave the go-ahead—and was one of the first on the ride when it opened.[5]

concept check

Distinguish between short- and long-term expenses.

What is the financial manager's goal in cash management? List the three key cash management strategies.

Describe the firm's main motives in making capital expenditures.

Obtaining Short-Term Financing

4 learning goal

How do firms raise the funding they need? They borrow money (debt), sell ownership shares (equity), and retain earnings (profits). The financial manager must assess all these sources and choose the one most likely to help maximize the firm's value.

Like expenses, borrowed funds can be divided into short- and long-term loans. A short-term loan comes due within one year; a long-term loan has a maturity greater than one year. Short-term financing is shown as a current liability on the balance sheet, and is used to finance current assets and support operations. Short-term loans can be unsecured or secured.

Unsecured Short-Term Loans

Unsecured loans are made on the basis of the firm's creditworthiness and the lender's previous experience with the firm. An unsecured borrower does not have to pledge specific assets as security. The three main types of *unsecured short-term loans* are trade credit, bank loans, and commercial paper.

unsecured loans
Loans for which the borrower does not have to pledge specific assets as security.

Trade Credit: Accounts Payable When Goodyear sells tires to General Motors, GM does not have to pay cash on delivery. Instead, Goodyear regularly bills GM for its tire purchases, and GM pays at a later date. This is an example of **trade credit:** the seller extends credit to the buyer between the time the buyer receives the goods or services and when it pays for them. Trade credit is a major source of short-term business financing. The buyer enters the credit on its books as an **account payable.** In effect, the credit is a short-term loan from the seller to the buyer of the goods and services. Until GM pays Goodyear, Goodyear has an account receivable from GM, and GM has an account payable to Goodyear.

trade credit
The extension of credit by the seller to the buyer between the time the buyer receives the goods or services and when it pays for them.

accounts payable
Purchase for which a buyer has not yet paid the seller.

Bank Loans Unsecured bank loans are another source of short-term business financing. Companies often use these loans to finance seasonal (cyclical) businesses. For instance, a swimwear manufacturer has strong sales in the spring and summer and lower sales during the fall and winter. It needs short-term bank financing to increase inventories before its strongest selling season and to finance accounts receivable during late winter and early spring, as shown in Exhibit 20.2. The company repays these bank loans when it sells the inventory and collects the receivables.

Unsecured bank loans include lines of credit and revolving credit agreements. A **line of credit** is an agreement between a bank and a business. It specifies the maximum amount of unsecured short-term borrowing the bank will make available to the firm over a given period, typically one year. A line of credit is not a guaranteed loan; the bank agrees to lend funds only if it has money available. Usually, the firm must repay any borrowing within a year. It must also either pay a fee or keep a certain percentage of the loan amount (10 to 20 percent) in a checking account at the bank.

line of credit
An agreement between a bank and a business that specifies the maximum amount of unsecured short-term borrowing the bank will make available to the firm over a given period, typically one year.

Exhibit 20.2 Swimwear Manufacturer's Seasonal Cash Flows

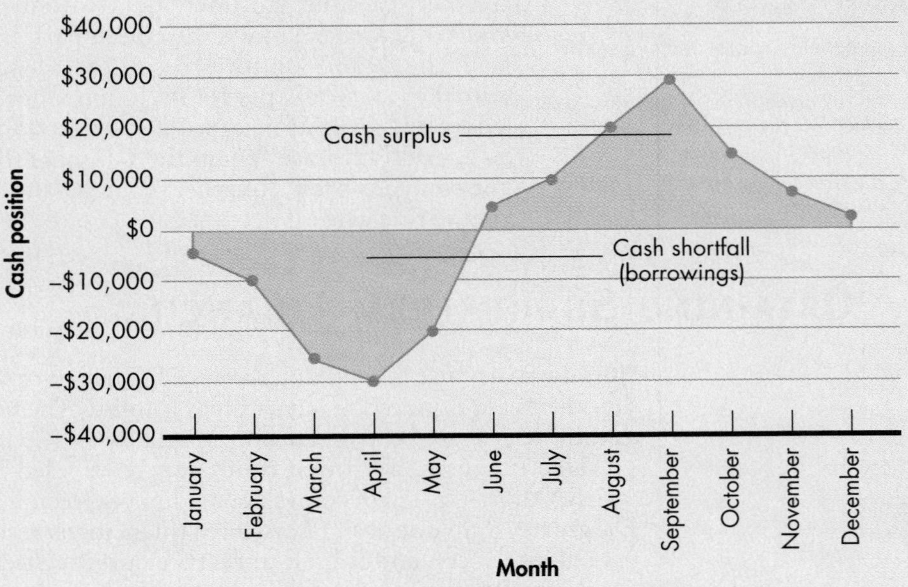

revolving credit agreement
A line of credit under which a bank guarantees that a certain amount of money will be available for a business to borrow over a given period.

Another bank loan, the **revolving credit agreement,** is basically a guaranteed line of credit. Because the bank guarantees that a certain amount of money will be available, it charges an extra fee in addition to interest. Revolving credit agreements are often arranged for a two- to five-year period. Finance companies as well as banks may provide these credit facilities. Clothing manufacturer Ecko, whose fashion companies include Physical Science and Sweat Equity, obtained a $56 million revolving credit facility from CIT Financial in early 2003. Ecko will use the funds to expand its product line and implement other growth initiatives.[6]

Firms often obtain annual lines of credit based on their expected seasonal needs. Then they can quickly borrow without having to reapply to the bank each time funds are needed. Suppose the swimwear manufacturer projected a cash shortfall of $80,000 for the period from February to June. The financial manager might get a $100,000 line of credit from the bank. (The extra $20,000 would be there to cover any unexpected outlays.) The firm could borrow funds as needed—$10,000 in February, $25,000 in March, $30,000 in April. Then it could gradually repay the loan as it collects cash during the summer months.

Commercial Paper As noted earlier, *commercial paper* is an unsecured short-term debt—an IOU—issued by a financially strong corporation. Thus, it is a short-term investment for firms with temporary cash surpluses, and it is a financing option for major corporations. Corporations issue commercial paper in multiples of $100,000 for periods ranging from 3 to 270 days. Many big companies use commercial paper instead of short-term bank loans because the interest rate on commercial paper is usually 1 to 3 percent below bank rates.

Secured Short-Term Loans

secured loans
Loans for which the borrower is required to pledge specific assets as *collateral*, or security.

Secured loans require the borrower to pledge specific assets as *collateral*, or security. The secured lender can legally take the collateral if the borrower doesn't repay the loan. Commercial banks and commercial finance companies are the main sources of secured short-term loans to business. Borrowers whose credit is not strong enough to qualify for unsecured loans use these loans.

Typically, the collateral for secured short-term loans is accounts receivable or inventory. Because accounts receivable are normally quite liquid (easily converted to cash), they are an attractive form of collateral. The appeal of inventory—raw materials or finished goods—as collateral depends on how easily it can be sold at a fair price.

factoring
A form of short-term financing in which a firm sells its accounts receivable outright at a discount to a *factor*.

Another form of short-term financing using accounts receivable is **factoring.** A firm sells its accounts receivable outright to a *factor*, a financial institution (usually a commercial bank or commercial finance company) that buys accounts receivable at a discount. Factoring is widely used in the clothing, furniture, sporting goods, and appliance industries. Factoring allows a firm to turn its accounts receivable into cash without worrying about collections. Because the factor assumes all the risks and expenses of collecting the accounts, firms that factor all of their accounts can reduce the costs of their credit and collection operations. Factoring is more expensive than a bank loan, however, because the factor buys the receivables at a discount from their actual value. But often a company has no choice because it has neither the track record to get unsecured financing nor other collateral to pledge as security for a loan.

Ecko, the fashion design company mentioned earlier, also has a factoring relationship with CIT. Because CIT and Ecko already had a relationship, CIT was willing to provide the larger revolving credit facility and include the factoring line of credit within it.[7]

concept check

Distinguish between unsecured and secured short-term loans.

Briefly describe the three main types of unsecured short-term loans.

Discuss the two ways that accounts receivable can be used to obtain short-term financing.

Raising Long-Term Financing

A basic principle of finance is to match the term of the financing to the period over which benefits are expected to be received from the associated outlay. Short-term items should be financed with short-term funds, and long-term items should be financed with long-term funds. Long-term financing sources include both debt (borrowing) and equity (ownership). Equity financing comes either from selling new ownership interests or from retaining earnings.

5 learning goal

Debt versus Equity Financing

Say that the Boeing Company plans to spend $2 billion over the next four years to build and equip new factories to make jet aircraft. Boeing's top management will assess the pros and cons of both debt and equity and then consider several possible sources of the desired form of long-term financing.

financial risk
The chance that a firm will be unable to make scheduled interest and principal payments on its debt.

The major advantage of debt financing is the deductibility of interest expense for income tax purposes, which lowers its overall cost. In addition, there is no loss of ownership. The major drawback is **financial risk:** the chance that the firm will be unable to make scheduled interest and principal payments. The lender can force a borrower that fails to make scheduled debt payments into bankruptcy. Most loan agreements have restrictions to ensure that the borrower operates efficiently.

Equity, on the other hand, is a form of permanent financing that places few restrictions on the firm. The firm is not required to pay dividends or repay the investment. However, equity financing gives common stockholders voting rights that provide them with a voice in management. Equity is more costly than debt.

Exhibit 20.3 Major Differences between Debt and Equity Financing

	Debt Financing	Equity Financing
Voice in management	Creditors typically have none, unless borrower defaults on payments. Creditors may be able to place restraints on management in event of default.	Common stockholders have voting rights.
Claim on income and assets	Debt holders rank ahead of equity holders. Payment of interest and principal is a contractual obligation of the firm.	Equity owners have a residual claim on income (dividends are paid only after interest and any scheduled principal payments are paid) and assets. The firm has no obligation to pay dividends.
Maturity	Debt has a stated maturity and requires repayment of principal by a specified maturity date.	The company is not required to repay equity, which has no maturity date.
Tax treatment	Interest is a tax-deductible expense.	Dividends are not tax-deductible and are paid from after-tax income.

Unlike the interest on debt, dividends to owners are not tax-deductible expenses. Exhibit 20.3 summarizes the major differences between debt and equity financing.

Financial managers try to select the mix of long-term debt and equity that results in the best balance between cost and risk. If a company's debt load gets too high, in the view of investors and securities analysts, the costs of borrowing will rise. Company policies about the mix of debt and equity vary. Some companies have high debt compared to equity. Debt as a percentage of equity is 177 percent at International Paper, a capital-intensive manufacturer. Others keep debt to a minimum. The long-term debt-to-equity ratio for Nike is about 19 percent; Pfizer, 17 percent; ExxonMobil, 10 percent; Oracle, 6 percent; Coach Inc., 1 percent; and Starbucks and Microsoft, 0 percent.

The media giant created when AOL and TimeWarner joined forces started its life with a legacy of debt. About two-thirds of the total debt in early 2003—about \$20 billion of \$27 billion—came along with Time Warner at the time of the January 2001 merger. Much of that debt resulted from the 1990 merger between Time Inc. and Warner Communications. Chief executive officer Dick Parsons acknowledged the dangers of such high debt levels. "While our balance sheet remains strong, we have a lot of debt," he said. His goal is to reduce debt by \$2 billion by year-end 2003 and to \$20 billion by 2005. Because AOL Time Warner's debt load is high for a company with a low cash position and net loss at year-end 2002, the company will have problems accessing the debt markets. If it finds willing lenders, it will have to pay higher interest rates to compensate for the additional risk lenders take. [8]

Long-Term Debt Financing

6 learning goal

term loan
A business loan with an initial maturity of more than one year; can be unsecured or secured.

Long-term debt is used to finance long-term (capital) expenditures. The initial maturities of long-term debt typically range between 5 and 20 years. Three important forms of long-term debt are term loans, bonds, and mortgage loans.

A **term loan** is a business loan with an initial maturity of more than one year. Term loans generally have 5- to 12-year maturities and can be unsecured or secured. They are available from commercial banks, insurance companies, pension funds, commercial finance companies, and manufacturers' financing subsidiaries. A contract between the borrower and the lender spells out the amount and maturity of the loan, the interest rate, payment dates, the purpose of the loan, and other provisions such as operating and financial restrictions on the borrower to control the risk of default. Term loans may be repaid on a quarterly, semiannual, or annual schedule. The payments include both interest and principal, so the loan balance declines over time. Borrowers try to arrange a repayment schedule that matches the forecast cash flow from the project being financed.

bonds
Long-term debt obligations (liabilities) issued by corporations and governments.

Bonds are long-term debt obligations (liabilities) issued by corporations and governments. Like term loans, corporate bonds are issued with formal contracts that set forth the obligations of the issuing corporation and the rights of the bondholders. Most bonds are issued in multiples of $1,000 (par value) with initial maturities of 10 to 30 years. The stated interest rate, or *coupon rate,* is the percentage of the bond's par value that the issuer will pay each year as interest.

mortgage loan
A long-term loan made against real estate as collateral.

A **mortgage loan** is a long-term loan made against real estate as collateral. The lender takes a mortgage on the property, which lets the lender seize the property, sell it, and use the proceeds to pay off the loan if the borrower fails to make the scheduled payments. Long-term mortgage loans are often used to finance office buildings, factories, and warehouses. Life insurance companies are an important source of these loans. They make billions of dollars' worth of mortgage loans to businesses each year.

Equity Financing

7 learning goal

Equity is the owners' investment in the business. In corporations, the preferred and common stockholders are the owners. A firm obtains equity financing by selling new ownership shares (external financing), or by retaining earnings (internal financing), or for small and growing, typically high-tech companies through venture capital (external financing).

common stock
A security that represents an ownership interest in a corporation.

Selling New Issues of Common Stock

Common stock is a security that represents an ownership interest in a corporation. The cover of the prospectus for a new issue of common stock is shown in Exhibit 20.4. It shows that in December 2002, Seagate Technology offered 72.5 million shares priced at $12 per share. Underwriters' fees totaled $0.51 per share, leaving $11.49 per share (a total of $833 million, of which Seagate received about $276 million and the selling shareholder, $557 million). The company also incurred several million dollars in issuance costs for printing, legal work, and accounting. Dividends, discussed below, are another potential cost of issuing common stock.

The Seagate offering is an example of a company *going public*—its first sale of stock to the public. Usually, a high-growth company has an *initial public offering (IPO)* because it needs to raise more funds to finance continuing growth. (Companies that are already public can issue and sell additional shares of common stock to raise equity funds.) An IPO often enables existing stockholders, usually employees, family, and friends who bought the stock privately, to earn big profits on their investment.

But going public has some drawbacks. For one thing, there is no guarantee an IPO will sell. It is also expensive. Big fees must be paid to investment bankers, brokers, attorneys, accountants, and printers. Once the company is public, it is closely watched by regulators, stockholders, and securities analysts. The firm must reveal such information as operating and financial data, product details, financing plans, and operating strategies. Providing this information is often costly.

Going public can be successful when a company is well established and market conditions are right. Strong equity markets in the late 1990s and into 2000 prompted many companies to go public, especially very young Internet-related companies. Frequently companies that were only a year or two old rushed to go public to take advantage of market conditions. Their prices popped up to what many believed were unrealistic levels. When the dot-com bubble burst and capital markets dried up, far fewer companies were willing to brave the IPO waters. Instead they turned to other financing sources to tide them over until the market for new issues picked up. IPO activity fell off sharply, and those that did issue stock, like Seagate, found that their

Exhibit 20.4 | Cover of the Prospectus for Seagate Technology's December 2002 Common Stock Offering

Filed Pursuant to Rule 424(b)(4)
Registration No. 333-10051

PROSPECTUS

72,500,000 Shares

Seagate
We turn on ideas

Common Shares

We are offering 24,000,000 of our common shares and the selling shareholder is offering an additional 48,500,000 shares. We will not receive any of the proceeds from the sale of common shares by the selling shareholder. This is our initial public offering and no public market currently exists for our common shares.

Our common shares have been approved for listing on the New York Stock Exchange under the trading symbol "STX".

Investing in our common shares involves risks. See "Risk Factors" beginning on page 14.

PRICE $12 PER SHARE

	Price to Public	Underwriting Discounts and Commissions	Proceeds to Seagate Technology	Proceeds to Selling Shareholder
Per Share	$12.00	$0.51	$11.49	$11.49
Total	$870,000,000	$36,975,000	$275,760,000	$557,265,000

The selling shareholder has granted the underwriters the right to purchase up to an additional 10,875,000 common shares to cover over-allotments.

The Securities and Exchange Commission and state securities regulators have not approved or disapproved these securities or determined if this prospectus is truthful or complete. Any representation to the contrary is a criminal offense.

The underwriters expect to deliver the common shares to purchasers on December 13, 2002.

MORGAN STANLEY **SALOMON SMITH BARNEY**

GOLDMAN, SACHS & CO. **JPMORGAN**
BEAR, STEARNS & CO. INC.
CREDIT SUISSE FIRST BOSTON
LEHMAN BROTHERS
MERRILL LYNCH & CO.
THOMAS WEISEL PARTNERS LLC

December 10, 2002

Crate & Barrel is a private company that has avoided raising money through an IPO in order to protect its independence. IPOs allow stockholders to potentially earn big profits on their investments.

dividends
Payments to stockholders from a corporation's profits.

stock dividends
Payments to stockholders in the form of more stock; may replace or supplement cash dividends.

retained earnings
Profits that have been reinvested in a firm.

shares traded well below the offer price. After the Seagate IPO, there were no other offerings until mid-February, marking the first January since 1974 without an IPO.[9]

Some companies choose to remain private. Housewares retailer Crate & Barrel, for example, is a private company. CEO Gordon Segal turned down offers from investment bankers to join the IPO crowd so the firm could expand more quickly. Instead he chose to continue his strategy of moving slowly and maintain his independence. When he needed to raise financing, he instead arranged for a private sale of equity to a private investor who bought 70 percent of the thriving $850 million company in 1998.[10]

DIVIDENDS AND RETAINED EARNINGS **Dividends** are payments to stockholders from a corporation's profits. A company does not have to pay dividends to stockholders. But if investors buy the stock expecting to get dividends and the firm does not pay them, the investors may sell their stock. If too many sell, the value of the stock decreases. Dividends can be paid in cash or in stock. **Stock dividends** are payments in the form of more stock. Stock dividends may replace or supplement cash dividends. After a stock dividend has been paid, more shares have a claim on the same company, so the value of each share often declines.

At their quarterly meetings, the company's board of directors (with the advice of its financial managers) decides how much of the profits to distribute as dividends and how much to reinvest. A firm's basic approach to paying dividends can greatly affect its share price. A stable history of dividend payments indicates good financial health. If a firm that has been making regular dividend payments cuts or skips a dividend, investors start thinking it has serious financial problems. The increased uncertainty often results in lower stock prices. Thus, most firms set dividends at a level they can keep paying. They start with a relatively low dividend payout ratio so that they can maintain a steady or slightly increasing dividend over time.

During the tough economic climate of 2002–2003, TECO Energy, parent company of Florida utility Tampa Electric, faced the possibility of reducing or not paying its dividend for the first time in 43 years. "We find ourselves more challenged than ever before to maintain the dividend and complete an extensive construction cycle," explained Gordon Gillette, TECO's CFO. The failure of a joint venture with Enron strained the company's cash position still further. To avoid sending a negative signal to investors, TECO's management cut costs, sold assets, and issued more equity to raise the funding for both dividends and construction.[11]

Retained earnings, profits that have been reinvested in the firm, have a big advantage over other sources of equity capital: they do not incur underwriting costs. Financial managers strive to balance dividends and retained earnings to maximize the value of the firm. Often the balance reflects the nature of the firm and its industry. Well-established and stable firms and those that expect only modest growth, like public utilities, financial-services companies, and large industrial corporations, typically pay out much of their earnings in dividends. For example, in the year ending January 31, 2003, Metropolitan Life paid dividends of $4.00 per share, Consolidated Edison paid $2.24 per share, and ChevronTexaco paid $2.80 per share.

Most high-growth companies, like those in technology-related fields, finance much of their growth through retained earnings and pay little or no dividends to stockholders. However, in January 2003, Microsoft and Qualcomm, two technology companies, began paying dividends.

In the case of Microsoft, its business throws off a huge amount of cash—about $1 billion a month— and its cash account had grown to more than $43 billion by 2003. However, it was not finding suitable growth companies and business

Making Ethical Choices

xtra! http://gitmanxtra.swlearning.com

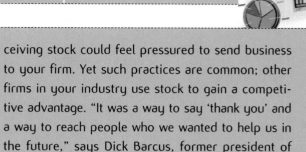

THE FRIENDS AND FAMILY IPO PLAN

As a financial analyst at an up-and-coming high-technology firm, you are involved in your most exciting project to date: helping to prepare pro forma financial statements for the prospectus for the firm's initial public offering.

During your visits to various departments, you hear rumors about promises of IPO shares for favored customers and suppliers. Researching if this is legal, you learn your company can give up to 5 percent of its offering to anyone it chooses. Because this price is not offered to the general public, inviting these "friends and family" to buy shares at the IPO price presents an attractive opportunity. At the height of the bull market, IPO stock prices were jumping an average of 65 percent on the first day. Even though times are more normal now, the growth prospects make these shares a good buy. "Companies are continuing to be approached for stock by analysts and others who wield influence," says David Helfrich, a venture capitalist in Silicon Valley.

However, some legal experts believe that allocating IPO stock to customers and vendors borders on bribery and creates conflicts of interest. Those receiving stock could feel pressured to send business to your firm. Yet such practices are common; other firms in your industry use stock to gain a competitive advantage. "It was a way to say 'thank you' and a way to reach people who we wanted to help us in the future," says Dick Barcus, former president of optical-networking company Tellium Inc.

If your company is only giving out small allocations of stock, such as 100 to 200 shares, and the offering price is $18 to $20, the profit from flipping the shares on the first days is negligible and the potential for conflicts of interest reduced. If the invitation is for larger amounts, at what point does it become a problem? "It's an ethical nightmare," says Richard Liebhaber, a former executive and board member at Qwest Communications International.

ETHICAL DILEMMA

Should you bring this situation to your superiors' attention and urge them to develop a corporate policy that covers offers to sell stock at special prices?

SOURCES: Linda Himelstein, "CEOs to Eliot Spitzer: 'Give It Back? No Way!'" *Business Week* (June 9, 2003), p.113; and Linda Himelstein and Ben Elgin, "High Tech's Kickback Culture," *Business Week* (February 10, 2003), pp. 74–77.

lines to acquire. The announcement also reflects Microsoft's coming of age in its company life cycle as it joins such notable dividend-paying tech firms as IBM, Hewlett-Packard, and Intel.[12] Qualcomm, on the other hand, had been using retained earnings to build up market share for its patented wireless technology. As its CDMA standard gained acceptance, licensing payments boosted its cash reserves to $3.7 billion. "The company can return some of its cash to shareholders without impacting future revenue and earnings growth or restricting strategic opportunities," said chairman and chief executive Irwin Jacobs.[13]

preferred stock
An equity security for which the dividend amount is set at the time the stock is issued.

Preferred Stock Another form of equity is **preferred stock**. Unlike common stock, preferred stock usually has a dividend amount that is set at the time the stock is issued. These dividends must be paid before the company can pay any dividends to common stockholders. Also, if the firm goes bankrupt and sells its assets, preferred stockholders get their money back before common stockholders do. Preferred stock is described in greater detail in Chapter 21.

Like debt, preferred stock increases the firm's financial risk because it obligates the firm to make a fixed payment. But preferred stock is more flexible. The firm can miss a dividend payment without suffering the serious results of failing to pay back a debt.

Preferred stock is more expensive than debt financing, however, because preferred dividends are not tax-deductible. Also, because the claims of preferred stockholders on income and assets are second to those of debtholders, preferred stockholders require higher returns to compensate for the greater risk.

Venture Capital As we learned in Chapter 6, *venture capital* is another source of equity capital. It is most often used by small and growing firms that aren't big enough to sell securities to the public. This type of financing is especially popular among high-tech companies that need large sums of money.

Venture capitalists invest in new businesses in return for part of the ownership, sometimes as much as 60 percent. They look for new businesses with high growth potential, and they expect a high investment return within 5 to 10 years. By getting in on the ground floor, venture capitalists buy stock at a very low price. They earn profits by selling the stock at a much higher price when the company goes public. Venture capitalists generally get a voice in management through a seat on the board of directors. For example, in March 2003, Matrix Semiconductor added another $52 million in funding, bringing its venture financing to $147 million. In addition to venture-capital funds, corporate investors Seagate Technology and Nintendo also invested in the company, which designs and manufactures a unique low-cost, high-density 3-D semiconductor chip for use in portable electronic devices.[14]

Getting venture capital is difficult, even though there are hundreds of private venture-capital firms in this country. Most venture capitalists finance only about 1 to 5 percent of the companies that apply. It was even more difficult than usual to get venture financing in 2002. During that year U.S. venture-capital firms invested $19.4 billion in young companies—down 44 percent from 2001 and 66 percent from peak 2000 levels. The types of companies receiving financing also changed after the technology bubble burst. Health care companies moved to the front of the pack, pushing aside the IT companies that led the way in prior years.

Venture-capital investors, many of whom experienced losses from their investments in failed dot-coms, are less willing to take risks on very early stage companies with unproven technology. They are looking for companies with high growth potential that are already on a demonstrated track to profitability. In 2002, only 30 percent of the deals funded represented the first investment in a company.[15]

As a result, other sources of venture capital, including private foundations, states, and wealthy individuals (called *angel investors*), are helping start-up firms find equity capital. These private investors are motivated by the potential to earn a high return on their investment. Accountants, attorneys, business associates, financial consultants, bankers, and others may help the small firm find an angel. While it's difficult to accurately estimate the size of this informal market, a study from the Center for Venture Research at the University of New Hampshire reveals that as many as 400,000 individuals currently invest $30 billion to $40 billion a year in 50,000 fledgling businesses. In 2001, 81 percent of angel investor financing was for the first three stages of funding: seed, start-up, and early stage.[16]

Trends in Financial Management

8 learning goal

Many of the key trends shaping the practice of financial management echo those in other disciplines. For example, technology is improving the efficiency with which financial managers run their operations. The "Customer Satisfaction and Quality" box, on page 655, describes how Dell Computer uses technology to improve its cash

Expanding Around the Globe

Benefits and Challenges of Centralizing Cash Management

If you think it's hard to balance your checking account, imagine trying to deal with 380 of them, in banks around the world! That's the job facing Lynn Younger, treasurer of Chiquita Brands International Inc. It's all part of being a financial manager at a company that operates globally. Because the Cincinnati, Ohio–based fruit company has facilities around the world, from Latin America to Asia, its treasury operations must do transactions in many different types of foreign currencies and manage the foreign-exchange risks they present. "We're making a big push to centralize things and reduce our huge number of legal entities," Younger says. Her goal is to cut the number of accounts to 150 or less and minimize the amount of cash not being put to use.

Many companies are joining Chiquita in the quest for more efficient global cash management systems. Enterprise-wide cash management has now taken on strategic implications and goes well beyond cutting costs and transaction fees. "There's a lot of emphasis now on cash flow, cash forecasts, and secure funding for the future—and on making sure analysts appreciate what you have done," says Martin Boyd, executive vice president for strategy and enterprise treasury at SunGard Treasury Systems in Calabasas, California. "Executives want to be able to see the current consolidated cash position of the enterprise and then drill down to see specific sources of exposure and risk and be able to take appropriate action quickly at the local level." Today's enterprise resource planning systems and banking software make it possible to deliver these reports almost in real time.

Developing the systems to centralize cash management worldwide may sound simple in theory, but in practice it's extremely complex. In addition to dealing with multiple foreign currencies, treasurers must understand and follow banking practices and regulatory and tax requirements in each country. Regulations may impede their ability to move funds freely across borders. Also, local managers may resist the shift to a centralized structure, because they don't want to give up control of cash generated by their units. Corporate financial managers must be sensitive to and aware of local customs and adapt the centralization strategy accordingly. As Jim O'Neill, head of global economic research at Goldman Sachs, says, "Employing a cookie-cutter prescription to global processes yields little success."

CRITICAL THINKING QUESTIONS

1. What are the benefits of centralizing cash management for a multinational company? Are there any disadvantages?
2. Suggest strategies that corporate financial managers can use to minimize local managers' resistance to new cash management policies.

SOURCES: Richard Gamble, "Now, the Only Choice Is to Go Global on Cash," *Treasury & Risk Management* (December 2002/January 2003), downloaded from http://www.treasuryandrisk.com; Blythe McGarvie, "Going Native," *CFO Europe* (March 21, 2003), downloaded from http://www.cfo.com; and Ann Queree and Abe De Ramos, "So Many Countries, So Few GTCs," *CFO* (November 2001), downloaded from http://www.cfo.com.

forecasts. And as the box "Expanding Around the Globe" explains, the increasing interdependence of the world's economies requires an international approach to finance. CFOs have taken center stage in the post-Sarbanes-Oxley-Act era, shifting from a strategic focus to overseeing corporate compliance with the act. The continued expansion of the financial manager's role in risk management is a natural outgrowth of the new regulations. In a surprising development, Coca-Cola and some other major companies have decided to stop releasing quarterly earnings forecasts.

The Changing Role of the CFO

Enron's Andy Fastow, Tyco's Mark Swartz, and WorldCom's Scott Sullivan focused the spotlight on CFOs—for the wrong reasons. Their misdeeds changed the public's perception of CFOs for the worse. Other holders of this title now find themselves on the defense, assuring board members, stockholders, and others that most CFOs are honest and operate with the highest standards of integrity. As Ed Moneypenny, 7-Eleven's CFO, says, "I've never had anyone put pressure on me to fudge the numbers."

During the 1990s, CFOs expanded their jobs beyond the ordinary finance responsibilities. No longer just numbers people, they joined top management in developing and implementing the firm's strategic direction. Negotiating billion-dollar mergers and finding creative financing vehicles were all part of the day's work. They were the company's face to the Wall Street analysts, who watched to see if the company would meet each quarter's earnings estimates.

The financial manipulations of Enron, Tyco, and WorldCom placed all CFOs under a magnifying glass. The Sarbanes-Oxley Act, discussed in detail in Chapter 18, clearly prohibited certain practices and established more stringent regulations for financial reporting. To avoid any suspicion of wrongdoing, companies often voluntarily ended strategies that were legal but could raise questions.

CFOs now must take the central role in reestablishing public trust, moving quickly to assure stakeholders that their company's transactions and reporting are honest. "My job is still to say, 'No, no, no!' whenever something doesn't make sense financially," says Home Depot CFO Carol Tomé. At the same time, the CFO should provide insight on the affairs of the company and its businesses to the CEO and the board.

"Every single aspect of my job is more difficult today than it was a year ago," says Dan Berce, CFO of AmeriCredit Corporation, a finance company. Investor relations now takes up 25 to 50 percent of his time, compared to almost none five years ago. He meets with investors, analysts, and mutual fund managers to review his company's business and financial statements. For example, he explains changes in accounting procedures to allay investor fears of possible impropriety.

In addition to all their additional responsibilities, however, CFOs are gaining a higher profile with their companies' boards. The increased status may mean higher compensation, as well as greater opportunities to move into a top executive job. [17]

Weighing the Risks after September 11, 2001

How can a company anticipate catastrophic events like September 11, 2001 and minimize the devastating impact on business? Many companies have created a new position, Chief Risk Officer, to study risk potential and coordinate risk management procedures throughout the company.

© AP / WIDE WORLD PHOTOS

The job of managing a company's risk became even more difficult after the September 11, 2001 terrorist attacks. No one had ever imagined an event of this magnitude, one that would bring business operations at New York companies to a halt. The ripple effect affected firms in all industries. Yet how do you prepare in advance for these events? Adding to the challenge were the volatility of the economy and financial markets at home and abroad.

Companies face a wide range of risks, including:

- *Credit risk.* Exposure to loss as a result of default on a financial transaction or a reduction in a security's market value due to decline in the credit quality of the debt issuer.
- *Market risk.* Risk resulting from adverse movements in the level or volatility of market prices of securities, commodities, and currencies.
- *Operational risk.* The risk of unexpected losses arising from deficiencies in a firm's management information, support, and control systems and procedures.

Ford Motor Company recently implemented new procedures and systems to consolidate the company-wide risk exposure of its many subsidiaries. It started with a Web-based tool to calculate credit exposure at different levels. Next came exposure limits and monitoring and reporting policies to identify problems and minimize risk. With the system fully operational, Ford can see its total credit risk exposure. This allows managers to forestall potential problems and be more proactive in managing risks.[18]

Because a failure in a company's risk control procedures can lead to substantial financial losses, financial managers continue to be key players in **risk management,** the process of identifying and evaluating risks and selecting and managing techniques to adapt to risk exposures. Many companies have created a new position, Chief Risk Officer (CRO), to coordinate risk management procedures throughout the company. Companies are also using risk management in response to new corporate governance

risk management
The process of identifying and evaluating risks and selecting and managing techniques to adapt to risk exposures.

guidelines. Better risk management procedures are important to stockholders in the post-Enron era. They want to know that companies have taken steps to minimize risks that would affect the company's values.[19]

In response to the September 11, 2001 attacks, one insurance company, Aon Re, has developed a terrorism exposure–analysis tool model. It uses its proprietary database of potential terrorism targets in the United States—for example, the top 500 skyscrapers, sports venues, major landmarks, and airports—and matches them to client locations. It can run different scenarios that give clients an estimate of the risk they face if terrorists attacked any of their locations. Clients that have used the service have been shocked at their potential exposure to business and financial risks. "They were not aware of the exposures they had both to loss of life, and injury and property damage," says Michael Bungert, Aon Re's chief executive. "When you have the ability to analyze what could happen based on different weapons that could be used, it is startling." By identifying total exposure, Aon Re's model helps companies see what types of insurance they need to cover such areas as workers' compensation, business interruption, and property damage.[20]

concept check

How has the role of CFO changed since the passage of the Sarbanes-Oxley Act?

Why are improved risk management procedures important to stockholders?

Great Ideas to Use Now

Whether you are a marketing manager, purchasing agent, or systems analyst, knowledge of finance will help you to do your job better. You'll be able to understand your company's financial statements, its financial condition, and management's investment and financing decisions. Financial information also provides feedback on how well you are doing and identifies problems. On a more practical note, you may be asked to prepare a budget for your department or unit. Employees who understand the financial decision-making process will be able to prepare proposals that address financial concerns. As a result, they will be more likely to get the resources they require to accomplish the firm's goals.

If you own a business, you must pay close attention to financial management. Without financial plans you may find yourself running out of cash. It's easy to get so caught up in growing sales that you neglect your billing and collection methods. In fact, managing accounts receivable is often one of the more challenging aspects of running a young company. But you can't rely on revenue increases to solve your cash flow problems. Good receivables practices start with credit policies. Be choosy when it comes to offering trade credit and check customers' credit references and payment history thoroughly. Set the initial credit limit fairly low until the customer establishes a prompt payment history. Here are some other ways to improve collections:

- Bill frequently, not just at the end of the month, so that money flows in throughout the month. Send bills when milestones are reached, such as making a presentation or completing a phase of a project.
- Clearly state payment terms, and make sure that the language on the invoice matches the contract.
- Establish regular and frequent follow-up procedures. Some companies call to notify the customer that the bill has been sent and to make sure the customer is satisfied. Weekly calls are in order for late payments.
- Try to get a firm date by which you will be paid, and be prepared to say what you will do if you aren't paid on time—for example, stopping work on a project or not shipping the next part of the order.

- Keep detailed notes of all conversations relating to a collection: your contact, date of the call, what was promised, and what you replied. You can then e-mail this as confirmation of your understanding and as another reminder.
- Monitor results of outstanding receivables collection.
- Don't fill new orders from customers who are continually delinquent.[21]

You can also apply financial management techniques to your personal life, as the budget exercise in the "Try It Now!" box demonstrates.

Try It Now

Prepare a personal budget. A personal budget is one of the most valuable tools for personal financial planning. It will help you evaluate your current financial situation, spending patterns, and goals. Use the following steps to create your budget:

1. Using credit-card receipts, check records, and other documents, record your income and expenses for the past 30 days. Based on this information, develop a personal budget for the next month. Record your budget in the "Planned" column of the worksheet in Exhibit 20.5. Include scholarships or grants as other income sources.
2. Track your actual income and expenses for one month. Write down *everything* you spend on a daily basis, or you will forget little things (like snacks) that add up over the course of a month. Record your actual totals in the "Actual" column of the worksheet.
3. At the end of the budget period, compare your budget to your actual results. Record any differences between the "Planned" and "Actual" values in the "Variance" column of the worksheet. How close were you to your budget estimates? In what categories did you overspend? Where did you underspend? Did creating the budget have any impact on how you allocated your money to different categories and how you spent your money?
4. Optional: Use the results of your first month's budget to project next month's income and expenses. And repeat the monitoring process.

Customer Satisfaction and Quality

Because an organization's finance department affects every other area of the firm, it must adhere to the highest quality standards. "Our decision-making needs to be near-perfect, if not perfect," says Ruth Ann M. Gillis, former CFO of Exelon Corp., an electric utility.[22]

Reliable and consistent financial reports and analyses are critical for managers throughout the firm and also to investors, creditors, suppliers, and customers. Because CEOs and CFOs must now certify the company's financial reports under the Sarbanes-Oxley Act, they are demanding that their managers adhere to strict quality control procedures and guidelines. To minimize risks of errors, companies are establishing formal rules and procedures for corporate finance. Some CFOs, including Home Depot's Carol Tomé and Consolidated Edison's Joan Freilich, ask key finance managers to sign personal statements that the financial statements they submit are correct.[23]

Financial managers are continually looking for ways to improve the quality of their forecasts and budgets. Unhappy with the level of accuracy in its cash forecasts, Dell Computer developed the Enzo Liquidity Forecasting Tool. It chose the name in honor of race car designer Enzo Ferrari, to underscore the speed of Dell's cash forecasts. Complex cash flow forecasts now take one person an afternoon to prepare, instead of three people working for two days. Accuracy is extremely high: the variance is less than $30 million on an accounts payable balance of $5 billion, a 99.4 percent accuracy level. Better cash forecasts were one reason Dell was able to raise its investment income about $1.5 million annually. In addition, Enzo's sophisticated analytical powers gives financial managers a broader view of the cash picture. "Any question you can have about a scenario, you can answer," says Nathan Brunner, senior finance consultant at Dell.[24]

Looking Ahead at Krispy Kreme

Krispy Kreme's financial condition remains strong as it continues to open new stores at a record pace. Sales growth has stayed in the 25 to 30 percent range, well above its retail restaurant industry peers, even during the economic slowdown. Net income and earnings per share (EPS) climbed as the company brought new franchised and company-owned stores online. It has reduced the capital investment required to open new stores from $1.4 million to about $1 million through improved engineering and purchasing economies of scale.

Exhibit 20.5 Monthly Budget Worksheet

Name: ____________________

Month of ____________________

	Planned	Actual	Variance
Income			
Wages (take-home pay)	______	______	______
Support from relatives	______	______	______
Loans	______	______	______
Withdrawals from savings	______	______	______
Other ________	______	______	______
Other ________	______	______	______
(1) Total Available Income	______	______	______
Expenses			
Fixed Expenses			
Housing	______	______	______
Automobile payment	______	______	______
Insurance	______	______	______
Loan repayment	______	______	______
Savings for goals	______	______	______
Tuition and fees	______	______	______
Other ________	______	______	______
Subtotal, Fixed Expenses	______	______	______
Flexible Expenses			
Food	______	______	______
Clothing	______	______	______
Personal care	______	______	______
Entertainment and recreation	______	______	______
Transportation	______	______	______
Telephone	______	______	______
Utilities (electricity, gas, water)	______	______	______
Cable TV	______	______	______
Medical and dental	______	______	______
Books, magazines, educational supplies	______	______	______
Gifts	______	______	______
Other ________	______	______	______
Other ________	______	______	______
Subtotal, Flexible Expenses	______	______	______
(2) Total Expenses	______	______	______
Cash Surplus (Deficit) [(1)–(2)]	______	______	______

Looking Ahead at Krispy Kreme *(continued)*

Even Krispy Kreme wasn't able to escape shareholder scrutiny about its accounting and financing methods. Press reports raised concerns about using a legitimate but complex financing technique called a synthetic lease to finance a doughnut mix plant. Investors, reading headlines like "Krispy Kreme Bites," worried that the off-balance-sheet financing could cause Enron-like problems. "In this new environment, it was shoot first and ask questions later," explained CEO Scott Livengood. He and CFO Randy Casstevens took a proactive stance to assure investors that the company's financial reporting and corporate governance procedures met the highest standards.[25]

Summary of Learning Goals

1 What roles do finance and the financial manager play in the firm's overall strategy?

Finance is the art and science involved in managing the firm's money. The financial manager must decide how much money is needed and when, how best to use the available funds, and how to get the required financing. The financial manager's responsibilities include financial planning, investing (spending money), and financing (raising money). Maximizing the value of the firm is the main goal of the financial manager, whose decisions often have long-term effects.

2 How does a firm develop its financial plans, including forecasts and budgets?

Financial planning enables the firm to estimate the amount and timing of the financial resources it needs to meet its business goals. The planning process begins with forecasts based on the demand for the firm's products. Short-term forecasts project expected revenues and expenses for one year. They are the basis for cash budgets, which show the flow of cash into and out of the firm and are used to plan day-to-day operations. Long-term forecasts project revenues and expenses over more than 1 year, typically 2 to 10 years. These strategic plans allow top management to analyze the impact of different options on the firm's profits.

3 What types of short-term and long-term expenditures does a firm make?

A firm invests in short-term expenses—supplies, inventory, and wages—to support current production, marketing, and sales activities. The financial manager manages the firm's investment in current assets so that the company has enough cash to pay its bills and support accounts receivable and inventory. Long-term expenditures (capital expenditures) are made for fixed assets such as land, buildings, machinery, and equipment. Because of the large outlays required for capital expenditures, financial managers carefully analyze proposed projects to determine which offer the best returns.

4 What are the main sources and costs of unsecured and secured short-term financing?

Short-term financing comes due within one year. The main sources of unsecured short-term financing are trade credit, bank loans, and commercial paper. Secured loans require a pledge of certain assets, such as accounts receivable or inventory, as security for the loan. Factoring, or selling accounts receivable outright at a discount, is another form of short-term financing.

5

How do the two primary sources of long-term financing compare?

Financial managers must choose the best mix of debt and equity for their firm. The main advantage of debt financing is the tax-deductibility of interest. But debt involves financial risk because it requires the payment of interest and principal on specified dates. Equity—common and preferred stock—is considered a permanent form of financing on which the firm may or may not pay dividends. Dividends are not tax-deductible.

6

What are the major types, features, and costs of long-term debt?

The main types of long-term debt are term loans, bonds, and mortgage loans. Term loans can be secured or unsecured and generally have 5- to 12-year maturities. Bonds usually have initial maturities of 10 to 30 years. Mortgage loans are secured by real estate. Long-term debt usually costs more than short-term financing because of the greater uncertainty that the borrower will be able to make the scheduled loan payments.

7

When and how do firms issue equity, and what are the costs?

The chief sources of equity financing are common stock, retained earnings, and preferred stock. The cost of selling stock includes issuing costs and potential dividend payments. Retained earnings are profits reinvested in the firm. For the issuing firm, preferred stock is more expensive than debt because its dividends are not tax-deductible and its claims are secondary to those of debt holders, but less expensive than common stock. Venture capital is often a source of equity financing for small and growing, typically high-tech, companies.

8

What trends are affecting the practice of financial management?

The role of the CFO has changed since the passage of the Sarbanes-Oxley Act, with CFOs taking the central role in overseeing corporate compliance with the Act and reestablishing public trust. They must balance the roles of corporate cop and strategic planner. The continued expansion of the financial manager's role in risk management is a natural outgrowth of the new regulations and September 11, 2001. Companies face a wide range of risks, including credit risk, market risk, and operational risk. More companies are adopting risk management to identify and evaluate risks and select techniques to control and reduce risk.

Some major companies have decided to stop releasing quarterly earnings forecasts.

Preparing for Tomorrow's Workplace

1. The head of your school's finance department has asked you to address a group of incoming business students about the importance of finance to their overall business education. Develop an outline with the key points you would cover in your speech.
2. As a financial manager at General Foods Company, you are preparing forecasts and budgets for a new line of high-nutrition desserts. Why should the

KEY TERMS

accounts payable 643
accounts receivable 641
bonds 647
budgets 639
capital budgeting 642
capital budgets 640
capital expenditures 642
cash budgets 640
cash flows 637
cash management 640
commercial paper 641
common stock 647
dividends 649
factoring 645
financial management 636
financial risk 645
line of credit 643
long-term forecasts 639
marketable securities 641
mortgage loan 647
operating budgets 640
preferred stock 650
retained earnings 649
return 638
revolving credit agreement 644
risk 638
risk management 654
risk-return trade-off 638
secured loans 645
short-term forecasts 639
stock dividends 649
term loan 646
trade credit 643
unsecured loans 643

finance department prepare these plans for the product development group? What factors would you consider in developing your projections and assessing their impact on the firm's profits?

3. You are the cash manager for a chain of sporting goods stores facing a cash crunch. To date, the chain has always paid accounts payable within the credit period. The CFO wants to consider extending payments beyond the due date. Write a memo that discusses the pros, cons, and ethics of stretching accounts payable as well as other cash-saving options to investigate.
4. You are the chief financial officer of Discovery Labs, a privately held, five-year-old biotechnology company that needs to raise $3 million to fund the development of a new drug. Prepare a report for the board of directors that discusses the types of long-term financing available to the firm, their pros and cons, and the key factors to consider in choosing a financing strategy.
5. Microsoft's announcement that it would begin paying dividends pleased investors and prompted other companies to consider following Microsoft's lead. However, some financial experts caution them to look long and hard before committing themselves to dividends. "If you lock yourself into a regular dividend, it reduces debt capacity and reduces financial flexibility, in exchange for which you get absolutely nothing," says Al Ehrbar, partner at consulting firm Stern Stewart. Also, paying dividends might signal that the company doesn't have good growth opportunities in which to invest. Others counter that dividends can help a company's stock. Siebel Systems CFO Ken Goldman believes that dividends "could decrease the volatility of your stock and it could help put a floor on your stock."[26] Standard & Poor's data supports this; in 2002 the 350 dividend paying stocks in the S&P 500 outperformed nonpayers. Divide the class into two teams to debate whether dividends add value to a company's stock.

WORKING THE NET

1. GetSmart (**http://www.getsmart.com**) is an information service that offers advice on business as well as personal loans. Click on Business Finance Center and move through the various types of loans. Try the questionnaires in each area, using different answers, to see what is necessary to qualify for that financing option.
2. If factoring accounts receivable is still a mystery to you, visit the 21st Financial Solutions site, **http://www.21stfinancialsolutions.com**. Follow the links on the home page to answer these questions: What are factoring's advantages? What are the additional benefits, and what types of companies can use factoring to their advantage? Then summarize the factoring process.
3. Visit the Wells Fargo Bank site, **http://www.wellsfargo.com**, to learn about the bank's products and services for corporate customers. Under the tab labeled Commercial, link to Business Financing. Describe briefly each type of loan Wells Fargo offers. Then do the same for Treasury Management services. How can the bank's Commercial Electronic Office help financial managers? What other services does the bank offer commercial clients.
4. Use the Venture Capital Resource Directory at vFinance, **http://www.vfinance.com**, to link to three different venture-capital firms. Compare the firms' investment strategies (industry specialization, age of companies in which they invest, etc.). Also do an AngelSearch to check out two angel investor firms. How do their requirements differ from the venture firms?
5. Want the latest headlines in management? Find news on market, credit, operational and other types of risk at RiskCenter, **http://www.riskcenter.com**.

Creative Thinking Case

Fitter International Keeps Its Balance

It was the breakthrough Louis Stack had been waiting for: a chance to sell his company's balance-related fitness products at Target Stores. Fitter International's high-end products, long popular with sports trainers and physical therapists, were starting to appear in specialty outdoor and sports stores. Adding Target as a channel would greatly increase Fitter's sales and profit potential.

As wonderful as the deal sounded, there was a catch: Target's buyers wanted a three-product, branded line priced at about half his current prices. Stack weighed the pros and cons. His company, located in Calgary, Canada, would have to change drastically to meet Target's price requirements. He would have to totally redesign his "wobble board" with lower-cost materials, find a new manufacturer for the board, negotiate better pricing for the "sitting disk" products, and find a less expensive supplier of fitness balls. The costs of moving to a larger facility, reengineering the wobble board, hiring more staff, developing new packaging, and marketing the products would run to $315,000 or more.

Spending such a large amount was daunting to Stack, who after 14 years of operating on a shoestring was finally on solid financial footing. On the other hand, greater sales volume and the new vendors would let him reduce the cost of his products by about 40 percent. "As long as we can keep our ratios in line, we can get debt financing," he figured. He also worried that the new lower-priced retail brand might pull sales away from his high-quality professional line.

Nike and Reebok had introduced similar balance products, indicating to Stack that there was a large market to tap. But there were definite risks as well. Would Target be calling all the shots? How would its payment terms affect Fitter's cash flow? Could the company handle the larger sales volume? He was worried that growing too quickly could throw the company off-balance, yet he realized that not doing so could cost him market leadership.

Stack decided to take the (fitness) ball and run with it. He increased his line of credit with Royal Bank of Canada from $150,000 to $225,000, obtained a $100,000 term loan, and moved ahead with his plans. Just as the pieces were coming into place, the buyer who was sponsoring Fitter products left Target, placing the deal in jeopardy.

Stack quickly regrouped, deciding to capitalize on Fitter's success with specialty stores. Sales took off, and Fitter products began appearing in a variety of stores, from Road Runner Sports, the world's largest running store, to the Discovery Channel Store. Yet the idea of working with Target still has some appeal, and Stack wonders about the impact on Fitter of entering the mass market.

CRITICAL THINKING QUESTIONS

1. How would Stack use capital budgeting techniques to analyze the original Target proposal? List the type of information he would need to evaluate whether or not to proceed.
2. Fitter International's revenues would go up significantly as a result of its agreement with Target. So why would the company need a larger bank credit facility?
3. What questions should Stack ask in deciding whether to go after Target's business again? What are the risks and rewards?

SOURCES: Donna Fenn, "The Offer You Almost Can't Refuse," Inc. (January 1, 2003), downloaded from http://www.inc.com; and Fitter International Web site, http://www.fitter1.com.

Video Case

Tweeter Sings a Different Tune

From a single store in Boston in 1972, Tweeter Home Entertainment Group has grown into a premier national chain with 200 stores and 2002 revenues of almost $800 million. It is not only profitable but still has plenty of growth potential. Unlike other national electronics chains, the company doesn't try to be all things to all people. It sells only mid- to high-end audio and video equipment—no low-end products, computers, home office equipment, or appliances.

"Tweeter has been successful because we have been true to our niche as a specialty retailer," says Joe McGuire, Tweeter's chief financial officer. "We are clear on who we are—and who we are not." Since 1996, when it began an aggressive expansion program of new-store openings and acquisitions, the company has grown at about 44 percent annually. By 2003 it had purchased 11 other small audio-video companies with a similar product mix and transformed itself into a national retailer of high-end consumer electronics. The company went public in July 1998.

"Being CFO of a company that's growing, and getting the chance to take the company public is a lot of fun," McGuire says. He points out that successful growth requires that the "back end of house" is in order. "You cannot grow a company at 50 to 60 percent if you do not have strong financial controls in place, run good management information systems, and provide decision support to people who are running the company."

Tweeter's rapid expansion through acquisitions has placed pressure on McGuire to maintain a strong profit picture. Reducing accounts receivable and inventory has been a priority. He also arranged for a larger asset-based bank credit facility in order to give Tweeter greater operating flexibility.

McGuire believes that the most important measure for a public company that wants access to the capital markets is net profits. "We can talk about cash flow or return on assets—and they all have their place in the process. But they must support our decision to grow net income." He continues, "We believe in keeping it simple. We spend a lot of time measuring net margins and knowing the components and also looking at return on equity. Someone who invested in Tweeter last year should be entitled to see that money grow this year."

Tweeter's marketing strategy is consistent with its financial objectives. "We haven't had a sale since 1995," says McGuire. Instead Tweeter features everyday competitive prices—an unusual strategy in the consumer electronics industry, which advertises sales almost daily. By selling higher-level items, Tweeter has more room to set prices at profitable levels. "Selling products below cost does not help gross margins," explains McGuire. "The gross margin to the retailer on a $299 20-inch Sony TV is 17 or 18 points gross margin, whereas a 36-inch Sony VGA TV selling for $3,000 has 28 or 29 points of gross margin attached to it."

CRITICAL THINKING QUESTIONS

1. Evaluate Joe McGuire's financial management practices based on what you have learned in the chapter about the financial manager's primary goal and key responsibilities.
2. What are the general and financial management implications of growing the company through acquisitions compared to opening new stores?
3. How does being a public company affect Tweeter's financial management decisions? What advantages does it bring?

SOURCES: Adapted from material in the video "Financial Management at Tweeter Home Entertainment Group" and on the Tweeter corporate Web site, http://www.tweeter.com, accessed June 9, 2003; Laura Heller, "Profit Picture Still Sharp Despite Rapid Acquisition," DSN Retailing Today (January 7, 2002); "Tweeter Home Entertainment Group Launches Phase One of a Major Strategic Repositioning Initiative," Business Wire (May 29, 2003); and "Tweeter Home Entertainment Group Reports Results for Its Second Fiscal Quarter Ended March 31, 2003," Business Wire (April 24, 2003), all downloaded from http://www.findarticles.com.

E-Commerce Case

Boston Beer Brews Up a New Finance System

Winner of more than 500 international awards for its high-quality beers, Boston Beer is one of the leading craft beer producers in the United States. Best known for its Samuel Adams Boston Lager, the company also brews other Samuel Adams brands, seasonal specialties, HardCore Crisp Hard Cider, and Twisted Tea Hard Iced Tea. Its financial systems, however, had not kept pace with the company's growth and were in need of upgrading.

For example, preparing budgets was a time-consuming process. Because sales personnel entered data manually, it took about five weeks to gather, consolidate, and review the information to develop budgets and plans. Shortening the planning cycle was a priority, so CFO Richard Lindsay and his team began looking at software applications to automate the process. He also included the salespeople in the selection process. "If it wasn't going to be easy for the users, it wasn't going to work," Lindsay said. "Our salespeople know the business best so we wanted to get them involved in the process."

Boston Beer chose Hyperion Planning, a Web-based tool, and implemented the system in just six weeks. About 52 salespeople and eight finance department staffers access the system over the Web. In addition to reducing the planning cycle to three weeks, the Hyperion application was easy to learn and use for both financial and nonfinancial employees. Not only was the entire budget process streamlined, but the software provided other features that the sales staff liked, such as instant profit and loss statements and better information on margins, pricing, and revenue.

The availability of better and more accurate financial information has been a great timesaver for the company's analysts. "The planning process is much smoother and the reporting is more flexible than prior solutions," reports Lindsay. Boston Beer now does annual enterprise-wide plans and monthly revisions of the financial forecasts but may switch to rolling six-quarter forecasts to improve the process even more. This would help the company focus on key drivers rather than budgeting at a low level of detail.

Prior to installing the new planning system, analysts spent 70 percent of their time on data collection and organization and only 30 percent on analysis and decision support. Now budget preparation takes only 30 percent of their time, leaving them many more hours to evaluate the plans and do resource planning and pricing analysis. "They can spend more time looking at what is in the plan, and it is easy for them to pick up errors, which are much more transparent," says Lindsay.

CRITICAL THINKING QUESTIONS

1. Why did Boston Beer choose a Web-based financial-planning system? What advantages does it have over a non-Web system?
2. What factors should a CFO like Richard Lindsay consider when choosing a financial-planning system?
3. How can the availability of better financial information help other departments, such as marketing and production? What types of analyses might these areas request?

SOURCES: "The Boston Beer Company Streamlines Finances with Hyperion Planning," Customer Success Stories, Hyperion corporate Web site, http://www.hyperion.com/customer_successes/boston_beer.cfm, accessed April 29, 2003; and Boston Beer Company corporate Web site, http://www.bostonbeer.com, accessed May 1, 2003.

Hot Links Address Book

When you come across a finance term you don't understand, visit the Hypertextual Finance Glossary at
http://www.duke.edu/~charvey/Classes/wpg/glossary.htm

What challenges do today's financial managers face? To find out, browse through recent issues of *CFO* magazine at
http://www.cfo.com

Find an introduction to the types of cash management services banks offer their customers at Centura Bank's site,
http://www.rbccentura.com/business/cashman/index.html

Learn about the services and current rates offered by 1st Commercial Credit, a factoring firm, at
http://www.1stcommercialcredit.com

Which companies are getting funding from venture capital firms? For this and other information, visit vFinance.com at
http://www.vfinance.com

Learn how Reuters Risk Management Services, at
http://risk.reuters.com
helps companies with global operations identify, measure, and manage financial risk.

appendix

MANAGING RISK AND INSURANCE

Overview

Every day, businesses and individuals are exposed to many different kinds of risk. Investors who buy stocks or speculate in commodities may earn a profit, but they also take the risk of losing all or part of their money. Illness is another type of risk, involving financial loss from not only the cost of medical care but also the loss of income.

Businesses, too, are exposed to many types of risk. Market risks, such as lower demand for a product or worsening economic conditions, can hurt a firm. Other risks involve customers, who could be injured on a company's premises or by a company's product. Like homes and cars owned by individuals, business property can be damaged or lost through fire, floods, and theft. Businesses must also protect themselves against losses from theft by dishonest employees. The loss of a key employee is another risk, especially for small firms.

It is impossible to avoid all risks, but individuals and businesses can minimize risks or buy protection—called insurance—against them. Although some risks are uninsurable, many others are insurable. Let's now look at basic risk concepts and the types of insurance available to cover them.

Risk Management

9 learning goal

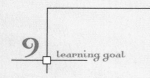

Every business faces risks like the ones listed above. **Risk management** involves analyzing the firm's operations, evaluating the potential risks, and figuring out how to minimize losses in a cost-efficient manner. In today's complex business environment, the concern for public and employee welfare and the potential for lawsuits have both increased. Risk management thus plays a vital role in the overall management of a business.

Types of Risk

Individuals and firms need to protect themselves against the economic effects of certain types of risk. In an insurance sense, **risk** (sometimes called *pure risk*) is the chance of financial loss due to a peril. Insurable risks include fire, theft, auto accident, injury or illness, a lawsuit, or death. **Speculative risk** is the chance of either loss or gain. Someone who buys stock in the hope of later selling it at a profit is taking a speculative risk and cannot be insured against it.

speculative risk
The chance of either loss or gain, without insurance against the possible loss.

Strategies to Manage Risk

Risk is part of life. Nevertheless, people have four major ways to deal with it:

- **Risk avoidance.** Staying away from situations that can lead to loss. A person can avoid the risk of a serious injury by choosing not to go skydiving. KinderCare, a nationwide day-care chain, could avoid risk by not transporting children to and from school or taking them on field trips. Manufacturers who wish to avoid risks could produce only goods that have a proven track record. But these risk-avoidance strategies could stifle growth in the long run. Thus risk avoidance is not good for all risks.
- **Self-insurance.** The willingness to bear a risk without insurance, also called *risk assumption.* This offers a more practical way to handle many types of risks. Many large firms with warehouses or stores spread out over the United States—Sears or Kmart, for instance—may choose not to insure them. They assume that, even if disaster strikes one location, the others won't be harmed. The losses will probably be less than the insurance premiums for all the loca-

tions. Many companies self-insure because it is cheaper to assume some risks than to insure against them. Some choose to pay small claims themselves and insure only for catastrophic losses. Others "go naked," paying for all claims from company funds. This is clearly the most risky strategy. A big claim could cripple the firm or lead to bankruptcy.

- **Risk reduction.** Adopting techniques to prevent financial losses. For example, companies adopt safety measures to reduce accidents. Construction workers are required to wear hard hats and safety glasses. Airlines keep their aircraft in good condition and require thorough training programs for pilots and flight attendants. Hotels install smoke alarms, sprinkler systems, and firewalls to protect guests and minimize fire damage.
- **Risk transference.** Paying someone else to bear some or all of the risk of financial loss for certain risks that can't be avoided, assumed, or reduced to acceptable levels. The way to transfer risk is through **insurance.** Individuals and organizations can pay a fee (a *premium*) and get the promise of compensation for certain financial losses. The companies that take on the risks are called *insurance companies.*

insurance
The promise of compensation for certain financial losses.

Insurance Concepts

10 learning goal

Companies purchase insurance to cover insurable risks. An **insurance policy** is the written agreement that defines what the insurance covers and the risks that the insurance company will bear for the insured party. It also outlines the policy's benefits (the maximum amount that it will pay in the event of a loss) and the premium (the cost to the insured for coverage). Any demand for payment for losses covered by the policy is a *claim.*

Before issuing a policy, an insurance company reviews the applications of those who want a policy and selects those that meet its standards. This **underwriting** process also determines the level of coverage and the premiums. Each company sets its own underwriting standards based on its experience. For instance, a life insurance company may decide not to accept an applicant who has had a heart attack within five years (or to charge a 50 to 75 percent higher premium). A property insurer may refuse to issue a policy on homes near brush-filled canyons, which present above-average fire hazards.

To get insurance, the applicant must have an **insurable interest:** the chance of suffering a loss if a particular peril occurs. In most cases, a person cannot insure the life of a friend, because the friend's death would not be considered a financial loss. But business partners can get life insurance on each other's lives because the death of one of them would have a financial impact on their firm.

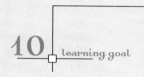

insurance policy
A written agreement that defines what the insurance covers and the risks that the insurance company will bear for the insured party.

underwriting
A review process of all insurance applications and the selection of those who meet the standards.

insurable interest
An insurance applicant's chance of loss if a particular peril occurs.

Insurable Risks

Insurance companies are professional risk takers, but they won't provide coverage against all types of risk. Some risks are insurable; some are not. For instance, changes in political or economic conditions are not insurable. An **insurable risk** is one that an insurance company will cover. For a risk to be insurable, it must meet these criteria:

- *The loss must not be under the control of the insured.* The loss must be accidental—that is, unexpected and occurring by chance. Insurance companies do not cover losses purposely caused by the insured party. No insurance company will pay for the loss of a clothing store that the insured set on fire. Nor will most companies pay life insurance benefits for a suicide.
- *There must be many similar exposures to that peril.* Insurance companies study the rates of deaths, auto accidents, fires, floods, and many other perils. They know about how many of these perils will occur each year. The **law of large numbers** lets them predict the likelihood that the peril will occur and then calculate premiums.

insurable risk
A risk that an insurance company will cover. It must meet certain criteria.

law of large numbers
Insurance companies' predictions of the likelihood that a peril will occur in order to calculate premiums.

Suppose that an insurance company has 150 policies in Morton, Iowa. The company knows from past experience that these policyholders are likely to have a total of 12 car accidents a year and that the average payment for a claim in Morton has been $1,000. The total claims for one year's car accidents in Morton would be $12,000 (12 accidents 3 $1,000). Thus the company would charge each policyholder a premium of at least $80 ($12,000 4 150). Profits and administrative expenses would make the premium somewhat higher.

- *Losses must be financially measurable.* The dollar amount of potential losses must be known so the insurance company can figure the premiums. Life insurance is for a fixed amount specified at the time the policy is bought. Otherwise, the company and the *beneficiary* (the one who gets the funds) would have to agree on the value of the deceased's life at the time of death. Premiums have to be calculated before then, however.
- *The peril must not be likely to affect all the insured parties at the same time.* Insurance companies must spread out their risks by insuring many people and businesses in many locations. This strategy helps minimize the chance that a single calamity will wipe out the insurance company.
- *The potential loss must be significant.* Insurance companies cannot afford to insure trivial things for small amounts. Many policies have **deductibles,** amounts that the insured must pay before insurance benefits begin.

deductibles
The amounts that the insured must pay before insurance benefits begin.

- *The company must have the right to set standards for insurance coverage.* Insurance companies can refuse to cover people with health problems like AIDS, cancer, or heart trouble, a poor driving record, or a dangerous job or hobby. They can also charge higher premiums because of the higher risks they are covering.

Premium Costs

Insurance policies must be economical—relatively low in cost compared to the benefits—so people will want to buy them. Yet the premiums must also cover the risks that the insurance company faces. Insurance companies collect statistics on many perils. Then specially trained mathematicians called *actuaries* use the law of large numbers to develop actuarial tables, which show how likely each peril is. Actuarial tables are the basis for calculating premiums. For example, actuaries use a mortality table showing average life expectancy and the expected number of deaths per 1,000 people at given ages to set life insurance premiums.

Almost every homeowner buys insurance to cover the perils of fire, theft, vandalism, and other home-related risks. With such a large pool of policyholders, homeowners policies are usually inexpensive. Annual premiums are about 0.5 percent (or less) of the value of the home. This low cost encourages people to buy policies and thereby helps spread the insurance companies' risk over many homes throughout the country.

When setting premiums, insurers also look at the risk characteristics of certain groups, in order to assess the probability of loss for those groups. For instance, smokers tend to die younger than nonsmokers do and thus pay higher life insurance premiums. Female drivers under the age of 25 have a lower rate of accidents than male drivers, so their car insurance premiums are lower.

Insurance Providers

Insurers can be either public or private. Public insurance coverage is offered by specialized government agencies. The federal government is in fact the largest single insurer in the United States. Private insurance coverage is provided by privately organized (nongovernment) companies.

Public Insurance

Government-sponsored insurance falls into two general categories: social insurance programs and other programs. Social insurance provides protection for problems beyond the scope of private insurers. These programs include:

unemployment insurance
Pays laid-off workers weekly benefits while they seek new jobs.

- *Unemployment insurance.* Every state has an **unemployment insurance** program that pays laid-off workers weekly benefits while they seek new jobs. Persons who terminate their employment voluntarily or are fired for cause are not eligible for unemployment insurance. These programs also provide job counseling and placement services. The benefits usually start a week after a person has lost a job and continue for 26 to 39 weeks, depending on the state. The size of the weekly benefit depends on the workers' previous income and varies from state to state. Unemployment insurance is funded by payroll taxes levied on employers.

workers' compensation
Covers the expenses of job-related injuries and diseases, including medical costs, rehabilitation, and job retraining if necessary.

- *Workers' compensation.* Every state has laws requiring employers to fund **workers' compensation** insurance to cover the expenses of job-related injuries and diseases, including medical costs, rehabilitation, and job retraining if necessary. It also provides disability income benefits (salary and wage payments) for workers who can't perform their job. Employers can buy workers' compensation policies or self-insure. A company's premium is based on the amount of its payroll and the types of risks present in the workplace. For instance, a construction company would pay a higher premium for workers' compensation insurance than would a jewelry store.

Social Security
Insurance that provides retirement, disability, death, and health benefits.

- *Social Security.* **Social Security** insurance provides retirement, disability, death, and health insurance benefits. Social Security is funded by equal contributions from workers and employers. These benefits go mostly to people over 65, although they are available to younger people who are disabled. More than 90 percent of all U.S. workers and their families are eligible to qualify for Social Security benefits.

Medicare
A health insurance program for those over 65.

- *Medicare.* A health insurance program for those over 65, **Medicare** was added to Social Security in 1965 and has two parts: hospital insurance, financed through the Social Security tax, and medical insurance, financed through government contributions and monthly premiums paid by those who want this coverage. Because Medicare pays only part of the insured's medical expenses, many people buy *supplemental insurance* from private insurance companies.

Private Insurance Companies

Private insurance companies sell property and liability insurance, health insurance, and life insurance. Life and health insurance companies dominate the industry, accounting for about 70 percent of total assets. Regulation of private insurance companies is under the control of the states and thus varies from state to state.

There are two basic ownership structures for private insurance companies: stockholder and mutual. Just like other publicly owned corporations, *stock insurance companies* are profit-oriented companies owned by stockholders. The stockholders do not have to be policyholders, and the policyholders do not have to be stockholders. Their profits come from insurance premiums in excess of claim payments and operating expenses and from investments in securities and real estate. Metropolitan Life Corporation is the largest stockholder-owned insurance company in the United States, with assets of about $257 billion. Other major stock insurance companies are Aetna, Allstate Insurance, Continental Insurance, Fireman's Fund Insurance, John Hancock, and Prudential. Of about 5,000 insurance companies in the United States, most are stock insurance companies.

The rest are *mutual insurance companies,* which are not-for-profit organizations owned by their policyholders and chartered by each state. Any excess income is returned to the policyholder-owners as dividends, used to reduce premiums, or retained to finance future operations. The policyholders elect the board of directors, who manage the company. Many of the large life insurance companies in the United States are mutuals, including New York Life, Masssachusetts Mutual, and Northwestern Mutual Life. State Farm, one of the largest auto insurers, is also a mutual company.

Types of Insurance

In Chapter 22, we will introduce several types of personal insurance coverage: property, liability, health, and life. Businesses also purchase insurance for these risks, but with some differences. Most companies offer group health and life insurance plans for their employees as a fringe benefit. Employers typically pay some of the health insurance premiums, and employees pay the rest. The cost is usually considerably less than for individual policies, although it pays to check before signing up. For example, companies may pay for the entire cost of life insurance equal to one or two times the employee's annual salary, with an option to purchase more under the group plan, but the premiums may be more expensive than buying an individual policy.

key-person life insurance
A term insurance policy that names the company as beneficiary.

Businesses often insure the lives of key employees, such as top executives, salespeople, inventors, and researchers, whose death could seriously limit the income or value of a firm. To protect themselves, businesses buy **key-person life insurance,** a life insurance policy that names the company as beneficiary. In the case of a partnership, which is dissolved when a partner dies, key-person insurance is often bought for each partner, with the other partner named as the beneficiary, so that the surviving partner can buy the partnership interest from the estate of the deceased and continue operating.

Property and Liability Insurance

More than 3,500 companies offer property and liability policies. This type of insurance is important for businesses, which wish to protect against losses of property and lawsuits arising from harm to other people. *Property insurance* covers financial losses from damage to or destruction of the insured's assets as a result of specified perils, while *liability insurance* covers financial losses from injuries to others and damage to or destruction of others' property when the insured is considered to be the cause. It also covers the insured's legal defense fees up to the maximum amount stated in the policy. Automobile liability insurance, which we will discuss in more detail in Chapter 22, is an example. It would pay for a fence damaged when the insured person lost control of his or her car. Commercial and product liability insurance also fall into this category.

Commercial liability insurance covers a variety of damage claims, including harm to the environment from pollution. In the case of *product liability,* if a defective furnace exploded and damaged a home, the manufacturer would be liable for the damages. If the manufacturer were insured, the insurance company would cover the losses or pay to dispute the claim in court.

Property and liability insurance is a broad category. Businesses buy many types of property and liability insurance. These protect against loss of property due to fire, theft, accidents, or employee dishonesty, and financial losses arising from liability cases. Landlords and owners of business property buy *building insurance,* a type of property coverage, for protection against both property damage and liability losses. For instance, if a person broke an arm slipping on a wet floor in a hardware store, the business's insurance policy would cover any claim.

coinsurance
Property insurance coverage that is equal to a certain percentage of the property's value.

Property insurance policies usually include a coinsurance clause. **Coinsurance** requires the property owner to buy insurance coverage equal to a certain percentage of the property's value. To cut premium costs, policyholders often insure buildings for less than their full value, in the hope that a fire or other disaster will damage only part of the property. But insurers limit the payout if the property is underinsured. They use coinsurance clauses as an incentive for businesses to maintain full insurance on their buildings. For instance, some fire insurance policies have an 80 percent coinsurance clause. If the owner of a building valued at $400,000 buys a policy with coverage equal to at least $320,000 (80% × $400,000), he or she will collect the full amount of any partial loss. If the owner buys a policy for less coverage, the insurance company will pay for only part of the partial loss.

Special Types of Business Liability Insurance

Businesses also purchase several other types of insurance policies, depending on their particular needs:

business interruption insurance

Covers such costs as rental of temporary facilities, wage and salary payments to employees, payments for leased equipment, fixed payments, and profits that would have been earned during that period.

theft insurance

A broad insurance coverage that protects business against losses for an act of stealing.

professional liability insurance

Insurance designed to protect top corporate management, who have been the target of malpractice lawsuits

- *Business interruption insurance.* This optional coverage is often offered with fire insurance. It protects business owners from losses occurring when the business must be closed temporarily after property damage. **Business interruption insurance** may cover such costs as rental of temporary facilities, wage and salary payments to employees, payments for leased equipment, fixed payments (for instance, rent and loans), and profits that would have been earned during the period. *Contingent business interruption insurance* covers losses to the insured in the event of property damage to a major supplier or customer.
- *Theft insurance.* Businesses also want to protect their property against financial losses due to crime. **Theft insurance** is the broadest coverage and protects businesses against losses from an act of stealing. Businesses can also buy more limited types of theft insurance.
- *Fidelity and surety bonds.* What if a firm has a dishonest employee? This situation is covered by a *fidelity bond,* an agreement that insures a company against theft committed by an employee who handles company money. If a restaurant manager is bonded for $50,000 and steals $60,000, the restaurant will recover all but $10,000 of the loss. Banks, loan companies, and retail businesses that employ cashiers typically buy fidelity bonds.

  A *surety bond,* also called a *performance bond,* is an agreement to reimburse a firm for nonperformance of acts specified in a contract. This form of insurance is most common in the construction industry. Contractors buy surety bonds to cover themselves in case the project they are working on is not completed by the specified date or does not meet specified standards. In practice, the insurance company often pays another contractor to finish the job or to redo shoddy work when the bonded contractor fails to perform.
- *Title insurance.* A title policy protects the buyer of real estate against losses caused by a defect in the title—that is, a claim against the property that prevents the transfer of ownership from seller to purchaser. It eliminates the need to search legal records to be sure that the seller was actually the owner of (had clear title to) the property.
- *Professional liability insurance.* This form of insurance covers financial losses (legal fees and court-awarded damages up to specific limits) resulting from alleged malpractice by professionals in fields like medicine, law, architecture, and dentistry. *Directors and officers insurance* is a type of **professional liability insurance** designed to protect top corporate management, who have also been the target of malpractice lawsuits. It pays for legal fees and court-awarded damages up to specific limits.

Chapter 21

© AP / WIDE WORLD PHOTOS

Understanding Securities and Securities Markets

learning goals

1. How do common stock and preferred stock differ as investments?
2. What are bonds, and what investment advantages and disadvantages do they offer?
3. What other types of securities are available to investors?
4. What is the function of the securities markets?
5. Where can investors buy and sell securities, and how are these securities markets regulated?
6. Which sources of investment information are the most helpful to investors?
7. What can investors learn from stock, bond, and mutual fund quotations?
8. What are the current trends in securities and securities markets?

Reinventing Charles Schwab & Co.

Like many corporate executives, Charles Schwab had every reason to be optimistic as the new millennium dawned in 2000. The stock market was booming, and so was demand for the discount brokerage services Charles Schwab & Co. (**http://www.schwab.com**) provided.

Since Schwab founded the company in 1975, Charles Schwab & Co. had catered to the needs of individual investors who preferred to do their own research and make their own decisions rather than pay the high prices charged by traditional brokerage firms. At Schwab's no-frills brokerage, the emphasis was on executing customer trades—not giving advice or pushing products.

As new investors flocked into the stock market in the 1990s, the company's customer base tripled in size. By 2000, Charles Schwab & Co. was making over 270,000 customer stock trades a day, many over its successful Internet site. Based on this success, the company's stock was also flourishing, selling for an all-time high of $44 a share.

After a decade of steady growth, however, the stock market "bubble" began to burst in mid-2000. As dot-com businesses began to fail and news of corporate scandals like Enron and WorldCom broke, investors began pulling out of the stock market. Economic uncertainty after September 11, also took a toll. Stock prices fell—and so did demand for brokerage services.

Charles Schwab & Co. was hit hard. The number of daily trades made by customers dropped below 130,000 by mid-2002, and the company posted a $13 million loss. Investors responded to the news by dumping their Charles Schwab stock. Soon, the stock was selling for only $7.50 a share.

In response, Schwab and his co-CEO David Pottruck were forced to make some tough decisions. To cut costs and boost profits, they fired more than 1,000 employees, closed several offices, and raised customer fees. Hoping to encourage customers to start trading stock again, the pair also decided to reinvent the company's services and marketing strategies.

First up: Build customer confidence by providing investment advice. In May 2002, Schwab announced the launch of the Schwab Equity Ratings. The fee-based research and advice service assigns a computer-generated letter grade of A through F to the stock of each publicly traded company. "This is perhaps the most significant moment in the company's history," said Schwab. "We are moving from the edges of client's investment decisions to helping them make those decisions."

Critical Thinking Questions

As you read this chapter, consider the following questions as they relate to Charles Schwab & Co.:

1. What external and internal factors have influenced the company's stock performance?
2. If you were advising Charles Schwab, what would be your major concerns? How would you resolve them?
3. How do you think investors will react to Charles Schwab's new strategies? Why?

Principles of Securities and Securities Markets

Charles Schwab & Co. is not the only company that has had to adapt to changing conditions in the securities industry. Record economic growth in the 1990s pushed the stock price of many firms to new levels and fueled tremendous structural changes in the securities markets. As 2000 dawned, however, a new cycle began. As the dot-com boom petered out, news of corporate scandals like those at Enron and WorldCom, and economic recession made investors wary. Uncertainty after September 11 sent securities markets around the world into a further tailspin. Faced with shrinking revenues and dropping stock prices, many corporate executives were forced to reevaluate company strategies in order to satisfy investors.

Today, more people have a direct stake in the stock market than ever before. While investing in the stock market was once the province of the wealthy, as the markets boomed in the 1990s, many smaller investors jumped into buying and selling stock. Almost half of all American households now hold stocks, compared to just 31 percent in 1989.[1]

Investors saw the value of their stock portfolios rise dramatically during the 1990s. Between year-end 1994 and 1998, the total value of U.S. common stocks increased an average of 25 percent a year. After peaking in March 2000, however, the stock market began a cyclical decline. By the start of 2003, the value of U.S. stocks had dropped 44 percent overall and investors had lost over $4.8 trillion.[2]

Historically, these recent events are not unique. The securities markets have a long history of rising and falling and ultimately rising again, affecting both corporate plans and investor pocketbooks. To capitalize on the cyclical nature of the securities markets, both business managers and investors must understand the basics of the securities traded and the securities markets. This chapter begins by describing the different types of securities available to investors: common and preferred stocks, bonds, mutual funds, futures contracts, and options. A discussion of the functions of the securities markets and the professionals that sell securities—investment bankers and stockbrokers—follows. Next, we'll examine the operation and regulation of securities exchanges and other markets. Discussions of the popular sources of investment information and security price quotations follow. Finally, we'll look at some important trends affecting the securities markets today.

Investor's Choice: Stocks and Bonds

securities
Investment certificates issued by corporations or governments that represent either equity or debt.

As we discussed in Chapter 20, a central concern of most businesses is raising capital to finance operations and expansion. Many corporations use securities as a source of long-term financing. **Securities** are investment certificates that represent either equity (ownership in the issuing organization) or debt (a loan to the issuer). Corporations and governments sell securities to investors, who in turn take on a certain amount of risk with the hope of receiving a profit from their investment. While we discussed equity and debt securities from the corporation's perspective in Chapter 20, let's review the advantages of these and other types of securities from an investor's viewpoint.

Sharing the Wealth—and the Risk: Stocks

1 learning goal

Equity securities, commonly called *stocks,* represent shares of ownership in a corporation. A share of stock is issued for each unit of ownership and the stockholder (owner) gets a stock certificate to prove ownership. If you own a share of stock in General Electric Corp., for example, you are a partial owner of GE. Your ownership interest isn't very big, because GE has billions of shares of stock outstanding, but your ownership gives you certain rights and potential rewards. The two types of equity securities are common stock and preferred stock. Each has advantages and disadvantages for investors.

Common Stock *Common stock* is the most widespread form of stock ownership. Common stockholders receive the right to vote on many important corporate decisions, such as who should sit on the company's board of directors and whether the firm should merge with another company. In most cases, common stockholders get one vote for each share of stock they own. Common stock also gives investors the opportunity to share in the company's success, either through dividends or stock price increases.

As discussed in Chapter 20, *dividends* are the part of corporate profits that the firm distributes to shareholders. Dividends for common stock can be paid either in cash or in additional shares of stock (called *stock dividends*). Common stock dividends are declared annually or quarterly (four times a year) by a corporation's board of directors. They are typically paid quarterly. However, common stock dividends are paid only after all other obligations of the firm—payments to suppliers, employees, bondholders, and other creditors, plus taxes and preferred stock dividends—have been met. Some firms, especially rapidly growing companies and those in high-technology industries, choose not to pay any dividends on their common stock. Instead, they reinvest their profits in more buildings, equipment, and new products in hope of earning greater profits in the future. As noted in Chapter 18, these reinvested profits are called *retained earnings.*

One advantage of common stock ownership is its liquidity: Many common stocks are actively traded in securities markets and can be quickly bought and sold. An investor can benefit by selling common stock when its price increases, or *appreciates,* above the original purchase price. For example, in 2000, Procter & Gamble's stock was trading at a low of $52 a share. Soon after, P&G chief executive A. G. Lafley launched a new strategy for the consumer products firm. Instead of constant—and costly—new-product introductions, P&G refocused its marketing efforts on its most successful and established products, including brands like Tide, Crest, and Pampers. As profits rose, so did the company's stock price. By early 2003, P&G's stock price had soared to $85 a share, a more than 60 percent increase.[3]

While the returns from common stock dividends and price appreciation can be quite attractive, common stockholders have no guarantee that they will get any return on their investment. Stock prices are subject to many risks related to the economy, the industry, and the company. Like any commodity, the price of a specific company's stock is affected by supply and demand. The supply of a stock is limited by the number of shares a company has issued, while demand is created by the number of investors who want to buy the stock from those who already own it. Factors that can increase demand for a stock—and its price—include strong financial reports, new product market opportunities, and positive industry trends. However, demand can fall—and a stock's price drop—when negative events occur.

The threat of a lawsuit or increased government regulation of a firm's industry can send stock prices downward. Market conditions can also affect a company's stock price. For example, videogame manufacturers have faced tough competition and a slowing market in the past few years. Electronic Arts, the publisher of popular games like Madden NFL and The Sims, saw its stock price drop nearly 33 percent in just three months in early 2003. The reason? Sales of Electronic Arts much-anticipated Sims Online interactive game didn't live up to sales expectations, forcing the firm to drastically cut the software's retail price.[4]

Factors like these can hold down a common stock's dividends and its price, making it hard to predict the stock's return. The "Focusing on Small Business" box on page 674 describes how investors in Rare Medium, an Internet-services firm, learned this lesson the hard way.

Focusing on Small Business

Rare Medium Investors Get Burned

At the time, the idea seemed brilliant: use the assets of an "old economy" business to get a stronger foothold into the booming market for Internet services. That was the plan in late 1998, when International Cogeneration Corp. (ICC), a small manufacturer of heating and air conditioning units, merged with Rare Medium, a fast-growing Internet consulting firm. ICC executives were anxious to cash in on the dot-com boom. After the merger, the new company took on the Rare Medium name and began selling off ICC's original business assets.

By 1999, the transformation was complete. The new company not only offered Internet design and consulting services to major clients like Nestlé, Microsoft, and MCI WorldCom, but it also began functioning as an "Internet incubator." As such, Rare Medium started investing in Internet start-ups. "As a result of the transformation that has taken place over the past year, our company is now well positioned for success and to share in the incredible growth opportunities of the Internet," read Rare Medium's 1999 annual report.

Investors, high on the promised profits of Internet companies, rushed to invest in Rare Medium. The company's stock soared from $4 just after the merger to a high of $94 in March 2000. Most investors, however, failed to spot two important trends that would affect Rare Medium's future: the stock market overall was peaking, and the dot-com boom was beginning to explode.

By the fall, Rare Medium was losing clients and cutting its staff. The firm's stock price fell to $3 a share by the end of 2000 and continued to slide throughout 2001 and 2002. Outside investors weren't the only ones who lost money. One Rare Medium executive had shares in the company worth $5 million at the height of the firm's rise. At the end of 2001, he sold those same shares for just $100,000.

By the end of 2002, Rare Medium's stock was virtually worthless and the company was dealing with a class action lawsuit filed by disgruntled investors. The final blow occurred when Nasdaq delisted Rare Medium's stock.

A handful of Rare Medium executives are now hoping to revive the company. They've exited the Internet-services industry completely and are trying to enter the satellite communications business. As of mid-2003, Rare Medium stock was still available for purchase by investors.

Critical Thinking Questions

1. Wall Street analysts warned as early as late 1998 that stock prices would eventually fall. Other analysts were also predicting the end of the dot-com boom. Why do you think investors continued to buy Rare Medium stock? What danger signs should investors have looked for?
2. Using the Internet, research Rare Medium's current stock performance. Do you agree or disagree with the decision of Rare Medium executives to try to revive the company by leaving the Internet-services industry completely? Why? Would you buy Rare Medium common stock in the next six months? Explain your anwer.

SOURCES: Sam Ames, "Investors See Nothing Hatching at Net Incubators," *CNET News.com* (October 19, 2000), downloaded from http://www.cnet.com; E. S. Browning and Ianthe Jeanne Dugan, "Aftermath of a Market Mania," *Wall Street Journal* (December 16, 2002), p. C1; Charles Cooper, "We Can Handle CEO Cheats," *CNET News.com* (July 11, 2002), downloaded from http://www.cnet.com; Rachel Konrad, "Hard Times See Exodus of CFOs," *CNET News.com* (March 26, 2001), downloaded from http://www.cnet.com; Lisa Rogak, "A Designer's Dilemma," *Business 2.0* (May 2000), downloaded from http://www.business2.com; Rare Medium corporate annual reports (1995–2002), downloaded from http://www.sec.gov.

Preferred Stock *Preferred stock* is a second form of corporate ownership. Unlike common stockholders, preferred stockholders do not receive voting rights. However, preferred stock does provide several advantages to investors that common stock does not, specifically in the payment of dividends and the distribution of assets if the firm is liquidated.

The dividend for preferred stock is usually set at the time the stock is issued, giving preferred stockholders a clearer picture of the dividend proceeds they can expect from their investment. This dividend can be expressed either in dollar terms or as a percentage of the stock's par (stated) value. As with common stock, the company's board of directors may decide not to pay dividends if the company encounters financial hardships. However, most preferred stock is *cumulative preferred stock,* which means that preferred stockholders must receive all unpaid dividends before any dividends can be paid to common stockholders. Suppose, for example, that a company with a $5 annual preferred dividend misses its quarterly payment of $1.25 ($5.00 ÷ 4). The following quarter, the firm must pay preferred stockholders $2.50—$1.25 in unpaid preferred dividends from the previous quarter plus the $1.25 preferred dividend for the current quarter—before it can pay any dividends to common stockholders. Similarly, if the company goes bankrupt, preferred shareholders are paid off before common stockholders.

Investors like preferred stock because of the fixed dividend income. Although companies are not legally obligated to pay preferred dividends, most have an excellent record of doing so. However, the fixed dividend can also be a disadvantage because it limits the cash paid to investors. Thus, preferred stock has less potential for price appreciation than common stock.

Cashing In with Bonds

2 learning goal

Bonds are long-term debt obligations (liabilities) of corporations and governments. A bond certificate is issued as proof of the obligation. The issuer of a bond must pay the buyer a fixed amount of money—called **interest,** stated as the *coupon rate*—on a regular schedule, typically every six months. The issuer must also pay the bondholder the amount borrowed—called the **principal,** or *par value*—at the bond's maturity date (due date). Bonds are usually issued in units of $1,000—for instance, $1,000, $5,000, or $10,000. The two sources of return on bond investments are interest income and gains from sale of the bonds. The average 20-year corporate bond had an average yield of 7.1 percent in 2002, down from 14.9 percent in 1982.[5]

interest
A fixed amount of money paid by the issuer of a bond to the bondholder on a regular schedule, typically every six months; stated as the *coupon rate.*

principal
The amount borrowed by the issuer of a bond; also called *par value.*

Unlike common and preferred stockholders, who are owners, bondholders are creditors (lenders) of the issuer. In the event of liquidation, the bondholders' claim on the assets of the issuer comes before that of any stockholders.

Bonds do not have to be held to maturity. They can be bought and sold in the securities markets. However, the price of a bond changes over its life as market interest rates fluctuate. When the market interest rate drops below the fixed interest rate on a bond, it becomes more valuable and the price rises. If interest rates rise, the bond's price will fall. (Bond prices will be discussed in greater depth in the section Security Price Quotations later in the chapter.)

Corporate Bonds *Corporate bonds,* as the name implies, are issued by corporations. They usually have a par value of $1,000. They may be secured or unsecured, include special provisions for early retirement, or be convertible to common stock. Approximately $594.4 billion in new corporate bonds were issued in 2002.[6] Exhibit 21.1 summarizes the features of some popular types of corporate bonds.

High-yield, or **junk, bonds** are high-risk, high-return bonds that became popular during the 1980s, when they were widely used to finance mergers and takeovers. Today, they are used by companies whose credit characteristics would not otherwise allow them access to the debt markets. Because of their high risk, these bonds generally earn 3 percent or more above the returns on high-quality corporate bonds.

Corporate bonds can be either secured or unsecured. **Secured bonds** have specific assets pledged as collateral, which the bondholder has a right to take if the bond issuer defaults. **Mortgage bonds** are secured by property, such as land, equipment, or buildings. **Debentures** are unsecured bonds. They are backed only by the reputation of the issuer and its promise to pay the principal and interest when due. In general, debentures have a lower risk of default than secured bonds and therefore have lower interest rates. Of course, a debenture issued by a financially shaky firm probably has greater default risk than a mortgage bond issued by a sound one.

Corporate bonds may be issued with an option for the bondholder to convert them into common stock. **Convertible bonds** generally allow the bondholder to exchange each bond for a specified number of shares of common stock. For instance, a $1,000 par value convertible bond may be convertible into 40 shares of common stock—no matter what happens to the market price of the common stock. Because convertible bonds could be converted to stock when the price is very high, these bonds usually have a lower interest rate than nonconvertible bonds.

high-yield (junk) bonds
High-risk, high-return bonds.

secured bonds
Corporate bonds for which specific assets have been pledged as collateral.

mortgage bonds
Corporate bonds that are secured by property, such as land, equipment, or buildings.

debentures
Unsecured bonds that are backed only by the reputation of the issuer and its promise to pay the principal and interest when due.

convertible bonds
Corporate bonds that are issued with an option that allows the bondholder to convert them into common stock.

Government Securities Both the federal government and local government agencies also issue bonds. The U.S. Treasury sells three major types of

Exhibit 21.1 Popular Types of Corporate Bonds

Bond Type	Characteristics
Collateral trust bonds	Secured by securities (stocks and bonds) owned by the issuer. Value of collateral is generally 25 to 35 percent higher than the bond's par value.
Convertible bonds	Unsecured bonds that can be exchanged for a specified number of shares of common stock.
Debenture	Unsecured bonds typically issued by creditworthy firms.
Equipment trust certificates	Used to finance "rolling stock"—airplanes, ships, trucks, railroad cars. Secured by the assets financed.
Floating-rate bonds	Bonds whose interest rate is adjusted periodically in response to changes in specified market interest rates. Popular when future inflation and interest rates are uncertain.
High-yield (junk) bonds	Bonds rated Ba or lower by Moody's or BB or lower by Standard & Poor's. High-risk bonds with high returns to investors. Frequently used to finance mergers and takeovers.
Mortgage bonds	Secured by property, such as land, equipment, or buildings.
Zero-coupon bonds	Issued with no coupon rate and sold at a large discount from par value. "Zeros" pay no interest prior to maturity. Investor's return comes from the gain in value (par value minus purchase price).

federal debt securities, commonly called "governments": Treasury bills, Treasury notes, and Treasury bonds. All three are viewed as risk-free because they are backed by the U.S. government. *Treasury bills* mature in less than a year and are issued with a minimum par value of $1,000. *Treasury notes* have maturities of 10 years or less, and *Treasury bonds* have maturities as long as 25 years or more. Both notes and bonds are sold in denominations of $1,000 and $5,000. The interest earned on government securities is subject to federal income tax but is free from state and local income taxes. According to the Bond Market Association, a total of $571.6 billion U.S. treasuries were issued in 2002, up 50.2 percent from 2001.[7]

municipal bonds
Bonds issued by states, cities, counties, and other state and local government agencies.

Municipal bonds are issued by states, cities, counties, and other state and local government agencies. More than $430 billion in municipal bonds—a record high—were issued in 2002, and analysts anticipated approximately $361 billion to be issued in 2003.[8] These bonds typically have a par value of $5,000 and are either general obligation or revenue bonds. *General obligation bonds* are backed by the full faith and credit (and taxing power) of the issuing government. *Revenue bonds,* on the other hand, are repaid only from income generated by the specific project being financed. Examples of revenue bond projects include toll highways and bridges, power plants, and parking structures. Because the issuer of revenue bonds has no legal obligation to back the bonds if the project's revenues are inadequate, they are considered more risky and therefore have higher interest rates than general obligation bonds.

Municipal bonds are attractive to investors because interest earned on them is exempt from federal income tax. For the same reason, the coupon interest rate for a municipal bond is lower than for a similar-quality corporate bond. In addition, interest earned on municipal bonds issued by governments within the taxpayer's home state is exempt from state income tax as well. In contrast, all interest earned on corporate bonds is fully taxable.

Exhibit 21.2 | Moody's and Standard & Poor's Bond Ratings

Moody's Ratings	S & P Ratings	Description
Aaa	AAA	**Prime-quality investment bonds:** Highest rating assigned; indicates extremely strong capacity to pay.
Aa A	AA A	**High-grade investment bonds:** Also considered very safe bonds, although not quite as safe as Aaa/AAA issues; Aa/AA bonds are safer (have less risk of default) than single As.
Baa	BBB	**Medium-grade investment bonds:** Lowest of investment-grade issues; seen as lacking protection against adverse economic conditions.
Ba B	BB B	**Junk bonds:** Provide little protection against default; viewed as highly speculative.
Caa Ca C	CCC CC C D	**Poor-quality bonds:** Either in default or very close to it.

Bond Ratings Bonds vary in quality, depending on the financial strength of the issuer. Because the claims of bondholders come before those of stockholders, bonds are generally considered less risky than stocks. However, some bonds are in fact quite risky. Companies can *default*—fail to make scheduled interest or principal payments—on their bonds.

Investors can use **bond ratings,** letter grades assigned to bond issues to indicate their quality or level of risk. Ratings for corporate bonds are easy to find. The two largest and best-known rating agencies are Moody's and Standard & Poor's (S&P), whose publications are in most libraries and in stock brokerages. Exhibit 21.2 lists the letter grades assigned by Moody's and S&P. A bond's rating may change with events.

concept check

What are the advantages and disadvantages of common stock for investors and corporations?

What is preferred stock, and how is it different from common stock?

Describe the common features of all bonds and the advantages and disadvantages of bonds for investors.

Playing the Market with Other Types of Securities

3 learning goal

In addition to equity and debt, investors have several other types of securities available to them. The most popular are mutual funds, futures contracts, and options. Mutual funds appeal to a wide range of investors. Futures contracts and options are more complex investments for experienced investors.

bond ratings
Letter grades assigned to bond issues to indicate their quality, or level of risk; assigned by rating agencies such as Moody's and Standard & Poor's (S&P).

Mutual Funds

Suppose that you have $1,000 to invest but don't know which stocks or bonds to buy, when to buy them, or when to sell them. By investing in a mutual fund, you can buy shares in a large, professionally managed *portfolio,* or group, of stocks and bonds. A **mutual fund** is a financial-service company that pools its investors' funds to buy a selection of securities—marketable securities, stocks, bonds, or a combination of securities—that meet its stated investment goals.

SOURCE: THE VANGUARD GROUP, INC. REPRINTED WITH PERMISSION.

Mutual funds pool investor funds into professionally-managed, diversified stock or bond portfolios which can reduce risk for investors. However, as this ad for the Vanguard Group discusses, investors should consider the fees and expenses charged by mutual fund companies before choosing a fund.

Each mutual fund focuses on one of a wide variety of possible investment goals, such as growth or income. Many large financial-service companies, like Fidelity Investments and The Vanguard Group, sell a wide variety of mutual funds, each with a different investment goal. Investors can pick and choose funds that match their particular interests. Some specialized funds invest in a particular type of company or asset: in one industry such as health care or technology, in a geographical region such as Asia, or in an asset such as precious metals.

Mutual funds appeal to investors for three main reasons:

- They are a good way to hold a diversified, and thus less risky, portfolio. Investors with only $500 or $1,000 to invest cannot diversify much on their own. Buying shares in a mutual fund lets them own part of a portfolio that may contain 100 or more securities.
- Mutual funds are professionally managed.
- Mutual funds may offer higher returns than individual investors could achieve on their own.

Futures Contracts

Futures contracts are legally binding obligations to buy or sell specified quantities of commodities (agricultural or mining products) or financial instruments (securities or currencies) at an agreed-on price at a future date. An investor can buy commodity futures contracts in cattle, pork bellies (large slabs of bacon), eggs, coffee, flour, gasoline, fuel oil, lumber, wheat, gold, and silver. Financial futures include Treasury securities and foreign currencies, such as the British pound or Japanese yen.

Futures contracts do not pay interest or dividends. The return depends solely on favorable price changes. These are very risky investments because the prices can vary a great deal.

Options

Options are contracts that entitle holders to buy or sell specified quantities of common stocks or other financial instruments at a set price during a specified time. As with futures contracts, investors must correctly guess future price movements in the underlying financial instrument to earn a positive return. Unlike futures contracts, options do not legally obligate the holder to buy or sell and the price paid for an option is the maximum amount that can be lost. However, options have very short maturities so it is easy to quickly lose a lot of money with them.

concept check

Why do mutual funds appeal to investors? Discuss some of the investment goals pursued by mutual funds.

What are futures contracts? Why are they risky investments?

How do options differ from futures contracts?

On the Trading Floor: Securities Markets

4 learning goal

Stocks, bonds, and other securities are traded in securities markets. These markets streamline the purchase and sales activities of investors by allowing transactions to be made quickly and at a fair price. They make the transfer of funds from lenders to borrowers much easier. Securities markets are busy places. On an average day, individual and institutional investors trade billions of shares of stock in more than 10,000 companies through securities markets. They also trade bonds, mutual funds, futures contracts, and options. *Individual investors* invest their own money to achieve their personal financial goals. **Institutional investors** are investment pro-

mutual fund
A financial-service company that pools its investors' funds to buy a selection of securities that meet its stated investment goals.

futures contracts
Legally binding obligations to buy or sell specified quantities of commodities or financial instruments at an agreed-on price at a future date.

options
Contracts that entitle holders to buy or sell specified quantities of common stocks or other financial instruments at a set price during a specified time.

institutional investors
Investment professionals who are paid to manage other people's money.

fessionals who are paid to manage other people's money. Most of these professional money managers work for financial institutions, such as banks, mutual funds, insurance companies, and pension funds. Institutional investors control very large sums of money, often buying stock in 10,000-share blocks. They aim to meet the investment goals of their clients. Institutional investors are a major force in the securities markets, accounting for about half of the dollar volume of equities traded.

Businesses and governments also take part in the securities markets. Corporations issue bonds and stocks to raise funds to finance their operations. They are also among the institutional investors that purchase corporate and government securities. Federal, state, and local governments sell bonds and other debt instruments to finance specific projects and cover budget deficits.

The Role of Investment Bankers and Stockbrokers

Two types of investment specialists play key roles in the functioning of the securities markets. **Investment bankers** help companies raise long-term financing. These firms act as intermediaries, buying securities from corporations and governments and reselling them to the public. This process, called **underwriting,** is the main activity of the investment banker, which acquires the security for an agreed-upon price and hopes to be able to resell it at a higher price to make a profit. Investment bankers advise clients on the pricing and structure of new securities offerings, as well as on mergers, acquisitions, and other types of financing. Well-known investment banking firms include Goldman, Sachs & Co., Merrill Lynch & Co., Morgan Stanley Dean Witter, First Boston, PaineWebber, and Salomon Smith Barney (a division of Citigroup).

A **stockbroker** is a person who is licensed to buy and sell securities on behalf of clients. Also called *account executives,* these investment professionals work for brokerage firms and execute the orders customers place for stocks, bonds, mutual funds, and other securities.

Stockbrokers are the link between public companies and the investors interested in buying their stock. Before investing in securities, investors must select a stock brokerage firm, select a stockbroker at that firm, and open an account. Investors are wise to seek a broker who understands their investment goals and can help them pursue their objectives. We'll discuss how individuals make securities transactions in Chapter 22.

Linking investors and public companies, stockbrokers serve a vital role in the securities marketplace. Today, most customer buy-sell orders are transacted electronically.

Brokerage firms are paid commissions for executing clients' transactions. Although brokers can charge whatever they want, most firms have fixed commission schedules for small transactions. These commissions usually depend on the value of the transaction and the number of shares involved.

Online Investing

Improvements in Internet technology have made it possible for investors to research, analyze, and trade securities online. Although traditional brokerage firms still dominate the investment industry, in the late 1990s many investors began using online brokerage firms for their securities transactions. At one time there were more than 170 online brokerage firms, accounting for about 50 percent of all trading activity. As the market slowed, however, many Internet brokerage firms went out of business or consolidated. A recent survey found only 27 online brokerages still operating.[9]

Online brokerages are popular with "do-it-yourself" investors who choose their own stocks and don't want to pay a full-service broker for these services. Lower transaction costs are a major benefit. Fees at online brokerages range from $8 to $20 to buy 200 shares of a $20 stock, compared to about $116 using a traditional firm's brokers. However, many traditional brokerage firms now have added online trading options to their list of services.

investment bankers
Firms that act as intermediaries, buying securities from corporations and governments and reselling them to the public.

Types of Markets

Securities markets can be divided into primary and secondary markets. The **primary market** is where *new* securities are sold to the public, usually with the help of investment bankers. In the primary market, the issuer of the security gets the proceeds from the transaction. A security is sold in the primary market just once—when it is first issued by the corporation or government.

Later transactions take place in the **secondary market,** where *old* (already issued) securities are bought and sold, or traded, among investors. The issuers generally are not involved in these transactions. The vast majority of securities transactions take place in secondary markets, which include the organized stock exchanges, the over-the-counter securities market, and the commodities exchanges. You'll see *tombstones,* announcements of both primary and secondary stock and bond offerings, in the *Wall Street Journal* and other newspapers.

concept check

How do securities markets help businesses and investors? How does an investment banker work with companies to issue securities?

How is online investing changing the securities industry?

Distinguish between primary and secondary securities markets.

Buying and Selling at Securities Exchanges

5 learning goal

The two key types of securities markets are organized stock exchanges and the over-the-counter market. **Organized stock exchanges** are organizations on whose premises securities are resold. They operate using an auction-style trading system. All other securities are traded in the over-the-counter market.

Trading in an organized stock exchange is done by exchange members who act as agents for individual and institutional investors. To make transactions in an organized stock exchange, an individual or firm must be a member and own a "seat" on that exchange. Owners of the limited number of seats must meet certain financial requirements and agree to observe a broad set of rules when trading securities.

underwriting
The process of buying securities from corporations and governments and reselling them to the public, hopefully at a higher price; the main activity of investment bankers.

stockbroker
A person who is licensed to buy and sell securities on behalf of clients.

Once a customer order is transmitted to the trading floor, getting the most competitive price for the customer is the job of the brokerage's floor broker. Floor brokers must act quickly and aggressively to outbid other brokers.

© AP / WIDE WORLD PHOTOS

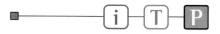

primary market
The securities market where *new* securities are sold to the public, usually with the help of investment bankers.

secondary market
The securities market where *old* (already issued) securities are bought and sold, or traded, among investors.

organized stock exchanges
Organizations on whose premises securities are resold using an auction-style trading system.

U.S. Stock Exchanges

The oldest and most prestigious U.S. stock exchange is the *New York Stock Exchange (NYSE)*, which has existed since 1792. Often called the Big Board, it is located on Wall Street in downtown New York City. The NYSE, which lists more than 300 billion shares of over 2,700 corporations, handles most of the shares traded on organized stock exchanges in the United States. Major companies like IBM, Coca-Cola, AT&T, Procter & Gamble, Ford Motor Co., and Chevron list their shares on the NYSE. In 2002, a total of $40.9 billion of stock was exchanged on the NYSE. The NYSE is also popular with non-U.S. companies. About 470 foreign companies now list their securities on the NYSE. On a typical day, more than 1.3 billion shares of stock are traded on the NYSE.[10]

The vast NYSE trading floor is where all NYSE transactions occur. Each of the companies traded at the NYSE is assigned to a trading post on the floor. When an exchange member receives an order to buy or sell a particular stock, the order is transmitted to a floor broker at the company's trading post. The floor brokers then compete with other brokers on the trading floor to get the best price for their customers. Exhibit 21.3 illustrates how a stock is bought and sold on the NYSE.

Another national stock exchange, the American Stock Exchange (AMEX), lists the securities of about 700 corporations. Because the AMEX's rules are less strict than those of the NYSE, most firms traded on the AMEX are smaller and less well known than NYSE-listed corporations. Some firms move up to the NYSE once they qualify for listing there. Other companies choose to remain on the AMEX. Well-known companies listed on the AMEX include Audiovox and Hasbro. Companies cannot be listed on both exchanges at the same time.

Exhibit 21.3 Anatomy of a Stock Trade

Buyer	**Seller**
1. Bill Jones of San Diego, California, decides to invest in the stock market by purchasing shares of IBM.	1. Sue Hastings of Austin, Texas, decides to sell 100 shares of IBM to help pay for home improvements.
2. Bill asks his stockbroker for a price quote on IBM stock.	2. Sue asks her stockbroker for a price quote on IBM stock.
3. Both brokers obtain quotes on the current trading price of IBM from the NYSE trading floor via the NYSE's electronic data system.	
4. Bill tells his broker to buy 100 shares of IBM.	4. Sue tells her broker to sell 100 shares of IBM.
5. The two orders are sent to the NYSE trading floor where they are directed to the trading post that handles IBM stock.	
6. At the trading post, the two transaction requests are entered into the system.	
7. The two floor brokers compete with other brokers on the trading floor to get the best price for their customers. The brokers for Bill and Sue agree on a price.	
8. Once the trades are executed, the brokerage firms are notified and the transaction is recorded into the NYSE system.	
9. Within three days, both Bill and Sue receive confirmations from their brokerage firms that their trades have been completed.	
10. Bill completes his purchase within three days by submitting payment to his brokerage firm.	10. Sue's trade is also settled within three days. Her broker credits her account with the sales proceeds, minus any commissions or brokerage fees.

SOURCE: Adaped from "How a Stock Is Bought and Sold," New York Stock Exchange, downloaded from http://www.nyse.com. Used with permission of NYSE.

In addition to the NYSE and AMEX, a number of regional exchanges in the United States list about 100 to 500 securities of firms located in their area. Regional exchange membership rules are much less strict than for the NYSE. The top regional exchanges are the Boston, Cincinnati, Chicago, and Pacific (in San Francisco) exchanges. An electronic network linking the NYSE and many of the regional exchanges allows brokers to make securities transactions at the best prices.

Global Trading and Foreign Exchanges

Improved communications and the elimination of many legal barriers are helping the securities markets go global. The number of securities listed on exchanges in more than one country is growing. Foreign securities are now traded in the United States. Likewise, foreign investors can easily buy U.S. securities.

Stock exchanges also exist in foreign countries. The London and Tokyo Stock Exchanges rank behind the NYSE and Nasdaq (described below). Other important foreign stock exchanges include those in Toronto, Montreal, Buenos Aires, Zurich, Sydney, Paris, Frankfurt, Hong Kong, and Taiwan. The number of big U.S. corporations with listings on foreign exchanges is growing steadily, especially in Europe. For example, more than 10 percent of the daily activity in NYSE-listed stocks is due to trades on the London Stock Exchange. The "Expanding Around the Globe" box discusses the Karachi Stock Exchange, currently one of the fastest-growing securities exchanges in the world.

EXPANDING AROUND THE GLOBE

Hot Times in Pakistan

Unimpressed with the returns on the NYSE? How about putting your money into a securities market growing at 112 percent a year? Founded in 1947, the Karachi Stock Exchange (KSE), **http://www.kse.net.pk**, in Karachi, Pakistan, has been the world's hottest securities market over the past several years, reaching record highs nearly every week over the past year.

With just 710 listed companies and a total capitalization of $10 billion, the KSE is tiny when compared to the likes of major exchanges in the United States, Europe, and Japan. Just five years ago, the Pakistani economy was in tatters and the KSE was struggling to show any gain at all. After September 11, however, when Pakistan joined forces with the United States in the fight against terrorism, the country's economy rebounded, helped along with an influx of U.S. aid money.

Pakistanis who once invested abroad began looking for opportunities to invest at home. The downturn on Wall Street convinced many Pakistanis to move their money to the KSE. Impressed with big returns, some institutional investors are also taking a closer look at the KSE. Stock price appreciation isn't the only gain for investors. The dividends of most KSE firms are rising at 10 percent a year or more.

Investors betting on the KSE, however, need to have a high tolerance level for risk. Most of the trading volume on the exchange centers on a handful of top firms. Smaller companies often see huge swings in the price of their stock. It's not unusual for listed stocks to gain or lose 10 percent of their value in a single day. Political and economic uncertainty in Pakistan remains high, as does the threat of nuclear war with neighboring India. Most U.S. investment analysts shy away from Pakistan. "It's not really even a country emerging-market investors pay attention to," says Bill Rocco, an analyst with Morningstar. "It's too small, too undeveloped, and too risky."

Still, the KSE continues to be the fastest-growing securities exchange in the world. Hoping to encourage more Pakistanis to invest at home, the exchange recently launched an aggressive educational campaign through schools and other forums. Pakistani stockbrokers have also entered the digital age, with several now offering online trading.

CRITICAL THINKING QUESTIONS

1. Explain how supply and demand has affected the Karachi Stock Exchange. Contrast the KSE's experience with the NYSE.
2. Would you be willing to invest in the Karachi Stock Exchange? Why or why not? What information would you need in order to change your mind?

SOURCES: Saeed Azhar Arshad, "Karachi Stock Market Hits Eight-Year High," *AP Worldstream* newswire (December 9, 2002); Tom Holland and Jason Singer, "A Year for Most Overseas Investors to Forget: Asia," *Wall Street Journal* (January 2, 2003), p. R16; Arshad Hussain, "Second Private Exchange Company Starts Operations," *Daily Times* (Pakistan) (March 22, 2002), downloaded from http://www.dailytimes.com.pk; John Lancaster, "Finding Opportunities in Post-9/11 Pakistan," *Washington Post* (February 12, 2003); Nicholas Stein, "Pakistani Premium," *Fortune* (March 2003), p. 60.

The Over-the-Counter Market

over-the-counter (OTC) market
A sophisticated telecommunications network that links dealers throughout the United States and enables them to trade securities.

National Association of Securities Dealers Automated Quotation (Nasdaq) system
The first electronic-based stock market and the fastest-growing part of the stock market.

Unlike the organized stock exchanges, the **over-the-counter (OTC) market** is not a specific institution with a trading floor. It is a sophisticated telecommunications network that links dealers throughout the United States. The **National Association of Securities Dealers Automated Quotation (Nasdaq) system,** the first electronic-based stock market, is the fastest-growing part of the stock market. It provides up-to-date bid and ask prices on about 3,500 of the most active OTC securities, with a 2002 market value totaling $5.2 trillion. An average of 1.75 billion shares were exchanged daily in 2002 through Nasdaq.[11] Its sophisticated electronic communication system is the main reason for the popularity and growth of the OTC market.

The securities of many well-known companies, some of which could be listed on the organized exchanges, trade on the OTC market. Examples include Apple Computer, Coors, Dell Computer, Intel, Microsoft, Nordstrom Department Stores, Qualcomm, and Starbucks. The stocks of most commercial banks and insurance companies also trade in this market, as do most government and corporate bonds. About 440 foreign companies also trade OTC.

What makes the Nasdaq different from an organized exchange? On the NYSE, one specialist handles all transactions in a particular stock, but on the Nasdaq system, a number of dealers handle ("make a market in") a security. For instance, about 40 dealers make a market in Apple Computer stock. Thus, dealers compete, improving an investor's ability to get a good price.

The Nasdaq merged with the AMEX in early 1999 to create what it termed a "market of markets." They operate as separate markets under the management of the Nasdaq-Amex Market Group, a subsidiary of the National Association of Securities Dealers, Inc. (NASD). This merger could pressure the remaining regional exchanges to find partners.

bull markets
Markets in which securities prices are rising.

bear markets
Markets in which securities prices are falling.

The NYSE and the Nasdaq face a competitive threat from the emergence of other electronic exchanges called *electronic communications networks (ECNs).* ECNs allow institutional traders and some individuals to make direct transactions, without using brokers, securities exchanges, or the Nasdaq, in what is called the *fourth market.* Because they deal mostly in Nasdaq stocks, ECNs are taking trading volume away from the Nasdaq. ECNs are most effective for high-volume, actively traded stocks. Money managers and institutions such as pension funds and mutual funds with large amounts of money to invest like ECNs because they cost less than other trading venues.

Investors dread "bear markets" when stock prices fall and investor profits dry up. Luckily, the U.S. stock market has seen more bull markets than bear markets in the past 50 years.

Market Conditions: Bull Market or Bear Market?

Two terms that often appear in the financial press are "bull market" and "bear market." Securities prices rise in **bull markets.** These markets are normally associated with investor optimism, economic recovery, and government action to encourage economic growth. In contrast, prices go down in **bear markets.** Investor pessimism, economic slowdown, and government restraint are all possible causes. As a rule, investors earn better returns in bull markets; they earn low, and sometimes negative, returns in bear markets.

Bull and bear market conditions are hard to predict. Usually, they can't be identified until after they begin. Over the past 50 years, the stock market has generally been bullish, reflecting general economic growth and prosperity. Bull markets tend to last longer than bear markets. The bull market that started in 1982 lasted a full five years, and the bear market that preceded it lasted just over a year and a half. The longest bull market on record began in October 1990 and peaked in early 2000. Since then, the market has been a bear market, with only very short periods of growth.

Regulation of Securities Markets

In the United States, both the federal government and state governments regulate securities markets. The states were the first to pass laws aimed at preventing securities fraud. However, most securities transactions occur across state lines, so federal securities laws are more effective.

Securities and Exchange Commission (SEC)
The main federal government agency responsible for regulating the U.S. securities industry.

In 1934, Congress established the **Securities and Exchange Commission (SEC),** as the main federal government agency responsible for regulating the U.S. securities industry. The SEC has five commissioners who are appointed by the president of the United States. In order to make sure the SEC remains nonpartisan, no more than three Commissioners may belong to the same political party. All Commissioners must be approved by a Senate vote. Each year, the SEC files between 400 and 500 civil enforcement actions against individuals and companies that break securities laws. The SEC can also order that the trading of a stock be suspended when a company is under investigation. In March 2003, for example, the SEC announced that it had filed accounting fraud charges against HealthSouth Corporation, the nation's largest outpatient surgery provider. The SEC charged that the company had overstated its earnings by at least $1.4 billion. The company's stock was suspended from trading while the investigation was under way.[12] Exhibit 21.4 highlights some of the common violations that may lead to SEC investigations and punishments.

The SEC also oversees the *Securities Investor Protection Corporation (SIPC).* The SIPC is a private, nonprofit corporation that insures the securities and cash in the customer accounts of member brokerage firms in the event those firms fail. However, it's important to keep in mind that investors do not have any insurance against losses due to market conditions or fraud.

In addition to legislation and government regulation, the securities industry has self-regulatory groups and measures to help protect investors.

SECURITIES LEGISLATION The *Securities Act of 1933* was passed by Congress in response to the 1929 stock market crash and subsequent problems during the Great Depression. It protects investors by requiring full disclosure of information about new securities issues. The issuer must file a *registration*

Exhibit 21.4 Securities Industry Violations Leading to SEC Investigations

- Insider trading
- Misrepresenting or omitting important information about securities
- Stealing customer funds or securities
- Violating broker-dealer responsibilities to treat customers fairly
- Selling securities without proper SEC registration

statement with the SEC, which must be approved by the SEC before the security can be sold.

The *Securities Exchange Act of 1934* formally gave the SEC power to control the organized securities exchanges. The act was amended in 1964 to give the SEC authority over the OTC market as well. The amendment included rules for operating the stock exchanges and granted the SEC control over all participants (exchange members, brokers, dealers) and the securities traded in these markets.

insider trading
The use of information that is not available to the general public to make profits on securities transactions.

The 1934 act also banned **insider trading,** the use of information that is not available to the general public to make profits on securities transactions. Because of lax enforcement, however, several big insider-trading scandals occurred during the late 1980s. The *Insider Trading and Fraud Act of 1988* greatly increased the penalties for illegal insider trading and gave the SEC more power to investigate and prosecute claims of illegal actions. The meaning of insider was expanded beyond a company's directors, employees, and their relatives to include anyone who gets private information about a company.

Other important legislation includes the *Investment Company Act of 1940,* which gives the SEC the right to regulate the practices of investment companies (such as mutual funds), and the *Investment Advisers Act of 1940,* which requires investment advisers to disclose information about their background. The SIPC was established in 1970 to protect customers if a brokerage firm fails by insuring each customer's account for up to $500,000.

Most recently, in response to corporate scandals that hurt thousands of investors, the SEC passed new regulations designed to restore public trust in the securities industry. We'll discuss some of these new regulations later in this chapter.

Self-Regulation The investment community also regulates itself, developing and enforcing ethical standards to reduce the potential for abuses in the financial marketplace. The individual stock exchanges, such as NYSE, have established strict rules, policies, and codes of conduct for their members. The National Association of Securities Dealers (NASD), the parent organization of the Nasdaq-Amex Market Group, oversees the nation's 5,600 brokerage firms and more than half a million registered brokers. It develops rules and regulations, provides a dispute resolution forum, and conducts regulatory reviews of member activities for the protection and benefit of investors.

circuit breakers
Measures that, under certain conditions, stop trading in the securities markets for a short cooling-off period to limit the amount the market can drop in one day.

In response to "Black Monday"—October 19, 1987, when the Dow Jones Industrial Average plunged 508 points and the trading activity severely overloaded the exchange's computers—the securities markets instituted corrective measures to prevent a repeat of the crisis. Now, under certain conditions, **circuit breakers** stop trading for a short cooling-off period to limit the amount the market can drop in one day. For instance, the NYSE circuit breakers stop trading for an hour if the Dow Jones Industrial Average drops 250 points and two hours if it falls another 150 points.

concept check

How do the organized stock exchanges differ from the OTC market?

What is insider trading, and how can it be harmful?

Briefly describe the key provisions of the main federal laws designed to protect securities investors.

Popular Sources of Investment Information

6 learning goal

Good information is a key to successful investing. Knowledge of current market conditions and investment options should increase returns. Individual investors can now benefit from the type of information formerly available only to investment professionals. The following sections describe commonly used sources of investment information.

Making Ethical Choices

xtra! http://gitmanxtra.swlearning.com

TRIALS AND MANIPULATIONS

You have just joined a prestigious investment banking firm as a junior securities analyst covering the pharmaceutical industry. Eager to make a good impression on your boss, you diligently monitor the companies your group follows and search for unique ways to get the scoop on new drugs currently under development. Rumor has it that a biotechnology firm has come out with a new drug for insomnia, with the potential to be a blockbuster. You've heard that other analysts, posing as doctors or patients, have called the managers of clinical trials to get inside information, or paid doctors involved in the trials to disclose confidential data. They then use what they learn in their stock reports, making recommendations that can significantly impact the price of the stock.

Why not go a step further, you wonder, and participate in the trial for the insomnia drug yourself? After all, you've had many sleepless nights and believe you'd qualify for the study. Not only would you help the cause of science, but you'd also get the chance to talk to doctors about the other patients in the study to find out more about the results of the trial so far.

With your boss's approval, you apply for the trial. When you arrive for your first appointment, you are asked to sign a confidentiality agreement not to disclose any treatment information based on your experiences or anything you learn about other patients.

ETHICAL DILEMMA

Should you honor the confidentiality agreement or share your findings with your boss to use in writing the stock report?

SOURCES: Getta Anand and Randall Smith, "Biotech Analysts Strive to Peek Inside Clinical Tests of Drugs," *Wall Street Journal* (August 8, 2002), pp. A1, A6; and Penni Crabtree, "Firm Fined for 'Creative' Research on Neurocrine," *San Diego Union-Tribune* (October 29, 2002), pp. C1, C2.

Company Financial Reports

All publicly traded companies are required by the SEC to file regular statements about their current financial conditions. Investors can access these statements by requesting a copy from a company's investor relations office. The SEC also maintains an online database of all company financial statements. The database, called EDGAR, is accessible from the SEC's main Web site. Annual reports are issued each year by publicly traded companies and include an annual financial statement. They usually also provide important information about the company's business strategies and operations. Many firms now publish an online version of their annual report at their corporate Web sites.

Economic and Financial Publications

Two of the best-known publications for economic and financial information are the *Wall Street Journal,* the weekday newspaper providing the most complete and up-to-date coverage of business and financial news, and *Barron's,* a weekly newspaper that carries detailed company analyses. Other excellent sources are magazines such as *Business Week, Kiplinger's Personal Finance, Forbes, Fortune, Smart Money, Worth,* and *Money.* Newspapers in most cities have sections with business news. Subscription advisory services also offer investment information and recommendations. Mergent, Standard & Poor's, Morningstar, and Value Line Invest-

Smart investors know information is power. Business publications, corporate annual reports, Internet sites, and other information sources keep investors and the business community on top of developments in the securities market.

© TERRI MILLER / E-VISUAL COMMUNICATIONS INC.

ment Survey are among the best known. Each offers a wide range of services. Numerous investment newsletters also give subscribers market analyses and make specific buy and sell recommendations. The major securities brokerage firms have their own analysts who issue reports on the companies they follow. While in many cases you must be a client of the firm to receive analyst reports, some Web sites have summaries or offer them for sale.

Online Information Resources

There has been a virtual explosion of online investment Web sites during the past five years. New sites appear every day, and many soon disappear. However, do not confuse this volume of information with good information! "Buyer beware" is certainly appropriate advice when using investment information from the Internet. Standards for accuracy and integrity are lax, and conflict-of-interest policies are rare. That glowing report on a stock investment could be written by owners of the stock who will profit by pushing up the price.

Despite these cautions, the Internet has many valuable investment resources, such as those listed in Exhibit 21.5. Most of these offer both information—current economic and business news, and educational articles—and tools that allow you to track investment performance, receive alerts of breaking news and specific stock price changes, and more. Some also provide databases of information that allow investors to screen (filter) vast amounts of information to make stock or mutual fund selections. The business publications mentioned in the preceding section frequently publish investment Web site recommendations and rankings. They can help you find reliable online information sources and learn more about how to use them wisely.

Security Price Quotations

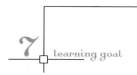

7 learning goal

The security price quotations in the *Wall Street Journal* and other financial media provide a wealth of current information. The quotations typically report the results of the previous day's trading activity. Stock brokerage firms have electronic quotation systems that give up-to-the-minute prices. Investors with a personal

Exhibit 21.5 Online Sources of Investment Information and Education

Popular Information, Education, and Tracking Sites	
CBS Marketwatch	**http://www.marketwatch.com**
CNNMoney	**http://money.cnn.com**
Excite	**http://money.excite.com**
FreeEdgar	**http://www.freeedgar.com**
Investor's Clearinghouse	**http://www.investoreducation.org**
MSN MoneyCenter Investor	**http://moneycentral.msn.com/investor/**
Morningstar	**http://www.morningstar.com**
The Motley Fool	**http://www.fool.com**
National Association of Investors Corporation	**http://www.better-investing.org**
Quicken	**http://www.quicken.com**
Thomson Investors Network	**http://www.thomsoninvest.net**
The Street.com	**http://www.thestreet.com**
The Wall Street Journal Interactive Edition	**http://www.wsj.com**
Yahoo! Finance	**http://finance.yahoo.com**
Stock and Mutual Fund Screening Sites	
CBS Marketwatch	**http://www.marketwatch.com**
Morningstar	**http://www.morningstar.com**
MSN MoneyCentral Investor	**http://moneycentral.msn.com**
Quicken	**http://www.quicken.com**
SmartMoney	**http://www.smartmoney.com**
StockWorm	**http://www.stockworm.com**
Wall Street City	**http://www.wallstreetcity.com**
Yahoo! Finance	**http://screen.yahoo.com/stocks.html**
Zacks Analyst Watch	**http://www.zacks.com**

computer can subscribe to special services, such as Dow-Jones News/Retrieval, that also give current stock quotations, and now many of the sites listed in Exhibit 21.5 provide up-to-the-minute quotations.

STOCK QUOTATIONS Prices for NYSE, AMEX, and Nasdaq stocks are all quoted the same way: in decimals. Exhibit 21.6 shows a portion of the March 27, 2003, stock quotations for NYSE-listed stocks, as they appeared in the *Wall Street Journal* on March 28, 2003. These quotations show not only the most recent (close) price, but also the percentage change in the stock's price since the beginning of the year, the highest and lowest price paid for the stock during the previous 52 weeks, the annual dividend, the dividend yield, the price/earnings ratio, the day's trading volume, and the change from the previous day's closing price. The **price/earnings (P/E) ratio** is calculated by dividing the current market price by annual earnings per share. A company's P/E ratio should be compared to those of other companies in the same industry.

price/earnings (P/E) ratio
The current market price of a stock divided by its annual earnings per share.

To understand how to read stock quotations, follow the listing for the common stock of Radio Shack (RSH) in Exhibit 21.6, highlighted in yellow. Since the first of the year 2003 the stock price (close) has increased 16.5%. Over the previous 52 weeks, the stock traded at a high of $36.21 and a low of $16.99. It paid annual dividends of $.22, a 1 percent dividend yield. (Note that these columns are blank for Railamer [RRA], a firm that doesn't pay a dividend.) On March 27, Radio Shack's P/E ratio was 15, and 1,808,600 shares (18,086 × 100) were traded. The closing price, or last price, of the stock on March 27 was $21.84, a 71 cent positive change from the previous day's closing price. Preferred stocks are listed

Exhibit 21.6 | Radio Shack Stock Quotation for March 27, 2003

YTD %CHG	52-WEEK HI	52-WEEK LO	STOCK (SYM)	DIV	YLD %	PE	VOL 100s	CLOSE	NET CHG
16.5	36.21	16.99	RadioShack RSH	.22	1.0	15	18086	21.84	0.71
−14.5	11.31	4.44	Railamer RRA		...	31	548	6.13	0.08
7.2	31.80	19.43	RalcpHlds RAH		...	15	1632	26.96	1.08

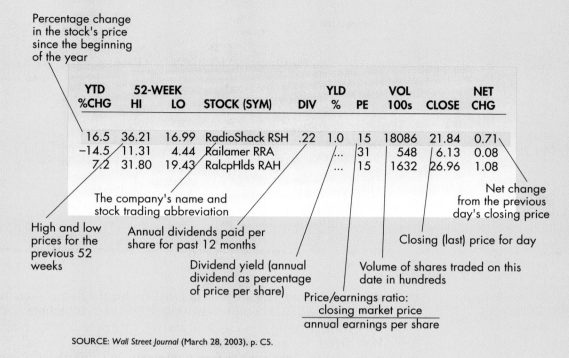

Percentage change in the stock's price since the beginning of the year

High and low prices for the previous 52 weeks

The company's name and stock trading abbreviation

Annual dividends paid per share for past 12 months

Dividend yield (annual dividend as percentage of price per share)

Price/earnings ratio: closing market price / annual earnings per share

Volume of shares traded on this date in hundreds

Closing (last) price for day

Net change from the previous day's closing price

SOURCE: *Wall Street Journal* (March 28, 2003), p. C5.

separately in the *Wall Street Journal* and many other publications. The letters *pf* or *pr* after the company's name identify a preferred stock. Other abbreviations are used by publications like the *Wall Street Journal* to indicate a variety of factors, including stock splits, dividend changes, new 52-week highs or lows, and many other conditions. A key to what these abbreviations mean is usually provided at the beginning of each publication's financial section.

BOND QUOTATIONS Bond quotations are also included in the *Wall Street Journal* and other financial publications. Exhibit 21.7 shows quotations for NYSE bonds trading on March 27, 2003. The labels indicate how to interpret the quotations. The numbers after the issuer's name are the coupon (interest) rate and maturity. If the bond is a convertible bond, a zero coupon bond, or another specialized issue, it will also be noted in this area. For the highlighted (in yellow) Duke Energy (trading abbreviation DukeEn) bond, 6⅞23 means that this bond has a stated annual interest rate—or coupon rate—of 6.875 percent and will mature in the year 2023.

Bond prices are expressed as a percentage of the face value (principal). A closing price above 100 means the bond is selling at more than its face value (at a *premium*). A closing price below 100 is less than the face value (the bond is selling at a *discount*). Duke Energy's bond closed at 102, so it is selling at a premium. The bond's value also had a net change of .50 since the previous trading day.

Treasury and other government bonds are also listed in the securities quotations pages. Their listings are similar to corporate bond listings.

net asset value (NAV)
The price at which each share of a mutual fund can be bought or sold.

MUTUAL FUND QUOTATIONS Mutual fund share prices are quoted in dollars and cents and trade at their **NAV,** or **net asset value,** the price at which each share of the mutual fund can be bought or sold. The mutual fund quotations

Exhibit 21.7 Duke Energy Corporate Bond Quotation for March 27, 2003

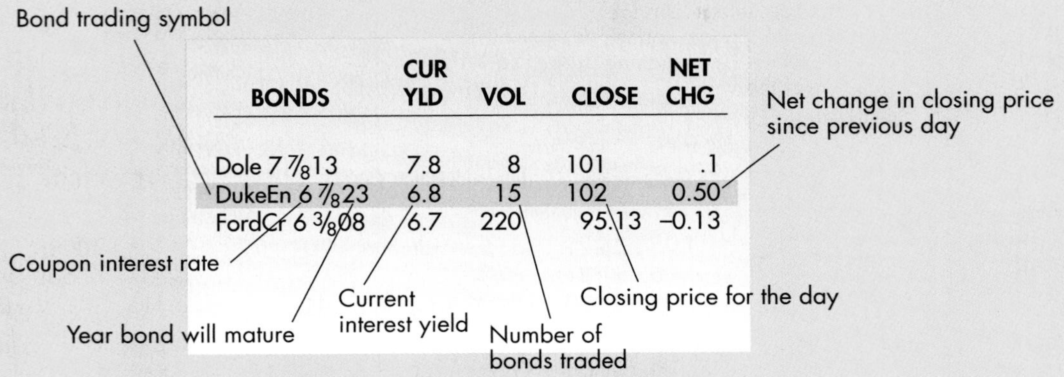

SOURCE: *Wall Street Journal* (March 28, 2003), p. C10.

shown in Exhibit 21.8 are the ones that appear the first of each month in the *Wall Street Journal.* Less comprehensive quotations that include NAV, net change in NAV from the previous day, and year-to-date percent return appear daily in the *Wall Street Journal* and in most major newspapers. The exhibit explains other items in the quotes, such as fees, total assets, and annual expense ratio.

market averages
Summarize the price behavior of securities based on the arithmetic average price of groups of securities at a given point in time; used to monitor general market conditions.

market indexes
Measures of the current price behavior of groups of securities relative to a base value set at an earlier point in time; used to monitor general market conditions.

Dow Jones Industrial Average (DJIA)
The most widely used market average; measures the stock prices of 30 large, well-known corporations that trade on the NYSE and Nasdaq.

Standard & Poor's (S&P) 500 stock index
An important market index that includes 400 industrial stocks, 20 transportation stocks, 40 public utility stocks, and 40 financial stocks; includes NYSE, AMEX, and Nasdaq stocks.

Market Averages and Indexes

"How's the market doing today?" This question is commonly asked by people interested in the securities market. An easy way to monitor general market conditions is to follow market averages and indexes, which provide a convenient way to gauge the general mood of the market by summarizing the price behavior of securities. **Market averages** use the arithmetic average price of groups of securities at a given point in time to track market movements. **Market indexes** measure the current price behavior of groups of securities relative to a base value set at an earlier point in time. The level of an average or index at any given time is less important than its behavior—its movement up and down over time.

The most widely used market average is the **Dow Jones Industrial Average (DJIA).** It measures the stock prices of 30 large, well-known corporations, listed along with the original 12 Dow Jones stocks in Exhibit 21.9 on page 692. The companies in the DJIA are chosen for their total market value and broad public ownership. It includes both NYSE and Nasdaq stocks. It is calculated by adding the closing price of each of the 30 stocks and dividing by the DJIA divisor, a number that changes over time to adjust for events such as stock splits.

The DJIA changes daily. If the DJIA closes at 9,500 one day and at 9,620 the next, the typical stock in the index would have moved up by about 1.25 percent [(9,620 − 9,500) / 9,500]. There are three other Dow Jones averages: a 20-stock transportation average, a 15-stock utility average, and a composite average based on the stocks in all three averages. Dow Jones introduced its World Index in January 1993 to provide a way to measure international stock performance. It tracks 2,200 companies in 120 industry groups.

An important market index is the **Standard & Poor's (S&P) 500 stock index.** The S&P 500 is broader than the DJIA. It includes 400 industrial stocks, 20 transportation stocks, 40 public utility stocks, and 40 financial stocks. It

Exhibit 21.8 | Dreyfus Balanced Mutual Fund Quotation for May 30, 2003

Fund Company

Investment objective

Additional sales charges to buy fund; this fund has none

Net asset value

Annual expense ratio

Fund name

NAV$ 5/30	FUND NAME	INV OBJ	MAY	TOTAL RETURN & RANK				MAX INT CHRG	EXP RAT
				YR	3YR	5 YR	10 YR		
	Dreyfus								
14.46	A Bond	AB	2.5	10.6 D	8.8 E	5.9 D	6.4 D	0.00	0.93
33.35	Aprec p	LC	4.6	−9.6 C	−7.5 A	0.0 A	10.9 A	0.00	0.97
12.33	Balanced	BL	4.2	−4.8 E	−4.7 D	−0.1 D	6.9 D	0.00	1.01
10.70	BdMktInv	IG	1.8	11.2 B	10.4 B	7.2 B	NS	0.00	0.40
15.28	CalTx r	SS	2.6	10.3 B	9.6 A	6.0 A	5.6 C	0.00	0.71
14.88	Cal Int r	IM	2.2	9.1 B	8.4 B	5.7 B	5.7 B	0.00	0.76
14.54	CT Int r	IM	2.3	8.8 C	7.8 D	5.3 D	5.5 C	0.00	0.77
26.37	Discp	LC	3.8	−10.7 D	−12.4 C	−2.9 C	8.8 B	0.00	1.00
28.21	Dr5000In t	SP	5.2	−8.5 C	−11.3 C	−1.6 C	9.3 D	0.00	0.50
8.40	Dreyf	LC	4.9	−10.5 C	−11.6 C	−3.1 D	4.4 E	0.00	0.76
19.36	DreyMid r	MC	8.3	−9.6 C	0.5 B	6.4 B	12.0 B	0.00	0.50
30.78	EmgLd	SC	8.0	−9.7 C	−4.5 E	4.3 B	NS	0.00	1.34
13.98	FL Int r	IM	2.4	9.9 A	8.1 C	5.4 C	5.4 C	0.00	0.80

Total return data from Lipper Analytical Services: month, year-to-date, periodic return, performance rank compared to peer group

SOURCE: *Wall Street Journal* (June 2, 2003), p. R3.

concept check

What are four popular sources of investment information?

What type of investment information can investors find on the Internet? What are the positive and negative aspects of using Internet sources of investment information?

What role do market averages and indexes play in the investment process?

includes NYSE, AMEX, and Nasdaq stocks. Many market analysts prefer the S&P 500 index to the DJIA because of its broad base. It is calculated by dividing the sum of the closing market prices of the 500 stocks by the sum of the market values of those stocks in the base period and multiplying the result by 10. Like the DJIA, the S&P 500 is only meaningful when compared to index values at other time periods. The S&P MidCap 400 Index tracks stocks of medium-size companies. It is composed of about 66 percent NYSE companies, 3 percent AMEX companies and 31 percent Nasdaq companies.

Trends in Securities and Securities Markets

8 learning goal

The 1990s were a euphoric time for many investors. Stock prices seemed to be on a never-ending upward spiral, fed by frenzied growth in the economy and the dot-com technology boom. As the old saw says, however, "all good things must come to an end." As we've discussed throughout this chapter, since the beginning of 2000 most investors have seen the value of their stock portfolios plummet. A slowing economy, the after-effects of September 11, and news of corporate scandals have brought the securities markets back to earth.

Exhibit 21.9 The Dow Jones Industrial Average Then and Now: The Original 12 and Current 30 Stocks

Original 12 Dow Jones Stocks	Today's 30 Dow Jones Stocks
American Cotton Oil	Aluminum Co. of America (ALCOA)
American Sugar Refining Co.	Altria Group
American Tobacco	American Express
Chicago Gas	AT&T
Distilling & Cattle Feeding Co.	Boeing
General Electric Co.	Caterpillar
Laclede Gas Light Co.	Citigroup
National Lead	Coca-Cola
North American Co.	Walt Disney
Tennessee Coal, Iron & Railroad Co.	DuPont
U.S. Leather	Eastman Kodak
U.S. Rubber Co.	ExxonMobil
	General Electric
	General Motors
	Hewlett Packard
	Home Depot
	Honeywell
	IBM
	Intel
	International Paper
	Johnson & Johnson
	J.P Morgan Chase
	McDonald's
	Merck
	Microsoft
	Minnesota Mining (3M)
	Procter & Gamble
	SBC Communications
	United Technologies
	Wal-Mart Stores

Many investors—both institutional and individual—are reevaluating their investment strategies. Some have moved their investment assets out of the stock market entirely and into bonds or bank savings products. Others have remained in the market, but become more cautious about making stock-purchasing decisions. Recently investor confidence in the stock market has begun to return slowly.

Disgruntled stockholders filed a record number of civil lawsuits against public companies in 2002 and the trend toward litigation is continuing. Many of these cases have led to multimillion-dollar settlements between public companies and their shareholders. Fifty-four shareholder lawsuits were filed against Lucent Technologies, for example, accusing the company of using financial fraud and aggressive sales tactics to sustain its stock price. In early 2003, Lucent agreed to pay $568 million in cash and stocks to its 5 million shareholders in order to settle the lawsuits.[13]

The most important trends in the securities industry, therefore, center around a simple question: "How can investor trust be rebuilt?" Increased government regulation and enforcement are attempting to provide better protection for investors, while the industry itself is redefining how it serves customer needs.

A Stronger Role for the SEC

The Sarbanes-Oxley Act of 2002, discussed in Chapters 18 and 20, has given the SEC more teeth when it comes to regulating how securities are offered, sold, and marketed. As a result, the SEC has been undergoing major reform, in both how it operates and its regulatory activities.

Sarbanes-Oxley redefined the roles and responsibilities of corporate auditors, executives, and boards by setting new standards for how company financial information is prepared and filed. The SEC is already actively pursuing companies that fail to comply with Sarbanes-Oxley requirements. New and proposed SEC regulations take additional steps in protecting investors from fraud and misinformation.

For example, many public companies traditionally held private briefings for institutional investors and investment analysts during which important information affecting investment decisions was shared. Unfortunately, individual investors were not always told the same information, giving unfair advantage to institutional investors and investment analysts.

Regulation FD
An SEC regulation that requires public companies to share information with all investors at the same time, leveling the information playing field.

In response, the SEC issued **Regulation FD** (for Fair Disclosure) in October 2000. Regulation FD requires public companies to share information with all investors at the same time, leveling the information playing field. In late 2002, the SEC announced its first Regulation FD enforcement actions. Defense contractor Raytheon and software maker Seibel Systems were among the companies the SEC found guilty of violating Regulation FD.[14]

The SEC is also extending its reforms beyond corporate executives and auditors. The SEC has announced plans to consider new rules that would tighten internal controls for mutual fund companies. Mutual funds must now tell investors how they vote on decisions at the companies whose common stock the fund holds. Additionally, the SEC has proposed creating a self-policing organization for the mutual fund industry that could potentially bring stricter oversight to how mutual funds are managed.

Many investors burned in the stock market since the late 1990s complained about receiving inaccurate or misleading information from stock brokerage firms. After the SEC began an investigation into alleged abuses at 10 major stock brokerage firms, the industry reached a $1.4 billion settlement with the agency in December 2002. Brokers must now provide at least one independent research report to investors for every stock they recommend. The firms in the settlement also agreed to repay unhappy investors for their losses.

In February 2003, the SEC also approved a rule that requires Wall Street analysts to certify the truthfulness of their research reports and public statements. Analysts must also disclose if they've received compensation related to their stock recommendations. The new rules were developed after high-profile analysts at companies such as Salomon Smith Barney and Merrill Lynch were accused of providing positive research reports even though they didn't favor the stock, in an attempt to win other business for their firms from the subject companies.

Rebuilding Investor Trust

Increased government regulation is an important first step in protecting investors and regaining their trust. However, the securities industry itself and public corporations are also being forced to voluntarily change in order to convince individual investors to return.

Major stock exchanges are tightening their rules for listed companies. The New York Stock Exchange, for example, recently adopted new recommendations for companies listing on the exchange. Under the new rules, companies must disclose insider stock purchases and sales faster and must report negative financial results more clearly.[15]

Technology is also being used to improve investor service and trading access. Nasdaq implemented a new trading system, SuperMontage, in late 2002 that allows brokers to post several buy or sell quotes at once. The system also displays detailed information about the amount of stock available and its price levels in order to show the best bid and ask prices.

Brokerage firms are adapting their services to investor needs as well. Investors in the booming 1990s turned to low-cost, no-frills brokerage services. Now, however, many investors are demanding more from their broker. Brokerages are responding by offering investors more information and guidance about their stock purchases. Like Charles Schwab in this chapter's opening vignette, even discount brokerage firms are now offering value-added services such as financial planning and educational programs.

Online brokers have also had to adapt. As already noted in this chapter, the number of online brokers dropped dramatically as investors who were burned by the stock market fall began looking for more service and guidance. For example, online broker Scottrade now promotes its 160 brick-and-mortar branches in addition to its online trading service.[16] Other online brokers have added new Internet services, allowing investors to buy and trade bonds, options, and other securities.

Public corporations themselves are also taking a proactive approach to building better relationships with shareholders. As discussed in the "Customer Satisfaction and Quality" box, investor relations are key to maintaining and building a strong reputation in the securities marketplace.

concept check

Describe the steps the SEC is taking to provide better protection for investors.

How are the securities industry and public corporations changing to rebuild investor trust?

Great Ideas to Use Now

After reading this chapter, you may be wondering if investing in stocks or bonds is right for you. Like millions of others, you've probably read headlines about the stock market's amazing rise during the late 1990s, as well as its slump since then. How can you minimize the risks while reaping the benefits of securities investments? The basic information presented in this chapter is a good starting point. It's also important to understand some of the key strategies used by successful investors.

The Time Is Now

As the Dow Jones Industrial Average fell after nearly a decade of nonstop growth, many investors panicked. They rushed to sell off their stock shares—often at a loss—because they believed doing otherwise would spell financial ruin.

These investors fell prey to some common mistakes of novice investors. For one thing, they got caught up in the mystique of the DJIA. Although it is the most publicized market indicator, it represents the activity of just 30 large industrial stocks. A milestone on the DJIA is just another number. It doesn't tell investors where their individual investments are going or how long the market will stay at a particular level.

Try It Now

1. **Compare brokerages.** Visit the sites of two online brokerages, such as E*Trade (**http://www.etrade.com**), Ameritrade (**http://www.ameritrade.com**), HARRIS direct (**http://www.harrisdirect.com**), or any others you know. Compare them for ease of use, quality of information, and other criteria you select. To check out the firms, use a ratings service such as Gomez Advisors' Internet Broker Scorecard, **http://www.gomez.com**, and Motley Fool Brokerage Center, **http://www.fool.com**. Summarize your findings. Which firm would you prefer to use, and why?
2. **Track stock prices.** Pick a portfolio of five companies in at least three different industries. Choose companies you know, read the financial press to find good candidates, or try one of the stock screening sites in Exhibit 21.5. Set up a table to track the stock prices. Record the end-of-month prices for the past six months and track the daily price movements for at least two weeks (longer is even better!). Visit the Web sites of these companies to view their investor relations information and go to the EDGAR database at the SEC Web site, **http://www.sec.gov**, to review recent company SEC filings. Finally, monitor economic and market trends and other events that affect market conditions. Share the performance of the portfolio with your classmates. Explain your basis for selecting each stock and analyze its price changes.

The stock market has always been cyclical in nature. Stock prices rise and fall depending on many factors. Bull markets are almost invariably followed by a bear market. Although every investor dreams of buying a stock at its low point and selling it at its peak, predicting the market's ups and downs is impossible.

Successful investors think of the stock market as a long-term investment. They know that it's important to let their investments grow over time and they avoid falling into the trap of thinking that they should sell their shares whenever there's a market downturn. They also recognize that the best time to buy stock is when the market is at a low point.

Financial advisers suggest investing small amounts over time. Start early and invest regularly, whether the market is up or down. Don't immediately panic if the market takes a nosedive. The highs and lows will average out over time, and you'll find yourself with long-term gains.

Another reason many investors lost money in recent years is that they failed to diversify their investment portfolios. Many poured money into technology stocks while ignoring the stock of businesses in other industries. When the technology boom ended, these investors were hardest hit. Building a portfolio of individual stocks in different industries can help cushion losses. Investing in mutual funds can also help spread your risk over a broad group of securities. Also, consider investing in a mix of stocks and bonds. Bonds tend to rise in value as stock prices drop and vice versa, further lessening the risk of losing it all when one investment vehicle declines. We'll discuss more strategies for successful investing in the next chapter.

Most important, do your homework. Don't make investment decisions based only on what you find on a Web site or in a single magazine. It's easy to be taken in by someone hyping a stock. To avoid investment scams, do your own research. Investigate the company's standing with the SEC and look at its historic performance over a number of years. Remember, if it sounds too good to be true, it probably is!

Looking Ahead at Charles Schwab & Co.

In late 2002, Charles Schwab was hopeful that investor confidence was beginning to return. Spurred on by an e-mail marketing campaign, the number of daily customer trades started to rise. The price of Charles Schwab & Co. stock topped $10 a share.

The stock market dipped again, however, in the first quarter of 2003 when investors worried about a possible war with Iraq. Once again, as daily trades and revenues fell, so did Charles Schwab & Co.'s stock price. Schwab responded with an aggressive advertising and e-mail marketing campaign designed to attract wealthier, and more profitable, customers. In fact, the company that Schwab founded to meet the needs of "average" investors no longer welcomes customers with investment accounts of less than $50,000.

Charles Schwab admits that it may be some time before the stock market and his company fully rebound, but he remains optimistic that a full recovery will occur. "Despite an almost daily litany of bad news, investors continue to have faith in the power of investing for building long-term financial security," he says.[17]

Customer Satisfaction and Quality

Corporate raider T. Boone Pickens once said that the first obligation of a public corporation is to make money for its shareholders. Of course, companies have many stakeholders—employees, customers, and the communities where they operate—but building shareholder value has been front and center of the concerns facing most corporate executives for the past 20 years.

As the stock market boomed in the 1990s, corporations faced tremendous pressure from stockholders to keep pace. Many CEOs made strategic decisions that were focused mainly on pushing the stock price. Unfortunately, as investors at companies like Enron and WorldCom eventually discovered, some corporate executives responded to the pressure by making unscrupulous choices.

Shareholder value will always be a central concern of publicly traded companies, but now many chief executives have discovered that providing shareholder value means more than just inflated stock prices. It also means serving investors with financial results built on honesty and realistic expectations. It means keeping an eye on the basic principle of business: Make your customers happy first.

Procter & Gamble's chief executive A. G. Lafley sums it up best when asked how P&G stock has soared nearly 60 percent in value since 2000. "Over the last half of the 1990s, we were a little bit too shareholder focused, too growth-at-any-cost focused," he says. "I tried to get people to flip that around. If we create brands that make a difference to our customers and focus on the fundamentals, ultimately shareholder growth will take care of itself."

SOURCES: Joseph Nocera, "Value Judgments," *Money* (December 2001), downloaded from http://www.business2.com; Nicholas Stein, "America's Most Admired Companies," *Fortune* (March 3, 2003), p. 81.

Summary of Learning Goals

1 How do common stock and preferred stock differ as investments?

Common and preferred stocks represent ownership—equity—in a corporation. Common stockholders have voting rights, but their claim on profits and assets ranks behind that of holders of other securities. Preferred stockholders receive a stated dividend. It must be paid before any dividends are distributed to common stockholders.

Common stocks are more risky than preferred stocks. They offer the potential for increased value through growth in the stock price and income through dividend payments. But neither price increases nor dividends are guaranteed. Preferred stocks are usually bought for their dividend income rather than potential price appreciation.

2 What are bonds, and what investment advantages and disadvantages do they offer?

Bonds are a form of debt and may be secured or unsecured. Bondholders are creditors of the issuing organization, and their claims on income and assets rank ahead of those of preferred and common stockholders. The corporation or government entity that issues the bonds must pay interest periodically and repay the principal at maturity. Bonds provide a steady source of income and the potential for price appreciation if interest rates fall below the coupon rate. However, investors also bear the risk that rising interest rates may erode the bond's price.

3 What other types of securities are available to investors?

Mutual funds are financial-service companies that pool the funds of many investors to buy a diversified portfolio of securities. Investors choose mutual funds because they offer a convenient way to diversify and are professionally managed. Futures contracts are legally binding obligations to buy or sell specified quantities of commodities or financial instruments at an agreed-on price at a future date. They are very risky investments because the price of the commodity or financial instrument may change drastically. Options are contracts that entitle the holder the right to buy or sell specified quantities of common stock or other financial instruments at a set price during a specified time. They, too, are high-risk investments.

4 What is the function of the securities markets?

Securities markets allow stocks, bonds, and other securities to be bought and sold quickly and at a fair price. New issues are sold in the primary market. After that, securities are traded in the secondary market. Investment bankers specialize in issuing and selling new security issues. Stockbrokers are licensed professionals who buy and sell securities on behalf of their clients.

5 Where can investors buy and sell securities, and how are these securities markets regulated?

Securities are resold on organized stock exchanges, like the New York Stock Exchange and regional stock exchanges, and in the over-the-counter market, a telecommunications network linking dealers throughout the United States. The most actively traded securities are listed on the Nasdaq system, so dealers and brokers can perform trades quickly and efficiently.

The Securities Act of 1933 requires disclosure of important information regarding new securities issues. The Securities Exchange Act of 1934 and its 1964 amendment formally empowered the Securities and Exchange Commission and granted it broad powers to regulate the organized securities exchanges and the over-the-counter market. The Investment Company Act of 1940 places investment companies such as mutual funds under SEC control. The securities markets also have self-regulatory groups like the NASD and measures such as "circuit breakers" to halt trading if the Dow Jones Industrial Average drops rapidly.

6

Which sources of investment information are the most helpful to investors?

The most popular sources of investment information are economic and financial publications like the *Wall Street Journal, Barron's, Business Week, Fortune, Smart Money,* and *Money*. The newest sources of information include the numerous Internet sites. Other sources are subscription services and investment newsletters and security price quotations.

7

What can investors learn from stock, bond, and mutual fund quotations?

Stock quotations show the percentage change in the stock's price since the beginning of the year, the highest and lowest prices paid for the stock during the previous 52 weeks, the annual dividend, the dividend yield, the price/earnings ratio, the day's trading volume, the closing price, and the change from the previous day's closing price. Bond quotations show the coupon interest rate, maturity date, current yield, trading volume, closing price, and change in closing price from the previous day. Mutual fund quotations provide the fund's net asset value, net change in NAV from the previous day, and year-to-date percent return.

8

What are the current trends in securities and securities markets?

After the investor euphoria of the 1990s, the securities markets and investment industry are in the midst of considerable change. Since the beginning of 2000, many investors have seen the value of their stock portfolios plummet due to slowing economic conditions, the after-effects of September 11, and news of corporate scandals. The SEC is taking a larger role in regulating the securities industry in order to rebuild investor confidence. In addition to the requirements of the Sarbanes-Oxley Act, the SEC has issued new regulations regarding fair disclosure of corporate financial information, mutual fund companies, and brokerage firms. In addition to government regulation, the securities industry and public companies are instituting changes to regain investor trust.

Preparing for Tomorrow's Workplace

1. Research the trends in the IPO marketplace from 1995 to 2003. Then select two IPO success stories and two failures. Prepare a report for the class on their performance. What lessons about the securities markets can you learn from their stories?
2. While having dinner at a Manhattan restaurant, you overhear two investment bankers at the next table. They are discussing the takeover of Bellamco Industries by Gildmart Corp., a deal that has not yet been announced. You have been thinking about buying Bellamco stock for a while, so the next day you buy 500 shares for $30 each. Two weeks later, Gildmart announces its acquisition of Bellamco at a price of $45 per share. Have you earned a profit fairly, or are you guilty of insider trading? What's wrong with insider trading?
3. What role do a CEO's actions/strategies have in influencing a company's stock performance? Prepare a class presentation that answers this question using both positive and negative examples from at least three companies covered in recent business news. In your presentation, discuss what your recommendations for each CEO would be.
4. Research the job responsibilities of a corporate Investor Relations Officer (IRO). If possible, try to interview an IRO, by either phone or e-mail. The Na-

tional Investor Relations Institute (**http://www.niri.org**), a trade association for IROs, is an alternate source of information. What types of experience and education does an IRO need in order to perform effectively? How are their roles changing? Write a paper summarizing your findings.

5. Learn what it's like to be a trader on the Nasdaq exchange. Divide the class into small groups of three or four students. Each group will play Nasdaq's "Head Trader" simulation as a team (**http://www.nasdaq.com/services/uo_hdtr.stm** or **http://www.academic.nasdaq.com/headtrader/**). Be sure to review the game's learning module before you begin and share decision making with all team members. After the game, share your results with the class in a presentation that evaluates the success of your team.

KEY TERMS

bear markets 683
bond ratings 677
bull markets 683
circuit breakers 685
convertible bonds 675
debentures 675
Dow Jones Industrial Average (DJIA) 690
futures contracts 679
high-yield (junk) bonds 675
insider trading 685
institutional investors 679
interest 675
investment bankers 680
market averages 690
market indexes 690
mortgage bonds 675
municipal bonds 676
mutual fund 679
National Association of Securities Dealers Automated Quotation (Nasdaq) system 683
net asset value (NAV) 689
options 679
organized stock exchanges 681
over-the-counter (OTC) market 683
price/earnings (P/E) ratio 688
primary market 681
principal 675
Regulation FD 693
secondary market 681
secured bonds 675
securities 672
Securities and Exchange Commission (SEC) 684
Standard & Poor's (S&P) 500 stock index 690
stockbroker 680
underwriting 680

WORKING THE NET

1. Choose a company currently traded on the NYSE (**http://www.nyse.com**). Find the company's Web site using a search engine such as Google.com. At the Web site, find the firm's investor relations information. Review the information, including, if available, the most recent online annual report. Follow up by researching if any SEC actions have been taken against the firm at the SEC Web site, **http://www.sec.gov**. Summarize your findings in a brief report that discusses whether you would recommend this company's stock as an investment.
2. Using the same company you researched in Question 1, research the company on several of the online resources discussed in this chapter. Look particularly for any analysts' evaluation of the stock, its potential, and trends in its trading history. Summarize your findings in a brief report. Based on this information would you recommend this stock as an investment? Did your evaluation change from Question 1 after further research? Why or why not?
3. At The Vanguard Group's site, **http://www.vanguard.com**, go to the page for Personal Investors, then to the Planning & Advice section. Click on Investment Basics and read Investment Basics and How to Select a Mutual Fund. After learning about the fundamentals of mutual funds, prepare a presentation for the class based on the materials.
4. You've been asked to address your investment club on socially responsible investing and how companies qualify as socially responsible. Research this topic at the Web sites of the Social Investment Forum, **http://www.socialinvest.org**, and Co-op America, **http://www.coopamerica.org**. Prepare a detailed outline of the key points you would include in the speech. How can your personal financial decisions have a positive impact on communities and the environment? Do you support socially responsible investing?
5. Using the information and links available at the Bond Market Association's Web site, **http://www.bondmarkets.com**, write a brief paper explaining the pros and cons of investing in corporate bonds. In your paper, provide at least three examples of currently available corporate bonds from a site such as **http://www.investinginbonds.com**, and explain why they would be good investments.
6. Would joining an investment club be a good way for you to learn about the stock market? Visit the National Association of Investors Corporation (NAIC) Web site at **http://www.better-investing.org.** Explore the site to learn more about the investment strategy the NAIC teaches, how investment clubs operate, and how to start an investment club. Summarize your findings. Would you prefer to start investing through an investment club or on your own? Explain your answer.

Creative Thinking Case

Opening Up Investor Relations

In March 2003, the Securities and Exchange Commission completed a review of the 10-K annual reports filed by Fortune 500 companies. The results were startling. According to the SEC, nearly 70 percent of the financial statements needed improvement. Among the SEC's recommendations: Companies should provide an executive summary of the information in their 10-K reports to make it easier for investors to make decisions.

Louis M. Thompson, Jr., president and CEO of the National Investor Relations Institute, agrees. "The road to restoring investor trust in corporate information must be paved with transparency, and transparency means more than disclosing sufficient information to meet the minimum regulatory requirements," he says. "Transparent information is that which is presented in a clear and understandable manner. The 'spirit' of good disclosure sometimes goes beyond the minimum requirements."

Shareholder.com is hoping more corporations listen to Thompson and the SEC. Founded 11 years ago, the Boston-based company specializes in investor communications, helping public companies touch base with investors. Want to get your investor relations message across on your company's Web site? Shareholder.com can create, host, and service your site. Need to get information about your firm's latest strategies and financial performance out to investors? Shareholder.com can set up and run a Webcast. Are your investors phoning in requests for your latest annual report? No problem, Shareholder.com can answer the phone for you and make sure the annual report is mailed out immediately.

Shareholder.com's clients include huge corporations like IBM, Coca-Cola, Sony, and Microsoft. Ron Gruner, Shareholder.com's CEO, says the company has seen double-digit revenue growth over the past three years and sees no sign of slowing as corporations increasingly recognize that they have a legal and ethical responsibility to communicate openly and effectively with their shareholders. "We think Sarbanes-Oxley is going to generate incredible revenue in the next year or two," he says. "With the total collapse of shareholder confidence, there's a lot more upside to communicating than there is a downside."

CRITICAL THINKING QUESTIONS

1. Do you agree with Thompson's statement that "the 'spirit' of good disclosure sometimes goes beyond the minimum requirements"? Discuss why some public corporations might not agree.
2. What are some of the potential advantages and disadvantages of outsourcing investor relations programs to a consulting firm like Shareholder.com?
3. Suggest other methods corporations can use to regain investor confidence.

SOURCES: "The Best Company Is an Open Company," *Fast Company* (April 2003), downloaded from http://www.fastcompany.com; Louis M. Thompson, Jr., "SEC Review of Annual Reports Shows Companies Need to Strengthen their MD&As," National Investor Relations Institute press release (March 17, 2003); Stephen Schultz, "Driving Shareholder Value through Investor Communication," *Corporate Communication*, National Institute of Investor Relations (February 2003), p. 1; Tom Witkowski, "Local Tech Cos. Capitalizing on Shift in Business Regs," *Boston Business Journal* (February 28, 2003), downloaded from http://boston/bizjournals.com.

Video Case

Morgan Stanley Plans for Its Own Financial Future

The Morgan Stanley name has a long history and a strong brand identity. Founded as an investment bank in 1935, the company ranks among Wall Street's elite. It has a number of securities industry firsts to its credit, including the first computer model for financial analysis, the introduction of automated processing for securities trading, and the creation of innovative new types of securities.

In 1997 Morgan Stanley merged with Dean Witter, combining Dean Witter's strong retail brokerage services with its investment banking and institutional securities operations. Today the combined firm's reach is global, with about 58,000 employees in more than 600 offices in 27 countries, and client assets under management totaling over $525 million.

Morgan Stanley is highly regarded for its financial advice and market execution in all aspects of the financial markets. The organization offers its clients a wide range of financial services through its four business segments: Institutional Securities (investment banking, institutional sales and trading, research), Individual Investor Group (investor advisory services, wealth management, individual investor services), Investment Management (global asset management products and services for individual and institutional investors), and Credit Services (Discover-branded cards and other consumer finance products and services). The combined firm continues to be on the cutting edge in its use of technology for its clients.

During the high-flying 1990s, Morgan Stanley and its Wall Street peers enjoyed a period of fast growth and increasing profitability as the stock market soared and corporate-financing activity was high. As the new century started, however, the 10-year bull market ended, bringing very different and volatile economic conditions. Few companies wanted to issue securities, merger activity fell off sharply, and individual investors retreated to the sidelines while stock prices tumbled. In response to the lower revenues from these changing financial markets, Morgan Stanley reduced staff and closed offices. The Institutional Securities unit channeled its resources to focus on building stronger relationships with its top clients and developing its own systems to automate its Nasdaq and options trading, offering clients improved execution at lower cost. The Individual Investor Group began emphasizing relationships in the form of fee-based accounts rather than transactional arrangements. In July 2002 Morgan Stanley held a national town hall meeting for 30,000 of the firm's clients. Chairman and CEO Philip J. Purcell and the firm's leading market strategists discussed the current outlook for stocks and the importance of having a smart asset allocation strategy.

Moving forward, the firm is committed to helping "One client at a time," as its new slogan states. Its emphasis is on growing by building individual client relationships, whether with a large corporation looking to raise financing or an individual investor saving for college or retirement. By helping clients evaluate their needs, develop financial plans, and implement strategies to reach their objectives, it will remain in the forefront of the securities industry.

CRITICAL THINKING QUESTIONS

1. How has Morgan Stanley adapted to the changing climate in the securities industry? Discuss also the impact of changes in securities industry regulations and how they affect the competitive environment.
2. Explain why is it important for Morgan Stanley's customers to understand their personal investment objectives. What might some of these be for a corporate client? As a potential individual client, list several of your financial goals.
3. Visit the Morgan Stanley Web site, **http://www.morganstanley.com**, and explore the pages for individual investors. Which of the features and benefits presented on the site appealed to you the most? Would you feel comfortable choosing Morgan Stanley as your investment adviser, and why?

SOURCES: Adapted from material in the video "Plan Now Pay Later: Financing and Investing at Morgan Stanley" and the Morgan Stanley corporate Web site, http://www.morganstanley.com, accessed June 19, 2003; Nelson D. Schwartz and Jeremy Kahn, "Can This Bull Run Again?" *Fortune* (December 30, 2002), pp. 68–82; Gregg Wirth, "Checkmate: How Dean Witter outmaneuvered Morgan Stanley," *Investment Dealers' Digest* (March 26, 2001), downloaded from http://www.findarticles.com.

E-Commerce Case

E*Trade Takes Stock

How do you sell stocks when you're a leading Internet broker and stock sales have crashed? Start selling stocks in the socks department. That's one strategy E*Trade has tried since the bear market sent online stock purchases into the cellar. E*Trade Internet kiosks are now located in 30 Target department stores, a move the company hopes will convince new customers to give online trading a try.

E*Trade isn't the only online brokerage firm looking for ways to lure customers. At the peak of online-trading popularity in early 2000, more than 45 percent of New York Stock Exchange and Nasdaq trades were made over the Internet. Now, just 22 percent of trades are made online. However, with an average customer balance of just $17,400, far less than that of competitors like Schwab ($108,000) or Merrill Lynch ($340,000), E*Trade has less room to absorb lost trading volumes.

After the stock market decline, Former CEO Christos Cotsakos tried to turn E*Trade into a financial-services powerhouse by adding online banking and other financial services. He opened five "investor center" offices in major U.S. cities, including New York and San Francisco, to attract larger, and more profitable, customers. Under his leadership, E*Trade expanded its operations to Japan, Europe, Hong Kong, Korea, and Israel. He also began moving E*Trade into institutional investment services.

In early 2003, Cotsakos left E*Trade. Soon after, company President Jarrett Lillien announced that E*Trade would make changes, including laying off employees, cutting costs, discontinuing noncore services, and closing some overseas operations. Although Lillien said E*Trade would continue its profitable banking business, "we want to make sure we focus on our core offerings, so that we exit anything that isn't core and isn't performing."

One strategy outlined by Lillien: Win market share among the important group of investors who make frequent stock trades by offering them low commission prices and fast trade guarantees. "The game on the brokerage side is to make it through the hard times making money, and pick up market share," he said.

CRITICAL THINKING QUESTIONS

1. Evaluate Cotsakos's decision to diversify E*Trade into a financial-services company instead of remaining focused solely as an online brokerage firm. Do you agree or disagree with this move? Explain.
2. What barriers might E*Trade face in attempting to win market share among active traders? Do you think this is the correct strategy to focus on? Why or why not?
3. Do you think online trading will ever again reach the same levels it achieved during the late 1990s? What does this mean for online brokers like E*Trade?

SOURCES: Ted David, "E*Trade Group—CEO Interview," *CNBC/Dow Jones Business Video* (April 8, 2003); Deborah Lohse, "E*Trade Posts Quarterly Profit, Scraps Unprofitable Lines," *San Jose Mercury News* (April 16, 2003), downloaded from http://www.elibrary.com; Timothy Mullaney, "Online Finance Hits Its Stride," *Business Week* (April 22, 2002), downloaded from http://www.elibrary.com; "E*Trade Group Increases Equity Stake in E*Trade Japan," Company press release (April 23, 2002), downloaded from http://www.etrade.com.

Hot Links Address Book

Start your online exploring at Yahoo! Finance, which offers everything from breaking business and world news to stock research, portfolio tracking tools, and educational articles, at
http://finance.yahoo.com

The Motley Fool is a favorite site for both novice and experienced investors. What can you learn at the Fool's School today? Go to its Web site at:
http://www.fool.com

You'll find a minicourse on different types of bonds at
http://www.investinginbonds.com

For the latest news about bond rating upgrades and downgrades, visit Moody's Investor Services at
http://www.moodys.com

What is the current level of outstanding Treasury securities? Find out at the Bureau of the Public Debt site,
http://www.publicdebt.treas.gov

How much is currently invested in mutual funds? The Investment Company Institute tracks these figures on a monthly basis at
http://www.ici.org

How many shares traded hands today? Find out at the New York Stock Exchange site,
http://www.nyse.com

Quickly find the latest news for different stock markets around the world at
http://quotes.nasdaq.com/asp/globalmarkets.asp

Thinking of investing in a particular company? Go to the SEC's Web site to access the EDGAR database of the financial reports filed by all public companies with the SEC:
http://www.sec.gov

Chapter 22

© MARK SCOTT / TAXI / GETTY IMAGES

Managing Your Personal Finances

learning goals

1 How does the financial-planning process facilitate successful personal financial management?
2 How do cash flow planning and management of liquid assets contribute to your financial goals?
3 What are the advantages and disadvantages of using consumer credit?
4 What types of taxes are individuals responsible for?
5 What factors should you consider in deciding what insurance to purchase?
6 What personal goals are important when making investment decisions?
7 How do investors open a brokerage account and make securities transactions?
8 What emerging trends affect the way you manage your personal finances?

An American Success Story

As the youngest son of hard-working immigrant parents, in a family of nine children, Carlos Vela learned from a young age the importance of making a dollar go a long way. Raised with a strong work ethic, he began working a newspaper route in his suburban New York neighborhood at the age of ten, saving his earnings in a metal cash box. His father told him if he worked hard and started saving early in life, by the time he reached his 40's he could amass $1 million. The young Carlos liked the sound of that, and decided to follow his father's advice.

Now a software designer, Carlos, 36, and his wife, Amy, 34, also an immigrant and a real estate agent, are approaching their first million. How did they do it? Their certified financial planner, Roy Jarrett, praises the Velas for earmarking 25 percent of their earnings—the highest rate he has seen—for savings. "We're pleased if our clients save 10 percent of their income," he says. He credits the couple with working and saving hard and spending little.

The Vela's disciplined approach to saving has increased their net worth to three-quarters of a million dollars, produced solely from savings and investments from their combined annual income of $155,000. Because Amy has an inside track on real estate in their area, the couple has been able to make savvy real estate investments, retaining both their former homes as rental properties. The properties have appreciated in value, while the rental income they generate covers their overhead.

Although they enjoy movies and trips to Hawaii, Carlos sees saving as their most important obligation after essential expenses, such as mortgages, utilities, and food, have been paid for. Fortunately Amy agrees with him. The couple does not squander money on clothing, and drives older cars. "I would like a Mercedes," says Carlos, "and I can afford one now, but it is not part of our plan at the moment." Instead, by shopping carefully and avoiding impulse buying, the couple is able to put away at least $3800 per month, ensuring their financial future will be secure.

Critical Thinking Questions

As you read this chapter, consider the following questions as they relate to Carlos and Amy:

1. What personal characteristics led Carlos and Amy to save almost three-quarters of a million dollars.
2. What specific financial and investment strategies did they follow to help them realize their financial goals?
3. How would you emulate Carlos and Amy to provide a secure future for yourself and your family.

Principles of Personal Finance

In today's highly competitive world, young couples like Carlos and Amy are increasingly aware of the need for early financial planning and its importance to their future security and success. Shifts in demographics have skewed the economic picture for many families, making proper financial planning essential. Some of these changes are:

- More families (now called sandwich families) find themselves caught in the middle financially, responsible for both their children (couples are having children later in life) and their aging parents (increasing longevity), at a time in their own lives when they're ready to retire.
- Increasing numbers of blended families result from divorce and remarriage.
- A significant number of single individuals are solely responsible for their own finances.
- Large numbers of people have experienced job losses due to a sluggish post–September 11 economy and corporate downsizing.
- The average cost for a middle-income family to raise a child to age 18 is now $177,700.[1]
- The average cost of a college education is $12,904 per year at a public university and $28,000 per year or more at a private one.[2]
- More employees are responsible for their own retirement funds.
- People have an overwhelming amount of information to consider when choosing suitable financial products.
- Changing financial obligations and world economics bring new challenges in preparing for the future. They can also bring confusion, frustration, and

Exhibit 22.1 Can Money Buy Happiness?

Money. Would life be sweeter if we all had more of it? The answer seems to be yes—and no. In a recent poll, 77 percent of adults believe America is the land of financial opportunity, yet 70 percent said the love of money is the root of all evil. And a full 76 percent of Americans believe money can't buy happiness. Here are some other American attitudes toward money:

81 percent said money is power.
79 percent said doing what they love is more important than making money.
76 percent said money is freedom.
75 percent of married adults say they and their mate share their money.
74 percent of adults say they are living paycheck to paycheck.
70 percent said it is just as easy to love a rich person as a poor one.
60 percent of women say they manage money better while 51 percent of men say they do.
54 percent of adults say one of their biggest money pressures is meeting bills.
49 percent prefer to be happy in their personal/family life than rich.
36 percent of women and 28 percent of men report spending conflicts.
30 percent want to be able to buy a house.
29 percent said they would rather be healthy than rich.
19 percent of women and 11 percent of men have a secret stash of cash.
14 percent said they'd rather be rich.

SOURCE: Gini Kopecky Wallace, "Can Money Buy Happiness," ***Family Circle*** **(March 15, 2003), pp. 64–68. Reprinted with permission of** ***Family Circle*** **magazine.**

worry about meeting financial goals. Exhibit 22.1 reveals how Americans think about money.

This chapter will provide an overview of the information and skills needed to meet the challenge of managing your own finances. We will demonstrate how the personal financial-planning process can help you manage your cash flow and meet your financial goals. We'll describe various types of checking and savings instruments, and explain how to use consumer credit wisely, manage taxes, and select insurance. Then we will outline how to set investment goals, develop an investment strategy, and make securities transactions. Finally, we review emerging trends in personal finance.

FINANCIAL PLANNING: THE FIRST STEPS

1 learning goal

personal financial planning
The process of managing one's personal finances to achieve financial goals.

In today's world financial planning is for everyone, not just the wealthy. As Carlos and Amy Vela know, you need personal financial planning whether you have too much money or too little. If you have enough money, planning can help you spend and invest it wisely. If your income seems inadequate, taking steps to control your financial situation could lead to an improved lifestyle.

Personal financial planning is the process of managing one's personal finances to achieve financial goals. Once you have established those goals, you can begin gathering information, analyzing the information, and then developing, implementing, and monitoring a financial plan designed to meet your goals. Exhibit 22.2 illustrates the personal financial-planning process.

Personal financial planning is a lifelong process. As your personal circumstances change, so will your needs and goals. By creating flexible plans and revising them on a regular basis, you will build a solid foundation for your financial future.

Exhibit 22.2 | Step Up to Achieve Your Financial Goals

6. **Monitoring your plan.** Regularly review and adjust your plan. Track the performance of the savings/investment components of the plan, and review and adjust the plan and your goals as necessary. Keeping up-to-date on the financial environment will help you monitor your plan effectively
5. **Implementing the plan.** Put your plan into action. Complicated plans may require the help of financial-planning experts.
4. **Developing a plan.** There may be several ways to achieve your goals, so consider various alternatives before arriving at the plan that works best for you.
3. **Analyzing the information.** Review the data you have collected and revise your goals if necessary.
2. **Gathering information.** Objective and subjective information are both important components of the decision-making process.
1. **Establishing financial goals.** Sound financial goals are the basis of your financial plan, a road map that guides spending, saving, and investment decisions.

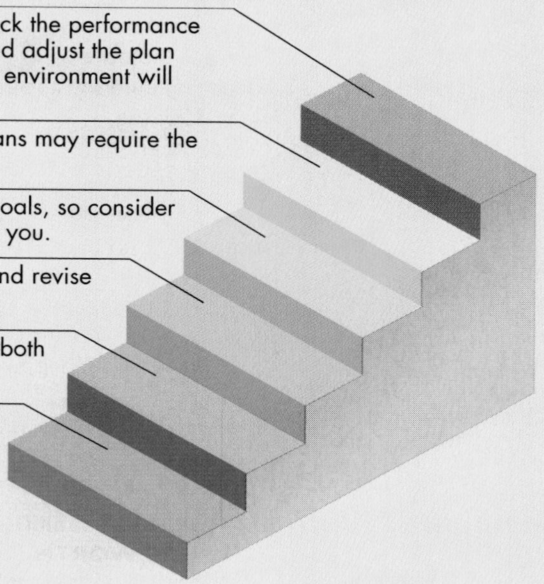

Before you set goals and develop financial plans for your future, you should assess your current financial situation. Just as corporations summarize their financial position on their balance sheets, preparing a **personal balance sheet** will present a summary of your financial position on a given day. *Assets*, the things you own, are valued at current market value on your balance sheet. *Liabilities* are what you owe. They are recorded at the amount you would have to pay if you paid off the entire debt immediately. **Net worth,** total assets minus total liabilities, measures your wealth at a given point in time.

Completing a personal balance sheet at regular intervals, such as every six months or each year, will help you track your progress toward achieving your goals. You'll be able to see how your assets are growing and your debt is—hopefully—going down. Exhibit 22.3 is an example of the personal balance sheets for Jay Martin. As you can see in the "change" column, he has significantly improved his net worth during calendar year 2005 by saving and investing more and paying off his auto loan.

concept check

What are the benefits of personal financial planning?

Describe the six steps in the personal financial-planning process. Develop four personal financial goals for yourself, two short-term (1–2 years) and two long-term (5–10 years).

How does a personal balance sheet help you track your progress toward your financial goals?

Exhibit 22.3 Personal Balance Sheets

Name Jay Martin

	Date 12/31/04	Date 12/31/05	Change
ASSETS			
Liquid assets			
Checking accounts	$ 1,230	$ 895	$ (335)
Savings/money market accounts	385	1,546	1,161
Money market mutual funds			
Certificates of deposit (6 months)			
Cash on hand	76	153	77
Other			
Other investment assets			
Certificates of deposit (>6 months)	500	1,000	500
Mutual funds		2,421	2,421
Stocks			
Bonds			
Other			
Personal assets			
Automobile	5,346	3,421	(1,925)
Furniture and appliances	3,460	8,000	4,540
Clothing	2,000	4,000	2,000
Other			
Other			
(1) Total assets	$ 12,997	$ 21,436	$ 8,439
LIABILITIES			
Bills past due			
Credit cards	$ 857	$ 472	$ (385)
Auto loans	2,569		(2,569)
Appliance/furniture loans			
Mortgage loans			
Education loans	9,365	8,593	(772)
Other			
Other			
(2) Total liabilities	$ 12,791	$ 9,065	$ (3,726)
NET WORTH (1–2)	$ 206	$ 12,371	$ 12,165

Cash Management: Where's the Money?

2 learning goal

personal balance sheet
A summary of a person's financial position on a given day; provides information about assets, liabilities, and net worth.

net worth
An individual's wealth at a given point in time, calculated as total assets minus total liabilities.

cash management
The day-to-day handling of one's liquid assets.

liquid assets
Cash and other assets that can be converted into cash both quickly and at little or no cost, such as checking accounts.

Assets listed on the personal balance sheet may include earnings from college students' summer jobs that are held in checking or savings accounts.

© AP / WIDE WORLD PHOTOS

Cash management is defined as the day-to-day handling of liquid assets. **Liquid assets** include cash, checking accounts, various savings instruments, and other assets that can be converted into cash quickly at little or no cost. A **cash flow plan** (also called a *budget*) is an important tool for cash management. It helps manage income and expenses, and the savings and investment contributions needed to accomplish one's financial goals. The following steps will help you develop and use a cash flow plan:

- *Establish your goals and calculate the savings you need to meet them.* It is helpful to prioritize your goals because you may have more goals than money. Identify each goal, estimate how much money is needed to accomplish that goal, and specify the time frame for achieving the goal.
- *Estimate your income and expenses, including contributions to savings.* Review your monthly income and estimate your monthly expenses. The monthly budget worksheet in Exhibit 20.5 in Chapter 20 on page 655 illustrates how to monitor your income and expenses, or you can create a spreadsheet covering several months.
- *Track actual income and expenses for a one-month period.* Carry a pad of paper with you so you don't forget small expenditures you make, and record all income and expenses. At the end of the month, total income and expenses for each category and enter them on the worksheet in Exhibit 20.5 in the "actual" column.
- *Compare planned and actual income and expenses.* Analyze each category that was above or below your estimate in the "planned" column and determine whether this was unusual. For example, if you needed a new suit for an unexpected interview you may have exceeded your clothing allocation for the month. But if you find the situation to be normal, decide whether to cut back your spending or increase your budget for that item. Of course, if you add to that category, you will need to reduce another by the same amount.
- *Modify estimates for the next month and repeat the process.* Depending on your analysis, you may want to make changes to your original plan. It may take several months before you are able to live within your cash flow plan so it is important to be flexible. But within a short period you will be in control of your spending and saving.

Checking Accounts

Checking and savings accounts are the most common liquid assets held by consumers, and a checking account is necessary to manage your income and expenses. A *check* is a written order, drawn on a depository institution by a depositor, ordering the depository institution to pay on demand a specific amount of money to a person or firm named on the check. Several types of checking accounts are available to meet the diverse needs of consumers. These were briefly noted in Chapter 19.

Electronic Fund Transfers Regardless of the type of checking account you select, you will probably be offered *electronic fund transfer (EFT) services.* EFT allows you 24-hour access to cash through an *automated teller machine (ATM),* and *point-of-sale (POS)* transfers for retail purchases with a debit card. With an ATM card and *personal identification*

cash flow plan
A cash management tool that includes a plan for managing income and expenses, including contributions to savings and investment needed to accomplish one's financial goals; often called a *budget.*

number (PIN), you can withdraw cash, make deposits, or transfer funds between accounts. You can pay for goods and services with a POS transfer using your *debit card*. It works very much like a credit card with one important exception: The money for the purchase is transferred immediately from your checking account to the vendor's account.

Using these cards requires good management skills. With both ATM and POS transactions, be sure to enter withdrawals in your check register. Failure to maintain an accurate record of your account balance may result in bounced checks. Guard your cards carefully so they are not stolen or fraudulently used. This is especially important with POS (debit) cards because they can be used without a PIN.

If your ATM or debit card is lost or stolen, federal regulations mandate that you may be responsible for up to $50 if the loss is reported within 2 business days, up to $500 if you report it between 3 and 60 days, and for an unlimited amount if the loss is reported after 60 days.

Be aware of ATM fees charged by your bank and the institutions that own the machines you use. Even small fees for withdrawing cash add up quickly if you make several withdrawals. You can usually reduce or eliminate ATM fees by using the ATMs at your own bank.

OVERDRAFT PROTECTION The Federal Reserve Board has been called upon to act quickly to stop banks from offering extremely expensive, deceptively advertised "bounce protection" targeted almost exclusively to low- and moderate-income consumers. Preliminary estimates indicate that more than 1,000 banks nationwide are earning 10s of millions of dollars annually for bounce protection, costing consumers as much as $2,000 a year. "Overdraft protection products are a deliberate, systematic attempt to hook consumers into overdrafts as a form of high cost credit," says Chi Chi Wu, staff attorney for National Consumer Law Center. "There is no question that these products are loans at outrageously high prices."

Banks are encouraging consumers to overdraw their accounts and charging penalty fees when they do. With bounce-protection plans, banks advertise to consumers that they will cover overdrafts up to a set dollar limit. They then charge the usual bounced-check fee, between $20 and $35 per transaction, as well as a per-day fee of $2 to $5 until the account has a positive balance. A $100 advance for 30 days would typically carry a minimum 243 percent annual percentage rate (APR). Bank customers are advised to view any overdraft protection offer from their bank very carefully before opting for what could be a very expensive way to borrow money.[3]

BALANCING YOUR CHECKBOOK This important task reveals possible mistakes you or the bank has made and helps you discover fraudulent debit-card withdrawals. It also helps to avoid bouncing checks, which can be expensive and embarrassing. Exhibit 22.4 lists the steps to follow in balancing your checkbook.

Savings Instruments

Checking accounts are appropriate for money you may need to access on a day-to-day basis, but savings instruments are a more appropriate way to accumulate money for short-term goals (a new television or a vacation) and for unexpected expenses (emergencies and opportunities). Banks, thrift institutions, and credit unions offer a variety of savings instruments, as noted in Chapter 19.

Before selecting your savings vehicle, consider your goals and how you will use it. Compare the interest rate you will receive with those paid by other institutions. Rates are always changing, but financial institutions, the Internet, and magazines such as *Kiplinger's Personal Finance* and *Money* are excellent sources of information. Exhibit 22.5 provides an overview of savings in the average young American's household by showing the percent in the group holding the given savings instrument and the average balance held.

Exhibit 22.4 | Seven Easy Steps to Balancing your Checkbook

1. If you receive canceled checks place them in numerical order.
2. Compare each check with the check entry on your bank statement and your checkbook record to make sure the amounts agree. Check off each correct item. Repeat the same process for all other withdrawals such as ATM, debit card, and cash.
3. List and total all outstanding withdrawals (withdrawals deducted in your checkbook but not yet reflected on your bank statement).
4. Repeat Steps 2 and 3 for all your deposits.
5. Subtract the total amount of any outstanding checks from your bank statement, and add any outstanding deposits to this balance to obtain your *adjusted bank balance*.
6. Subtract bank service charges and add interest earned to your checkbook balance to find your *adjusted checkbook balance*.
7. Your adjusted bank balance and adjusted checkbook balance should be the same. If not, recheck your math and the deposits and withdrawals listed in your checkbook. If you cannot find an error, you will need to consult with your bank to see if an error was made in your account.

Using Consumer Credit

3 learning goal

What if you want (or need) to make a purchase before you have accumulated the money? You might use a credit card or a loan to make the purchase, paying interest to the lender for the privilege of borrowing the money. We have discussed how to set goals and use various types of instruments to save for your future needs, but using credit to make purchases is the opposite of saving money to buy things. In this section, we will investigate the pros and cons of using consumer credit, look at various types of credit, and learn how to build a positive credit rating.

The Pros and Cons of Using Credit

There are a number of very good reasons for using consumer credit:

- Convenience.
- Immediate use of a good or service.
- Bargain prices on sale merchandise.
- Opportunity to establish a credit rating.
- Convenient record keeping.

Exhibit 22.5 | Savings of Households Headed by an 18- to 34-Year-Old

Savings Instrument	Holding Instrument Percent	Average Balance
Retirement account	45%	$6,600
Certificate of Deposit	6%	$4,000
Savings bond(s)	13%	$ 300
Stock	17%	$5,700

SOURCE: "Tip Sheet Financial Guide," *Newsweek Magazine* (March 24, 2003), p. 63.

Making Ethical Choices

xtra! http://gitmanxtra.swlearning.com

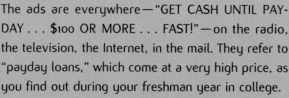

PAYDAY LOANS ARE COSTLY CASH

The ads are everywhere—"GET CASH UNTIL PAYDAY . . . $100 OR MORE . . . FAST!"—on the radio, the television, the Internet, in the mail. They refer to "payday loans," which come at a very high price, as you find out during your freshman year in college.

Your parents are always after you to be responsible about money and manage the budget you have worked out together. Then your car unexpectedly breaks down and you need to get it repaired. To pay for the repairs you borrow $200 from a loan store. You plan to pay back the loan with money from your student loans and the allowance from your parents. You are proud of yourself for not asking your parents for the extra money, and begin making $50 biweekly payments to roll the loan over. You have paid more than $500 and still owe the original $200 loan amount when the owner of the loan store approaches you with a proposition.

Promote his loan store on campus, and for every "referral" you send him, $25 will be deducted from your loan balance until it is paid off. You are very anxious that your parents not find out what you have done—you do not want to disappoint them . . . again. While you realize that encouraging fellow students with temporary money problems to use this loan store could place them in financial jeopardy with potentially damaging consequences, you also see it as the best way to extricate yourself from the financial mess you are in. Although it goes completely against your character, you are so desperate that you agree to do it.

ETHICAL DILEMMA

Do you have a greater obligation to do the right thing for:

- Yourself?
- Your parents?
- Your fellow students?
- All of the above?

Is it ever appropriate to ignore your conscience in order to save yourself? In what other way might you have resolved your financial problems without compromising your personal integrity?

SOURCES: Stephen Rothman, "Officials Call Payday Financing 'Loan Sharking,'" downloaded from Web site http://www.bankrate.com on April 16, 2003; "Payday Loans = Costly Cash," downloaded from Web site of the Federal Trade Commission—Consumer Alerts, at http://www.ftc.gov, on April 15, 2003; Michelle Samaad, "Payday Loans—An Expensive Choice for Borrowers with No Options," downloaded from http://www.bankrate.com, on April 16, 2003.

- Payment for financial emergencies.
- Perks such as rebates and frequent-flyer miles.

Although not as numerous, there are also important disadvantages to using consumer credit:

- It's easy to overspend.
- Most types of credit cost money in the form of interest charges.
- Merchandise may cost more.
- The legal commitment to repay debt reduces future discretionary income.

The ability to overspend, especially because credit cards are so convenient to use, can be the most devastating disadvantage. The financial and psychological stress created by this debt forces some students to drop out of college altogether, or work long hours, often causing their grades to suffer. A recent poll showed that the top financial goal of 71 percent of Americans is getting out of debt.[4]

The secret to using credit responsibly is your cash flow plan. Don't use credit to buy anything that does not fit into your plan. Use your credit card for convenience,

Exhibit 22.6 | Debt Inventory

Name Becky Sampson **Date** 10/15/2005

Type of Debt	Creditor	Annual Rate of Interest	Current Monthly Payment	Latest Balance Due	Comments
Auto Loans	1 University Federal				
	2 Credit Union	8%	$315	$6,893	Car will be
	3				repossessed if loan
					is not repaid
Education Loans	1				
	2				
Home Mortgage Loan					
Home Improvement Loan					
Other Installment Loans	1				
	2				
Single-Payment Loans	1				
	2				
Credit Cards	1 MasterCard	18%	$22	$716	$1,000 credit line
	2 Visa	21%	$40	$1,608	$2,000 credit line
	3				
	4				
	5				
	6				
	7				
Personal Line of Credit	First National Bank	12%	–	–	$3,500 credit line
Home Equity Credit Line					
Overdraft Protection Line					
Loan on Life Insurance					
Margin Loan from Broker					
Other Loans	1				
	2				
	3				
TOTALS			$377	$9,217	

using it instead of cash for purchases so that you have to write only one check for all you buy. Then be sure to *pay the total bill at the end of the month.* Use a credit card for credit (meaning that you will not pay it off monthly) only when really necessary, revising your cash flow plan to repay the debt as quickly as possible.

If you currently have outstanding debt, use a form like Exhibit 22.6 to inventory your debt and develop a debt repayment strategy. For Becky Sampson, whose debt inventory is presented in this exhibit, an effective strategy might be to borrow from her personal line of credit (at 12 percent) to pay off her high-interest loans—the credit-card balances (18 percent and 21 percent). But she must be careful not to run up her credit-card balances again after paying them off.

open-end credit
Any type of credit where the borrower applies for the credit and then, if approved, is allowed to use it over and over again; for example, credit cards.

line of credit
For credit cards, the maximum amount a person can have outstanding on a card at any one time.

Credit Cards

Credit cards are the most used type of open-end credit. **Open-end credit** is any type of credit where once your application for credit is approved you may use it over and over again. Your **line of credit** is the maximum amount you can have

It's fun to have an impulsive side.
Just don't send it to the mall with your credit card.
A credit card is a powerful tool.
By all means have fun, just don't go overboard.
usecreditwisely.com is one of the many resources Citi offers to help you know the rules,
be informed, and spend wisely.
1-888-CITICARD
citi.com
citi
Live richly.
aol keyword: citi citi.com

COURTESY OF CITIGROUP, INC.

When something calls to you, you can buy it with your credit card. But without first consulting your budget you run the risk of overspending and getting into debt. Learning to balance the benefits of convenience against the downside of temptation is important when using consumer credit.

revolving credit cards
Credit cards that do not require full payment upon billing.

outstanding at any one time. Some cards require the entire balance to be paid upon billing, but most require a minimum monthly payment. Cards that do not require full payment upon billing are called **revolving credit cards.** Some credit cards carry an annual fee while others do not.

When you receive your monthly bill and do not pay the entire balance, you are charged interest. Some credit cards offer a **grace period,** a period of time after making a purchase when interest is not owed if the entire balance is paid on time. Those cards with no grace period will charge interest even if you pay the entire bill monthly.

Depending on how they are used, credit cards can be either one of the most or one of the least expensive ways to make purchases. Those individuals who pay off their entire credit-card balance each month are called convenience users of credit cards. If they select cards with a grace period and no annual fee, they have free use of money for the period of time until the bill must be paid. On the other hand, credit-card users who pay only the minimum monthly payment can incur high interest charges, as Exhibit 22.7 shows. The average credit-card late fee has more than doubled from $13 in 1995 to nearly $29 today.[5]

Here are some other tips to help you pay off those credit cards:

- *Don't wait until the last minute.* Many issuers now use a "hair-trigger" for assessing late fees. In some cases you could get hit with a $35 to $40 penalty if the payment is just a few hours late.
- *Talk back.* If you are a customer who carries a balance and pays on time, ask for a lower interest rate and removal of any fees. Tell the issuer you are tempted to switch to another issuer who is offering 0 percent interest. If the bank won't bargain, shop for a new card.
- *Check your statement.* Credit-card fraud is widespread, so it is important to protect your credit cards and review your monthly statement carefully. Federal legislation limits your responsibility up to a maximum of $50 per card before you report the problem. Even though your direct loss is rather low, the thief may tie up your total line of credit for months until the issue is resolved, and may use one card to get other cards. All credit card users pay indirectly for fraudulent charges with higher interest rates and fees.

Exhibit 22.7 Minimum Payments Don't Pay

Making minimum payments on your credit cards can cost you a bundle over a number of years. Here's what would happen if you paid the minimum—or more—every month on a $2,705 card balance, with an 18.38 percent interest rate.

Monthly Payment	How Long to Pay Off	Interest Paid
2% of balance	27 years, 2 months	$11,047
4% of balance	8 years, 5 months	$ 2,707
8% of balance	2 years, 1 month	$ 594

grace period
The period of time after a purchase is made on a credit card during which interest is not owed if the entire balance is paid on time.

Other Card Tricks

Minimum monthly payments used to be around 4 percent of the outstanding balance. But today many credit-card issuers set them so low they do not cover the interest or added fees such as late-payment penalties, or fees for exceeding your credit limit. So even though cardholders pay the minimum every month, their balance continues to grow.

Federal bank regulators have issued a new set of guidelines designed to prevent this "negative amortization." The new rules, which apply to all banks, say that credit-card issuers must set the minimum monthly payment at an amount that will allow the cardholder to pay off the debt within a "reasonable period of time."

So although monthly minimum payments may actually increase, straining the budgets of those cardholders who regularly pay the minimum due, it will free them of debt sooner.[6]

Loans

principal
The total amount borrowed under a loan.

Loans differ from credit cards because they are closed-end agreements. You borrow an amount of money called the **principal** for a specific period of time and agree to pay it back by the end of the term, by paying in installments or as a lump sum. Interest is charged on the amount of principal borrowed, and you may also be required to secure the loan with something of value. An auto loan is a good example of a secured installment loan: Payments on the loan are due in equal monthly installments, and if you default on the debt the lender, who initially files a lien against the auto, has the legal right to repossess the car. Loans are also used to finance a college education, fix up a home, or purchase appliances.

Before you apply for a loan, shop around to get the best deal just as you would for any product you are purchasing. There are numerous sources of consumer loans. Banks and savings and loan associations offer relatively low interest rates to low-risk borrowers. Credit unions generally offer even lower interest rates, but you have to be a member of the credit union to get a loan there. Consumer finance companies specialize in borrowers who are higher risk, and captive finance companies (Ford Credit Corp. and GMAC) offer credit when you are making a specific type of purchase. Online lending is a relatively new way to find a loan; the "Applying Technology" box on page 716 has more information on this growing segment of online banking services.

A family member may charge the lowest interest rate, but if you decide to borrow money from Grandma treat the transaction in a businesslike manner. Draft a loan repayment agreement specifying the amount being borrowed, the interest rate to be paid (if any), and how the debt will be repaid. Both Grandma and you should sign the agreement and keep a copy. This will help to avoid misunderstandings about the terms of the loan.

prepayment penalties
Additional fees that may be owed if a loan is repaid early.

security requirements
Provisions that allow a lender to take back the collateral if a loan is not repaid according to the terms of the agreement.

credit life insurance
Insurance that will repay a loan if the borrower dies while the loan is still outstanding.

Three of the most important factors to consider when comparing loans are the dollar cost of credit (finance cost), the annual percentage rate of interest (APR), and the monthly payment. According to the federal Truth-in-Lending Law, lenders must calculate the APR in a standardized way, so, other things being equal, a loan with a lower APR will be less expensive.

But when the term of the loan varies, loans with the same APR will have different monthly payments and finance costs. As you can see from Exhibit 22.8, the longer the term of the loan, the lower the monthly payment but the higher the finance cost. Selecting a shorter repayment term will save you money in the long run.

In addition to these factors, check a loan for **prepayment penalties,** additional fees owed if you decide to repay the loan early, and **security requirements,** which allow the lender to take back the collateral if you do not repay the loan according to the terms of the agreement. Also beware of add-ons a lender may offer. For example, **credit life insurance** will repay the loan if you die while the loan is

Applying Technology

Banks Branch Out on the Internet

After its first month of operations, the Internet banking site for First National Bank of Amarillo had nearly 1,000 customers. Amarillo is a highly competitive market for online banking with six other banks offering online services. First National chose to differentiate its site so users can obtain real-time balances on their account as transactions occur, rather than waiting for the end-of-day totals of traditional banking.

In addition to banks wanting to take advantage of the substantial cost savings—estimates place the average teller or telephone transaction at $2.36 as compared with 10 cents for an online transaction—advances in technology and competition for business among financial institutions assures consumers of an ever more stunning array of online banking services 24/7.[7]

One of the newest of these is Internet consumer lending. According to the U.S. Census Bureau, this service tends to appeal to households with more than $75,000 in annual income. Projections by Meridien Research estimate that traditional lending transactions will stay close to their current number of 75 million through 2005. Internet loan transactions, on the other hand, are expected to increase from a current 26 million to close to 60 million by 2005.

Sites such as Compubank.com and LendingTree.com are unique online marketplaces where lenders compete for your business. You can obtain information on a wide range of loans including mortgage, car, and student loans, supported by plenty of glowing satisfied customer testimonials.

But if not managed properly, Internet lending can work too well, producing more loan originations than a traditional loan-processing system can handle. A West Coast bank, eager to jump on this new business opportunity, advertised their online lending services with enticing marketing slogans touting "instant decisions" and a "quick turnaround." In the space of two months it was swamped with close to 350 transactions, while its internal systems were only designed to handle 75, stressing their staff and, worst of all, disgruntling their customers.[8]

What does all this mean for the consumer? As tempting as it may be to test the wonders of Internet lending, be warned that some financial institutions may be setting up unrealistic expectations for their customers. Find out how long a particular lender has been offering Internet lending—longer is better, giving the bank more time to iron out the wrinkles. But if you are at all concerned about a lender's Internet service ability, either choose to go the traditional route with your loan application and processing, or choose another bank.

CRITICAL THINKING QUESTIONS

1. What are some of the advantages and disadvantages of Internet banking?
2. What should you look for when selecting an Internet source for an important financial transaction like obtaining a loan?

SOURCES: Greg Rohloff, "First National Enters Internet Banking Market," *Amarillo Daily News*, Web posted July 21, 2000; John Ginovsky, "Internet Consumer Lending—Do It, But Do It Right," *Bankers News* (October 29, 2002).

still outstanding. Although this sounds like a good idea, consider whether you really need life insurance for this purpose. And if you do, find out what the coverage would cost from an insurance agent rather than the lender. The lender offers convenience, but that convenience generally comes at a cost. It is not uncommon to pay 10 times as much for credit life insurance compared to a term life policy purchased through an insurance agent!

Credit History and Credit Ratings

Don't do what Daniel did—finish college with $20,000 in student loans and $9,500 in credit-card debt. Now aged 23 and a recent graduate of the University of Cali-

Exhibit 22.8 Comparisons of a $20,000, 8-Percent Loan

Number of Payments	Monthly Payment	Finance Cost
36	$627	$2,572
48	488	3,424
60	406	4,360

fornia, Riverside, he says, "I know all the temptations and traps that got me where I am now. I wish I'd had this information available to me before." Daniel has been working with Consumer Credit Counseling Service in California for more than three years and is now their College Outreach Coordinator. As someone who has "been there and done that—over and over again," he looks forward to sharing his experiences with other students, in the hope it will help them avoid making the same mistakes he did. Go to CollegeDebt.net (**http://www.collegedebt.net**) to meet Daniel and get out of debt.[9]

One of the reasons for using credit is to build a good credit rating. Three national credit bureaus—Equifax (800-685-1111), Experian (888-397-3742), and TransUnion (800-888-4213)—collect credit information and make it available for a fee to retailers, banks, and other organizations that are subscribers or approved recipients of this highly confidential information. Credit bureaus do not evaluate the data; they report the following types of credit information for each lender: the date the account was opened; the highest amount of credit extended; the current outstanding balance; the number of times the account has been 30, 60, and 90+ days overdue; and the number of inquiries there have been for this account information. Negative account information can stay in the file for no more than 7 years, 10 years in the case of bankruptcy. Information from the three credit bureaus does not always match so you should check all three.

Lenders use information from your credit report as well as other information from your credit application to decide whether to grant credit and under what terms. The better "score" you receive, the more likely you are to be approved for a credit card or loan, and be offered lower rates of interest. Because the information in your credit bureau file is so important, you should periodically check your own file for accuracy. If you are applying for a loan, or have been in a dispute with a creditor, request a copy of your credit report from all three major credit bureaus.

concept check

What are the pros and cons of using consumer credit?

How can an inventory of your debt help you make better decisions about debt repayment?

What is a credit bureau, and what function does it perform in the granting of credit?

If you find inaccurate information in your credit file, report it to the credit bureau. The credit bureau must investigate your dispute within 30 days or remove the disputed item from your file. If the investigation does not resolve your dispute, you may add a brief statement to your file, which must be included in future reports. In addition, credit bureaus must prevent deleted information from reappearing in a credit report, and creditors are liable if they neglect to correct errors.

MANAGING TAXES

4 learning goal

Although taxes represent the largest expenditure in the average American family's budget, a whopping 91 percent say they have never cheated on their taxes.[10] Because the tax code is very complex, some knowledge on the subject is important. In this section we will briefly discuss the four types of taxes that are paid directly by individuals: income, Social Security and Medicare, sales, and property taxes.

Income Taxes

progressive tax
An income tax that is structured so that the higher a person's taxable income, the higher the percentage of income paid in taxes.

The federal income tax is a **progressive tax,** meaning the higher your taxable income the higher the percentage of your income paid in taxes. In 2003, taxpayers in the lowest tax bracket pay 10 percent on the first $7,000 of taxable income ($14,000 for married taxpayers filing jointly), while higher income taxpayers pay at rates of 15, 25, 28, 33, and 35 percent.[11] Because of the progressive structure and certain *tax deductions* (the personal exemption and the standard deduction), people with low incomes may pay little or no federal income taxes.

PAY-AS-YOU-GO SYSTEM The federal government expects us to pay both federal income taxes and Social Security taxes (discussed later) as we earn income.

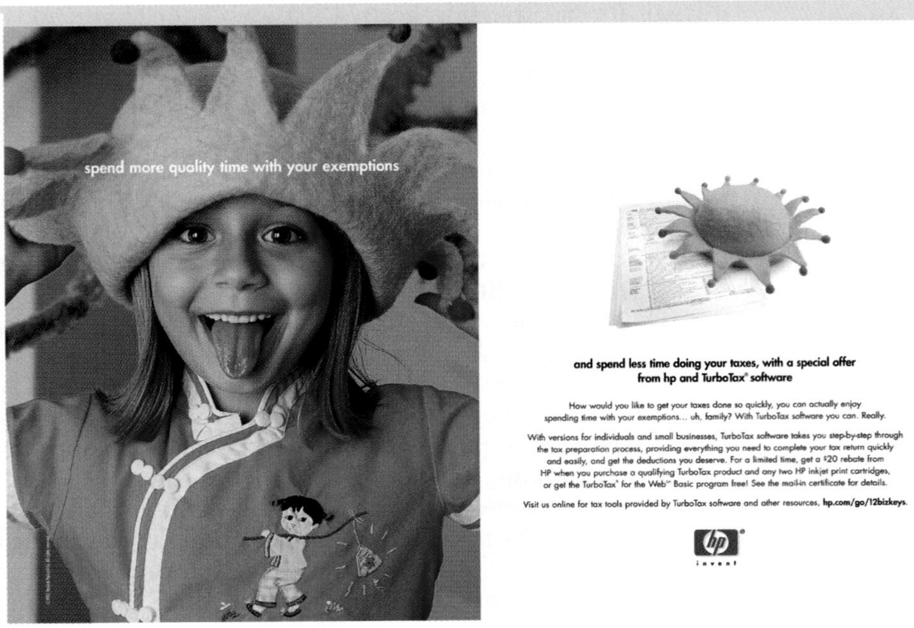
spend more quality time with your exemptions
and spend less time doing your taxes, with a special offer from hp and TurboTax® software
How would you like to get your taxes done so quickly, you can actually enjoy spending time with your exemptions... uh, family? With TurboTax software you can. Really.
With versions for individuals and small businesses, TurboTax software takes you step-by-step through the tax preparation process, providing everything you need to complete your tax return quickly and easily, and get the deductions you deserve. For a limited time, get a $20 rebate from HP when you purchase a qualifying TurboTax product and any two HP inkjet print cartridges, or get the TurboTax® for the Web℠ Basic program free! See the mail-in certificate for details.
Visit us online for tax tools provided by TurboTax software and other resources, **hp.com/go/12bizkeys**.
invent

COURTESY OF HEWLETT-PACKARD. PHOTOGRAPHER STEPHANIE RAUSSER

Don't let your dependents down—learn to manage your taxes with professional tax software. Proper tax planning will help to minimize your tax burden while maximizing your health.

This is accomplished through tax withholding by employers, or by filing quarterly tax estimates on self-employment income, investment income, and other income that is not subject to withholding. When you start a new job, your employer will ask you to fill out a W-4 form on which you report your **filing status** (similar to your marital status) and the number of **withholding allowances** you want to claim. The more withholding allowances you claim, the less your employer will withhold from each paycheck. However, the goal is to have the right amount withheld, so use the W-4 worksheet for guidance.

MINIMUM FILING REQUIREMENTS The federal government does not require all income earners to file federal income tax returns. If your income is below the minimum filing requirement in a given year, you do not have to file. If you are entitled to a tax refund, however, you must file to receive the refund.

Taxpayers can claim **personal exemptions** that reduce the amount of their taxable income. You can take a personal exemption for yourself, your spouse, and each of your dependents. If you are a taxpayer who is claimed as a dependent by someone else, however, you cannot claim the personal exemption. In 2003 a personal exemption was worth $3,050. The **standard deduction** is another amount that most taxpayers can automatically deduct from their gross income. In 2003 the standard deduction was $4,750 for single people and $9,500 for married couples filing jointly. If a taxpayer elects to itemize deductions, the standard deduction would not apply.

FILING A FEDERAL INCOME TAX RETURN Individuals may use one of three basic forms when filing their income tax returns: the 1040EZ, the 1040A, and the 1040. The 1040EZ and the 1040A are limited to taxpayers with relatively simple finances. Taxpayers can also use the TeleFile system to file their returns by punching in their data on touch-tone phones, or file online at the Internal Revenue Service Web site at **http://www.irs.gov/efile/**.

When completing a tax return, you start by listing your gross income, which includes **earned income**, income earned through employment (wages, tips, self-employment income), and **unearned income** (interest, dividends, other investment income). Students must include scholarship and grant proceeds in their gross income if these exceed the direct cost of the education. After totaling your gross income from all sources, subtract any legal deductions you are eligible to take: adjustments to

filing status
The marital status of a taxpayer specified on the income tax return.

withholding allowances
Allowances claimed with an employer that determine the amounts that are withheld from each of the employees' paychecks.

personal exemptions
Deductions that reduce the amount of income on which income tax is paid. Each taxpayer is entitled to a personal exemption, for himself, his spouse, and each of their dependents; a personal exemption can be used only once.

standard deduction
An amount that most taxpayers can automatically deduct from their gross income in computing their income tax; not permitted if the taxpayer elects to itemize deductions.

earned income
Income that is earned from employment such as wages, tips, and self-employment income.

unearned income
Income that is not earned through employment such as interest, dividends, and other investment income.

gross income, itemized deductions, personal exemptions, and tax credits. You may claim adjustments for interest paid on student loans, job-related moving expenses, and contributions to Individual Retirement Arrangements (IRAs). In addition, a new tax credit of $2,000 for the Clean-Fuel Vehicle Deduction is available on the purchase of certain hybrid gas/electric motor–powered vehicles.[12]

The tax-filing deadline is April 15. Tax returns filed on April 15, 2005, applied to income earned in the calendar year 2004. If the 15th falls on a weekend, the filing date is the next business day.

TAX PLANNING As long as your financial life is relatively simple, your biggest tax-planning issues will be having the correct amount of money withheld and keeping the appropriate tax records. However, once you purchase a home, begin investing, and earn a larger income, more sophisticated tax planning becomes important. You will probably need a good accountant, perhaps someone who specializes in taxation. You should also learn more about the federal income tax laws and keep up with the frequent changes made to those laws. Exhibit 22.9 offers some useful advice about organizing your taxes.

Social Security and Medicare Taxes

Like income taxes, Social Security and Medicare taxes are payroll taxes—taxes deducted from each employee's paycheck. Social Security taxes, often seen on a payroll stub as FICA (Federal Insurance Contributions Act), are paid at a uniform rate on a specified amount of earned income (the wage base). Both the percentage and the wage base can change annually.

Your employer matches your Social Security and Medicare paycheck withholding with company funds, and sends the total to the Internal Revenue Service (IRS). Self-employed people are responsible for paying both the employee's and the employer's share of this tax by making quarterly estimated payments. They are

Exhibit 22.9 IRS Stress Relief Tips

It's a taxing life. Here's how to be more organized at tax time.

Get Organized – Keeping your records organized throughout the year takes little time and lots of pressure off at tax time. Use an 8" x 11" envelope for each month to keep receipts and other tax related documents where you can find them.

Get Going – Don't leave yourself too little time—you're more likely to overlook something. Besides, the sooner you file, the sooner that refund will find its way back into your pocket.

Get Help – Decide whether you'll be doing the job yourself or using a tax preparer. The IRS sponsors Volunteer Income Tax Assistance (VITA) for taxpayers who need help but are unable to afford a preparation service.

Get Online – The IRS web site **http://www.irs.gov** has forms and publications for downloading and interactive calculators.

Get Smart – Keep tax returns and supporting documentation for seven years, when supporting documentation can be disposed of and tax returns placed in permanent storage. Shred monthly bank, brokerage, mutual fund, or 401(k) statements when you receive year-end statements, which should be kept for at least three years.

SOURCES: Robert Longley, "*U.S. Gov Info/Resources,*" downloaded from Web site http://www.usgovinfo.about.com/library/weekly/bltaxstress.htm, October 21, 2003; Deborah Fowles, "Making Tax Filing Easier," downloaded from Web site http://www.financialplan.about.com/library/weekly, October 21, 2003.

then allowed to deduct one-half of their Social Security tax as an adjustment to their gross income on their federal income tax returns.

Sales and Property Taxes

Two additional taxes are sales tax and property tax. All but five states (Alaska, Delaware, Montana, New Hampshire, and Oregon) currently have *sales tax* on retail goods and some services. In certain states, items like food consumed in the home, prescription drugs, and services such as doctor's fees, haircuts, and laundry bills are not taxed. Generally, sales tax rates range from 4 to 7 percent for the state's share with an additional 1 to 2 percent added by some cities.

The biggest single property tax for most individuals is on real estate, including a home. *Property tax* (real estate tax) is generally divided among the city, the county, the school system (which gets the largest portion), and in some cases the state government. The annual property tax (often paid in two installments) is calculated by multiplying the appraised (or assessed) value of the property by the tax rate. A house appraised at $100,000 could be taxed at 2 percent of its assessed value, resulting in an annual property tax of $2,000. Some state and local governments also impose personal property taxes on items such as automobiles, boats, and even the fixtures, furniture, and fittings belonging to a business.

concept check

What is a progressive tax? Explain why the federal income tax is progressive.

What are the personal exemption and the standard deduction? How do these amounts differ for taxpayers who are dependents as compared with independent taxpayers?

Briefly describe three types of taxes other than the income tax.

SELECTING INSURANCE

5 learning goal

While financial planning helps us meet our financial goals, we need to make provision for life's other uncertainties. We could suffer major losses from a serious illness, an auto accident, or a fire. Assessing these risks and purchasing the appropriate insurance to protect against them is an important part of a sound financial plan. Insurance planning involves learning about various types of insurance, such as property and liability insurance, health and disability income insurance, and life insurance, and setting priorities for your individual insurance needs.

Setting Insurance Priorities

Robert Hartwig, chief economist at the Insurance Information Institute, predicts the cost of insuring cars and homes could continue to rise,[13] so before buying an insurance policy, it is important to identify, evaluate, and prioritize your insurance needs. Start by identifying the types of insurable risks you face. For example, if you own a car, you face the risk of being in an accident that is your fault, injuring the other driver and damaging his or her car. Your own car could also be damaged and you could be hurt. Some of the everyday insurable risks people face include:

- Property damage to personal property such as automobiles, homes, and boats.
- Liability losses due to negligent actions.
- Medical expenses due to illness or accidents.
- Loss of income due to disability or premature death.

The key to managing your insurance needs in a cost-effective way is to budget (have funds set aside) to cover minor losses, and to purchase property, health, and life insurance to cover potential major losses.

Property and Liability Insurance

Property insurance covers financial losses from damage to or destruction of the insured's property as a result of specified perils, such as fire or theft. *Liability insurance* covers financial losses from injuries to others and damage to or destruction of others' property when the insured is considered to be the cause. It also covers the insured's legal-defense fees. The property and liability policies most often purchased by individuals are automobile insurance and homeowners/renters insurance.

automobile liability insurance
Insurance that protects the insured from financial losses caused by automobile-related injuries to others and damage to their property.

AUTOMOBILE INSURANCE Auto insurance covers financial losses from such perils as accident, theft, fire, and liability lawsuits. The two main types of automobile insurance are liability coverage and physical damage coverage. **Automobile liability insurance** protects the insured from financial losses caused by automobile-related injuries to others and damage to their property. Each policy specifies maximum payment limits. For example, a $50,000/$100,000/$25,000 policy will pay up to $50,000 for each person injured in an accident but a total of no more than $100,000 per accident for personal injuries, no matter how many people are involved. In addition, it will pay a maximum of $25,000 for damage to other people's property.

All 50 states have financial responsibility laws that require drivers to show proof of liability insurance, the ability to pay the costs (up to a limit) of any accidents for which they are responsible.

automobile physical damage insurance
Insurance that covers damage to or loss of the policyholder's vehicle from collision, theft, fire, or other perils; includes collision coverage and comprehensive (other-than-collision) coverage.

comprehensive (other-than-collision) coverage
Automobile insurance that covers damage to or loss of the policyholder's vehicle due to perils such as fire, floods, theft, and vandalism; part of automobile physical damage insurance.

Automobile physical damage insurance covers damage to or loss of the policyholder's vehicle from collision, theft, fire, or other perils. It includes collision coverage for damage caused by crashing into another vehicle or object, and **comprehensive (other-than-collision) coverage** for losses due to perils such as fire, floods, theft, and vandalism.

Automobile insurance rates generally depend on the driver's age, marital status, gender, area of residence, and driving record, as well as the characteristics of the automobile being insured. Young male drivers who live in cities, have more than one traffic ticket, and drive expensive, high-horsepower automobiles are charged the highest rates. Historically this group is involved in the most accidents.

actual cash value
The market value, determined by subtracting the amount of depreciation from its replacement cost, of personal property; the amount paid by standard homeowners and renters insurance policies.

replacement cost coverage
Homeowners and renters insurance that pays enough to replace lost and damaged personal property.

HOMEOWNERS/RENTERS INSURANCE It is advisable for homeowners and renters to purchase insurance for protection against property damage and liability losses. These policies cover losses due to fire, riots, windstorms, lightning, hurricanes, vandalism, frozen water pipes, and even falling airplanes. Special federally subsidized insurance provides coverage for earthquakes and floods. Homeowners insurance covers both the dwelling and personal property (furniture, clothing, etc.) while renters insurance covers personal property but not the dwelling. A standard policy pays out the **actual cash value** (similar to market value), determined by subtracting the amount of depreciation for its replacement cost, for personal-property losses. Policies that provide **replacement cost coverage,** enough money to replace lost or damaged personal property, costs about 10 to 15 percent more.

Homeowners and renters should also carry liability coverage to protect against financial losses arising from their liability for the injury of others. For example, if one of your inebriated guests was injured in a fall after attending a party where you served liquor, you could be legally liable for the subsequent medical expenses. Comprehensive personal-liability coverage purchased as part of a homeowners policy protects against a wide range of occurrences, both on and off your property. But it does not protect you when driving a motor vehicle, for slander or libel, or for professional malpractice.

Health Insurance

Elizabeth McKenty wanted a new treatment for her congenital heart defect. Her insurer said no. She appealed, and got another refusal. But McKenty, a 43-year-old librarian in Philadelphia, didn't give up. With the help of a company that fights denials such as these she appealed again, supporting her request with medical

COBRA
A federal regulation that allows most employees and their families to continue group health insurance coverage at their own expense for up to 18 months after leaving an employer.

indemnity (fee-for-service) plans
Health insurance plans that reimburse the insured for medical costs covered by the insurance policy. The policyholder selects the health care providers.

managed care plans
Health insurance plans that generally pay only for services provided by doctors and hospitals that are part of the plan.

The most common types of managed care plans are health maintenance organizations and preferred provider organizations. Managed care health insurance plans help control soaring medical costs by focusing on preventive care.

literature showing why the new treatment would give her better odds than open-heart surgery. This time she won.[14]

Health insurance is a vital component of financial stability. Many families and individuals obtain health insurance coverage through group policies offered as part of employment fringe-benefit plans. Group policies usually include comprehensive coverage at low cost. If you leave your job, your group coverage will terminate, although a federal regulation called **COBRA** allows most employees and their families to continue group health coverage at their own expense for up to 18 months. You should also be aware that coverage through a parent's policy usually ends around ages 23 to 25.

There are two basic types of health insurance coverage, available in combination and with variations. Traditional health insurance plans, called **indemnity (fee-for-service) plans,** reimburse the insured for medical costs covered by the insurance policy. The policyholder may select the physician, hospital, and other health care providers to obtain the required services. The patient pays for the services and files for reimbursement from their health insurance company. The primary advantage of this type of plan is a greater choice of health care providers for the patient.

The fastest-growing segment of the health insurance market is **managed care plans.** They became popular in the late 1980s as a way to control the spiraling cost of health care. Unlike traditional health insurance plans, managed care plans generally pay only for services provided by doctors and hospitals that are part of the plan. They may pay a smaller portion of the cost if the insured uses providers that are not part of the plan.

MAJOR MEDICAL INSURANCE **Major medical insurance** can be sold as a stand-alone product or combined with a managed care plan. It typically covers a wide range of medical costs with few exclusions and high maximum limits ($250,000 to $1 million). The insured pays a deductible and a percentage of the covered expenses. This **coinsurance (participation)** is typically 15 to 25 percent. Most policies include a limit, or cap, on the total amount the insured must pay.

© ROB LEWINE / CORBIS

MANAGED CARE PLANS Unlike traditional health insurance, managed care plans cover preventive care. The insured typically pays a small copayment ($10 to $20) each time he or she needs care. There is generally no cost for hospitalization. The most common types of managed care plans are health maintenance organizations and preferred provider organizations.

Health maintenance organizations (HMOs) provide comprehensive health care services for a fixed periodic payment. *Primary-care physicians (PCPs),* also known as "gatekeepers," are responsible for decisions about their patients' health care and for referrals to specialists when necessary. Except in the case of an emergency, the HMO will not pay for care that is given by non-HMO providers.

Preferred provider organizations (PPOs) combine major medical insurance with a network of health care providers, contracted to provide services at discounted prices. If you choose to go to a physician who is not a preferred provider, your out-of-pocket costs (deductibles and coinsurance) will be higher than if you receive care from a preferred provider. In some plans you pay only a small copayment (as with an

major medical insurance
Health insurance that covers a wide range of medical costs with few exclusions and high maximum limits. The insured pays a deductible and a coinsurance portion.

coinsurance (participation)
A percentage of covered expenses that the holder of a major medical insurance policy must pay.

health maintenance organizations (HMOs)
Managed care organizations that provide comprehensive health care services for a fixed periodic payment.

preferred provider organizations (PPOs)
Networks of health care providers who enter into a contract to provide services at discounted prices; combines major medical insurance with a network of health care providers.

disability income insurance
Insurance that will replace a portion of your earnings, typically 60 to 70 percent of your monthly income if you are unable to work due to illness or accident.

HMO) if you use a preferred provider, thus reducing your paperwork as well as your out-of-pocket cost.

Disability Income Insurance

Some insurable risks, such as a long-term illness, can have devastating financial consequences. If you are unable to work due to illness or accident, **disability income insurance** will replace a portion of your earnings, typically 60 to 70 percent of your monthly income. There is generally a **waiting period (elimination period)** after the onset of the disability, ranging from 3 to 12 months, before insurance coverage payments begin. The shorter the waiting period, the more expensive the insurance premiums will be. The policy will have a stated **duration of benefits,** the length of time the insurance coverage payments will continue. Under short-term policies, benefits are paid for periods ranging from 13 weeks to two years; long-term policies provide payments for periods of five years through the insured's lifetime.

One of the most important considerations in this type of insurance is the policy's definition of disability. With some policies you are considered disabled if you cannot perform the functions of your own occupation; with others you are disabled only if you cannot work at all. Exhibit 22.10 lists some of life's riskier career choices.

Life Insurance

Life insurance provides a specific amount of money upon the death of the policyholder, which is paid to a beneficiary of the policy owner's choice, or to the deceased's estate if there is no named beneficiary. The primary reason to purchase life insurance is to provide income for surviving family members, but life insurance can also be used to save for the future. The most common types of life insurance are term life, whole life, and universal life insurance.

Term life insurance provides the maximum amount of life insurance coverage for the lowest premium. It covers the insured's life for a fixed amount and a specific time period, typically 5 to 20 years. It has no **cash value** (a dollar amount paid to the policy owner if the policy is canceled before the death of the insured). When the policy term ends, protection stops, unless the policy is renewed or a new policy is purchased.

Exhibit 22.10 Top 10 Most Dangerous Jobs

According to the Bureau of Labor Statistics, the 10 most dangerous jobs are:

1. Timber cutters
2. Airplane pilots
3. Construction laborers
4. Truck drivers
5. Farm occupations
6. Groundskeepers
7. Laborers
8. Police and detectives
9. Carpenters
10. Sales occupations

SOURCE: Downloaded from the Web site http://www.insurance.com, March 25, 2003.

Whole life insurance (also called **straight life, cash value,** or **continuous pay insurance**) covers the insured for his or her entire life, as long as the premiums are paid. In addition to death protection, it has a cash value that increases over the life of the policy. Whole life is much more expensive than term insurance and the interest rate used to determine its cash value is low—usually 4 to 6 percent. But it does provide a way to save for the future.

Developed in the 1980s to help insurance companies compete with other financial institutions for investment funds, **universal life insurance** combines term life insurance with a tax-deferred savings plan. The portion of the premium not used to pay for the term life coverage, commissions, and other business expenses, is invested in short- and medium-term securities. It earns interest, at current market rates, that contributes to the policy's cash value.

concept check

Distinguish between property and liability insurance coverage. Why should families and individuals have both?

What are the primary differences between traditional indemnity health insurance and managed care plans?

What are the two main reasons for buying life insurance? Which types of policies meet each need?

Making Investment Decisions

6 learning goal

People invest money for a variety of reasons. Some want to save for a new home, their children's education, or a vacation. Others invest to build up a nest egg to supplement their retirement income. The "Focusing on Small Business" box describes the additional financial-planning and goal-setting challenges faced by people who are self-employed. **Investing** is the process of committing money to various *investment instruments* in order to obtain future financial returns. It

Focusing on Small Business

Why Good Business Owners Make Bad Investors

Who brings more baggage to the task of personal investing than a small-business owner? Visions for their companies can interfere with the personal goal setting that is a prerequisite for making sound investment decisions. In other words, personal financial goals may be subordinated to business objectives, reducing choices in investing to either building up their core asset, their business, or committing those dollars to an investment portfolio. The business often wins.

The dilemma facing many small-business owners is how to successfully juggle the financial needs of their business, while adequately meeting their personal investment goals. The temptation to place all their financial eggs in one basket—their business—is huge. It is a quandary many small-business owners face, even those in the financial planning business.

Richard Stanley is a good example. He knows that a well-balanced portfolio is a thing of beauty and a bulwark for the future. As a financial planner he understands that diversification, and keeping a level head, is part of a solid investment strategy. But Stanley, 58, would rather take the money his business generates and plow it right back into the business. "I'm betting that by the time I get to retirement age the business will be worth more than I could earn in the market," he says.

Stanley is like many small-business owners except for one thing—he earns a living by helping his clients act on the very precepts that he has put on hold for himself. And when it comes to planning for the future, the entrepreneur trumps the planner. Following the expansion goals outlined in his business plan, Stanley next plans to fund a move to larger business premises, with the addition of several more associates to his business.

Personal financial decisions are complicated-for everyone. But for small-business owners they are about so much more than money. As a small-business owner, investing in your business is investing in yourself, which, in turn, can provide the satisfaction of realizing your dreams. It's difficult to place a monetary value on that.[15]

Critical Thinking Questions

1. Why does being a small-business owner present unique challenges to investing for the future?
2. According to traditional financial planning guidelines, what should Richard Stanley be doing to prepare for his retirement?
3. How could Richard Stanley contribute to both the continued growth of his business and his personal investment portfolio? Explain.

waiting period (elimination period)
In disability income insurance, the period between the onset of the disability and the time when insurance payments begin.

duration of benefits
In disability income insurance, the length of time the insurance coverage payments will continue.

term life insurance
Life insurance that covers the insured's life for a fixed amount and a specific period and has no *cash value*; provides the maximum amount of life insurance coverage for the lowest premium.

cash value
The dollar amount paid to the owner of a life insurance policy if the policy is canceled before the death of the insured; *term life insurance* has no cash value.

whole life (straight life, cash value, continuous pay) insurance
Life insurance that covers the insured for his or her entire life, as long as the premiums are paid; has a cash value that increases over the life of the policy.

universal life insurance
A combination of term life insurance and a tax-deferred savings plan. Part of the premium is invested in securities, so the cash value earns interest, at current market rates, that contributes to the policy's cash value.

investing
The process of committing money to various investment instruments in order to obtain future financial returns.

emergency fund
Liquid assets that are available to meet emergencies.

should be considered a long-term strategy, and as Chapter 21 describes, the most common investments used by individuals are stocks, bonds, and mutual funds.

Investment Goals

Realistic investment goals are based on the investor's financial resources, age, family situation, and investment motives, so every investor needs to first ask themselves: "What do I want to achieve with my investment program?" Setting investment goals is the basis for developing a sound investment strategy. Your investment goals will relate to certain goals in your financial plan, such as saving for a home, your children's education, and your retirement. Investment goals also play a role in determining how conservative or aggressive you want to be in making investment choices.

Investors can tolerate different levels of risk, and it is important to determine how much risk you can withstand when making investment decisions. The more risk you are willing to take, the higher the potential return on an investment. The investment risk pyramid shown in Exhibit 22.11 on page 726 depicts the relationship between risk and reward.

The most common investment goals are income, growth, and safety. Investors wishing to *supplement their income* will choose securities that provide a steady, reliable source of income from bond interest, stock dividends, or both. Good choices include low-risk securities such as U.S. Treasury issues, high-quality corporate bonds, preferred stock, and common stock of large, financially sound corporations that regularly pay dividends (called *income stocks*).

Another important investment goal is growth, *increasing the value of the investment.* Many investors look for securities that are expected to increase in price over time. Generally, they choose stocks that expect to continue above-average rates of growth in earnings and price. For instance, the earnings of so-called *growth stocks* might increase 15 to 20 percent or more at a time when the earnings of most common stocks are increasing only 5 to 6 percent.

Safety is yet another investment goal. Investors who opt for safety do not want to risk losing the money they've invested. They generally choose government and high-grade corporate bonds, preferred stocks, and mutual funds. They avoid common stock because of its frequent price fluctuations.

Developing an Investment Strategy

Although much is written about various investment strategies, as Carlos and Amy Vela discovered, the secret to success is to start investing early. But before putting money into investments it is a good idea to establish an adequate **emergency fund** (liquid assets that are available to meet emergencies), obtain necessary insurance coverage, and reduce debt. Then diversify your investments and invest regularly.

Start Early to Enjoy the Benefits of Compounding

Financial-planning practitioners and educators believe starting to invest early so returns can compound is the most important element in a successful savings/-investment program. Consider attorney Jeff Stier, who at 27 years old had already invested $32,000 for his retirement. With no additional contributions to this investment and assuming a 10 percent annual return, Jeff's $32,000 will grow to $1,196,939 by the time he is 65 years old! If Jeff had waited until age 45 to start saving for his retirement, he would have to invest $20,898 a year for 20 years (a total of $417,962) in order to accumulate $1,196,939.

Start early and let your investments work for you, but remember that you need to protect your assets with the appropriate insurance. And because the interest you

Exhibit 22.11 | Investment Risk Pyramid

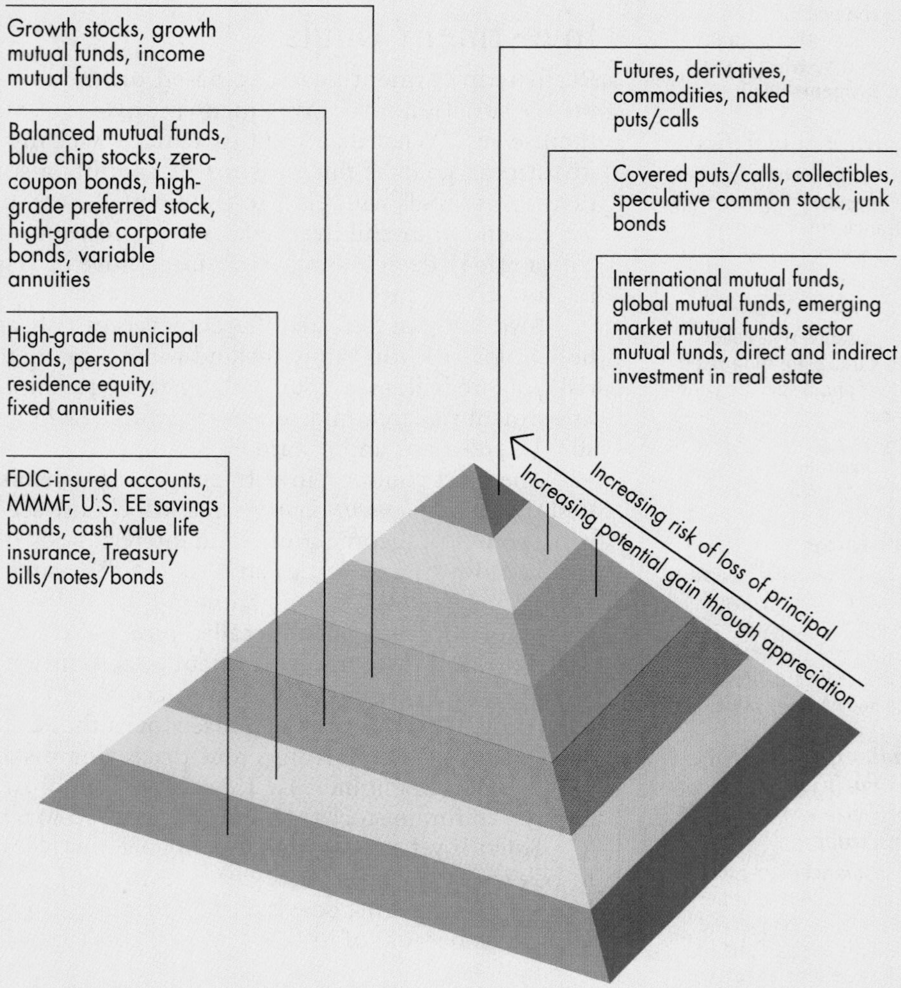

pay on debt is usually more than you can earn on your investments, it is important to reduce your debt first.

diversification
An investment strategy that involves investing in different classes of assets, such as cash equivalents, stocks, bonds, and real estate, and purchasing securities with different risk patterns and rates of return.

portfolio
A collection of investments.

DIVERSIFY Another important element of a successful investment strategy is **diversification.** This means you should invest in different classes of assets—cash equivalents, stocks, bonds, real estate—and purchase securities with different risk patterns and rates of return. A diverse **portfolio,** or collection of investments, is more likely to meet your investment goals than a single security is. A portfolio that includes preferred stocks paying high dividends and growth stocks paying modest dividends increases the potential of achieving both income and growth. Investing in 5 to 10 different companies in different industries is another way to diversify. Diversification is an important method of spreading your risk and increasing your potential for achieving your investment goals.

INVEST REGULARLY Make investing for your goals part of your cash flow plan. Decide how much to invest, then purchase the investments monthly, quarterly, or annually. Or, better yet, set up automatic transfers from your checking account to a mutual fund or stock **dividend reinvestment plan (DRIP)** so that a preplanned amount is regularly invested in the investment vehicles of your choice.

Most mutual funds welcome monthly contributions of $50 or more through their automatic investment plans, and more stock can now be purchased regularly in small increments. Originally, stock DRIPs were set up to automatically reinvest dividend income paid on stocks, but many companies have also made stock purchase plans available to investors who own as little as one share of the company stock.

concept check

What is investment risk? What is the relationship between risk and return?

What steps should be taken before starting an investment program? Why?

Discuss three strategies for implementing a successful investment program.

Securities Transaction Basics

7 learning goal

The traditional approach to investing in securities is through a stockbroker at a stock brokerage firm. Investors should seek a broker who understands their investment goals and will help them pursue those objectives.

Investors can open two basic types of accounts at a brokerage firm: cash accounts and margin accounts. With a *cash account,* purchases of securities are paid for in full by the investor (cost of the securities plus brokerage commissions). In a *margin account,* the investor puts up as little as 50 percent of the cost of the securities, borrowing the balance from the broker and paying interest on the loan. The broker holds the securities as collateral for the loan.

dividend reinvestment plan (DRIP)
A program in which dividends paid by a stock are automatically reinvested in that stock along with any additional stock purchases submitted by the stockholder.

Typically when an investor decides to buy or sell securities, they place an order with their broker who handles the transaction on their behalf. The broker transmits a buy or sell order to the appropriate stock exchange, like the New York Stock Exchange (NYSE), where it is sent to the exchange trading floor for execution. To make transactions in the Nasdaq/OTC market, the broker must find out via computer who deals in the security and contact the dealer, offering the best price to make the transaction.

Stocks are usually bought and sold in blocks of 100 shares, called *round lots.* But if an investor can't afford 100 shares of a stock, he or she may purchase less than 100 shares, called an *odd lot.* Because only round lots are traded on the exchanges, odd lots are grouped together by brokers to make up a round lot. An extra fee is charged for odd-lot transactions.

Investors can place three types of orders when buying or selling securities. A *market order* is an order to buy or sell a security immediately at the best price available. A *limit order* is an order to buy a security at a specified price (or lower) or to sell at a specified price (or higher). The trade is executed only if the requested limit is reached. With a *stop-loss order,* the stock is sold if the market price reaches or drops below a specified level. A stop-loss order limits an investor's losses in the event stock prices rapidly decline.

Brokerage firms are paid commissions for executing clients' transactions. Although brokers can charge whatever they want, most firms have fixed commission schedules for small transactions. The value of the transaction and the number of shares involved helps to determine the amount of brokerage commission you are charged. Today many investors are using on-line brokerage firms to execute their securities transactions.

concept check

Differentiate between cash and margin accounts.

What are the three types of orders investors can place to trade securities?

Trends in Personal Finance

8 learning goal

The protection of your good name and credit rating is critical to sound financial health, so two important trends need to be recognized: the dramatic increase in identity theft and the increasing "debt load" of the Gen-X generation.

Getting Downright Personal

Chapter 17 introduced you to the rising problem of identity theft and for the third straight year the Federal Trade Commission (FTC) confirmed that it topped their list of consumer fraud complaints, accounting for 43 percent of all the complaints it receives. The total number of fraud complaints jumped from 220,000 in 2001 to 380,000 in 2002, costing consumers $343 million, more than double 2001's figure of $160 million. Some of the top categories of consumer fraud complaints in 2002 included:

• Internet auctions	13 percent
• Internet services and computer complaints	6 percent
• Catalog sales	5 percent
• Business opportunities/work-at-home plans	3 percent

As you can see from this partial list, Internet fraud is one of the fastest-growing segments of consumer fraud, which includes identity theft. Online e-commerce has opened up a whole new world of opportunity for crooks. Eighty-five percent of students now own a PC, and more than half of all students made online purchases last year. In fact student online spending totaled $1.4 billion in 2002.

In one notorious case of Internet identity theft, the criminal not only incurred more than $100,000 of credit-card debt, he obtained a federal home loan and bought homes, motorcycles, and handguns in the victim's name. To make matters even worse he called the victim to taunt him, as identity theft was not a federal crime at that time. It was this case and others like it that prompted Congress to pass the Identity Theft and Assumption Deterrence Act in the fall of 1998.

Most people do not realize how easily criminals can obtain our personal data, without having to break into our homes or steal our wallets. In public places they may engage in "shoulder surfing," watching you punch in a telephone calling-card number, or listening in as you give your credit-card number over the phone. Others engage in "dumpster diving," going through trashcans or communal dumpsters to obtain copies of checks, credit-card, or bank statements. Buy a shredder and make sure your personal financial papers are destroyed before you throw them in the trash.

Connectivity comes at a cost, with crooks and hackers getting online access to everything. Guard your personal financial information carefully at all times and know to whom and why you are giving it out.

Exhibit 22.12 Keep Your Identity to Yourself

With Internet fraud and identity theft dramatically on the rise, how can you protect yourself from this silent scourge that could target you next? Here are some tips from the FTC to protect yourself, your identity, and your money while online:

- Never disclose private information unless you are sure who's collecting it and why.
- Never give out your passwords.
- Be wary of any online business that does not give an e-mail address or have a customer service Web page.
- If it sounds too good to be true, it probably is.
- When using a credit card for online purchases, make sure it is to a secure server.
- Install an antivirus program and keep it updated.
- Be wary of downloading ".EXE" program files unless you know their source and what they are going to do.
- Avoid responding to "spam" mail, which is very often nothing more than an attempt by Internet criminals to obtain large amounts of personal data . . . about you.

If despite your best efforts you still become a target of identity thieves, you can call the Federal Trade Commission toll free at 1-877-FTC-HELP or file a complaint online at **http://www.consumer.gov/idtheft**.

SOURCE: Robert Longley, "How to Not Get E-Taken," January 30, 2003, downloaded from Web site http://www.usgovinfo.about.com.

As Exhibit 22.12 shows, there are other precautions you can take to recognize threats and protect your personal information at all times; it's a valuable commodity.[16]

For the Gen-X Generation the Future Is Now

Who doesn't have piles of credit-card debt when they're young? It's practically a rite of passage. But many Gen-X households are also buried under car loans and student loans; a third carry an installment-loan balance of at least $9,500. Even more worrisome, nearly 25 percent have fallen seriously behind in their payments.

The average annual income (before taxes) for single men ages 25–34 is $36,766 and for single women, $31,640, with average annual expenditures of $28,925 and $28,267, respectively. Although 29 percent of the men and 33 percent of the women have college degrees, 41 percent of them do not know their credit-card interest rate, and 24 percent do not review their monthly statements. It is easy to see why so many young adults fall into debt that quickly spirals out of control.[17]

Following the suggestions in this chapter with respect to financial goal setting, budgeting, and investing, will help to make sure you can pay your bills and enjoy a financially secure future.

concept check

How do the emerging trends of increased Internet fraud and identity theft place more responsibility on the individual?

Explain the concept of identity theft and what it means to the victim.

How can you avoid falling into the Gen-X "debt trap"?

Great Ideas to Use Now

As this chapter clearly demonstrates, you will need to make financial-planning decisions throughout your life. Financial knowledge allows you to manage your financial resources to best meet your goals now and in the future, while lack of knowledge may cost you dearly in money, time, and missed opportunity. You will

Try It Now

1. **Choose a bank.** Select three different financial institutions: one that you actually use for checking and/or savings and two others. Determine what checking and savings accounts are available that suit your needs and find out how these accounts are structured (minimum opening deposits, minimum required balances, fees, and other limitations). Look at the institution's complete list of fees, not just the cost of the checking account. Get a written copy of all account descriptions and fees if possible. Which one would be best for you given your needs? Be sure to discuss your needs as well as the characteristics of the institutions.
2. **Select a credit card.** How do you choose the best credit card and use it wisely? Compare three different credit cards. If you already have a credit card(s), use your own in addition to those offered through local banks or flyers you see on campus. Compare annual fees, APRs, methods of calculating finance costs, grace periods, and other terms. Get a written copy of the credit-card terms if possible. Which one would be best for you given your needs and the way you intend to use a credit card? Be sure to discuss your needs as well as the characteristics of the cards.

make your money work for you by spending it in a way that gives you the most satisfaction for the dollar, and investing it so that you get the most return for the amount of risk. The key to making the best use of your money overall is the knowledge to make informed decisions. Let's look specifically at some areas of financial planning discussed in this chapter.

We are all faced with unexpected expenses from time to time. You cannot know when emergencies may strike or how much they will cost. You may need a new set of tires, or have an opportunity to go skiing over the holiday break. In or-

Customer Satisfaction and Quality

It seems wherever you look nowadays, people have been replaced by technology. And as technology services more and more of our everyday needs, we have lost the "human touch," which is so important, especially in the area of customer service.

Perhaps the most dramatic example of this phenomenon is the banking industry, where ATMs and online banking have made any contact with your friendly local banker a thing of the past. In their never-ending quest for new business, and in an attempt to keep and build loyalty with the customers they have, some banks are rethinking the role of automation, and ATMs in particular, with respect to their customer service function. Kate Harris was urged by her bank to try the bank's newly installed ATM machine to make her deposit, saving herself a 20-minute wait inside. Kate was uncertain. She liked to give her paycheck to a real person, which seemed safer than feeding it into a machine. But the young man assured her it was quite safe and helped her make the transaction. Kate rarely went inside the bank after that; she preferred the convenience of using the ATM for her regular banking needs. When a competing bank in town solicited her business with offers of free checking and other enticements, she made the switch without a second thought. Her only bond with her bank was with a machine!

So have banks trained their customers too well? Although having customers use ATMs saves the bank money—ATM transactions cost banks pennies compared with several dollars for an "inside transaction"—the banks are losing something much more valuable in the process, "face time" with their customers. Face time helps build customer loyalty and trust. More important, it allows bank staffers to promote other (profitable) products and services the bank has to offer. These might include upgraded checking and savings vehicles, investments, and loans, including home refinancing. Nowadays when customers approach Kate's old bank, they are greeted at the door by a bank staffer, welcoming them inside.

der to structure your cash flow so that money is put aside for unexpected expenses, you need a spending plan and the discipline to follow it.

The cash management section of this chapter describes liquid assets, such as money market accounts, that could be used for an emergency fund. Financial experts recommend that you keep sufficient financial resources in your emergency fund to cover two to six months of expenditures, including unexpected emergencies and investment opportunities. You will want to choose the best savings vehicle at the best interest rate for your emergency fund. Putting this money into a two-year certificate of deposit would be a mistake if your tires need replacing in 14 months, because there is a penalty for early withdrawal. Putting the money into a money market deposit account at 3 percent, rather than a money market mutual fund paying 5 percent, will cost you $20 a year for each $1,000 in the account. You can probably find something fun to do with $20.

Where credit is concerned, if it sounds to good to be true it usually is! Advertisements that invite purchases with no money down and no payment for months or even years sound wonderful, but you need to read the fine print and understand exactly what is required. Most require a minimum monthly payment and are only "interest free" as long as you continue to make those payments in a timely manner. Or at the end of the term the entire balance may become due in a lump sum, carrying huge interest penalties if you are not able to pay it all on time. And remember—don't be afraid to call your credit-card company to negotiate lower rates, more miles, better terms. And calling more than once may trigger greater gains as you may not be advised of all your options on the first call. A brief mention that you are considering switching to a lower-rate card with more benefits will usually produce results.

In the tax area, you can be assessed significant penalties if you don't pay what you legally owe in taxes, but you need to take legitimate deductions that could save you tax dollars. Not having the proper insurance will cost you if you suffer a loss. No car insurance may mean you take the bus to work. Homeowners and renters insurance is needed to protect against property damage and liability losses. Lack of health insurance can put families on welfare. And buying too much insurance, or insurance from the wrong company, can be expensive.

Looking Ahead at Carlos and Amy Vela

Carlos hopes to retire in 5 to 10 years to run his own software consulting business, but not before the couple has set aside enough money for their 4-year-old daughter, Jillian's, college education. In addition, the dramatic downturn in the stock market following September 11, 2001, prompted the couple to re-evaluate how they will meet their future financial goals.

Financial planner Jarrett advised them to diversify their investments into different kinds of stocks as well as bonds, believing this will increase their returns while lowering their risks. Carlos, who has always managed his own investment portfolio, believes his risk tolerance to be high—he's not planning to tap into his investments until age 57 or older—so he wants to purchase more stock while the market is low. His single-minded focus is to secure his family's financial future, even if the Mercedes has to wait a while longer.

Once you have met the necessities with regard to financial planning, cash flow, credit, taxes, and insurance, you should develop an investment program that will allow you to achieve your goals. Start early to benefit from compounding, diversify, and invest regularly. Be sure to find a broker who understands your investment goals and will help you achieve them.

Even in areas such as banking and credit, knowledge about how accounts are structured and the fees associated with their use is very important. Take the case of the student who wondered why his checking account cost him so much. With the help of his personal-finance instructor, he discovered that he had made 23 ATM withdrawals from ATMs not owned by his bank—and each one had cost him $1. The monthly checking account fee was only $3, but the total cost for that month was $26! By walking one more block to use his own bank's ATM, he could have saved the $23 and spent it on something more enjoyable.

Summary of Learning Goals

1

How does the financial-planning process facilitate successful personal financial management?

Financial planning is a six-step process that includes establishing financial goals, gathering objective and subjective information, analyzing the information, developing a financial plan, implementing the plan, and monitoring your plan. The process starts with your goals and provides a road map to meet those goals.

2

How do cash flow planning and management of liquid assets contribute to your financial goals?

A cash flow plan manages income and expenses. Based on your financial goals, it includes saving for those goals. With money set aside regularly to pay for these goals, you are more likely to achieve them. Liquid assets such as checking and savings accounts are important for day-to-day spending, to meet short-term goals, and for unexpected or emergency expenditures. Liquid assets can be held in safe, accessible accounts so the money is readily available when needed.

3

What are the advantages and disadvantages of using consumer credit?

The benefits of consumer credit include convenience, the ability to purchase a good or service when you need it and take advantage of bargains, establish a credit rating, convenient record keeping, meeting financial emergencies, and perks such as rebates and frequent-flyer miles. Using consumer credit has some important disadvantages including the ease of overspending, the cost of credit (interest charges), the possibility that merchandise may cost more, and the reduction in future discretionary income due to the legal commitment to repay debt.

4

What types of taxes are individuals responsible for?

The major taxes paid by individuals are income, Social Security and Medicare, sales, and property taxes. Income and Social Security and Medicare taxes are called payroll taxes because they are based on income and deducted from an employee's paycheck. Sales tax is assessed on purchases made, and property tax is based on the value of property owned, usually real estate.

5

What factors should you consider in deciding what insurance to purchase?

The key to managing your insurance needs in the most cost-effective way is to budget to cover minor losses and purchase insurance to cover potential major losses. Set aside money in savings so that you can pay for the loss when it happens, and buy good insurance policies to cover major losses.

6 What personal goals are important when making investment decisions?

Investment decisions should be based on your goals and your risk tolerance. Examples of investment goals include the desire for income from interest and dividends, the need for growth (capital gains), and the need for safety.

7 How do investors open a brokerage account and make securities transactions?

Investors must choose a brokerage firm and a stockbroker in that firm. Then they open a cash account or a margin account. In a cash account, all securities transactions are paid in full by the investor. Margin accounts allow investors to put as little as 50 percent of the price of the securities and borrow the rest from the broker. The investor gives an order to buy or sell securities to the broker, who sends it to the stock exchange to be carried out or, in the case of an over-the-counter stock, finds the dealer with the best price. Today many investors are using online brokerage firms to execute their securities transactions.

8 What emerging trends affect the way you manage your personal finances?

The dramatic increase in identity theft means you need to take precautions to protect your good name. Don't fall victim to the increasing "debt load" of the Gen-X generation—protect your credit rating as well.

Preparing for Tomorrow's Workplace

1. Use the six-step financial-planning process to develop a financial plan for yourself for the next year. List your financial goals and gather the appropriate information needed to analyze your situation. Develop your plan and explain how it will be implemented.
2. Use the steps detailed in this chapter to balance your most recent checking account statement. After completing this process, analyze your use of the checking account, EFT services, and so on. Are you satisfied with the way you are handling your account? If not, what changes would you make in how you use it?
3. College junior Andy Jung overused his credit cards last year. He currently has the following outstanding debt on two credit cards plus an auto loan and a student loan:

    - MasterCard—$984 outstanding debt, $40 minimum monthly payment, 18 percent interest rate, no annual fee, $25 late-payment fee, 2 percent cash-advance fee ($20 maximum), $1,000 line of credit.
    - Visa—$569 outstanding debt, $17 minimum monthly payment, 14 percent interest rate, $20 annual fee, $20 late-payment fee, 1.5 percent cash-advance fee ($20 maximum), $800 line of credit.
    - Auto loan—$3,490 outstanding balance, $257 monthly payment, 8 percent interest, 15 more payments.
    - Student loan—$15,490 outstanding balance, deferred payments, 7.5 percent interest (unsubsidized).

    Andy has $450 a month to use for debt repayment. Divide into small groups and advise Andy on how best to pay off his debt obligations. Start by completing a debt inventory for Andy. Then write a one- to two-page memo explaining how Andy should allocate the $450. Support the rationale for your recommendations.

4. You have just won $100,000 in your state lottery. In light of your personal situation (age, finances, family status, and so on), what types of securities would you choose, and why? Now you also have to find a broker to execute the transactions. Should you use a traditional full-service brokerage, a discount broker, or an online brokerage? Using the Internet and personal-finance publications to gather information, compare the services of these types of firms. Summarize the pros and cons of each and decide which best meets your needs. Justify your choice.
5. Form a team of four or five classmates to evaluate employer fringe-benefit plans. Gather written information on the insurance and retirement benefits offered by at least two employers. This information may be available directly from an employer, from your parents, or from senior classmates who are interviewing with companies. After reviewing the information write a brief summary evaluating the insurance and retirement plans offered, and what investments are available through the retirement plans. Present your findings to the class.

KEY TERMS

actual cash value 721
automobile liability insurance 721
automobile physical damage insurance 721
cash flow plan 710
cash management 709
cash value 725
COBRA 722
coinsurance (participation) 723
comprehensive (other-than-collision) coverage 721
credit life insurance 715
disability income insurance 723
diversification 726
dividend reinvestment plan (DRIP) 727
duration of benefits 725
earned income 718
emergency fund 725
filing status 718
grace period 715
health maintenance organizations (HMOs) 723
indemnity (fee-for-service) plans 722
investing 725
line of credit 713
liquid assets 709
major medical insurance 723
managed care plans 722
net worth 709
open-end credit 713
personal balance sheet 709
personal exemptions 718
personal financial planning 707
portfolio 726
preferred provider organizations (PPOs) 723
prepayment penalties 715
principal 715
progressive tax 717
replacement cost coverage 721
revolving credit cards 714
security requirements 715

Working the Net

1. Finance Center (**http://www.financecenter.com**) is a comprehensive, highly rated financial-planning Web site that includes more than 100 online calculators to help with the number crunching involved in personal finance decisions. Click on Calculators to see how to budget for college living expenses. Input your information and click on Results to tally your monthly living expenses. Then click on Graph to view what percentage of funds you have allocated to various types of expense. Use the site's calculator to analyze whether living on campus or at home would save you money. If you decide to live at home, perhaps a college meal plan would be a good idea to cover your lunches each day. While at the site check it out, as well as other applications that may interest you.
2. At Bankrate (**http://www.bankrate.com**) you will find the current average rates on standard, gold, and platinum credit cards. To find the best rate for you, fill in the required information based on your wants and needs in a credit card. Planning to move? Use the site's calculator to compare the cost of living between two cities. Summarize your findings.
3. Wells Fargo (**http://www.wellsfargo.com**) offers one-stop shopping for all your banking needs. Click on Education Center and Paying for College to see their full range of college-financing options.
4. Go to Tax Cut (**http://www.taxcut.com**) for information on taxes and tax preparation software. Click on Tax Resources for information regarding tax planning, including information on deductions, how to treat investment and dividend income, and family dependents. Also find and analyze one other topic that is of interest to you.
5. SmartMoney (**http://www.smartmoney.com**) provides information to assist you with your personal investing. Go to My Portfolio to create your own investment portfolio. Click on Tools to find the information you need to track your investments. Select a company you would like to know more about, perhaps one you might like to work for. Click on Stocks to get the current stock quote for the company and see if there is any breaking news about it.

Creative Thinking Case

The Credit-Card Trap

In your first week at college a major credit-card company offers you your very first credit card. You are excited about the financial freedom this represents as your par-

KEY TERMS

standard deduction 718
term life insurance 725
unearned income 718
universal life insurance 725
waiting period (elimination period) 725
whole life (straight life, cash value, continuous pay) insurance 725
withholding allowances 718

ents were always strict with money. You use the card to buy some new clothes and the state-of-the-art sound system you have been wanting for your dorm room. You also join a group on a visit to a local casino and get swept away in the headiness of the moment. Soon you owe $4,500, and although you struggle to make the minimum monthly payment from the allowance your parents give you, your balance never seems to get any lower. Feeling trapped, you decide to take advantage of an on-campus debt-counseling service where they instruct you to destroy your credit card. They also negotiate with the credit card issuer on your behalf for a reduction in the balance due. They ask you to share your experience with other students to help them avoid falling into the credit-card trap.

CRITICAL THINKING QUESTIONS

1. In speaking with students, what is the first thing you would tell them?
2. What can a student expect to feel when she receives her first credit card? What types of risks is she exposed to?
3. How would you recommend a student control her spending?

VIDEO CASE

The Edward Jones Approach to Personal Finance

Unlike firms like Morgan Stanley (see Chapter 21 video case), whose client base includes wealthy individuals and large, institutional investors, and Ameritrade, whose clients conduct most of their brokerage business online, the Edward Jones Company (**http://www.edwardjones.com**) focuses on smaller individual investors and business owners who want highly personalized, face-to-face service. The only major financial-services firm that exclusively targets retired investors, working investors, tax professionals and attorneys, and small-business owners, Edward Jones's approach appeals to investors in smaller communities as well as larger metropolitan areas. In fact, about three-quarters of its offices are in major cities.

Edward Jones provides investment services to its targeted clientele through a branch-office network and a comprehensive IT system. Its more than 8,000 branch offices in all 50 states, plus another 700 in Canada and the United Kingdom, are located in neighborhoods where people live and work rather than in center-city high-rises. Account representatives focus on building long-term relationships with their clients. They also strive to ensure that clients are comfortable with and confident about their investment decisions. As managing partner John Bachman says, "We want our people touching customers."

The brokerage firm implements its strategy of one-on-one, personalized investment services through three key elements:

- Customizing financial strategies and solutions to each client's needs and goals.
- Providing a Full Service Account (FSA) to simplify customers' financial management needs.
- Focusing on customers who are interested in long-term, relatively high-quality, low-risk investments.

For instance, the company provides small-business owners with retirement plan choices, cash flow management, and information on legislative issues. For working investors, the company focuses on managing personal finances, saving for retirement, and financing their children's college education. Its stock reports are written in easy-to-understand language, and its fees are lower than most other full-service brokerage firms.

Edward Jones's Full Service Account helps clients simplify their financial lives. This cash and investment management account coordinates their savings and investments into an organized portfolio that simplifies record keeping and streamlines transactions. Investors can borrow money through an automatic line of credit and open a money market account.

A third element of the company's strategy is its focus on clients who are interested in relatively high-quality, low-risk investments that are held for the long term. These investments include certificates of deposit; mutual funds; government, municipal, and corporate bonds; common stocks of companies with histories of sound management and solid growth; retirement plans and individual retirement arrangements (IRAs); and life insurance products, including annuities.

A few years ago, its lack of online trading and other Internet-based services made Edward Jones seem stodgy and out of step with the times. Its recent growth shows that Jones is doing something right. The number of offices has more than doubled in recent years, to about 9,000, and it manages more than $250 billion in assets for its 6 million-plus customers.

CRITICAL THINKING QUESTIONS

1. How can Edward Jones's strategy of one-on-one, personalized investment services help a customer develop a personal financial plan and an investment strategy?
2. Suppose that you are looking for investment management services. Would you be inclined to become a client of the Edward Jones Co.? Why or why not?

SOURCES: Adapted from the material in the Edward Jones video; the Edward Jones Web site, http://www.edwardjones.com, accessed June 17, 2003; and David Landis, "Street Smart," *Kiplinger's Personal Finance* (May 2003), downloaded from http://www.edwardjones.com.

E-Commerce Case

Can You Plan on Online Financial Advice?

Financial planning was once considered a luxury item for those wealthy enough to pay high fees for personal advice from a financial professional. Today, financial advice is just a click away for most Americans, courtesy of specialized Web sites that provide advice ranging from retirement planning to diversifying your assets. Many sites have automated financial advisers. T. Rowe Price (**http://www.troweprice.com**), a mutual fund company, offers investors a variety of planning tools in its individual investor Tools and Calculators pages. These cover investment, retirement, and college. Many other mutual fund Web sites have extensive online financial planning advice sections; The Vanguard Group (**http://www.vanguard.com**) and American Century Funds (**http://www.americancentury.com**) are two. You'll find broader planning capabilities at independent advice sites, including Financial Engines, and Morningstar.com's ClearFuture service.

Let's see how one of these sites approaches the financial-planning process. Financial Engines (**http://www.financialengines.com**) is one of the most sophisticated online advisers, specializing in tax-deferred investment planning for retirement. It is available to individual participants in employer-sponsored programs. A recent survey revealed that Financial Engines helped users increase their average savings from 6 percent to 10 percent of income

It offers a free forecast based on your financial profile—including demographic information, current income, investments in your portfolio, savings rate, risk tolerance, retirement age, tax status, retirement income goal, and other criteria. Rather than asking you to make estimates about future inflation rates, interest rates, or investment returns, the planning model runs thousands of possible economic scenarios to simulate many different future financial climates. After taking into account your personal variables like retirement age, savings rate, and investment return, it charts the probability that you will achieve your goals. It suggests possible mutual funds to help you improve your results and even sends quarterly updates with new recommendations and reminders to review your plan.

You can view a demo, and if you decide to proceed, the advice costs $39.95 a quarter or $149.95 a year, which includes multiple accounts. (For $300 a year, you receive more comprehensive portfolio advice.) You can experiment with your forecast and make changes to your portfolio or goals by adjusting portfolio risk, retirement age goal, ideal retirement income goal, or your annual contribution to a tax-deferred account. It's easy to run what-if scenarios with different assumptions to quickly see a new portfolio with recommended changes. It also shows the trade-offs between risk and reward.

CRITICAL THINKING QUESTIONS

1. What are the pros and cons of using an online financial adviser? List the major differences between these services and a traditional financial adviser.
2. Visit the Financial Engines (**http://www.financialengines.com**) site and Morningstar.com's ClearFuture (**http://www.morningstar.com/Cover/ClearFuture.html**). Compare the features and ease of use. Would you use an online advisor, and if so, which one?

SOURCES: Financial Engines Web site, http://www.financialengines.com, accessed June 15, 2003; Wayne Harris, "Plan on the Web," *Mutual Funds* (September 2000), pp. 60–63; Philip J. Longman, Kathy Yakal, "Investing in (Your) Futures," *Barron's Online*, March 24, 2003, downloaded from http://online.wsj.com/barrons.

HOT LINKS ADDRESS BOOK

For helpful information on budgeting and credit counseling, go to
http://www.collegedebt.net
and
http://www.studentcredit.com

For mortgage, personal loan, and bank interest rates visit the Web site at
http://www.banxquote.com

In too deep? For information on digging yourself out of debt, check out the Web site at
http://www.center4debtmanagement.com

How good is your credit? Check your credit score at
http://www.experian.com

Answers to your tax questions are available at the IRS Web site:
http://www.irs.gov

Compare quotes and analyze your insurance needs at
http://www.insurance.com

Need guidance on health care organizations? Visit
http://www.healthfinder.gov/organizations

To help you plan your investment goals, use the personal finance and investing calculators at
http://www.investorguide.com

your career

in Finance

If you have an interest in the dollars and cents of running a business, like to follow the daily ups and downs of the securities markets, or have a knack for numbers, the world of finance may be for you. Because businesses and individuals need many different financial services, you can choose from a wide variety of positions.

There are two basic career paths in finance. The first is managerial finance, which involves managing the finance function for manufacturing and service businesses that make or sell consumer and commercial products or provide nonfinancial services. The second is a career in the financial services industry, which creates and sells financial products and services. Banking, insurance, and securities are all financial service industries.

Until recently, the financial services area was the fastest growing area of finance. But the many changes in these industries—for example, mergers and financial difficulties—have slowed the growth of employment opportunities. Although fewer new jobs are now available in this sector, business graduates will still find many interesting and challenging positions.

As you've seen in the chapters in this part, information technology now plays a major role in finance. The ability to access databases, create spreadsheets, perform "what if" analyses, and run computer models are skills that will help you advance your career.

Dream Career: Financial Planner

Today's financial world is more complex than ever. Americans constantly face new investment opportunities, changes in tax laws, and revised employee benefit plans. The variety of savings plans, securities, mutual funds, insurance policies, real estate investments, and other options confuses and frustrates many people. They are concerned with preserving or increasing their financial assets, protecting their families, and planning for their retirement. In addition, many people do not have the time to do all the research needed to make wise savings and investment decisions.

Enter the financial planner. He or she asks clients specific questions about their financial needs. The planner then advises them about budgeting, securities, insurance, real estate, taxes, and retirement and estate planning and prepares a comprehensive financial plan to meet their goals. The financial planner is paid a straight fee or a fee plus commission on the dollar amount handled.

Financial planning is a growing field. More and more people seek professional advice on managing their personal financial assets. Financial planners should be good at dealing with people, communicating, and problem solving. The two main certification programs for financial planners are the Certified Financial Planner (CFP)® or the Chartered Financial Counselor (CFC) credential. Each requires approximately two years of study and several tests. The accounting and banking fields also have certification programs.

- **Places of Employment:** Large securities or insurance companies such as Merrill Lynch or Prudential in medium to large size cities throughout the United States; financial planners can also work independently in any area, although a population base of 50,000 or more is desirable.
- **Skills Required:** Four-year degree is generally required, although it is possible to enroll in the CFP® program without a bachelor's degree. Three years' professional experience in personal financial planning or a related field such as banking or accounting is required to enroll in the CFP® program. To establish an independent practice, a CPA (certified public accountant), CFP®, or CFC credential is helpful.
- **Employment Outlook through 2010:** Excellent
- **Salaries**: $25,000 for an entry-level position with a large firm; planners with experience and a good reputation can earn more than $145,000. The median salary for a financial planner is $66,000.

Where the Opportunities Are

Credit Manager

Over the years, buying on credit has become a common way of doing business. Consumers use credit to pay for houses, cars, appliances, and travel, as well as for everyday purchases. Most business purchases are also made on credit.

Credit managers set the firm's credit policies, decide whether to accept or reject credit applicants, and oversee the collection of accounts receivable. In extending credit, the credit manager or credit analyst evaluates and analyzes detailed financial reports submitted by the applicant and reviews credit agency reports to determine the applicant's history in repaying debts. Credit managers usually start as credit analysts and advance as they gain experience.

- **Places of Employment:** Throughout the country.
- **Skills Required:** Generally a four-year degree in accounting or finance, but sometimes a two-year degree is acceptable.
- **Employment Outlook through 2010:** Good.
- **Salaries:** $24,400–$37,500 for credit analysts; $49,900–$79,100 for credit managers.

Corporate Financial Manager

There are many positions of financial responsibility in corporations of all types—manufacturing, trade, service, and financial institutions. The highest positions are finance manager, controller, vice president of finance, and treasurer. Assistant managers and financial analysts work with finance managers.

Financial managers are concerned with raising and spending money for the firm's operations. They prepare financial plans to determine what funds will be required for payroll, raw material purchases, other operating expenses, loan payments, and so on. Financial managers work closely with the accounting department.

Most people starting out in financial management begin as financial analysts in the planning and budgeting area. Larger firms tend to have financial analysts who specialize in one area such as forecasting, short- or long-term borrowing, or capital budgeting. Smaller firms may assign the analyst several areas of responsibility.

Financial managers should have math aptitude, analytical ability, communications skills, computer skills, and the ability to work independently.

- **Places of Employment:** Throughout the United States.
- **Skills Required:** Four-year degree in business, with accounting or finance major preferred; many employers require an MBA for advancement.
- **Employment Outlook through 2010:** Above average.
- **Salaries:** $30,000 for entry-level financial analysts; $55,000–$102,000 for higher-level positions. The range for chief financial officers is $100,000 to $300,000, with an average of $143,600.

Stockbroker or Securities Account Executive

Stockbrokers and securities account executives handle orders for clients who wish to buy and sell securities. They also advise customers on financial matters, supplying the latest stock and bond quotations and analyst reports. Stockbrokers are usually hired by brokerage firms, investment banks, mutual funds, and insurance companies. Job opportunities for brokers are also emerging in other financial institutions such as banks.

In addition to knowledge of financial analysis and investments, successful account executives have good sales and interpersonal skills, self-confidence, and a high energy level. Most large brokerage firms offer a training program at the entry level that prepares the stockbroker to take a licensing examination.

- **Places of Employment:** Opportunities are available in all medium and large cities.
- **Skills Required:** Generally a four-year degree, but two-year degree may be acceptable at some smaller firms.
- **Employment Outlook through 2010:** Average.
- **Salaries:** $24,800 average for trainees, who are usually paid a salary until they develop a client base, after which they receive commissions: $15,000–$20,000 plus commissions for trainees; $50,000–$145,600+ for experienced brokers.

Securities Analyst

Securities analysts are experts who study stocks and bonds and make recommendations on what to buy or sell. They usually specialize in certain industries (such as energy, utilities, automotive, telecommunications, or high technology) and follow selected firms in those industries. They prepare reports on these industries and securities that take into account the competitive, economic, and political environments. They are employed by and act as advisers to securities brokerage firms, investment bankers, mutual funds, insurance companies, and other financial institutions. The Chartered Financial Analyst (CFA) designation is important to success in this field. It requires passing a series of tests.

- **Places of Employment:** Principally New York, although securities analysts work for institutions throughout the United States.

- **Skills Required:** Four-year degree; an M.B.A. is often required.
- **Employment Outlook through 2010:** Above average.
- **Salaries:** $35,400–$69,200 for junior analysts with an MBA; experienced analysts can earn $100,000+.

SOURCE OF SALARY INFORMATION: *CareerJournal*, downloaded from http://www.careerjournal.com, accessed June 30, 2003; and *Occupational Outlook Handbook 2002–2003*, Bureau of Labor Statistics, downloaded from http://www.bls.gov/oco/, accessed July 3, 2003.

glossary

A

absolute advantage The situation when a country can produce and sell a product at a lower cost than any other country or when it is the only country that can provide the product.

accounting The process of collecting, recording, classifying, summarizing, reporting, and analyzing financial activities.

accounts payable Purchase for which a buyer has not yet paid the seller.

accounts receivable Sales for which a firm has not yet been paid.

acid-test (quick) ratio The ratio of total current assets excluding inventory to total current liabilities; used to measure a firm's liquidity.

acquisition The purchase of a corporation by another corporation or by an investor group; the identity of the acquired company may be lost.

activity ratios Ratios that measure how well a firm uses its assets.

actual cash value The market value of personal property; the amount paid by standard homeowners and renters insurance policies.

administrative distribution system A vertical marketing system in which a strong organization takes over as leader and sets policies for the distribution channel.

advertising Any paid form of nonpersonal presentation by an identified sponsor.

advertising agencies Companies that help create ads and place them in the proper media.

advertising media The channels through which advertising is carried to prospective customers; includes newspapers, magazines, radio, television, outdoor advertising, direct mail, and the Internet.

advocacy advertising Advertising that takes a stand on a social or economic issue; also called grassroots lobbying.

affirmative action programs Programs established by organizations to expand job opportunities for women and minorities.

agency shop A company where employees are not required to join the union but must pay it a fee to cover its expenses in representing them.

agents Sales representatives of manufacturers and wholesalers.

American Federation of Labor (AFL) A national labor organization made up of numerous craft unions; founded in 1881 by splinter groups from the Knights of Labor. In 1955, the AFL merged with the Congress of Industrial Organizations (CIO) to form the AFL-CIO.

angel investors Individual investors or groups of experienced investors who provide funding for start-up businesses.

annual report A yearly document that describes a firm's financial status and usually discusses the firm's activities during the past year and its prospects for the future.

application service providers (ASPs) A service company that buys and maintains software on its servers and distributes it through high-speed networks to subscribers, for a set period and price.

apprenticeship A form of on-the-job training that combines specific job instruction with classroom instruction.

arbitration The process of settling a labor-management dispute by having a third party—a single arbitrator or a panel—make a decision, which is binding on both the union and the employer.

assembly process A production process in which the basic inputs are either combined to create the output or transformed into the output.

assets Things of value owned by a firm.

attitude Learned tendency to respond consistently toward a given object, idea, or concept.

audience selectivity An advertising medium's ability to reach a precisely defined market.

auditing The process of reviewing the records used to prepare financial statements and issuing a formal auditor's opinion indicating whether the statements have been prepared in accordance with accepted accounting rules.

authority Legitimate power, granted by the organization and acknowledged by employees, that allows an individual to request action and expect compliance.

autocratic leaders Directive leaders who prefer to make decisions and solve problems on their own with little input from subordinates.

automobile liability insurance Insurance that protects the insured from financial losses caused by automobile-related injuries to others and damage to their property.

automobile physical damage insurance Insurance that covers damage to or loss of the policyholder's vehicle from collision, theft, fire, or other perils; includes collision coverage and comprehensive (other-than-collision) coverage.

B

baby boomers Americans born between 1946 and 1964.

backward integration The acquisition of the production process by a wholesaler or retailer.

balance of payments A summary of a country's international financial transactions showing the difference between the country's total payments to and its total receipts from other countries.

balance of trade The difference between the value of a country's exports and the value of its imports during a certain time.

balance sheet A financial statement that summarizes a firm's financial position at a specific point in time.

bank charter An operating license issued to a bank by the federal government or a state government; required for a commercial bank to do business.

bargaining unit The employees who are eligible to vote in a union certification election and who will be represented by the union if it is certified.
barriers to entry Factors, such as technological or legal conditions, that prevent new firms from competing equally with a monopoly.
batch processing A method of updating a database in which data are collected over some time period and processed together.
bear markets Markets in which securities prices are falling.
belief An organized pattern of knowledge that an individual holds as true about the world.
benefit segmentation The differentiation of markets based on what a product will do rather than on customer characteristics.
bill of material A list of the items and the number of each required to make a given product.
board of directors A group of people elected by the stockholders to handle the overall management of a corporation, such as setting major corporate goals and policies, hiring corporate officers, and overseeing the firm's operations and finances.
bond ratings Letter grades assigned to bond issues to indicate their quality, or level of risk; assigned by rating agencies such as Moody's and Standard & Poor's.
bonds Long-term debt obligations (liabilities) issued by corporations and governments.
brainstorming A method of generating ideas in which group members suggest as many possibilities as they can without criticizing or evaluating any of the suggestions.
brand A company's product identifier that distinguishes the company's products from those of its competitors.
brand equity The value of company and brand names.
brand loyalty A consumer's preference for a particular brand.
breakeven point The price at which a product's costs are covered, so additional sales result in profit.
breaking bulk The process of breaking large shipments of similar products into smaller, more usable lots.
brokers Go-betweens that bring buyers and sellers together.
budgets Formal written forecasts of revenues and expenses that set spending limits based on operational forecasts; include cash budgets, capital budgets, and operating budgets.
bull markets Markets in which securities prices are rising.
bundling The strategy of grouping two or more related products together and pricing them as a single product.
business An organization that strives for a profit by providing goods and services desired by its customers.
business cycles Upward and downward changes in the level of economic activity.
business plan A formal written statement that describes in detail the idea for a new business and how it will be carried out; includes a general description of the company, the qualifications of the owner(s), a description of the product or service, an analysis of the market, and a financial plan.
buyer behavior The actions people take in buying and using goods and services.
buyer cooperative A group of cooperative members who unite for combined purchasing power.
buy-national regulations Government rules that give special privileges to domestic manufacturers and retailers.

C

C corporation Conventional or basic corporate form of organization.
CAD/CAM systems Linked computer systems that combine the advantages of computer-aided design and computer-aided manufacturing. The system helps design the product, control the flow of resources, and operate the production process.
capital The inputs, such as tools, machinery, equipment, and buildings, used to produce goods and services and get them to the customer.
capital budgeting The process of analyzing long-term projects and selecting those that offer the best returns while maximizing the firm's value.
capital budgets Budgets that forecast a firm's outlays for fixed assets (plant and equipment), typically covering a period of several years.
capital expenditures Investments in long-lived assets, such as land, buildings, machinery, and equipment, that are expected to provide benefits that extend beyond one year.
capital products Large, expensive items with a long life span that are purchased by businesses for use in making other products or providing a service.
capitalism An economic system based on competition in the marketplace and private ownership of the factors of production (resources); also known as the private enterprise system.
cash and carry wholesaler A limited-service merchant wholesaler that does not offer credit or delivery services.
cash budgets Budgets that forecast a firm's cash inflows and outflows and help the firm plan for cash surpluses and shortages.
cash flow plan A cash management tool that includes a plan for managing income and expenses, including contributions to savings and investments needed to accomplish one's financial goals; often called a *budget*.
cash flows The inflows and outflows of cash for a firm.
cash management The process of making sure that a firm has enough cash on hand to pay bills as they come due and to meet unexpected expenses.
cash value The dollar amount paid to the owner of a life insurance policy if the policy is canceled before the death of the insured.
category management Suppliers manage the inventory of a category of products for a retailer.
cellular manufacturing Production technique that uses small, self-contained production units, each performing all or most of the tasks necessary to complete a manufacturing order.
centralization The degree to which formal authority is concentrated in one area or level of an organization.

certified management accountant (CMA) A managerial accountant who has completed a professional certification program, including passing an examination.
certified public accountant (CPA) An accountant who has completed an approved bachelor's degree program, passed a test prepared by the American Institute of Certified Public Accountants, and met state requirements. Only a CPA can issue an auditor's opinion on a firm's financial statements.
chain of command The line of authority that extends from one level of an organization's hierarchy to the next, from top to bottom, and makes clear who reports to whom.
chief information officer (CIO) An executive with responsibility for managing all information resources in an organization.
circuit breakers Measures that, under certain conditions, stop trading in the securities markets for a short cooling-off period to limit the amount the market can drop in one day.
circular flow The movement of inputs and outputs among households, businesses, and governments; a way of showing how the sectors of the economy interact.
closed shop A company where only union members can be hired; made illegal by the Taft-Hartley Act.
COBRA A federal regulation that allows most employees and their families to continue group health insurance coverage at their own expense for up to 18 months after leaving an employer.
code of ethics A set of guidelines prepared by a firm to provide its employees with the knowledge of what the firm expects in terms of their responsibilities and behavior toward fellow employees, customers, and suppliers.
coercive power Power that is derived from an individual's ability to threaten negative outcomes.
cognitive dissonance The condition of having beliefs or knowledge that are internally inconsistent or that disagree with one's behavior.
coinsurance (participation) A percentage of covered expenses that the holder of a major medical insurance policy must pay.
collective bargaining The process of negotiating labor agreements that provide for compensation and working arrangements mutually acceptable to the union and to management.
comarketing Where two or more companies promote each others products or services.
command economy An economic system characterized by government ownership of virtually all resources and economic decision making by central-government planning; also known as communism.
commercial banks Profit-oriented financial institutions that accept deposits, make business and consumer loans, invest in government and corporate securities, and provide other financial services.
commercial paper Unsecured short-term debt—an IOU—issued by a financially strong corporation.
committee structure An organizational structure in which authority and responsibility are held by a group rather than an individual.
common stock A security that represents an ownership interest in a corporation.
comparative advertising Advertising that compares the company's product with competing, named products.
competitive advantage A set of unique features of a company and its products that are perceived by the target market as significant and superior to those of the competition; also called differential advantage.
component lifestyle A lifestyle made up of a complex set of interests and choices.
comprehensive (other-than-collision) coverage Automobile insurance that covers damage to or loss of the policyholder's vehicle due to perils such as fire, floods, theft, and vandalism; part of automobile physical damage insurance.
computer network A group of two or more computer systems linked together by communications channels to share data and information.
computer virus A computer program that copies itself into other software and can spread to other computer systems.
computer-aided design (CAD) The use of computers to design and test new products and modify existing ones.
computer-aided manufacturing (CAM) The use of computers to develop and control the production process.
computer-integrated manufacturing (CIM) The combination of computerized manufacturing processes (like robots and flexible manufacturing systems) with other computerized systems that control design, inventory, production, and purchasing.
conceptual skills A manager's ability to view the organization as a whole, understand how the various parts are interdependent, and assess how the organization relates to its external environment.
concession bargaining Unions giving contract gains back to management.
conciliation A method of attempting to settle labor disputes in which a specialist from the Federal Mediation and Conciliation Service helps management and the union focus on the issues and acts as a go-between.
conglomerate merger A merger of companies in unrelated businesses; done to reduce risk.
Congress of Industrial Organizations (CIO) A national labor organization made up of numerous industrial unions; founded in 1935. In 1955, the CIO merged with the American Federation of Labor (AFL) to form the AFL-CIO.
consensual leaders Leaders who encourage discussion about issues and then require that all parties involved agree to the final decision.
consultative leaders Leaders who confer with subordinates before making a decision, but who retain the final decision-making authority.
consumer price index (CPI) An index of the prices of a market basket of goods and services purchased by typical urban consumers.
contingency plans Plans that identify alternative courses of action for very unusual or crisis situations; typically stipulate the chain of command, standard operating procedures, and communication channels the organization will use during an emergency.

contingent workers Persons who prefer temporary employment, either part-time or full-time.
continuous improvement A commitment to constantly seek better ways of doing things in order to achieve greater efficiency and improve quality.
continuous process A production process that uses long production runs lasting days, weeks, or months without equipment shutdowns; generally used for high-volume, low-variety products with standardized parts.
contract manufacturing The practice in which a foreign firm manufactures private-label goods under a domestic firm's brand name.
contractionary policy The use of monetary policy by the Fed to tighten the money supply by selling government securities or raising interest rates.
contractual distribution system A vertical marketing system in which a network of independent firms at different levels (manufacturer, wholesaler, retailer) coordinate their distribution activities through a written contract.
controlling The process of assessing the organization's progress toward accomplishing its goals; includes monitoring the implementation of a plan and correcting deviations from the plan.
convenience products Relatively inexpensive items that require little shopping effort and are purchased routinely without planning.
convertible bonds Corporate bonds that are issued with an option that allows the bondholder to convert them into common stock.
cooperatives A legal entity typically formed by people with similar interests, such as suppliers or customers, to reduce costs and gain economic power. A cooperative has limited liability, an unlimited life span, an elected board of directors, and an administrative staff; all profits are distributed to the member-owners in proportion to their contributions.
corporate campaign A union strategy in which a union disrupts a corporation's relations with its shareholders or investors as a means of attacking the company.
corporate culture The set of attitudes, values, and standards that distinguishes one organization from another.
corporate distribution system A vertical marketing system in which one firm owns the entire distribution channel.
corporate open house Persons are invited to an open house on the premises of the corporation. Qualified applicants are encouraged to complete an application before leaving.
corporate philanthropy The practice of charitable giving by corporations; includes contributing cash, donating equipment and products, and supporting the volunteer efforts of company employees.
corporation A legal entity with an existence and life separate from its owners, who therefore are not personally liable for the entity's debts. A corporation is chartered by the state in which it is formed and can own property, enter into contracts, sue and be sued, and engage in business operations under the terms of its charter.
corrective advertising An advertisement run to correct false impressions left by previous ads.
cost competitive advantage A firm's ability to produce a product or service at a lower cost than all other competitors in an industry while maintaining satisfactory profit margins.
cost of goods sold The total expense of buying or producing a firm's goods or services.
cost per thousand (CPM) Cost per thousand contacts is a term used in expressing advertising costs; refers to the cost of reaching 1,000 members of the target market.
cost-of-living adjustment (COLA) A provision in a labor contract that calls for wages to increase automatically as the cost of living rises (usually measured by the consumer price index).
cost-push inflation Inflation that occurs when increases in production costs push up the prices of final goods and services.
costs Expenses incurred in creating and selling goods and services.
countertrade A form of international trade in which part or all of the payment for goods or services is in the form of other goods and services.
craft union A union that represents skilled workers in a single craft or occupation such as bricklaying, carpentry, or plumbing.
credit life insurance Insurance that will repay a loan if the borrower dies while the loan is still outstanding.
credit unions Not-for-profit, member-owned financial cooperatives.
critical path In a critical path method network, the longest path through the linked activities.
critical path method (CPM) A scheduling tool that enables a manager to determine the critical path of activities for a project—the activities that will cause the entire project to fall behind schedule if they are not completed on time.
cross-functional teams Teams of employees who are from about the same level in the organizational hierarchy but from different functional areas; for example, engineering, finance, and marketing.
crowding out The situation that occurs when government spending replaces spending by the private sector.
culture The set of values, ideas, attitudes, and other symbols created to shape human behavior.
current assets Assets that can or will be converted to cash within the next 12 months.
current liabilities Short-term claims that are due within a year of the date of the balance sheet.
current ratio The ratio of total current assets to total current liabilities; used to measure a firm's liquidity.
customer departmentalization Departmentalization that is based on the primary type of customer served by the organizational unit.
customer satisfaction The customer's feeling that a product has met or exceeded expectations.
customer value The ratio of benefits to the sacrifice necessary to obtain those benefits, as determined by the customer; reflects the willingness of customers to actually buy a product.
customization The production of goods or services one at a time according to the specific needs or wants of individual customers.

customs regulations Nonstandardized product rules and specifications created to block imports.
cyclical unemployment Unemployment that occurs when a downturn in the business cycle reduces the demand for labor throughout the economy.

D

data mart Special subset of a data warehouse that deals with a single area of data and is organized for quick analysis.
data mining Sophisticated database applications that look for hidden patterns in a group of data to help track and predict future behavior.
data warehouse An information technology that combines many databases across a whole company into one central database that supports management decision making.
database An electronic filing system that collects and organizes data and information.
dealer brands Brands that are owned by the wholesaler or retailer rather than the name of the manufacturer.
debentures Unsecured bonds that are backed only by the reputation of the issuer and its promise to pay the principal and interest when due.
debt A form of business financing consisting of borrowed funds that must be repaid with interest over a stated time period.
debt ratios Ratios that measure the degree and effect of a firm's use of borrowed funds (debt) to finance its operations.
debt-to-equity ratio The ratio of total liabilities to owners' equity; measures the relationship between the amount of debt financing following and the amount of equity financing (owner's funds).
decentralization The process of pushing decision-making authority down the organizational hierarchy.
decertification election An election in which workers vote, by secret ballot, on whether they want to continue to be represented by their union.
decision support system (DSS) A management support system that helps managers make decisions using interactive computer models that describe real-world processes.
decisional roles A manager's activities as an entrepreneur, resource allocator, conflict resolver, or negotiator.
delegation of authority The assignment of some degree of authority and responsibility to persons lower in the chain of command.
demand The quantity of a good or service that people are willing to buy at various prices.
demand curve A graph showing the quantity of a good or service that people are willing to buy at various prices.
demand deposits Money kept in checking accounts that can be withdrawn by depositors on demand.
demand-pull inflation Inflation that occurs when the demand for goods and services is greater than the supply.
democratic leaders Leaders who solicit input from all members of the group and then allow the members to make the final decision through a vote.
demographic segmentation The differentiation of markets through the use of categories such as age, education, gender, income, and household size.
demography The study of people's vital statistics, such as their age, race and ethnicity, and location.
demotion The downgrading or reassignment of an employee to a position with less responsibility.
departmentalization The process of grouping jobs together so that similar or associated tasks and activities can be coordinated.
depreciation The allocation of an asset's original cost to the years in which it is expected to produce revenues.
detailing The physical stocking of merchandise at a retailer by the salesperson who delivers the merchandise.
devaluation A lowering of the value of a nation's currency relative to other currencies.
differential competitive advantage A firm's ability to provide a unique product or service with a set of features that the target market perceives as important and better than the competitor's.
direct foreign investment Active ownership of a foreign company or of manufacturing or marketing facilities in a foreign country.
disability income insurance Insurance that will replace a portion of your earnings, typically 60 to 70 percent of your monthly income if you are unable to work due to illness or accident.
discount rate The interest rate that the Federal Reserve charges its member banks.
distribution centers Warehouses that specialize in changing shipment sizes, rather than in storing goods.
distribution channel The series of marketing entities through which goods and services pass on their way from producers to end users.
distribution strategy Creating the means by which products flow from the producer to the consumer.
diversification An investment strategy that involves investing in different asset classes, such as cash equivalents, stocks, bonds, and real estate, and combining securities with different patterns and amounts of return.
dividend reinvestment plan (DRIP) A program in which dividends paid by a stock are automatically reinvested in that stock along with any additional stock purchases submitted by the stockholder.
dividends Payments to stockholders from a corporation's profits.
division of labor The process of dividing work into separate jobs and assigning tasks to workers.
double-entry bookkeeping A method of accounting in which each transaction is recorded as two entries so that two accounts or records are changed.
Dow Jones Industrial Average (DJIA) The most widely used market average; measures the stock prices of 30 large, well-known corporations that trade on the New York Stock Exchange.
dumping The practice of charging a lower price for a product in foreign markets than in the firm's home market.

duration of benefits In disability income insurance, the length of time the insurance coverage payments will continue.

E

earned income Income that is earned from employment such as wages, tips, and self-employment income.
earnings per share (EPS) The ratio of net profit to the number of shares of common stock outstanding; measures the number of dollars earned by each share of stock.
economic growth An increase in a nation's output of goods and services.
economic system The combination of policies, laws, and choices made by a nation's government to establish the systems that determine what goods and services are produced and how they are allocated.
economics The study of how a society uses scarce resources to produce and distribute goods and services.
efficient consumer response (ECR) A method of managing inventory and streamlining the movement of products from supplier to distributor to retailer; relies on electronic data interchange to communicate information such as automatic shipping notifications, invoices, inventory data, and forecasts.
electronic data interchange (EDI) Computer-to-computer exchange of information, including automatic shipping notifications, invoices, inventory data, and forecasts; used in efficient consumer response systems.
electronic data interchange (EDI) The electronic exchange of information between two trading partners.
embargo A total ban on imports or exports of a product.
emergency fund Liquid assets that are available to meet emergencies.
employee orientation Training that prepares a new employee to perform on the job; includes information about job assignments, work rules, equipment, and performance expectations, as well as about company policies, salary and benefits, and parking.
empowerment The process of giving employees increased autonomy and discretion to make decisions, as well as control over the resources needed to implement those decisions.
enterprise portal A customizable internal Website that provides proprietary corporate information to a defined user group, such as employees, supply chain partners, or customers.
enterprise resource planning (ERP) A computerized resource-planning system that incorporates information about the firm's suppliers and customers with its internally generated data.
entrepreneurs People who combine the inputs of natural resources, labor, and capital to produce goods or services with the intention of making a profit or accomplishing a not-for-profit goal.
environmental scanning The process in which a firm continually collects and evaluates information about its external environment.
e-procurement The process of purchasing supplies and materials online using the Internet.
equilibrium The point at which quantity demanded equals quantity supplied.
equity A form of business financing consisting of funds raised through the sale of stock in a business.
equity theory A theory of motivation that holds that worker satisfaction is influenced by employees' perceptions about how fairly they are treated compared with their coworkers.
ethics A set of moral standards for judging whether something is right or wrong.
European Union Trade agreement among fifteen European nations.
exchange The process in which two parties give something of value to each other to satisfy their respective needs.
exchange controls Laws that require a company earning foreign exchange (foreign currency) from its exports to sell the foreign exchange to a control agency, such as a central bank.
exclusive distribution A distribution system in which a manufacturer selects only one or two dealers in an area to market its products.
executive information system (EIS) A management support system that is customized for an individual executive; provides specific information for strategic decisions.
expansionary policy The use of monetary policy by the Fed to increase the growth of the money supply.
expectancy theory A theory of motivation that holds that the probability of an individual acting in a particular way depends on the strength of that individual's belief that the act will have a particular outcome and on whether the individual values that outcome.
expense items Items, purchased by businesses, that are smaller and less expensive than capital products and usually have a life span of less than one year.
expenses The costs of generating revenues.
experiment A marketing research method in which the investigator changes one or more variables—price, packaging, design, shelf space, advertising theme, or advertising expenditures—while observing the effects of these changes on another variable (usually sales).
expert power Power that is derived from an individual's extensive knowledge in one or more areas.
expert system A management support system that gives managers advice similar to what they would get from a human consultant; it uses artificial intelligence to enable computers to reason and learn to solve problems in much the same way humans do.
exporting The practice of selling domestically produced goods to buyers in another country.
exports Goods and services sold outside a firm's domestic market.
express warranty A written guarantee about a product, such as that it contains certain materials, will perform a certain way, or is otherwise fit for the purpose for which it was sold.
extensive decision making Purchasing an unfamiliar, expensive, infrequently bought item.

F

factoring A form of short-term financing in which a firm sells its accounts receivable outright at a discount to a factor.

factors of production The resources used to create goods and services.

federal budget deficit The condition that occurs when the federal government spends more for programs than it collects in taxes.

Federal Deposit Insurance Corporation (FDIC) An independent, quasi-public corporation backed by the full faith and credit of the U.S. government that insures deposits in commercial banks and thrift institutions for up to a ceiling of $100,000 per account.

Federal Reserve System (Fed) The central bank of the United States; it consists of 12 district banks, each located in a major U.S. city.

Federal Trade Commission (FTC) An agency of the U.S. government that works to prevent deception and misrepresentation in advertising.

filing status The status of a taxpayer as single, married, or some other situation on the income tax return.

Financial Accounting Standards Board (FASB) The private organization that is responsible for establishing financial accounting standards in the United States.

financial accounting Accounting that focuses on preparing external financial reports that are used by outsiders such as lenders, suppliers, investors, and government agencies to assess the financial strength of a business.

financial intermediation The process in which financial institutions act as intermediaries between the suppliers and demanders of funds.

financial management The art and science of managing a firm's money so that it can meet its goals.

financial risk The chance that a firm will be unable to make scheduled interest and principal payments on its debt.

fiscal policy The government's use of taxation and spending to affect the economy.

fixed assets Long-term assets used by a firm for more than a year such as land, buildings, and machinery.

fixed costs Costs that do not vary with different levels of output; for example, rent.

fixed-cost contribution The selling price per unit (revenue) minus the variable costs per unit.

fixed-position layout A facility arrangement in which the product stays in one place and workers and machinery move to it as needed.

flexible manufacturing system (FMS) A system that combines automated workstations with computer-controlled transportation devices—automatic guided vehicles (AGVs)—that move materials between workstations and into and out of the system.

floating exchange rates A system in which prices of currencies move up and down based upon the demand for and supply of the various currencies.

focus group A group of 8 to 12 participants led by a moderator in an in-depth discussion on one particular topic or concept.

formal organization The order and design of relationships within a firm; consists of two or more people working together with a common objective and clarity of purpose.

forward integration The acquisition by a market intermediary of another marketing intermediary closer to the customer.

four Ps Product, price, promotion, and place (distribution), which together make up the marketing mix.

franchise agreement A contract setting out the terms of a franchising arrangement, including the rules for running the franchise, the services provided by the franchisor, and the financial terms. Under the contract, the franchisee is allowed to use the franchisor's business name, trademark, and logo.

franchisee In a franchising arrangement, the individual or company that sells the goods or services of the franchisor in a certain geographic area.

franchising A form of business organization based on a business arrangement between a franchisor, which supplies the product concept, and the franchisee, who sells the goods or services of the franchisor in a certain geographic area.

franchisor In a franchising arrangement, the company that supplies the product concept to the franchisee.

free trade The policy of permitting the people of a country to buy and sell where they please without restrictions.

free-rein (laissez-faire) leadership A leadership style in which the leader turns over all authority and control to subordinates.

free-trade zone An area where the nations allow free, or almost free, trade among each other while imposing tariffs on goods of nations outside the zone.

frequency The number of times an individual is exposed to an advertising message.

frictional unemployment Short-term unemployment that is not related to the business cycle.

fringe benefits Indirect compensation such as pensions, health insurance, and vacations.

full employment The condition when all people who want to work and can work have jobs.

full warranty The manufacturer's guarantee to meet certain minimum standards, including repair or replacement of the product or refunding the customer if the product does not work.

full-service merchant wholesalers Wholesalers that provide many services for their clients, such as providing credit, offering promotional and technical advice, storing and delivering merchandise, or providing installation and repairs.

functional departmentalization Departmentalization that is based on the primary functions performed within an organizational unit.

futures contracts Legally binding obligations to buy or sell specified quantities of commodities or financial instruments at an agreed-on price at a future date.

G

Gantt charts Bar graphs plotted on a time line that show the relationship between scheduled and actual production.

general partners Partners who have unlimited liability for all of the firm's business obligations and who control its operations.
general partnership A partnership in which all partners share in the management and profits. Each partner can act on behalf of the firm and has unlimited liability for all its business obligations.
generally accepted accounting principles (GAAP) The financial accounting standards followed by accountants in the United States when preparing financial statements.
Generation X Americans born between 1965 and 1978.
Generation Y Americans born after 1979.
generic products Products that carry no brand name, come in plain containers, and sell for much less than brand-name products.
geographic departmentalization Departmentalization that is based on the geographic segmentation of the organizational units.
geographic segmentation The differentiation of markets by region of the country, city or county size, market density, or climate.
global management skills A manager's ability to operate in diverse cultural environments.
global vision The ability to recognize and react to international business opportunities, be aware of threats from foreign competition, and effectively use international distribution networks to obtain raw materials and move finished products to customers.
goal-setting theory A theory of motivation based on the premise that an individual's intention to work toward a goal is a primary source of motivation.
goods Tangible items manufactured by businesses.
grace period The period after a purchase is made on a credit card during which interest is not owed if the entire balance is paid on time.
grievance A formal complaint, filed by an employee or by the union, charging that management has violated the contract.
gross domestic product (GDP) The total market value of all final goods and services produced within a nation's borders in a year.
gross profit The amount a company earns after paying to produce or buy its products but before deducting operating expenses.
gross sales The total dollar amount of a company's sales.
group cohesiveness The degree to which group members want to stay in the group and tend to resist outside influences.
guerilla marketing Proactive efforts to spread positive word-of-mouth information and to encourage product usage.

H

Hawthorne effect The phenomenon that employees perform better when they feel singled out for attention or feel that management is concerned about their welfare.
health maintenance organizations (HMOs) Managed care organizations that provide comprehensive health care services for a fixed periodic payment.
high-yield (junk) bonds High-risk, high-return bonds.
horizontal merger A merger of companies at the same stage in the same industry; done to reduce costs, expand product offerings, or reduce competition.
human relations skills A manager's interpersonal skills that are used to accomplish goals through the use of human resources.
human resource (HR) planning Creating a strategy for meeting future human resource needs.
human resource management The process of hiring, developing, motivating, and evaluating employees to achieve organizational goals.
hygiene factors Extrinsic elements of the work environment that do not serve as a source of employee satisfaction or motivation.

I

ideal self-image The way an individual would like to be.
implied warranty An unwritten guarantee that a product is fit for the purpose for which it is sold.
import quota A limit on the quantity of a certain good that can be imported.
imports Goods and services that are bought from other countries.
income statement A financial statement that summarizes a firm's revenues and expenses and shows its total profit or loss over a period of time.
indemnity (fee-for-service) plans Health insurance plans that reimburse the insured for medical costs covered by the insurance policy. The policyholder selects the health care providers.
industrial distributors Independent wholesalers that buy related product lines from many manufacturers and sell them to industrial users.
industrial union A union that represents all of the workers in a particular industry, such as auto workers or steel workers.
inflation The situation in which the average of all prices of goods and services is rising.
informal organization The network of connections and channels of communication based on the informal relationships of individuals inside an organization.
information technology (IT) The equipment and techniques used to manage and process information.
informational labeling A type of product label that provides product information to aid consumers in making product selections and minimize cognitive dissonance after the purchase.
informational roles A manager's activities as an information gatherer, an information disseminator, or a spokesperson for the company.
infrastructure The basic institutions and public facilities upon which an economy's development depends.
injunction A court order barring certain union activities.

insider trading The use of information that is not available to the general public to make profits on securities transactions.
institutional advertising Advertising that creates a positive picture of a company and its ideals, services, and roles in the community.
institutional investors Investment professionals who are paid to manage other people's money.
intangible assets Long-term assets with no physical existence, such as patents, copyrights, trademarks, and goodwill.
integrated marketing communications (IMC) The careful coordination of all promotional activities—media advertising, sales promotion, personal selling, and public relations, as well as direct marketing, packaging, and other forms of promotion—to produce a consistent, unified message that is customer focused.
intensive distribution A distribution system in which a manufacturer tries to sell its products wherever there are potential customers.
interest A fixed amount of money paid by the issuer of a bond to the bondholder on a regular schedule, typically every six months; stated as the *coupon rate.*
intermittent process A production process that uses short production runs to make batches of different products; generally used for low-volume, high-variety products.
International Monetary Fund (IMF) An international organization, founded in 1945, that promotes trade, makes short-term loans to member nations, and acts as a lender of last resort for troubled nations.
interpersonal roles A manager's activities as a figurehead, company leader, or liaison.
intranet An internal corporate-wide area network that uses Internet technology to connect computers and link employees in many locations and with different types of computers.
intrapreneurs Entrepreneurs who apply their creativity, vision, and risk taking within a large corporation, rather than starting a company of their own.
inventory The supply of goods that a firm holds for use in production or for sale to customers.
inventory management The determination of how much of each type of inventory a firm will keep on hand and the ordering, receiving, storing, and tracking of inventory.
inventory turnover ratio The ratio of cost of goods sold to average inventory; measures the speed with which inventory moves through a firm and is turned into sales.
investing The process of committing money to various instruments in order to obtain future financial returns.
investment bankers Firms that act as underwriters, buying securities from corporations and governments and reselling them to the public.
involvement The amount of time and effort a buyer invests in the search, evaluation, and decision processes of consumer behavior.
ISO 14000 A set of technical standards designed by the International Organization for Standardization to promote clean production processes to protect the environment.
ISO 9000 A set of five technical standards of quality management created by the International Organization for Standardization to provide a uniform way of determining whether manufacturing plants and service organizations conform to sound quality procedures.

J

job analysis A study of the tasks required to do a particular job well.
job description The tasks and responsibilities of a job.
job enlargement The horizontal expansion of a job by increasing the number and variety of tasks that a person performs.
job enrichment The vertical expansion of a job by increasing the employee's autonomy, responsibility, and decision-making authority.
job fair An event, typically one day, held at a convention center to bring together thousands of job seekers and hundreds of firms searching for employees.
job rotation Reassignment of workers to several different jobs over time so that they can learn the basics of each job.
job sharing A scheduling option that allows two individuals to split the tasks, responsibilities, and work hours of one 40-hour-per-week job.
job shop A manufacturing firm that produces goods in response to customer orders.
job specification A list of the skills, knowledge, and abilities a person must have to fill a job.
joint venture Two or more companies that form an alliance to pursue a specific project for a specified time period; also considered a strategy for entering the global marketplace when a dometic firm buys part of a foreign firm or joins with a foreign firm to create a new entity.
justice What is considered fair according to the prevailing standards of society; in the 20th century, an equitable distribution of the burdens and rewards that society has to offer.
just-in-time (JIT) A system in which materials arrive exactly when they are needed for production, rather than being stored on site.

K

Knights of Labor The first important national labor organization in the United States; founded in 1869.
knowledge The combined talents and skills of the workforce.
knowledge management (KM) The process of researching, gathering, organizing, and sharing an organization's collective knowledge to improve productivity, foster innovation, and gain competitive advantage.

knowledge worker A worker who develops or uses knowledge, contributing to and benefiting from information used in performing planning, acquiring, searching, analyzing, organizing, storing, programming, producing, distributing, marketing, or selling functions.

L

labor union An organization that represents workers in dealing with management over disputes involving wages, hours, and working conditions.
Landrum-Griffin Act A statute enacted in 1959 to regulate the internal affairs of unions; contains a bill of rights for union members, rules for electing union officers, and safeguards to keep unions financially sound.
layoff A temporary separation of an employee from the organization; arranged by the employer, usually because business is slow.
leader pricing The strategy of pricing products below the normal markup or even below cost to attract customers to a store where they would not otherwise shop.
leadership The process of guiding and motivating others toward the achievement of organizational goals.
leadership style The relatively consistent way that individuals in leadership positions attempt to influence the behavior of others.
lean manufacturing Streamlining production by eliminating steps in the production process that do not add benefits that customers are willing to pay for.
legitimate power Power that is derived from an individual's position in an organization.
leveraged buyout (LBO) A corporate takeover financed by large amounts of borrowed money; can be started by outside investors or by a company's own management.
liabilities What a firm owes to its creditors; also called debts.
licensing The legal process whereby a firm agrees to allow another firm to use a manufacturing process, trademark, patent, trade secret, or other proprietary knowledge in exchange for the payment of a royalty.
limited decision making Consumer has previous product experience but is unfamiliar with the current brands available.
limited liability company (LLC) A hybrid organization that offers the same liability protection as a corporation but may be taxed as either a partnership or a corporation.
limited partners Partners whose liability for the firm's business obligations is limited to amount of their investment. They help to finance the business, but do not participate in the firm's operations.
limited partnership A partnership with one or more general partners, who have unlimited liability, and one or more limited partners, whose liability is limited to the amount of their investment.
limited-service merchant wholesalers Wholesalers that typically carry a limited line of fast-moving merchandise and do not offer many services to their clients.
line extension A new flavor, size, or model using an existing brand name in an existing category.
line of credit An agreement between a bank and a business that specifies the maximum amount of unsecured short-term borrowing the bank will make available to the firm over a given period, typically one year; for credit cards, the maximum amount a person can have outstanding on a card at any one time.
line organization An organizational structure with direct, clear lines of authority and communication flowing from the top managers downward.
line positions All positions in the organization directly concerned with producing goods and services and that are directly connected from top to bottom.
line-and-staff organization An organizational structure that includes both line and staff positions.
liquid assets Cash and other assets that can be converted into cash both quickly and at little or no cost, such as checking accounts.
liquidity The speed with which an asset can be converted to cash.
liquidity ratios Ratios that measure a firm's ability to pay its short-term debts as they come due.
local area network (LAN) A network that connects computers at one site, enabling the computer users to exchange data and share the use of hardware and software from a variety of computer manufacturers.
local union A branch or unit of a national union that represents workers at a specific plant or in a specific geographic area.
lockout An employer tactic in a labor dispute in which the employer refuses to allow workers to enter a plant or building to work, which means that the workers do not get paid.
long-term forecasts Projections of a firm's activities and the funding for those activities over a period that is longer than 1 year, typically 2 to 10 years.
long-term liabilities Claims that come due more than one year after the date of the balance sheet.
loss leader A product priced below cost as part of a leader pricing strategy.
loyalty cards Cards issued by a manufacturer, service organization, or retailer that give discounts to loyal and frequent shoppers.

M

M1 The total amount of readily available money in the system, that includes currency and demand deposits.
M2 A term used by economists to describe the U.S. monetary supply. Includes all M1 monies plus time deposits and other money that are not immediately accessible.
macroeconomics The subarea of economics that focuses on the economy as a whole by looking at aggregate data for large groups of people, companies, or products.
major medical insurance Health insurance that covers a wide range of medical costs with few exclusions and high maximum limits. The insured pays a deductible and a coinsurance portion.

make-or-buy decision The determination by a firm of whether to make its own production materials or buy them from outside sources.

Malcolm Baldrige National Quality Award An award given to recognize U.S. companies that offer goods and services of world-class quality; established by Congress in 1987 and named for a former secretary of commerce.

managed care plans Health insurance plans that generally pay only for services provided by doctors and hospitals that are part of the plan.

management The process of guiding the development, maintenance, and allocation of resources to attain organizational goals.

management information system (MIS) The methods and equipment that provide information about all aspects of a firm's operations.

management support system (MSS) An information system that uses the internal master database to perform high-level analyses that help managers make better decisions.

managerial accounting Accounting that provides financial information that managers inside the organization can use to evaluate and make decisions about current and future operations.

managerial hierarchy The levels of management within an organization; typically, includes top, middle, and supervisory management.

managing diversity Fully utilizing the potential of all employees in a work environment.

manufacturer A producer; an organization that converts raw materials to finished products.

manufacturer brands Brands that are owned by national or regional manufacturers and widely distributed; also called national brands.

manufacturers' representatives Salespeople who represent noncompeting manufacturers; function as independent agents rather than as salaried employees of the manufacturers.

manufacturing resource planning II (MRPII) A complex computerized system that integrates data from many departments to allow managers to better forecast and assess the impact of production plans on profitability.

market averages Summarize the price behavior of securities based on the arithmetic average price of groups of securities at a given point in time; used to monitor general market conditions.

market indexes Measures of the current price behavior of groups of securities relative to a base value set at an earlier point in time; used to monitor general market conditions.

market segmentation The process of separating, identifying, and evaluating the layers of a market in order to identify a target market.

market structure The number of suppliers in a market.

marketable securities Short-term investments that are easily converted into cash.

marketing The process of discovering the needs and wants of potential buyers and customers and then providing goods and services that meet or exceed their expectations.

marketing concept Identifying consumer needs and then producing the goods or services that will satisfy them while making a profit for the organization.

marketing database Computerized file of customers' and potential customers' profiles and purchase patterns.

marketing intermediaries Organizations that assist in moving goods and services from producers to end users.

marketing mix The blend of product offering, pricing, promotional methods, and distribution system that brings a specific group of consumers superior value.

marketing research The process of planning, collecting, and analyzing data relevant to a marketing decision.

markup pricing A method of pricing in which a certain percentage (the markup) is added to the product's cost to arrive at the price.

Maslow's hierarchy of needs A theory of motivation developed by Abraham Maslow; holds that humans have five levels of needs and act to satisfy their unmet needs. At the base of the hierarchy are fundamental physiological needs, followed in order by safety, social, esteem, and self-actualization needs.

mass customization A manufacturing process in which goods are mass-produced up to a point and then custom tailored to the needs or desires of individual customers.

mass production The ability to manufacture many identical goods at once.

master brand A brand so dominant that consumers think of it immediately when a product category, use, attribute, or customer benefit is mentioned.

materials requirement planning (MRP) A computerized system of controlling the flow of resources and inventory. A master schedule is used to ensure that the materials, labor, and equipment needed for production are at the right places in the right amounts at the right times.

matrix structure (project management) An organizational structure that combines functional and product departmentalization by bringing together people from different functional areas of the organization to work on a special project.

mechanistic organization An organizational structure that is characterized by a relatively high degree of job specialization, rigid departmentalization, many layers of management, narrow spans of control, centralized decision making, and a long chain of command.

mediation A method of attempting to settle labor disputes in which a specialist from the Federal Mediation and Conciliation Service serves as a mediator.

mentoring A form of on-the-job training in which a senior manager or other experienced employee provides job- and career-related information to a protégé.

merchant wholesaler An institution that buys goods from manufacturers (takes ownership) and resells them to businesses, government agencies, other wholesalers, or retailers.

Mercosur Trade agreement between Peru, Brazil, Argentina, Uruguay, and Paraguay.

merger The combination of two or more firms to form a new company, which often takes on a new corporate identity.

microeconomics The subarea of economics that focuses on individual parts of the economy such as households or firms.

middle management Managers who design and carry out tactical plans in specific areas of the company.

mission An organization's purpose and reason for existing; its long-term goals.

mission statement A formal document that states an organization's purpose and reason for existing and describes its basic philosophy.

mixed economies Economies that combine several economic systems; for example, an economy where the government owns certain industries but others are owned by the private sector.

monetary policy A government's programs for controlling the amount of money circulating in the economy and interest rates.

money Anything that is acceptable as payment for goods and services.

monopolistic competition A market structure in which many firms offer products that are close substitutes and in which entry is relatively easy.

mortgage bonds Corporate bonds that are secured by property, such as land, equipment, or buildings.

mortgage loan A long-term loan made against real estate as collateral.

motivating factors Intrinsic job elements that lead to worker satisfaction.

multinational corporations Corporations that move resources, goods, services, and skills across national boundaries without regard to the country in which their headquarters are located.

municipal bonds Bonds issued by states, cities, counties, and other state and local government agencies.

mutual fund A financial-service company that pools investors' funds to buy a selection of securities that meet its stated investment goals.

mutual-aid pact An agreement by companies in an industry to create a fund that can be used to help cover fixed costs of any member company whose workers go on strike.

N

National Advertising Division (NAD) A subdivision of the Council of Better Business Bureaus that investigates complaints about advertising from consumers and other advertisers.

National Advertising Review Board (NARB) A board that hears appeals from the decisions of the National Advertising Division (NAD) of the Council of Better Business Bureaus or resolves issues if the NAD is deadlocked.

National Association of Securities Dealers Automated Quotation (NASDAQ) system The first electronic-based stock market and the fastest-growing part of the stock market.

national debt The accumulated total of all of the federal government's annual budget deficits.

National Labor Relations Board (NLRB) An agency established by the Wagner Act of 1935 to enforce the act and investigate charges of employer and union wrongdoing and supervise elections for union representatives.

national union A union that consists of many local unions in a particular industry, skilled trade, or geographic area and thus represents workers throughout an entire country.

nationalism A sense of national consciousness that boosts the culture and interests of one country over those of all other countries.

net asset value (NAV) The price at which each share of a mutual fund can be bought or sold.

net loss The amount obtained by subtracting all of a firm's expenses from its revenues, when the expenses are more than the revenues.

net profit (net income) The amount obtained by subtracting all of a firm's expenses from its revenues, when the revenues are more than the expenses.

net profit margin The ratio of net profit to net sales; also called *return on sales*. It measures the percentage of each sales dollar remaining after all expenses, including taxes, have been deducted.

net sales The amount left after deducting sales discounts and returns and allowances from gross sales.

net working capital The amount obtained by subtracting total current liabilities from total current assets; used to measure a firm's liquidity.

net worth An individual's wealth at a given point in time, calculated as total assets minus total liabilities.

niche competitive advantage A firm's ability to target and effectively serve a single segment of the market within a limited geographic area.

nonprogrammed decisions Responses to infrequent, unforeseen, or very unusual problems and opportunities where the manager does not have a precedent to follow in decision making.

Norris-La Guardia Act A statute enacted in 1932 that barred the use of injunctions to prevent strikes and other union activities and made yellow-dog contracts unenforceable; also called the Anti-Injunction Act.

North American Free Trade Agreement (NAFTA) A 1993 agreement creating a free-trade zone including Canada, Mexico, and the United States.

not-for-profit organization An organization that exists to achieve some goal other than the usual business goal of profit.

O

observation research A marketing research method in which the investigator monitors respondents' actions without interacting directly with the respondents; for example, by using cash registers with scanners.

odd-even (psychological) pricing The strategy of setting a price at an odd number to connote a bargain and at an even number to suggest quality.

office automation system An information system that uses information technology tools such as word processing systems, e-mail systems, cell phones, PDAs, pagers, and fax machines to improve communications throughout an organization.
oligopoly A market structure in which a few firms produce most or all of the output and in which large capital requirements or other factors limit the number of firms.
one-to-one marketing Creating a unique marketing mix for every customer.
on-line (real-time) processing A method of updating a database in which data are processed as they become available.
on-the-job training Training in which the employee learns the job by doing it with guidance from a supervisor or experienced coworker.
open market operations The purchase or sale of U.S. government bonds by the Federal Reserve to stimulate or slow down the economy.
open shop A company where employees do not have to join the union or pay dues or fees to the union; established under right-to-work laws.
open-end credit Any type of credit where the borrower applies for the credit and then, if approved, is allowed to use it over and over again; for example, credit cards.
operating budgets Budgets that combine sales forecasts with estimates of production costs and operating expenses in order to forecast profits.
operating expenses The expenses of running a business that are not directly related to producing or buying its products.
operational planning The process of creating specific standards, methods, policies, and procedures that are used in specific functional areas of the organization; helps guide and control the implementation of tactical plans.
operations management Management of the production process.
opinion leaders Those who influence others.
options Contracts that entitle holders to buy or sell specified quantities of common stocks or other financial instruments at a set price during a specified time.
organic organization An organizational structure that is characterized by a relatively low degree of job specialization, loose departmentalization, few levels of management, wide spans of control, decentralized decision making, and a short chain of command.
organization chart A visual representation of the structured relationships among tasks and the people given the authority to do those tasks.
organized stock exchanges Organizations on whose premises securities are resold using an auction-style trading system.
organizing The process of coordinating and allocating a firm's resources in order to carry out its plans.
outsourcing The assignment of various functions, such as human resources, accounting, or legal work, to outside organizations; the purchase of items from an outside source rather than making them internally.
over-the-counter (OTC) market A sophisticated telecommunications network that links dealers throughout the United States and enables them to trade securities.
owners' equity The total amount of investment in the firm minus any liabilities; also called net worth.

P

participative leadership A leadership style in which the leader shares decision making with group members and encourages discussion of issues and alternatives; includes democratic, consensual, and consultative styles.
partnership An association of two or more individuals who agree to operate a business together for profit.
penetration pricing The strategy of selling new products at low prices in the hope of achieving a large sales volume.
pension funds Large pools of money set aside by corporations, unions, and governments for later use in paying retirement benefits to their employees or members.
perception The process by which we select, organize, and interpret stimuli into a meaningful and coherent picture.
perfect (pure) competition A market structure in which a large number of small firms sell similar products, buyers and sellers have good information, and businesses can be easily opened or closed.
performance appraisal A comparison of actual performance with expected performance to assess an employee's contributions to the organization.
perpetual inventory A continuously updated list of inventory levels, orders, sales, and receipts.
personal balance sheet A summary of a person's financial situation on a given day; provides information about assets and liabilities.
personal exemptions Deductions that reduce the amount of income on which income tax is paid. Each taxpayer is entitled to a personal exemption, for himself, his spouse, and each of their dependents; a personal exemption can be used only once.
personal financial planning The process of managing one's personal finances to achieve financial goals.
personal selling A face-to-face sales presentation to a prospective customer.
personality A way of organizing and grouping how an individual reacts to situations.
persuasive labeling A type of product label that reinforces or repeats a promotional theme or logo.
physical distribution (logistics) Efficiently managing the acquisition of raw materials to the factory and the movement of products from the producer to industrial users and consumers.
picketing Union members parade in front of the employer's plant carrying signs and trying to persuade nonstriking workers to stop working and customers and suppliers from doing business with the company.

planning The process of deciding what needs to be done to achieve organizational objectives; identifying when and how it will be done; and determining by whom it should be done.

portfolio A collection of investments.

power The ability to influence others to behave in a particular way.

preferential tariff A tariff that is lower for some nations than for others.

preferred provider organizations (PPOs) Networks of health care providers who enter into a contract to provide services at discounted prices; combine a major medical insurance plan with a network of health care providers.

preferred stock An equity security for which the dividend amount is set at the time the stock is issued.

prepayment penalties Additional fees that may be owed if a loan is repaid early.

prestige pricing The strategy of increasing the price of a product so that consumers will perceive it as being of higher quality, status, or value.

price skimming The strategy of introducing a product with a high initial price and lowering the price over time as the product moves through its life cycle.

price/earnings (P/E) ratio The current market price of a stock divided by its annual earnings per share.

pricing strategy Setting a price based upon the demand and cost for a good or service.

primary data Information collected directly from the original source to solve a problem.

primary market The securities market where *new* securities are sold to the public.

principal The amount borrowed by the issuer of a bond; also called *par value*.

principle of comparative advantage The concept that each country should specialize in the products that it can produce most readily and cheaply and trade those products for those that other countries can produce more readily and cheaply.

private accountants Accountants who are employed to serve one particular organization.

problem-solving teams Teams of employees from the same department or area of expertise and from the same level of the organizational hierarchy who meet regularly to share information and discuss ways to improve processes and procedures in specific functional areas.

process departmentalization Departmentalization that is based on the production process used by the organizational unit.

process layout A facility arrangement in which work flows according to the production process. All workers performing similar tasks are grouped together, and products pass from one workstation to another.

producer price index (PPI) An index of the prices paid by producers and wholesalers for various commodities such as raw materials, partially finished goods, and finished products.

product In marketing, any good or service, along with its perceived attributes and benefits, that creates value for the customer.

product (assembly-line) layout A facility arrangement in which workstations or departments are arranged in a line with products moving along the line.

product advertising Advertising that features a specific good or service.

product departmentalization Departmentalization that is based on the goods or services produced or sold by the organizational unit.

product life cycle The pattern of sales and profits over time for a product or product category; consists of an introductory stage, growth stage, maturity, and decline (and death).

product manager The person who develops and implements a complete strategy and marketing program for a specific product or brand.

product strategy Taking the good or service and selecting a brand name, packaging, colors, a warranty, accessories, and a service program.

production The creation of products and services by turning inputs, such as natural resources, raw materials, human resources, and capital, into outputs, which are products and services.

production orientation An approach in which a firm works to lower production costs without a strong de-sire to satisfy the needs of customers.

production planning The aspect of operations management in which the firm considers the competitive environment and its own strategic goals in an effort to find the best production methods.

production process The way a good is made.

productivity The amount of goods and services one worker can produce.

profit The money left over after all expenses are paid.

profit maximization A pricing objective that entails getting the largest possible profit from a product by producing the product as long as the revenue from selling it exceeds the cost of producing it.

profitability ratios Ratios that measure how well a firm is using its resources to generate profit and how efficiently it is being managed.

program evaluation and review technique (PERT) A scheduling tool that is similar to the CPM method but assigns three time estimates for each activity (optimistic, most probable, and pessimistic); allows managers to anticipate delays and potential problems and schedule accordingly.

programmed decisions Decisions made in response to frequently occurring routine situations.

programmed instruction A form of computer-assisted off-the-job training.

progressive tax An income tax that is structured so that the higher a person's taxable income, the higher the percentage of income paid in taxes.

promotion An upward move in an organization to a position with more authority, responsibility, and pay; the attempt by marketers to inform, persuade, or remind consumers and industrial users to engage in the exchange process.

promotion strategy The unique combination of personal selling, advertising, publicity, and sales promotion to stimulate the target market to buy a product or service.

promotional mix The combination of advertising, personal selling, sales promotion, and public relations used to promote a product.
prospecting The process of looking for sales prospects.
protected classes The specific groups who have legal protection against employment discrimination; include women, African Americans, Native Americans, and others.
protectionism The policy of protecting home industries from outside competition by establishing artificial barriers such as tariffs and quotas.
protective tariffs Tariffs that are imposed in order to make imports less attractive to buyers than domestic products are.
psychographic segmentation The differentiation of markets by personality or lifestyle.
public accountants Independent accountants who serve organizations and individuals on a fee basis.
public relations Any communication or activity designed to win goodwill or prestige for a company or person.
publicity Information about a company or product that appears in the news media and is not directly paid for by the company.
pull strategy A promotional strategy in which a manufacturer focuses on stimulating consumer demand for its product, rather than on trying to persuade wholesalers or retailers to carry the product.
purchasing The process of buying production inputs from various sources; also called procurement.
purchasing power The value of what money can buy.
pure monopoly A market structure in which a single firm accounts for all industry sales and in which there are barriers to entry.
push strategy A promotional strategy in which a manufacturer uses aggressive personal selling and trade advertising to convince a wholesaler or retailer to carry and sell its merchandise.

Q

qualifying questions Inquiries used by salespeople to separate prospects from those who do not have the potential to buy.
quality Goods and services that meet customer expectations by providing reliable performance.
quality control The process of creating standards for quality, producing goods that meet them, and measuring finished products and services against them.
quality of life The general level of human happiness based on such things as life expectancy, educational standards, health, sanitation, and leisure time.

R

ratio analysis The calculation and interpretation of financial ratios using data taken from the firm's financial statements in order to assess its condition and performance.
reach The number of different target consumers who are exposed to a commercial at least once during a specific period, usually four weeks.
real self-image How an individual actually perceives him- or herself.
recession A decline in GDP that lasts for at least two consecutive quarters.
recruitment The attempt to find and attract qualified applicants in the external labor market.
reengineering The complete redesign of business structures and processes in order to improve operations.
reference groups Formal and informal groups that influence buyer behavior.
referent power Power that is derived from an individual's personal charisma and the respect and/or admiration the individual inspires.
Regulation FD An SEC regulation that requires public companies to share information with all investors at the same time, leveling the information playing field.
relationship management The practice of building, maintaining, and enhancing interactions with customers and other parties in order to develop long-term satisfaction through mutually beneficial partnerships.
relationship marketing A strategy that focuses on forging long-term partnerships with customers by offering value and providing customer satisfaction.
reminder advertising Advertising that is used to keep a product's name in the public's mind.
replacement cost coverage Homeowners and renters insurance that pays enough to replace lost and damaged personal property.
reserve requirement Requires banks that are members of the Federal Reserve System to hold some of their deposits in cash in their vaults or in an account at a district bank.
resignation A permanent separation of an employee from the organization, done voluntarily by the employee.
retailers Firms that sell goods to consumers and to industrial users for their own consumption.
retained earnings The amounts left over from profitable operations since the firm's beginning; equal to total profits minus all dividends paid to stockholders.
retirement The separation of an employee from the organization at the end of his or her career.
return on equity (ROE) The ratio of net profit to total owners' equity; measures the return that owners receive on their investment in the firm.
return The opportunity for profit.
revenue The money a company earns from providing services or selling goods to customers.
revenues The dollar amount of a firm's sales plus any other income it received from sources such as interest, dividends, and rents.
revolving credit agreement A line of credit under which a bank guarantees that a certain amount of money will be available for a business to borrow over a given period.
revolving credit cards Credit cards that do not require full payment upon billing.
reward power Power that is derived from an individual's control over rewards.

right-to-work laws State laws that allow employees to work at a unionized company without having to join the union.
risk The potential for loss or the chance that an investment will not achieve the expected level of return.
risk management The process of identifying and evaluating risks and selecting and managing techniques to adapt to risk exposures.
risk-return trade-off A basic principle in finance that holds that the higher the risk, the greater the return that is required.
robotics The technology involved in designing, constructing, and operating computer-controlled machines that can perform tasks independently.
routine response behavior Purchase of low-cost, frequently bought items with little search or decision making.
routing The aspect of production control that involves setting out the work flow—the sequence of machines and operations through which the product or service progresses from start to finish.

S

S corporation A hybrid entity that is organized like a corporation, with stockholders, directors, and officers, but taxed like a partnership, with income and losses flowing through to the stockholders and taxed as their personal income.
sales promotions Marketing events or sales efforts—not including advertising, personal selling, and public relations—that stimulate buying.
sales prospects The companies and people who are most likely to buy a seller's offerings.
Sarbanes-Oxley Act Act passed in 2002 that sets new standards for auditor independence, financial disclosure and reporting, and internal controls; establishes an independent oversight board; and restricts the types of nonaudit services auditors can provide audit clients.
savings bonds Government bonds of relatively small denominations.
scanner-based research System for gathering information from a single group of respondents by continuously monitoring the advertising, promotion, and pricing they are exposed to and the things that they buy.
scheduling The aspect of production control that involves specifying and controlling the time required for each step in the production process.
scientific management A system of management developed by Frederick W. Taylor and based on four principles: developing a scientific approach for each element of a job, scientifically selecting and training workers, encouraging cooperation between workers and managers, and dividing work and responsibility between management and workers according to who can better perform a particular task.
seasonal unemployment Unemployment that occurs during specific seasons in certain industries.
secondary data Information that has already been collected for a project other than the current one, but that may be used to solve the current problem.
secondary market The securities market where *old* (already issued) securities are bought and sold, or traded, among investors.
secured bonds Corporate bonds for which specific assets have been pledged as collateral.
secured loans Loans for which the borrower is required to pledge specific assets as collateral, or security.
Securities and Exchange Commission (SEC) The main federal government agency responsible for regulating the U.S. securities industry.
securities Investment certificates issued by corporations or governments that represent either equity or debt.
security requirements Provisions that allow a lender to take back the collateral if a loan is not repaid according to the terms of the agreement.
selection The process of determining which persons in the applicant pool possess the qualifications necessary to be successful on the job.
selection interview An in-depth discussion of an applicant's work experience, skills and abilities, education, and career interests.
selective credit controls The power of the Federal Reserve to control consumer credit rules and margin requirements.
selective distribution A distribution system in which a manufacturer selects a limited number of dealers in an area (but more than one or two) to market its products.
selective exposure The process of deciding which stimuli to notice and which to ignore.
selective strike strategy A union strategy of conducting a strike at (shutting down) a critical plant that supplies parts to other plants.
self-concept How people perceive themselves.
self-managed work teams Highly autonomous teams of employees who manage themselves without any formal supervision and take responsibility for setting goals, planning and scheduling work activities, selecting team members, and evaluating team performance.
seller cooperative Individual producers who join together to compete more effectively with large producers.
separation The departure of an employee from the organization; can be a layoff, termination, resignation, or retirement.
services Intangible offerings of businesses that can't be held, touched, or stored.
shop steward An elected union official who represents union members to management when workers have complaints.
shopping products Items that are bought after considerable planning, including brand-to-brand and store-to-store comparisons of price, suitability, and style.
short-term forecasts Projections of revenues, costs of goods, and operating expenses over a one-year period.
sick-out A union strategy in which a group of employees claim they cannot work because of illness, thereby disrupting the company.

Six Sigma A quality control process that relies on defining what needs to be done to ensure quality, measuring and analyzing production results statistically, and finding ways to improve and control quality.
Small Business Administration (SBA) A government agency that helps people start and manage small businesses, helps small business owners win federal contracts, and speaks on behalf of small business.
Small Business Investment Company (SBIC) Privately owned and managed investment companies that are licensed by the Small Business Administration and provide long-term financing for small businesses.
small business A business that is independently owned, is owned by an individual or a small group of investors, is based locally, and is not a dominant company in its industry.
social investing The practice of limiting investments to securities of companies that behave in accordance with the investor's beliefs about ethical and social responsibility.
social marketing The application of marketing techniques to social issues and causes.
social responsibility The concern of businesses for the welfare of society as a whole; consists of obligations beyond those required by law or contracts.
socialism An economic system in which the basic industries are owned either by the government itself or by the private sector under strong government control.
socialization process The passing down of cultural norms and values to children.
sole proprietorship A business that is established, owned, operated, and often financed by one person.
span of control The number of employees a manager directly supervises; also called span of management.
specialization The degree to which tasks are subdivided into smaller jobs.
specialty products Items for which consumers search long and hard and for which they refuse to accept substitutes.
staff positions Positions in an organization held by individuals who provide the administrative and support services that line employees need to achieve the firm's goals.
stakeholders Individuals or groups to whom a business has a responsibility; include employees, customers, the general public, and investors.
Standard & Poor's 500 stock index An important market index that includes 400 industrial stocks, 20 transportation stocks, 40 public utility stocks, and 40 financial stocks; includes NYSE, AMEX, and NASDAQ stock.
standard deduction An amount that most taxpayers can automatically deduct from their gross income in computing their income tax; not permitted if the taxpayer elects to itemize deductions.
standard of living A country's output of goods and services that people can buy with the money they have.
statement of cash flows A financial statement that provides a summary of the money flowing into and out of a firm during a certain period, typically one year.
stock dividends Payments to stockholders in the form of more stock; may replace or supplement cash dividends.
stockbroker A person who is licensed to buy and sell securities on behalf of clients.
stockholders or shareholders The owners of a corporation who hold shares of stock that provide certain rights.
strategic alliance A cooperative agreement between business firms; sometimes called a strategic partnership.
strategic giving The practice of tying philanthropy closely to the corporate mission or goals and targeting donations to regions where a company operates.
strategic planning The process of creating long-range (one to five years), broad goals for the organization and determining what resources will be needed to accomplish those goals.
strike replacements Nonunion employees hired to replace striking union members; also known as scabs.
structural unemployment Unemployment that is caused by a mismatch between available jobs and the skills of available workers in an industry or region; not related to the business cycle.
supervisory management Managers who design and carry out operation plans for the ongoing daily activities of the firm.
supply The quantity of a good or service that businesses will make available at various prices.
supply chain The entire sequence of securing inputs, producing goods, and delivering goods to customers.
supply chain management The process of smoothing transitions along the supply chain so that the firm can satisfy its customers with quality products and services; focuses on developing tighter bonds with suppliers.
supply curve A graph showing the quantity of a good or service that a business will make available at various prices.
survey research A marketing research method in which data is gathered from respondents, either in person, by telephone, by mail, at a mall, or through the Internet to obtain facts, opinions, and attitudes.

T

tactical planning The process of beginning to implement a strategic plan by addressing issues of coordination and allocating resources to different parts of the organization; has a shorter time frame (less than one year) and more specific objectives than strategic planning.
Taft-Hartley Act A statute enacted in 1947 that defined unfair union practices, outlined the rules for dealing with strikes of major economic impact, broadened employer options for dealing with unions, and further defined the rights of employees as individuals.
target market The specific group of consumers toward which a firm directs its marketing efforts.
target return on investment A pricing objective where the price of a product is set so as to give the company the desired profitability in terms of return on its money.
tariff A tax imposed on imported goods.

technical skills A manager's specialized areas of knowledge and expertise, as well as the ability to apply that knowledge.
technology The application of science and engineering skills and knowledge to solve production and organizational problems.
telecommuting An arrangement in which employees work at home and are linked to the office by phone, fax, and computer.
term life insurance Life insurance that covers the insured's life for a fixed amount and a specific period and has no cash value; provides the maximum amount of life insurance coverage for the lowest premium.
term loan A business loan with an initial maturity of more than one year; can be unsecured or secured.
termination A permanent separation of an employee from the organization, arranged by the employer.
test-marketing The process of testing a new product among potential users.
The process of managing one's personal finances to achieve financial goals.
Theory X A management style, formulated by Douglas McGregor, that is based on a pessimistic view of human nature and assumes that the average person dislikes work, will avoid it if possible, prefers to be directed, avoids responsibility, and wants security above all.
Theory Y A management style, formulated by Douglas McGregor, that is based on a relatively optimistic view of human nature; assumes that the average person wants to work, accepts responsibility, is willing to help solve problems, and can be self-directed and self-controlled.
Theory Z A theory developed by William Ouchi that combines U.S. and Japanese business practices by emphasizing long-term employment, slow career development, moderate specialization, group decision making, individual responsibility, relatively informal control over the employee, and concern for workers.
thrift institutions Depository institutions formed specifically to encourage household saving and to make home mortgage loans.
time deposits Deposits at a bank or other financial institution that pay interest but cannot be withdrawn on demand.
top management The highest level of managers; includes CEOs, presidents, and vice presidents, who develop strategic plans and address long-range issues.
total cost The sum of the fixed costs and the variable costs.
total profit Total revenue minus total cost.
total quality management (TQM) The use of quality principles in all aspects of a company's production and operations.
total revenue The selling price per unit times the number of units sold.
trade credit The extension of credit by the seller to the buyer between the time the buyer receives the goods or services and when it pays for them.
trade deficit An unfavorable balance of trade that occurs when a country imports more than it exports.
trade surplus A favorable balance of trade that occurs when a country exports more than it imports.
trademark The legally exclusive design, name, or other identifying mark associated with a company's brand.
training and development Activities that provide learning situations in which an employee acquires additional knowledge or skills to increase job performance.
transaction processing system (TPS) An information system that handles the daily business operations of a firm. The system receives and organizes raw data from internal and external sources for storage in a database using either batch or online processing.
transfer A horizontal move in an organization to a position with about the same salary and at about the same organizational level.

U

underwriting The process of buying securities from corporations and governments and reselling them to the public; the main activity of investment bankers.
unearned income Income that is not earned through employment such as interest, dividends, and other investment income.
unemployment rate The percentage of the total labor force that is actively looking for work but is not actually working.
union certification election An election in which workers vote, by secret ballot, on whether they want to be represented by a union; conducted by the National Labor Relations Board.
union shop A company where nonunion workers can be hired but must then join the union.
universal life insurance A combination of term life insurance and a tax-deferred savings plan. Part of the premium is invested in securities, so the cash value earns interest at current market rates.
unsecured loans Loans for which the borrower does not have to pledge specific assets as security.
unsought products Products that either are unknown to the potential buyer or are known but the buyer does not actively seek them.
Uruguay Round A 1994 agreement by 117 nations to lower trade barriers worldwide.
utilitarianism A philosophy that focuses on the consequences of an action to determine whether it is right or wrong; holds that an action that affects the majority adversely is morally wrong.

V

value pricing A pricing strategy in which the target market is offered a high-quality product at a fair price and with good service.

value-stream mapping Routing technique that uses simple icons to visually represent the flow of materials and information from suppliers through the factory and to customers.
variable costs Costs that change with different levels of output; for example, wages and cost of raw materials.
venture capital Financing obtained from investment firms that specialize in financing small, high-growth companies and receive an ownership interest and a voice in management in return for their money.
vertical marketing system An organized, formal distribution channel in which firms are aligned in a hierarchy such as from manufacturer to wholesaler to retailer.
vertical merger A merger of companies at different stages in the same industry; done to gain control over supplies of resources or to gain access to different markets.
vestibule training A form of off-the-job training in which trainees learn in a scaled-down version or simulated work environment.
virtual corporation A network of independent companies linked by information technology to share skills, costs, and access to one another's markets; allows the companies to come together quickly to exploit rapidly changing opportunities.
virtual private networks (VPNs) Private corporate networks connected over a public network, such as the Internet. VPNs include strong security measures to allow only authorized users to access the network.
volume segmentation The differentiation of markets based on the amount of the product purchased.

W

Wagner Act A statute enacted in 1935 that established that employees have a right to organize and join labor unions and to engage in collective bargaining; also known as the National Labor Relations Act.
waiting period (elimination period) In disability income insurance, the period between the onset of the disability and the time when insurance payments begin.
warranty A guarantee of the quality of a good or service.
whole life (straight life, cash value, continuous pay) insurance Life insurance that covers the insured's entire life, as long as the premiums are paid; has a cash value that increases over the life of the policy.
wholesalers Firms that sell finished goods to retailers, manufacturers, and institutions.
wide area network (WAN) A network that connects computers at different sites via telecommunications media such as phone lines, satellites, and microwaves.
wildcat strike A strike by a group of union members or an entire local union without the approval of the national union while the contract is still in effect.
withholding allowances Amounts that are withheld from each paycheck vary according to the number of allowances claimed and other criteria.
work groups Groups of employees who share resources and coordinate efforts so as to help members better perform their individual duties and responsibilities. The performance of the group can be evaluated by adding up the contributions of the individual group members.
work teams Groups of employees who not only coordinate their efforts, but also collaborate by pooling their knowledge, skills, abilities, and resources in a collective effort to attain a common goal; causing the performance of the team to be greater than the sum of the members' individual efforts.
World Bank An international bank that offers low-interest loans, as well as advice and information, to developing nations.
World Trade Organization (WTO) An organization established by the Uruguay Round in 1994 to oversee international trade, reduce trade barriers, and resolve disputes among member nations.

Y

yellow-dog contracts Contracts in which employees agreed not to join a labor union as a condition of being hired.
yield management systems (YMS) Mathematical software that helps companies adjust prices to maximize revenue

endnotes

Prologue

1. Marlene Caroselli, *Interpersonal Skills* (South-Western, a division of Thomson Learning, 2003), 1. The section entitled "Getting Ahead in Business and Life" is also adapted from the above text.
2. The section on planning is adapted from: *Investing in Your Future* (South-Western, a division of Thomson Learning, 2001), pp. 1–10.
3. The material on "going to college" is adapted from Abby Marks-Beale, *Success Skills: Strategies for Study and Lifelong Learning* (South-Western, a division of Thomson Learning, 2002).
4. Julie Griffin Levitt, *Your Career: How to Make It Happen,* 5th edition (South-Western, a division of Thomson Learning, 2003), pp. 2–4.
5. "Understand What Employers Want" is from: Levitt, p. 36.
6. "Get Your Career in Site," *Fast Company* (March 2000), pp. 218–230.
7. Barbara Ling, Creator of the RISE Internet Recruiting Seminars. http://www.riseway.com
8. "Web Largely Untapped by Job Seekers," CBS MarketWatch.com (January 24, 2003).
9. "Get Your Career in Site."
10. Levitt, p. 100.
11. Levitt, pp. 189–205.
12. Levitt, p. 205.

Chapter 1

1. Emily Nelson, "Marketers Push Individual Portions and Families Bite," *Wall Street Journal* (July 23, 2002), pp. A1, A6. © 2002 by Dow Jones & Co. Inc. Reproduced with permission of Dow Jones & Co. Inc., in the format Textbook via Copyright Clearance Center.
2. *Worldwide Quality of Life Survey* (London: Mercer Consulting Group) March 11, 2002.
3. Michael J. Ybarra, "Miami: Connecting Latin America's Entrepreneurs," *Upside* (March 2001), pp. 144–154.
4. Lester Thurow, "Changing the Nature of Capitalism," in *Rethinking the Future,* ed. Rowan Gibson (London: Nicholas Brealey, 1997), p. 228.
5. "Fast-Food Chains Vie to Carve Out Empire in Pricey Sandwiches," *Wall Street Journal* (February 5, 2002), pp. A1, A10.
6. "High Style In a Tiny Package," *Wall Street Journal* (October 17, 2001), pp. B1, B4.
7. "Work Experience Rises Again," *Bureau of Labor Statistics* (November 22, 2000).
8. "SEPs for Female Owned Business," *New York Life* (2003).
9. http://www.mediapost.com, "Research Briefs," (July 16, 2002).
10. "The Roxy Echo-It's A Girl Thing," *The Star Ledger* Newark, New Jersey (September 9, 2001), p. 5.
11. Christy Harvey, "A Guide to Who Holds the Purse Strings," *Wall Street Journal* (June 22, 2000), p. A14.
12. Linda Morten, "Targeting Generation Y," *Public Relations Quarterly* (Summer 2002), pp. 46–49.
13. "Keeper of the Flame," *Advertising Age* (September 23, 2002), p. 18.
14. "The Gen-X Budget," *American Demographics* (July/August 2002), S5.
15. "The Younger Boomer Budget," *American Demographics* (July/August 2002), S6.
16. Ibid.
17. Ibid.
18. "The Older Boomer Budget," *American Demographics* (July/August 2000), S7.
19. Ibid.
20. "The Senior Budget," *American Demographics* (July/August 2002), S10.
21. "Diversity In America," *American Demographics* (November 2002), pp. S1–S15.
22. Ibid.
23. *UNCTAD Commerce and Development Report*, 2002.
24. David Lynch, "CEO Pushes China's Haier As Global Brand," *USA Today* (January 3, 2003), pp. 6A-7A. © January 3, 2003. Reprinted with permission.
25. This section is adapted from: Bruce Nussbaum, "9.11.02," *Business Week* (September 16, 2002), pp. 21–28.
26. "Too Many Workers? Not for Long," *Business Week* (May 20, 2002), pp. 126–130.
27. "Getting A Sense of Purpose Along With Their Paychecks," *Adweek Western Edition* (April 15, 2002), p. 62.
28. Ibid.
29. Elliot Spagat, "Like, What's a Spin Cycle?" *Wall Street Journal* (June 4, 2002), pp. B1, B4. © 2002 by Dow Jones & Co. Inc. Reproduced with permission of Dow Jones & Co. Inc., in the format Textbook via Copyright Clearance Center.

Chapter 2

1. Walter Mossberg, "An $8,000 Conversation Piece," *Wall Street Journal* (October 23, 2002), pp. D1, D12. © 2002 by Dow Jones & Co. Inc. Reproduced with permission of Dow Jones & Co. Inc., in the format Textbook via Copyright Clearance Center.
2. "The World's Factory," *Wall Street Journal* (October 10, 2002), pp. A1, A8; and "High Tech in China," *Business Week* (October 28, 2002), pp. 80-91.
3. Noah Rothbaum, "Leg Work," *Smart Money* (September 2002), pp. 128–129.
4. Olga Chudakova, "Executive Commentary," *Academy of Management Executive* (November 2001).
5. Don Clark, "In Setting Up Its New Plants, Chip Maker Clones Older Ones Down to the Paint on the Wall," *Wall Street Journal* (October 28, 2002), pp. B1, B4. © 2002 by Dow Jones & Co. Inc. Reproduced with permission of Dow Jones & Co. Inc., in the format Textbook via Copyright Clearance Center.

Chapter 3

1. Nicholas Varchaver, "The Big Kozlowski," *Fortune* (November 18, 2002), pp. 123–126. © 2002 Time Inc. All rights reserved.
2. Marianne Moody Jennings, *Case Studies in Business Ethics*, 2nd ed. (St. Paul: West Publishing Company, 1996), pp. xx-xxiii.
3. "Four Businesses Honored with Prestigious International Award for Outstanding Marketplace Ethics," *PR Newswire* (September 23, 2002).
4. "More Employees Are Cheating," *Leadership for the Front Lines* (March 15, 2003), p. 6.
5. J. N. Bradley, "Attitudes on Ethics in Small Business: Employer versus Employee," *Journal of Small Business Strategy* (Fall 2002); and Tim Fulton, "Four Ways to Prevent Yourself from 'Enroning' Your Small Business," http://www.workplacespirituality.info.
6. "NBC Refuses to Booze It Up," *E! Online News* (March 21, 2002).
7. Betsy McKay, "Drinks for Developing Countries," *Wall Street Journal* (November 27, 2001), pp. B1, B6. © 2001 by Dow Jones & Co. Inc. Reproduced with permission of Dow Jones & Co. Inc., in the format Textbook via Copyright Clearance Center.
8. http://www.capitalresearchcenter.org (August 2002).

9. http://home3.Americanexpress.com/corp/philanthropy (November 20, 2002).
10. http://www.Aetna.com/foundation/main
11. http://www.Adobe.com/aboutadobe/pressroom
12. http://www.business-ethics.com
13. http://www.business-ethics.com
14. *JP Morgan Chase Corporate Responsibility Annual Report* (2002), p. 2.
15. "Twenty-Four Towns Ponder Life As 'Got Milk?' California," *Associated Press Newswires* (November 1, 2002). Reprinted with permission of the Associated Press.

Chapter 4

1. Steven Erlanger, "Ach! The Viennese Lap Up Starbucks," *International Herald Tribune* (June 3, 2002), pp. 1, 4.
2. Gillette Annual Report, 2002.
3. "Armchairs, TVs and Expresso—Is It McDonald's?" *Wall Street Journal* (August 30, 2002), pp. A1, A6. © 2002 by Dow Jones & Co. Inc. Reproduced with permission of Dow Jones & Co. Inc., in the format Textbook via Copyright Clearance Center.
4. Charles Lamb, Joe Hair, and Carl McDaniel, *Essentials of Marketing* (South-Western, a division of Thomson Learning, 2003), p. 95.
5. What's At Stake," *Business Week* (October 22, 2001), pp. 34–37.
6. http://www.ita.doc.gov
7. http://www.tradealert.org
8. http://www.research.stlouisfed.org
9. "Anti-Trade/Pro-Poverty," *Fortune* (January 10, 2000), p. 40.
10. "Anti-Trade/Pro-Poverty," 4D.
11. "The Pros and Cons of Globalization," *Business Week* (April 24, 2000), p. 41.
12. "Globalization: What Americans Are Worried About," *Business Week* (April 24, 2000), p. 44.
13. "Toy Story," *Fortune* (June 26, 2000), p. 270.
14. "So Far, Steel Tariffs Do Little of What President Envisioned," *Wall Street Journal* (September 13, 2002), pp. A1, A12.
15. "Clinton Signs Africa-Caribbean Trade Benefits into Law," Dow Jones Newswire (May 18, 2000).
16. "Preserving and Expanding Our Important NAFTA Trading Relationships in Light of September 11," *Business Credit* (September 2003), pp. 53–60.
17. "NAFTA's Scorecard: So Far So Good," *Business Week* (July 9, 2001), pp. 54–56.
18. "European Union Gets Ready to Grow," *Wall Street Journal* (October 10, 2002), p. A12.
19. "Increasingly, Rules of Global Economy Are Set in Brussels," *Wall Street Journal* (April 23, 2002).
20. http://www.business.gov (international trade) January 31, 2003.
21. Cait Murphy, "The Hunt for Globalization That Works," *Fortune* (October 28, 2002), pp. 163–176. © 2002 Time Inc. All Rights Reserved.
22. McDonald's Annual Report, 2002.
23. "How the Chevy Name Landed on a SUV Using Russian Technology," *Wall Street Journal*, February 20, 2001, pp. A1, A8.
24. "How Well Does Wal-Mart Travel?" *Business Week* (September 3, 2001), pp. 82–84.
25. "War of the Superstores," *Business Week* (September 23, 2002), p. 60.
26. "Wal-Mart's European Beachhead," *International Herald Tribune* (March 13, 2001).
27. Dalia Marin, "The Economic Institution of International Barter," *Economic Journal* (April 2002), pp. 293–316.
28. Joel Millman, "Mexican Chain Thrives Selling U.S. Surplus," *Wall Street Journal* (May 10, 2002), pp. B1, B4. © 2002 by Dow Jones & Co. Inc. Reproduced with permission of Dow Jones & Co. Inc., in the format Textbook via Copyright Clearance Center.
29. "Does Globalization Have Staying Power? *Marketing Management* (March/April 2002), pp. 18–22.
30. "Payment System Lets Customers Choose Currency," *Information Week* (April 2, 2001), p. 33.
31. Hal Lancaster, "Global Managers Need Boundless Sensitivity, Rugged Constitutions," *Wall Street Journal* (October 13, 1998), p. B1.
32. "To Keep Up the Growth It Must Go Global Quickly," *Business Week* (September 9, 2002), pp. 101–105.
33. T. R. Reid, "Buying American? It's Hard to Know," *International Herald Tribune* (May 21, 2002), p. 2.

Chapter 5

1. 180s Web site, http://www.180s.com; Donna Fenn, "The B-School Boys," *Inc.*, September 2002, p. 78; and Ann S. Kim, "Earmuffs? Ear Warmers? A Rose Is a Rose . . . ,"*San Diego Union Tribune*, January 19, 2003, p. E8.
2. Anne Stuart, "Where Do Great Ideas Come From?" *Inc.*, October 2002, pp. 43, 45.
3. Personal interview with Linda Ravden, January 3, 2003.
4. Mike Hofman, "The Bad Boy," *Inc.*, September 2002, pp. 78–80.
5. "Fast-Growth Entrepreneurs Seek Niche Markets, E-Commerce Opportunities Closer to Home," *Business Wire*, August 2001, downloaded from http://www.ask.elibrary.com; and George Mannes, "Don't Give Up on the Web," *Fortune Small Business*, March 2001, downloaded from http://www.ask.elibrary.com.
6. Ace Hardware Web site, http://www.AceHardware.com.
7. Jeff Bailey, "Co-ops Gain as Companies Seek Competitive Power," *Wall Street Journal*, October 2002.
8. Penni Crabtree, *San Diego Union-Tribune*, December 2002, "Neurocrine, Pfizer join in $400 million alliance" downloaded from http://www.SignOnSanDiego.com.
9. Tahl Raz, "Berries Jubilee," *Inc.*, September 2002, pp. 34–35.
10. Geoff Williams, "Keep Thinking," *Entrepreneur Magazine*, September 2002.
11. Stephen D. Solomon, Julie Sloane, "The Brain Trust," *Fortune Small Business*, December 2002, downloaded from http://www.ask.elibrary.com.
12. Cynthia E. Griffin, "Ladies in Waiting," *Entrepreneur Magazine*, November 2002, downloaded from http://www.Entrepreneur.com.
13. *Franchise Zone*, December 2002, downloaded from http://www.Entrepreneur.com.
14. *Franchise Zone*, December 2002, downloaded from http://www.Entrepreneur.com.
15. "Letter to Shareholders," *ConocoPhillips 2002 Annual Report*, published March 2003, downloaded from corporate Web site, http://www.conocophillips.com, accessed July 15, 2003.
16. David Henry, "Mergers—Why Most Big Deals Don't Pay Off," *Business Week*, October 2002.
17. Nick Wingfield, "Roxio Agrees to Acquire Napster Assets," *Wall Street Journal*, November 18, 2002.
18. Rob Wherry, "Pedal Pushers," *Forbes Magazine*, October 2002, pp. 204–205.
19. Tom Lowry, Amy Barrett in Philadelphia, Ronald Grover in Los Angeles, "A New Cable Giant," downloaded from *Business Week Online*, November 2002.
20. Devlin Smith, "You Bought What on eBay?", *Entrepreneur Magazine*, January 2003, downloaded from http://www.entrepreneur.com.
21. Amanda C. Kooser, "Testing the Waters," *Entrepreneur Magazine*, January 2003, downloaded from http://www.entrepreneur.com.
22. Amanda C. Kooser, "Explore Your Auctions," *Entrepreneur Magazine*, January 2003, downloaded from http://www.entrepreneur.com.
23. Cynthia E. Griffin, "Ladies in Waiting," *Entrepreneur Magazine*, November 2002, downloaded from http://www.entrepreneur.com.
24. Devlin Smith, "One Big Happy Family," January 2003, downloaded from http://www.entrepreneur.com.

25. Geoff Williams, "Keep Thinking," *Entrepreneur Magazine,* September 2002.
26. Devlin Smith, "Have You Heard the Latest," *Entrepreneur Magazine,* January 2003, downloaded from http://www.entrepreneur.com.
27. David Henry, "Mergers—Why Most Big Deals Don't Pay Off," *BusinessWeek,* October 2002.
28. Robert Frank, "Merger Market Gets Year-End Jump Start," *Wall Street Journal,* January 2, 2003, p. R6
29. Kenneth Klee, "Mergers and Accusations," *Inc.,* October 2002, pp. 48–49.
30. Caliber Collision Centers Web site, http://www.calibercollision.com; and Justin Martin, David Birch, "Slump? What Slump?" *Fortune Small Business,* December 2002/January 2003, downloaded from http://www.ask.elibrary.com; Robert McGarvey, "When It Comes to Customer Service Actions Speak Louder Than Words," *Entrepreneur Magazine,* January 1997, downloaded from http://www.entrepreneur.com.
31. 180s Web site, http://www.180s.com, and Donna Fenn, "The B-School Boys," *Inc.,* September 2002, p. 78.
32. Jane Applegate, "Novelty Pillow Catches Manufacturer's Eye," February 2002, downloaded from http://www.entrepreneur.com; Carolyn Morton, e-mail correspondence, January 17 and 24, 2003; and Peeramid Web site, http://www.peeramid.com.

Chapter 6

1. Ben Elgin and Jim Kerstetter, "Why They're Agog over Google," *Business Week,* September 24, 2001, pp. 83, 88; "Google Corporate Information," *Google.com,*" downloaded December 16, 2002, http://www.google.com; Sarah J. Heim, "Vroom Vroom," *Brandweek,* November 27, 2000, downloaded from http://www.findarticles.com; Jennifer Lee, "Postcards from Planet Google," *The New York Times,* November 28, 2002, downloaded from http://www.nytimes.com; Steven Levy, "The World According to Google," *Newsweek,* December 16, 2002, pp. 46–51.
2. "Small Business by the Numbers," Advocacy Office of the Small Business Administration, downloaded November 7, 2002, from http://www.sba.gov/advo/stats/sbfaq.html.
3. "The 411 on OGIO," OGIO International Web site, http://www.ogio.com; and Anne Stuart, "Where Do Great Ideas Come From?" *Inc. 500,* October 15, 2002, pp. 40, 42, 43.
4. John Case, "Trading Places," *Inc.,* November, 2002, p.76.
5. Paul D. Reynolds , Nancy M. Carter, William B. Gartner, Patricia G. Greene, and Larry W. Cox. *The Entrepreneur Next Door: Characteristics of Individuals Starting Companies in America.* (Kansas City, MO: E. M. Kauffman Foundation, 2002).
6. April Y. Pennington, "Entrepreneurial Snapshot: Katrina Markoff," *Entrepreneur,* November 2002, downloaded from http://www.entrepreneur.com.
7. David Shook, "Jeff Bezos: Finally Relaxing?" *Business Week Online,* October 1, 2002, downloaded from http://www.businessweek.com.
8. "Company Bios," Proflowers.com, downloaded from http://www.proflowers.com.
9. Dean Takahashi, "Reinventing the Intrapreneur," *Red Herring,* September 2000, downloaded from http://www.red_herring.com
10. Michael Arndt, "Whirlpool Taps Its Inner Entrepreneur," *Business Week Online,* February 7, 2002, downloaded from http://www.businessweek.com.
11. "Got ID?" *Entrepreneur,* November 2002, downloaded from http://www.entrepreneur.com.
12. "Are You Building an Inc. 500 Company?" *Inc. 500,* October 15, 2002, downloaded from http://www.inc.com/inc500.
13. "Are You Building an *Inc.* 500 Company?" *Inc. 500.*
14. Lucile Reid and Terry Lonier, *Bigstep–Working Solo Portrait of Small Business USA,* November 2001, downloaded from http://www.bigstep.com/company/img/SB_Portrait_Study.pdf.
15. "Employer Firms, and Employment by Employment Size of Firm by NAICS Codes, 1999," Office of Advocacy, U.S. Small Business Administration, based on data provided by the U.S. Census Bureau, Statistics of U.S. Businesses, downloaded from http://www.sba.gov/advo/stats/us99_n6.pdf; and Reid and Lonier, *Bigstep—Working Solo Portrait of Small Business USA.*
16. Justin Martin; David Birch, "Slump? What Slump?" *Fortune Small Business,* December 2002/January 2003, downloaded from Electric Library, http://ask.elibrary.com.
17. Leigh Buchanan, "A Little Down. Far from Out," *Inc. 500,* October 15, 2002, downloaded from http://www.inc.com; and Martin and Birch, "Slump? What Slump?"
18. April Y. Pennington, "Entrepreneurial Snapshot: Steve Richardson, Stave Puzzles," *Entrepreneur,* September 2002, downloaded from http://www.entrepreneur.com; Stave Puzzles Web site, http://www.stave.com; and "Unwrapper's Delight," *Fortune,* December 9, 2002, p. 236.
19. "D&B 21st Annual Small Business Survey Summary Report," Dun & Bradstreet, downloaded from http://www.dnb.com.
20. Joel Skolnick, "My Business: A Demanding Mistress," *Businessweek Online,* November 19, 2002, downloaded from http://www.businessweek.com.
21. Much of the statistical information for the SBA section is from the Small Business Administration Web site, http://www.sba.gov.
22. "History of the SBA," Small Business Adminstration, updated December 23, 2002, downloaded from http://www.sba.gov/aboutsba/.
23. "Historical SBIC Program Financing to Small Businesses-March Year End," Small Business Administration, downloaded December 26, 2002, from http://www.sba.gov/INV/stat/2002.html.
24. Stephen Barlas, "Muscle-Bound," *Entrepreneur,* November 2002, downloaded from http://www.entrepreneur.com.
25. "Announcing the Launch of Groove-EVERYWHERE by GrooveJob.com," October 7, 2002 and "Groovejob.com Launches New Job Board Site Targeted for Teens and College Students," GrooveJob.com, December 3, 2001, downloaded from http://www.GrooveJob.com; and Kathy Showalter, "Executive Search Firm Finds New Biz Niche," Columbus Business First, downloaded from columbus.bizjournals.com.
26. Ellen Roseman, "The Vision Thing Helps When Starting a Business," *Toronto Star,* May 5, 2002, downloaded from Electric Library, http://ask.elibrary.com.
27. "Are You Building an Inc. 500 Company?" *Inc. 500.*
28. "Small Business by the Numbers."
29. David Noonan, "Be Your Own Master," *Newsweek,* September 23, 2002, p. 61.
30. Kimberly McCall, "Then There Were Two: Should You Hire a Staff?" *Startup Journal.com,* November 4, 2002, downloaded from http://www.inc.com.
31. Cara Cannella, "Keeping It Flexible," *Inc. 500,* October 15, 2002, p. 76.
32. Online Success: More Than a Dream," *Costco Connection,* December 2001, p. 22.
33. Jeff Bailey, "Growing Up," *Wall Street Journal,* March 27, 2002, p. R6; Case, "Trading Places," pp. 74–82; Brenda L. Moore, "Changing Classes," *Wall Street Journal,* March 27, 2002, p. R8; and Noonan, "Be Your Own Master,".
34. Martin and Birch, "Slump? What Slump?"
35. Reynolds et al., *The Entrepreneur Next Door.*

36. Roger Franklin, "The Surge in Female Entrepreneurs," *Business Week Online*, May 15, 2003, downloaded from http://www.businessweek.com.
37. Gisela M. Pedroza, "Survival of the Fittest," *HomeOffice*, November 2002, downloaded from http://www.entrepreneur.com.
38. "Minority Share of U.S. Business Ownership Nears 15 Percent," Office of Advocacy, U.S. Small Business Administration, press release (February 4, 2002), downloaded from http://www.sba.gov/advo.
39. Thomas Brady, " Small Contractor Keeps Moving Up," *Philadelphia Enquirer*, October 19, 2002, pp. C1, C2.
40. "2001 Entrepreneurial Spirit Awards: Color Coordinated," *Hispanic Business*, December 4, 2001.
41. Stephen D. Solomon and Julie Sloane, "The Brain Trust," *Fortune Small Business*, December 1, 2002, downloaded from Electric Library, ask.elibrary.com
42. "D&B 21st Annual Small Business Survey Summary Report"; and "Internet Important Tool for Most Small Businesses, Study Finds," Small Business Administration, press release, October 10, 2002, downloaded from http://www.sba.gov.
43. Noonan, "Be Your Own Master."
44. Geoff Williams, "Looks Like Rain," *Entrepreneur*, September 2002, downloaded from http://www.entrepreneur.com.
45. "Got ID?"
46. Kate O'Sullivan, "Six Ways to Outrun the Competition," *Inc. 500*, October 15, 2002, pp. 56–58.
47. "Google Corporate Information," *Google.com*, downloaded December 16, 2002 from http://www.google.com; Jennifer Lee, "Postcards from Planet Google," *The New York Times*, November 28, 2002, downloaded from http://www.nytimes.com; Steven Levy, "The World According to Google," *Newsweek*, December 16, 2002, pp. 46–51; Mary Anne Ostrom, "Google Adds Froogle, a Shopping Search Site," *San Jose Mercury News*, December 12, 2002, downloaded from http://www.siliconvalley.com.
48. Eleni's NYC Web site, http://www.elenis.com; and "Got ID?" *Entrepreneur*, November 2002, downloaded from http://www.entrepreneur.com.

Chapter 7

1. Rebecca Buckman, "Soft Spot at Microsoft: Power Still Revolves Around Gates and Ballmer," *Wall Street Journal* (April 8, 2002), pp. A-1, A-8.
2. "Now for the Hard Part," *Fortune* (November 18, 2002), pp. 95–106.
3. Katrina Brooker and Julie Schlosser, "The un-CEO," *Fortune* (September 16, 2002), pp. 88–94.
4. "Jim Kilts Is Old-School Curmudgeon," *Fortune* (December 30, 2002), pp. 95–102.
5. Denise Bedell, "Con Ed Sticks to the Straight and Narrow," *Corporate Finance* (April 2002), pp. 24–27.
6. Jeffrey Garten, "Jack Welch: A Role Model for Today's CEO," *Business Week* (September 10, 2001), p. 32.
7. "Jim Kilts Is. . . . ," *Fortune*.
8. Mark Borden, "How to Succeed at Succeeding Dad," *Fortune* (September 4, 2002), pp. 381–386.
9. Max Messmer, "Surviving and Thriving as a New Manager," *National Public Accountant* (June 2000), pp. 22–24.
10. Steve Hamm, "CEO on the Spot," *Business Week* (September 30, 2002), p. 88.
11. Jay Green, "Ballmer's Microsoft," *Business Week* (June 17, 2002), p. 66.
12. Mark Miller, Daniel Klaidman, Tom Masland, Mark Hosenball, Howard Fineman, Michael Isikoff, John Barry, Eleanor Clift, and Mide Cadman, "The Hunt for the Anthrax Killer," *Newsweek* (August 12, 2002), pp. 22–28.
13. Jill Rosenfled, "Down-Home Food, Cutting-Edge Business," *Fast Company* (April 2000), pp. 56, 57.
14. Jeff Bailey, "The Supporting Cast Makes All the Difference," *Wall Street Journal* (October 28, 2002), p. R3. © 2002 by Dow Jones & Co. Inc. Reproduced with permission of Dow Jones & Co. Inc. in the format Textbook via Copyright Clearance Center.
15. Orit Gadiesh, "Transforming Corner-Office Strategy into Frontline Action," *Harvard Business Review* (May 2001), pp. 72–90.
16. Andy Raskin, "Are You Geek Enough?" *Business 2.0* (December 2001), pp. 95–98. © 2001-Time Inc. All rights reserved.
17. Tom McDonald, "A World of Challenges," *Successful Meetings*, (July 2002), p. 25.
18. Robert Ramsey, "What Will You Do If the Worst Case Scenario Really Happens?" *Supervision* (June, 2002), pp. 6–7.
19. "The Shiniest Reputations in Tarnished Times," *Fortune* (March 4, 2002), pp. 70-72.
20. Cora Daniels, "The Last Taboo: It's Not Sex. It's Not Drinking. It's Stress—and It's Soaring," *Fortune* (October 28, 2002), pp. 136–140. David Noonan, Jill Sieder, and Kevin Peraino, "Stop Stressing Me," *Newsweek* (January 29, 2001), pp. 54–56.
21. Betsy Morris, "Can Ford Save Ford?" *Fortune* (November 18, 2002), pp. 52–60. © 2002 Time Inc. All rights reserved.

Chapter 8

1. Brian Garrity and Carolyn Horwitz, "BMG Realigns Management Units," *Billboard* (October 2001), p. 5; and Wolfgang Spahr, "BMG Is Fit and Ready for Expansion," *Billboard* (April 2002), p. 49.
2. Timothy Aeppel, "On Factory Floors, Top Workers Hide Secrets to Success," *Wall Street Journal* (July 1, 2002), pp. A1, A10.
3. "Building the Right Team," *Maclean's* (October 28, 2002), p. 31.
4. Kemba Dunham, "Telecommuters' Lament," *Wall Street Journal* (October 31, 2000), pp. B1, B18.
5. Michael Allen, "As Dot-Coms Go Bust in the U.S., Bermuda Hosts an Odd Little Boomlet," *Wall Street Journal* (January 8, 2001), p. A1.
6. Paul Sweeney, "Ford's Better Idea: A Centralized Treasury," *Treasury & Risk Management* (March 2000), p. 12.
7. Stephane Fitch, "Reengineering 101: Phil Condit Sees Salvation in Services," *Forbes* (May 13, 2002), pp. 82–84.
8. *Five Challenges to Virtual Team Success: Lessons from Sabre, Inc.*, by Bradley L. Kirkman, Benson Rosen, Cristina B. Gibson, Paul E. Tesluk and Simon O. McPherson, Academy of Management Executive, 10795545, August 2002, Vol. 16, Issue 3.
9. "Managing Virtual Teams," *Workforce* (June 2001), pp. 60-65.
10. Frederick Reichhold, "Putting Customers First Is Rewarded," *Wall Street Journal* (September 10, 2002), p. A1.
11. Kelly Barron, "Stormy Weather," *Forbes* (February 19, 2001), p. 66.

Chapter 9

1. Michelle Neely Martinez, "Get Job Seekers to Come to You," *HR Mazagine*, Vol. 45 (August 2000), pp. 44–52.
2. Sacha Cohen, "High Tech Tools Lower Barriers for Disabled," *HR Magazine*, Vol. 47 (October 2002), pp. 60–65.
3. "Gore-Text," *Fast Company* (January 1999), p. 160.
4. Carla Joinson, "No Return," *HR Magazine*, Vol. 47 (November 2002), pp. 70–77.
5. Frank Jossi, "Successful Handoff," *HR Magazine*, Vol. 47 (October 2002), pp. 48–52.
6. Betty Sosnin, "Is a Video in Your Vision?" *HR Magazine*, Vol. 46 (February 2001), pp. 100–106.
7. Janice Revall, "Mo' Money, Fewer Problems," *Fortune* (March 31, 2003), p. 34.
8. "The Looting of Kmart, Part 2," *Fortune* (February 17, 2003), p. 30.

9. Bill Leonard, "Reflecting the Wide World of HR," *HR Magazine*, Vol. 47 (July 2002), pp. 50–56.
10. Terry Chapko and John English, "Paid Family Leave—It Could Happen to You," *HR Magazine*, Vol. 47 (December 2002), pp. 89–96.
11. Carla Joinson, "Strength in Numbers," *HR Magazine*, Vol. 45 (Novembr 2002), pp. 42–49.
12. Diane Cadrain, "An Acute Condition: Too Few Nurses," *HR Magazine*, Vol. 47 (December 2002), pp. 69–71.
13. Susan J. Wells, "Stolen Identity," *HR Magazine*, Vol. 47 (December 2002), pp. 30–38.

Chapter 10

1. Keith Hammonds, "Handle with Care," *Fast Company* (August, 2002), pp. 102–107.
2. Kim Clark, "No Pink Slips at the Plant," *U.S. News & World Report* (February 2002), p. 40.
3. Clint Willis, "The 100 Highest Rollers," *Forbes* (April 2, 2001), p. 78.
4. Kayte Vanscoy, "The Hiring Crisis," *Smart Business for the New Economy* (July 2000), pp. 84–94.
5. Iris Taylor, "You're the Boss, Now Motivate Your Workers," *Richmond Times-Dispatch* (August 19, 2002).
6. Cecil Pearson and Lynette Tang Yin Hui, "A Cross-Cultural Test of Vroom's Expectancy Motivation Framework," *International Journal of Organizational Theory and Behavior* (Summer 2001), pp. 307–327.
7. The section on "Motivation Is Culture Bound" is from Nancy J. Alder, *International Dimensions of Organizational Behavior*, 4th ed. (South-Western, a division of Thomson Learning, 2002), pp. 174–181.
8. From Alder, *International Dimensions*, pp. 174–181.
9. John Izzo and Pam Withers, "Balance and Synergy: The Greatest Benefit," *Compensation & Benefits Management* (Summer 2001), pp. 23–28.
10. Izzo and Withers, "Balance and Synergy."
11. Timothy Mullaney, "The Wizard of Intuit CEO Bennett Has Crafted a Nifty Turnaround. Now He's Challenging the Company's Corporate Culture," *Business Week* (October 28, 2002), pp. 60–61.
12. "Preventive Medicine," *Wards Auto World* (June 1, 2002).
13. Martin Rosenthal, "High-Performance Teams," *Executive Excellence* (October 2001), p. 6.
14. Julie Filatoff and Thomas Zamiara, "Secrets of Teambuilding Gurus," *On Wall Street* (October 2000), pp. 10–16.
15. Robert Levering and Milton Moskowitz, "The 100 Best Companies to Work for in America," *Fortune* (January 20, 2003), pp. 127–144.
16. Theodore Spencer, "Brainy Builders," *Fortune* (January 8, 2001), p. 154.
17. Laird Harrison, "We're All the Boss," *Time* (April 8, 2002), pp. 10–11.
18. "ESOP Companies Outperform Stock Market," *PR Newswire* (August 19, 2002).
19. "RTM Restaurant Group," *Datamoniter Company Profiles* (2003).
20. "Knowledge Work," *Executive Excellence* (October 1, 2002), p. 12.
21. Okey Chigbo, "The Dollars and Cents of Absence," *CA Magazine* (March 1, 2002), p. 13.
22. "Strategies for Developing an Effective Employee Absenteeism Policy," *HR Focus* (September 11, 2001), p. 5.
23. Jeffrey Marshall, "Employee Retention Linked to Better Customer Service," *Financial Executive* (March/April 2001), pp. 11–12; Gary Wallace, "Satisfied Employees Help Attract and Retain Members," *Credit Union Magazine* (September 2002), p. 32.
24. Hammonds, "Handle with Care."
25. Hillary Stout, "TD Industries Faces Realities of the Economic Slowdown," *Wall Street Journal* (May 15, 2001), p. B5.

Chapter 11

1. Paul Wilborn, "West Coast Port Lockout Takes Toll on Truck Drivers," *Fort Worth Star-Telegram* (October 3, 2002), p. 2C.
2. Daniel Machalaba, Carlos Tejada, Thomas M. Barton, and Queena Sook Kim, "Talks Break Down in Lockout of Dockworkers," *Wall Street Journal* (October 2, 2002), p. A2.
3. Thomas M. Burton, Daniel Machalaba, and Andy Pasztor, "Dock Lockout Spurs Shortages Concern," *Wall Street Journal* (October 1, 2002), pp. A3, A6.
4. Leigh Strope, "Unions to Target Key Campaigns for Pro-Labor Candidates," *Fort Worth Star-Telegram* (October 13, 2002), p. A8; Greg Hitt, "This Union Label is 'GOP Ally,'" *Wall Street Journal* (October 5, 2002), p. A4.
5. Jeanne Cummings and Carlos Tejada, "U.S. Judge Switfly Orders End to Lockout at West Coast Ports," *Wall Street Journal* (October 9, 2002), pp. A1, A2.
6. Jeanne Cummings and Carlos Tejada, "Taft-Hartley Could Bloody Labor and Bush," *Wall Street Journal* (October 11, 2002), p. A4.
7. J. Lynn Lunsford, "Boeing Union Fails in Strike Vote," *Wall Street Journal* (September 16, 2002), p. A11; Peter Robison, "Boeing Refuses to Resume Talks; Machinists Agree to Stay on Job," *Fort Worth Star-Telegram* (August 30, 2002), p. 2C.
8. Dan Piller, "Engineers, Teamsters Oppose Use of Unmanned Locomotives," *Fort Worth Star-Telegram* (September 26, 2002), p. 2C.
9. Wendy Zellner, "How Wal-Mart Keeps Unions at Bay," *Business Week* (October 28, 2002), pp. 94–96.
10. Mark Heinzl and Norihiko Shironzu, "Canadian Union Reaches Accord with Ford Motors," *Wall Street Journal* (October 1, 2002), pp. A2, A14.
11. Harry C. Katz, John Paul MacDuffie, and Fritz K. Pil, "Autos: Continuity and Change in Collective Bargaining," in *Collective Bargaining in the Private Sector*, Industrial Relations Research Association, 2002, pp. 55–90.
12. Marc Champion, "British Labor's New Militancy," *Wall Street Journal* (October 23, 2000), p. A16.
13. "Citgo Refining and Chemical Co.," *Labor Arbitration Reports*, Vol. 115, pp. 65–71, Bureau of National Affairs, 2002.
14. "Saint-Gobain Container Inc.," *Labor Arbitration Reports*, Vol. 116, pp. 572–576, Bureau of National Affairs, 2002.
15. Ellen Lyon, "Protestors Abandon Really at HIA; Organizers Fail to Get Required Permit," *The Harrisburg Patriot* (February 4, 2003).
16. Brian Lockett, "Skilled Worker Shortage, Training among Workforce Issues Facing Industry," *Daily Labor Report* (January 8, 1999), pp. C1, C2.

Chapter 12

1. Mark Haines, David Farber, "Harley-Davidson—CEO Interview," *CNBC/Dow Jones Business Video* (October 11, 2002); Tim Stevens, "Technologies of the Year—DFM Concurrent Costing Version 2.0," *Industry Week* (December 12, 2002), downloaded from http://www.industryweek.com; John Teresko, "Technology Leader of the Year—Fueled by Innovation," *Industry Week* (December 1, 2002), http://www.industryweek.com; John Teresko, "Driven by Cost," *Industry Week*, September 1, 2002, downloaded from http://www.industryweek.com.
2. Traci Purdum, "Best Practices—Fast-Track Furniture," *Industry Week* (August 1, 2002), downloaded from http://www.industryweek.com.
3. John Teresko, "Locations—Nebraska's Innovative Polymer Plant," *Industry Week* (October 1, 2002), downloaded from http://www.industryweek.com.

4. Jill Jusko, "Locations—Globe Motors Turns to Portugal," *Industry Week*, (November 1, 2002), downloaded from http://www.industryweek.com.
5. Jill Jusko, "Locations."
6. John S. McClenahen, "The World's Best," *Industry Week* (April 16, 2001), downloaded from http://www.industryweek.com.
7. John S. McClenahey, "The World's Best."
8. Barbara Hagenbaugh, "U.S. Manufacturing Jobs Fading Away Fast," *USA Today* (December 13, 2002), p. 1B.
9. Michael A. Verespej, "E-Procurement Explosion," *Industry Week* (March 1, 2002), downloaded from http://www.industryweek.com.
10. Michael A. Verespej, "E-Procurement."
11. John S. McClenahen, "Best Plants 2002," *Industry Week* (undated), downloaded from http://www.industryweek.com.
12. John S. McClenahen, "Best Plant Winners 2002," *Industry Week* (undated), downloaded from http://www.industryweek.com.
13. Chris Costanzo, "Celebrated Six Sigma Has Its Critics, Too," *American Banker* (August 28, 2002), p. 1.
14. "Malcom Baldrige National Quality Award Winners Announced," NIST press release (November 19, 2002), downloaded from http://www.nist.gov/public_affairs/releases/baldrige2002.htm.
15. "First U.S. Winery to Achieve Certification to New International Standard," Company press release (October 8, 2002).
16. Tonya Vinas, "JIT Still A-OK," *Industry Week*, (December 1, 2002), downloaded from http://www.industryweek.com.
17. Doug Bartholomew, "Faster CAD Design Called a Lifesaver," *Industry Week* (June 4, 2001), downloaded from http://www.industryweek.com.
18. John Teresko, "Robots Evolution," *Industry Week* (April 1, 2002), downloaded from http://www.industryweek.com.
19. Barbara Hagenbaugh, "U.S. Manufacturing Jobs."
20. Lisa Singhania, "Manufacturing Activity Contracts for Third Straight Month," *Associated Press Business Wire* (December 2, 2002).
21. Gene Bylinsky, "Elite Factories: They're Setting Lofty Standards in Quality Control, Preventive Maintenance, and Automation," *Fortune* (September 2, 2002) p. 172B.
22. Gene Bylinsky, "Elite Factories."
23. Tim Stevens, "Factories of the Future—Integrated Product Development," *Industry Week* (June 1, 2002), downloaded from http://www.industryweek.com.
24. Tim Stevens, "Factories of the Future."
25. Mark Haines and David Farber, "Harley-Davidson—CEO Interview"; Tim Stevens, "Technologies of the Year," John Teresko, "Technology Leader of the Year"; John Teresko, "Driven by Cost."

Chapter 13

1. Sally Beatty, "Avon Is Set to Call on Teens," *Wall Street Journal* (October 17, 2002), pp. B1, B7. © 2002 by Dow Jones & Co. Inc. Reproduced with permission of Dow Jones & Co. Inc., in the format Textbook via Copyright Clearance Center.
2. "Caring for the Customer Pays Off for Lexus Again," *Essex Chronical Series* (May 10, 2002).
3. http://www.marketingpower.com (August 28, 2003).
4. Adapted from Louise Lee, "If You Also Want to Buy a Crock-Pot, This Isn't the Place," *Wall Street Journal* (August 26, 1997), pp. A1, A11.
5. "Hard Core Shoppers," *American Demographics* (September 1998), p. 49.
6. Carl McDaniel and Roger Gates, *Marketing Research*, 5th Ed. (New York: John Wiley and Son, 2002), pp. 15–16.
7. Ann D'Innocenzio, "Stores Putting Data from Loyalty Cards to Work," *Fort Worth Star Telegram* (March 25, 2003), p. 12C.
8. "GM's Winning Vision: Staff First, Profit Follows," *Hotels* (March 2003), p. 14.
9. "The Persuaders—Cold Is Hot," *Business 2.0* (November 2002), p. 115. © 2002-Time Inc. All rights reserved.

Chapter 14

1. "Less Power to You," *Newsweek* (January 27, 2003), p. 72; "Kids Need to Brush Up on Oral Care Habits, Crest SpinBrush Survey Finds," *PR Newswire* (January 16, 2003); "Why P&G's Smile Is So Bright," *Business Week* (August 12, 2002), p. 58; Daniel Eisenberg, "A Healthy Gamble; How Did A. G. Lafley Turn Procter & Gamble's Old Brands into Hot Items?" *Time* (September 16, 2002).
2. "Quaker Oats Raises Cereal Prices; Brand Loyalty May Give a Lift to Profit," *Washington Post* (May 23, 1998), p. D1.
3. "Brand Loyalty Loses to Price, Quality and Promotions in All Categories but Pet Food," *Research Alert* (October 18, 2002).
4. Carl Franklin, "The Last 30 Years Have Seen Great Advances in Marketing Techniques," *The Business* (April 7, 2002).
5. Elliot Spagat, "A Web Gadget Fizzles, Despite a Salesman's Dazzle," *Wall Street Journal* (June 27, 2001), pp. B1, B4. © 2001 by Dow Jones & Co. Inc. Reproduced with permission of Dow Jones & Co. Inc., in the format Textbook via Copyright Clearance Center.
6. Yumiko Ono, "Overcoming the Stigma of Dishwashers in Japan," *Wall Street Journal* (May 19, 2000), pp. B1, B4. © 2000 by Dow Jones & Co. Inc. Reproduced with permission of Dow Jones & Co. Inc., in the format Textbook via Copyright Clearance Center.
7. Conversation with Jerry Thomas, CEO of Decision Analyst, April 14, 2003.
8. Michael Mendano, "Priced to Perfection," *Business2.com*, March 6, 2001, pp. 40–41.
9. "Color by Numbers," *American Demographics* (February 2002), pp. 31–35.
10. "Color by Numbers," pp. 31–35.
11. Ron Lieber, "How to Beat Priceline: Now Sites Post Secret Bids," *Wall Street Journal* (April 19, 2002), pp. D1, D16.
12. "Making the Most of eBay," *Business 2.0* (June 2002), pp. 129–130. © 2002-Time Inc. All rights reserved.
13. Cris Prystay and Meeyoung Song, "Fragrant Fabrics: Peppermint 3-Piece Is Hot in Hong Kong," *Wall Street Journal* (October 21, 2002), pp. A1, A8. © 2002 by Dow Jones & Co. Inc. Reproduced with permission of Dow Jones & Co. Inc., in the format Textbook via Copyright Clearance Center.

Chapter 15

1. Shirley Leung and Alexei Barrionuevo, "Fast-Food Chain Makes a Move Out of the Box," *Wall Street Journal* (October 29, 2002), pp. B1, B4. © 2002 by Dow Jones & Co. Inc. Reproduced with permission of Dow Jones & Co. Inc., in the format Textbook via Copyright Clearance Center.
2. Maureen T. Kacik, "How Young Dealers of Rare Sneakers Challenge Nike," *Wall Street Journal* (August 20, 2002), pp. A1, A8. © 2002 by Dow Jones & Co. Inc. Reproduced with permission of Dow Jones & Co. Inc., in the format Textbook via Copyright Clearance Center.
3. Kevin J. Delany, "Beyond Bar Codes," *Wall Street Journal* (September 23, 2002), pp. R10, R13. © 2002 by Dow Jones & Co. Inc. Reproduced with permission of Dow Jones & Co. Inc., in the format Textbook via Copyright Clearance Center.
4. Part of the section on supply chain management is adapted from: Charles Lamb, Joe Hair and Carl McDaniel, *Marketing*, 7th Ed. (South-Western, a division of Thomson Learning, 2002), pp. 392–394.

5. David Maloney, "Rite Place, Rite Time, Rite Aid," *Modern Materials Handling* (May 2002), pp. 6–9.
6. Andrew Raskin, "Who's Minding the Store," *Business 2.0* (February 2003), pp. 70–74.
7. Kim Cross, "Fill It to the Brim," *Business 2.0* (March 6, 2001), pp. 36–41.
8. "Oracle Puts Priority on Customer Service, *Wall Street Journal* (January 21, 2003), p. B5.
9. Kevin Helliker, "Rare Retailer Scores by Targeting Men Who Hate to Shop," *Wall Street Journal* (December 17, 2002), pp. A1, A11. © 2002 by Dow Jones & Co. Inc. Reproduced with permission of Dow Jones & Co. Inc., in the format Textbook via Copyright Clearance Center.

Chapter 16

1. Suzanne Vranica, "New Beetle Takes on a Bug Problem," *Wall Street Journal* (October 31, 2002), p. B8. © 2002 by Dow Jones & Co. Inc. Reproduced with permission of Dow Jones & Co. Inc., in the format Textbook via Copyright Clearance Center.
2. "The Top 5 Rules of the Ad Game," *Business Week* (January 20, 2003), pp. 72–75.
3. "World Ad Outlays Seen Rising 2.9% During Next Year," *Wall Street Journal* (December 9, 2002), p. B8.
4. http://www.advertisingage.com, Leading National Advertiser's database.
5. Jung Jeon and Sharon Beatty, "Comparative Advertising Effectiveness in Different National Cultures," *Journal of Business Research* (November 2002), pp. 908–913.
6. "NARB Upholds NAD Costco Decision," *National Advertising Division Press Release* (December 13, 2002).
7. Deborah Vence, "Match Game," *Marketing News* (November 11, 2002), pp, 1, 11–12.
8. "Doan's Decision Sets Precedent for Corrective Ads," *Advertising Age* (September 6, 2000), p. 7.
9. Charles Lamb, Joe Hair, and Carl McDaniel, *Marketing*, 7th ed. (South-Western, a division of Thomson Learning, 2002), p. 537.
10. Bob Oros, "Remove the Roadblock to a Successful Sale," *ID: The Information Source* (March 2002).
11. "Promotion Trends 2002: A Glass Half Full," *Promo Magazine* (March 14, 2002).
12. "General Motors and Genmar Holdings to Develop Co-Marketing Programs," *PR Newswire* (January 21, 2003).
13. Sarah Ellison, "On the Table in the Cafes of France, Logo du Jour," *Wall Street Journal* (June 2, 2002), pp. B1, B4. © 2002 by Dow Jones & Co. Inc. Reproduced with permission of Dow Jones & Co. Inc., in the format Textbook via Copyright Clearance Center.
14. "Online Ads Proven to Boost Brand Awareness and Sales," *New Media Age* (April 18, 2002), p. 18.
15. "Major Offline Advertisers Lead Advance in Web Ads," *New Media Age* (January 2003).
16. "Click and Clip," *Wall Street Journal* (October 21, 2002), p. R8.
17. "Advertisers Hope Fragrant Posters Are Nothing to Sniff At," *Wall Street Journal* (October 10, 2002), pp. B1, B4.
18. "High Tech Billboards Tune in to Driver's Taste," *San Francisco Chronicle* (December 22, 2002).
19. "That Guy Showing Off His New Phone May Be a Shill," *Wall Street Journal* (July 31, 2002), pp. B1, B4.
20. Jonah Bloom, "Sky-High Marketing Excellence: Jet Blue Named Ad Age Marketer of the Year," *Advertising Age* (December 12, 2002).
21. Maureen Tkacik, "Quiksilver Keeps Marketing to a Minimum," *Wall Street Journal* (August 28, 2002), p. B4. © 2002 by Dow Jones & Co. Inc. Reproduced with permission of Dow Jones & Co. Inc., in the format Textbook via Copyright Clearance Center.

Chapter 17

1. "Home Depot Launches a Major Computer Initiative—'Key Partner' IBM Provides Technology and Services," Home Depot Web site; September 30, 2002, "Home Depot to Invest $4 Billion in Stores, Associates, Technology, and Merchandising in 2003," Home Depot, January 17, 2003, both downloaded from http://www.homedepot.com; Janice Revell, "Can Home Depot Get Its Groove Back?" *Fortune*, February 3, 2003, pp. 110–112; Marc L. Songini, "Home Depot's Next IT project: Data Warehouse," *Computerworld*, October 7, 2002, downloaded from http://www.computerworld.com; and Harry R. Weber, "Retailer Adding Self-Serve Checkouts," *San Diego Union-Tribune*, December 3, 2002, p. C2.
2. Section based on Danielle Dunne, "The ABCs of Wireless Communications," *CIO.com*, http://www.cio.com/communications/edit/120701_abc_wireless.html; "Executive Guides: Wireless," *Darwin Executive Guides*, downloaded January 31, 2003, from http://guide.darwinmag.com/technology communications/wireless/index.html.
3. Drew Robb, "Case Study: Care Group Health System," *Computerworld*, December 16, 2002, downloaded from http://www.computerworld.com.
4. "Executive Guides: Intranet/Extranet," *Darwin Executive Guides*, downloaded January 30, 2003, from http://guide.darwinmag.com/technology/web/intranet/index.html.
5. "Executive Guides: Wireless," *Darwin Executive Guides*, downloaded January 31, 2003, from guide.darwinmag.com/technology/communications/wireless/index.html; and "Wi-Fi," Webopedia, downloaded from http://www.webopedia.com.
6. "(VPN) Virtual Private Network FAQs," Find VPN.com, downloaded January 31, 2003, from http://findvpn.com/articles/faq.php; and "VPN Tutorial," *About.com: Computer Networking*, downloaded January 24, 2003, from http://compnetworking.about.com/library/weekly/aa010701a.htm.
7. "Executive Guides: Data Warehouse," *Darwin Executive Guides*, downloaded February 3, 2003, from http://guide.darwinmag.com/technology/enterprise/data/index.html
8. Thomas Hoffman, "Healing Touch of a One-Company View," *Computerworld*, December 2, 2002, downloaded from http://www.computerworld.com.
9. David Haskin, "Years After Hype, 'Expert Systems' Paying Off for Some," IT Management, January 16, 2003, downloaded from http://itmanagement.earthweb.com/netsys/article.php/1570851.
10. Kathleen Melymuka, "Far from the Mother Ship," *Computerworld*, December 9, 2002, downloaded from http://www.computerworld.com.
11. Jaikumar Vijayan, "How Will You Optimize Your Infrastructure?" *Computerworld*, January 6, 2003, downloaded from http://www.computerworld.com.
12. Section based on "Executive Guides: Knowledge Management," *Darwin Executive Guides*, downloaded January 31, 2003, from http://guide.darwinmag.com/technology/enterprise/knowledge/index.html.
13. "The Water Cooler Goes Virtual," *Tech Trends 2002 Annual Report*, published by Deloitte & Touche LLP, Technology, Media and Telecommunications Group, p. 17.
14. Tom Standage, "When the Door Is Always Open," Survey of Digital Security, *Economist*, October 26, 2002, Special Section pp. 16–17.
15. "Tech Industry Responds to Rise in Computer Crime," *PR Newswire*, November 7, 2002, downloaded from http://www.bigchalk.com.
16. "CERT/CC Statistics 1988–2002," CERT Web site, http://www.cert,org; and Neal Katyal. "How to Fight Computer Crime," *New York Times*, July 30, 2002, p. A19.

17. "Egghead Files for Chapter 11," *New York Times*, August 6, 2001, p. C4; and Daniel F. Lohmeyer and Jim McCrory, "Managing Information Security," *Inc.*, July 1, 2002, downloaded from http://www.inc.com.
18. Donna Howell, "New Tactics Could Stave Off Digital Pirates," *Investor's Business Daily*, Monday, December 16, 2002, downloaded from http://www.investors.com.
19. Michael Liedtke, " Critics See Turbo-Tax's Anti-Piracy Activation Code as Anti-Consumer," *San Diego Union-Tribune*, January 13, 2003, p. C1.
20. Jon Surmacz, "Ante Virus," *Darwin*, January 29, 2003, downloaded from http://www.darwin.com.
21. Alex Salkever, "The Big Lessons of a Little Worm," *Business Week Online*, January 31, 2003, http://www.businessweek.com.
22. "Cost of Junk Email to Exceed $10 Billion for American Corporations in 2003," *Internet Wire*, January 6, 2003, downloaded from http://www.bigchalk.com.
23. "Security Policies 101," *Intranet Journal*, January 6, 2003, downloaded from http://www.intranetjournal.com.
24. Tom Standage, "The Weakest Link," Survey of Digital Security, *Economist*, October 26, 2002, Special Section, pp. 11–16.
25. Dan Verton, "Data Mining Raises Privacy Concerns," *Computerworld*, January 17, 2003, downloaded from http://www.computerworld.com.
26. *Tech Trends 2002*, Volume 2, published by Deloitte & Touche LLP, Technology, Media and Telecommunications Group, downloaded from http://www.deloitte.com
27. Spencer E. Ante, "The New Blue," *Business Week*, March 17, 2003, pp. 80–88; Bruce V. Bigelow, "Gateway Launches On-Demand Computing," *The San Diego Union-Tribune*, December 11, 2002, p. C-1; Sami Lais, "Grid Computing," *Computerworld*, December 23, 2002, downloaded from http://www.computerworld.com; Darnell Little and Ira Sager, "Who Needs Supercomputers?" *Business Week Online*, June 3, 2002, pp. 82–83; Irving Wladawsky-Berger and Ira Sager, "Info Tech's 'Post-Technology Phase'," *Business Week Online*, December 31, 2002, downloaded from http://www.businessweek.com.
28. Linda Foley, "Refocusing the Fight Against Identity Theft," *San Diego Union-Tribune*, February 7, 2003, p. B7; Ann Perry, "Identity Theft Takes Alarming Turn for Worse," *San Diego Union-Tribune*, February 2, 2003, p. I1
29. Tony Fong, "Bridge Medical Is Healthy Again," *San Diego Union-Tribune*, November 23, 2002, pp. C1, C7; and Terri Somers, "Bar Codes May be a Boon for S.D. Firms," *San Diego Union-Tribune*, March 15, 2003, pp. C1, C2.
30. "Home Depot Launches a Major Computer Initiative—Key Partner' IBM Provides Technology and Services," September 30, 2002; and "Home Depot to Invest $4 Billion in Stores, Associates, Technology, and Merchandising in 2003," Home Depot, January 17, 2003, both downloaded from http://www.homedepot.com.

Chapter 18

1. Peter Behr and April Witt, "Visionary's Dream Led to Risky Business," July 28, 2002, "Dream Job Turns into a Nightmare," July 29, 2002, and "Concerns Grow Amid Conflicts," July 30, 2002, *Washington Post*, all downloaded from http://www.washingtonpost.com; John R. Emshwiller, "Enron Improperly Transferred Up to $5 Billion, a Report Finds," *Wall Street Journal*, downloaded from http://www.wsj.com, March 6, 2003, "Enron's Accounting" (graphic), *HoustonChronicle.com*, downloaded February 25, 2003, from http://www.chron.com/content/news/photos/02/03/18/enron/popup2/htm; Tom Fowler, "The Pride and the Fall of Enron, *Houston Chronicle*, October 20, 2002, downloaded from http://www.houstonchronicle.com; "Understanding Enron's Partnerships" (graphic), *HoustonChronicle.com*, downloaded February 25, 2003, from http://www.chron.com/content/news/photos/02/01/25/partnership/popup2/htm.
2. Brad Foss, "Pain of Scandals May Yield Benefits," *San Diego Union-Tribune*, January 1, 2003, pp. C1, C8; Jesse Drucker and Henry Sender, "Strategy Behind Accounting Scheme," *Wall Street Journal*, June 27, 2002, p. A9; "KPMG: Bitten by the Watchdog," *Business Week*, February 10, 2003, p. 40; Andrew Ross Sorkin and Alex Berenson, "Tyco Used Gimmicks to Cook the Books," *San Diego Union-Tribune*, December 31, 2002, pp. C1, C4; and "Year Marked by Corporate Scandal," *Augusta Chronicle*, December 29, 2002, p. D2.
3. Stephen Taub, "Big Five Get Low Grades for Performance," *CFO.com*, July 12, 2002, downloaded from http://www.cfo.com.
4. Robert Durak, "Audit Risk Alert—2002/03: Current Risks" (New York: American Institute of Certified Public Accountants, Inc., 2002), p. 14.
5. Robert Durak, "Audit Risk Alert—2002/03: Current Risks."
6. Brad Foss, "Pain of Scandals May Yield Benefits," *San Diego Union-Tribune*, January 1, 2003, pp. C1, C8.
7. Eric Krell, "Auditors on Red Alert," *Business Finance*, March 2002, downloaded from http://www.businessfinancemag.com.
8. Brad Foss, "Pain of Scandals May Yield Benefits."
9. "In the Name of the Dollar: A Closer Look at the Sarbanes-Oxley Act of 2002," *California CPA*, September 2002, downloaded from http://www.findarticles.com.
10. Andrew Osterland, "No More Mr. Nice Guy," *CFO*, September 1, 2002, downloaded from http://www.cfo.com.
11. Andrew Osterland, "No More Mr. Nice Guy."
12. "Foxhunt Staffing Predicts a Growth Market for Internal Auditors in Wake of Sarbanes-Oxley Act," *PR Newswire*, August 14, 2002, downloaded from http://www.findarticles.com.
13. "CFOs and Finance Executives Favor More, Not Less, Regulation," *PR Newswire*, December 12, 2002, downloaded from http://www.findarticles.com; and Andrew Osterland, "No More Mr. Nice Guy."
14. "AICPA Takes Stand on Sarbanes-Oxley Implementation," Accounting WEB News, December 3, 2002.
15. Fay Hansen, "Outlook 2003: More Changes, Greater Challenges," *Business Finance*, December 2002, downloaded from http://www.businessfinancemag.com.
16. Amey Stone and Robert Herz, "It's Like When Someone Robs a Bank," *Business Week Online*, August 19, 2002, downloaded from http://www.businessweek.com; and Andrew Osterland, "No More Mr. Nice Guy."
17. Fay Hansen, "Outlook 2003: More Changes, Greater Challenges."
18. Fay Hansen, "Outlook 2003: More Changes, Greater Challenges."
19. David Cay Johnston, "Enron Is Accused of 'Drilling' the Tax Code," *San Diego Union-Tribune*, February 14, 2003, pp. C1, C4; and William L. Watts, "Enron Used Tax Code as 'Profit Center,' *CBS.MarketWatch.com*, February 13, 2003, downloaded from http://www.marketwatch.com.

Chapter 19

1. Julie Creswell, "Banking's Not-So-Secret Weapon," *Fortune* (October 14, 2002), pp. 158–166; Carol Loomis, "Whatever It Takes," *Fortune* (November 25, 2002), pp. 74–86; Melanie

Shanely, "A Golden Deal for Citi Shareholders?," *Fortune* (June 24, 2002), p. 178; and All Star Banking Team 2002 Top 5 Chief Marketing Officers," *US Banker* (November 1, 2002), http://www.americanbanker.com.
2. Federal Reserve, http://www.stlts.frb.org/fred/data/reserves/currcir.
3. Federal Reserve, U.S. Monetary System, http://www.stlts.frb.org/fred/data.
4. John M. Berry, "Fed to Cut 400 Jobs as It Processes Fewer Checks," *Washington Post*, (February 7, 2003), p. E01.
5. "QBP-Stats at a Glance," Federal Deposit Insurance Corporation (September 30, 2002), downloaded from http://www.fdic.gov.
6. "QBP-Stats at a Glance," Federal Deposit Insurance Corporation, (September 30, 2002), downloaded from http://www.fdic.gov.
7. Credit Union Statistics, Credit Union National Administration, http://www.cuna.org.
8. "Frequently Requested U.S. Credit Union/Bank Comparisons," Credit Union National Administration research report, http://www.cuna.org.
9. "Top U.S. Bank and Thrift Holding Companies by Assets," *American Banker* (February 10, 2003), http://www.americanbanker.com.
10. Karen Krebsbach, "Citgroup's Big Bet on China," *U.S. Banker* (October 2002), http://www.usbanker.com.
11. William R. Keeton, "The Transformation of Banking and Its Impact on Consumers and Small Businesses," Federal Bank of Kansas City, http://www.kc.frb.org.
12. William R. Keeton, "The Transformation of Banking and Its Impact on Consumers and Small Businesses," Federal Bank of Kansas City, http://www.kc.frb.org.
13. Dean Calbreath, "Bucking a Trend," *San Diego Union-Tribune* (October 13, 2002), p. H-1.
14. Riva D. Atlas, "Wachovia to Acquire Prudential Brokerage," *San Diego Union-Tribune* (February 20, 2003), p. C-1.
15. David Breitkopf and Kate Gibson, "Double Play: E-Trade Adds ATMs, Eyes Credit Cards," *American Banker*, (February 5, 2003), http://www.americanbanker.com.
16. Brian Deagon, "Banks Put Cash into their Web Sites," *Wall Street Journal*, (December 12, 2002), p. A6.
17. Forrester Research, "Statistics for Online Banking," reported on http://epaynews.com, 2002.
18. Jennifer Gordon, "Bank Industry Takes 'Clicks-and-Mortar' Approach," *Business First-Louisville* (February 1, 2002), http://louisville.bizjournals.com.
19. Charles Fishman, "This is a Marketing Revolution," *Fast Company* (May, 1999), http://www.fastcompany.com.
20. Chuck Salter, "Customer Service: Commerce Bank," *Fast Company* (May 2002), http://www.fastcompany.com.
21. Julie Creswell, "Banking's Not-So-Secret Weapon," *Fortune* (October 14), 2002, pp. 158–166; Carol Loomis, "Whatever It Takes," *Fortune* (November 25, 2002), pp. 74–86.

Chapter 20

1. Carlye Adler "Would You Pay $2 Million for This Franchise?," *Fortune Small Business* (May 1, 2002), downloaded from http://www.fortune.com; Krispy Kreme corporate Web site, accessed March 28, 2003 and June 9, 2003, http://www.krispykreme.com; Scott Livengood and David Shook, "His Doughnut Stores Are His 'Children,' " *Business Week Online* (December 9, 2002), downloaded from http://www.businessweek.com; Amey Stone and David Shook, "The Rise—and Rise—of Krispy Kreme," *Business Week Online* (September 4, 2001), downloaded from http://www.businessweek.com; and "Yahoo!/Market Guide—Krispy Kreme" and "Yahoo! Finance Restaurants Industry," *Yahoo! Finance* (June 9, 2003), downloaded from http://www.biz.yahoo.com.
2. David Deeds, "Extra! Extra!" *Inc.* (September 2002), pp. 110–112.
3. Kris Frieswick, "The Five-Year Itch," *CFO*, (February 1, 2003), downloaded from http://www.cfo.com.
4. Jay Sherman and Susan Kelly, "Uphill Racer—The 2002 Alexander Hamilton Award Winners," Treasury & Risk Management (October 2002), downloaded from http://www.treasuryandrisk.com.
5. Scott Kirshner, "How Do You Spell Value?" *Newsweek* (June 20, 2002), pp. 32F–32H.
6. "CIT Commercial Services Provides $56 Million to Fashion Design House Ecko," *PR Newswire* (January 9, 2003), downloaded from Big Chalk Library, http://www.bigchalk.com.
7. "CIT Commercial Services Provides $56 Million to Fashion Design House Ecko," *PR Newswire* (January 9, 2003), downloaded from Big Chalk Library, http://www.bigchalk.com.
8. "Profile: AOL Time Warner," *Yahoo! Finance*, downloaded March 26, 2003 from biz.yahoo.com/p/a/aol.html; and Doug Tsuruoka, "AOL's Real Bogeyman Is Debt, Not Its Ailing Internet Service." *Investor's Business Daily* (February 25, 2003), downloaded from http://www.investors.com.
9. Kate Kelly and Raymond henessey, "Finally, an IPO! But It Surely Isn't a Mania," *Wall Street Journal* (February 13, 2003), pp. C1, C5.
10. Susan Chandler, "A Barrel of Fun," *San Diego Union-Tribune* (January 3, 2003), pp, C1, C4.
11. Craig Schneider, "Dividends Are Forever," *CFO* (March 1, 2003), downloaded from http://www.cfo.com.
12. Steve Lohr, "Microsoft Says It Will Start Paying Dividend," *San Diego Union-Tribune*, (January 17, 2003), pp. C1, C8; and Amey Stone, "Microsoft's Lonely Dividend Bandwagon," *Business Week Online* (January 28, 2003), downloaded from http://www.businessweek.com.
13. Jennifer Davies, "Qualcomm to Reward Shareholders with Dividend," *San Diego Union-Tribune* (February 12, 2003), pp. E1, E9.
14. "VC Watch: Matrix Semi Secures $52 Million," *CNET News.com* (March 21, 2003), downloaded from http://www.news.com.
15. "2002 U.S. Venture Investment Higher than '98, but Falling," VentureOne press release (January 27, 2003), downloaded from http://www.ventureone.com.
16. Thomas Zizzo, "Bands of Angels," *Electronic Business* (February 1, 2003), downloaded from http://www.e-insite.net/eb-mag/.
17. Section based on "Deloitte Consulting/BusinessWeek Survey Finds Ambiguity in Who Leads Charge in Response to New Disclosure Rules," Deloitte Consulting (March 7, 2003), downloaded from http://www.dc.com; Jeremy Kahn, "The Chief Freaked-Out Officer," *Fortune* (December 3, 2002), downloaded from http://www.fortune.com; and Joseph Weber, "CFOs on the Hot Seat," *Business Week* (March 17, 2003), pp. 67–70.
18. "A Long-Range Radar for Risk," in Jay Sherman and Susan Kelly, "Uphill Racer—The 2002 Alexander Hamilton Award Winners," *Treasury & Risk Management* (October 2002), downloaded from http://www.treasuryandrisk.com.
19. Jerry Miccolis, "ERM Lessons Across Industries," *IRMI.com* (March 2003), downloaded from http://www.irmi.com.
20. Michael Bungert and Amey Stone, "Modeling Terrorism Risks for Business," *Business Week Online* (February 20, 2003), downloaded from http://www.businessweek.com.
21. Ilan Mochari, "How to Collect from Anyone (Even Enron)," *Inc.* (September 1, 2002), pp. 67–68."

22. Joseph Weber, "CFOs on the Hot Seat," *Business Week* (March 17, 2003), pp. 67–70.
23. Joseph Weber, "CFOs on the Hot Seat," *Business Week* (March 17, 2003), pp. 67–70.
24. "Stand Back! Enzo Has Arrived," in Jay Sherman and Susan Kelly, "Uphill Racer—The 2002 Alexander Hamilton Award Winners," *Treasury & Risk Management* (October 2002), downloaded from http://www.treasuryandrisk.com.
25. Jeremy Kahn, "The Chief Freaked-Out Officer," *Fortune* (December 3, 2002), downloaded from http://www.fortune.com; "Krispy Kreme Buying Montana Mills Bread," *AP Online* (January 24, 2003), downloaded from Big Chalk Library, http://www.bigchalk.com; Jerry Useem, "In Corporate America, It's Cleanup Time," *Fortune* (September 2, 2002), downloaded from http://www.fortune.com; and "Yahoo!/Market Guide—Krispy Kreme" and "Yahoo! Finance Restaurants Industry," *Yahoo! Finance* (March 28, 2003), downloaded from http://www.biz.yahoo.com.
26. Quotes from Craig Schneider, "Dividends Are Forever," *CFO* (March 1, 2003), downloaded from http://www.cfo.com.

Chapter 21

1. Adam Lashinsky, "A Nation of Investors," *Fortune* (September 30, 2002), downloaded from http://www.fortune.com.
2. Allan Sloan, "Bull? Bear?," *Newsweek* (March 17, 2003), p. 44.
3. Nicholas Stein, "America's Most Admired Companies," *Fortune* (March 3, 2002), p. 81.
4. Adam Lashinsky, "Game Over?," *Fortune* (March 3, 2003), p. 156.
5. "Moody's Corporate Bond Yield Averages, 1980–2002," downloaded from The Bond Market Association, http://www.bondmarket.com/Research/C3.shtml.
6. "Highlights," *Research Quarterly*, The Bond Market Association (February 2003), downloaded from http://www.bondmarket.com.
7. "Treasury Coupon Issuance Surges in 2002," *Research Quarterly*, The Bond Market Association (February 2003), downloaded from http://www.bondmarket.com.
8. "Municipal, Mortgage and ABS Issuance Expected to Decrease in 2003," *Research U.S. Market Outlook*, the Bond Market Association (January 2003), downloaded from http://www.bondmarket.com.
9. Theresa W. Carey, "The Electronic Investor: Squeezed Down," *Barron's* (March 3, 2003), p. T4.
10. NYSE corporate Web site, http://www.nyse.com, downloaded March 17, 2003.
11. "NASDAQ Full-Year and Fourth Quarter 2002 Results," Nasdaq corporate press release (March 10, 2003), downloaded from http://www.nasdaq.com.
12. "SEC Charges HealthSouth Corp., CEO Richard Scrushy with $1.4 Billion Accounting Fraud," Securities and Exchange press release, March 20, 2003.
13. Dennis K. Berman, "Lucent Settles Shareholders' Suit for $568 Million," *Wall Street Journal* (March 28, 2003), p. A3
14. Adam Lashinsky, "Hey SEC, Is That All You Got?," *Business 2.0* (December 4, 2002), downloaded from http://www.business2.com.
15. Jim Bohman, "Local Companies Face Tough, New Rules," *Dayton Daily News* (July 7, 2002), downloaded from http://www.elibrary.com.
16. Jane Haseldine, "Bruised Online Investors Return to Full-Service Financial Firms," *Centre Daily Times* (September 22, 2002), downloaded from http://www.elibrary.com.
17. Amy Collins, "Schwab's Fortunes Sink," *Business 2.0* (March 15, 2001), downloaded from http://www.business2.com; John Kador, "Requiem for Charles Schwab's Past," *BusinessWeek Online*, (January 21, 2003), downloaded from http://www.businessweek.com; Adam Lashinsky, "Schwab Gets an E for Effort," *Business 2.0* (May 20, 2002), downloaded from http://www.business2.com; Amy Stone, "Schwab: Pick It While It's Down?," *BusinessWeek Online* (January 31, 2003), downloaded from http://www.businessweek.com; "Schwab Investment Sentiment Survey Reveals Mixed Emotions," Charles Schwab & Co. company press release, (July 24, 2002), downloaded from http://www.schwab.com.

Chapter 22

1. "How Much Will It Cost to Raise a Child?" Downloaded from Web site http://www.kiplinger.com, (March 5, 2003).
2. Based on data reported by the College Board from Annual Survey of Colleges in Trends in College Pricing, 2001, downloaded from Web site http://www.collegeboard.com, (March 17, 2003).
3. Chi Chi Wu, "Consumer Groups Urge Federal Reserve Board to Stop Abusive Bank Overdraft Charges," (January 28, 2003), downloaded from Web site http://www.consumerfed,org,
4. Gini Kopecky Wallace, "Can Money Buy Happiness?" *Family Circle* (March 15, 2003).
5. Paul J. Lim, "Unearthing the Best Deals—Credit Cards," *U.S. News & World Report* (December 9, 2002).
6. Ronaleen R. Roba, "Avoid the Minimum Payment Trap," *Kiplinger Magazine* (January 22, 2003), downloaded from Web site http://www.kiplinger.com.
7. Greg Rohloff, "First National Enters Internet Banking Market," *Amarillo Daily News*, Web posted, July 21, 2000.
8. John Ginovsky, "Internet Consumer Lending—Do It, But Do It Right," *Bankers News* (October 29, 2002).
9. Downloaded from Web site http://www.studentdebt.net/askdaniel2.htm, March 10, 2003.
10. Gini Kopecky Wallace, "Can Money Buy Happiness?" *Family Circle* (March 15, 2003).
11. "2002 Tax Changes: Individuals," January 2003, downloaded from Web site http://www.irs.gov., March 25, 2003.
12. "2002 Tax Changes: Individuals," January 2003, downloaded from Website http://www.irs.gov, March 25, 2003.
13. Leonard Wiener, "Unearthing the Best Deals—Insurance," *U.S. News & World Report* (December 9, 2002).
14. Peter Landers and Amy Dockser Marcus, "You *Can* Make Them Pay," *Wall Street Journal* (September 17, 2002), pp. D1, D4.
15. Kenneth Klee, "Why Good Entrepreneurs Make Bad Investors," *Inc.* (November 1, 2002), downloaded from Web site http://www.inc.com/magazine/20021101/24821.html.
16. Robert Longley, "Top Consumer Fraud Complaints in 2002," (January 30, 2003), downloaded from Web site http://www.usgovinfo.about.com; "Identity Theft and Fraud," downloaded from Web site http://www.usdoj.gov/criminal/fraud/idtheft.html, on March 27, 2003.
17. "TipSheet, Gen X: A Snapshot," *Newsweek* (March 24, 2003).

subject index

A

Absenteeism, 327
Absolute advantage, 121
Accountability, 251, 591–592
Accountants
  accountability for, 591–592
  explanation of, 573–574, 605
  private, 574
  public, 574, 605
Accounting
  accounting equation and, 577–578
  balance sheet and, 579–583
  careers in, 605
  computers in, 578–579
  cycle for, 578
  explanation of, 571–572
  financial, 572
  financial statement analysis and, 586–590
  income statement and, 583–585
  managerial, 571–572
  overview of, 570–571
  reforms in, 575–577
  scandals in, 569, 570, 574–575
  statement of cash flows and, 585, 586
  trends in, 590–593
Accounts payable, 643
Accounts receivable, 641
Acid-test ratio, 587
Acquisitions
  banking, 621–622
  effects of, 173–174
  explanation of, 167
Acronyms, 10, 11
Active Corps of Executives (ACE), 192
Activity ratios, 589
Actual cash value, 721
Adamson, James, 286
Administrative agencies, 105, 106
Administrative distribution systems, 479
Administrative law, 104
Advantage, 121
Advertising
  corrective, 511–512
  cost and reach of, 508, 509
  explanation of, 505, 506–507
  regulation of, 111, 509–512
  tobacco, 512
  types of, 507–508
  web, 522–523
Advertising account managers, 533
Advertising agencies, 509, 511
Advertising media
  explanation of, 508–509
  strengths and weaknesses of, 510
Advertising media planners, 534–535
Advocacy advertising, 508
Affirmative action, 294
Africa, globalization and, 122
African Americans
  color preferences and, 462
  demographic trends of, 32
  recruitment of, 295
  as small-business owners, 203
Age Discrimination Act, 292
Agency shop, 348
Agents, 474
Albers, Rolf, 642
Alcohol Labeling Legislation, 112
Allen, Paul, 311
Alliances, 2
Allin, Cheryl, 334
Altschul, Randice-Lisa, 210–211
Americans for Tax Reform, 70
Americans with Disabilities Act (ADA), 112, 278, 292
Andersen, Arthur, 599
Angel Capital Electronic Network (ACE-Net), 191
Angel investors, 196, 651
Angelidis, Kathy, 233
Annual reports, 573
Antidumping laws, 124
Antitrust cases, 67
Antitrust regulation, 110
Appellate courts, 105
Application service providers (ASPs), 543–544
Apprenticeship, 281
Arbitration, 106, 351
Assault and battery, 109
Assembly process, 371
Assembly-line techniques, 377
Asset management, 389
Assets
  current, 580
  explanation of, 577
  fixed, 580–581
  intangible, 582
  liquid, 709
  personal, 708
Attitudes, 418
Auctions, Internet, 380–381
Audience selectivity, 508
Auditing, 574
Authority, 251
Autocratic leaders, 224–225
Automated teller machines (ATMs), 709, 710
Automation, 388
Automobile liability insurance, 721
Automobile physical damage insurance, 721
Automotive industry, 27–29

B

Baby boomers, 27, 28, 31
Background checks, 279
Backward integration, 479
Badaracco, Joseph, 99
Balance of payments, 120
Balance of trade, 119
Balance sheets
  assets and, 580–582
  explanation of, 579
  liabilities and, 582
  owners' equity and, 583
  personal, 708
Ballmer, Steve, 217, 227, 237
Bank charters, 615
Bank Insurance Fund (BIF), 618
Banking Act of 1933, 618
Bankruptcy, 110
Bankruptcy law, 99, 110
Bankruptcy Reform Act of 1978, 110
Banks. *See also* Financial institutions
  commercial, 613–615
  function of, 611, 613, 616
  insuring deposit accounts in, 618–619
  international, 619–620
  mergers and acquisitions of, 621–622
  savings, 615, 710
  services provided by, 623–625, 716
Barbash, Barry, 575
Bargaining unit, 345
Barlow, Richard G., 428
Barriers to entry, 65
Bear markets, 683
Beardsley, Peter, 102
Bechtolsheim, Andy, 181
Becker, Mike, 186–187
Beliefs, 418
Bell Helicopter, 324
Benefit segmentation, 422
Benefits. *See also* Employee compensation
  collective bargaining and, 350
  types of, 285–286
  work-life, 326
Bennett, Mike, 580
Bennett, Stephen, 321
Berce, Dan, 653
Bezos, Jeff, 183, 184, 235
Bill of material, 377
Birch, David, 190, 201
Blair, Tony, 35, 351
Blakely, Sara, 61
Blashack, Jill, 190
Blaustein, Lawrence A., 437
Bleustein, Jeffrey, 367, 392
Board of directors, 157–158
Bobo, Paul, 388
Body language, 2, 19
Bonds
  corporate, 675, 676
  explanation of, 647, 675
  issued by government, 675–676
  municipal, 676
  quotations for, 689
  ratings for, 677
Bonuses, 284, 321
Bookkeeping, 577, 578
Boyd, Martin, 652
Bracken, Josh, 409
Bracken, Michael, 409
Brady Law, 112
Brainstorming, 449

Brand equity, 442
Brand recognition, 506–507
Branding
  benefits of, 441–442
  building loyalty to, 442–443
  explanation of, 441
  facilitating new-product sales through, 443
Brands
  building loyalty to, 442–443
  explanation of, 441
  master, 442, 443
  types of, 444
Bratton, William, 253
Breach of contract, 107–108
Breakeven analysis, 456–457
Breaking bulk, 477
Breen, Edward D., Jr., 97
Bribery, 119
Brin, Sergey, 181, 182
Brokerage firms, 617
Brokers, 474
Brown, Marc, 212
Brunner, Nathan, 655
Budgets, 639–640
Building insurance, 668
Build-to-order, 490
Bull markets, 683–684
Bundling, 458
Bungert, Michael, 654
Burk, Martha, 427
Burke, Greg, 168
Burman, Mitchell, 199
Burton, Jake, 45, 46
Bush, Barbara, 190
Bush, George W., 123, 230, 337, 343, 359
Business. *See also* Global marketplace; Small businesses
  demographic trends and, 30–33
  environment of, 28
  explanation of, 24
  factors of production for, 25–27
  global competition and, 38–39
  global economic systems and, 33–36
  knowledge-based, 326–327
  learning the basics of, 1
  role of, 25
  social factors and, 28–29
  technological trends and, 36–38
  terrorism and, 39–40
  trends in, 27–28
Business cycles, 52–53
Business interruption insurance, 669
Business law, 99, 104–105
Business liability insurance, 669
Business market, consumer vs., 419–420
Business organization
  cooperatives, 160–162
  corporations, 155–161
  forms of, 150
  franchises, 130–131, 162–166, 169–170
  joint ventures, 131–132, 162
  limited liability companies, 149, 160
  mergers and acquisitions, 166–171
  partnerships, 152–155, 161
  sole proprietorships, 150–152, 161
  trends in, 169–171
Business plans
  explanation of, 194
  outline for, 195
  use of, 195–196
Buyer cooperatives, 162
Buying behavior. *See* Consumer buyer behavior
Buy-national regulations, 123

C

C corporations, 159
CAD/CAM systems, 387
Cain, Jim, 258
Canada, 36, 126
Capital, 26
Capital budgets, 640, 642–643
Capital expenditures, 642–643
Capital products, 440
Capitalism, 34–35, 37
Career Employment Opportunities Directory—Business Administration, 15
Career Mosaic, 16, 40
Careers. *See also* Employment; Jobs
  computer/information systems, 603–605
  financial, 738–740
  management, 400–403
  marketing, 533–535
  selection of, 1
  self-assessment to help choose, 13–14
  sources of information on, 15–16
Casares, Wenceslao, 26
Cash and carry wholesalers, 482, 483
Cash budgets, 640
Cash flow plans, 709
Cash flows, 637
Cash management
  explanation of, 640–641, 652
  personal, 709–711
Cash value, 723, 725
Category management, 492
Cease-and-desist orders, 110
Celler-Kefauver Act, 110
Cellular manufacturing, 377
Center for Women's Business Research, 202
Centralization, of decision making, 252–253
Certified management accountants (CMAs), 574, 605
Certified public accountants (CPAs)
  explanation of, 574, 575, 605
  small businesses and, 198
Chain of command, 250
Chambers, Jeff, 312
Changing Times Annual Survey: Jobs for New College Graduates, 15
Chapman, Judy, 233
Chapter 7 bankruptcy, 110
Chapter 11 bankruptcy, 110
Chavez, Cesar, 354
Checking accounts, 709–711
Chief financial officers (CFOs)
  changing roles of, 652–653
  function of, 636, 637
Chief information officers (CIOs), 538
Chief risk officers (CROs), 653
Child Protection Act, 112
Children's Television Act, 112
China
  banking market in, 620
  economic growth in, 52, 70
  entrepreneurial spirit in, 68–69
  global competition and, 38, 39
  human rights and, 95
Chirac, Jacques, 35
Chudakova, Olga, 69
Cigarette Labeling Act, 112
Circuit breakers, 685
Circular flow, 52
City managers, 401
Civil Rights Act of 1964, 292, 293
Clark, Kim B., 235
Class action lawsuits, 294
Classic entrepreneurs, 183–184
Clayton Act of 1914, 110
Clean Air Act, 296
Clinton, Bill, 69
Closed shop, 348
Clyde, Rob, 552
COBRA, 722
Code of ethics, 85, 86
Coercive power, 223
Cohen, Ben, 83
Cohesiveness, group, 322
Coinsurance, 668, 722
Collective bargaining
  explanation of, 338
  process of, 347–350
College
  community, 10
  concentration tips for, 8–9
  financial aid for, 9–10
  learning to concentrate in, 8–9
  memory devices for, 10–11
  money sources for, 9–10
  studying tips for, 10–11
  test-taking strategies for, 11–12
  time management in, 9
College education, benefits of, 1
The College Board College Costs and Financial Aid Handbook, 10
Color, products and, 460–462
Comarketing, 516
Command economy, 35, 37
Commercial banks, 613–615
Commercial liability insurance, 668
Commercial paper, 641, 644
Commission, 284
Committee structure, 256–257
Common law, 104
Common stock, 647–649, 673
Communications, 38. *See also* Body language
Communism, 35, 50
Comparative advantage, 121, 122
Comparative advertising, 507
Competition. *See also* Global competition
  laws to promote fair, 110–112
  monopolistic, 65–66
  perfect, 64–65
  trends in, 138–139
Competitive advantage
  cost, 411–412

differential, 412
diversity as, 290–291
explanation of, 290, 411
niche, 412–413
Component lifestyles, 29
Comprehensive coverage, 721
Computer network administrators, 605
Computer networks
application programs for, 543–544
explanation of, 539–540
Intranet, 541–542
types of, 540
virtual private, 542–543
wireless, 540, 542
Computer programmers, 604
Computer-aided design (CAD), 387, 388
Computer-aided manufacturing (CAM), 387
Computer-integrated manufacturing (CIM), 388
Computerized resource planning, 378–380
Computers
accounting using, 578–579
confidentiality issues related to, 555–556
protection of, 552–555
viruses affecting, 553–554
Conaway, Charles, 286
Concentration, 8–9
Conceptual skills, 232
Concession bargaining, 356–357
Conciliation, 293, 344
Condit, Phil, 259
Conflict, 4–5
Conflict of interest, 82
Conglomerate mergers, 169
Consensual leaders, 225
Consultative leaders, 225
Consumer buyer behavior
business-to-business market and, 419–420
explanation of, 415
influences on, 415–418
types of decisions and, 418–419
Consumer credit
credit cards and, 713–715
history and ratings and, 716–717
loans and, 715–716
pros and cons of using, 711–713
Consumer Credit Protection Act, 112
Consumer price index (CPI), 55, 56
Consumer Products Safety Act, 112
Consumer Products Safety Commission, 106
Consumer protection laws, 111, 112
Consumerism, 111
Contingency plans, 220–222
Contingent workers, 275
Continuous improvement, 385
Continuous pay insurance, 724
Continuous process, 371
Contract manufacturing, 131
Contractionary policy, 57
Contracts
breach of, 107–108
explanation of, 99, 106
requirements for, 107
types of, 106–107
Contractual distribution systems, 479
Controlling, 228–229
Convenience products, 439
Convertible bonds, 675
Cooper, Russ, 164
Cooperative education programs, 10
Cooperatives
explanation of, 160–161
types of, 162
Copyrights, 108, 582
Corporate bonds, 675, 676
Corporate campaigns, 354
Corporate culture, 226–227
Corporate distribution systems, 478–479
Corporate financial managers, 739
Corporate philanthropy
explanation of, 92
trends in, 93–94
Corporate trainers, 402
Corporations. *See also* Multinational corporations
advantages of, 158, 161
disadvantages of, 158–159, 161
explanation of, 155–156
list of largest, 156
process for setting up, 156, 157
structure of, 156–158
types of, 159–160
virtual, 260–261
Corrective advertising, 511–512
Cosi, 27
Cost competitive advantage, 411–412
Cost of goods sold, 583
Cost per thousand (CPM), 508
Cost-of-living adjustment (COLA), 349, 350
Cost-push inflation, 55
Costs, 25
Cotsakos, Christos, 702
Countertrade, 132–133
Court system, 105
Courts of appeal, 105
Courville, Mary, 530
Craft unions, 339
Credit
consumer, 711–717
open-end, 713
setting rules on, 611–612
trade, 643
Credit cards, 609, 713–714
Credit life insurance, 715–716
Credit managers, 739
Credit risk, 653
Credit unions, 615–616, 715
Crime, 109
Crisis management, 235
Critical path method (CPM), 383, 384
Cross-functional teams, 324
Crow, Bob, 351
Crowding out, 58, 59
Culture. *See also* Diversity
buyer behavior and, 415–416
corporate, 226–227
explanation of, 415
global marketplace and, 133–135
motivation and, 318
Cunningham, Lawrence, 171
Currency
changing values of, 120
distribution of, 612
explanation of, 609
Current assets, 580
Current liabilities, 582
Current ratio, 587
Customer departmentalization, 248
Customer satisfaction
employee motivation and, 328–329
financial reporting and, 594
financial-services industry and, 627
information technology and, 561
in Japan, 141
managers' role in, 236
marketing concept and, 407
marketing research and, 430
products and, 465
small businesses and, 206–207
through service leadership, 173
Customer service, 41, 89, 97, 388
Customer value, 70–71, 407
Customization, 370, 371
Customs regulations, 123–124
Cyclical unemployment, 54

D

Daniels, John L., 639
Data
analysis of, 424–425
security issues related to, 553–554
types of, 424
Data marts, 547–548
Data mining, 556
Data warehouse, 547
Database management systems (DBMS), 539
Database managers, 604–605
Databases, 539
Dealer brands, 444
Debentures, 675
Debt, 196
Debt financing
equity financing vs., 645–646
explanation of, 646–647
Debt ratios, 589
Debt-to-equity ratios, 589
Decentralization, of decision making, 253
Decision Analyst, 460
Decision making
centralization of, 252–253
decentralization of, 253
extensive, 419
group, 323
human resources, 297
limited, 418–419
as managerial function, 229–231
Decision support systems (DSSs), 548
Decisional roles, 229, 230
Deeds, David, 638
Defamation, 109
Delegation of authority, 251
Dell, Michael, 26–27
Demand
changes in, 63, 65
explanation of, 60

interaction between supply and, 61–63
Demand curve, 60
Demand deposits, 609
Demand forecast, 275
Demand-pull inflation, 55
Deming, W. Edwards, 385
Democratic leaders, 225
Demographic segmentation, 420–421
Demographic trends
baby boomers and, 31
business opportunities created by, 42–43
diversity and, 32–33
franchising and, 169
Generation X and, 31
Generation Y and, 30
mobility and, 32
older consumers and, 31–32
Demography, 30
Demotion, 288
Departmentalization, 247–248
Depository institutions
commercial banks, 613–615, 621–623
credit unions, 615–616
explanation of, 613, 614
thrift institutions, 615
Depreciation, 580–581
Deregulation, 111
DeRodes, Bob, 537
Detailing, 521
Devaluation, 120
Differential advantage, 504
Differential competitive advantage, 412
DiPiazza, Samuel, Jr., 592–593
Direct foreign investment, 132
Disability income insurance, 723
Discount rate, 611
Distribution
category management and, 492
customer satisfaction and, 494
exclusive, 479
explanation of, 474
intensive, 480
selective, 479–480
sharing information and load and, 492–493
strategies for, 414
Distribution centers, 491
Distribution channels
function of, 475–478
market coverage intensity and, 479–480
marketing intermediaries in, 474–475
vertical marketing systems and, 478–479
Distribution systems, corporate, 478–479
Distribution traffic managers, 535
Diversification, 726
Diversity. *See also* Culture
best companies for managing, 291
color preferences and, 461–462
as competitive advantage, 290–291
immigration and, 32–33
management of, 234–235, 289–291, 296
trends resulting in, 32
Dividend reinvestment plan (DRIP), 727
Division of labor, 246–247
Doppelmeyer, Arthur, 412
Double-entry bookkeeping, 578
Dow Jones Industrial Average (DJIA), 690–692
Downsizing, 39
Drop shippers, 483
Drucker, Peter, 88
Dual-income families, 29
Dumping, 124
Duration of benefits, 723, 725

E

Earned income, 718–719
Earnings
of college graduates, 1
retained, 583, 649–650, 673
Earnings per share (EPS), 589
e-commerce cases
Alliance Web site and, 364
Boston Beer Company, 662
Calbert Group, 334
CCBN, 601
DoubleClick, 530–531
E*Trade Group, 702
First Capital International, 146–147
Geekcorps, 102–103
General Motors, 398
Lands' End, 470–471
MaidPro, 178–179
NetBank, 632
Netflix, 499–500
online financial advisors, 736–737
Oracle, 268–269
Orbitz, 75–76
Powell's Books, 46–47
PrintingForLess.com, 212–213
Staples, 242–243
Taco John's, 304
U.S. Army, 434–435
Wineaccess.com, 566
Economic environment, 134–136
Economic growth, 52–53
Economic publications, 686–687
Economic systems
capitalism and, 34–35
command economy and, 35
description of, 33, 37, 43, 50
mixed, 36
socialism and, 35
trends in, 67–69
Economics. *See also* Macroeconomics; Microeconomics
as circular flow, 52
explanation of, 50
subareas of, 50–51
EDGAR, 686
Edmondson, David, 450
Education. *See also* College
benefits of, 1
employee motivation and, 325–326
loans for, 9
Effective consumer response (ECR), 486
Elderly individuals, 31–32
Electronic communications networks (ECNs), 683
Electronic data interchange (EDI), 381, 486
Electronic fund transfers (EFTs), 709–710
Elimination period, 723
Ellison, Larry, 268, 269
El-Mansy, Youssef Aly, 74
Embargos, 123
Emergency funds, 725
Emotional intelligence, 279
Employee absenteeism, 327
Employee compensation
collective bargaining and, 349–350
executive, 286–287
factors affecting, 283–284
motivation and, 321
types of, 284–286
Employee motivation. *See* Motivation; Motivation theory
Employee ownership programs, 326
Employee Retirement Income Security Act, 292
Employee testing, 278–279
Employee training
employee motivation and, 325–326
on ethics, 83–84
function of, 280–281
off-the-job, 282
on-the-job, 281
Employees
demotion of, 288
disabled, 278
empowerment of, 89, 226, 234, 320–321
incentives for, 321
in overseas assignments, 280
performance planning and evaluation of, 282–283
promotion of, 287
recognition of, 320
recruitment of, 276–277
redefining employer relationship with, 94
responsibility to, 89
scheduling options for, 319–320
selection of, 277–280
separation of, 288–289
in small businesses, 198–199
transfer of, 287
Employment. *See also* Careers; Job interviews; Jobs
during college, 10
full, 53
interviewing for, 17–20
making choices for, 20
part-time, 275
relocating for, 20
skills for, 14
tips for finding, 14–16
using Internet to search for, 16–17
Empowerment
of employees, 89, 226, 234
methods to gain, 3
motivation and, 320–321
Enterprise portals, 557
Enterprise resource planning (ERP), 380, 397, 539
Entrepreneurs. *See also* Small businesses
characteristics of successful, 185–187
classic, 183–184
entrepreneur, 184
explanation of, 26–27, 182

immigrant, 33
motives of, 184–185
multipreneur, 184
in Russia and China, 68–69
Entrepreneurship. *See also* Small businesses
explanation of, 182
small business vs., 183
statistics regarding, 182
trends in, 182–183, 200–204
Environmental protection, 92
Environmental Protection Agency (EPA), 106
Environmental scanning, 410
E-procurement, 380–381
Equal Credit Opportunity Act, 112, 618–619
Equal Pay Act, 292
Equilibrium, 61–63
Equity, 196
Equity financing
common stock and, 647–649
debt financing vs., 645–646
dividends and retained earnings and, 649–650
preferred stock and, 650–651
venture capital and, 651
Equity theory, 316–317
e-quotient, 279
Essay tests, 12
Ethics
codes of, 85, 86
explanation of, 80
individual rights and, 80
influence of organizations on, 83–85
justice and, 81
purchasing power and, 66
recognizing breaches in business, 81–83
resolving problems related to, 96, 98
responsibilities to stakeholders and, 89–94
social responsibility and, 85, 87–88, 94–95
utilitarianism and, 80
Ethics-training programs, 83–84
European Commission, 128
European Community Bank, 128
European Union (EU)
explanation of, 126–127
objectives of, 127–128, 139
Event sponsorships, 520
Eways, Eric, 485
Exchange, 406
Exchange controls, 124
Exchange rates, 120
Excise taxes, 113
Exclusive distribution, 479
Executive compensation, 286–287
Executive information systems (EISs), 549
Executive management information system (EMIS), 549
Expansionary policy, 57
Expectancy theory, 316–318
Expense products, 440
Expenses
long-term, 642–643
operating, 584–585, 640–642
short-term, 640–642
Experiments, 424
Expert power, 223
Expert systems, 549
Export management companies (EMCs), 199–200
Exports. *See also* Trade
explanation of, 38, 118
United States and, 129–130
Express contracts, 106
Express warranties, 108, 446
Extensive decision making, 419
External environment, 409–410

F

Factoring, 645
Factors of production, 25–26
Factory-simulation tools, 390–391
Fair Credit Reporting Act, 112
Fair Debt Collection Practice Act, 112
Fair Labor Standards Act, 291–293
Fair Packaging and Labeling Act, 112
Families, dual-income, 29
Family and Medical Leave Act, 292, 293
Farid, Teriq, 162
Fast-food industry, trends in, 27
Fastow, Andy, 652
Federal budget deficit, 58–59
Federal Deposit Insurance Corporation (FDIC), 615–619
Federal Insurance Contribution Act (FICA), 719
Federal Mediation and Conciliation Service, 344
Federal Open Market Committee (FOMC), 610
Federal Reserve Districts, 610
Federal Reserve System (Fed)
check clearing role of, 612–613
credit rule-setting by, 611–612
currency distribution by, 612
function of, 56–57, 609–610, 618
policy of, 610–611
Federal Savings and Loan Insurance Corporation (FSLIC), 618
Federal Trade Commission Act, 110
Federal Trade Commission (FTC)
explanation of, 105, 106
franchising and, 172
Federal Trade Commission Improvement Act, 446–447
Federal Universal Service Fund, 105
Fidelity bonds, 669
Field, Andrew, 212–213
Filing status, 718
Finance. *See* Personal finance
Finance companies, 617–618
Financial accounting, 572
Financial Accounting Standards Board (FASB), 572, 592, 594
Financial aid, 9–10
Financial careers, 738–740
Financial institutions
customer satisfaction and, 627
depository, 613–616
explanation of, 613
insuring bank deposits and, 618–619
international banking and, 619–620
nondepository, 616–617
services provided by, 623
trends in, 621–625
Financial intermediation, 613, 614
Financial management
capital expenditures and, 642–643
explanation of, 636–637
goals of, 638
long-term financing and, 645–651
operating expenses and, 640–642
planning process and, 638–640
responsibilities and activities of, 637–638
short-term financing and, 643–645
trends in, 651–654
Financial managers, function of, 637–638
Financial planners, 738–739
Financial planning
budgets and, 639–640
explanation of, 638–639
forecasting and, 639
personal, 707–708
Financial publications, 686–687
Financial Services Modernization Act, 623
Financial statements
analysis of, 586–590
balance sheets, 579–583
income statements, 583–585
statement of cash flows, 585, 586
Fine, Deborah I., 405
Fiorina, Carly, 219, 556
Firmaini, Mark, 315
Fiscal policy, 57–59
Fisher, Dan, 235
Fixed assets, 580
Fixed-position layout, 377
Flammable Fabrics Act, 112
Flexible manufacturing system (FMS), 387
Flextime, 319–320
Floating exchange rates, 120
Focus groups, 449
Food, Drug, and Cosmetic Act, 112
Food and Drug Administration (FDA), 106
Ford, Bill, 240
Forecasting, 275–276
Forecasts, 639–640
Formal organization, 246
Forward integration, 478–479
Four Ps, 414
Framework for Global Electronic Commerce, 112
France
economic system in, 35
trade and, 117
trade policies and, 123–124
Franchise agreements, 164
Franchise World Magazine, 172
Franchisees, 163–164
Franchises
advantages of, 164
disadvantages of, 164–165
examples of, 162
explanation of, 130–131, 162–163
gaining information about, 172
in global marketplace, 130–131, 165–166
growth of, 165
list of low-investment, 163
online auctions for, 168

trends in, 169–170
Franchisors, 163
Free trade, 121
Freeman, Douglas, 632
Free-rein leadership, 225
Free-trade zones, 126
Freilich, Joan, 655
Frequency, 508
Frictional unemployment, 54
Fringe benefits, 285–286
Full employment, 53
Full warranty, 448
Fulton, Tim, 85
Functional departmentalization, 247
Futures contracts, 678

G

GAAP Convergence 2002 project, 573
Gaffney, Paul, 242
Gain-sharing plans, 321
Gannon, Bill, 84
Gantt charts, 382–383
Gates, Bill, 27, 190, 217, 237
Geller, Matthew, 162
General Agreement on Tariffs and Trade (GATT), 125, 591
General obligation bonds, 676
General partners, 153
General partnerships, 153
Generally accepted accounting principles (GAAP), 572, 573, 592
Generation X, 31
Generation Y, 30
Generic products, 444
Genin, Alex, 147
Geographic departmentalization, 248
Geographic segmentation, 421
Germany, trade and, 117
Gifford, Charles, 621
Gillis, Ruth Ann M., 655
Givens, Beth, 302
Glass-Steagall Act of 1933, 623
Global competition. *See also* Competition
human resource management and, 296–297
laws to promote fair, 110–112
productivity and, 38–39
technology and, 38
terrorism and, 39–40
trends in, 138–139
Global managers
role of, 141–142
skills for, 232–233
Global marketplace
accounting issues and, 573
background of, 116–117
competition in, 110–112, 138–139
contract manufacturing and, 131
countertrade and, 132–133
cultural issues and, 133–135
direct foreign investment and, 132
economic environment and, 134–136
exporting and, 129–130
franchises in, 130–131, 165–166
international economic communities and, 126–128
joint ventures and, 131–132
licensing and, 130–131
manufacturing issues and, 374–375
multinational corporations and, 136–138
political issues and, 133
small businesses and, 199–200
terrorism and, 117–118
trade and, 118–125 (*See also* Trade)
United States and, 117
unity of command and, 251
Globalization, 121, 122
Goal-setting theory, 317
Goizueta, Roberto, 281
Golden parachute, 287
Golisano, B. Thomas, 233
Gonzalez, Tony, 295
Goodnight, James H., 241
Goods, 24
Goodwill, 582
Gore-Tex, 279
Gourdon, Jean, 430
Grace period, 714
Gramm-Leach-Bliley Act of 1999, 623
Grants, 9
Gray, Diana, 194
Gray, Douglas, 194
Great Britain
economic system in, 35, 36
labor unions in, 351
trade and, 117
Grenier, Jim, 321
Grid computing, 557–559
Grievance, 350–352
Gross domestic product (GDP), 38, 52
Gross profit, 584
Gross sales, 583
Group behavior
cohesiveness and, 322
explanation of, 321–322
teams and, 323–325
Group norms, 260
Grove, Andrew, 290
Gruner, Ron, 700
Gryfe, Shelly Glick, 434
Guerrero, Joe, 485
Guerrilla marketing, 523

H

Halsall, Peter, 250
Hand, Learned, 104
Harkins, Ana Marie, 102
Harp, Autumn, 315
Harper, Kevin, 315
Harris, Margrit, 325
Hart, Myra M., 202
Hastings, Reed, 500
Hawthorne effect, 310
Hawthorne studies, 309–310
Hazen, Paul, 162
Health insurance
explanation of, 721–722
major medical insurance, 722
managed care, 722–723
Health maintenance organizations (HMOs), 722
Hebert, Michelle, 155, 160
Helfrich, David, 650
Henley, Jeff, 268
Herscovitz, Marcia, 152
Herz, Robert, 592–593
Herzberg, Frederick, 313, 314
Herzenberg, Stephen, 364
Hierarchy of needs, 31–311, 318
Higgins, Glenn, 278
High-yield bonds, 675
Hillman, Sidney, 339
Hispanics
color preferences and, 462
demographic trends of, 32, 33, 294
recruitment of, 295
as small-business owners, 203
HIV/AIDS, 292
Hoefler, Brent, 304
Holzschuh, Franz, 115
Homeowners insurance, 721
Horizontal mergers, 168
Horn, Julie, 304
Hotel and motel management, 400–401
Hughes, Christine, 141
Human relations skills, 232
Human resource (HR) planning
explanation of, 273–274
forecasting and, 275–276
job analysis and design and, 274
Human resource management
careers in, 402
diversity and, 289–291, 296
employee compensation and benefits and, 283–287
employee recruitment and, 276–277, 295
employee selection and, 277–280
employee training and development, 280–282
explanation of, 272–273
laws affecting, 278, 291–295
organizational career management and, 287–289
performance planning and evaluation and, 282–283
technology and, 296–297
whistleblower protection and, 295
Human rights, 80, 95
Hund, Gerg, 170
Hunegnaw, Dave, 193
Hunt, Isaac, 575
Hunter, Billy, 354
Hurt, Brett, 198
Hygiene factors, 313–314

I

Iacocca, Lee, 2
Ideal self-image, 417
Identity theft, 302–303
Identity Theft and Assumption Deterrence Act of 1998, 302, 728
Image, creation of, 486–487
Immigration
demographic shifts in, 32–33
terrorism and, 117–118
Immigration Reform and Control Act, 292

Implied contracts, 106–107
Implied warranties, 108, 446
Imports, 118–119, 123. *See also* Trade
Incentive programs, 321
Income statements
expenses and, 583–585
explanation of, 583
net profit or loss and, 585
revenues and, 583
Income taxes, 113, 717–719
Indemnity plans, 722
Individuals rights, 80
Industrial distributors, 474
Industrial production management, 401–402
Industrial unions, 339
Inflation, 55–56
Informal organization, 259–260
Information technology (IT)
careers in, 603–605
computer networks and, 539–544
customer satisfaction and, 561
explanation of, 538
function of, 538–539
management and planning for, 234, 550–552
management information systems and, 544–550
protecting computers and information and, 552–556
trends in, 556–559
Informational labeling, 445–446
Informational role, 229, 230
Infrastructure, 134, 136
Initial public offering (IPO), 647, 649, 650
Injunctions, 341, 343
Inputs
availability of production, 373–374
converted to outputs, 371, 372
Insider trading, 685
Insider Trading and Fraud Act of 1988, 685
Institutional advertising, 507–508
Institutional investors, 678–679
Insurable interest, 665
Insurable risks, 665–666
Insurance
business liability, 669
disability income, 723
explanation of, 664–666
government-sponsored, 666–667
health, 721–723
life, 723–724
premium costs and, 666
property and liability, 668, 720–721
public, 666–667
selecting personal, 720–724
self-, 664–665
unemployment, 667
Insurance companies, 616, 667
Intangible assets, 582
Integrated marketing communications (IMC), 506
Intensive distribution, 480
Interest, 675
Intermittent process, 371
Internal Revenue Code, 104
International Accounting Standards Board (IASB), 573
International Accounting Standards Committee, 572–573
International Financial Reporting Standards (IFRS), 573
International Monetary Fund (IMF), 121, 125
Internet. *See also* e-commerce cases; Web sites
advertising on, 522–523
banking services on, 623–625, 716
connecting appliances to, 49
global marketplace and, 138–139
investing on, 679–680, 736–737
labor unions and, 362, 364
legal issues related to, 199
marketing research using, 426
procurement using, 380–381
regulation of, 111–112
retailing on, 485
small business formation and, 189, 203–204
Interpersonal role, 229, 230
Interpersonal skills, 2–5
Interviews, employment, 279
Intranets, 541–542
Intrapreneurs, 184
Inventory
management of, 378
as short-term expense, 641–642
turnover ratios for, 589
Investment Advisers Act of 1940, 685
Investment bankers, 679
Investment Company Act of 1940, 685
Investment information
company financial reports, 686
economic and financial publications, 686–687
importance of, 685
market averages and indexes, 690–691
online, 687
security price quotations, 687–690
Investors
decision making by, 724–727
rebuilding confidence of, 693–694
responsibility to, 93
Involuntary bankruptcy, 110
Involvement, 418
ISO 9000, 386
ISO 14000, 386
Ivester, Douglas, 281

J

Jacobs, Harvey, 199
Jain, Susan, 397
Japan
customer satisfaction and quality issues in, 141
dishwashers in, 453
dumping and, 124
management approaches in, 312, 313
Job analysis, 274
Job boards, online, 17
Job description, 274
Job enlargement, 319
Job enrichment, 319
Job fairs, 276, 277
Job hopping, 42
Job interviews
preparation for, 17–18
tips for, 18–20
Job promotion, 287
Job rotation, 281, 319
Job security, 350
Job sharing, 320
Job shop, 370
Job specification, 274
Jobs. *See also* Careers; Employment
gaining first, 14–16
getting promoted in, 21
interviews for, 17–20
making choices for, 20
skills for, 14
starting first, 20–21
starting new, 20–21
using Internet to search for, 16–17
JobTrak, 16
Johnson, Dana, 84
Johnson, Rachetta, 26
Johnson, Ricardo, 26
Joint ventures
explanation of, 131, 162
in global marketplace, 131–132
Jones, Charles, 45
Jones, Tim, 333
Jospin, Lionel, 35
Judiciary, 105
Junk bonds, 675
Justice, 81
Just-in-time (JIT), 386

K

Katz, Jeff, 76
Kaucic, Lou, 232
Keirsey Character Sorter, 14
Kelleher, Herb, 287
Kershner, Robin, 580
KhiMetrics, 460
Kilts, Jim, 221
King, Stephen, 190
Kinzel, Dick, 643
Knautz, Cynthia, 392
Knights of Labor, 338
Knowledge, 27
Knowledge management (KM), 551
Knowledge workers, 326–327, 538
Kozlowski, Dennis, 79, 95, 97
Kruse, Douglas, 326
Kuhlmann, Arkadi, 630
Kurth, George, 236
Kurtz, Jeff, 379
Kushinsky, Mark, 179

L

Labeling, 445–446
Labor, 26
Labor force
shortage of skilled workers in, 356
trends in, 40–41
women in, 29, 42

Labor strikes, 343, 352–354
Labor unions
contract negotiation and, 347–350
explanation of, 338
in Great Britain, 351
grievance procedure and, 350–354
historical background of, 338–339
legal environment of, 341–345
local, 340
membership in, 356
national and international, 340–341
organizing campaigns of, 345–347
strategies of, 352–354
Labor-management relations
customer satisfaction and, 358
managing conflict in, 351–355
trends in, 355–356
Labor-Management Relations Act (Taft-Hartley Act), 343, 344, 348, 359
Labor-Management Reporting and Disclosure Act (Landrum-Griffin Act), 345
Lafley, A. G., 220–221, 437, 673, 696
Lagman, Randy, 287–288
Laissez-faire leadership, 225
LaManchusa, Kathy, 461
Landrum-Griffin Act, 345
Lane, Ray, 268–269
Language, 134
LaPrade, Burch, 203, 204
Lauren, Dylan, 186, 187
Law of large numbers, 665
Laws. *See also* Legal system
administrative, 104
bankruptcy, 99, 110
business, 99, 104–105
common, 104
contract, 106–108
explanation of, 104
product-liability, 99, 109–110
to promote fair competition, 110–112
statutory, 104
tort, 99
Lay, Kenneth L., 34, 569
Layoffs, 288
Le Gette, Brian, 149, 174
Leader pricing, 458
Leadership
corporate culture and, 226–227
empowerment by, 226
explanation of, 223–224
styles of, 224–225
Leadership power, 223
Lean manufacturing, 386
Legal rights, 80
Legal system. *See also* Laws
arbitration and, 106
bankruptcy and, 110
contracts and, 106–108
fair competition and, 110–112
function of, 99, 104
judiciary and, 105
mediation and, 106
patents, copyrights, and trademarks and, 108–109
product liability and, 109–110
torts and, 109
types of law and, 104–105
warranties and, 108
Legitimate power, 223
Lekwa, Neal, 334
Leveraged buyouts (LBOs), 169
Levy, Jack, 171
Lewis, David, 724
Lewis, John L., 339, 340
Liabilities, personal, 708
Liability
current, 582
explanation of, 577, 578
long-term, 582
product, 109–110
strict, 109
Liability insurance, 668, 669, 720–721
Libel, 109
Library of Congress, 65
Licensing, 130–131
Life insurance, 723–724
Lifestyles, 29
Limited decision making, 418–419
Limited liability companies (LLCs), 149, 160
Limited liability partnerships (LLPs), 154
Limited partners, 153
Limited partnerships, 153
Limited-service merchant wholesalers, 482, 483
Lindsay, Richard, 662
Line extension, 447, 448
Line of credit, 643, 713–714
Line organization, 255, 256
Line positions, 255, 256
Line-and-staff organization, 255–256
Liquid assets, 709
Liquidity, 579
Liquidity ratios, 587
Listening skills, 2
Litow, Stan, 93
Livengood, Scott, 657
Loans
bank, 643–644
consumer, 715–716
explanation of, 9
mortgage, 647
secured, 645
term, 646–647
unsecured, 643
Local area networks (LANs), 540
Local unions, 340
Location
production planning and, 372–375
retail, 488
Lock, Tony, 564
Lockouts, 337, 343, 354
Logistics, 489–490
Long-term forecasts, 639
Long-term liabilities, 582
Loyalty cards, 427–428
Lullien, Jarrett, 702

M

M1, 609
M2, 609
MacKay, Gene H., III, 565–566
Macroeconomics
economic growth and, 52–53
employment and, 53–54
explanation of, 50, 52
fiscal policy and, 57–59
monetary policy and, 56–57
prices and, 55–56
Madden, Orval, 315
Magnuson-Moss Warranty Act, 112, 446
Maiffret, Mark, 155
Mail Fraud Act, 112
Major medical insurance, 722
Make-or-buy decisions, 377–378
Malcolm Baldridge National Quality Award, 385
Managed care plans, 722–723
Management. *See also* Human resource management
city, 401
college recruiting, 402–403
corporate training, 402
of diversity, 234–235, 289–291, 296
explanation of, 218
hotel and motel, 400–401
industrial production, 401–402
middle, 223
plant health and safety, 402
purchasing, 401
quality control, 401
scientific, 308–309
supervisory, 223
top, 222
trends in, 234–235
Management information systems
decision support, 548
executive, 549
expert, 549
explanation of, 544–546
management support, 547–548
office automation, 549–550
transaction processing, 546–547
Management information systems (MIS), 538–539
Management support systems (MSSs), 547
Managerial accounting, 571–572, 605
Managerial hierarchy, 248–251
Managers
controlling function of, 228–229
crisis management and, 235
cultural diversity and, 234–235
decision-making function of, 229–231
employee empowerment and, 234
entrepreneurs as, 186–187
information technology and, 234
leading function of, 223–227
organizing function of, 222
planning function of, 218–222
skills of, 231–233
time management by, 236–237
Mancuso, Mary, 541–542
Mandell, Steve, 170
Mangan, Mona, 363
Manufacturer brands, 444
Manufacturer's representative, 534
Manufacturing
cellular, 377
contract, 131
environment for, 374
explanation of, 474

facility design and, 375–377
in foreign locations, 374–375
lean, 386
process, 371
technology applications for, 386–388
Manufacturing resource planning II (MRPII), 379–380
Margin requirements, 612
Market averages, 690
Market indexes, 690–691
Market researchers, 533–534
Market risk, 653
Market segmentation
benefit, 422
demographic, 420–421
explanation of, 420
geographic, 421
psychographic, 422
volume, 422
Market structures
explanation of, 63, 67
monopolistic competition, 65–66
oligopoly, 66–67
perfect competition, 64–65
pure monopoly, 65
Marketable securities, 641
Marketing
careers in, 533–535
explanation of, 406
guerrilla, 523
location and, 374
one-to-one, 428
social, 414–415
Marketing concept
customer satisfaction and, 407
customer value and, 407
explanation of, 406–407
relationship building and, 407–409
Marketing database, 428
Marketing mix
distribution strategy and, 414
explanation of, 412
in not-for-profits, 414–415
pricing strategy and, 413
product strategy and, 413
production strategy and, 414
Marketing research
customer satisfaction and, 430
explanation of, 423
Internet use for, 426
scanner-based, 426–427
steps in, 423–425
types of, 423–425
Marketing strategy
buyer behavior and, 415–420
competitive advantage and, 411–413
creating marketing mix and, 413–415
defining target market and, 410–411
external environment and, 409–410
market segmentation and, 420–422
Markfield, Roger, 251
Markhoff, Katrina, 183–184
Markup pricing, 456
Marshall, Colin, 407
Martinez, Arthur, 290–291
Maslow, Abraham, 310, 311
Mass customization, 370, 371, 490–491
Mass production, 370, 371
Master brands, 442, 443
Materials requirement planning (MRP), 379, 380
Materials-handling systems, 491
Matrix structure, 257–258
Mayo, Elton, 309
McClelland, Geoff, 543
McCorey, William E., Jr., 551
McCullough, Stuart, 407
McGregor, Douglas, 312
McGuire, Joe, 660
McKenty, Elizabeth, 721
Mechanistic organization, 253–254
Mediation, 106, 344
Medicaid, 286
Medicare, 285–286, 667, 719
Medina, Tom, 204
Melancon, Barry, 592
Memory devices, 10–11
Mentoring, 281
Merage, Paul, 23
Merchant wholesalers
explanation of, 481–482
full-service, 482
limited-service, 482, 483
Mercosur, 126, 139
Mergers
banking, 621–622
effects of, 173–174
emerging truths regarding, 170–171
explanation of, 166–167
list of large, 167
motives for, 167–168
structuring for global, 262–263
types of, 168–169
Messmer, Max, 226
Mexico, 126
Miami, Florida, 26, 27
Microeconomics
demand and, 60, 63
explanation of, 50–51, 59–60
market equilibrium and, 61–63
supply and, 60–61, 63–64
Microelectromechanical systems (MEMS), 37
Micromarketing, 428
Middle management, 223
Minnesota Clerical Test, 278
Minorities. *See also* Diversity; *specific minorities*
in accounting, 605
affirmative action and, 294
recruitment of, 295
as small-business owners, 192, 203
Mission, 219
Mission statement, 219
Mitnick, Kevin, 555
Mitterrand, François, 35
Mixed economy, 36, 37
Mnemonic sentences, 10–11
Mobility, trends in, 32
Modular production, 390
Monetary policy
explanation of, 56–57
Fed and, 610–611
Money
characteristics of, 608
explanation of, 608
function of, 608–609
supply of, 609
Moneypenny, Ed, 652
Monopolistic competition, 65–66
Monroe, Charlene, 26
Moore, Gordon, 74
Morgan, Carl, 454–455
Morgan, Kelly, 101
Morrison, Nettie, 642
Morse, Larry, 203
Mortgage bonds, 675
Mortgage loans, 647
Morton, Jill, 462
Motivation
absenteeism and, 327
customer satisfaction and, 328–329
education and training and, 325–326
employee ownership and, 326
empowerment and, 320–321
group behavior and, 321–322
incentives and, 321
job design and, 319
knowledge workers and, 326–327
recognition and, 320
in small businesses, 315
teams and, 323–325
tips for, 12
work groups vs. work teams and, 323
work-life benefits and, 326
work-schedule options and, 319–320
Motivation theory
culture and, 318
equity theory, 316–317
expectancy theory, 316
goal-setting theory, 317
Hawthorne studies, 309–310
hierarchy of needs, 310–311
motivator-hygiene theory, 313–314
scientific management, 308–309
theory X and theory Y, 312
theory Z, 312–313
Motivator-hygiene theory, 313–314
Multinational corporations. *See also* Corporations; Global competition; Global marketplace
advantages of, 137–138
banking services for, 619–620
explanation of, 136
list of largest, 137
Multipreneurs, 184
Municipal bonds, 676
Murray, Carolyn, 279
Mutual funds
explanation of, 677–678
quotations for, 689
Mutual insurance companies, 667
Mutual-aid pact, 355
Myers-Briggs Type Indicator, 278

N

Nadhirz, Saad, 136
Napoleonic Code, 104
Nardone, Paul, 211, 212
Nasser, Jacques, 240
National Advertising Division (NAD) (Council

of Better Business Bureaus), 509–511
National Advertising Review Board (NARB), 509, 511
National Association of Securities Dealers Automated Quotation (Nasdaq) system, 682, 683
National Credit Union Share Insurance Fund, 618
National debt, 59
National Environmental Policy Act, 104
National Labor Relations Act (Wagner Act), 342–343
National Labor Relations Board (NLRB), 343, 345
National unions, 340–341
Nationalism, 133
Natural resources, 26
Net asset value (NAV), 689–690
Net loss, 585
Net profit, 585
Net profit margin, 588–589
Net sales, 583
Net working capital, 587
Network administrators, 605
New Markets Venture Capital Program, 192
Niche competitive advantage, 412–413
Niche job boards, 17
Nondepository institutions, 616–618
Nonprogrammed decisions, 229–231
Norris-LaGuardia Act, 342
North American Free Trade Agreement (NAFTA), 126, 128, 139
Not-for-profit organizations
  explanation of, 25
  marketing mix and, 414–415
  standard of living and, 42
Nottingham, John R., 437
Nussbaum, Ed, 592
Nutrition, 8
Nutrition Labeling and Education Act of 1990, 112, 445–446

O

Objective tests, skills for, 12
Observation research, 424
Occupational Outlook Handbook, 15
Occupational Safety and Health Act, 292
O'Connell, Susan, 289
Odd-even pricing, 459
O'Donnell, James, 251
Office automation systems, 549–550
Offshore virtual corporations, 255
Off-the-job training, 282
Ohrstein, Matthew, 173
Older Boomers, 31
Oldroyd, David, 564–565
Oligopoly, 66–67
On-demand computing, 557–559
One-to-one marketing, 428
Online investing, 679–680, 687, 688
On-the-job training, 281–282
Open houses, recruitment, 277
Open market operations, 611
Open shop, 348
Operating budgets, 640
Operating expenses
  explanation of, 584–585
  management of, 640–642
Operational planning, 220–222
Operational risk, 653
Operations management
  asset management and, 389
  automation and, 388
  customer satisfaction and, 392
  explanation of, 368–369
  lean manufacturing and, 386
  production efficiency and, 390–391
  production planning and, 369–381 (*See also* Production planning)
  quality and, 384–386
  routing and, 381
  scheduling and, 382–384
  technology and, 386–388
Opinion leaders, 416–417
Options, 678
Ore, Norbert, 389
Organic organization, 253–254
Organization chart, 247
Organizational career management
  job change with organization and, 287–288
  separations and, 288–289
Organizational structures
  centralization of decision making and, 252–253
  committee, 256–257
  departmentalization and, 247–248
  division of labor and, 246–247
  explanation of, 246, 263
  flat, 253, 254
  global mergers and, 262–263
  informal, 259–260
  line, 255
  line-and-staff, 255–256
  managerial hierarchy and, 248–251
  matrix, 257–258
  mechanistic vs. organic, 253–254
  reengineering, 258–259
  span of control and, 251–252
  tall, 253, 254
  trends in, 260–263
Organizing
  explanation of, 222
  function of, 246
Osher, John, 437
Ouchi, William, 312
Outputs, converting inputs to, 371, 372
Outsourcing
  explanation of, 296, 377, 378
  trends toward, 190
Over-the-counter (OTC) market, 683, 685
Owners' equity, 577, 583

P

Packaging
  functions of, 444–445
  labels on, 445–446
Page, Larry, 181, 182
Panel Study on Entrepreneurial Dynamics (PSED), 183, 202
Panic pushers, 11
Parker, Michael, 203
Parsons, Dick, 646
Participative leadership, 225
Partnerships
  advantages of, 153, 161
  disadvantages of, 153–155, 161
  explanation of, 152–153
  general, 153
  individual characteristics for, 154
  limited, 153
Patents, 108, 582
Paull, Lindy, 595
Payroll taxes, 113
Penetration pricing, 457–458
Pension funds, 616–617
Pension Reform Act, 292
Perception, 418
Perfect competition, 64–65
Performance appraisal, 282–283
Performance bonds, 669
Perpetual inventory, 378
Personal exemptions, 718
Personal finance
  cash management and, 709–711
  consumer credit and, 711–717
  decision making regarding, 724–727
  insurance selection and, 720–724
  investing and, 727
  overview of, 706–707
  planning steps in, 707–708
  tax management and, 717–720
  trends in, 727–729
Personal identification number (PIN), 709–710
Personal selling
  advantages of, 512–513
  employment opportunities in, 513
  explanation of, 505, 512
  process of, 514–516
  professional, 513
Personality, 417
Persuasion, 2
Persuasive labeling, 445
Peru, 133–134
Peterson's Business and Management Jobs, 15
Philanthropy, corporate, 92–94
Philyaw, J. Jovan, 450
Physical distribution. *See* Distribution; Distribution channels
Physical exams, for job candidates, 280
Pianalto, Antonella, 76
Pickens, T. Boone, 696
Picketing, 354
Piece-rate pay plans, 321
Piecework, 284
Pinochot, Gifford, 184
Planning
  contingency, 220–222
  effects of, 220
  life, 6–8
  operational, 220, 221
  role of, 5
  strategic, 219, 220

tactical, 219–221
Planning process, 5–6
Plans, 5, 7
Plant health and safety officers, 402
Point-of-sale (POS) transfers, 709, 710
Polis, Jared, 184, 185
Politics
effective handling of organizational, 3
in global marketplace, 133
Polonetsky, Jules, 531
Portfolios, 726
Positive thinking, 12–13
Pottruck, David, 671
Poverty, trade and, 122
Powell, Michael, 46–47
Powell, Walter, 46
Power, 223–224
Praise, importance of, 2
Pratt, Dale, 262
Pratt, Mike, 182, 183
Preferential tariffs, 126
Preferred provider organizations (PPOs), 722–723
Preferred stock, 650–651, 674–675
Pregnancy Discrimination Act, 292
Premium costs, 666
Prepayment penalties, 715
Prestige pricing, 459
Price skimming, 457
Price/earnings (P/E) ratios, 688
Pricing. *See also* Product pricing
inflation and, 55–56
leader, 458
markup, 456
odd-even, 459
penetration, 457–458
prestige, 459
regulation of, 111
retail, 488
strategies for, 413
value, 455
Primary data, 424
Primary markets, 680
Principal, 675, 715
Principle of comparative advantage, 121
Private accountants, 574
Process departmentalization, 248
Process layout, 375, 376
Process manufacturing, 371
Producer price index (PPI), 56
Producers' cooperatives, 483
Product advertising, 507
Product departmentalization, 248
Product development
Internet use and, 459–460
organizing for, 447
process of, 447–451
role of product manager in, 451
Product layout, 377
Product liability, 668
Product managers, 451, 534
Product offering, development of, 486
Product pricing. *See also* Pricing
bundling and, 458
leader, 458
objectives of, 454
odd-even, 459
overview of, 452–454
penetration, 457–458
prestige, 459
price skimming and, 457
profit maximization and, 454–455
target return on investment and, 455
techniques for, 455–457
value, 455
yield management systems and, 460
Product strategy, 413
Production
customization, 370–371
explanation of, 368
mass, 370, 371
mass customization, 370
modular, 390
Production orientation, 406–407
Production planning
explanation of, 369–370
facility design and, 375–377
location issues and, 372–375
production process and, 370–372
resource planning and, 377–380
supply chain management and, 380–381
Production process, 370
Production scheduling, 490–491
Production strategy, 414
Productivity
comparative advantage and, 122
explanation of, 36
technology to improve, 388
trends in, 38–39
Product-liability law, 99, 109–110
Products
branding of, 441–444
business, 440–441
capital, 440
color and, 460–462
consumer, 439–440
convenience, 439
expense, 440
explanation of, 438–439
generic, 444
life cycle of, 451–453
packaging of, 444–447
shopping, 440
specialty, 440
unsought, 439
Professional employer organization (PEO), 276
Professional liability insurance, 669
Profit, 25
Profit maximization, 454–455
Profit sharing, 284–285
Profitability ratios, 588–589
ProfitLogic, 460
Profit-sharing plans, 321
Program evaluation and review technique (PERT), 383–384
Programmed decisions, 229
Programmed instruction, 282
Progressive tax, 717
Promotion. *See also* Sales promotion
explanation of, 504
goals of, 504–505
job, 287
strategy for, 486–487
technology use in, 523
trends in, 522–523
Promotional mix
advertising and, 506–512
explanation of, 505–506
factors affecting, 520–521
personal selling and, 512–516
public relations and, 519–520
sales promotion and, 516–518
Property insurance, 668
Property taxes, 720–721
explanation of, 113
Prospecting, 514
Protected classes, 294
Protectionism, 121
Protective tariffs, 122
Psychographic segmentation, 422
Psychological pricing, 459
Public accountants, 574, 605
Public Company Accounting Oversight Board (PCAOB), 576
Public relations
explanation of, 506, 519
functions of, 519–520
role of, 414
Public utilities, 65
Publicity, 519, 520
Public-relations agents, 534
Pull strategy, 521, 522
Purcell, Philip J., 701
Purchasing, 377, 490
Purchasing management, 401
Purchasing power, 55, 66
Pure Food and Drug Act, 112
Pure monopoly, 65
Push strategy, 521, 522

Q

Qualifying questions, 514–515
Quality
explanation of, 384
global marketplace and, 141
importance of, 41
Quality control
Baldrige Award and, 385
explanation of, 384–385
methods of, 385
standards for, 386
Quality control managers, 401
Quality of life, 25
Quick-Books, 578

R

Rack jobbers, 483
Radio frequency identification (RFID) tags, 487
Ramani, Srinivasan, 130
Ramirez, Monica, 203
Ratio analysis, 586–587
Ravden, Linda, 152
Reach, 508
Reagan, Ronald, 69

Real GDP, 52
Real self-image, 417
Recession, 52
Recruitment, 276–277
Reengineering, 258–259
Reference checks, 279
Reference groups, 416–417
Referent power, 223
Regulation FD, 693
Reitzle, Wolfgang, 28, 240
Relationship management, 67–68
Relationship marketing, 407–409
Reminder advertising, 507
Renters insurance, 721
Replacement cost coverage, 721
Reserve requirements, 611
Resource planning
computerized, 378–380
inventory and, 378
make-or-buy decisions and, 377–378
Résumés
posting digital version of, 16, 17
software to create, 16
tips for preparing, 16
Retail buyers, 533
Retailers
components of successful, 485–488
explanation of, 475, 483
return policies of, 494
types of, 483–485
Retained earnings, 583, 649–650, 673
Retirement, 289
Return on equity (ROE), 589
Returns, 638
Revenue, 25
Revenue bonds, 676
Revenues, 583
Reverse auctions, 380–381
Revolving credit agreements, 644
Revolving credit cards, 714
Reward power, 223
Reyes, George, 181
Richardson, Steve, 190
Right-to-work laws, 348
Riley Guide, 277
Risk
avoidance of, 664
credit, 653
explanation of, 25, 638, 664
financial, 646
insurable, 665–666
market, 653
operational, 653
reduction of, 665
speculative, 664
transference of, 665
Risk management
business liability insurance and, 669
explanation of, 664–665
insurance concepts and, 665–667
private insurance companies and, 667
property and liability insurance and, 668
terrorism and, 653
Risk-return trade-off, 638
Robinson-Patman Act, 111
Robotics, 387
Robson, Mike, 150, 151
Rocca, Mike, 297
Rogers, Steven, 170
Rollout, 450
Roosevelt, Franklin D., 618
Roughgarten, Trish, 74
Routine response behavior, 418
Routing, 381
Rowe, Derek, 132
Rubin, Jeff, 186, 187
Ruether, Walter, 339
Russia
devaluation in, 120
entrepreneurial spirit in, 68–69
Ryan, Kevin, 531

S

S corporations, 159
Salaries, 284. *See also* Employee compensation
Sales promotion. *See also* Promotion
explanation of, 516–517
objectives of, 517, 518
Sales prospects, 514
Sales taxes, 113, 720
Sarbanes-Oxley Act, 576–577, 590–592, 594, 601, 653, 655, 693, 700
Savings and loan associations (S&Ls), 615
Savings Association Insurance Fund (SAIF), 618
Savings bonds, 59
Savings instruments, 710, 711
Scanner-based research, 426–427
Schacht, Jack, 315
Scheduling
critical path method and, 383
explanation of, 382
Gantt charts and, 382–383
PERT and, 383–384
Scheele, Nick, 240
Schmidt, Eric E., 181
Schmidt-Holtz, Rolf, 245, 264
Scholarships, 9
Schwab, Charles, 671, 696
Scientific management, 308–309
Screening interviews, 19
Seasonal unemployment, 54
Secondary data, 424
Secondary markets, 680
Secured bonds, 675
Secured loans, 645
Securities. *See also specific securities*
equity, 672–675
explanation of, 672
government, 675–676
price quotations for, 687–688
Securities account executives, 739
Securities Act of 1933, 684–685
Securities analysts, 739–740
Securities Exchange Act of 1934, 685
Securities exchanges
explanation of, 680
foreign, 482
U.S. stock, 681–682
Securities markets
bull vs. bear, 683–684
explanation of, 678–679
online investing and, 679–680
over-the-counter, 683
regulation of, 684–685
role of investment bankers and stockbrokers and, 679
sources of information on, 685–691
stock exchange, 680–682
trends in, 691–694
types of, 680
Security requirements, 715
Segal, Gordon, 649
Selection interviews, 279
Selective credit controls, 612
Selective distribution, 479–480
Selective exposure, 418
Selective strike strategy, 353–354
Self-assessment, guidelines for, 13–14
Self-concept, 417
Self-insurance, 664–665
Self-knowledge, importance of, 13–14
Seller cooperatives, 162
Semel, Terry, 268
Seniority, 350
Separations, employee, 288–289
Service Corps of Retired Executives (SCORE), 192
Servicemarks, 108
Services, 24
Shareholders, 156–157
Sheets, Mary Ellen, 202–203
Sherman Antitrust Act of 1890, 110
Shop steward, 340
Shopping products, 440
Short-term forecasts, 639
Short-term loans, 645
Shroeger, Jennifer, 307
Sick-out, 354
Sifontes, Don Miguel, 101
Simpson, Derek, 351
Sinelli, Jeff, 163, 168
Six Sigma program, 384, 385
Skidmore, Rick, 206
Skilling, Jeffrey, 34, 569
Skolnick, Joel, 191
Slack, Michele, 531
Slander, 109
Small Business Investment Companies (SBICs), 191
Small businesses. *See also* Entrepreneurs; Entrepreneurship
advantages of, 190–191
characteristics of, 182, 188
employee motivation in, 315
entrepreneurship vs., 183
financial assistance for, 191–192, 625–626
global marketplace and, 199–200
hiring and retaining employees for, 198–199
impact of, 188–190
management assistance programs for, 192
outside consultants for, 198
relationships between banks and, 617
statistics regarding, 188, 189
steps to start, 192–198
trends for, 187–188, 200–204
working for, 205–206

Smith, Frederick, 236
Smith, Marty, 333
Social change
    component lifestyles and, 29
    effects of, 42
    explanation of, 28
    two-income families and, 29
Social investing, 93
Social marketing, 414–415
Social responsibility
    corporate, 87
    dimensions of, 88
    explanation of, 85, 87–88
    to stakeholders, 89–93
Social security, 285, 667
Social Security Act, 292
Social Security tax, 719–720
Socialism, 35, 37
Socialization process, 417
Society, responsibility to, 90–91
Software
    accounting, 578–579
    application service providers and, 543–544
    database management systems, 539
    language translation, 138–139
    logistics, 493
    WebResume, 16
Software piracy, 553
Sole proprietorships
    advantages of, 151, 161
    disadvantages of, 151–152, 161
    explanation of, 150–151
    women and, 202
Solheim, Karsten, 498–499
Sourcing, 490
Soviet Union, former, 35
Spam, 554
Span of control, 251–252
Spanx, 61
Specialization, 246–247
Specialty products, 440
Speculative risk, 664
Spirk, John W., 437
Stack, Louis, 660
Staff positions, 255–256
Stafford, Dan, 334
Stakeholders, responsibility to, 89–93
Standard & Poors 500 stock index, 690
Standard deductions, 718
Standard of living, 24, 42
Stanley Group, 320
Statement of cash flows, 585, 586
Statuatory law, 104
Stern, David, 354
Stevens, Robert, 178
Stock dividends, 649, 673
Stock insurance companies, 667
Stock options, 286
Stockbrokers, 679, 739
Stockholders, 156–157
Stocks
    common, 647–649, 673
    explanation of, 672–673
    preferred, 650–651, 674–675
    quotations for, 688–689
Stoklosa, Gregory A., 592
Straight life insurance, 724
Strategic alliances, 68
Strategic giving, 93
Strategic planning, 219, 220
Stress management, 237
Strict liability, 109
Strike replacements, 354–355
Structural unemployment, 54
Study skills, 10–11
Sullivan, Scott, 652
Sullivan, Thomas, 631
Supervisory management, 223
Supply
    changes in, 63–65
    explanation of, 60–61
    interaction between demand and, 61–63
Supply chain, 475
Supply chain management
    explanation of, 380–381, 474
    function of, 488–490
    materials handling and, 491
    production scheduling, 490–491
    sourcing and procurement and, 490
    transportation decisions and, 491, 492
    warehouse location and type and, 491
Supply curve, 61, 62
Supreme Court, U. S., 105
Surety bonds, 669
Survey research, 423, 425
Sutton, Michael H., 591
Swanson, Harold, 565
Swanson, Ruth, 565
Swartz, Mark, 79, 652
Sweeny, John, 340
Systems analysts, 604

T

Tactical planning, 219–221
Taft-Hartley Act. *See* Labor-Management Relations Act (Taft-Hartley Act)
Talbot, Robert, 84
Target market, 410–411, 485–486
Target return on investment, 455
Tariffs
    arguments for and against, 123
    explanation of, 122
    preferential, 126
    protective, 122
Taxes
    business, 112–113
    by country, 57
    income, 113, 717–719
    managing personal, 717–720
    offshore virtual corporations and, 255
    sales and property, 720
Taylor, Andy, 264
Taylor, Frederick, 308–309
Taylor, Lisa, 200
Taylor, Michael, 164
Technical skills, 231
Technology. *See also* Computer networks; Information technology (IT); Internet; Software
    to aid disabled individuals, 278
    cash management, 641
    change resulting from, 36–38, 43
    developing nations and, 93
    economic growth and, 52, 53
    employee recruitment using, 277
    explanation of, 36
    global communications and, 38
    human resource management and, 296
    manufacturing applications for, 386–388
    promotion using, 523
    small-business creation and, 203–204, 210–211
    telecommuting and, 250
    wireless, 540, 542, 552
Technology planning, 551–552
Telecommuting, 250, 296, 298, 320
Term life insurance, 723, 725
Term loans, 646–647
Terrorism
    decision making for responses to, 229–231
    impact on global business, 39–40, 42, 117–118
    risk management and, 653–654
Test marketing, 450
Testing, employee, 278–279
Tests, skills for taking, 11–12
Theft insurance, 669
Theory X, 312
Theory Y, 312
Theory Z, 312–313
Thompson, Louis M., Jr., 700
Thrift institutions, 615
Thurow, Lester, 27
Thursfield, David, 240
Time deposits, 609
Time management, 9, 236–237
Title insurance, 669
Tobacco advertising, 512
Toffler, Barbara Ley, 599
Tomé, Carol, 653, 655
Top management, 222
Tort law, 99, 109
Torts, 99, 109
Total quality management (TQM), 385
Trade
    antidumping laws and, 124
    balance of, 119
    balance of payments and, 120
    barriers to, 122–124
    changing value of currencies and, 120
    fear of, 121
    free, 121
    institutions for fostering, 124–125
    reasons for, 120–122
    small businesses and, 199–200
    terrorism and, 117–118
    United States and, 117–119
Trade and Development Act of 2000, 123
Trade credit, 643
Trade deficit, 119
Trade surplus, 119
Trademarks, 108–109, 441, 582
Training. *See* Employee training
Transaction processing systems (TPSs), 546–547
Transfer, job, 287–288
Transportation, criteria for chosing, 491, 492

Treasury bills, 676
Treasury bonds, 611, 676
Treasury notes, 676
Trial courts, 105
Truck wholesalers, 483
Trust, importance of, 2
Tschohl, John, 173
Tuchman, Robert, 205

U

Underwriting, 665, 679
Unearned income, 718
Unemployment, 40, 53–54
Unemployment compensation, 285
Unemployment insurance, 667
Unemployment rate
  explanation of, 53–54
  monetary policy and, 57
Uniform Commercial Code (UCC), 105
Uniform Franchise Offering Circular (UFOC), 172
Union certification election, 345
Union shop, 348
United States, trade and, 117–119, 126, 129–130
Universal Commercial Code for Electronic Commerce, 112
Universal life insurance, 724, 725
Unsecured loans, 643
Unsought products, 439
Uruguay Round, 124–125
Utilitarianism, 80

V

Value pricing, 455
Value-stream mapping, 381
Variable pay, 321
Vela, Carlos and Amy, 705
Venture capital, 196, 651
Vertical marketing systems, 478–479
Vertical mergers, 168
Vestibule training, 282
Vidaguren, Ignacio, 26
Viekeman, Marvin, 91
Vietnam Veterans Readjustment Act, 292
Vincent, Terri, 334
Virtual assistants, 334
Virtual corporation, 260–261
Virtual organization, 255
Virtual private networks (VPNs), 540, 542–543
Virtual work teams, 261–262, 324
Vision, 2, 116
Visualization, 11
Volte, Lee, 211
Volume segmentation, 422
Voluntary bankruptcy, 110
Voluntary reduction in pay, 288

W

Wade, David, 617
Wages, 284, 349–350. *See also* Employee compensation
Wages, Robert, 341
Wagner Act, 342–343
Wainstein, Deborah, 199
Waiting period, 723, 725
Wallace, Gary, 328
Wallace, Ray, 224–225
Wardynski, Casey, 434–435
Warehouses, location and types of, 491
Warranties, 108, 446–447
Watanabe, Miwa, 453
Watkins, Sherron C., 81
Web site designers, 603–604
Web sites
  on business ethics, 100
  career-related, 15
  for college costs and financial-aid information, 10
  for company information, 17–18
  for posting résumés, 17
  for relocation information, 20
  for self-assessments, 14
  for test-taking information, 12
WebResume software, 16
WebVan, 25
Weekly project planners, 9
Weill, Sandy, 607, 627
Welch, Jack, 128, 222
Wheeler, James E., II, 631
Wheeler-Lea Act of 1938, 111
Whistleblowers, 295
Whitwam, David R., 184
Whole life insurance, 724, 725
Wholesaler sales representative, 534
Wholesalers
  explanation of, 475, 480–481
  types of, 481–483
Wide area networks (WANs), 540
Wi-Fi, 542, 552
Wildcat strikes, 352
Wilson, Ron, 149, 174
Wireless LANs (WLANs), 540
Wireless technology, 540, 542, 552
Wireless WAN (WWAN), 540
Withey, Annie, 211, 212
Withholding allowances, 718
Wolf, Amy, 205
Women
  in accounting, 605
  franchise ownership by, 169
  in labor force, 29, 42
  as small-business owners, 192, 202–203
Wonderlic Personnel Test, 278
Woods, Tiger, 427
Work aid, 10
Work groups, 323
Work teams
  building high-performance, 326–327
  cross-functional, 324
  explanation of, 323
  goals for building, 4
  group behavior and, 321–322
  types of, 323–324
  virtual, 261–262, 324
Worker's compensation, 285
Workers' compensation, 667
Work-life benefits, 326
Workplace, interpersonal skills for, 2–5
Work-scheduling options, 319–320
World Bank, 121, 125
World Trade Organization (WTO), 121, 125, 139
World Wide Web. *See* Web sites
Worthington, Bob, 545
Wu, Chi Chi, 710

Y

Yates, Davin, 437
Yellow-dog contracts, 342
Yield management systems (YMS), 460
York, Tanya, 186
Younger, Lynn, 652
Younger Boomers, 31

Z

Zarate, Steve, 234
ZEOM.net, 388
Zhang Ruimin, 39
Zuckerman, Ethan, 102, 103
Zweig, Mark, 315

company index

A

Abacus, 531
ABN Amro, 619–620
Ace Hardware, 161
Activision, 254
ACT-UP, 94
Adelphia, 570
Adidas, 29
Adobe Systems, 90, 92
Aetna, 92
Aetna Inc., 549
AFLAC, 311
AFL-CIO, 340
Aim Services of Tennessee, 549
Allegheny Ludlum, 447
Allied Van Lines, 541
Alston & Bird, 90
AltiTunes Partners LP, 205
Altria Group, 166, 169
Amazon.com, 46–47, 111, 139, 183, 184
American Airlines, 279, 280, 282, 320
American Building Restoration Products, 129–130
American Cancer Society, 25
American Cast Iron Pipe, 90
American Eagle Outfitters, 251
American Express, 83, 92, 287, 428
American Federation of Labor (AFL), 339, 340
American Freightways, 236
American Information Systems, Inc., 184
American Institute of Certified Public Accountants (AICPA), 574, 577, 592
American Red Cross, 92
American Society of Chartered Life Underwriters, 85
American Stock Exchange (AMEX), 681
America Online Inc., 166, 234, 268, 646
AmeriCredit Corp., 652
Analytics Operations Engineering, 199
Arthur Andersen, 570, 575, 599
Anheuser-Busch, 94
Ann Taylor, 460
AOL, 646
Aon Re, 654
Applebee's Restaurants, 232
Archway Cookies, 565–566
Arista Records, 245
AT&T, 39, 90–91, 94, 129, 167, 294, 540
AT&T Capital Business Finance, 617
Atwood Richards Co., 133
Auto Workers of Canada, 349
Aventis, 545
Avon Products Inc., 405, 406, 414, 430
Avtovaz, 131

B

Bank of Alma, 631
Bank of America Corp., 281, 385, 554, 639
Bank of Montreal, 620
Bank of New York, 138
BASF, 137
Beecham, 137
Beijing Genomics Institute, 53
Bell Labs, 412
Beneficial Corp., 617
Ben & Jerry's, 83, 219, 220, 234
Bio-Rad Laboratories, 254
Black Forest Motors, 75
Blockbuster, 500
Bloor Research, 564
Blue Diamond, 162
Bluemountain.com, 184
BMG, 245, 264
BMW, 27–28, 490–491
Boeing Corp., 38, 39, 66, 68, 100, 118, 133, 247, 259, 344, 378
Bombardier, 396
Borders Books, 492
Boston Beer Company, 662
BP, 473
Branch-Smith Printing Division, 385
Briazz, 27
Bridge Medical, 561
Brightroom, 203–204
British Airways, 407
Burger King, 388
Burlington Northern Santa Fe Railroad, 280, 294, 344
Burton Snowboards, 45–46
Buy.com, 460

C

Cadbury Schweppes, 29, 71
Calavo, 162
Calbert Group, 334
Caliber Collision Center, 173
California Closets, 170
California Milk Producer Board, 100–101
CAMI Automotive, 132
Campbell Soup Company, 83, 447, 479
Capital One Financial Corp., 627
Capital Research Center, 94
Cardianove Inc., 387
CareerMosaic.com, 277
CareerPath.com, 277
Cargill Dow LLC, 373
Carnival Cruise Lines, 410
Caterpillar, 287, 296
CCBN, 601
Certa ProPainters, 170
Chapparal Steel, 412
Chartered Financial Consultants, 85
Chase Manhattan Bank, 167
Chef America Inc., 23
Chemlawn, 479
Chevrolet, 421
Chevron, 167
ChevronTexaco, 389, 473, 649
Chiquita Brands International Inc., 652
Circuit City Stores, 551
Cisco Systems, 261, 296, 641
CIT Financial, 644, 645
Citgo Petroleum Corp., 473
Citgo Refining and Chemicals Co, 351
Citibank, 166–167, 619
Citicorp, 428, 607
Citigroup, 84, 138, 167, 522, 607, 608, 620, 627
Club Med, 30
CMP Media, 89
Coca-Cola Company, 39, 91, 94, 109, 128–129, 133, 136, 277, 281, 287, 294, 447, 480
Colby Care Nurses, Inc., 87
Colgate-Palmolive, 71, 459
Comcast, 167–168
Commerce Bancorp, 627
Commonwealth Credit Union, 328
Compaq, 219, 282
Computer Store, 191
The Computer Forum, 191
Con Edison, 221–222, 649
Congress of Industrial Organizations (CIO), 340
Conoco, 166
Container Store, 90
Control Data Corp., 288
Corner Bakery Cafe, 27
Corning, 296
Costco Wholesale Corp., 85, 86, 473, 482, 510–511
Council of Better Business Bureaus, 509–511
Crate & Barrel, 649
CVS Corp., 428
Cyprus Amac Mineral Co., 36

D

DaimlerChrysler, 28, 390, 455
Dana Corporation, 381
Dean Witter, 701
DeBeers Consolidated Mines Ltd., 65
Dell Computer, 129, 219, 234, 322, 419, 488, 490–491, 651–652, 655
Deloitte & Touche Tohmatsu International (DTT), 574
Department of Education, 10
Department of Labor, 293
Deutsche Bank, 619
DHL, 139
Dieceland Technologies, 211
Dillard's, 486
R. R. Donnelley, 592
DoubleClick, 530–531
Dow Chemical, 137, 447
Duke Energy, 690
Dunkin' Donuts, 333
Du Pont Merck Pharmaceutical, 33
Dylan's Candy Bar, 187

E

Eastman Kodak, 65, 94, 125, 184, 410–411
eBay, 1, 11, 111, 168
Ecko, 644, 645
Edible Arrangements, 162, 163
Edward Jones, 90, 735–736
Edy's Ice Cream, 639
eEye Digital Security Inc., 155, 183
Electrical Innovations, 26
Electrolux, 39
Electronic Acts, 673
EMI, 245
Enron Corporation, 34, 81, 83, 88, 89, 93, 97, 569, 575, 595, 642, 652, 653, 672
Enterprise Rent-A-Car, 264
Epic Rus, 69
Equal Employment Opportunity Commission (EEOC), 293–294
Equal Exchange, 101–102
Equifax, 717
ESPN, 145–146, 522–523
Esprit, 83
Ethics Officer Association (EOA), 85, 99
E*Trade Group, 623, 702
E4X, Inc., 139
Expedia, 75, 76, 254
Experian, 717
Exxon Corporation, 39, 136
ExxonMobil, 296, 646

F

Fairview Capital Partners, 203
Family Dollar Stores Inc., 136
Farmland Industries, 162
Federal Communications Commission (FCC), 104, 106
Federal Reserve Board, 710
Federal Trade Commission (FTC), 302, 511
FedEx, 89, 139, 236, 281, 296
Fidelity Investments, 678
Fiji Film, 125
Firstbank Corporation, 631
First Capital International, 146–147
First National Bank of Amarillo, 716
Fisher-Price, 433–434
Fitter International, 660
FleetBoston, 621
Food Lion, 428
Foot Locker, 182
Ford Motor Company, 28, 39, 41, 82, 118, 129, 240–241, 258, 326, 348, 349, 370, 421, 428, 639
Foresight, 642
Fort Howard Paper, 412
Fort James, 493
Fox & Hounds, 580
The Franchise Company, 170
Frito-Lay, 23, 25, 421, 445
Front Range Bank, 617
Fruit-of-the-Loom, 130
Funko, Inc., 186–187

G

Gallo, 68
The Gap, 83
Gateway Computer, 557
GE Capital Small Business Finance, 617
Geekcorps, 102–103
Geek Squad, 178
General Electric Corp., 39, 41, 94, 129, 133, 167, 222, 234, 276, 277, 280, 283, 287, 348, 385
General Foods, 169
General Mills, 492, 493
General Motors Corp., 28, 35, 39, 118, 129, 131, 132, 133, 136, 289, 354, 372, 381, 387, 398, 440, 459, 506, 517, 643
Genghis Grill, 163, 168
Gillette, 38, 116–117, 136, 221, 421, 479
GlaxoSmithKline, 66
Global Crossing, 88, 93
Global Motors, 374, 375
Glycomed Inc., 302
GNC, 163
Goodyear, 643
Google, Inc., 181, 183, 207
W. C. Gore and Associates, 279
Grant Thornton LLP, 592
Graphic Packaging, 493
Gray Matter Holdings, 149
Green Mountain, 102
Green Mountain Bank, 617
Greenpeace, 25
GrooveJob.com, 193
Guangdong Galanz Enterprise Group Co., 53
Gymboree, 460

H

Häagen-Daz, 38
Haier Group, 39
Halsall Associates, Ltd., 250
Hanes, 479
Harley-Davidson, 367, 387, 392, 422
HarperCollins, 492
Hart Schaffner and Marx, 479
Health-South Corporation, 684
H. J. Heinz, 71
Hershey Foods, 71
Hertz, 164
Hewlett-Packard (HP), 44, 94, 130, 219, 289, 410, 556–559, 650
Hilton Hotels, 294
Hire.com, 277
Holiday Inn, 164
Home Depot Inc., 41, 161, 295, 476, 537, 561, 652
Homegrown, 211, 212
Honda, 136, 137, 138, 282
Honeywell, 297, 392
Hotjobs.com, 277
Hot Topic, 315
Household International, 617
Houston Astros, 288
HSBC, 620
Huawei Technologies Co., 53
Huffy, 167
Hyundai Motor America, 236

I

IBM, 91, 93–94, 118, 129, 184, 219, 278, 289, 296, 364, 447, 558
Information Resources, Inc. (IRI), 426
ING, 630
Ingersoll-Rand, 280
Intel Corporation, 68, 74, 184, 290
Interactive Travel Services Association (ITSA), 75–76
Internal Revenue Service (IRS), 719
International Association of Machinists and Aerospace Workers, 344
International Cogeneration Corp. (ICC), 674
International Executive Service Corps (IESC), 103
International Franchise Association, 165
International Longshore and Warehouse Union (ILWU), 337, 343
International Organization for Standardization (ISO), 386
Intuit, 321
i2Technologies Inc., 159

J

Jack in the Box, 473
Jacobs & Associates, 199
Jamba Juice, 163
Jantzen, 88
JC Penney, 32, 279, 460
JD Powers and Associates, 407
JetBlue, 275
Jiffy Lube, 163
Johnson Controls Inc. (JCI), 390
Johnson & Johnson, 41
JP Morgan, 167
Jungle.com, 564–565

K

Karachi Stock Exchange, 682
Keds, 31
Keep America Beautiful, 25
Kellogg, 128–129, 136, 419
Kentucky Fried Chicken (KFC), 165, 169
Kimberly Clark, 428
Kinko's, 163
Kinsley Construction Company, 355
Korn Ferry, 277
KPMG, 375, 574, 591
Kraft General Foods, 169, 428, 447, 459
Krispy Kreme, 635, 636, 656-657
Kroger Co., 282, 473

L

Labatt Brewing Company, 130
Laborer's International Union, 355
Land O'Lakes, 162, 493
Land's End, 139, 287–288, 470–471
Levi Strauss, 83, 105, 131, 490–491
Lexus, 71, 407, 504

LG Electronics, 49, 71
Liebherr, 39
Ligand Pharmaceuticals Inc., 302
The Limited, Inc., 411
Lockheed Martin, 273
Logitech, 254
London Stock Exchange, 682
Lowe's, 161
LT Designs, 200
Lucent Technologies, 88

M

MaidPro, 178–179
Mail Boxes Inc., 170
Mandarin Oriental Hotel Group (MOHG), 543
Manufacturers' agents, 482
Manufacturers' representatives, 482
Marion Merrell Dow, 521
Mariott International, 96, 411
Mars Corp., 53, 71
Massachusetts Mutual, 667
Matrix Semiconductor, 651
Mattel, 491
Maytag, 71
Mazda, 507
McDonald's Corp., 39, 96, 116, 117, 128, 163, 165, 284, 293, 414, 473, 479
McDonnell Douglas, 66, 259
MCG, 83
MCI WorldCom, 540
McLane Co., 479
Medina Cycleworks, 204
Medtronic, Inc., 381
Men's Warehouse, 279
MercadoLibre.com, 26
Mercedes-Benz, 71, 74–75
Merck, 296
Merrill Lynch, 281
Metropolitan Life, 649
Microsoft Corporation, 27, 35, 39, 128, 217, 218, 227, 237, 279, 282, 296, 311, 649–650
Miller Brewing Company, 169, 284
Mitsubishi Motor Manufacturing, 134, 294
ML Parker Construction, 203
Molly Maid, 170
The Money Store Commercial Lending, 617
Monsanto Company, 558–559
Monster.com, 277, 304
Moody's, 677
Morgan Stanley, 700–701, 735
Motive Communications, 277
Motorola, 41, 54, 294, 385, 591
Mr. Handyman, 170
MTV, 419

N

Nabisco, 169
Napster Inc., 167
Nasdaq, 682
National Association of Securities Dealers (NASD), 683, 685
National Cooperative Business Association, 162
National Federation of Independent Businesses, 188–189
National Geographic Society, 296
National Trade Association (NTA), 315
NationsBank, 277
NBA, 354
NBC, 88
Nescafe, 136
Nestlé, 138
NetBank, 632
Netflix, 500
Neurocrine Biosciences, 162
New Era Cap, 373
New United Motor Manufacturing Inc. (NUMMI), 381, 386
New York Life, 667
New York Stock Exchange (NYSE), 577, 681, 682, 685, 694, 727
NFL Players Association, 349
Niagra Mohawk, 84
Nicholson-Hardie Nursery & Garden Center, 409
A.C. Nielsen Company, 426
Nike, 68, 138, 427, 660
Nintendo, 651
Nordstrom, 182, 623
Nortel Networks Corporation, 262
Northwestern Mutual Life, 667
Novartis Seeds, Inc., 428

O

OCB, 518
Occupational Safety and Health Administration (OSHA), 291, 293
Ocean Spray, 162
Office of Federal Contract Compliance Programs (OFCCP), 294
OGIO, 182–183
Oil, Chemical and Atomic Workers Union (OCAW), 340–341
Onesage.com, 184
Online Reporting Services, 304
Oracle, 268–269
Orbitz, 75–76
Otis Elevator, 91, 137–138
Outboard Marine Corp. (OMC), 396
Owens Corning, 381

P

Pacific Cycles, 167
Pacific Maritime Association (PMA), 337, 343–344
Paine Webber, 277
Pal's, 385
Pampers, 136
Panera Bread Co., 27, 28
Paper, Allied-Industrial, Chemical and Energy International Union (PACE), 341
Party City, 170
Patagon.com, 26
Paul Davis Restoration, 170
Pawsenclaws & Co., 170
Paychex, Inc., 233, 234
PeopleSoft, 234
PepsiCo, 133, 136, 271, 298, 479, 506
PetFoodDirect.com, 254
Petroleum Geo-Services (PGS), 558
Pfizer, 27, 68, 162, 263, 522, 646
Pharmacia, 66, 263
Philip Morris Company, 94, 130, 136, 166, 169
Phillips Petroleum, 166, 289
Pillsbury, 493
PING-Karsten, 498–499
Pizza Hut, 164, 421
Planned Parenthood, 94
Playcentric.com, 255
Polaroid, 65, 530
Pop Culture, 155, 160
Powell's Books, 46–47
Priceline.com, 254
Pricewaterhouse-Coopers (PWC), 574
PrintingForLess.com, 212–213
Priority Staffing Solutions, 199
Procter & Gamble, 91, 129, 137–138, 220, 290, 296, 405, 437, 447, 457, 466, 673, 696
Proflowers.com, 184

Q

Quaker Oats Co., 71, 410, 443
QVC, 149, 174
Qwest, 570

R

RadioShack Corp., 450, 688, 689
Ralston Purina Co., 445
Rand Corporation, 254
RCA Records, 245
Reebok, 660
Renault, 465
Rent-A-Center, 294
Republic Engineered Products, 326
Resource Advisory Services, Inc., 724
Rite Aid, 491
Robert Half International, 226
Rocket Electric Co., 117
Roxio Inc., 167
Royal Dutch/Shell, 473
RPS, 236
RTM Restaurant Group, 326

S

Sabre, Incorporated, 261–262
Saint-Gobain Container, Inc., 351
Salomon Brothers, 166–167
Sam's Clubs, 482
SAP Software, 27
Sara Lee, 522
SAS Institute, Inc., 241, 312
Saturn, 30
SBC Communications Inc., 268
Charles Schwab & Co., 671, 672, 694, 696, 735
Schwinn/GT Bicycle Company, 167
SC Johnson, 311

Seagate Technology, 647, 648, 651
Sears, 278, 290–291, 294, 445
Secure Computing, 141
Securities and Exchange Commission (SEC), 93, 569, 575, 592, 594, 627, 684, 685, 693, 700
Securities Investor Protection Corporation (SIPC), 684
7-Eleven, 139, 169, 473
Shareholder.com, 700
Sherwin-Williams, 479
Siemens A. G., 39, 136
Sierra Club, 25
SIGMA Marketing Group, 289
Simplex Nails, 379
Small Business Administration (SBA), 183, 190–192, 196, 197, 199
Smartfood, 211
SmithKline, 137
J.M. Smucker Company, 23, 24, 25, 41, 90
Snap-on Tools, 294
Solera Capital, 212
Sony Erikson, 523
Southwest Airlines, 96, 234, 276, 287, 311, 358
Spaulding Company, 130
Sprint, 540
SSM Health Care, 385
Stained Glass Overlay, 170
Standard & Poor's, 677
Staples, 242–243
Starbucks, 102, 115, 142, 277, 314
State Farm, 667
Stave Puzzles, 190
STI Music Private Bank, 413
Stryker, 447
Sunkist, 162
Suzuki, 131–132
Swatch Group AG, 518
Synovus, 90

T

T. Rowe Price, 736
Taco Bell, 163
Taco John's, 304
Tampa Electric, 649
Tandy, 279
Target Stores, 660
Tastefully Simple, 190
TD Industries, 90, 279, 332–333
TECO Energy, 649
TE Corp., 53
Telcom, 83
Telus, 311
Texaco, 167, 281
Texas Instruments, 96, 184, 277
3M, 41, 134
Thrifty Car Rental, 169
Timberlane Woodcrafters, 206
Time Inc., 646
Time Warner Inc., 128, 166, 168, 646
T.J.Maxx, 321
Tokyo Stock Exchange, 682
Toronto Blue Jays, 469–470
Toyota Motors, 29, 71, 92, 134, 228–229, 381
TransUnion, 717
Travelers Group, 607
Travelers Insurance Company, 108, 166
Travelocity, 75, 76
Travelodge, 67–68
Trinity Industries, 224–225
TriZetto Group, Inc., 545
TSE Sports and Entertainment, 205
Tweeter Home Entertainment Group, 661
Two Men and a Truck, 202–203
Tyco, 79, 88, 95, 97, 570, 652, 653

U

Umum Provident Corporation, 278
Unifi Network, 328
Union Pacific Railroad, 344
United Airlines, 275, 288, 320, 356, 357
United Auto Workers (UAW), 241, 348
United Farm Workers Union, 354
United Food and Commercial Workers (UFCW), 345
United Papermakers International Union (UPIU), 340–341
United Parcel Service (UPS), 139, 276, 307, 309, 329, 542
United Transportation Union (UTU), 344
United Way, 25
Universal Studios, 141
UPR, Inc., 288
UPS Stores, 165–166
U.S. Army, 434–435
U.S. Patent Office, 108
U.S. Postal Service, 65, 280
U.S. Small Business Administration (SBA), 129
U.S. Treasury Department, 611, 612, 615, 675–676
USX, 66

V

Valassis Communications, Inc., 303–304
Vanguard Group, 678
Vespa Scooters, 523
Virgin Group, 518
Volkswagen, 503, 522, 526
Vosges Chocolate, 184

W

Waldo's $ Mart, 136
Wal-Mart Stores, Inc., 39, 132, 234, 276, 287, 345, 347, 473, 479, 486, 500, 623
Walt Disney Company, 30, 279
Warner Communications, 646
Weathervane Terrace Inn and Suites, 600
Wegmans, 90
Western Electric, 309
Westinghouse, 479
Weyerhaeuser Company, 166, 508
Whirlpool Corporation, 39, 45, 184
Wick's 'n' Sticks, 163
Willamette Industries, 166
Wineaccess.com, 566
Winn-Dixie Stores, 428
Workforce Solutions, 296
WorldCom, 81, 88, 93, 97, 570, 652, 653, 672
Wrench Science, 204
Wrigley, 87
Writers Guild of America, 363

X

Xerox Corporation, 137, 138, 184, 289, 570
Xilinx, 90

Y

Yahoo!, 9, 267–268, 287
Yoplait, 89
York Entertainment, 186
Young Americans Business Network, 40
Young Entrepreneurs Network, 40

Z

Zalia International, 203
ZTE Corp., 53
Zweig White & Associates, 315